in

EUROPE

Hanging out in Europe

in

Europe

Second Edition

Hungry Minds

Best-Selling Books • Digital Downloads • e-Books • Answer Networks
e-Newsletters • Branded Web Sites • e-Learning

New York, NY ◆ Cleveland, OH ◆ Indianapolis, IN

Project Editor: Kristen Couse
Production Manager: Maria Fernandez
Production Editors: Mike Walters, Paul Paddock, Simon Sullivan
Proofreaders: Donna Stonecipher, Shoshanna Wingate
Associate Editors: Nathaniel Knaebel
Cartographers: John Decamillis, Elizabeth Puhl, Roberta Stockwell, Nick Trotter
Map artist: Michael Matos
Editorial Interns: Emily Reid, Gloria Ahn, Kristine Eco, Leah Arabia

Published by
Hungry Minds, Inc.
909 Third Avenue
New York, NY 10022

ISBN: 0-7645-6471-4
ISSN: 1531-1546

Book design: Sue Canavan and Mike Walters

Special Sales: For general information on Hungry Minds' products and services please contact our Customer Care Department within the U.S. at Tel 800-762-2974, outside the U.S. at Tel 317-572-3993 or Fax 317-572-4002.

For sales inquires and reseller information, including discounts, premium and bulk quantity sales, and foreign-language translations, please contact our Customer Care Department at Tel 1-800-434-3422 or Fax 317-572-4002.

CONTENTS

europe

u.k. and ireland

scandinavia

northern europe

southern europe

maps

a disclaimer

Please note that prices fluctuate over the course of time, and travel information changes under the impact of the many factors that influence the travel industry. We therefore suggest that you write or call ahead for confirmation when making your travel plans. Every effort has been made to ensure the accuracy of information throughout this book, and the contents of this publication are believed correct at the time of printing. Nevertheless, the publishers cannot accept responsibility for errors or omissions or for changes in details given in this guide or for the consequences of any reliance on the information provided by the same. Assessments of attractions and so forth are based upon the author's own experience and therefore, descriptions given in this guide necessarily contain an element of subjective opinion, which may not reflect the publisher's opinion or dictate a reader's own experience on another occasion. Readers are invited to write the publisher with ideas, comments, and suggestions for future editions.

Your safety is important to us, however, so we encourage you to stay alert and be aware of your surroundings. Keep a close eye on cameras, purses, and wallets, all favorite targets of thieves and pickpockets.

an invitation to the reader

In researching this book, we discovered many wonderful places—hotels, restaurants, shops, and more. We're sure you'll find others. Please tell us about them, so we can share the information with your fellow travelers in upcoming editions. If you were disappointed with a recommendation, we'd love to know that, too.

Please write to:
Hanging Out in Europe
Hungry Minds, Inc.
909 Third Avenue
New York, NY 10022

introduction

most of us have had the experience of going to a new school or moving to a new neighborhood and not knowing a soul there, not knowing the laws of the land, feeling lost and uncool. But if you're lucky, someone comes along who invites you in and shows you where the action is. The same can be said for travel—unless you're committed to seeing Europe through the moving tinted window of a tour bus, pretty soon you're going to want to get past the initial strangeness and get with it. And to really be able to do that, you need someone or something to help you along, so that what could have been just another cute postcard turns into a new chapter in your life. We created the *Hanging Out* guides to be that thing.

Going to Europe is infinitely more complicated—and ultimately more rewarding—than just going on your standard road trip. Without some help, you may repeatedly find yourself surrounded by a numbed-out tour group, scratching your head and wondering what all the fuss is about. We sent out our team of 15 writers with just that in mind. Go to where the action is, we instructed them, and tell us how to find it.

Of course we tell you how to see all the cultural and historical goodies you've read about in art history class and heard about from your folks, but we also tell you where to find the party, shake your butt, and make friends with the locals. We've tried to find the hottest scenes in Europe—where traditions are being reinvented daily—and make this guide into the equivalent of a hip friend to show you the ropes.

So, welcome to the new Europe, on the verge of mighty unification. The European Union (EU)—and the euro's arrival as a common currency—is already making many happy, others nervous, and the entire continent abuzz with a different kind of energy. As the Grand Tour of Europe meets the Info Age, the old ways are having to adjust to a faster tempo.

But even as the globe is shrinking to the size of a dot com, Europe remains a vast place with enough history and art and monuments to fill endless guides—so we had to make a choice. We wanted the *Hanging Out Guides* to live up to their title, so we decided to specialize and not only show you the best spots to eat, shop, sightsee, party, and crash, but also give you a real feeling for each place, and unique but do-able ways to get to know it better. So we don't cover *every single* European city—instead, we picked what we felt were the best and served them up with plenty of detail. We felt it was crucial to have the room to go deeper, and to tip you off as to how to do the same, so that after you see the sights, you'll almost certainly end up in a place where you'll get to know the secret to the best travel—the locals.

Aside from the basics—**neighborhoods, eats, crashing, stuff** (shopping), **culture zoo** (sightseeing stuff), and **need to know** (the essentials)—we cover **the bar scene, the live music scene, the club scene, the gay scene, the visual arts scene,** and **the performing arts scene,** always giving you the scoop on where to chill out and where to get wild. We take you on some beautiful walks and show you great places to hang (sometimes for no money). "Things to Talk to a Local About" actually gives you some fun conversation openers. "Fashion" tells you what people are wearing. "Wired" lists websites for each city—some general, some cool, some out-of-the-way—so you can start checking things out immediately; it also takes you to the best cybercafes in each place. "Rules of the Game" lays out local liquor and substance laws and also gives you the vibe on the street. "Five-0" does a quick sketch of cops in each city. "Boy Meets Girl" dares to speculate on that most mysterious of travel adventures. And "Festivals and Events" lists just that.

Our adventurous team of writers (average age, 24) and editors let you in on the ongoing party. We want to make sure that your time abroad is punctuated by moments when you've sunk deep enough into the mix (or danced long enough to it), that you suddenly get it, you have that flash of knowing what it's like to actually *be* somewhere else, to live there—to hang out in Europe.

u.k. and ireland

London

Having given birth to the Swinging '60s, the Sex Pistols, and all-night raves, London could easily rest on its party laurels, but instead the city is the pacesetter for the 21st century—and now you don't even have to know some secret password to find the good parties. Those days are done, as are the days of the strict 11pm shutdown of bars and pubs that gave London nightlife its peculiar character. Beginning in 1993, late-night licenses were granted to a few bars, starting what many hope will be a complete overhaul of London's ancient drinking laws. It was around the same time that the government also started cracking down on E-fueled warehouse parties, passing a law against people dancing to "repetitive beats," moving raves into clubs and special-event halls. The outcome of this epic battle between the forces of youth culture and the status quo is still undecided, but the lines of division are pretty clear.

London is in fact two cities in one: an exciting, fast-paced, international center of fashion, music, and club culture; and the remains of one of Europe's most powerful empires, trying to preserve (and promote) some of its former glory. And while the government looks to the future, eagerly throwing money at wacko monuments to England like the Millennium Dome, most Londoners take greater national pride in the treble victory of the football (soccer) powerhouse, the Manchester United. The two Londons coexist, creating a weird rhythm between them, as thousands of partiers and barflies run from pub to bar to club before everything shuts down around midnight. Sometimes the two faces of the city can even intersect, as when the austere **National Portrait Gallery** [see *culture zoo,* below] hosted a huge show of rock 'n' roll photography.

four things to talk to a local about

1. **Middle America:** The English are absolutely intrigued by the vast, flat expanse of America that's just overflowing with homicidal/suicidal kids, hysterically ignorant yokels, and guys with big mullet hairstyles. True or not, the stereotype comes up a lot when locals realize you're from across the pond.
2. **Football:** Just don't call it soccer. Ask a local to explain the special thrill when a big game ends in a tie.
3. **Movies:** Most kids have a recent favorite, whether it be American extravaganzas or local flicks.
4. **Raving Back in the Day:** Many Londoners enjoy reminiscing about the heady days before everybody figured out that lots of sketchy drugs and loud music probably aren't that good for the head.

But in the city that now modestly calls itself the "New Capital of Europe" (perplexing the European Union even further), the relentless bone of contention for revelers is still the absurd curfew. Happily, a bunch of spots do have late-licenses, letting them stay open until 1am, 3am, and sometimes 6am: **The End, Ministry of Sound,** and **Bar Rhumba** [see *club scene,* below] are all there for diehards.

Despite the shortage of early-morning action, London's shockingly vibrant nightlife has only expanded and diversified in recent years, with tons of clubs, concerts, and bars ready to drain your wallet. Jazz, rock, punk, techno, trance, tribal, neo-psychedelic-whatever—all co-exist happily side by side, in addition to a rapidly developing Asian and world-beat scene. The new London is as cosmopolitan as it's ever been, back on the cutting edge of the art, music, and fashion worlds—and there's actually good food now (some of it even English, for chrissake). The vibe is definitely upbeat. To get the lowdown on just about everything, pick up a copy of ***Time Out*** at any newsstand. It lists everything from films to special sales and comes out each Wednesday. Smaller magazines like ***Sleaze Nation*** also contain listings and can be found in many of the trendy shops off Oxford Street. The 411 on raves and one-off parties is generally publicized on fliers, which get stuck on walls and piled high by the doors of many shops. Just remember though, this city ain't cheap, so keep an eye on what you spend (definitely in pubs, where it's easy to lose track) if you want to get to know London's myriad personalities.

The English have a reputation for being standoffish, but they're actually generally friendly and love to talk, especially to people from the "colonies," and *especially* after a few pints. You've really got nothing to lose striking up a conversation, and hey, they speak English! Your only risk might be getting snagged on the end of a sharp wit. Just don't get too riled up if you think someone's picking on you; they're probably just "taking the piss out of you"—a national sport. Favorite subjects to ridicule Americans about include our penchant for oversize clothing and our slang—but, like, *duuude,* people in glass houses...[see *say what?,* below].

neighborhoods

While it appears to have been built with little to no planning, there is some semblance of structure within London's sprawl. The city center is usually divided into the City (to the east), the spot where London began, and the **West End,** a cluster of neighborhoods most people consider the city's true center. Many of the major tourist spots are in a small area just north of the Thames River and are easily walkable. **Trafalgar Square** is a good place to orient yourself, with the **National Gallery,** the **National Portrait Gallery** [see *culture zoo,* below, for both], **Nelson's Column,** and all that other good stuff (including pesky pigeons) at hand. To the north is **Soho,** thronged both day and night by a mix of tourists and locals. The acknowledged center of London's gay scene, Soho is lined with hundreds of quirky little boutiques, record stores, pubs, and clubs to check out. Due south is **Whitehall,** home to all the grand official buildings including **No. 10 Downing Street** (home of the Prime Minister), and further south is **Westminster** of **Westminster Abbey** fame [see *culture zoo,* below].

Southwest takes you past the **ICA** [see *arts scene,* below] and beautiful **St. James Park** to **Buckingham Palace;** you keep going south to reach stylish **Chelsea,** where famous artists from Oscar Wilde to Mick Jagger lived once, and where rich yuppies live now, in spectacular houses. Northwest of Chelsea is **Kensington,** named for the palace nearby. Some of London's best shops, and its only Urban Outfitters, are along **Kensington High Street.** For a funky bit of shopping, **Portobello Road,** in nauseatingly famous **Notting Hill,** west of Kensington, has a weekend market as well as a host of cool shops and bars.

West of Trafalgar is the super-swanky shopping area bordered by **Regent** and **Piccadilly** streets. Further west there's more luxurious living and shopping in **Mayfair** and **Park Lane** until you reach the truly enormous **Hyde Park** [see *great outdoors,* below].

Just north of Trafalgar, **Theaterland**—a clot of big, glitzy theaters along **Shaftesbury Avenue** and **Leicester Square**—also has more than its fair share of bars, restaurants, and tourists. London's small but lively **Chinatown** is just north of Leicester Square, and a short walk east gets you to trendy **Covent Garden,** crammed with bars and shops appealing to teenagers and upscale artsy-fartsy types alike. **Bloomsbury,** home of the **British Museum** [see *culture zoo,* below] and London University,

12 hours in London

1. Skip the tourbuses, climb atop the nearest **double decker** and let it show you London's sometimes cluttered and confusing charm from on high.
2. Visit the **Victoria and Albert** [see *culture zoo,* below] so you can appreciate the finer side of the city.
3. High-speed and pretty damn good, **Wagamama** [see *eats,* below] is a citywide favorite for noodles and the like.
4. Narrow and unassuming, Berwick Street, in the heart of Soho, is lined with some of London's best record shops, like **Selectadisc** [see *stuff,* below].
5. No trip to London is complete without purchasing some ludicrously priced clothes, the best of which can be found in and around Covent Garden's **Neal Street** [see *stuff,* below].
6. Not even the East Village compares to the slightly played-out freak scene at the **Camden Market** [see *stuff,* below].
7. Go see some legit. With literally more theaters than one could visit in a year, there's bound to be something worthwhile being performed [see *arts scene,* below].
8. An integral part of the English social fabric, drinking in the pub is critical to seeing England as the locals do—slightly blurry and spinning [see *bar scene,* below].
9. The birthplace of rave culture, London's clubs top America's biggest and best with both hands tied. **The End** [see *club scene,* below] is one of the coolest, not to mention the loudest.
10. Wind up the night with a few friends and some beers on top of **Primrose Hill** [see *hanging out,* below], a popular park with a kick-ass view of the city's historic skyline.

sits just north of Covent Garden and Soho. Kind of dull at the moment, the neighborhood owns a place in literary history as home to the moody, randy geniuses of the Bloomsbury Group, including Virginia Woolf, Bertrand Russell, and John Maynard Keynes. Farther north, popular with crusty punkers as well as colorful ravers, the streets of **Camden Town** (aka Camden) are cluttered with young people shopping the crowded market or stumbling from one local pub to another.

To the east, on the south side of the Thames, **Bankside** houses big draws like the **Museum of the Moving Image,** the **Design Museum,** the spankin' new **Tate Gallery of Modern Art** [see *culture zoo,* below, for all three], and the **Globe Theatre** [see *arts scene,* below].

For its gritty appeal and a bounty of hipster hangouts like **Dogstar** [see *bar scene,* below], **Brixton,** in South London—at the very end of the Victoria line of the Tube—is well worth the schlep. A largely Caribbean neighborhood, Brixton is notoriously dangerous, but the relative absence of handguns makes it seem less so in comparison to equally famous spots in New York or L.A. Also worth checking out are some neighborhoods on the make, including North London's **Islington,** a grownup version of Camden, and nearby **Stoke Newington,** which has a multi-culti vibe along **Church Street.**

The city is sectioned into boroughs and postal districts, delineated by combinations of letters and numbers posted on the wall-mounted signs about town (W6, SE4, etc.). They're actually directional markers telling you where a place is in relation to London's original post office—W6-West 6, for example. Not that it's going to help you all that much, because actual addresses don't seem to be regulated in any way. Some places don't even have numbers. To make matters worse, most people just use the neighborhood name to locate themselves. That's why people mean Camden Town, not the larger borough of Camden, when they tell you to check out the shopping in Camden.

Thankfully, the omnipresent Tube goes just about everywhere (but shuts down at around midnight—check times of last train in the tube station), and buses will get you to the more secluded sections of the city. Just tell the driver your destination, and he'll not only stop at the appropriate spot, but point you in the right direction. Walking can be a pain, but it's your best bet in clogged and crowded Soho, Leicester Square, and Covent Garden. All too familiar with the difficulties of finding and getting to where they need to be, Londoners rely on their beloved taxi drivers—not to be confused with minicab drivers [see *need to know,* below]—who must spend two whole years in training to gain *The Knowledge* of the streets. For those without the time or inclination to memorize every back alley in town, there is the *London A-Z.* Known as the "A to Zed," this indispensable book maps out the whole city, with a street-finding index in the back. Don't worry about looking like a tourist whipping yours out on the street; most locals have at least one copy, too. If you really can't find what you're looking for, just ask somebody; Londoners live in a heavily touristed city, but they're secretly proud of it and bear few grudges against confused travelers.

hanging out

Sprawling as well as plagued by lousy weather, London lacks landmark hangouts like Astor Place and St. Mark's in New York's East Village. Sure, there are places like Leicester Square and Neal Street, always crammed with mad people, but there are few places famous for just plain chillin'. Fortunately, people are friendly for the most part, and often quite interested in what visitors think of their town. A note to Yanks: Curiosity aside, many English people assume young American tourists

only here

So, you know the steering wheel is on the right side, chips are fries, crisps are chips, and there's more nudity on TV. But a lesser-known idiosyncratic attraction is London's pirate radio scene. Anyone with a cell phone and a transmitter can set up shop *Pump Up the Volume*-style. While few of the stations have broadcasters as scandalous as Hard Harry, most play different types of dance music, interspersed with shout-outs and commercials for upcoming events. Pirate radio enjoys de facto legitimacy by virtue of its popularity. **Freak FM 101.8** and **Kool FM 94.6** are two popular broadcasts specializing in garage and jungle, but new stations come and go on a weekly basis, so just spin the dial…

are uncouth goofballs (now, where would they get *that* idea?), so try to muster a little polish when making new friends.

For skaters, there's **South Bank,** which is right opposite the Strand on the Thames by Waterloo Bridge. This patch of concrete underneath the National Film Theater is an all-weather favorite of skateboarders, in-line skaters, and their hangers-on, who artfully outmaneuver the corporate types out for their lunchtime jog.

If the risk of grievous bodily harm is too much to stomach, another nice place to relax and enjoy a spot of good weather is **Regents Park.** Accessible by Tube (*Regents Park* stop), this expanse of gardens houses the London Zoo as well as a boating lake. Oh yeah, and you can drink beer in public in this country, so why not unwind with a nice cold one?

Or try North London's **Primrose Hill,** just across Prince Albert Road from the northern edge of Regents Park. Much smaller and significantly less spectacular, the hill sports one of the best views of downtown London you can find. The view does the skyline justice only at night, though, when the park becomes home to lots of small groups of young people getting wasted one way or the other. The only catch is getting there directly. While the *Swiss Cottage, St. John's Wood,* and *Chalk Farm* Tube stops all put you within a few blocks, a visit requires a short walk and your trusty *A-Z.*

For meeting people late at night, nothing really compares to a wander through **Soho.** Convenient to just about every night bus and minicab operator in the city, the Soho streets between Tottenham Court Road and Leicester Square stay crowded long after most bars have closed. Both locals and tourists wander around in search of munchies at the Chinese restaurants on Lisle Street, the many kebab stands, the 24-hour **Café**

Bohème [see *bar scene,* below], or the **Burger King** on Tottenham Court Road and Oxford Street.

Despite the range of places to go at all hours, London is still mostly an early city. The social hub of the city, its pubs, are the places to schmooze for most locals, even those too young to drink. Many pubs (stylish theme bars aside) are local joints visited by regulars who've been drinking and watching football (soccer) together year after year. For the indispensable English experience, head to the neighborhood pub on the night of an important football match. The crowds, the cheers, and the beer raining out of upheld pint glasses is a truly pagan religious experience. If the dive around the corner is just too awful to bear, try **Flask** *(77 Highgate West Hill; Tel 0208/340-72-60; Tube to Highgate; 11am-11pm Mon-Sat, noon-10:30pm Sun; AE, MC, V)* by Hampstead Heath, or **Sir Richard Steele** *(97 Haverstock Hill; Tel 0207/483-12-61; Tube to Belsize Park or Chalk Farm; 11am-11pm Mon-Sat, noon-10:30pm Sun; No credit cards).* Both of these North London pubs capture the multigenerational community vibe in the comforting surroundings of traditional English pub decor.

bar scene

Drinking verges on sport for the English, who consume alcohol to such excess that bars' taps sometimes actually go dry before midnight. No great pastime is without its shrines, and London has thousands of bars and pubs that elevate getting wasted to new heights. Pubs are also, of course, the places to sample pub grub, which varies in quality but almost always seems to have some kind of internal organ in it.

A scuzzy, dingy pub right in midst of the Camden Market **The Elephants Head** *(224 Camden High St.; Tel 0207/485-31-30; 11am-11pm Mon-Sat, till 10:30pm Sun; No credit cards)* is a punk version of the traditional local, serving greasy sandwiches alongside beer and booze. It's populated by a hodgepodge of elderly alcoholics and mohawked punks trapped in 1977, so there's little chance of bumping into a group of camera-toting tourists while sipping a pint here (so stash that camera!).

The World's End *(174 Camden High St.; Tel 0207/482-19-32; Tube to Camden Town; 11am-11pm Mon-Sat, noon-10:30pm Sun; No credit cards)* is an oft-mentioned, classic piece of the Camden scene. Catering to a raucous and inexplicably immense mob of indie-rocking teens and college-age misanthropes, the pub serves the standard food and drinks. But after the quaint front area, the decor veers into the bizarre—the back bar resembles some sort of dream town with mock storefronts and streetlights. As at all pubs, the hours favor compulsive and early drinking, both rooms filling up with throngs of punters by early evening.

Housed in a truly amazing space, **Dogstar** *(389 Coldharbour Lane; Tel 0207/733-75-15; Tube to Brixton; Noon-2:30am Mon-Thur, noon-4am Fri, Sat, noon-12:30am Sun; AE, MC, V)* puts most bars to shame and is well worth the trip to Brixton. High ceilings, a large bar, a good

boy meets girl

Since so much of London's social scene revolves around getting pissed, pickups are often heavy-handed. If the club is loud, you can even forget about pickup lines. From the boy's perspective, the modus operandi is basic:
1) Casual chitchat shouted into the woman's ear
2) A drink is offered
3) Maybe a dance (if venue permits)
4) If steps 1-3 have gone well, numbers are exchanged.

But it's important to remember that English gals aren't shy about getting what they want, either. Though many expect the man to make a move, British women are less reserved than many puritanical Americans when it comes to romance. All that said, it's important to recognize when to kick game and when to step back. For starters, neighborhood pubs are not the place to aggressively mack. Save the James Bond act for a bustling club or bar, where the vibe is more conducive to meeting and greeting. If the bar scene is too intimidating, raves and clubby spots are filled with eager and inebriated people of all persuasions looking for love—or at least its convincing imitation.

number of spacious tables, and an *X-Files* pinball machine all make for a comfortable, uncramped vibe. Well-priced double shots and a wide selection of standard beers are the main attractions—and the rotating lineup of DJs never hurts. The tunes tend toward house, with a smattering of techno and electronica thrown in, although Dogstar neither looks nor feels like a rave. Beware of bigger crowds and cover charges on weekends.

Known mostly as a nightclub, **Bar Rhumba** [see *club scene,* below] also has a fantastic happy hour from 5pm till 9pm, before things get really swinging at night. Both the bar and the nearby booths get packed with cool and friendly regulars drawn by reasonable prices and excellent music, ranging from soul to hip-hop to jungle and back. The decor is pretty plain, but the nice vibe makes Bar Rhumba a worthwhile stop for a drink or three. A smartly fashionable dress code is enforced only on Saturday nights.

Dark and airy, the **Beat Bar** (*265 Portobello Rd.; Tel 0207/792-20-43; Tube to Ladbroke Grove; 11am-11pm daily; No credit cards*) is a long and narrow hipster pub near the end of trendy Portobello Road. Even with quirky art exhibits and a slew of DJs spinning anything from hip-hop to jungle to Latin jazz, this bar is mysteriously uncrowded. The simple food is good, the staff groovy, and the few customers funny and amicable. Ideal for catching a drink while scouring the markets and shops in Notting Hill.

Attracting a diverse, clubby clientele, **Junction** (*242 Coldharbour*

Lane; Tel 0207/738-40-00; Laughborough Junction Rail or Bus P4, 35, 45, 345; 4pm-midnight Mon, till 11pm Tue, Wed, till 2am Thur, Fri, noon-2am Sat, noon-midnight Sun; AE, MC, V) serves up a good range of well-priced beers, especially during the lengthy happy hours: all day on Mondays and from 4pm to 8pm all other nights. Music runs the gamut of DJ-driven styles, with regular appearances by both lesser-known talents as well as big names like Bassment Jaxx. The huge crowds are always up for it, and their enthusiasm seems to have taken a toll on the scruffy interior. Most nights have no cover charge, and it's pretty reasonable when it's required.

london pub crawl

One of the dandiest ways to explore the city, other than aimless wandering around the West End, is to set aside an evening for a classic, leisurely pub crawl. This one begins at Piccadilly Circus and ends in Covent Garden. After exiting the Tube station, head right on Shaftesbury Avenue. A block and a half along, on the righthand side, **Bar Rhumba's** evening happy hour beckons. Crowded with cool and friendly locals of the New Media, scenester variety, Rhumba exudes a vibe of cultivated hipness. Soak it up over a pint or two, then bounce out the door and continue right until you hit Wardour Street. Hang a left and keep going until you reach gay Soho's main drag, Old Compton Street; take a right. Keep going till you come to Frith Street; go left and walk a couple of blocks until you reach **Garlic and Shots,** on the right. Stop in for a quick "bloodshot" against a background of grinding industrial tunes, then head back out to Old Compton Street to resume your course toward Charing Cross Road. One block before you get to that bustling avenue, stop in at **Café Bohème** to rinse the garlic taste out of your mouth with the after-work crowd. Then head back out to Charing Cross Road and take a left. Cross at the circle and walk down Earlham Street for about two blocks until you come upon the busy shopping area around Neal Street. Just before you get to that pedestrian walkway, duck into the basement space of the **Freedom Brewery** to sample some of London's finest microbrews amid stark modern surroundings. By the time you've had enough of the elitist brew, not to mention the elitist patrons, it may be time to call it a night. Just hang a right on Neal Street, walk two blocks to Covent Garden station and head home, drunk and not, mind you, too disorderly [see *bar scene*, above and below, for all bars mentioned].

five of the best pubs

Hitting the local pub is as much a part of your average Brit's lifestyle as eating and sleeping, and even though London is much more sophisticated than the rest of Britain, the same applies here when it comes to passion for the pub. And although you can't swing a dead cat without hitting a pub in the city, there are a few that are just superior when it comes to ambience, location, and/or history. **Freemason's Arms** *(32 Downshire Hill; Tel 0207/433-68-11; Tube to Hampstead; 11am-11pm weekdays and Sat, noon-10:30pm Sun)* is right next to the Hampstead Heath and down the road from Hampstead High Street. It has a wonderful garden with benches that is perfect for a sundowner or a lazy weekend mid-afternoon pint. **The Clifton** *(96 Clifton Hill; Tel 0207/624-52-33)*, in nearby St. John's Wood, is much more formal in decor with drapes and armchairs, lending the feel of sitting in a library. Another North London suburb, Maida Vale, has the **Warrington** *(93 Warrington Crescent; Tel 0207/286-29-29; Tube to Maida Vale; 11am-11pm Mon-Sat, noon-10:30pm Sun; All major credit cards)* as its local. Apart from the fussy decorative lamps, porch columns and glazed tiles at the entrance, the huge saloon bar inside is a great place to grab a pint and take it outside to the many small tables and chairs on the sidewalk. **Ye Olde Cheshire Cheese** *(145 Fleet St.; Tel 0207/353-61-70; Tube to Blackfriars; Open till 9pm daily)* is olde England at its best. This 1667 tavern is set in the heart of what used to be London's newspaper hub. Once there, take a stroll down Fleet Street, which has a lot of great old buildings. And finally, the **Cow Saloon Bar** *(89 Westbourne Park Rd.; Tel 0207/221-00-21; Tube to Bayswater, Edgeware Rd., or Lancaster Gate)* is a popular one for its buzzy ambience attributable to its small size, as well as the outdoor garden.

The somewhat precious microbrew craze sweeping the States has hit England now, too. **Freedom Brewery** *(41 Earlham St.; Tel 0207/240-06-06; Tube to Covent Garden; 10:30am-midnight Mon-Sat, noon-11:30pm Sun; www.freedombrew.com; MC, V)* offers four different kinds of boutique beers brewed on site, in the basement of the Thomas Neals shopping center in trendy Covent Garden. The bar's staff seem hipper than the yuppie customers. But the beers are quite good, as is the low-key, moderately priced Italian food.

Down along the banks of the Regents Canal, off Camden High Road, **Dingwalls** *(Camden Lock; Tel 0207/267-15-77; Tube to Camden Town; 7:30pm-12:30am Mon-Thur, 7pm-midnight Fri, Sat; No credit cards)* is a massive indoor/outdoor bar with a bumping nightclub and an upstairs comedy club on the premises. It's lovely on a warm summer night, with a number of outdoor tables set under parasols, and if the weather or crowds seem inhospitable, there's plenty of room indoors. The club space, which has a separate entrance, is sweaty and crowded, drawing scruffy dudes and women in various states of undress. Check out the long-running Metalheadz party on Sundays for a good sampling of London's drum 'n' bass scene.

Smack-dab in the thick of Soho's thriving bar scene on Old Compton Road is **Café Bohème** (13-17 Old Compton St.; Tel 0207/734-06-23; Tube to Leicester Sq.; 8am-3am Mon-Wed, 24 hours Thur-Sat, 9am-midnight Sun; AE, MC, V), a classy little Paris-style brasserie that's a relaxed alternative to the packed bars that abound in the area. People lounge on comfy couches, as well as on chairs on the sidewalk, and the bar offers a respectable assortment of drinks plus tasty French food. Blessed with a late-night license, the bar stays open till 3am during the week and all night long on weekends. Although the fashion police aren't manning the door, the music and crowd tend toward an upscale sophistication, typified by the regular evening jazz performances.

Catering to the seemingly incompatible yuppie and goth crowds, **Garlic and Shots** (14 Frith St.; Tel 0207/439-19-11; Tube to Tottenham Court Rd.; 5pm-midnight Mon-Wed, 6pm-1am Thur-Sat, 5-11:30pm Sun; MC, V) serves a huge selection of beer, booze, and garlic-saturated Swedish food. Cramped seating and a soggy downstairs bar serve it up, while a scary mix of goth and industrial music blares from the speakers. The vodka of choice is Black Death, and the bar's most popular shot is the super-spicy "bloodshot." A vampire's nightmare, this indoor/outdoor bar sounds much weirder than it really is.

Celebrated restaurateur Terence Conran is known for his love of space when it comes to designing the latest hipster food spot (i.e., all of his restaurants are massive). **Mezzo** (100 Wardour St.; Tel 0207/314-40-00; Fax 0207/314-40-40; Tube to Leicester Sq./Piccadilly Circus; AE, MC, V) is no exception. It's fairly pricey to eat here and the food is nothing spectacular, so have a drink or two at the bar, as the atmosphere is unbeatable. There is a large bar upstairs and a smaller one downstairs, where the chances of snagging a table are higher. It's a great spot for meeting friends and it's right in the heart of Soho.

If you're a cocktail fanatic, do not waste your time on flash bars. Go straight to **Nam Long-Le Shaker** in South Kensington (159 Brompton Rd.; Tel 0207/373-19-26 or 0207/370-35-81) which, although primarily a Vietnamese restaurant, has a bar that is a lot less lethal looking than the drinks it serves. Enter the Flaming Ferrari. This bad boy, consisting of every imaginable spirit that will get you wasted and quickly, will not bring you fond memories the following day.

Browns (82-84 St. Martin's Lane; Tel 0207/497-50-50; Tube to Leicester Sq.) is another of London's very popular chain restaurants but the atmosphere is still great, and the bar area of this particular Browns in

London bars, clubs and culture zoo

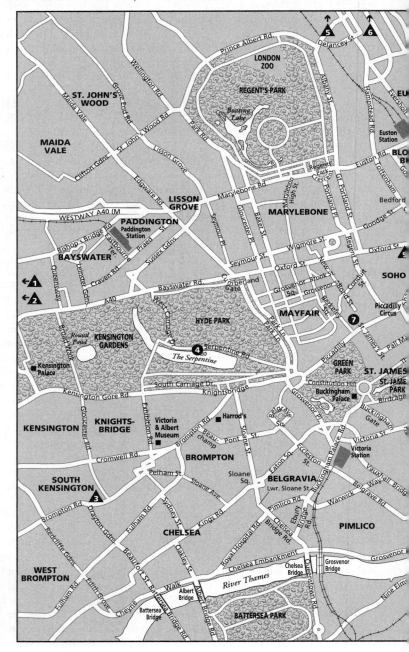

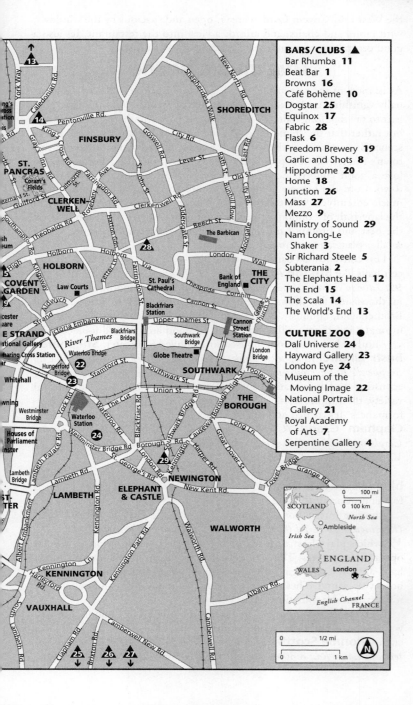

BARS/CLUBS ▲

Bar Rhumba **11**
Beat Bar **1**
Browns **16**
Café Bohème **10**
Dogstar **25**
Equinox **17**
Fabric **28**
Flask **6**
Freedom Brewery **19**
Garlic and Shots **8**
Hippodrome **20**
Home **18**
Junction **26**
Mass **27**
Mezzo **9**
Ministry of Sound **29**
Nam Long-Le
  Shaker **3**
Sir Richard Steele **5**
Subterania **2**
The Elephants Head **12**
The End **15**
The Scala **14**
The World's End **13**

CULTURE ZOO ●

Dalí Universe **24**
Hayward Gallery **23**
London Eye **24**
Museum of the
  Moving Image **22**
National Portrait
  Gallery **21**
Royal Academy
  of Arts **7**
Serpentine Gallery **4**

the West End/Covent Garden area is open and spacious by the windows, with tables and chairs, and affords a view into the restaurant. It's also a good central spot for pre-theater or after-theater drinks.

LIVE MUSIC SCENE

As in most of the rest of the world, London's rock 'n' roll scene is gradually vanishing underneath a massive pile of records and samplers. That isn't to say that long hair and power chords have completely disappeared, but rather that they're no longer at the heart of London's massive music scene. But a glance at the listings for concerts and shows in any of this town's numerous newspapers and magazines proves that Londoners do love a good concert. Seemingly every band of import passes through town, from the biggest arena-rock groups to the most way-out world-music ensembles. While shows take place in small clubs tucked away in the labyrinth of London's streets, several major venues consistently book the best and brightest on the national and international scene. At the smaller places, expect to pay £3 to £10.

Less conventional bands avoid the über-venues in favor of cooler concert halls like **Brixton Academy** *(211 Stockwell Rd.; Tel 0207/924-99-99; Tube to Brixton; Hours vary; MC, V)*, in South London, which packs in thousands for shows ranging from Lauryn Hill to the Chemical Brothers and, famously, Mrs. Ritchie's 2000 NYE concert. The space is intimate, but there's still enough of it to stand around and look cool in.

Another London venue housed in a converted theater, **Shepherds Bush Empire** *(Shepherds Bush Green; Tel 0207/771-20-00; Tube to Shepherd's Bush; Hours vary; MC, V)* offers a decent atmosphere, better acoustics, and box seats available for booking. Dedicated to musical variety, the Empire hosts everything from Sebadoh to world music performances. It's owned and operated as a counterpart to South London's **Clapham Grand** *(Clapham Junction, St. John's Hill; No phone; Clapham Junction train station via Waterloo or Victoria; Hours vary; MC, V)*, a fairly standard rock venue.

One of the biggest of England's concert arenas, the legendary **Wembley** *(Empire Way; Tel 0208/902-09-02; Tube to Wembley Park)*, is closed for renovation until 2002.

Another internationally known venue is the **Royal Albert Hall** *(Kensington Fore; Tel 0207/589-82-12; Tube to S. Kensington; AE, MC, V)*, which plays host to loads of big-name acts in addition to regular opera performances. The venue itself is an enormous Victorian concert hall, suitably extravagant for the range of glitzy, heavy-hitting events it hosts year-round. They're in the process of a renovation, and many hope it'll sharpen the sometimes spacey acoustics.

Everything from swing to free jazz can be found in London, but two venues consistently get recommended by the locals. The first is the legendary **Ronnie Scott's** *(47 Frith St.; Tel 0207/439-07-47; Tube to Tottenham Court Rd.; 8:30pm-late daily; £5-20 cover; AE, MC, V)*, London's

fIVE-O

The English hear all the stories about lawlessness and police brutality and wonder how Americans manage to stay alive. Their own impressions of the police are far more benign. While Scotland Yard doesn't have the reputation of being the friendliest police force on Earth, the officers are generally courteous and patient with tourists. Nevertheless, they can and will bust people for their misbehavior. If you don't wind up drunk and pantless in Leicester Square, or decide to roll joints on the Tube, you shouldn't have any trouble. Use your head, don't steal, and treat the officers with the respect they will probably accord you, even as they arrest you.

most respected jazz venue. Small and hazy with cigarette smoke, the club hosts two nightly shows by some of jazz's leading heavyweights. Vibes virtuoso of the '70s Roy Ayers recently held down two weeks of nightly gigs, but the music often treads less funkified territory.

If the traditional jazz-joint vibe at Ronnie Scott's doesn't tickle your fancy, head to the **Jazz Café** *(5 Parkway; Tel 0208/963-09-40; Tube to Camden Town; 7pm-1am Mon-Thur, 7pm-2am Fri-Sat, noon-4pm/7pm-midnight Sun; Cover £6-18; www.jazzcafe.co.uk; MC, V)* for a more new-school experience. While still booking big names like McCoy Tyner, the Jazz Café will also reel in performers like Fred Wesley and Lynn Collins of James Brown fame. The smooth, modern space is cool and accessible, as is the balcony restaurant. The food is equally modern (European) and pretty good.

club scene

While mainstream pop music has spiraled down into Boyband Hell, London's underground scene has created some of the most progressive and exciting music of the past decade. Styles ranging from tech-house to neurofunk aren't just for ravers in wacky clothes any more. Clubbing is a national pastime for the English, and London is unquestionably the place. *Time Out* lists what's on where, but less commercial events advertise via fliers, which can be had at pretty much every club/bar/shop in the city. Dress codes, attitudes, and door policies vary from place to place, as do the peak times to groove. For more options, check out the mixed parties listed in the Gay Scene [see below].

A good number of London's most beloved DJs work at dance record shops like **Black Market** [see *ground zero of the club scene,* below], so a visit to any one of London's gazillion vinyl emporiums may offer the chance to rub elbows with a spinning star.

Bar Rhumba *(36 Shaftesbury Ave.; Tel 0207/287-69-33; Tube to Piccadilly Circus; 5pm-3:30am Mon-Thur, till 4am Fri, 7pm-6am Sat,*

genrefication

Unless you've taken some interest in the whole electronica frenzy, the array of musical styles, from house to hardcore, is really confusing. Evolved out of the dance music of the '70s and '80s, today's styles derive from disco, hip-hop, and early electronic geniuses like Kraftwerk and Stockhausen. Here's a simple breakdown of some of dance music's ever-multiplying subgenres:

House: A direct descendant of disco, house music is named after the Chicago club where its earliest fans went dancing. Today, house can be soulful and smooth or hard and futuristic. It's always recognizable by strong, disco-y beats.

Techno: Also imported from America's Midwest, techno has taken London by storm. Utilizing all sorts of electronic gadgetry, producers have married synthetic sounds and rhythms to the steady bounce of house music.

Garage: House music's soulful cousin, garage is currently all the rage in London. Using soulful vocals, MC raps, and deep bass lines, garage is faster and more in-your-face than house.

Big Beat: Fusing techno production with the funky beats of hip-hop, big beat/breakbeat is the most accessible style of dance music. Artists like Prodigy and Fatboy Slim have made this style extremely popular.

Jungle/Drum 'n' Bass: Drawing from sources as diverse as dub, reggae, hip-hop, jazz, and techno, jungle and drum 'n' bass utilize staccato beats and tearing bass lines to devastating effect. The lighter sounds known as intelligent are a good deal easier on the ears of the uninitiated.

Trance: Recognizable by its trademark buildups, trance is like melodramatic techno, energetic but often repetitive.

Hardcore: Lost somewhere between techno and jungle, hardcore is fast and pounding. Less funky than drum 'n' bass, it's like techno on speed.

8pm-2am Sun; Cover £3-12; MC, V) heats things up until well after midnight with a fantastic sound system, top talent, and a clientele of cool regulars. Movement Thursdays, hosted by drum 'n' bass luminaries Bryan G and Ray Keith, is one of the best in England. While things get moving on the dance floor, the bar keeps up a mellower blend of hip-hop and soul. Also check out the Monday night party hosted by James Lavelle of UNKLE fame, who spins jazz and funky stuff to a less rowdy crowd. The vibe is chilled-out, focusing more on the music and social scene than on fashion or connections. Cool but within reach of those tired of the relentless pursuit of trendiness, Bar Rhumba is a standout.

Another venue with a strong reputation among the party people is **The End** (*18 West Central St.; Tel 0207/419-91-99; Tube to Tottenham Court Rd.; 10pm-3am Tue-Thur, till 5am Fri, till 7am Sat, 8pm-4am Sun; No credit cards*), the undisputed clubber's club, boasting one of the best sound systems in England. Massive crowds jam the dance floor each night. The music tends toward the rave-oriented, with house, jungle, techno, and garage all well represented alongside chiller sounds and hip-hop. Its location not far from Soho and the rest of the West End guarantees a slightly pricey cover (£8 to £13), but it's well worth it.

Another destination for those in search of well-heeled hedonism is the world-famous **Ministry of Sound** (*103 Gaunt St.; Tel 0207/378-65-28; Tube to Elephant and Castle; 10:30pm-6am Fri, midnight-9am Sat; Cover £10-15; No credit cards*), London's answer to the bygone New York superclub. Featuring internationally renowned DJs spinning uptempo house, techno, trance, and breaks, Ministry attracts a decked-out mob of seriously intoxicated clubbers stoked to dance until dawn. The downsides include occasionally brutal cover charges and choosy bouncers enforcing the smart dress code.

The Scala (*275 Pentonville Rd.; Tel 0207/833-20-19; Tube to King's Cross/St. Pancras; 8pm-2am Mon-Thur, 10pm-5am Fri, Sat, 7pm-midnight Sun; www.scala-london.co.uk; No credit cards*) does it all—food, drinks, cinema, theater—but it remains best-known for its club nights. Just north of collegiate Bloomsbury in a drab part of town, Scala's multiple floors and varied attractions draw a down-to-earth crowd of punters and hotties. The club's featured musical styles are eclectic, with Thursday night *Scratch* parties bringing top hip-hop to London, complete with some of the best break dancing this side of *Beat Street*. Other nights offer up anything from reggae to alt theater.

Subterania (*12 Acklam Rd.; Tel 0208/960-45-90; Tube to Ladbroke Grove; 8pm-2am Mon-Thur, 10pm-3am Fri, Sat, 8pm-midnight Sun; AE, MC, V*), deservedly has a strong rep for booking quirky acts in its unusual space. Located underneath the elevated train tracks at the tail end of Portobello Market, this club aggressively supports up-and-coming talent like hip-hoppers Company Flow and also established acts like Israel Vibration. It's one of London's more consistently bumping venues, featuring a strong roster of hip-hop, dance, and R&B nights as well as one-off concerts and parties. When they aren't drinking, the patrons throng to the circular dance floor. There are a few tables and chairs set in odd nooks and crannies along the walls for those too shy to get funky.

Housed on an upper floor of what was once a gigantic church, **Mass** (*St. Matthews Church, Brixton Hill; Tel 0207/738-52-55; Tube to Brixton; 10pm-6am Fri-Sat, 6pm-1am Sun; MC, V*) is split into two rooms, one of which has a large stage. The other room features a balcony overlooking a downstairs dance floor and DJ booth. The dress code is street style and the

rules of the game

Although England's drinking age is 18, the only aspect of the liquor law that's strictly enforced regards drunk driving. So it looks like you can take a beer onto the streets without fear. As for recreational drugs, they're all illegal. Hash is commonplace, since it's relatively cheap, and hard drugs are around, but most party-goers seem to be happy with some drinks and the old club favorite, E. Needless to say, drugs of any type are risky. Most clubs either provide EMTs or can sort you out with the medical attention you need. Scary, huh?

diverse crowd couldn't care less. The music tends towards the dark and gritty, with both DJs and bands representing on the weekends. Known for going late, the party doesn't even get really packed until after other bars and pubs have closed down for the night. Highlights include the monthly installment of Bar Rhumba's *Movement* party, as well as the funky hybrid of Indian instrumentation and electronic energy at *Air Swaraj*.

Hit happenin' EC1 with a night at **Fabric** *(77A Charterhouse St.; Tel 0207/490-04-44; Tube to Farringdon; Open regular club days and hours; www.fabric-london.com)*, which, along with Home, are two of the newer clubs to hit London's larger-than-life clubbing scene, with the intention of seducing a range of clubbers not only in the 18-24 division. The three dance floors are outfitted with audiovisual technology to make the most jaded DJ weep, including satellite-ready plasma screens. If you need a break from the deep house, U.S. garage, breakbeats, and drum 'n' bass, there's an escape route via an elevator to the roof terrace.

Home *(1 Leicester Sq.; Tel 0207/964-19-99; Tube to Leicester Sq.; Open regular club days and hours)* is spread luxuriously over seven floors, with a top-floor restaurant, a members bar below—named aptly enough for the cooler-than-thou 'At Home'—a club bar, and the main event, a double-volume, 1,200 capacity dance space. There's also another dance floor as well as a multimedia cafe (why not?), but the devoted 'homies' go Home more for the trancey house and garage, not to mention the appeal of Saturdays with resident DJ Paul Oakenfeld.

If you're not a lover of garage, and perhaps are not even too sure what that means when it doesn't refer to the place where you put your car, and are longing for some good, old-fashioned disco (i.e., mainstream dance tunes), both the **Hippodrome** *(Charing Cross Rd.; Tel 0207/437-43-11; Tube to Leicester Sq.; Thur-Sat)* and **Equinox** *(Leicester Sq.; Tel 0207/437-14-46; Tube to Leicester Sq.; Open regular club days and hours)* on Leicester Square, have going what you're craving. The Hippodrome is majorly untrendy when it comes to what's hot in London now, but it can't be beat for a larger-than-life laser, lights, dancers-in-a-cage-type feel. You'll probably bump into more tourists here than at Fabric, for instance, but at least when the Backstreet Boys come on the sound system, you'll know you're among kindred spirits.

ARTS SCENE

Having spent the past decade dragging itself out of the doghouse, London has rebounded big time. Art, music, film, fashion, and food have become some of London's hottest cultural exports—including Saatchi's *Sensation* that created all the hoopla in New York—attracting all manner of artists and fashionistas to its galleries, boutiques, and special events, like the incomparably stylish biannual London Fashion Week.

▸▸VISUAL ARTS

In addition to the major museums and galleries, London has established itself as a place of contemporary innovation. When bad boys like Damien Hirst are already part of the art establishment, the door opens even further for new talent to push the boundaries.

One of the biggest of these edgy arts spaces is the **Slaughterhouse Gallery** *(63 Charterhouse St.; Tel 0207/490-08-47; Tube to Farringdon or Barbican; 11am-6pm daily; Free admission).* Located opposite a meat market in Clerkenwell, the gallery's name is a reminder of the underground space's former use.

Slightly more pleasant is the massive studio complex **Delfina** *(50 Bermondsey St.; Tel 0207/357-66-00; Tube to London Bridge; 10am-5pm Mon-Fri, 2-5pm Sat, Sun; Free admission).* This relatively new studio/gallery/restaurant grants free studio spaces to international as well as British artists, which has its obvious risks as well as rewards....

Whitechapel Open Studios *(Whitechapel High St.; Tel 0207/522-7878; Tube to Aldgate East; 11am-5pm Tue-Sun, 11am-8pm Wed; Free)* is a great place to check out East London's edgy talent. They show a variety of media, most of it cool, some of it sexy, and all of it provocative.

The **White Cube** *(2 Duke St.; Tube to Green Park; www.white cube.com)* and now the **White Cube 2** *(48 Hoxton Sq., Shoreditch; Tube to Liverpool St., bus to Shoreditch)* are two ultra-white, ultra-bright modern little art exhibition spaces. White Cube 2 consists of one very brightly top lit room in the lovely, tucked-away Hoxton Square, with two giant brick and glass front doors making a dramatic opening statement. Much like the **Saatchi Gallery** [see *culture zoo*, below], they both showcase lots of the controversial contemporary British artists, such as the aforementioned Hirst.

While not strictly on the artistic fringe, the **Cartoon Art Trust** *(67-68 Hatton Garden; Tel 0207/405-47-17; Tube to Chancery Lane or Farringdon; 10am-5pm Mon-Sat, noon-5pm Sun; Free admission)* has a cool schedule of rotating shows dedicated to historic as well as modern cartoon art.

▸▸FASHION

As one of the world's most fashionable cities, London starts trends and creates styles. Top designers like Jean-Paul Gaultier regularly scope out what the kids are wearing on the street for inspiration, and the rest of the world looks to the biannual **London Fashion Week** *(for information and tickets: Tel 0120/342-64-12, Fax 0120/342-64-11; www. londonfashionweek.co.uk)*

Taking place in February and September, London's biggest fashion event features around 140 designer collections worn by the world's top models. Held in a large tent, this three-ring fashion circus has become the most important style event outside Paris or Milan, featuring luminaries such as Alexander McQueen, Hussein Chalayan, Nicole Farhi, and Tristan Webber. Although attendance at many shows is by invitation only, some events organized around Fashion Week are open to the public.

▶▶**PERFORMING ARTS**

It's no surprise there's a full range of theater and dance in London, for every budget and taste. And if that's not for you, there are plenty of movie theaters. Listings can be found in *Time Out* as well as the

bookworms

Though the literary scenes London once hosted—like Dr. Johnson's or Virginia Woolf's—no longer exist, the city does have a bookish side. In addition to being more articulate than most Americans, it would appear that the English read more, too. One of the newer and cooler celebrations of the English scene is the **Clerkenwell Literary Festival** *(www.clerkenwell.barts.com)*, held each July. Sponsored by artsy heavy hitters like David Bowie, the festival is a multimedia celebration of new and old works and their connections to the rest of London's vibrant arts scene. Held in venues as diverse as Dickens' house and **Turnmills** [see *gay scene,* below], the festival includes films and performances by DJs and groups like the Beta Band. Readings and the like take place every day in a variety of changing venues all over the city. Check *Time Out* or **Waterstone's** bookstore [see *stuff,* below] for specs.

The highbrow and lowbrow mix pretty comfortably here, as witnessed by the yearly furor over the prestigious Booker prize. Everyone argues over the final outcome—in 1977, Chairman Philip Larkin threatened to jump out a window if Paul Scott's *Staying On* didn't win (it did)—and the result is almost always unpopular with the critics. This distinctly eggheaded passion is matched only by the excitement generated at betting shops when people wager on the outcome of this literary event. Booker and bookies—a match made in England's green and pleasant land.

ELEMENTS of design

From the outrageous window displays of Carnaby Street to the sleek interiors of Ian Schrager's latest hotel, London cool is never more present than when it involves interior design. There are a coupla spots to check out on a day's wandering that offer a taste of what some of the hottest designers about are up to. The aforementioned Ian Schrager has two hotels in the city: **St. Martin's Lane** *(45 St. Martin's Lane, off Trafalgar Square)* and the **Sanderson** *(50 Berners St, off Oxford St.).* The windows in the rooms of St. Martin's change color according to the preference of each guest, so at night you're ensured a dazzling rainbow effect from the street below. At his other hotel, off Oxford Street, the lobby and Purple Bar are definitely worth a scope. From sparsely placed funky bits of furniture, including a replica of Dali's lips, to the reception counter that has some kind of luminescent screen covering it with a naked figure that walks across, to the elevators that feel as if you've stepped into the galaxy, the Sanderson has so many novelties and gimmicks that you can be entertained without even checking in. Off Brick Lane [see *five of the best ethnic eats,* below] is a cluster of stores selling clothes, furniture, and housewares but, above all, selling design elements. **Eat my Handbag Bitch** *(6 Dray Walk, 91-95 Bridge Lane; Tel 0207/375-31-00; www.eatmyhandbagbitch.co.uk)* is certainly not your most conventional of store names, and the 20th-century vintage stuff inside isn't either. Two doors down is the **World Design Laboratory,** which is more like a carnival ride than a shop. In order to actually get inside, you have to walk through a dark tunnel (with musical accompaniment) into a room lit so brightly you might need to grab some ultra-trendy sunglasses in one of the cabinets to shield your eyes. In this temple of weirdness, the odd pair of jeans hangs on a rack from plastic, see-through pipes that make it appear as if they're floating in mid-air. For some more conventional consumer fun, the chain store **Muji** (which means 'no brand goods' in Japanese) *(187 Oxford St.; Tel 0207/437-75-03 and 77 King's Rd.; Tel 0207/352-71-48; Branches all over; Prices vary for goods from £1 to over £100)* sells everything from tank tops to erasers. The rich display of stationery, kitchenware, furniture, and toiletries illustrates typical Japanese flair when it comes to effortlessly combining minimalism, functionality, and elegance in anything.

festivals and events

Although annual street festivals like the **Caribbean Notting Hill Carnival** (*3 days during the Bank Holiday Weekend in late Aug; Tel 0208/964-05-44*) and **Greenwich and Docklands Festival** (*Mid-July; Tel 0208/305-18-18*) and music festivals such as the **London Fleadh** (*One day in mid-June; Finsbury Park; Tube to Finsbury Park*), modern Irish and Celtic extravaganza, and the South Bank's **Coin Street Festival** (*Through July and Aug, along the South Bank in venues such as Oxo Tower Wharf, Gabriel's Wharf, and the Riverside Walkway; Tel 0207/401-22-55*) promise mayhem in certain parts of the city, the real action lies in the English countryside, which hosts several Woodstock-scale festivals between May and September.

Touted as the best of the festivals, **Homelands** (*End of May; The Bowl in Matterley Estate, Winchester; Tel 0208/963-09-40; www.homelands-uk.com*) has eight arenas featuring the freshest European and American electronic acts like the Chemical Brothers and DJ Shadow.

Glastonbury (*End of June; Worthy Farm, Pilton, Somerset; Tel 0906/708-08-08; www.glastonbury-festival.co.uk*): A rock 'n' roll extravaganza hosting 200,000 fans, Glastonbury is the most diverse of the summer jams. The festival features music ranging from indie rock to jazz to reggae on nine stages. Other attractions include food stalls, a kids' area, and acres of muddy English farmland. Sadly, the 2001 festival was cancelled, but it should be back bigger and better than ever in 2002.

Big Day Out (*Second week of July; The National Bowl, Milton*

weekend supplements of London's major newspapers. Prices vary from reasonable to astronomical, but discounts are often available to students and young people. Booking through services like **Globaltickets** (*Tel 0207/734-45-55*) can sometimes get you into sold-out West End events, but often with a hefty premium. For bargain tickets, check the **Half-Price Ticket Booth** in Leicester Square on the day of show. Your best bet is to call the venue ahead of time to book (this applies to movies, too).

London's crawling with theaters. Big, glitzy productions take place in the West End, which stretches from Piccadilly Circus, along Shaftesbury Avenue, to Covent Garden and the Strand. If Andrew Lloyd Webber doesn't light your wick, loads of Shakespearean theater, opera, and fringe events provide excellent alternatives.

The **Barbican Centre** (*Silk St.; Tel 0207/638-88-91; Tube to Moorgate or Barbican; £12-42; AE, MC, V*) has regular seasons by both the Royal

Keynes): While heavy metal may have suffered a severe loss of popularity in the States, English fans still turn out in droves to feel the noise. Located 45 minutes outside of London, Big Day Out books big names like Metallica and Marilyn Manson alongside their English counterparts.

Womad *(End of July; Rivermead Centre, Reading; Tel 01225/744-494; realworld.on.net/womad):* Started by Peter Gabriel, Womad is a multiday world-music smorgasbord. In addition to performers from across the globe, the festival features international food and art displays. More family-friendly than most, Womad features a children's area and swimming pool.

Be aware that these festivals face steep competition from at least a dozen similar events scheduled each summer. Due to the scale and quantity of the festivals, locations, lineups, dates, and even the events themselves are subject to change or cancellation. **National Express** *(Tel 08705/010-104, www.nationalexpress.co.uk)* runs special bus trips to and from many of the bigger events, with prices included in the entry fee.

The **Bishopstock Blues Festival** *(Last week of May for a couple of days; Bishop's Court Palace, Exeter, Devon; Tel 01392/875-220, Fax 01392/876-528)* is billed as the UK's premier blues festival and is set in the grounds of an 850-year-old Gothic Revival palace. Last year's highlight was John Lee Hooker, and the organizers set a limit on allowing only 5,000 people in per day, so you gotta know this is a fairly sought-after event. The relaxing vibe comes catered and with full bar facilities.

Shakespeare Company and the London Symphony Orchestra. The monolithic arts complex also houses a three-screen cinema and gallery spaces.

Funky and unconventional performances combine with avant-garde art, photography, dance and cinema at the **ICA** *(The Mall; Tel 0207/930-36-47; Tube to Charing Cross or Piccadilly Circus; MC, V),* which also hosts lectures and club nights. Recent events included a showing of Swedish director Roy Anderson's *Songs from the 2nd floor* and the regular digital arts event *Cybersalon.*

Serious theatergoers stick to the off-West End scene. **The Bush** *(Shepherds Bush Green; Tel 0208/743-33-88; Tube to Goldhawk Rd.; MC, V)* has a reputation as a top theater committed to up-and-coming writers. Getting seats can be tricky, due to the theater's tiny size and its immense popularity.

Maybe the most significant off-West End theater, the **Royal Court** *(Sloane Sq.; Tel 0207/565-50-50; Tube to Sloane Sq.; MC, V),* has now returned to its home in Sloane Square after a lengthy exile for renovations. Known as the top venue for new writers, the works performed here often raise a few eyebrows.

Virtually all of England's professional dancers make their living in London. Among the many dance troupes and companies, standouts include the Royal Ballet, the Adzido Pan-African Dance Ensemble, and the Richard Alston Dance Company.

The top venue for ballet is the **Royal Opera House** *(Bow St.; Tel 0207/304-40-00; Tube to Covent Garden; AE, MC, V)*, a gorgeous, grand old theater that is the home of the Royal Ballet. Be prepared to pay up big-time (over £40) for tickets.

Contemporary and brand-new works are consistently strong at **The Place** *(17 Duke's Rd.; Tel 0207/387-00-31; Tube to Euston; MC, V)*, which hosts the Richard Alston Dance Company as well as performers from around the world.

The newly renovated **Sadler's Wells Theatre** *(Rosebery Ave.; Tel 0207/863-80-00; Tube to Angel; £8-35; AE, MC, V)* also has a strong reputation built on its eclectic schedule of local and international talent. The theater also hosts seasons by the English National Ballet.

Smokers and the people who love them should check listings to see if there's a movie worth seeing at the **Notting Hill Coronet** *(Notting Hill Gate; Tel 0207/727-67-05; Tube to Notting Hill Gate; MC, V)*. This theater is probably the last in London to allow smoking in the auditorium. It shows mostly American flicks, which debut a couple of months after their Stateside premieres.

For all the blockbusters, check out the **Odeon Marble Arch** *(10 Edgware Rd.; Tel 0870/505-00-07; Tube to Marble Arch; MC, V)*, home of London's largest screen.

Art-house pictures and foreign films are fixtures at the Barbican Centre and the ICA [see above for both]. Both of these multimedia venues feature film series as well as one-off oddities.

gay scene

When there was a terrorist attack on the popular Admiral Duncan bar in the heart of gay Soho, there was a public outpouring of sympathy and rage. So, while intolerant lunatics can exist everywhere, the general attitude toward gay life here is accepting and supportive. London's queer population is visible and vocal, and the gay community has loads of bars, clubs, shops, and services in and around Soho. Although there are plenty of exclusively gay clubs and bars around town, mixed nights are currently enormously popular, allowing circuit boys and the straight girls who love them (and every other combo) to party together. In addition to *Time Out* and the handful of widely available free gay mags, hotlines like the **Gay and Lesbian Switchboard** *(Tel 0207/837-73-24; 24 hours)* and the **London Lesbian Line** *(Tel 0207/251-69-11; 2-10pm Mon, Fri, 7-10pm Tue-Thur)* provide info on all types of goings-on around town.

Organizations like **Outrage** *(Tel 0207/439-23-81)* and **Stonewall**

(Tel 0207/336-88-60) are very active on issues like legal inequality and homophobia. Additionally, large events like the annual **Gay and Lesbian Mardi Gras** *(Tel 0906/302-27-79; www.londonmardigras.com for dates and info)* and the **Lesbian and Gay Film Festival** *(National Film Theatre, South Bank; Tel 0207/928-32-32; Tube to Waterloo)* provide ample opportunities to party with a purpose (who could ask for more?). Check the free weekly *Pink Paper*, available at newsstands and many shops in Soho, for more info.

As one of the battlefields in the struggle for gay rights, the **Admiral Duncan** *(54 Old Compton St.; Tel 0207/437-53-00; Tube to Leicester Sq.; 11am-11pm Mon-Sat, noon-10:30pm Sun; V, MC, AE)* stands as a rainbow-festooned declaration of gay resistance to intolerance. Reopened after the tragic bombing that tore the place apart, this traditional gay bar is a lively and crowded refuge for gay London.

Noted as one of the few gay bars with a happy hour, **Bar Code** *(3-4 Archer St.; Tel 0207/734-33-42; Tube to Picadilly Circus; 1pm-midnight Mon-Sat; V, MC)* gets really out of control between 5:30 and 6:30pm. Packed with young folks getting as trashed as possible, so you'll never notice the lack of decor. While some might mind the scuzzy upstairs, few seem to mind the downstairs dance floor, which is lit mainly by a charmingly sorry set of disco lights.

Walking the length of the bar at **Compton's of Soho** *(51-53 Old Compton St.; Tel 0207/479-79-61; Tube to Leicester Sq.; Noon-11pm Mon-Sat, noon-10:30pm Sun; MC, V)* almost guarantees a visual undressing by other patrons, as the place is overwhelmingly patronized by men on the prowl. With loud music and aggressive come-ons aplenty, this place will disappoint those in search of a quiet pint and good conversation.

Known mostly as a gay man's hangout, Soho also has a few lesbian-only haunts. The first and best-known is **Candy Bar** *(4 Carlisle St.; Tel 0207/494-40-41; Tube to Tottenham Court Rd.; 5pm-midnight Mon-Thur, till 2am Fri, 2pm-2am Sat, 1-11pm Sun; No credit cards)*. Occupying two floors, this compact and stylish bar is teeming with friendly dykes enjoying the uncommonly man-free surroundings.

Some of the most popular DJs in London are regulars at gay clubs and club nights. One venue which consistently draws top talent to its gay nights is **Heaven** *(Villiers St.; Tel 0207/930-20-20; Tube to Charing Cross or Embankment; 10:30pm-5am daily; No credit cards)*. Renowned for its dance floor, this 2,000-capacity club attracts way more boys than girls, though that may not be the case on mixed nights.

Ranking a close second on the gay club-ometer are the Trade parties rocking the **London Astoria** *(157 Charing Cross Rd.; Tel 0207/734-69-63; Tube to Tottenham Court Rd.; 5am Sat night till late Sun afternoon; No credit cards)*. A massive and legendary party renowned in gay and straight circles, *Trade* is a fierce end to a debauched weekend, full of sweaty, wide-eyed clubbers hoping Monday never comes.

The ever-popular **Turnmills** *(63 Clerkenwell Rd.; Tel 0207/250-34-*

09; Tube to Farringdon; Late-license hours; No credit cards), one-time host of Trade, still has the occasional gay event. A staple of London's club scene, Turnmills has several different hangs, from classy coffee bar to a two-level dance floor in the big room.

Capitalizing on the current trend toward mixed clubbing, **Freedom** (60-66 Wardour St.; Tel 0207/734-00-71; Tube to Tottenham Court Rd.; 11am-3am Mon-Sat, till 11pm Sun; MC, V) attracts a super-trendy mob of fashion types with its futuro-loungey interior and posh cocktails. The sweaty dance floor downstairs comically mixes shirtless men flexing their pecs and girls attempting to dance in too-tight dresses.

CULTUre ZOO

If culture could kill, you'd be dead in London. The Empire stretched far and wide, grabbing loads of great loot along the way. So it's all here, and your greatest problems will be time and money. There's so much history and culture here, you could spend your whole life exploring it. Here are the greatest hits—plus a few old & moldies we had to throw in, against our better judgement.

The little-known White Card, which can be purchased at Tourist Info booths [see *need to know*, below], entitles you to wander a slew of museums freely for three or seven days and might end up saving you a bundle. You can probably sneak out (if so inclined) and see all the corny royal stuff while your hip friends are still sleeping off a hangover.

The most recent exciting cultural news in London has been the development of the city's South Bank. Much press has been devoted to the new Tate Museum of Modern Art, the Millennium Bridge (the first Thames crossing built in a century), by Sir Norman Foster, that links Bankside with St. Paul's Cathedral, and the London Eye (the massive big wheel that moves continuously very slowly). Shakespeare's Globe has also recently undergone a refurbishment and the oldest working theater in the United Kingdom, the Old Vic, is also here. There's also no shortage of trendy places to have a bite, a beer, or do some shopping. Oxo Tower Wharf and Gabriel's Wharf are two spots for these sorts of pursuits. To get to Bankside, get out at the Black Friars, London Bridge, Southwark, or Monument Tube stops.

In Shakespeare's time, there were tons of pubs, theaters, and inns here, making the South Bank area a lot more bustling and seedy. People would look across the Thames River (as the masses couldn't read in those days) and if there was a flag on the flagpole, that meant that there was a show on that day. Today, you can just pick up a program from the Globe Theatre, or check on the Web.

Tate Modern (Bankside Power Station, The Queen's Walk; Tel 0207/887-88-88, Fax 0207/887-88-98; 10am-6pm Sun-Thur, 10am-10pm Fri-Sat; www.tate.org.uk/modern; Free admission except for special shows): This behemoth of a building is matched inside by quadruple-volume spaces and massive iron sculptures by Louise Bourgeois. The

down and out

In a city as expensive as London, keeping amused without breaking the bank is pretty difficult. Window shopping never costs a penny, and just walking around markets like Camden is an activity unto itself. Plenty of the museums and galleries, like the **Slaughterhouse Gallery,** the **Cartoon Art Trust**, the **Tate Gallery,** the **National Gallery,** and the **British Museum** [see *arts scene*, above, and *culture zoo*, below] charge no entrance fee, providing culture on the cheap. Weather permitting, London's parks are ideal for walks or lazy picnics. At night, the view from **Primrose Hill** [see *hanging out*, above] will take your mind off any and all financial problems. Then there are bars like **Dogstar** [see *bar scene*, above], with no cover during the week and double shots for the price of a single. Imagination and some self-restraint go a long way in London. If your budget is still getting you down, find an orange crate to stand on and vent your frustrations at **Speakers Corner,** where whining (and shouting and gesticulating wildly) have become a cultural institution [see *culture zoo*, below]. Then, after dark, head to the center of **Piccadilly Circus** and sit by the fountain. Either gaze at the huge electronic billboards and watch the moveable feast go by, or strike up a chat with some other West End wanderer. The fountain is always brimming with hangers-out.

actual gallery rooms on the third and fifth floors are by and large a bit pokey, though. Divided up into themes (instead of in chronological order or according to 'isms'), the paintings and sculptures deal with History/Memory/Society, Nude/Action/Body, Landscape/Matter/Environment, Still Life/Object/Real Life, and 'Between Cinema and a Hard Place.' At times, the magnificent panoramic views visible through the floor-to-ceiling glass windows outdo the art on display. Especially the sight of St. Paul's Cathedral directly ahead.

Shakespeare's Globe Theatre *(21 New Globe walk, opposite the Bankside Pier; Tel 0207/401-99-19 or Tel 0207/887-88-88, Fax 0207/902-15-15; 9am-noon daily May-Sept, 10am-5pm daily Oct-Apr; Performances May 12-Sept 24; www.shakespeares-globe.org; £7.50, £6 students; Tickets £5-£26):* Here you'll find the biggest exhibition devoted to the world of Shakespeare from Elizabethan times to today. Documenting everything from blueprints to corsets, the more interesting part of the building is the actual theater, which is open only in summer, when the Shakespeare productions are performed. The original site of the theater is around the corner, where there is a plaque and

not your average religious experience

Hawksmoor's Christ Church in Spital-fields, near the market, is considered by many to be one of London's most beautiful churches. It was designed by Nicholas Hawksmoor and Sir Christopher Wren, one of England's most famous architects (he was responsible for St. Paul's Cathedral). Constructed between 1715 and 1759, the church falls into the English Baroque style and features a dramatic Georgian steeple rising from a grand portico. The Parish church **St. Martin-in-the-Fields** *(Trafalgar Sq., Tube to Charing Cross; Open daily 10am-6pm, free lunchtime concerts daily at 1pm, candlelit recitals in the evenings)* was designed by James Gibbs and dates from the 18th century. However, there has been a church on this site since the 13th century, so the name derives from the time when the site actually was in the fields, between Westminster and the City. The white stone exterior and elaborate spire come into their own at night when floodlit. **Shri Swaminarayan Mandir** *(105-115 Brentfield Rd., Neasden, just off the North Circular Rd.; Tube to Neasden; Tel 0208/965-26-51; Open 9am-noon and 4-6pm Apr-Oct and Nov-Mar; £2)* is Europe's first traditional Hindu Temple. Built in 1995, it is a replica of the Akshardam temple in western India. It was created with 26,300 pieces of limestone and marble crafted by over 1,500 sculptors in India, and then shipped to London to be erected, all at a cost of about £10 million. The **Central Mosque** *(Tube to St. John's Wood),* on the western side of Regents Park, is the largest Islamic Center in Britain. First opened in 1978, the building has a minimalist design with a couple of dazzling touches such as the minaret and the golden dome, which was designed by Frederick Gibberd. The oldest surviving Parish church in London, built between 1123 and 1250, and possibly the most beautiful, **St. Bartholomew The Great** *(Enter through Tudor-style gate called Smithfield Gate, at the cloth fair; Tube to Barbican)* also has a movie star résumé: It made appearances in *Four Weddings and a Funeral* and *Shakespeare in Love.*

some informational boards. The Globe has been reproduced as closely as possible to an Elizabethan theater, and the tour guides will tell you (since they're often asked) that *Shakespeare in Love* was not filmed here. For the movie, the theater was reproduced in Shepperton Studios.

The Rose *(56 Park St., off the Globe walk; Tel 0207/593-00-26; Open daily; www.rdg.ac.uk/Rose/; £3, £2.50 students):* Just around the corner from the Globe Theatre is the archaeological site of the theater where plays by Henslowe, Shakespeare, and Marlowe were performed. Built in 1587, this was the first theater on Bankside. Its remains were discovered in 1989 and are being excavated and conserved. Since there is only a sound and light show at the site illustrating the story of The Rose, a brief walk by would probably suffice.

London Eye *(Riverside Building, County hall, Westminster Bridge Rd.; Tel 0870/500-06-00 for pre-bookings; 9am-10pm Apr 1-Sept 10, 10am-6pm Sept 11-Mar 31; www.british-airways.com/londoneye; £7.45 Jan-May, £7.95 June-Dec):* The big wheel you see looming over the Thames with cable cars attached to it is not a temporary carnival attraction, it's the spanking new observation wheel, which turns continuously all day long and provides panoramic views of the city. Arrive early or prepare to languish in endless lines for a chance to hop on the contraption.

Dalí Universe *(County hall, Riverside Building; Tel 0207/620-24-20; Tube to Waterloo or Westminster; 10am-5:30pm daily; www.daliuniverse.com; £8.50, £6 students):* If you're a Dalí enthusiast, this is definitely worth a visit since it is the first permanent commercial Dalí exhibition in the world, comprising four galleries of over 30,000 square feet. The collection of about 500 sculptures and drawings includes the Mae West sofa (the giant red lips), and a selection of dripping clocks. Located right next to the London Eye, the galleries make for a surreal contrast to the super-symmetrical engineering of the big wheel.

Hayward Gallery *(Tel 0207/960-42-42; 10am-6pm daily, till 8pm Tue-Wed, 10pm Fri; www.hayward-gallery.org.uk; £6, £4 students):* This modern art gallery merits a mention since it is the largest public art space in the UK. It features everything from modern masters to contemporary names, showcasing controversial exhibits similar to those at the Saatchi Gallery.

The **Design Museum** *(Butler's Wharf, Shad Thames; Tel 0207/378-60-55; www.designmuseum.org; Tube to Tower Hill or London Bridge, then short walk; 10:30am-6pm Mon-Fri, noon-6pm Sat, Sun; £5.25, £4.50 students):* A monument to all things usefully beautiful (i.e., functional art), it is vastly more appealing than the over-touristed Tower of London, which sits just across the Thames. Unless you have a thing for old prisons, you creepy thing. (If you do, however, make sure to go first thing in the morning so you don't get crushed with the other creepies.)

Serpentine Gallery *(Kensington Gardens; Tel 0207/298-15-15; Tube to Knightsbridge, Lancaster Gate or South Kensington; 10am-6pm daily; www.serpentinegallery.org; Free admission):* Back in the center of the city and certainly worth a detour if you're in Hyde Park, this gallery is the exhibition site for contemporary artists. The structure was a tea pavilion in 1934 and now houses modern art exhibits that change every two to three months. A recent, particularly interesting exhibit, called *The Greenhouse Effect,* illustrated the links between the display of nature in the gardens and the display of nature in the gallery by turning the Serpentine into a conceptual greenhouse. Sculptures included *Bird*, a small skeleton of a bird made from the artists' fingernail parings and superglue, as well as a full-size apple tree in a mound of dirt in the entrance. The most interesting exhibit, though, was an aviary with live parrots inside that were trained to learn the sounds of an extinct language. These are the only living 'speakers' of the language of the Maypure—a Caribbean Indian tribe that was annihilated by a neighboring tribe.

Saatchi Gallery *(98a Boundary Rd.; Tel 0207/624-82-99; Tube to Swiss Cottage or St. John's Wood; Noon-6pm Thur-Sun; £4):* Bankrolled by ultra-wealthy advertising kingpin Charles Saatchi, the gallery exported its *Sensations* and hosts bizarre exhibitions and installations, including a room half-filled with sump oil. The tree-filled suburban location of this venue (in the quiet, upmarket St. John's Wood) stands in contrast to its wide-open space of oddities, illusions, and eye-openers.

St. Paul's Cathedral *(St. Paul's Churchyard; Tel 0207/236-41-28; Tube to St. Paul's; Open 8:30am-4pm Mon-Sat, galleries open 9:30am-4pm Mon-Sat; Cathedral £4 adults, galleries £3.50 adults):* Famous for the wedding of Charles and Diana in 1981 (watched by over 900 million people all over the world), this cathedral is an indelible part of the London skyline. The present building dates back to 1675. In 1666, the great fire of London destroyed St. Paul's and, as a result, the great architect of the day, Sir Christopher Wren, was appointed to design a new cathedral. The great dome became the symbol of English survival during the blitz or WWII.

Westminster Abbey *(Parliament Sq.; Tel 0207/222-51-52; Tube to Westminster or St. James's Park; 9:15am-3:45pm Mon-Fri, 9:15am-1:45pm and 4pm-4:45pm Sat; £5 adults, £3 students):* A tour through this focal monument of English political and religious life will teach you more than you ever wanted to know about medieval British history. Most of England's kings and queens have been crowned here and many have been buried here, including Elizabeth I.

Kensington Palace *(Kensington Palace Gardens; Tel 0207/937-95-61; Tube to High St. Kensington, Queensway, or Bayswater; 10am-5pm daily in summer, 10am-4pm daily in winter; £8.50 adults, £6.70 students):* Supremely luxurious and rich with history, this is the one-time home of Princess Diana and well worth a visit for royal buffs and those with delusions of grandeur.

Houses of Parliament and **Big Ben** *(Bridge St. and Parliament Sq.; Tel 0207/219-42-72 House of Commons, Tel 0207/219-31-07 House of Lords; Tube to Westminster; House of Commons: from 2:30pm Mon, Tue, from 3:30 Thur, from 9:30am Wed, from 11:30am Thur; House of Lords: from 2:30pm Mon-Wed, from 3pm Thur; Free admission):* Standing gloriously on the Thames, these buildings add another striking aspect to the city's skyline. Benjamin Clock is about as characteristic of England as the Statue of Liberty is of New York. Visiting the House of Commons is a unique experience. The debates are certainly colorful and watching Tony Blair in action is a somewhat surreal experience.

British Museum *(Great Russell St.; Tel 0207/636-15-55; Tube to Tottenham Court Rd. or Holborn; 10am-5pm Mon-Sat, noon-6pm Sun; www.britishmuseum.ac.uk; Free admission):* There's something for everyone in this giant storehouse of goodies gotten (and misbegotten) during the days of the Empire. It features around six million exhibits, not to mention the mummies!

Victoria and Albert Museum *(Cromwell Rd.; Tel 0207/938-84-41; Tube to S. Kensington; Noon-5:45pm Mon, 10am-5:45pm Tue-Sun; £5 adults, £3 students, free admission after 4:30pm):* Possibly the biggest museum devoted to applied arts, here is housed a gigantic collection of Asian art, modern design objects, and seven legendary tapestries by Raphael.

Museum of the Moving Image *(South Bank; Tel 0207/928-35-35; Tube to Waterloo; 10am-6pm daily; £6.25):* Beginning with shadow puppetry and optical toys from back in the day, the campy chronology is re-created in the flesh by costumed actors, and is at once informative and bizarrely entertaining.

Barbican Centre *(Silk St.; Tel 0207/382-71-05; Tube to Moorgate or Barbican; 10am-6:45pm Mon, Thur-Sat, till 5:45pm Tue, till 7:45pm Wed, noon-6:45pm Sun; £5):* Despite being written off as a wannabe Pompidou Center, here you will find some high-caliber contemporary art and photography exhibits in its main galleries. A recent David Bailey exhibit had huge Rolling Stones portraits staring down.

The Wallace Collection *(Hertford House, Manchester Sq., just north of Oxford St.; Tel 0207/935-06-87; Tube to Bond St. or Baker St.; 10am-5pm Mon-Sat, 2-5pm Sun; www.demon.co.uk/heriatge/wallace; Free admission):* Housed in a historic London town house, and not that well known to the visiting masses, this is formerly one of the world's most extensive private collections. It was made public in 1897 and contains an eclectic combination of work from several centuries: medieval and renaissance, European and Oriental arms and armor, Dutch genre painting, 18th and 19th English and French painting, furniture, and porcelain. However, the highlight of the museum is *The Swing* by Fragonard, painted in 1767. If you've ever studied art history, you've probably heard of this little, sparkling gem. Upon order of the family who bequeathed the collection, nothing has ever been added or loaned, thus reserving it as one of the greatest collections ever made by an English family.

National Gallery *(Trafalgar Sq.; Tel 0207/747-28-85; Tube to Charing Cross, Leicester Sq., Embankment, or Piccadilly Circus; 10am-6pm daily, till 9pm Wed; Free admission except for special shows):* Sure it's old hat, but what a hat! This is truly one of the great art museums of the world, with spectacular stuff spanning eight centuries. Da Vinci, Rembrandt, Van Gogh, they're all here, struttin' their stuff.

National Portrait Gallery *(St. Martin's Place; Tel 0207/306-00-55; Tube to Charing Cross, Leicester Sq.; 10am-6pm daily; Free admission):* A fine art album, this gallery displays a broad range of headshots, from the old and stodgy to the new and wacky. Check out Warhol's take on Queen Elizabeth.

Royal Academy of Arts *(Piccadilly; Tel 0207/300-80-00; Tube to Green Park or Piccadilly Circus; 10am-6pm daily, until 8:30pm Fri; www.royalacademy.org.uk; £7-8 admission, £5 students):* If you're in London during the months of May till August, check out the annual Summer Exhibition. Featured are rooms with hundreds of little paintings cluttered together on the walls as well as modern sculptures, drawings, and architectural models. One room is usually dedicated to the work of an individual artist while another sculptor is chosen to exhibit a large piece or pieces in the front courtyard of the building. The majority of the works are for sale and there are prizes awarded to the artists.

Tate Gallery *(Beside the Thames, Millbank; Tel 0207/887-80-00; Tube to Pimlico; 10am-5:50pm daily; Free admission):* Along with the new Tate Gallery of Modern Art, the entire contents of the original have been reorganized, so that instead of the conventional art-museum struc-

by foot

London may be one of Europe's largest cities, but the interesting sections of the city are within walking distance of one another. One of the best routes begins at the **Museum of the Moving Image** [see *culture zoo,* above] on the South Bank of the Thames. After zipping through the chronology of cinema, head out the door and down to the Millennium Mile, a park along the river's edge. Before heading off to the right, check out the skateboarders at **South Bank** [see *hanging out,* above]. The first big draw is the **Oxo Tower** *(Tel 0207/401-22-55; 11am-6pm daily),* directly accessible from the footpath. This arts development houses several galleries, shops, and restaurants. The best attraction, however, is the observation gallery on the eighth floor (open until 10pm). A few more minutes' walk down the path takes you by the **Tate Gallery of Modern Art.** Occupying an enormous space along the river bank, the museum houses the modern art collection of the **Tate Gallery** [see *culture zoo,* above, for both Tates]. Next comes the historic **Globe Theatre** [see *arts scene,* above], Shakespeare's famed playhouse. Still farther along, a few twists and and turns take walkers past **The Clink** *(Clink St.; Tel 0207/378-15-58; Tube to London Bridge; 10am-6pm daily; £4; No credit cards),* a prison-turned-museum full of displays about torture. The last stop along the Mile is the **Design Museum** [see *culture zoo,* above]. Cross the Tower Bridge to the north bank and zip past the dreadful lines at the **Tower of London** to reach the nearby Tube station.

ture that follows chronological order, the two Tates are designed thematically. In addition, the Tate Gallery now houses only British art—as well as work by some famous visitors to the city—as the modern art collection has been moved to the new Tate. Be sure to catch the misty Turners and the God-drunk Blakes.

modification

If pain (the good kind, silly) is on your travel itinerary, stop by **Hair By Fairy** *(8-10 Neal's Yard; Tel 0207/497-07-76; Tube to Covent Garden; 10am-6pm Mon-Sat, noon-5pm Sun; No credit cards)* for ear work or body piercing. Don't worry, the shop is registered with the local health authorities and the piercers all have first-aid training.

Or try **Into You** *(244 St. Johns St.; Tel 0207/253-50-85; Tube to Farringdon; Noon-7pm Tue, Wed, Fri, noon-9pm Thur, till 6pm Sat; AE, MC, V for jewelry, piercing, no credit cards for tattoos)*, an East London clearinghouse for all things pointy and primitive. This specialty studio will pierce or tattoo you almost anywhere, for a price.

Still another alternative is **Sacred Art** *(148 Albion Rd.; Tel 0207/254-22-23; Tube to Angel, bus 73; 11:30am-6:30pm Mon-Fri, 11am-6pm Sat; No credit cards)* in Stoke Newington. Located in North London, this modern mecca for all types of body-mod is known as the best in London.

Traveling takes its toll on one's appearance. Luckily, **Theorem** *(4 Cross St.; Tel 0207/354-97-13; Tube to Angel or Highbury Islington; 9am-7pm Mon-Sat; No credit cards)* can transform the wack-est hairstyle into something special. Phone ahead for an appointment and prices.

great outdoors

While lunch-break joggers usually hit the Millennium Mile on the South Bank of the Thames, the paths of **Regents Park** *(Tube to Regents Park)*, **Hyde Park** *(Tube to Knightsbridge)*, and **Hampstead Heath** *(Tube to Hampstead)* are where non-corporate joggers jog. A run, a power walk, or even a plain old saunter through Regents or Hyde Park will not only be a good dose of oxygen to counter London's pollution, but it's also an aesthetic treat. Regents is one of London's most genteel parks, offering boating, a bandstand, a cafe, and an open-air theater, which dates back to 1932. At the center is a lovely rose garden surrounding a small duck-filled pond with connecting Japanese bridges. The London Zoo is located in Regents Park, and even if you don't go in, the sight of giraffes sticking out of the top of the fence as you walk by is a weird sight in the middle of London. To the north of Regents Park, the 206-foot-high **Primrose Hill** *(Prince Albert Rd.; Tube to Camden Town)* is good for a quick climb and sharp intake of oxygen. Once at the top, it's prime positioning for kite-flying, picnicking, or just checking out the view of the city. Hyde Park, one of the biggest in the world, also has its fair share of gardens, ponds, trees, and a 41-acre lake called the Serpentine, where you can row or (ye gads!) swim. In-line skating is very big in Hyde Park. Not only is there a wide, flat stretch along the Serpentine, but also on many other paths that diverge into the green. Hampstead Heath is great for walking and the patches of grass get packed with picnickers, particularly on Sundays. Some of the heath is very wild, which makes for a nice contrast to London's heavily manicured parks, such as Regents. If you saw *Notting Hill* with Hugh Grant and Julia Roberts, you'll remember **Kenwood House** *(Hampstead Lane, Hampstead Heath; Tube to Hampstead; Open daily 10am-6pm Apr-Oct, 10am-4pm Nov-Mar; Free admission)* as the setting of the Henry James movie that Julia's character was starring in. Dating from the 17th century, the house was re-vamped in the 1760s for the Earl of Mansfield. The last private owner of the house was the Earl of Iveagh, an avid collector of 17th and 18th century art. When he died, he bequeathed the Rembrandts, Vermeers, van Dycks, and Gainsboroughs to the nation and they're now on public display here. Other highlights include the oval library, dating from the 18th century. The gardens, apart from acting as Hollywood locations, are also used for the occasional music concert. **Green Park** is very small in comparison to the ones mentioned above, but it's a convenient spot to walk through if you're at the Royal Academy [see *culture zoo*, above] and want to get to Buckingham Palace, since it links Piccadilly with The Mall. In summer, there are stripy deck chairs laid out. Not to mention that the park is situated right next to The Ritz Hotel, so it's worth a quick look for the associated glamour, at any rate. Linked to Green Park is **St. James's Park,** an equally beautiful stretch of manicured gardens with black swans in the river. The best feature of St. James's is the bridge: If you stand in the middle of it, you have a unique view of Buckingham Palace on one side and Whitehall on the other. Rental bikes are available at **Bikepark** [see *need to know,* below] in Covent Garden for £10 the first day, £5 the second, and £3 each successive day. And if all that sounds too tiring to your hungover ears, you can always chill out in one of the deck chairs scattered around the lawns.

Head to **Slam City Skates** *(16 Neal's Yard; Tel 0207/240-09-28; Tube to Covent Garden; 10am-6pm Mon-Sat; MC, V)* for info on events and competitions, and rentals.

If and when all the pubs, clubs, and bars start to get boring, call **Adrenalin Village** *(Chelsea Bridge Tower, Queenstown Rd.; Tel 0207/731-59-58; Tube to Sloane Sq., then bus 137; Noon-5pm Wed, Fri, 11am-6pm Sat, Sun; MC, V)* to book a bungee jump over Battersea Park. The price tag is £50.

If you suddenly get the hankering to glide on water, both **Docklands Watersports Club** *(Gate 16, King George V Dock, Woolwich Manor Way; Tel 0207/511-70-00; Tube to N. Woolwich Station)* and **Royal Docks Waterski Club** *(Gate 16, King George V Dock; Tel 0207/511-20-00; Tube to N. Woolwich Station)* provide all the necessary equipment. The former rents jet skis, while the latter has wakeboards as well as plain old water skis. Given the proximity to central London, don't expect crystal-blue waters or beautiful, bikini-clad beachgoers.

CITY WITHIN A CITY

Once the seat of the British Empire, London has a diverse population from all corners of the globe. While many internationals have assimilated seamlessly into English society, ethnic communities still pepper the city, creating their own rhythms and keeping London lively.

Concentrated in the north, London's Jewish community is visible in Golder's Green, where most of the city's Orthodox population resides. Aside from the synagogues and religious resources available in the area, this neighborhood beyond Hampstead also has the best bagels and delis in all of London. Sites of interest include the **Jewish Cemetery** *(Hoop Lane; Tube to Golder's Green; 8:30am-5pm Mon-Fri, Sun)*, a burial ground in use since 1895.

Much of London's Arab community shares the area around Queensway in Bayswater with the city's second-largest Chinese community (Chinatown is the biggest). Busy and prosperous, this stretch of shops and cafes is minutes from the big thoroughfare of Edgeware Road. The closest Tube station is Paddington.

On the way out of the prosperous central region of London, beyond the City, lies the infamous East End. Though renowned as a rough-and-tumble area plagued by crime and racism, London's eastern sectors aren't all dangerous. Spitalfields, an East End neighborhood, is home to much of the city's Indo-Pak population, as well as a bunch of artists. Accessible from Liverpool Street station, the area's markets, shops, and restaurants are among the best in East London. Check out Brick Lane on a weekend, when it's jammed with the local subcontinentals shopping and hanging out.

Most visible in Brixton, London's West Indian population is among the largest outside the Caribbean. Having come in the 1950s, the Afro-Caribbean community has kept a foothold in the area, which has become a hot spot for London's hipsters. The site of riots during the '80s, Brixton, located in South London, is plagued by racial problems and has a reputation for being dangerous. Both of these impressions seem a bit off when you visit the busy market along Electric Avenue just a few feet from the Brixton Tube station. The **Brixton Market** is open every day but Sunday, from 8:30am to 5:30pm, till 1pm Wednesdays.

STUff

The good news: London offers unbelievable shopping. The bad news: Everything costs way, way, too much money. Numerically, prices are equivalent to those in the U.S., only the currency is nearly twice as precious. So, unless you're a trust-fund baby or a newly minted web tycoon, shopping can be dangerous to your finances.

Although it's famed for its markets, there's more to London's shopping scene than the funky threads hawked at the Camden and Potabello markets. Boutiques from Soho to Covent Garden peddle the newest styles and designers, while bigger shops on Oxford Street and Kensington High Road offer more civilized shopping. And shoe fanatics and fetishists of all stripes will find their salvation on Neal Street, which sells footwear unlike anywhere else on earth.

If clothes aren't your bag, the mecca of DJ culture has everything for music junkies, from rare funk to unreleased promo vinyl. London's music superstores, like **Virgin** [see *stuff, below*], sell current albums alongside thousands of high-priced CDs. For more cutting-edge stuff, stick to the specialty shops.

▶▶USED AND BRUISED

For 18-hole oxblood Docs or the most outlandish orange nylon drawstring cargo pants, look no farther than **Camden Market** (*Camden High Rd. and Chalk Farm Rd.; Tube to Camden Town; 9am-6pm weekends; No credit cards at most stalls*), a hipster version of Marrakech. Visiting this indoor/outdoor market is an experience, not an activity. If all the bustle makes you hungry, dozens of vendors sell falafel, pad thai, and French fries for cheap.

Portobello Market (*Portobello Rd.; Tube to Notting Hill Gate; All day Fri and Sat*) in trendy Notting Hill (if you've seen the movie *Notting Hill*, it's the market that Hugh Grant walks through) is a great market to browse after brunch on a weekend. Head to the end of the market, away from the gate, to rummage for more vintage clothes and less fussy antiques.

The two lesser known markets, Brick Lane and Old Spitalfields, also offer some good finds. **Brick Lane** (*Brick Lane; Tube to Liverpool St.; market on Sun only*) sells vintage clothes and cheap cleaning products (not exactly the most likely of combos). It's also a good opportunity to check out the old Truman Brewery, which has now become a hangout and workspace for the local fashion, arts, and design crowds. Even though this is a primarily Bangladeshi community, there are an inordinate amount of funky design and furniture shops [see *elements of design,* above] on and off this strip.

Old Spitalfields (*Columbia Rd.; Sun*) is on the site of a once famous fruit and veggie market but now sells arts and crafts, old clothes, young designer labels, candles, organic produce, books, flowers, furniture, and food. If it's flowers you're after, though, head to Columbia Road, which on Sunday morning, comes alive with flowers, herbs, and all types of greenery.

▶▶DUDS

Skipping preppiness for the edgy looks of London's youth scenes, **Mash** *(73 Oxford St.; Tel 0207/434-96-09; Tube to Tottenham Court Rd.; 10am-6pm Mon-Sat, noon-5pm Sun; MC, V)* stocks a complete array of street, skate, and club clothing for both men and women. In addition to jeans, cargos, combats, fleeces, hoodies, and workwear, Mash sells skateboards, sneakers, videos, backpacks, and jewelry.

Keeping it real on the streetwear tip, but going for a more fashionable market, is the perennially cool **Red Or Dead** *(41-43 Neal St.; Tel 0207/379-75-71; Tube to Covent Garden; 10:30am-7pm Mon-Fri, 10am-6:30pm Sat, noon-5:30pm Sun; www.redordead.co.uk; MC, V)*. Selling shoes, accessories, and the clothes to go with them, Red Or Dead is a favorite of London's trendoid women, but they sell a small assortment of men's clothes too.

In the same vein, **Diesel** *(43 Earlham St.; Tel 0207/497-55-43; 10:30am-7pm Mon-Wed, Fri, Sat, till 8pm Thur, till 6pm Sun; AE, MC, V)* also works hard to make exceptional versions of everyday clothing. Housed on three floors abutting the pedestrian chaos of Neal Street, Diesel is always crowded with fashion-hungry men and women frantically racing to grab up the wares.

Importing the latest baggy and expensive gear from New York, **Home** *(39 Beak St.; Tel 0207/240-70-77; Tube to Oxford Circus; 10:30am-6:30pm Mon-Wed, Fri-Sun, 11am-7pm Thur; homesoho@aol.com; No credit cards)* sells American labels like Triple 5 Soul and cartoony designs by Paul Frank alongside courier bags and a selection of sneakers from the past 20 years.

The French are looking to hip-hop style! Run by a French hip-hop enthusiast, **Regular Store** *(Earlham St.; Tel 0207/240-26-25; Tube to Leicester Sq.; 11am-7pm Mon-Sat, 1-5:30pm Sun; www.regular_store.co.uk; MC, V)* sells a range of futuristic urban streetwear, watches, bags, and kicks. The basement record shop provides the perfect soundtrack—in French or English.

▶▶FOOT FETISH

The English may rate poorly regarding dental hygiene, but they outclass the competition when it comes to footwear of all varieties. While Camden High Street has its fair share of shoe stores, any serious shoe shopper should head to Neal Street, which has more cool shoe stores than any other strip in town.

The first name in shoe stores, **Shelly's** *(14 Neal St.; Tel 0207/240-37-26; Tube to Covent Garden; 10am-6pm Mon-Sat, 11am-5pm Sun; AE, MC, V)* sells a wild array of footwear. The styles are current, but the futuristic sneakers and boots, from Acupuncture to Vans, aren't quite cutting-edge by the time they reach Shelly's.

The clunky and crazy designs available just down the street at **Swear** *(61 Neal St.; Tel 0207/240-76-73; Tube to Covent Garden; 10am-6:30pm Mon-Sat, noon-5pm Sun; MC, V)* are at times out of this world. Wide, bubbling soles are a must, and the shoes feature unusual accents like

ground zero of the club scene

London may have hundreds of vinyl and dance specialty shops, but only one enjoys the loyal following of **Black Market Records** *(25 D'Arblay St.; Tel 0207/437-04-78; Tube to Tottenham Court Rd.; 11am-7pm Mon-Sat; MC, V)*. Started in 1987, this Soho shop has been at the center of the rave scene from the beginning. While the upstairs section specializes in house, garage, and hip-hop, the basement area sells a top selection of jungle and drum 'n' bass. Five daily deliveries of fresh stock flesh out the selection to include the joints every DJ needs to have.

With a staff that includes top DJs like Nicky Blackmarket, Clarkie, and Ray Keith, Black Market is an important testing ground for new styles and sounds. Staffers know what works in the mix, and patrons often rely on them for advice. On the rare occasions when the store doesn't stock what you are looking for, staffers often volunteer to sell their personal copies—and if that isn't love, what is?

Adding to Black Market's phenomenal reputation, staffers run two record labels out of the upstairs offices. Azuli Records is the house imprint, while Kartoonz releases drum 'n' bass. Releases are available in the shop and other dance outlets. Other draws include the huge number of fliers and advertisements for the best raves and clubs in London, a selection of underground mix tapes, the army of celebrity customers, and the loudest shop sound system in the United Kingdom.

liquid-filled bubbles emblazoned with the Swear logo. Not for the faint of heart or feet.

JD Sports *(33-34 Carnaby St.; Tel 0207/287-40-16; Tube to Oxford Circus; 10am-6:30pm Mon-Fri, till 7pm Sat, 11am-5pm Sun; MC, V)* carries the newest Air Jordans, but its strength is the selection of classic Adidas, Nike, New Balance, and Puma trainers. JD's stock of old-school sneakers and running shoes is absolutely unbeatable.

▶▶LOTIONS AND POTIONS

The idea of **Lush** *(123 King's Rd.; Tel 0207/376-83-48; Tube to Sloane Sq.; 10am-7pm Mon-Sat, noon-6pm Sun; www.lush.co.uk)*, a chain of stores across England selling fresh, handmade cosmetics, is not one whose product idea is supremely original, yet Lush has perfected it. With bowls of chunky mixtures that resemble oatmeal more than face masks, and huge rounds of soap that look like giant cheeses, you will be enraptured by the multi-sensory experience to be had here—even if you're faithful to Neutrogena.

▶▶BOUND

From Shakespeare to Johnson to Orwell, London has always fostered a love of words. For the latest readings and such, check *Time Out* for listings. Some events will, of course, be advertised in bookstores, and one of the best for info and also for its stock is **Waterstone's** *(121-129 Charing Cross Rd.; Tel 0207/324-42-91; Tube to Tottenham Court Rd.; 9:30am-8pm Mon-Sat, noon-6pm Sun; MC, V)*, which has branches everywhere in addition to the one listed here. Charing Cross Road (between Tottenham Court Road and Leicester Square) is lined with bookstores, and everything from the latest bestsellers to antiquarian and second-hand books can be found on these sometimes sleek, sometimes dusty shelves. All the major names are here: Waterstone's, Foyle's, Blackwell's and Borders, as well as some lesser known ones such as Bookends and Lovejoys. Head lower down toward Leicester Square, for the rare books.

For those with a taste for traditional English lunacy, **Foyle's** *(113-119 Charing Cross Rd.; Tel 0207/437-56-60; Tube to Tottenham Court Rd.; MC, V)*, hasn't changed much in 50 years and has some out-of-the-way titles.

The American megastore **Borders** *(203-207 Oxford St.; Tel 0207/292-16-00; Tube to Tottenham Court Rd.; 8am-11pm Mon-Sat, noon-6pm Sun; AE, MC, V)* is good, if predictable, and has a cafe and music store to boot.

The cramped and chaotic **Compendium** *(234 Camden High St.; Tel 0207/485-89-44; Tube to Camden Town; 10am-6pm Mon-Sat, noon-6pm Sun; MC, V)* has everything from obscure poetry to critical theory on the shelves. The staff is knowledgeable and polite, so don't be shy.

Another beloved London bookshop is **Murder One** *(71-73 Charing Cross Rd.; Tel 0207/734-34-85; Tube to Tottenham Court Rd. or Leicester Sq.; 10am-7pm Mon-Wed, till 8pm Thur-Sat; AE, MC, V)*, the one-stop crime and suspense specialty store. The land that gave us Sherlock Holmes is still enthralled by whodunits and mysteries of all stripes.

▶▶TUNES

The 'zines and fliers that pile up in heaps by the cashiers in **Selectadisc** *(34 Berwick St.; Tel 0207/734-32-97; Tube to Tottenham Court Rd.; 9:30am-7pm Mon-Sat; AE, MC, V)* are important documents of London's music scene. To find the records people buzz about, just browse the racks of CDs and vinyl.

For more historic sounds, try **Reckless Records** *(30 Berwick St.; Tel 0207/437-42-71; Tube to Tottenham Court Rd.; 10am-7pm daily; MC, V)*, two adjacent storefronts devoted to used and hard-to-find vinyl. The first shop sells soul, funk, reggae, hip-hop, and dance music, while the second sells jazz, blues, and rock.

Ray's Jazz Shop *(180 Shaftesbury Ave.; Tel 0207/240-39-69,*

Fax 0207/240-73-75; 10am-6:30pm Mon-Sat, 2-5:30pm Sun; rays. jazz@dial.pipex.com; Access, V, MC) is a superb place for a jazz lover. You can feel the store's history as you walk in, among the stacked shelves and racks of new and used LPs and CDs. The shop stocks everything from early jazz to funk records, and there are also books, magazines, and cassettes. Ray's is also a good place to find out about upcoming gigs and to pick up listings (look for the free *Jazz Guide*).

When time is of the essence, just stop by the gargantuan **Virgin Megastore** (14-16 Oxford St.; Tel 0207/631-16-14; Tube to Tottenham Court Rd.; 10am-9pm Mon-Sat, noon-6pm Sun; AE, MC, V). This behemoth of a record store has not only a gazillion CDs, tapes, and records, but a fun selection of fiction and nonfiction, movies, and video games too. Located right outside the exit from the Tube, the store could very well bankrupt you before the shopping trip along Oxford Street even begins.

EATS

While the younger, trendier contingent may have put London back on the global culinary map, huge segments of the population turn up their noses at organic radicchio salad, preferring a greasy plate of fried fish and chips. Most of the good restaurants still steer well clear of traditional English cuisine, and London's diverse population offers ample alternatives to the almighty pub grub. In addition to countless Indian restaurants and balti houses, London has a fair number of Chinese restaurants in Soho. Kebab stands abound, often outselling their Western fast-food competition through larger portions and later hours. A good one to check out is the Cafe Metro on Camden High Street, right by Camden Town Tube.

Healthy stuff like organic produce and noodley dishes have become wildly popular here, the new health awareness even sparking national hysteria over genetically modified food (hmmm, maybe there is something wrong with eight-pound talking tomatoes...). The change in attitude has created a vast market for healthful California-esque cuisine, but ironically, the rising health consciousness of English diners hasn't convinced most restaurants to prohibit smoking at the table. And make sure to see if service is included in the check before tipping the waiter (usually 10 to 15 percent, depending).

▶▶CHEAP

Although a virtual infinity of kebab restaurants peppers London's commercial streets, they occupy wildly varying culinary territory.

Blending the cuisine of the Middle East with the cafe vibe of Paris, **Cafe Diana** (5 Wellington Terrace, Bayswater Rd.; Tel 0207/792-96-06; Tube to Notting Hill Gate or bus 12, 52, 94; Entrees from £5; No credit cards) is perfect for a quick lunch before heading toward Portobello Road or into Kensington Gardens. Cafe Diana also looks Parisian, until you notice that the walls are completely concealed behind a mass of portraits of Princess Di. With mostly indoor seating and just a couple of small

say what?

Cockney isn't the only kind of slang in England. Everyday conversation is full of words and phrases that are meaningless to the uninformed. To sound like a local, fake an accent and be sure to drop the following sayings:

Geezer: No, it's not a senior citizen. A "geezah" is the English equivalent of "dude." Achieve "Diamond Geezer" status, and you have hit the big time.

Bloke: A person of the male persuasion, as in: "That bloke is a geezer."

Bird: The English term for people of the female persuasion, as in: "Did you see that bird kick that bloke in the huevos?"

Draw: Also known as chuff, gear, spliff, or marijuana, as in: "That bird stole my draw and ran off with me brother!"

Bloody: An English substitute for "damn," as in "Where's me bloody draw, dammit?"

Safe: Not used as an umpire's judgment in England—something is "safe" when it's cool.

Sorted: A slang term originally used in an antidrug campaign, the situation is "sorted" when all is going well.

Wicked: Slightly different than its usage in New England, as in: "That party was safe, I mean it was bloody wicked!"

Mate: You know you're in when someone calls you "mate" instead of "that Yank bastard."

Shag: If a hottie wants to shag you senseless, be very happy. That means they want to do the wild thing all night.

Snog: Make out.

Tosser (pronounced 'tos-sa'): If someone calls you a tosser or, even worse, a "giant tosser," you are clearly not making friends down at the local pub.

Nutter (pronounced 'nut-ta'): A nutter is someone a few sandwiches short of a picnic. If you have a tendency to do tequila slammers in your spare time, you may be deemed by some to be a nutter.

Taking the piss: If you're taking the piss out of someone, you're making fun of him or her because they're a big, fat wanker (equivalent to tosser).

Bollocks: Bullshit. But, if something is "the dog's bollocks," that means it's very cool indeed.

five of the best ethnic eats

London is just as multicultural as New York, and the same dazzling array of ethnic restaurants can be found here. But if you're in the mood for a casual, quick bite but still want an international flavor, head to these ethnic gems: **Yo! Sushi** (*O2 Centre, Finchley Rd.; Tel 0207/431-44-99; Noon-11pm daily; www.yosushi.co.uk; £2.50 and up depending on color-coded dish*) is a ubiquitous chain of eat-and-run sushi restaurants. There is a circular bar along which a conveyer belt runs carrying a variety of color-coded (according to price) dishes. If the one you want isn't there, one of the chefs in the center of the bar will be happy to whip it up for you. Highlights include the salmon maki rolls, the chicken yakitori, and the salmon yakitori. The other novelty of this place is the motorized drink cart that winds its way around the restaurant making comments, such as "OK, OK, I'm here. Do you think I'm a bus or something?" But be sure you don't step in its path because it won't hesitate in exclaiming "Out of my way, sucker!"

Solly's (*148A Golders Green Rd.; Tel 0208/455-21-21; Tube to Golder's Green; Less than £5 for take-out orders*) in Golders Green is the always busy archetypal Israeli food joint set in a predominantly Jewish neighborhood. It is only because the falafels are to-die-for that anyone would put up with the abuse that comes with ordering at Solly's. (Think Soup Nazi.)

Ranoush Juice (*43 Edgeware Rd.; Tel 0207/723-59-29; Tube to Marble Arch; 9pm-3am daily; £4 starter*) is one of those Lebanese quickie hot spots that only locals know about. This is because it's well hidden

sidewalk tables, Cafe Diana attracts mostly local folks and probably more than a few royal-watchers.

Another unusual take on the kebab shop is the studenty **Groovy Grub** (*52 Tavistock Place; Tel 0207/713-09-03; Tube to Russell Sq.; "Morning"-midnight daily; Entrees from £3.50; No credit cards*). Keeping things copacetic, the staff serve up the obligatory falafels and gyros, with chicken, burgers, and a rainbow trout in "groovey sauce" (whatever that is) for the more adventurous. Located on a boring street in a neighborhood lacking streetlife, Groovy Grub is ideal for those staying at the **Generator** or **Crescent Hotel** [see *crashing*, below, for both], but probably doesn't warrant a schlep across town (which defeats the purpose of budget eating).

If something more well-rounded tickles your fancy, London has a good number of all-you-can-eat buffet joints in Soho's compact Chinatown. **Mr. Au** (*47-49 Charing Cross Rd.; Tel 0207/437-74-72; Tube to Leicester Sq.; 11am-11:30pm daily; Entrees from £4.90; No credit cards*) is a good choice for gluttons and tightwad tourists. Right in the thick of it at Leicester Square, Mr. Au is where the action is. For a reasonable price,

in a clump of similarly sounding restaurants (all ending in 'noush'), in the not too aesthetically enhanced Edgeware Road. The spread of Mediterranean fare to be found here, not to mention the freshly squeezed fruit juices, is, simply put, out of this world. Rush there as soon as you can. If you're craving more Lebanese, Shepherd's Market in Mayfair is a good little area to bounce from one spot to the next. **Brick Lane,** very near Petticoat Lane, is the strip to sate all your Bangladeshi and Indian cravings. The road is home not only to one curry joint after another, but also to an outdoor market on the weekends [see *used and bruised,* above]. For the most misshapen but delicious pizza, go to **La Pizzeria** *(Sydney St., off the King's Rd.; Tel 0207/376-76-00; Tube to Sloane Sq.; Open daily; No credit cards)* in the Chelsea Farmer's Market. The open kitchen also doles out big bowls of pasta and risotto. The only catch with this restaurant is that on weekends the line stretches around the block and there is a ridiculous cover charge of £1 per person (which is usually reserved for a tablecloth charge or coat keeping, not for a casual pizza picnic setup), but do take it off the bill if you see fit (a 12.5 percent tip is also included).

The other ultra-popular spot in the Chelsea Market is **The Market Place** *(Chelsea Farmer's Market; Tel 0207/352-56-00; 9:30am-5pm daily winter; 9:30am-11pm daily summer).* Especially good on a sunny weekend afternoon, the menu is casual and homely with sprinklings of South African culinary tidbits.

you can gorge yourself on a variety of soups, rolls, stir-fries, and noodle dishes. Of course, you sacrifice any semblance of atmosphere—unless, that is, you consider the sound of chewing ambience. Mr. Au is a favorite of drunken tourists racing to gobble their food to get back onto the streets of the West End.

Yet, sometimes you need a real meal for not a lot of loot. For good, cheap food made to order, head to South London's **Noodle House** *(426 Coldharbour Lane; Tel 0207/274-14-92; Tube to Brixton; Noon-11:30pm Mon-Thur, till midnight Fri, Sat; Entrees from £5; No credit cards).* This super-cheap Vietnamese restaurant on one of Brixton's most happening streets is both popular and delicious, serving a wide variety of appetizers and entrees, noodled or noodle-free, for veggies and omnivores alike. The food, like the restaurant, is simple and no-nonsense, with a couple of little flourishes, like a fresh juice selection, to distinguish it from the run-of-the-mill noodle spot. A popular stop before a night of drinking or clubbing, Noodle House gets a bit crowded in the later evening, so come early to avoid the crunch.

Within the maze of streets that inhabit Covent Garden lies tranquil Neal's Yard. The square is lined with stores selling alternative products and outdoor cafes, the best of which is **Neal's Yard Salad Bar** *(2 Neal's Yard; Tel/Fax 0207/836-32-33; Tube to Covent Garden; About £4)*. This tiny restaurant with its rickety outdoor tables and heated lamps was the first vegetarian cafe in the Yard, opening in 1982, and the daily variety of veggie and vegan dishes are soul food par excellence, not to mention outstanding value.

The Portuguese fast food chicken chain **Nando's** *(O2 Centre, Finchley Rd.; Tube to Finchley Rd.; Tel 0800/975-8181; About £3 for burgers, £6 for meal combos; www.nandos.co.uk)* was brought over to the UK after enormous success in South Africa, where the restaurant is based. As a result, you're bound to hear more than one or two South African accents if you pop in to sample the delicious combos on offer with their signature *peri peri* sauce. There are also delicious veggie burgers.

▶▶DO-ABLE

While the budget eats in London are nothing to get too excited about, there is plenty of excellent food available for just a few pounds more. Ground rules for finding good food at decent prices: Eat adventurously, and avoid all American chain restaurants. While most pubs serve food during the day and evening, similarly priced, significantly better fare can be found in restaurants around the city. Operating a four-restaurant chain, **Wagamama** *(11 Jamestown Rd.; Tel 0207/428-08-00; Tube to Camden Town; Noon-11pm Mon-Sat, 12:30-10pm Sun; www.waga mama.com; Entrees £10 and under; AE, MC, V)* presents itself as the restaurant of the future: fast, cheap, and delicious. Located off the main streets of Camden, the newest branch of this fantastically popular chain (the name means "selfish" in Japanese) is just as "Futurama" as the other three, featuring an undulating green metal and glass wall. Inside, staff takes orders on handheld Trekkie computers, whisking generous portions of Japanese noodles and dumplings to your place at the crowded picnic-style tables within minutes. While the quasi-cafeteria thing is a bit wacky, the hordes of hipsters mobbing the restaurant don't seem to mind at all.

Tactical *(27 D'Arblay St.; Tel 0207/287-28-23; Tube to Tottenham Court Rd. or Oxford Circus; 9am-11pm Mon-Fri, noon-11pm Sat; Entrees £10-18; No credit cards)* serves up more conventional eats in cool sur-roundings. A bar, cafe, coffeeshop, and bookstore in one, Tactical's eclecticism makes it a standout. Serving a rotating menu of sandwiches, beers, and coffees alongside a motley assortment of edgy and subversive books, Tactical is a hipster's paradise. Don't plan on getting too much reading done, unless you can concentrate while the freshest New York hip-hop booms out of the speakers. Definitely a cool place to chill while in the neighborhood, especially on Sundays, when they have a live DJ.

The ubiquitous **Pizza Express** *(39 Abbey Rd.; Tel 0207/624-55-77; Tube to Kilburn Park; 11:30-midnight daily; www.pizzaexpress.co.uk; Entrees from £10-18; AE, MC, V)*, with dozens of branches across

to die for desserts

The Hampstead High Street is one of the nicer high streets in London, and this is in part due to **La Creperie de Hampstead** *(Perrin's Lane, midway off the High Street; Tube to Hampstead; 11:45am-11pm Mon-Thur; 11:45am-11:30pm Fri-Sun; Savory crepes £3; sweet crepes £2),* a tres petite creperie that has been selling crepes that melt perfectly in your mouth available with milk, dark, or white Belgian chocolate, for 20 years. A sign on the stand warns: 'Belgian chocolate is absolutely divine but may ooze out when you bite.' Mmmm.

For sticky toffee pudding that you simply will not believe, **The House on the Hill** *(Rosslyn Hill, lower Hampstead High St.; Tel 0207/435-80-37; Tube to Hampstead; Daily till midnight; Dessert £5; All major credit cards)*—also in Hampstead—is the place to get it. The House, as it is referred to by locals, is also a restaurant and bar serving the North London hipsters. The best time to drop in, however, is after dinner for a cappuccino and the aforementioned heavenly sticky stuff. The ubiquitous restaurant chain **Dome** *(35A-B Kensington High St; Tube to High Street Kensington; Tel 0207/937-66-55; Daily till 10:30pm; Dessert £4; All major credit cards)* serves a dessert called Banoffi Pie. Now, you will find Banoffi Pie at other London eateries, but do not be fooled. None of these pathetic attempts will in any way compare to the real deal on offer at Dome. An orgasmic combination of caramelized condensed milk and bananas balancing precariously on a ginger cookie–type base, this is *the* stuff.

London, sounds like a chain of takeout joints—but Pizza Hut it ain't. This hugely popular chain fully deserves its good rep. The menu offers a range of personal pizzas as well as salads topped with the fine house dressing (which is also sold in bottles). It's popular with most Londoners, so expect to see all sorts dining together in London's original pizzeria. The upscale St. John's Wood location is near to both the happening **Saatchi Gallery** [see *culture zoo,* above], and the legendary Abbey Road crossing, immortalized on the cover of the Beatles album.

Also in the area is **Sauce** *(214 Camden High St.; Tel 0207/482-07-77; Tube to Camden Town; Noon-11pm Mon-Sat, till 4pm Sun; Entrees from £6; MC, V)* an organic bar and restaurant. Minimal and white, the restaurant is warmed by colorful tablecloths and excellent paintings. The bar is willing and able to amuse the odd twenty- or thirtysomething put off by veggie burgers with lentils, nuts, and seeds.

Cranks *(17-19 Great Newport St.; Tel 0207/836-52-26; Tube to Leicester Sq.; Open daily)* is London's well-known health food restaurant chain. Cranks used to be much more organic in feel, with long wooden benches and huge buffets with loads of mushy bowls, whereas now it's much more sleek and colourful in that bright and plastic way. But despite the fact that the quality of the grub has deteriorated somewhat, it's still a sure thing for healthier fast food, although it is fairly costly.

Similar to Pizza Express, **Ask** *(121-125 Park St., off Oxford St.; Tel 0207/495-77-60; Tube to Bond St. or Marble Arch; 5:30-10:30pm; £10; All major credit cards)* is also one of the usual suspect restaurants that seems to have a branch or two in every suburb of London. The food is as imaginative as can be expected from a run-of-the mill pizza/pasta spot, but it is consistently delicious. The restaurants are minimalist, but elegantly decorated with a modern, bright feel. Although the pizza Fiorentina at Pizza Express can't be beat, the penne with tuna at Ask is just as good.

▶▶**SPLURGE**

As with anywhere else, it usually takes lots of money to get a first-class meal in London. **Mr. Kong** *(21 Lisle St.; Tel 0207/437-73-41; Tube to Leicester Sq.; Noon-3am daily; Entrees £10-25; MC, V),* on Chinatown's main drag, is an exception to the rule. Serving Cantonese food, it makes its reputation on the daily and chef's specials. Talk things over with the waiter, who can recommend obscure and tasty dishes. Although the decor is equivalent to any ghetto wok in America, authentic Chinese food of this caliber is a rare find in London or anywhere else.

For those wanting something posh, London has no shortage of trendy gourmet restaurants. A standout is **Axis** *(1 Aldwych; Tel 0207/300-03-00; Tube to Temple, Covent Garden, or Charing Cross; Noon-3pm Mon-Fri, 5-11:30pm Mon-Sat; Avg entree £25; AE, MC, V),* housed in the **One Aldwych** hotel. Blending influences from Europe and Asia, Axis (though its name is odd in a city that got Blitzkrieged) serves an excellent selection of fusion cuisine. A meal may be costly, but the service and the exquisite ambience, complete with a vertigo-inducing cityscape mural, confirm that it's money well spent. As in the rest of One Aldwych, simplicity and good taste prevail.

An expanse of cream and gold with giant palms in brass urns and slowly revolving fans greets you as you enter. To the right is a conservatory with more greenery, and all around the walls are lined with original photos of gents on elephant-back out to bag a tiger. The air is laden with the sweet, sour, and heady scents of a thousand spices. Yes, you're in curry heaven. **The Bombay Brasserie** *(Courtfield Rd.; Tel 0207/370-40-40; £10-20 per entree)* is the restaurant of **Bailey's Hotel,** on Gloucester Road, conveniently located directly opposite the Tube station. The menu is exquisite, so the best time to visit is at the all you can eat Sunday lunchtime buffet (book early). True, there are better curries in London, and at better prices, but the atmosphere here is like nowhere else, so you don't resent the price.

Beach Blanket Babylon *(45 Ledbury Rd; Tel 0207/229-29-07; Open daily; Starters £4.95-11, Entrees £11.50-35)* in trendy Notting Hill is a candlelit Gaudiesque paradise complete with multicolored, glistening, mirrored mosaics, twisting spiral staircases held together by chains, and a cavernous seating arrangement that juts out of the stone walls. The menu is pretentious in the extreme, but certainly varied (rabbit, Thai, prawn curry, squid, gravlax, foie gras, red meat, and chicken), and the atmosphere is superb and surreal. This is a perfect spot to hide away with that desirable someone in its many nooks and crannies. If your wallet is not busting at the seams, at least down a drink in the overcrowded bar and take a peek around.

Tucked behind London's answer to Madison Avenue—Sloane Street—is a kitchen serving some of the best Italian in town. **Sale e Pepe** *(9/15 Pavilion Rd.; Tel 0207/235-00-98 or Tel 0207/235-01-14; Tube to Knightsbridge)* is run by actual Italians, and the taste of the heaped bowls of spaghetti and endless breadsticks will stay with you long after you've paid the check.

crashing

Even the thriftiest travelers will find it next to impossible to survive on less than about £50 a day in London. Much of that money will inevitably go toward lodgings, which of course range from simple to opulent. If the latter is to your liking, understand that you're gonna drop some cash for that luxury. Luckily, even London's least expensive accommodations are comfortable and fairly convenient. The tourist office will help you make a reservation if you show up without a plan.

▶▶CHEAP

The cozy **Ashlee House** *(261-265 Gray's Inn Rd.; Tel 0207/833-92-48, Fax 0207/833-96-77; Tube to King's Cross/St. Pancras or Bus 10, 46, 91, 73, 214, 19 to King's Cross; info@ashleehouse.co.uk; £36 single, £24 double, £15 dormitory; No credit cards)* is just blocks from the King's Cross/St. Pancras Station, which has seven different subway and train lines and a number of city buses. It hosts loads of young tourists from all over the world, so there's no lack of company in the clean-but-styleless dorms or the smoky lobby. Breakfast of the cereal-and-coffee variety is included, and kitchen facilities are available for other meals. Coin laundry, common showers, and single-sex bathrooms let you preserve some dignity while living out of a backpack.

Situated in a neighborhood that's a favorite among both Australian tourists and leather-clad gays, the **YHA Earl's Court Youth Hostel** *(38 Bolton Gardens; Tel 0207/373-70-83, Fax 0207/835-20-34; Tube to Earl's Court, Bus C1, N97 to Earl's Court; Desk open till 11pm; earlscourt_@yha.org.uk, www.yha.org.uk; £21 dormitory; AE, V, MC)* is sure to be a blast. The hostel features a smoky little common room with cable TV and a pay-per-use Internet station as well as a garden, kitchen, laundry facilities, phone cards, tickets, and money exchange. The bathrooms and showers are shared, though they aren't coed. Drawbacks

London Eats and Crashing

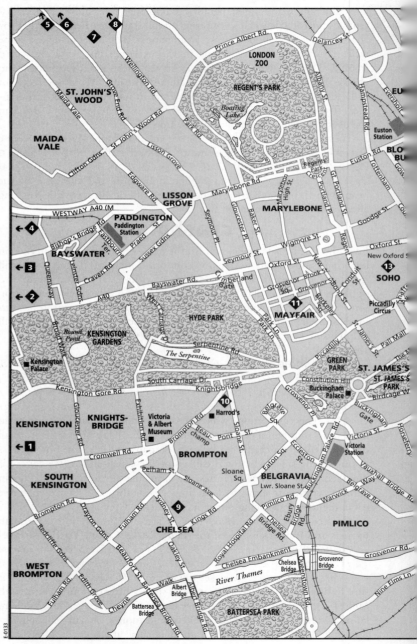

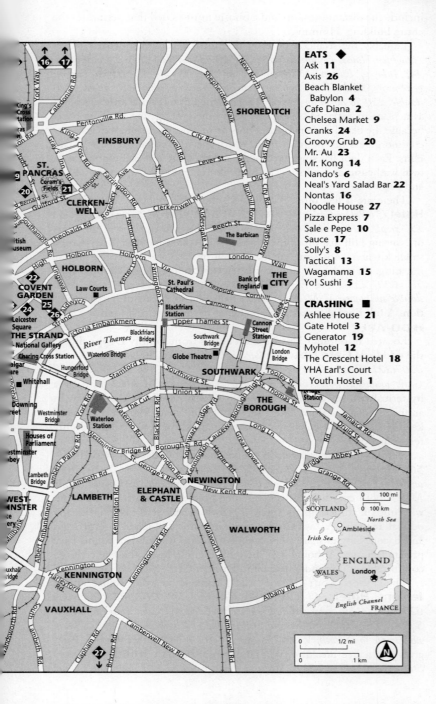

EATS ◆
Ask **11**
Axis **26**
Beach Blanket
  Babylon **4**
Cafe Diana **2**
Chelsea Market **9**
Cranks **24**
Groovy Grub **20**
Mr. Au **23**
Mr. Kong **14**
Nando's **6**
Neal's Yard Salad Bar **22**
Nontas **16**
Noodle House **27**
Pizza Express **7**
Sale e Pepe **10**
Sauce **17**
Solly's **8**
Tactical **13**
Wagamama **15**
Yo! Sushi **5**

CRASHING ■
Ashlee House **21**
Gate Hotel **3**
Generator **19**
Myhotel **12**
The Crescent Hotel **18**
YHA Earl's Court
  Youth Hostel **1**

include the distant location and a bizarre musty smell that permeates the entire building. Hmmm....

Probably the strangest hotel in the universe, the **Generator** *(Mac-Naughten House, Compton Place; Tel 0207/388-76-66, Fax 0207/388-76-44; Tube to Euston or Russell Sq., or Bus 10, 30, 73, 91 to Euston; generator_@lhdr.demon.co.uk, www.lhdr.demon.co.uk; £38 single, £26 double, £20.50 dormitory; V, MC)* is decorated in industrial style. It's billed as a place to meet and hang out with other young travelers—probably because the bland and cramped rooms drive most patrons to retreat to the common areas on the main floor, which include several bars and restaurants. Each floor has single-sex toilets and showers, and each dorm has its own washbasin and mirror. The hotel also offers breakfast, tourist advice, and packed lunches.

There are a few other reliable and affordable options: **The Palace Hotel** *(31 Palace Court; Tel 0207/22--5628, No Fax; £12 dorm, £15 quad, £17 triple, £18 double; shared bathrooms; No credit cards)* is in the heart of Notting Hill just off of the Notting Hill Gate tube stop. They have a small kitchen and game room, as well as free tea and coffee in the morning. Or park your bones at **Enrico House** *(77079 Warwick Way; Tel 0207/233-7538, Fax 0207/233-9995; £45 double w/o bath, £450 double w/shower; V, MC)*, around a half-mile southeast of Victoria Station. A full English breakfast is included in the price of a room.

▶▶DO-ABLE

Located in popular Notting Hill across from Johnny Depp's digs is the odd little **Gate Hotel** *(6 Portobello Rd.; Tel 0207/221-07-07, Fax 0207/221-91-28; Tube or Bus 12, 27, 28, 31, 52, 94 to Notting Hill Gate; www.gatehotel.com; £65 single, £85 double; V, MC)*. Run by a hysterically funny couple, the Gate is a most pleasant place to stay. In addition to attractions like the Portobello Road Market, the hotel keeps its very own celebrity, a parrot named Sergeant Bilko. Highly recommended.

Definitely not a swingers' paradise, the staid **Crescent Hotel** *(49-50 Cartwright Gardens; Tel 0207/387-15-15, Fax 0207/383-20-54; Tube or Bus 10, 30, 73, 91 to Euston; £45 single, £85 double, £95 triple; AE, V, MC)* is both cozy and convenient. The hotel features a common room with info on attractions, as well as a knowledgeable staff to help with any oddball requests. A stay includes breakfast buffet and made-to-order eggs and bacon. Singles share a common bathroom, while larger rooms have private facilities. Although not the most exciting hotel, the Crescent is a comfortable and friendly bargain in a pricey city.

These spots won't do too much damage to your wallet either: **Jenkins Hotel** *(45 Cartwright Gardens; Tel 0207/387-2067, Fax 0207/383-3139; reservations@jenkinshotel.demon.co.uk; Tube to Russell Square, Kings Cross, or Euston; £62 double w/o bath, £72 double w/bath, £83 triple with bath; V, MC)*, around 1 1/2 miles east of Regents Park, gives you a free breakfast with your room. **Arofsk Hotel** *(83 Gower Street; Tel 0207/636-2115; Tube to Goodge Sgreet; £44 double w/o bath,*

£58 double w/bath; V, MC), is in the heart of Bloomsbury and will also feed you in the morning. **Rusking Hotel** *(23-24 Montague Street; Tel 0207/636-7388, Fax 0207/323-1662; Tube to Russel Square or Holborn; £60 double w/o bathroom, £75 double w/bathroom, £75 triple w/o bathroom, £85triple w/bathroom; AE, DC, MC, V)*, is just south of the Jenkins Hotel.

▶▶**SPLURGE**

A spectacular space, **Myhotel** *(11-13 Bayley St.; Tel 0207/667-60-00, Fax 0207/667-60-01; Tube to Tottenham Court Rd. or Goodge St., Bus 10, 24, 29, 73; guestservices@myhotels.co.uk; £170 single, £205 double; AE, V, MC)* is convenient to collegiate Bloomsbury as well as Soho. Blending Eastern and Western elements, every space in Myhotel is decorated in accordance with feng shui. In addition to this polar reassurance, you are also provided with access to a fitness room, a stylish lounge, and an East/West fusion restaurant, **MyChi.**

The greatest asset of the **Shaftesbury Hotel** *(65-73 Shaftesbury Ave.; Tel 0207/871-60-01, Fax 0207/871-60-01; Tube or Bus 14, 19, 38 to Piccadilly Circus; £165 single, £185 double, £205 single suite; AE, V, MC)* is its location, smack-dab in the heart of Theaterland and Soho. The rooms are clean and conservative, but there are ample distractions outside the windows, which open onto crowded streets lined with theaters and restaurants.

need to know

Currency Exchange Money can be changed at **Bureaux de Change** around town or at most banks. Make sure to ask about the commission, which often takes a sizable chunk out of your funds. ATM machines will also dispense pounds, at a much better rate.

Tourist Information A wealth of tourist information can be found at the **Tourist Information Centre** *(Victoria Station Forecourt; Tube to Victoria; 8am-7pm Mon-Sat, till 5pm Sun),* which can help you out with hotel reservations, or the smaller info desks in **Heathrow Terminals 1-3, Harrods** *(87-135 Brompton Rd.; Tel 0207/730-12-34; Tube to Knightsbridge; 10am-6pm Mon, Tue, Sat, till 7pm Wed-Fri),* and **Selfridges** *(400 Oxford St.; Tel 0207/629-12-34; Tube to Bond St.; 10am-7pm Mon-Wed, till 8pm Thur, Fri, 9:30am-7pm Sat, noon-6pm Sun).* Bus and rail info can be found by calling the **Travel Information Centre Hotline** *(Tel 0207/222-12-34),* or by visiting their desks at Heathrow, Victoria, Piccadilly Circus, Oxford Circus, Euston, and King's Cross/St. Pancras stations.

Public Transportation Most attractions are accessible by subway or bus. The subway, known as the **Tube,** is fast and convenient, but it's closed after midnight. A series of night buses, designated by the prefix "N," pick up the slack. Fares for the Tube vary from 80p to £3.10 depending on how many of the six zones you plan to travel through. Multi-day passes called **Travelcards** *(£17.60-34.90 for unlimited use),* available at the Tube stations, grant varying degrees of flexibility. The

wired

Along with all the porn and bootleg music on the Internet, a number of excellent websites about London are floating around in cyberspace.

www.bta.org.uk: The official site of the British Tourism Authority, regarding all things touristy in London and the rest of England.

www.timeout.co.uk: The web version of the omnipresent bible of London culture.

www.london.eventguide.com: Listings of arts events, restaurants, and hotels.

www.albemarle-london.com: Dedicated to London's glitzier West End productions, this site has listings, top-ten lists, news, and online booking.

www.s-h-systems.co.uk/london.html: In addition to comprehensive hotel listings by neighborhood, this site has local weather, car rental service, and exclusive discounts on accommodations.

www.sorted.org/london: A website devoted to London's hedonistic nightlife. Listings and info are provided alongside DJ bios and loads of links to related sites.

www.guardian.co.uk: The online version of London's popular daily, *The Guardian.*

www.multimap.com: Organized by postal code, this site can provide comprehensive street maps of the entire city.

www.grafcafe.com: A cool site with tons of cool flicks of London's finest aerosol villains.

www.urban75.com: "Underground" website with info on raves, drugs, direct action (protests), and lots of other cool shit to read.

www.neonlit.co.uk: A comprehensive site devoted to England's literary scene brought to you by the good folks at *Time Out.*

www.hostels.com: For a complete listing of hostels in London.

best deal is the weekly travel pass, which grants access to the Tube and all buses. Bus fares are £1 for all trips in zone 1 and 70p for all others. Taxis are widely available, and the drivers are legendary for their knowledge of the city. Look for the taxi's distinctly large silhouette barreling down the road and flag it down—they're available if the yellow bar on top is lit. Many taxis accept credit cards in lieu of cash. Still another option is London's minicabs, private car services that vary wildly in price and dependability. An excellent service is **Addison Lee** *(Tel 0207/387-88-88).*

American Express Presuming you accidentally left home without it, get a replacement card here *(192 Victoria St.; Tel 0207/828-45-67; Tube to Victoria; 9am-5:30pm Mon-Fri, till 4pm Sat).*

www.hotelnet.co.uk: For a complete listing of hotels in London.

www.thisislondon.com: Updates, listings, events guides, and info on everything London-related.

www.londontransport.co.uk: This site deals with the Tube and bus network, and includes useful maps.

www.pti.org.uk: This website deals with the entire UK transport system, including info on rail, coach, air, ferry, and metro travel.

www.artsfestivals.co.uk: Directory of all the arts festivals in the UK with dates and useful contact numbers.

www.uktw.co.uk: Online theatre bookings for the forward planner.

www.countryside.gov.uk: Good assemblage of info on national trails, areas of beauty, wilderness areas, and national parks in the country.

For e-mail and a Vampire (beet, carrot, and orange juice), try **Juice** *(7 Earlham St.; Tel 0207/836-73-76; Tube to Leicester Sq.; 10am-10pm Mon-Sat, till 8pm Sun; No credit cards)* a Covent Garden juice bar and cybercafe. Because of the natural food and juice selection, the regular customers look less pasty than your average Net-head.

From the creator of easyJet.com and easyRentacar.com comes the ultra-cheap, super-easy chain of Internet cafes **easyEverything.com** *(9-16 Tottenham Court Rd., Oxford St. end; Tel 0207/907-78-00; Tube to Tottenham Court Rd.; Open daily 24 hrs; www.easyeverything.com).* With five supermarket-sized stores open in central London all the time offering computer access for as little cash as £1, this is revolutionizing the concept of the Internet cafe internationally. In addition to web surfing, Microsoft Office 2000 software is available now as well, at the same price.

Health and Emergency For emergencies: *999.* Call *0208/900-10-00* for doctors on-call 24 hours a day. **Charing Cross Hospital Emergency Room** *(Fulham Palace Rd., Hammersmith; Tel 0208/846-12-34)* is also open 24 hours.

Pharmacy Get the pills for all types of chills or spills at **Bliss** *(5 Marble Arch; Tel 0207/723-61-16; Tube to Marble Arch; 9am-midnight daily).*

Telephones Country code: *44,* city codes: *207* and *208;* Directory assistance: *192;* International operator: *155.* Pay phones accept coins or calling cards, available at any off-license (convenience store). **AT&T:** *0800/890-011;* **MCI:** *0800/444-44-44;* **Sprint:** *0800/877-46-46.*

Airports London's three main international airports are **Heathrow** *(Tel*

0208/759-43-21; www.baa.co.uk), **Gatwick** (Tel 01293/535-353; www.baa.co.uk) and **Stansted** (Tel 01279/680-500; www.baa.co.uk). By far the largest and busiest, Heathrow is connected to town by both the Tube and the speedy **Heathrow Express** (Paddington Station; Tel 0845/600-15-15; £10; Trip takes 15 minutes; 5:10am-11:40pm daily every 15 minutes). On your way out of town, additional time can be saved by checking in for your flight at Paddington Station. From Gatwick, get into town via the **Gatwick Express** (Victoria Station; Tel 0990/301-530; Trip takes 35 minutes; 5am-11:45pm daily, then hourly through the night; £9.50). While this is the most expensive way to the airport next to taxis (which will run you £35-45 plus tip from any of the airports), it is both fast and reliable. The speediest route from Stansted is via **Stansted Skytrain** (Liverpool St. Station; Tel 0345/484-950; Trip takes 45 minutes; Every 30 minutes 5am-midnight Mon-Sat, 7am-midnight Sun; £10.70).

Trains The first step for any rail journey out of London is a call to the **National Rail Enquiry Line** (Tel 0345/484-950). Schedule information for all of England's numerous rail services can be found there. Fares tend to be very reasonable, and even the most distant points are accessible within a few hours. Trains to the south coast of England leave from **Charing Cross Station.** Those bound for the east, from **Fenchurch Street.** Those heading to the northeast and Scotland, from **King's Cross.** Trains to East Anglia leave from **Liverpool Street.** Trains to the Midlands leave from **Euston. Paddington** serves the southwest and South Wales. **St. Pancras** sends trains out to the north of England. The south, Kent, and the Sussex coast are accessible via **Victoria.** Lastly, trains for the Dorset coast, the south, and the **Eurostar** (Tel 0990/186-186) train to Paris and Brussels can be caught at **Waterloo Station.** Tickets can be booked in advance or purchased at the station with cash, check, or credit card. However, prices and ticketing are complicated and are subject to change without notice.

Bus Lines Out of the City The main bus service to points outside London is **National Express** (Tel 0990/898-989). Buses depart from **Victoria Coach Station** (Buckingham Palace Rd.; Tel 0207/730-34-66). As with most services in England, special pricing is available for students. The bus service also provides special coaches to and from some of Britain's major summer festivals and concerts [see *festivals and events,* above].

Bike Rental Bikes can be rented from **Bikepark** (14 Stukeley St.; Tel 0207/430-0083; Tube to Covent Garden; 7:30am-8:30pm Mon-Fri, 8:30am-6:30pm Sat; AE, MC, V). It's £10 the first day, £5 the second, and £3 each successive day.

Scooter Rental There's something European about getting around by moped. To get putting, call **Scootabout** (King's Cross; Tel 0207/833-46-07; Tube to King's Cross; 9am-6pm Mon-Fri, till 1pm Sat; MC, V). Thankfully, insurance and a helmet are included in the rental fee.

Laundry Convenient location and standard coin-operated facilities make **Duds 'n' Suds** *(49-51 Brunswick Shopping Centre; Tel 0207/837-11-22; Tube to Russell Sq.; 8am-9pm Mon-Fri, 9am-8pm Sat, Sun; No credit cards)* the ideal laundromat near Soho and the rest of the West End.

Internet See *wired,* above.

edinburgh

It makes sense that the author of *Dr. Jekyll and Mr. Hyde* hailed from Edinburgh. By day, the city still maintains its reputation as the slightly stuffy capital of Scotland, but by night the number of blissfully hammered souls stumbling around town is truly staggering. Major clubs like **The Venue** [see *club scene*, below] aren't just places to go dancing, they've become national institutions. Dance music is king, with rock largely replaced by techno, trance, and (never can say goodbye) disco—seemingly every pub and club in town has at least one '70s night a month. And Edinburgh's bars, showing some sanity, stay open later than those in England, further fueling an already healthy nightlife scene.

Edinburgh is a far cry from urban centers like Glasgow and London—it's got much more of a comfortable, small-town thing going on. The locals are so friendly your paranoid mind might be suspicious of their sincerity, but they honestly enjoy the visitors who flood the city all year—especially during the world-class, three-week **Edinburgh International Festival** [see *festivals & events*, below], a bonanza of arts, culture, and pandemonium. The good vibes are so infectious that tons of foreigners never leave, held captive by the beauty of the city, the surrounding countryside, and the easy hospitality of the locals.

Traveling to Edinburgh and ignoring the sights and museums would be a mistake; visiting and never seeing the city like a native would be even worse. While the folks back home may be impressed by photos of medieval buildings and people in tartan (will they *never* tire of it?), the truly awesome Edinburgh experience is clutching a pint in the pub and happily waiting for somebody to strike up a conversation. To find out about the local events, check the biweekly *The List*, which features club and music listings, theater reviews, and articles about the Scottish scene. The happenings-du-jour are publicized through highly visible posters and fliers.

neighborhoods

Still standing after a millenium, the hulking silhouette of **Edinburgh Castle** [see *culture zoo*, below] looms over **New Town**, which is a comparatively (constructed during the 18th century) recent addition to the city on the north side of the castle. Built on a rocky cliff smack-dab in the center of town, the castle is joined to the rest of medieval Edinburgh by the **Royal Mile**, which starts at the southwest side of the castle and stretches east through **Old Town**. To the south of the Old Town and **Waverly Station**, **Edinburgh University** marks the beginning of the grassy playground of the **Meadows** [see *hanging out*, below]. A favorite when weather permits, the park comes alive with cricket games, football matches, and vagrant students.

Up in New Town, tourists and locals clog the sidewalks of **Princes Street** shopping and sightseeing. On one side of Princes Street lies the **West End**, the only part of town filled with modern office buildings, and not much to draw the casual visitor, while on the east end, **Leith Walk** runs north to the historic port of **Leith**. Rough and desolate after dark, Leith is slowly gentrifying thanks to waterfront development and flocks of artsy residents. Also on the east end of New Town is the already-hip **Broughton Street**, both the center of gay Edinburgh and a favorite hangout for college students fleeing University-dominated **Marchmont** in droves in favor of Broughton's stylebars, bistros, and restaurants. The bustling scene includes hotspots like **The Outhouse** [see *bar scene*, below] and **Cafe Graffiti** [see *club scene*, below].

hanging out

Edinburgh is breathtaking on a sunny day, but those can be rare around here. When the rain stops and the skies do clear, people tend to get giddy, making hanging out here even more fun than in relentlessly sunny places. Skaters congregate at Old Town's **Bristo Square** (*Lothian St. immediately south of Charlotte Square*), a little stone plaza crowded with students, skaters, and spectators. Crowded all day with dog walkers, joggers, jocks, and students, the nearby **Meadows** (*Melville Dr. south of N. Meadow Walk*), adjacent to the University, also hosts special events during the summer. Another park, New Town's **Princes Street Gardens** (*Princes St. about two blocks from Charlotte Square*), is popular with tourists attracted by a nice picnic spot and **Castle** [see *culture zoo*, below] views towering overhead. In the heart of Princes Street, Edinburgh's busiest strip, there's always musical accompaniment, compliments of kilt-clad Scots pumping at their bagpipes for change.

The after-hours scene is paltry in Edinburgh. Once the bars and clubs let out, partiers head to afterparties held in somebody's place. Just ask

around as the night winds down to find out where the early-morning action is—the gregarious locals will be happy to fill you in. If a late-night snack is all you really need, **Pizza Paradise** (*South Bridge at Hunter Sq.; Tel 0131/557-49-05; Bus 3, 7, 8, 9, 14, 21, 33, 36, 64 to Royal Mile; 5pm-5am daily; AE, MC, V*) is probably the highest quality almost-all-night restaurant in town. The takeout section is no great shakes, but the restaurant proper serves decent Italian food. The place gets crowded with rowdy, inebriated customers, so beware or be one of them.

bar scene

They don't call it *scotch* for nothing. Whiskey is the cherished national drink, and bars here stay open until 3 in the morning to give it its due respect. You'll see packs of comically drunk citizens stumbling down the street singing, screaming, or puking *all night long*. The Scots love to share their magic elixir with the throngs of unwitting tourists who crowd into town each year, so be sure to ask at least one bartender to recommend a brand to sample in traditional 50ml "nips."

Despite the new competition, Edinburgh's most popular pre-club drinking den remains **EH1** (*197 High St.; Tel 0131/220-52-77; Bus 3, 7, 8, 9, 14, 21, 33, 36, 64 to Royal Mile; 9:30am-1am daily; AE, MC, V*), down in Old Town. Popular with visitors and business folk during the week, DJs ensure a clubbier crowd on weekends. The interior is painted in cool hues illuminated by funky light fixtures and an unbelievable chandelier. All manner of drinks and food are available, allowing trendy waifs to carbo-load before hitting the dance floor.

Among the competition, **Pivo** *(2-6 Calton Rd.; Tel 0131/557-29-25; Bus 2, 7, 10, 11, 12, 14, 16, 17, 22, 25, 87, 88 to top of Leith Walk, then short walk; 12pm-1am daily; pivocafe@yahoo.com;)*, a Czech bar, is popular with a slick young crowd attracted by the excellent beers and pumping house music. Ideal for a pre-club drink before heading over to **The Venue** [see *club scene*, below] across the street, Pivo is cool enough to stay at for the duration, too.

Over in the hot Broughton Street area, **The Outhouse** *(12a Broughton St. Lane; Tel 0131/557-66-68; Bus 2, 7, 10, 11, 12, 14, 16, 17, 22, 25, 87, 88 to top of Leith Walk, then short walk; 12pm-1am daily; MC, V)* is the most popular of the local bars, boasting a beer garden with Sunday bbq at noon in the summer, and two floors of indoor seating. The crowd, which sticks around until closing, is cool and sophisticated, flashing a more cosmopolitan style than most locals in this part of town. Thankfully, the regulars aren't as pretentious as they look.

Iguana *(41 Lothian St.; Tel 0131/220-42-88; Bus 23, 27 28, 37, 45, 47; 9am-1am daily; MC,V)*, in Old Town, attracts students and other young folk with Thursday evening drink specials and DJs Wednesday through Sunday, including Friday night jazz funk. Most of the time, the music remains chill, perfect for the mellow patrons downing drinks at the comfy tables and booths.

While some places clamor to keep pace with the vagaries of style, **Henry's Cellar Bar** *(8-16a Morrison St.; Tel 0131/538-73-85; Bus 2, 2a, 3, 3a, 4, 5n, 12, 21, 25, 30, 61 to Haymarket Station; 12pm-3am daily; No credit cards)*, in Old Town, remains a laid-back, pub-ish space

angus meets bonnie

The Scottish are very warm and reasonably polite given the amount of alcohol they knock down, and the bar scene definitely offers many opportunities to become better aquainted with other revelers. Starting conversations is pretty easy, especially if you look like an out-of-towner. Dead giveaways include oversize clothing or non-white ancestry. Just keep in mind that a nice conversation and a friendly kiss might just be a drunken flight of fancy and not a come-on. Real romance takes more than a drink and the bat of an eyelash (doesn't it?). A good place to troll for easy romance would be the ever-popular **Negociants** [see *bar scene*, below] which is usually the last stop of the night while out getting bent. Other potential pimping grounds include **The Venue** and the coed-filled **Potterow** [see *club scene*, below, for both].

filled with groups of friends enjoying the nightly jazz, drum 'n' bass, and hip-hop open mikes. The interior is nothing to get excited about, but the bohemian atmosphere definitely is—a good place to bring your honey.

Surprisingly cool despite its scruffy, diner-style appearance, Old Town's **City Cafe** *(19 Blair St.; Tel 0131/220-01-27; Bus 3, 7, 8, 9, 14, 21, 33, 36, 64 to Royal Mile, then short walk across Hunter Sq.; 11am-1am daily; No credit cards)* gets packed with a mix of grungy and trendy young people every evening. A favorite meeting place before going out large, everyone seems to know each other. More sophisticated surroundings are available in the clubby downstairs area, open Thursday through Sunday for pre-club shenanigans.

Attracting a devoted late-night crowd of freaks, drunks, and party people, Old Town's **Negociants** *(45-47 Lothian St.; Tel 0131/225-63-13; Bus 23, 27 28, 37, 45, 47; 9am-3am daily; AE, MC, V)* is among the most hysterically amusing places in Scotland. While the restaurant remains subdued, the downstairs dance floor becomes a drunken mess of friendly people trying to disco dance while clutching their cocktails.

Technically a restaurant with a bar, **Three Quarters Sports Cafe** *(4 Grassmarket; Tel 0131/622-16-22; Bus 2, 2a, 12, 12a; 11am-1am Mon-Sat, 12:30pm-1am Sun; MC, V)* is the closest thing to an American sports bar in Scotland. Perfect for watching Scotland's warring football teams, the Rangers and the Celtics, the giant screens also show foreign and international events like the World Series or the Olympics.

LIVE MUSIC SCENE

Edinburgh's live music scene suffers at the hands of Glasgow. Just under an hour away, Glasgow boasts bigger crowds and venues, leaving Edinburgh to commute to the biggest shows and tours. So you can't catch too many arena rock shows in the capital, but then again, what arena shows are worth the trouble these days, anyway? What Edinburgh does have is a number of smallish clubs featuring a range of fresh live bands from punk to jazz to hip-hop. Yes, there is Scottish hip-hop (which should come as no surprise, considering some of the mean rhymes busted out by Scottish poet-icon, Robert Burns). Listings of concerts and shows make up a large portion of *The List*, (which also includes Glasgow, for those willing to travel). For info on up-and-coming local acts, the staff of record shops like **Fopp** and **Avalanche Records** [see *stuff*, below, for both] are happy to educate the ignorant.

For purists uninterested in the out-there fusions of jazz, hip-hop, and electronica that are in vogue these days, the **Tron Tavern and Ceilidh House** *(9 Hunter Square; Tel 0131/226-09-31; Bus 3, 7, 8, 9, 14, 21, 33, 36, 64 to Royal Mile; 11am-12pm Mon-Thur, 11am-1am Fri, Sat, 12:30pm-12pm Sun; MC, V)*, in Old Town, hosts the city's best straight-up jazz on Thursday evenings. The place for folk as well as jazz, this traditional-looking bar is a hangout for local talent and their fans, with an entire floor devoted to *Satchmo's Jazz Cafe*.

Sharing space with Old Town's **Henry's Cellar Bar** [see *bar scene*, above], **Kulu's Jazz Joint** *(8 Morrison St.; Tel 0131/538-73-85; Bus 2, 2a, 3, 3a, 4, 5n, 12, 21, 25, 30, 61 to Haymarket Station; Noon-3am daily; No credit cards)* is a basement club favoring a heady brew of jazz, dance, and DJ-spun funk. Bands take the stage each night around 9pm, followed by DJs spinning until closing. The space doesn't really get rammed with scruffy hipsters until almost midnight.

Despite the best efforts of MTV and the music press to forget about rock, loud guitars still excite a small but diehard constituency. One of the biggest venues for rock music as well as electronic beats, **La Belle Angele** *(11 Hasties Close, Cowgate; Tel 0131/225-75-36; Bus 3, 7, 8, 9, 14, 21, 33, 36, 64 to Royal Mile; 9pm-1am for live music; £3-£6; No credit cards)*, in Old Town, is a favorite for major industry showcases and events. Long and concrete, the main room isn't all that special, but the shows are among the best in town.

club scene

In keeping with the laid-back spirit of the city, nightlife denizens don't pigeonhole themselves but go for everything from disco to trance to techno on consecutive nights. In keeping with the flexible vibe, most clubs have little to no dress code or door policy. They can also be intimate places to see big acts, free from the security needed at bigger venues. Don't even think about getting to the club before 10pm—the crowds are still out for pre-club drinks until around 11:30pm. Unfortunately, clubs close at 3am, leaving plenty of prime hours for private after-parties. Getting the lowdown is a simple matter of striking up a conversation with a local and not being scary. Piles of fliers are all over town, and comprehensive listings can be found in *The List*, Scotland's answer to *Time Out*.

Part of the Edinburgh University's student center, **Potterrow** *(Bristol Square; Tel 0131/650-91-95; Bus 23, 27 28, 37, 45, 47; 9pm-3am daily; £2.50-£8; No credit cards)* is one of the largest venues in town, hosting a mix of club nights that attract big names like Goldie and Boy George (yes, *that* Boy George!). Admission to this Old Town

rules of the game

Strictly speaking, the drinking age is 18, but no one asks for ID. Kids under 16 are barred from many drinking institutions, with the exception of those serving food. The penalties for driving under the influence are strict. As for drugs, the Scottish take the same pragmatic attitude as the English. While all the fun stuff is strictly illegal, the government provides lots of information and rehabilitation instead of draconian punishments. There's even a drug info shop on crowded Cockburn Street, which posts info on bad pills.

edinburgh bars, clubs and culture zoo

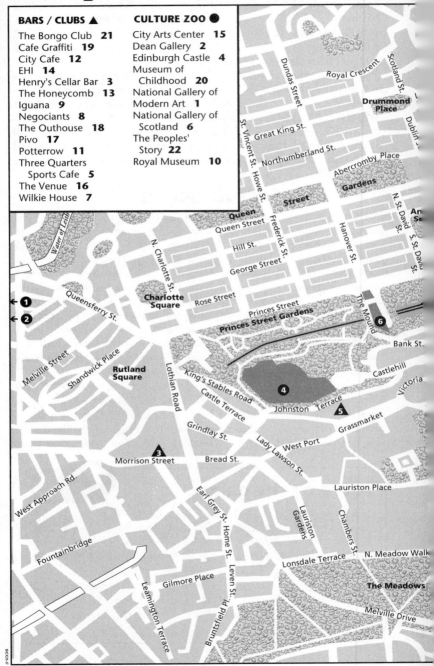

BARS / CLUBS ▲

The Bongo Club **21**
Cafe Graffiti **19**
City Cafe **12**
EHI **14**
Henry's Cellar Bar **3**
The Honeycomb **13**
Iguana **9**
Negociants **8**
The Outhouse **18**
Pivo **17**
Potterrow **11**
Three Quarters
  Sports Cafe **5**
The Venue **16**
Wilkie House **7**

CULTURE ZOO ●

City Arts Center **15**
Dean Gallery **2**
Edinburgh Castle **4**
Museum of
  Childhood **20**
National Gallery of
  Modern Art **1**
National Gallery of
  Scotland **6**
The Peoples'
  Story **22**
Royal Museum **10**

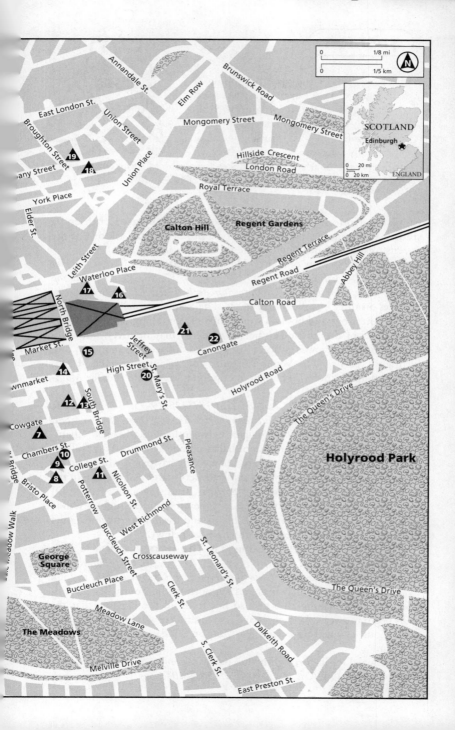

fashion

Good news or bad news depending on who you are: Edinburgh doesn't seem to give a rat's ass about keeping up with the style police. Most folks schlep around in what's comfortable, like jeans, chinos, and nice woolly sweaters when it cools down. The generally unaffected vibe makes for a relaxed time, even venturing out into nightlife. If you're comfy, they're comfy.

club is limited to students and their guests, so you'll have to befriend a student to get in, but that shouldn't be a problem—just ask one of the dozens of students hanging outside to sign you in.

Built in the shadow of Calton Hill, **The Venue** *(15 Calton Rd.; Tel 0131/557-30-73; Bus 2, 7, 10, 11, 12, 14, 16, 17, 22, 25, 87, 88 to top of Leith Walk, then short walk; 10pm-3am daily; Free-£12; No credit cards)* operates on three equally scuzzy levels. The Venue's actually in the same vein as Potterrow, and books a similar mix of acts, along with live shows by the likes of the Jungle Brothers. The decor may be divey, but that's not keeping the crowds away. Hosting loads of weekly, monthly, and fortnightly parties, The Venue is a must for serious partygoers. Highlights include the Scottish branch of London's *Scratch* and the free *Motherfunk* on Tuesdays.

Wilkie House *(207 Cowgate; Tel 0131/225-29-35; Bus 3, 7, 8, 9, 14, 21, 33, 36, 64 to Royal Mile then short walk; 10:30pm-3am Wed-Sat; £3-£10; No credit cards)*, on Cowgate between Lawnmarket and Chambers St., features a large dance floor balanced out by an upstairs chillout room. The monthly *Joy* is a sweaty and frenetic gay party, while Friday's *Vertigo* is a showcase for indy and punk rockers marooned up here in the land of dance music. The weekly *Shebang*, featuring an all-female DJ crew, is generally considered the place to be on Saturday nights. Wilkie House is also home to several club nights and theater events during the **Edinburgh Festival** [see *festivals & events*, below].

The attractive and well-heeled head to **The Honeycomb** *(36 Blair St.; Tel 0131/220-43-81; Bus 3, 7, 8, 9, 14, 21, 33, 36, 64 to Royal Mile, then short walk; 11pm-3am Thur-Sun; Free-£10; No credit cards)* to look fly together. Housed in two arches supporting the South Bridge, this small but breathtaking club gets so hot from all the dancing that the walls begin to sweat. With two bars, a smattering of tables and sofas, and voluptuous, cranked-up parties like *Taste* on Sundays, what more could you want?

Renowned for its fortnightly dub party, *Messenger Sound System*, **The Bongo Club** *(14 New St.; Tel 0131/558-76-04; Bus 1, 6; 10pm-3am*

Wed, Fri, Sat, Sun; £3-£5; No credit cards) also features Latin music that it mixes with clubbier fare. The club doubles as a multimedia arts space and offers the occasional dance class. Unsurprisingly, the out-of-the-way, warehousey space is a favorite among wildly varying cliques and scenes.

Housed in what was once the Mansfield Place Church, **Cafe Graffiti** *(East London St.; Tel 0131/557-80-03; Bus 7a, 8, 8a, 9, 9a, 19, 39; 9:30pm-2am Fri, Sat; £4-£6; No credit cards)*, in New Town, holds "services" on weekends, when hipster sophisticates crowd this crypt to enjoy a diverse roster of soul, jazz, and world music artists—call ahead for schedule and detailed directions to this out-of-the-way venue. This definitely beats Sunday school.

ARTS SCENE

The performing arts get more attention in Edinburgh because of the Festival, but there's a happening visual arts scene too. Always patriotic, Edinburgh's art community continues to support and show the work of Scottish artists, though the range represented is becoming less and less conservative. While many of the larger museums and galleries stick to conventional material, the annual degree shows of Edinburgh College of Art, Duncan of Jordanstone College of Art and Design, and Napier University reveal a range of styles and subjects, from the familiar to the way-out. Having caught the buzz around young British talent, the spaces in the Gallery Quarter south of Market Street exhibit material produced by the nation's best and brightest, including locals like Dalziel and Scullion, and Stephanie Smith. The closest thing to hangouts for the otherwise elusive artsy set are the cafes attached to The Fruitmarket and Stills galleries and the shelves of Beyond Words.

▶▶VISUAL ARTS

Occupying a former produce market, **The Fruitmarket Gallery** *(45 Market St.; Tel 0131/225-23-83; Bus 6n, 8n, 100, 154, 199; 10am-6pm Mon-Sat, 12pm-5pm Sun; AE, MC, V)* exhibits cutting-edge works in a space that incorporates a lefty bookshop and a restaurant.

Situated just a few hundred yards away, the **Stills Gallery** *(23 Cockburn St.; Tel 0131/622-62-00; Bus 3, 7, 8, 9, 14, 21, 33, 36, 64 to Royal Mile, then short walk; 10am-5pm Tue-Sat; www.stills.org; MC, V in gallery only)* strives to combine a beautiful but compact gallery space with a cafe, a digital imaging lab, and public art facilities. Bright and airy, the space is suited to the minimalist-leaning paintings, prints, and installations within.

Surrounded by the serene beauty of the Royal Botanic Gardens, about a mile north of the city center, the **Inverleith House** *(Royal Botanic Garden, Inverleith Row; Tel 0131/552-71-71; Bus 8, 8a, 9, 9a, 19, 23, 27; 10am-5pm Wed-Sun; www.rbge.org.uk/inverleith-house; No credit cards)* goes the extra mile to bedazzle. Work focusing on nature by hot local and international talent in a range of media is displayed inside this intimidating mansion.

The gallery at the **Edinburgh College of Art** *(Lauriston Place; Tel*

FESTIVALS and EVENTS

The Edinburgh International Festival may get all the attention, but there are lots of other special events, from traditional Scottish shindigs to big rock shows, to get your panties in an uproar.

Edinburgh International Festival *(mid Aug-early Sept; throughout Edinburgh; Tel 0131/473-20-00; ww.edinburghfestivals.co.uk)*: Touted as the biggest arts festival in the world, the Festival takes over Edinburgh, jamming every venue, hotel, and restaurant with attendees and artists. Featuring hundreds of performers from all over the world, the schedule is particularly strong in dance and theater, with touring companies and artists flooding in and staging everything from operas to naked avant-dance performances.

Fringe Festival *(mid Aug-early Sept; throughout Edinburgh; Fringe Box Office, 180 High St.; Tel 0131/475-23-60; www.edfringe.com)*: Having started as an edgier companion to the main festival, the Fringe has grown into a massive event in its own right. Emma Thompson, John Cleese, Eric Idle, and Rowan Atkinson all performed here early in their careers. With too many off-the-beaten-track performances to count, plus concerts, club nights, and comedy to boot, the Fringe satisfies anybody too cool for mainstream fare. Highlights include the **Flux Festival** *(0181/694-80-40; www.fluxfestival.com)* classical concert series.

Scotland Homelands *(early Sept, Royal Highland Centre, Ingliston; 0181/963-09-40; www.homelands.co.uk)*: The Scottish incarnation of Britain's premiere dance music gathering, Homelands brings a massive lineup of international performers and DJs up to Scotland for a two-day rave near Edinburgh.

T In The Park *(mid July; Balado, Kinross; 0141/339-83-83; www.tinthepark.com)*: Held halfway between Glasgow and Edinburgh, this two-day rock, dance, and world-music extravaganza draws bands of all styles and audiences from all across Britain, making it one of the best events of the summer.

0131/221-60-32; Bus 23, 27, 28, 37, 45, 47; 10am-8pm Mon-Thur, 10am-5pm Fri, 10am-2pm Sat; www.eca.ac.uk; No credit cards) exhibits year-round, but it's a hot spot come summer with the arrival of the annual degree shows. While these student shows are the most popular, their other year-round exhibits also number among the coolest in town.

▶▶**PERFORMING ARTS**

Performing arts in Edinburgh do exist beyond the world-class Festival—really. While year-round there is neither the money nor the scale of the

London scene, a number of excellent theaters put on groundbreaking new works, revivals, and local productions. The city also has a lively fringe centered around Edinburgh University. While larger companies like the Scottish Opera and the Royal Scottish National Orchestra (RSNO) are based in Glasgow, regular visits to the capital ensure that Edinburgh gets its fill of culture. The local **Scottish Chamber Orchestra** is also popular. Tickets should be booked at the box office, or by calling **Ticketline** *(Tel 0131/220-43-49)*. And despite a lack of local product, Edinburgh's screens show a happy mix of English, American, and foreign films all year long. Tickets can be bought at the door, or booked by phone.

Offering mainstream theater plus visits from touring companies, the **Royal Lyceum** *(Grindlay St.; Tel 0131/248-48-48; Bus 11, 15, 16, 17, 23, 37, 45; 10am-7pm Mon-Sat; AE, MC, V)* mixes it up—integrating a few new works and writers—into a diet of classics. The theater produces about seven shows during its spring and autumn seasons, along with a holiday program and a special summer season.

For slightly less traditional fare, the **Traverse Theatre** *(10 Cambridge St.; Tel 0131/228-14-04; Bus 11, 15, 16, 17, 23, 37, 45; 10am-6pm Mon, 10am-11pm Tue-Sun; AE, MC, V)* serves up touring productions, dance, and its own productions on two stages. The theater

only here

Not normally known for outrageous behavior, Edinburgh cuts loose each year at the end of winter during **Beltane** *(late April; on Calton Hill, Bus 2, 7, 10, 11, 12, 14, 16, 17, 22, 25, 87, 88)*, in a truly bizarre fertility ritual. From 10pm until the crack of dawn, revelers join a procession behind the May Queen, which is followed by the symbolic death and rebirth of the Green Man. Following the creation of a bonfire, large crowds of semi-clothed, drum-carrying revelers perform wacky rituals, many involving lots of the ceremonial whisky. Now, that's a *real* rite of spring.

Weird in a totally different way, the **Playfair Pathology Museum** *(18 Nicolson St.; 0141/527-16-49; Bus 2, 12, 23, 27, 28, 37, 40, 41, 42, 45, 46; By appointment; Free admission)* is definitely unholy. Part of the Royal College of Surgeons, this museum of medical oddities is a freak show of deformity and disease. Creepy mutations preserved in glass jars full of formaldehyde are displayed for examination by medical students or anyone else willing to book ahead. Definitely skip this place if you have a weak stomach.

is loyal to Scottish talent, a policy popular with the nationalist artsy set hanging in the theater's bar.

Housed in a deconsecrated church, the **Bedlam Theatre** *(2a Forrest Rd.; Tel 0131/225-98-93; Bus 23, 27, 28, 37, 45, 47 to Bristol Square, then short walk; 9:30am-12am during productions; No credit cards)*, in Old Town, looks as fringe as the works it produces. With a stoop popular with hobos, one could easily mistake the theater for its namesake asylum. Affiliated with Edinburgh University Theatre Company, the Bedlam also hosts student productions.

Edinburgh's most technically sophisticated venue, the **Edinburgh Festival Theatre** *(13-29 Nicolson St.; Tel 0131/529-60-00; Bus 3, 7, 8, 9, 14, 21, 33, 36, 64; 11am-8pm Mon-Sat, 4pm-8pm Sun; AE, MC, V)* shines when hosting performances by the Scottish Opera, which shares the schedule with orchestral events by the RSNO and a host of dance performances.

The largest venue in Edinburgh, with 3,100 seats, the **Playhouse Theatre** *(18-22 Greenside Pl.; Tel 0131/557-25-90; Bus 2, 7, 10, 11, 12, 14, 16, 17, 22, 25, 87, 88 to top of Leith Walk; 10am-6pm Mon-Sat; AE, MC, V)* is the home of the Scottish Ballet and Scottish Opera. The theater also hosts concerts, musical comedies, and Festival events.

The lone art-house movie theater in Edinburgh, Old Town's **The Filmhouse** *(88 Lothian Rd.; Tel 0131/228-26-88; Bus 11, 15, 16, 17, 23, 37, 45; MC, V)* shows foreign films, indy flicks of the moment, and classic movies, and hosts themed series as well as the Edinburgh International Film Festival, which runs in conjunction with the larger Festival [see *festivals and events*, above, for both] each August.

ABC Film Centre *(120 Lothian Rd.; Tel 0131/228-16-38; Bus 11, 15, 16, 17, 23, 37, 45; AE, MC, V)* shows the biggest Hollywood flicks on their monster main screen. To get you in the mood, the theater provides two separate bars, which can only be a good thing.

gay scene

Despite its conservative legacy, Edinburgh has a vibrant gay community. Centered in the so-called Pink Triangle, Edinburgh's gay life happens around New Town's Broughton Street. With the advent of the Scottish Parliament, gay groups are stepping up their political actions, hoping to make their presence felt electorally as well as socially. But things are looking up already: The Lothian and Borders Police have a **Gay and Lesbian Liaison Committee**, and it has an actual liaison, who is a direct community contact supervising police patrols of known cruising areas, stationed at the **Gayfield Square Police Station** *(2 Gayfield Square; Tel 0131/556-92-70; Bus 2, 7, 10, 11, 12, 14, 16, 17, 22, 25, 87, 88; 24 hours daily)* near the Pink Triangle. Those areas outside the patrols, such as Calton Hill, are best avoided after dark.

Edinburgh's gay scene has much to offer year-round, but the mammoth **Pride Scotland** each June is the biggest event. Information about this and other goings-on are widely available via newspapers like the monthly *Gay Scotland* and the weekly *Scotsgay*, which are both free. Basic info is available by phone at the **Lesbian Line** *(Tel 0131/557-07-51; 7:30pm-10pm)* and **Phone Gay Switchboard** *(Tel 0131/556-40-49; 7:30pm-10pm Mon-Thur).*

The Blue Moon *(36 Broughton St.; Tel 0131/557-09-11; Bus 7a, 8, 8a, 9, 9a, 19, 39; 9am-11:30pm Sun-Thur, 9am-12:30am Fri, Sat; £7; MC, V)* is one of the best places in town to get the lowdown on current events, parties, and activities. In addition to the friendly atmosphere, there's a good menu with a diverse mix of snacks and bistro cuisine that has plenty for vegetarians.

Just down the street, on a block full of funky bars and cafes, the friendly **Nexus Cafe Bar** *(60 Broughton St.; Tel 0131/478-70-69; Bus 7a, 8, 8a, 9, 9a, 19, 39; 11am-11pm daily; £7-£10; No credit cards)* serves more than food. Sharing space with a clubby, flamboyant clothing shop [see below] and the Lesbian, Gay, and Bisexual Centre, Nexus serves as a clearing house for info relevant to the gay community.

If The Blue Moon is the biggest gay cafe in town, then **CC Blooms** *(23 Greenside Place, Leith Walk; Tel 0131/556-93-31; Bus 2, 7, 10, 11, 12, 14, 16, 17, 22, 25, 87, 88; 6pm-3am Mon-Thur, 11am-3am Fri, Sat; No cover; No credit cards)* is the biggest—and most outrageous—gay bar. Packing crowds in every evening, the seating area and upstairs bar remain more civilized than the downstairs club, which features striptease and other tawdry attractions (use your imagination…).

Tucked away in an alley, **French Connection** *(89 Rose St. Lane North; Tel 0131/225-76-51; Bus 2, 3, 4, 11, 12, 15, 17, 21, 25, 26, 30, 33, 36, 38, 43, 44, 63, 85, 86; 12pm-1am daily; No credit cards)* is the tiny but trusty home of Edinburgh's transvestite and transsexual scene.

Over in the Pink Triangle, you can't miss the wildly popular, straight-friendly **Planet Out** *(6 Baxter's Place; Tel 0131/524-00-61; Bus 2, 7, 10, 11, 12, 14, 16, 17, 22, 25, 87, 88; 4pm-1am Mon-Fri; 12:30pm-1am Sat, Sun; MC, V)*—the exterior of the bar is painted an outlandish shade of orange. Prices for drinks and the usual bar snacks are tame in comparison to the raucous animal-print interior.

Edinburgh's lasting affinity for '70s tunes has kept its nightlife scene as gay-friendly as the Paradise Garage. With no gay-only clubs besides CC Blooms, Edinburgh's gay scene has successfully integrated itself, heavily patronizing a bunch of club nights that cater to its needs and interests. **Wilkie House** [see *club scene*, above], has several gay parties each month, such as *Joy*, and *Luvely*, a girls-only glamfest.

Another women-only shindig goes down each month at **The Venue** [see *club scene*, above]. *Divine Divas* is undoubtedly Edinburgh's biggest female fiesta. Call *Tel 0131/556-89-97* for info and schedule.

Tackno, held at **Club Mercado** *(36-39 Market St.; Tel 0131/226-42-24; Bus 6n, 8n, 100, 154, 199, ns101, ns201, ns106; 10pm-3am Wed, 5pm-3am Fri, 11pm-4am Sat, Sun; No credit cards)* is a freaky-themed

12 hours in edinburgh

1. The views from **Arthur's Seat** [see *great outdoors*, below] are unbeatable. The hike is fun, too.

2. Among the best records stores around, **Fopp** [see *stuff*, below] sells the crucial selection of CDs and vinyl for that definitive track to remember Edinburgh by.

3. Not popular for the decor, the **City Cafe** [see *bar scene*, above] is thronged on weekends with tons of psyched-up clubbers getting ready to paint Edinburgh red.

4. If you decide to check out Edinburgh's club scene only once, do not overlook the wild and crazy *Taste* parties held on Sundays at **The Honeycomb** [see *club scene*, above].

5. There are too many good reasons to justify why Edinburgh's **Festival** [see *festivals & events*, above] is the world's largest arts and performance bash.

6. **T In The Park** [see *festivals & events*, above] may not be precisely in Edinburgh, but the heavyweight lineups guarantee that it's the area's most infamous mega-concert.

7. Good food at reasonable prices is hard to find anywhere, espe-

tribute to '70s kitch trends too ridiculous to forget. The crowd comes dressed in appropriately silly get-ups (think wide-lapeled lime-green leisure suits) to get into the spirit of things.

Rubbing elbows with Nexus Cafe Bar at the **Lesbian, Gay, and Bisexual Centre, PJ's** *(60 Broughton St.; Tel 0131/558-81-74; Bus 7a, 8, 8a, 9, 9a, 19, 39; 11am-7pm daily; MC, V)* sells everything from flamboyant club gear to books, toys, and silly gifts.

CULTURE ZOO

Touristed year round, with crowds ballooning during the **Festival**, some of Edinburgh's most famous attractions cater to the lowest common denominator: The nostalgia and ghost tours, kilt purveyors, and historic museums along the Royal Mile between the Castle and the Palace of Hollyrood House are largely a waste of time and money. Nevertheless, amazing art museums and a handful of worthwhile historic attractions offer plenty of culture to squeeze between binges at the pub.

Edinburgh Castle *(Castlehill; Tel 0131/668-88-00; Bus 1, 6, 34, 35; 9:30am-6pm daily; AE, MC, V)*: The medieval buildings clustered at the top of the Royal Mile offer history and views, plus a renewed appreciation for modern amenities.

Museum of Childhood *(42 High St.; Tel 0131/529-41-42; Bus 1,*

cially in Edinburgh. Luckily the subterranean **Chez Jules** [see *eats*, below] fits the bill perfectly, with damn good French food convenient to much of the nightlife in Old Town.

8. While most of Edinburgh's museums try to out-Scottish one another with endless retrospectives of national heritage and art, the **Tate Gallery** [see *culture zoo*, below] demonstrates its patriotism by dedicating much of its exhibition space to an impressive collection of sculptures done by the nation's foremost artist, Sir Eduardo Paolozzi.

9. Have something battered and fried and douse it in salt and brown sauce.

10. Known for blending hip-hop, dub, and jazz into a funky brew, Blacka'nized is Scotland's illest hip-hop group. They make regular appearances at **Harry's Cellar Bar** [see *bar scene*, above] and **The Bongo Club**'s *Messenger Sound System* parties [see *club scene*, above].

6; *10am-5pm Mon-Sat; Free admission; MC, V*): Crammed with old toys and weird mechanical amusements, this museum could be a 19th-century Toys "R" Us.

The Peoples' Story (*163 Canongate; Tel 0131/529-40-57; Bus 1, 6; 10am-5pm Mon-Sat; Free admission; No credit cards*): Packing several hundred years of anthropology into a small row house, this very cool site gives some idea of what life in Edinburgh was like for everyone from the peasants of the 18th century to the punk rockers of the '70s.

Royal Museum (*Chambers St.; Tel 0131/225-75-34; Bus 3, 7, 8, 9, 14, 21, 33, 36, 64; 10am-5pm Mon, Wed, Sat, 10am-8pm Tue, 12pm-5pm Sun; MC, V*): The architecturally stunning addition, known as the **National Museum of Scotland**, is almost cooler than the natural history exhibitions within.

National Gallery of Scotland (*The Mound; Tel 0131/624-62-00; Bus 2, 3, 4, 11, 12, 15, 17, 21, 25, 26, 30, 33, 36, 38, 43, 44, 63, 85, 86; 10am-5pm Mon-Sat, 2pm-5pm Sun; Free, except for visiting exhibitions; AE, MC, V*): Set back from the action of Princes Street, the museum distracts lots of camera-wielding tourists with its collection of Italian Renaissance and French Impressionist art.

National Gallery of Modern Art (NGoMA) (*Belford Rd.; Tel 0131/624-62-00; Bus 13; 10am-5pm Mon-Sat, 2pm-5pm Sun; Free,*

by foot

While aimless wandering can turn up plenty, a more organized approach to Edinburgh's confusing streets is also a good idea. Take a stroll on the secluded **Water of Leith Walkway**, where you'll pass the Inverleith House in the Royal Botanic Gardens (accessible by Inverleith Row), the National Gallery of Modern Art, and the Dean Gallery (accessible by a path to Belford Road), and end up at Sandport Place, where a right turn leads to the Shore, Leith's most pleasant street [see *culture zoo*, below]. Stop in at **Kavio's** *(63 Shore; Tel 0131/467-77-46; Bus 1, 6, 7, 14, 14a, 25, 25b, C3 to Ferry Rd., then short walk; £15; MC, V)* for great Italian food. Then follow the Shore to **Commercial Street**, take a left and continue a short way to **Dock Place**. Stop in at upscale Bar Sirius *(Dock Pl.; Tel 0131/555-33-44; Bus 1, 6, 7, 14, 14a, 25, 25b, C3 to Ferry Rd., then short walk; 11:30am-12am Mon-Wed, 11:30am-1am Thur-Sun; MC, V)* for a stylish martini with the arty set.

Less charming but just as much fun, a shopping/scouting mission may unearth unlikely finds. Starting at **Waverly Bridge**, head up **Cockburn Street**, which has plenty of cool record stores like Underground Solu'shun [see *stuff*, below] to peruse. About halfway up the short street, stop at Whiplash Trash *(53 Cockburn St.; Tel 0131/226-10-05; Bus 3, 7, 8, 9, 14, 21, 33, 36, 64 to Royal Mile; 10:30am-5:30pm Mon-Sat; No credit cards)* which sells fetish gear and pot paraphernalia. After picking out a bong and bull whip, head to the **Royal Mile**, hanging a right. Check out the tourist traps along the way, keeping an eye open for **George IV Bridge**, where you take a left. Go right onto **Victoria Street**, which has lots of funky little shops like **Kool** [see *stuff*, below], and a Cuban bar called Baracoa *(7 Victoria St.; Tel 0131/225-58-46; Bus 2, 12, 23, 27, 28, 37, 40, 41, 42, 45, 46; 11am-1am daily; MC, V)*. At the bottom of the hill, take a left onto **Grassmarket**, which quickly becomes the medieval-looking **Cowgate**. After about five minutes of walking, turn left onto **Blair Street**, which is lined with bars, clubs, and restaurants, such as the gritty City Cafe [see *bars*, above]. At the top of the street, cross **Hunter Square** to the intersection of Royal Mile and **North Bridge**. Go left along North Bridge, where a few short steps take you to Cult Clothing and Schuh [see *stuff*, below].

except for visiting exhibitions; AE, MC, V): Massive and impressive, NGoMA houses an eclectic array of 20th-century art: works by Warhol, Pollack, Magritte, and the renowned artists of the Glasgow School.

Dean Gallery *(Belford Road; Tel 0131/624-62-00; Bus 13; 10am-5pm Mon-Sat, 2pm-5pm Sun; Free, except for visiting exhibitions; AE, MC, V):* Across the road from the NGoMA, this new space houses a large portion of the works of Sir Eduardo Paolozzi (a very hip modern Scottish sculptor), including the Iron Giant-esque *Vulcan,* which looks ready to bust down a wall and wreak havoc on the city beyond.

City Arts Centre *(2 Market St.; Tel 0131/529-39-93; Bus 6n, 8n, 100, 154, 199; 10am-5pm Mon-Sat; www.cac.org.uk; Free admission; MC, V):* Five floors show anything from cutting-edge textile design and video installations to mundane displays documenting the history of Scotland through its art. Hit or miss.

modification

With the city's biggest range of jewelry and best reputation, **Tribe Body Manipulations** *(248 Canongate; Tel 0131/558-94-60; Bus 1, 6; 12pm-6pm Mon-Sat; No credit cards)* is the place to get tattooed and pierced while in Edinburgh.

If changing your appearance doesn't appeal, how about your aura? **The Whole Works** *(Jackson's Close, 209 Royal Mile; Tel 0131/225-80-92; Bus 1, 6, 34, 35; 9am-8pm Mon-Fri, 9am-5pm Sat; No credit cards)* offers New Age-y services like acupuncture and dream therapy.

Another option is to get the full treatment from the **Edinburgh Floatarium** *(29 North West Circus Place; Tel 0131/225-33-50; Bus 20, 28, 80; 9am-8pm Mon-Fri, 9am-6pm Sat, 9:30am-4pm Sun; MC, V).* With services including sea salt floats, this is Edinburgh's answer to the Dead Sea.

great outdoors

If you can't afford airfare to Asia, try **Kagyu Samye Ling Monastery and Tibetan Centre** *(For information, contact Eskadale-muir, near Langholm, Dumfriesshire, Scotland, UK; 0138/737-32-32),* the first Tibetan center in the Western world. Primarily a monastery and temple, the center also coordinates international humanitarian efforts, and it's also a place to meditate or receive traditional Tibetan medicine. Phone in advance for info and reservations.

Less transcendental, but still cool, **Arthur's Seat**, a large craggy mound looming over the Palace of Hollyrood House, makes for a fun twenty minute hike. Take a right after the gates of the palace at the foot of the Royal Mile; paths wind up to a plateau of sorts, while the peaks require some minor rock climbing and scrambling. Only a (lazy) fool would pass up the free and spectacular views of the rolling hills ringing the city and the sea glinting to the east.

A cultural activity in its own right, golf is a source of national pride to the Scots, who are credited with creating the game. **Braids** *(Braid*

Hills Approach Rd.; Tel 0131/447-66-66; Bus 11, 15, 15a; 7am-8:45pm daily; No credit cards) is the nicest and most convenient of the two municipal courses in Edinburgh.

While the city proper lends itself to walking, the countryside offers flats and hills for your cycling pleasure. Bikes can be rented at **Central Cycle Hire** [see *need to know*, below]. Ask the employees for routes out of the city and into the hills.

STUff

Edinburgh is not what you would call a fashion hot spot. Avoiding the expensive labels that abound in London, the natives seem to prefer casual clothes. Most stores offer the standard fare, but often at prices that are lower than those found in bigger cities. Prices on records and CDs are also better, though still steep. Thanks to the aforementioned Scottish love of '70s music, there are oodles of collectible and hard-to-find albums.

▶▶**CLUB GEAR**

The best of the few streetwear retailers, **Cult Clothing** *(7-9 North Bridge; Tel 0131/556-50-03; Bus 3, 7, 8, 9, 14, 21, 33, 36, 64; 9:30am-6pm Mon-Wed, Fri, Sat, 10am-7pm Thur, 12pm-5pm Sun; AE, MC, V, DC)* sells men's and women's clothes, shoes, and accessories of the skater/clubbish ilk, plus more Carhartt workwear than Sears.

In a similar vein, though veering off toward the campy, **Kool** *(22-24 Victoria St.; Tel 0131/225-44-13; Bus 2, 12, 23, 27, 28, 37, 40, 41, 42, 45, 46; 10am-5:30pm Mon-Fri, 10am-6pm Sat, 1pm-6pm Sun; MC, V, DC, AE)* stocks a staggering selection of clothing and bags, given the tiny size of the shop. Now united with Wacky Enterprises next door, it also sells funky home items, makeup, and toys.

▶▶**DEPARTMENT STORES**

Not just the oldest, but among the biggest department stores in town, **Jenners** *(48 Princes St.; Tel 0131/225-24-42; Bus 2, 3, 4, 11, 12, 15, 17, 21, 25, 26, 30, 33, 36, 38, 43, 44, 63, 85, 86; 9:30am-5:30pm Mon-Wed, Fri, Sat, 9am-7:30 pm Thur, 12pm-a5pm Sun; AE, MC, V)* is a taste of what mainstream shopping was like before malls. Serving up just about everything from a snack to a wig, the store makes for hours of conspicuous consumption or just inconspicuous browsing.

For shopaholics who need to compare then and now, leave Jenners and stroll down Princes Street to the **St. James Centre** *(Leith St.; Tel 0131/557-00-50; Bus 2, 7, 10, 11, 12, 14, 16, 17, 22, 25, 87, 88; 7:30am-6:30pm Mon-Sat, 12pm-5pm Sun)*, the most central of Edinburgh's several shopping centers. In addition to the **John Lewis** *(Tel 0131/556-91-21; Closed Sun; AE, MC, V)* department store, there are athletic shops, a pharmacy, and a record store.

▶▶**GIRLIE**

If Delia's were British and had a store, it would look like **Miss Self-ridge** *(13-21 Hanover St.; Tel 0131/220-12-09; Bus 2, 3, 4, 11, 12, 15, 17, 21, 25, 26, 30, 33, 36, 38, 43, 44, 63, 85, 86; 9:30am-6pm*

Mon-Wed, Fri, 9:30am-8pm Thur, 9am-6pm Sat, 12pm-5pm Sun; AE, MC, V), a shiny happy shop with all the stuff the teen magazines recommend to get hot boys to *like* like you.

▶▶HOT COUTURE

Decorated in the all-white style often reserved for hair salons and art galleries, **Cruise** *(94 George St.; Tel 0131/226-35-24; Bus 13, 19, 34, 35, 39, 40, 41, 43, 47, 55, 82; 10am-6pm Mon-Wed, Fri, 10am-7pm Thur, 9am-6pm Sat, noon-5pm Sun; AE, MC, V)* cultivates sophistication and elegance with attentive service and the trendiest designer clothes in Edinburgh.

▶▶FOOT FETISH

Schuh *(32 North Bridge; Tel 0131/225-65-52; Bus 3, 7, 8, 9, 14, 21, 33, 36, 64; 9am-6pm Mon-Sat, 12pm-5pm Sun; www.schuh.co.uk; AE, MC, V)* is the preeminent shoe store here. Good prices on shoes of all styles make this the only place you need visit. While the sneaker selection favors old-school and skater varieties, the shoes range from futuristic moon boots to strappy sandals.

▶▶TUNES

While Princes Street has all the giant corporate retailers like **Virgin Megastore** *(124-125 Princes St.; Tel 0131/220-22-30; Bus 2, 3, 4, 11, 12, 15, 17, 21, 25, 26, 30, 33, 36, 38, 43, 44, 63, 85, 86; 9am-6pm Mon-Wed, Fri, Sat, 9am-8pm Thur, 11am-6pm Sun; www.virgin.co.uk; AE, MC, V),* Cockburn Street is Edinburgh's indie retail strip. **Underground Solu'shun** *(9 Cockburn St.; Tel 0131/226-22-42; Bus 3, 7, 8, 9, 14, 21, 33, 36, 64 to Royal Mile; 10am-6pm Mon-Wed, Sat, 10am-7pm Thur, Fri, 12pm-5pm Sun; MC, V)* stands as Edinburgh's top dance specialty emporium, featuring tons of hip-hop, house, jungle, and old-school records, CDs, mix tapes, and T-shirts.

Located just up the street, **Fopp** *(55 Cockburn St.; Tel 0131/220-37-81; Bus 3, 7, 8, 9, 14, 21, 33, 36, 64 to Royal Mile; 9:30am-7pm Mon-Sat, 11am-6pm Sun; www.fopp.demon.co.uk; AE, MC, V)* sells a wide variety of styles. While the vinyl selection in the basement endears the shop to DJs, the unbelievable number of sale CDs attracts all kinds.

Selling new and used CDs, plus some records, **Avalanche** *(63 Cockburn St.; Tel 0131/225-39-39; Bus 3, 7, 8, 9, 14, 21, 33, 36, 64 to Royal Mile; 9:30am-6:45pm Mon-Sat; MC, V)* hides gems in its highly subdivided but disorganized racks. With every style represented, there is something for everyone, especially those willing to scour the bargain bins.

▶▶BOUND

The Scottish literary superstore, **James Thin** *(53-59 South Bridge; Tel 0131/556-67-43; Bus 3, 7, 8, 9, 14, 21, 33, 36, 64; 9am-10pm Mon-Fri, 9am-5:30pm Sat, 11am-5pm Sun; AE, MC, V),* in Old Town, competes with big guns like **Waterstones** *(128 Princes St.; Tel 0131/226-26-66; Bus 2, 3, 4, 11, 12, 15, 17, 21, 25, 26, 30, 33, 36, 38, 43, 44, 63, 85, 86; 9:30am-9pm Mon-Fri, 9:30am-8pm Sat, 11am-6pm Sun; AE, MC, V)* by offering an exceptional selection of mainstream books alongside cultish titles and secondhand copies in a cool building away from the hordes on Princes Street.

Beyond Words *(42-44 Cockburn St.; Tel 0131/226-66-36; Bus 3, 7, 8, 9, 14, 21, 33, 36, 64 to Royal Mile then short walk; 10am-8pm Tue-Sat, 9am-5pm Sun, Mon; MC, V)* is the place to go for great photography books and treatises on the art of snapping pictures. Built for browsing, the shelves ringing the shop have benches built in.

▶▶**GIFTS**

And you thought it was just a skit on "Saturday Night Live".... **All Things Scottish** *(9 Upper Bow; No phone; Bus 1, 6, 34, 35; 9am-6pm daily; AE, MC, V)* is a real store selling a hysterically cheesy assortment of gifts festooned with tartan plaids. Worth a visit for a good laugh if nothing else.

ЄATS

With national dishes like haggis (which nobody's borrowing or fusing with anything) [see *deconstructing haggis*, below], Scotland is not known for its contributions to the culinary world. Fortunately, a lot of locals can't stand the fried and fatty grub either, preferring restaurants dedicated to cuisine that does not rely on brown sauce and salt. Unfortunately, anything beyond a baked potato or slice of pizza comes at a premium. Local favorites include French, Mexican, Thai, Indian, and anything with meat in it. Most restaurants don't require reservations, and few have high standards regarding dress. The tip is often included, so investigate before shelling out the 15 percent gratuity twice.

▶▶**CHEAP**

Sitting right off Leith Walk, the **Salsa Hut** *(3a Albert St.; Tel 0131/554-43-44; Bus 2, 7, 10, 11, 12, 14, 16, 17, 22, 25, 87, 88; 6pm-late Tue-Sun; Avg. £6 per entree; No credit cards)* sticks out like a sore thumb. This cramped and funky restaurant serves up Mexican staples to a young crowd drawn by the cheap prices, cool staff, and the excellent soul and hip-hop pumping out of the kitchen.

The **Baked Potato Shop** *(56 Cockburn St.; Tel 0131/225-75-72; Bus 3, 7, 8, 9, 14, 21, 33, 36, 64 to Royal Mile; 9am-9pm daily; £.1-3.50 per entree; No credit cards)* is among the cheapest restaurants in Edinburgh and is conveniently located just off the Royal Mile on the busy shopping strip of Cockburn Street. While seating is scarce and the deli counter unattractive, the salads, potatoes, fritters, and yes, vegetarian haggis, keep packin' em in.

Set beneath the **Edinburgh Backpackers Hostel** [see *crashing*, below], the **Southern Cross Cafe** *(963a Cockburn St.; Tel 0131/622-06-22; Bus 3, 7, 8, 9, 14, 21, 33, 36, 64 to Royal Mile; 8:30am-5pm Mon, 8:30am-11pm Tue-Fri, 11am-11pm Sat, 11am-5pm Sun; £5-£8 per entree; MC, V)* offers a menu of superbly presented sandwiches and entrees alongside coffees, beers, and homemade pastries. Both the

deconstructing haggis

A quintessential part of Scottish culture, haggis is even the subject of an ode by poet Robert Burns, "Address to a Haggis." Yet to the outsider, few things seem more disgusting than this national culinary treasure. While most Scots eat it only around Burns's birthday in late January, haggis is always available from fish and chips shops, butchers, and tons of restaurants.

So what the hell is it, anyways? Made from finely chopped sheep's heart, lungs, and liver; oatmeal, and pepper cooked within a batter-fried sheep's stomach, haggis is customarily served with "tatties and neeps," or potatoes and turnips. *Mmm mmm good.* Vegetarians should wipe the smug, relieved smiles off their faces: Though far from cruelty-free—to the eater—meatless version is also available.

recently renovated space and the food are comforting and attractively arranged.

▶▶**DO-ABLE**

With loads of restaurant/bars offering food at reasonable prices, you can easily eat where you drink. One such spot in New Town is **The Basement** (*10a-12a Broughton St.; Tel 0131/557-00-97; Bus a, 8, 8a, 9, 9a, 19, 39; 12pm-1am, service until 10:30pm daily; www.thebasement.org.uk; Avg. £8 per entree; AE, MC, V*), with their rotating menu of fusion cuisine heavy on Thai and Mexican flavors. The food is more sophisticated than you might expect judging by appearances, with homemade pâté and burritos proving perennial favorites.

Known as a late-night spot to get your freak on, **Negociants** [see *bar scene,* above] also serves an eclectic menu in the upstairs restaurant, with entrees around £9. With a capacity as large as the number of offerings, this is the perfect place for big groups who can't agree on what to eat. Try the kiwi-marinated lamb in rosemary sauce.

Chez Jules (*1 Craigs Close, Cockburn St.; Tel 0131/225-70-07; Bus 3, 7, 8, 9, 14, 21, 33, 36, 64 to Royal Mile; 5:30pm-10:30pm Mon-Thur, Sun, 5:30pm-11pm Fri, Sat; MC, V*) is easy to miss, due to its sneaky cellar location in a narrow pedestrian alley. Don't! The menu changes daily, offering up yummy French comfort foods like salade Niçoise and boeuf bourguignon. Options for vegetarians and health nuts are offered, too.

▶▶**SPLURGE**

Although it was opened as a low-key alternative to the posh Baan

edinburgh eats and crashing

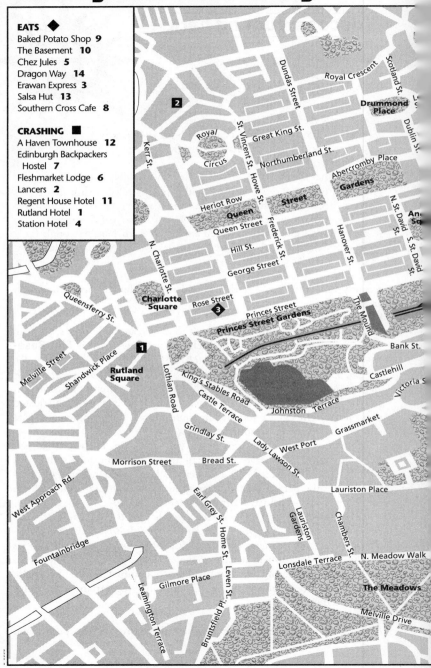

EATS ◆
Baked Potato Shop **9**
The Basement **10**
Chez Jules **5**
Dragon Way **14**
Erawan Express **3**
Salsa Hut **13**
Southern Cross Cafe **8**

CRASHING ■
A Haven Townhouse **12**
Edinburgh Backpackers
 Hostel **7**
Fleshmarket Lodge **6**
Lancers **2**
Regent House Hotel **11**
Rutland Hotel **1**
Station Hotel **4**

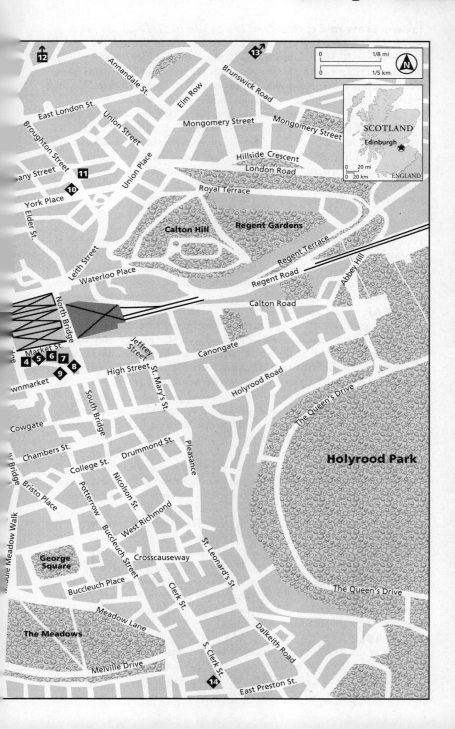

Erawan, **Erawan Express** *(176 Rose St.; Tel 0131/22-00-59; Bus 2, 3, 4, 11, 12, 15, 17, 21, 25, 26, 30, 33, 36, 38, 43, 44, 63, 85, 86; 12pm-2:30pm/6pm-10:30pm daily; £11-£13 per entree; MC, V)* is still pricey, despite the simple dining room adorned only by a few Thai tchotchkes. Thankfully, the menu justifies the expense with superb dishes like the ever-popular char-grilled satays and scorching curries.

Keeping in the vein of sophisticated Asian dining, **Dragon Way** *(74 South Clerk St.; Tel 0131/668-13-28; Bus 3, 7, 8, 9, 14, 21, 33, 36, 64; 12pm-2:30pm/5pm-12am Mon-Fri, 5pm-12am Sat, 6pm-12am Sun; MC, V)* looks like it was swept out of Hong Kong and set down in Edinburgh by some bizarre tornado. The red and gold pillars covered in serpentine dragon sculptures cultivate luxury, as does the extravagant menu, which offers dozens of entrees, starters, and soups.

crashing

Here in the land of the bed and breakfast, it's easy to find charming accommodations inside peoples's houses. While some are luxurious, many practically define the term budget, offering little more than a bed and some cereal. If you crave more privacy, there are thankfully also plenty of hotels in Edinburgh.

▶▶**CHEAP**
Visited by gajillions of backpackers and nature buffs on their way to the Highlands—or to the Festival—Scotland's capital has no shortage of cheap lodgings aimed at the young and the unpretentious. The best of the budget is the **Edinburgh Backpackers Hostel** *(65 Cockburn St.; Tel 0131/220-17-17, Fax 0131/539-86-95; Bus 3, 7, 8, 9, 14, 21, 33, 36, 64 to Royal Mile; info@hoppo.com, www.hoppo.com; £12 dorm, £40 double or twin; MC, V)*, where high-rolling backpackers can rent rooms in a duplex apartment complete with private baths and a kitchen instead of sleeping and showering with the common folk staying in the main dormitories. Centrally located on Cockburn Street, the hostel is surrounded by head shops, record stores, boutiques, and restaurants. Lively and well run by a young staff, the top draw for most is the weekly organized pub crawl from one end of town to the other (in the summer season only).

Though the name is disturbing, the **Fleshmarket Lodge** *(16 Fleshmarket Close; Tel 0131/226-51-55, Fax 0131/220-50-50; Bus 3, 7, 8, 9, 14, 21, 33, 36, 64 to Royal Mile; hostel@fleshmarketlodge.co.uk, www.fleshmarketlodge.co.uk; £14.50 dorms, £25 single, £50 twin; MC, V)*, near Waverly Bridge, is nicer than it sounds with comfortable, sparse-but-simple rooms. Dorms and singles share the facilities, doubles have en-suite bathrooms. The place is militantly non-smoking, but there are steps outside for nic fits.

▶▶**DO-ABLE**
Located at the west end of Princes Street, the **Rutland Hotel** *(1 Rutland St.; Tel 0131/229-34-02, Fax 0131/228-53-22; Bus 16, 18, 19, 22, 25, 26, 26a, 28, 31, 31a, 33, 36, 36a to west end of Princes St.; £29.50*

down and out

Edinburgh has plenty for the spendthrift visitor to do and see, from sights to nights. When the weather is good, trips to **Arthur's Seat** [see *great outdoors*, above] are tough to beat. A short walk from Old Town, it has unbelievable views and enough rocks to climb around on for hours. When the weather isn't favorable, stick to the museums—most of them are free. Clustered near Waverly Station, the **Fruit-market Gallery**, **Stills**, and the **City Arts Centre** take several hours to cover [see *arts scene* and *culture zoo*, above]. Further out, the **National Gallery of Modern Art** and the **Dean Gallery** [see *culture zoo*, above] sit opposite one another. After closing time, head to the student-oriented bars near the university [see *bar scene*, above]. Most have nightly DJs and dancing with no cover charge, and **Pivo**, **Negociants**, and **Iguana** [see *bar scene*, above] don't seem to care if you don't even get something to drink—though a good scotch whiskey might be just the thing to blunt the sting of the no-money blues.

single, £59.50 double; AE, MC, V) is near some forgettable shops and offices, but the city's cooler attractions require a brief (15 min.) walk. Rooms have TV and tea and coffee contraptions, although some lack private facilities. The hotel restaurant serves food and drink all day, not just between 8 and 9am like B&B's.

The recently remodeled **Regent House Hotel** *(3-5 Forth St.; Tel 0131/556-16-16, Fax 0131/556-16-16; Bus 7a, 8, 8a, 9, 9a, 19, 39 to Broughton St.; £20-45 per person depending upon single, double, or family rooms; MC, V)* is filled with antiques that cringe every time a drunken guest bumbles past returning from the bars around the corner on Broughton Street. Homey and convenient to the hipness of New Town.

▶▶**SPLURGE**

Conveniently situated within a hundred yards of the train station, the **Station Hotel** *(9-13 Market St.; Tel 0131/226-14-46, Fax 0131/226-14-47; Bus 6n, 8n, 100, 154, 199; £47 single, £75 double; MC, V)* rents nonsmoking rooms devoid of aggressively antique furniture. Perks include breakfast, laundry, and a restaurant.

A standout B&B, the **A Haven Townhouse** *(180 Ferry Rd.; Tel 0131/554-65-59, Fax 0131/554-52-52; Bus 1, 6, 7, 11, 14, 14a, 17, 17a, 25, 25b, C3 to Ferry Rd. and New Haven court; £40-70 single, £64-98 double; AE, MC, V)* is warm and abundantly Scottish, thanks to the proprietors, Ronnie and Moira Murdoch. The smaller rooms are very cramped, but the doubles are pretty normal in size and layout. The early breakfast is well attended by older couples and diehard tourists, confirming the Haven's status as a romantic little guesthouse, not a party palace. A short bus ride out of the center, to the north.

Need To KNOW

Currency Exchange: Scotland's currency is the same **pound sterling (£)** used in England, and while the Scottish issue their own banknotes, they're interchangeable with the British bills. Exchange your dough at places called **Bureau de Change** all around town or in most banks, or at the abundant ATMs. To do it with no commission, head to the **Edinburgh and Scotland Information Centre** [see below].

Tourist Information: The official regional tourist association, the **Edinburgh and Lothians Tourist Board**, operates two public centers that are packed with all manner of information and advice for the wayward traveler, and sell maps, books, stamps, and trinkets for tourists. To get the skinny before you arrive, check out *www.edin burgh.org.* Otherwise head to the **Edinburgh and Scotland Information Centre** *(Waverly Market, 3 Princes St.; Tel 0131/473-38-00; Bus 2, 3, 4, 11, 12, 15, 17, 21, 25, 26, 30, 33, 36, 38, 43, 44, 63, 85, 86; 9am-6pm Mon-Sat, 10am-6pm Sun)* or the **Edinburgh Airport Tourist Information Desk** *(Edinburgh Airport; Tel 0131/333-21-67; 8:30am-9:30pm Mon-Sat, 9:30am-9:30pm Sun).*

Public Transportation: Operated by a number of companies, Edinburgh's **bus system** is comprehensive and fairly inexpensive at 50p-£1.50 per ride, depending on the distance traveled, or £10 for a one-week **Travelcard**. Buses run erratically after midnight, if at all. For maps, schedules, and travelcards, visit either of the two **Travelshops** *(Waverly Bridge; Tel 0131/225-38-58; Bus 6n, 8n, 100, 154, 199, ns101, ns201, ns106; and 27 Hanover St.; Tel 0131/554-44-94; Bus 2, 3, 4, 11, 12, 15, 17, 21, 25, 26, 30, 33, 36, 38, 43, 44, 63, 85, 86; 8:30am-6pm Mon-Sat for both)*, both run by a knowledgeable and courteous staff. **Taxi** drivers are competent and can be hailed on the street or at queues around the central parts of Old Town and New Town. Minicabs operate for less money, but rides must be booked by telephone. One reliable service is **Persevere Private Hire** *(Tel 0131/552-23-22).*

Bike Rental: Bike Irax Cycle Hire *(13 Lochrin Place; Tel 0131/228-63-33; Bus 10, 10a, 27, 47, 102, 202 to Home Street, then short walk; 9:30am-6pm Mon-Sat, noon-5pm Sun in summer; www.bikeirax.co.uk; MC, V)* is one of the city's most knowledgeable outlets. Rentals run about £10-£15, with a £100 deposit refunded upon the safe return of the cycles.

Car Rental: Only requiring that the renter be a licensed driver age 21 or older, **National Car Rental** *(0900/996-699; 24 hours daily; AE, MC, V)* rents cars at the airport as well as within the city center. Rates begin at about £40 and get much higher for weekends, pickups, and deliveries.

American Express: *(139 Princes St; Tel 0131/718-25-01; Lost travelers*

wired

To check the Edinburgh sites listed below, or to meet other wayward travelers, try **Cyberia** *(88 Hanover St.; Tel 0131/220-44-03; Bus 2, 3, 4, 11, 12, 15, 17, 21, 25, 26, 30, 33, 36, 38, 43, 44, 63, 85, 86; 10am-10pm Mon-Sat; 12am-7pm Sun; www.cybersurf.co.uk; No credit cards)*. Terminal access is sold in half-hour chunks for £2.50, and sandwiches run about £3. The scene is like that of a neighborhood hangout, only nobody inside is actually from Edinburgh.

www.scotsman.com: The online version of Scotland's biggest paper. The site has news, weather, sports, and even a live camera feed showing Waverly Station and Princes Street from the roof of the paper's Old Town offices.

www.edinburgh.org: The official website of the **Edinburgh and Lothians Tourist Board**. The site is chock full of advice, accommodations info, links, and schedules of special events.

www.go-edinburgh.co.uk/main_set.html: All the info one could ever need on Edinburgh's lively festival schedule, from Fringe to Hogmanay.

www.dcs.ed.ac.uk/home/jhb/whisky: This in-depth site is devoted to Edinburgh's favorite beverage, malt whisky, lovingly compiled by the Department of Computer Science at the University of Edinburgh.

www.veg.org/veg/orgs/edvegans.html: The "cruelty-free guide to Edinburgh," from drinking spots to hotels to staying healthy without dairy or meat.

www.insideout.co.uk/ed/index2.htm: A search engine specializing in Scottish sites, with a focus on the nation's capital.

checks: 0800/521-313; Lost or stolen credit cards: 0127/369-69-33; Bus 2, 7, 10, 11, 12, 14, 16, 17, 22, 25, 87, 88; 9am-5:30pm Mon-Fri, 9am-4pm Sat) right in New Town is the local outpost of the credit card giant.

Health and Emergency: Medical emergencies: *999,* For 24-hour emergency care, the **Royal Infirmary of Edinburgh** *(Lauriston Place; Tel 0131/536-40-00; Bus 23, 27, 28, 37, 45, 47)* is the primary hospital facility here.

Pharmacy: For prescriptions, head to **Boots the Chemist** *(101-103 Princes St.; Tel 0131/225-83-31; Bus 2, 7, 10, 11, 12, 14, 16, 17, 22, 25, 87, 88; 9am-6pm Mon-Wed, Fri, Sat, 9am-7:30pm Thur, 12pm-5pm Sun; AE, MC, V),* which has many area branches.

Telephone: Country code: *44;* city code: *131;* information (politely called Directory Inquiries in Britain): *192;* international operator:

155. Pay phones accept calling cards and coins, with a minimum charge of 10p. **Calling cards** are available at tourist shops and tobacco shops. **AT&T:** *0800/890-011*; **MCI:** *0800/444-44-44*; **Sprint Express:** *0800/877-46-46.*

Airport: Just 10 miles west of the central Royal Mile, **Edinburgh Airport** *(Tel 0131/333-10-00; Airbus, Airline 100 Buses)*, handles flights from all over England as well as continental Europe. The **Airline 100 Bus** *(Waverly Bridge; Tel 0131/555-63-63; 6:30am-10:30pm Mon-Fri, 7:30am-10:30pm Sat, Sun; £3.20; No credit cards)* runs between the airport and Waverly Station. The **Airbus** *(Waverly Bridge, Tel 0131/556-22-44; 7:45am-8pm Mon-Fri, Sun, 7:45am-7pm Sat; £3.50; No credit cards)* operates a similar service. For more direct service downtown, try **Edinburgh Airport Taxis** *(Tel 0131/344-33-44; 5am-11pm daily; £12)* who will zip you there in about 15 minutes, longer during rush hour.

Airlines: All major airlines have their main facilities in Edinburgh at the airport. Call **Edinburgh Airport** [see above] for directions and the phone numbers.

Trains: All trains coming into Edinburgh stop at **Waverly Station** *(Waverly Bridge; 0345/484-950; Bus 6n, 8n, 100, 154, 199, ns101, ns201, ns106)*; many also stop at **Haymarket Station** *(Haymarket; 0345/484-950; Bus 2, 3, 4, 12, 18, 21, 25, 26, 30, 33, 37, 43, 61, 69, 85, 86)*, the city's smaller terminal.

Buses: Just off Princes Street, the **Saint Andrew's Square Bus Station** *(Clyde St.; Bus 2, 7, 10, 11, 12, 14, 16, 17, 22, 25, 87, 88)* provides service throughout Britain via the **National Express** *(0990/808-080)* and the **Scottish Citylink** *(0990/505-050)* coach companies.

Laundry: Get the smell of too many nights in smokey bars out of your clothes at **Bendix Self-Service Launderettes** *(342 Leith Walk; Tel 0131/554-21-80; Bus 2, 7, 10, 11, 12, 14, 16, 17, 22, 25, 87, 88; 8am-6pm Mon-Fri, 8am-5pm Sat, 9am-4pm Sun; No credit cards).*

glasgow

Despite persistant perceptions of Glasgow as a decadent drug- and crime-infested city, the 1999 UK City of Architecture and Design has (for the most part) left the days of razor gangs and heroin epidemics behind. Now, Scotland's biggest burg is one of the coolest destinations in Europe, a hot spot for music, performance, art, and of course, architecture. Inexpensive and highly livable, Glasgow is popular with students drawn by the Glasgow School of Art and University of Glasgow, Scotland's second-oldest university. Located in the West End, the University is surrounded by Glasgow's own funky version of San Francisco's Haight, a great place to chill out.

While the rest of Scotland gets more than its fair share of cold and rain, Glasgow, located near the west coast, enjoys slightly milder temperatures and a bit less rainfall, making it seem comparatively tropical. Glasgow is an industrious city, home to a hard-working blue collar populace that is enormously down-to-earth and friendly. In fact, some say the city's industrial past has helped free it from all that fluffy antiquity that can make Edinburgh a wee bit precious.

That doesn't mean that the local arts and culture scenes have been given short shrift. On the contrary, the city houses most of Scotland's classical music and dance companies, several great museums, both its football teams, and its largest concert venues. It's also famous for being home to numerous architectural marvels produced by the Art Nouveau genius Charles Rennie Mackintosh. A city rehab campaign begun in the '80s succeeded dramatically in restoring the area called Merchant City, now a trendy central district filled with shopping, nightlife, and sights.

Not only is Glasgow a different place than it was in the dark, depressed days of the '60s and '70s, it's now a northern outpost for cutting-edge artists and performances, fashions, and soon-to-be trends. From the impressive degree shows held by the **School of Art** each spring to the very layout of the **Gallery of Modern Art** [see *arts scene*, below, for both], art and aesthetics swirl together into unexpected and exciting mixes of tastes and styles. Glasgow is also at the center of the happening Scottish film industry, and music notables from here include earnest post-rockers like Mogwai and the Beta Band. All of which has made Glasgow a popular stop for travelers. Still, the new prosperity and tourism seem largely limited to the City Center and West End. The eastern and southern sections of the city continue to struggle with lingering crime and smack problems.

For all the culture available here—both high and low—just hanging out is a constant temptation. Glasgow's killer clubs and venues, DJs, and international acts keep the nightlife jumping. If banging techno and smooth, lounge-y house doesn't light your wick, the city is cluttered with enough cool stylebars, pubs, and restaurants serving the best food in Scotland, to leave you plenty of options. As in Edinburgh, all the relevant info on current parties, concerts, and exhibits can be found in *The List*, which comes out biweekly. For the skinny on the bar and restaurant scene, *Bite* magazine has all the news that fits into its pocket-size pages.

neighborhoods

Bigger and less concentrated than Edinburgh, Glasgow is easier to get around, thanks to its grid of streets. Making things even easier, many attractions, from bars to museums, are within walking distance of each other, clustered in the **City Center** and around the **West End**. Pick up a free *Visitor's Transport Guide* at the **Strathclyde Travel Centre** [see *need to know*, below] for help finding your way around these two areas.

Within the City Center, the architecturally stunning and slightly snooty **Merchant City**, near geographically-central **George Square**, the bohemian **School of Art** [see *arts scene*, below], and most of Glasgow's nightclubs, offer plenty to amuse besides museums and the like. A circular subway line joins downtown to the West End, where the **University of Glasgow** sits in the middle of a groovy mecca. Quirky little shops, cafes, bars, and other hangs clutter **Byres Road**.

Taxi rides are an easy and affordable alternative to the early-closing subway system, the **Underground** (aka the "clockwork orange" for its bright orange cars and circular route). The rail system, the **Low Level**, runs through the city and out to the suburbs. The cheapest public transport, the buses, would be convenient if only you could find a route map—the bus system is going through deregulation and things are a bit messy. Luckily, the underground, rail system, and taxis can put you within walking distance of everywhere important for about £5.

hanging out

Other than the pub, the best places for hanging out are in the parks in the West End or the squares and plazas in the city. **Kelvingrove Park**, a lush, sloping park tucked into the northwest corner of the city has space to frolic, a tiny skate park, and plenty of lounging folk. Near the Kelvinhall Underground station, the park is in the shadow of the University of Glasgow. Also nearby, the **Botanic Gardens** (*Great Western Rd.; 0141/334-24-22; Underground to Hillhead or Kelvinbridge; 7am-dusk; Free admission*) are a favorite with locals, who picnic on the lawns instead of checking out the greenhouses.

Central Glasgow has its share of places to people-watch, lounge, or soak up the sun between museums. Down the road from Queen Street Station, George Square is in the thick of things, convenient to sights and shopping, as well as to the bustling business district. On nice days, workers and visitors clog the square during lunchtime. Just a couple of blocks away, off Queen Street, the coffee shops and benches ringing the **Gallery of Modern Art** [see *arts scene*, below] provide refuge from the rigors of tourism. Visitors can lose themselves among the locals hanging out at the outdoor tables and benches, buried in cups of espresso and highbrow books.

For late-night hangouts, Glasgow favors the after party over the after-hours club. Once the bars stop serving, which tends to be—steady, now—between 11pm and midnight, people head to a friend's house if clubbing for whatever reason is out of the picture. For food, the comfy and vibrant **Insomnia Cafe** (*38-42 Woodlands Rd.; Tel 0141/564-17-00; Underground to Charing Cross, then short walk; 24 hours daily; Avg. £4-7 per entree; No credit cards*) is open all night. Halfway between the University and the School of Art, it attracts students, misanthropes, and weirdos trying to get off the streets. Other pickings for nocturnal snacking are kebabs, fish and chips, and convenience store junk.

Glasgow's weekend market, **The Barras** (*Between Gallowgate and London Rd.; Rail to High St.; 9am-6pm Sat, Sun*), over on the east side of town, is a contrast to the Glasgow tourists generally see. Both indoors and out, the market is filled with random junk, bootleg clothes, pipes, CDs, and snacks. More practical than cool, this is where bargain hunters and working-class families come to shop. The resultant atmosphere is one of utility—there are no punks hanging around sullenly smoking fags while club kids search for next week's outfit.

bar scene

Drinking establishments here fall into two basic categories: cool and conventional. Leaving the standard set for the old folks and teenage drinkers, Glasgow's young people prefer the style-y bars and pubs dotting the West

End and Merchant City, many of which are so near to each other that pub crawling means walking around the block.

Called **The Living Room** *(5-9 Byres Rd.; Tel 0141/339-85-11; Underground to Kelvinhall; 11am-11pm Mon-Thur, 11am-12am Fri, Sat, 12pm-11pm Sun; MC, V)* for good reason, this bar and bistro is a favorite with students and hipsters. The main room features exposed brick walls and a fireplace, and the music keeps up the vibe with plenty of soul and funk for color. Right off Kelvingrove Park.

Classier, but still homey, the east side's **Bar 91** *(91 Candleriggs; Tel 0141/552-52-11; Underground to Queen St., then short walk; 11am-12am daily; No credit cards)* has effortless flavor, combining a stylebar with a coffee shop. Its like a "Central Perk" that serves alcohol to media types instead of lattes to those oh-so-lovable scamps.

Bargo *(80 Albion St.; Tel 0141/553-47-71; Underground to Queen St., then short walk; 11am-12am Mon-Sat, 11:30am-12am Sun; MC, V)* is the quintessential Merchant City stylebar. The glass wall facing the street lets passersby gawk at the trendy customers quaffing martinis and looking swell. While locals typically man the turntables, visitors like Chicago's Green Velvet have spun a tune or two.

Removed from the prime drinking area in the heart of the city, hiding over on the east side, **Spy Bar** *(153 Bath St.; Tel 0141/221-77-11; Underground to Buchanan St.; 11am-12am Mon-Sat, 6pm-12am Sun; MC, V)* is all red and silver hues, recently revamped but maintaining its lanky, lounge-y vibe with music spinning every night. Soul and funk are staples. The drinks selection highlights cocktails, with martinis being the obvious choice for the dressed-up crowd of young professionals.

Simultaneously catering to young Merchant City drinkers and those in search of superb Scottish cuisine, **Rab Ha's** *(83 Hutcheson St.; Tel 0141/571-04-00; Underground to Queen St., then short walk; 12pm-3pm, 5:30pm-11pm Mon-Fri, 12pm-11pm Sat, Sun; AE, MC, V)* is a fresh take

lad meets lass

As in Edinburgh, Glaswegian mating rituals are closely related to the omnipresent social traditions of drinking. With the exception of traditional blue-collar drinking pubs, most bars get crowded nightly with eager and intoxicated groups of young people. While this is not unique to Scotland, many visitors are stunned by the brazen behavior of severely bent bargoers. An unfortunate consequence of a social scene so captivated with drinking is that a, shall we say, *lack of subtlety* is an infrequent but no less unfortunate spectacle. Clubs witness more effective macking, filled as they are with swarms of dressed-up fed-up people shaking their money-makers.

on the gastro-pub. The atmosphere is cozy and more like a regular pub, but the trip-hop on the stereo and the groovy clientele distinguish it from the run of the mill.

LIVE MUSIC SCENE

The center of the Scottish scene, Glasgow gets most of the big tours. There are plenty of all-star locals like Belle and Sebastian, Teenage Fanclub, and Arab Strip to play homecoming shows, too. It's got the usual mix of smaller clubs and venues where the local bands play, and a few places suitable for big acts and their elaborate stage shows. Hip-hop and reggae shows are few and far between, with most bands tending towards the loud and fuzzy or soft and intricate. Catch musicians hunched over a beer in Merchant City's cooler bars or flipping through the racks at **Fopp** [see *stuff*, below]. Check *The List* for info on upcoming shows and concerts. Tickets can be purchased at the **Ticket Centre** *(Candleriggs between Ingram and Trongate; Tel 0141/287-55-11; Underground to Queen St., then short walk; 9:30am-6:30pm Mon-Sat, 10am-5pm Sun; AE, MC, V)* in person or by phone.

Capable of housing 2,000 concert-goers, **Barrowland** *(244 Gallowgate; Tel 0141/552-46-01; Rail to High St.; 7pm-11pm; Ticket prices vary and must be purchased in advance; No credit cards)* is Glasgow's biggest concert hall. Big-name acts like Suede come through to rock the student crowd. Hence this drab-looking east side venue is busiest when school is in session.

The riverside mega-venue **SECC** *(Finnieston Quay; Tel 0141/248-30-00; Exhibition Centre rail; 9am-5:30pm Fri; Admission varies; AE, MC, V)* is the only place for arena rock. As with most venues capable of hosting the Stones, the acoustics are horrible. Nevertheless, bands keep coming and tickets keep selling....

Merchant City's **King Tut's Wah Wah Hut** *(272a St. Vincent St.; Tel 0141/221-52-79; Underground to Charing Cross; 12pm-1am Mon-Sat, 6pm-1am Sun; Admission varies; MC, V)* is the most legendary rock venue in Glasgow. This 350-capacity club hosts all types of bands from traditional rock acts to the reunited Sugar Hill Gang for one-off shows and runs.

About the same size, in the same neighborhood, but catering to an edgier audience, **The Cathouse** *(15 Union St.; Tel 0141/248-66-06; Underground to St. Enoch; 11pm-3am Wed, Thur, 10:30pm-3am Fri-Sun;*

five things to talk to a local about

If you think you can decipher the answers you'll get in the nasal accent prevalent in Glasgow, mention the following for a couple of guaranteed laughs:

1. **Edinburgh**: Glaswegians all seem to have a witty diss for the citizens of the nearby capital.

2. **Groundskeeper Willie**: While Barney may drink like one, Groundskeeper Willie is the one and only actual Scot on "The Simpsons"—if not all of American television (excluding, of course, the iconic Scottie of "Star Trek").

3. **Fat Bastard**: While you're talking idiotic stereotypes, why not mention Mike Myers' alarmingly accurate (yipes!) portrayal from *The Spy Who Shagged Me.*

4. **Glasgow's Razor Gangs**: If you happen to find yourself at a divey drinking pub, chatting with a fortysomething Scot who looks tough as nails, see if he'll reminisce about Glasgow's infamous and bloody gang battles of the 1960s.

5. **Local Music**: From banging hard techno to lounge-y house, Glasgow's electronic music scene is among the best in Europe. Ask the locals about any up-and-coming artists on the verge.

£1.50-4; No credit cards) books everything loud and fast. Throw on your Docs and a Nirvana T-shirt and come to mosh.

A vegan restaurant and a venue for shows and club nights, **The Thirteenth Note** *(50-60 King St.; Tel 0141/553-16-38; Underground to St. Enoch; 12pm-12am Mon-Sat, 12:30pm-11:30pm Sun; Free-£6; V, MC)* is at the heart of Glasgow fringe music scene—and in the heart of the city. Popular with artsy types and punky kids, concert-goers come for the food [see *eats*, below], and then head downstairs to hear anything from punk to jungle.

club scene

Long a presence in the global dance music scene, Glasgow has a club scene to match its creative output. Labels like Soma and artists like Freq Nasty get serious respect all over the world, and the strength of their reputations has generated interest in the Glasgow sound, typified by a hypnotic vibe of chilled-out house and trance grooves and the jarring thump of hard techno. Glasgow's style sense is "smart casual," excluding sneakers and wife-beaters—many venues openly discourage athletic gear or shabby streetwear. Clubs open later in the evening, staying open until 3am for the most part, and the few that stay open until 5am stop serving drinks at 3.

The crowds tend not to arrive before 11:30 or midnight, preferring pre-club cocktails elsewhere to empty dance floors. Fliers, which can be found at any record store, announce gigs, as does *The List*.

Probably the best club in Scotland, **The Arches** *(Midland St. between Oswald and Jamaica streets; Tel 0141/221-40-01; Central Station rail, Underground to St. Enoch; 11pm-3am Thur-Sat; £5-15; No credit cards)* holds thousands of sweaty clubbers dancing, drinking, and smoking fiendishly in a superbly frenetic atmosphere. Events rotate weekly in this centrally located club, with the monthly highlight being the house and techno of Pressure.

A few blocks away, snotty-as-can-be, **The Tunnel** *(84 Mitchell St.; Tel 0141/204-10-00; Underground to St. Enoch; 10:30pm-3:30am Thur, 11pm-3:30am Fri, 10:30pm-4am Sat; £2.50-12; No credit cards)* tries harder than any other club to rival London's megaclubs. A strict door policy ensures a sophisticated crowd hot to hear top international DJs. If you're interested, look and act rich, famous, or both.

Out of the running for best club due to its size, the **Sub Club** *(22 Jamaica St.; Tel 0141/240-46-00; Underground to St. Enoch; 11pm-3am Wed-Fri, Sun, 10:30pm-5am Sat; £3-10; No credit cards)* is still a perennial Merchant City favorite, with low ceilings and loads of booths to hide in. The smooth Saturday house party is one of the latest-closing nights in town. Knowing crowds of stylish low-key hipsters stay till closing regularly.

Just to the east, **Yang** *(31 Queen St.; Tel 0141/248-84-84; Underground to St. Enoch; 5pm-3am Thur-Sun; Free before midnight, £5 after; No credit cards)* plays a variety of musical styles simultaneously in separate rooms connected by winding corridors. While smartly dressed punters relax in booths in one room, B-boys headspin in another.

ARTS SCENE

Taking enormous pride in the current international interest in local architectural hero Charles Rennie Mackintosh, Glaswegians are eager for the rest of the world to take note of their entire national art scene. Celebrated in the newspapers and in *The List*, Glasgow's designation as the 1999 UK City of

RULES OF THE GAME

Under-18s aren't supposed to drink, but the only places that ever seem to card are nightclubs. As with everywhere in the UK, stiff penalties await anyone dumb enough to drink and drive, while people can stumble about in a drunken haze unmolested. Recreational drugs are illegal, but they're around to some degree. The city's had its share of problems with hard drugs and has managed to clean up a bit, while hash is ubiquitous among students and young people.

glasglow bars, clubs and culture zoo

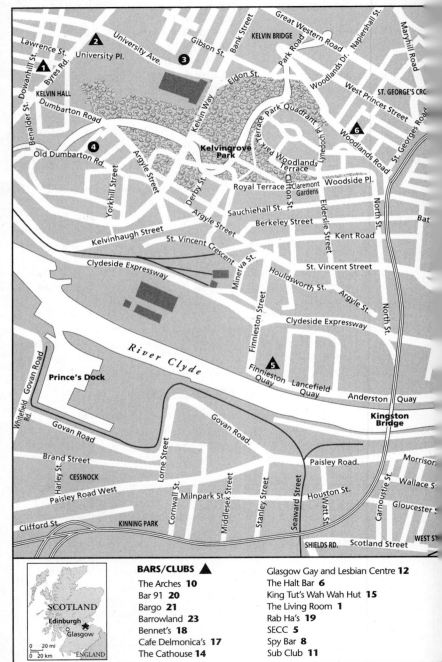

BARS/CLUBS ▲

The Arches **10**
Bar 91 **20**
Bargo **21**
Barrowland **23**
Bennet's **18**
Cafe Delmonica's **17**
The Cathouse **14**

Glasgow Gay and Lesbian Centre **12**
The Halt Bar **6**
King Tut's Wah Wah Hut **15**
The Living Room **1**
Rab Ha's **19**
SECC **5**
Spy Bar **8**
Sub Club **11**

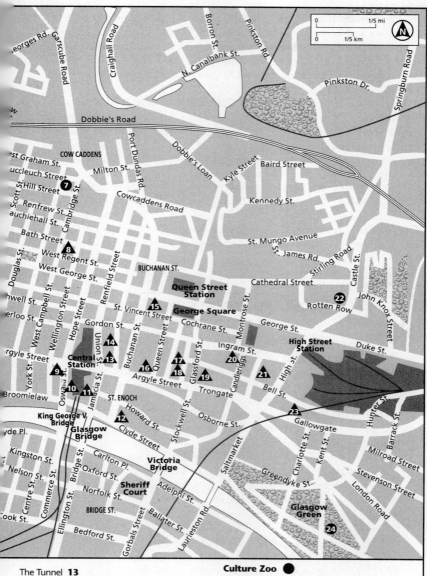

The Tunnel **13**
The Ubiquitous Chip **2**
Waterloo Bar **9**
Yang **16**

Culture Zoo ●

Hunterian Art Gallery and Museum **3**
Kelvingrove Art Gallery and Museum **4**
The People's Palace **24**
Tenement House **7**
Saint Mungo Museum of Religious Life and Art **22**

Architecture and Design has increased the fervor for all things inventive and original.

Aside from the elegant Mackintosh, the other golden child of Glasgow's architectural scene is Alexander "Greek" Thompson, famous for his take on the Victorian style of the city. As for more recent architectural standouts, the "armadillo" addition to the **SECC** [see *live music scene*, above] is an arresting site on Glasgow's River Clyde.

▶▶**VISUAL ARTS**

A jewel of a museum, the **Burrell Collection** *(Pollok Park, 2060 Pollokshaws Rd.; Tel 0141/649-71-51; Pollokshaws East rail, then short walk; 10am-5pm Mon-Sat, 11am-5pm Sun; Free admission; AE, MC, V)* houses excellent exhibits along with the treasures of Sir William Burrell. In addition to the Greco-Roman artifacts and Degas paintings, the museum recently curated a more-is-more retrospective of Mies van der Rohe.

The **Gallery of Modern Art** *(Queen St.; Tel 0141/229-19-96; Underground to Buchanan St.; 10am-5pm Mon-Thur, 11am-5pm Fri, 10am-5pm Sat, 11am-5pm Sun; Free admission; AE, MC, V)*, aka **GoMA**, has a consistently cutting-edge program of exhibits on top of its stunning permanent collection just east of Merchant City. Lacking

FESTIVALS AND EVENTS

Scotland Homelands *(Early Sept, Royal Highland Centre, Ingliston; 0181/963-09-40; www.homelands.co.uk)*: The Scottish incarnation of Britain's premiere dance music festival, Homelands brings a passel of international performers and DJs to Scotland for a gigantic two-day rave.

T In The Park *(Mid-July; Balado, Kinross; Tel 0141/339-83-83; www.tinthepark.com)*: Held halfway between Glasgow and Edinburgh, this rock, dance, and world music extravaganza lasts for two whole days, drawing attendees from all across the U.K.

Glasgow International Jazz Festival *(Late June-early July; Throughout Glasgow; Tel 0141/552-35-52; www.jazzfest.co.uk)*: Begun in the mid-'80s, the local jazz festival has grown more diverse over the years. Usually representing a variety of musical styles, performers in the last couple of years include George Benson, Joe Lovano and the queen of salsa herself, Celia Cruz.

West End Festival *(Mid-June; throughout the West End; Tel 0141/341-08-44; www.westendfest.demon.co.uk)*: With almost 200 events held all over the trendy West End, the celebration is one big self-congratulatory party in honor of Glasgow's swingingest section. Club nights, concerts, and performances of poetry and theater make the festival an exciting couple of weeks.

works by celebrity artists, the main galleries house exciting works by more obscure talents.

Serving as the temporary home of the **Centre for Contemporary Arts** *(350 Sauchiehall St.; Tel 0141/332-75-21; Underground to Cowcaddens; 11am-6pm Mon-Sat, 12pm-5pm Sun; Free admission; MC, V)*, the **McLellan Galleries** *(270 Sauchiehall St.; Tel 0141/331-18-54; Underground to Buchanan St.; 10am-5pm Mon-Sat, 11am-5pm Sun; Free admission; AE, MC, V)* are the focal point for Glasgow's art community. While the Centre is being remodeled to allow for even better art and multimedia exhibitions, the Galleries have stepped up to serve as a home away from home for all manner of progressive work from paintings to multimedia wackiness. There is also a coffee/snack/hangout space here with excellent people watching facilities!

▶▶ARCHITECTURE

A favorite Mackintosh building, the **Glasgow School of Art** *(167 Renfrew St.; Tel 0141/229-19-96; Underground to Cowcaddens; Tours begin at 11am, 2pm Mon-Fri, 10:30am Sat; Free admission; AE, MC, V)* is open for tours. Blending form and function to aesthetic perfection, Mackintosh created a lasting work made stronger by the collection of his drawings and designs contained within. This space also serves as a venue for live music and dance performances which tend to be young, fun, and energetic; mainly drawing students and longer-term travelers in Glasgow. Call for info or times and covers.

Only recently realized, Mackintosh's award-winning plans for the **House for an Art Lover** *(Bellahouston Park, 10 Dumbreck Rd.; Tel 0141/353-47-91; Underground to Ibrox; 10am-5pm Sat, Sun; £3.50; No credit cards)*, over on the west side, sat unused for nearly 90 years. While only four rooms have been faithfully re-created, the masterful dining room alone shows Mackintosh's genius.

The best thing to come out of the whole 1999 UK City of Architecture and Design thing is **The Lighthouse** *(11 Mitchell Lane; Tel 0141/221-63-62; Underground to Buchanan St.; 10:30am-6pm Mon, Wed, Fri, Sat, 11am-6pm Tue, 10:30am-8pm Thur, 12pm-5pm Sun; £2.50; www.thelighthouse.co.uk; No credit cards)*, a centrally located center dedicated to architecture, design, and the city of Glasgow. The space incorporates five galleries and an education center into one of Mackintosh's first public commissions.

▶▶PERFORMING ARTS

In the shadow of the Edinburgh International Festival, Glasgow's performing-arts scene is used to taking a back seat—even though the city boasts most of Scotland's major classical music, dance, and opera companies. In addition to the big companies and the annual visits by London's Royal Shakespeare Company, Glasgow has several small theaters and companies committed to innovative work. The center of the national film industry—which boomed following successes like *Trainspotting*—Glasgow is something of a cinematic hot spot. To find out what's hot, look in *The List* for reviews and schedules. Tickets should

12 hours in glasgow

1. The **Centre for Contemporary Arts** [see *arts scene*, above] consistently curates exhibitions of current artists making waves in Scotland and beyond.

2. **The Necropolis** [see *culture zoo*, below] is among the most breathtaking cemeteries on earth.

3. Possibly the most popular restaurant in town, **Air Organic** [see *eats*, below] has a fantastic menu and outdoor seating ideal for evening cocktails in the summer.

4. Tucked away below street level, the **Spy Bar** [see *bar scene*, above] is all style, from the colored wall panels and luminescent glass tables to the tall martini glasses in everyone's hands.

5. **The Sub Club** [see *club scene*, above] may not be the biggest club in Glasgow, but it is consistently the most fun, thanks to a loyal crowd of cool young people, great music and a relatively casual atmosphere.

be purchased by phoning the box office or by contacting the **Ticket Centre** [see *live music scene*, above].

Sharing its home with one of Glasgow's most popular nightclubs, **The Arches Theatre** (*30 Midland St.; Tel 0141/221-40-01; Underground to St. Enoch; 12pm-8pm Mon-Sat; £3.50-6.50; MC, V*) stages cool, youthful shows alongside a bevy of touring productions right in the center of town.

The **Citizens' Theatre** (*119 Gorbals St.; Tel 0141/429-00-22; Underground to Bridge St.; 10am-5pm Mon-Fri; £2-9; MC, V*), in the south end of town, is among the best in Scotland. The main theater, seating 600, shows bigger productions and reinterpreted classics, and the two smaller stages serve the more experimental productions.

For song and dance, the **King's Theatre** (*294 Bath St.; Tel 0141/287-55-11; Underground to Buchanan St.; 9am-9pm Mon-Sat, 10am-5pm Sun; Ticket prices vary; AE, MC, V*) is, indeed, king. Anything from cabaret to Andrew Lloyd Webber is performed at this Merchant City spot.

Just a block north, the **Glasgow Royal Concert Hall** (*2 Sauchiehall St.; Tel 0141/353-41-31; Underground to Buchanan St.; 10am-6pm daily; Ticket prices vary; MC, V*) is the home of orchestral music in Glasgow. Hosting international tours and the regular season of the Royal Scottish National Orchestra in its 2,500-person auditorium, this venue is lavishy comfortable and has excellent acoustics.

Over toward the east side, one of the only places to see ballet in Glasgow, the **Theatre Royal** (*282 Hope St.; Tel 0141/332-90-00; Underground to Cowcaddens; 10am-6pm Mon-Sat; Ticket prices vary; AE, MC, V*) is a spectacular venue. An annual schedule of productions by the Scottish Opera and visits by touring theater and dance companies provide lots of stellar performances.

The multiplexes can have the Hollywood fare, the **Glasgow Film Theatre** *(12 Rose St.; Tel 0141/332-81-28; Underground to Charing Cross or Buchanan St., then short walk; £2-4.25; MC, V)* specializes in art-house independents and foreign films. Art deco flourishes and a central location make this theater the perfect place to check out film series and festivals throughout the year. Also worth checking out is the coffee house to the left of the main lobby where you can hang out and discuss the merits of the flick you just saw/give away the surprise ending, etc.

gay scene

Although Glasgow is bigger and more populous than Edinburgh, the city has a much smaller gay community. Plagued by occasionally violent religious conflicts between Protestants and Catholics, the city in general is more anxious around questions of difference than its laid-back neighbor. The local gay community is spread out, and there is not much in the way of gay clubbing. Major annual events include **Pride Scotland** [see *gay scene* in *Edinburgh* chapter] and **Glasgay!**, a biennial gay and lesbian arts fest in late October and early November. Information, listings, and news relevant to the gay scene can be found in the free monthly *Gay Scotland*, or via the **Gay and Lesbian Switchboard** *(Tel 0141/332-83-72; 7pm-10pm daily)*.

With drag shows in a deceptively traditional-looking pub-style space, **Cafe Delmonica's** *(68 Virginia St.; Tel 0141/552-48-03; Underground to St. Enoch; 12pm-12am daily; No credit cards)* is a big hit with Glasgow's younger gay set, who come for the lengthy happy hours and stay to laugh at the karaoke.

Maybe it's the central location that makes **Waterloo Bar** *(306 Argyle St.; Tel 0141/221-73-59; Underground to St. Enoch; 12pm-12am daily; No credit cards)* so popular. Then again, maybe it's the cheap double shots during the 9pm-midnight happy hour. It surely ain't the garish decor. The knowledgeable staff is happy to provide info on the scene.

Run by the same folks as **Cafe Delmonica's, Caffe Latte** *(58 Virginia St.; Tel 0141/553-25-53; Underground to St. Enoch; 12pm-1am Mon-Thur, 12pm-3am Fri-Sun; MC, V, D)* is low-key and friendly during the day, more live, loud and trendy at night, especially on the weekends. The tasty food and eclectic music draws a 20ish, 30ish gay and straight crowd.

With a cafe and a bar, the **Glasgow Gay and Lesbian Centre** *(11 Dixon St.; Tel 0141/221-72-03; Underground to St. Enoch; 10am-11pm Mon-Sat, 11am-6pm Sun; MC, V)* is one of the best resources the gay community has and a center for gay life in Glasgow. The Centre also functions as ground zero for the organization of Glasgay!

One of the only gay clubs in town, the tried-and-true **Bennet's** *(80-90 Glassford St.; Tel 0141/552-57-61; Underground to St. Enoch; 11:30pm-3am Tue-Sun; No credit cards)* wins Miss Popularity. Attracting large throngs of gays and lesbians (mainly gays) of all ages, the club also squeezes in a popular straight night.

Glasgow's gay community moves in to take over the best and biggest dance floors in town when *Love Boutique* hits the ever-popular **Arches** [see *club scene*, above] on the first Saturday of the month.

CULTURE ZOO

From the eclectic collection of the Kelvingrove Art Gallery and Museum to The Necropolis, Glasgow has no shortage of alternatives to the crowds jostling to view the latest maverick of the art scene.

Kelvingrove Art Gallery and Museum *(Kelvinhall; Tel 0141/287-27-00; Underground to Kelvinhall; 10am-5pm Mon-Sat, 11am-5pm Sun; Free admission; AE, MC, V in gift shop)*: Built by an architect who is rumored to have killed himself when he noticed it faced backwards, this gigantic stone building houses a wild collection, from dead insects to a storm trooper's uniform from *Star Wars*.

Hunterian Art Gallery and Museum *(University of Glasgow, Hillhead St.; Tel 0141/330-54-30; Underground to Hillhead; 9:30am-5pm Mon-Sat; Free admission; AE, MC, V in gift shop)*: Home to a vaguely fuddy-duddyish collection of 19th-century artwork and a massive number of antiquities and fossils, this is Scotland's oldest public museum.

by foot

The Merchant City Pub Crawl: The true Glasgow walking tour, done the way the locals do it, is the Merchant City pub crawl. Starting at the upscale **Babbity Bowster** [see *crashing*, below], get your drunk on with a buttoned-up-but-arty crowd before exiting onto quiet **Blackfriars Street**, heading right. When you reach **Albion Street**, go left, and walk to **Bargo** [see *bar scene*, above] for drinks with Glasgow's coolest and best-connected. After leaving, continue left, making a right onto **Bell Street**. Walk one block to **Candleriggs**, where the cozy **Bar 91** [see *bar scene*, above] is located, to the right. After a cocktail with the relaxed bunch of regulars, head back the way you came, turning right onto **Wilson Street**. Two blocks up, on the corner, **Rab Ha's** [see *bar scene*, above] is waiting. After mingling with the intergenerational crowd enjoying drinks and delicious food, stumble back out to Wilson and continue one block further. At **Glassford Street**, turn right and walk up to the more studenty **Bacchus** *(80 Glassford St.; Tel 0141/572-00-80; Underground to Buchanan St.; 11am-12am Mon-Sat, 12:30pm-12am Sun; MC, V)*, where you can down yet another drink and some affordable eats at the last stop of the crawl.

Saint Mungo Museum of Religious Life and Art (*2 Castle St.; Tel 0141/553-25-57; Underground to High St.; 10am-5pm Mon-Sat; 11am-5pm Sun; Free admission; AE, MC, V*): Aside from the enormous Dalí painting, the stained glass and Zen garden are top draws in this monument to the world's religions.

The People's Palace (*Glasgow Green; Tel 0141/554-02-23; Bridgeton rail; 10am-5pm Mon-Sat, 11am-5pm Sun; Free admission; AE, MC, V in gift shop*): Built at the twilight of the 19th century, this one-time municipal building has become a repository for Glasgow's social and industrial history. Cool if you're into that sort of thing.

Tenement House (*145 Buccleuch St.; Tel 0141/333-01-83; Underground to Cowcaddens; 2pm-5pm daily Mar-Oct; £3.15; No credit cards*): Once somebody's actual home, this small attraction is a reminder of life in Glasgow's tenements. Good reality/perspective check.

The Necropolis (*Glasgow Necropolis Cemetery; Tel 0141/552-31-45; Underground to Queen St. Station; 24 hours daily; Free admission*): Inspired by Père Lachaise in France, this is Glasgow's premiere boneyard, the resting place of choice for many of the city's notables since 1832. Sounds macabre, but trust me, this place is spectacular and remarkably chilled, for a spot of self-contemplation.

modification

Before leaving Glasgow for warmer destinations, it helps to work out the kinks brought on by hard living. **City Beach** (*29 Royal Exchange Sq.; Tel 0141/248-82-82; Underground to Buchanan St.; 9am-10pm Mon-Fri, 9am-9pm Sat, 10am-7pm Sun; MC, V*) provides all the necessary services, from massage to tanning to an assortment of hair-removal techniques, in a convenient central locale.

great outdoors

When the thought of seeing one more house designed by Charles Rennie Mackintosh makes you want to shoot yourself, take a break and spend the morning learning qi kung (*chee kong*) at the **Patrick Burgh Hall** (*9 Burgh St.; Tel 0141/946-78-18; Underground to Partick; 10am-11am Wed; Free and open to the public, reservations recommended*), over on the west side. An ancient Chinese art of mind/body harmonizing, qi kung is a new craze in Scotland.

Glaswegians aren't really health nuts, but the few that bother to exercise do so in the parks around town. West Enders favor **Kelvingrove Park** [see *culture zoo*, above] with its tree-lined paths and grassy slopes, plus a path along the small but pretty River Kelvin. For jogging near the city center, choose the spacious **Glasgow Green**. Located by **The Barras** [see *hanging out*, above], it's Britain's first public park.

When the rains come, power-walk over to the West End and work some traveling stress out at **Kelvin Hall International Sports Arena** (*Argyle St.; Tel 0141/357-25-25; Underground to Kelvinhall; 9am-9:30pm daily; No credit cards*), the biggest public fitness facility in

Glasgow. It's got tracks and weights, and also hosts boxing matches and other athletic events.

STUff

Glasgow is the most cosmopolitan place in all of Scotland, and its shopping is unrivaled. Hundreds of mainstream shops augmented by nearby malls line Sauchiehall Street and Argyle Street, with smaller boutiques and shops tucked away in Merchant City and the West End selling cool club and streetwear, graffiti mags, and funky vintage gear. Prices are reasonable, with only the serious designer items costing too much. As in Edinburgh, record stores gravitate towards edgy CDs and hard-to-find vinyl, with enormous catalogues of reggae, soul, and funk that you won't find at mainstream outlets.

▶▶HOT COUTURE

You know a city has arrived when it gets its own **Diesel** *(116-120 Buchanan St.; Tel 0141/221-52-55; Underground to Buchanan St.; 10am-6pm Mon-Wed, Fri, 10am-7pm Thur, 9:30am-6pm Sat, 11:30am-5:30pm Sun; AE, MC, V)*. This particular outlet is long on women's clothing, with just a handful of men's items and the regular assortment of slickly hip tops and jackets and perfect jeans. In Merchant City, of course.

Other designer labels can be found for sky-high prices at **Cruise** *(180 Ingram St.; Tel 0141/552-99-89; Underground to Buchanan St.; 10am-6pm Mon-Fri, 9am-6pm Sat, 1pm-5pm Sun; AE, MC, V)*. Specializing in less mainstream labels, this chain delivers one of the largest selections of men's and women's fashions in town.

only here

Scotland's two biggest football teams, the Catholic **Celtic** and the Protestant **Rangers** are long-time combatants. Competing not just for victory but for sectarian pride, the teams—and their fans—are fanatics. When they play, age-old religious rivalries erupt both at matches and in the streets, often resulting in injury and death. Such hooliganism is increasingly discouraged these days, and while lasting peace is nowhere in sight, the growing tranquility has lured families back into attendance at local matches. The season lasts from August to May. **Celtic** plays at **Celtic Park** *(95 Kerrydale St.; Tel 0141/551-86-53; Bridgeton rail; 9am-5pm Mon-Fri; MC, V)* and the **Rangers** at **Ibrox Stadium** *(Edmiston Dr.; Tel 0141/427-88-00; Cardonald rail; 9am-5pm Mon-Fri; MC, V)*. Home games usually sell out, so check for availability and book in advance.

▶▶STREETWEAR

Taking inordinate pride in being the sole importer of Stussy clothing in Scotland, **Dr. Jive's** *(111-113 Candleriggs; Tel 0141/552-54-51; Underground to Buchanan St., then short walk; 10am-6pm Mon-Sat; www.drjives.com; AE, MC, V)* is a more than an emporium for surf and skate duds. With a superb collection of futuristic outfits for men and women, bags, shoes, and jewelry, the shop rates among the cooler—though more expensive—outlets in Glasgow.

With several different retailers setting up shop in the basement beneath its expansive anchor store, **Flip of Hollywood** *(70-72 Queen St.; Tel 0141/221-20-41; Underground to Buchanan St.; 9:30am-5:30am Mon-Wed, 9:30-6pm Thur-Sat, 12pm-5pm Sun; MC, V)* is a three-ring retail circus that has everything for retro dressers, trenchcoat mafiosi, and candy ravers in its central location.

Shoes and the clothes to match, from old-school Pumas to Tommy Jeans, can be found at the **Original Shoe Company** *(Queen St.; Tel 0141/248-75-10; Underground to St. Enoch; 9am-5:30pm Mon-Wed, Fri, Sat, 9am-7pm Thur, 12pm-5pm Sun; MC, V).* Selling men's and women's sneakers, shoes, and boots plus a preppy selection of pants, shirts, and jackets, the store draws Glaswegians in droves to get the clothes they see on "Dawson's Creek." (God only knows why.)

▶▶USED AND ABUSED

Relics *(Downside Lane; Tel 0141/341-00-07; Underground to Hillhead; 10:30am-6pm Mon-Sat, 12pm-6pm Sun; No credit cards)* is long on *Star Wars* memorabilia and short on anything useful. This campy little shop offers a special collection of books, records, and home decorations.

Although not quite as cool as Telly Savalas, the west side's **Kojak** *(116 Dunbarton Rd.; No phone; Underground to Kelvinhall; 10am-6pm Mon-Sat; No credit cards)* is a funky shop filled with outrageous outfits from the '60s and '70s. Leather jackets, boots, and corduroys line the walls and burst from the overstocked racks.

▶▶TUNES

A tiny shop stuffed with old-school hip-hop, house, techno, jungle, and reggae, out near the **Botanic Gardens** [see *hanging out,* above] **The Beat Museum** *(639 Great Western Rd.; Tel 0141/579-50-34; Underground to Hillhead; 11am-6pm daily; MC, V)* has a knowledgeable staff of self-professed soundboys.

Selling a more conventional selection of CDs, **Missing Records** *(685 Great Western Rd.; Tel 0141/334-79-66; Underground to Hillhead; 10am-7pm Mon-Sat; AE, MC, V)* is a West End institution. Well-organized, it also features numerous titles for £2 or less.

▶▶BOUND

Offering the same solid selection of books, plus a schedule of special events, **Borders** *(98 Buchanan St.; Tel 0141/222-77-00; Underground to Buchanan St.; 8am-11pm Mon-Sat, 11am-10pm Sun; AE, MC, V)* brings the American-style bookshop on steroids to Scotland. Even if you don't have the time to read a book, visit just to check out its fantastic

fashion

Glasgow is certainly trendier than Edinburgh, but it doesn't have any particularly discernable individual style-vibe going on. Whatever is popular and chic everywhere else at the moment is popular and chic here. So, for the moment—or was that five minutes ago?—break out the running shoes, cargo pants, cuffed jeans, minimalist gear, and Prada knockoffs.

location at the center of the public square surrounding the **GoMA** [see *arts scene*, above].

eats

Glasgow has some of the best food in all of Scotland. Drawing most prominently from Japanese cuisine, a number of new restaurants are generating a whirlwind of interest in authentic sushi, sashimi, and hearty noodle dishes in a faddish dash for foodie fame. Excellent Indian cuisine, wood-fired pizza, and authentic Thai adds up to a full range of culinary styles and price ranges.

▶▶CHEAP

The University Cafe (*87 Byres Rd.; Tel 0141/339-52-17; Underground to Kelvinhall; 9am-10pm Mon, Wed-Fri, 9am-10:30pm Sat, 10am-10pm Sun; £4; No credit cards*) looks and tastes straight out of the '50s. The food is cheap and the desserts are swell. As the name implies, there's a big student crowd here, 'cause it's near the University.

Leave the fur coat behind when you eat at **The Thirteenth Note** [see *live music scene*, above]. Serving vegan food on the cheap, this cozy restaurant/club attracts the obligatory students and scruffy audience members.

Technically a coffeeshop, **Tinderbox** (*189 Byres Rd.; Tel 0141/339-31-08; Underground to Hillhead; 8am-10pm daily; Avg. £4 per entree; No credit cards*) serves way more than coffee at its west side locale. Snacks, sandwiches, and everything from trendy CDs to 'zines like *Too Much Coffee Man* are on offer inside the sharply modern seating area.

▶▶DO-ABLE

Glasgow's first sushi bar, **Fusion** (*41 Byres Rd.; Tel 0141/339-39-66; Underground to Kelvinhall; 12pm-3pm, 6pm-12am Tue-Sat, 6pm-12am Sun; Avg £4-11 per entree; MC, V*), up by Kelvingrove Park, also serves gigantic bowls of noodles and delicate tempuras. Every dish is perfectly presented, a work of art prepared before your eyes in the open kitchen.

Too mature for its location in the student section of the West End, **Firebird** (*1321 Argyle St.; Tel 0141/334-05-94; Underground to Kelvin-*

hall; 12pm-11pm Sun-Thur, 12pm-1am Fri, Sat; £9; MC, V) is a subdued restaurant/bar with a cozy fireplace. The house specialty is wood-oven pizza; also try the mussels or the roast duck. The best time to visit is during happy hour (5pm-7pm), when a beer and pizza cost £6.

Also on the West End, the only all-Thai restaurant in all of Scotland, **ThaiSiam** *(1191 Argyle St.; Tel 0141/229-11-91; Underground to Kelvinhall; 12pm-2pm, 6pm-11pm Mon-Fri, 6pm-11:30pm Sat; Avg. £10 per entree; AE, MC, V)* teaches the Scots the true meaning of spicy. The menu has the ubiquitous pad thai and the other dishes that made Thai food popular, but there are also some tasty entrees that most won't recognize. Just ask.

▶▶**SPLURGE**

Air Organic *(36 Kelvingrove St.; Tel 0141/564-52-00; Underground to Kelvinhall; 11am-11pm Mon-Thur, Sun, 11am-12am Fri, Sat; Avg. £16 per entree; MC, V)* serves light, healthy, trendy fusion cuisine in a West End space both spare and striking. Futuristic tables and chairs are arranged in a cool white interior livened by lush plants and large, sunny windows. The wildly diverse menu covers everything from sushi to chicken noodle soup. Confusingly, not everything on the menu is actually organic—the owners use the best ingredients available, even if they sometimes happen to be doused with pesticides.

whiskey-a-go-go

Diehard Glaswegians rarely look happier than when they are clutching a "dram," whether single-malt or blended, straight or with soda. Though the subtleties of the many varieties of Scotch remain meaningless to most visitors, the curious traveler should take note of some elementary particulars.

Single-malt Scotch comes from one point of origin, giving it an unadulterated flavor. It is typically sipped without ice or dilutants, so that you can truly appreciate the clean, distinct taste—which varies dramatically from Scotch to Scotch. Given the purity of single-malts, it's no surprise that many find them too strong. Thus, blended varieties combine single-malt whiskey with other ingredients like corn, water, and coloring, to produce a milder (and much yuckier-tasting) liquor. No visit to Glasgow is complete without a sampling of Scotland's finest. **The Ubiquitous Chip** *(12 Ashton Lane; Tel 0141/334-50-07; Underground to Hillhead; 11am-11pm Mon-Thur, 11am-12am Fri, Sat, 12:30pm-11pm Sun; AE, MC, V)* is an energetic and smart hangout with plenty of malts to choose from.

glasgow eats and crashing

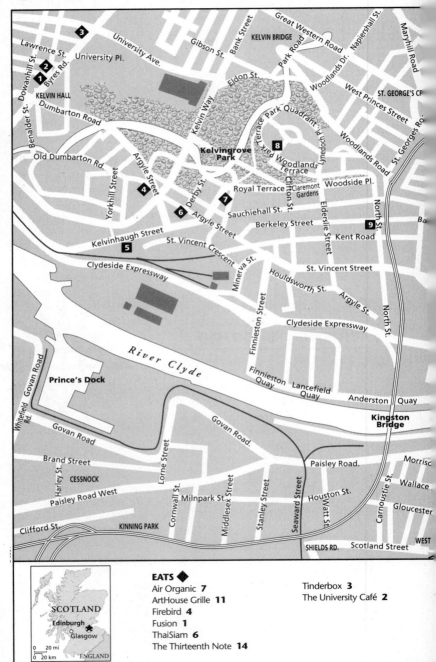

SCOTLAND
Edinburgh
Glasgow
0 — 20 mi
0 — 20 km
ENGLAND

EATS ◆
Air Organic **7**
ArtHouse Grille **11**
Firebird **4**
Fusion **1**
ThaiSiam **6**
The Thirteenth Note **14**

Tinderbox **3**
The University Café **2**

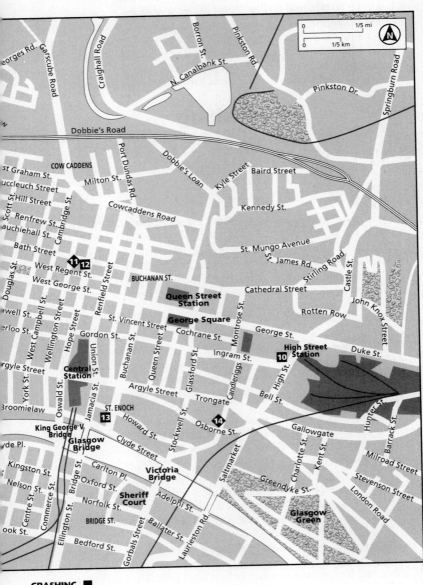

CRASHING ■

ArtHouse Hotel **12**
Babbity Bowster **10**
Berkeley Globetrotters Hostel **9**
Conference and Vacation Office, University of Glasgow **5**
Glasgow Youth Hostel **8**
St. Enoch Hotel **13**

Taking up the basement of the **ArtHouse Hotel** [see *crashing*, below], the **ArtHouse Grille** (*Same address and phone as the hotel; Avg. £17 per entree; AE, MC, V*) defies categorization. Offering a menu of Italian cuisine as well as a *teppanyaki* bar, and an oyster bar to boot, the kitchen seeks to satisfy the picky assortment of wealthy folks and celebrities staying upstairs. As with the rest of the hotel, the decor is eclectic to the point of confusion, jumping from bar to restaurant and back again within a single basement space.

crashing

Not as jam-packed with guesthouses as Edinburgh, Glasgow has its share of bed-and-breakfasts. This Scottish cottage industry competes with other accommodations varying in cost from ultracheap to extravagant. In addition to hostels and hotels, many of Glasgow's universities rent out dormitories when school is out.

▶▶CHEAP

As inexpensive as they come, the **Berkeley Globetrotters Hostel** (*63 Berkeley St.; Tel 0141/221-78-80; Underground to Charing Cross; £7.50 with own bedding, £9.50 shared, £12.50 per person for double; MC, V*) offers a good location between the West End and the City Center, plus laundry, Internet access (at a not very generous L1 per 15 mins.), and satellite television. Like most other things in the hostel, bathrooms and showers are of the shared variety.

A hotel disguised as a hostel, **Glasgow Youth Hostel** (*7-8 Park Terrace, Tel 0141/332-30-04, Fax 0141/332-50-07; Underground to St. George's Cross, then short walk; www.syha.org.uk; £13 nightly; No credit cards*) provides rooms of about six beds, each with complete private facilities. This amenity, along with the game room, common room, and television, and location near the University are big draws. The 2am curfew is not.

▶▶DO-ABLE

Used by businesspeople and students in town for conferences at the university, the rooms rented out by the **Conference and Vacation Office, University of Glasgow** (*Office: 81 Great George St.; Rooms: 5 Kelvinhaugh Gate, 115 Kelvinhaugh St.; Tel 0141/330-53-83, Fax 0141/334-54-65; £35 per room; MC, V*) are comfortable in that sterile way. The rooms at both locations are suites with a common kitchen/sitting room. A simple breakfast is included in the cost.

A block away from Central Station, the **St. Enoch Hotel** (*44 Howard St.; Tel/Fax 0141/221-24-00; Underground to St. Enoch; £35 single, £55 double; AE, MC, V*) provides simple accommodations in the shadow of the most enormous glass shopping center in the universe, the St. Enoch Centre, and is convenient to tons of bars and clubs. The hotel restaurant looks pretty unappetizing but is open 24 hours.

▶▶SPLURGE

The **ArtHouse Hotel** (*129 Bath St.; Tel 0141/572-60-00, Fax 0141/221-67-77; Underground to Buchanan St., then short walk; £50* *single, £80 double, £130 suite; www.arthousehotel.com; AE, MC, V)* favors the kind of opulence that includes stained glass and purple velvet wallpaper. Posh and flamboyant, this is where movie stars stay in Merchant City. With a hair salon and several restaurants, including the **ArtHouse Grille** [see *eats*, above], first-class service and comfort are inevitable.

need то кnow

Currency Exchange Scotland's currency is the same **Pound Sterling** (£) used in England. While the Scottish issue their own bank notes, they are interchangeable with British bills. Change your money in the places marked **Bureau de Change** that are all around town, or in most banks. The latter tend to offer better rates, though it pays to check around. Try **Barclays Bank** *(90 St. Vincent St.; Tel 0141/221-95-85; Underground to Buchanan St.)* or **Thomas Cook Travel** *(Unit 19, Central Station; Tel 0141/204-44-96; Underground to St. Enoch).*

Tourist Information Information and advice can be obtained at the **Greater Glasgow and Clyde Valley Tourist Board** *(11 George Sq.; Tel 0141/204-44-00, Fax 0141/221-35-24; Underground to Buchanan St.; 9am-7pm daily; tourismglasgow@ggcvtb.org.uk; MC, V).* Phone ahead *(Tel 0141/221-00-49)* to utilize the reservation service, which costs £2 plus 10 deposit. Pick up maps, leaflets, and public transport timetables at the **Strathclyde Travel Centre** *(over the St. Enoch Underground Station on Buchanan St.; 9:30am-5:30pm Mon-Sat).*

Public Transportation Walking is the quickest way around the center and West End. The city's buses are convenient as long as you know which one to take. For route and fare information, call or visit **St. Enoch Travel Centre** *(St. Enoch Sq.; Tel 0141/226-48-26; Underground to St. Enoch; 9am-5pm Mon-Sat).* Underground info is also available. Rides on the circle line connecting the city center to the West End cost 65p, and the subway closes around 10pm (6pm Sun). Thankfully, taxis are affordable, costing under £5 to go from Queen Street to Kelvingrove [see *hanging out*, above].

Car Rental The cheapest around is **Arnold Clark** *(459 Crow Rd.; Tel 0141/434-04-80; Bus 6, 6a, 16, 16a to Crow St.; 8am-6pm Mon-Fri, 8am-5pm Sat, 11am-5pm Sun; AE, MC, V),* which charges around £18 a day.

American Express *(115 Hope St.; Tel 0141/226-3077; 8:30am-5:30pm Mon-Fri, 9am-12noon Sat Aug-May, 9am-4pm Sat Jun-Jul; Underground to Buchanan St.)*

Health and Emergency Emergency: *999*. The **Western Infirmary NHS Trust** *(Dunbarton Rd.; Tel 0141/211-40-00; Underground to Kelvinhall)* has 24-hour emergency services.

Pharmacy Boots *(200 Sauchiehall St.; Tel 0141/332-19-25; Underground to Buchanan St.; 8:30am-6pm Mon-Wed, Fri, Sat, 8:30pm-7pm Thur; AE, MC, V)* has everything from antihistamines to condoms.

Telephone Country code: *44*; city code: *141*; information: *192*; international dialing code: *00*; international operator: *155*. Pay phones accept

wired

www.virtualglasgow.com: Complete tourist information with accomodations, shopping, and a web cam to show you the city.

www.fives.com: An online travel guide to Glasgow, download-able for easy printing.

www.rainbowrhythm.co.uk/glasweb.html: A funky city guide that covers club listings, style info, and the arts.

www.gglc.org.uk/gglc/: The online resource for Glasgow's gay and lesbian community.

To check these or other sites out (or to catch up on all that *news* from home), head to **Link Internet Cafe** *(569 Sauchiehall St.; Tel 0141/564-10-50; Underground to Charing Cross; 9am-11pm Mon-Fri, 10am-11pm Sat, Sun; AE, MC, V).* Offering internet access, instruc-tion, Web design, and Internet business advice in a central location, Link is more than the average cybercafe. While they do provide many small-business services, the staff are approachable and helpful to casual Net users too—and they give good directions. Close to the **Globe-trotter Hostel** [see *crashing*, above].

calling cards (available at tourist shops and off-licenses) and coins, with a minimum charge of 10p. **AT&T:** *0800/890-011;* **MCI:** *0800/444-44-44;* **Sprint:** *0800/877-46-46.*

Airport Glasgow Airport *(Tel 0141/887-11-11)* is 10 miles southwest of the city. Flight schedules available by phone.

Train Queen Street Station *(West George St.; 0345/484950; Under-ground to Buchanan St.),* and **Central Station** *(Union St.; 0345/484-950; Underground to St. Enoch)* are within walking distance of one another in the city center.

Bus Buchanan Street Bus Station *(Killermont St.; Tel 0141/332-71-33; Underground to Buchanan St.)* is the place to go for trips by coach.

Laundry Park Launderette *(14 Park Rd.; Tel 0141/337-12-85; Under-ground to St. George's Cross; 8:30am-7:30pm Mon-Fri, 9am-6:30pm Sat, Sun; No credit cards)* offers dry cleaning in addition to the stan-dard coin-op machines.

dublin

If you're young and out for a good time, the new Dublin beckons. This place is completely awash in money, and over half its population is under the age of 25. It'd be hard to find this kind of youthful, optimistic, hedonistic energy anywhere else on earth. In the past decade, an unprecedented economic boom started to sweep through Ireland, and things are moving along as strong as ever, with the capital city at the heart of it. Justifiably famous for its friendly, laid-back people, beautiful pubs, and small-city charm, the now cosmopolitan Dublin is even more inviting with packed clubs, vibrant theater and music scenes, great bars, and quiet cafes where you can kick back and watch Europe's wild west unfold.

You'll hear a lot of noise about Dublin's pubs, and though the hype can get a little overdone, the truth is that these establishments are, and always have been, the living heart of the town. Check out the special kind of friendly living-room vibe in a few comfy little beauties, and you'll see what all the fuss is about. The number of great places is astounding—the ones listed here only scratch the surface—and finding your own special pub is a Dublin rite. A lot of new places (often either slick "theme" bars or sort of Euro-loungey places) are also opening all over town, some say at the rate of dozen a day. Many Dubliners haven't quite decided what to make of these, but the international hipster contingent in town flocks to the best of them. The newer bars also usually offer more of a pickup/mingling vibe than the older pubs.

Dublin's generally a safe city, but the standard problems everywhere else are standard here, too: Just don't be careless. Pickpockets and purse-snatchers have been known to work busy shopping districts and crowded pubs, and it's not a good idea to embark on solo explorations down those temptingly dark, deserted side streets after hours. Lately, the local authorities have set up a pretty impressive network of 24-hour street surveillance cameras around town, so you might want to think twice about your own behavior under Big Brother's watchful eye.

Sources for arts and entertainment happenings in Dublin are legion: The glamour-glossy *In Dublin,* published bi-weekly and sold everywhere for £1.95, contains listings and articles on bars, music, clubs, flicks, theater, the gay scene, galleries, museums, and restaurants (plus the added bonus of always displaying a gratuitously bare, contorted babe and the word "SEX" splashed on the cover, not to mention the dominatrix ads in the back). The *Event Guide,* a free listings paper you'll find lying around most cafes and bars, does as good a job as In Dublin, minus the price, gloss, gay scene, and naked chick. The *Hot Press,* another £1.95 investment, also contains listings but is more of an organ for music-industry propaganda. The hefty *GCN* (Gay Community News), published monthly, can be found in gay-friendly places about town.

neighborhoods

Whatever you're up to, the city center will usually be the place for doin' it. The slow, walled-in **River Liffey** flows east-west through Dublin's core, and most main streets either flow from bridges at right angles to the Liffey, or branch out from these main thoroughfares and run parallel to its bending path. **O'Connell Bridge** lies at the heart of the center. **O'Connell Street,** the old commercial guts of the town, stretches north from the bridge and past the monumental **General Post Office** to **Parnell Square.** This is one of the most soulful parts of Dublin, with a lot of grand old architecture gone a little seedy and not a lot going on (although new development is brightening things up rapidly). To the south, there's **Temple Bar,** a web of cobblestone streets once a funky haven for artists, now a Disneyfied hotbed of touristy bars, clubs, shops, and restaurants. To the east, in the network of winding streets within the borders formed by **Grafton Street, Trinity College, Dublin Castle,** and Temple Bar, is one of the city's heaviest clusters of great bars, pubs, cafes, and live music: The Dublin where Dubliners party. To the southeast,

fIVE-O

Dublin police, called Gardai (that's "Gardee" or usually just "the Gard"), are a pretty straightforward, helpful bunch. Feel confident going to them if you need assistance, but also keep in mind that they can search anyone on reasonable suspicion of drug possession and hold them in jail for seven days without charge.

five things to talk to a local about

Dubliners need about as much prodding to talk as hemophiliacs do to bleed. A hearty "hello" should get you an earful with most any representative of this most friendly, loquacious race. Still, if you're worried, give the following openers a try:

1. The Irish seem generally obsessed with any and all of their **famous fellow-citizens,** especially the musicians: U2, the Cranberries, Samantha Mumba, Boyzone, Ronan Keating, the Corrs, Sinead O'Connor, etc. Drop a name and see where it takes you.

2. Anything touching on **drink:** Irish beers, Irish whiskey, and, of course, the great old pubs of Dublin.

3. Ask somebody about **Gaelic football** and/or hurling [see *gaelic games,* below].

4. These days, **the Celtic Tiger** is on everyone's lips. What is it, where did it come from, and how will it thrive in the future?

5. **Ireland** itself seems an inexhaustible subject for the locals. Ask someone to tell you what you should know about this fair island, but only if you've got a comfortable seat.

down Grafton Street, there's **St. Stephen's Green** [see *hanging out,* below]. Here you get a lot of the fancier hotels and expensive shopping, plus the national gallery, museum, and the library complex. Further to the east of the Green, there are long, elegant rows of brick-faced townhouses arranged around well-manicured squares. Not a hot spot, sure, but something to see.

Public transportation in Dublin is in a bit of a transitional period at the moment. The current bus-centered system just can't keep up with the huge load brought in by Dublin's boomtown economy, nor do those big and beautiful double deckers exactly fly through the city's near-constant gridlock. To make matters worse, Dublin's regular transit routes shut down by 11:30pm, just when the party's getting started for most people. The DART system, which connects the suburbs to the north and south of Dublin, runs til midnight. A new system is currently in the government pipeline, but don't hold your breath. Fortunately, the bulk of stuff to see and do in town lies within a 20 minutes' walk of O'Connell Bridge. So save yourself a lot of wasted time and aggravation, book your digs as near as possible to the city center and take to the streets by foot. Bicycle rental is also an option [see *need to know,* below], but in Dublin's kind of urban mayhem, it's only for those who like to walk that fine line between bravery and stupidity.

how to score really good craic

First thing you gotta know when you come to Ireland is about *craic*. You may be shocked to hear people talking about how much good crack they have. You'll hear things like, "ooh, boy, did I have great *crack* last night!" You may wonder, since when did Dublin get hooked on the pipe? Well, don't fret, they're actually talking about *craic*, not *crack*. *Craic* (pronounced "crack") is not a *thing*, it's more of a feeling. When you go out with friends, sit around, have a couple pints, talk, gossip, laugh, maybe listen to music, well, that's *craic*. When you smoke a purified form of cocaine out of a little glass pipe, well that's just stupid. *Craic* is what makes Ireland the place it is. It's the resilient attitude that keeps the Irish Irish, the invisible glue that binds people together. How do you get local *craic*? It's really second nature, it's just a bit different in Ireland. Go out with friends old or new, spark up a conversation with a local, talk, laugh, drink and you'll be having *craic* in no time.

For info about where to find good *craic*, go to ***www.wheresthe craic.com.*** This entertainment guide features up-to-date listings of music gigs in Dublin, Cork, Kilkenny, Limerick and other places.

hanging out

Dublin's streetlife is kind of manic-depressive, with full bipolar swings depending on the weather's whims. Of course, the wet days can turn the outdoor hangout spots bleak and lifeless, but that's the perfect time to join everybody else in a cozy corner of the nearest pub. Meanwhile, even just an hour of warm sunshine guarantees crowds in the parks, cafes, and plazas. Spring fever comes on something fierce for the ray-starved Irish. You've got to get yourself to a park on these rare days: The vibe is electric.

The very best place in town for collective, ecstatic sun worship has got to be the **Trinity College Park** (*back of Trinity College, near corner of Leinster St. S. and Lincoln Place*). On sunny weekday mid-afternoons, the young and over-privileged gather to drink beer, watch cricket, and mingle. This is the best to pretend you're local or meet someone who is. The good times come complete with a patio of (sometimes) sun-kissed picnic tables at Trinity's **Pavilion Bar,** gorgeously manicured grass, and leafy colonnades of trees. If you get tired of gazing on white linens and melanin-deprived flesh, there's always the glowering imperial architecture for eye candy.

For that universal "My God, small world!" run-in with your old college roommate or to mix with other travelers from around the world, go sit on the steps of **Temple Bar Square,** right in the heart of Temple Bar. On a sunny afternoon, there'll always be someone here you'll want to talk to, even if you can't speak the same language. To add to the circus feel, summertime brings street theater to the square every weekday from noonish to 3pm.

For the local skate rats, it's gotta be the **Central Bank Plaza,** just down from Trinity College on Dame Street.

At the south end of Grafton Street, **St. Stephen's Green** is the most popular park in Dublin. Once a great spot for grisly public executions, now it's a tranquil haven for groping lovers. A mixed, anonymous, all-city crowd frolics here, amidst the landscaped flower beds, duck ponds, bridges, gazebos, and shady groves. Usually full of folks, but big enough so there's always a spot free.

Since this is Dublin, the key thing about **The Bailey** *(Duke St., D2; Tel 01/670-49-39; Bus 32X, 39X, 41X, 66X, 67X; Noon-11:30pm Mon-Sat, 4-11pm Sun; AE, V, MC, DC)* is those big heat lamps set up above the outdoor tables. In a pedestrianized enclave just off shoporama-central Grafton Street, these are the best (and most popular) sidewalk views in town. Regulars cultivate that "just slightly overdressed" look, both day and night. Lunch in leopardskin? They've done it—without raising an eyebrow. Slightly gay, pickings are good for all persuasions in the evenings, especially if you like trophy-wife-in-training types.

A more casual choice, on the other side of Grafton Street, behind Powerscourt Shopping Centre, smack-dab in a people-watching-friendly cluster of outdoor cafes, is the mellow **Metro Café** *(43 S. William St., D2; Tel 01/679-45-15; Bus 32X, 39X, 41X, 66X, 67X; 8am-8pm daily; No credit cards)*. The outdoor tables here wrap into an alley that gets a direct solar hit in the afternoon.

Turning into an all-night party on weekends after the clubs close, **@ Home Cafe** [see *eats,* below] draws an international, gay-straight mixed crowd of hipsters in for grooves, tapas, and wine. This place can be hard to find and sometimes hard to get into (but definitely worth the effort), so make sure you know the where's and how's before you get wasted. Drop in during the day and get the lowdown from the ultra-friendly staff.

rules of the game

Public drinking gets you unfavorable attention, as does walking down the street with a joint. They don't mess around here when it come to drugs [see *five-o,* above]. Even so, the streets of Temple Bar crawl with sweat-suited teenage touts selling hash and E of questionable quality. Hard drugs, particularly cocaine, are getting bigger all the time in the clubs around here.

dubun bars, clubs and culture zoo

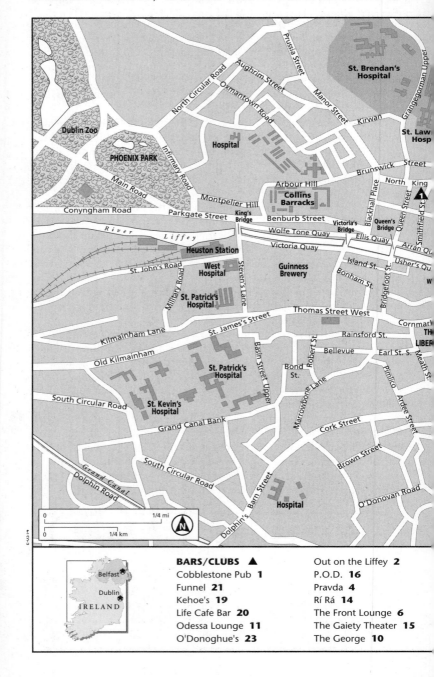

BARS/CLUBS ▲

Cobblestone Pub **1**	Out on the Liffey **2**
Funnel **21**	P.O.D. **16**
Kehoe's **19**	Pravda **4**
Life Cafe Bar **20**	Rí Rá **14**
Odessa Lounge **11**	The Front Lounge **6**
O'Donoghue's **23**	The Gaiety Theater **15**
	The George **10**

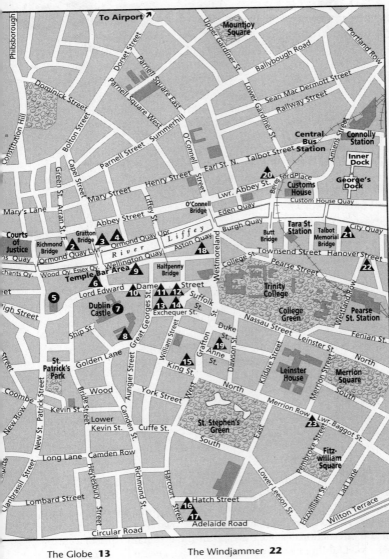

The Globe **13**
The Kitchen **9**
The Long Hall **8**
The Odeon **17**
The Palace Bar **18**
The Stag's Head **12**

The Windjammer **22**
Zanzibar **3**

CULTURE ZOO ●
Christ Church Cathedral **5**
Dublin Castle **7**

lad meets lass

The first thing you gotta know is that Dublin is undergoing a sexual revolution, plain and simple. Back in the day, Dublin's nightlife wasn't exactly centered around carousing and arousing with the opposite sex. Everyone went out with their "mates"—boys over here, girls over there. Things are changing rapidly, and if you really feel the need to know the Irish intimately, you probably should get yourself to the established meat markets. Anyone in Dublin can tell you where they are, but they'll probably all deny they ever go. They lie. Anyway, perhaps the most infamous place for local action is **Copper-Faced Jack's** *(Jackson Court Hotel, 29-30 Harcourt; 10pm-2:30am Fri, Sat, 11pm-2:30am Sun-Thur; £5 cover; V, MC)*, full of the Irish equivalent of the Biff and Muffy crowd. There's no cover before 11pm on Friday and Saturday. For a slightly less intense experience, **The Bailey** [see *hanging out,* above] sees good cruising both day and night, and the same goes for **Café en Seine** [see *live music scene,* below]. As a rule, the newer pubs in town are better for mingling [see *bar scene,* below]. As for clubs, it's mostly a bust, but the vibe at **Rí-Rá** [see *club scene,* below] seems the most comfortable for meeting people. For the backpacker set, it's gotta be sunny afternoons at Temple Bar Square—flirt with that statuesque Swede and then set a date for a drink that night. Otherwise, all of Temple Bar's mass-tourism super-pubs have a rep for libidinous behavior, most satisfying if your taste runs in the direction of rowdy English-soccer-fan-types and/or the women who love them.

So, just how do you do get yourself "in process" with a prospective lust object around here? Make sure you have a drink and keep the conversation *light.* Superficial is the key: witty banter, plays on words, jokes.

Lots of Latin jazz and some techno fills the night at **Kaffe Moka** *(39-40 S. William St., D2; Tel 01/679-84-75; Bus 32X, 39X, 41X, 66X, 67X; 8am-4am daily; No credit cards)*. Check out the big couches and coffee tables in the third-floor "library." The crowd here is mostly young, stylish, and international—like the easy-on-the-eyes staff. Kind of a clearinghouse for Dublin's newest arrivals, this place gives a lot of folks their first job in town.

If you're feeling more philosophical on a Saturday at 3am, try **Sufi's Café** *(48-50 Lower Stephen St., D2; Tel 01/679-85-77; Bus 16, 16A, 19, 19A, 22, 22A, 155; 8am-11pm Mon-Thur, till 4am Fri, Sat, 10am-11pm Sun; No credit cards)* just up the street from Kaffe Moka, but with a much mellower, quiet-conversation vibe, with Persian poetry decorating the walls.

Another sweet, very social late-night spot is the ultra-modern **Juice** (*73-83 S. Great George's St., D2; Tel 01/475-78-56; Bus 16, 16A, 19, 19A, 22, 22A; 9am-11pm Mon-Wed, till 4am Thur, Fri, 11am-4am Sat, noon-11pm Sun; No credit cards*), serving a hip, post-club crowd till the late hours. Just across from **The Globe** [see *bar scene,* below].

bar scene

Dublin's bars generally serve beer and liquor, but most don't do much in the way of cocktails beyond a vodka tonic or two. Ask for a martini, and you're probably gonna get a blank stare. Beer is generally sold and drunk by the pint. For lightweights, there's a measurement called "a glass," which is something like a half-pint but not exactly. Prices are pretty uniform in the city center: A shot of whiskey runs around £2.10, a pint of stout about £2.30, and lager £2.50. Late bars, clubs, or any especially swank place will often tack on another 30p or more to the price of a drink. The downstairs bar at **J.J. Smyth's** [see *live music scene,* below] serves the most affordable pint of stout (£2.15) in Dublin city center. Remember, when ordering a pint of Ireland's famous stout, patience is the key. Go freshen up in the bathroom, strike up a conversation with the drinker next to you, or scan the room for talent—the pouring process will take at least a few minutes.

Bar hours in Dublin get a little complicated. Most pubs follow the nationwide standard pub hours (10:30am-11pm Mon-Sat or till 11:30pm in summer and 12:30-2pm/4-11pm Sun), but there are a few "early houses" in town that start up at 7 or 7:30am all week and some selected "late bars" that pour until 12:30 or even 1:30am, mostly on weekends.

the tart with the cart

Dubliners love cheeky nicknames, especially when they mock public figures. They call the famous monument to fishmonger Molly Malone at the end of Grafton Street (around the corner from where she was baptized) "the tart with the cart" and the women at the Ha'penny Bridge "the hags with the bags." The O'Connell Street statue of Anna Livia, James Joyce's sensual symbol of the River Liffey in *Finnegan's Wake,* is better known as "the floozy in the Jacuzzi." And Joyce himself, who stands immortalized with his cane, frozen in cement across from the General Post Office on O'Connell Street, is lovingly referred to as "the prick with the stick" or "the dick with the stick." Take your pick.

dublin eats and crashing

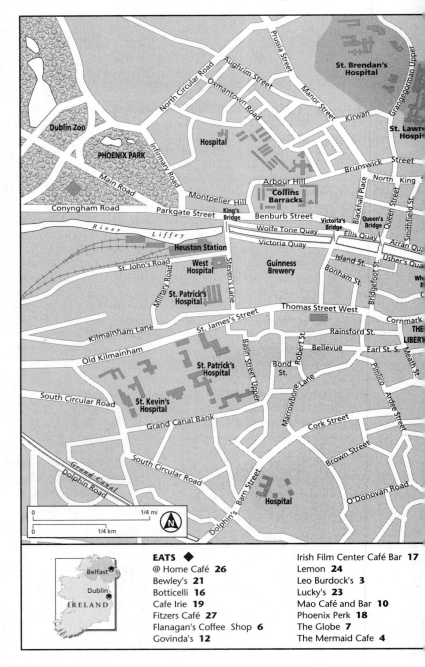

EATS ◆
@ Home Café **26**
Bewley's **21**
Botticelli **16**
Cafe Irie **19**
Fitzers Café **27**
Flanagan's Coffee Shop **6**
Govinda's **12**

Irish Film Center Café Bar **17**
Lemon **24**
Leo Burdock's **3**
Lucky's **23**
Mao Café and Bar **10**
Phoenix Perk **18**
The Globe **7**
The Mermaid Cafe **4**

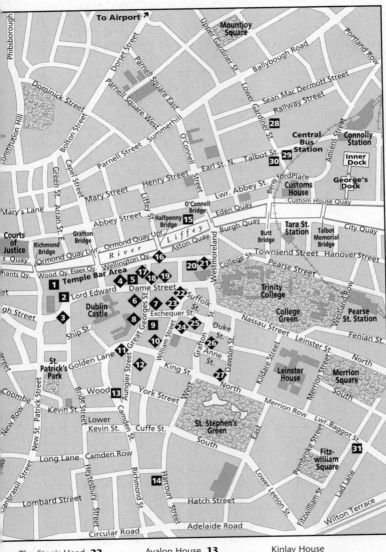

The Stag's Head **22**
Tosca **25**
Yamamori Noodles **8**
Wagamama **11**

CRASHING ■
Abbey Hostel **15**
Abraham House **28**

Avalon House **13**
Barnacles Temple
 Bar House **5**
Fitzwilliam Hotel **31**
Glen Court **29**
Harding Hotel **1**
Kelly's Hotel **9**

Kinlay House
 Christchurch **2**
Oliver St. John Gogarty's
 Temple Bar Penthouse
 Apartments **20**
Russell Court Hotel **14**
The Townhouse **30**

These closing hours mean last call; the courteous Irish lawmakers allow you a half hour to finish up afterwards. A few further exceptions: If you're staying in a hotel with a bar, you can usually stay in the bar for as long as your bartender is willing to stay awake. Also, there are a few restaurants that have started to play with the law by staying open and serving wine (and food, at least theoretically) until 4am or later [see *hanging out,* above], thereby offering the added thrill of the very real possibility of a police raid. (Don't worry, you're not the one who's going to be arrested.) Then there's the old late-night standby: A row of basement dives on Leeson Street, just up from St. Stephen's Green, where the truly desperate go after the clubs close to buy bottles of rotgut wine for the ridiculous price of £20. But the expansion of pub and club hours has been a big issue in Dublin government for years now, so all this may change any minute....

Unless otherwise noted, all bars have the same hours, as stated above, and are within walking distance of Tara Street DART Station.

Don't leave town without having a pint or three at **O'Donoghue's** *(15 Merrion Row, just off St. Stephen's Green; Tel 01/661-43-03; 2pm-11:30pm daily; No credit cards).* A Dublin institution, this pub is the center of Irish folk music in Dublin, close to the hearts of the festive crowd that gathers here each night. The music is sing-songy, and visitors have been known to get dragged from their barstools onto the middle of the floor to jig with the locals. Just smile and act like you know how. The aforementioned locals are generally older, though there's a handful of twentysomethings hanging around. The atmosphere is rustic and the lighting is a little too bright, but it's the kind of place where accidentally spilling a drink is not a major faux pas, but a likely way to have someone buy you a new one. The only problem with O'Donoghue's is that it's so dense with harsh cigarette smoke that the clouds have almost condensed into liquid or solid masses. But it's almost worth getting laryngitis just to experience the fun of this place. Who says north of the Liffey ain't all that?

For those brave enough to walk the deserted streets after dark, or for those who can spare a couple quidros for a cab, the **Cobblestone Pub** *(North King St. on main square in Smithfield; Tel 01/872-17-99; Open daily 'til 11:30pm; No credit cards)* is an absolute must. Lacking the glammy grunge of Temple Bar's pubs, Cobblestone is a place for locals and those who love them. Enlightened and casual-cool students chat loudly amidst old-timers who look like they've been glued to the bar since the 1950s. There is superb traditional music here almost every night in one, two, or all three of its rooms. The main room is always busy, and musicians usually set up by the end of the bar and play acoustic only. The side bar on the first floor gets busy, but is darker and more atmospheric. If you come before 10pm, you may be lucky enough to catch a trad session with only a handful of people sitting around, wallowing in the beauty of a sad old melody. Upstairs the mood varies and is only open a few nights a week. If you want to see the Dublin that residents of Dublin see, come here.

Set in a stone courtyard off Dame Street that becomes an open street party in the summer months, the **Stag's Head** (*1 Dame Court, D2; Tel 01/679-37-01; Bus 16, 16A, 19, 19A, 22, 22A, 155; Open till 12:30am Thur, Fri; No credit cards*) is one of those great Dublin pubs that welcomes just about anybody, from students to construction workers. You couldn't find better atmosphere for lunch or a contemplative pint than the eerie, stained-glass-lit back room, accompanied by the resident stuffed fox-in-a-box. Weekends always get packed here, but so does everywhere else Dublin.

Some say the **Palace Bar** (*21 Fleet St., D2; Tel 01/677-92-90; Bus 46, 46A, 46B, 63, 150; No credit cards*), on the edge of Temple Bar, pours the best pint of stout in town. Behind those huge, swinging, frosted glass and wood doors, preside some of the finest old-school barmen in Dublin, always there to greet your order with a smile and a nod of the head. God bless 'em—they know how to make a body feel right at home. No wonder your drink tastes better.

The Long Hall (*51 S. Great George's St., D2; Tel 01/475-15-90; Bus 16, 16A, 19, 19A, 22, 22A, 155; No credit cards*) is the pub for nostalgic purists. There ain't much here that hasn't been in place since Queen Victoria ruled: from the ornate, hand-carved wood, to the dozens of filigreed mirrors, and to the crowd of friendly geezers. Take in a few pints at the extra-long bar and see if you can get anybody talking.

The upstairs at **Kehoe's** (*9 S. Anne St., D2; Tel 01/677-83-12; Bus 32X, 39X, 41X, 66X, 69X; V, MC, AE*) looks just like what it is: an old family home converted into a pub. Even the threadbare red wall-to-wall is still in place. First floor wins for coziest digs in town. The regular crowd shuffling up to the unvarnished bar is mostly made up of scruffy-looking arty types, perhaps because the **Kerlin** [see *arts scene,* below], Dublin's big-name gallery, is just up the street.

For those who need to know such things, and you know who you are, things are usually downright lively at **The Windjammer** (*111 Townsend St., D2; Tel 01/677-25-76; DART to Pearse Station; Open at 7:30am daily; No credit cards*) at the otherwise ungodly drinking hour of 8am. Behind the portholes and under the pictures of sailing ships, Dubliners regularly partake in an alcoholic salutation to the dawn. Many here haven't had a job in years, but that just means they've had time to perfect their conversation skills.

Frequented by music industry folks, **The Globe** (*11 S. Great George's St., D2; Tel 01/671-12-20; Bus 16, 16A, 19, 19A, 22, 22A, 155; No credit cards*) is also Grand Central Station for Dublin's student/hipster community, somehow managing to be cool while still being unpretentious and friendly. Ever wanted to meet an A&R man? Now's your chance. A laid-back vibe, with big ol' wooden tables and a broad-beamed barn floor, plus a few Roman busts for no particular reason. Good coffee, great lunches, and a mellow Sunday afternoon jazz session. The Globe becomes part of **Rí Rá** [see *club scene,* below] after closing time.

The Front Lounge (*33 Parliament St., D2; Tel 01/670-41-12; Bus 46, 46A, 46B, 63, 150; V, MC*) is as Gotham as it gets in Dublin. The modern, art-museum interior fills with a fab-dressed, bite-me-I'm-beautiful crowd, given more flavor than your average Dublin watering hole by the presence of **The Back Lounge** [see *gay scene,* below], a second bar mostly for men who like men.

Housed in the old Harcourt train station, **The Odeon** *(57 Harcourt St., D2; Tel 01/478-20-88; Bus 14, 14A, 15A, 15B, 48A; 12:30pm-midnight Mon-Wed, till 1:30am Thur-Sat, 1pm-midnight Sun; V, MC, AE)* has to be one of the biggest bars in town, and it's packed with young, professional, late-twenties suburbanites every weekend, when the DJs bring in everything from jazz to disco. And they don't just come for the minimalist decor and cool Sunday afternoon cult movies in the winter—they come because this is the most likely spot to meet your Hibernian lover-to-be.

So, you like vodka and big, beautiful Soviet art? Make your way to the north side of the Ha'Penny Bridge, comrade. Cavernous, but still full of little nooks, **Pravda** *(3-5 Lower Liffey St., D1; Tel 01/874-00-90; Bus 25, 25A, 26, 37, 39, 39A, 66, 66A, 66B, 67, 67A, 60, 70X, 134; Noon-11:30pm Mon-Wed, Sat, till 1:30am Thur, Fri, 4-11:30pm Sun; V, MC, AE)* features about 20 different vodkas and DJs spinning mostly hip-hop and funk on weekends starting at 8:30pm. Food, too.

Just around the back of The Globe is the **Odessa Lounge** *(13-14 Dame Court, D2; Tel 01/670-76-34; Bus 16, 16A, 19, 19A, 22, 22A, 155; 5:30-11:30pm Mon-Sun; Noon-4:30pm Sun; V, MC, AE)*. Head down into the basement dimness for "young, modern urbanites" sinking into leather couches and doin' the chill cocktail lounge thang. Very comfy but a little more expensive than most. Did we mention they do cocktails? Come for the hangover-curing Sunday brunch of stuffed sausages, Bloody Marys, and people-watching. Reservations recommended.

Remember how mellow watching your little aquarium used to make you feel? The people at the "late bar" **Life Cafe Bar** *(Irish Life Mall, off Lower Abbey St., D1; Tel 01/878-10-32; DART to Connolly Station or Bus 27B, 42, 43, 53, 53A; Noon-11:30pm Sun-Wed, till 1:30am Thur-Sat, till 12:30am; V, MC)* know all about that. The mid-twenties crowd lazing on the continuous blue wall couch under the big tropical fish mural are here for relaxing, conversing, and late-night drinking, but not for straining themselves while DJs spin loungey, laid-back grooves. One downside: Pints are pricey to begin with, at £2.50 to £2.75, and they do a 20p hike during the late hours.

LIVE MUSIC SCENE

What Dublin's music scene lacks in variety it makes up for in atmosphere. More than a few Dublin pubs have grown from neighborhood locals to major city venues hosting international acts without losing their classic pub character. These intimate places naturally spark those indispensible connections between bands and crowds, and their general manage-ment style seems to follow a love of music, not specializing in any one musical style, so you'll often see weekly lists ranging from jazz to grunge to trad (traditional Irish music), and nobody seems to mind. Free jazz performances on Sundays are pretty standard in Dublin, so be on the lookout. Unless otherwise noted, these places follow the standard pub hours [see *bar scene*, above].

Whelans *(25 Wexford St., D2; Tel 01/478-24-20; Bus 16, 16A, 19, 19A, 22, 22A, 155; Bands play 8:30pm daily; No credit cards)*, down near St. Stephen's Green, is the scruffy little place in town every band wants to play and then play again, just to bathe in that certain special vibe that lives around the wooden stage in the back room. Unvarnished and unpretentious, seven nights a week here can be a musical education in itself: Gypsy fiddle players, salsa, pop, and rock, it's all here, and the talent (and crowd) is consistently the best in town.

The International Bar *(23 Wicklow St., D2; Tel 01/677-72-90; Bus 32X, 39x, 41X, 66X, 67X; No credit cards)*, off the west side of the Trinity College Green, is just a real vintage Dublin pub and a superb one for so many reasons. Simon's been behind the bar here for 30 years, pulling pints under seven beautifully carved heads representing the rivers of Ireland. The nightly acts upstairs could be blues, R&B, acoustic folk, or even comedy and theater. David Murphy's Tuesday open-mike acoustic is an institution: More than a few who started here have been signed to the majors, and Friday's blues regulars back B.B. King when he's in town. Definitely a musician's hangout.

Trad has experienced a new blossoming in Dublin's music scene over the last decade. Listening to a really good trad jam is like listening to great jazz: It's wild, primal, and intoxicating. But forget the cheesy tourist trad sessions drowned out by drunken crowds in Temple Bar. The place to go if you want the real deal is the **Harcourt Hotel** *(60 Harcourt St., D2; Tel 01/478-36-77, Bus 10, 10A, 11B, 13, 20B; V, MC)*, a classy old Georgian job just down the street from **P.O.D.** [see *club scene*, below]. They serve up the best in town for free (well, almost always) seven nights a week in one of their two wood-lined hotel bars. It's another musician's favorite, especially since they can drink after hours at the "residents only" bar. They're planning an expansion of their gigging space, so the intimate feel here may change some.

Black and beautiful, **J.J. Smyth's** *(12 Aungier St., D2; Tel 01/475-25-65; Bus 16, 16A, 19, 19A, 22, 22A, 155; No credit cards)* is another classic, family-owned local doing jazz and blues upstairs in a low-lit, smoky old bar with a no-nonsense, casual feel—no snooty twits here. All their nights are good, but the jazz on Thursdays is the real standout. Tuesday's an open jam session, so sign up in the afternoon for a spot. The benevolent J.J. may serve the cheapest pint of stout in the city center: £2.15 downstairs, 5p more upstairs.

Right between Trinity and St. Stephen's Greens, **Café en Seine** *(40 Dawson St., D2; Tel 01/677-43-69; Bus 32X, 39X, 41X, 66X, 67X; V, MC, AE)* does a deliciously mellow brunch/detox session at 1:30pm. Local

legend Herbie fronts the Red Hot Jazz Trio, crooning out hypnotic renditions of Ella's and Billie's favorites under the twirling metallic vegetation
of the Parisian Art Nouveau decor. Try **The Globe** [see *bar scene*, above]
after 5pm for another particularly good Sunday jazz fix.

For info on the small jazz scene in Dublin, contact the **Improvised
Music Company** *(Tel 01/670-38-85; imcadmin@tinet.ie),* a government-funded organization charged with developing jazz in Ireland. Cool
job, eh? They arrange gigs around city and bring in a lot of international
acts, as well as host the Pendulum jazz night at J.J. Smyth's every Sunday.

For people who prefer high-decibel electronic enthusiasm (i.e. feedback), **Eamonn Doran's** *(3A Crown Alley; Tel 01/679-91-14; Bus 46,
46A, 46B, 63, 150; V, MC)* is just off Temple Bar Square. This is more of
a loud, grungy, young guitar-band venue than you'll find in the rest of the
city; clashing chords are belted out downstairs in a vaguely honky-tonk
looking bar done up in copper-chrome and red velvet. The place to go if
you think no Irishman wears his hair long.

club scene

Dublin's club scene is small, but the town's clubbers more than make up for
it with gung-ho drive—no blasé crowds here. Keep on the lookout for the
frequent "one-offs": One-time special events often supplying the month's
best party. For the real news, ask the folks at **Big Brother** or **TAG** [see
stuff, below]. Something you may notice if you get around is that the
postage-stamp-size dance floors at Dublin's "big clubs" suffer from long-
bar-envy; drinking space is the priority here. If you dance, you gotta love
the crush of bodies, and the open, promiscuous exchange of bodily fluids
(mostly sweat but also the standard Irish public display of deep-tongue
skills) is rampant. As The Man currently dictates, clubs are open 11pm-
2am. Crowds move in around 12:30am.

P.O.D. *(35 Harcourt St., D2; Tel 01/478-01-66; Bus 14, 14A, 15A,
15B, 48A; 11pm-2am daily; Cover £5-8; V, MC, AE)* stands for Place Of
Dance, in case there was a question about what people do here. A house-
dominated joint in a former train tunnel, this one's a killer to get into. On
weekends, it's regulars and their suppliers only, mate. Always dress to
impress, but save yourself the poser-posturing aggravation and try the
easier techno-driven Thursdays or free-entrance Sundays (if you arrive
before 10pm in the adjoining, wrought-iron and blue-neon Chocolate
Bar). Fridays claim a "totally queer" door policy, but some hets manage to
slip in. Worth it for bragging rights more than anything else, and to test
your mettle in the terrifying installation-art bathrooms.

As every Dubliner will tell you in tones of hushed sacredness: *"It's
part-owned by U2."* Bono and the gang tried hard on the basement
makeover of **The Kitchen** *(Clarence Hotel basement, E. Essex St., Temple
Bar, D2; Tel 01/677-66-35; Bus 46, 46A, 46B, 63, 150; Cover £3-8; No
credit cards),* coming up with a kind of Jabba's palace look; there's not a
straight wall in the place, and this is probably the only dance floor in the
world with a moat. Already damn tiny anyway but it's made smaller by

12 hours in dublin

1. Do what everybody else does. Take the bus tour to ease your guilt over squandering yet another opportunity to broaden yourself through enlightening intercultural exchange, then get to pub crawling with a vengeance. The open-topped double-deckers of **Dublin Bus Tour** (*59 Upper O'Connell St., D1; Tel 01/873-42-22; Departs every 15 minutes 9:30am-4:45pm daily; £6; V, MC*) tour the town and stop at most of the major cultural sites [see *culture zoo*, below]. One ticket lets you get on and off as much as you like during the day.

2. Check out the spectacular *Book of Kells* [see *culture zoo*, below].

3. Have a pint or two in the magisterial tranquillity of the **Palace Bar** [see *bar scene*, above].

4. Take in some great live music at **Whelans,** the **International Bar,** or the **Harcourt Hotel** [see *live music scene*, above].

5. Expose yourself to some good theater at **Project @ The Mint** [see *arts scene*, above].

6. Ease that hangover with some Billie Holiday, eggs Benedict, and a Bloody Mary at **Café en Seine** [see *live music scene*, above].

7. Dance 'round the tulips in **St. Stephen's Green** [see *hanging out*, above].

8. Learn the words to *Molly Malone* by heart. (Check out her well-endowed statue at the north end of Grafton Street.)

a cordoned-off part to keep the quality away from the peasantry. The no-nonsense techno-babies' favorite, the place cooks on Tuesdays, fires fueled by £2 vodka and Redbull hits.

If you just want a fun, hip place that won't turn you away, head for **Rí Rá** (*Dame Court; Tel 01/677-48-35; Bus 16, 16A, 19, 19A, 22, 22A, 155; No credit cards*). It's the enlightened middle road in relaxed cool, playing everything from hip-hop to disco. Dance floor thing in the basement; cult movies, projections, and mellower grooves in the upstairs **Globe Bar** [see *bar scene*, above]. Another good thing about this place: Unlike the other two "big rep" clubs in town, romantic encounters actually happen regularly here.

Humming with that unbeatable underground buzz, the two floors of **Funnel** (*24 City Quay; Tel 01/677-03-40; DART to Pearse Station or Bus 5, 7, 7A, 7X, 8; Bar 9am-6pm Mon-Fri, club 8:30pm-2am Wed-Sat; Cover £6-8; V, MC*) tuck into redeveloped riverside warehouses opposite the Custom House. Warm up in the curvy, uncannily vulva-like downstairs bar, then ascend to the heights of pleasure in the blacked-out upstairs dance floor and stage. There's a superb performer-audience vibe here, as

fESTIVALS and EVENTS

St. Patrick's Festival *(Mar 13-17; Tel 01/676-32-05):* Parades and festivities in celebration of Ireland's favorite snake-charmer.

Dublin Film Festival *(Mar; in the IFC, Savoy, and Screen cinemas; Tel 01/679-29-37):* Film screenings, lectures, seminars, and industry schmoozarama.

Bloomsday *(June 16; Tel 01/878-85-47; www.jamesjoyce.ie):* An annual, 24-hour-long party for James Joyce worshipers and anyone else who cares to join in.

Temple Bar Blues Festival *(Late July; Tel 01/677-22-55):* International blues acts pack the pubs and streets of Temple Bar. Films and workshops, too.

International Puppet Festival *(Mid Sept; Tel 01/280-09-74):* Puppeteers from around the world descend on Monkstown, County Dublin. Madness ensues.

Dublin Fringe Festival *(Late Sept-mid-Oct; Tel 01/872-90-16; www.fringefest.com):* The best of international off- and off-off-Broadway theater hits town.

Dublin Theatre Festival *(Early Oct; Tel 01/677-84-93; www.iftn.ie/dublinfestival):* Irish and international theater at its best.

the best in up-and-coming local DJs give their all, and the crowd gets down. The door staff is actually friendly.

An old Victorian theater full of salsa, reggae, and world music on three levels—how can you go wrong? **Salsa Palace @ the Gaiety Theatre** [see below] *(11:30pm-2am Fri; Cover £7)* is just a big funhouse; five Bogart-and-Bacall-classy antique bars, a couple dance floors, live bands, and cult movies in the vast theater, which incidentally is kept quite dark and is a "great place to snog." (That's "make out" to us Yanks) This place is a maze, so watch out: Get too hazy and you probably won't surface 'til morning.

Yes, they're beautiful and dress damn fine in **Zanzibar** *(34-35 Lower Ormond Quay, Tel 01/878-72-12; DART to Tara St. Station or Bus 25, 25A, 26, 37, 39, 39A, 66, 66A, 66B, 67, 67A, 70, 70X, 134; 10:30am-1:30am Mon-Fri, 11am-1am Sat, Sun; No cover; V, MC),* a 1,500-capacity, over-the-top, African-themed late bar replete with palms, mosaics, giant urns, and Arabian Nights-evocative paintings. A little cheesy, but hey, sometimes we all want that, especially since you don't have to pay to party. Also, it's a good place for meeting members of the opposite sex. Popular with foreign university students, who carouse and arouse to anything from techno to ABBA on one of the larger dance floors in Dublin. Get there before 10pm, it fills up fast.

ARTS SCENE

Dublin's art, fashion, and design world is just now starting to gain momentum. You've got to realize that it's only been in the last four or five years that there was any significant population in Ireland with money to spend, period. Some say this is the reason Ireland has had more than its share of great writers: Paper and ink are cheap; canvas, silver, or silks are not. Well, as a wise man said, money is the grease for creativity's wheels, and the wheels are spinning in Dublin. You're sure to get an earful on the subject, and perhaps an introduction to a few of Ireland's future groundbreakers at **The Clock** *(110 Thomas St., D8; Tel 01/677-55-63; No credit cards),* the local pub for Dublin's College of Art and Design, a few minutes walk west of the Temple Bar. Another spot drawing in a picture-peddling crowd is the venerable **Kehoe's** [see *bar scene,* above], just around the corner from Dublin's top gallery, the Kerlin.

▶▶VISUAL ARTS

Irish contemporary art is a little subdued compared with works from other parts of Europe. You'll see lots of subtle grays and blacks, muted colors, and straightforward, museum-like presentations. There's not much showboating going on. That wouldn't be the Irish way.

If art drama is what you're looking for, the most experimental of the big-name contemporary galleries in town is the warehouse-sized **Green On Red Gallery** *(26-28 Lombard St. East, D2; Tel 01/671-34-14; 11am-6pm Mon-Fri, till 3pm Sat; greenred@iol.ie; No credit cards),* a few blocks south of **Dublin Castle** [see *culture zoo,* below]. Here you're likely to see more installation art, from found materials to video, with a mixture of Irish and international artists.

Being the big cheese of the Dublin art scene, the **Kerlin Gallery** *(Anne's Lane, off S. Anne St., D2; Tel 01/670-90-93; 10am-5:45pm Mon-Fri, 11am-4:30pm Sat; gallery@kerlin.ie, www.kerlin.ie; No credit cards)* has the most impressive stable of established Irish artists working in photography, painting, sculpture, and prints. They also have the most impressive prices on works ranging from charcoal sketches of magnified clustered sperm to photographs of bleak urban wastelands. Don't be afraid to drop in for a look: The staff here are down-to-earth and friendly. Conveniently located between Trinity College and St. Stephen's Green.

For an edgier feel, try **Temple Bar Gallery and Studios** *(5-9 Temple Bar, D2; Tel 01/671-00-73; 10am-6pm Tues-Sat, till 7pm Thurs, 2-6pm Sun; tbgs@indigo.ie; No sales)* a big concrete and industrial steel complex founded by a group of artists back in '94 in the hope of giving first-timers a chance. Mostly a publicly funded workspace for 30 artists, this is where they get up to those sometimes ground-breaking, sometimes "Screw your petty bourgeois conventions of taste! This filthy rag thrown in the corner is art!" kind of shenanigans.

Where the local DJs who do projection effects hang out, **Arthouse Multimedia Center for the Arts** (*Curved St.; D2; Tel 01/605-68-00; 9:30am-6:30pm Mon-Fri, 10am-5pm Sat; www.arthouse.ie, info@ arthouse.ie; Free admission*), in Temple Bar, is about as hip as it gets in Dublin. Inside a big Bauhaus steel-and-glass fish tank, their official line is to "further the use of digital technologies in Irish artistic practice." According to them, they are the keepers of the "Artifact," a sinister object with unspeakable powers with which they will enslave the Earth. Actually, it's a CD-ROM of the work of over 800 local artists working in multi-media. They also do exhibitions, performance art, training, publishing, the whole digital kit-and-caboodle. Definitely worth a look-see, then kick back in their upstairs cafe [see *wired*, below].

▶▶PERFORMING ARTS

Irish theater seems to be a little obsessed with rural nostalgia these days. That means a lot of what you'll see on the main stages will be set in the same little thatched-farm kitchen with lines like: "Cup of tea?"; "Cow's gotten out again"; "It's the priest, the priest!"; and "Johnny's gone off to America, oh, how will we manage?!" repeated ad nauseam. Hopefully, it's just a phase. Thankfully, there's plenty of edge-cutting going down, too.

If you really want the whole footlights shebang in a nutshell, drop £10 on the *Irish Theatre Handbook,* a comprehensive guide to Irish drama and dance with descriptions of all known venues and companies. For the latest skinny on what's hot and what's not in local theater, check out *Irish Theatre Magazine,* a £4 quarterly. Both are available in **Waterstone's** [see *stuff,* below].

For the post-curtain crowd, the formula is to look for the comfiest pub nearest the theater. Practically connected to the back door of the Gaiety, **Neary's** (*1 Chatham St., D2; Tel 01/677-85-96; Bus 10, 11A, 11B, 13, 16A; No credit cards*) gets most all their thespian trade. **Brogan's Bar** (*75 Dame St., D2; Tel 01/679-95-70; Bus 50, 50A, 54, 56A, 77, 77A, 77B; No credit cards*) is convenient to the Olympia. And for a pow-wow of the big heads from the Gate and the Abbey, try the **Flowing Tide** (*9 Lower Abbey St., D1; Tel 01/874-41-06; DART to Connolly Station; No credit cards*).

The never-boring 3-person **Barabbas** group (*7 South Great George St.; Tel 01/671-20-13*) specializes in outrageous "what will they do next?" physical theater. Wunderkind Mikel Murfi was last seen talking out of his ass, artfully done up as a face and thrust through a stage floor. (It's a lot better than it sounds, really.) **The Corn Exchange** (*43-44 Temple Bar; Tel 01/679-64-44*), a theater, dance, and performance group, does a lot with stylish, experimental stagings. They're regular favorites at fringe festivals worldwide. **Rough Magic** (*Tel 01/671-92-78*) is the big deal in town for new Irish plays.

Otherwise, for consistently good stuff there's always the **Project Arts Center** (*39 E. Essex St., Temple Bar, D2; Tel 01/679-66-22; DART to*

Connolly Station; Shows 8pm; Tickets £5-8; www.project.ie, info@project.ie; V, MC). Founded in '66 by artists wanting an alternative venue, the Project does theater, music, dance, and performance art. They've helped foster the likes of U2, Gabriel Byrne, Liam Neeson, and Neil Jordan, to name a few. In June 2000, they moved into a big, newfangled, Euromoney building, complete with 250-seat auditorium, gallery, bar, garden, and bookshop.

For theater on the cheap, there's the **Players Theatre** *(Upstairs in the Samuel Beckett Centre, Trinity College; Tel 01/608-22-42; DART to Tara St. Station or Bus 5, 7A, 8, 15A-C, 46, 55, 62, 63, 83, 84; Shows 1pm, 8pm Mon-Sat Oct-May; £3.50, £2.50 members, matinee £2.50/1.50; No credit cards)* showing works produced, directed, and performed by Trinity students.

The **Abbey and Peacock Theatres** *(26 Lower Abbey St.; Tel 01/878-72-22; DART to Connolly Station; Performances 8pm; Tickets £8-16; www.abbey-theatre.ie, abbey@indigo.ie; V, MC),* Ireland's national theater, were founded by Celtic revivalists back in 1904, and some might say things haven't progressed since then. Ground zero for Irish nostalgic self-absorption and the tourists who flock to see it. The Peacock is the Abbey's little studio, intended for more adventurous programming. Overall, this is not an exciting place, but the acting and production standards are truly world-class. They're getting a new (as yet undetermined) artistic director soon, so who knows what the future holds?

The Gate *(Cavendish Row, D1; Tel 01/874-43-68; DART to Connolly Station; Box office 10am-7pm Mon-Sat, shows 8pm Mon-Sat; Tickets £12-14; V, MC, AE, DC)* is where a young Orson Welles cut his teeth. Same story as the Abbey: These days it's for suburban upper-middle-class consumption. Uh, I mean, this is where you can see definitive productions of the Irish classics.

John Scott's **Irish Modern Dance Theater** *(SFX City Theater, Upper Sherrard Street; Tel 01/874-96-16, Fax 01/878-77-84; imdt@iol.ie, www.adnet.ie/imdt)* is a contemporary theater specializing in offbeat and innovative productions and stagings of original works. Using Irish talent from around the world, the company strives to take dance in new directions, and is now incorporating multimedia into their work. In this year's *Off the Wall,* massive still images of dancers in motion were projected on top of trippy, ambient lighting effects on the wall of a Temple Bar lot. It's all a bit pretentious and who knows if it means anything at all, but it's cool as hell to see giant, half-naked girls and boys arabesqueing on a wall. They put on about two shows a year, generally in late fall and winter, but check their Web site or give them a ring when you're in town. They perform all over Ireland and Europe as well. It's a good place to let the Guinness haze inside your head interact with the world.

You'll never know what's up at the **Gaiety** *(S. King St.; Tel 01/677-17-17; Box office 11am-7pm Mon-Sat, shows 8pm Mon-Sat, matinee 3pm Sat; Tickets £7-46; V, MC),* Dublin's oldest theater, set in a gorgeous old

Victorian. Could be opera, ballet, concerts, or theater. Some good, some bad. It's worth the price of a ticket just to sit in the Dangerous Liaisons-like gilt-and-velvet splendor of the 1,000-seat hall. Same holds for Dublin's other, slightly smaller old Vic, the **Olympia Theatre** *(72 Dame St. D2; Tel 01/677-77-44; Bus 50, 50A, 54, 56A, 77, 77A, 77B; Tickets £15-30; V, MC, AE).*

Despite what the international phenom of Riverdance might lead you to assume, dance ain't so big in Dublin. For news, check in with the **Dance Theatre of Ireland** *(Tel 01/280-24-55).*

The place for film geeks has got to be the **Irish Film Center** *(6 Eustace St., D2; Tel 01/679-34-77; Bus 21A, 78A, 78B; Screenings 2-11pm daily; Membership £10 per year, £1 weekly; Tickets £4.50 adults, £3 students; fii@ifc.ie, www.iftn.ie/ifc; V, MC).* It's the only place in town for art-house cinema and a pretty cool one at that, with a tasty restaurant and bar added in [see *eats,* below]. There's just one catch: You have to be a member. Fortunately, weekly memberships only cost £1 and can be purchased up to 10 minutes before any screening. Don't miss Flashback, their survey of Irish filmmaking, shown for free Wednesday through Sunday at noon.

For the latest Hollywood schlockfest, get your rocks off at the **Savoy** *(Upper O'Connell St., D1; Tel 01/874-88-22; DART to Connolly Station; Tickets £4.75, £3 before 6pm; V, MC)* a five-screener on the city's main drag, with the biggest screen in Ireland.

▶▶LITERARY SCENE

The history of Dublin's literary life is legendary. We all know that more than a few of the greatest European writers of this century came out of this little town. Well, times have changed, and the local talent these days seems less likely to be found sitting next to you at the pub and more likely to be heading for cities outside of Ireland, where them big publishers roam. A lot of what goes on these days amounts to ancestor worship with the venerable James Joyce getting the most flattering offerings made to his dead white maleness. If you want to sample some local authors still among the living, pick up The *Stinging Fly,* Dublin's literary journal, available at local bookstores. For other news, the free, bi-weekly *Event Guide* has a literary events section called "Literary Live" with all upcoming events listed. The *Irish Times* runs a definitive lit listings section every Saturday. To talk to another human being about it, contact the Irish Writers' Centre *(Tel 01/872-13-02; iwc@iol.ie, www.iol.ie/~iwc/).* The staff here are so lethargically boho cool, they come off like those pesticide junkies in the movie *Naked Lunch.*

The place where things word-wise go down, the **Winding Stair Bookshop & Café** *(40 Lower Ormond Quay, D1; Tel 01/873-32-92; Bus 70, 80; 10am-6pm Mon-Sat, 1-6pm Sun; Cover £1.50-5; V, MC)* is the most frequent host for readings of contemporary poetry and prose in Dublin, usually in the evenings. The place has a great vibe, a chill cafe overlooking the Liffey, and...a very windy old staircase. Who knows? Maybe you'll meet tomorrow's Seamus Heaney scribbling away over a cup of joe.

Looking like the basement conversion Grandpa did for the benefit of his poker buddies, **Grogan's Castle Lounge** *(15 S. William St.; Tel*

01/677-93-20; Bus 32X, 39X, 41X, 66X, 67X; No credit cards) is an old man's pub where Dublin's bookish types come a-slumming. Actually, it's quite cool; darn attractive local artwork hangs on the walls above the green 1950s-vintage upholstery. The dominant color being green, calm meditativeness sets in pretty quickly here, especially after a pint or two. So come and lay the groundwork for your next novel or something.

gay scene

Compared with other European capitals, the gay scene in Dublin is none too big. Actually, with only two officially "gay" bars, it's pretty small. Even so, an enlightened Irish government gave the legal go-ahead to homosexuality a few years ago, and gay culture is thriving. For listings and other info, pick up the *GCN* (Gay Community News) at **Waterstone's** [see *stuff*, below]. *Dublin* magazine also has a gay happenings section. There are a few places around town that regularly draw a good gay crowd: **Juice** [see *hanging out*, above] just up the street from the George; **@Home Café** [see *eats*, below], which hosts a gay night on Sundays; and **The Front Lounge** [see *bar scene*, above]. Some good numbers to know: Dublin Lesbian Line, Tel 01/872-99-11; Gay Switchboard Dublin, Tel 01/872-10-55; LOT (Lesbians Organizing Together), Tel 01/872-04-60; LEA (Lesbian Education and Awareness), Tel 01/872-04-60; and Out House, Tel 01/670-63-77.

The George *(89 S. Great George's St.; Tel 01/478-29-83; Bus 22A; 12:30-11pm Mon-Tue, till 2:30am Wed-Sun; V, MC)* holds the honor of being the first gay bar established in Dublin. Actually a bar and nightclub, the crowd here is mostly gay men, with some lesbians and an increasing number of straights walking on the wild side. The Sunday evening bingo here with dancing drag queen Penny Bridge has become a fine old Dublin institution.

Just downriver from the Four Courts, **Out on the Liffey** *(27 Upper Ormond Quay; Tel 01/872-24-80; DART to Tara St. Station or Buses 34, 70, 80)* is more of a lesbian hangout, in an old-style stained wood and bric-a-brac pub.

Gay nights in Dublin hot spots are not well-established. *HAM (Homo Action Movies)* at **P.O.D.** [see *club scene*, above] (£8) is probably the best night in town these days, drawing a ridiculously well-manicured, fab-dressed, mixed crowd. For the most up-to-date listings, check out *GCN*.

culture zoo

Trinity College and the Book of Kells *(College Green, D2; Tel 01/608-16-88; Bus 5, 7A, 8, 15A-C, 46, 55, 62, 63, 83, 84; 9:30am-5pm Mon-Sat, noon-4:30pm Sun Oct-May, 9:30am-4:30pm Sun Jun-Sept; Admission £3.50 adults, £3 students):* One of the funkiest illuminated picture books ever made, housed in a city-center, green haven of a campus.

National Gallery *(Merrion Square West, D2; Tel 01/661-51-33; DART to Pearse Station or Bus 5, 6, 7, 7A, 8, 10, 44, 47, 47B, 48A, 62; 10am-5:30pm Mon-Sat, till 8:30pm Thur, 2pm-5pm Sun; Free tours 3pm*

Sat, Sun; www.nationalgallery.ie, artgall@tinet.ie; Free admission): Easy to get to and chock-full of old Irish art. Nice on a rainy day.

National Museum *(Kildare St. near St. Stephen's Green; Tel 01/677-74-44; 10am-5pm Tue-Sat, 2pm-5pm Sun; Free admission):* The National Museum is a must-see for those seeking knowledge about the history of this island. Particularly enticing to the curious visitor is the extensive collection of pre-Christian artifacts. These bronze- and stone-aged relics bring to life the religious customs and burial practices of the ancient Irish, and even shows how they ate. Check out the iron-age grave with a remarkably intact body that was found in a bog. Metalwork that dates from the introduction of Christianity in the 5th century onward is also incredible. The metal has distinct Celtic swirls and ornamentation; check out the biggest draw, the truly beautiful Tara Brooch. The good thing about the museum is that it's filled with booty from other parts of the country, so you can get an excellent picture of the cultural and archaeological history of the whole of Ireland without leaving Dublin.

Irish Museum of Modern Art *(Military Rd., Kilmainham; Tel 01/671-86-66; Bus 78A, 79, 90; 10am-5:30pm Tue-Sat, noon-5:30pm Sun; Free admission):* Beautiful building, nice garden, so-so art.

Chester Beatty Library and Gallery of Oriental Art *(20 Shrewsbury Rd., Ballsbridge, D4; Tel 01/269-23-86; DART to Sandymount Station or Bus 5, 6, 6A, 7A, 8, 10, 46, 46A, 46B, 64; 10am-5pm Tue-Fri, 2-5pm Sat; Free admission, free guided tours 2:30pm Wed, Sat; mryan@cbl.ie):* One of the finest collections of Asian art in Europe.

Dublin Castle *(Dame St. at Castle St.; Tel 01/677-71-29; 10am-5pm Mon-Fri, 2pm-5pm Sat-Sun; Admission £3 Adults, £2 Students):* Let's put it this way: do you enjoy torture? If your answer to this question is yes, plunk down the pound and take the guided tour of Dublin Castle. Even if your answer is no, the castle does have one thing going for it: the couches look very comfortable, so if you're about to fall asleep, maybe you can ask nicely and the tour guide will let you curl up on one. Better yet, just stick to the outside and read our brief history: Built in 1204 by Norman King John, it was the seat of British power in Ireland until the early 20th century. The Easter Uprising led to 50 defeated insurgents being executed within the castle's walls. In 1938, the first President of Ireland was sworn in here. Nowadays, it's used as a government office and is the formal reception area for powerful political visitors to Ireland. The architecture is a questionable hodgepodge of 800 years of additions.

Christ Church Cathedral *(Christ Church Place; Tel 01/677-80-99; 10am-5:30pm daily; £2 suggested donation):* Dean John Patterson and his wacky band of clerics have cooked up a riotous helping of Cathedral zaniness sure to satisfy your appetite for the Big Man. But seriously, folks, the Christ Church Cathedral has a fascinating history and exudes an intimacy and sense of peace that you will find in few churches anywhere. It's much cooler than its neighbor down the street, the more grandiose St. Patrick's Cathedral. Perhaps it's because they don't have braggin' rights to St. Patrick having baptized people on their grounds, or maybe it's because of the church's history that they all seem more down-to-earth about the whole eternal salvation racket. In 1038, a group of Vikings, who had apparently taken a break from pillaging Ireland, saw fit to construct a little wooden church here. In 1171, the original structure was buffed out in stone. The present cathedral structure dates from the 1870s, when a massive restoration took place.

Bank of Ireland/Parliament House *(2 College Green, D2; Tel 01/661-59-33 x2265; All city centre buses; 10am-4pm Mon-Fri, 2-5pm Sat, 10am-1pm Sun; Free admission):* Come see the opulent former chambers of the only parliament that ever voted itself out of existence. The stylish place to change money. With guided tours of the House of Lords Chamber *(10:30am, 11:30am, 1:45pm Tue, Thur).*

The General Post Office (GPO) *(O'Connell St., D1; Tel 01/872-88-88; DART to Connolly Station or Bus 25, 26, 34, 37, 38A, 39A, 39B, 66A, 67A; 8am-8pm Mon-Sat, 10:30am-6:30pm Sun; Free admission):* A symbol of Irish freedom. Story has it you can still see bullet holes from the 1916 Easter Rising in the pillars out front.

The Custom House *(Custom House Quay, D1; Tel 01/878-77-60; Bus 27A, 27B, 53A; 10am-5pm Mon-Fri, 2-5pm Sat, Sun; Admission £2):* One of Ireland's most dramatic architectual sites, more than slightly screwed up by a misplaced, hulking DART bridge: Beauty and the Beast. Check out the octagonal room on the first floor.

St. Patrick's Cathedral *(Patrick's Close, Patrick St., D8; Tel 01/475-48-17; Bus 50, 50A, 54, 54A, 56A; 9am-6pm Mon-Sat, 9am-4:30pm Sun; Admission £2 adults, £1.75 students):* The former haunt of Saint Patrick and Jonathan Swift—you find the connection.

Kilmainham Gaol Historical Museum *(Inchicore Rd., Kilmainham,*

fashion

For a European capital, Dublin's a pretty casual town. The basic youth uniform looks like a Gap ad, minus the khakis (a piece of clothing curiously absent from Ireland, perhaps as a result of the long, cruel occupation by khaki-wearing British). Two things stand out in Dublin street fashion; the omnipresence of "combats" (known to folks in the U.S.A. as "cargo pants") and the absence of "runners" (aka sneakers). Everybody wears some kind of leather shoe. Sporting sneakers will probably get you barred from more than a few of the places mentioned in this guide. Seems many pubs have bouncers just to enforce the "no-runners" rule. Otherwise, you look great. Don't worry.

D8; Tel 01/453-59-84; Bus 21, 78, 78A-B, 79, 123; 9:30am-4:45pm daily Apr-Sept, 9:30am-4pm Mon-Fri, closed Sat, 10am-4:45pm Sun Oct-Mar; Admission £2 adults, £1 students): A fascinating and sometimes gruesome presentation of Irish prison history.

Guinness Hopstore *(St. James' Gate, D8; Tel 01/408-48-00; Bus 51B, 78A, 123; 9:30am-5pm Mon-Sat, 10:30am-4:30pm Sun Apr-Sept, 9:30am-4pm Mon-Sat, noon-4pm Sun Oct-Mar; www.guinness.ie; Admission £5 adults, £4 students or certified alcoholics (har, har)):* A tour of this site is obligatory for anyone who partakes of the dark stuff. Free pint (or two!) with admission.

The Old Jameson Distillery *(Bow St., D7; Tel 01/807-23-55; Bus 67, 67A, 68, 69, 79, 90; 9:30am-6pm daily, last tour at 5pm; Admission £3.50 adults, £3 students):* Get to know your whiskey history at this former distillery.

The Joyce Tower Museum *(Sandycove, County Dublin; Tel 01/280-92-65; DART to Sandycove Station or Bus 8; 10am-1pm/2-5pm Mon-Sat, 2-6pm Sun Apr-Oct; Admission £2.50 adults, £2 students):* James Joyce slept here.

great outdoors

If you want to work the physique in Dublin city center, your best bet is a gym. Otherwise, to avoid the constant congestion on the downtown sidewalks and streets, you could run with the deer in the vastness of Phoenix Park at the edge of the city or maybe do laps around St. Stephen's Green. There are two gyms in town that offer short-term memberships.

Right in the heart of Temple Bar, **Pulse Fitness Center** *(1-2 Temple Bar, D2; Tel 01/679-96-20; DART to Tara St. Station or Bus 46, 46A, 46B, 63, 150; 7:30am-10pm daily; Membership £7 per day, £15 per week, £55 per month; Classes £3 at lunchtime, £3.50 evenings; V, MC)* offers a smallish weight room with the basic machines and classes, plus a unisex sauna.

Why run when you can trot? **Ashtown Riding Stables** *(Navan Rd., Castleknock, D15; Tel 01/838-38-07; Bus 37, 38, 39, 70; 9am-5pm daily in summer; £15/hr riding or lesson; No credit cards)* will rent you a horse and let you wander as you please through the hills, forests, and fields of Phoenix Park, just at the edge of Dublin. (Don't worry, the park is quite safe and innocuous, except for Ireland's rampant public indecent exposure problem.) Don't know how to ride? Don't worry, they offer lessons, too. (Just kidding about the indecent exposure.)

Ah, a romantic row in a brightly painted, handmade boat, out to an uninhabited island, followed by a picnic by one of the old ruins.... Sure, 'tis a recipe for lovin'. Find **Aidan Fennel** (aka **The Ferryman**) *(Coliemore Rd., Dalkey, Co. Dublin; Tel 01/283-42-98; Ferry £3, rowboat rental £5/hour Jun-Aug, weather permitting; DART to Dalkey Station)* on the stone wharf next to the Dalkey Island Hotel.

If you're in town sometime during May and June, you owe it to

gaelic games

If you want to experience something truly, authentically Irish, without any mass-tourism b.s., you'll have to check out a **Gaelic football** or **hurling** match.

Dubliners, as well as the rest of Ireland, are madly passionate about these two sports. Both are considered home-grown, are played on an amateur basis only in Ireland, and evoke happy feelings of national identity. There's some history here: The **GAA** (Gaelic Athletic Association) was founded in 1884, as part of the Irish independence movement. But whatever the history, both sports also embody the kind of fast-paced, high-skill, and high-scoring events that any sports fan will immediately respond to. Gaelic football could be called a cross between soccer and rugby, while hurling looks something like lacrosse spliced with field hockey: The players carry big wooden sticks, which they can use like bats, but they can also handle the ball, called a *sliothar* (that's "shlither"). You're sure to see these sports on any pub TV screen in the summer.

For live blood, sweat, and tears, check out the elite inter-county games taking place in Dublin from mid-March to mid-September at **Croke Park** *(Jones Rd., D9; 01/836-32-22; Bus 3, 11, 16; Times and teams listed in Evening Herald; £2-6)*. This is the finest Gaelic sport to be seen in the land, and the intense inter-county rivalry makes for an electric atmosphere. The season culminates in the All-Ireland Hurling and Football Finals, Ireland's Superbowl.

yourself to check out the **Howth Castle Rhododendron Gardens** *(Howth, Co. Dublin; Tel 01/832-22-12; DART to Howth Station or Bus 31; 8am-sunset daily Apr-Jun; Free admission)*, where 2,000 varieties of rhododendron will be blooming like heaven fallen to Earth in this 30-acre garden. Just checking out pretty little Howth Harbor and the view from the headlands above the town is worth the 20 minute DART ride.

Only a block south of St. Stephen's Green, but worlds away in atmosphere, is the serene, walled-in **Iveagh Gardens** *(Clonmel St., off Harcourt St.)*. So few people come to its broad lawns, shady walkways, and fountains, it's almost spooky. You can feel like it's your own private garden in the middle of a sunny afternoon. Great for a picnic with a special friend; it closes at 6pm.

STUff

The places for a mainstream shopping fix in Dublin are around the pedestrianized Grafton and Henry streets. Grafton Street, on the south side of the Liffey at the edge of Temple Bar, is definitely more expensive and upmarket; it's Dublin's equivalent of Fifth Avenue. It's also much more touristy than Henry Street, where Dublin's north-siders go bargain shopping. But if you're trawling for goodies with some real character, you'll have to wander off the main track.

▶▶DUDS

If you want to blend with the in crowd at the clubs, get your socially acceptable uniform at **Hobo** (*4 Exchequer St.; Tel 01/670-48-69; 9:30am-6pm Mon-Wed, Fri, till 8pm Thur, till 7pm Sat, noon-6pm Sun; £1-150; V, MC*), which sells streetwear ("combats"—basically cargo pants—and tight T-shirts) to every hipster and skate rat in town.

Ten doors down, **Sabotage** (*14 Exchequer St.; Tel 01/670-48-69; 10am-6pm Mon-Sat, 2-6pm Sun; V, MC, AE*) does the phattest hip-hop wear.

One great thing about being a female is **No-Name** (*11 Suffolk St.; Tel 01/677-37-99; 9:30am-6pm Mon-Sat, till 8pm Thur, 2-6pm Sun; 99p-£24.99; V, MC*) a women's-only shop for labels like Calvin Klein and Kookai at discount prices. Snatch up two little numbers for £5 in the bargain basement.

You'll find the who's-who at the **Design Centre** (*Powerscourt Townhouse Centre, top floor, D2; Tel 01/679-57-18; 9:30am-6pm Mon-Sat, till 9pm Thur; www.designer-place.ie; £100-250; V, MC, AE*), a ready-to-wear "group showcase" for up-and-coming women's designers.

Oakes (*8 Dawson St., D2; Tel 01/670-41-78; 10am-6pm Mon-Fri, till 5pm Sat; oakes@tinet.ie; £70-350; V, MC*) specializes in collection-based, custom-fit high fashion at ready-to-wear prices. Calling their concept "customized-to-order," young design partners Donald Brennan and Niall Tyrell have attracted a worldwide following. Check it out.

For a slightly younger take on classic Hibernian beauty, try Marc O'Brien, upstairs at **Awear** (*26 Grafton St., D2; Tel 01/671-72-00; 9:30am-6:30pm Mon-Sat, till 8:30pm Thur, noon-6pm Sun; £85-130; V, MC*).

Definitely doing the iconoclastic side of local fashion, **Sé Sí** (*13 Temple Bar; Tel 01/679-05-23; 10am-6pm daily, till 8pm in summer; £15-90; V, MC*) features the kind of stuff that will stand out in any crowd. Pronounced "shay-shee," the name means "him and her" in Gaelic. Vibrant and innovative are the words for their clothing and accessories. The place to go for that purple velvet backpack with the fuzzy technicolor horns sticking out all over.

▶▶BOUND

Easons (*40 Lower O'Connell St., D1; Tel 01/ 873-38-11; DART to Connolly Station or Bus 25, 34, 37, 38A, 39A, 39B, 66A, 67A; 8:30am-7pm Mon-Wed, till 8:45pm Thurs and 7:45pm Fri, 1-6pm Sun; V, MC*) is Ireland's big chain bookstore, with branches all over the country. This particular one, off the Henry Street shopping area, has all the atmosphere you would expect of a big chain, but the selection, including imported newspapers and magazines, just goes on and on.

Hodges Figgis (*56-58 Dawson St., D2; Tel 01/677-47-54; Bus 10, 11A, 11B, 13, 20B; 9am-7pm Mon-Fri, till 8pm Thur, 9am-6pm Sat,* noon-6pm Sun; V, MC)—say that one five times fast. Just a hop south of Trinity College, this is the grand old man of Dublin's bookshops, now going all trendy with a comfy cafe inside. The stained wood interior is a great place for a free read on a rainy day.

Across the street from Hodges Figgis is **Waterstone's** *(7 Dawson St., D2; Tel 01/679-141-5; Bus 10, 11A, 11B, 13, 20B; 9am-8pm Mon-Fri, till 8:30pm Thur, till 7pm Sat, 11am-6pm Sun; V, MC)*. This one has dark wood too, plus a slightly more piquant stock than its neighbor, doing gay stuff, New Age, and Women's Studies. These folks also host frequent, free readings by authors.

Dandelion Books *(74 Aungier St., D2; Tel 01/ 478-47-59; Bus 16, 16A, 19, 19A, 22, 22A, 155; 10:30am-6:30pm Mon-Sat; No credit cards)* is just a horde of cheap, used paperback thrillers. Pulp-lover's heaven.

Part of the host of book peddlers next to Trinity, **Hannas** *(27-29 Nassau St., D2; Tel 01/677-12-55; Bus 5, 7A, 8, 62; 9am-6pm Mon-Sat, till 8pm Thur; V, MC)* feels like a real bookshop, with high-shelved, oodles-o-books chaos and slightly naughty erotic art on the wall. Does new stuff too, but it's the secondhand we're interested in.

Don't let the creepy entrance tunnel scare you—**The Secret Book and Record Store** *(15A Wicklow St., D2; Tel 01/679-72-72; Bus 32X, 39X, 41X, 66X, 67X; 11am-6:30pm daily; V, MC)* is quite friendly, stocking secondhand and antique books in a small, comfortable space. You'll never know what you'll find here. They even have some old vinyl (hence the name).

▶▶**THRIFT**
The big mama of Dublin flea markets has gotta be **Mother Red Caps Market** *(Back Lane, off High St., D8; Tel 01/453-83-06; Bus 21A, 78A, 78B; 10am-5pm Fri-Sun)*. "Da Mutha" lies sprawled in a big roofed-in space just a little trot past Christchurch Cathedral. You know the drill: Stalls selling anything from framed portraits of John Wayne to floral-print couches, henna tattoos, or your fortune. Good luck, and don't forget to haggle.

Dublin also has a slew of charity secondhand shops. There are a couple just around the corner from **Trinity College** [see *culture zoo*, above], including **Oxfam** *(S. Great George's St., D2; 10am-5pm Mon-Sat; 99p-£7; AE, V, MC)*. Down the street is **Cerebral Palsy** *(Unit 8, S. Great George's St., D2; 9:30am-5pm Mon-Sat; £2.50-10; No credit cards)*. On the north side, there's **C.A.S.A.** *(26 Capel St., D1; Tel 01/872-85-38; 9:30am-5pm Mon-Sat; Most items under £5; No credit cards)*, which benefits the Caring and Sharing Association. Sounds nice, doesn't it?

Two parts of town have sprung up as secondhand zones, conveniently close to one another. **George's Street Arcade** *(S. Great George's St. near the corner of Exchequer St., D2; Bus 16, 16A, 19, 19A, 22, 22A, 155; 10am-6pm Mon-Sat)* hosts no fewer than three shops: **Jenny Vander** *(Tel 01/677-04-06; £10-250; V, MC)* has serious, Great Gatsby-esque vintage clothes and jewelry for women at some serious prices. Just up Jenny's stairs, **Rufus the Cat** does more men's clip-on ruffles, jumbo afro wigs, glittery gold platforms with 6-inch heels, and full '60s- and '70s-style suits. Both shops regularly equip the discerning partygoer with stylish rental outfits. Across the arcade, the **Big Whiskey** *(Tel 01/677-92-99; V, MC)* does your more standard secondhand stuff very well, and very cheaply, mostly for £5 or under.

There are even a couple of cheap secondhand shops in the well-touristed environs of Temple Bar *(Bus 46, 46A, 46B, 63, 150)*. **The Eager Beaver** *(17 Crown Alley; Tel 01/677-33-42; 9:30am-5:30pm Mon-Fri, 9:30am-6pm Sat, till 7pm Thur in summer; £3.95-17.95; V, MC)* has two floors of unisex secondhand. **Damascus** *(2 Crown Alley; Tel 01/679-70-87; 10am-6pm Mon-Sat; Clothes £1-20; V, MC)* has men's and women's secondhand, plus some creepy totems from Indonesia and a fleet of wind chimes that's threatening to collapse the ceiling.

▶▶**FOOT FETISH**

Need some new treads? Try **DV8 Shoes** *(4 Crown Alley; Tel 01/679-84-72; Mon-Sat 10am-6pm, till 8pm Thur; £19.99-110; V, MC, AE)*. They're all here: Shelly's of London, Bunker, Yellow Cab, Diesel, Vagabond, those yummy f—k-me boots, platform sneakers, and blue suede shoes. Stomp in style, baby.

▶▶**TUNES**

Remember, most of the records in Ireland are like the wine: brought in by

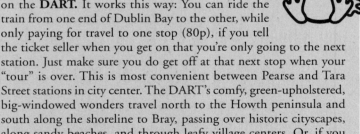

down and out

Got no money? Take the poor man's tour of Dublin on the **DART.** It works this way: You can ride the train from one end of Dublin Bay to the other, while only paying for travel to one stop (80p), if you tell the ticket seller when you get on that you're only going to the next station. Just make sure you do get off at that next stop when your "tour" is over. This is most convenient between Pearse and Tara Street stations in city center. The DART's comfy, green-upholstered, big-windowed wonders travel north to the Howth peninsula and south along the shoreline to Bray, passing over historic cityscapes, along sandy beaches, and through leafy village centers. Or, if you know you'll want to get off a few times, you can always get an all-day pass for £3.50.

Or take in a free flick. During July and August, there's a free screening every Saturday night in Temple Bar's Meeting House Square. Tickets (free but required) are available at **Temple Bar Information Centre** *(18 Eustace St., D2; Tel 01/671-57-17)*.

Otherwise, most of the major cultural sites in Dublin are free entry [see *culture zoo,* above]. You got no money for anything else, you might as well feed your head.

ship. Still, there's a pretty good selection outside of those multinational-owned, pop-dominated megastores (which we won't talk about). The two floors of **Chapters Music Store** (*54 Middle Abbey St.; Tel 01/873-04-84; 9:30am-6:30pm Mon-Sat, till 8pm Thur, 1:30-6:30pm Sun; V, MC*) offer a wide selection of new and secondhand CDs and videos, plus vinyl and DVD.

Vinyl junkies and beat freaks, **Big Brother Records** (*Basement of 16B Fade St.; Tel 01/672-93-55; 11am-6pm Mon-Sat, till 6:30pm Thur; www.bigbrotherrecords.ie, bigbrother@connect.ie; V, MC*) is your home for everything in hip-hop, jazz, and electronica. In a cozy basement just a stone's throw from George's Street Arcade [see above], owner Killian "Heart-O-Gold" Murphy is ever-present, amicable, and knowledgeable, like a regular Bodhisattva of Beats.

Upstairs at the same address, **Road Records** (*16B Fade St.; Tel 01/671-73-40; 10am-6pm Mon-Sat; www.groov.ie/road, road@groove.ie; V, MC*) has what's new in indie vinyl, Chicago "post-rock," reggae, and ska in your basic hole-in-the-wall record shop.

For the drum 'n' bass, techno, and trance you heard the DJs spinning last night, head down the banks of the Liffey to small but slick **TAG Records** (*5 The Cobbles, Wellington Quay; Tel 01/677-97-05; 11am-7pm Mon-Sat; V, MC*). The staff here are so obliging, it's almost eerie.

Just north of the Ha'Penny Bridge, **Abbey Discs** (*3 Meller Court, Lower Liffey St.; Tel 01/873-37-33; 9:30am-6:30pm Mon-Sat, till 8pm Thur; V, MC*) carries a very respectable selection of dance music, new vinyl, and budget CDs.

Pick up your black roses and Marilyn Manson key rings at **Rhythm Records** (*1 Aston Quay; Tel 01/671-95-94; 11am-6pm Mon-Sat; V, MC*). On Temple Bar's river side, this chaotic tourist bazaar features hard rock, punk, and goth secondhand, collectible CDs and vinyl.

EATS

All the money flowing around Ireland, combined with a surge of immigration into the country from abroad, has brought some real cosmopolitan variety and quality to the Dublin restaurant scene. You can get anything from Mongolian to Mexican, but unfortunately you're likely to wait long stretches for just about everything. There's no such thing as snappy service in Ireland. Glacially slow is more like it. Your best strategy is to do like the Irish and keep a sense of humor. One tip: The wait staff will usually ignore you completely after they've dropped off your meal. If you want your check before the third millennium, it's probably better to go up to the "cash" and ask to pay there. Otherwise, resign yourself to gathering dust. If you do get a good waiter, tip as you would at home. They'll appreciate it. Unless noted, all spots below are within walking distance of Tara Street DART Station.

▶▶CHEAP

For a real Dublin pubgrub lunch done right, take a pilgrimage to the **Stag's Head.** Try the daily special for £4.50. **The Globe** serves up tasty and trendy lunchtime fare for under £5 between noon and 3pm [see *bar scene*, above, for both].

Eat lunch with the last of the independents in the cafe/bar at the **Irish Film Center** [see *arts scene*, above] a chill, almost homey bar connected to the IFC art-house cinema complex. The soup of the day (with a hearty slice o' bread) makes a good light lunch for under £2. Don't wait for the waiters to come to your table—place your orders at the bar, and you'll get the food faster.

Staffed by an international collection of friendly freaks, the **@ Home Cafe** *(Creation Arcade, off Duke St., D2; Tel 01/672-90-10; Bus 32X, 39X, 41X, 66X, 67X; 9am-11pm Mon-Thur, till 3am Fri-Sun; £1.20-7.95 all items; V, MC)* is a real gem. It's a laid-back, informal cafe with a kind of hip East Village feel, tucked away in a little mall between Grafton and Dawson streets, that serves absolutely delicious Mediterranean-style food, doing morning breakfast, lunchtime soups, killer salads, sandwiches, and exotic tapas in the evening. The Sunday brunch is great, too. Check it out anytime but especially late-night, after the clubs close.

A little upstairs hole-in-the-wall with a constant rock-steady and reggae soundtrack, **Cafe Irie** *(11 Upper Fownes St., Temple Bar, D2; No phone; Bus 46, 46A, 46B, 63, 150; 10am-6pm Mon-Wed, Fri, Sat, till 8pm Thur, noon-6pm Sun; 80p-£3.75 breakfast and lunch items; No credit cards)* might actually persuade you that the tourist-laden Temple Bar is still funky. Serving it up fresh and creative, they also have prices that can't be beat: A meal of soup, sandwich, and tea here can cost you well under £5. Go before the lunch rush at 1pm.

Doin' the cheapest Irish breakfast in town, **Flanagan's Coffee Shop** *(10 Castle House, S. Great George's St., D2; Tel 01/475-02-25; Bus 16, 16A, 19, 19A, 22, 22A, 155; 7:30am-4:30pm daily; All breakfasts under £3; No credit cards)* comes through with an egg, a sausage, and a rasher (Irish bacon), plus toast and tea, all for £1.50. Beat that. Tiny and purple, it's just across from **The Globe** [see *bar scene*, above].

For the best (and probably cheapest) slice of deep-dish 'za in town, made by Italians, naturally, hit Temple Bar's **Botticelli** *(3 Temple Bar, D2; Tel 01/672-72-89; Bus 46, 46A, 46B, 63, 150; V, MC)*. For £1.50 to £1.80, they've got anything from sausage to smoked salmon on those slabs, and slices are available from noon to 3pm.

Eat your way to cosmic consciousness without dropping too much of your material world in the process at **Govinda's** *(4 Aungier St., D2; Tel 01/475-03-09; Bus 16, 16A, 19, 19A, 22, 22A, 155; 11am-9pm Mon-Sat; £1.25-4.50; MC, V)*, just south of Temple Bar. One of a constellation of cheap, cafeteria-style, tofu-and-salad eateries connected to a meditation center/Krishna commune/what-have-you. Physical manifestations tastefully decorated in auras of red, green, and yellow.

The best thing at **Yamamori Noodles** *(71-72 S. Great George's St.; Tel 01/475-50-01; Bus 16, 16A, 19, 19A, 22, 22A, 155; 12:30-11pm Sun-Wed, till 11:30 Thur-Sat; £6.50-9.50 per entree; V, MC, AE)* is the 12:30

to 5:30pm lunch special: £5 for any dish of noodles (14 choices of ramen, soba, or udon) with a choice of tea, coffee, or fresh carrot juice. Their huge bowl of ramen, chock-full of veggies, meat, and seafood, never disappoints. It's "cool food, cool jazz, and sushi," and they get packed later for their more expensive, but still reasonable, dinners. Around the block from **Dublin Castle** [see *culture zoo*, above].

If you're in Dublin and you don't go to **Bewley's** *(78 Grafton St; Tel 01/676-761; 7:30am-11pm daily. 11/12 Westmoreland St.; Tel 01/676-761; 7:30am-7:30pm daily. 40 Mary St.; Tel 01/677-671; 7am-9pm Mon-Wed, 7am-2pm Thu-Sat, 10am-10pm Sun)*, then you must be too high to know what's good for you. Bewley's is another Dublin institution—think of it as the yin to Starbuck's evil yang. The place is elegant while still being ultra-chill and inexplicably cheap (the all-day Irish breakfast of eggs, tea, toast, bacon, sausage, more sausage, and beans is only £3.95). The crowd is diverse, surprisingly so for a place that looks like only confirmed teetotalers would dare step inside. Angsty teens defiantly cloud the smoking section with their incessant puffing while little old ladies read the papers and sip tea. There are three locations in downtown Dublin, so wherever you are, you can find relaxation only minutes away.

Noodles are status symbols at **Wagamama** *(South King St.; Tel 01/478-21-52; Noon-11pm Mon-Sat, 12:30-10pm Sun; £6-8)*. This elbow-to-elbow style eatery is slick and attracts people who definitely want to be seen slurping their soba, but damn if the food isn't tasty. It's not even that expensive; a huge bowl of noodle soup could fill at least 1.5 people.

Lucky's *(39 Dame St.; 8am-5pm Mon-Sat; £3.95 for a large breakfast)* is a great spot for whiling away the morning hours over greasy slabs of rashers (like bacon only thicker) and white pudding (hockey-puck-like sausage filled with god-knows-what). The "Big Breakfast" (fatty meats, anyone?) features tea, eggs, sausage, rashers, white pudding, and toast for a paltry £3.95—enough fatty acids to keep you trekking for hours. On a lighter note, you can get coffee and cappuccinos as well as a hearty assortment of pastries and croissants. The crowd is diverse in age, level of hep, and working status, but lands on the proper side of things. The comfy but smoky backroom has attractive ceiling windows to let in the sun, diffused by Dublin's ubiquitous clouds.

You've tried the rest, now stop messing around at those pretentious Temple Bar cafes and come to **Leo Burdock's** *(2 Werburgh St; Tel 01/454-03-06; Noon-midnight Mon-Sat, 4pm-midnight Sun; £3-4.50; No credit cards)*, hands down the best chip shop in the known universe. You'll recognize it by the queues running around the corner most days. Spitting distance from the Christ Church Cathedral, it's a toss-up as to which place will do more for your soul. An enormous filet of battered and fried cod is £3; chips are £1.20. Easily enough food for two adults, but with stuff this good, get your own, dammit. Get 'em with salt and vinegar or splurge for ketchup or tarter sauce (£0.15 for a little packet that you could probably

wired

www.ireland.travel.ie : Irish Tourist Board
www.eventguide.ie : The Event Guide Site
www.iol.ie/~smytho/dublin/ : Hedonist's guide to Dublin
www.geocities.com/sunsetstrip/club/3008/ : Dublin clubbing

Most hostels have at least one computer available, and Internet cafes seem to be taking over every basement in town. Try going well before noon or late evening unless you're OK with waiting.

Central Cybercafe *(6 Grafton St., D2; Tel 01/677-82-98; 8am-11pm Mon-Fri, 9am-11pm Sat, 10am-10pm Sun; www.centralcafe.ie; £5/hr, £4 students; No credit cards)* is a bright, second-story cafe with lots of big art and stained-glass windows, just packed with the latest equipment: 15 flat-monitored Pentium III's, plus a printer, scanner, and fax service. Plenty of food and designer coffee too, all on the menu for under £4. Basement-housed **Planet Cyber Café** *(23 S. Great George's St., D2; Tel 01/679-0583; 10am-10pm Sun-Wed, 10am-midnight Thur-Sat; £1.50/15 mins, £5/hr; £0.80-2.35 all food items; No credit cards)* offers 17 fast PCs, a scanner, and color printing; as well as coffee, sandwiches, pizza, and sweet stuff to munch on. Head north of O'Connell's statue to find **Global Internet Café** *(8 Lower O'Connell St., D1; Tel 01/878-02-95; 8am-11pm Mon-Fri, 9am-11pm Sat, 10am-10pm Sun; £5/hr; www.globalcafe.ie; No credit cards)*. It's the bright and happy California vegetable still-life theme in yet another basement, this time with a mixture of swift PCs and iMacs, plus color printing, scanning, and faxing. **Béta-café** *(Curved St.; Dublin 2; Tel 01/605-68-00; 10am-6pm Mon-Sat, noon-6pm Sun; £5/hr, £4 students; www.betacafe.com; No credit cards)*, in the second-floor atrium of Temple Bar's Arthouse [see *arts scene,* above], is the cybercafe with the best ambiance but the worst hardware. The videoheads from Arthouse come here to sip cappuccinos but not necessarily to surf, so the crowd is more arty and sociable. The old black Macs here are only for the desperate. Otherwise, there's a printer and seven slightly aged PCs, built by Hyundai. When the others are full, try the north side's **Interpoint** *(67 O'Connell St., upstairs at Funland, D1; Tel 01/878-34-55; 9am-10pm daily; £5/hr, £4.50 students; V, MC)*. No caffeine here but there's always a few speedy PCs open, and you can make cheap international calls from the phone booths, then play some pinball downstairs. A fax and laser printer are available as well.

get for free from Burger King). About the only thing Burdock's doesn't have is hot girls behind the counter. Too much of a good thing could kill you, after all.

Lemon *(66 S. William St.; Tel 01/672-90-55; 8am-late; £1.80-3.50 for crepes; No credit cards)* is a welcome addition to the new, gastronomically enlightened Dublin. Enjoy crepes sweet and savory in this slick, ultra-modern café. Imagine a lovely crepe with butter and sugar. Or tuna and cheddar. Or smoked salmon . Or Canadian maple syrup and bananas. Eat in the small back dining area or bask in the infrequent Dublin sun at outdoor café tables. The staff is friendlier than you'd expect for a trendy place in a trendy neighborhood.

Ah yes, the **Phoenix Perk** *(50 Dame Street; Tel 01/679-96-68; 10:45am-8:00pm Mon-Fri, 10:15am-8pm Sat-Sun; Sandwiches £3-4; No credit cards)*. Is there *anywhere* American pop culture has not laid a reminder of its ubiquitousness in the lonesome backpacker's path? Hard to say for sure. Phoenix Perk's logo is based on the logo for the coffee shop on TV's *Friends, Central* Perk, get it? Inside, it's pretty much the same as the show, except you won't see Chandler, Monica, Rachel, Joey, Phoebe, or Ross, and all the furniture is different, and the lay-out of the building is nothing like the set they show on TV. Nonetheless, the people that work here make you want to stay and hang out with your...friends! Kick it over tea and coffee, pretty good baguette and Panini sandwiches filled with a wide assortment of meats, cheese, and veggies, £3-4.

▶▶DO-ABLE

Taking Ireland's communist chic craze to its extreme, **Cafe Mao** *(2-3 Chatham Row; Tel 01/670-48-99; Noon-late daily; Entrées under £10; V, MC)* attracts everyone from 40-year-old-mom-types on a Saturday out to fresh-faced coolios who like wearing sunglasses indoors. The noisy, busy, trendy spot has a well-lit interior thanks to large garage-style windows. Décor is a bit like an Ikea showroom, with brilliant bands of reds, blues, and yellows wrapping around mostly unadorned white walls. Warhollian silk screens in neon colors embellish the back walls and entrance (The staff is darn attractive, too). Try the Malaysian chicken with saffron rice and a side order of delicious, hot Lemongrass Nan bread. Finding good food that's not meat-based in Dublin is like trying to get high on Sleepy Time Tea, so this place should be a find for all of you hippie-dippy veggie-types. If you don't salivate over the flesh of caged animals, go for the red pumpkin curry with butternut squash and lemongrass, with vegetable spring roles as an appetizer.

The old standby for young Dubliners going out on the town, the popular local chain **Fitzers Café** *(51 Dawson St., D2; Tel 01/677-11-55; Bus 10, 11A, 11B, 13, 20B; 9am-11:30pm daily; £6.95-13.95 per entree; V, MC, AE)* serves everything from tandoori to chili in attractive, modern surroundings. This one is just south of Trinity College; another branch is at Temple Bar Square.

▶▶SPLURGE

The atmosphere at **Tosca** *(21 Suffolk St., D2; Tel 01/679-67-44; 10:30am-*

11pm Mon-Fri, 11am-11:30pm Fri, Sat, 1-4pm Sun; £8.95-15.95 per entree; V, MC, AE) puts it in a category of its own. Everybody who thinks they're anybody comes here to rub shoulders with supermodels, rock stars, and any other young gods and goddesses of our media-obsessed world. Still, it's a comfortable place for mere mortals, conveniently right off Grafton St., and the Italian-style food is darn good. Best for dinner or the *Elvis Loves Eggs* Sunday brunch with live DJs.

The Mermaid Cafe *(69-70 Dame St., D2; Tel 01/670-82-36; Bus 15, 15A 15B, 83, 155; 12:30-2:30pm/6-11pm Mon-Sat, 12:30-3:30pm/6-9pm Sun; £8.75-13.75 per entree; V, MC)* is one of the places in town food critics flock to for the pleasure of it. On a sunny Temple Bar corner, and with lots of windows, chef/owner Ben Gorman puts up a different menu of creative seafood dishes every week. Try the giant seafood casserole with Thai aromatics or tuna tartare with white horseradish slaw and wasabi mayonnaise: It's craft cooking at its best.

crashing

Dublin city-center lodgings have been springing up like toadstools after a rain these last few years, responding to the massive influx of partying weekenders. Unfortunately, although many places are mediocre, even the dirty, overcrowded, and poorly run places are guaranteed full houses in summer because of the heavy demand. To avoid getting stuck in a dive, book well in advance, especially for weekends. Irish hotels are known to have a quirk about beds; budget or big-bucks makes no difference. They all seem to have a stock of mattresses strangely reminiscent of the island's geography: pointy at the corners, bog-soft in the middle, and generally ancient. If you want a firm mattress, make sure you insist on one. And one more thing: There's lots of street noise in the presently construction-frenzied Dublin, so ask for a bed away from the road if that bothers you.

▶▶**CHEAP**

The hostels listed here all have comfy TV lounges, well-equipped kitchens, and serve a small breakfast (generally toast and tea) included in the crashing price.

Painted yellow and white, every window full of blooming flowers, the **Abbey Hostel** *(29 Bachelor's Walk, D2; Tel 01/878-07-00; DART to Tara St. Station or Bus 51, 51B, 68, 68A, 69, 69X, 78A, 79, 90, 210; info@abbey-hostel.ie, www.indigo.ie/~abbeyhos; £40-60 double, £13-17 4-bed, £11-16 6-bed, £8-14 10-bed; V, MC)* takes the prize as prettiest hostel in city center. Overlooking the Liffey at O'Connell Bridge, this hostel is about as central as it gets. With bathrooms in every room, the real power showers feel pretty damn good in comparison to the usual whimpy 30-seconds-a-push jobs. Friendly, clean, and relatively small, you can even practice your piano playing in the TV room. BBQ-o-rama on the back patio in the summer, charcoal provided.

Avalon House *(55 Angier Street; Tel 01/475-00-01, Fax 01/475-03-03; info@avalonhouse.ie; www.avalon-house.ie/index.shtml; £9-15 dorm)* is the Grand Central Station of hostels. This 300-bed backpacker Mecca welcomes the budget traveler with clean sheets, and free "breakfast in a bag" (a muffin, yogurt, and fruit). Avalon House sees over 100,000 guests a year and does so with remarkable efficiency. The place is giant, and so by its nature is a bit impersonal; some people complain about the service. But it has a full kitchen, 24-hour access, secure locker storage (£1), no curfew, pay Internet kiosks and helpful staff. Online reservations can be made at their web site and you can book ahead for other hostels here too. Doubles and singles are available, though they fill up fast; book well in advance.

Located in the heart of the hedonist's paradise, **Barnacles Temple Bar House** *(19 Temple bar, corner of Cecelia Street; Tel 01/671-62-77, Fax 01/671-659; templeba@barnacles.iol.ie; £18-25 per person twin room, £13-17 4-bed dorm, £11.50-£14 6-bed dorm, £10.50-13 10-bed dorm, £9-11 12-bed dorm)* is super-friendly and clean; it seems to be popular with gay and lesbian backpackers. This new hostel features en suite bathrooms, gratis continental breakfast, and moins cher laundry facilities. There is also a self-catering kitchen to boil your spaghetti.

Located just around the corner from the central bus station, **Abraham House** *(82 Lower Gardiner St., D1; Tel 01/855-06-00; DART to Connolly Station; Bus 27B, 42, 43, 53, 53A; £7.50-10.50 dorm, £13.50 quad, £18.50-19.50 double; V, MC, AE)* is everything it should be: clean, secure, and cheap. Most rooms have attached bathrooms, and everybody gets a towel.

The Dublin branch of the USIT NOW empire, **Kinlay House Christchurch** *(2/12 Lord Edward St., D2; Tel 01/679-66-44; DART to Tara St. Station or Bus 21A, 50, 50A, 78, 78A, 78B; kindub@usit.ie; £9-14 dorm, £14 quad, £14-17 double; V, MC)* has a great location in Temple Bar, attractive interior, and clean communal bathrooms—so don't let the name scare you off. The big, cheap, sky-lit dorm rooms on the top floor are by far the nicest in Dublin.

The best of the super-cheap B&B's on Gardiner Street, **Glen Court** *(67 Lower Gardiner St.; Tel 01/836-40-22; DART to Connolly Station or Bus 27B, 42, 43, 53, 53A; £16 single, £30 double, £42 triple, £52 quad; No credit cards)* takes up a high-ceilinged old Georgian all done in dainty, light pink paint. It's hard to believe the hostel-comparable prices for private rooms include a full Irish breakfast plus soap and a towel, but it's true. The sparse rooms need a paint job and the furniture's secondhand, but it's all clean. Yep, you get a sink and phone booth-like shower all to yourself, too. The shared toilets are in the hall. There's also a nice little breakfast room and a chill satellite-fed TV lounge (pink, of course).

▶▶DO-ABLE

Right on Great George's nightlife strip and just over from Grafton Street, **Kelly's Hotel** *(36-37 S. Great George's St., D1; Tel 01/677-92-77; DART to Tara St. Station or Bus 16, 16A, 19, 19A, 22, 22A; kellyshtl@iol.ie; £30-45 single, £68-76 double; V, MC, AE)* has budget prices but gives you Old-World class and atmosphere. With its banistered staircases, mellow blue-and-white floral wallpaper, dark wood, and frosted glass, the place has a real "tranquil haven" feel. A small "student" single, with shared bathroom, goes for £30, breakfast included.

Harding Hotel *(Copper Alley, Christchurch, D2; Tel 01/679-65-00; Bus 21A, 50, 50A, 78, 78A, 78B; www.iol.ie/usitaccm, harding@usit.ie; £45 single; £50-£60 double or triple; V, MC)* has bright, spotless, and spankin'-new rooms complete with bathrooms, TV, and coffee/tea makers—smack dab in the middle of tourist central. No breakfast, but there is Darkey Kelly's, the hotel's restaurant/bar named after a famous old Dublin whore who had a heart of gold (but was unfortunately burned to death for murder). Connected by an inner courtyard to Kinlay House Hostel [see above], so sly use of their kitchen may be an option.

The Townhouse *(46-48 Lower Gardiner St., D1; Tel 01/878-88-08; DART to Connolly Station or Bus 27B, 42, 43, 53, 53A; gtrotter@indigo._ie; £40-52.50 single, £56-86 double, £72-96 triple, £12-17 hostel dorms, all including full breakfast; V, MC)* gives a lot of bang for the buck. Their rooms are truly stylin' (each one individually decorated by the owner), if small, and the huge breakfast is the best coronary-inducing Irish grub around. The tranquil little back garden has a Japanese look to it (Lafcadio Hearn, the "Supreme Interpreter of Japan to the West, and Vice Versa" lived here in the 19th century) and the staff is great. Private bathrooms with every room.

Other do-able options include **Kilronan House** *(70 Adelaide Rd.; Tel 01/475-52-66, Fax 01/478-28-41; info@dublinn.com, www.dublinn.com; Single £55, double/twin £96, breakfast included, private baths; V, MC, AE)* in the city center; **Charleville Lodge** *(268/272 North Circular Road; Tel 01/838-66-33, Fax 01/838-58-54; Bus 10 to N. Circular Rd. and Rathdown Rd.; charleville@indigo.ie, www.charlevillelodge.ie; Nov-Apr: Single £35, Twin/Double: £27.50/person, Triple/family £25/person; May-Oct: Single £60, Twin/Double £45/person, Triple/family £35/person; Full Irish breakfast included, private baths; V, MC, AE)* 10-15 minutes from the city center; and **Aston Hotel** *(7-9 Aston Quay; Tel 01/677-93-00, Fax 01/677-90-07; stay@aston-hotel.com, www.aston-hotel.com; Nov-Feb: Sun-Thur £34/person, Fri-Sat £40/person; Mar-Oct Sun-Thur £40/person, Fri-Sat £48/person; V, MC, AE)* in the Temple Bar area.

▶▶**SPLURGE**

Not the Ritz, but damn charming in its own way is the **Fitzwilliam Hotel** *(83 St. Stephen's Green South; Tel 01/478-21-33; Fax 01/478-22-63; £55-85 per person; AE, V, DIN)*. With only a handful of rooms (all with private bath), staying here makes you feel you're at someone's house. High Georgian ceilings give the small rooms a spacious feeling. The location can't be beat, a beautiful quiet street two seconds from St. Stephen's Green and nearby one of the best traditional pubs in Dublin, **O'Donnoghue's** [see *bar scene*, above]. Breakfast is served up hot and delicious downstairs in the dining room.

Russell Court Hotel *(Harcourt St., D2; Tel 01/478-49-94; DART to Tara St. Station or Bus Bus 14, 14A, 15A, 15B, 48A; £65 single, £100* *double, £115 triple; V, MC, AE, DC)* is a big, classy, old-world hotel on a pretty Georgian street just off St. Stephen's Green, and it just happens to look like some beautiful fantasy bordello in a Hollywood movie. And you might even be able to afford it. In addition to the regular rates, there's a weekend special: two nights, one dinner, and two full breakfasts, all for £89 per person sharing. A lot of their rooms are actually (get this) suites, chock-full of old, faux-Chinese antique furniture, couches, canopy beds, and gas fireplaces. Rooms 111, 112, and 300 are especially sweet. There's a great beer garden in back, a superb residents' bar inside, and free entrance to the Vatican nightclub in the basement every night.

What could be better to start your party weekend than watching the sunset from a downtown Pimp Daddy rooftop penthouse? At the **Oliver St. John Gogarty's Temple Bar Penthouse Apartments** *(18-21 Angelsea St., Temple Bar, D2; Tel 01/671-18-22; DART to Tara St. Station or Bus 46, 46A, 46B, 63; £70-80 1-bedroom, £120-130 2-bedroom, £130-140 3-bedroom; V, MC, AE)*, the dream becomes reality. These modern, lots-o-glass-and-hardwood apartments do the full kitchen, dining room, living room (with TV, video, and leather couches, no less), and bedrooms deal, plus there's a rooftop deck and balconies with sweeping views of the city. For this price (each bedroom is a double), it's a steal.

need to know

Currency Exchange The local currency is the **Irish pound (£),** aka the *punt.* A Bureau de Change within any bank will have the best rates.

Tourist Information Best bet is the centrally-located **Dublin Tourism Centre** *(St. Andrew's Church, Suffolk St.; Tel 01/605-77-00; 8:30am-7:30pm Mon-Sat, 11am-5:30pm Sun June-Sept, 9am-5:30pm Mon-Sat Sept-June; information@dublintourism.ie, www.visit.ie/dublin).* Other offices include: **Irish Tourist Board** *(Baggot St. Bridge; Tel 01/602-40-00; 9:15am-5:15pm Mon-Fri; www.ireland.travel.ie)* and branches at the airport and ferry terminal. **USIT NOW** *(Aston Quay; Tel 01/677-81-17; 9am-5:30pm Mon-Fri, 10am-1pm Sat)* will help you find a hostel.

Public Transportation The primary public transit is **Dublin Bus** *(55p-£1.25),* operating between 6am and 11:30pm, with special NiteLink (£2.50) service from the center to outer areas on Thur, Fri, and Sat at midnight, 1am, 2am, and 3am. Free maps, schedules, etc., are available at **Dublin Bus Head Office** *(59 Upper O'Connell St., D1; Tel 01/873-42-22; 9am-5:45pm Mon-Fri; till 1pm Sat).* **DART** trains run through town and out to Dublin's suburbs. Tickets can be bought at the DART stations and at the **Rail Travel Centre** *(35 Abbey St. Lower, across O'Connell Bridge on the north side; Single trip £3-12, weekly £12.50).* If you buy a single-trip ticket, you must specify your exact destination. Taxis are expensive and in short supply around town. It's especially bad late-night, when you can easily wait for an hour or more to get a ride. The standard taxi practice, with tourists and locals alike, is to take the most out-of-the-way route possible to jack up the fare, then play politely dumb if called on it—Dublin's maze-like setup makes this an easy scam. When getting in a cab, try to have an idea of how best to get where you're going or at least have a map handy to check that you're not being given the runaround. If you want vengance, take the taxi's roof sign number and call the **Garda Carriage Office** *(Tel 01/475-58-88)*.

Bike Rental Rent a two-wheeler at **Cycle Ways** *(185-186 Parnell St., three blocks north of the Liffey; Tel 01/873-47-48)*.

American Express *(116 Grafton St.; Tel 01/677-28-74)*.

Emergency Emergency *999*. **The Mater Hospital** *(Eccles St.; Tel 01/453-79-41)*, **St. Vincent's Hospital** *(Elm Park; Tel 01/209-43-58)*, and **St. James' Hospital** *(James St.; Tel 01/830-11-22)*, will all stitch you up.

Pharmacies **O'Connell's Late Night Pharmacy** *(21 Grafton St.; Tel 01/679-04-67; 8:30am-8:30pm Mon-Sat, 11am-6pm Sun)* and **Hamilton Long Late Night Pharmacy** *(5 Lower O'Connell St., Tel 01/874-84-56; Mon-Fri 8am-8pm, Sat 8:30am-6pm)* aren't that late-night, but they're open later than most.

Telephone Country code: 353. Area code: *01;* information: *1190;* international operator: *114.* If you're going to be making many local calls, save yourself some money and aggravation and pick up a phone card. Both local and international calling cards can be purchased in almost any shop. **AT&T:** *1/800/550-000;* **MCI:** *1/800/551-001;* **Sprint:** *1/800/552-001.*

Airports **Dublin International Airport** *(Tel 01/704-42-22)*. *Dublin Bus Airlink,* with a stop outside the arrivals terminal, will run you directly into the city center, Connolly Station or Heuston Station, departing about every 10-12 minutes *(7am-11pm daily; £3 adults, £1.50 students)*. **Dublin Bus CitySwift 41** also goes from the airport to Eden Quay in the city center with many local stops in between. It's cheaper, at £1.10, but much slower. Taxis to the center cost around £12.

Trains **Heuston Station** *(Kingsbridge, off St. John's Rd.)*, out on the west side of town, serves south, west, and southwest. Take Stationlink Bus 90 into town. **Connolly Station** *(Amiens St.)* serves north and north-west, take a left out of the station, walk down Amiens Street, and you'll be smack in the middle of Temple Bar. **Pearse Station** *(Westland Row, Tara St.)*, just east of **Trinity** College Green, serves southeast. **Irish Rail** *(Tel 01/836-62-22)* provides the trains.

Bus Lines Out of the City **Bus Eirann** *(Busárus, Store St.; Tel 01/836-61-11)* is right in the city center.

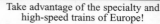

Take advantage of the specialty and high-speed trains of Europe!

Thomas Cook timetable with railpass orders over $1,000   Check out our European railpasses

Your search for the perfect railpass and backpack has ended

The Backpack Traveler offers expert advice and service on railpasses, backpacks, youth hostels and travel gear

Our goal is to make your trip safe, comfortable and easy while saving money.

With your Eurail/Europass you'll receive the lowest price available plus the following special offers:

- **Free** 2nd day railpass shipping
- **Free** Eurail video
- **Free** timetable
- **Free** rail map
- **Free** 500 page rail guide
- **Free** Thomas Cook Timetable on rail orders over $1,000

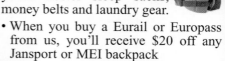

That's not all. We carry a great selection of backpacks and over a hundred travel products including youth hostel sleep sacks, money belts and laundry gear.

- When you buy a Eurail or Europass from us, you'll receive $20 off any Jansport or MEI backpack
- Youth hostel memberships and ISE Student Discount Cards are available to help keep your expenses down
- Our entire catalog is now online at: www.europebytrain.com

We specialize in Eurail, Europass, Britrail, Eurostar and country passes

Call today for a FREE catalog and railpass brochure

1-800-688-9577

The Backpack Traveler

PO Box 1386, San Juan Capistrano, CA 92693

www.europebytrain.com

Catalog and rail brochure

@angingout

The coolest guides
to the hottest spots in Europe

What to see
Where to hang
How to party . . .
While traveling abroad

galway

Galway is to Ireland what California is to the States: the wild and beautiful west where the disaffected free thinkers from the east came to start over. By the early '80s, the influx of artists and other boho types, combined with the presence of a major university, had transformed this once-grand medieval port of derelict buildings into the most happening hotbed of the arts in Ireland: Experimentation is the norm, partying is a serious occupation, and the cast of local characters is a lot wilder, more diverse, and a helluva lot more fun than you'd expect from a little town of 60,000 souls.

With stunning surroundings, scores of bars and cafes, tons of live music, packed clubs, internationally renowned theater, plus a summer-long schedule of kick-ass festivals, Galway's not lacking much. The pubs are the heart of this city, and you'll find them full of former travelers who came here for a weekend, loved the vibe, and never left. The general welcome for young globe-trotters goes something like this: "You're from out of town? That's nice. Let's party." It's more than likely you won't want to leave, either.

neighborhoods

Most everything in Galway is centered around two parks: **Eyre Square**, by the train station in the east end of the city, and **Spanish Parade**, to the west of Eyre Square by **Galway Bay.** The parks are connected by a half-mile of the pedestrian-only **Shop Street** (as per usual in Ireland, this street changes names five times, but we'll stick with this one). The maze of medieval streets to either side of Shop Street is where you'll find the more tourist-oriented cafes and pubs. Just west of the Spanish Parade, you'll cross the **River Corrib,** which, in this stretch, is a spectacular network of stonework canals, bridges, and waterfalls, full of hundreds of gliding swans, crisscrossed by footpaths and bordered by banks of flower gardens. The other side of the Corrib is slightly less touristic,

portrait of the artist

James Joyce has long been hailed as one of Ireland's finest writers, possibly *the* finest of them all; critics say Joyce is Shakespeare's sole rival when it comes to a mastery of the English language. But although every story he wrote took place in Ireland, he left Ireland in his early twenties and only came back twice—both times to see Nora Barnacle, the Galway woman he later married; you can read their love letters at the Barnacle family house on Bowling Green [see *culture zoo,* below]. Joyce made no secret of his quarrels with his native land, yet Ireland was always at the very heart of his novels, short stories, and poems.

With spells in Paris, Rome, Trieste, and Zurich, Joyce's life reads like an exciting, romantic adventure. In reality, he was plagued by rotten health, money troubles, censorship, and family strife throughout his now much-celebrated life.

Joyce's most famous works include *Dubliners, Finnegan's Wake,* and *A Portrait of the Artist as a Young Man.* But it was the notorious 1922 publication of *Ulysses* that catapulted him into the international literary spotlight, principally because the novel was sensationally banned from the United States on grounds of obscenity. (There, that got your attention, didn't it?) But before you lasciviously plunge in, be forewarned that Joyce's dense, allusive, wordy writing is hard to crack (many's the college student who's dismissed it as mere drink-inspired gobbledygook). Don't give up, though: Joyce's subtle plots, psychologically vivid characters, and stream-of-consciousness narrative style, all radical in their day, get to the heart of human reality in a way no mere fiction ever had before. Highbrow academics now fight over who can come up with the "deepest" analyses of the many hidden meanings and complex symbolism in James Joyce's work, and Joyce himself once said that a reader could easily spend a lifetime studying only *Finnegan's Wake.* But on another day, and in another mood, Joyce also said, "I'm afraid I'm more interested in Dublin street names than in the riddle of the universe." Contradictions, ambiguities, and sly Irish humor—that's James Joyce for you.

five things to talk to a local about

1. **"Know any cute hoors?"** The word is pronounced scandalously, like "whores," but has nothing to do with the world's oldest profession. Rather, it's an expression better left to the Irish for explanation.

2. **"What's up with this town's obsession with JFK and Ché Guevara?"** [see *by foot,* below].

3. **"Who's this Ming character?"** (A minor local celeb/politician. Look for the guy who's the spitting image of Ming the Merciless.)

4. **"Do fairies really exist?"** Late one night outside a chip shop, a perfectly lovely, and otherwise sane, worldly, and intelligent undergrad spent an hour and a half trying to convince me of the existence of the wee little people.

5. As per usual, anything touching on the subject of **drinking** will get you along like a house on fire.

more student-ish. Things peter out quickly here, into a big housing development on the bay side, and the university campus upriver.

Since Galway is so small, the best public transit is your feet and a good map: You'll definitely need one to find your way around here. For info on local happenings, pick up the free bi-weekly *Galway List,* scattered around most cafes, or the west country's monthly arts and culture mag, *Magpie (£1.50),* on sale at any newsstand. Another good one, with more "real news," is the weekly *Galway Advertiser.*

hanging out

Hands down the best gathering place in town is **Eyre Square** (aka JFK Park, named after the president's visit in June '63 and home of a bust of the man himself). On a sunny afternoon, droves of merry Galwegians join the usual cast of resident winos and stretch out on nature's goodness. You can almost always count on a good vibe and a spontaneous guitar or drum session.

The multitudes gathered at the riverside park and plaza by the **Spanish Arch** usually seem deeply mellowed, perhaps lulled by the drifting swans, swirling seagulls, and beautiful view of Galway Bay.

Just out of town, **South Park** is the favorite spot for kite flyers, with lots of beachfront grass; it's never crowded, and often gusting like a wind tunnel.

Disheveled students, wayfaring street performers, or bermudas-and-baseball-cap tourists all drop in at people-watching central outside **Tigh**

galway bars, clubs and culture zoo

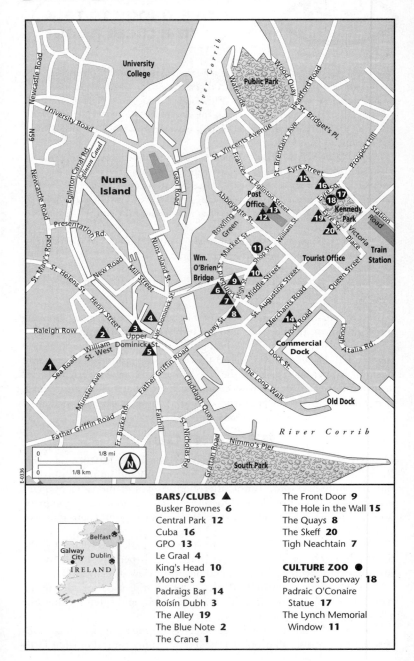

BARS/CLUBS ▲

Busker Brownes **6**
Central Park **12**
Cuba **16**
GPO **13**
Le Graal **4**
King's Head **10**
Monroe's **5**
Padraigs Bar **14**
Roísín Dubh **3**
The Alley **19**
The Blue Note **2**
The Crane **1**

The Front Door **9**
The Hole in the Wall **15**
The Quays **8**
The Skeff **20**
Tigh Neachtain **7**

CULTURE ZOO ●

Browne's Doorway **18**
Padraic O'Conaire
  Statue **17**
The Lynch Memorial
  Window **11**

Neachtain [see *bar scene*, below], one of the best pubs in Galway. **Café du Journal** (*The Halls, Quay St.; Tel 091/568-426; 8:45am-9:30pm daily; No credit cards*) features stone-topped cafe tables and wooden church pews under chaotic piles of books and the daily papers. As the name suggests, it's a bit of a literary intellectual/journalist hangout, but everyone goes—and goes by—here.

Two cafes reign over Galway's late-night scene. Both serve good cafe food, with soundtrack, to a student/backpacker crowd. **Apostasy** (*56 Lower Dominick St.; Tel 091/561-478; 10am-4am daily; No credit cards*) is a funky little chamber with a wall shrine to the genius of espresso and other incarnations of the divine bean. **Java** (*17 Upper Abbey St.; Tel 091/567-400; 10am-4am Mon-Sat, noon-4am Sun; No credit cards*) takes up two floors. The long kitchen-style tables upstairs are great if you're doing the late shift with posse in tow. Last time I was here, a soft-spoken guy wearing a spiked dog collar served me chamomile tea.

For late-night wine, candles, and weirdness, try **O'Ché's** (*3 Francis St.; Tel 091/585-126; Noon-4am daily; info@e-maginet.com, www.e-maginet.com/jazz; £2 after 11pm; No credit cards*), a landmark of Galway's bizarre Ché obsession [see *by foot*, below]. Check out the cosmic-erotic entrance mural starring that darling "Commie Christ," his pal Fidel, and dancing showgirls, then submerge yourself in the slightly eerie underground atmosphere of this up-all-night wine bar. The two candlelit rooms won't fill up with the usual revolutionary leftists until well after midnight. Glasses of house wine run £2.30, pitchers of sangria keep the crowd happy, and the little stage hosts live acts almost every night, starting around midnight.

bar scene

Sure, and the Irish love the drink—and the music. There's no such thing as a dead night out, or a night without music. Seems every pub in town hosts nightly gigs, usually trad sessions or cover bands [see *live music scene*, below]. Most young travelers in Galway gravitate toward the

lad meets lassie

Galway's a college town, so if you're young, comely, and nocturnal, you shouldn't have any trouble getting the affection you (perhaps) so richly deserve. For the locals, hookups mostly happen at the clubs, while the touristy "superpubs" fill the bill for the backpacker set. Crossover is frequent and not a problem. Mating here remains in the classic collegiate style: It's just as likely the object of your lust will end the night by barfing all over your shoes or hopping into bed with you (or both).

tourist-oriented "superpubs" of Shop and Quay streets. Sardine-packed with drunken hordes of university students in winter months and drunken hordes of tourists in summer, they're definitely a blast, in that beer-blast kind of way. For a more mellow, local feel, try the cluster of bars around Dominick Street, on the west side of the River Corrib.

Galway's drink prices are country-cheap, compared with Dublin. The general price for a pint in a pub hovers around £2.20, or £1.85 for a shot. Drink prices at clubs are around 20p higher across the board. Pub hours are the same as in the rest of Ireland *(10:30am-11:30pm Mon-Wed, 10:30am-12:30am Thurs-Sat, 10:30am-11pm Sun)*, but it's standard publican practice in "the country" to shut the front doors at the prescribed closing time, then let the party roll on inside for another hour or so. You won't get in off the street anywhere after legal closing, so if you're still doing the crawl at 11pm, give it up quick and settle into your favorite pub.

Despite its ground-zero location in Galway's teeming tourist hub, the scrappy little **Tigh Neachtain** *(17 Cross St.; Tel 091/568-820; No credit cards)* maintains an old-timey, wooden snugs-and-stools character. The crowd is a mix of locals and scruffy beatnik travelers. Allen Ginsberg was known to enjoy a pint (and maybe a joint) here, when in town. On sunny afternoons, drinkers take to the tables outside, resting their chair backs against the cool blue of "Knocktan's" wall.

The Hole in the Wall *(9 Eyre St.; Tel 091/586-146; No credit cards)*, right on Eyre Square, is the kind of chill, friendly pub where you wish you could be a regular: Low-beamed ceiling, a jukebox with the standard rock classics, a sunny beer garden out to the side, and just enough off the beaten track so you can always find a seat. The Hole ain't too fashionable, but it fits. One warning: The owner is big into horses, so madness reigns during the late July races.

Just to confuse you, the **Front Door** *(Cross St.; No phone; 10:30am-11:45pm Mon-Sat, 4-11:30pm Sun; No credit cards)* presents itself as "Tomás ó Riada: Draper, Grocer, Matchmaker" over its other entrance on High Street (which turns into Shop Street). The best bar in town for playing hide-and-seek with its maze-like layout, it's also the mellowest of the superpubs, catering to an unpretentious post-university crowd.

The other, interchangeable "superpubs" include **The Quays** *(Quay St.; Tel 091/568-347; V, MC)* done in "seagoing church" decor; **The King's Head** [see *live music scene,* below]; **The Skeff** *(Eyre Sq.; Tel 091/563-173; V, MC)* with six different bars on two floors, and **Busker Brownes** *(Cross St.; Tel 091/563-377; www.failte.com/king-buskers; V, MC)* featuring an impressive, medieval "Hall of Tribes" on the third floor that's definitely worth a look. These are the pubs with the highest pickup potential. Come'n git it!

On the alternative side of town, there's the **Le Graal** *(38 Lower Dominick St.; Tel 091/567-614; 6pm-12:30am daily, plus extra summer hours of noon-3pm Mon-Fri, 9am-12:30am Sat, Sun; V, MC)*, whose motto is "atmosphere in action." Popular with Galway's international and gay crowds, who come to drink wine and lounge about on the red felt couches while candelabras flicker against the rough stone walls. Dance to sounds of Latin, jazz, salsa, and world music, or grab a bite—the tropically relaxed staff also serve up food until last call. Sometimes there's a cover of two to three punts.

In the same neighborhood, the **Blue Note** *(William St. West; Tel 091/568-347; 5-11:50pm Mon-Thur, 3-11:50pm Fri, Sat, 4-11:30pm Sun; No credit cards)* is the committed clubber's pre-club hangout. Here, in the murky blue shadows, you'll find the town's greatest density of green hair. Local DJs spin hip-hop, house, and techno on weekends. Go for the great BBQ deal on Tuesday nights in the summer: Buy a Heineken, get a free burger, repeat.

Padraigs Bar *(The Docks; Tel 091/563-696; 7:30am-11:30pm Mon-Sat; No credit cards)* defines the classic Irish "early": right on the docks, maybe a little sketchy, and always full of hearty, salt-of-the-earth types exuding 80-proof perfume from every pore. Best on a weekend morning, when all walks of life can be seen crawling in for "just the one more" under the smoke-stained collection of classic film posters. There's a pool table in the back and a spinning ceiling fan to help patrons further lose their bearings.

LIVE MUSIC SCENE

For the most part, trad rules the night in Galway. Other than that, your standard rock cover bands fill the bills at pubs all around town. Sort of like college parties all over again—which makes sense, given the overwhelming university crowd in Galway. No matter what's playing, everyone's out for a good time. One exception to the cover-band rule is Róisín Dubh, a live joint with enough character (and incoming talent) to stand out in any city. **BarCuba*** [see *eats*, below] spices up the week with jazz on Saturdays and occasional imported Latin-flavored bands.

You can hear tourist-trap trad almost anywhere in town, but the place to go for the real stuff is **The Crane** *(2 Sea Rd.; Tel 091/587-419; No cover; No credit cards)*. It's an old man's pub a little out on the west side of town, so the dress code is a lot of old tweed and a weather-beaten face

fashion

The fashion in Galway? Grunge is dominant. Really, nobody cares what you're wearing. Relax.

galway eats and crashing

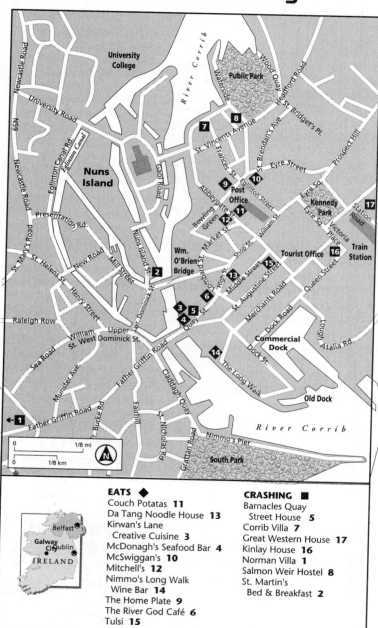

EATS ◆

Couch Potatas **11**
Da Tang Noodle House **13**
Kirwan's Lane
  Creative Cuisine **3**
McDonagh's Seafood Bar **4**
McSwiggan's **10**
Mitchell's **12**
Nimmo's Long Walk
  Wine Bar **14**
The Home Plate **9**
The River God Café **6**
Tulsi **15**

CRASHING ■

Barnacles Quay
  Street House **5**
Corrib Villa **7**
Great Western House **17**
Kinlay House **16**
Norman Villa **1**
Salmon Weir Hostel **8**
St. Martin's
  Bed & Breakfast **2**

behind a scruffy beard. A session could occur at any time, but a good bet is the one casually "scheduled" nightly at 9:30pm. The Sunday afternoon session here can be a religious experience.

The wood-lined pub **Roísín Dubh** *(Dominick St.; Tel 091/586-540; Free-£10; info@roisindubh.net, www.roisindubh.net; No credit cards)*—that's "rawsheen dove" to you—happens to be one of the best places in Ireland for all that other music, hosting local and international names in rock, folk, R&B, blues—and trad—on the little stage in back. Definitely a musicians' hangout, the bar fills with what one local rocker called "a good, healthy bohemian blend." The all-fun house band Full Trousers jams with reggae and ska every Sunday; no cover.

The King's Head *(High St.; Tel 091/566-630; No cover; No credit cards)* is elbow-to-elbow most nights with the young and drunk, all staggering along to the daily parade of (actually, pretty good) cover bands. Summer meat market provided by weekly package bus tour shipments of eager young backpackers. Their chill Dixieland jazz session, Sunday afternoons at 12:30pm, has become a local institution.

Catch an excellent (and very well attended) set-dancing session at **Monroe's** *(Upper Dominick St.; Tel 091/583-397; Mon-Sat from 9:30am, Sun from 12pm; No credit cards)* every Tuesday night. And you can hear trad, trad, and more trad every night of the week, beginning at 9:30pm Irish time, which is to say "very approximately." Although relatively spacious for a pub (and charming, too, with murals of the countryside gracing the walls), there's almost never any room to sit down when the music starts, so get here early, around 8-9pm, for a prime seat. Monroe's also serves good pub grub during breakfast and lunch times, and you can get above-average pizzas beginning at 4pm at the little hole-in-the-wall pizzeria they operate next door. Aside from a few well-informed hostellers, the crowd here's exclusively local.

club scene

As you might expect in such a laid-back town, Galway clubs are a no-stress affair. Some fashion victims don the full get-up, but the guy in Birks just behind them gets in just the same. With a little straightening, your grungy travel gear might even pass muster. Sounds too good to be true, but bouncers are (relatively) mellow, and the mainly undergrad clubbers are out to drink, dance, drink some more, then hook up—not pose or critique. The size of these places may surprise you—there's no shortage of floor space here. For a night-by-night breakdown, pick up the ever-present *Galway List*. Covers run from £4 mid-week to £6 weekends. Clubs are open from 11pm till 2am, but the crowds, and the lines, arrive after the pubs clear out at midnight. Make an early dash out of the pub on weekends, or take the chance of waiting in line half the night.

GPO *(Eglinton St.; Tel 091/563-073)* does its best to keep the western flame of trendiness alive, trying just a little harder than the rest to be hip. Wear black to match the inky dark interior and the rest of the patrons.

Rules of the game

Public drinking, locally called "bushing," doesn't
seem to get anyone *too* nervous in Galway. Still, it's best to keep it
mellow, and in a paper bag. Favorite spots include Eyre Square and
along the banks of the Corrib, preferably on the down-low. As with
the rest of Ireland, the drinking age is 18, all recreational drugs are
illegal, and walking down the street with a joint will likely get you
in big trouble.

The "Drum Bar" is downstairs, a dance space the size of a four-car garage
is upstairs. Home of local heroes, the Disconauts duo, spinning soul and
funk-infused house to loving crowds, GPO also regularly hosts hip-hop
and drum 'n' bass nights. Daytime barstaff often have free passes hidden
behind the jungle-gym piping—just ask sweetly.

Big and blue and three stories high, **Cuba** *(Eyre Sq.; Tel 091/565-991)*
has a lounge bar on one, DJs on two, and live bands on three. Indie Mondays, Latin jazz, funk, and soul Saturdays, and a healthy mix of chart,
disco, and dance for the rest of the week. The crowd is youngish and, as
far as Galway goes, hip—you'll be pleased to hear the smurfy lighting and
Latin rhythms seem to get the co-eds *en fuego* so a smooch may be in
order. Public displays of lust abound. Passes behind the bar during daytime hours; ask the bartender to give you a few.

The Alley *(Ball Alley Lane, off Williamsgate St.; Tel 091/563-173)* is
youthquake central in a converted warehouse. They claim to be over-21-
only at the door, but the dance floor and three bars are packed with the
youngest club crowd in town—seems to be a don't-ask-don't-tell policy.
Once in, you don't have to be off your face, but it would definitely help
you blend....Mostly college pop tunes, with the dance stuff coming on
later in the night. To sum up: The theme to "Friends" played in here one
night, and the crowd loved it. Yikes!

Rumor has it that **Central Park** *(Upper Abbeygate St.; Tel 091/565-
974; www.indigo.ie/~cpbran)* is a big ol' meat market for dirty old clubbers over 23, which in this town means over the hill. The standard diet
of chart and dance applies under space-age molded plywood and tin. You
may want to get here early: It's pretty big, but fills up fast.

Arts Scene

▶▶VISUAL ARTS

Like the little government-funded bohemian paradise that it is, Galway
is home to a number of established artists, and a few contemporary galleries. As you would expect from a city set between two national parks,
local art tends towards landscapes, but the constant influx of art pilgrims
can bring all sorts of unexpected global variety.

A quiet little gallery on a quiet little lane, the **Logan Gallery** *(4a St. Anthony's Place; Tel 091/563-635; 9am-6pm Mon-Sat; No credit cards)* is *the* commercial gallery for contemporary fine art in Galway (which might be because it's the only one...). There's no predominant style or medium here, but the work is of a uniformly high standard. The friendly, laid-back owner is always up for a chat about the Irish art scene.

The **Galway Arts Centre** *(47 Dominick St.; Tel 091/565-886; 10am-9:30pm Mon-Sat; gac@indigo.ie)* has two galleries on two floors of an airy restored mansion. Government-funded and committee-run, the GAC shows about 24 exhibitions a year of what they call "leading and emerging Irish artists," as well as some international stuff. This is the only space in town for installations with giant seesaws made from railroad ties featuring in one memorable exhibition.

You can also take your hungry artist's soul to the restaurants and cafes in town hanging regular exhibitions of local work. If you dig around, maybe you'll find that fabled diamond in the rough at **Kirwan's Lane Creative Cuisine** or **Le Graal** [see *eats,* below]; **Apostasy** or **Kenny's Book Shop and Gallery** [see *stuff,* below].

For an eyeful of the big names in contemporary Irish design and fashion, try **Design Concourse Ireland** *(Kirwan's Lane; Tel 091/566-016; 9am-6pm Mon-Thur, Sat, 9am-7pm Fri; V, MC, AE, DC).* This place is pricey, but it's fun just to drool over the jewelry, clothing, furniture, sculpture, and prints.

▶▶PERFORMING ARTS

For such a small town, Galway's theater scene is kickin'. Some of Ireland's finest have come out of this artistic hotbed. If you're lucky enough to be in Galway when the **Druid Theatre Company** *(Chapel Lane; Tel 091/568-617; Box office noon-8pm, shows 8pm; druid_@iol.ie; Tickets £8-10; V, MC, AE)* is here, go to a show. They're old hands in London and on Broadway, have recently won several Tonys, and are considered by many to be the best theater company in Ireland. Their own theater is pretty small, so the Town Hall Theatre on Courthouse Square usually hosts their larger productions.

Based in Galway but traveling worldwide, **Macnas** *(Fisheries Field, Salmon Weir Bridge; Tel 091/561-462; macnas@iol.ie, www.failte.com/macnas; No credit cards)* is another company you should catch if they're in town when you are. Known for mind-blowing costumes and sets, these are the people who put on the surreal parade at **Galway Arts Fest** [see *festivals and events,* below].

Town Hall Theatre *(Courthouse Sq.; Tel 091/569-777; Box office 10am-7:30pm Mon-Sat, shows 8pm Mon-Sat; tht@tinet.ie, home_page.tinet.ie.~tht; Tickets £5-13; V, MC)* is the big newish theater in town, just across from the courthouse. Hosts anything that fills seats: Irish or international theater, dance, opera, music, and readings, and serves as main venue for the **Cúirt** [see *festivals and events,* below]. The Town Hall people also run the **Studio** (on the same site), for smaller productions, and the **Black Box** *(Dyke Rd.; Tel 091/568-151)* which does everything from theater to music to comedy to circus in a big school gymnasium—looking space.

gay scene

Galway's no gay mecca, but it does have a small scene. Your best bet for a comfortable place to check out the local talent, or just be yourself, is probably **Le Graal** [see *bar scene,* above]. Keepers of the faith often congregate in other hip spots, such as **Café du Journal** and **Apostasy** [see *hanging out,* above], and **Nimmo's** [see *eats,* below].

The **Galway Gay Help Line** *(Tel 091/566-134)* and **Galway Lesbian Line** *(Tel 091/564-611)* are good resources, or check out the monthly freesheet, *GCN (Gay Community News)* and look for listings on Galway in the back.

Friday and Saturday nights, Club Mix in The Attic at **Liquid** *(Salthill; Tel 088/269-14-12; Doors open 10:30pm; £4 cover)* draws every lonely farm boy and maybe an incognito village priest or two from the homophobically oppressed western hinterlands.

Jazz Juice brings a mixed crowd of hipsters, trendy folks, and gay and straight undergrad bohos to **GPO** [see *club scene,* above].

culture zoo

As you might have guessed, there are no cavernous art museums tucked into Galway's quaint little streets. But there are a few gorgeous churches and other neat old structures.

Galway Cathedral *(University and Gaol Rds.; Tel 091/563-577; 8am-6pm daily; Free admission):* A 1960s-vintage cathedral with saintly mosaic of JFK, obscured in darkness since those shocking revelations of his lecherous character. The hopelessly tacky mishmash of architectural styles make for an art history student's worst nightmare.

Cathedral of Our Lady Assumed in Heaven and Saint Nicholas *(Lombard St.; Tel 091/564-648; 9am-5:45pm Mon-Sat, 1-5:45pm Sun Apr-Sept, 10am-4pm Mon-Sat, 1-5pm Sun Oct-Mar; Free admission):* This 14th-century Protestant church features a crusader's tomb with Norman inscription. Cromwell kept his horses here and destroyed every other church in Galway. It's the largest still-used medieval church in Ireland.

Galway City Museum *(Next to Spanish Arch; Tel 091/567-641; 10am-1pm/2:15-5:15pm daily Apr-Sept, Tue-Thur only Oct-Mar; Admission £1):* A walk around this tiny museum is sure to inspire a nap in the park out front.

Nora Barnacle House *(8 Bowling Green; Tel 091/564-743; 10am-1pm/2-5pm Mon-Sat mid-May to mid-Sept; Admission £1):* Ireland's westernmost outpost of James Joyce worship, being the former home of the Great One's in-laws [see *portrait of the artist,* above].

Lynch's Castle *(Allied Irish Bank; Corner of Abbeygate St. and Shop St.; 10am-4pm Mon-Wed, Fri, till 5pm Thur; Free admission):* Witness the

calling all yeats fans

Poetry lovers won't want to miss a visit to **Thoor Ballylee** *(N18, Gort; Tel 091/631-436; 10am-6pm Easter-Sept; Admission around £3.50)*, the 16th-century residence that William Butler Yeats purchased in the 1920s for a mere £35. Usually referred to as a castle, although it's really more of a tower house, Thoor Ballylee provided inspiration for much of Yeats's finest poetry, such as *The Winding Stair* and *The Tower*.

The price of admission entitles you to the run of the house, which offers some fine views of the surrounding countryside—the tower is a lot taller than it looks from the outside. There is also a short audio-visual presentation on Yeats's life and work. Gort is right on the Bus Éireann line (routes 51 and 55) between Ennis and Galway (37 km from Galway) and buses pass through literally dozens of times a day, so you'll have no trouble getting here. Call the **Galway Bus Station** *(Tel 091/562-000)* for information.

march of civilization: Intricately carved medieval stones once harboring Galway's richest clan now house ATMs supplying booze money to pub crawlers.

Spanish Arch *(End of Quay St.; Free admission):* Once part of the city wall through which Spanish ships bearing exotic spirits could unload. In short: Sexy name, uninteresting structure.

Padraic O'Conaire Statue *(Eyre Sq.):* This monument commemorates one of Ireland's most revered writers, a Galway native controversial for his thoroughly grim depictions of "realistic" everyday Irish life. Though O'Conaire is acknowledged as an initiator of the Gaelic Revival, most folks pass right by the western end of this public square without acknowledging the debt owed, so pause a moment for Paddy.

Browne's Doorway *(Eyre Sq.):* Right next to O'Conaire's statue stands this imposing example of a townhouse of the once-powerful shipping classes of Galway. It's an elaborate and rather creepy structure, decorated with family seals and hand-carved stonework, dating from the early 17th century.

Lynch Memorial Window *(Market St., north of St. Nicholas's Cathedral):* The story goes that a man named Lynch, mayor of Galway in the late 1400s, condemned his own son to death—and when no one else in the city would serve as executioner, he personally followed through on his order. The Window supposedly marks the spot where the gallows stood.

by foot

The most important part of this walk is to somehow find a way to announce to anyone who will listen that you are either of "Clan Kennedy" or descended from the mighty Ché, or both. How and where you do this is entirely up to you. It's only fitting that two of the most charismatic ideological enemies of the cold war should be united in the geography of friendly, neutral Galway. (Of course, we all know it was Ché's idea to assassinate Kennedy for trying to assassinate Castro, and Kennedy's successors in Washington repaid the favor.) May old foes rest in peace, and may we get to drinking, please?

First, we must start at JFK's *Freeman of the City* monument next to the fountain at **Eyre Square.** This special honor was granted (on this very spot) by the publicans of Galway, involving a promise to supply lifelong "free" pints to our young Prez. Feels historic, no? Now, for a drink: Walk south across the square, past the **Tourist Office** [see *need to know,* below], and take a left onto **Queen Street** (becoming **Dock Road**), where you'll find **Padraigs Bar** [see *bar scene,* above]. Legend has it ol' Jack and Co. stopped in here the morning after the "Freeman" ceremony for one last free pint before catching an early Air Force One back to D.C. Can you spot his special friend Marilyn among the movie posters? Next, take a right out the door, a right again onto **New Dock Street,** then a left on **Flood Street,** which brings us to Jury's Inn at **Wolfe Tone Bridge.** Take in the view, and the swans, and the fresh sea air, then continue north by the path running along the riverside just on the left of Jury's. Continue up past **William O'Brien Bridge,** looking

great outdoors

For a nice place to run, try the path along the Corrib starting beside Jury's Hotel in front of the Spanish Arch, going up to the **Salmon Weir Bridge** [see *by foot,* above], or cross the Wolfe Tone bridge and head out along the coast to Salthill, via **South Park** [see *hanging out,* above].

If paddling away up the River Corrib in a little wooden boat to picnic in the ruins of an old castle surrounded by fields of grazing horses sounds like good exercise to you, drop by **Corrib Boat Hire** *(Brando Screen Printing, Waterside St. across from the old Galway Rowing Club; No phone; 9am-8pm daily; Rowboats £4 per hour, £25 per day; No credit cards).* The whole trip, including about 45 minutes for a picnic, takes about 2 hours.

For everything else, you really ought to get out of the city. If beaches good for prancing and showing off your nonexistent tan will satisfy, you can take a 20-minute walk out to **Salthill,** a hotel- and amusement-gorged suburb west of the city center and across the bridge, home to

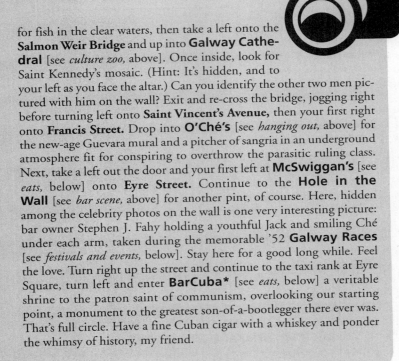

for fish in the clear waters, then take a left onto the **Salmon Weir Bridge** and up into **Galway Cathedral** [see *culture zoo*, above]. Once inside, look for Saint Kennedy's mosaic. (Hint: It's hidden, and to your left as you face the altar.) Can you identify the other two men pictured with him on the wall? Exit and re-cross the bridge, jogging right before turning left onto **Saint Vincent's Avenue,** then your first right onto **Francis Street.** Drop into **O'Ché's** [see *hanging out,* above] for the new-age Guevara mural and a pitcher of sangria in an underground atmosphere fit for conspiring to overthrow the parasitic ruling class. Next, take a left out the door and your first left at **McSwiggan's** [see *eats,* below] onto **Eyre Street.** Continue to the **Hole in the Wall** [see *bar scene,* above] for another pint, of course. Here, hidden among the celebrity photos on the wall is one very interesting picture: bar owner Stephen J. Fahy holding a youthful Jack and smiling Ché under each arm, taken during the memorable '52 **Galway Races** [see *festivals and events,* below]. Stay here for a good long while. Feel the love. Turn right up the street and continue to the taxi rank at Eyre Square, turn left and enter **BarCuba*** [see *eats,* below] a veritable shrine to the patron saint of communism, overlooking our starting point, a monument to the greatest son-of-a-bootlegger there ever was. That's full circle. Have a fine Cuban cigar with a whiskey and ponder the whimsy of history, my friend.

Galway's closest beach. It's almost always teeming with humanity's ritzier half. That said, you can probably find nicer strands among Galway's outermost reaches [see **Connemara,** below], or try the beach at **Spiddal,** a short Bus Éireann (route 424) ride west of Galway, past Salthill. It's actually nicer than Salthill's beach: clean, sandy, and perfect for swimming.

You can also take the bus to the **Aille Cross Equitation Centre** *(Aille Cross, Loughrea; Tel 091/841-216; Approx. £12 per hour),* positioned 32 km (20 mi) east of Galway. This is one of the largest horseback riding centers in the country, with 50 mounts and 20 Connemara ponies available; you can ride down forest trails, through farm lands, and over mountains. Week-long riding trips throughout Connemara are conducted regularly. Take Bus Éireann (route 70) from the Galway Bus and Train Station to Loughrea; it's about a half-hour ride.

STUFF

Galway ain't your shopper's mecca. We're talking a town of 60,000 folks. If you gotta have that shopping fix, check out a few of the 50 shops in

festivals and events

The schedules on these festivals vary, so call for exact dates.

Cúirt International Festival of Literature *(Apr, flexible dates; Most events in Town Hall Theatre, Courthouse Sq.; Tel 091/569-777):* An eclectic migration of world-renowned scribblers letting it all hang out, literally. Past greats have included Seamus Heaney and Allen Ginsberg, presumably stoking the flames of culture, creativity, and lust.

Galway Early Music Festival *(Three days in mid-May; Tel 091/846-366):* Pageantry, theater, and music from those vibrant Dark Ages.

Galway Film Fleadh *(Early July; Tel 091/569-777):* Your standard film festival, with past appearances by famous Irish actors, including Gabriel Byrne.

Galway Arts Festival *(Mid-July; Tel 091/562-480; info@gaf.iol.ie; www.galwayartsfestival.ie):* The Big One. Famous for its street carnival, music, theater, and much more. Could be the best summer festival in Europe.

Galway Races *(Late July; Tel 091/753-870):* A Bukowski-like horse-racing bacchanal that utterly transforms the town. Many businesses shut down for the week as everybody goes to the track and/or pub. You won't find a vacancy in a Limerick broom closet, let alone in Galway.

Galway International Oyster Festival *(Late Sept; Tel 091/527-282):* Besides lots of oyster-eating, this festival includes, among other things, a golf tournament and yacht race to celebrate Ireland's favorite bottom-feeding mollusk.

Eyre Square Centre *(Eyre Sq.; Tel 091/568-302; 9am-6:30pm Mon-Wed, Sun, 9am-9pm Fri, Sat).* This mall features a real scratch 'n' sniff medieval wall.

▶▶**VINTAGE**

For funky vintage '70s stuff, mostly for women, climb the stairs to **Idol Angel** *(24 Upper Abbeygate St.; Tel 091/562-240; 12-6pm Mon-Sat; £2-30 price range; No credit cards).*

▶▶**BAZAAR**

Try the **Galway Market** *(Market St.; 9am-5pm Sat)* for stands of fruit, organic veggies, pottery, clothes, jewelry, and trinkets. They've got good eats here: Look for the famous "Curryman" and the stand selling sweet and savory crêpes.

In the taxi rank area at the top of Eyre Square, stalls sell clothes, jewelry, and even horse and bridle stuff from 9am till 5pm every Monday through Saturday.

▶▶BOUND

Don't let the slightly precious exterior fool you, 'cause **Kenny's Book Shop and Gallery** (*Corner Middle and High Sts.; Tel 091/562-507; 9am-6pm Mon-Sat; www.kennys.ie, queries@kennys.ie; V, MC, AE*) is the grand old man of Galway books. The three floors are packed with all sorts of subjects and titles, both rare and budget-bin, with a specialty in (what else?) Irish literature.

Conveniently opposite the back door of Kenny's, there's **Charlie Byrne's Bookshop** (*The Cornstore, Middle St.; Tel 091/561-766; 9am-6pm Mon-Thur, 9am-8pm Sat; chabyrne@iol.ie; No credit cards*). Just a big, comfy ol' horde of used, remaindered, and discounted books. Books, books, and more books, from Behan to Dewey, line every inch of wall space. This is the one in town with that stay-all-day vibe. Mmm...it even smells like a good bookshop.

For rock-bottom pulp fiction, it's gotta be **Book Exchange** (*23 Lower Abbeygate St; Tel 091/562-225; 10am-6pm Mon-Sat; No credit cards*), a tiny hole-in-the-wall used bookshop full of those cheap, trashy novels and spy thrillers you just need on a trip through Europe.

Your best bet to find out what's up here in a literary way is to check in with local author **Fred Johnston** (*Upstairs at Galway Center for the Unemployed, Canavan House, Nun's Island St.; Tel 091/567-438; 9am-5pm Mon-Fri*). Fred founded the **Cúirt** festival [see *festivals and events*, above] back in '86 and currently works in community literary arts development. You could also check for literary news in Markings and Bookview West, Fred's pages in the weekly *Galway Advertiser*.

▶▶TUNES

Besides being the only place in town where you can score secondhand vinyl, **Mulligan** (*5 Middle St. Court, Middle St.; Tel 091/564-961;*

surf's up

Since Ireland hosted the European surfing championship in '98, word's gotten around about the good Irish surf. The Atlantic swells come year-round, but the best are in April/May and September/October.

For the lowdown on surfing from Galway locals, talk to the staff at **Great Outdoors Sports Centre** (*Eglington St.; Tel 091/562-869*) or contact the **Irish Surfing Association** (*Tel 096/49428*). For gear, check out the **Lahinch Surf Shop** (*The Promenade, Lahinch; Tel 065/708-15-43; 11am-6pm Tue-Sun; V, MC*). Owners Tom and Rosemarie Buckley rent beginner surfboards, boogie boards, and full-length wetsuits all for £5 per 2 hours each, and offer instruction for £5 per hour.

10am-7pm Mon-Thur, till 9pm Fri, till 6pm Sat, 2-6pm Sun; mulligan@ indigo.ie, indigo.ie/~mulligan; V, MC, AE) boasts of having "everything" in Irish and Scottish trad, along with respectable collections of jazz, blues, soul, and ethnic music. Tickets for Róisín Dubh [see *live music scene,* above] shows, other biggish local gigs, and charity events are all on sale here.

Half-looking like yet another cheesy tourist-drag souvenir shop, **Zhivago** *(5 Shop St.; Tel 091/509-960; 9am-6pm Mon-Wed, Sat, till 9pm Thur, Fri, 10am-6pm Sun; www.musicireland.com, info@musicireland._com; V, MC, AE)* has the Ticketmaster outlet for all major shows nationwide. And you can pick up a "Guinness Is Good For You" T-shirt while you're getting your tix.

Eats

For a small town, Galway has an impressive number of cafes and restaurants. Unfortunately, like most of Ireland, the wait service here is uniformly bad, which verges on spoiling your meal, no matter how good it tastes. The cafes and restaurants listed below are usually pretty good with the service, among other things.

▶▶CHEAP

The Home Plate *(13 Mary St.; Tel 091/561-475; Noon-9:30pm daily; £1.95-4.95 per entree lunch, £4.75-6.95 per entree dinner; No credit cards)* is possibly the best place for lunch in Galway. Huge, fresh, tasty helpings of pasta, curry, or sandwiches for next to nothing in a homey little place across from the post office with checked tablecloths, friendly staff, and good service.

McSwiggan's *(3 Eyre St., Woodquay; Tel 091/568-917; Normal pub hours, Carvery lunch noon-3pm; £4.50; V, MC, AE, DC)* is a little off the tourist path, in the Eyre Square area, but the meat-and-potatoes food is plentiful, tasty, and reasonably priced. Plus, you can eat your grub under the looming presence of a huge, shellacked, indoor tree. Get here before 1pm, and beat the hordes.

Also on Eyre Square, **BarCuba*** *(Eyre Sq.; Tel 091/565-991; 10:30am-11pm Mon-Sat, or till 11:30pm in summer, 12:30-2pm/4-11pm Sun; £5 or under per entree; V, MC)* has tasty Caribbean food, killer coffee, and folks toking on fat stogies of a kind embargoed in the States. Just what you expected from an Irish pub, right? This spacious, loungey bar may well have Ireland's finest collection of wall-sized photos, Ché memorabilia, and potted shrubbery. They've definitely got good eats, and possibly the strongest cup of joe in Galway.

You want some fish and chips with your grease? **McDonagh's Seafood Bar** *(22 Quay St.; Tel 091/565-001; Noon-12am Mon-Sat, 5-11pm Sun; £5-14 per entree; V, MC, AE, DC)* serves it up right, over by the William O'Brien Bridge. There's eats outside on picnic tables come sunny days. The lunch is a better value than dinner.

A languorous and well-endowed mermaid on the first-floor mural points you to **The River God Café** *(2 Quay St.; Tel 091/565-811; 12:30-10pm; therivergod@eircom.net, www.therivergod.com; £4.95 two-course lunch; V, MC)*, as does the menu board outside proclaiming that a delicious two-course lunch is available for just £4.95 until 4pm. Sound good? Dude, it's *more* than good! This chow nearly merits the "divine" description the restaurant gives it—and it'll feed you for dinner as well. Try the roasted aubergine and red lentil soup, followed by salmon and lemon rice fajitas with a side salad. Dinner main courses here go for £6.50 to £12.50, and of course they're equally mouth-watering, but as usual the lunch is a better value. All in all a splendid afternoon hangout with fantastic service, a classy yet casual atmosphere, and great views overlooking Galway's eccentrics doing what they do best on Quay Street.

More than any other place in town, the relatively new **Mitchell's** *(Lower Abbeygate St.; Tel 091/66441; Hours vary; All items under £8, most under £5; No credit cards)* resembles a typical American diner. The menu's similar too, with nice hefty Irish breakfasts for around £3.50, a veggie option for a mere £2.50, sandwiches for well under £2, and cheap main courses. The hours are still rather erratic; at some point the owner aims to be open 24-7, but a lack of help makes that goal a tad difficult to achieve. At any rate, the place'll stay open for as long as you choose to hang out, which means that if you're still alert and hungry after closing time at **Java's** or **Apostasy** [see *hanging out*, above], and you don't feel badly about further darkening the bags under the poor proprietor's eyes, it's the perfect place.

And here's what you've been waiting for: an homage to Ireland's favorite tuber. The folks at **Couch Potatas** *(Upper Abbeygate St.; Tel 091/561-664; Noon-10pm Mon-Sat, 1-10pm Sun; All items under £5; No credit cards)* offer nice big spuds with a ton of different fillings. (But don't come here if you don't like potatoes.) Try the Hawaii 5-0, with ham, onion, pineapple, peppers, and melted cheddar cheese. Every 'tater comes with a generous side salad, as well. It's a great spot for lunch, although it does get quite crowded at midday.

▶▶DO-ABLE

A tiny place on a quiet street off Shop Street, **Da Tang Noodle House** *(2 Middle St.; Tel 091/561-443; Noon-3pm/5:30-10pm Mon-Thur, till 10:30pm Fri, Sat, 5:30-10pm Sun; £5-10 per entree; V, MC)* has just a few tables inside, but it's got that great hole-in-the-wall atmosphere. And great noodles.

Also in the Shop Street area, **Tulsi** *(3 Buttermilk Walk, off Middle St.; Tel 091/564-831; £5.95-12.95 per entree, 20 percent discount on takeout; V, MC)* is your standard Indian restaurant: lots of dark tapestry and rattan, and lots of excellent vegetarian options. Go for the takeout and save a bunch.

▶▶SPLURGE

Set on the river in an old stone house just behind the Spanish Arch,

Nimmo's Long Walk Wine Bar (*Spanish Arch; Tel 091/561-114; Winebar: lunch 12:30-3pm, dinner 6:30-10pm, open till 11:30pm; Restaurant: 7-10pm Tue-Sat, 5-11:30pm Sun; £6-13 per entree; No credit cards*) is the little romantic bistro all the others wish they could be. Local fishermen bring in the daily catch for your wine-soaked soirée in a cozy alcove. If this place don't set fire to your love life, give it up.

How 'bout some balsamic roasted duck with sweet pear and sage dressing, or perhaps a couple of pan-seared lamb's kidneys in honey and black pepper? Chef Padraic Kielty, who has the helm at the famous **Kirwan's Lane Creative Cuisine** (*Kirwan's Lane; Tel 091/568-266; 12:30-2:30pm/6:30-10:30pm Mon-Sat; £6.95-16.95 per entree; V, MC, AE*) won't disappoint. Enjoy the extensive wine list in this stylish space by the William O'Brien Bridge.

crashing

Being the festival capital of Ireland, Galway naturally has a wide range of good digs, from super-cheap to absolutely opulent. Still, you definitely need to book ahead for weekends, during festivals [see *festivals and events,* above], or anytime in the summer, or you might end up in some dingy dive. If you do find yourself bedless on a packed weekend, give your feet a rest and try the reservations center upstairs at the Tourist Office [see *need to know,* below]. For a measly punt, they'll call around until they find you something.

▶▶**CHEAP**

For the most part, the hostels in Galway are clean and well-run. The ones listed here all have laundry services, comfy TV lounges, and well-equipped kitchens.

Directly opposite the train station, **Great Western House** (*Frenchville Lane, Eyre Sq.; Tel 091/561-139; shaungwh@iol.ie, www.iol._ie/~shaungwh; £8.50-9.50 large dorm, £11.50-12.50 4- and 6-bed dorm, £26-32 double, £36 triple, £45-60 3-bed quad; V, MC*) has to be one of the best-equipped hostels in Ireland. Get this: In addition to the spacious and immaculate kitchen, dining room, TV lounge, laundry service, billiard room, and access for disabled travelers, they've got a sauna. Price includes a small breakfast and discount entrance to **The Alley** [see *club scene,* above], but the staff here can be a little cold, and there's not much of a social vibe.

Like a black hole of fun, like a soap opera with a laugh track, the **Salmon Weir Hostel** (*3 St. Vincent's Ave., Woodquay; Tel 091/561-133; £7.50-8 10-bed, £8-8.50 6-bed, £8.50-9 4-bed, £20-22 double/twin; No credit cards*) has that welcoming, party-loving atmosphere. Up near the Public Park, this place has such a good vibe, one-time guests long since settled into Galway regularly come by just to hang out. A clean and cozy converted house, the "Sadly Weird" features B.J. McKay shower curtains, a Scott Baio shrine, free-flowing tea and coffee, and mucho mayhem. The whole place, including the slacker-paradise TV room with VCR, is totally nonsmoking. Not for introverts.

Barnacles Quay Street House *(10 Quay St.; Tel 091/568-644; qshostel@barnacles.iol.ie, www.iol.ie/~lalco; £8-9.50 dorm, £10.50-13 4-bed, £15-18 twin/double; V, MC)* takes the prize for bravest paint job in town. Something in "Radioactive Tang" covers the facade, entrance hallway, and reception area of this clean, well-managed hostel right on the main pub drag. Most rooms are bright, white, and airy, and come with the added ambience of busker music drifting up from the street. There's bike storage, and the price of a bed includes a small breakfast.

By far the coolest hostel in town, by general consensus, is **Corrib Villa** *(4 Waterside; Tel 091/562-892; Open 24 hours; 6-bed dorms £8.50; No credit cards)*, which epitomizes the fun, laid-back, boho lifestyle for which Galway is renowned. A Georgian townhouse with festively painted walls, cool artwork, a cozy atmosphere, and an ultra-friendly staff, Corrib Villa is located right on the river, convenient for boat rental and just across the street from the **Town Hall Theatre** [see *arts scene*, above]. This is the hostel where all backpackers eventually end up after

12 hours in galway

This town ain't so big. No need to rush.

1. Chill.
2. Call your mother. She'll be relieved you're in such a safe, happy little village instead of one of those big, bad European mega-metropolises full of strange people who can't speak English and rip the roofs off McDonald's with their tractors.
3. Hang out outside **Tigh Neachtain's,** and check out the human circus [see *bar scene*, above].
4. Find the Corrib River's alpha swan, and pick a fight with him. Legend has it the hero who defeats this mighty swan will break an evil spell and raise the merry medieval Iberian sailors from their slumber under the Spanish Arch, who will in turn show their gratitude by delivering up the lost treasure of Lynch's Castle (now a bank). A thousand years of peace and prosperity will follow.
5. Do a pub crawl and try not to crawl by the end of it [see *by foot*, above].
6. Walk the beautiful banks of the Corrib and fine-tune your soul.
7. Keeping with the soulful, but livening it up a bit, go hear some good trad [see *live music scene*, above].
8. Chill some more.

enduring bad—or at least lukewarm—experiences at almost every other hostel in town. It's the kind of place you'll hate to leave when your sojourn in Galway has ended.

▶▶**DO-ABLE**

St. Martin's Bed & Breakfast *(2 Nun's Island St.; Tel 091/568-286; £20 single, £36 double; No credit cards)* is your fantasy B&B made reality. With a house set in a flower garden overlooking the river just 5 minutes out from the center of town, super-friendly owners Mary and Donie Sexton have a real gem here. You'll fall asleep to the sound of little waterfalls, and awake to freshly squeezed OJ, Mary's homemade brown bread, and a full Irish breakfast, made to order. Sounds good, no? Just remember this is a family home, so it won't be robo-pound in the breakfast room at 4am, but you may be able to talk Donie into going out for a pint. Make sure you book advance though, as Mary & Donie are extremely popular with a lot of regular visitors.

Some other reasonably priced spots include **Roncalli House** *(24 Whitestrand Ave.; Tel 091/584-159, Fax 091/584-159; £20-29.50, all rooms include private baths and complimentary breakfast; V, MC)*, a 10-minute walk from the city center, **Knockrea B&B** *(55 Lower Salthill Rd.; Tel 091/520-145, Fax 091/529-985;www.galway.net/pages/knockrea/, knockrea@eircom.net; £20-25 single, £25-30 double, all rooms have private baths; V, MC)*, a nice 10-minute walk from the city center; and the **Adare Guesthouse** *(9 Father Griffin Place; Tel 091/582-638, Fax 091/583-963; adare@iol.ie; July-Sept £45 single, £30 per person double, £37.50 per person suite, Oct-June £27.50 single, £25 per person double, £27.50 per person suite, all rooms have private baths; V, MC)*, 5 minutes from the city center and only a 15-minute walk from the bus station.

▶▶**SPLURGE**

For a crash course on the best in contemporary Irish art, check into **Norman Villa** *(86 Lower Salthill; Tel 091/521-131; £37 single, £64-70 double; V, MC)*. Only 10 minutes' walk from downtown, Dee and Mark Keogh's impressive Victorian is pure class, with pine floors, flagstone dining room, and art pieces hung over the brass beds in every room. Made-to-order breakfast is included. You want smoked salmon, kippers, and poached eggs? No problem. On a sunny morning, take it in the beautiful, quiet garden out back.

Looking for another place to blow all of your money? Try **Great Southern Hotel** *(Eyre Sq.; Tel 091/564-041, Fax 091/566-704; res@galway.gsh.ie; www.gsh.ie; Summer £117 single, £170 double, rest of the year £105 single, £190 double, all rooms have private baths; V, MC, AE)*, located right downtown.

WİTHİN 30 MİNUTES

All right, so it's gonna take you longer than a half-hour to get out to **Connemara National Park** or some of the cool little towns on the coast that make perfect sporting spots, but they still make excellent trips out of Galway

City. **Oughterard** is a 35-minute bus ride (via Bus Éireann routes 416 or 419); this little town is usually just a passing-through spot on the way out to Connemara, but there's actually plenty to do here: canoeing on **Lough Corrib,** hiking in the **Maam Turk Mountains,** and visiting **Inchagoill Island,** with its incredible ancient ruins [see *everywhere else, below,* for both]. And, of course, there's always **Salthill** [see *great outdoors, above*].

need to know

Currency Exchange A Bureau de Change within any bank will have the best rates.

Tourist Information Ireland West Tourism *(Forster St., off Eyce Sq.; Tel 091/537-700; 9am-5:45pm Mon-Fri, 9am-12:45pm Sat, 9am-7:45pm Mon-Sat July, Aug).*

Public Transportation Buses to Salthill and other suburbs depart from the **Bus Éireann Travel Centre** *(Tel 091/562-000)* in Ceannt Station (get your bus maps here) and Eyre Square. The flat rate is 70p. Within the city, you really don't need public transportation.

Bike Rental Mountain Trail Bike Shop *(St. Augustine St.; Tel 091/569-888)* or **Celtic Cycles** *(Queen St., Victoria Place; Tel 091/566-606)* are good options.

American Express Northwest side of Eyre Square *(Tel 091/562-316).*

Health and Emergency Emergency: *999.* **Galway University College Hospital** *(Newcastle Rd.; Tel 091/580-580),* **Merlin Park Regional Hospital** *(Merlin Park; Tel 091/757-631).*

Pharmacies Flanagan's Pharmacy *(32 Shop St.; Tel 091/562-924;*

wired

For web access, try **Net@ccess Cyber Café** *(The Olde Malte Arcade, High St.; Tel 091/569-772; 10am-10pm Mon-Fri, 10am-7pm Sat, noon-6pm Sun; www.netaccess.ie; £5 per hour, £4 students),* and don't forget to ask for your free coffee! Trekkie murals spout interstellar wisdom above the 14 fast PCs. Equipped with friendly staff, scanner, fax, and printer. A lesser-known late-night option, just over the Corrib, is **Jamie Starlights** *(Upper Dominick St.; Tel 091/588-710; 9am-12am Mon-Sat, noon-midnight Sun; £2.50 per half-hour, £2 students).* Five PC carrels line one side of this video library-cum-cybercafe. They don't sell "real" food anymore, but there's plenty of candy store rotgut for your munchies. Monitors here spew a constant stream of those action movie explosions so beloved by video clerks the world over. Neither of these places has much of a social vibe.

9am-6pm Mon-Sat; V, MC) or **Whelan's Chemist** *(Williamsgate St.; Tel 091/562-291; 9am-6pm Mon-Sat; V, MC, AE).*

Telephone City code: *(0)91;* information: *1190;* international operator: *114.* International and local phone cards can be purchased in almost any shop. The green-and-pink "Spirit" cards have the best international rates.

Airports Galway Airport *(Tel 091/755-569)* is out in Carnmore, just 6 km from the city center; cabs to Galway cost around £12; the bus is £2.50.

Airlines Aer Lingus *(Tel 018/868-888)* offers service into Galway Airport.

Trains Irish Rail *(Tel 091/562-000)* trains run into **Ceannt Station** *(Tel 091/562-000),* just off Eyre Square in the city center.

Bus Lines Out of the City Bus Éireann *(Bus Éireann Travel Centre, Ceannt Station; Tel 091/562-000)* or **CityLink** *(Forster Court; Tel 091/564-163).*

scandinavia

Reykjavík

You stare out the airplane window at the boulder-strewn landscape and wonder if your plane has slipped through a wormhole and is landing on Mars. Actually, you're setting down in Iceland, conveniently located in the middle of the Atlantic Ocean, a logical and delightful stopover point on your way to or from mainland Europe. Reykjavík, Iceland's small-but-booming capital, is a new hot spot for young travelers. Reykjavík is very safe (there are less than 200 incarcerated in all of Iceland), sophisticated, impeccably clean, and the Viking-spirited inhabitants party like rock stars. Weirdly, beer has only been legal here for the past decade, and Icelanders are still making up for lost time. Hard alcohol was always legal, but the sky-high prices for spirits certainly put a damper on things. Now, with an explosion of bars and clubs, things can get pretty rowdy on weekends.

The world you're used to gets turned upside down in Reykjavík. First, there's the climate. The warm air of the jet stream brings surprisingly mild temperatures to a country so close to the North Pole; the average temperature in July is about 58°F, in January about 31°F. (However, the weather changes very rapidly, so be prepared. High winds and cold rain can suddenly wipe out a sunny day.) During summer months, nights stay incredibly bright with sunlight—for much of the short warm season, the sun goes below the horizon for only a few hours each day, and the sky never gets completely dark. And of course, for all you vampires, the opposite is true in winter, when the sun is in hiding for much of the day. Second, there's the landscape. Outside city limits, Iceland unfurls all its strange natural splendor: geysers, fjords, glaciers, waterfalls, hot springs, volcanoes, and bizarre moonscapes. A quick bus ride from Reykjavík will take you there, and several non-cheesy day trips are available from **Reykjavík Excursions**, but to really experience the landscape, a chartered **Mountain Taxi** tour is the way to go [see *great outdoors,* below, for both].

When you take your first stroll around town, you'll immediately notice how quiet and reserved Icelanders are as they go about their daily business. But by Friday night, they're ready to kick it out in a huge way. The natives may initially seem like ice-cold robot types, but if you make the first move, you may not be able to get them to shut up. Practically everyone here speaks English like they live in the 51st state, and seem enthused to practice foreign language skills on any friendly English (or American) speaker, so it's relatively easy to meet locals, especially during a night out. And the people are *beautiful*—most of them look like they come from the Tribe of the Nordic Supermodel.

If you think Reykjavík is totally out of your way, check this out: Icelandair offers customers whose trans-Atlantic flights have a stopover in Reykjavík the opportunity to take a 3-day layover at no additional fee. Another way to save yourself some bucks is to check out ***www.icelandair.com*** and sign up to become a "Lucky Fare" member—news about incredibly low deals is e-mailed to members only. There are no strings attached; the service is free.

five things to talk to a local about

1. **Icelandic Genetics**: What happens when a private company is granted the exclusive right to construct a database containing DNA profiles of every Icelander? A dangerous invasion of privacy or an important step in studying how genes and disease work? [see *icy genes,* below].

2. **The Weather**: Considering the northerly latitude of Iceland, it's not a boring subject here. What strange effects does the lack of sunlight in winter (and/or extra sunlight in summer) produce?

3. **The truth about beauty**: What the hell? Why is everyone so gorgeous here? A common theory begins: "Well, the Vikings stole all of the beautiful women from Europe and brought them to Iceland...." Agreeing is a good idea, since obvious flattery rarely fails.

4. **The American military base at Keflavik**: Should the U.S. military stay in Iceland even though the Cold War ended years ago? Should the Yanks go home?

5. **Why are things so damn expensive?** Attempt to get an acceptable answer (good luck). Caution: Never to be used in an attempted pickup [see *drengur meets stúlka,* below].

Be forewarned, though—Iceland is quite expensive in comparison to the rest of Europe, and a stay of more than a few days can be financially painful. (It's no big secret that almost everyone who arrives from an international flight at Keflavík stocks up on alcohol at the duty-free shop at the airport and pre-games before they hit the bars.) Plan your visit around a weekend, unless you have a ton of cash and time to burn—the nightlife is quiet during the middle of the week, and you'll be bored and broke by the time Thursday comes around. Of course, there are plenty of ways to keep yourself busy if you arrive mid-week: Hit some of the museums and geothermal swimming pools, head for the natural surroundings just outside of town [see *great outdoors*, below, for both], and, most importantly, pick up a copy of **What's On in Reykjavík** and **Reykjavik This Month** at the Tourist Information Center [see *need to know*, below] or at any hotel or hostel to see what the coming days will bring. But be sure to be ready at midnight on Friday, or you could miss out on one of the better-kept secrets in Europe.

Neighborhoods

Reykjavík is tiny for a European capital (population: 150,000), and looks more like an overgrown village than a city. Several streets in the downtown area house the bulk of the bars, cafes, restaurants, and pricey fashion-oriented stores. But as you move away from the center of the city, the prosperous, modern Scandinavian/Baltic look quickly fades. Gray concrete-slab housing dominates, leaving you wondering if the outskirts of the city were purposely designed to depress.

Reykjavík is still out of the way and overlooked, so having to venture out of the central area to get away from cheesy tourist traps isn't necessary (yet). And since Reykjavík is so small, most of the areas you'll frequent can be easily reached on foot. Scoring a youth hostel, hotel, or guesthouse close to the center of town is a huge plus, since all the nightlife that's worth living happens in the space of the dozen or so central blocks.

hanging out

You're not in mainland Europe yet—there aren't any cafe-lined streets where locals and travelers alike while the day away. Tourism isn't an enormous industry here, so there just aren't as many places or activities based on killing time as there are in, say, Paris. Most of the hanging out gets done after dark—*way* after dark—when the bars and clubs spill out into the streets, making an instant outdoor party.

However, Reykjavík does have more kids on skateboards per capita than anywhere outside southern California, and unlike in some countries, the cops don't interfere with the skate scene here. Check it out on a sunny day at **Ingolfstorg**, around the corner from the **Salvation Army Guesthouse** [see *crashing*, below] where the skaters drag picnic tables and bike racks into the square for rail slides off the stairs. This is a great way to meet fellow travelers hanging around and watching the action.

bar and club scene

The line between bar and club is not so heavily drawn in Reykjavík, and there are only a handful of places that can be described exclusively as nightclubs. This makes the vibe more relaxed even when it turns posh. Icelanders' romance with beer is still going strong, so most places offer several Icelandic and Danish choices, with a few imports rounding out the options. Expect the possibility of getting bumped, pushed, or shoved in a bar—don't take it personally, and don't think anyone's trying to start a fight with you, it's just the way things can get here. But this beer-bash mentality doesn't apply to personal style—Icelanders pride themselves on being "with it," and they dress to prove it. So if your daily travel uniform consists of ripped jeans and old sneakers, you may want to get out of them for the night. The clubs aren't super-selective, though, and if you aren't dressed like Ronald McDonald, you shouldn't have much of a problem getting in. And overdressing is next to impossible.

The club scene is all but dead during the week, and showing up before 11pm is foolish. By Thursday night, things begin picking up at places such as Rex Bar or Kaffi Thomsen, which sport the best DJs in town, spinning the latest hits on Nordic charts. As Friday evening approaches, a small hurricane of young adults slams downtown Reykjavík, creating total havoc. The clubs peak from 1am until the last drunken kid is forced to leave at closing, usually around 3 or 7 am, depending on the bar's liscence. One tip: Do as the Icelanders do, and warm up (and save some big bucks) with your duty-free booze before heading out. If you forgot to stock up at the airport, keep in mind that the liquor stores are only open from 11am-2pm on Saturdays, and not at all on Sunday.

Iclandic for "Ugly Duckling Inn," **Lilli Ljoti Andarunginn** (*Laekjargata 6B; Tel 552-98-15; Bus 2, 3, 4, 5, 6, 7, 110, 111, 112, 115 to Laekjartorg; Noon-1am Sun-Thur, 1:30pm-3am Fri, Sat; MC, V*) is a charming, candle-lit bar with a quiet atmosphere, wooden beams stretching across the ceiling, and Muddy Waters on the stereo. This is the perfect place to take that hot Icelandic specimen you met the night before, especially if you're staying at the guesthouse upstairs [see *crashing*, below] wink wink, nudge nudge...say no more. Chances are good that there's a cheap beer special to get the night started, and it's one of the few places

five-o

The police here are low-profile and pretty trustworthy. As long as you're not flaunting illegal drugs and are basically peaceful, you should have no cause for worry. After all, if public intoxication was punished without any exceptions, everyone in the street at 3am would be in jail.

drengur meets stúlka

Yes, the people are foxy, especially if you dig the tall, blond, and fair-skinned. So, when attempting to insinuate yourself with a yummy local, please keep the following tips in mind:

Icelanders are very direct, and you'll know from the outset if they're interested in you or want you to get lost. "Get lost," here means get lost.

You can't be turned out too fine when you go out here. Try to blend in: You're always safe in Johnny Cash black.

If you're not from a major city, lie (a small lie). Always say you're from New York, L.A., London, Chicago, etc.

Never complain about how expensive Iceland can be...hardly anybody's turned on by a cheapskate. Since drinks are crazy expensive, offer to buy your new friend a drink and let them see you're a class act.

where you can order a Colt 45 (plus or minus—you decide...). During the day and evenings it serves up a tasty pasta salad for 590ISK. The patrons are reserved and of mixed age, with couples chatting at little tables making up much of the crowd.

Question: What's black and black and blond all over? Answer: The ultramodern and trendy **Rex Bar** (*Austurstræti 9; Tel 551-91-11; Bus 2, 3, 4, 5, 6, 7, 110, 111, 112, 115 to Laekjartorg; 11:30am-1am Mon-Thur, 11:30am-3pm Fri, 5:30pm-3:30am Sat, closed Sun; MC, V*), just a block off Ingolfstorg Square. It's all about short spiky hair, cell phones, and wire-rimmed glasses. Recognized for its roomy, well-lit neoclassical/space age look and attentive service, the Rex is the hottest place in town on Thursday nights, when the best local DJs do their thing from around 10pm until 1am. People are actually friendly, provided you abide by the unofficial black-only dresscode strictly followed by the late-twenties to mid-thirties crowd. The huge variety of cocktails are as popular as the 500ISK beers. It's also a great place to chow, if you opt to suck it up and throw down some loot [see *eats*, below].

If you're looking for beautiful people, head for the teeny **Kaffi Barinn** (*Bergstaðastræti 1; Tel 551-15-88; Bus 2, 3, 4, 5, 6, 7, 110, 111, 112, 115 to Laekjartorg; 11am-1am Mon-Thur, 11am-3am Fri, Sat, 3pm-1am Sun; MC, V*), one of the loudest, most popular, and densely populated places on a Friday or Saturday night. Legend has it that this place was a brothel back in the day, and the rugged Dodge City decor does its best to keep the rumor going—the only thing missing here is a player piano and cheap whiskey. You need to be 22 to get in when the DJs are spinning hip-hop, Latin, funk, and house on weekend nights the place is jumping. Standard beer prices are 500ISK here, which isn't bad considering what a hot spot it is. Of course, the best time to slink around in the cruisy atmosphere is well after midnight on Friday or Saturday nights. Rumor has it that part-time Reykjavik resident and lead singer of Blur, Damon Albarn, is also part-owner of Kaffi Barinn...which would explain why he's a regular customer come summertime.

Kaffi Brennslan *(Pósthússtræti 9; Tel 561-36-00; Bus 2, 3, 4, 5, 6, 7, 110, 111, 112, 115 to Laekjartorg; 11am-1am Mon-Thur, 11am-3am Fri, 12pm-3am Sat, 2pm-1am Sun; MC, V)* is another top place in town, busy both night and day. If you're not down with the beer selection elsewhere, come on over. Brennslan boasts perhaps the largest beer menu in the city, as well as one of the most fully stocked bars. This split-level restauraunt/cafe is younger, more laid-back, less packed, and not quite as dressy as most places. The food is terrific—great vegetarian sandwiches for 600ISK, big bowls of French onion soup for 450ISK, and "blackboard" bar food available until late-night. The generous bread basket that comes with each order is a meal in itself, not to mention the house specialty. Don't come if you're in a rush. Service is extraordinarily slow, keeping with the relaxed attitude, but with a 290ISK bottled beer special every day, who's complaining?

A hip-yet-casual crowd of twentysomethings comes roaring into **Vegamot Bistro and Bar** *(Vegamotastigur 4; Tel 511-30-40; Bus 2, 3, 4, 5, 6, 7, 110, 111, 112, 115 to Laekjartorg; 11:30am-1am Sun-Thur, 11:30am-3am Fri, Sat; 690ISK-990ISK per entree; Kitchen closes at 9pm weekdays, 10pm weekends; Large beer 500ISK; V, MC)* on Friday and Saturday nights for the cold Tuborgs, great DJs spinning soul/funk, and the unpretentious atmosphere. With outdoor seating, an extensive and comparatively inexpensive menu, daily beer specials, two bars, and two floors, this is one of the most hopping spots in town. After 10pm, the energy picks up and the bistro/bar is transformed into one of the hottest nightspots in the city.

Nelly's *(Þingholtsstræti 2; Tel 562-12-50; Bus 2, 3, 4, 5, 6, 7, 110, 111, 112, 115 to Laekjartorg; Noon-1am Sun-Thur, noon-6am Fri, Sat; MC, V)* is perfect if you're low on dough and ready to get down. Its got a clubby feeling on the upstairs dance floor and a packed bar downstairs. The decor is nothing special, but that keeps the drink prices down and the crowd young. That crowd can be pretty diverse, too—you'll meet anyone from drag-queen divas to the occasional American soldier—but for the most part it's a young, straight, drink-till-you-drop kinda atmosphere. After midnight on the weekends there's a 500ISK cover to get in, but the half-price beer price that's in effect until 1am more than makes up for the door tax. The party peaks around midnight, giving you ample time to fuel up on their wide selection of Irish and British beers on tap before getting your groove on upstairs.

Kaffi Thomsen *(Hafnarstræti 17; Tel 561-57-57; Bus 2, 3, 4, 5, 6, 7, 110, 111, 112, 115 to Laekjartorg; 9pm-1am Thurs, 12am-7am Fri, Sat; www.thomsen.is; V, MC)* became one of Reykjavík's two superclubs (Astro

rules of the game

The legal drinking age is 20, but some clubs impose a 22-and-over rule on certain nights. Drinking on the street is not allowed, but this rule is frequently broken once the bars/clubs let out early on a weekend morning.

Illegal drug laws are strict here, both at customs and in the city. Drug use is well hidden from the public eye in Reykjavík. Just a few years ago, some of the clubs had a reputation for being rife with speed, acid, and ecstasy. But the word on the street is that drug use is down here as a result of increased enforcement, and also simply because it's going out of style. The locals also stress that you may be hassled at customs if you look suspicious and your flight originated in naughty Amsterdam. Travelers flying through Iceland from Europe to North America should note that a stamp in your passport from Amsterdam or anywhere in the Netherlands is a red flag for customs officials. Do not attempt to smuggle any kind of drug, no matter how small the amount, into Iceland.

But Icelanders do like their drinks, and in general, the cops are tolerant of drunken behavior on weekend nights. This doesn't give you an excuse to act like a moron, but staggering around the streets belting out "Hotel California" with your pals won't land you in the slammer (although, God knows, it probably should).

being the other) under the previous ownership because Björk, the members of Gus Gus, and other local bigwigs conspired to bring in overseas DJs once a month. Though the venue was sold and renovated in February 2000, there is still top-flight talent from abroad, only now DJs call the club, asking or begging to be booked to play alongside the local talent. Dimitry from Paris, Kevin Saunderson, and Adam Freeland have all spun there since the remodeling, probably without so much of the begging. The new-look Thomsen features two levels with clean lines, orange plastic retro chairs, and dim white lights set in the blond hardwood floor. The lower level has a second bar and is dedicated to the more hardcore crowd (techno, breakbeat, hard house) while the main floor keeps it real with hip-hop, trip-hop, house, and the occasional disco remix. The cover runs from 500-1000ISK, depending on what's on that night and pints of beer are 500ISK. You don't want to be there before 2 am—and never before 1, dahling—but once you're in, you'll probably stay and see the wrong end of the morning with the flood of jittery and hoarse Norse who stumble out between 7 and 8 am.

When Jerry Seinfeld came here on his reported pilgrimage to Iceland to bag a Nordic babe (pre-marriage, of course), he got his name etched into the pillar in front of the bar at **Astro** (*22 Austurstræti; Tel 552-92-22; Bus 2, 3, 4, 5, 6, 7, 110, 111, 112, 115 to Laekjartorg; 9pm-*

3am, Fri, Sat only; AE, MC, V), the trendiest club in town. You can etch your name right next to his: All you gotta do is spring for a 40,000ISK bottle of champagne. With two floors, five large rooms that pack in 550 people nightly, three bars, a large dance floor, and plenty of semi-circular couches, this is as swanky as it gets in a small city. Beer is the drink of choice, going for the standard 550ISK. The patrons are generally somewhere in their 20s and dressed to kill. A 500ISK cover charge is levied when you enter the building. If want to do the club thing with less hassle and less of an assault on your wallet, walk up the hill towards Nelly's.

LIVE MUSIC SCENE

Reykjavík's location and size limit its ability to draw international musical talent—not many big names come this far north. It's more common for most venues to have DJs on a regular basis, so folks can dance to both the *Grease* soundtrack and the latest Euro club hits. But don't completely count out seeing great live music here—the international attention garnered by Björk has spurred a renaissance of sorts on the Icelandic pop scene. Just keep your eyes and ears open, and don't be shy to ask around at some of the places mentioned below. The live music in town is especially active on weekend nights, beginning somewhere around 10pm and peaking around midnight. The music is usually done before 1am, but you should check with individual venues for specific show times.

Gaukur Á Ströng *(Tryggvagata 22; Tel 551-15-56; Bus 2 through 7, 110 through 112, 115 to Laekjartorg; 8pm-1am Sun-Thur, 8pm-6am Fri, Sat; After midnight, cover varies depending on bands, which start 10pm;*

fashion

The people at the top of the world definitely take fashion seriously. Disheveled travelers who only feel comfortable in jeans, sneakers, and a polar fleece over a ratty plaid shirt are going to stick out. Young Icelandic adults seem to have perfected every detail of their personal appearance. Outfits tend to be dark, sharp, and sleek, kind of like in *The Matrix*. Men keep their hair heavily gelled, and ponytails on guys are as common as Icelandic heat waves. An incredible amount of young people sport cell phones, and sitting in a cafe may make you worry for your health with all those rays flying around. Wacky, over-the-top club kid uniforms are uncommon in Reykjavík. The dress code in the clubs gravitates towards the polished and classy.

MC, V), the oldest pub in Iceland, is your best bet for blues or rock any night of the week. The front part has the look and feel of a Herman Melville novel set to a Pearl Jam soundtrack—it's no surprise that the dark hardwood interior was once the preferred hangout for thirsty Icelandic shipmates. The pub was an important player in the legalization of beer here: In order to circumvent the weak-beer-only laws in Iceland, the bartenders would simply dump liters of vodka into the half-empty kegs. It's much more casual and chill than most of the popular scenes here in town. Both electric and acoustic bands play in a sprawling, garage-like room out back—you might see an unknown queen of Icelandic blues singing her heart out as her keyboardist pounds away on his old Hammond organ—and the crowd varies with the kind of band that's playing. Recent renovations more than tripled the size of this place, and they're planning on opening a restaurant on the top floor. The atmosphere may be a little more upscale, but the beers are still 500ISK.

ARTS SCENE

Although Reykjavík isn't automatically thought of as a huge player in the world of contemporary art and theater, don't let the locals know it. The scene is growing all the time—there were over 36 art galleries in Reykjavík at last count—and very cool. After all, unusual and bizarre creations are bound to spring from artists who live in a place where sometimes day is night and night is day....

▶▶**VISUAL ARTS**

The most under-appreciated art museum in town has to be the **Living**

FESTIVALS AND EVENTS

National Day *(June 17)*: This is the big day for Iceland, marking the country's official independence from the Kingdom of Denmark on June 17, 1944. All over the country, people celebrate with traditional costumes, parades, speeches, and parties. This is hands-down the best weekend of the year to visit Reykjavík: A midsummer pinnacle evening for that famed Icelandic party scene.

Midsummer's Day *(June 24)*: The longest day of the year in Iceland is not a public holiday but still a traditionally spirited day for the sunlight-deprived Icelanders.

Seamen's Day *(June 6)*: A day to remember all of the Icelandic men lost at sea, it is yet another reminder of how important the sea and its sailors are to both Icelandic history and economy. Boats and ships of all sizes come into port carrying modern Vikings (also of all sizes) eager to try their hands at the strongman competitions.

Art Museum *(Vatnsstigur 3b; Tel 551-43-50; Bus 2, 3, 4, 5, 6, 7, 110, 111, 112, 115 to Laekjatorg; 2pm-6pm Tue-Sun; www.nylo.is/nylo@nylo.is; Free admission; No credit cards)*, a mind-bending, non-profit contemporary art gallery located just off Laugavegur. Without a doubt, this is the place for the not-so-mainstream art crowd, offering a wide range of exhibitions by young up-and-coming Icelandic and foreign artists. Expect film, video, mixed media, and installation art.

▶▶PERFORMING ARTS

Iðno (Icelandic Theater Company) *(Vonarstræti 3; Theater Tel 530-30-30, Restaurant Tel 562-97-00; www.idno.is; Bus 2, 3, 4, 5 ,6,7 , 110, 111, 112, 115 to Laekjartorg; Noon-6pm daily, upstairs restaurant/bar 6pm-1am Sun-Thur, 6pm-3am Fri, Sat, cafe noon-6pm daily; idno@idno.is; 2,200ISK for 8:30 daily evening show, 1300ISK for 12 afternoon show; MC, V)* has an unbelievably cheerful atmosphere, and the ambiance is unbeatable. This 150-seat, privately run playhouse, frequented by a great international mix of people, is one of the hidden jewels of Reykjavík. A vast majority of the performances here are written by Icelandic playwrights, with an occasional performance in English. It's worth seeing just for the Victorian decor, which was recently renovated with exacting detail. The rather formal dining room stops serving around 10pm, but the third-floor lounge and bar, which has a wonderful overlook of "the pond," a man-made lake in the city center, is a cozy place to hang out till the wee hours of the evening. Keep an eye out for the occasional rock or pop concert played here as well.

gay scene

The hub of the local scene is **Samtökin '78** *(3 Langaveger, 4th floor; Help line 522-78-78 Fax 552-78-20; 2-4pm Mon-Fri only, cafe 2-4pm Mon-Fri, 8-11pm Thur, 10pm-2am Sat, library 8-11pm Mon, Thur; For more info: www.gayiceland.com/reykjavik is a great resource)*. The group, started in 1978 by 13 gay men, now has 500 members and has fought for—and won—advances like the legalization of same-sex marriages (homosexual couples have the same legal rights as hetero couples), the right of gay couples to adopt, an anti-discrimination law that can land bigots in jail for up to two years, and a local climate that looks down on homophobia. So that's yer history. The present? The scene is still small but thriving and very open, with as many lesbians as gays packing the discos. Stop by the Samtökin '78 cafe Thursday evenings, where a big crowd converges to warm up for the gay nights at the clubs listed here.

22 *(22 Laugavegur; Tel 551-36-28; Bus 1, 2, 3, 4, 5, 6, 7, 110, 111, 112, 115 to Laekjartorg; Noon-1am Sun-Thur, noon-7am Fri, Sat; 500ISK cover on Fridays and Saturdays; V, MC)* plays host to a mixed-age, leather-wearing crowd. On very busy weekend nights, you may have a problem getting in if you're under 22, but things are lax during their most popular hours (4-6am). Classic disco keeps people grooving in the barn-like upstairs, and the great view of the main drag keeps those seated at tables on the lower level more than content. There's a daily beer special for

200ISK, and a double vodka and coke—the drink of choice here—goes for 700ISK. The scene isn't strictly gay or lesbian; everyone's welcome.

The Web site for **Spotlight** *(8-10 Hverfisgata (look for the rainbow flag over the door); No phone; 11pm-1am Thur, 11pm-4am Fri, 11pm-5am Sat; www.spotlight.hie.is)* claims that the club is "70 gay on weekends, 100 gay on Thursdays." You just gotta love those odds! Thursdays, as you may have guessed, play host to *GAY Night* (18 and over, please), a mixed affair—men and women, hardcore (cage dancing!) and mainstream—presided over by local fave DJ Ivar. There's a nightly happy "hour" from opening til 1am, when the cutie bartenders will sell you 350ISK large beers from the long wooden bar.

CULTUre ZOO

This is a rather small city, so don't come here expecting that blockbuster Impressionist or Egyptian Art show (who needs 'em anyway?). But this place does have its fair share of cultural attractions. Sculpture and photography, both closely linked to the beautiful landscapes in Iceland, are particularly big in Reykjavík. There are enough unusual choices here to be worth a brake from clubbing, napping, or snowboarding. The **Reykjavík Car** *(900ISK for 24 hrs/1200ISK for 48 hours)*, available at the super-helpful tourist info office [see *need to know*, below], grants access to all of the museums, galleries, and thermal pools in town. The pass also includes free bus rides, not that you can't walk anywhere you need to go.

National Gallery of Iceland *(Fríkirkjuvegur 7; Tel 562-10-00; Bus 2, 3, 4, 5, 6, 7, 110, 111, 112, 115 to Laekjartorg; 11am-5pm Tues-Sun; 300ISK, free on Wednesdays; www.listasafn.is, list@natgall.is; V, MC):* This is a beautifully designed modern gallery with four exhibition rooms that focus on Icelandic and international art from the nineteenth and twentieth century. The watercolor and oils of the Icelandic landscape sometimes seem more otherworldly than the featured paintings by Picasso and Munch. Other highlights include works by Richard Serra, Icelandic Pop Art, and occasional installations and digital art exhibits.

Icelandic Museum of Natural History *(Hlemmur 3, entry from Hverfisgata; Tel 562-98-22; Fax 562-08-15; Bus 1, 2, 3, 4, 5, 6, 10, 11, 12, 14, 15 to Hlemmur; 1pm-5pm June-Aug, 1:30pm-4:30pm Sept-May; Closed Mon, Wed, Fri; 300ISK admission; www.ni.is; No credit cards):* Exhibitions of every stuffed Icelandic critter you ever wished to know about—or even knew existed.

The Icelandic Phallogical Museum *(Laugavegur 24; Tel 561-66-63; Bus 1, 2, 3, 4, 5, 6, 110, 111, 112, 115 to Laekjartorg; 2-5pm Tue-Sat Sept-April, 2-5pm Tue and Sat May-Aug; 300ISK; www.rvik.ismennt.is/~phallus, phallus@ismennt.is; MC, V):* A little more focused than the above, this small, backstreet museum has an impressive collection of over 80 penises, representing almost all the land and sea animals of Iceland. Wow!

The Reykjavík Museum of Photography *(Tryggvagate 15; Bus 1, 2, 3, 4, 5, 6, 10, 11, 12, 14, 15 from Hlemmur; 9am-4pm Mon-Fri; Free*

reykjavík city center

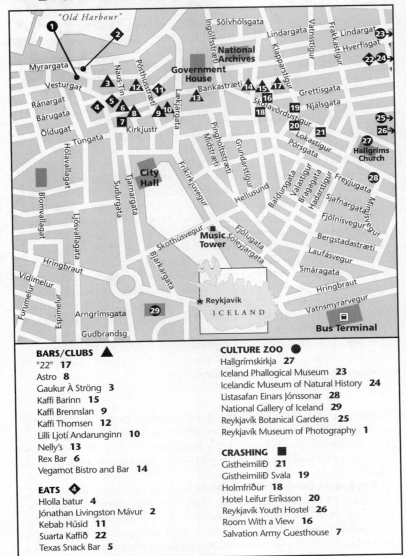

BARS/CLUBS ▲
"22" 17
Astro 8
Gaukur À Ströng 3
Kaffi Barinn 15
Kaffi Brennslan 9
Kaffi Thomsen 12
Lilli Ljotí Andarunginn 10
Nelly's 13
Rex Bar 6
Vegamot Bistro and Bar 14

EATS ◆
Hlolla batur 4
Jónathan Livingston Mávur 2
Kebab Húsid 11
Suarta Kaffið 22
Texas Snack Bar 5

CULTURE ZOO ●
Hallgrímskirkja 27
Iceland Phallogical Museum 23
Icelandic Museum of Natural History 24
Listasafan Einars Jónssonar 28
National Gallery of Iceland 29
Reykjavík Botanical Gardens 25
Reykjavík Museum of Photography 1

CRASHING ■
Gistheimilið 21
Gistheimilið Svala 19
Holmfriður 18
Hotel Leifur Eiríksson 20
Reykjavík Youth Hostel 26
Room With a View 16
Salvation Army Guesthouse 7

admission; www.reykjavik.is/ljosmynasdafn; photomuseum@reykjavik.is; No credit cards): 1.5 million photographs by Icelandic shutterbugs, covering everything from history to photojournalism to school pictures.
Hallgrímskirkja (Hallgrim's Church) *(On the top of the hill on*

ICY GENES

Iceland is a geneticist's dream. First of all, the small population has been virtually cut off from the rest of the world since the original settlers came here over 1,000 years ago, and these first Vikings came largely from the same background.

The population—along with a small influx of Irish slaves—was kept in check by harsh weather conditions, hunger, and outbreaks of disease. It's no wonder that many first-time visitors comment that "everyone kinda looks alike here."

Anyway, scientists have discovered that genetic diseases here can be easily traced to some of the first Viking settlers, and geneticists are interested in the Icelandic gene pool, convinced that studying it will allow them to help solve some of the mysteries around genetically transmitted diseases.

Now, here comes the controversial part. In 1998, Icelanders voted to pass a law that grants a biotech company rights to construct a database with access to every Icelander's health records. Although the people who voted it in feel that this research could be an important leap forward for the future well-being of all Icelanders, many worry about the potential abuse of this most private information. For example, what if an employer or health insurance company somehow got hold of your DNA records? Hey, there's that *Gattaca* theme again. For more info on both viewpoints, check out ***www.decode.is/newsroom/index.html.***

Skólavörðustígur; Tel 510-10-00; Bus 1 to Laekjartorg; 9am-6pm daily May-Sept, 10am-5pm daily Oct-Apr; 200ISK to go up the tower; V, MC): This, Iceland's biggest church, is *the* landmark of Reykjavík, rising high above all other buildings in the city to offer a magnificent view from its 75-foot steeple.

Reykjavík Botanical Gardens *(Skulatun 2; Tel 553-88-70; Bus 2, 5, 10, 12, 15 to Laugardalur; 8am-11pm Mon-Fri, 10am-11pm Sat, Sun Apr-Sept; 8am-3pm Mon-Fri, 10am-6pm Sat, Sun Oct-Mar; Free admission; botgard@rvk.is; No credit cards):* A huge variety of flora, both arctic and subarctic (in the greenhouse, of course), in a tranquil setting just a 10-minute bus ride from the concrete sprawl surrounding Reykjavík.

great outdoors

If you just want to work out in order to de-tox, you have some choices: swims in the naturally heated swimming pools, walks in the botanical gardens [see *culture zoo*, above] or along the harbor. But anyone who comes to Reykjavík without taking a day trip to see the incredible land-scape that begins just outside of town is really missing the point. There are many ways to see the backcountry that fit every budget and physical condition, all while exercising your body, or just your eyes, and your soul.

There are reasons why there are not many bikes on the street in Reyk-javík. The weather can change instantaneously, and a pleasant little bike ride could leave you cold and soggy. Bike rental is an option, just be ready to brave the often-blustery winds. Still, when the weather is beautiful in the summer, a pedal around town can be the perfect way to clear your head the morning after….The best place to pick up some wheels is **Borgarhjól** [see *need to know*, below].

Hardcore mountain-bikers will want to meet their Viking cousins at the Thursday night meeting of the **Icelandic Mountain Bike Club** *(Brekkustigur 2; Tel 354-562 0099; Bus 2, 3, 4, 5, 6, 7, 110, 111, 112, 115 to Laekjartorg; Meetings 8pm Thurs, plus 2pm on 1st and 3rd Sat of month in summer; www.mmedia.is/~ifhk/tourist.htm, ifhk@mmedia.is).* These fanatics will be happy to give advice and plan rides.

Or you could head out to the far east end of town to **Breiðholtslaug Swimming Pool** *(Austurberg 5; Tel 557/55-47; Bus 8, 12, 112 to Breiðholtslaug; 7am-10pm Mon-Fri, 8am-10pm Sat, Sun; 200ISK entrance fee, 200ISK towel rental; V, MC)* and take a tourist-free dip in the outdoor geothermal lap pool or one of the three heated sitting pools. Don't come expecting to meet the Nordic supermodel of your dreams: Most of the swimmers will be heavy-set Icelandic men wondering—in a friendly way, of course—what the hell you're doing here.

Sundholl Reykjavíkur *(Baronsstigur; Tel 551-40-59; Bus 1 to Sund-*

by foot

This walk takes you along the western side of the city. It parallels the ocean at all times, so it may be chillier than a stroll within the city itself. A well-kept walking path is underfoot the entire way, so don't worry about hiking boots. Taking this route is a great way to get a feel for the importance of the maritime tradition here in Reykjavík.

Start at the intersection of **Nesveger** and **Granaskol**. Walk east-ward, heading towards the Reykjavík Airport. Along the way, you'll see the makeshift shacks that are used by fishermen to hang their catch. Looking out across the other side of the fjord, you can see small incoming planes touching down at the airport, and, depending on the visibility, the president of Iceland's house. The walk ends at **Heidmork**, the popular outdoor park, where you can sit, relax, and eat a packed lunch in peace.

holl; 200ISK entrance fee, 200ISK towel rental; V, MC) is the only indoor geothermal swimming pool in town, accompanied by three outdoor heated sitting pools. The crowd is more diverse here, ranging from Icelandic kids taking swimming lessons to those wishing to get a quick dip in before work.

The most unique landscape in the world surrounds Reykjavík. Although many tours in Iceland can (surprise!) be pretty expensive, there are some mind-blowing trips at sensible prices. Tours range from standard bus tours, to horseback riding over gorgeous pastures and rolling hills, to a stroll through a charming Icelandic fishing village, to renting a super-jeep 4x4, to snowmobiling on a glacier.

Take the road less traveled. Kristján Kristjánsson is the burly neo-Viking owner of **Mountain Taxi** (Álfholt 10-Hafnarfir_i; Tel/Fax 565-5695; Year-round by request; Tours leave in the morning and pick you up at your hotel or hostel; mountain@centrum.is; www.mountain-taxi.com; V, MC). His company has a small fleet of large SuperJeeps (the local word for jacked-up and reinforced 4x4 SUV snow yachts) and a merry band of English-speaking, fear-challenged drivers culled from the area's 4x4 enthusiasts. Every Jeep is equipped with enough communications and locating devices to fly a jet (some of them even have auto-pilot) and tires big enough to ford the mightiest fjord. Mountain Taxi runs many of the same tours as other companies (The Golden Circle, for example), but they go over what the buses go around. The drivers pride themselves on their local knowledge and willingness to share stories with the three to four passengers per vehicle. If on the way to see Geysir, you express interest in rock carvings, don't be too surprised to find the driver taking you off-road to find some runes carved by a reclusive local artist. The most popular tour is the 8-9 hour "Iceland in a Nutshell" and consists of careening over a high mountain road, an intense spin on the massive Langjökull glacier, splashing though creeks, lava caves, hot springs, a waterfall and finally a relaxing drive back to town along a fjord. The drivers get out and adjust the air pressure in the tires every time the terrain changes (you're not going to see a bus driver doing *that*). At 12,000ISK, it's way more expensive than a bus tour, but so very worth it. There are 10 other trips on the Mountain taxi menu, including kayaking, volcano-scaling, and Highland trekking and last from 8 hours for 4 days. Some areas are so remote that they fly you to the jeeps, and others are extreme enough that the ads warn, "The tour might be disturbing for those who are sensitive to heights". Kristján will also design custom tours if you want to go snowboarding, ice-fishing, inner-tubing behind a jeep, or whatever other crazy shit you can dream up. Like most tour companies here, they will pick up and drop off at your guesthouse. Unlike most, they will also play your CDs in the jeep.

For a more laid-back experience, take an Icelandic horse ride with **Ishestar Riding Tours** (Sörlaskeió 26, IS-220 Hafnarfjöróur; Tel 555-7000, Fax 555-7001; Office hours 8am-5pm daily; Hotel pick up at 9 and 12am, depending on tour; http://www.ishestar.is; info@ishestar.is V, MC).

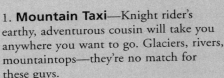

12 hours in reykjavik

1. **Mountain Taxi**—Knight rider's earthy, adventurous cousin will take you anywhere you want to go. Glaciers, rivers, mountaintops—they're no match for these guys.

2. **Texas Snack Bar**—The cheap hot dogs here can't be beat. The trashy atmosphere and weird name will make you want to sing out "the stars at night are big and bright deep in the heart of Iceland." Yee-haw!

3. **Kolaportið**—Experience what is probably the world's northernmost flea market. Maybe you'll stumble across that Viking helmet you've secretly dreamed of [see *stuff*, above].

4. **National Gallery of Iceland**—See the sea, then see the seascapes at Reykjavík's most impressive cultural attraction [see *culture zoo*, above].

5. **Hallgrímskirkja** (Hallgrim's Church)—Take a hike up the hill, check out the statue of Leif Eiríksson and climb up the church tower for a great view of the entire city [see *culture zoo*, above].

6. **Kaffi Brennslan**—Re-energize yourself with a cup of coffee or two, and let your eyes wander the cafe and feast on the pretty people [see *bar and club scene*, above].

7. **Vegamot Bistro and Bar**—Kick back with several pints of Tuborg and a tasty snack [see *bar and club scene*, above].

8. **Gaukur Á Stöng**—Float on down here and investigate the nightly drink special. Hang out and check out the band (quality of band and number of drinks should be inversely proportional) [see *bar and club scene*, above].

9. **Astro**—'Round midnight, join the swishy line of people waiting to get into Astro. You're gonna dig deep to get in and tie one on, but hey, when are you going to be in Iceland again? [see *bar and club scene*, above]

10. Follow the mating suggestions in our sidebar [see *drengur meets stúlka*, above]—It's no mystery what's on your mind by now if you've followed this itinerary. Spot your intended mark, collect yourself, and move on in there, baby.

Short, shaggy, and docile, Icelandic horses are all descended from the stock the Vikings introduced in the 900's. They have a special gait, lost in all other breeds, that allows a rider to stay level with no bouncing in the saddle even over rough terrain. Ishestar offers several riding tours from their riding center 15 minutes outside of town, starting with the Lava Tour around the moonlike landscape around the Helgafell volcano (3 hours total, 2 hours riding) for 3,000ISK. All tours include pickup from any accommodation in Reykjavík. Read the brochures carefully, many of the longer tours include driving for sightseeing after a ride, not galloping around geysers.

For those on a budget, the cheapest option is the one most traveled by: **Reykjavík Excursions** *(Sales office Bankastræti 2; Tel 562-10-11; Bus 2, 3, 4, 5, 6, 7, 110, 111, 112, 115 to Laekjartorg; 8:30am-5pm Mon-Fri; 8:30am-1:30pm Sat, Sun; www.re.is; main@re.is; V, MC;)* goes to the big tourist destinations in big buses in their "Golden Circle Tour." It's very popular, and you'll see signage for it everywhere (like half the country, Reykjavík Excursions is owned by IcelandAir). To put it nicely, though, this is the trip your Mom would take if she were here. Most of the other companies have their own tour of the Golden Circle, and Super Jeeps and horses are just cooler modes of transport than tourist buses. If you truly can't afford any of the other trips, at 5,400ISK, this trip is much better than not seeing the spooky beauty of the landscape at all.

And there's always public transport. **Thórsmörk**, a rugged area in southern Iceland that includes the climber's-dream 458-metre-high Valahnjúkur cliff, and **Landmannalaugar**, the largest geothermal formation in the country, can be reached by B.S.I. buses [see *need to know*, below]: Buses to Thorsmork leave Reykjavik at 8:30am daily and arrive in Húsadalur, the largest village in the Thorsmork area, at noon; the return bus leaves at 3:30pm. In the summer, there is also a weekend bus that leaves at 8:30pm on Friday nights. Buses run to Landmannalauger daily between July 15 and August 31, weather permitting, leaving Reykjavík at 8:30am and arriving at 12:30; the return bus leaves at 2:30pm. You can stay overnight in the Landmannalauger hut, which, though it holds 115 people, often fills up during the summer, so reserve ahead of time or pitch a tent at the free camping area, which is adjacent to the hut and shares it's facilities. One of the great Icelandic hikes is the three-day trek between Thórsmörk and Landmannalaugar. The Tourist Information Center [see *need to know*, below] can give you more info on the hike and the towns, and make reservations for the hut.

Stuff

Shopping in this town can easily break you, even if you aren't on the I-live-on-beer-and-bread-and-cheese-and-I-love-it! traveler's budget. If that trust fund is itching to bust loose, you should still give some serious thought before embarking on a shopping spree in this mark-up-happy town. If you feel you absolutely *have* to come home with something, you might be able to pick up some nice souvenirs in the main downtown pedestrian shopping area without emptying your wallet. For those who manage to get their jollies just by looking, Bankastræti and Laugavegur are great window-shopping streets, and all these major shopping streets are confined in an easily walkable area. The big tourist purchase here are the Icelandic wool sweaters (and socks and gloves and so on), which are gorgeous, if bulky knits are your thing. Look for them downtown on Hafnarstræti and Austurstaeti, and avoid the ones being hawked at the airport, where the prices are wildly inflated.

▶▶MALL RATS

If your homesick cravings for fluorescent lighting, recirculated air, and elevator music become overwhelming, **Kringlan** (*Kringlan 8-12; Tel 568-92-00 general phone, 588-08-00 movie theater; Bus 5, 6, 110 through 112 to Kringlan; 10am-6:30pm Sat-Thur, 10am-7pm Fri, 1-5pm Sun; service@kringlan.is; MC, V*), on the east side of town, is the place to go. It's an upscale version of your common mall: cleaner, classier, quieter, and more expensive. There's also a multiplex here if you want to catch a movie. The latest American releases aren't dubbed over—just ignore the Icelandic subtitles at the bottom of the screen.

▶▶I BRAKE FOR YARD SALES

Perhaps the sole affordable alternative is the indoor flea market, **Kolaportið** (*corner of Tryggvagata and Geirsgata; Tel 561-70-63; Bus 2 through 7, 110 through 112, 115 to Laekjartorg; 11am-5pm Sat, Sun only; No credit cards*). From Norse jewelry to used reindeer skins, this is the place to find that never-to-be-found-again piece of memorabilia. Your haggling skills can also be put to the test at this weekend-only giant garage sale, at the northwest end of the city center.

▶▶BOUND

The highly educated Icelanders are avid readers, and the large international bookstore **Mál og Menning** (*Laugavegur 18; Tel 515-25-00; Bus 2 through 7, 110 through 112, 115 to Laekjartorg; 9am-10pm Mon-Fri, 10am-10pm weekends; www.mm.is., bokabud@mm.is; V, MC, AE, DC*) handles their needs. This busy emporium boasts a variety of books on Icelandic culture, language, and geography, as well as large sections of English fiction and nonfiction. The small cafe here also hosts poetry readings, some of which are in English, so swing by to inquire about scheduled events.

EATS

Although food is costly here, there are other options besides making do on hot dogs. For instance, it's normal for a place to be considered a cafe and restaurant during the day and a hopping bar at night [see *bar and club scene*, above], and places like that serve decently priced meals. When you do finally cave in and shell out for a good meal, maybe you can take small comfort in the fact that a tip is already included in the price.

▶▶CHEAP

Well, nothing is *cheap*...but the pre-made sandwiches and hot dogs sold at corner stores aren't that expensive. Two safe bets are both located on Ingolfstorg Square. The **Texas Snack Bar** (*Ingolfstorg; No phone; Bus 2 through 7, 110 through 112 to Stoppistod or Bidstod; 8am-9pm Mon-Fri,*

reykjavík

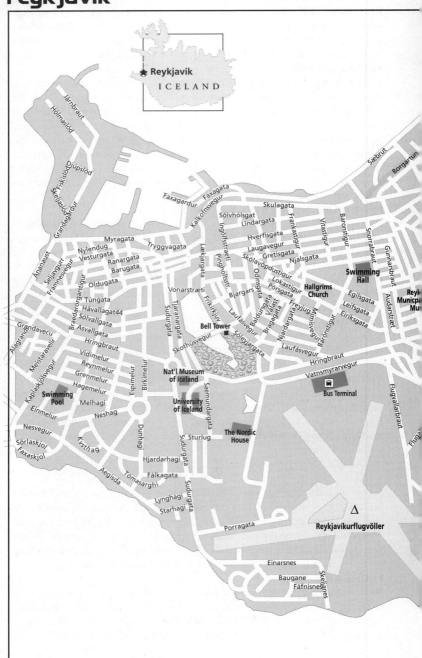

10am-9pm Sat, 12-6pm Sun; Hot dog 140ISK, wrapped sandwiches 200ISK-330ISK; V, MC) is a funky, inexpensive place to grab a meal. It's not gourmet, not even close, but it ain't dog food either. The electronic gambling machines in the corner add to the charm here. You can sit at one of the stools along the counter, or do as most prefer and eat on the street outside.

Hlolla batar *(Ingolfstorg; No phone; Bus 2 through 7, 110 through 112 to Stoppistod or Bidstod; 10am-2am weekdays, 11am-6am weekends; V, MC)*, across the square, is one notch above Texas Snack Bar. It's also open late-night and bakes its own bread daily. This place is basically Iceland's version of a retro diner, and you can grab a hamburger or a sub (try the "pizza boat") for 450ISK. The counter here has plenty of room to make yourself comfortable.

A sure bet for satisfying grub is **Kebab Húsid** *(Laekjargata 2; Tel 561-30-70; Bus 2 through 7, 110 through 112, 115 to Laekjartorg; 11am-midnight Sun-Thur, 11am-7am Fri, Sat; 470ISK-500ISK per meal; V, MC)*, a late-night, stuff-your-face greasy kebab-and-shwarma shack. If you look past the grease, though, you'll see that the ingredients are all fresh, the bread is baked daily, and it's squeaky clean. The interior has your run-of-the-mill fast food look, with a few tables strewn about for seating.

▶▶DO-ABLE

Eventually, you gotta venture out and get a mid-priced meal, and **Veg-amot Bistro and Bar** [see *bar and club scene,* above] should be at the top of your list. Both Mediterranean and Mexican food are in abundance here, all at prices that won't make you feel guilty for finally going out and strapping on the feed bag. Outdoor seating is available when it's nice enough to hang outside, and it's a great place to people-watch.

Suarta Kaffið Cafe Bar *(Laugavegur 54; Tel 551-29-99; Bus 1 through 7, 110 through 112, 115 to Laekjartorg; 11:30am-1am Mon-Thur, 11:30am-3am Fri, Sat, 2pm-1am Sun; 500ISK-1,300ISK per meal, 500ISK for a large Icelandic beer; V, MC)*, a small second-floor bar/restaurant/cafe, has the best soup in the city, which is served in edible bread bowls. African masks and drums decorate the place, Guinness beer signs hang over the bar, Bob Marley or Peter Tosh is usually on the stereo, and there are views of the ocean and mountains from certain seats. The crowd is a mixed bag; doctors can be seen hanging out next to bums. An added bonus: 400ISK beer every day from 6 till 9pm! And the soup and pint combo is just 1000ISK.

You'll probably find yourself returning to **Kaffi Brennslan** [see *bar and club scene,* above] again and again. The food is some of the best around at these prices (600ISK for soups and sandwiches) and the English menu really helps.

▶▶SPLURGE

If you're gonna shell out the big bucks here, you might as well go Icelandic. **Jonathan Livingston Mávur** *(Tryggvagata 4-6; Tel 551-55-*

20, Fax 354-562-1482; Bus 2 through 7, 110 through 112, 115 from Laek-jartorg; 5:30pm until guests leave daily; 1,600ISK-3,900ISK per entree; www.livingston.is; V, MC, AE) is numero uno, top notch, A-1, no one else even close. An excellent Lebanese chef serves up fresh Icelandic seafood, reindeer, mountain lamb, goose, puffin, dolphin, and even whale meat (bad! bad! bad!!). There are roses on every table, Cuban cigars for sale, and candlelight is the rule, illuminating the tasteful paintings on the walls. Reservations are a must.

Another good call for upscale food is **Rex Bar** [see *bar and club scene*, above], where a great lunch entree starts at 900ISK and dinner entrees go for around 2000ISK. The grilled tuna is spectacular. The kitchen stays open till 10pm, which is later than most bar/restaurant type places here. Reservations are a good idea.

crashing

Finding that perfect combination of location, comfort, and price is next to impossible here when it comes to crashing. But if you're a little creative and more than a little flexible, you should do fine. And think of it this way: After a night in downtown Reykjavík, you probably won't care too much where you sleep.

▶▶**CHEAP**

Finding a good, cheap place to check in for the night here is as likely as *not* spotting an attractive Icelander in downtown Reykjavík late on Friday night. One decent option is **Salvation Army Guesthouse** (*Kirkjus-træti 2; Tel 561-32-03, Fax 561-33-15; Bus 2, 3, 4, 5, 6, 7, 110, 111, 112 to Stoppistod or Bidstod; 1,400ISK sleeping bag accommodation, 2,900ISK single, 4,100ISK double, 5,300ISK triple, 6,500ISK quad Sept-Apr; 1,400ISK sleeping bag accommodation, 3,700ISK single, 5,000ISK double, 6,200ISK triple, 7,500ISK quad May-Aug; http://guesthouse.is; MC, V*). Don't let the name throw you—all in all, it's not a bad place: located in the downtown area, clean, and sufficiently comfortable. One annoyance is having to share the single shower and toilet with everyone on your floor. Breakfast, consisting of bread, milk, cheese, salami, and coffee, is an extra 700ISK per day, and the reception is open until 1am (after that you can ring the bell and the porter will let you in).

Although this place grows on you the longer you stay, you may feel more comfortable at the **Reykjavík Youth Hostel** (*Sundlaugavegur 34; Tel 553-88-10; Bus 5 to Farfuglaheimili or the fly bus from the airport; 8-midnight Mon-Fri, 8am-11am and 4pm-midnight Sat, Sun; 1,450ISK, HI members 1,200ISK May-Sept, 1,000ISK, HI member 900ISK Oct-Apr; 108 beds, 3 doubles, 3 quads; www.hostel.is, info@hostel.is; MC, V*). Located a bit out of the center of town, but right next to the public pool, it's still only a 10-minute bus ride from the action, and there's no curfew. Situated in the back of the hostel is the **Reykjavík Botanical Gardens** [see *culture zoo*, above] as well as one of Reykjavík's thermally heated outdoor swimming pools. This is the only hostel in Reykjavík,

wired

If you are looking to go online in Reykjavík, you might want to bring your laptop. Even though Icelanders are very tech-oriented, there's a major lack of public access to computers in the city. All of the cyber-cafes have gone under, so there is only one option available: the **National and University Library of Iceland** (*Arngrímsgata 3; Tel 525-56-15; Bus 5 to Haskoli Islands; 8:15am-7pm Mon-Thur, 8:15am-5pm Fri, 10am-5pm Sat Sept-May; 9am-5pm Mon-Fri, 1pm-5pm Sat June-Aug; www.bok.hi.is).* Located across the traffic circle from the National Museum, you can go online on one of their 70 PCs free of charge.

www.whatson.is: cyber version of *What's on in Reykjavík.*
www.icetourist.is or **www.goiceland.org**: Icelandic Tourist Board.
www.Reykjavik.is: shopping guide to Iceland and Reykjavík.
www.icelandair.com: Iceland Air.
tourist.reykjavik.is: basic tourist info.

so its a good idea to book in advance. A decent 600ISK buffet breakfast, an extensive kitchen facility, a large dining room overlooking the botanical gardens, and clean communal showers and bathrooms make this a good deal for your *kroner*. Single and double rooms can be requested at an additional charge.

▶▶**DO-ABLE**

Guesthouses in Reykjavík tend to be homey, family-run places, and there are quite a few of them. A good compromise between hotels and bottom-of-the-barrel places, they often draw an older, more middle-aged crowd. **Gistheimilið Svala** (*Skólavörðustíg 30; Tel 562-35-44; Bus 2 through 7, 110 through 112, 115 to Laekjartorg; Front desk hours vary; 2,500ISK single, 3,000ISK double, 4,500ISK triple Oct-Apr, 4,000ISK single, 6,000ISK double, 7,500ISK triple May-Sept; V, MC)* is a cozy, clean mom-and-pop place, with a superb served-with-a-smile breakfast (bread, cheese, hard-boiled egg, jam, coffee, milk, juice) included in the price. Located halfway between Hallgrímskirkja and Bankastræti, it puts you right in the thick of things. Sinks in every room, sparkling shared bathrooms, and a big kitchen and dining room make it feel like Grandma's house—only Grandma hands you a bill on your way out.

The view is the thing at **Holmfriður** (*Skólavörðustígur 16, fourth floor; Tel 896-52-82; Bus 2 through 7, 110 through 112, 115 to Laekjartorg; Front desk hours vary; 4,000ISK single, 6,000ISK double, 7,500ISK triple June-Oct, 2,500ISK single, 3,000ISK double, 4,500ISK triple Nov-*

April, closed May; V, MC). The 8 spacious rooms all have huge windows, and there are even full-body-length windows in the bathrooms so you can see the city while you shower. Plus, it's right around the corner from the nightlife, and the buffet breakfast kicks butt.

▶▶SPLURGE

The family-ran **Hotel Leifur Eiríksson** *(Skólavörðustígur 45; Tel 562-08-00; 8,800ISK single, 12,900ISK triple May-Sept, 6,500ISK single, 8,500ISK triple Oct, 4,500ISK single, 7,000ISK triple Nov-Mar, closed Dec 19-27; hotel-leifur@Islandia.com; V, MC)* has a terrific location—it's just a five-minute walk down the hill to all the bars. A big fat 500ISK buffet breakfast accompanies the genuinely cheerful service at this small hotel, and some rooms have a terrific view of Hallgrímskirkja. Self-serve tea and coffee are available in the lobby. One slightly odd drawback is the lack of anything larger than a twin bed, but the private bathrooms with killer showers can balance things out.

need To KnOW

Currency Exchange The local currency is the **Icelandic Krona (ISK)**. **Islandbanki** and **Sparisjoður** don't charge commission for currency exchange or travelers checks, and branches are located throughout the city. There is also a currency exchange at the **Tourist Information Center**, and **ATMs** all over down town that will spit out *krona*.

Tourist Information The **Tourist Information Center** *(Bankastræti 2; Tel 562-30-45, Fax 354-562-3057; Bus 2 through 7, 110 through 112, 115 to Laekjartorg; 8:30am-7pm daily May 11-Sept 15; 9am-5pm Mon-Fri, 9am-5pm Mon-Sat, closed Sunday Sept 16-May 10; tour info@tourinfo.is, www.tourist.reykjavik.is)* has heaps of brochures and maps, plus you can purchase foreign currency and travelers checks, get cash advances on credit cards (subject to a fee of 630ISK), and exchange currency.

Public Transportation The public bus system is called **SVR**. Buses run 7am-12am Mon-Sat, 10am-12am Sun, holidays; night buses run Fri, Sat 2:30am-4am. Bus maps are available at the **Tourist Information Center**. Bus fare is 150ISK, bus drivers aren't permitted to give change. **Reykjavík Tourist Cards** can be purchased at the **Tourist Information Center**, many hotels, and the bus station on a one-day *(900ISK)*, two-day *(1,200ISK)*, or three-day *(1,500ISK)* basis, and give you unlimited bus service in the city; admission to several city pools and museums is included in the purchase.

Bike Rental Borgarhjól *(Hverfisgotu 50; Tel 551-56-53; 1,500ISK per day, 900ISK half a day; MC, V)*, conveniently located downtown, will hook you up.

American Express Currently there are no **American Express** offices in Reykjavík.

Health and emergency Emergency: *112.* **Hospital-Landspitalinn:**

(Tel 560-10-00), **Hospital-Sjukrahus Reykjavíkur:** *(Tel 525-10-00)*, **Police Station:** *(Tryggvagata 19; Bus 2, 3, 4, 5, 6, 110, 111, 112, 114, 115; Tel 569-90-25).*

Pharmacies Laugavegs Apotek *(Laugavegi 16, Tel 552-40-45)*, **Vesturbaejar Apotek:** *(Melhaga 20-22, Tel 552-21-90).*

Telephone Country code: *354* (no city code); information: *118*, international operator: *533-50-10.* Phonecards are available at the Tourist Information Center for 500ISK or 1000ISK, but aren't really a necessity—only a few pay phones take them. **AT&T:** *800-900-1*; **MCI:** *800-900-2*; **Sprint:** *800-900-3.*

Airport Keflavik International Airport is 45 minutes out of town. The **Flybus** will take you into town for 750ISK; buses leave every half hour.

Airlines Iceland Air International Services/Reservations Head Office *Tel 505-720*; Located at Hotel Esja, Sudurlandsbraut 2. Bus 5 to hotel. **Arrival and departures info (24-hour)** *Tel 505-05-00.* Tickets *(Tel 505-01-00; 8am-7pm Mon-Fri; 8am-4pm Sat).*

Bus Lines Out of the City B.S.I. coach bus terminal *(Vatnsmyrarvegur, Tel 552-23-00, Bus 7, 110, 111, 112, 115 to BSÍ terminal).* For destinations and timetables, call the terminal.

copenhagen

A millennium ago, Danish Vikings pillaged, looted, and terrorized their European neighbors to the southwest. Once the feared scourge of Europe, the Danes of today could be described as Vikings Lite. They're gentle, highly educated, cosmopolitan, well-traveled, egalitarian, reserved, and rather...hushed. The speaking tone of Copenhageners in public is incredibly *low*, and an unofficial code of silence seems to be in effect on buses and S-trains. But when the booze comes out, the old-school Viking is back: The Danes transform into unrestrained, boisterous, outgoing, sloppy maniacs. On Sunday mornings, when car traffic is nonexistent, the sidewalks fill up with pedestrians who'll wait and wait rather than break the jaywalking law. And yet hookers and hash, though technically illegal, are openly available (in separate parts of the city) every day. Thus are some of the contradictions inherent in the mighty Danish nation.

Denmark has one of the highest standards of living in the world, accompanied by very liberal attitudes towards sex, marriage, religion, domestic spending, the environment, and social solidarity. There's an extensive "cradle-to-grave" welfare state, which of course means mad taxes (like 50 percent income tax!), but it gets them a free university system, universal health insurance, generous pension benefits, and an extensive public transit system. Poverty and homelessness are rare, and the rate of violent crime is one of the lowest in Europe. It feels so safe here, Danish mothers don't think twice about leaving their babies in carriages on busy sidewalks while they run into stores, and you'll feel comfortable walking home alone in nearly every neighborhood at 4am. And this safety hasn't been achieved through beefing up a security presence—you can walk around here for a whole day and not see a single cop. This near-perfection is marred only by how outrageously expensive everything is here.

The language barrier is basically nonexistent—English is the de facto common tongue in town. Although communication won't be a problem with the Copenhageners, don't necessarily expect a gregarious reception when you introduce yourself to a typical local. It takes some time to warm up the average Dane on the street, but when you finally get one going, it's worth the effort. Danes are notorious sarcastic wise-asses, always ready to make a crack.

Meandering cobbled streets, laid-back locals, a relatively low rate of tourism, and summer sunsets at 11pm all help make Copenhagen one of Europe's most livable cities...until Mother Nature steps in and does her thing. The dark, cloudy, cold, and rainy weather that sets in here from October to April can make you feel like your head's stuck in a peat bog. Danes retreat indoors to ride out the seemingly endless winter, but during the few warmer months they come wildly to life, taking in all the precious warm sunlight they possibly can. You can pretty much look at the sky here and figure out the what the collective mood of the city is going to be for the day.

The tourist agencies are well-organized, very helpful, and English-speaking, providing you with anything from hotel bookings to a wealth of pamphlets about events in the city. Pick up a copy of the extensive *Playtime*, aimed at young budget travelers, from **Use It** [see *need to*

dreng meets pige

　　Danes have a reputation for 1) Being tall, blond, and beautiful, 2) Speaking English well, and 3) Having very liberal attitudes towards nearly everything, including the two magic ingredients of most one-night stands, alcohol consumption and premarital sex. Among Norwegians and Swedes, Denmark is known as a bastion of porn, cheap alcohol, and, to a certain extent, soft drug toleration. All of this may be true, but it doesn't make it any easier to pick up a Danish hottie when you're out on the town. Most young Danes go out in groups, and picking up "new" people is usually not a high priority. So how is this difficult task accomplished? First of all, the sharper and darker you dress, the better. Next, never insult Denmark. Yeah, it's small, it's flat, the weather ain't so hot, and it's pricey, but Denmark is the center of the universe in the minds of the Danes. You love it here, the Danes are great, you can't get enough of Copenhagen. Finally, be persistent. You may have to drive the conversation for a long while, but your hard work can pay off—keep pushing, and eventually you'll pull that bashful Dane into a conversation.

know, below], or, for a schedule of upcoming events, grab a copy of **Copenhagen This Week** from **Wonderful Copenhagen Tourist Information** [see *need to know*, below]. If you plan to visit several museums and sights in Copenhagen, get your hands on a Copenhagen Card [see *need to know*, below].

neighborhoods

Helpful, frequent, and heavily used city buses and S-trains (local metro trains) are both clean and punctual [see *need to know*, below]. But the Danes come in a close second to the Dutch for their love of bicycles, so do like the natives and use a bike to get around town [see *need to know*, below].

Høvedbanegården, or **Central Railway Station**, is located in the center of town, just to the east of **Tivoli Gardens** [see *culture zoo*, below] and **Rådhuspladsen**. When you walk out of the main doors of the station onto **Vesterbrogade**, head right to reach the city center.

The first thing you should check out is what Danes have begun calling the "city" section: the town center, the heart of which is **Strøget**, an area of long pedestrian walking streets. Rådhuspladsen, Denmark's version of Times Square, is at the west end of the longest section of Strøget. When Denmark won the European soccer championships in 1992, this square was filled with 100,000 drunken, screaming Danes. The area has also been shrunken a bit by the widely despised, unsightly black bus station that was plopped at the north end of the square in 1996. The large neon Carlsberg Beer ad facing the square is perhaps the most fitting example of Danish modesty. Instead of declaring that their product is #1, the best, or "the king," the sign simply reads, "Probably the best beer in town." On the south side of the square is the **Rådhus**, Copenhagen's city hall [see *culture zoo*, below]. For over 150 years, the Danes have been frequenting the festive Tivoli Gardens, just a two-minute walk west down Vesterbrogade from Rådhuspladsen. At the east end of the longest stretch of Strøget lies **Kongens Nytorv**, or Kings Square. The **Royal Theater** [see *arts scene*, below] sits across Kongens Nytorv from **Nyhavn**, a popular seaside place to get a drink [see *hanging out*, below]. Across the harbor from Nyhavn is the area known as **Christianshavn**. Accessible to the city center by **Knippelsboro Bridge**, Christianshavn has the port feel of an old shipyard and reminds you of the rich Danish seafaring tradition. Finally, there is **Christiania**, the roughly 1,000-member-strong alternative community, just a few steps away.

The area across the small lakes just north of the city center is known as **Nørrebro**. Artists, students, and anybody else searching for energy and 24-hour action have traditionally called this area home. The epicenter of life in Nørrebro is at **Sankt Hans Torv**. Here are numerous cafés which lack the hint of pretension which sometimes prevails in other parts of the city. Great for Sunday hangin' out or when the weather's not so hot. **Østerbro**, east of the city at the northeast end of the "lakes," is quieter, with older and calmer residents, and is generally more green, clean, and spacious than the rest of Copenhagen. Still, one of Copenhagen's most popular options for a great night out can be found here at **Park Cafe and Restaurant** [see *club scene*, below]. **Vesterbro**, just west of the Central Train Station, doesn't exactly have the best reputation. You'll find the somewhat depressing red light district here in this old working-class neighborhood, and a few blocks on one of its streets, **Istedgade**, are often littered with junkies. But this is as close as Denmark comes to a slum, and it doesn't even begin to compare to the more run-down areas in most large European cities. The rest of Vesterbro is tough to pin down: There are respectable residential areas, affordable ethnic takeout places, sections with a large population of Muslim immigrants, and a rapidly emerging trendy nightlife scene. You may also notice occasional "Thai massage parlors" under red lights scattered throughout the area. Put it this way: the girls aren't always Thai, the girls aren't always *girls*, and the massages aren't always massages.

hanging out

When it's warm and the sun is shining, Copenhageners are outdoors—sitting on benches, relaxing at the cafes, and strolling in the parks. If you've been through a Danish winter, you'll certainly understand why sunlight is worshipped here.

Just beyond the eastern end of Kongens Nytorv lies **Nyhavn**, the most popular and scenic spot for hanging out along the harbor. Once a run-down seamen's district, the drunken sailors and prostitutes have now been cleared out, and Nyhavn is now a semi-touristy, yet still appealing, spot for an afternoon beer. A beer at one of the pricey outdoor bar/cafes lining the waterfront will run you 35Dkr, so do like the local kids: Grab a cold one from the supermarket and sit down next to the water. Those boisterous drunken Swedes often show up here, fresh off the ferry and getting completely annihilated on cheap Danish beer.

When in Christiania, join the Greenlanders, Danish hip-hop kids, rasta men, Danish families, and other assorted international characters watching the day slip by at **Cafe Nemoland** (*Bådsmandsstræde 43; Tel 32/95-89-31; Bus 8; 10am-2am daily; No credit cards*). Bottled Tuborg and Carlsberg beers will run you only 15Dkr, and small drafts are an amazingly cheap 10Dkr. Sit at one of the two dozen outdoor picnic tables, complete with patio umbrellas advising, "Say No to Hard Drugs." This obviously doesn't include hash, which most patrons are smoking.

Arguably the most beautiful park in the city center is **Rosenborg Slot**. Adjacent to **Rosenborg Palace and Gardens** [see *culture zoo*, below], these beautiful gardens and well-kept lawns sit in the middle of Copenhagen's most upscale residential area. If it's midsummer and exceptionally warm, don't be shocked to see Danish men and women alike hanging out in their underwear. This park is the perfect place for a picnic, so take along a blanket or towel and a packed lunch. And wear your good panties.

bar scene

If there's one thing Danes love, it's beer. Danish beer. The two biggies are Carlsberg and Tuborg, both tasty pilsners. The Christmas and Easter holidays are celebrated with the release of special seasonal brews. Young Danes drink more alcohol than any other youth in Europe. It's not uncommon for parents to allow their kids to start drinking in their early teens, but the bars are somewhat strict about the age-18 entrance requirement. A typical Danish night out starts with some drinks at home, then out to the bar around 11, and finally a stumble home around 4 or 5am.

Just south of the lakes in the city center is the popular bohemian cafe/bar **Bankerât** *(29 Ahlefeldtsgade; Tel 33/93-69-88; S-train to Nørreport Station, Bus 5, 14, 16 to Nørreport Station; 9:30am-midnight Mon-Fri, 10:30am-midnight Sat, Sun; 49-69Dkr per entree, 35Dkr sandwiches; No credit cards)*, made up of two smallish rooms, one cafe/food oriented and another more fixated on Tuborg. Funky decor, including animal heads on human mannequins, and walls decorated with paintings from local artists draw a somewhat unconventional crowd, as do the reasonable drink prices *(20Dkr for bottled Tuborg)* and kick-ass nachos *(29Dkr)*.

The happy "hour" at Christiania's oldest and weirdest bar, **Woodstock** *(Pusherstreet, Christiania; Tel 31/54-55-86; Bus 8 to Prinsessegade; 9am-5am daily; No credit cards)*, when Tuborg bottles are only 12Dkr, runs from 9am-9pm. If you have a problem with open hash/marijuana sales,

four things to talk to a local about

1. **Bad neighbors**: The Swedes have to deal with a government-controlled alcohol monopoly in their own country, so they come to Copenhagen to get smashed on cheap booze, basically using the city as a resort for indulging in drunken Swedish idiocy. The indignant Danes view the Swedes as immature brats who can't hold their liquor.

2. **Germans don't do comedy**: The Danes, who pride themselves on their humor, see the Germans as lacking any inkling of a sense of humor and singled them out as the lamest people in Europe (tied with the Swedes, of course). If you've ever seen a German sitcom, you'll agree with the Danes....

3. **Can't stand the rain**: Locals are obsessed with the weather, maybe because it's so rotten in Denmark.

4. **Yanks**: Danes have a pretty big interest in American culture. American movies are huge, and American music runs a close second to British in terms of influence.

free-running large dogs, or sharing a table with a motley crew (I said crew, not crüe—get your mind out of the '80s!), this isn't the place for you. But if you *enjoy* meeting freaks, and we do mean freaks, from all over the world, drop on by. The scene here at 4am takes the word "zombie" to a whole new level. Live music happens on an occassional basis but is never planned (!). Other bars in Christiania are more tourist friendly but not much to write home about.

If your tastes run more to whiskey and absinthe, **Krut's Karport** (*Øster Farimagsgade 12; Tel 35/26-86-38; Bus 14, 40 to Øster Farimags-gade; 11am-2am Mon-Sat, noon-1am Sun; MC, V*) is calling for you. This small, cozy Østerbro bar/cafe offers the only legal absinthe in Scandinavia (yes, it's the real deal) and the largest selection of whiskeys in Denmark. Young, casual, laid-back patrons chat to the tune of light jazz as they sip down one of the 114 brands of whiskey available and snack on the small selection of sandwiches. For 700Dkr, you can get your hands on a large bottle of the mildly hallucinogenic licorice of death known as abinsthe—it will send your head spinning and your taste buds pleading for mercy.

The focal point of the rapidly emerging trendy Vesterbro night scene is **Bang & Jensen** (*Istedgade 130; Tel 33/25-53-18; Bus 16 to Istegade; 8pm-2am Mon-Fri, 10am-2am Sat, 10am-12am Sun; No credit cards*). For two years now, this pharmacy-turned-bar has been jammed with a relaxed, under-thirty crowd. The front room has a standard cafe-bar atmosphere, but the back room's got more of a lounge thing going on, with larger tables. Pinball machines, down-to-earth bartenders, a Saturday-only cocktail bar, and music ranging from classic rock to jazz make this a tough place to beat. Drink prices are surprisingly low for such a hot spot, with 22Dkr Tuborg bottles and cocktails at about 50Dkr. Like clock-work, the weekend patrons pack it up at 2am and head over to nearby **Vega** [see *club scene*, below].

The best outdoor terrace for people-watching in the lively Nørrebro district is at **Pussy Galore's Flying Circus** (*30 Sankt Hans Torv; Tel 35/24-53-00; Bus 3 to Blegdamsvej; 8am-2am Mon-Fri, 9am-2am Sat, Sun; 45-118Dkr per dinner entree; MC, V*) Prices are higher than the norm, but, hey, you're paying for trendy atmosphere and professional ser-vice (not to mention the name)! The predominately twentyish crowd is blatantly here to see and be seen. Excellent chow is served: Breakfast buffet, brunch till 4, sandwiches, burgers and a menu of Danish/French street food are served all day, traditional Danish specials come in at lunchtime. If the weather is cooperating when you make your way up to Nørrebro, this is the place to be.

LIVE MUSIC SCENE

What Copenhagen is really known for, musically, is the jazz scene. Blues and rock bands have their place here too, but the quality of the music will vary from night to night. The highlight of the year is the **Copenhagen Jazz Festival** [see *festivals & events*, below] featuring dozens of indoor and outdoor concerts at the peak of the summer season. There's also the **Roskilde Festival** [see *festivals & events*, below], typically held in early July, the largest annual musical event in northern Europe.

On a little street right off Strøget, the **Copenhagen JazzHouse** *(Niels Hemmingsensgade 10; Tel 33/15-26-00; By foot from Strøget; 6pm-5am Thur-Sat; 60-90Dkr usual cover charge for concerts, www.jazzhouse.dk; 50Dkr club entrance fee; MC, V, AE)* is the primo jazz club in Denmark. Various styles of jazz, world music, and improv are performed by talented Danish and international artists every Thursday, Friday, and Saturday, and additional shows are held during the week from September to April. During the **Jazz Festival** [see *festivals & events*, below] this club plays host to a major concert or two daily. Shows begin on Friday and Saturday at 9:30pm and on weeknights at 8:30pm. The space becomes a welcoming and decently priced nightclub at 1am Thursday–Saturday, playing just about everything but techno to the capacity crowd of casual, twentysomething Danes.

Also in the Strøget area, the small, cozy, and candle-lit **Mojo Blues Bar** *(Løngangstræde 21C; Tel 33/11-64-53; Bus 2, 6, 8, 11, 14, 16, 28, 29, 30, 34, 67, 68 to Rådhuspladsen, then a five-minute walk; 8pm-5am daily; www.mojo.dk; Usually a 30-50Dkr cover charge Fri-Sat; No credit cards)* features mostly Scandinavian blues every night of the week. Get here early—drafts are half price from 8 to 10pm, and you might actually score one of the precious few seats. The music is mostly classic Delta blues covers played by guys with names like Lars or Anders. Blues tunes sung in Danish don't usually make the cut—somehow "This weather sucks, I'm out of Tuborg, and my herring jar is empty, baby" just doesn't sound right. The mixed-age, unassuming, and friendly crowd focuses on drinking and the music at hand and are sometimes known to dance in a happy drunken stupor all night.

Passersby on Strøget can hear the live American-style rock blaring from **Lades Kœlder** *(Kattesundet 6; Tel 33/14-00-67; By foot from Strøget; 5pm-4am Sun-Thur, 5pm-5am Fri, Sat; www.lades.dk; 20Dkr cover charge after 10pm; No credit cards)* seven days a week. The decor of this smoky basement bar is simple, with bare walls and sturdy benches around thick wooden tables. The crowd is a mix of foreigners and Danes who prefer screeching guitar solos to techno. On weekends, if you don't

fIVE-0

The cops are pretty cool in Copenhagen, so you don't have to worry about police brutality, corruption, or any of that bad stuff. And you only have to deal with cops if you come across them—and there aren't many cops in the first place, so the law of averages is on your side.

copenhagen bars, clubs and culture zoo

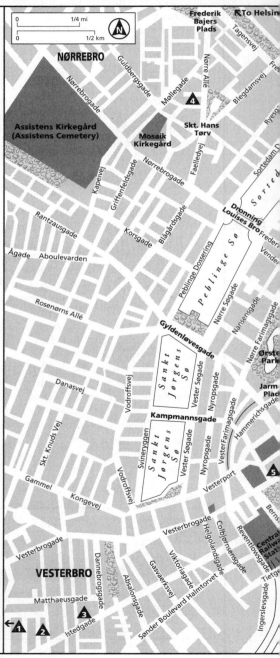

BARS/CLUBS ▲
Bang & Jensen **3**
Baron & Baroness **5**
Copenhagen Jazz-
  house **12**
Ideal Nightclub **1**
Mojo Blues Bar **10**
NASA/Fever **18**
Pussy Galore's
  Flying Circus **4**
Tivoli **7**
Woodstock **2**

CULTURE ZOO ●
Amalienborg Palace **21**
Botanisk Have **16**
Christiansborg Castle **11**
Danish Museum
  of Decorative Art **20**
The Little Mermaid **19**
Museum Erotica **14**
Ny Carlsberg
  Glyptotek **9**
Rådhus **6**
Rosenborg Palace
  and Gardens **15**
Rundetaarn **13**
Statens Museum
  for Kunst **17**
Tivoli Gardens **8**

get there before the band goes on at 10:30pm, you'll be left without a seat—and you'll miss the cheap 20Dkr drafts that are sold until 10pm.

It's not every night you can hang out in a Renaissance castle, complete with thick stone walls, carved wooden ceilings, suits of armor, and mounted game trophies. Okay, so it's not a real castle, but the 38 million Danish kroner used to renovate the **Baron & Baroness** *(Vesterbrogade 2E; Tel 33/16-01-01; S-train to Central Railway Station or Vesterport, or Bus 2, 6, 8, 11, 14, 16, 28,29, 30, 34, 67, 68 to Rådhuspladsen; 11am-2am Sun-Wed, 11am-5am Thur, 11am-6am Fri, 11am-9am Sat; 40-50Dkr cover charge after 11pm Fri, Sat; 99-179Dkr per entree; MC, V, AE)* did an excellent job of imitating one in this bar/restaurant/club. Located across the street from **Tivoli Gardens** [see *culture zoo,* below] acoustic folk guitar is played here nightly until about 11pm, and on Friday and Saturday nights the "everything but techno" second-floor disco gets packed. From Thursday through Saturday nights, the rules tighten up: You can't be wearing sneakers, jeans, or shorts, or be under 21. The international crowd is generally between 21 and 35, and a pint of Tuborg will run you about 38Dkr. They serve two kinds of food: cuisine fit for a baron, including steak, lamb, and salmon; and a wide range of Asian dishes. Try one of their excellent wines or champagnes.

One of the most active venues in Scandinavia for live music, the **Vega-House of Music** *(40 Enghavevej; Tel 33/25-70-11; Bus 3, 16 to Enghave Plads; www.vega.dk; 50-200Dkr for concerts; MC, V)* was designed by renowned Danish architect Vilhelm Lauritzen, giving it a '50s look and high-quality acoustics. Vega's top-notch and varied repertoire includes the likes of Björk, George Clinton, Prince, and Burning Spear. Look for their promotional flyers plastered on walls all over town, or check out their website. Slightly out of the way, west of Vesterbro, but worth a trek.

CLUB SCENE

Clubbing in Copenhagen is not for those low on kroner—drinks are more expensive than the norm, and you'll pay a pretty hefty cover charge just to get inside. Danish club kids drink at home for several hours before heading out, and don't even think of going out before midnight or so. Most clubs here don't shut down till about 5am and continue to serve alcohol right up to closing. On Thursday nights, some clubs drop their cover charges, bringing out a more student-age crowd. Dress codes are relatively relaxed, but shorts, sneakers, and jeans are definite no-nos at most of the venues. At most of the more popular clubs, beefy, shaved-head Viking wannabes man the doors, enforcing the moderately snobby door policies.

You enter **Park Cafe and Restaurant** *(79 Østerbrogade; Tel 35/42-62-48; Bus 6, 14 to Østerbrogade; 11am-1am Sun-Wed, till 4am Thur, till 5am Fri, Sat; 50Dkr cover charge Fri, Sat after 10pm; 68-74Dkr brunch, 52-95Dkr per lunch entree; MC, V, AE)* to the tune of chandeliers, hardwood floors, Persian rugs, and a small stage where, if you're there on a Thursday, Friday, or Saturday night, a live funk, soul, rock, or jazz band

Rules of the Game

You'll only be hassled by the police if you're very drunk and your behavior is incredibly obnoxious or endangering the welfare of other people—and even then, the chances that they'll bother with you are pretty remote. There is no open-container law in Copenhagen—but if you're drinking in the train station, you may be politely asked by police to keep your beer under your jackets. The drinking age is 18, but the age restrictions are only enforced at bars—12-year-old kids sucking on lollipops can buy bottles of whiskey in the supermarket, all they have to do is tell the cashier that they're buying it for Daddy. No questions asked! Things get a little tougher when it comes to drugs. Hard and soft, they're all illegal in Copenhagen, and, technically, you can get in big trouble with the authorities if you get snared with anything—even a gram or so of hash. The situation in Christiania is complicated and somewhat risky too [see *only here*, below].

will be playing. Make your way past the bar and up the winding stairs, and you come to the large outdoor terrace. The surprises continue as you come upon two disco floors and six more bars beyond that. This Vesterbro favorite holds 1,500 people, and it *constantly* gets packed on the weekends with a semi-trendy, over-21, and overwhelmingly Danish crowd. Thursday nights, when the cover charge goes away, see a less chic, student-heavy crowd. Drink prices are steep—45Dkr half liters of Tuborg, and 35Dkr import bottles—and the excellent restaurant, serving everything from sandwiches, stuffed peppers, and huge burgers to creative salads, is tough on the wallet, too. The popular Sunday brunch is relatively manageable, though.

Packed, unpretentious, and cutting-edge, the **Ideal Nightclub** *(40 Enghavevej; Tel 33/25-70-16; Bus 3, 16 to Enghave Plads; 6pm-4am Thur, till 5am Fri, Sat; 30Dkr cover charge after 1am Fri, Sat; MC, V)* caters to the crowd that's making its way into the newly trendy Vesterbro neighborhood where it's located: chic but not dressed to kill, friendly, mainly under thirty, and from all types of backgrounds. The first floor plays laid-back Latin or jazz, and house music dominates on the second level, keeping the dance floor boiling until the wee hours. The focus of the club is not image but music, bringing in the latest trends in the global club scene. You have to be over 20 to enter, but there's absolutely no dress code, and the cover charge doesn't kick in until after 1am. Ideal is connected to **Vega-House of Music** [see *live music scene*, above].

Okay, so maybe one in 50 of you'll actually get in, but we've gotta tell you about this place. If you're on the hunt for a lavish, trendy, futuristic, and exclusive private party atmosphere, say your prayers, meet some influential people, buy new clothes, and head to the Kongens Nytorv area to **NASA** *(Baron Boltens Gård, Gothersgade 8f; Tel 33/93-74-15; Bus 1, 6, 9, 10, 19, 29, 31, 42, 43 to Kongens Nytorv; Midnight-6am Fri, Sat only; 3,000Dkr to reserve a table; AE, V, MC)*. There is no way to get in to NASA without a connection—the five-star hotels and high-end limo services in town are sometimes allowed to send over guests, but that's it. With a sterile, all-white latex interior straight out of *2001: A Space Odyssey*, NASA attracts the most gorgeous and pretentious people in town. Rumored to be a favorite hangout for the Crown Prince of Denmark, and a regular stop for celebrities when they happen to find themselves in Copenhagen, the club is a living manifestation of conspicuous consumption...and it's also one hell of a party. If you fail to make a connection to get in to NASA, a more reasonable option is **Fever** *(Baron Boltens Gård, Gothersgade 8f; Tel 33/93-74-15; Bus 1, 6, 9, 10, 19, 29, 31, 42, 43 to Kongens Nytorv; Midnight-6am Fri, Sat only; 50Dkr; AE, V, MC)*, located directly underneath NASA. Local DJs play hip-hop and house until 6am for a younger crowd that lacks most—but not all—of NASA's exclusivity or snootiness. You can float upstairs to the side room of NASA so that, in the words of the owner, "people can get just a taste" of what lies next door. As you can imagine, drinks are pretty steep at both places: Beers run around 40Dkr, and mixed drinks start at 60Dkr.

arts scene

The contemporary art scene here is surprisingly lively and well-supported for such a small capital. Over 100 galleries and museums dedicated to all aspects of contemporary art have set up shop within the Copenhagen metro area. Most famous for contemporary furniture design in the postwar era, Danish design is typically associated with soft, rounded lines and ergonomic structure. Pick up the small brochure containing a detailed listing and map of all contemporary art venues in *Copenhagen and Environs* at museums and galleries or get it online at *www.KultuNaut.dk.* To mingle with the artsy crowd, try **Bankeråt** [see *bar scene*, above].

▶▶VISUAL ARTS

Five exhibitions are shown annually at **Kunstforeningen** *(48 Gl. Strand; Tel 33/36-02-60; Bus 5, 29 to Nybrogade, or five-minute walk from Rådhuspladsen; 11am-5pm Tue-Sun, closed Mon; www.kunstforeningen.dk; 30Dkr adult, 20Dkr students; No credit cards)*, including video, multi-media, Modernist painting, installations, glass, and animation. This centrally located multiple-floor 19th-century exhibition hall is an excellent place to start your gallery crawl.

Next door to the Kunstforeningen, the small **Fotografisk Center** *(48 Gl. Strand; Tel 33/93-09-96; Bus 5, 29 to Nybrogade, or five-minute walk from Rådhuspladsen; 11am-5pm, closed Mon; www.photography.dk; 20Dkr adults, 15Dkr students; No credit cards)* mostly displays photographs by Scandinavian artists, but other internationally renowned photographers sometimes pop up here too. Unconventional black and white nudes are common.

Leave it to the resourceful Danes to find good use for yet another empty church. Located right off Strøget, the **Nikolaj Copenhagen Contemporary Art Center** *(Nikolaj Plads; Tel 33/93-16-26; By foot from Strøget; Noon-5pm daily; 20Dkr entrance fee, Wed free admission; No credit cards)* displays photography, mixed media, video, and installations from international artists for one to two months at a time.

▶▶PERFORMING ARTS

The season for both the Royal Danish Ballet and the Royal Danish Opera concludes in late May and starts up again in early August. For information on performances during the summer, call or stop by **Use It** [see *need to know*, below], where the staff can fill you in on both English and Danish performances on other stages. At **Tivoli Gardens** [see *culture zoo*, below,] there is also **Pantomime Theatre, Children's Theatre, Tivoli's Concert Hall**, and an **Open Air Stage** with a variety of performances. For gay theater, check out what's planned at **Bøssehuset** [see *gay scene*, below].

Completed in 1748, the **Royal Theatre** *(Kongens Nytorv; Tel 33/69-69-69; Bus 1, 6, 9, 10, 19, 29, 31, 42, 43 to Kongens Nytorv; Box office 1pm-7pm Mon-Sat, performances 8pm Mon-Sat; www.kgl-teater.dk; MC, V, AE)*, near Kongens Nytorv, is home to both the world-famous Royal Danish Opera and the Royal Danish Ballet. You can get discounted tickets at the theater after 5pm on the day of the performance, but in the winter months, when Danes of all ages commonly frequent the ballet and opera, it might pay to book in advance. The Opera's repertoire includes Mozart, Verdi, and Wagner, and Jerome Robbins, Bournonville, and Balanchine are favorites of the Ballet.

gay SCENE

Without question, Copenhagen is one of the most gay-friendly cities in the world. Since 1989, gay marriage has been permitted by civil ceremony, granting homosexuals the same legal rights as married heteros. The sizable, flourishing gay community has plenty of options in terms of bars and clubs to frequent. **Ørstedsparken**, a beautiful park located near Nörreport Station, is a well-known gay cruising location. Pick up a copy of *PAN* magazine at any gay club or bar, published by the **National Danish Organization for Gays and Lesbians**, or check out their website at *www.lbl.dk.*

Bøssehuset (Gay Men's Liberation Front) *(Christiania, Refshalevej; Tel 32/95-98-72; Bus 8 to Prinsessegade; Hours vary)* organizes gay theater productions, gay film festivals, drag queen beauty contests, and a gay a capella group. Call ahead and see what is planned or stop by Bøssehuset when you take a stroll around Christiania.

But the first stop for a gay traveler in Copenhagen should be **Sebastian Café Bar** *(Hyskenstraede 10; Tel 33/32-22-79; Noon-2am daily, restaurant closes at 9pm; V, MC, AE)*, a large sprawling cafe popular with a gay and lesbian crowd of all ages. Weekend evenings draw a younger crowd for the pre-party hours.

Just around the corner is **heaven** *(Kompgnistraede 18; Tel 33/15-19-*

00; *Noon-2am daily, restaurant closes at 10pm; No credit cards)*, drawing a slightly older crowd than Sebastian. It also gets more crowded on the weekends, maybe because of its proximity to Pan Disco. The soundtrack can lean a little heavily on camp classics, but that doesn't detract from the all-around pleasant atmosphere.

If you're after a quiet night, **Pan Disco** *(Knabrostraede 3; Tel 33/11-37-84; www.pan-cph.dk; Cafe 8pm-5am daily, till 6 Fri, Sat; Club from 11pm Wed-Sat; closed Mon, Tue in winter)* is not for you. With two floors (pop and 80s upstairs, hard house and techno downstairs), three bars, and a cushy chill-out zone, it's no suprise that Pan is the city's favorite gay nightspot—not that there's much competition....

CULTURE ZOO

On the plus side, the quality of the museums and castles here is excellent in nearly all instances. On the minus side, the admission prices are usually sky-high, and navigating a day on the bus going from museum to museum can be a big pain in the rump—getting around by bike will prove be much less of a hassle.

Rundetaarn (Round Tower) *(52 Købmagergade 52a; Tel 33/73-03-73; By foot from Strøget; 10am-8pm Mon-Sat, noon-8pm Sun June-Aug, 10am-5pm Mon-Sat, noon-5pm Sun Sept-May; 15Dkr admisson; No credit cards)*: Located in the city center, this 17th-century tower/observatory gives you an excellent panoramic view of Copenhagen, the Øresund Bridge, and the Swedish coastline. It'll quickly make you realize that the Øresund, the new link between Denmark and Sweden, is one hell of an engineering feat.

Tivoli Gardens *(Vesterbrogade 3; Tel 33/15-10-01; S-Trains to Central Railway Station or Bus 1, 8, 11, 12, 13, 30, 34, to Tivoli Gardens; Season Apr 23-Sept 26, 11am-midnight Sun-Thur, till 1am Fri, Sat; www.tivoli.dk; 45Dkr admission June 14-Aug 15, 39Dkr admission Apr 23-June 13 and Aug 16-Sept 26; Multi-ride ticket Tivoli Pass 178Dkr)*: This magical amusement park and garden features rides, illuminated fountains, theater, concerts, 30 places to eat, and...fireworks! To find out the daily program of events, visit the Tivoli Gardens homepage, ask at the Tivoli reception desk, look for the promotional posters at the front entrance on Vesterbrogade, or check in *Copenhagen This Week.*

Ny Carlsberg Glyptotek *(7 Dantes Plads, Tel 33/14-82-41; Bus 1, 8, 10, 30, 32 to Dantes Plads; 10am-4pm daily, closed Mon; www.glyptoteket.dk; 30Dkr admission, free Wed, Sun; No credit cards)*: An example of Carlsberg beer money put to good use, this museum is a magnificent display of Egyptian, Greek, Roman, Etruscan, French Impressionist, and 19th-century Danish art. A beautiful winter garden connects to neighboring rooms with works by Van Gogh, Manet, Monet, Degas, Cezanne, and Gauguin.

Museum of Danish Resistance *(Churchillparken, Tel 33/13- 77-14; Bus 1, 6, 9 or S-train to Østerport Station; 10am-4pm Tue-Sat, till 5pm Sun May 1-Sept 1; 11am-3pm Tue-Sat, till 4pm Sun Sept 2-Apr 30; Free*

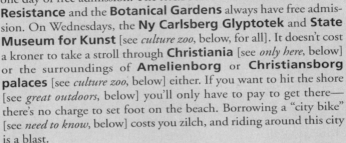

down and out

If you're not careful here, you'll find yourself collecting empty Tuborg bottles for the deposit. If it comes to that, hit some of the museums when they have their one day of free admission. The **Museum of Danish Resistance** and the **Botanical Gardens** always have free admission. On Wednesdays, the **Ny Carlsberg Glyptotek** and **State Museum for Kunst** [see *culture zoo*, below, for all]. It doesn't cost a kroner to take a stroll through **Christiania** [see *only here*, below] or the surroundings of **Amelienborg** or **Christiansborg palaces** [see *culture zoo*, below] either. If you want to hit the shore [see *great outdoors*, below] you'll only have to pay to get there—there's no charge to set foot on the beach. Borrowing a "city bike" [see *need to know*, below] costs you zilch, and riding around this city is a blast.

If you still insist on the party lifestyle when you're broke, buy beer at the supermarket and sit along the water's edge at **Nyhavn** [see *hanging out*, above]. Or get an early start at **Woodstock**'s [see *bar scene*, above] all-day happy hour. From there, you can walk to the end of Pusherstreet and slurp down a few 10Dkr draft beers from **Cafe Nemoland** [see *hanging out*, above]. When darkness falls and you want to hit the clubs, **Ideal Nightclub** [see *club scene*, above] doesn't charge a cover until after 1am.

admission): Well-done tribute to the Danish resistance against the Nazi occupiers, a highlight being the rescue of Danish Jews from German hands. Hitler may have had Denmark in mind as a kind of Aryan sperm bank, but the Danes worked to shuttle Jews to safety in Sweden.

Christiansborg Castle (*Christiansborg Slotspads; Tel 33/92-64-92; Bus 1, 2, 6, 8, 9, 10, 19, 28 to Christiansborg Palace; www.slotte.dk; 20Dkr admission; No credit cards*): The current Christiansborg Castle was completed in 1928, following fires that destroyed the three previous castles that stood on this spot. The founding father of Copenhagen, Bishop Absalon, had the original castle completed in 1167. Guided tours of the original castle ruins (*Castle ruins and history exhibition 9:30am-3:30pm daily May-Sept, same hours Tue, Thur, Sat, Sun Oct-Apr*) and the lavish royal state reception rooms (*Tel 33/92-64-92; 11am, 3pm daily May-Sept; 11am, 3pm Tue, Thur, Sat, Sun Oct-Apr; 40Dkr admission; No credit cards*) are available year round.

Rådhus (City Hall) and **Olsen's World Clock** (*Rådhuspladsen; Tel 33/66-25-82; Bus 2, 6, 8, 11, 14, 16, 28, 29, 30, 34, 67, 68, to Rådhuspladsen; 9:30am-3pm Mon-Fri; Free admission to Rådhus; Clock tower 10am-4pm Mon-Fri, till 1pm Sat; 20Dkr admission; No credit cards*):

fESTIVALS and EVENTS

Every year, **Tivoli's Christmas Market** *(Christmas season; Tivoli Gardens; Tel 33/15-10-01)* turns **Tivoli Gardens** [see *culture zoo*, above] into a bustling holiday marketplace, complete with ice skating, ornate decorations, and Christmas luncheons.

Every Christmas Eve, **Christmas for the Homeless** *(5pm Dec 24; Den Grå Hall, Christiania)* volunteers from the Christiania community [see *only here*, below] organize and throw a holiday dinner party for the homeless of Copenhagen. All are welcome to join, and the party continues into Christmas morning with live music and dancing.

For info on the annual **Copenhagen Carnival** *(Late May; Tel 33/11-13-25)* contact the **Wonderful Copenhagen Tourist Office** [see *need to know*, below]. Celebrated in various venues throughout the city, this festival has parades, dancing, and music, with an emphasis on entertaining the kiddies.

The annual **Midsummer's Eve** *(Late June)* celebration brings bonfires throughout the city, particularly in Nyhavn, Amager, and Bellevue beaches. Huge Midsummer's Eve bonfires really bring out the old Viking spirit in the Danes.

One of Europe's largest annual rock events, the **Roskilde Festival**, takes place in Roskilde, west of Copenhagen *(Late June-early July; Tel 46/36-66-13; www.Roskilde-festival.dk.)*, drawing 60,000-plus people for a four-day outdoor party that over the past decade has featured everybody from Al Green to Nashville Pussy.

The musical highlight of the year in Copenhagen is the **Copenhagen Jazz Festival** *(Early July annually; Tel 33/93-20-13)*, with several hundred indoor and outdoor concerts held in various venues throughout the city over 10 days. Some of the open-air concerts are free.

The **International Summer Theatre** *(Late Aug; Tel 33/15-15-64)* at various venues throughout the city, featuring over a dozen theater, music, circus, dance, and multimedia performances by artists from several nations.

The annual **Copenhagen International Fashion Fair** *(Early Aug; Bella Center; Tel 32/47-21-11)* highlights the latest fashions in men's and women's clothing, with an emphasis on Danish and other Scandinavian designers.

Completed in 1905, Copenhagen's city hall contains a highly precise astronomical clock and a 346-foot tower.

Statens Museum for Kunst *(48-50 Sølvgade; Tel 33/74-84-94;*

Bus 10, 14, 40, 42 to Statens Museum for Kunst; 10am-5pm Tue, Thur-Sun, till 8pm Wed, closed Mon; www.smk.dk; 40Dkr adults, 25Dkr students, permanent collection free Wed; No credit cards): Denmark's recently renovated national gallery, displaying Danish and international works of art from the 17th century to the present.

The Little Mermaid (Langelinie; Bus 1, 6, 9, 19, 29 to Esplanaden): she's very small, has had her head stolen twice, and stands against a backdrop of an industrial shoreline. It may be a great story, but it's been a long time since anyone has walked away from this tourist attraction in a state of awe.

Danish Museum of Decorative Art (68 Bredgade; Tel 33/14-94-52; Bus 1, 6, 9, 10, 19, 29, 31, 42, 43 to Kongens Nytorv; 10am-4pm Tue-Fri, noon-4pm Sat, Sun, closed Mon; www.mus-kim.dk; 35Dkr adults, 20Dkr students; No credit cards): An extensive exhibition of contemporary Danish and international furniture, ceramics, textiles, silver, and glass, plus an impressive collection of foreign and Danish decorative art from the Middle Ages to the 20th century.

Amalienborg Palace (Slotspads; Tel 33/12-21-86; Bus 1, 6, 9, 19, 29 to Amelienborg Palace; 11am-4pm Tue-Sun, closed Jan-Apr, 11am-4pm daily during May , 10am-4pm daily June-Aug, 11am-4pm daily Sept 1-Oct 31, 11am-4pm Tue-Sun, closed Mon Nov 1-mid-Dec, closed mid-Dec-Jan 2; www.slotte.dk; 35Dkr adults, 25Dkr students; No credit cards): Part of the residence of the Danish Royal Family is now open to the public, giving a rare opportunity to get a glimpse of recently refurbished Glucksborg family royal apartments. The beautiful brick courtyard in the middle of four palaces is itself worth the visit—especially since it's open 24 hours and *free*. The changing of the guard is at 11am daily.

Botanisk Have (Botanical Gardens) (128 Gothersgade; Tel 35/32-22-40; Bus 31, 42, 43 to Botanisk Have; 8:30am-6pm Apr-Sept, till 4pm Oct-Mar; www.nathimus.ku.dk; Free admission): Outside, the gardens present you with an enormous variety of cold-weather plants and trees, walking paths, and a beautiful pond. Indoors, the palm house is the perfect way to escape a rainy day, pretending you're in the tropics.

Rosenborg Palace and Gardens (4A Øster Voldgade; Tel 33/15-32-86; Bus 31, 42, 43 to Kongens Have; 11am-2pm Tues, Fri, Sun Jan 2-Apr 30, 10am-4pm daily May-Sept, 11am-3pm Oct, 11am-2pm Tues, Fri, Sun Nov 1-Dec 17, closed Dec 18-Dec 27, 11am-3pm Dec 27-30; 40Dkr adults, 30 Dkr students; No credit cards): A 17th-century Renaissance castle, with the honor of being the official home of the crown jewels and treasury of the Danish royal family. Cool in a Robin Leach kinda way.

Museum Erotica (Købmagergade 24; Tel 33/12-03-11; By foot from Strøget; 10am-11pm daily May-Sept, 11am-8pm daily Oct-Apr; www.museumerotica.dk; 59Dkr admission; No credit cards): A detailed historical look at the evolution of human sexuality and a glimpse into the sex lives of famous philosophers, celebrities, and others (ooh!). After the sex museum in Amsterdam, this one receives the silver medal in the contest for Northern Europe's top sex museum.

only Here

In the early '70s, an abandoned military barracks in Christan-shavn was squatted by a bunch of hippies who wanted to build a communal lifestyle. The number of people resettling in the greater Copenhagen area was so high, the police were unable to evict the squatters (there was no place for them to go), and eventually, in 1971, the hippies declared their enclave a "free city." Since then, the Danish government's position toward what has become Christiania has been inconsistent. Initially, they accepted this "social experiment," but soon they started making threats of closure. Meanwhile the community became better-organized and set up successful collective shops, musical events, and garbage disposal and recycling programs, and they eventually filed a lawsuit against the Danish government to stop the continued threats. In 1978 the case was lost in the Supreme Court, mainly because there were signs of a growing heroin problem in the district. So by 1980, Christiania-ites banned heroin and all other hard drugs from the area, but throughout the '80s and '90s, the controversy surrounding Christania raged on. Pressure from the police, conservative politicians, and neighboring countries threaten its independence, and now there's the added factor of increasing pressure from the EU to shut it down. (There is a vehement anti-EU sentiment within Christiania—the sign on the wooden gate that marks the exit of Freetown warns, "You are now entering the EU" as you step back into Copenhagen proper.) But for now the experiment stands.

So what is it, exactly? Well, it's *not* a violent, junkie-ridden district

modification

The only things more popular than herring in Copenhagen appear to be tattoos and/or piercings, so you'll come across lots of needle-jockeys in your wanderings around town. And the fashion-conscious Danes are *always* in search of a trendy haircut, so there's no end of cool chop shops here.

Located in the alternative "Latin Quarter," Mette Hintze's **Piercing-klinik** *(Studiestr de 16; Tel 33/32-31-13; By foot from Strøget; 11am-5:30pm Wed-Fri, 10am-2pm Sat; No credit cards)* is your best option for any type of professional body piercing. Known as the "mistress of the rings," Mette has an incredibly extensive collection of body piercing paraphernalia in her "clinic," including glow-in-the-dark tongue rings, nose bones from Borneo, and instructional videos. Barbed wire criss-crosses the ceiling, and framed photographs of pierced hot dogs and pacifiers where you have to be constantly worried about your personal safety. And it's not really a mini-Amsterdam: Although "Pusherstreet" in Christiania is lined with small stands selling hash and marijuana, they are technically illegal. If people wander out of Christiania with their newly acquired stash, they're breaking Danish law. And though the Danish soft drug laws may not be enforced on a regular basis in Christiania, police raids do occur on Pusherstreet. They're not nearly as frequent as they once were, but there's always a remote possibility that they'll occur. Hard drugs are absolutely forbidden anywhere in Christiania, and picture-taking in the area of Pusherstreet may result in a smashed camera. In other areas of Christiania, always ask before you take pictures. Weapons and violence are banned, and running on or near Pusherstreet is frowned upon. The rest of Christiania is a basically a quaint, modern, self-governing village. Bars, restaurants, clubs, stores, workshops, bike shops, a post office, an outdoor trinket market, a soccer field, a picturesque lake, kindergartens, and playgrounds are just a few of the things you should expect to see. And you won't see cars—Christiania is a pedestrian-friendly area. Dogs (some of which are huge) run free throughout Christiania, especially around Pusherstreet. Den Grå Hall occasionally holds a big-name concert, with performers like Bob Dylan, Gwar, Phish, and Rage Against the Machine making recent appearances.

give you a clue as to what goes on behind the curtain when Mette gets her hands on you.

Holed away in a seedy basement in Nyhavn, **Tattoo Bob** (*Lille Strandstræde 3; Tel 33/15-19-47; Bus 1, 6, 9, 10, 19, 29 to Kongens Nytorv; Noon-9pm daily; No credit cards*) is the type of place a where a drunken sailor would get a tattoo on his chest. One of the oldest tattoo shops in town, with over 50 years' experience, most of the designs seem focused around Vikings and the Danish flag. However, the artists are quite flexible and can also do a variety of designs, from Japanese characters and Celtic motifs to biomechanical weirdness.

The young trendies get their hair done at **Kaiser Schnitt Frisør** (*Istedgade 99; Tel 33/22-00-56; Bus 16 to Istedgade; 10:15am-7pm Thur-Tue, closed Wed; No credit cards*), a small, professional, and affordable neighborhood salon in Vesterbro. Cuts will run you 250Dkr or so, and an appointment is absolutely mandatory.

great outdoors

In the summer, when the Danes emerge from their wintertime hibernation, the bikers, joggers, rollerbladers, and skaters come out in full force, the canal tours start up again, and the parks fill up with ecstatic sunbathers. Located just north of Strøget, **Street Machine** *(Kronprinsensgade 3; Tel 33/33-95-11; By foot from Strøget; 10am-6pm Mon-Fri, till 5pm Sat; MC, V)* leans more heavily towards clothing and the "skater look" but also has a decent supply of decks, trucks, etc. The workers always know if an upcoming competition is planned or where to find the current hot spots in the city for skating—which, for now, are the halfpipe/bowl in Christiania and at Ølledparken in Østerbro.

Jogging along the uncrowded, smooth, wide, and well-groomed paths that wrap around the scenic lakes north of the city center should inspire you. The air is clean, the view is terrific, and it may be hard to believe you're actually in a capital city.

If you're here in summertime, the beaches near Copenhagen should not be missed. The best "strip" of sand near the city is **Bellevue Beach** *(Bus 6 or S-train to Klampenborg Station)*, just under 12 kilometers out of town. Full of partially naked and non-naked Danes soaking up as much sun as possible, this beach is frequented by those (whose gender will go unnamed) who like to gawk, gaze, and (attempt to) pick up members of the opposite sex. On a sunny weekend afternoon, it may be a challenge to locate a piece of sand large enough for your blanket.

A canal tour through Copenhagen is worth it. Most of the tours are about an hour long and are conducted in several languages. The routes of the sightseeing boats are fairly similar, passing by several castles, churches, the Holmen area, and **The Little Mermaid** [see *culture zoo*, above], and the season lasts from early April till mid-October. Tours depart from Nyhavn [see *hanging out*, above] every half hour from 10am till 7pm in midsummer, till 5pm in the slower months. The two major companies are **Canal Tours** *(Tel 33/13-31-05; 45Dkr for a guided tour)* and **Netto Boats** *(Tel 32/54-41-02; 20Dkr for a guided tour)*. Besides the prices, there's little difference between the two.

stuff

Wise travelers know that Scandinavia is not the place to do your European souvenir shopping—the prices are insane, although nothing like as bad as London, for example! On a more positive note, there are clusters of centrally located streets where you can find cheap secondhand clothes, records, and CDs. The vast majority of stores accept all major credit cards and the shopping hours are generally 10am till 6pm Monday through Friday and 10am till 4pm on Saturday.

▶▶**BREAKING THE BANK**

The area of Strøget closest to Kongens Nytorv is the main area for upscale shopping, with stores like **Benneton, Gianni Versace**, **Gucci**, **Bang & Olufsen**, and **Royal Copenhagen Crystal**. You'll also find Estée

bike wars

So you think you know the Danes: a fairly reserved, buttoned-down group that, while they have some liberal ideas and cut loose every once in a while, certainly couldn't be called "wild." Right? Then explain this: In October of 1996, 18 people were injured and two killed when a mortar rocket was fired at a Hell's Angels hangout by a rival motorcycle gang. And this was not an isolated incident. The infamous Biker War—among the Angels, a group called Bullshit (which disbanded and then reformed as the Banditos), and several other groups—has been going on for decades. In the '70s everything was fine, with the bikers peacefully going about their drug smuggling and petty theft. But since a falling-out between the Angels and Bullshit in the early '80s, they've been bickering and shooting and ambushing. Since the mortar rocket incident, though, you won't see bikers around much. A "Biker Law" was passed, prohibiting public biker gatherings and shutting down their main hangs.

Things seem to be pretty peaceful now, and the police are back to investigating the biker gangs for their shady business deals rather than their machine-gun attacks.

Lauder, Revlon, L'Oréal, and Christian Dior at the elegant **Magasin** (*Kongens Nytorv 13; 10am-7pm Mon-Thur, till 8pm Fri, 9am-5pm Sat*) department store. As you move away from Kongens Nytorv towards Rådhuspladsen on Strøget, the stores become more mainstream. The prices tend to come down, with shops lke **Levi's**, **The Sweater Market**, and **The Amber Specialist** popping up.

▶▶**THRIFT**

All of the following shops are located on the small streets just to the north and northwest of Strøget, where there are tons of great alternatives to the pricy options on the main walking street. **5th Avenue Copenhagen** (*Larsbjørnsstræde 8; Tel 33/13-02-88; By foot from Strøget; 11am-6pm Mon-Thur, till 7pm Fri, till 4pm Sat; MC, V, AE*) is the polar opposite of Fifth Avenue, New York. Most of the clothes are leftovers from the '70s and '80s, like used Boy Scout uniforms, secondhand hats, coats, jackets, the ugliest (and thus the coolest) Hawaiian shirts ever created, and old army/navy gear. There are also bell bottoms and a selection of new clothes that tend to imitate the funky styles of the past.

▶▶**TUNES**

2nd Hand Records (*Larsbjørnsstræde 20; Tel 33/15-00-03; By foot from Strøget; Noon-5:30pm Mon-Thur, till 7pm Fri, 11am-3pm Sat; No credit*

12 hours in copenhagen

1. **Tivoli Gardens**: Okay, so it's the biggest tourist attraction in Denmark—it's still got an overwhelmingly charming allure that makes Disneyland look like a plastic rip-off [see *culture zoo*, above].

2. **Copenhagen Jazz Festival**: A pint of Tuborg Classic in hand, the Danish summer, and dozens of world-class jazz performers: oh, baby [see *festivals & events*, above].

3. **Copenhagen by bike**: The bike lanes are well-maintained, the streets are as flat as a pancake, and it's a hell of a lot more fun than walking!

4. **Base Camp Holmen**: A bizarre yet somehow attractive blend of a former military-industrial complex, club, and salsa bar. A unique time is always in store, whether you go for brunch, clubbing, or to grill your meal with your feet in the sand [see *eats*, below].

5. **Christiania**: An oasis of self-government, collective spirit, and individual freedom, just a five-minute bike ride from the center of town.

6. **Ideal Nightclub (Vega)**: Come join the legions of hip-yet-down-to-earth twentysomethings at this hip-yet-unassuming club [see *club scene*, above].

7. **Nyhavn**: Old wooden sailboats, the setting sun, a drink in hand, and lots of smiles. Soak up those precious rays and grab a seat along Copenhagen's beautiful waterfront.

8. **Kaffesalonen**: Mouth-watering '50s-style food, old-school decor, exceptional service, and lakefront seating [see *eats*, below].

9. **Bang & Jensen**: The young hipsters hang at the bar in the quickly-rising Vesterbro area. Come rap with beautiful Scandinavian kids in their fun, trendy neighborhood [see *bar scene*, above].

10. **Copenhagen JazzHouse**: A no-nonsense, risk-free option for a night on the town. The place is packed, unassuming, affordable, and pure Copenhagen [see *live music scene*, above].

cards), just next door to **5th Avenue**, can provide you with all kinds of used CDs and LPs from only 5Dkr. The staff is very friendly in this small basement shop and will help you locate the used CD you have always wanted. Artists range from Milli Vanilli to the Grateful Dead. Located off Larsbjørnsstrœde, **Sex Beat Records** (*Studiestrœde 18; Tel 33/12-82-*

92; By foot from Strøget; 10:30am-6pm Mon-Thur, till 7pm Fri, 10am-3pm Sat; MC, V) is the authority on alternative, rock, metal, and punk in Copenhagen. The second-floor shop has a decent selection of both new and used CDs and vinyl. Tickets for concerts and sporting events throughout Copenhagen are also sold here. **Jazz Kælderen** (Gråbrødre Torv 5; Tel 33/91-22-45; By foot from Strøget; 11am-5:30pm Mon-Fri, till 3pm Sat; MC, V) is the only strictly jazz music shop in Copenhagen. This tiny basement store has an excellent selection of jazz CDs from the early '50s to the present day. Sheet music and books are also sold here, and the workers are well-versed in jazz happenings in the city.

▶▶CLUB KIDS

For club gear and information on local club happenings, make an effort to stop by **Subwear** (Vestergade 18; Tel 33/11-51-16; By foot from Rådhuspladsen; 11am-6pm Mon-Thur, till 7pm Fri, 10am-4pm Sat; MC, V, AE). Two floors of club attire, including platform sneakers, bug-eyed shades, neon pants and vests, spiked plastic backpacks, and Day-glo jewelry. The staff is very helpful and will give you a detailed rundown on every club in the city.

▶▶BOUND

Denmark is among the world's leaders in published authors per capita. Danes are also quick to point out that Hans Christian Anderson's works have been translated into more languages than any other book except the Bible. Since most Danes speak fluent English, bookstores with English titles are common throughout the city, but books here are notoriously expensive.

Boghallen (Rådhuspladsen 37; Tel 33/47-25-60; Buses 2, 6, 8, 11, 14, 16, 28, 29, 30, 34, 67, 68 to Rådhuspladsen; 9:30am-5:30pm Mon-Thur,

fashion

Denmark is sometimes referred to as "the Paris of the North." While that's not a totally accurate description, the Danes do take fashion every bit as seriously as countries to the south. The style used to be simple but formal, with black blazers and solid dark colors prevailing, and while the preppy look does live on, the younger generation are a bit hipper than thou—FUBU, porn star, and Diesel being among the labels of choice. Expect to see your fair share of faashion disasters and remember—you can wear what you want, but only if the crowd permits. While there may be some snazzy threads in the cheaper shops, clothing tends to be pretty pricey.

till 6:30pm Fri, 10am-2pm Sat, closed Sun; MC, V, AE) is a large, centrally located book store with a vast selection of titles in English: a large selection of hardcover and paperback fiction and nonfiction, biographies, maps, and guides.

EaTS

Most Copenhageners don't eat out at fine restaurants very often, opting instead to have small dinner parties. No, they're not agoraphobic—it's just that the check for a meal in a classy restaurant may leave you speechless. If you're not looking for style, reasonable prices for takeout food can be found. Always keep an eye out for establishments with excellent "all you can eat" deals.

▶▶CHEAP

Copenhagen is a wiener-lover's paradise. **Pølser wagons** can be found on numerous corners, particularly in the areas near Rådhuspladsen and Strøget, and Copenhageners devour the famed "fransk hot dog" *(franskie danskie* in the vernacular) like there's no tomorrow. Stuffed into a closed bun and covered with a mayo-like dressing, the *franskie danskie* will run you about 18Dkr.

If dogs aren't your thing, walk west on Vesterbrogade to **Manar Grill & Pizzeria** *(Vesterbrogade 65; Tel 33/23-00-35; Bus 3, 6, 16 to Vesterbrogade, or 10-minute walk from Central Railway Station; 11am-10pm Mon-Fri, noon-10pm Sat, 1pm-10pm Sun; 10Dkr falafel, 22Dkr big burger, 30Dkr plain pizza pie; No credit cards)* to the Vesterbro neighborhood for an inexpensive-but-filling falafel, pizza, or burger. The place is tiny, but the food comes fast, and is one of the cheapest deals in town. It's strictly a takeout place—most patrons devour their meal on the sidewalk just outside the door.

Lille Istanbul Pizzeria *(Larsbjørnsstræde 25; Tel 33/14-28-14; Five-minute walk from Rådhuspladsen; 10:30am-10pm Mon-Sat, noon-10pm Sun; 11-18Dkr slices; No credit cards)*, operated by Turkish Danes, is another option for a quick cheap slice, just north of Rådhus Plads. There are a few tables and chairs crammed in front of the ordering counter, but most customers eat on the run. The standard veggie, Hawaiian, and pepperoni options are among your choices. If you do eat inside, a picture of Geronimo with his rifle in hand will stare down at you from the wall.

Near Kongens Nytorv, **The Bagel Co.** *(Gothersgade 17; Tel 33/13-13-10; Bus 1, 6, 9, 10, 19, 29 to Kongens Nytorv; 8am-8pm Mon-Fri, 9am-6pm Sat-Sun; 12Dkr bagel w/cream cheese; No credit cards)* does a damn good job of imitating a typical tiny takeout bagel shop on a corner in Manhattan—only the workers here probably speak better English. The first and only bagel shop in Copenhagen, it has won over the residents of the city with its excellent bagels of all kinds and inexpensive, tasty, filling bagel sandwiches.

▶▶DO-ABLE

The most famous Danish dish is *smørrebrød*, basically an open-faced sandwich on rye or white. Toppings like herring, liver paste, hard-boiled eggs, salami, sausage, tomato, pork, and potatoes are common. The conveniently located **Bon Appetit Smørrebrød** (*Vesterbrogade 15; Tel 31/31-17-02; Five-minute walk east on Vesterbrogade from Central Railway Station; 7am-4pm Mon-Thur, till 1pm Fri, closed Sat, Sun; 25-37Dkr per smørrebrød; No credit cards*) has the largest selection of smørrebrød within walking distance of the city center.

For something more unique, head on up to Nørrebro and pull up a seat at **Kaffesalonen** (*Peblinge Dossering 6; Tel 35/35-12-19; Bus 5, 16 to Nørrebrogade; Mon-Fri 8am-midnight, Sat and Sun 10am-midnight; 32Dkr for breakfast buffet, 85Dkr for weekend brunch, 75-95 Dkr for lunch/dinner entrée; MC, V*). The '50s decor and fair prices will transport you back several decades. A top spot for a sunny morning breakfast overlooking Peblinge Lake, with terrace seating available on the water. Enjoy the friendly waitresses here—table service at a cafe is a rarity in Copenhagen. A pictorial sequence of how coffee arrives in Denmark decorates the longest interior wall, and a sign above the counter suggests that you *drik et glas økologisk maelk*: "drink a glass of organic milk."

If the sun is out, you can't beat dining on picturesque Kompagnistræde **Riz Raz** (*20 Kompagnistræde; Tel 33/15-05-75; By foot from Strøget; 11:30am-10pm daily; 49Dkr lunch buffet, 59Dkr dinner buffet, 89-179Dkr per entree w/buffet included; MC, V, DC*) offers up an affordable and tasty vegetarian buffet and prime outdoor seating in the Strøget area. If the weather isn't cooperating, the basement seating area of this Mediterranean restaurant is a good consolation prize. Pasta salads, falafel, pizza, and a ton of vegetable dishes and salads are included in the buffet, and non-buffet entrees (i.e. the meat and fish) include couscous, lamb, grilled fish, calamari and shwarma. Of course, various types of wine and beer are available—after all, this is Denmark.

Base Camp Holmen (*Building 148, Holmen; Tel 70/23-23-18; Bus 8 to Holmen; 11am-midnight Sun-Wed, till 5am Thur-Sat; www.base camp.dk; 90-140Dkr per entree, 80Dkr brunch; MC, V, AE*) wins handsdown for the most original, coolest, and largest eatery in Copenhagen. Just down the road from Christiania, this former military canon repair shop/warehouse seats 600 in an environment that marries the artsy with an army mess hall. Outside, you can ignore the fact you're in northern Europe and grill meat from deck chairs at the sand-floored salsa bar. The weekend buffet brunch (*11am-3pm*), perfect after an exhausting night at the bars and clubs, loads you up with omelets, bacon, cereals, OJ, coffee, cheeses, bread, fruit, fish, and a whole lot more. Friday and Saturday nights, the old warehouse becomes a relaxed disco club, bringing in a friendly, twentyish, fun-loving Danish crowd.

An equally cool atmosphere can be found just a few steps further out in Holmen at the **Thorsen** (*Street #13 Holmen; Tel 40/93-39-63; Bus 8 to Holmen; 11am-3am daily, June 1-Sept 1 only; 35Dkr sandwiches, 100Dkr grilled platter; No credit cards*), also in an industrial setting, with tables strewn about right on the waterfront under ship-loading cranes and huge metal scaffolding. The crowd's a bit older than that at Base

copenhagen eats and crashing

DENMARK

Copenhagen

EATS ◆
The Bagel Co. **13**
Base Camp Holmen **15**
Bon Appetit
  Smørrebrød **5**
Kaffesalonen **8**
Kamel's Spisehus **1**
Lille Istanbul Pizzeria **11**
Manar Grill & Pizzeria **3**
Riz Raz **12**
Thorsen **16**

CRASHING ■
City Public Hostel **4**
Hotel Cab Inn
  Copenhagen **6**
Hotel Jørgensen **10**
Neptun Hotel **14**
Sleep in Green **9**
Sleep in Heaven **7**
YMCA Interpoint **2**

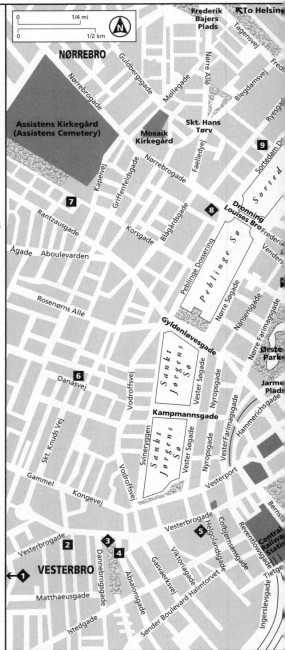

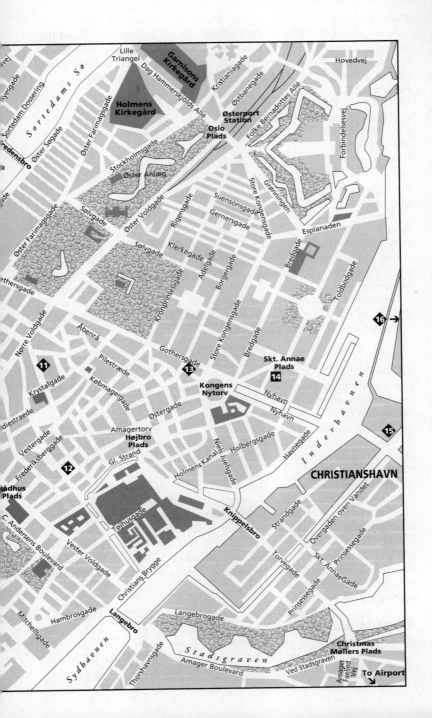

Camp Holmen [see above], sipping 35Dkr Heinekens and taking in the terrific view of **Amalienborg Palace** [see *culture zoo*, above] and the setting sun over the harbor. When the wind picks up and a chilly breeze comes across the water, wrap yourself up in one of the old army blankets that they stash behind the bar.

▶▶**SPLURGE**

Restaurant Divan 2 Tivoli *(Vesterbrogade 3; Tel 33/12-51-51; Bus 1, 8, 11, 12, 13, 34, to Tivoli Gardens; 11am-11:30pm daily; 125-295Dkr per entree; MC, V, AE)*, in the heart of **Tivoli Gardens** [see *culture zoo*, above] has been pleasing customers with its excellent French cuisine and flawless service since 1843 (yes, that's *1843*). Dine on salmon, tuna, eel, venison, beef, or lamb, or go straight for the Danish specialties like fjord shrimp and fresh berries with cream. An overwhelming assortment of international wines is available.

Kamel's Spisehus *(Sundevedsgade 4; Tel 33/25-32-41; Bus 6 to Vesterbrogade; 5:30pm-midnight Tue-Sun, closed Mon; 190Dkr and up per entree; No credit cards)* specializes in French fusion cuisine and draws a young upscale clientele. Although the brightly-colored interior of this small Vesterbro establishment is somewhat boring, that doesn't slow the stampede of young well-to-do folk into the place—the forgettable decor more than made up for by the delicious entrees. Veggie options are available. Reservations are a must, and be prepared to sit through an excellent four-course meal spanning several hours.

crashing

The hospitable Danes have set up some of the best-quality hostels of any large European city, most of which are right in the city center. The center also contains dozens of somewhat overpriced upscale hotel options, catering to older tourists and businesspeople, but the "middle-of-the-road" hotel option is harder to come by. "Budget" hotels do exist, but they aren't very cheap, and are concentrated in the only semi-sketchy area of town—you'll be hard-pressed to find a decent hotel for under 370Dkr a night.

Use It [see *need to know*, below] will happily call around and locate a private room for you. Prices for these rooms are about 25 percent less than rooms arranged through **Wonderful Copenhagen Tourist Information** [see *need to know*, below], and Use It won't charge you the 40Dkr service fee. Singles run between 125 and 150Dkr, doubles between 225 and 250Dkr, and breakfast isn't included. Most of the rooms are close to the city center, although some of them may be located a few stops away from the city on the S-train.

▶▶**CHEAP**

The most cost-effective option for a few nights in Copenhagen is at the **YMCA Interpoint** *(15 Valdemarsgade; Tel 33/31-15-74; Bus 3, 6, 15, 16 to Vesterbrogade, or 15-minute walk from Central Railway Station; Open June 25-Aug 7 only; 75Dkr for dorm bed; No credit cards)*. Located just down the Vesterbrogade from the train station, the "Y" is jammed with an international mix of young travelers. Hardwood floors, a small kitchen, and clean, simple, bunk-style rooms are the pluses; the fact that the doors are locked between 12:30am and 7am is a minus. A simple 25Dkr breakfast is served by the friendly international staff in a large lounge/living room. The bathrooms and showers are located outside the rooms, and showers for guys and girls are restricted to separate times of day. No hanky-panky at the Y!

Out in the quieter district of Østerbro lies the **Copenhagen Sleep-In** *(132 Blegdamsvej; Tel 35/26-50-59; Bus 1, 6, 14 to Blegdamsvej; Open July-Aug only; www.sleep-in.dk; 80Dkr for dorm bed; No credit cards).* You may initially feel like a recent flood victim sleeping in this large converted gymnasium. But you get over that pretty quickly once you realize that this place has got Internet access, a small cafe that serves a variety of breakfast options, 24-hour access, kitchen facilities, a young international crowd, free condoms (hey!), clean bathrooms, showers right outside the main sleeping area, wall maps of Christiania, close proximity to both the city center and Nørrebro, and an organized, friendly, and accommodating staff. This place has been operating since 1971, and it's clearly got it together.

Located in the heart of energetic Nørrebro, **Sleep in Green** *(18 Ravnsborggade; Tel 35/37-77-77; Bus 5, 16 to Nørrebrogade; open May 25-Sept 25 only; 80Dkr for dorm bed; No credit cards)* is a friendly, mellow, eco-oriented hostel. Grab a simple organic breakfast for an extra 30Dkr, use their Internet connection, and hang out in the spacious lounge with other young international travelers. The three-bunk rooms have an intimate, homey feeling to them, though the bathrooms and showers, located outside the rooms, have a reputation for being a bit on the grungy side. 24-hour access is a huge plus, as is the fact that it's in an area surrounded by ample nightlife spots—plus there's a laundry across the street. Reservations a few days in advance are recommended.

True to its name, there are glow-in-the-dark stars lighting up the high ceilings at **Sleep in Heaven** *(7 Struenseegade; Tel 35/35-46-48; Bus 8, 12, 13 to Rantzausgade; Open year round except Jan; http://hjem.get 2net.dk/sleepinheaven/; 100Dkr for dorm bed; No credit cards).* This 24-hour-access hostel recently moved from an inconvenient location outside Copenhagen into an old bread factory in Nørrebro. The service is exceptionally warm, and the place prides itself on its high standard of cleanliness, with immaculate bathrooms and showers. The airy split-level lounge comes complete with a small bar serving 20Dkr half liters of beer, Internet access, a pool table and an outdoor terrace. A small continental breakfast can be had for an extra 25Dkr. Reservations probably aren't a bad idea.

City Public Hostel *(8 Absalonsgade; Tel 33/31-20-70; Bus 6, 16 to Vesterbrogade, or seven-minute walk from Central Railway Station; Open May 5-Aug 20; 100Dkr, 130Dkr w/breakfast for dorm bed; No credit cards)* is the largest hostel in the city center, with a rowdy young international crowd, 24-hour access, and a busy reception/lounge area. There are

by foot

Copenhagen sights

1. This first walk takes you past some of the more worthwhile Copenhagen sights. Start at Rosenborg Have [see *culture zoo*, above], where sunny days attract scantily clad Danes attempting to recreate the Garden of Eden. Check out the Rosenborg Palace and Gardens [see *culture zoo*, above]. From here, head back towards the city center, cutting up **Landemœrket** to the trendy **Købmagergade**. Make a left on **Købmagergade**, and the Round Tower [see *culture zoo*, above] will be on your left. Built by Christian IV, it was once visited by Peter the Great, who opted to ride his horse all the way up the spiraling ramp. Continuing down **Købmagergade**, you'll soon come to **Amager Torv**, a bustling square with a recently renovated tiled pedestrian plaza. In the center of the square is the **Storkspringvandet** fountain. If you're lucky, you'll witness a Danish bride-to-be wading in the fountain, continuing the old tradition of trying to catch a live eel with her bare hands. Hmmm....Continuing in the same direction, you'll pass the *statue of Bishop Absalon*, Copenhagen's founding father. As you cross the bridge, look down in the canal for perhaps Denmark's only underwater statue, *The Merman with Seven Sons*. Cross the street and you're on **Slotsholmen**, home to Christiansborg Palace [see *culture zoo*, above], the **Folkitinget**, the **Supreme Court**, and the **Royal Library**. Walk around the front of the imposing palace to **Tøjhusgade**, where you should make a right underneath the arches of the **castle** and into the side square of the Palace. Follow the street to just past the second set of arches and you'll come to a small passageway on your left leading to **Den Kongelig Bibliotek** (the Royal Library). The *statue of Søren Kierkegaard* may be your only company in this little hidden nook.

Christiana

2. And now for something completly different...a stroll through Copenhagen's own social experiment, Christiania. Take Bus 8 going towards Christiania. After crossing over the large Knippelsbrro bridge, the bus will make a left onto Prinsessegade. Get off at the **entrance to Christiania**, which is marked by an arched wooden gate on the right.

kitchen facilities, a BBQ terrace in the backyard, and plenty of low-end ethnic takeout joints in the area. As a result of the heavy traffic passing through the hostel, the bathrooms can be a bit scary at times. Reservations are strongly suggested, since so many travelers make their way over less than 10 minutes after stepping off the train.

Cut through the small alleyway directly across the street from the Christiania entrance until you run into the street called **Overgaden oven Vandet**. Make a left onto **Overgaden oven Vandet**, walking on the brick sidewalk along the small canal. Make a right over the small bridge over the canal on **Skt. Annæ Gade**. Continue on until the street dead-ends at **Asiatisk Plads**, and go straight through the archway towards the waterfront. There is usually a large wooden sailboat tied up on the right-hand side, and the most of the city's spires are visible from the water's edge. Make a left after a short rest on the concrete wall over the harbor, and head back over **Knippelsbro bridge** on the right. Walk over the bridge, and picture this: In a recent winter storm, an empty city bus driving across the bridge was hit by an unusually strong gust of wind that actually forced the bus over the side of the bridge into the water below. Once safely over the bridge, make a right down the first set of stairs and continue walking straight on **Niels Juels Gade**. Make a right at the first light onto **Havnegade**, passing the ferries to Sweden (and their drunken occupants) on your right. At the end of the street lies **Nyhavn** [see *hanging out*, above]; make your way over to the opposite side of the canal, and if you feel a bit dried-out, sit down with a cold Tuborg Classic from a supermarket. Hans Christian Anderson once lived in **Nyhavn**, so stop and take a look at #67, his residence for two decades. Continue walking along **Nyhavn** and make a left on **Toldboldsgade**. Down the road a bit, Amelienborg Palace [see *culture zoo*, above] will be on your left. Its courtyard is worth a quick stroll, and if you have the time and the kroner, the Glucksborg family apartments can be visited [see *culture zoo*, above]. Head out the way you entered, across **Toldboldsgade**, through **Amelienhavn** and past the large fountain. Make a left at the waterfront, and continue on towards **Langelinie**. Now just continue down the waterfront until it either ends or you're too tired to go on any longer. You'll pass the Museum of Danish Resistance [see *culture zoo*, above] on the left, stumble upon the Little Mermaid [see *culture zoo*, above], see moored cruise ships, and walk out onto the pier surrounded by open harbor.

▶▶**DO-ABLE**

Hotel Jørgensen *(11 Rømersgade; Tel 33/13-81-86; S-train to Nørreport Station or Bus 5, 14, 16, 31, 42 to Nørreport Station, or 15-minute walk north from Central Railway Station; Open year round; www.hotel-joergensen.aok.dk; Dorm bed 115Dkr, single 425-525Dkr, double 525-*

wired

The Danes are on top of their shit technologically, so Internet access is very accessible and popular. Several of the hostels and hotels have terminals [see *crashing*, above], Internet cafes with fast connections are scattered through out the city, and it seems as if *everything* here has its own Web site.

www.useit.dk—Use It Tourist Office

www.ctw.dk—*Copenhagen This Week*: what's going on

www.copenhagen.now.dk—*Copenhagen Now*: bars, clubs, and other nightlife and cultural goodies.

www.cjf.dk—Copenhagen Jazz Festival

For 100Dkr, you can be wild and crazy and surf the Web all night long at **Gamestation PC & Internet Cafe** *(Vesterbrogade 115; Tel 33/25-97-96; Bus 6, 28 to Vesterbrogade; Noon-2am Sun-Thur, noon-8am Fri-Sat; www.gamestation.dk; 35Dkr one hour, 15Dkr 15 minutes).* A simple breakfast is even served at 8am. It's right near Rådhus Plads, the service is friendly, you'll wait in line for a computer only in the evening, and the machines here have superfast connections, but you'll be hanging with a mainly teenage male gamer crowd.

650Dkr; MC, V, DC for hotel rooms, cash only for dorm rooms) is a pleasant hotel-hostel combination with lots of perks. All rooms have TVs, plus there are two basement lounges, one with drinks and snack machines and internet access at 1Dkr per minute and the other has a pool table, pinball and table football, there's a decent buffet breakfast included in the price of all rooms, and it's located in the city center, just south of Botanisk Have [see *culture zoo*, above]. Predictably, the hostel section sees younger and more carefree guests, and the hotel section houses tourists with more money. The hotel rooms are very clean and well-furnished, and both twin and queen-size beds are available. All singles and doubles have ensuite (hit and miss) showers and a communal WC, while wash facilities in the hotel are obviously communal. The breakfast and the more upscale service makes this the best deal in town.

Each room at the **Hotel Cab Inn Copenhagen** *(Danasvej 32-34; Tel 33/21-04-00; Bus 29 to Kampmannsgade, or 15-minute walk northwest from Central Railway Station; All rooms w/ private bathroom and shower, www.cab-inn.dk; 425Dkr single, 550Dkr double, 675Dkr triple, 800Dkr quad; MC, V, AE)* has a mini-cafe with free tea and coffee, TV, air conditioning, telephone, and a comfortable sofa-like pull-out bed. A buffet breakfast will cost an extra 45Dkr, and sandwiches, coffee, and snacks are served at the cafe on the ground floor. The furniture in the rooms is modeled after that found on an upscale Scandinavian ocean liner. Service is both courteous and helpful, and the hotel is within a stroll of the city center.

▶▶**SPLURGE**

Just around the corner from **Nyhavn** [see *hanging out*, above], **Amalien-borg Palace** [see *culture zoo*, above], and the **Royal Theatre** [see *arts scene*, above], the location of **Neptun Hotel** *(Sankt Annæ Plads 18-20; Tel 33/96-20-02; Bus 1, 6, 9, 19, 21 to Bredage; All rooms W/ private bath-room and shower; www.neptun-group.dk; 1,400Dkr single, 1,600-1,900Dkr double; MC, V, AE, DC)* is tough to beat. The service here is courteous and helpful, as you would expect from a four-star hotel. All light-colored, well-furnished rooms include two telephones, radio, cable TV, hair dryer, iron, safe, mini-bar, voicemail, PC plug, and a delicious buffet breakfast. A restaurant specializing in Danish cuisine with a French twist adjacent to a first-class library room. You'll eat breakfast in an enclosed courtyard with a retractable glass roof and have a chance to look at the stars from the rooftop terrace. As if that wasn't enough, Neptun has also won a prestigious award for its environmentally aware operations.

need to know

Currency Exchange The local currency is the **Danish Kroner (Dkr)**. Expect to pay either a flat fee or a percentage commission for currency exchange anywhere in the city. **Strøget** is lined with currency exchange outlets, most with fairly similar high rates. **Forex**, in the Central Railway Station, tends to have the most competitive rates. Most banks charge a hefty per-check fee.

Tourist Information Wonderful **Copenhagen Tourist Information** *(1 Bernstorffsgade, adjacent to the main entrance to Tivoli Gardens; 33/25-38-44; www.woco.dk; 9am-4:30pm Mon-Fri, till 1:30pm Sat, closed Sun Sept-Apr, 9am-9pm daily May-Sept)* provides free maps, hotel booking service, advice on tours, and brochures; it sells the Copenhagen Card [see below] and creates and distributes the free monthly publication *Copenhagen This Week*, which provides a detailed monthly events calendar and basic tourist info.

Use It *(13 Rådhusstræde; Tel 33/73-06-20; www.useit.dk; 9am-7pm daily mid-June-mid Sept, 11am-4pm Mon-Wed, till 6pm Thur, till 2pm Fri, closed Sat, Sun mid-Sept-mid-June)*, a budget-oriented informa-tion center aimed at the student-age traveler, will book private rooms, refer you to hostels, provide free daytime luggage storage and Internet access, and answer every possible question you have about the city. They also provide a complimentary comprehensive English budget guide to Copenhagen called *Playtime*. The service is very friendly, and since this is not a private agency, these guys are here to help you, not drain your bank account.

The **Copenhagen Card**, sold at **Wonderful Copenhagen Tourist Information**, the **Central Railway Station**, and **Kastrup Airport**, can be bought in increments of 24 *(155Dkr)*, 48 *(255Dkr)*, or 72 *(320Dkr)* hours. It gives you free travel on all trains and buses in the

Copenhagen metro area and much of the rest of North Sjælland, plus free admission to over 60 museums and sights, and 25 to 50 percent savings on ferry crossings to Sweden.

Public Transportation Copenhagen's public transport is very comprehensive, and bus tickets are also good for travel on the **S-trains**, the local metro trains. Trains run from 5am to just before midnight; night buses run every couple of hours after midnight. Night buses cost double unless you have a **Copenhagen Card** or a 24-hour ticket. Public transport is run on a zone system—the entire Copenhagen area is divided into 95 zones—and your fare depends on how many zones you travel through. If you don't think you'll be going beyond the city center and its adjacent neighborhoods, get a two-zone ticket *(11Dkr for one hour)*. If you plan on riding the buses or S-trains more, grab a "clip card" *(75Dkr for 10 trips)* at any train station or supermarket. Just validate the card in the yellow box on the bus or at the train station before getting on. A 24-hour ticket *(115Dkr)* is also available, allowing you to travel in most of North Sjælland. It is expensive, but worth it if you are planning to travel a lot. The bus drivers will make change for you, and you can purchase tickets at the automated machines at the train station. Bus stops are really hard to recognize—the yellow signs are extremely small. If you get on a bus and are unsure of what the stop you're heading for looks like, or where it is, ask the driver to let you know when you're nearing it. Overall, the drivers are really courteous and helpful, although not all speak English.

Bike Rental Copenhageners take bicycling very seriously: Stay to the right, use hand signals, obey traffic signs, and, after dark, use front and rear bike lights, or you'll be pulled over and fined. **Københavns Cyker** *(11 Reventlowsgade; Tel 33/33-86-13; Regular bikes 50Dkr per day, 90Dkr two days; 225Dkr per week, deposit necessary; MC, V, AE)* or **Københavns Cykelbørs** *(157 Gothersgade; Tel 33/14-07-17; Mountain bikes 100Dkr per day, 500Dkr per week, deposit necessary; MC, V, AE)* will rent you a ride. Or you can borrow one: A few thousand "city bikes" are scattered throughout the city center for anyone to use. On a sunny day, locating a city bike is tough, but if you look hard enough, you'll probably come across one. These bikes are stored at about 150 special bike racks in the city center. A 20Dkr piece dropped in the slot unlocks the bike, and when you lock your bike up at another specialized rack, the 20Dkr pops back out. If you steal one of these bikes, you are a complete loser and an embarrassment to your country.

American Express The American Express office in Copenhagen was indefinitely closed in the summer of 1999.

Health Emergency: *112*. **Bispebjerg Hospital** *(23 Bispebjerg Bakke; 3531-35-31)*, **Frederiksberg Hospital** *(57 Nordre Fasanvej; 38-16)*.

Pharmacies **Steno Apotek** *(6c Vesterbrogade; Tel 33/14-82-66)* and **Sønderbro Apotek** *(158 Amagerbrogade; Tel 32/58-01-40)* are open 24/7.

Telephone Country code: *45*; information: *118*; international operator:

114; no city codes. Phone cards available at train stations, supermarkets, and kiosks. **AT&T**: *8001-0010*; **MCI**: *8001-0022*; **Sprint**: *8001-0877*.

Airport Kastrup International Airport is located on the island of **Amager**, about 15 kilometers from the center of Copenhagen. Trains depart for **Amager** from the **Central Railway Station** every 20 minutes *(Tel 32/47-4747; www.cph.dk)*.

Airlines SAS *(1 Hammerichsgade; Tel 32/54-17-01; www.sas.dk)*, **IcelandAir** *(1 Vester Farimagsgade; Tel 33/12-33-88; www.icelandair.is)*, **KLM** *(Kastrup Airport; Tel 32/52-74-11; www.klm.com)*, **United Airlines** *(7 Mitermolen; Tel 35/25-81-00; www.ual.com)*.

Trains The **Central Railway Station**, **Høvedbanegården** *(Tel 70/13-14-15; www.dsb.dk)*, located just west of Rådhuspladsen, has hourly connections to the rest of the country.

Bus Lines Out of the City Eurolines *(8 Reventlowsgade; Tel 33/25-12-44)* offers cheap bus tickets to destinations all over Europe.

STOCKHOLM

Stockholm is a miserable place in winter. It's dreary and cold, beset with arctic winds and endless nights. But then the sun comes back, and everything changes. Come April, like a Jenny Craig client dropped into a chocolate factory, the Swedes break their winter fast and go at it with gusto. Coats are peeled back to reveal gorgeous blondes in sleek fashions. Where, the locals muse, have these babes been hiding all winter? Streetside cafes fill with revelers. Festivals and celebrations take over the avenues. Lush parks overflow with frolickers and sunbathers. And, as if reluctant to give up all this attention, the summer sun dips below the horizon for only a few hours every night. If the party rallying cry in Los Angeles and New York is: "I can sleep tomorrow," then here it's: "I can sleep in winter."

Spread across a gorgeous network of islands, Stockholm is one of the most beautiful and refined cities in the world. Its citizens aren't bad to look at, either. The city is remarkably clean, smelling of fresh sea air. Stores like **Ordning & Reda** [see *arts scene*, below] showcase the country's famous minimalist designs; and the Stockholm Jazz & Blues Festival [see *festivals & events*, below] is among the most celebrated anywhere, having drawn legendary performers for more than three decades.

Stockholm's elegance is also one of its weaknesses: An air of self-consciousness permeates everything. It's as if the city is afraid to look scruffy or really cut loose. Although there are plenty of trendy watering holes, fancy-schmancy restaurants, stylish nightclubs, and hip live music joints, there's a strange uptight vibe lurking beneath the scene. It doesn't help that everything is ludicrously expensive, thanks to the stable

Swedish economy and a pants-wetting 25 percent sales tax. Liquor is expensive, food is expensive, crashing is expensive.

But this place ain't Paris, so don't interpret the slight snootiness as xenophobia. Swedes worship English speakers and have adopted the language as their second tongue (ask someone here if they speak English, and prepare for a severe "duh" look), which is good because Swedish is thoroughly incomprehensible to most outsiders. And once you get past their slightly chilly facades, the Swedes are super-friendly and welcoming. Even their greeting—*hej*, pronounced like "hey"—will make you feel like Norm walking into Cheers every time.

neighborhoods

Stockholm is small and defined really simply by the natural landscape. The practical and commercial center of the city, which houses the **T-Centralen** train station, is called **Norrmalm**. Most department stores are around **Hötorget**, a medium-sized square that holds a street market [see *by foot*, below] and a subway stop. The big gallerias run down **Drottninggatan** (*gatan* = street), a pedestrian drag that goes from northeast to southeast a block west of Hötorget. **Kungsgatan**, running east-west and forming the top edge of Hötorget, plays host to a bunch of bars and clubs, though most tend to be a little cheesy.

It's hard to tell where Norrmalm ends and **Östermalm**, the area just to the east, begins. The **Stureplan** area between them, where Kungsgatan meets **Biblioteksgatan** and **Birger Jarlsgatan**, is basically the stomping grounds for the stinking rich and super-stylish, with swank nightclubs like **Sture Compagniet** [see *club scene*, below] and **Sophie's Bar** [see *bar scene*, below].

To the north of Norrmalm is **Vasagatan**, a pretty residential area with lots of families. But two of its streets, **Odengatan**, and **Sankt Eriksplan**, both up to the northwest by the **Vasaparken** [see *hanging out*, below], are worth checking out for **Tranan** [see *bar scene*, below], a trendy drinkers' hang, and rock joint **Studion** [see *live music scene*, below].

If you head down Drottninggatan from Norrmalm, you'll cross a few stone bridges to the cobblestoned **Gamla Stan** (**Old Town**), which is charming despite its usual congestion of tourists.

Keep going south, cross the **Centralbron bridge** at the east end of Gamla Stan, and you'll hit **Södermalm**, a working-class neighborhood gone trendy in a young, studenty sort of way. It's the closest thing you'll find to scruffy in Stockholm and can be a much-needed respite from the pretension of Stureplan. There are tons of great bars along **Götgatan**, which runs north to south, and **Skånegatan**, which runs east to west. Just make sure Söder is your first stop, since almost everything there closes down at 1am.

Långholmen and **Skeppsholmen**, just east of Södermalm are small islands dominated by famous youth hostels. Långholmen is greener; Skeppsholmen has the **Moderna Museet** [see *culture zoo*, below].

The lushest part of Stockholm is the **Djurgården**, a tree-hugger's paradise to the south of Östermalm across the **Djurgbron bridge**. This national park houses the **Vasa Museum** [see *culture zoo*, below] and **Skansen**, a living-history museum with actors playing the part of villagers.

Public transportation is a breeze to use. The **Tunnelbana** subway, known as the **T-Bana**, runs beneath the water from island to island. The T-Bana stops running around midnight, but night buses continue until the crack of dawn. You can buy T-Bana tickets at the information desk in most stations. You shouldn't need to take public transportation much, though. Stockholm is really small and very manageable on foot (a 20-minute walk from one hangout to the next is the most you'll find). Plus, you can't see how beautiful the city is when you're underground.

For coverage of the newest, trendiest restaurants and clubs on the scene, check out the English-language magazine *Stockholm New*, which comes out every six months. It's a pretty thick mag, and it'll give you a good sense of what Swedes are into. For more timely info, like concerts and parties, check the events listing in *Dagens Nyheter* (Stockholm's daily paper) on Fridays.

hanging OUT

If NBC chose Stockholm for a "Friends" spin-off, they'd surely tag **String** (*Nytorgsgatan 38; Tel 08/714-85-14; T-Bana to Medborgarplatsen; 9:30am-9pm Mon-Fri, till 6 Sat, Sun; 22-45SEK sandwiches and salads; No credit cards*) as the replacement for Central Perk. Easily the funkiest java shop in the city and a great late-afternoon hang, this place is your best bet for finding a speed chess game, cutting edge Swedish music, a young crowd of "interestingly" dressed hipsters, retro chairs, and some angst-ridden guy scribbling away in his journal (guidebooks always say that, but we *really* saw him here).

Another good place to chill out is at Götgatan 31, which houses a **Wayne's Coffee** (*Götgatan 31; Tel 08/644-45-90; T-Bana to Medborgarplatsen; 10am-8pm Mon-Sat, 11am-8pm Sun; No credit cards*) and a **Press Stop** (*Götgatan 31; Tel 08/644-35-10; T-Bana to Medborgarplatsen; 10am-6:30pm Mon-Fri, till 4pm Sat, noon-4pm Sun; press-stop.soder@swipnet.se; V, MC, AE*), where you can pick up the new *Harry Potter* or the latest copies of *People, Premiere, The Source*, whatever. Wayne's is self-service, and the wait can be a bit rough on weekends; but if you've got the time to burn, this is a mellow spot to camp out in the comfy chairs and listen to hyper-caffeinated music with a young, international crowd. And, as it's a chain, no one is going to hassle you if you stay the whole day.

Stockholm's fashion set lives and breathes out of Stureplan, and the many surrounding cafes in this area offer great vantage points for the voyeur. These places do tend to be a bit upscale, so don't expect to make yourself at home on an order of water. A step down the snobbery scale, the crowd that hangs out on the steps behind art mecca **Kulturhuset** [see

five things to talk to a local about

1. The **cellular phones** surgically attached to the ears of most Swedes provide great fodder for conversation. Ericsson, the Swedish mobile-phone giant, is a source of national pride, but Nokia is making a serious run at the champion of airwaves. It's all about accessories: battery power, colored face plates, standby time....

2. Nothing riles up a Swede quite as much as mention of the dreaded **winter**. The dark and dreary season saps life from the population, turning everyone into a bunch of zombies until the spring thaw. Ask how bad Swedish winters really are, and you won't be wanting for chat-up subject matter for hours. And if you happen to hail from a place where winter rivals theirs, you've made a friend for life.

3. Before the Internet globalized the nudie industry, Sweden was pumping out **blue movies** faster than...never mind, we won't go there. Anyhow, use your visit to, um, probe the history of the skin-flick and the culture that, um, spawned it.

4. Night doesn't fall until the wee hours during the summer. So what's up with so many **bars closing at 1am**? Most Swedes haven't even booted and rallied by then!

5. Really, it doesn't matter what you talk about—**English** is music to a Swede's ears and will draw new friends to you from a two-block radius to practice their already perfect pronunciation.

arts scene, below] is less dressy, more chatty, and generally younger. Just inside Kulturhuset is **Lava** *(Sergels Torg 3; Tel 08/508-31-44; T-Bana to T-Centralen; 2-9pm Tue-Fri, 1-6pm Sat, Sun; www.kulturhuset.stockholm.se/lava; No credit cards)*, an all-purpose activity room supporting Stockholm's youth culture, complete with cafe, video lounge, poetry corner, CD listening stations, computers, magazines, newspapers, and a stage open to performers of all ilk. This is definitely the place to come if you're looking for feedback on that indie film script you just happened to bring along on your trip to Scandinavia.

And, for you sporty types, take a breath of fresh air at **Rålambshov** [see *great outdoors*, below], a popular park on Kungsholmen. On a sunny day you'll have to hop, skip, and jump your way around the abundant bodies crammed onto the lush green. If you're feeling overcrowded, you can always dive into the Riddarfjärden—Rålambshov's popular swimming hole. Also, anywhere along the water's edge in the Djurgården is likely to be an attractive spot for both swimmers and sun-seekers. For you landlubbers, **Vasaparken**, a small shoreline-impaired piece of turf in Vasastaden, is a cheery family hangout but also sports a skate park where bladers and local skate rats bleed the ground red practicing new tricks.

A market that no one from the States can ignore is **Gray's American Food Store** [see *eats*, below], where expats and Ameriphiles come to stock up on Pringles, Bubblicious, Jif, and Campbell's soups. Seriously, this place is more American than most places in the U.S.

bar scene

Finally, a chance to trade the "Can I see some ID, please?" culture of the United States for Europe, where the drinking age is achieved somewhere during embryonic development! Um, *wrong*. Stockholm has strict age policies, and they're enforced by the clubs as a way to weed out youngsters with short bankrolls. Most places have an 18-year-old minimum, but some roll out minimum age requirements of 20, 23, 25, and even 27 (of course, any place where you have to be 27 doesn't draw anyone younger than 40).

As if the age requirement wasn't enough to worry about, there's also the matter of closing times. Barhopping in Stockholm is an art form: You've got to plan your excursions well, because places shut down according to the crankiness and density of the neighborhood. Start your night in Södermalm, which completely shuts down at 1am. If you haven't had your fill, head to Stureplan or Kungsgatan, where most places close at 3.

And no matter where you go, if you plan on getting drunk, do your wallet a favor and buy a bottle at a shop—liquor is stupid expensive.

Stockholm's high-rollers blow their dough wooing the city's finest women at **Sophie's Bar** (*Biblioteksgatan 5; Tel 08/611-84-08; T-Bana to Östermalmstorg, Bus 41, 46, 55 to Stureplan; 11:30am-1am Mon-Wed, 11:30-3am Thur-Sat; AE, MC, V, DC*), the swankest spot north of Miami. With Latin music pumping and magnums of Moët sweating in ice buckets, you almost expect to see Will Smith gettin' jiggy widdit beside the Swedish film stars and name-brand athletes. The blood-red walls frame a bizarre mix of stuffed elk's heads and antique mirrors, perfect for the self-conscious Stureplan crowd. Look for the tip-hungry bartenders to light the bar aflame every few minutes when the mood takes them. Unless you're a hot stylish woman or can adopt one to help get you in the door, don't even try to come here on a Friday or Saturday night; the doormen are just too choosy. Good luck getting in, but if you do...Gah-damn! A loose 25-year-old minimum age rule.

Kind of a Stureplan-in-training, Ofenplau is home to **Tranan** (*Karlbergsvågan 14; Tel 08/30-07-65; T-Bana to Odenplan; 5pm-1am daily; V, MC, AE*), perfect for those who aren't quite old or rich enough to get into Sophie's Bar. Fear not, there are still more hotties here than should be legally allowed in one place. Getting in the door is no problem, but making your way across the room can be a real challenge, especially when local DJs spin on Fridays and Saturdays. The bar is in the basement of a

fIVE-O

New York City cops could take some major courtesy lessons from Stockholm's finest. With little major crime to turn them into bitter vigilantes, police in Stockholm do their job and do it well. As long as you respect their authority, they're generally happy to help change a tire or give directions. That is, except when things get out of hand during soccer matches. Then cops can become ass-whoopin' hooligan-stompers. The major complaint about Stockholm PD is that there simply aren't enough of them. You could spend a week here and never see a cop. In a pinch, you can always turn to the ever-present door guards: the large, badge-wearing bouncers who stand post outside most bars and clubs. They all certify through the city and are legally required to help damsels in distress (OK, guys too).

well-respected restaurant by the same name; as you're facing the restaurant, the bar's entrance is to the right, down the stairs. Cocktails will run you 72-85SEK, and beers cost 43-49SEK, a limited menu is offered from the restaurant upstairs, try the meatball and mashed potatoes for 105SEK. Over 23 only.

For a less trendy drinker's hang, head to **Fenix** *(Götgatan 40; Tel 08/640-45-06; T-Bana to Slussen or Medborgarplatsen; 4pm-1am Mon-Sat, till midnight Sun; www.fnx.se; V, MC)*, a noisy and dark bar on Södermalm with a frisky college crowd. The steamy basement is a maze of crumbling brick walls, but the disco ball and soul music are enough to get the crowd groovin' wherever there's room. Upstairs is more of a pure bar, where the people are hotter and more interested in being seen than the booty-shaking cellar-dwellers. Try to go around 9pm, before the crowds prompt the bouncer to shut the doors. Well drinks cost 66SEK.

Club Bonden *(Bondegatan 1C; Tel 08/642-99-13; T-Bana to Medborgarplatsen; 5pm-1am bar, 9pm-1am club; No cover; V, MC)* is a bar/club that's all the rage, with lines of the city's alterna-kids curling out the door at, like, 9pm on a Wednesday. There's no dress code per se, just that stylishly scruffy, retro-'70s, funk hipster look: heavy-framed glasses, hooded sweatshirts, dark jeans with fat cuffs, courier bags. Most nights are 20-plus, but almost no one is older than 30. The ceilings are barely eight feet high, making the music louder, and the frantic dancers seem more in-your-face. Thursday nights feature techno, Saturday nights offer R&B and soul classics, and other nights are mixed. If you get here after 8pm and the line's too big, try telling the bouncer that you came all the way to Stockholm because you heard this place was just so great and please, can't I come in?

Hey, all you chowda'-heads out theah, this is the bah for ya! Beantown's in the house at Södermalm's **O'Learys** *(Götgatan 11; Tel 08/644-*

POJKE MEETS FLICKA

First, the bad news: When it comes to appearance, Swedes kick the crap out of most foreigners. The usual traveler's skanky duds just won't cut it in Stockholm's chic hookup scene; grungy jeans and ripped T-shirts should stay in your backpack if you want any chance of getting some booty. But now for the good news: Swedes dig English-speakers. Whether it's tinged with an Aussie, British, or American accent, your voice will turn some heads in most bars. Moreover, the sheer exuberance of Swedish drinking virtually guarantees high libidos and low inhibitions. Whether you can take advantage of those depends on your skills. Play it cool, don't act like shagging a Swede would make you a legend back home, and stay more sober than your local competition.

69-01; *T-Bana to Slussen; 5pm-midnight Sun-Tue, till 1am Wed-Sat; www.olearys.se; V, MC, AE, DC*), a classic Irish-American sports bar that's popular with the local rugby players. Bruins, Celtics, and Pats merchandise blanket the walls, TVs are tuned in to international sporting events, and guys will find the *USA Today* sports section posted at eye level in the latrine. Drink pitchers of beer (165SEK) or try the good, though way expensive (94-178SEK per entree), pub food, such as the Bobby Orr bacon and mushroom burger, the Larry Bird club sandwich, and the Doug Flutie strawberry sundae. Expect nothing less than Heinz ketchup for your fries. No regular age requirement.

LIVE MUSIC SCENE

The electronica revolution hasn't yet taken over the land that spawned ABBA, Robyn, and the Cardigans. Pop, jazz, and rock still reign supreme, and there are tons of good local bands that sing mostly in English ('cause it's the only way to get famous). Music students hang out with the jazz cats at Fasching, while your more blue-collar, alternative musicians chill at Tre Backar. Don't expect eardrum-liquefying noise levels anywhere, Stockholm has a city ordinance restricting music to 100 decibels.

No matter who you ask—young or old, hip or square—the jazz club **Fasching** (*Kungsgatan 63; Tel 08/21-62-67; Bus 41 to Vasagatan; 8pm-2am Sun-Thur, till 5am Fri, Sat; 80-250SEK cover; www.fasching.se; V, MC, AE, DC*) is the place to go in Stockholm. Founded in the early '70s by local jazzmen looking for a place to gig, this place has become the stuff of legends, drawing big-name performers from Chick Corea to Joshua Redman. The space, just a block north of the T-Centralen Station, is intimate, and so narrow you'd better duck when the trombonists reach for their low notes. The summer season is slower, with most big-time musicians playing outdoor jazz festivals, but talented local cats are happy to step in and show their chops. The late-night dancing shoes come out for salsa early Saturday and soul disco classics early Sunday (both midnight-5am).

For lesser-known and less costly groove music, try **Mosebacke** (*Mosebacke Torg 3; Tel 08/55-60-98-90; T-Bana to Slussen; 5pm-2am; Free-80SEK cover; www.mosebacke.se; V, MC*) in Södermalm. A recent change in owners brought a change in 'tude, and the place that was once best known for its mellow jazz setting is now pulling in groovy local musicians and their butt-shaking hipster groupies. Sure bets are Tuesdays, when the Jazztified record label showcases its hot young ska bands and Stevie Wonder–laced R&B acts. "Club Cornelis," a tiny red-curtained room off the main hall, is still the best scene around for cheap jazz, with its free gigs Thursday to Sunday.

Another live music joint worth a visit is the cocktail lounge in the lobby of the hopelessly hip **Lydmar Hotel** [see *crashing*, below]. It's a great place to catch funky international acts; Maceo Parker, Roy Ayers, Isaac Hayes, and Jimmy McGriff have gigged here, as well as Swedish lounge crooners and jazz acts.

A grungy Irish-pub-turned-local-musicians'-hang up in Vasastaden, **Tre Backar** (*Tegnérgatan 12-14; Tel 08/673-44-00; T-Bana to Rådmans-gatan; Music 9 or 10pm-midnight, closed July; 20-50SEK cover; www.tre backar.se, V, MC, AE, Diners*) no longer gigs in Gaelic, but still has enough Mick in it to serve up a satisfying pint of Guinness, Kilkenny, or Caffrey's (only 38SEK from 2 till 8pm). A lineup of mostly young, local rock bands draws a similar crowd, who cram into and wreck the sweltering broom closet–esque performance space. On Saturdays a crew of more accomplished Swedish artists cook up old-school Chicago and New Orleans–style blues.

With a pretty even mix of local and international artists, **Studion** (*Sankt Eriksplan 4; Tel 08/34-44-54; T-Bana to Sankt Eriksplan; Music from 9 or 10-11pm, days vary, closed July, Aug; 20-150SEK depending on band; www.studion.net; No credit cards*) is your best bet for hearing a well-known band in a small venue. In the five years it's been around, Studion has brought in names like Verve Pipe, Natalie Imbruglia, the Pixies, Sean Mullins, and Supergrass. The crowd depends on the act, but it's generally a jeans-and-T-shirt kind of crew.

When the Backstreet Boys, Andrea Bocelli, Iron Maiden, or Whitney Houston are in town, they play to 16,000 screaming fans at **Globen** (*Globentorget 2; Tel 08/725-10-00; T-Bana to Globen; Box office 9am-6pm Mon-Fri, 10am-3pm Sat, closed Sun; www.globen.se; V, MC, AE*), down in Södermalm, which doubles as a hockey rink.

CLUB SCENE

When you look as good as people do in Sweden, you go out and flaunt it. And with over 50 clubs open on any given weekend, Stockholm provides plenty of choice. If you're eager to roll with the "in" crowd, hit the Sture-

STOCKHOLM bars, clubs and culture zoo

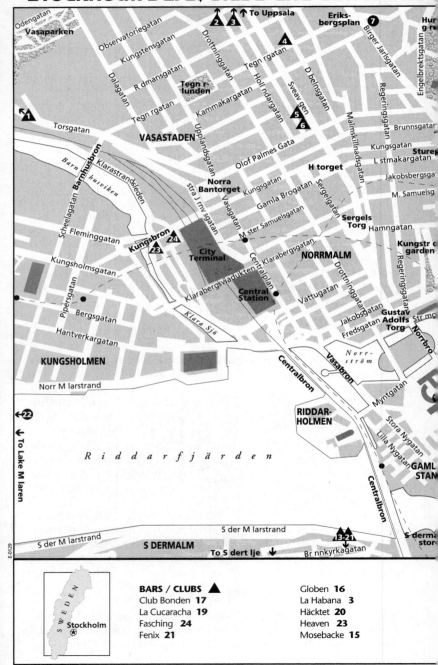

BARS / CLUBS ▲
Club Bonden **17**
La Cucaracha **19**
Fasching **24**
Fenix **21**

Globen **16**
La Habana **3**
Häcktet **20**
Heaven **23**
Mosebacke **15**

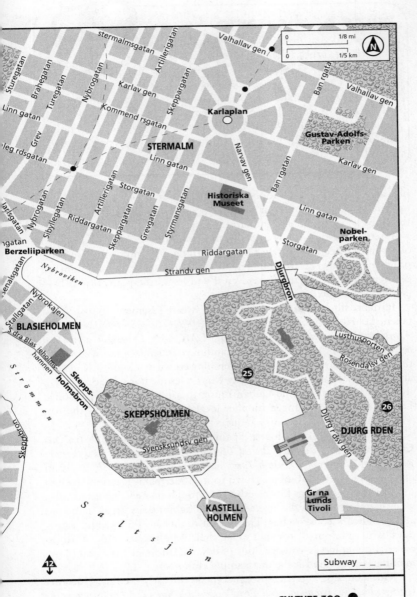

O'Learys **18**
Patricia **12**
Rosa Rummet **5**
Sophie's Bar **10**
Spy Bar **8**

String **13**
Studion **1**
Sture Compagniet **9**
Tip Top **6**
Tranan **2**
Wayne's Coffee **14**

CULTURE ZOO ●
Drottningholm Palace **22**
Kungliga Slottet **11**
Moderna Museet **7**
Skansen **26**
Vasa Museum **25**

Rules of The Game

In the land that invented schnapps, alcohol is the drug of choice. The legal drinking age is 18, but drinking in a club can be a little tricky because of age requirements. It's arbitrary: Some places say you have to be 18 to get in, while others say you have to be 21, 23, or 27. Cops are really tough on drunk drivers. Checkpoints aren't uncommon on weekend nights, so be careful with that rented Yugo if you've been slopping down the sauce. The drug scene is pretty low-key—people usually get high as a recreational alternative to booze.

plan area, where the velvet rope–burn is the nastiest. Don't bother showing up here in anything but your Saturday best. For a more laid-back scene, the clubs on Götgatan and the surrounding streets in Södermalm play to a more dressed-down crowd. Sadly, most nightlife in highly residential Söder has a strict 1am curfew. General warning: The most common party pitfall in S'holm is the age thing; many clubs here enforce a minimum age of anywhere from 18 to 27, so even if you've got the years, bring ID— getting sent home early sucks.

Its dance floor hidden away in a small, sweaty basement up past Vasastaden, **La Habana** (*Sveavägen 108; Tel 08/16-64-65; T-Bana to Rådmansgatan; 5pm-1am daily; No cover; V, MC, AE, Diners*) is a tropical retreat in an otherwise barren Scandinavian landscape. Wednesday through Saturday a mixed twentysomething crowd drinks 68SEK *mohitos* and *Cuba Libres* as a DJ spins Ricky Martin–esque hot salsa. Sundays, a live band plays traditional Cuban music to a lively older set of skilled Latin dancers and younger, blonder locals, who hang back at the bar. There's no dress code to worry about.

Another good spot for a Spanish/Latin inter-cultural fix, **La Cucaracha** (*Bondegatan 2; Tel 08/644-39-44; T-Bana to Medborgarplatsen; Club from 10:30pm-1am daily; No cover; V, MC, AE*) draws an older but energetic suburban crowd to its Södermalm location. Techno remixes of Gypsy Kings hits reverberate through the twisting catacombs, washing over stucco walls littered with bullfighter dolls, Jesus statuettes, and metalwork cockroaches. The busiest nights are Fridays and Saturdays, when the out-of-townies make their way into the city. With no cover and a come-as-you-are door policy, La Cucaracha is a solid low-maintenance option for the unassuming club-goer.

With a buzzing and friendly bar scene in the early evening, **Heaven** (*Kungsgatan 54; No phone; Bus 41 to Vasagatan, Bus 47, 69 to Kungsgatan; Opens 11:30pm Fri, Sat; No credit cards*) opens its doors to a crush of club-goers bent on storming the dance floor. Before you can say "Soul Train flashback," girls wearing teeny backpacks crowd onto raised platforms and fog machines cloud up the room. If you really want to make an impression, wear white—the dance floor is heavily black-lit. Eighteen to enter on Fridays, Saturdays are a bit stiffer: 23 for women, 25 for guys. Either night, know that sneakers and jeans are gonna buy you trouble at the door. Just down the road from **Fasching** [see *live music scene*, above] near the T-Centalen station.

Come to Stureplan and bask in the glow of the genetically fortunate at **Sture Compagniet** (*Sturegallerien 30; Tel 08/611-78-00; T-Bana to Östermalmstorg, Bus 41, 46, 55 to Stureplan; Midnight-5am Thur-Sat; 60-80SEK Thur, 100SEK Fri, Sat; www.sturecompagniet.se; V, MC, AE, Diners*), where a finger-lickin' crowd populates a five-bar complex. Most of the dancing takes place in the main hall, which moves to the loud sounds of house remixes. For more of a *Swingers* vibe, head upstairs for some jazz and fusion and chill with the dressier element. A second bar above the main floor plays Stax and Motown records. And for a really different experience, check out the rock 'n' roll bar on the ground level, which seems intent on bringing bands like Kiss, AC/DC, and Van Halen back from the black. While the door policy is sympathetic to travelers, your best bet is to put in an appearance before 1am. And however old you are, make sure your ID reads at least 23.

Spy Bar (*Birger Jarlsgatan 20; Tel 08/611-65-00; T-Bana to Östermalmstorg, Bus 41, 46, 55 to Stureplan; 10pm-5am Wed-Sat; No cover Wed, Thur, 100SEK Fri, Sat; V, MC, AE*), Stockholm's hot spot du jour, is mainly a members-only joint for the Swedish yuppie brigade. Situated in a lavish Stureplan apartment, the rooms in Spy Bar are cozy and loungey in a Bruce-Wayne-mansion sort of way. Several dance floors offer a choice of house, techno, reggae, and standard dance tracks; the hallways are a good place to cool down and mingle, especially by the wall of TV screens flashing vids of fashion shows and extreme snowboarding. If you try to get in on a weekend, show up as early as possible, dress slick, and bring women.

ARTS SCENE

▶▶VISUAL ARTS

You'll most likely be visiting Stockholm in the summertime (assuming you don't have a thing for 24-hour darkness), which, interestingly, may not be the best time to enjoy the arts scene—most galleries go into hibernation during the tourist season. But, wherever the city falls short in visual media, it easily makes up for in wearable media. The Swedish passion for shopping has served as subsidy to their thriving fashion marketplace, and the city boasts an understandably high number of designers per capita [see *stuff*, below].

Founded 25 years ago to serve as sort of a cultural supermarket, **Kulturhuset** (*Sergels Torg; Tel 08/508-31-508; Noon-6pm Mon-Fri, Noon-5pm Sat, Sun; 40SEK admission for major exhibitions; www.kulturhuset.stockholm.se*) does just that. Nearly one million visitors flood through the building each year to take in the various exhibits and use the numerous facilities. Two large galleries house shows ranging from interactive filmmaking exhibits to international collections of Harley-Davidson motorcycles. Smaller displays often line the hallways. Kulturhuset's resources also include an Internet cafe [see *wired*, below], a library with audio listening stations, video rental, magazine racks featuring most major publications, and Lava [see *hanging out*, above].

If you're around in the chillier months, when the fun gallery scene comes alive, be sure to pop into **Galleri Index** *(Sankt Paulsgatan 3; Tel 08/640-94-92; T-Bana to Slussen; Noon-4pm Tue-Sun)*, a noncommercial space in Södermalm dedicated to young contemporary Nordic and international artists. The main showroom downstairs houses mainly painting,

festivals and events

As if to show the rest of the world how stunning and refined they are, the Stockholmians open their city for a seemingly endless number of festivals during the spring, summer, and fall.

The most celebrated of them all is the **Stockholm Jazz & Blues Festival** *(Mid-July, www.stockholmjazz.com)*. Think about all the great live albums that came out of here: *Miles and Coltrane in Stockholm, Sonny Rollins in Stockholm,*...we could go on. And the repertoire has expanded to include heavy backbeats and Chicago shuffles. How's this for a roster: Ray Charles, George Clinton and the P-Funk All-Stars, Roy Hargrove, Tito Puente, Clark Terry, the Johnny Lang Blues Band, Maynard Ferguson, and Chick Corea. We have one word for you: Go.

The Stockholm Film Festival *(Mid-November, www.film festivalen.se)* pulls in as many as 50,000 guests to see roughly 160 films from three dozen countries. This is one of the earliest places to have recognized the jaded genius of Todd Solondz: He won the best script award for the comically bitter *Happiness.*

Still in its nascent years, the **Stockholm Pride festival** *(Late June to early July, www.stockholmpride.org)* has already become the leading celebration of queer-dom in Scandinavia, and it's building steam every year. Buy yourself a dogtag pass at **Rosa Rummet** [see *gay scene*, below], which gets you into all the parties, debates, theater performances, films, and concerts. Check out the official Web site for people willing to put up travelers, though you should be prepared for the possibility of some lovin' if you accept a free room—many guys ask for photos of their potential guests. This festival demonstrates how open this city is to gay life: The tourist office backs the event, hotels and taxi companies offer discounts to pass-bearers, and the Swedish national airline is an official sponsor, offering reduced fares.

photography, and video installations. One recent exhibit featured a darkly comical collection of silhouettes depicting African pilgrims in twisted configurations of sex and torture. Upstairs is a lounge area, formally dubbed the "sit-down-TV-magazine-corner," where you can relax, drink coffee, and watch the available video magazines.

Perched on the raised walkway on the Eastbound side of Hornsgatan, down in Södermalm, Stockholm's densest gallery strip, **Grafiska Sällskapet** (*Hornsgatan 6; Tel 08/643-88-04; T-Bana to Slussen; Noon-7pm Tue, till 6pm Wed-Thur, till 4pm Fri-Sun Sept-May,; www. grafiskasallskapet.pp.se; V, MC*) is devoted entirely to resident Swedish graphic artists. The styles and techniques represented by the huge number of contributors vary widely, from etchings to silkscreens to drypoints to lithographs. The gallery has geared itself towards the young collector, with prints starting at around 500SEK.

If you can't seem to find what you're looking for, why not make it yourself? The stationery and art supplies at **Ordning & Reda** (*Götgatan 32; Tel 08/714-96-01; T-Bana to Medborgarplatsen; 10am-6:30pm Mon-Fri, till 4pm Sat, noon-4pm Sun; www.ordning-reda.com; V, MC, AE, Diners*) are so cool-looking, you'll almost want to leave them untouched. O&R stocks notebooks, photo albums, and sketch pads in all shapes and sizes and all in bright, beautiful primary colors. There are other branches throughout Stockholm.

▶▶PERFORMING ARTS

Seeing films in Stockholm is a piece of cake; every Hollywood blockbuster is shown here in its original language and not long after the stateside release. The two largest cinemas are **BioPalatset** (*Medborgarplatsen; Tel 08/64-43-100; T-Bana to Medborgarplatsen; www.sandrews.se*) and **Filmstaden Sergel** (*Hötorget; Tel 08/56-26-00-00; T-Bana to Hötorget; www.sfe.se*), but there are dozens of others, so check listings in local newspapers. And be prepared for one cultural difference: Movie tickets come with assigned seats.

If you're more keen on Fellini and Kurosawa, you must swing by **Biografteatern Fågel Blå** (*Skeppargatan 60; Tel 08/661-80-35; T-Bana to Karlaplan or Bus 42, 44 to Skeppargatan; 70SEK; No credit cards*). Legendary Swedish director Ingmar Bergman, who used to live just up the block—and who still lives nearby and often strolls past—saw his first films here and brought his first dates here. To celebrate its most famous client, the 85-year-old Art Deco cinema usually shows about a dozen Bergman films, with English subtitles, during the summer.

For its size, Stockholm has a crazy amount of interesting dance going on. The leading supporter of the modern scene is **Dansenshus** (*Barnhusgatan 12-14; Tel 08/796-49-10; T-Bana or Bus 47, 69 to Hötorget; Box office noon-6pm in season, Aug-Dec, Jan-May; www.dansenshus.se, biljett@dansenshus.se; 160-270SEK , 50 percent discount if under 26; V, MC*), which is actually one of the biggest venues in Europe committed strictly to contemporary dance. The 800-seat main hall (which once held 35,000 liters of water for an experimental performance) plays host to troupes from the United States, Japan, and Scandinavia. The Blue Box (a small black-box theater painted, you guessed it, blue) features big-name international stars doing their thing solo, plus such varied styles as street funk, flamenco, and traditional Korean dance.

The Moderna Dansteatern (*Torpedverkstan, Skeppsholmen; Tel 08/611-14-56 information, 08/611-32-33 tickets; Bus 65 to af Chapman, after 6pm take T-Bana to Kungsträdgården; www.mdt.a.se, info@mdt.a.se; 150SEK, 100SEK students; V, MC*) is slightly more progressive and experimental, giving creative voice to established and struggling choreographers, dancers, and performance artists. The 130-seat auditorium is housed in a former military torpedo repair shop on Skeppsholmen.

If you're into the whole tutu scene, **Dansmuseet** (*Gustav Adolfs torg 22-24; Tel 08/441-76-50; T-Bana to T-Centralen or Kungsträdgården; 11am-8pm Tue, till 4 Wed-Fri, noon-5 Sat, Sun, closed Mon; 50SEK, 30SEK students; www.dansmuseet.nu; No credit cards*) is worth a visit. This unique museum, the first of its kind, traces the history of global dance through costume, video, art, and books.

gay scene

Stockholm's queer scene is open and happening, with beautiful dykes and the gorgeous men of Swedish porn fame holding court. Unfortunately, the hot spots can be a bit tricky to pin down; though a few shops and cafes have clustered on Hornsgatan, in Södermalm, and Sveavägen, in Vasastaden, there are no real gay neighborhoods, and places open and close quicker than even the locals can keep up with. Upon arrival in town, your first stop should be **Rosa Rummet** (*Sveavägen 57; Tel 08/736-02-15; T-Bana to Rådmansgatan; Noon-8pm Mon-Thur, noon-6pm Fri, 1pm-4pm Sat, Sun; www.rfsl.se/rosarummet; V, MC*), a gay and lesbian bookstore where you can find queer mags, books, videos, and music. Pick up a free copy of the annual *Gaymap*, which lists hot clubs, bars, restaurants, clothing and piercing shops, etc., or check them out online at ***www.gaymap.com***. If you get the map shortly before July 1, when the new edition is published, the bookstore's clerk can also cross out the roughly 50 percent of the places that no longer exist.

It ain't the Love Boat's "Pacific Princess," but on Sunday nights the good ship **Patricia** (*Stadsgårdskajen 152; Tel 08/743-05-70; T-Bana Slussen; 6pm-3am Sun; 50SEK cover after 9pm if you don't have dinner; www.ladypatricia.se; V, MC, AE, DC*) houses more queens than a royal convention. The boat, docked just off the northern coast of Södermalm, sponsors a weekly Sunday-night ritual for a diverse crowd of regulars, both gay and lesbian. Start the evening with a fine meal at half-price (50-90SEK per entree, fajitas are de riguer, tables are sometimes booked two weeks ahead) or hold off until later—food is served until 2am. Non-diners start filing in by 10:30 and sip drinks at one of three bars, five in summer, including an outdoor cocktail lounge above-deck. Deep in the hold, techno and house spin from 11:30pm to 3am, bringing young stallions, dykes, femmes, and drag queens to the dance floor.

Get more boner for your kroner at **Häcktet** (*Hornsgatan 82, at Restaurant Bysis; Tel 08/84-59-10; T-Bana to Slussen or Bus 55 to Timmermansgatan; 7pm-1am Wed, Fri; V, MC, AE, DC*), a cramped little restaurant that opens its doors for an award-winning gay party twice weekly. Wednesday draws a good mix of queers, both men and women, while Friday is more male and a bit younger. The graying old guard lingers around the fringes, sipping T&Ts, while the young'uns, under the influence of stellar house and Latin tunes, get hot and slippery on impromptu dance floors. Come before 10pm to beat the line.

Get as sleazy as you wanna be at **Tip Top** (*Sveavägen 57; Tel 08/32-98-00; T-Bana to Rådmansgatan; 4pm-3am; 20SEK cover Wed, Thur, 70SEK cover Fri, Sat; V, MC, AE, DC*), which is a bit more skanky than swanky. Despite having the decor of a run-down disco, Tip Top does bring in a crowd—mostly gay, but part lezzie—that ranges in age from teens to the old men who love them. The stray partygoer will shake a tail feather in the enclosed glass dance space, but most mingle around the various bars. They also serve Pad Thai (100SEK per entrée) from 6pm til 10pm.

CULTURE ZOO

Swedish culture, steeped in tradition, makes plenty of room for monuments to days gone by and remembrances of things past. A simple walk through Gamla Stan is as rich in history as most museums. Here are some of our favorite sight in and outside of Stockholm.

Skansen (*Djurgärden 49-51; Tel 08/442-80-00; Bus 47 to Djurgärden; 10am-8pm daily in May, 10am-10pm daily June-August, 10am-4pm daily in September, 11am-3pm daily in winter; www.skansen.se; 60SEK admission*): This place is like a zoo, a museum, and a Swedish Colonial Williamsburg all rolled into one. The 19th century workshops come complete with workers, in period peasant costumes, who toil and sweat for your amusement. In addition to the livestock kept on the farm, Skansen is also home to a wide variety of other beasties, ranging from wolves to wolverines to bears.

Moderna Museet (*Skeppsholmen; Tel 08/666-42-50; Bus 65 to Skeppsholmen; 11am-10pm Tue-Thur, 11am-6pm Fri-Sun; 60SEK admission; www.modernamuseet.se*): From surrealism to pop art, this museum has got the 20th century covered. With major works by artists like Dalí, Picasso, Brancusi, Matisse, Warhol, and a recent addition from Damien Hirst, Stockholm's Modern Museum is a must-see.

Vasa Museum (*Galärvarvet, Djurgärden; Tel 08/666-48-00; Bus 47 to Djurgärden; 9:30am-7pm daily June-August, hours vary rest of year; 50SEK admission*): This tremendous 17th-Century warship is the world's oldest surviving seagoing vessel. It's surprisingly well-preserved, having spent over three hundred years at the bottom of Stockholm harbor, where it sank several hundred feet into its maiden voyage. But, however dubious and unwarship-like its history, the sheer size of it makes the Vasa something worth seeing.

12 hours in Stockholm

1. Coffee Break: String [see *hanging out*, above] makes a groovy pit stop during a shopping excursion along Götgatan. One part coffee shop, one part dive, this mellow local hangout is ideal for catching up on reading or overdue postcard writing.

2. ...two if by sea: Rent yourself a boat at **Skepp & Höj** [see *great outdoors*, below] and cruise around the waters of Stockholm. It's a beautiful way to see the city, and the traffic is a hell of a lot smoother.

3. Absolut American: Savor the best that America has to offer—mostly junk food—at **Gray's American Food Store** [see *eats*, below]. In addition to the steady flow of expats that stream in for their Fritos fix, great gobs of Swedes who have tasted the fruits of America's splendor make a regular pilgrimage as well.

4. Roll with GenNext: Explore the work of the next generation of Swedish artists at **Lava** [see *hanging out*, above]. With a stage, recording equipment, computers for desktop publishing, and all sorts of other publicly available resources, Lava provides a forum for self-expression for Stockholm's youth culture. It's also a good place to just crash out and read.

5. Grab some grub in Thailand: Decked out like a tropical paradise, complete with thatch huts and the chirping of crickets, an evening at **Koh Phangon** [see *eats*, below] is about as close to the

---

Kungliga Slottet (*Kungliga Husgeradskammaren; Tel 08/402-61-32; T-Bana to Gamla Stan; Hours vary; 30-45SEK admission*): The official residence of the Swedish royal family, the Royal Palace's deceptively austere exterior disguises a lavish Italian Baroque interior. While here, you're welcome to check out the crown jewels, the palace armory, and you can even wander through the royal apartments—but don't expect to run into their royal highnesses, they mostly chill at nearby Drottningholm Palace.

Drottningholm Palace (*Lovön Island, Drottningholm; Tel 08/402-62-80; T-Bana to Brommaplan, then connect to any Mälar bus to Drottningholm; Hours vary; 40SEK admission*): About seven miles west of Stockholm, Drottningholm Palace is worth the trip. The palace grounds, a magnificent stretch of fountains, parks, and gardens, are commonly compared with Versailles, and the 18th century theater, one of the best-preserved in the world, hosts a number of performances, mostly opera, during the summer. The palace is also open to the public, but please remember this is where the blue bloods hang out, so stand up straight and definitely don't go rummaging through Her Royal Highness's knickers.

real deal as you're going to get in Scandinavia. Bring an appetite, and you might want to consider a fire extinguisher, because they like their food hot, hot, hot!

6. Do the high-profile lounge thing: Tip 'em back in style at the ultra-swank bar in the **Lydmar Hotel** [see *crashing*, below], where more often than not there will be live music to nod to. You'll pay an arm and a leg for drinks, but it just might be worth it for the celebs that stay and play here, like the Chemical Brothers and the Beastie Boys.

7. Trip the light fantastic: Shake your sacroiliac with the hotties at **Sture Compagniet** [see *club scene*, above]. You can get your swerve on at any of the four bars that crowd this triplex club; just be sure to show up early if you want to avoid the gnarly lines.

8. Break Out: One of the best things you can do when visiting Stockholm is leave...and take in a day in the **Swedish Archipelago** [see *great outdoors*, below]. Between the tens of thousands of islands off Sweden's eastern coast, there's plenty of wild countryside to explore, so grab a swimsuit and head out for some prime biking, hiking, camping, and cliff diving (yeah, you heard right...they love that shit here).

modification

When you arrive in Stockholm, you may wonder what the secret to the staggering Nordic beauty is. Unfortunately, it's genetics; so, for those of us who have some catching up to do, here are a few local recipes for quick-fix beautification.

Whatever look you're going for, from au naturel to Tammy Faye Baker, the makeup masters at **Face Stockholm** *(Biblioteksgatan 1; Tel 08/611-00-74; T-Bana to Östermalmstorg; 10am-7pm Mon-Fri, till 5 Sat, noon-4 Sun; V, MC, AE, Diners)* can help you hit the scene with your best face forward at any of their seven locations around town.

A total blast from the past, **R. Göller's** *(Hälsingegatan 2; Tel 08/31-39-04; T-Bana to Odenplan; 9am-6pm Mon-Fri; 180SEK for a wash and cut, men only; No credit cards)* is a '50s-style gentlemen's barbershop with everything but a striped pole outside. Disappointingly, after 26 years in business, this one-horse salon no longer uses the hair tonic and straight razor displayed in the window. But, if a simple, clean cut is all you need, a haircut here, for 180SEK, is one of the best deals in Stockholm.

Far more funky is **Hair Studio** *(Mäster Samuelsgatan 1; Tel 08/611-*

by foot

Stockholm is a city of beauty—in its architecture, its people, and its natural surroundings. This walk takes you through the city's different phases, starting in the modern center of commerce and ending in Gamla Stan, the old city.

Start at **Hötorget**, the city square where merchants set up stands of fruit, vegetables, and crafts. Take **Gamla Brogatan** south, then turn left on **Drottninggatan**. You're now walking down the busiest shopping street in the city, which, especially during the lunch hour, feels like a people zoo. This is a pedestrian street; notice the lion statues used to keep traffic out. As you cross **Klarabergsgatan**, look on your left for Kulturhuset [see *arts scene*, above], a cultural center like the Centre Pompidou in Paris, with exhibitions, an Internet cafe, and a chill youth center open in the summer. Keep going down Drottninggatan and cross over the cobblestoned **Riksbron bridge**. Stop for a view of the sea and the city's islands. Next, you'll cross the **Stallbron bridge**, where enterprising Swedish massage therapists set up portable massage chairs for weary travelers. Continue straight into Gamla Stan ("Old Town" in Swedish), where the streets narrow and the tourist density skyrockets. After Kåkbrinken, an ice cream shop that sells gigantic waffle cones, take a left down the alley of the same name. This side street takes you up a hill to **Stortorget square**, a popular visitors' hangout where you

11-60; *T-Bana to Östermalmstorg; 9am-7pm Mon-Fri, 10-4 Sat; 325-450SEK depending on the style; www.hairstudio.nu.se; V, MC, AE, Diners*), a Stureplan salon that plays Dennis Rodman to R. Göller's Mr. Rogers. Pretty stylists mold snappy head-sculpture in a vibrant atmosphere notable for its loud pop radio tunes and a profusion of blow-up alien dolls. Inflated martians aside, expect to have the air taken out of your billfold.

For your flesh-puncturing needs, head over to **Plain Pain** (*Gamla Brogotan 27; Tel 08/411-26-30; T-Bana to T-Centralen; Noon-6pm Mon-Fri; No credit cards*), where a vaguely reassuring sign on the wall attests to the proprietor's successful completion of a course on blood-borne pathogens. We recommend that you try not to look at the stomach-turning photos of exotic piercings behind the counter. Prices range from 200SEK for an ear pierce to 550SEK for a bar through the nuts. A tattoo artist also does tribals and custom renderings for around 500SEK and up.

great outdoors

While the Swedes' activity of choice in the winter is to leave Scandinavia for warmer climes, blond bodies crawl over every inch of the Swedish can snap photos of old Stockholm and eat your ice cream. Where Kåkbrinken meets Stortorget, turn onto **Skomakargatan** and look up. On the corner of the building on your left, a cannonball is embedded in the wall. No one knows if it's genuine or a restauranteur's gimmick, but most travelers don't notice it anyway. Walk down Skomakargatan to the end and turn left on **Tyska Brinken**. Continue straight as it turns into **Kindstugatan**. You're now off the beaten path, between two heavily trafficked streets. You'll come to a little green square called **Brända Tomten**, where locals sit in the shade with their dogs. Head left on **Själagårdsgatan**, right on **Köpmangatan**, and right down the hill at the **statue of Sankt Göran**, onto **Österlånggatan**. As you head south down the street, peer into the tiny alleys on the left, which lead down to the water. You'll finally reach **Järntorget**, where you'll find more masseuses and masseurs. From the square, take a left onto **Södra Bankogränd**, then right on **Skeppsbron**, and immediately look at the door frame above restaurant **Züm Franziskaner**. Locals swear that a former owner had a representation of his mistress' naughty bits engraved in stone above the front door, but we just don't see it. You be the judge. Finish your walk by continuing to walk down Skeppsbron along the waterfront until you reach **Slussen**, where there's a T-Bana stop.

countryside in the summertime. After spending six months in virtually perpetual darkness, Swedes turn sunworship into an extreme sport, taking every opportunity to expose their bare flesh to the searing rays of our stellar center...but in a good way.

For starters, upgrade your mode of transportation and rent a bike or some blades at **Skepp & Höj** [see *need to know*, below]. They rent by the hour *(50SEK first hour, 40SEK/hour thereafter)* or by the week *(500SEK)*. If you're really feeling adventurous, hire a canoe or a rowboat for an hour *(60SEK/hour and 80SEK/hour, respectively)* and check out Stockholm from its waterways.

Easily the most popular of the city's many green spaces, **Djurgården** [see *neighborhoods*, above], previously a royal hunting ground, is now an island paradise for Stockholm's fresh-air fanatics. The expansive park grounds offer hours of trails for walking and biking and plenty of shoreline for swimmers, picnickers, and sunbathers. **Rålambshov**, a park to the west on Kungsholmgaten, is wall-to-wall people at the first sign of sun. You can enjoy a good swim off the shore here and maybe catch a game of frisbee, and people are welcome to join in the muscle beach–style workouts that often happen on the green.

Stockholm is built on only a handful of the thousands of islands that are scattered throughout the Swedish archipelago—so if you're eager to get away from the crowds in the city, an island-hopping excursion should top your list. Many islands, like **Utö**, have hosteling or camping facilities, and some rent bikes or kayaks. **Vaxholm** is a quick trip, but if you want a little privacy, you'll need to put aside at least a day for outings as far as Sandham or Dalarö. Ferries leave regularly from Nybrohamnen and Strömgatan; for information call **Waxholmsbolaget** *(Tel 08/679-58-30; Prices and departure times vary)* or **Strömma Kanalbolaget** *(Tel 08/587-140-00; Prices and departure times vary)*.

Another popular Swedish pastime is fishing, which is legal and common both in and out of Stockholm. The waters coursing through the city are rich with pike, perch, trout, and salmon—and we're talking healthy specimens...these puppies aren't like the mutated freaks you pull out of New York's Hudson River. For equipment rental and some quick pointers, try **Fiskarnas Redskapshandel** *(Sankt Paulsgatan 4; Tel 08/644-21-29)*.

STUFF

The only thing Swedes defend with as much vigor as their summers is their right to consume conspicuously. The local retail motto: If you sell it, they will come. Stockholm has enough indoor shopping arcades and department stores to chew through your credit cards in a hurry, so pace yourself. Just about every neighborhood in Norrmalm is wall-to-wall shopping—you half-expect to see American Express stickers in apartment windows. Norrmalmstorg makes for good middle-of-the-road-to-upscale shopping, with **Sisley, InWear/Matinique**, **DKNY**, and **Esprit** outlets within shouting distance of each other. For high fashion and more genuine Swedish styles, take a stroll down Grev Turegatan or saunter down Biblioteusgaten and grab an Irish coffee at Biblios [see *bar scene,* above]. If you're counting your pennies, you might want to relocate your shopping efforts to Götgatan, where the merchants won't bleed you quite as dry as the bankroll bandits in Norrmalm.

▶▶MALL RATS

Attention K-Mart shoppers: This is not the store for you. The Bloomingdales of Stockholm, **NK** *(Hamngatan; T-Bana to T-Centralen; 10am-7pm Mon-Fri, till 5pm Sat, noon-5pm Sun; V, MC, Diners)* is the most upscale shopping center in town, complete with designer clothing outlets, perfume and makeup counters, leather goods shops, a glass and crystal store...well, you get the gist. There's even a Forex booth on the ground floor in case your money runs out. How thoughtful. Don't miss the bakery on the lower level: It's our favorite part.

▶▶HOT COUTURE

Stockholm's busiest strip for fashion seekers is the southern stretch of Grev Turegatan, just a block off of Stureplan. **Anna Holtblad** *(Grev Turegatan 13; Tel 08/545-02-220; T-Bana to Östermalmstorg; 11am-7pm Mon-Fri, till*

4pm Sat; V, MC, AE, Diners), a well-known Swedish designer of women's clothing, recently set up shop on Grev Turegatan. Holtblad's colorful styles and airy materials are particularly popular with young girls. Just up the street, **Filippa K** *(Grev Turegatan 18; Tel 08/662-20-15; T-Bana to Östermalmstorg; 11am-7pm Mon-Fri, till 5pm Sat, noon-4pm Sun; www.filippa-k.com; V, MC, AE, Diners)* has evolved into more of a consumer label, offering increasingly practical clothes for both guys and gals. Filippa K's collections cover the technicolor rainbow from gray to black...very typical of Swedish designs.

Inside **NK** [see above], **NK Independent** *(Regeringsgatan 55; Tel 08/762-89-45; T-Bana to T-Centralen; 10am-7pm Mon-Fri, till 5pm Sat, noon-5pm Sun; V, MC, AE, Diners)* showcases Sweden's established and up-and-coming designers. For women's clothing, **Elizabeth Yanagisawa**'s uniquely blended European-Japanese aesthetic is stunning. Reminiscent of Japanese paper lanterns, the sheer, crumpled fabrics she uses are even more startling as pants. Also be sure to check out **Nygårdsanana**, Sweden's most well-known women's designer, who represents a very Swedish taste, offering subtle variations in tone and stitching to alter the lay of her clothing. NK Independent also houses a selection of menswear from Swedish minds. **J. Lindberg** has gone very, very retro. '50s-style shirts are on the make again, with plenty of wide-collared, short-sleeved plaids to go around. And, apparently, the terrycloth craze has finally hit Scandinavia. For a complete change of pace, get out of the old and get dressed with the Jetsons: **Whyred?** offers sleek, synthetic, skintight garments in stark black, red, and yellow with randomly placed zippers for a futuristic effect. For a happy medium, **Tiger** offers a trendy, suit-heavy, European look.

▶▶CLUB GEAR

Bursting at the seams with Day-glo tops, leopard print stretch pants, and sequin g-strings, **C.U.M.** *(Klara Norra Kyrkogatan 21-23; Tel 08/10-40-18; to T-Centralen; 11am-6pm Mon-Fri, noon-4pm Sat; V, MC, AE)*, a clubwear/divawear outlet, attracts a big transvestite and stripper crowd. They actually sell Austin Powers–style, British flag–decorated crotch huggers. Watch underfoot for FiFi, the resident chihuahua—drop the chalupa, man.

Serving the rhythmically advantaged among the local white-bread population, **Home Boy** *(Gamla Brogatan 32; Tel 08/411-42-78; T-Bana to T-Centralen; www.homeboyonline.com; V, MC, Diners)* sells a complete line of hip-hop clothing, from low-riding jeans to the latest in next gen sneaker design. The proprietors of Home Boy live by their motto, "Listen loud and dress accordingly," bringing over bands from New York like the Black Star and Wu-Tang Clan. They also sell over a hundred colors and styles of spray paint for graffiti artists.

▶▶SKATE RATS

Truly a thrasher's paradise, **08** *(Norrlandsgatan 18; Tel 08/679-80-08; T-Bana to Östermalmstorg; 10am-6:30pm Mon-Fri, till 4pm Sat, noon-4pm Sun; www.nollatta.com; V, MC, AE)* offers a complete complement of boards and threads, from Kangol hats to Fox street gear to Globe sneaks. The counter dudes are down with the local scene and can show you where the best halfpipes are and which streets offer the gnarliest rails to grind.

▶▶BACK IN BLACK

Blue Fox (*Gamla Brogatan 27; Tel 08/20-32-41; T-Bana to T-Centralen; 11am-6:30pm Mon-Fri, 10am-4:30pm Sat; V, MC*) is the local purveyor of metalhead clothing, providing row upon row of black long-sleeved shirts with emblems from every big-hair band that ever featured a strong "lyrics advisory" on their albums. In addition, Blue Fox boasts a full line of steel-toed shitkickers and an overstock of blacklight-friendly stoner tees.

▶▶BOUND

The shops at **Sture Gallerian**, an indoor gallery just off Stureplan, are also for the well-heeled but offer a tad more by way of variety. **Hedengrens** (*Stureplan 4; Tel 08/611-51-28; T-Bana to Östermalmstorg; 10am-8pm Mon-Fri, till 5pm Sat, noon-5pm Sun; hedengrens@hedengrens.se; V, MC, AE, Diners*) bookstore, at the entrance of the Sture Gallerian, is your best bet for non-Swedish reading in Stockholm. The downstairs stocks predominantly English materials, which constitute a fairly decent collection of fiction, nonfiction, and academic titles across several disciplines.

▶▶TUNES

Just next door to Blue Fox, **Pitch** (*Gamla Brogatan 27; Tel 046/822-56-40; T-Bana to Hötorget; 11am-6pm Mon-Fri, till 4pm Sat; pitch@telia.com; V, MC, AE, DC*) outfits DJs for everything from weddings to raves. This place stocks top 40, hip-hop, and electronic dance, as well as record needles and DJ bags.

▶▶BAZAAR

Småsmulor (*Skånegatan 75; Tel 08/642-53-34; T-Bana to Medborgarplatsen; 9:30am-6pm Mon-Fri, 10am-3pm Sat; No credit cards*) is more like an indoor flea market than a secondhand shop. Here you can find anything from old Jordaches to Swedish Harlequin novels. Boxes of LPs store titles like *Brahms' Greatest Hits* and Hall and Oats' *H2O*. Beneath the teddy bears with missing eyes and the fluorescent unitards is some good stuff...just keep digging.

EATS

Stockholm's culinary scene has seen an explosion in the last decade, leaving locals startled by the number and variety of new restaurants springing up around the city. Swedish food is robust; its culinary staples, fish and meat, are often smothered in cream sauces. But international favorites—Thai, Indian, Chinese, American, Japanese—are also making a surge, and many have become the hottest restaurants in their respective neighborhoods.

Take our advice: If you want to drop a little money and eat well, do it during lunch. Places competing for the business crowd whip together full meals, including salad, bread, and water or juice, for less money than

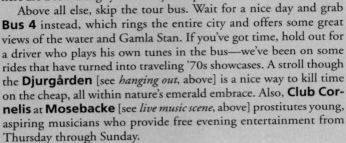

down and out

If you've come to Stockholm on a tight budget, fuggedaboudit. But, if you've just watched some horribly gleeful merchant cut your last credit card in two, here are a few things you can try in a pinch:

Above all else, skip the tour bus. Wait for a nice day and grab **Bus 4** instead, which rings the entire city and offers some great views of the water and Gamla Stan. If you've got time, hold out for a driver who plays his own tunes in the bus—we've been on some rides that have turned into traveling '70s showcases. A stroll though the **Djurgården** [see *hanging out*, above] is a nice way to kill time on the cheap, all within nature's emerald embrace. Also, **Club Cornelis** at **Mosebacke** [see *live music scene*, above] prostitutes young, aspiring musicians who provide free evening entertainment from Thursday through Sunday.

most dinnertime appetizers. That is, unless you have the ducats to back up your tastes, in which case you should skip ahead to the delectable *splurge*, below. P.S. Tipping isn't necessary in Sweden.

▶▶CHEAP

If you're traveling through Europe as the last hurrah of a semester abroad, let us lead you to the promised land: **Gray's American Food Store** (*Odengatan 39; Tel 08/612-30-40; T-Bana to Odenplan; 10am-6pm Mon-Fri, 11am-4pm Sat, noon-4pm Sun; V, MC, AE*). This place features the most essential in American junk food, including Bubblicious gum, Whatchamacallit candy bars, Pepperidge Farms goldfish, and Kool-Aid. Young Swedes shop here like crazy: Guys come to chug caffeine-loaded Jolt cola (picture them with a T-shirt pulled over their blond heads sputtering "I need TP for my bunghole!" à la Beavis), and au pairs just back from the States come to fuel their recently acquired Doritos habit.

We highly recommend a stop at **Saluhall** (*Östermalmstorg; 9:30am-6pm Mon-Thur, till 6:30pm Fri, 9:30am-2pm Sat; No credit cards*), a large indoor food market selling high-quality meats, fish, pastas, dairy, baked goods, coffee, and fine cigars. Go on an empty stomach, because you'll definitely want to sample the wares: A small cafe area offers instant gratification for hungry shoppers.

For the cheapest chow around, wade through the teenyboppers at **Kungshallen** (*Kungsgatan 44; T-Bana 1 to Hötorget; 9am-11pm Mon-Fri, 11am-11pm Sat, noon-11pm Sun; 50-70SEK per entree; Credit cards vary*) for the international offerings that have become standard in food courts: Greek, Japanese, Mexican, Italian. For huge portions of not-bad Chinese, stop at Hot Wok Cafe, where they'll sizzle up a pork, chicken, or vegetarian dish with noodles or rice right in front of you. There are also

STOCKHOLM EATS AND CRASHING

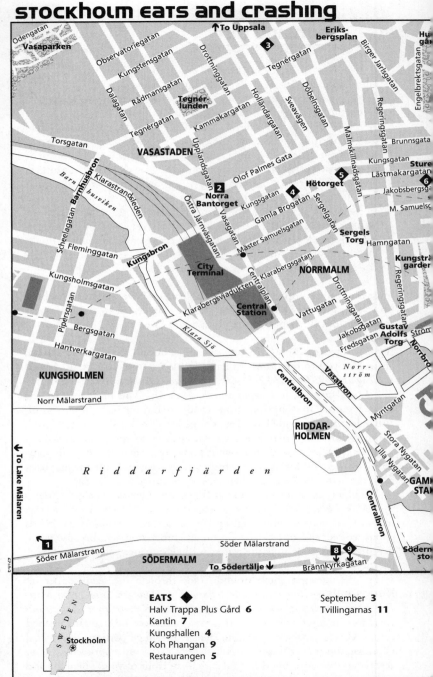

EATS ◆
Halv Trappa Plus Gård **6**
Kantin **7**
Kungshallen **4**
Koh Phangan **9**
Restaurangen **5**

September **3**
Tvillingarnas **11**

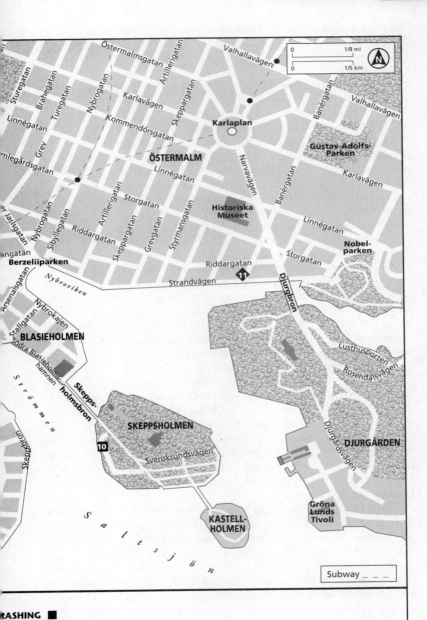

Östermalmsgatan
Artillerigatan
Valhallavägen
Sturegatan
Brahegatan
Turegatan
Nybrogatan
Karlavägen
Skeppargatan
Banérgatan
Valhallavägen
Linnégatan
Grev
Kommendörsgatan
Karlaplan
Gustav-Adolfs-Parken
rmlegårdsgatan
ÖSTERMALM
Linnégatan
Narvavägen
Banérgatan
Karlavägen
r Jarlsgatan
Nybrogatan
Sibyllegatan
Artillerigatan
Storgatan
Skeppargatan
Grevgatan
Styrmansgatan
Historiska Museet
Linnégatan
Nobel-parken
angatan
Riddargatan
Storgatan
Berzeliiparken
Riddargatan
Nybroviken
Strandvägen
Djurgårdbron
Arsenalsgatan
Stallgatan
Nybrokajen
BLASIEHOLMEN
Lusthusporten
Södra Blasieholms-
hamnen **holmsbron**
Skepps-
Rosendalsvägen
Strömmen
SKEPPSHOLMEN
Djurgårdsvägen
DJURGÅRDEN
Skeppsbron
Svensksundsvägen
KASTELL-HOLMEN
Gröna Lunds Tivoli
S a l t s j ö n

0   1/8 mi
0   1/5 km

Subway _ _ _

CRASHING ■
Chapman & Skeppsholmen **10**
ty Backpackers **2**
ngholmen **1**
nkensdamm Vandrarhem & Hotell **8**

Hot Wok Cafe branches at Hantverkargatan 78 *(Tel 08/654-42-02; T-Bana to Rådhuset)* and Nortullsgatan 11 *(Tel 08/33-71-81; T-Bana to Odenplan or Bus 46).*

▶▶**DO-ABLE**

For a stellar Swedish-style lunch, stop by **September** *(Luntmakargatan 99; Tel 08/14-44-70; T-Bana to Rådmansgatan; 11am-2pm/5pm-1am Mon-Fri, 5pm-1am Sat, closed Sun; 59-62SEK per lunch entree, 95-162SEK per dinner entree; www.restaurang-september.se; V, MC, AE),* a tiny little place that feels more like a bar than a restaurant. The menu changes daily, depending on the market, but you always have a fish, a meat, and a veggie dish to choose from. Ask for a translation, and expect something like cod with sour cream and tomato sauce served on a bed of ratatouille. Pay first, then stop by the lunch table for salad, water or lingonberry iced tea (a Swedish classic), and slices of spongy bread slathered with cheese, perfect for sopping up the thick sauces.

It's not easy to make a salad feel like a heavy meal, but **Kantin** *(Norrlandsgatan 24; Tel 08/611-88-10; T-Bana to Hötorget or Östermalmstorg, or Bus 46, 55 to Stureplan; 11:30am-midnight Mon-Thur, till 2am Fri, Sat, 50-60SEK; kantin@matovin.com; V, MC, AE, DC)* pulls it off with style. Choose between the ever-changing veggie plate (offering stuff like greens with avocado and red peppers with hot new potatoes smothered in butter) or the meat plate (think ground lamb patty with capers, red onions, and herb butter). Sit at communal tables beside the city's trendy young business crowd in their designer eyewear and three-button suits. Go there between 12:30pm and 2pm, and the lunch is only 50SEK.

If the great outdoors is just a-callin' your name, dine where the summer yuppies (suppies?) go to see and be seen: **Tvillingarnas** *(Strandvägskajen 27; Tel 08/663-37-39; Bus 47, 69 to Strandvågan; 8am-1am May-Sept, lunch 11-4, closed winter; 67-72SEK prix-fixe lunch, 69-115SEK per dinner entree; www.tvillingarnas.com; V, MC, AE),* located on a dock by the bridge to Djurgården. Go for lunch, when the value is as good as the people-watching. The meal of fish or pasta comes with bread, salad, beer, and coffee. Bring sunscreen and shades on a bright day, when the sun kicks up hot off the water.

The chirping crickets, thatch huts, and stereophonic thunderstorms at **Koh Phangan** *(Skånegatan 57; Tel 08/642-50-40; T-Bana to Medborgarplatsen or Skanstull; 11am-midnight Mon-Thur, till 1am Fri, 2pm-1am Sat, Sun; 90-220SEK per entree, lunch at about 60SEK; www.kohphangan.nu; V, MC, AE, DC)* will make you forget that the restaurant's island namesake, off the coast of Thailand, is 11,340km away (according to a sign in the bar)—that's some 7,000 miles to you Yanks. The food is as legit as the atmosphere, a new menu is now coming into action with such delicacies as chicken in scorchingly hot Thai curry with baby eggplant, sweet basil, and noodles, or sweet chicken with cashews and snow peas and the house specialty, a phenomenal seafood platter. Ask for a menu in English. The bar is cozy and lively, with DJs playing roots and reggae Tuesday–Sunday, which is key, 'cause you'll be spending some serious time here—the restaurant doesn't take reservations, and the wait for a table can often stretch to two hours.

▶▶SPLURGE

Opened in 1997 by a popular Swedish restauranteur, **Halv Trappa Plus Gård** (*Lästmakargatan 3; Tel 08/611-02-77; T-Bana to Hötorget or Östermalmstorg, or Bus 46, 55 to Stureplan; 5pm-1am Mon, Tues, 5pm-3am Wed-Sat, closed Sun; 135-215SEK per entree; V, MC, AE, DC*) features a bombastic, mainly mediterranean, cuisine that scores big more often than it goes over the top. The menu changes monthly and is set to include more traditional fare alongside the southern European staples. Filled with the balding hip, this is the type of place that leaves you debating whether the walls are more of a burnt sienna than an umber. The outdoor terrace is a hugely popular drinker's hang on warm nights, packing them a dozen deep at the bar. New developments for 2002 include live jazz and funk nights—apply directly for details.

Gimmicky restaurants have a tendency to crash and burn, but **Restaurangen** (*Oxtorgsgatan 14; Tel 08/22-09-52; T-Bana to Hötorget; 11:30am-1am Mon-Fri, 5pm-1am Sat, closed Sun; 190-250SEK per meal; V, MC, AE, DC*) backs up its schtick with refined food and elegance. Here's their bag: Diners choose meals of three or five "tastes" (three is enough for most people) such as "saffron" (a paella dish with chorizo and prawns), "kaffir lime" (a tangy Thai mussel soup), or "barbecue" (a boneless rib brisket). With a long list of delectable-sounding tastes, you'll probably find yourself second-guessing your choices...that is, until the food is served. Each dish presented is stunning in its color, symmetry, and flavor. The decor is even more stylish than the food: Bare white walls set off by mammoth abstract paintings, a ceiling sculpture looks like a giant Pick Up Sticks game, and the projected wall clock all give the feeling that you're dining in a modern art gallery.

crashing

So here's the problem with Swedish hostels: They're clean, but they're pretty expensive and have no age limit. That's a deadly combination for the budget traveler, because penny-pinching families who plan their vacations months in advance Bogart all the rooms. Your best bet for a short-notice bed is to stop by **Hotell Centralen** (*Central Station, main floor; Tel 08/24-24-25; 7am-9pm daily May-Sept, 9am-6pm Mon-Fri Oct-Apr*), the tourist office's reservation service, or ring up the City Backpackers hostel. If they don't have a room free, they might be able to refer you somewhere else. Also, City Backpackers is one of the only hostels in the city that doesn't charge more if you're not a member of the International Youth Hostel Federation. If you want to save money, get an IYHF membership, and bring sheets and a padlock so you don't have to rent them.

▶▶CHEAP

Stockholm is just too sophisticated for the *Animal House* shenanigans and all-night bashes of youth hostels in Amsterdam, Berlin, and the like. Nowhere is this more evident than in **Zinkensdamm Vandrarhem**

(Zinkens Väg 20; Tel 08/616-81-00; T-Bana to Zinkensdamm; 135SEK-175SEK/person quad, 225SEK-265SEK/person single or double for IYHF members, 40SEK extra for non-members; info.zinkensdamm@swedenho tels.se; V, MC, AE, DC), the biggest and probably most boring hostel in the city. That said, the rooms are clean, each with cheesy flower-print curtains and small bunk beds. There's also a communal kitchen, laundry machines, a TV room, and bike rentals. This place is on the western part of Södermalm, a 10-minute walk from the T-Bana station past verdant gardens. Bring your own breakfast; theirs costs 60SEK.

For more ambience, hipper travelers, and a central location, head to **City Backpackers** *(Upplandsgatan 2A; Tel 08/20-69-20; T-Bana to T-Centralen; 150SEK/person 8-bed room, 180SEK/person quad, 225SEK/person double, no private bathrooms; city.backpackers@swipnet.se, www.svif.se/57.htm; No credit cards)*, a cozy, well-worn hostel in an old house. Staff members are in their twenties, so they can recommend places to go out. There's a communal living room with cable TV, a stocked kitchen complete with coffeemaker, and a dry sauna for 10SEK. Sweeet! Beware: The main entrance has the funk of 40,000 years going on— management makes all travelers leave their shoes in the front hall to save on cleaning bills.

Only the chosen few (in other words, those who plan ahead) get to stay in Stockholm's most famous youth hostel, **af Chapman & Skeppsholmen** *(Västra brobänken; Tel 08/463-22-66; Bus 65 to af Chapman, after 6pm take T-Bana to Kungsträdgården; 100SEK/person in 15-bed dorm for IYHF members, 140SEK for non-members, 130SEK/person in 4- to 10-bed rooms for IYHF members, 170SEK for non-members, 150SEK/person double for IYHF members, 190SEK for non-members; www.stfurist.se/van drarh/chapman.htm, info@chapman.stfurist.se; V, MC, AE)*. Af Chapman is a gorgeous, turn-of-the-century clipper ship, with an on-deck cafe and 136 sleeping berths, while Skeppsholmen is a cozy, ancient building overlooking the harbor. If you haven't made reservations months in advance, you still have a slim chance if you're an early bird: Management holds onto some nonreservable beds during the summer, but they start offering them at 7am, and lines are already curling out the door by then; the rooms are gone by 9am.

▶▶**DO-ABLE**

Attached to the youth hostel on Södermalm is **Zinkensdamm Hotel** *(Zinkens Väg 20; Tel 08/616-81-10; T-Bana to Zinkensdamm; info.zinkens damm@swedenhotels.se; 1,130SEK double weekdays, 850SEK double weekends, 845SEK single weekdays, 595SEK single weekends, all w/ private bathroom; V, MC, AE, DC)*, a plain-'ol three-star hotel with comfortable, though pretty institutional, rooms. The hallways and rooms are a little dark. On the plus side, it's clean, in a quiet spot with a suburban feel, and the price includes breakfast and a sauna.

For a *Jailhouse Rock* vibe, try **Långholmen** *(Island of Långholmen; Tel 08/668-05-10; T-Bana or Bus 40, 54, 66 to Hornstull; 1,195SEK double weekdays Sept-May, 895SEK single weekdays Sept-May, 895SEK*

All you digerati out there can research your trip before leaving by logging on to Stockholm's official website, ***www.stoinfo.se***. Here you'll find links to hotels, restaurants, and festivals, as well as information about the tourist office. Check out ***www.stonight.com***, an unofficial site run by a bunch of young scrubs, to find out all you need to know about the current club and bar scene. It's very cool and very candid.

When you get to Stockholm and need to satisfy your online jonesing, you have plenty of choices:

Nine *(Odengatan 44; Tel 08/612-90-09; T-Bana to Odenplan; 10-1am Mon-Fri, 11-1am Sat, Sun; V, MC, AE)* is a high-tech Internet cafe in the basement of an excellent coffee shop. With enormous monitors on its 30 new computers, this place attracts gamers like ants to watermelon. Grab a brick of maple syrup-soaked corn bread from the cafe and surf the Net for 1SEK per minute.

Miss the feeling of playing hooky from school? Live vicariously through the young hooligans at **Cafe Tilt** *(Birgr Jarlsgatan 9; Tel 08/678-04-24; T-Bana to Östermalmstorg; 10am-11pm Mon-Fri, 1pm-11pm Sat, Sun; No credit cards)*, a video arcade that also has eight computers for surfing. The place seems a bit seedy, but it's perfectly safe (high-fashion boutiques are its neighbors), so venture in if you want to refine your Pac-Man skills before you check your e-mail. Internet prices are 1SEK per minute or 50SEK per hour.

Downtown holds two Internet joints. **Internet C@fe** *(Drottninggatan 63; Tel 08/555-412-00; T-Bana to Hötorget; 10-7 Mon-Fri, till 5 Sat, noon-4 Sun; No credit cards)* is a run-of-the-mill place, on the top floor of the P.U.B. department store on Hötorget. They charge 1SEK per minute. Much funkier, and closer to the train station, is **Café Access** *(Sergelstorg 31; Tel 08/508-31-489; T-Bana to T-Centralen; 10am-7pm Tue-Fri, 10am-5pm Sat, Sun, closed Mon; www.cafeaccess.se; No credit cards)*, in **Kulturhuset** [see *arts scene*, above]. They also charge 1SEK per minute.

double weekends, holidays, and June-Aug, 595SEK single weekends, holidays, and June-Aug; www.langholmen.com, vandrarhem@langholmen.com; V, MC, AE, DC), an old prison where the only guillotining in Sweden's history went down in 1910. Lucky you get to sleep behind reinforced wooden doors in an actual cell, with a locker, a small table, and bunk beds. OK, you might feel a little claustrophobic, but it's not every day you get to sleep where murderers, thieves, and oppressed writers once did their time (unless you happen to be from New York). The former prison yard is now an outdoor cafe, with a dummy guard keeping his post. There's also a little sand beach outside the front door, where you can hit the waters that flow between Stockholm's islands. Management has a few rooms set aside for backpackers at youth hostel prices *(IYHF members: 155SEK/person single, double, or quad w/o private bath, 175SEK/person single, double, or quad w/private bath, 40SEK extra for non-members).*

▶▶**SPLURGE**

Visiting artists and musicians (the likes of Chaka Khan and Paula Abdul) inevitably find themselves crashing at **Lydmar Hotel** *(Sturegatan 10; Tel 08/566-113-00; T-Bana or Bus 46, 55 to Stureplan; 1,450-1,700SEK single weekdays, 975-1,215SEK single weekends and holidays, 1,700-2,900SEK double or suite weekdays, 1,215-2,400SEK double or suite weekends and holidays, all with private bath or shower; www.lyd mar.se, info@lydmar.se; V, MC, AE, DC).* Man, is it refreshing to find a classy hotel that doesn't take itself too seriously: The lobby is a cocktail lounge with live music most nights and risqué photo exhibits; the five clocks above the reception each say "Stockholm" beneath and tell the same time; and—the *pièce de resistance*—the lift has choose-your-own elevator music, with hip choices ranging from ambient to Latin to jungle. Each room has Ralph Lauren wallpaper, a minibar, Internet connections, and free movie channels on TV. The less expensive rooms are a bit small but still stylish.

need to know

Currency The **Swedish Krona (SEK)** is the national currency, which is subdivided into 100 *ore.* Most banks offer currency exchange services, but **Forex** exchange bureaus, in the airport and **Centralstationen**, the main rail station, provide the best rates.

Tourist Offices The main tourist information center in Stockholm is on the ground floor of **Sverigehuset** *(Hamngatan; Tel 08/789-24-95; 8am-6pm Mon-Fri, 9am-5pm Sat-Sun June-Aug, 9am-6pm Mon-Fri, 9am-3pm Sat, Sun rest of the year; www.stoinfo.com).*

Public Transportation Stockholm and its surrounds are linked by a network of subways (called the **T-Bana**) and **buses**, run by **Storstockholms Lokaltrafik** *(Tel 08/600-10-00).* T-Bana stops can be identified by signs with the letter T on a blue background. Maps are available at the tourist offices and are displayed in subway stations and at most bus stops. Tickets are available as one-day and three-day passes, in single rides or in strips, and can be purchased from bus drivers or at booths in the T-Bana stations. At 19.50SEK for a single ticket, buying reduced fare tickets in bulk makes sense. Ships often offer the best value around. With each trip you are given a stamp that validates your ticket for one hour (including multiple journeys therein). The ticket is valid forever as long as it is stamped prior to each journey.

Bike and Car Rental For bike and rollerblade rentals, try **Skepp & Höj** *(Galärvarvsvägen 2; Tel 08/660-57-57; Bus 47 to Djurgården;*

9am-9pm on days it isn't raining May-mid-Sept; 50SEK first hour, 40SEK/hour thereafter).

American Express *(Birger Jarlsgatan 1; Tel 08/679-52-00; 9am-5pm Mon-Fri.).*

Health and Emergency Police, Fire, Paramedic: *112*; if you need an ER, head for **Sankt Görans Hospital** *(Sankt Göransplan 1; Tel 08/672-10-100; T-Bana to Fridhemsplan).*

Pharmacies C.W. Scheele *(Klarabergsgatan 64; Tel 08/454-81-00; T-Bana to T-Centralen)* is open 24 hours, seven days a week.

Telephone Country code: *46*; city code: *08*; local operator: *07-975*; international operator: *07-977*. **AT&T**: *020/79-56-11*; **MCI**: *020/79-59-22*; **Sprint**: *020/79-90-11*.

Airports Approximately 30 minutes by car from Stockholm is **Arlanda Airport** *(Flight information Tel 08/797-61-00)*. **Buses** run regularly to and from outside the terminal, stopping in Stockholm at **Centralstationen**. One-way fare is 60SEK and takes around 40 minutes.

Airlines American Airlines *(Nybrogatan 3; Tel 08/781-59-99)*, **British Airways** *(Hamngatan 11; Tel 08/679-78-00)*, **Delta Airlines** *(Kungsgatan 18; Tel 08/796-96-00)*, **Qantas** *(Kungsgatan 64; Tel 08/24-25-02)*, **United Airlines** *(Kungsgatan 3; Tel 08/678-15-70)*.

Trains Trains in and out of Stockholm stop at **Centralstationen** *(on Vasagatan in Norrmalm; Tel 08/696-75-09 from outside Stockholm, Tel 020/75-75-75 from within the city).*

Buses Buses also arrive and depart from **Centralstationen** *(Tel 08/440-85-70)*. Tickets can be purchased at designated offices in the terminal.

northern europe

amsterdam

Yes, it really is everything your older brother/cousin/aging hippie neighbor said it would be. Amsterdam is to twentysomething hedonists what Disneyland is to five-year-olds: It's somewhere over the rainbow, it's never-never land, it's where Alice landed when she followed the rabbit down the hole. It's one of the few places around that can really qualify for that lame tourism catchphrase, "like nowhere else on earth." Case in point: There's a museum dedicated to the history and usage of hemp and marijuana. Dig?

But what makes Amsterdam so unique isn't just the fact that you can buy pot in a store or see prostitutes in storefront windows motioning for you to step up to the plate—it's the mentality behind these things. It's the whole Dutch *attitude*—laid-back, tolerant, practical, friendly, fun—that makes Amsterdam such a great place to hang out. (Way back when, Amsterdam flourished as the center of Euro-commerce, and the whole free-market mentality created and sustained this attitude of free thinking.) There's an overwhelming feeling of relaxation, where people who just want to do nothing are completely welcomed. Tons of Amsterdam locals are actually former travelers who decided they never wanted to go home again. And when you wander through this city of small arched bridges, gabled brick buildings, concentric canals, and gorgeous houseboats, you'll understand why.

Clearly, marijuana and live sex shows aren't the only things Amsterdam has going for it. There's a happening live music scene, with every-thing from jazz to punk. Club kids can take their pick of strobe-lit hot spots, propelled by DJs spinning techno, trip-hop, house, Goa, funk, drum 'n' bass, garage, jungle, or classic disco. You can find a bar to fit any purpose, from searching for your Dutch soulmate to those nights when you don't want to talk to anyone but the beer in front of you.

Dutch tolerance made Amsterdam a refuge for those free-lovin', dope smokin', patchwork wearin' children of the '60s. The radical upheaval that went down in the U.S. was just as active in Amsterdam, but the Dutch had a higher level of success with some issues—most notably in 1975, when marijuana was for all intents and purposes decriminalized. Thus the smoking coffeeshop was born, and the pilgrimage to Amsterdam became a wastoid college-age rite of passage. A few words of warning on the sketchy legality of marijuana in A'dam: Though it's *tolerated*, it's still technically *illegal*. In plain English: If you're over 18, have a relatively small amount of dope (five grams or less), and aren't peddling it or blatantly smoking it on the street, you're unlikely to get any hassle from the law. Also, coffeeshops are the *only* establishments that welcome smokers. If you light up a joint in a cafe or in certain bars you'll probably get the boot, or worse—just ask first. Not fun to hear, but hey, nobody wants to spend their beer money on a fine [see *rules of the game*, below].

The infamous sex industry is well-regulated, with health and zoning laws in place to keep it as safe as possible, but that doesn't *guarantee* anything. Even though prostitutes are checked out for STDs frequently, there is still no such thing as "totally safe sex," especially if your partner is a person who has multiple encounters with strangers on a regular basis. So...whatever.

Dutch free thinking also manifests itself in ways that don't inspire such phrases as, "*duuude*, you wouldn't be*lieve*...." Amsterdam has always been a magnet for creative types. Rembrandt and Van Gogh are the most famous, but native sons Mondrian, Vermeer, and Jan van Eyck are no small potatoes either. Even if you're dead-set on avoiding the standard cultural hoopla in your travels, the **Rijksmuseum** and the **Van Gogh Museum**, two of Amsterdam's three biggies, all of which are great, are worth making an exception for [see *culture zoo*, below, for both]. The contemporary art scene in Amsterdam is just as impressive, with a tradition of young designers who for the past half-century have been turning out fashion and furniture that's light years ahead of what's been done anywhere else (ask your folks about Dutch Modern furniture). The experimental dance, music, and theater scenes rival New York's in their size and level of brilliant insanity. For information on upcoming events, you can pick up a copy of VVV Tourist Information's publication, **What's on in Amsterdam** for 4Dfl [see *need to know*, below].

Amsterdam is one of the more traveler-friendly places in Europe, and many Dutch speak English better than most of your friends. Locals seem pretty cool with the fact that their city is an obvious tourist attraction. (Note: If you want to avoid tourist overload, come here in the winter. Summers are a little overwhelming.) Apparently, that famous Dutch tolerance applies to soused backpackers as easily as it does to refugee artists. This, of course, doesn't give you permission to act like a big loser, partying beyond your limit and puking into the tulips. Also, don't go wandering around zonked-out with your wallet taped to your forehead. Pickpocketing and petty theft are a problem in a few sections of town, and young, dazed travelers are naturally easy targets. This is particularly true of the Centraal Station and somewhat the case in the Dam Square area and red-light district, so don't be a dope.

One small drawback is that the weather here can quickly turn miserable, with a damp, chilly drizzle making an appearance almost daily during the cooler months. But on a warm sunny afternoon, the streets are packed with locals, along with a hefty contingent of tourists of all ages and persuasions, drinking little beers at outdoor cafes and watching the day float by in classic laid-back Amsterdam fashion. What could be simpler?

neighborhoods

For newcomers, getting around Amsterdam can be a bit dubious at times. Extensive use of a street map is absolutely necessary if you don't want to end up pissed off and walking in circles. Probably the best thing to keep in mind is that if you follow the **canals** you probably won't be dumped onto a different street. Since most of the major canals are laid out in concentric circles, you can actually walk from one end of the city to another following a single canal. Still confused? Envision the following picture in your mind: You toss a stone into the far end of a small, still pond. Consider the point where the stone hits the water as the Centraal Station, and the ripples that the stone caused as the canals. If you get off track, just remember the line from that epic film, *Happy Gilmore*: "It's circular, Happy, harness the good energy and block out the bad, think circular." The major problem here is that so many canal-street-bridge combos look remarkably identical. Just be patient and have a map handy, because at some point you're gonna need it.

The center of the city (locals will tell you it's only the center to tourists) is the area of **Dam Square**, which is surrounded by such notable attractions as the **Royal Palace** and the **Nieue Kerk** [see *culture zoo*, below]. For the most part, this area is packed full of tourists trying to figure out where they are on the map. The large, white, phallic-looking statue is the **National Monument** [see *hanging out*, below] paying homage to those who died in WWII. Just around the corner from the monument (to your left as you face the monument with your back at the Royal Palace) is the infamous **red-light district** [see *red light*, below].

The main section of the red-light district shouldn't be missed. It can look a lot seedier than it actually is. If you stay alert, and keep your money tucked away—especially after dark, when the streets fill up with gawking onlookers and "shoppers"—you shouldn't have a problem. If you like looking (*just* looking, of course) at hookers, browsing porno shops, or attending a live sex show, this is your scene. Definitely ignore the surreptitious men on the canal bridges offering you cocaine or E. Then again, you *deserve* to get crushed baby aspirin if you flash money at a stranger on the street.

In the southern part of the city lies the **Museumplein** area. As the name suggests, the big three art museums in Amsterdam—the **Rijksmuseum**, the **Van Gogh Museum**, and the **Stedelijk Museum**—are found here [see *culture zoo*, below, for all three]. Near the "big three" is the lovely **Vondelpark**, Amsterdam's version of New York's Central Park [see *great outdoors*, below].

The **Jordaan** district, situated to the west of Dam Square, is a semi-trendy, up-and-coming neighborhood. Formerly an exclusively blue-collar district, it's now a magnet for students and the young starving-artist kind of crowd (although, with comfy state subsidies for artists, they can't be *too* starving...). Fortunately, the Jordaan has continued to preserve its individual character despite the small influx of outsiders—to wit: It's still working-class and run-down, but in that good way. It's also the best area for finding an out-of-the-way art gallery or a cozy brown cafe [see *bar scene* and *arts scene*, below].

The best way to get to know Amsterdam is on foot. Get acquainted with the major landmarks, canals, and streets by hoofing it. But be careful—crossing the street here can cause major Frogger flashbacks, with bike lanes, car lanes, and tram lanes all lumped together on the major streets. If you have a momentary lapse of clear judgment (in Amsterdam? Never!) and get hit by a bike, you will look like an idiot and get a loud lecture in Dutch. And a car or a tram could not only bring you back to earth in a jiffy, but take you away from it just as quick.

Cruising around on the trams is also an easy, popular, and fast way to get from one end of the city to the next. They save time, energy, and are cute like trams are [see *need to know*, below]. Zipping around Amsterdam by bike or moped is also fun, plus it makes you look like and feel like a local. It's no coincidence that almost everyone here appears to be fit and trim—Amsterdammers and their bikes are totally inseparable, and you will sometimes see people riding two or three on a bike. If you're too damn lazy to pedal—or you just enjoy zooming around at higher speeds—moped rental is your best option [see *need to know*, below].

hanging out

Amsterdam is all about the slow pace, light on the hustle and bustle, heavy on hanging out. **The Rookies** (*Korte Leidsedwarsstraat 145-147; Tel 639-09-78; Tram 1, 2, 5-7, 10, 20 to Leidseplein; 10am-1am Sun-Thur, 10am-3am Fri, Sat; No credit cards*) is a bar—no, wait, it's a cof-feeshop—well...it's hard to define. The first thing you see as you enter is a poster of Hendrix, a pool table, and lots of twentysomething characters chatting, reading the paper, and killing time. The crowd ranges from dread-heads to frat boys, but they all share the distinct goal of smoking themselves into oblivion. The Rookies is known in the neighborhood (out near Museumplein) for its pre-rolled "joints to go," which come in small plastic tubes. The bartender explained—insisting that this was a perfect example of "modern Dutch ingenuity"—that the tubes let you smoke half your joint, throw it in the tube, and save the rest for a rainy day. Uh-huh...

four things to talk to a local about

The Dutch are friendly and incredibly multilingual—many can switch seamlessly from conversations in Dutch to English, French, and German. Here are a few topics to get things going:

1. **The European Union**: There is a feeling of inevitability concerning Holland's controversial social policies as a member of the EU. Many fear that it is merely a matter of time before the EU clamps down on the soft drug and sex industry. Good topic to get a native all riled up.

2. **Football (soccer)**: If you know anything about the world of European football, finding an interested party to chat about the sport shouldn't be difficult. Always a good lead-in topic.

3. **The Germans and the French**: Holland's big bad neighbors are looked on with disdain by many Amsterdammers. The Germans are seen as uptight, regimented, and lacking a sense of humor, while the French are rude, demanding, and always insisting on speaking French when most Dutch would prefer to speak English. Stoke 'em up with some good old-fashioned cultural animosity!

4. **International Travel**: Ask a local where they've been, plan to go, or if they've ever been to your country, etc. The Dutch travel *everywhere*.

Here's the situation: It's a weeknight around 1am, and the bar you've been in all night is closing, as most of the bars do at this hour on weeknights. You want the night to move on, but you don't want to deal with the snotty attitudes, dress competitions, expensive drinks, and deafening dance music of a club. Come, join the other like-minded souls at the **Bamboo Bar** (*Lange Leidsedwarsstraat 64; Tel 624-39-93; Tram 1, 2, 5-7, 10, 20 to Leidseplein; 9pm-3am Sun-Thur, till 4am Fri, Sat; No credit cards*), just a couple of blocks from The Rookies. A friendly group of regulars and greenhorns—best described as a no-nonsense, jeans-and-T-shirt, under-30 crowd—rolls down here after 1am, and the place is full up by 2am. The Stones or Beatles keep things moving, and you can even munch on Dutch sausage and cheese at the bar.

If you want to people-watch, and even people-meet, head to Dam Square, and chill on the steps of the **National Monument** (*Tram 1, 2, 4, 5, 9, 13, 14, 16, 17, 20, 24, 25 to Dam*). Weather permitting, young people come here to bask in the sun. It's also a preferred spot for newcomers to slouch and take a load off. Come by and strike up a conversation, which is never hard to do at this particular spot.

Head to **Leidseplein** or **Rembrandtplein** to spend an entire day doing absolutely nothing. In the warmer months, a variety of outdoor cafes in both squares call to you for that great ritual, the afternoon beer. Rembrandtplein, a stone's throw from the Amstel River, is a predominantly dingy area, overwhelmed by a heavy stream of pedestrian traffic. Unfortunately, many of the restaurants, coffeeshops, and bars here can be frequented by uninspiring flocks of tourists (not our kind, the cheeseball variety). But the sheer *number* of these outdoor cafes makes Rembrandtplein a great attraction. The cafes form a ring around a lovely small garden in the middle of the square with a statue of Rembrandt at its center. Leidseplein, another large square not far from Museumplein, is a better bet. There are excellent street performances, a livelier, younger crowd, and finer choices of close-by restaurants, bars, and clubs. One side of the square, split in half by tram tracks, is dominated by street performers and their enthusiastic crowds. When the weather cooperates, the opposite end of the square is packed with comfortable, shady, outdoor cafe seating. In short, it's an excellent environment for a long chat with a traveling buddy or an old friend. Attempting to strike up a conversation with your neighbor can be a challenge in both squares, since most of the patrons are usually in groups of two or more, but a couple rounds of beer usually gets the conversation going. Before you know it, the sun's going down, your face is red from a slight case of Dutch sunburn, and five hours have whizzed by.

bar scene

The overall chill vibe of Amsterdam spills into the bar scene, resulting in a casual, low-attitude atmosphere at most watering holes. To add to the take-your-time ambience, beer is served in tiny quarter-liter glasses (with an inch or so of foamy head!), giving you not much more than a few shots of beer per serving. For outsiders, this system may seem illogical and inconvenient, but hey, that's the way it is. If you want the big beers, Moose, jump on the next overnight train to Bavaria! Or you can order a "large" non-Dutch-size beer (as many foreigners do), but you might as well just wear a neon sign flashing "I am a pig-headed tourist." The bars are generally open till 1am on weekdays, and 2 or 3am on the weekends.

If you dig the fraternity basement scene, from the smell of stale beer to rooms packed with young, rowdy boozers, **Mr. CoCo's** *(Thorbeck-plein 8-12; Tel 627-24-23; Tram 4, 9, 14, 20 to Rembrantplein; Noon-1am Sun-Thur, till 3am Fri, Sat, closed Mon; 10.50-36Dfl per entree; MC, V, AE)* will satisfy your soul with its graffiti-covered walls and ceilings, massive 300-gram burgers, and several well-stocked bars under one roof. Between the beer-bellied bouncers and the poor choice of puke-yellow and green decor, the outdoor seating arrangement here is reminiscent of stretches of the New Jersey shore. An all-draft-beer happy hour from 5 till 6pm will get you two beers for the price of one. Come late-night, tables are dragged out of the way and the jukebox keeps the

jongen meets meid

If you're here with the idea of picking up a local Amsterdammer, you'd better have some skills. A huge number of tourists and travelers come to Amsterdam with a similar agenda, so courting the locals can get super-competitive. You're going to have to somehow separate yourself from being seen as "just another goony tourist." First order of business: Don't be an American college kid, even if you are. The T-shirt, khaki shorts, and sandals/sneakers uniform will render you another member of the undistinguished herd, as will traveling in a large, obnoxious group of identically dressed English speakers, and shouting.

Of course, the flip side of having massive numbers of young travelers come together in one place is that you can easily hook up with one of them!

international crowd grooving with a wide variety of rock tunes. Located right off Rembrandtsplein.

Here's how a group of nearly identical, tight-clothes-wearing, full-bosomed Dutch bartenders describe the scene here: "Well, ya know, there's a lot of pretty blonde girls and at least three cell phones at each table." Welcome to **Cafe Palladium** (*Kleine Gartmanplantsoen 7-9; Tel 626-65-66; Tram 1, 2, 5-7, 10, 20 to Leidseplein; 10am-1am Sun-Thur, till 2am Fri, Sat; 19.50-32.50Dfl per entree; V, MC, AE).* During the day, it's all about the food—particularly the tasty finger sandwiches—and the attitude is toned down a few notches. The largely local, chic patrons flood in come sundown, when the over-22, no-sneakers-or-hats policy kicks in. Gives you the impression that the patronage may be rehearsing for Amsterdam's version of "Melrose Place." Most of the customers prefer to sit in the abundant outdoor seating or under the glass terrace, shying away from the large bar and single dining room. There's an insane stereo system, and it's right off the action of Leidseplein. Best as an early-part-of-the-night option, since the drinks are predictably more expensive than the norm.

There comes a time when you only have one thing on your mind: Guinness! Many of the Irish bars in Amsterdam completely suck, especially the ones close to the Dam Square area where mainstream tourists rule and the bartenders treat you like a number. **Mulligan's Irish Music Bar** (*Amstel 100; Tel 622-13-30; Tram 4, 9, 14, 20 to Rembrantplein; 4pm-1am Mon-Fri, 2pm-3am Sat, 2pm-1am Sun; No cover; No credit cards),* on the Amstel just north of Rembrantsplein, is a whole other story. This is a *real* Irish bar, not part of some wannabe chain. The homey feel of the split-level place—with photos of Ireland scattered on the walls—is made complete with a staff that greets you with a gracious smile. You'll be in the company of an older (say, over 25) mixed Irish, Dutch, British, and American crowd and will find it hard to avoid being cornered by a talkative Irishman or Irishwoman. On Wednesday, Friday, and Saturday nights, they host acoustic Irish, Celtic, and Scottish music, and Sunday is open mike night.

You've committed a cardinal sin if you don't chill in a brown cafe during your stay in Amsterdam. The name "brown cafe" comes from the color of the walls, which are completely stained from centuries of thick tobacco smoke. Yum. These distinctively Dutch, cozy, and simple neighborhood cafes are the most untrendy hangouts in the city, many remaining virtually unchanged for centuries. The oldest of these is a great corner hangout called **Cafe Chris** *(Bloemstraat 42; Tel 624-59-42; Tram 13, 14, 17, 20 to Westerkerk; 2pm-1am Sun-Thur, till 3am Fri, Sat; No credit cards).* Born in the Jordaan in 1624, this dark, all-wood-interior bar is still keeping the locals happily singing Dutch drinking songs. At first, the regulars may be a bit skeptical of boisterous outsiders. But if you're outgoing in a *nice* way, and don't act like a bozo, they'll quickly warm up to you. A pocketless billiard table is the center of attention, but the locals will demolish you if you choose to test your snooker skills. Another classic Jordaan brown cafe, **Cafe Hegeraad** *(Noodermarkt 34; Tel 624-55-65; Tram 13, 14, 17, 20 to Westerkerk; 11am-1am Sun-Thur, till 3am Fri, Sat; No credit cards),* right behind Noordkerk, covers its tables with spongy red rugs for those of us who can get a little clumsy after a few beers. An overwhelmingly Dutch, mixed-age crowd happily drinks and listens to recorded Dutch drinking songs. Vintage Amsterdam, baby.

LIVE MUSIC SCENE

The locals in A'dam agree that the city has an energetic, well-rounded, and somewhat talent-deficient music scene. You should find whatever kind of music you're looking for, but that doesn't guarantee it's going to be any good. Jazz is probably the biggest of the scenes here, and you can catch a decent show every day of the week. If you're a huge jazz fan, try to arrange your trip to coincide with the **North Sea Jazz Festival** [see *festivals & events*, below]. Blues, rock, folk, funk, hip-hop, and world music also have established footholds in the city, and shows are performed in English more than 90 percent of the time. In general, the music usually begins just before midnight or so, the energy levels peak around 2am, and things are winding down by 4am. For a daily combo of rock, blues, and a coffeeshop, try the **Last Waterhole** [see *crashing*, below]. Unless otherwise noted, smoking hash/pot in these venues is a no-no.

On the window facing the street, the sign at **Bourbon Street Jazz & Blues Club** *(Leidsekruisstraat 6-8; Tel 623-34-40; Tram 1, 2, 5-7, 10, 20 to Leidseplein; 10pm-4am Sun-Thur, till 5am Fri, Sat; 5Dfl cover Fri-Sat, 2.50Dfl cover Sun-Thur; No credit cards)* reads: "Who needs New Orleans?" Hmmm...with talk like that, they better be *damn* good, right?

Sorry, no contest. The semi-touristy, late-twenties-to-early-forties crowd sometimes appears to be more into the Bryan Adams blasting between sets. And forget about the "jazz" promised in the name, 'cause it ain't here. The local and international bands are usually blues or rock, with the occasional funk or soul show thrown in to keep things interesting, and the place is consistently packed and fully charged with energy until closing. Ask the staff when the Santana cover band is scheduled to come back—they're definitely worth your time. For real.

It's hard to get the blues in A'dam, but that shouldn't stop you from going to the hugely underrated **Maloe Melo** (*Lijnbaansgracht 163; Tel 420-45-92; Tram 7, 10, 17, 20 to Elandsgracht; 9pm-3am Sun-Thur, till 4am Fri, Sat; people.a2000.nl/rstam/mm_home; No cover; No credit cards*) A bit off the beaten path (a five- to ten-minute walk from Leidseplein), it's got a mostly local, blue-collar, hard drinkin', no-gimmick atmosphere with live blues six nights a week. Both black and white musicians perform, many in town from the U.S. for a show or two. When you take a seat at the front room bar, you'll see a large Texas state flag hanging alongside a Jack Daniels flag, which gives you a pretty accurate representation of the scene. Things stay hot until around 2 or 3am, when the crowd starts to thin out. Strike up a conversation with Jur, the amiable owner/bartender, who looks like he just stepped out of a trailer park in the Ozarks. The pinball-loving patrons are laid-back, friendly, and easy to meet. Friday is rockabilly night.

Just round the corner from Bourbon Street Jazz & Blues Club is the more relaxed **Alto Jazz Cafe** (*Korte Leidsedwarsstraat 115; Tel 626-32-49; Tram 1, 2, 5-7, 10, 20 to Leidseplein; 9 pm-3am Sun-Thur, till 4am Fri, Sat; No cover, minimum age 23; V, MC, AE, D*), where a young, diverse, casual, and mellow crowd jams into the very small space to hear some of the best jazz acts in town. Get there early if you want to get a seat. The Alto Jazz Ensemble, a top-caliber group playing in a largely conservative style, perform regularly. An occasional guest sits in and mixes up the schedule. Holland's Hans Dulfer, a funky and way talented tenor sax player, takes the stage every Wednesday night.

Bimhuis (*Oude Schans 73-77; Tel 623-33-73; Tram 9, 14, 20 to Waterlooplein; 8pm-4am Thur-Sat; www.bimhuis.nl; 15-35Dfl; No credit cards*), just east of the city center, has been providing Amsterdam with superb jazz and improvisational music for 25 years. A mid-twenties and up, classy, attentive, and reserved crowd makes up a majority of the audience. An upscale cafe/bar is situated on the upper level, and the musicians play on a lower-level stage encircled by stadium-like seating. Famous names in innovative jazz from all over the world, from Sun Ra to Dexter Gordon, made this their stop in Holland. The slightly narcissistic patrons smoke their rolled cigarettes very slowly and gently bob their heads to the music. Concerts start at just after 9pm and continue until the early morning hours. The cafe/bar opens up at 8pm, just in time for a few pre-concert cocktails. For the best shows, it's a good idea to book your tickets in advance through the **Uit Boro** [see *need to know*, below].

If the damp, rainy, and cloudy weather is ruining your Dutch vacation, **Brasil Music Bar** (*Lange Leidsedwarsstraat 68-70; Tel 626-15-00; Tram 1, 2, 5-7, 10, 20 to Leidseplein; 10pm-4am Sun-Thur, till 5am Fri, Sat; No cover Mon-Wed, 10Dfl cover w/ free drink Thur, Fri, 10Dfl cover w/o free drink Sat*) will brighten up your mood. The crazy quotient for the night is a direct function of the number of overenthusiastic Brazilian girls who show up to dance—who, by the way, are more than happy to dance with an outgoing English speaker. Live bands from Brazil or the Netherlands Antilles play seven days a week. The Brazilian flag is all over the walls, along with autographed photos of famous Brazilian soccer stars, and a painting of the late Formula One hero Ayrton Senna raising his arms in victory watches over the large dance floor. The crowd is very multicultural, with Brazilians, Dutch, Africans, and everyone else downing the powerful *caipirinhas*. If the Brazilian national soccer team is playing a match, this place is packed like sardines till the sun comes up. Just down the street from the **Bamboo Bar** [see *bar scene*, above].

The jumpin' **De Duivel** (*Reguliersdwarsstraat 87; Tel 626-61-84; Tram 4, 9, 14, 20 to Rembrandtplein; 8pm-3am Sun-Thur, till 4am Fri, Sat; deduivel@xs4all.nl; No cover; No credit cards*), over near Rembrandtsplein, has DJs spinning and scratching hip-hop seven days a week. Big players like Public Enemy, Wu-Tang Clan, and The Roots have performed here. Smoking a spliff at the bar is fine, as long as you don't abuse the privilege and chain-smoke all night. A surprisingly mixed crowd congregates here—from baggy jean–wearing skaters to the occasional lawyer in a suit—and it's usually packed.

coffeeshop scene

The term "coffeeshop" here basically means "hash and pot emporium." They're all over town, so finding one is definitely not going to be a problem. What may turn into a problem is standing, walking, and talking—all that normal stuff. Proceed with caution: The quality here is very, um, high.

It's generally assumed that the non-Dutch visitors prefer to smoke the so-called "jolly green giant," which is famous (or infamous) for packing a knockout punch, and the Dutch (and most other Europeans) prefer hash which they claim is clearer and more coherent. Prices start at about 10Dfl a gram, and people can smoke pot/hash purchased from one coffeeshop in another as long as they buy a drink at the bar.

Run by gringoes from the States, **Grey Area** (*Oude Leliesstraat 2; Tel 420-43-01; Tram 1, 2, 5, 13, 20 to Magna Plaza; Noon-8pm daily, closed Mon; www.greyarea.nl; No credit cards*), just a few blocks west of Homegrown Fantasy, is plastered with all sorts of Grateful Dead/Garcia memorabilia and is said to sell the best of the best. It has won over a dozen **Cannabis Cup** [see *festivals & events*, below]. The crowd here is mostly young Americans and other English-speaking travelers stopping by to drain a few tubes.

As the verging-on-cheesy name suggests, **Global Chillage** (*Kerk-

RULES OF THE GAME

As Vincent Vega says in *Pulp Fiction*: "It breaks down like this: It's legal to buy it, it's legal to own it, and if you're the proprietor of a hash bar, it's legal to sell it. It's legal to carry it, which doesn't really matter, 'cause—get a load of this—if the cops stop you, it's illegal for them to search you. Searching you is a right that the cops in Amsterdam don't have."

There have been some recent tweaks to the law, as the goverment is bearing down a little bit in order to disassociate coffeeshops with the shady criminal world that had supposedly controlled many of them, but they're not changing things too much. Licenses are now distributed only to coffeeshops that are "deemed lawful" by the government, and the personal legal limit of marijuana and hash people can buy at a time, and can legally carry, has been lowered from 30 grams to 5 grams. For the most up-to-date drug laws, check out ***www.trimbos.nl/ukfsheet/index.html***. This government-imposed "licensing" has slightly decreased the overall number of coffeeshops in the city, but A'dammers do see a bright side: Since the government now officially sanctions coffeeshops, the future of the coffeeshops has been secured. Note: *You can't just light up anywhere in town outside the coffeeshops.* If you're unsure whether it's okay to light up somewhere, just ask. Don't be shy: The workers in these places are used to these questions. Also keep in mind that if a cop is having a *really* bad day, smoking in public can result in a fine. On the other hand, drinking on the street is legal as long as you're over 18 and don't act like a loud, drunken, belligerent jackass (at least *try*, dammit).

straat 51; Tel 779-97-77; Tram 1, 2, 3 to Leidsplein; 10am-midnight daily; www.globalchillage.com; No credit cards) delivers a mellow mood. The comfy little room over by the Leidsplein is decked out with lava lamps, funky mismatched lounge furniture (and we mean *loounge*—it's all pretty low to the ground), and Dali-esque murals, and is watched over by one of the more friendly staffs in A'dam. On the weekends, DJs spin Goa, trance, and ambient.

Those who prefer to eat their THC can head to **Homegrown Fantasy** (Nieuwe Zijds Voorburgwal 87a; Tel 627-56-83; Tram 1, 2, 5, 13, 20 to Magna Plaza; 9am-midnight daily; www.homegrownfantasy.com; No credit cards), a groovy blend of art gallery/coffeeshop right in the center of town. Patrons claim it's a great place to contemplate the pretty paintings on the wall…. With super-friendly service, an aquarium, outdoor seating, and an all-blacklight bathroom, it's easy to get stuck here for the whole day. One of A'dam's most sophisticated smoke shops.

STIX (Utrechtstraat 21; Tel 638-33-25; Tram 4, 9, 14 to Rembrandtplein; 11am-1am daily; No credit cards), to the south of Rembrantsplein,

red light

Some find it degrading and disgusting, while others find it pretty entertaining. Hey, whatever floats your boat. During the day, the neighborhood is not as active—its less appealing and more sordid aspects are more apparent in natural light. Of course, the nights are when the district comes to life, the peak action heating up at around 11pm, when the crowds throng and the colored lights flash. It continues to thrive until around 2 or 3am, when the streets empty and everything shuts down. Middle-aged men stand in front of live sex shows, trying to get you in the door with shouts of, "Live f—ing, right on stage before your eyes." Surrounding these erotic theaters, scantily dressed women—old, young (but over 18), black, white, Asian, fat, skinny, ugly, beautiful—pose in windows, lick their lips, and try to lure you inside. Stores full of hardcore videos, magazines, and sex toys complete the attractions in this sexual amusement park.

If you're really hankering to see a live sex show, **Theater Cassa Rosso** *(Oudezijds Achterburgwal Tel 106; 627-89-54; Tram 4, 9, 16, 20, 24, 25 to Dam Sq.; 8pm-2am Sun-Thur, till 3am Fri, Sat; 50Dfl admission; MC, V, AE)* should do you fine. Located just next to the Erotic Museum, this is the "classiest" venue for a nonstop erotic show. Women should feel as comfortable as men here, since they seem to make up a good percentage of the audience. The place is rather large and clean, with waiters taking drink orders. Use your imagination to figure out what happens on stage.

At the **Banenenbar** *(Oudezijds Achterburgwal 37; Tel 622-46-70; Tram 4, 9, 16, 20, 24, 25 to Dam Sq.; 8pm-2am Sun-Thur, till 3am Fri, Sat; 75Dfl admission; MC, V, AE)*, located across the canal from the **Erotic Museum** [see *culture zoo*, below], drinks are included with your entrance fee, and bananas are an integral part of the erotic show. Women might not feel comfortable in this environment (and who would? we wonder), as their female counterparts will be completely nude and well, you know...going bananas.

is classier than most, with a squeaky-clean, modern interior. Follow the tight spiral staircase (*before* ingestion, doofus!) to the second floor for a better view of the street. The crowd is pretty local and mainstream, so don't be shocked if you run into the guy who checked you into your hotel puffing on some hash.

Just when you think you've seen it all, A'dam can still surprise. The **Magic Mushroom Gallery** *(Singel 524; Tel 422-78-45; Tram 16, 24,*

25 to Muntplein; 9:30am-6pm Mon-Sat, closed Sun; www.pulse.nl/mush room; No credit cards), just across the canal from **iT** [see *club scene*, below], sells a mind-blowing assortment of natural drugs, from funky fungi to herbal sex enhancers. But, you know, mind-altering drugs can have many effects—both pleasant and unpleasant—depending on the mind you start out with. So be careful.

For more options, check out ***www.stiltskin.com/coffee.html*** or ***www. geocities.com/augusta/5173/index.html***, or pick up the English-language ***Mellow Pages*** at almost any bookstore.

club scene

A'dam's nightlife suffered a major blow recently when its biggest and best nightclub, ROxY, burned to the ground from a fireworks show gone awry during the wake that was being held for its former owner. But there's still a mongo club scene, with DJs spinning the full spectrum. Most places have bouncers, and if you look like a slob, you'll be one of those poor, undesirable souls left outside. It's customary here to tip the doorman a few guilder on the way out, especially if you want to have a prayer of getting in on another night. A few pointers: Be patient, go early (around 11) on an off night, don't advertise that you're not Dutch, blend in dress-wise with the rest of the crowd, and, perhaps most important, *look supremely confident*. And of course, if you're a guy, do your best to bring a female date or three. Some places even have "membership" requirements, but it's often amazingly unclear as to what the hell that actually means. If you don't think your coolest threads will make the cut, get some new ones at **ClubWear-House** [see *stuff*, below], also a great source of flyers for raves and other underground parties.

If you're worried that you won't be able to locate a prime-time, semi-elitist club now that the ROxY is no more, fear not. **Escape** *(Rembrantplein 11; Tel 622-11-11; Tram 4, 9, 14, 20 to Rembrantsplein; 10pm-4am Thur, Sun, 11pm-5am Fri, Sat; www.escape.nl; 25Dfl cover; No credit cards)* is a viable substitute for its former competitor. The weekly *Chemistry*, Amsterdam's largest Saturday night party, is three levels of eclectic insanity right on Rembrandtsplein, complete with chill-out zones and deafening trance, house, and jungle music. The door is unpredictable, with that annoying "membership policy" sometimes getting in the way of entry—mostly it's applied to groups of males dressed like dorks. On Sunday nights Escape throws a party called *Hour Power*, which is less hyped than *Chemistry*, so getting in isn't as tough. The club's over-2,000 capacity can mean super-long lines at the door, but your patience should pay off, as top DJs like Marcello and Dimitri will be heading up the party inside.

When you feel the urge to be completely blown away by a no-holds-barred, over-the-top techno dance club overrun with lavish transvestite and gay clientele, **iT** *(Amstelstraat 24; Tel 625-01-11; Tram 4, 9, 14, 20 to Rembrandtplein; 11pm-4am Thur, Sun, till 5am Fri, Sat; 12.50-17.50Dfl cover; No credit cards)* is it. The black warehouse interior makes iT—one of

fashion

Generally, the fashion scene in Amsterdam is, like nearly everything else, relaxed and unassuming. Attempting to characterize or classify the dress code in a city this diverse is a tough thing to do, especially with all the travelers and expats wandering around. The massive influx of young travelers from around the world has added to the color and flash on the streets, but all in all, the relaxed, carefree, whatever's-comfortable mode seems to dominate. You won't stand out and feel like a bum tramping around town in jeans, shorts, sneakers, whatever. Most of the other young people you'll encounter will be in a similar uniform, and the vibe on the street is that people don't really care what you're wearing. The club scene, of course, always has its own rules, with outfits ranging from the completely outrageous to the all-black, wealthy-yuppie look. Naturally, a pot-headed, neo-hippie aesthetic also exists in a city where soft drugs are easily available, but the grungy-crunchy-long-hair-and-Birkenstocks stoner style isn't as prevalent as it used to be. The new anti-establishment style is the "slick intellectual" look: thick-rimmed eyeglasses, short haircuts, and a more mature, neater, and cleaner line.

the larger clubs in town—seem even more monstrous. It's also got that hard-to-define "members only" policy, so get there early and bust out that feather boa. Glance at the photos of nights past on the outside of the building to get a clue about the intensity inside. Saturdays are "gay only," and the rest of the nights are mixed. Seriously wacky debauchery, right on the Amstel.

In 1967, hippies squatted an abandoned Protestant church just off Leidseplein. Since that time, that church has evolved into one of the coolest scenes in town, **Paradiso** *(Weteringschans 6-8; Tel 626-45-21; Tram 1, 2, 5, 6, 7, 10, 20 to Leidseplein; Hours vary; Office open 10am-6pm Mon-Fri; www.paradiso.nl; 10-40Dfl cover; MC, V, AE)*. The shows usually center around pop concerts, but can also include multimedia events, DJ dance theme nights, and political lectures. The interior of the church remains largely unaltered, making events here a bit more divine. Big names like Iggy Pop put on occasional shows, and the DJ dance nights are pretty casual and unassuming. To find out about scheduled events, call the office; book tickets through **Uit Boro** [see *need to know*, below].

There's good reason why a stylish pack of 25-and-under Dutch kids choose **Odean** *(Singel 460; Tel 624-97-11; Tram 1, 2, 5 to Konigsplein; 10pm-4am Sun-Thur, till 5am Fri, Sat; 5Dfl cover Sun-Thur, 10Dfl Fri, Sat; No credit cards)*. Admittedly, this 17th-century canal house just to the south of the city center doesn't look too appealing from the outside. But behind the walls lies a tri-level, multi-music extravaganza. The "cellar" concentrates on a jazz/funk mix, the ground level "mirror room" on R&B, and the stunning classical-style main room on house music. Drift around as your moods shift. You don't have to be dressed like the Pope to get in, but the sportswear thing ain't gonna get you past the ropes.

Not every traveler has the right trendy club gear stashed in the old backpack, and not everybody wants to splurge on that neon latex one-piece jumpsuit to gain entry for a night. Don't despair, there are still quality clubs that have very easy dress codes. **Mazzo** *(Rozengracht 114; Tel 626-75-00; Tram 13, 14, 17, 20 to Westerkerk; 11pm-4am Wed, Thur, Sun, till 5am Fri, Sat; No cover before midnight, 10Dfl after midnight; www.mazzo.nl; No credit cards)* is the old faithful of Amsterdam's nightclubs, with an airy, shoebox-shaped room with a large dance floor, lots of comfy seating, and a sizable bar out in the Jordaan. Wednesday nights are the coolest, with a tremendously popular *Jazzadelic* theme keeping everyone very happy until 4am. A casual, twenty-ish, mostly Dutch crowd makes this venue a regular stop. And the man at the door lets everyone in—what a concept!

Another reliable choice for a hassle-free good time is **The Melkweg** *(Lijnbaansgracht 234 A; Tel 531-81-81; Tram 1, 2, 5-7, 10, 20 to Leidseplein; Hours vary; Cover 10-40Dfl, plus membership fee of 5Dfl; melkweg@melkweg.nl, www.melkweg.nl; No credit cards)*, which mixes all the fun stuff—theater, club, cinema, restaurant, photo gallery, and varied live music acts—in one multicultural setting right off Leidseplein. The Melkweg tends to promote experimental, cutting-edge film, theater, and photography, by both Dutch and foreign artists. Of course, the crowd varies depending on the type of performance, band, DJ, or whatever happens to be taking place. For example, musical guests can range from acts like Stephan Malkmus to *Soundclash-100% Jamican Crossover* nights, which feature DJs and crossover bands. Come in the early evening (the gallery/restaurant usually opens at 8pm). If you're short on time, or too beat to deal with club-hopping, The Melkweg is the one-stop place to go.

ARTS SCENE

▶▶VISUAL ARTS

As it has been since the middle of the last century, Holland is currently a hot spot for photography, modern art, and contemporary design. The Jordaan seems to have a gallery or showroom on every other corner, and an easygoing, amiable, neighborly vibe still permeates the district. Maybe this is because of the historically working-class character of the Jordaan, or the fact that the area is farther away from the traditional tourist centers of town. In any event, where nonconformity is basically the norm, you can be sure to find a contemporary art scene that will challenge your imagination.

The Reflex Modern Art Gallery *(Weteringschans 79a; Tel 627-28-32; Tram 6, 7, 10 to Weteringplantsoen; 11am-6pm Tue-Sat, closed Sun,*

amsterdam bars, clubs and culture zoo

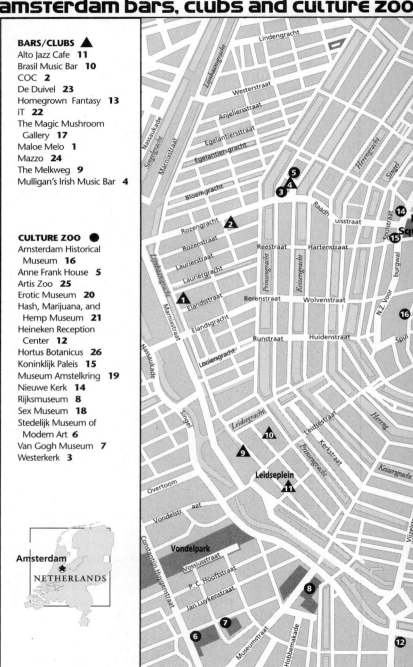

BARS/CLUBS ▲
Alto Jazz Cafe **11**
Brasil Music Bar **10**
COC **2**
De Duivel **23**
Homegrown Fantasy **13**
iT **22**
The Magic Mushroom
  Gallery **17**
Maloe Melo **1**
Mazzo **24**
The Melkweg **9**
Mulligan's Irish Music Bar **4**

CULTURE ZOO ●
Amsterdam Historical
  Museum **16**
Anne Frank House **5**
Artis Zoo **25**
Erotic Museum **20**
Hash, Marijuana, and
  Hemp Museum **21**
Heineken Reception
  Center **12**
Hortus Botanicus **26**
Koninklijk Paleis **15**
Museum Amstelkring **19**
Nieuwe Kerk **14**
Rijksmuseum **8**
Sex Museum **18**
Stedelijk Museum of
  Modern Art **6**
Van Gogh Museum **7**
Westerkerk **3**

Amsterdam ★
NETHERLANDS

Openhaven Front

Prins Hendrikkade

de Rujterkade

Het IJ

IJ-Tunnel

CITY CENTER

18

Damrak

19

Zeedijk

Ouderkerksplein

Oosterdok

Geldersekade

Kromme

Waal

Oudezijds Voorburgwal

Damrak

Uuwendijk

20

Nieuwe Markt

Eilandgracht

Oude Waal

21

Oude Schans

Nieuwe Uilenburgerstraat

Prins Hendrikkade

Kattenburger-straat

Kloveniersburgwal

Uilenburgerstraat

Valkenburgerstraat

Hoogtekadijk

Rapenburgerstraat

Entrepotdok

Groenburgval

Waterlooplein

Mr. Visserplein

Plantage Doklaan

Muntplein

22

26

Plantage Kerklaan

Artispark

Rembrandtplein

23

Nieuwe

Plantage Middenlaan

25

Plantage Muidergracht

Utrechtsestraat

Nieuwe *Keizersgracht*

Plantage Muidergracht

Nieuwe Kerkstraat

Nieuwe *Prinsengracht*

Amstel River

Nieuwe *Achtergracht*

Weesperstraat

Nieuwe Weesperstraat

Sarphatistraat

Falckstraat

Sarphatistraat

Frederiksplein

Mauritskade

Ooster-park

Singelgracht

adhouderskade

Ruyschstraat

Blasiusstraat

FESTIVALS and EVENTS

The **High Times Cannibus Cup** *(Late November annually; www.hightimes.com/ht/eve/cup for info and to purchase a judge's pass)* is six days of music, events, forums, and tastings taking place at Pax Party House, The Melkweg, and various coffeehouses...

Queen's Day *(April 30 annually; Call VVV 0900/400-40-40)* is the definitive Dutch nationwide celebration, when Amsterdam turns into a drunken open-air market.

Liberation Day *(May 5 annually; Call VVV 0900/400-40-40)* is the festive anniversary of the liberation of Holland from the Germans in WWII.

Holland Festival *(Month of June annually; Tel 530-71-11)* offers several productions highlighting new developments in theater, dance, opera, pop music, film, and photography in various locations throughout the city.

Amsterdam Roots Festival *(June 5-13 annually; Call Uit Boro 621-12-11)* is a wide range of music, theater, and cultural events with an international flavor happening in several different locations in the city.

North Sea Jazz Festival *(Mid-July annually; Tel 015/215-77-56; www.northseajazz.nl)* is a three-day music festival in The Hague (the Netherlands' capital, to the south of Amsterdam) with a top-notch assembly of jazz performers.

Grachtenfestival *(Third week in August annually; Tel 523-52-35)* is an evening classical music concert that now draws 20,000 spectators in front of Hotel Pulitzer on Prisengracht.

Mon; www.reflex-art.nl) is just across Singelgracht from the Rijksmuseum. The exhibits include work influenced by the *nouveau réalisme* movement, and inspired by the likes of the CoBrA group, a now-famous group of Western European artists from the '50s. Sculpture, painting, and installation art are routine exhibition items. The work of the brilliant young artist Dadara is definitely a highlight.

The **Jordaan's Torch** *(Lauriergracht 94; Tel 626-02-84; Tram 13, 14, 17, 20 to Westerkerk; 2pm-6pm Thur-Sat, and by appointment; a.c.van.der.have@cable.a2000.nl, www.ccc.nl/artg/torch)* is a magnet for young and quickly rising talents. A majority of the exhibits feature progressive photography, video, film, CD-Roms, and fashion. Not much painting and sculpture here—probably a bit passé for this crowd.

If you're searching for paintings and a bit of sculpture, take a short walk west of the city center to **Galerie Zilver** *(Prisengracht 234; Tel 624-33-95; Tram 13, 14, 17, 20 to Westerkerk; 1-5:30pm Thur, Fri, noon-*

5pm Sat, and by appointment; MC, V, AE). Most of the works here are that of Erik Zilverberg, an Amsterdam native influenced by Chagall, Picasso, and Blackner. Born a Jew in Amsterdam in 1941, his early childhood was filled with tragedy, loss, and turbulence. Bright colors, emotional tension, and dynamic movement are key elements to his paintings.

Galerie Carla Koch *(Prisengracht 510; Tel 639-01-98; Tram 1, 2, 5 to Leidestraat; Noon-6pm Wed-Sat, 2-6pm first Sun of every month, and by appointment; ckoch@xs4all.nl, www.artsite.nl/galerie/koch.htm; MC, V, AE),* down by the Leidsplein, is a premier gallery for internationally recognized talents and young Dutch/Belgian artists concentrating in modern glass and ceramics. The gallery has 10 exhibitions a year, alternating between ceramics and glassware. The work here is refreshingly different, daring, and utterly impressive.

Contemporary furniture enthusiasts flock to the **Frozen Fountain**, *(Prisengracht Tel 629; 622-93-75; Tram 1, 2, 5 to Leidsestraat; 1-6pm Mon, 10am-6pm Tue-Fri, 10am-5pm Sat, closed Sun)* an interesting blend of a furniture shop and exhibition center. This spacious two-floor facility places an emphasis on creative (read: impractical) modern design. Cool designs of lamps, chairs, couches, rugs, pillows, clocks, ceiling fans, and just about every other home accessory can be found here. The work of the talented Dutch designer Piet Hein Eek stands above the rest. You may just think you wandered into "Futurama."

▶▶PERFORMING ARTS

When all the coffeeshops, bars, and clubs start blending in your mind into an intoxicated haze, take a night off for a glimpse into *civilized* Dutch life. Call or stop by the **Uit Boro** [see *need to know,* below] to check out what's happening and to book tickets.

The Concertgebouw *(Concertgebouwplein 2-6; Tel 671-83-45; Tram 2, 3, 5, 12, 20 to Concertgebouwplein; www.concertgebouw.nl; Ticket prices vary drastically, call for info and reservations; V, MC, AE)* is one of the busiest and most acoustically perfect classical music halls on the planet. It is home to the Royal Concertgebouw Orchestra, which is famous in its own right. In addition, some of the most talented and recognized orchestras in the world make this a regular stop. If you're even remotely interested in classical music, find the time to visit this place.

Both the Dutch National Ballet and the Netherlands Opera operate out of the **Muziktheater** *(Waterlooplein 22; Tel 625-54-55; Tram 9, 14, 20 to Waterlooplein; Tickets from 25-115Dfl, call for info and reservations; V, MC, AE).* The opera has always been, and continues to be, a big deal in the Netherlands. A repertoire consisting of works by the likes of Wagner and Stravinsky is more common than the occasional production by less famous composers. The Dutch National Ballet has equally impressive international prominence. Its repertoire is also quite varied and can range from classic ballets like *Romeo and Juliet* to more innovative works like Balanchine's *Symphony in C.*

The revitalized **Leidseplein Theater** is home away from home for a wacky young crew of Chicago-area improvisational actors calling themselves the *Boom Chicago Comedy Show (Leidseplein 12; Tel 423-01-01; Tram 1, 2, 5-7, 10, 20 to Leidseplein; Shows 8:15pm Mon-Fri, plus 11:30pm Fri, 7:45pm, 11:15pm Sat, 8:15pm Sun after May 9; office@boomchicago. nl, www.boomchicago.nl; 27.50Dfl, Sun-Thur, 29.50Dfl Fri, Sat; MC, V, AE).* Tasty steaks, chicken, lamb, and salads are served as you laugh it up while drinking large pitchers of Heineken. Attentive service, an unpretentious atmosphere, and the first Pinball 2000 machine on the European continent make this hilarious English-language comedy venue a can't-miss attraction. The shows sell out often, so get there early for dinner and the best seats.

gay scene

Homosexuality was legalized in A'dam in 1811! So, it's no surprise that the gay/lesbian scene is thriving and unabashed, with the full range of choices from smurfy to hardcore. Check out ***www.gayamsterdam.com*** for even more options.

COC *(Rozenstraat 14; Tel 623-40-79; www.cocoamsterdam.nl; Tram 13, 17, 20 to Westerkerk; Office 11am-8pm Mon-Fri, bar/cafe 10pm-4am Fri, Sat; Cover 5dfl for women only; No credit cards)*, in the Jordaan, is the main office of the Organization of Homosexuals, and they'll be happy to help you find your particular scene. This place is also a relatively clean-cut gay/lesbian bar-cafe and disco filled with calm, cappuccino-sipping patrons (except on the S&M nights...).

April *(Reguliersdwarsstraat 37; Tel 625-95-72; Tram 1, 2, 5 to Konigsplein; 2pm-1am Sun-Thur, till 3am Fri, Sat; No credit cards)* is the gay male bar of the moment. A youngish, multicultural crowd frequents the shiny, bright, roomy interior. There's also a large circular bar in the dimmer back room. Across the street, **Club Exit** *(Reguliersdwarsstraat 42; Tel 625-87-88; www.april-exit.com; Tram 1, 2, 5 to Konigsplein; 11pm-4am Sun-Thurs, till 5am Fri, Sat; 5-10Dfl cover; No credit cards)* is one of the oldest and biggest gay (and friends) clubs in Amsterdam. With four floors of different tunes (pop, R&B, house, and techno) you're bound to find something or someone for you. There is a "dark room" on the 4th floor

If that isn't enough action for you, stop in at **iT** [see *club scene,* above], which is gay-only on Saturdays and gay-friendly always.

The lesbian bar **Saarein** *(Elandstraat 119; Tel 623-49-01; Tram 7, 10 to Elandsgracht; 3pm-1am Tue-Thur, Sun, till 2am Fri, Sat; No credit cards)* was opened as a political spot in the early '70s, but has since mellowed into just a low-key women's hang, out to the west of the city center. Watch for the weed-grower's contest the last Friday in November.

On Sunday nights, line up with the rest of the mixed gay-only crowd to get in to **De Trut** *(Bilderdijkstraat 165; Tel 612-35-24; Tram 3 to Marnixplein; Tram 7, 17 to Elandsgracht; 11pm-4am Sun only; 2.50Dfl cover; No credit cards)*, where it's all about alt sounds, cheap drinks, underground art, and good causes: The staff is all-volunteer and the profits go to charity. Gets full fast, so go around 10:30 if you want in. A bit out of the way, out past Lesidsplein, but worth the trip.

CULTURE ZOO

From a hash museum to a Bible museum, there's something here for everyone. If you only have a limited amount of time, don't miss the "big three": the Stedelijk Museum, the Van Gogh Museum, and the Rijksmuseum.

Museum Amstelkring *(Oudezijds Voorburgwal 40; Tel 624-66-04; Tram 4, 9, 16, 20, 24, 25 to Dam; 10am-5pm Mon-Sat, 1pm-5pm Sun, holidays; 7.50Dfl admission; No credit cards)*: An enchanting 17th-century Catholic church hidden in the attic of a canal house, from a time when the Dutch were less tolerant of other views.

Amsterdam Historical Museum *(Kalverstraat 92; Tel 523-18-22; Tram 1, 2, 4, 5, 9, 14, 16, 20, 24, 25 to Spui; 10am-5pm Mon-Fri, 11am-5pm Sat, Sun; 8Dfl admission; No credit cards)*: A meticulously detailed museum on the history of Amsterdam that is really as much fun as it is informative. Really!

Anne Frank House *(Prisengracht 263; Tel 556-71-00; Tram 13, 14, 17, 20 to Westerkerk; 9am-5pm daily, till 9pm Apr-Sept; 10Dfl admission; www.annefrank.nl; No credit cards)*: If you're willing to wait in the very long lines, you can see where the Frank family hid from the Nazis. Even with the crowds, this place has the power to shake you up.

Artis Zoo *(Plantage Kerklaan 38-40; Tel 523-34-00; Tram 9 to Artis Zoo; 9am-5pm daily; 25Dfl admission; www.artis.nl; V, MC, AE)*: The oldest zoo in Europe, with a collection of over 750 different animal species. Rumored to be a popular destination for tripping travelers.

Dutch Resistance Museum *(Plantage Kerklaan 61; Tel 620-25-35; Tram 9 to Artis Zoo; 10am-5pm Tue-Fri, noon-5pm Sat, Sun and public holidays, closed Mon; 8Dfl admission; No credit cards)*: A recently opened, eye-opening museum devoted to the Dutch resistance to Nazi occupation. Gives you a detailed background on why many of the Dutch aren't too fond of the Germans.

Erotic Museum *(Oudezijds Achterburgwal 54; Tel 627-89-54; Tram 4, 9, 16, 20, 24, 25 to Dam; 11am-1am daily, till 2am Fri, Sat; 5Dfl admission; No credit cards)*: Five floors of photos, dildos, sex cartoons, sculptures, sketches, and an entire floor dedicated to S&M paraphernalia. Yikes!

At the **Hash, Marijuana, and Hemp Museum** *(Oudezijds Achterburgwaal 148; Tram 4, 9, 16, 20, 24, 25 to Dam; 11am-10pm daily; 19Dfl admission; www.sensiseeds.com; No credit cards)*: Dude, it's all about the *hemp*. All the history and uses, plus a "live marijuana grow room." An optional free taste test is included in admission price.

Heineken Reception Center *(Stadhouderskade 78; Tel 523-96-66; Tram 16, 24, 25 to Stadhouderskade; Guided tours 9:30am, 11am Mon-Fri, 9:30am, 11am, 1pm, 2:30pm Mon-Fri June 1-Sept 15, plus 11pm, 1pm, 2:30pm Sat July 1-Aug 31; 2Dfl admission)*: They don't brew it here anymore, but who cares? A guided tour of the history of beer and the Heineken Brewery precedes a short free beer-drinking session.

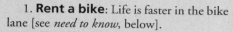

12 hours in amsterdam

1. **Rent a bike**: Life is faster in the bike lane [see *need to know*, below].

2. **Paradiso**: Have mercy! This old church is just too damn cool! Hit this venue for its one-of-a-kind atmosphere and extraordinary nightlife offerings [see *clubs*, above].

3. **Take a canal cruise that doesn't suck**: Don't waste your time and money at the other cruises; they don't even compare [see *great outdoors*, below].

4. **The "big three"**: Your appetite for Dutch culture and art will be more than satisfied at the famed trio of Holland's finest art museums [see *culture zoo*, above].

5. **Boom Chicago**: Funny, creative, and guaranteed to give you the giggles: Find the time for an evening at Amsterdam's top English-language comedy show [see *performing arts*, above].

6. **Maleo Melo**: Stuck inside Amsterdam with the Memphis blues again. Best place in town to sip whiskey in a smoky bar and nod along to wailing guitars [see *live music scene*, above].

7. **Vondelpark**: No chaos, no trams, no cars, no crowds, few tourists, and a little peace of mind [see *great outdoors*, below].

8. **The Rookies**: The preferred watering hole for all types of young adults who like to puff, play pool, and shoot the shit [see *hanging out*, above].

9. **Brown cafes**: no games, no gimmicks, no nonsense, just locals and beer [see *bar scene*, above].

10. **Bimhuis**: A no-brainer for a great night of impressive live music [see *live music scene*, above].

Hortus Botanicus *(Plantage Middenlaan 2a; Tel 625-90-21; Tram 9, 14, 20 to Plantage Middenlaan; Apr 1-Sept 30: 9am-5pm Mon-Fri, 11am-5pm Sat, Sun; Oct 1-Mar 31: 9am-4pm Mon-Fri, 11am-4pm Sat, Sun; hortus.amsterdam@wxs.nl; 7.50Dfl admission; No credit cards)* is one of the oldest botanical gardens in the world, with a collection of over 8,000 types of indoor and outdoor plants. Sorry, no marijuana grow room here.

newMetropolis *(Oosterdok 2; Tel 919-11-00; Five-minute walk from Centraal Station; 10am-6pm daily, closed Mon; 22Dfl admission, 14Dfl after 4pm; www.newmet.nl, info@newmet.nl; MC, V, AE)* is a good rainy day option. This massive science and technology center welcomes you with a bunch of unique interactive exhibits. A good choice for video-game addicts in withdrawal.

Nieuwe Kerk *(Dam Sq., across from the Royal Palace; Tel 638-69-90; Tram 1, 2, 4, 5, 9, 13, 14, 16, 17, 20, 24, 25 to Dam; 11am-5pm daily; Free admission, except for special exhibitions)*: Although the name means "new church," this marvelous, centrally located Gothic gem was completed some 600 years ago.

Rijksmuseum *(Stadhouderskade 42; Tel 673-21-21; Tram 2, 5, 6, 7, 10, 20 to Rijksmuseum; 10am-5pm daily; 15Dfl admission; www.holland museums.nl, ukinfo@rijksmuseumamsterdam; No credit cards)*: Holland's largest art museum, houses a grand assortment of paintings by the likes of Rembrandt, Van Dyck, and others. The Vermeers are beautiful enough to crawl into. A must-see.

Koninklijk Paleis *(Dam Square; Tel 624-86-98; Tram 1, 2, 4, 5, 9, 13, 14, 16, 17, 20, 24, 25 to Dam; 12:30pm-5pm daily, 11am-5pm daily July, Aug, but hours are very irregular, call before going; 7Dfl admission; No credit cards)*: A Golden Age–era building that was originally a city hall, but Louis Napoleon converted it into the majestic Royal Palace and filled it with ornate junk.

Sex Museum *(Damrak 8; Tel 622-83-76; Across from Centraal Station; 10am-11:30pm daily; 4.50Dfl admission; No credit cards)*: Not to be confused with the Erotic Museum [see above], this is a 2,000-year history lesson on everything you ever wanted to know (and didn't want to know) about sex.

Stedelijk Museum of Modern Art *(Paulus Potterstraat 13; Tel 573-29-11; Tram 2, 3, 5, 12, 16 to Stedelijk Museum; 11am-6pm daily; 9Dfl admission; No credit cards)*: Amsterdam's best modern art museum, with works ranging from Nordic industrial design to Cezanne and Monet. An absolute must.

Van Gogh Museum *(Paulus Otterstraat 7; 570-52-00; Tram 3, 5, 12, 16, 20 to Museumplein; www.vangoghmuseum.nl; 12.50Dfl admission; No credit cards)*: An entire museum dedicated to one nutty genius. You need to see these babies live to understand just how scary beauty can get. Another must-see.

Westerkerk *(Prisengracht 281; Tel 624-77-66; Tram 13, 14, 17, 20 to Westerkerk; 11am-3pm daily, tower tour leaves every hour on the hour 10am-5pm Apr-Sept; 3Dfl admission to tower, free admission to church; No credit cards)*: The highest church tower in Amsterdam provides an impressive bird's-eye view of the entire city.

modification

After too many space cakes, you might be inspired to tattoo a pot leaf on your chin. Fortunately, **Tattoo Palace** *(Reguliersdwarsstraat 91; Tel 638-44-48; Tram 4, 9, 14, 20 to Rembrantplein; Noon-7pm Mon-Sat, 2pm-7pm Sun; www.tatoopalace.com; No credit cards)* will discourage you from such a well-considered plan. These guys aren't out to dip deep into your wallet, and will help you make the best body art decision. The motto here is "the body is a temple and we are the decorators." If you can't find them, look for the green dragon on the front of the building, and listen for loud heavy metal. They've got super-high hygienic standards and two majorly talented artists that go by the monikers "King Ferry" and "Raw."

great outdoors

Hands down, the best place to take a run, a long walk, or a bike ride is the beautiful **Vondelpark** (Tel 673-14-99; Tram 2, 5, 710 to Leidseplein, then a five-minute walk; www.nl/vondelpark). Ponds, trees, and great green lawns offer ample lounging options. The park is big enough to make you temporarily forget you're in Europe's so-called city of sin, and it doesn't have a reputation for being unsafe for women. On Wednesday through Sunday from May 30 to August 22, musicians play free of charge here at the open-air theater. Call **Uit Boro** for details [see *need to know*, below].

The skaters in Amsterdam have good reason to be angry at the world. Ever since their skate park was closed back in 1998, they have had to stick to the streets. Problem is, many of the streets are brick, which makes for a really uncomfortable ride. A petition has been started by the crew at **Sub-liminal** (Nieuwendijk 134; Tel 428-26-06; Five-minute walk from Centraal Station; Noon-5pm Sun, till 6pm Mon, 10am-6pm Tue-Sat; MC, V, AE) to get a new skate park. Stop in to see if the situation has improved at all, or to stock up on gear. This is the only pure skate shop in town, and it carries tons of decks, equipment, shoes, and clothes.

If your battered body is telling you to give it a break, do it in style at **Koan Float** (Herengracht 321; Tel 625-49-70; Tram 1, 2, 5 to Konigsplein; 9:30am-10pm Mon-Thur, till 11pm Fri-Sun; info@koan-float.com, www.koan-float.com; 55Dfl for a 45-minute session; MC, V, AE). A 45-minute "float" session in your own personal pool-like cabin atop a 35 (cel) pool of salt water will make you new once again. All outside distractions—sound, sight, temperature fluctuations, and gravity—are eliminated, so your sense of time and space is delightfully altered. Reservations recommended.

If you'd like to stare through a glass window while sitting between a whining eight-year-old and a bitchy French couple listening to boring tour-guide drivel repeated in four different languages, never even making eye contact with the driver, please ignore the following two canal tours.

The **MS Avontuur** (Docked next to Amstel Kerk, at the intersection of Reguliersgracht and Prisengracht; Captain's cell phone number 06-553-387; Tram 4 to Utrechtstraat; Day trips 10am-8pm, evening trips 6-10pm; 175Dfl an hour, can be split up to 12 ways) is a beautifully restored, flat-bottomed transport ship built in 1913. You're able to completely customize your trip: Just tell the captain where you want to go, and he plans it accordingly. You'll chat with the captain, sit and drink beers on the carpeted deck, and help navigate some of the tight spaces. Call the captain to inquire about possible openings on an upcoming tour, or gather up to 12 new friends together for a private adventure.

by foot

A lovely stroll along the canal **Prisengracht** and through some of the quieter and more traffic-free areas of the **Jordaan**: Walk or take the tram out to **Westerkerk** [see *culture zoo*, above], go inside, and check it out. Take a right out of the church, heading along Prisengracht. If the line is short at the **Anne Frank House** [see *culture zoo*, above] you should absolutely stop in. Continue along the canal and make a quick left at **Leliegracht**, crossing the canal. Continue on, heading away from the church, and maybe pop in and poke around any of the **small art galleries** [see *arts scene*, above] on your left. **Noordkerk** will now be directly in front of you. Go around the left side of the church; on your left is **Cafe Hegeraad** [see *bar scene*, above], one of the best brown cafes in the city. Stop in for a quick beer or relax for a few. Make a left as you head out of the cafe, and then a quick right onto **Noodermarkt** (you have now almost circled Nooderkerk) and take a look at the architecture of the houses on your left. The hooks at the top of the houses were used for pulleys, enabling owners to get furniture to the upper levels of the house. Make a left back onto Prisengracht, and then a quick left onto **Brouwersgracht**. Make a another left, after the second of the two green drawbridges, onto **Palmgracht**. Walk down to the end of the street, make a left onto **Lijnbaansgracht**, where houseboats are "bumper-to-bumper" throughout the canal, and continue past yet another drawbridge. Make a left onto **Bloemstraat**, and there it is! Westerkerk, off in the distance! You can now see the colorful clock side of the church. As you make your way back to Westerkerk on your left is the **Cafe Chris** [see *bar scene*, above], the oldest brown cafe in A'dam, calling your name for one more beer.

The **Saint Nicolaas Boat Stichting** (*Info available at Boom Chicago Comedy Show; Leidseplein 12; Tel 423-01-01; Tram 1, 2, 5, 6, 7, 10, 20 to Leidseplein; 15Dfl donation encouraged*) is an informal, not-for-profit organization committed to the preservation of two small, open-air Dutch Tuindervelt boats. With no scheduled times of departure, the best advice is to head down to **Boom Chicago** [see *arts scene*, above] and see what's up. The tour takes you to the smaller, less-traveled, out-of-the-way canals that the big, monster boats can't dream of entering. The captain doesn't have to speak through a microphone, and seems to know every tidbit of Amsterdam historical trivia. The other alternative tour-goers in the boat will generally be young, fun-loving, and laid-back.

There are also a variety of both guided and unguided bike tours available. Once you get somewhat familiar with the layout of the city, a sunny day on a bike could be your finest day yet [see *need to know*, below].

STUff

If you're shopping for a new wardrobe in this city, you better have some ducats. The area for designer-type clothing is **P.C. Hoofdstraat** *(Tram 3, 5, 12, 16, 20 to Museumplein; Store hours are generally 1pm-6pm Mon, 10am-6pm Tue, Wed, Fri, 10am-9pm Thur, 10am-5pm Sat, noon-5pm first Sunday of the month)*, where you'll find some of the usual suspects—Hugo Boss, DKNY, Benetton—and if you get your hands on Daddy's gold card, there's always Gianni Versace.

Heading up **Leidsetraat** away from Leidseplein *(Tram 1, 2, 5 to Leidsetraat)*, the prices come down and the looks become more casual. Continue browsing such shops as Timberland, Shoebaloo, and House of Claire. After a short walk, you end up on **Kalverstraat** *(Tram 1, 2, 4, 5, 9, 13, 14, 16, 17, 20, 24, 25 to Dam)*, the main pedestrian shopping street in Holland, where every other shop is a shoe, clothing, or leather-goods store. Behind the **Royal Palace** on Dam Square [see *culture zoo*, above] there is indoor shopping at **Magna Plaza** *(10am-5pm daily, noon-5pm Sun)*. This American-looking (maybe a bit nicer) three-floor mall has an enormous Virgin megastore in the basement.

▶▶BOUND

The most comprehensive of all the English-language bookstores in A'dam is the **American Book Center** *(Kalverstraat 185; Tel 625-55-37; Tram 16, 24, 25 to Muntplein; 10am-8pm Mon-Sat, 11am-6pm Sun; info@abc.nl; MC, V, AE)*, a one-stop shop for American and English books and magazines, with a wide selection ranging from architecture to shamanism to biography to horror. Holders of a valid student ID get a 10 percent discount on all books.

▶▶BAZAAR

Antiques, used records, Army/Navy gear, clothes, hardcore porn videos, old books, cheap grub on the run: **Waterlooplein Flea Market** *(Waterlooplein; No phone; Tram 9, 14, 20 to Waterlooplein; 9am-5pm daily; No credit cards)* is a small tent city of locals hawking everything you can imagine. 95 percent of the stuff sold here is crap, but the ever-elusive 5 percent of treasure makes it worth it. See *this little piggy went to market*, below, for more market options.

▶▶CLUB GEAR

The ratty T-shirt-cargo-shorts-and-sneakers look is not the current trend at the clubs here in Amsterdam, so stop by **ClubWear-House** *(Herengracht 265; Tel 622-87-66; Tram 1, 2, 5 to Konigsplein; 11:30am-6pm Tue-Wed, Fri, till 8pm Thur, noon-6pm Sat, closed Sun, Mon; cwh@xs4all.nl, www.xs4all.nl/~cwh; MC, V, AE)* if you're hell-bent on hitting a hot club. They'll throw a new outfit on you and point you in the right direction. You might walk out of the store in an electronic lightshirt and belt, with a few secondhand DJ records under your arm. If you prefer feathers, latex,

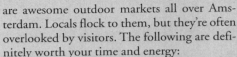

THIS LITTLE PIGGY WENT TO MARKET

There are awesome outdoor markets all over Amsterdam. Locals flock to them, but they're often overlooked by visitors. The following are definitely worth your time and energy:

Albert Cuypmarkt *(Albert Cuypstraat; 9:30am-5pm Mon-Sat)* is a few streets behind **Heineken Reception Center** [see *culture zoo*, above]. This giant outdoor bazaar has a flea market–style setup. Secondhand and new clothes, plants, international foods, and a whole lot more.

Bloemenmarkt *(Singel, between Konigsplein and Muntplein; 9:30am-5pm Mon-Sat)* is a colorful, sweet-smelling flower and plant market floating on the Singel.

Waterlooplein is a flea market [see *stuff*, above].

At **Boekenmarkt** *(Spui, 10am-6pm Fri)*, used hardcover and paperback books are sold outdoors in a tranquil setting on Spui.

Boeren/Vogelmarkt *(Noordermarkt, outside Nooderkerk, 9am-4pm Sat)* is an outdoor farmer's market loaded with cheese, organic vegatables, fruits, grains, and spices. There is also a small collection of cool tapestries, secondhand clothes, and furniture.

rubber, or plastic, there's plenty of that. The groovy staff has the knowledge on underground and unannounced parties, raves, and shows.

▶▶**TUNES**

If you dig the funked-up thang, **Back Beat Records** *(Egelantiersstraat 19; Tel 627-16-57; Tram 13, 14, 17, 20 to Westerkerk; 11am-6pm daily, closed Sun; No credit cards)* will do you right. Run by a group of mellow Dutch musicians who admit that "freaks from all over the world come here," the specialty here is soundtracks from blaxploitation movies like *Trouble Man*, *Superfly*, and *Black Ceasar*. They also have an impressive collection of soul, jazz, modern R&B, and blues.

Jazz nuts will dig **Blue Note from Ear to Eye** *(Gravenstraat 12; Tel 428-10-98; Tram 4, 9, 16, 20, 24, 25 to Dam Sq.; 11am-7pm Mon-Sat, noon-5pm Sun; www.eareye.nl; MC, V, AE)*. Just around the corner from **Homegrown Fantasy** [see *coffeeshop scene*, above] and right behind **Nieue Kerk** [see *culture zoo*, above], this hep joint carries all types of jazz, from mainstream to avant-garde, from Latin to Dutch. Killer CD system lifts you off the ground as you enter.

Musiques du Monde *(Singel 281; Tel 624-13-54; Tram 1, 2, 5 to Konigsplein; 1-6pm Mon, 10am-6pm Tue, Wed, Fri, 10-8pm Thur, 10-5pm Sat; musdumon@euronet.nl, www.euronet.nl-musdumon; MC, V)* is

down and out

Amsterdam's unofficial motto could be: "Anything you want, as long as you pay for it," so trying to hang here when you're totally broke can be rough. Of course, there are common-sense ways to spend time and not money. On the top of your list should be a stroll around the red-light district at night. It doesn't cost a guilder to gaze and gawk at the sex shops, prostitutes, and characters who gravitate to such places. Free concerts are given at **Vondelpark** [see *great outdoors*, above], and **Leidseplein** [see *hanging out*, above] usually has excellent street performers during the day. There are also free concerts at the Concertgebouw on Wednesdays from October to June at 12:30pm—arrive early for a seat. The **Muziktheater** [see *arts scene*, above] also holds short free performances on Tuesdays at the same time of the day and year. If you want to get out on the water, you can also do that free of charge. The city operates a small ferry service running across the river IJ. The ferry leaves from behind Centraal Station frequently, but the entire trip takes less than 10 minutes. Then again, if you really like the view of the river—and you're flat broke—they don't care if you take the ferry back and forth all day long. For another cheap activity you can do over and over again, take the tour at the **Heineken Reception Center** [see *culture zoo*, above]. For only two guilder, you will be able to drink four or five Dutch-size beers per tour. But remember, you'll have to put up with brainwashing sessions about the history of the brewery each time through....

just that, with a collection ranging from the Mississippi blues to Tajikistan folk, and everything in between.

It's vinyl, vinyl everywhere at **Fat Beats** *(Singel 10; Tel 423-08-86; Five-minute walk from Centraal Station; 11am-7pm daily; www.fatbeats.nl; MC, V).* With pictures of Chuck D, Slick Rick; and Run DMC on the walls, you know you're in hip-hop heaven. They also have the latest in DJ equipment and magazines, and a down-to-earth staff.

For the generic selection of everything, try the Virgin megastore in **Magna Plaza** [see above].

EATS

Cheese or herring, herring or cheese: Which would you like? Remember, the herring is raw and must be devoured in one bite. Okay, so not everyone has eagerly embraced Dutch cuisine. Fortunately, almost every conceivable type of ethnic food—from Argentinean to Thai—is represented here. Catering to the young, stoned, low-budget crowd are the seemingly infinite falafel, kebab, and french-fry joints. (Yes, they do eat their french fries with mayonnaise here.) The restaurants' prices range from reasonable to ridiculous, and tips are customarily included in the bill.

▶▶CHEAP

Don't be fooled by imitators—always look for the original **Maoz Falafel** (*Reguliersbreestraat 45; Tel 676-76-12; Tram 4, 9, 14 to Rembrantsplein; 11am-1am Sun-Thur, till 4am Fri, Sat; 6Dfl falafel; No credit cards*), over by Rembrandtsplein, where you get the best guilder-to-fullness ratio in the city. A self-serve veggie bar will help dress up your delicious falafel with fresh condiments.

If you prefer to go native and still want to eat an inexpensive meal, stop at one of the large, no-name, daytime-only, fish-smelling stands on any street. The best one in town is on the bridge at Harlemeer Straat and Singel, right down the road from Centraal Station. You can grab smoked eel or herring in a hot dog–like bun for 6.50Dfl. And yes, it tastes much better than it sounds.

Gary's Muffins (*Prisengracht 454; Tel 420-14-52; Tram 1, 2, 5 to Leidsetraat; 9am-5:30pm Mon-Fri, till 6pm Sat-Sun; 3Dfl muffin, 27Dfl large bagel with cream cheese and lox; No credit cards*) will do the trick for a kick-ass breakfast or lunch. All kinds of fresh bagels, muffins, cookies, and brownies at low, low prices. The 7.75Dfl tuna melt gets a big vote from the regulars. The scenic outdoor seating along Prisengracht makes up for the slow, understaffed service.

▶▶DO-ABLE

Top Thai (*Herenstraat 22; Tel 623-46-33; Tram 13, 14, 17, 20 to Westerkerk; 4:30-10:30pm daily; 20-35Dfl per entree; MC, V, AE*) is a premium choice for dinner, where gracious service is backed by flavorful plates and reasonable prices. Vegetarian entrees start at just 20Dfl, and are alone guaranteed to stuff you silly. The restaurant is small but tidy and tucked away on a relatively quiet street west of the city center. Watch out when you ask for it spicy—they mean it. Try the "James Brown": prawns roasted in Thai brown chili sauce. I feel nice, like sugar and spice!

It's an entirely different scene at **Walem** (*Keizersgracht 449; Tel 625-35-44; Tram 1, 2, 5 to Keizersgracht; 10am-1am Mon-Thur, till 3am Fri, Sat; www.dinersite.nl; 16.50-38.50Dfl per entree, sandwiches from 7.50Dfl; MC, V, AE*), just off Leidstraat. When the menu boasts of "a fusion of senses," you know you've entered attitudeville. A well-dressed yuppie-ish crowd stops in here mid-day to gossip and compare designer clothing. To its credit, the sandwiches are terrific and the service better than the Amsterdam norm. Maybe the crowd seated indoors is afraid that the breeze will muss their trendy new haircuts.

For an nice Italian food fix, do lunch at **Panini** (*Vijzelgracht 3-5; Tel 626-49-39; Tram 16, 24, 25 to Prisengracht; 9:30am-10:00pm daily; 6.75-15Dfl per lunch entree, 20-35Dfl per dinner entree; MC, V*). This understaffed split-level cafe/restaurant with limited outdoor seating is the King of Italian in A'dam. Customers keep coming back for the

amsterdam eats and crashing

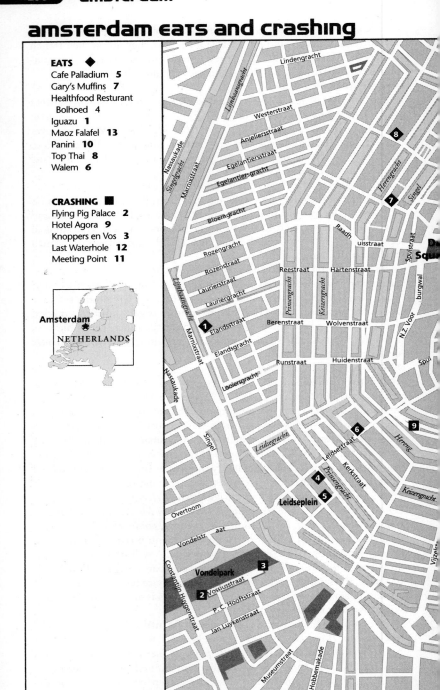

EATS ◆
Cafe Palladium **5**
Gary's Muffins **7**
Healthfood Resturant
  Bolhoed **4**
Iguazu **1**
Maoz Falafel **13**
Panini **10**
Top Thai **8**
Walem **6**

CRASHING ■
Flying Pig Palace **2**
Hotel Agora **9**
Knoppers en Vos **3**
Last Waterhole **12**
Meeting Point **11**

Amsterdam
NETHERLANDS

delightful homemade bread and soup of the day. An English-only menu is available upon request, catering to the significant tourist crowd that makes its way here.

An old Dutch sailor would feel comfortable at **Eetcafe Blauwbrug** *(Waterlooplein 403; Tel 638-14-62; Tram 9, 14, 20 to Waterlooplein; 10:30am-1:30am Sun-Thur, till 3am Fri, Sat; 14.50-26.75Dfl per entree; MC, V)* Holland's version of "The Rusty Barnacle" on "The Simpsons"—you just want to yell out, "Arrghhh...matey!" The life vests, oars, props, nets, and boat engines hanging from the ceiling say it all. The atmosphere keeps you entertained, so you don't mind the traditional unhurried service. A mostly family-oriented Dutch crowd is found here, as the tourists shy away (somewhat understandably) from the native food. Of course, the best bet here is the fish—be it pickled, fried, or baked—washed down with several little beers.

▶▶**SPLURGE**

You don't have to be vegetarian to enjoy the phenomenal grub at **Health-food Restaurant Bolhoed** *(Prisengracht 60-62; Tel 626-18-03; Noon-10pm daily; 24.50-28.50Dfl per entree; No credit cards)*, one of the coolest places to sit down and dine in the city. Located across the canal from the Anne Frank house, it's all about a super-chill, free, and welcoming atmosphere. All ingredients are organic, with the emphasis on a pure, clean, powerful, and nutritious meal, and great vegan dishes are also available. The interior is roomy, colorful, and peaceful. An international mix of crunchy/veggie types make their way over here.

crashing

Even with the huge number and variety of places to stay in Amsterdam, finding the right digs during high season *(May 15-Sept 15)* can be a challenge, to say the least, especially on a Friday or Saturday night. Beware: Some places overbook, those creeps. Reserving in advance is strongly suggested, or you may just find yourself catching the tram out to Vondelpark and using your backpack as a pillow. If you do show up and can't find a bed, head for the **VVV** or **GWK Tourist Services** in the Centraal Station [see *need to know*, below]. For 5Dfl, they'll find you that much-needed place to lay your head.

Youth hostels here are clean, basic, relatively safe, popular, wild, and affordable. Most of the patrons tend to be young, on a tight budget, and in Amsterdam with the distinct goal of losing as many brain cells as possible. There are also several lower-end hotels, B&Bs, etc., that provide a homier atmosphere, a hearty breakfast, and a good night's sleep without costing you an arm and a leg.

▶▶**CHEAP**

If you like young, high-energy, yet paradoxically burned-out roommates, the **Flying Pig Downtown** *(Nieuwendijk 100; Tel 420-68-22; Five-minute walk from Centraal Station; downtown@flyingpig.nl; 55Dfl doubles, 25Dfl dorm bed in 26-bed room; MC, V)* is the place for you. The summer season here is crazy busy, but the staff remains extremely friendly and keeps the place clean. Here's the scene: no curfew, a central location, a free no-frills breakfast, showers and toilets in the rooms, a bar filled with dope smoke, a lounge area filled with giant cushions, pool and foosball tables, kitchen facilities, lockers, and a crazy international mix of guests. Quoting the hostel's beautiful and sweet-tempered manager, "Those who stay here are young, wild, and want to have a good time." To the point, no?

Located right on Vondelpark, the **Flying Pig Palace** *(Vossiusstraat 46; Tel 400-41-87; Tram 1, 2, 5 to Leidseplein, walk towards Vondelpark; palace@flyingpig.nl; 47.25Dfl double, 27.30Dfl for a bed in a 12-bed room; MC, V)* has just about the same setup as the downtown location, but the crowd is a little calmer, quieter, and more conservative (read: no dope smoke in the air here). It's very well-maintained and right near the major museums.

The best option for a nonstop party is the **Last Waterhole** *(Oudezijds Armsteeg 12; Tel 624-48-14; Five-minute walk from Centraal Station; 30Dfl for a bunk-style bed in a 64-bed room; www.lastwaterhole.nl; No cover for music; No credit cards).* The front side of the staff's T-shirts read "bar.coffeeshop.hostel.the red-light district." The back side of the T-shirt reads "hole lotta shakin' goin on." What they forgot to put on the T-shirts was "live rock/blues played here seven days a week," and "decent food available from lounge restaurant." The bartender here claims that people come for a week and don't leave the building. With free lockers, a clean, coed, dorm-style sleeping room, 24-hour access, and hot showers available 24 hours a day, you almost believe him.

If you can't live without ESPN, the NBA, or the NFL, The **Globe** *(Oudezijds Voorburgwal 3; Tel 421-74-24; Five-minute walk from Central Station; www.theglobe.demon.nl; 40Dfl for a bed in a dorm-style room; 140-180Dfl double, triple, or quad room; No credit cards)* eagerly awaits you. This beautiful family-run bar, hostel, and restaurant is a haven for the jock American or Brit. Most rooms have both a view of the canal and a private bathroom. The bar area serves up over 20 different types of beers, has the clearest big-screen TV in town, a pool table, and dart boards. The rooms are modest but clean, and breakfast will cost you a bit extra. The kitchen is open from 8am till 10pm weekdays, 8am till 11pm weekends.

Five years ago, two brothers from Surinam took over the **Meeting Point** *(Warmoesstraat 14; Tel 627-74-99; Three-minute walk from Central Station; 25Dfl Nov-Mar, 30Dfl Apr-Oct, for a bed in dorm-style accommodation; No credit cards),* and since then these two guys have gone out of their way to make sure their guests have a blast in A'dam. It's damn close to the train station, a basic breakfast is included, and beer prices in the marijuana-tolerant bar are cheap *(pints 5Dfl).* A pool table and a few dart boards keep the beer drinkers amused. Rooms are on par with the standard clean-but-boring theme of Amsterdam hostels. But the lockers are cool: 50-gallon drums keep your luggage secure.

▶▶**DO-ABLE**

The lovely canal house **Hotel Prisenhof** *(Prisengracht 810; Tel 623-17-*

72; Tram 4 to Utrechtstraat; prisnhof@xs4all.nl, www.xs4all.nl/~prinshof; 85Dfl single, 125Dfl double w/o bathroom, 165Dfl double w/ bathroom, 175Dfl triple, 210Dfl triple w/ bathroom; MC, V, AE), one of Amsterdam's best bargains, is highly recommended—if you can get a room before they're booked solid. Located just a few hundred meters from Rembrandtplein, it's tucked away overlooking the canal Prisengracht. A filling breakfast of toast, cheese, jam, coffee, OJ, and a hard-boiled egg is graciously served. Comfortable box-spring beds, immaculately clean rooms, and cordial service are all included. The likeable manager uses an odd pulley contraption to help you out with your bags.

If you are searching for the intimately cozy, the charming B&B **Knoppers en Vos** (Vossiusstraat 26; Tel 671-60-09; Tram 2, 3, 5, 12 to Vondelpark; 135Dfl double; No credit cards) is what you are looking for. Run by two hatmakers, this tiny B&B will make you feel like you're staying with a long-lost Dutch relative. High ceilings, well-worn rugs, hallways cluttered with hatmaking equipment, and clean rooms all add to the homespun flavor. A breakfast of eggs, bread, cheese, coffee, and jam is served by a bay window overlooking the garden as classical music fills the air. The front room has a small balcony overlooking Vondelpark. Showers are inside the rooms, and the bathroom is shared with the other double. Book ahead to avoid disappointment.

▶▶SPLURGE

If you want a top-of-the-line room in the heart of the action, try **Hotel Amsterdam** (Damrak 93-94; Tel 622-85-26; Tram 1, 2, 4, 5, 9, 13, 14, 16, 17, 20, 24, 25 to Dam Sq., or a 400-meter walk from Centraal Station; drhotel@wxs.nl, hotel_amsterdam@wxs.nl; 260Dfl single, 320Dfl double, 390Dfl triple Mar 15-Nov 14, 240Dfl single, 260Dfl double, 330Dfl triple Nov 15-Mar 14; MC, V, AE). For a high-end hotel, it's a bit short on character, but it's long on amenities. The ho-hum interior is more than made up for by all the toys, including a new computer with Internet access in every room. Of course, all rooms have a bathroom, safe, shower, radio, TV, direct-dial telephone, and mini-bar. The front rooms have large balconies peering down onto the heavy pedestrian traffic of Damrak, and everybody gets a delicious buffet breakfast with a wide selection of eggs, meats, juices, and coffee.

Hotel Agora (Singel 462; Tel 627-22-00; Tram 1, 2, 5 to Konigsplein; agora@worldonline.nl, home.worldonline.nl/~agora; 110-180Dfl single, 120-215Dfl double, 235-275Dfl triple, 270-325Dfl quad, depending on season and amenities; MC, V, AE) prides itself on a pleasant staff, comfortable and well-decorated rooms, and a location that can't be any better. This renovated family-run canal house hotel warmly welcomes visitors of all ages from every corner of the globe. A lovely breakfast room adjacent to the garden adds to the enchantment. An overabundance of traditional and modern furniture fills the bedrooms. The charm just oozes out of every inch of this place.

need to know

Currency Exchange The Dutch unit of currency is the *guilder (Dfl)*. Of the most visible change offices here, **GWK** *(Centraal Station; Tel 0800/05-66; 24-hour service)* has the best commission rates in town.

Tourist Information There are four locations of **VVV Amsterdam** *(Leidseplein office open 9am-7pm daily, other offices 9am-5pm daily; Phone service 0900/400-40-40 9am-5pm Mon-Fri at 1Dfl per minute)*, the city's pleasantly helpful tourist information organization; the best and most convenient being on the second floor of Centraal Station. The others are: across the tram tracks from Centraal Station at Stationsplein 1, at Leidseplein 1, and in the south at Stadionplein and Van Tuyll van Serooskerkenweg. All are pleasant and helpful, and can book hotel rooms, theater, ballet, opera, and concert tickets; and bike, canal, and guided tours to nearby towns and villages.

The **Uit Boro** *(Leidseplein 26; Tel 621-12-11; 10am-6pm Mon, Tue, Wed, Sat, 9am-9pm Thur, closed Sun; www.amsterdamarts.org)* can make reservations for almost every show or concert scheduled in Amsterdam from its very helpful information desk.

Public Transportation The public transportation system consists of **trams**, **metros**, and **buses**. Stick to the trams—the metros mainly run to the suburbs for commuters, and the buses are slow and infrequent—except after 12:30am, when the trams stop and the night buses take over. There are 11 public transport fare zones in the greater Amsterdam area, but it's unlikely you'll ever venture beyond the sizable city center *(Zone 5700, or centrum)*. You must be sure that your ticket is validated for the number of zones you are entering, plus one extra zone. So, since most trips are all within one zone *(centrum)* validate your ticket for two zones. If there's a conductor on the train, he/she will validate your ticket, and if not, validate it yourself at the machine on the tram. Fold over the section twice (one for each zone), watch the rest of the passengers stick their tickets in the machine, and follow suit. The ticket is good for one hour after you validate it, and you can jump on any other tram in the same zones until that hour is up. You can buy a 15-zone "strip card" for 11.50Dfl from the GVB tram office in front of Centraal Station, VVV Tourist Offices, post offices, and some news vendors. It's much more expensive to buy your tickets on the tram: A single costs 3Dfl, and an all-day pass *(dagkaart)* costs 10Dfl. Tram maps are on the walls of most tram shelters, and are available at the **VVV Tourist Offices**.

Bike/Moped Rental Don't leave Amsterdam without renting a bike. This is the best way to get around once you're decently acquainted with the city. **Mac Bike** *(Mr. Visselplein 2; Tel 620-09-85; Tram 9, 14, 20 to Mr. Visserplein; 9am-6pm daily; Passport and 50Dfl deposit)* will rent you wheels and suggest itineraries for day trips in the city and its

Internet access machines have been popping up lately on the streets of Amsterdam (usually next to phone booths). You can't send e-mail from these terminals, but you can read incoming messages.

A few Internet cafes/coffeeshops offer cheap Internet services. The original of these is **Cafe Internet Free World** *(Nieuwendijk 30; Tel 620-09-02; 10am-1am Sun-Thur, till 3am Fri, Sat; 2.50Dfl per 30 minutes)*. Only 150 meters from the Centraal Station, this coffeeshop has computers that are a bit faster than the competition, but you have to buy a drink to get onto a computer and probably have to wait in line for a little while to get on. **Internet Cafe "Tops" Coffeeshop** *(Prisengracht 480; Tel 638-41-08; 10am-1am Sun-Thur, till 3am Fri, Sat; 3.50Dfl per 20 minutes)* is a two-minute walk from Leidseplein, right on the canal Prisengracht. It's a bit more expensive, and the computers are kinda slow, but the lines are shorter and the atmosphere's a lot cooler. The bartenders constantly have joints hanging out of their mouths and like to keep the music (from Led Zep to techno) pretty loud. If for some inexplicable reason, you're having a difficult time finding other travelers from home, the Internet cafes are always a good bet.

www.visitamsterdam.com, ***www.amsterdam.nl:*** good basic info.

www.amsterdamhotspots.nl: nightlife and stuff.
www.amsterdamfordummies.nl: lots of links.

surroundings. There's another Mac Bike office next to **XXX Moped Rental** [see below].

For a guided bike tour in English, try **Mike's Bike Tours** *(Meet at west entrance of Rijksmuseum; Tel 622-79-70; Three to four-hour tours 11:30am, 4pm daily, noon only from Apr 15-May 15, Sept 1-Oct 31; 37Dfl)*. These guys are the authority on getting around Amsterdam by bike. They stay away from the traffic, take it easy, and stop at some cool spots.

For wheels with more power, try **XXX Moped Rental** *(Marnixstraat 208; Tel 422-02-66; Tram 7, 10, 20 to Elandsgracht; Helmets available and suggested; 500-1,000Dfl deposit; MC, V)*.

American Express Amex is easy to find here, right on **Damrak 66** *(Tel 520-77-77)*.

Health and Emergency Emergency: *112*. Two reliable hospitals are **Ziekenhuis** *(De Boelelaan 1117; Tel 444-44-44)*, and **Slotervaartziekenhuis** *(Louwesweg 6; Tel 512-93-33)*, both out past Vondelpark.

Pharmacies The centrally-located **Apotheek Dam** *(Damstraat 2; Tel 624-43-31)* or **Apotheek Koek Schaeffer & van Tijen** *(Vijzelgracht 19; Tel 623-59-49)*, down by the museums, are friendly.

Telephone Country code: *31*; city code: *020*; information: *0900/80-08*; international operator: *0900/84-18*. Phone cards are available at post offices, supermarkets, Centraal Station, **GWK**, the occasional corner deli/tobacco stores, and news vendors. **AT&T**: *0800/022-91-11*; **MCI**: *0900/022-91-22*; **Sprint**: *0900/022-91-19*.

Airports Schiphol Airport *(Flight information 0900/141)*. The **KLM Hotel Shuttle** *(17.50Dfl)* bus runs between the airport and the city center, stopping at 16 top hotels and near many others. Leaves every 20 minutes. Or take a 20-minute train ride from Schiphol Station *(Downstairs from Schiphol Plaza; 6.25Dfl)* to Centraal Station. Good during peak hours, otherwise might wait up to an hour. Taxis line up out front of the Arrivals Hall, but they'll run you about 60Dfl to the city center.

Airlines KLM Airlines *(Postbus 7700; Tel 474-77-47)*; **Northwest Airlines** *(Amsterdamweeg 55; Tel 555-999)*.

Trains Centraal Station *(Stationsplein; Netherlands railway info 0900/92-92)*. Trains depart for **Schiphol Airport** from **Centraal Station**. From here you can just walk out onto the town, or grab a tram from one of the tram stops that flank the main entrance.

Buses Eurolines *(Julianaplein 5; Tel 560-87-87)*. The terminal is opposite Amstel Station; you can grab a train, metro, or tram into the city center from there.

brussels

Brussels may not be the heavyweight party center of Europe, but don't write the European Union capital off as a complete bureaucratic wasteland. The best of Brussels is *well hidden* from the pinstriped lemmings who shuffle their way through its vast government complexes. In fact, the EU-capital thing has done wonders to spice up the local flavor by attracting visitors and immigrants from around the globe. Truly a multicultural, cosmopolitan city, Brussels is a fine place to taste the rainbow. And taste the food. And taste the chocolate. And did we mention the beer? With over 400 native brews, and as many bars, Brussels has cornered the market on insobriety. Belgians take their drinking very seriously and make nightly pilgrimages to their local bars religiously. Clubbing doesn't happen with the same vigor and is confined mainly to weekends, but the scene is picking up steam and has a true heavyweight contender in **Le Fuse** [see *club scene*, below]. Substance-wise, young *Bruxellois* pretty much stick to the current standards—mostly Mary Jane and E—and, of course, their suds.

Outside a few inflammatory subjects (food, parking, the EU), Belgians are a modest, soft-spoken people. Unfortunately, they're mainly a French-speaking people, too, so don't be surprised if your average conversation plays like a game of charades. (No, speaking English with a French accent doesn't help, and keep that Lady Marmalade *voulez-vous-coucher* shit to yourself.) Fortunately, unlike the famous snooty Parisians, *les Bruxellois* remain friendly in their complete inability to understand a word you're saying.

As far as getting around goes, the only transportation device you need is a map, which you can snag at any newsstand. Though it's a maze of narrow streets, Brussels is tiny and totally walkable. Public transportation is necessary only for cross-city trips—which is fortunate, since the metro and trams are pretty limited, and the bus system is not so much elaborate as indecipherable. When picking up a map, be sure to snare a copy of *The Bulletin*, a weekly magazine for English speakers, also available at most newsstands. The center section, *What's On*, has an indispensable listing of upcoming events throughout Belgium. For all you rock 'n' roll groupies, *The Ticket*, a free monthly listing of music events (yeah, it's in French...deal), can be your key to finding a reprieve from the constant barrage of electronic music that Belgian youngsters seem hard-wired to crave. You can pick one up at music stores and most venues.

neighborhoods

Here's a quick geography lesson: To the east of **Boulevard Anspach**, the main drag that runs north-south through the city center, is the **Bourse**, Brussels' stock exchange *and* teen meeting place, as well as **Grand Place** (the equivalent of New York's Times Square minus the neon), which is surrounded by streets packed with assorted tourist snares. Note: Anspach is called **Boulevard M. Lemmonier** to the south and **Boulevard Adolphe Max** to the north. The less-developed area to the west of Anspach is far more residential, but is home to the rapidly-gentrifying **Rue Antoine Dansaert**, running northwest-southeast, where the city's avant-garde fashion design scene is digging in its heels, and trendy hangouts like **Bonsoir Clara** [see *eats*, below] and **L'Archiduc** [see *live music scene*, below] are following suit. Just south of Dansaert is the **Place Saint-Géry** area, where a number of bars, like **Zebra** [see *bar scene*, below], and a booming vinyl trade are attracting a young, hip crowd.

Rue Neuve, which runs parallel to Anspach on its east side, is Brussels' busiest shopping street, filled with clothing and shoe stores that won't take your wallet for a ride. If you're just dying to indulge your inner millionaire, **Boulevard de Waterloo**, which runs along the southeastern perimeter of the city, and **Avenue Louise**, which branches off Waterloo to the south, can outfit you in a diamond-studded evening gown faster than you can say "Chapter 11." The Avenue Louise crowd can be followed back to the swarm of upscale restaurants and antiques boutiques around the **Place du Grand Sablon**, just a 10 minute walk south of Grand Place. In the southwest quadrant of the city, the **Marolles**, a less moneyed neighborhood where many of Brussels's Arabs and North Africans have settled, is speckled with hole-in-the-wall antiques shops and crafts stores.

hanging out

Grand Place is truly the heart of the Brussels jungle, through which all the city's wildlife ends up at one time or another. At night you can find groups of high-school and college-age tourists sitting in large circles in the middle of the square, beating bongos and singing songs in whatever language they do best. To spend an evening trading battle stories with fellow travelers, settle in with the backpack rats at **Sleep Well** or **Vincent Van Gogh** [see *crashing*, below for both], the liveliest of the city's many youth hostels. Even if you're not staying there but just want to put your feet up for a few, you can grab some real estate in a busy common area and not worry about being hassled. And if you're traveling solo, the hostels are good places to pick up a drinking partner...or twelve.

If you want to ingratiate yourself with the locals, make an appearance at the huge Sunday morning flea market at the **Place du Jeu de Balle** [see *stuff*, below] in the Marolles and share a good laugh with the hip young crowd that comes to marvel at the truly bizarre collection of wares. If you're into the juvie thing, a younger high-school crowd can be found, day and night, slouching on the steps of the Bourse, blowing cigarette smoke at passing traffic. For a less sedentary experience, grab a board and head to where the skate rat scene lives, at the **Palais des Congrès** [see *great outdoors*, below], about a ten-minute walk northeast of the Gare Centrale. In the late-late night, join fellow red-eyed bar/club fiends outside of **Fritland** [see *eats*, below] to munch on fries and other greasy morsels.

For some quality down time, **La Vache Qui Regarde Passer Les Trains** [see *eats*, below] (literally, "The Cow Who Watches the Trains Go By") is a cozy place to sip your *pressé* and let the upscale tourist traffic in Galerie Saint-Hubert, Europe's first covered shopping arcade, flow by. The benches outside the grafitti-stained 18th-century **Eglise Notre Dame du Finistère** on Rue Neuve are slightly less lounge-friendly, but offer a great vantage point for people-watching on this bustling east side avenue.

bar scene

Only a country that loves beer this much would have a peeing boy as its national hero [see *culture zoo*, below]. Trendy cafes, dives, and traditional beer halls (almost all with outdoor seating) line every street, bringing together suits and students, punks and parishioners, in pursuit of the perfect brew. Ask for a citrusy, sweet *blanche*, a pungent *gueuze*, or a sturdy *lambic* to save yourself the mocking heaped upon a young American traveler who recently asked a bartender for "anything that tastes like Coors Light." If you're out with Belgians, the custom is to take turns buying rounds, so, drinking in large groups...well, you do the math.

From his perch on the blood-red wall, the divinely mustachioed Salvador Dali grins over his namesake, **Dali's Bar** (*Petite Rue des Bouchers 35; Tel 02/511-54-67; Tram 23, 52, 55, 56, 81 to Bourse; 10pm-4am Mon-Thur, 9pm-6am Fri, Sat; No credit cards*), right near Grand Place. Surrealism abounds, from the melting cardboard clock that greets visitors to the scruffy guys who tote Prada-bedecked models on their arms. The best spots in the house are the red velvet lip-shaped love seats. "The Shaker," a house cocktail, costs 500BF and contains precious little mixer—this should be shared; drink one alone and the walls will probably start melting, too. Pretty, underage teenyboppers populate Dali's until transportation stops running at midnight, so plan to arrive late...unless jailbait is your bag.

rules of the game

Belgians take their boozing very seriously, and they start training early: 18 is the legal age to buy. You may see the patrons of a crowded bar spilling into the street, but lower that concerned eyebrow—hittin' on a brew in public is A-OK here. Hittin' on the pipe, on the other hand, is not so legal—though the laws are not so strictly enforced.

For a taste of the traditional Belgian cafe, visit **A la Mort Subite** (*Rue Montagne-aux-Herbes Potagères 7; Tel 02/513-13-18; Premetro 1a, 1b to De Brouckère; 11am-1:30am Mon-Thur, 11am-2am Fri, Sat, 12:30pm-1am Sun; No credit cards*), which has been serving up the sauce for nearly 90 years. This is the one you'll find on every travel agent-planned itinerary, but somehow it doesn't feel too touristy. Choupette, the resident cat, weaves around the boot-clad feet of twentysomething Bruxellois, the splendid wingtips of the city's businessmen, and the Nikes of plaid-shirted Americans, alike. Great *gueuze*, *lambic*, and *kriek* (cherry-flavored) draught beers brewed exclusively for **A La Mort Subite** ("Sudden Death") cost 75-115BF.

Zebra (*Place Saint-Géry 33-35; Tel 02/511-09-01; Tram 23, 52, 55, 56, 81 to Bourse; Noon-2am daily, till 3am Fri, Sat*) is a place of harmonious contradictions, where local hipsters mix with cigarillo-smoking construction workers, and velvet curtains soften the industrial sheet-metal decor. Brooders fill the cafe during the day, crowded around the tiny tables as they nod to the mellow trip-hop; old-school funk energizes the place after 9pm. The cheap, though limited, food menu includes decent grilled mozzarella-and-veggie panini sandwiches. Just a short walk from the Bourse.

French and Flemish become foreign languages again at **O'Reilly's** (*Place de la Bourse 1; Tel 02/552-04-80; Tram 23, 52, 55, 56, 81 to Bourse; 11am-2am, Sun-Thur, 11am-4am Fri, Sat; www.oreillys.com; with 500BF minimum V, MC, AE*). The city's young anglophiles pack this enormous wood-paneled pub, right off the Bourse, to seek refuge from thumping electronica amid American and British pop. The scene is casual, but still kickin'—the Irish know how to throw a party. Navigating your way through the crowds is tough on weekend nights and during televised English soccer matches on Sunday afternoons. A tiny widow's walk overlooks the Bourse and Anspach.

Tiki-torch kitsch meets standard-issue college bar at **Le Sphinx** (*Rue Marché aux Fromages 20; Tel 02/514-24-38; Tram 23, 52, 55, 56, 81 to Bourse; 2pm-4am Sun-Thur, 2pm-6am Fri, Sat; V, MC, AE*). Under the ubiquitous house-techno blend, schlumpy university students come to get bombed and hook up. Black lights and a television perpetually tuned to a sports channel might make you feel like you never left home. It's nestled between shwarma stands [see *eats*, below] behind the Grand Place, which makes the late-night sodium binge easy. Belgian beers, which will cost you 70-95BF, are obscured by an array of faux-exotic cocktails. The house drink, boldly titled "Le Sphinx," looks like Smurf juice and tastes like teen spirit.

The look-at-me-I'm-an-artist crowd flocks to **Au Soleil** *(Rue Marché au Charbon 86; Tel 02/513-34-30; Tram 23, 52, 55, 56, 81 to Bourse; 10am-1am Mon-Thur, 10am-2pm Fri, Sat, 11am-1am Sun; No credit cards)*, which sits on one of Brussels' busiest gay drags, just paces from the Bourse. With a little soul, a little '70s funk-fusion jazz, and a little angsty guitar rock as your sound track, you can sit down with a cheap glass of Jupiler beer and stew about The Man who's always trying to keep you down.

LIVE MUSIC SCENE

With a plethora of cramped, smoky venues, the Brussels scene is well suited for jazz. But several great venues have closed during the last decade, and now musicians bemoan the decline of the city's jazz scene. Rockers don't fare so well in the land of the mix-masters, either. Brussels manages to pull in some big-name international and hip-hop acts, but the city suffers from a lack of quality, mid-sized joints.

The last hardcore jazz hangout is **Le Travers** *(Rue Traversière 11; Tel 02/217-60-58; Metro 2 to Botanique; 8pm-2am Mon-Fri, 9pm-2am Sat; travers@cyclone.be, www.cyclone.be/travers; No credit cards)*, a smoky dive lit by Christmas lights and candles. Your best bet is Monday night, when a free jam session draws young lions eager to show their chops, older expat jazzmen, and a legendary pair of groupie sisters who have practiced their amateur (though impressive, we're told) dominatrix skills on most musicians in the city. The packed crowd is a mix of local and international, helped by heavy advertising at the youth hostel across the street. Concerts on other days cost 150-400BF, depending on the caliber of performer. Check the schedule in *The Ticket* for relatively big names—you might get lucky.

Marcus Mingus *(Impasse de la Fidelité 10; Tel 02/502-02-07; Premetro 1a, 1b to De Brouckère; 8:30pm-2am, closed Sun; V, MC)* is a newer, more sterile jazz club that suffers from a lack of marketing. The club is hit-or-miss most nights, but Thursday night's free jam session is a sure bet. Find the club just off Rue des Bouchers and next to *Jeanneke-Pis*, the diminutive (in both size and stature) squatting sister of *Manneken-Pis* [see *culture zoo*, below].

Make sure you're not down to your last *centime* when you stop at **L'Archiduc** *(Rue Antoine Dansaert 6; Tel 02/512-06-52; Tram 23, 52, 55, 56, 81 to Bourse; 4pm-4am daily; V, MC, AE)*, a sleek Art Deco bar dedicated to jazz that caters to the upstart Rue Antoine Dansaert crowd. With the air of a private club, it's the perfect spot to sip a cosmopolitan and feel sophisticated. The "Round About Five" live music series every Sunday is on the pricey side (500BF), even for the privilege of hearing the happening local Eric Boeren Kwartet.

five things to talk to a local about

1. You don't need to put a Belgian behind the wheel to incite a nasty case of road rage. Just mention traffic, parking, or road conditions—Bruxellois get so heated about **anything auto-related** you may have to keep a hose handy.

2. You can't go wrong asking for **the lowdown, re: food or beer**. The Belgians' stomachs are near and dear to their hearts, and with hundreds of bars serving as many different types of brew and new restaurants going in and out of style daily, every local has an opinion they're dying to share.

3. One of the things that really cheeses the locals off about having the EU capital in Brussels is the steady rape of the city's architectural monuments in order to make room for a glut of **ugly office buildings**. Most older Bruxellois will be happy for the chance to bitch about the loss of native treasures like Victor Horta's Maison du Peuple and the Quartier Léopold.

4. A rather boring lot, the members of the Belgian royal family are at minimal risk of having a version of "Candle in the Wind" dedicated to them. However, **the recent marriage of Prince Philippe**, heir to the throne, has created some uncharacteristic excitement in the young, female community. Hey, there are worse ways to start a conversation.

5. And, of course, there's **football (aka soccer)**. It is important to realize that in Europe, where the next best sports are cricket and rugby, you've got to make the best of what you have. If you do try to talk sports with a local, the most important thing to know is: Anderlecht rules! Rooting for anyone else could be hazardous to your health.

Ancienne Belgique (*Blvd. Anspach 110; Tel 02/548-24-24; Tram 23, 52, 55, 56, 81 to Bourse; www.abconcerts.be; 400-900BF cover; V, MC, AE*), the only concert venue downtown, recently reopened its doors after a long hiatus. AB, as it's called, features a wide range of music, from bluegrass to hip-hop to alterna-rock, and only holds about 2,000 people, so you never need binoculars to see the stage.

Go even smaller with **La Botanique** (*Rue Royale 236; Tel 02/226-12-11; Metro 2 to Botanique; 9am-7pm Mon-Fri, 10am Sat, Sun, open later for performances; botanique@arcadis.be; V, MC, AE*). This former botanical garden has three rooms, the biggest of which holds 700 standing people. Despite its tiny size and designation as a cultural center for French language, this venue has seen Jeff Buckley, Oasis, and the Cranberries

brussels bars, clubs and culture zoo

BARS / CLUBS ▲
A La Mort Subite **12**
Au Soleil **5**
Dali's Bar **10**
Le Fuse **1**
Le Sphinx **7**
Le Sud **11**
O'Reilly's **4**
Zebra **2**

CULTURE ZOO ●
Cathédrale des Saints
   Michel et Gudule **13**
Centre Belge de la
   Bande Déssinée **14**
Hôtel de Ville **6**
Mannekin-Pis **3**
Musée d'Art Ancien **8**
Musée d'Art
   Moderne **9**

Brussels
BELGIUM

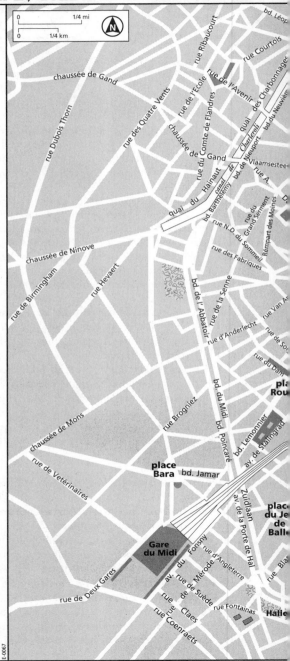

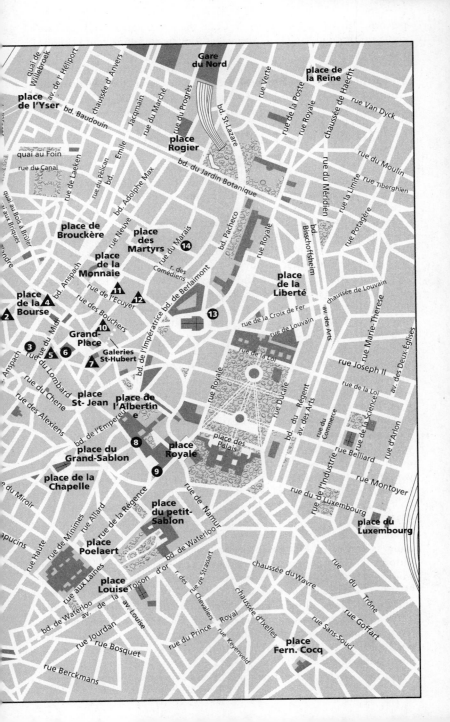

perform. It's also a good place to catch the few Belgian bands that do come up through the music scene—as long as you don't mind singing along *en français*.

Perhaps best known as the home of the **International Cartoon and Animated Film Festival** [see *festivals & events*, below], **Auditorium 44** *(Passage 44, Blvd. du Jardin Botanique; Tel 02/201-06-03; Metro 2 to Botanique; Hours and cover vary; No credit cards)* also hosts some of the better folk and world music acts that have become popular in Brussels's expat-heavy scene.

club scene

Pop quiz: Given that the average Brusselian drinks roughly three pints of beer per day, consumes 10 ounces of mayonnaise per week, and sharpens pencils for exercise at their desk jobs, how do they not all look like Cartman on Weight-Gain 2000? Answer: They go clubbing on the weekends. And not the half-cocked, home-by-3 kind of clubbing. When the Belgians put on their club gear, it generally doesn't get peeled off until after daybreak (though it usually doesn't see action until after midnight). But before you squeeze into those vinyl pants, there's a few need-to-knows: The vast majority of Belgians worship at the altar of electronic music, so what you can expect to grind to on most dance floors (and in most cafes, restaurants, and shops for that matter) is techno, house, trip-hop, trance, drum 'n' bass...anything with a digital beat. This love affair with electronica has landed the DJ at the functional center of the music scene, and crowds follow good ones around Belgium like a pack of tripped-out lemmings. A good place to check where the groove is going on is **Doctor Vinyl** [see *stuff*, below], a record shop that's always stocked with flyers for events mainstream and underground, near and far. Many bars and most other music stores also carry the latest news on upcoming jams. The regular parties are a bit more hit-and-miss, but there are a few scenes you can take to the bank. General tip on getting into Belgian clubs: doormen are pretty laid-back and will only hassle you if you look totally wrong for the crowd, but if you decide not to grease them on the way out—around 50BF is standard—don't expect to get back in.

The Taj Mahal of techno clubs, **Le Fuse** *(Rue Blaes 208; Tel 02/511-97-89; Bus 20, 48 to Jeu de Balle; 10pm-7am Sat only; 300BF cover, free before 11pm; www.fuse.be; No credit cards)*, just south of place du Jeu de Balle, is known by DJs far and wide as one of the top spots in all of Europe. The cavernous main dance floor is a true shrine to the disc jockey, who spins from a platform elevated above hundreds of grungy club kids. "Motion," a separate dance floor, sports the latest in timed strobe lighting and fog machines, all set to kitschy blue and orange '70s decor. You can watch the dancers' spastic movements from a lounge area where people retire to make out or pass out. Though showing up before 11pm avoids the 300BF cover, things don't really jump until well after 1am or wind down until sunrise.

An early-twenties crowd of students and hip North African émigrés

fIVE-O

On the heels of a long series of kidnappings, rapes, and murders back in the mid-'90s, allegations of corruption and misconduct have shredded the local police's public image. Searing press accounts aside, Brussels is a relatively safe city where ticket-happy cops spend most of their time scolding naughty, illegally parked cars. Though there is some racial tension between the police and resident North Africans, it's not nearly as serious as in Antwerp. As a visitor, your main safety concern should be holding on to your wallet—pickpockets haven't yet made it onto the endangered species list.

Oh, one annoying quirk of Belgian law: you're required to carry your passport or some form of national identification at all times. Unless you want to risk a police escort to your hotel to retrieve your ID, don't leave home without it.

sneak down a back alley off of Rue de l'Ecuyer to get their freak on every Friday and Saturday night at **Le Sud** (*Rue de l'Ecuyer 45; Tel 02/514-37-03; Premetro 1a, 1b to De Brouckère; 10pm-6am, Fri, Sat only; 100BF cover; www.lesud.net; No credit cards*), where three completely different rooms will give you the best bang for your franc. On the main dance floor, crumbling walls scrawled over with Arabic confine a capacity crowd yelling along to Gloria Gaynor and the *Grease* soundtrack. The place jams solid by midnight, when traditional Middle Eastern dance music cuts off the golden oldies and a local belly dancer climbs onto the bar to shake her money-maker for an hour or so. Downstairs in the "Clo Clo Club," a dank cellar that makes the main floor seem upscale, shit-faced Belgians sing along to the vocal stylings of this dungeon's namesake, cheesy French disco singer Claude François. A third room in the back dedicated to commercial house and techno is a good place to escape the suffocating heat of the main floor and the freaky (but fun) Clo Clo cult.

Tour & Taxis (*Rue Picard 5; Tel 02/420-95-50; Metro 2 to Ribacourt; 11pm-7am, Fri, Sat; 200BF cover; tour&taxi@place.to.be; No credit cards*), a customs warehouse complex turned dance venue, throws passable parties every weekend, but don't miss the standout *Union Jack* party, the first Saturday of the month, when crowds of hardcore techno junkies turn out to sample the skills of London's DJ du jour.

aRTS SCENE

▶▶VISUAL ARTS

The country that bred Rubens, Brueghel, and Magritte also reveres its cartoon art icons, Tintin and Astérix. Prismatic murals, most based on popular characters from comic book lore, are splashed upon the walls of aging buildings across the city [see below]. Keep your head up and prepare to be startled by Lucky Luke staring down at you.

The underground art scene in Brussels is small, but squatters sometimes toss together exhibits. Police generally leave them alone in the most regular of their illicit venues, such as **Tour & Taxis** [see *club scene*, above], which hosts the occasional loosely organized film or art exhibit. Advertising is done by flyer or word of mouth. The best place to tap into the scene is at Nova, which is also run by a group of squatters. Express interest, and they're more than likely to invite you to the Hungarian performance piece being thrown in the loft someone swiped.

For more mainstream fare, head for the road that snakes up to the **Palais des Congrès** [see *great outdoors*, below]. Most of the snooty, pee-your-pants-expensive art galleries are run by cigarette-waving matrons who sit at their desks waiting for the big spenders. These paintings are meant for buying, so tuck in your shirt and finish your waffle before heading inside.

One of these galleries, **Horizons** *(59 Rue de la Madeleine; Tel 02/512-86-42; Premetro 1a, 1b to Gare Centrale; 11am-6:30pm Tue-Sat, 11am-1pm Sun)* hawks works by up-and-coming artists from Europe, Asia, and North America. Especially keep an eye out for one of the owner's favorites, Belgian painter Marcel Lucas. His distorted, undulating cityscapes look like a trippy Escher-Magritte combination.

▶▶**PERFORMING ARTS**

You would think the international contingent in Brussels would give birth to some sort of regular English-language theater, but you would be wrong. An amateur comedy troop looking for an audience is usually the most you'll find advertised in the English section of *The Bulletin*, which lists plays by language. Check to see if your visit happens to coincide with a visiting performance.

The thirst for culture is better quenched by catching a dance performance. The Brussels dance scene is lively and innovative, as small venues draw contemporary dance troops from across the world. The 743-seat **Lunatheater** *(Place Sainctlette 20; Tel 02/201-59-59; Metro 2, tram 18 to Yser; 480-800BF, 300-500BF for those under 26; info@kaaithe ater.be, www.kaaitheater.be; V, MC)*, known also by its Dutch name Kaaitheater, regularly features stars from renowned troops who are just splitting off on their own projects. Its smaller companion theater, **Kaaitheater Studios** *(Rue Notre Dame du Sommeil 81; Tel 02/201-59-59; Tram 18 to Porte de Ninove)*, with only 100 seats, hosts lesser-known faces in an intimate setting. Performance art also finds a home in the two venues, with the likes of New York's Wooster Group tripping out audiences with technology-pumped dance/theater.

Not as much fun as actually *being* John Malkovich, but great fun nonetheless can be had watching puppeteer José Géal's marionettes bust a wooden move in **Théâtre Toone VII** *(Impasse Schuddeveld 6, off Petite Rue des Bouchers; Tel 02/217-27-53; Premetro 1a, 1b to De Brouckère; 8:30pm Tue-Sat; 400BF, students 250BF except Fri, Sat; No credit cards)*, just a block north of Grand Place. Performing the satirical stylings of *Faust*, *The Three Musketeers*, and *Hamlet*, the performances

festivals and events

The up-and-coming **Brussels International Film Festival** *(Mid- to late-Jan; 02/227-39-80)* owes its recent recognition mainly to the roster of famous guests it has cajoled into attendance in recent years, like Tim Robbins and Dennis Hopper. But it *is* in January...and much better than being outside in the cold and damp Brussels winter.

The **International Cartoon and Animated Film Festival** *(Mid-Feb; Auditorium 44, Blvd. du Jardin Botanique; 02/534-41-25)* screens new and old international cartoons, both features and shorts. Attention all *anime* fetishists—reserve your tickets now.

The **Royal Hothouses** *(Late Apr, early May; 61 Ave. du Parc Royal; 9:30am-4pm Wed-Thur, 9pm-11pm Fri-Sun; Tel 02/513-89-40)*, a spectacular group of eleven greenhouses, are home to dense copses of exotic plants and flowers. If you're around for the few weeks the plants are in bloom, it's a must-see.

For three days, the **Brussels Jazz Marathon** *(Late May; Tel 02/456-04-85; info@jazztronaute.be)* kicks the city's nightlife into overdrive, with jazz from fundamental to funk drawing crowds to dozens of indoor and outdoor venues.

Festival Couleur Café *(Late June; Tour&Taxis, Rue Picard 2; Tel 02/672-49-12; www.couleurcafe.org)* brings out Brussels' truly multiculti side, with a nonstop weekend of theater, exotic dancing, world music, ragga, funk, acid jazz, and hip-hop.

Unless you've got wicked hay fever, check out the **Tapis des Fleurs**, or flower carpet, *(Mid-Aug; Grand Place; Tel 02/513-89-40)*, which blankets Grand Place in thousands of ornately patterned begonias for a weekend every other year (2000, 2002...).

are usually in French or Flemish, but are not too difficult to follow. Now in its seventh generation under the control of the Toone family, this puppet show has become one of Brussels' most famous (if most clichéd) attractions.

Brussels is one of the best cities in Europe in which to catch a flick. The huge international community ensures that films are nearly always shown in their original languages with French and Flemish subtitles. Must-see films come in from Brazil, France, Germany, and the States (though a few months after their original release, for the U.S. flicks).

For the least-outdated American blockbusters, head for **UGC de Brouckère** *(Place de Brouckère 38; Tel 02/218-57-25; Premetro 1a, 1b to De Brouckère; 250BF admission; www.cinebel.com/ugc; No credit cards)*. For you film buffs, the **Musée du Cinéma** *(Rue Baron Horta 9; 02/507-83-70; Premetro 1a, 1b to Gare Centrale; Bus 30, 60, 71 to*

Beaux-Arts; From 5:30pm daily; 90BF entry fee, 60BF if you reserve ahead; No credit cards) brings back the timeless classics by the world's preeminent filmmakers. Black-and-white masterpieces by Fritz Lang, Frank Capra, Akira Kurosawa, and Federico Fellini fill one tiny theater, while the other features silent movies accompanied by a live pianist. The entry fee also gains you entry to the museum, which exhibits equipment from the first days of film. Unfortunately, most displays are only in French and Flemish.

For the latest in indy celluloid, the bomb shelter-esque back-alley venue **Nova** *(3 Rue d'Arenberg; Tel 02/511-27-74; www.nova-cinema.com; 200BF, 150BF for students; No credit cards)* screens mostly foreign projects in formats ranging from 35mm to VHS. Once a month Nova offers a free *Open Screen* event, where you get to watch Joe Wannabe fill 15 minutes with sometimes brilliant home movie bytes. Below the cinema is a bar, about as underground as you can hope for, where Nova's turtleneck-clad, bed-headed artist crowd talk shop and listen to discordant borderline-demented industrial music.

gay scene

Gay life in Brussels is a little like the Artist Formerly Known as Prince: It's flamboyant, compact, and a little stale at times, but definitely capable of going crazy with the best of them. Like most things in Brussels, the best neighborhoods thrive after midnight around the Bourse. Rue du Marché au Charbon, Rue des Pierres, and Rue des Riches-Claires hold small, lively clubs and cafes for the man's man and woman's woman. Some of the best parties are held on the fringes of Brussels [see *La Démence* and **Strong**, below], but for daily fun, you don't have to go far.

A good first stop is **Tel Quels** *(Rue du Marché au Charbon 81; Tel 02/512-32-34; Tram 23, 52, 55, 56, 81 to Bourse; 5pm-2am Mon, Tue, Thur, 2pm-2am Wed, 5pm-4am Fri, 11am-4am Sat, 6am-2am Sun)*, a gay and lesbian community center by day and bar by night. Ask for the free gay map/guide, which lists every association, nightclub, clothing store, sauna, or sex shop you could possibly need during your stay—in French, but decipherable. The bartender will be happy to tell you which places fit your wants: young, hardcore, leather, whatever. Monday and Tuesday nights draw more women than men. A post-clubbing breakfast is held every Sunday at 6am.

Held in clubbing tour-de-force **Le Fuse** [see *club scene*, above], the occasional *La Démence (11pm-7am every Sunday; www.fuse.be/lademence; No credit cards)* party is hailed by many as the best gay party in Belgium. And since what's good for the gander is good for the goose, Le Fuse also throws a women-only party, subtly titled *Pussy Galore (11pm-dawn second Fri of each month; No credit cards)*.

A close second to Le Fuse's offerings is the recently launched **Strong** *(Rue de la Loi 155; Tel 02/375-93-96; Tram 1a, 1b to Maalbeek; 11pm-dawn as announced; strongbrussels@hotmail.com; No credit cards)*, a raging scene where erotic guest entertainers from Ibiza and other hedonist havens get freaky-deaky and whip the crowd into a randy frenzy.

CULTURE ZOO

Brussels is eager to sit at the table with the world's great cities, and its cultural accomplishments should be enough to guarantee it a comfy chair. The city's buildings glisten with florid Art Nouveau architecture, and works of the country's master painters hang in the ample museums.

One of many legends has it that **Manneken-Pis** *(corner of Rue de l'Etuve and Rue du Chêne; Tram 23, 52, 55, 56, 81 to Bourse)* used the only thing handy to defuse a bomb: his willy. Everyone goes crazy over this fountain of a kid peeing.

The ornately Gothic **Hôtel de Ville** *(Grand Place; Tel 02/279-43-65; Tram 23, 52, 55, 56, 81 to Bourse; 9:30am-12:15pm/1:45pm-4pm Tue-Fri, 10am-1pm Sun; 80BF; No credit cards)*, still the seat of local government, houses Baroque decoration and intricate 17th-century tapestries for those who care.

Good luck finding finer stained-glass windows than in the **Cathédrale des Saints Michel et Gudule** *(Blvd. de l'Impératrice; Tel 02/217-83-45; Premetro 1a, 1b to Gare Centrale; 7am-7pm daily, closes at 6pm Oct-Mar; Free entrance, 40BF for crypts; No credit cards)*, a breathtaking Gothic cathedral from 1226.

Visit the **Musée d'Art Ancien** *(2 Rue de la Régence; Tel 02/508-32-11; Tram 92-94; 10am-1pm/2pm-5pm Tue-Sun; 150BF; No credit cards)* if only for Brueghel's spectacular *Adoration of the Magi* and *Fall of the Rebel Angels*, not to mention works by Rembrandt, Bosch, and Rubens. In the same **Musées Royaux des Beaux-Arts** complex, the **Musée d'Art Moderne** houses a staggering collection of modern surrealist works by Dali, Magritte, Delvaux, and others.

Astérix and Tintin are the gods of the **Centre Belge de la Bande Déssinée** *(20 Rue des Sables; Tel 02/219-19-80; Metro 2 to Rogier or Botanique; 10am-6pm Tue-Sun; 150BF; No credit cards)*, which is housed in a gorgeous Art Nouveau building. Enjoy a glimpse into the goofy, cartoon-crazed Belgian mind.

The far-reaching collection of archaeological artifacts and relics from antiquity at the **Musée Royal d'Art et d'Histoire** *(Parc du Cinquantenaire 10; Tel 02/741-72-11; Tram 1a, 1b to Merode; 9:30am-5pm Tue-Fri, 10am-5pm Sat, Sun; 150BF admission, 100BF for students, free Wed; No credit cards)* is so huge they alternate: one half of the museum is open one day and the other half the next. If you're into big half-empty provincial museums, this is your place.

A brilliant view of the city makes the **Atomium** *(Heysel; Tel 02/477-09-91; Tram 1a to Heysel; Open daily Apr-Aug 9am-7pm, Sept-Mar 10am-5:30pm; 200BF; No credit cards)*, a 335-foot-tall molecular reproduction built for the 1958 World's Fair, a worthwhile trip on a sunny day. Tell them you're going up to the restaurant at the top, and they won't charge you admission.

modification

A turf war has broken out between the alterna-shops of Passage Saint-Honoré and the nearby Galerie du Centre (both in the center of town, near the Bourse). The fiesty and prodigiously pierced young owner of **Arkel Piercing** (*Passage Saint-Honoré 16; Tel 02/223-02-94; Tram 23, 52, 55, 56, 81 to Bourse; 11am-7pm Tue-Sat, 1pm-7pm Mon; arkelpiercing @hotmail.com; No credit cards*) is so dedicated to her craft that the entire second floor of her shop is devoted to paintings of body art. Her store sits across from **Hannya Tattoo** (*Passage Saint-Honoré 9; Tel 02/219-22-76; Tram 23, 52, 55, 56, 81 to Bourse; Noon-7pm, closed Sun; No credit cards*), which offers three specialty artists: Shad for Japanese, Psychopat for tribal, and Patrice for custom designs. **Ritual** (*Galerie du Centre 21; Tel 02/218-1440; Tram 23, 52, 55, 56, 81 to Bourse; 11am-7pm, closed Sun; www.supergids.be; No credit cards*), is more of a pierce-and-tattoo-in-the-box, but it's been around for seven years and is always filled with young alterna-teens.

In his florid studio just off the Bourse, **Yvan David** (*Rue de la Bourse 24; Tel 02/511-47-53; Tram 23, 52, 55, 56, 81 to Bourse; 9am-6pm Mon-Fri; V, MC*) has coiffed the likes of Ace of Base, INXS, and Gerard Depardieu! Though he colors and cuts all lengths of hair, his specialty is *la coiffe chignone*, which he describes with a bouffant wave of his hands around his feathered mane. A stylist to the stars won't come cheap: expect to pay at least 1,000BF for a man's cut and 1,950BF for a woman's. At least he offers a nice cup'a joe with each styling.

For a less flamboyant haircut, head to **Toni & Guy** (*Ave. de la Toison d'Or 12; Tel 02/515-11-11; Metro 2 to Louise; 9am-6pm Mon-Wed, 9am-8pm Thur, Fri, 8:30am-6pm Sat; www.toniandguy.co.uk; V, MC, AE, Diners*), an upscale Avenue Louise salon where you can spend anywhere from 950-3,500BF for a simple chop job, depending on which stylist is at the shears. The royal treatment, including tea, biscuits, and a long shampoo and scalp massage, helps excuse the royal damage to your pocketbook.

great outdoors

Cycling is a national sport for the Belgians (lord knows they haven't been in the running for any other championships recently), so bike paths are set up throughout the city and its surroundings. Spin your wheels in the **Bois de la Cambre** (*Main entrance on Ave. Louise, 1050; Tram 23, 90, 93, 94*), a lush green forest about a half-hour's pedal to the southeast of the city. **Pro Vélo** [see *need to know*, below] rents bikes and gives guided tours. Road bikes will run you 100BF for an hour, 400BF for a day, and 2,000BF for a week.

The closer **Parc de Bruxelles** (*Between the Palais du Roi and Rue de la Loi, one block east of Gare Centrale*) is one of the few patches of green within city limits, good for emergency sunbathing or a quick jog around the mile-long perimeter.

The terrace in front of the **Palais des Congrès** (*on Rue Royal at Rue de Congres*), near the Gare Centrale, draws the skate rats. Those little rebels love to show off under the nation's political hero, riding their rails along the base of King Albert I.

Brussels has a few indoor pools, but the summer swelter brings the city to the **Océade** (*Bruparck, 20 Blvd. du Centenaire; Tel 02/478-43-20; Premetro 1a to Heysel; 10am-6pm Tue-Fri, 10am-10pm Sat, Sun Apr-June, 10am-10pm daily July-Aug, 10-6 Wed-Fri, 10am-10pm Sat, Sun Sept-Mar; 470BF for four hours; V, MC*). This is mostly a family crowd, but it could be worth an afternoon trip if the heat's wilting your spirits.

STUFF

If Brussels' bevy of businessmen and bureaucrats bring one thing to Belgium, it's bucks. While the average resident's budget is devoted first and foremost to food and drink, the impressive size of most Belgians' bank accounts leaves plenty of room for aggressive shopping habits.

The snobby world of haute couture has entrenched itself in the local fashion scene, with the Avenue Louise area practically choking on its sartorial stature. But formality spawns rebellion, and the young breed of Belgian designers have set up camp on the once-seedy Rue Antoine Dansaert. Heavily influenced by the young upstarts of the Antwerp Fashion Academy to the north, the area's shops offer footwear and ready-to-wear clothing with sleek lines and price tags that won't make you cry.

▶▶HOT COUTURE

Designer **Kaat Tilley** (*Galerie du Roi 4; Tel 02/514-07-63; Premetro 1a, 1b to Gare Centrale; 10am-6pm Mon, 10am-6:30pm Tue-Fri, 10:30am-6:30pm Sat, closed Sun; V, MC, AE*) has installed her costly *Escape* line in the haughty and tourist-laden Galerie Saint-Hubert, just south of Grand Place. One look at her fantastical, airy clothes, and it's easy to guess that she started out in theatrical costume design.

If you want to roll with the fashion set at **L'Archiduc** [see *live music scene*, above] and are willing to max out your remaining credit cards, the creamy tones and European cut of the men's collection at **(cacharel)** (*Ave. Louise 39-41; Tel 02/534-73-87; Metro 2 to Ave. Louise; 10am-6:30pm Mon-Sat; V, MC, AE, Diners*) can help perfect your image as a Belgian Don Juan. If Don Johnson is more your style, check out the threads at **Olivier Strelli** (*Ave. Louise 72; Tel 02/512-56-07; Metro 2 to Ave. Louise; 10am-6:30pm Mon-Sat; www.strelli.be; V, MC, AE, Diners*), a Belgian fashion designer who has made stylish use of viscose. Strelli's line for women is a bit more runway than the rest of the Avenue Louise shops, which tend toward the conservative.

For a younger vibe, stroll down Rue Neuve for more frugal clothing and shoe shopping. The off-the-rack yet stylish Euro fashions of **InWear/Matinique** (*Rue Neuve 66; Tel 02/218-66-76; Premetro 1a, 1b to De Brouckère; 10am-6:30pm Mon-Fri, 10am-7pm Sat; V, MC, AE*) provide a quick remedy for acute Banana Republic withdrawal. **M.A.G. Collections** (*Rue Neuve 114-116; Tel 02/231-18-94; Metro 2 to Rogier;*

by foot

Beginning at the steps of the **Bourse**, cross **Boulevard Anspach** to **O'Reilly's** [see *bar scene*, above]. With **O'Reilly's** on your left, walk down **Rue de la Bourse**, the street with the city's highest concentration of Thai and Vietnamese restaurants. Continue straight through **Place Saint-Géry**. The row of colorfully painted facades on your right represents a neighborhood protest against the tide of real estate speculation that has left many buildings similarly gutted. As you come to **Rub-A-Dub**, an all-reggae-and-dub vinyl shop, take a left around the back of **Place Saint-Géry**. To the right is one of many public murals, a testament to Brussels' preoccupation with comic art. Brochures describing a walking tour that passes all 18 murals can be picked up free at the tourist office and most hostels.

Take your next left at **Le Lion Saint Géry**, then two quick rights, first onto **Rue du Borgval** then onto **Rue Saint-Géry**. On your right you will pass a doorway, covered in crayon scribblings, leading to **La Cantina** [see *eats*, below], a well-hidden Brazilian restaurant with "simple food for complicated people." Continue straight through an intersection, and about 100 feet down **Grand Ile** take a peek into **Totem Café**, where, according to a sign in front, "narcotics will be stuffed in your ass." Should you skip that tempting offer, continue on until the road opens onto a large playground, then head right. At the next intersection, hang a right onto **Rue Van Artevelde**, and after 100 yards or so, take **Rue Saint-Christophe** to the left. Take the following right onto **Rue de Chartreux**, and about halfway down the block, on the left, look for **Espace Bizarre**, a design store with a funky Japanese aesthetic. Pass the store and turn around. Above you to the right is another moodier, more artful example of the city's art murals.

Continue along **Rue de Chartreux**, go straight through an intersection and follow **Rue Auguste Orts** to return to the **Bourse**.

9:30am-7pm Mon-Fri, 9:30am-8pm Sat; V, MC, AE) is a solid outlet for club gear with an industrial feel, complete with silver stretch pants, lycra fatigues, and heavy foam jackets. Nearby the Place de la Monnale.

▶▶**TUNES**

In a town where everyone under the age of 30 seems to be working toward their PhDJ, vinyl shops do a ton of business. Most record stores in town can be found in and around the Place Saint-Géry area, including **Doctor Vinyl** *(Grande Ile 1; Tel 02/512-73-44; Tram 23, 52, 55, 56, 81 to Bourse; 11:30am-6:30pm Tue-Sat; V, MC, AE)*, whose collection of house and classic techno attracts many of **Le Fuse**'s [see *club scene*, above] DJs.

For a more grab-bag assortment of both LPs and 45s, check the centrally-located **Goupil-O-Phone** (*Blvd. Anspach 101; 02/511-00-74; Tram 23, 52, 55, 56, 81 to Bourse; 10:30am-7pm Mon-Sat; V, MC, AE*), which sells new and secondhand vinyl. Browsing through their electronic database makes their broad selection a bit more manageable.

If you're just trying to get hold of the latest Madonna CD, your best bet is (Like a) **Virgin Megastore** (*Blvd. Anspach 30; Tel 02/219-90-04; Tram 23, 52, 55, 56, 81 to Bourse; 10am-7pm daily, till 8 Fri; Brussels@vre.co.uk; V, MC, AE*), an old standby right in the heart of Brussels.

▶▶BAZAAR

Perhaps the most interesting, if not the most useful, shopping can be done at one of Brussels' many outdoor markets. On any given morning, some square or other will be populated with natives sifting eagerly through piles of assorted junk in search of bargains. The **antiques market at Place du Grand Sablon** (*Place du Sablon; Sat 8am-6pm, Sun 9am-2pm*) is the kind of affair Robin Leach might slum at. Possessing all the charm of a street fair, but without the riff-raff, long boulevards of open tents display beautifully arranged collections of well-preserved junk.

The city's true heavyweight is the **flea market at Place du Jeu de Balle** (*Place du Jeu de Balle; 7am-2pm daily*), where young hipsters amuse themselves as older eccentrics snoop hungrily through the deer antlers, old tubas, and broken-in bras. Come early and claim a seat at one of the many surrounding cafes to take in the sound of accordion music and the scent of *escargots* wafting through the square.

If you prefer a little funk with your junk, check out **Candar** (*Rue Blaes 164; Tel 02/514-58-77; Metro 2 to Ave. Louise; 10am-6pm Tue-Sat, 10am-4pm Sun; V, MC, AE, Diners*), right off Place du Jeu de Balle. Groove to R&B and hip-hop as you browse through nifty design items like giant floor candles embedded with mirror fragments.

▶▶BOUND

With the Walloons and the Flemish duking it out for linguistic superiority, Brussels has little time to cater to the needs of English bookworms and beat poets. Anglophones in search of intellectual stimulation should look away from the world of literature; English-language poetry readings in Brussels happen about as often as *Manneken-Pis*'s bladder dries up.

For a do-it-yourself literary fix, head to one of Brussels' two English language book shops. **Waterstone's** (*Blvd. Adolph Max 71-75; Tel 02/219-27-08; Metro 1a, 1b to De Brouckère; 9:30am-7pm Mon, 9am-7pm Tue-Sat, 11:30am-6pm Sun; www.waterstones.co.uk; V, MC, AE*) stocks about 60,000 titles, with everything from Grisham to DeLillo to Dickinson. **Sterling** (*Rue du Fossé aux Loups 38; Tel 02/223-62-23; Metro 1a, 1b to De Brouckère; 10am-7pm Mon-Sat, noon-6:30pm Sun; V, MC, AE*), equally well stocked with English classics and best-sellers, also sponsors the occasional book signing and works with the British Council on sporadic readings.

L'Imaginaire (*Place du Jeu de Balle; Tel 02/511-22-23; Metro 2 to Porte de Hal, Bus 20, 48 to Jeu de Balle; 10am-2pm, closed Mon; No credit cards*) is a dusty secondhand book shop just off the Jeu de Balle marketplace. In addition to French lit classics from Proust to Sartre, this tiny bookseller sometimes has a few English titles in the store.

EaTS

It's been said that the best French food in the world is in Belgium. Ground zero for Belgian restauranteurs, Brussels is a gourmet's wet dream and Jenny Craig's worst nightmare (mayonnaise is considered a salad dressing here). It is a city where *frites*, aka french fries, come with a choice of 10 or more different sauces (*la sauce américaine* = le ketchup), where run-down hole-in-the-wall shwarma shacks have hand-scripted leather-bound menus, and patrons of Häagen-Dazs sit on leather sofas and are served by sharply uniformed waiters. Suffice it to say that the Bruxellois take their cuisine awfully seriously, and you should too. A well planned restaurant tour in Brussels can be an experience to remember, and a poorly planned restaurant tour can be an experience for your *credit card* to remember.

▶▶**CHEAP**

Starting at 180BF, sandwiches at **La Vache Qui Regarde Passer Les Trains** (*Galerie de la Reine 29; Tel 02/513-33-36; Premetro 1a, 1b to Gare Centrale; 8am-7pm daily; 140-375BF per entree; lavachequi...@skynet.be; V, MC, AE*) are relatively cheap, but ingredients like *foie gras* and goat cheese still give that European flavor. The coffee is great, served in a cow-adorned bowl with a pitcher of steamed milk.

Just a short walk from the Bourse, **Fritland** (*Rue Henri Maus 49; Tel 02/514-06-27; Tram 23, 52, 55, 56, 81 to Bourse; 11am-6am daily; 50-100BF; No credit cards*) is moderately busy during the day but explodes in the wee hours, bringing in all the club kids and endurance drinkers for their nightly dose of solids—they sell burgers and other greasy damnations to go with the fries. You can cop a squat in the back of the restaurant and eat in relative peace or become part of the action out front on the street, where a more boisterous crowd clamors for their grub at the takeout window.

For meatier late-night fare, head over to Rue Marché aux Fromages, the red light district of gyro joints behind Grand Place, where waiters beckon persistently to passing tourists from open shop windows. The cheapest of the pita pushers, **Pitta's Gold** (*Marché aux Fromages 17; Tel 02/503-32-03; Tram 23, 52, 55, 56, 81 to Bourse; 11am-6am Mon-Sun; 120-350BF per entree; No credit cards*) serves up good, if somewhat unfamiliar, variations on the standard Greek gyro, tossing things like sausage, cole slaw, and pineapple into the mix.

▶▶**DO-ABLE**

The interior of **iNDIgo** (*Rue Blaes 160; Tel 02/648-16-00; Metro 2 to Louise; Tue-Fri 10am-4pm, weekends 9am-3pm; 285-295BF per entree; No credit cards*), a hippy-dippy hole-in-the-wall brunch restaurant, looks like a first-grade art project, covered in messy, colorful flower drawings. A friendly mix of sleepy natives and wide-eyed tourists pass the menu, hand written on the inside cover of an old French novel, from table to table, and listen to Motown hits and French disco as they wait (and wait, and

12 hours in brussels

1. **Pastries and waffles and chocolates, oh my:** Can you say "sugar high"? What better excuse to rot your teeth than engaging in an indigenous cultural practice? Park yourself at one of the chocolatiers around Grand Place and go cuckoo for Cocoa Puffs with the natives.

2. **Go on a walkabout:** Brussels is so charming and Old World you could just puke. Wander around and do some exploring, but wear comfy shoes—cobblestones are rough on the feet. We've planned out a little something special for you [see *by foot*, above], but you could always try something else—see if we care.

3. **Get pissed:** Or watch a little kid do it. Yes, it's cheezy and touristy...but could you really come all this way and not check out *Manneken-Pis*, the world's most famous monument to incontinence? [see *culture zoo*, above].

4. **OK, actually get pissed:** Brussels is a town that rewards the drinker...with another round! The beer here is tasty, plentiful, and damn cheap. Everybody's doing it. And if everybody's doing it...everybody's doing it.

5. **The mother of all garage sales:** Usher in the day by rooting through someone else's shit. For the most part, the **flea market at Place du Jeu de Balle** [see *stuff*, above] is chock-full-o'-useless-crap, but the crowd is hip, lively, and out mainly for kicks.

6. **Try your hand as a film critic:** You can catch the latest international indy pics at **Nova** [see *performing arts*, above]. But, before you do, muss your hair, grow some scruff, if that's an option, and throw on a turtleneck. Nova is (quite literally) a true underground artists hang—we swear the single-screen theater was a bomb shelter in a former life.

7. **Jump around:** Party like it's 2999 at **Le Fuse** [see *club scene*, above], techno mecca of Europe. This place is wall-to-wall dancing, and the beats come fast and furious, so get ready to sweat out all that chocolate.

8. **Get your finger-lickin' on:** Dine in swanky style at **Bonsoir Clara** [see *eats*, below], where the wait staff is as yummy as the food. A popular spot for local glitterati, keep your eyes open for gossip-worthy attendees.

wait...service happens at a snail's pace here) for salads and tasty home-made quiches. A good place to relax after a **Jeu de Balle** [see *stuff*, above] excursion.

Le Pain Quotidien (*Rue Antoine Dansaert 16; Tel 02/502-23-61;*

Metro 1a, 1b to Ste Catherine; 7:30am-7pm daily, till 6pm Sun; 130-395BF; No credit cards) is a more upbeat brunch spot; as quaint as iNDIgo, minus the flowers. There are a few private seatings, but most people sit at the large communal table and converse energetically in French. The food is simple bakery fare, ranging from quiche to smoked salmon sandwiches.

With ham hocks and strings of garlic cloves hanging from the yellowed walls and ceiling, **Le Bar à Tapas** *(Rue Borgval 11; Tel 02/502-66-02; Tram 23, 52, 55, 56, 81 to Bourse; Noon-2:30pm/5pm-1am, no lunch Sat, closed Sun; 80-295BF per entree; V, MC)* pulls off an authentic Spanish feel in a very livable atmosphere. A mix of Belgian yuppies and Spanish expats nibble delectable tapas dishes (the *jambon sec serrano* and the *beignets de poulet miel* are our personal faves) to the sounds of traditional Spanish and Portuguese music in the afternoons; after 9pm the rhythm of salsa takes over the restaurant and a younger crowd follows. Look for heavy burlap drapes and heavy iron slat blinds on the windows.

▶▶**SPLURGE**

Through a small unsigned door along a back street near the Bourse, colored candles lead the way up a rickety set of stairs to one of Brussels' best-kept secrets. The second-story dining room of **La Cantina** *(Rue Saint-Géry 31; Tel 02/513-42-76; Tram 23, 52, 55, 56, 81 to Bourse; Noon-3pm/7pm-late, Mon-Sat, no lunch Sat; 300-850BF per entree; No credit cards)* is set adrift to the sweet sounds of Portuguese love songs as couples savor the exotic Brazilian cuisine by soft candle light. The chef manages to evoke delicately sensuous flavors using combinations of exotic, yet simple, ingredients like olives, mangos, and red beans. All told, La Cantina gets our vote for best hand-holding spot in Brussels.

If you're willing to endure the easy-listening soundtrack, conservative decor, and business-oriented crowd, **Le Jardin de Catherine** *(Place Ste Catherine 5-7; Tel 02/513-92-62; Metro 1a, 1b to Ste Catherine; Noon-2:30pm/7pm-11pm daily, No lunch Sat; julie.r@glo.be; 500-900BF; AE, V, MC, Diners)* is one of the best places for lobster or mussels hereabouts. In the warmer months, skip the drab interior and grab a table in the courtyard, where soft lighting and an overgrowth of grapevines set a romantic mood.

Bonsoir Clara *(Rue Antoine Dansaert 22-26; Tel 02/502-09-90; Metro 1a, 1b to Ste Catherine; Noon-2:30pm Mon-Thur; 7pm-midnight Fri, Sat; 560-760BF per entree; AE, V, MC)* is home to the resident hip fashion set on Rue Antoine Dansaert, so this is the place to flaunt any Donna Karan, Calvin Klein, or Gucci artefacts you may have brought along. The ultra-trendy setting comes complete with flashy yet tasteful Hollywood Hills décor, black-clad waitress slash models, and a menu of fine modern European fare—if you're a carnivore, the beef carpaccio is not to be skipped. For the economically challenged, a *prix fixe* lunch seating on weekdays can be had for only 450BF. If you have the means, we highly recommend it. It is so choice.

crashing

The wealth pumped into hotels that cater to the business and political elite seems to have trickled down into the budget pensions and youth hostels, so in this city, cheap rooms certainly don't mean crappy rooms. Most hostels offer Internet access, free luggage storage, breakfast, and single or double rooms. If you have some money to spend, the Friday-to-Sunday exodus of the business crowd can play to your advantage. Hotel owners often offer special weekend discounts, so don't be afraid to ask nicer places about their deals. The tourist office [see *need to know*, below] can provide a full list of accommodations and help you book rooms.

▶▶CHEAP

The **Centre Vincent Van Gogh/C.H.A.B.** *(8 Rue Traversière; Tel 02/217-01-58; Metro 2 to Botanique; 24-hour access; 685BF single, 570BF/person double, 460BF/person quad, 300-400BF dormitory; chab@ping.be, www.ping.be/chab; No credit cards)* is in many ways your typical youth hostel, but it realizes that hostel-crashers aren't always dolts who love sleazy digs and oversized cartoon characters on the walls. Walls are sponge-painted in tasteful hues, and prints of real art are peppered around the place. The glassed-in sun porch is a great place to meet people, play pool, or watch a video. The little courtyard in back is beautiful in the spring and summer—just sit with your back to the 20-foot mural of the tricked-out skateboarder (even this place couldn't resist one juvenile touch). The happening **Travers** jazz club [see *live music scene*, above] is across the street, and the center of Brussels is only three Metro stops or 20 minutes away on foot.

Rising five stories in a newly renovated building, **Sleep Well Auberge du Marais** *(23 Rue du Damier; Tel 02/218-13-13; Metro 2 to Rogier; 24-hour access; 695BF single, 570BF/person double, 500BF/person triple, 470BF/person quad, 330-410BF dormitory; info@sleepwell.be, www.sleepwell.be; No credit cards)* has a slightly more institutional feeling. But Sleep Well wins the location contest, sitting atop shopper's-haven Rue Neuve. This place fills up quickly, so book ahead.

▶▶DO-ABLE

An Old World hotel with an Asian fetish, **Hotel Pacific** *(Rue Antoine Dansaert 57; Tel 02/511-84-59; Tram 23, 52, 55, 56, 81 to Bourse; 1,100BF single w/o shower, 1,900BF double w/o shower, 2,300BF double w/ shower, 2,650BF triple w/o shower; No credit cards)* ranks as one of the sweetest deals in town. It's like checking into Mr. Wizard's world: the charming owner uses his Art Nouveau hotel as a prop for little lessons in everything from Buddhist philosophy to Western science. Splatter-art paintings, done by a friend who also teaches a free Tai Chi Chuan/yoga class every Friday, cover the elevator, floors, and most walls, and a 75-foot Foucault's Pendulum twisting in the stairwell reminds you that the world indeed continues to rotate around us. The hearty breakfast, included in the price, features overstuffed omelets. The only drawbacks are the occasional saggy bed (a few need Viagra worse than Bob Dole), and the midnight curfew imposed after some foreign guests were mugged a few years back—the curfew can be relaxed if you ask nicely....

The cozy, though somewhat drab, **Hotel Opéra** *(Rue Grétry 53; Tel*

brussels eats and crashing

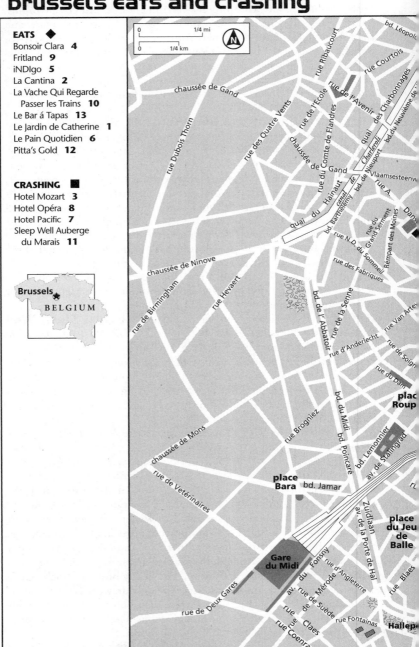

EATS ◆
Bonsoir Clara **4**
Fritland **9**
iNDIgo **5**
La Cantina **2**
La Vache Qui Regarde
  Passer les Trains **10**
Le Bar á Tapas **13**
Le Jardin de Catherine **1**
Le Pain Quotidien **6**
Pitta's Gold **12**

CRASHING ■
Hotel Mozart **3**
Hotel Opéra **8**
Hotel Pacific **7**
Sleep Well Auberge
  du Marais **11**

Brussels
BELGIUM

E-0067

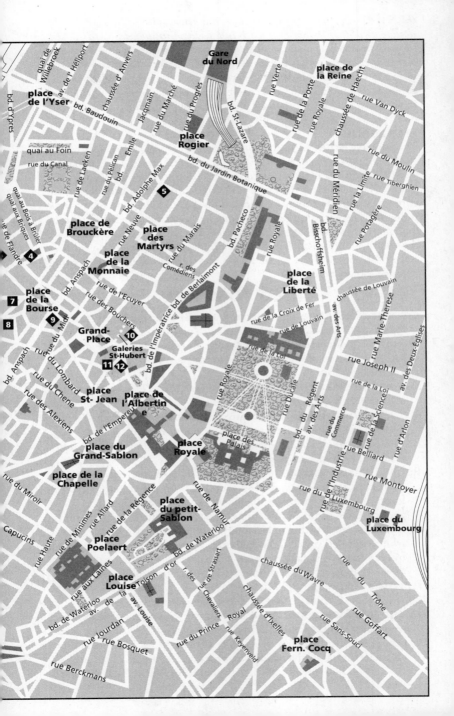

place de l'Yser

quai de Willebroek

av. de l'Héliport

bd. d'Ypres

bd. Baudouin

chaussée d'Anvers

Jacqmain

Emile

rue du Marché

rue du Progrès

Gare du Nord

place de la Reine

rue Verte

rue de la Poste

rue Royale

chaussée de Haecht

rue Van Dyck

quai au Foin

rue du Canal

rue de Laeken

bd.

rue du Pélican

place Rogier

bd. St-Lazare

bd. du Jardin Botanique

rue du Moulin

rue du Méridien

rue la Limite

rue Tiberghien

quai au Bois à Brûler

quai aux Briques

de Flandre

5

bd. Adolphe Max

rue Neuve

place de Brouckère

place des Martyrs

rue du Marais

bd. Pacheco

rue Royale

bd. Bischoffsheim

rue Potagère

4

7

place de la Bourse

8

9

bd. Anspach

rue de l'Ecuyer

place de la Monnaie

r. des Comédiens

bd. de Berlaimont

place de la Liberté

chaussée de Louvain

rue Marie-Thérèse

av. des Arts

rue des Bouchers

rue du Midi

bd. de l'Impératrice

rue de la Croix de Fer

rue de Louvain

rue Joseph II

av. des Deux-Eglises

Grand-Place

10

Galeries St-Hubert

11 **12**

rue de la Loi

place St- Jean

rue du Lombard

rue du Chene

bd. Anspach

rue des Alexiens

place de l'Albertine

rue Royale

bd. de l'Empereur

place du Grand-Sablon

place Royale

place des Palais

bd. du Régent

av. des Arts

rue du Commerce

rue de la Loi

av. d'Arlon

rue Belliard

rue de la Science

place de la Chapelle

rue du Miroir

rue du Ducale

rue de l'Industrie

rue du Luxembourg

rue Montoyer

Capucins

rue Haute

rue de Minimes

rue Allard

rue de la Régence

place du petit-Sablon

rue de Namur

place du Luxembourg

place Poelaert

bd. de Waterloo

chaussée du Wavre

rue du Trône

place Louise

rue aux Laines

Toison d'or

r. des Chevaliers

rue de Strassart

chaussée d'Ixelles

rue Sans-Souci

rue Goffart

bd. de Waterloo

av. de la

av. Louise

Royal

rue du Prince

rue Keyenveld

place Fern. Cocq

rue Jourdan

rue Bosquet

rue Berckmans

02/219-43-43; Premetro 1a, 1b to De Brouckère; 2,300BF single, 2,700BF double, 3,450BF triple, 3,950BF quad, all with shower; V, MC, AE), located smack-dab in the middle of town, caters to visiting suits and tourists. Each room has a television, private bathroom or shower, and telephone. Rooms with bathtubs are available. Breakfasts of croissants, coffee or tea, and bologna and cheese are all-you-can-eat—you will learn to appreciate plentiful breakfast meats (yes, bologna qualifies as a meat) on the scant occasion that you find them.

▶▶**SPLURGE**

The adorable **Hotel Mozart** *(Rue Marché aux Fromages 15a; Tel 02/502-66-61; 2,500BF single; 3,000BF double, 4,000BF triple, all with shower; V, MC, AE)* hides between pestering shwarma vendors just behind the Grand Place. The tiny entrance is deceiving; rooms cascade down the entire block in a sweeping labyrinth of dark carpeting and salmon-pink walls, with neo-classical paintings and statuettes scattered throughout. Some rooms overlook a peaceful courtyard in back; others gaze out over the rooftops above Rue Marché aux Fromages. The hotel also features some of the best showers around, with blissfully hot water and pulsating massage shower heads.

need to know

Currency Exchange The **Belgian Franc (BF)** is the national currency. Banks *(9am-1pm/2pm-4:30pm Mon-Fri)* give the best exchange rates, but their hours are limited. The street *bureaux de change* are open late, but beware of sneaky commission costs and low rates. ATMs are plentiful in Brussels.

Tourist Information The **Belgian Tourist Office** *(Rue du Marché aux Herbes 63; Tel 02/504-03-90; 9am-7pm Mon-Fri, 9am-1pm/2pm-7pm weekends)* and **Tourist Information Brussels** *(ground floor, Hôtel de Ville, Grand Place; 9am-6pm daily in summer, 9am-6pm Mon-Sat, 10am-2pm Sun in winter)* both offer brochures and maps, make hotel reservations, and arrange guided tours.

Public Transportation A network of **metro**, **tram**, and **bus lines** gives easy access to the city and its surroundings. All public transportation begin running at around 5:30am and stop about midnight. Get maps and schedules from metro stations or the tourist office. Metro stations, most decorated with contemporary art, are marked by signs with a white letter "M" on a blue background. Tram and bus stops are marked by red and white signs. Even at designated stops, raise your hand to flag down an approaching tram or bus; they might not stop if you don't.

American Express *(100 Blvd. de Souverain; Tel 02/676-21-11; Metro to Hermann Debroux; 9am-1pm/2pm-5pm Mon-Fri).*

Health and Emergency Accidents or fire: *100*; police assistance: *101*; emergency medical service: *02/479-18-18* or *Tel 02/648-80-00*; emergency dental service: *02/426-10-26* or *02/428-58-58*. The main hospitals are **Hôpital Universitaire Saint Luc** *(10 Ave. d'Hippocrate; Tel 32-2-764-11-11; Metro to Alma),* **Hôpital Saint Pierre** *(322 Rue Haute;*

down and out

There are still a few things you can do when you're down to the Belgian coins that have been collecting in your pocket.

Take in the **antiques market on the Place du Grand Sablon** [see *stuff*, above], a few minutes' walk south of Grand Place, and rub elbows with society matrons as you browse through tables of polished junk that looks as though it were plundered from the set of *Shakespeare in Love*. A more ghetto alternative is the **Jeu de Balle flea market** [see *stuff*, above], where the action is much more hands-on and the spread more closely resembles an ACME garage sale. Camping down at one of Brussels' innumerable outdoor cafes is a great way to kill an afternoon—or drown one, if you've got a few bucks left for a Duvel or two. If you're planning to make camp for a while, sip your drink s-l-o-w-l-y, so the waiters don't hassle you to move along. **La Vache Qui Regarde Passer Les Trains** [see *eats*, above] is best for peeping at the upper-crusties, while the view from **O'Reilly's** [see *bar scene*, above] is of a younger, more down-to-earth crowd. If you can resist the urge to binge drink with the rest of the crowd at **Travers** [see *live music scene*, above], you can take in a full night of jazz without dropping a nickel at their Monday jam session, which kicks off at 9pm and goes until at least 2am. **Marcus Mingus** [see *live music scene*, above] has a similar offering on Wednesday evenings, minus the youth hostel crowd. A more touristy event, though equally free, is the nightly **Music and Light Show** (*Grand Place; After dusk June-Sept*), where families crowd into Grand Place and crane their necks to watch the surrounding buildings light up to the sounds of classical music.

Tel 02/535-31-11; Metro to Porte de Hal), and **Hôpital Brugmann** (*2 Place Van Gehuchten; Tel 02/477-21-11; Metro to Houba-Brugmann*).

Pharmacies Green neon crosses indicate pharmacies. One pharmacy in each neighborhood is open 24 hours. A sign on the door of each pharmacy will tell you which one is on call late night.

Telephone Country code: *32*; area code: *02*; international operator: *0800-100-10*. Pay phones are operated with phone cards, which you can buy at the tourist office, train station, or post office. **AT&T**: *0800-11-0010*; **MCI**: *0800-10012*; **Sprint**: *0800-10014*.

Airports Brussels National Airport (*Tel 02/753-39-13 for flight info, 7am-10pm daily*) is in Zaventem, about 9 miles northeast of the city center. Trains (*90BF*) run to the Gare du Nord, Gare Centrale, and Gare du Midi every 20 minutes.

wired

A few websites can help plan your trip. Started for the English-speaking contingency living in or visiting Brussels, ***www.plug-in.be*** lists some suggestions for heading out at night in style; ***www.xpats.com***, a forum for English-speaking expatriates in Belgium, is a good way to tap into the local anglo scene. The tourist office also maintains two sites: ***www.agenda.be*** (in French and Flemish) lists specific events and festivals, while ***www.belgique-tourisme.net*** (English) lists museums, attractions, and places to stay.

Once you hit Brussels and the e-mail tremors begin to set in, get your fix at **Cybertheater** *(4-5 Ave. de la Toison d'Or; Tel 02/500-78-11; Metro to Porte de Namur; 10am-1am Mon-Thur, Sun, 10am-2am Fri, Sat; www.cybertheater.net; No credit cards).* An hour at one of the 100 terminals in this mod computer mecca off Avenue Louise will run you 250BF, or 200BF per hour for students. The cavernous cafe *(7pm-1am Thur-Sat)* situated within the three-level establishment plays frequent host to movie screenings, ethnic music concerts, and sometimes even bigger-name acts, like Simple Minds.

When cheap and dirty will do the trick, the far less elegant and trendy (though more centrally located) **Point Net** *(Petite Rue des Bouchers 16; Tel 32/2-513-14-15; Premetro 1a, 1b to Bourse; 9am-7pm Mon-Fri; info@pointnet.be; V, MC)* will run you 200BF per hour (150BF per hour if you're a student or simply say you are). Be sure to ask for a computer with an American keyboard; Belgian keypads are all FUBAR.

Airlines Sabena *(110 Rue du Marché aux Herbes; Tel 32-2-723-31-11)*, **American Airlines** *(98 Rue du Trône; Tel 32-2-714-49-04)*, **British Airways** *(98 Rue du Trône; Tel 02/548-03-36)*, **United Airlines** *(350 Ave. Louise; Tel 02/646-55-88)*, **Continental Airlines** *(240 Ave. Louise; Tel 02/752-52-52)*.

Trains The three main stations are: **Gare Centrale** *(Carrefour de l'Europe 2)*, **Gare du Midi** *(Rue de France 2)*, and **Gare du Nord** *(Rue du Progrès 86)*. The system offers two telephone information lines, one in **French** *(Tel 02/555-25-25)* and one in **Flemish** *(Tel 02/555-25-55)*. The Flemish operator will likely speak English.

Buses Eurolines *(Tel 02/218-29-93)* services destinations outside of Belgium.

Bike Rental Pro Velo *(Rue de Londres 13-15; Tel 02/502-73-55; Metro 2 to Porte de Namur or Trone; 9-6 Mon-Fri, closed weekends; No credit cards).*

antwerp

If life were a game of hide-and-seek, Antwerp would be winning. This little city sits holed away in the Flemish part of Belgium, somewhere between the staid elegance of Brussels and the chilled-out zaniness of Amsterdam. It likes to give young travelers lots of reasons to scoot on by without a second glance. Did you know, for example, that Antwerp is one of the world's most prolific diamond manufacturing centers? Yawn. But hey, get this—Antwerp is the fourth-largest port in the world! Zzzzz. But before you shake the sleep out of your eyes and turn the page, ye dubious groovster, consider one thing: Antwerp is the place where Brussels and Amsterdam come to party.

Believe it or not, Antwerp's nightlife kicks ass. The cobblestone streets are lined with dark pubs where locals drink themselves into blissful stupors. Antwerpians may come off as shy, but plop down to say hey, and you'll find them highly hospitable and quick to give you the latest dirt on cool hangouts. The nightlife tends to have a cozy vibe, and pockets of conversation are simple for travelers to infiltrate. And don't worry about language barriers: Though it's the country's official tongue, French just isn't parlayed here. Since no one else in the world speaks Flemish, everyone, from the little shopkeeper on the corner to the boarder hanging out in the park, speaks excellent English. By the way, they don't do any of that European kissy stuff when meeting or greeting; a simple handshake will do just fine.

In some ways Antwerp feels like an extension of Brussels, its big sibling 45 minutes to the south. The flyers for concerts and parties in Antwerp that plaster record shops in Brussels (and vice versa) give the

five things to talk to a local about

1. **The Frogs**: French is the official language, but it's just not spoken in this part of Belgium. While too bad for the hoity-toity *Bruxellois*, it's cool for us English-speakers. Drop a few anti-French slurs, and you're in like Flynn.

2. **Couture?**: Runway chic rules the city's formidable fashion schools, but sartorial taste doesn't seem to have trickled down to the masses. Most locals see it as either a passing fad among the artsy-fartsy or as the wave of the future.

3. **A Girl's Best Friend**: Seeing as how Antwerp is the diamond capital of the world, here's the topic: Diamonds. Artificially price-inflated lumps of glorified coal mined using labor enforced by child mercenaries, OR the scintillating embodiment of two hearts beating as one? Discuss amongst yourselves.

4. **Beer**: Dark or light? What the hell is a *bolleke*? Ask your neighbor to decipher a menu or recommend a frothy brew, and you'll find yourself on the receiving end of a treatise. Avoid mention of Budweiser at all costs.

5. **Canvases:** Nothing stirs civic pride like mention of the Flemish master painters who made their fortunes in Antwerp. Ask them what painters Brussels has produced.

impression of one big old roof-raising family. You'll quickly find, though, that it's mainly the misfits of Brussels (those *salops* who dare to speak Flemish instead of French, sniff sniff!) who thrive in the Antwerpian scene. Mix that rebellion with the tons of young people here, and you've got a laid-back little city that knows how to get funky. But the youth barrage hasn't penetrated much past the nightlife and music scenes—cool kids from Amsterdam and Brussels come to Antwerp to party, not to check out the art galleries. Antwerp is still an old city with an old soul, and aside from fashion design, its best art is in its stellar museums.

That said, Antwerp isn't a particularly beautiful city, with its brooding old-world architecture mixed with the grit and grime of an industrial seaport. Not that it really matters, though, when you drop in for an evening of sweaty salsa dancing at **La Bodeguita** [see *bar scene*, below]; or wrap yourself in a blanket and munch on incredible pad thai at **Farine** [see *eats*, below]; or spend an afternoon picking through the couture that spills out of the acclaimed **Antwerp Fashion Academy** [see *fashion*, below], then pose with the pretty people at **Café d'Anvers** [see *club scene*, below].

Like everywhere else, the cool kids get bored easily and move often.

Ask around about the flyers you see, and pick up a copy of the free publication **Week Up**. It's in Flemish, but listings for movies, concerts, and club parties are easily decipherable. For more standard fare, buy the overpriced **Cultural Bulletin** from the tourist office for listings of museum exhibits, concerts, and performances. Home of both an astounding Gothic cathedral and of that master painter of the flesh, Rubens, Antwerp has more than enough cultural attractions to feed your brain by day before you fry it at night.

neighborhoods and hanging out

The evil urban planner who laid out the center of Antwerp somehow designed streets that never seem to lead in the same direction twice, and most are tighter than Ricky Martin's pants. Luckily, getting lost in Antwerp is much less frightening than in, say, Paris, for a simple reason: There's not that far you can go. Most hangouts are clustered between the **River Scheldt** (aka the Schelde River) and the city's two main squares, **Groenplaats** and **Grote Markt** (use the towering spire of **Our Lady's Cathedral**, which sits between the two squares, as a landmark). Antwerp isn't much of a lounge-in-the-great-outdoors kind of city, but **Groenplaats** (tram stop of the same name) and **Grote Markt** (a few blocks to the northwest) are where you're most likely to find grungy teens and travelers strewn under the Rubens monuments on sunny days. Overpriced cafes along the squares also offer decent people-watching for the patient pickup artist (the place isn't crawling with hotties, but they're around). A notable exception to the between-the-river-and-the-squares rule is the **Meir** (running west from Grote Markt to Central Station), the city's main shopping drag. **Ernest Van Dijkckkaai** (a block east of Grote Markt, along the river) offers a stroll along the disappointingly homely river, but the strip throbs with Latin and disco clubs at night. The **red light district** (four blocks north of Grote Markt) [see *boy meets girl meets wallet*, below] is the seedier cousin of Amsterdam's famed district. Aside from beckoning, half-naked women and the subsequent droves of ogling men, there's not much up in this former sailors' strip except two great clubs, **Café d'Anvers** and **Red & Blue** [see *club scene*, below, for both]. During the day, you'll have better luck in **Kammenstraat** (two blocks south of Groenplaats), where Alternative Nation is taking over. An influx of new tattoo parlors, clubwear stores, and record shops have made this street one of the best places to find out about the local club and music scene, especially tripped-out electronica.

For a cool place to chill, head about a mile south of Groenplaats to **Het Zuid** (*Tram 8*), which means the South District. The quays on this industrial zone-turned-artists'-quarter-turned-hot-spot are lined with bars, restaurants, and clubs. The district is walking a tightrope between laidback hipness and yuppified gentrification, but the total sellout shouldn't hit full swing for another decade, so enjoy it while you can. It offers the best views of the sun setting over the **River Scheldt**, and the **Royal Museum of Fine Arts** [see *culture zoo*, below], with its collection of Rubens and Van Dyck, is just around the corner.

Since the city is so small, it's hard to tell when you've left one neighborhood and entered another (with the glowing exception of the red light district). Nearly everything is walkable, but trams run within a few blocks of virtually any place you'd want to go. They stop running at midnight. Bikes are usually a better (and much more fun) way to go [see *need to know*, below].

This city feels like a big college campus on weekend nights, with people milling around the streets in search of the next watering hole. Keep a hand on your wallet or bag, especially on the trams, but otherwise there's little to worry about from the locals on the crime front. The train station and the red light district are among the few shady parts of town, and should be avoided if you're going solo.

bar scene

An Antwerp local was recently heard to declare: "The more pubs we have, the less shrinks we need." If so, with 2,000 bars serving fewer than half a million people, Antwerpians must be Europe's poster children for mental health. Older Antwerpians tend to be all-day drinkers, sipping their brews in outdoor cafes, but the younger element doesn't show its face in pubs until the sun sets. With so many cafes to choose from, and with the rowdy Dutch hordes driving locals from their favorite watering holes, the hot spot du jour is constantly changing, so keep an ear to the ground. There's a great mix of vibes in this city; you'll find everything from frat-house rowdy (University of Antwerp students in pegged jeans and baggy T-shirts) to trip-hop smooth (slackers in oversized jeans and tight T-shirts) to guzzle-and-gab (young professionals in button-down shirts and khaki pants). By the way, if the beer menu reminds you of your high-school physics textbook, just ask for a *bolleke* (a dark beer served in a glass shaped like a light bulb). Bars start hopping after 9pm, hit their peak after midnight, and don't close down until the barkeeps kick people out, usually around 4am.

jongen meets meisje

People in Antwerp, as in most of Europe, aren't nearly as uptight about s-e-x as your standard-issue American. This does not mean you can just stroll into a bar with a chocolate bar and a smile and expect to get laid. What it does mean is no one is going to stamp "skeezer" on your forehead for trying out one of your Grade-E pickup lines. It means a gal can make the first move without earning the social rank of Chia Slut. It means ads with visible nipples, and open, liberated conversations that don't mask matters of the flesh as matters of the heart. Another added help: Antwerp youngsters are in thrall to all things American, so having a mailing address in the 50 states is like instant sex appeal.

Of all the crazes to rip through the Antwerp scene, the latest is, disappointingly, crime. The recent insurgence of Albanians and other Eastern Europeans has coincided with an upswing of car jackings, purse snatchings, and other naughtiness. As a result, immigration and race have become rather explosive local issues—the Vlaams Blok, an ultra-conservative political party, nearly succeeded in a recent movement to exile the city's immigrant population. To the dismay (and puzzlement) of the restless natives, Antwerp PD has responded to all this public pressure with a frenzy of parking tickets (hey, maybe fewer cars will mean fewer jackings). To their discredit, the fuzz have taken to rolling suspicious (aka ethnic)-looking foreigners. Bottom line: No need for paranoia, but it's best to watch your back in some of the shadier areas of town....Antwerp can be a city that does not play well with others.

Named for Kapitein Zeppos, a Belgian Mr. Rogers–like TV hero, **K. Zeppos** *(Vleminckveld 78; Tel 03/231-17-89; 10am-4am Mon-Fri, 11am-4am Sat, Sun; No credit cards)* draws a late-twenties to early-thirties crowd, whose gray wool hacking pants and manicures betray their yuppie origins. Despite the crowd, K. Zeppos is a comfortably Spartan, out-of-the-way tavern (a few minutes' walk down Kammenstraat from Groenplaats) where you can drink in peace outside the Antwerp spotlight. They also offer a simple dish of the day, like spaghetti and meatballs, that's a good dinner option at 295BF.

A mellow re-creation of the oh-so-typical Parisian smoke shop down in Het Zuid, **Bar Tabac** *(Waalse Kaai 43; Tel 03/238-19-37; Tram 8 to Museum; 6pm-6am daily; No credit cards)* is an enjoyably laid-back dive, where candles burn slowly in Perrier bottles and DJs come in and spin (mostly relaxed funk, soul, and Latin tunes) when they feel like it. After midnight, cozy becomes crowded becomes claustrophobic as artsy twentysomethings and fashionistas parade in. In the warmer months, an outside seating area offers refuge from intoxicated late-night revelers.

Perhaps the liveliest of Antwerp's bars, the riverside **La Bodeguita** *(Ernest Van Dijckckaai 21; Tel 03/260-112; 9pm-5am Thur-Sat, open Sun afternoons May-Sept; No credit cards)* is a nonstop dervish of salsa music and Latin dancing. Tables and chairs are perpetually pushed against the walls of this spacious saloon, providing the maximum floor space for the older South American crowd to rip it up. A younger contingent hangs by the bar, eyeing the bolder ones dancing; if you join the movers and hip-shakers, be prepared to get tossed about by some feisty older Brazilian. It's your best shot in Antwerp of finding an off-white crowd.

Ready for a dose of raw, American college–style debauchery? **Café T'Veurleste** *(Lijnwaadmarkt 4; Tel 03/231-97-92; 4pm-late and days;*

No credit cards) is probably Belgium's best version of a frat party. Loud, crowded, and full of spastic drunken dancers ready to spill beer on you, the pickup scene here is probably the most promising in Antwerp...as long as you know how to say "nice shoes" in Flemish. Conveniently just a block away from Grote Markt.

LIVE MUSIC SCENE

Antwerp rocks...but live music lovers will be disappointed to learn that we don't mean that *literally*. In general, if it don't relate to electronica, it don't belong in this city. Sure, garage bands try their hands at guitar rock...but it just doesn't fly. A lot of venues do not host things regularly, so check out posters and flyers around town for the latest info.

Since trip-hop, drum 'n' bass, and much of the laid-back DJ genre claim jazz as their roots, it's no surprise that Antwerp hosts thoroughly passable swing and modern jazz. The best combos in the city gig at **De Muze** *(Melkmarkt 15; Tel 03/226-01-26; Premetro or any tram to Groen-plaats; Noon-4am daily; No credit cards)*, just off Groenplaats, where wooden terraces three stories high overlook a smoky little stage, and the bar is usually packed three deep. Hep cats turn out for regular Thursday night jam sessions, where you're likely to run into the same musicians you caught in Brussels earlier in the week. Antwerp doesn't draw many big-namers, but this brick-walled joint offers a nice place to kick back for a mellow night of recovery, or a warmup for the wildness ahead.

CLUB SCENE

From the plaid-shirted preppie to the Dieseled-out cool chick, Antwerp is a clubbing city. Nonetheless, on any given night, picking the venue that's right for you requires a little homework—lest you wind up looking like Blossom at a goth party. Check out ***www.amphion.be*** for 100 prime, Grade-A club reviews and rave announcements. Also look for flyers at **Fish and Chips** [see *stuff*, below] or ask around the record shops on Kammen-straat. Things don't get kickin' until at least 1am, and wind down some-time around sunrise; showing up before midnight may bring out the agoraphobe in you, but it will ensure you a spot inside. The hottest Latin dancing in town, by the way, is at **La Bodeguita** [see *bar scene*, above].

That is to say, if the fear-inducing Belgian doorman deems you worthy of entrance. In general, Antwerpian clubs don't have much patience for the traveler's costume; avoid sneakers, baseball caps, and blue jeans, and you're probably golden. "Sorry, private party tonight," is doorman-speak for, "You total scrub," and should be taken as a not-so-subtle hint to go change into something a little sleeker, or find a more relaxed place to hang out—ask a member of the staff for the current hot spots as they change hourly. Much like a troll under a bridge, the Belgian bouncer does little but look mean and collect money for his troubles. They'll expect to be tipped at least 50BF when you leave. Some will offer an outstretched palm as a gentle reminder—others won't let you leave without coughing up the green.

antwerp bars, clubs and culture zoo

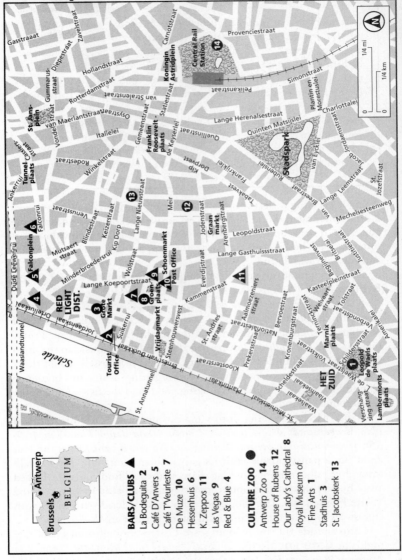

Friday night at **Café d'Anvers** *(Verversrui 15; Tel 03/232-47-12; 11pm-dawn Fri, Sat; 250-500BF cover; www.fiesta.be; No credit cards)*, a former monastery on the edge of the red light district, is the trendiest (and most difficult to get in to) party in town, where glassy-eyed, Guess-clad clubbers mingle with regal drag queens and undulate to techno and

rules of the game

In a country that prides itself on its beer above all else, it's not really surprising that there's no official drinking age—so, if you have a younger sibling along, you can legally be the bad influence he/she has always needed. As for the other flavors of the substance rainbow, Antwerp is not quite as forthcoming as its Netherlandic neighbors. Hash is technically illegal, but cops don't expend much energy pursuing dope smokers. Naturally, in the city's heavy rave scene there's a lot of E around. A word to the wise: True, you're not in Singapore, and in general, Antwerp PD isn't looking to hassle tourists, but be careful about where and with whom you expand your mind—nobody wants to end up a miniseries.

drum 'n' bass. Big with students at the Antwerp Fashion Academy. Expect a distinctly underground feel, with expensive cocktails served up at the bar. The "it's-all-about-me" scene gives way to a relaxed crowd on Saturday, when The List gets put away, the happy house music comes out, and sneakers will do fine.

Steel cages come out on Saturday nights in the red light district at **Red & Blue** (*Lange Schipperskapelstraat 11-13; Tel 03/232-47-12; 11pm-7am; 250BF cover; www.fiesta.be; No credit cards*), for a wild gay party; the first Saturday of each month is *Club Flesh*, attracting a kinkier crowd for on-stage showering and general hanky-panky. Taking over on Friday nights is *The Fill Collins Club*, named after the lamest musician the organizer (who also founded the legendary Le Fuse in Brussels) could think of. The largely hetero crowd is more into getting drunk and bouncing around like pogo sticks than in looking good, and the fist-waving house DJs respond in kind.

Dance Mecca to young Euro-yuppies from across Belgium, **Zillion** (*Jan Vangenstraat 4; Tel 03/248-15-16; 10pm-dawn Thur-Sat; 150-350BF; www.zillion.be, info@zillion.be; No credit cards*) tints the Het Zuid sky a pansy purple with its gargantuan neon sign. Try to walk through the door without looking sharp, and you'll find yourself whisked away by Terminator-like bouncers faster than a baldy in camo on the White House lawn. The thousands who make it inside this mammoth club sweat to mainstream house and dance. Expect an 18–25 crowd.

Latin sounds fill the swinging pre-Castro-era ballroom on Friday nights at **Café Local** (*Waalse Kaai 25; Tel 03/238-50-04; Tram 8 to Museum; 9pm-3am Fri, 10pm-4am Sat; 250BF cover, free before midnight Sat; www.whib.be/cafe_local; No credit cards*), also in the trendy Het Zuid. A Cuban cantina leads into a decent-sized dance floor, with catwalks above offering a view for scoping muchachos or muchachas. Costa Rican DJ Mario Rumba spins salsa and merengue—show up at 9 for an hour-long lesson if your hips can't get with the beat without help. Saturday nights, when youngsters dance the white man's overbite to everything from the Jackson Five to Madonna, are hokier and emptier.

gay scene

San Francisco has the Castro. New York City has Christopher Street. Antwerp has, well...nothing. There is no geographic or metaphoric center of Antwerp's gay scene—a few gay and lesbian bars are tucked in between straight bars, and the best dance parties find their homes on certain nights in come-one-come-all clubs just to the west of the red light district. Many of the city's hotties have split for Amsterdam, so, with the exception of the raging weekend club nights when those hotties come back, the scene tends to be a little bit older and mellower. Also, Antwerp is not the greatest place to go walking hand-in-hand; the narrow, dark streets of this conservative city offer easy hiding spots for those whose attitudes are as ancient as the architecture.

The staple of the scene is **Hessenhuis** (*Falconrui 53; Tel 03/231-13-56; Bus 6, 9, 34 to Falconplein or Tram 4, 7 to Huikstraat; 10am-4am Sun-Thur, 10am-6am Fri, Sat; MC, V*), a bar in an old museum that draws the most chiseled features in town. The crowd is often a bit mature and a lot upscale, loitering around the bar with martinis surgically attached to their hands. If this place is too swank for you, the bartenders will be happy to turn you on to the best underground gay party or newest trendy gay bar. A few scant blocks from **Café D'Anvers** [see *club scene*, above].

Saturday nights, **Red & Blue** hosts what locals consider the city's most consistent gay soirée. **Café d'Anvers** doesn't host any gay-specific fêtes, but it's certainly gay-friendly and perpetually overrun with gorgeous trannies [see *club scene*, above, for both].

culture zoo

For its size, Antwerp packs an impressive cultural punch. You'll find Gothic cathedrals, statues of such native Flemish master painters as Rubens and Van Dyck, and portraits of fat naked ladies all over the place. Most museums are cheap, and students get discounts. If you're looking to stay downtown, hit the Stadhuis, Our Lady's Cathedral, St. Jacobskerk, and House of Rubens (*not* a plus-size clothing store). The Antwerp Zoo and Diamondland are near each other, next to Central Station, where you'll also find one of the largest Hasidic Jewish communities in Europe. The Middelheim Open-Air Sculpture Museum is a good 20-minute bus ride from Antwerp's center, but it's worth the trip on a sunny, feelin' groovy kind of day.

Royal Museum of Fine Arts (*Leopold de Waelplaats; Tel 03/238-78-09; Tram 8 or Bus 23 to Museum; 10am-5pm, closed Mon; 150BF, 120BF students, free under age 18, free Fri; No credit cards*): You best believe the city of Rubens has a great Rubens collection—plus works by Rembrandt and Magritte—in its top museum. In the Het Zuit district and near the **Boomerang Hostel** [see *crashing*, below], the museum is a good late-afternoon stop before hitting the bars along the quays at night.

Our Lady's Cathedral *(Hanschoenmarkt; Tel 03/231-30-33; Metro to Groenplaats; 10am-5pm Mon-Fri, 1-4pm Sat, 1-9pm Sun, holidays, 1-3pm the day before a church holiday; 60BF; No credit cards):* This majestic 14th-century Gothic church houses four Rubens masterpieces, stunning stained-glass windows, and an appealing, if unlikely, abstract sculptural representation of the stations of the cross.

Stadhuis *(Grote Markt 1; Tel 03/220-82-11; Metro to Groenplaats; 9am-3pm Mon-Sat; Tours begin at 11am, 2pm, and 3pm daily; 30BF; No credit cards):* The Spanish burned it down. The Belgians rebuilt it. The French burned it down. The Belgians rebuilt it again—now this city hall is one of the oldest examples of the Flemish-Italian Renaissance style.

St. Jacobskerk *(Lange Nieuwstraat 73; Tel 03/232-10-32; 9am-noon Nov-Mar, 2-5pm Apr-Oct, closed Sun; 50BF, 30BF for students; No credit cards):* If you've seen everything else Rubenesque in Antwerp, you might as well check out the Gothic church where he's taking a dirt nap.

House of Rubens *(Wapper 9-11; Tel 03/232-47-47; Tram 2, 15 to House of Rubens or Metro to Meir; 10am-4:45pm, closed Mon; 100BF, 50BF under age 18; No credit cards):* Clearly, Rubens' models weren't starving, and neither was he; the painter's lavish 17th-century home is filled with his Roman sculpture collection and several of his own works.

Antwerp Zoo *(Koningin Astridplein 26; Tel 03/232-45-40; Tram to Central Station; 9am-6:30pm daily in summer, 9am-4:45pm daily in winter; 450BF; No credit cards):* Just to the east of Central Station, this 25-acre zoo houses a startling range of animals in beautiful Art Nouveau surroundings.

Diamondland *(Appelmasstraat 33A; Tel 03/234-36-12; Tram to Central Station; 9:30am-5:30pm Mon-Sat, open 10am-5pm Sun Apr-Oct only; Free admission):* Learn how stones are polished into gems in the largest diamond showroom in Antwerp.

Middelheim Open-Air Sculpture Museum *(Middelheimlaan 61; Tel 03/828-13-50; Bus 17, 18, 27, 32; 10am-5pm Oct-Mar, 10am-7pm Apr and Sept, 10am-8pm May and Aug, 10am-9pm June and July; Free admission):* Pick a sunny day to check out this park's 300 statues, which include works by Rodin and Zadkine.

STUFF

Let's face it, you didn't come all the way to Antwerp to shell out dough for stuff you could get elsewhere. And unless you're into high-quality diamonds, Antwerp doesn't offer much in the way of unique wares. The Meir, a ritzy pedestrian street running from the Central Station to Groenplaats, features most of your basic chain stores, from Armani to European Gap knockoffs. The Groenplaats end of the Meir, on such streets as Steenhouweenvrsvest, Nationalestraat and Lombardest, plays host to Antwerp's famed fashion houses [see *fashion*, below], where you can gaze in the windows and: a) marvel at the stylish threads only the rich and famous can afford or b) wonder where you can score some of the crack they were smoking when they designed it. Fashion-conscious

boy meets girl meets wallet

Prostitution in Belgium is technically illegal, but the government tolerates it as long as it stays in one place: the red light district. Once home to the scurviest ruffians just into port, the area hasn't come far. A quick jaunt up **Sint-Paulusstraat** will take you into the lion's den, a small ganglion of miscreancy that's less campy and more down-to-business than its Amsterdam counterpart. Lingerie-clad women of all races, ages, and degrees of heft roost in closet-sized window cabins, leering back at the groups of men that saunter up the sidewalk. A male passerby with an averted gaze will incite the prostitutes to rap their rings on the glass in a shrill chorus of ill repute. Potential customers (there are more than you'd think) wave the women from the window to a side door, where prices can be haggled over. If successful, the curtain is drawn over the front window and, well, the deal is sealed. The district, which dates back to the city's rise as an international port centuries ago, is most densely concentrated around **Oude Manstraat**, **Leguit**, and **Verversrui**.

Exuding a different breed of bad karma is the neighborhood just to the east of the red light district, which locals have dubbed "Red Square." The Mercedes quotient skyrockets on **Falconplein**, a shabby street where enterprising Russian immigrants (read: mobsters) have built up a bargain-basement shopping street *de résistance*. Browsing through the convincing knockoffs of name-brand televisions, video recorders, and purses is a lesson in intimidation, as heavily jeweled front men scowl from their stoops. If you're interested in logos, not quality, hit Red Square before night falls, when the border between red lights and Red Square blurs even more. Not for the nighttime—this place can get properly scary.

tourists have no difficulty finding their way to the contemporary and avant-garde clothing stores in the chic shopping streets around Huidevetterstraat, Schuttershofstraat, Lombardenvest, and Steenhouwersvest. Nearly every store in Belgium closes on Sunday, so don't expect to do much shopping aside from the window variety then.

▶▶REALISTIC RETAIL

Head down Kammenstraat to **Fish and Chips** (*Kammenstraat 36-38; Tel 03/227-08-24; Tram 8; 10am-6:30pm Mon-Sat; www.fishand chips.be; V, MC, AE*), a virtual smorgasbord of gear and grub for the grungy alterna-kid. The first floor is packed with clubwear, messenger bags, and down vests. Trying on a pair of pants can leave you feeling a bit naughty:

fashion

When it comes to style in Antwerp, you'll find two types of people: the minority haves and the majority have-nots. Unlike other fashion meccas like Paris and Milan, Antwerpians in general don't have much style. They seem pretty happy in ripped jeans or simple Oxford shirts. OK, so the revolutionary styles coming from the Academy of Fine Art's fashion division haven't spawned a citywide revolution. Who cares, when the city has such an influence on the world's catwalks? Antwerp began its reign as the little-city-that-could-sew in the early 1980s, when a group of young designers, dubbed "The Antwerp Six," took the British Designers Show by storm. The most famous of the Six, Dries Van Noten and Walter Van Beirendonck (who designed the wacky duds for U2's Pop-Mart tour), have remained true to their roots, setting up fashion houses downtown even while their lines expanded to Paris, London, and Japan. Make sure to look for the Antwerp Watch from G-Shock, designed by a group of academy grads. The Antwerp Six—which also includes Ann Demeulemeester, Martin Margiela, Dirk Van Saene, and Dirk Bikkembergs—have been followed by new waves of designers, including Kaat Tilley [see *Brussels*] and An Vandevorst, Bernard Willems, and Raf Simmons.

360° curtains in the center of the floor make for dressing rooms, so you'll be stripping down to your knickers in the middle of rush hour (yeah, baby, yeah!). The second floor holds a coffee shop with Internet access for free and *croque-monsieur* (ham and cheese on toasted bread) and turkey sandwiches. And, good Lord, if you're looking for rave party and club flyers, go no farther. The sales staff is the hottest, trendiest (in an early-twenties sort of way), and snootiest the city has to offer. There is also now a good hairdresser and a DJ spinning on Saturdays.

▶▶TUNES

The centrally located **Taboo Records** *(Kammenstraat 66; Tel 03/233-39-73; Tram 8 to Kammenstraat; 11am-6:30pm, closed Sun; www.tabooproductions.com, aorta@tabooproductions.com; V, MC)*, owned by DJ Aorta, serves as headquarters for the local Goa and psychedelic trance scene, one of the few underground music movements left in Antwerp. The place is tiny, with a few racks of CDs on the main floor and milk crates of albums in the brick-walled basement. It also has one of the best gimmicks in town: three Roswell-looking aliens, each about five feet tall, floating in preservation tanks on the wall. We think they're fake, but listening to the music pumping from the monstrous speakers makes anyone wonder whether they're the owner's relatives. Definitely a niche-market crowd, but very cool.

A few doors down, **Stereophonic Records** *(Kammenstraat 70; Tel 03/232-98-70; Tram 8 to Kammenstraat; Noon-6:30pm Mon, 11am-6:30pm Tue, Wed, 11am-7pm Thur-Sat, closed Sun; V, MC)* specializes in indie electronic music that doesn't quite fit into categories. But they also have your standard electronic fare, catering to local DJs and drum 'n' bass heads. Don't expect any aliens here—it's just a no-nonsense record shop with posters on the walls and lines at the registers.

For R&B, hip-hop, and a twist of everything else, look no farther than **Metrophone** *(Kammenstraat 47; Tel 03/231-18-65, Tram 8 to Kammenstraat; 10am-6pm Mon-Sat; V, MC, AE, DC)* a few doors farther still. Mainly CD format with intelligent and knowledgable staff.

EATS

Antwerp is heaven for the budget gourmand. There are dozens of places serving up tasty square meals (they even serve veggies for you backpackers at high risk of coming down with scurvy) for prices that won't break the bank. Now the bad news: Ultra-cheap eats are a bit harder to come by. Brussels' omnipresent kebab stands have relegated themselves to one street called Paardenmarkt, just below the red light district. During the day, the best place to grab an inexpensive bite is at one of the little shops around Grote Markt or Groenplaats. They feature simple Belgian and French classics, from *frites* to omelets to *croque-monsieur*. Almost every bar also serves up its own menu, though they tend to be a little rough on the bankroll.

▶▶CHEAP

Serving up the late-night chow is **Las Vegas** *(Melkmarkt 26; Tel 03/233-64-01; 11am-1am Mon-Thur, till 2am Fri, till 4am Sat; Snacks 20-120BF; No credit cards)*, a grease shack just next to **Café T'Veurleste** [see *bar scene*, above]. The standard deep-fried products (e.g., burgers and *frites*) are nummy and definitely suitable for the economically challenged.

▶▶DO-ABLE

Spaghetti World *(Oude Koornmarkt 66; Tel 03/234-38-01; Tram to Groenplaats; 3pm-3am daily; 350-525BF per entree; V, MC)* dishes up simple Italian food in a scene that feels more like a bar than a restaurant. A wild array of milkshake-cocktails (*Superman's Fast Favorite* is a Red Bull energy drink laced with vodka and apricot brandy) and beers pull in a young crowd of after-dinner bar-hoppers. The flamboyant decor features Keith Haring–influenced doodles of spaghetti strands that are tangled tighter than the Gordian Knot. The kitchen is open 4-11:30pm, serving up hearty salads and a not-bad pesto dish.

The deliciously homely **Farine** *(40 Vlaamse Kaai; Tel 03/238-37-76; Tram 8 to Museum; 7am-10:30pm, closed Tues; 150-400BF per entree; V, MC)* offers one the finest meals per franc you'll find in Antwerp. The pad thai tastes as though it were made in a heavenly realm. Daily specials include banana soup and a dessert of chocolate-drenched crêpes. The toughest choice is where to sit: If you're into making eyes at some Het Zuid

12 hours in antwerp

1. Liquid lunch: Find a seat at one of the outdoor cafes surrounding Grote Markt and the cathedral and pour any of (or many of) Belgium's plethora of brews down your hatch as you watch the not-so-local crowd bum about the square.

2. Shop till you drop: Even if you go easy on the liquid and heavy on the lunch, the wares on Kammenstraat will appear no less funky. A veritable strip mall of psychedelica, this run of music stores, clothing shops, and tattoo parlors is most notable for **Fish & Chips** [see *stuff*, above]—so ignore the beat-up Woolworth's-style storefront and dive in.

3. Dine in Nouveau Impressionist style: Claim a spot at **Farine** [see *eats*, above], and watch the sun set over the River Scheldt at the most happening hangout for hungry hipsters. If you can find a date, bring one—sitting out amidst the hay bales and gazing toward the horizon is like walking into a Monet.

4. You vs. the Sauce, Round II: Just across the street from **Farine,**

hipster or watching the sun setting over the quays, grab a seat at the wicker tables outside (wool blankets are at the ready when there's a nip in the air). Or, to fully savor the sounds of sizzling vegetables and the intoxicating smells drifting from the open kitchen, camp down at the communal table indoors. From November to April, they feature an "Empty the Fridge" special, where hearty dishes from their winter menu are all 275BF. And, for added measure, afternoons in the summer feature DJs spinning ambient trip-hop, energy, house, and techno.

▶▶**SPLURGE**

Just down the block from Farine, the cell-phone-for-pleasure-not-business crowd heads to **Table d'Anvers** (*43 Vlaamse Kaai; Tel 03/248-51-51; Tram 8 to Museum; 350-750BF per entree; Noon-2:30pm/6-11pm Tue-Fri, no lunch on weekends; www.amphion.be/table-d-anvers, table.d.anvers@skynet.be; V, MC*), for fine French cuisine like rack of lamb and filet of sole. Exposed brick, light woods, and faux cracked ceilings give the place a casually elegant feel. Situated along the trendy southern quays, and with only 40 seats inside and 12 outside, this place books solid days in advance, so call for reservations.

crashing

The old phrase "a diamond in the rough" holds true in Antwerp: The proliferation of diamond shops is overshadowed only by the sheer number of hotels. Hoteliers have set up shop around the Central Station to catch every traveler fresh off the train. Some are good, some are not so good, but either way, you're only a 5-minute Premetro ride from the bars and museums in the city center. The centrally located hotels are generally

Bar Tabac [see *bar scene*, above], a retro Parisian dive, is a cozy place to sip red wine and mingle with the Euroflash. So you're a few hundred miles north of Paris—let's pretend.

5. Take a stab at La Vida Loca: La Bodeguita [see *bar scene*, above] is just a quick stroll up the river from Het Zuid. This South American retreat just might be the freshest salsa party this side of the Atlantic. Bring your dancing shoes and check your ego at the door—unless you were born with castanets in your hands, the older dudes here will show you up, my friend.

6. Let it all hang out: Spend a few minutes browsing the red light district (or 15, depending on how lonely you are), then head over to former-monastery-cum-disco **Red & Blue** [see *club scene*, above]. *Friday's Fill Collins Club* (house music) and Saturday's legendary gay party whip the all-monkey-business crowd into a frenzy.

more expensive, and not usually worth the extra money since Antwerp is so small. For a full list of city lodgings, check out *www.roomz. com/da/eu/beantwerp.html*.

▶▶CHEAP

Compared to its counterparts in Brussels, **Boomerang Youth Hostel** *(Volkstraat 49; Tel 03/238-47-82; Bus 23 to Volkstraat; 360BF dormitory bed; No credit cards)* is the true ghetto option. Business cards describing the rooms as "cozy and artistic" should read "dingy and crappy." Memo to the staff: Buy a broom. But, if you're short on cash and don't mind sharing a room with a dozen other stinky travelers, this cheap-as-dirt hostel is the place. The grubby ambiance breeds a jovial atmosphere among the guests, and the money you save on sleeping can buy you drinks or dinner on the quays of the hip Het Zuit, just down the street. A simple bread, jam, and coffee breakfast will cost you only 25BF extra. No single rooms or private bathrooms.

▶▶DO-ABLE

Only a short stumble from the train station, the **Tourist Hotel** *(Pelikaansstraat 20; Tel 03/232-58-70; Any bus or tram to Central Station; 1,500BF single w/public toilet in hall; 1,900BF single w/toilet, 2,200BF single w/shower; 1,900BF double w/public toilet in hall, 2,600BF double w/toilet, 2,950BF double w/shower; V, MC, AE)* is far more sightly inside the rooms than it is outside. Beds are comfortable, the included breakfast is hearty, and the range of prices will fit most budgets, especially if you don't mind trekking into the hallway to use the public bathroom. This is a popular place to crash for visiting soccer and rugby teams. The location makes this hotel fill up fast, so try to call ahead.

antwerp eats and crashing

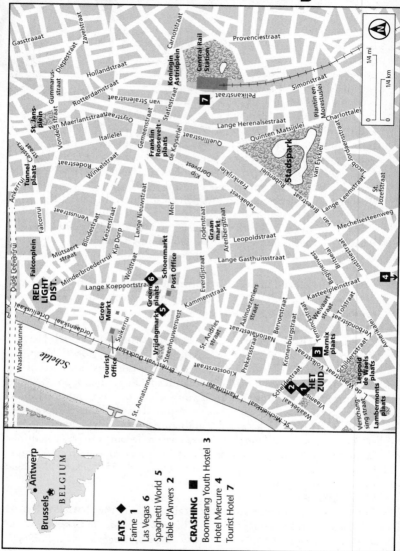

EATS ◆
Farine **1**
Las Vegas **6**
Spaghetti World **5**
Table d'Anvers **2**

CRASHING ■
Boomerang Youth Hostel **3**
Hotel Mercure **4**
Tourist Hotel **7**

▶▶SPLURGE

Hotel Mercure *(Desguinlei 94; Tel 03/244-82-11; Tram 2, Bus 18 or 25 to Jan van Rijswijcklaan-de Singel; 6,500BF singles and doubles Sun-Thur, 3,500BF Fri, Sat; V, MC, AE)* is very sweet if you can afford the lush life. All rooms have TVs, air conditioning, and private baths, but the outdoor pool, sauna, and fitness center are prime pampering devices. The buffet breakfast costs 590BF extra. Located south of the city center, about 10 minutes by car or bus. You can find deals on weekends (3,500BF per room), when the business crowd clears out and management is eager to fill the rooms.

need to know

Currency Exchange The local currency is the **Belgian Franc (BF)**. Banks give the best exchange rates, but they are only open 9am-1pm/2-4:30pm Mon-Fri. The street bureaus are open late, especially around the train station, but be careful about sneaky commission costs and low rates.

Tourist Information The **Antwerp Tourist Office** is smack in the middle of things *(Grote Markt 15; Tel 03/232-01-03; Premetro to Groenplaats; toerisme@antwerp.be; 9am-6pm, closed Sat).*

Public Transportation An underground subway, called the **Premetro**, and aboveground trams will take you pretty much wherever you need to go. The **Premetro** has only one line, running from **Central Station** to **Groenplaats**, then underneath the **River Scheldt**. **Tickets** *(book of 10: 300BF, single ride: 40BF, day pass: 115BF)* are available in the **tourist office** and on the trams; **maps** are available at the **tourist office** and **Central Station**. Most trams run 5:30am-11:30pm, select lines run later; ask at a station for details. Fri and Sat, night buses run on the tram routes.

American Express There are no AMEX offices in Antwerp, we're sorry to say.

Health and Emergency Medical emergency: *101*; fire or police: *100*. The main hospital is **St. Elizabeth** *(Leopoldstraat 26)*.

Pharmacies Look for neon green crosses. They rotate the 24-hour shift; check any pharmacy's door for a sign pointing you to the all-night establishment of the moment.

Telephone Country code: *32*; area code: *03*; operator: *1207*; international operator: *1204* (both operators are Flemish-speaking, but will likely speak English). Most pay phones accept only phone cards, which you can buy at the tourist office, train station, or post offices. **AT&T**: *0800-100-10*; **MCI**: *0800-100-12*; **Sprint**: *0800-100-14*.

Airports Antwerp doesn't have its own airport; the closest is **Brussels National Airport** *(Tel 02/753-45-50)*, about 40 minutes away by train, which you can catch at Central Station. The **Sabena Airport Express Bus** *(Tel 02/511-90-30; 250BF)* runs to and from Antwerp every hour.

Airlines Sabena *(Appelmansstraat 12-14; Tel 03/231-68-25 for information, 02/723-23-23 for ticket reservations).*

Trains Central Station is the main station, about one mile east of the city center. To get to the tourist office, take Premetro to Groenplaats, then walk up Blomstraat until you hit Grote Markt. On foot, it's a straight shot into town: Walk along De Keyserlai, which turns into Teniersplaats, then Leystraat, then Meir, then Meirbrug, then Schoenmarkt.

wired

In Antwerp, the easiest place to get your e-mail fix is at **2Zones** *(Wolstraat 15; Tel 03/232-24-00; Tram 10 or 11 to Wolstraat; 11:30am-midnight Sun-Thur, 11:30am-1am Fri, Sat, closed Mon; www.2zones.s-dreams.net; Internet access 240BF/hour, 60BF minimum charge).* Only two minutes on foot from Groenplaats, this place offers no-frills access to the Internet and meets most basic computer needs, such as printing and word processing. Business is usually pretty plodding, with only the occasional traveler and the casual Antwerpian e-mailer occupying the comfy seats. Be warned that European keyboards suck big time—the letters just aren't where they're supposed to be.

For cheaper prices, you might have to wrestle a terminal away from shrieking Tomb Raiders. The gamer-to-grownup ratio at **Warp Factor 9** *(Kasteelpleinstraat 6; Tel 03/288-60-51; 11am-3am daily; Access 150BF/hour; No credit cards)* is on the high side, but if your blood pressure can withstand the constant stream of battle sounds, the price is right. This place is a good walk from the city center, but well placed if you're hanging out on the southern quays. WF9 is quite the pickup scene...if you're a Klingon. Otherwise, come here just to e-mail and get in a few games of Quake.

Two tourist office-maintained websites can help you plan a trip to Antwerp: *www.dma.be* provides basic information about the city, its museums, and how to book hotels. The tourist office can answer questions by e-mail if you drop them a line at *Toerisme@Antwerp.be*. The other official site, *www.antwerpenopen.be*, lists cultural events and festivals. For the underground scene, check out *www.amphion.be*, which posts dates and locations of local raves and special club nights.

When you hit Groenplaats, turn right on Blomstraat and walk until you hit Grote Markt.

Bike Rental Bikes are the way to go in this itty-bitty city. For rentals, try **De Windroos** *(Steenplein 1; Tel 03/480-93-88; 9am-6pm daily; 75BF/hour, 300BF/day; No credit cards)* or **Cyclorent** *(Sint-Katelijnevest 19; Tel 03/226-95-59; Tram 7, 4; 10am-6pm Mon-Sat, Sun by appointment; cyclorent@ping.be; 75BF/hour, 300BF/day, plus 1,000BF deposit; MC, V).*

berlin

A long long time ago, before the Iron Curtain, before the Nazis—and way before tepid cheeseheads like Marilyn Manson—Berlin of the Weimar Republic was ground zero for *real* drug-addled, cross-dressing decadence. In the Cold War days, youngsters from all over the world looking to live the anarcho-alternative life shaved their heads, donned black, and flocked to West Berlin, but now the action is shifting east, and the farther east you go—from the more touristic Mitte to the funky Prenzlauer Berg—the edgier the scene gets. Since the infamous wall crumbled more than a decade ago, the city's reunification has released a lot of fresh energy and has made the city's youth culture more diverse than it's ever been, ready to accommodate every stripe of 21st century cool, from anti-establishment punk and eco-hippie to clubkid and freshly minted ex-communist entrepreneur.

Every bombed-out tenement in East Berlin seems to be at some stage of conversion to a hotel or shopping center. The city has so many construction sites, the skyline looks like an overgrown Erector set. Bars and restaurants come and go like shooting stars. Clubs are here today and gone tonight. Yet, surprisingly, the rapid pace of change hasn't fostered the kind of anxious urgency you might expect it would. The scene is definitely more fractured and varied, catering to the increasing presence of both Western travelers and Eastern immigrants, but everyone seems okay with it. So many millions of people have come rubbernecking through Berlin since the wall crumbled, the city seems to belong as much to the tourist as to the native. This seems to be improving local English skills, but the average locals still have a long way to go before they'll be reading

five things to talk to a local about

1. People here complain a lot about the amount of **attitude** most salespeople, waiters, and public servants dish out—Germans haven't yet conquered the concept of service with a smile. You have a couple of tactics here: Initiate a gripe session with someone about rude servers or speak mock-German-accented English with a cashier and see how sassy they get with you.

2. There are a host of unlicensed, underground **squat bars** that regularly flash in and out of existence in East Berlin. Bring up the subject with any students you meet, and, if you're lucky, they might tell you about one—they're cheaper than other bars, and because it's all word-of-mouth, the crowds tend to be more intimate.

3. **East vs. West Berlin:** Pretty much everyone here expects you, as a foreigner, to ask about this, but deep down they also really want to be asked. Berliners all have an opinion about the differences between the old Communist and American sectors, and if you give them the airtime, they'll give you an earful.

4. Many Berliners and plenty of unwitting travelers ride the city's public transportation without tickets, risking spot checks by *kontrolleure*, sort of like plainclothes traffic cops who can fine you on the spot. Ask locals where they stand on the practice of *schwarz fahren* ("driving black"), or riding illegally, and see which side of the law they fall on.

5. Play fun **German trivia games:** Who said, "Touch my monkey. Love him. Feel him."
a) Dieter Sprockets b) Mike Myers c) Bill Clinton d) All of the above.

any Shakespeare in the original (making them not so different from the average American, come to think of it). You'll have better luck with younger Germans, who've had to study English in school and tend to be more interested in hanging out with travelers anyway. If you approach them, most will be happy to extend their circle to include you. Overall, Berlin is a friendly and inviting place, and despite nasty stories of xenophobic neo-Nazi movements, you don't need to be too concerned here. Yes, there's definitely a contingent of stuffy old cranks who can get belligerent with you for no good reason, but the Nazi thing is really not a presence in the city (at least not for short-term visitors). Berlin has just become too international for skinhead freaks to get too much play. Travelers from all over the globe have become a welcome ingredient in the melting pot that is Germany's capital.

So how exactly do you get around in a melting pot? Public transportation is the key. Berlin is gargantuan; it can take over an hour to get from the east to the west, even using the Metro. Walking is simply not an option. Many people get around by bike, but for sizable trips, they make use of the city's extensive network of subways (the U-Bahn and the S-Bahn), trams, and buses. That said, Berlin *is* a city that rewards the walker. Every alleyway and back door seems to be concealing some little-known gallery or underground jazz jam. Some of Berlin's liveliest nightspots are squat bars: courtyards or apartments where illegally organized parties are held until they get too busy and the fuzz move in. The beer is cheap, the crowd is young and neighborhoody, and there's live music more often than not. Five-O usually kills these gigs after a few weeks, so it's not worth our publishing specific names and locations. A good strategy for finding the newest spot is to troll through residential areas in the East at night, like Prenzlauer Berg and Friedrichshain, and look for bunches of bicycles parked outside a doorway/alley/staircase, then just follow the music.

To clue into more mainstream attractions, pick up a copy of *Tip* or *Zitty*, biweekly mags similar to *Time Out*, available at newsstands. They're in German, but the event listings are easily decipherable and can help you navigate the turbulent waters of Berlin nightlife. Same deal for *Flyer*, a bite-sized biweekly handout, available at bars and stores throughout Berlin.

neighborhoods

The city is most commonly divided into **East** and **West**, but the whole of Berlin is further broken up into precincts. In the West, **Charlottenburg** is the busiest and most tourist laden. At its easternmost edge is the city's main train station, **Bahnhof Zoo**. Just to the south lies the beginning of West Berlin's main street, **Kurfürstendamm** (which runs roughly east-west, and is called **Ku'Damm** locally), along which you can find gobs of outdoor cafes and some of the city's most expensive shopping. North of Ku'Damm is the **Savigny Platz** area, Charlottenburg's youngest neighborhood, home to a pile of trendy bars and restaurants, and also Berlin's better jazz joints, **A Trane** and **Quasimodo** [see *live music scene*, below].

To the southeast of Charlottenburg is **Schöneberg,** home to a hip young bar scene centered around **Nollendorf Platz**. This is also the epicenter of gay Berlin, which lives mostly on and about **Motz Strasse**. Farther south is **Rathaus Schöneberg**, site of JFK's infamous "jelly-donut"/Berliner blooper (ask your folks).

North of Schöneberg is **Tiergarten**, which includes both the park (also called Tiergarten) and the residential districts north of it. The park known as **Tiergarten** [see *great outdoors*, below] is bisected by **Strasse des 17 Juni** [see *stuff*, below], the location of the city's most popular weekend flea market.

Directly to the east is **Mitte**, East Berlin's answer to Charlottenburg, attracting almost as many tourists, but a generation or two younger.

Rebuilt faster than the rest of the East, streets like **Friedrich Strasse** and **Unter den Linden** have again become major commercial strips, full of upscale shopping centers, theaters, and concert halls. To the north, the area between **Oranienburger Strasse** and **August Strasse** is another hotbed of shops, galleries, bars, restaurants, and clubs. A visit to **Potsdamer Platz**, in the southwest corner of Mitte, is necessary to truly appreciate the uninhibited pace of change in East Berlin. Skyscrapers, multi-screen cineplexes, and a good old American-style mall—complete with Swatch, Gap, and Eddie Bauer outlets—have grown like fresh mold on an old sausage on the site of this former checkpoint. It's so far removed from the style and culture of the rest of the city, native Berliners stagger around, gazing skyward like tourists.

Prenzlauer Berg, northeast of Mitte, is Berlin's feistiest up-and-comer. The neighborhood around **Kollwitz Platz**, often called hippietown because of an aging, crunchy element and a preponderance of organic food stores, is bursting with trendy and increasingly expensive restaurants like **Pasternak** [see *eats*, below]. Still edgy, the **Lychener, Schliemann,** and **Duncker Strasse** area, often shortened to **LSD**, is a less-gentrified stomping ground for a younger, funkier set eager to escape the crowding on **Oranienburger Strasse**.

Friedrichshain, to the east of Mitte, remains an urban shambles, but is beginning to show signs of life in the form of a number of bars and nightspots along **Simon-Dach Strasse** and the surrounding avenues.

Just south of Mitte is **Kreuzberg**, home to Berlin's huge Turkish population and a radical mix of alternative elements centered around the **Oranien Strasse**.

hanging out

A good spot to mingle with fellow travelers in West Berlin's Charlottenburg is Breitscheid Platz, at the intersection of Ku'Damm and Budapester Strasse by the Kaiser Wilhelm Gedädachtniskirche, the blasted remains of a 19th-century neo-Romanesque church. Street performers, mostly teenagers doing throwback breakdancing routines and board and bike tricks, do well off the steady flow of traffic from the nearby Bahnhof Zoo station. Behind the large and unusual fountain is also a popular skate-rat practice ground.

For some good East Berlin crowd watching, the view from any of the outdoor cafes on Oranienburger Strasse is one of the most entertaining. If you linger into the early evening, you'll see prostitutes reporting for duty. In the afternoon, the nearby Tacheles Courtyard is popular with a student and young artist crowd. Grab a drink at **Café Zapata** [see *wired*, below], head out back and camp down on one of the benches, rocks, or old tires strewn about the mammoth sandlot. On Friday and Saturday nights, starting at 11pm, this transforms into an outdoor jam (with a 1DM cover) that's frighteningly reminiscent of the beach party in *The Lost Boys*. A freaky teens and twenties crowd half-dance-half-shuffle around listening to heavy-bassed reggae, while others perch on

fIVE-O

Cops in Berlin are more likely to be a pain than a problem. Generally, the only time you'll see them is when you have incurred the minor wrath of the state, at which point they'll suddenly appear to collect money from you. This is most common on public transportation, where *kontrolleure*, undercover officers, conduct random sweeps of subways or buses, and impose a stiff 60DM penalty on anyone riding without a ticket. Don't even bother playing the dumb foreigner—they'll escort you to a bank machine and watch you take out the money. An additional warning should be made about jaywalking (New Yorkers beware!), which is not tolerated and will get you slapped with a spot fine of 10DM. This habit may also get you dirty looks from locals waiting patiently on the curb, so cross on the green...not in between.

abandoned trailer beds and puff up. Be wary of climbing up into the bridge of the bizarre metalwork rocket, as it has become a popular lover's lane of sorts.

Another East Berlin hangout on a warm weekend night is the corner of Tucholsky Strasse and August Strasse, where young, hip-dressing, good-looking types take expensive mixed drinks out of trendy local bars to mingle in the street.

If you pull a Friday night endurance run, stay up for the Winterfelder Platz Market, just south of the **Tiergarten**. Saturday mornings from 8am till 2pm, the entire Nollendorf Platz neighborhood, which is very young and very gay, comes out to savor the sights and smells of all manner of baked goods, produce, meats, cheeses, olives, and other goodies lined up in the large square. This is a fine place to do some people-watching and grab a cheap lunch at one of the many Turkish, Chinese, Thai, and other exotic food stands around. If you're looking for less architecture and more Mother Nature, the Tiergarten, right in the center of Berlin, attracts large crowds of locals on sunny days. Look out for bunny rabbits—there are so many of them, the city government at one point commissioned hunters to invade the park and exterminate them. Run, Flopsy, run!!

bar scene

What good is sitting alone in your room? No really, what good is it? There are so many bars in Berlin, we guarantee you'll be able to find a cure for whatever ails you. Here's the trick: In a town with no statutory last call, everything starts *late*. Berlin is not a city to experience on an early-to-bed regimen. Most bars don't busy up until 10 or 11, so catch a nap after dinner if you plan to go the distance.

In the Berlin bar scene, you can't get any more upscale and trendy than

Bar Am Lützowplatz (*Lützowplatz 7; Tel 030/262-68-07; U-Bahn 1, 2, 4, 12 to Nollendorf Platz, Bus 100, 129, 187 to Lützowplatz; 3pm-3am daily; V, MC, AE*), playground of the über-chic in the heart of the Nollendorf Platz neighborhood, where six-figure salaries and six-foot models meet. Seven bartenders line Germany's longest bar, hand-crafting what may be Germany's most expensive drinks (from 6.75DM to 35DM for cocktails). A daily happy hour from 3 to 9 halves the hurt, but be warned of the 150-item champagne list, where a wayward slip of the tongue can cost you 1,300DM. A final word to the wise: Wear black and look sharp or be ready to play the role of loser.

Located on Mitte's youngest and liveliest strip, **Obst & Gemuse** (*Oranienburger Str. 48-49; Tel 030/282-96-47; S1, S2 to Oranienburger Str., U-Bahn 6 to Oranienburger Tor; 8:30am-4am; No credit cards*) (literally, "fruits and vegetables") attracts a crowd as varied as its name implies, from dashing to dorky to dirty. The intimate yellow and orange decor gives the bar a pleasantly warm and mellow atmosphere. At 12DM, mixed drinks are reasonable, but the house special "Hemingway Sour," an exotic gin-and-juice variation, is a better deal for 10DM. Bring your glass back to the bar to reclaim your 1DM deposit.

Bringing a taste of Bavaria to Berlin is **Cafe Am Neuen See** (*Lichtensteinallee 2; Tel 030/254-49-30; S-Bahn 3, 5, 7, 75, 9 or U-Bahn 2, 9, 12 to Zoologischer Garten, then Bus X9 to Budapester Str., or Bus 100, 187, 341 to Stüler Str.; 10am-11pm daily; No credit cards*), a beer garden in the Tiergarten, just next to the city zoo. Sip a half-liter of beer (6.50DM) in this picturesque setting, enjoy the lake view, and ignore the the suits-and-shades business-lunch crowd. Beer gardens aren't a way of life here like they are down south, so neither the food nor the atmosphere are quite as delicious. The charm of this place is in finding a slice of quiet nature in this massive industrial city.

Pray for a bull market at **Broker's Bier Borse** (*Schiffbauerdamm 8; Tel 030/30-87-22-93; S-Bahn 1, 2, 25 to Friedrich Str.; Restaurant from 9am, Stock exchange from 5pm till 1 or 2am weekdays, 5am weekends; V,*

junge meets fräulein

Berlin wants your sex. No joke, this is one sexed-up city. Home of the Love Parade, cabaret, Sprockets, and other sexual oddities, Berlin has more mojo than Mike Myers. While queer culture is at the head of the class as far as publicly visible fornication is concerned, the straight crowd earns itself a gold star for general sketchiness. The rules for the pickup are just about the same as they are in most places—schmooze 'em, booze 'em, and use 'em— it's just a lot easier here. Happy hunting.

MC, AE), also in Mitte, where brew prices follow the capitalist doctrine of supply and demand: Order a beer and watch that brand's price go up on the digital screen listing the up-to-the-minute costs. The cheapest beers are the ones no one's ordering, so why not try bargain beers you've never heard of, like the Berlin pilsner *Jubilaums Kindl*. Budget drinkers win on the usually dead weekday evenings, when low demand keeps prices at rock bottom. The gimmick wears thin, as does the un-relaxed crowd of nondescript students and professionals, so come here early when prices are down, then move on.

LIVE MUSIC SCENE

Berlin's live music scene is about music in the same way Sprocket's is about dance—that is, not at all. Gimmick outweighs melody, pretense obscures harmony, and weirdness transcends quality. As a preeminent metropolis, Berlin does of course pull in great bands large and small. But cruise the local circuit, and you're likely to find German death metal next to ragtime, country western next to Turkish rap, and Indian trance next to klezmer. Yeah, so the scene is bizarre, but you're sure to find your niche no matter what your taste may be.

On the mezzanine level of the **Volksbühne** *(Rosa Luxemburg Platz; Tel 030/247-67-72; U-Bahn 2 to Rosa Luxemburg Platz, Bus 157 to Memhard Str.; Box office noon-6pm daily; No credit cards)*, Berlin's largest avant-garde theater venue, are two small railroad-style lounges. On Fridays, the Roter Salon (Red Saloon), with a 100 percent crimson interior, hosts "Nachtrock," a live performance featuring bands with names like Poems For Lilah and Killercouch. The music ranges anywhere from run-of-the-mill guitar rock to acoustic Goa. Wednesdays, the Roter Salon features "Tangonacht," a night of dancing to live Latin music. Across the hall, the Grüner Salon, an exact replica of Roter Salon, only...green, is a completely different experience. Performances here are mostly jazzy *chansons*, '20s and '30s showtune-style numbers led by aspiring Sinatra-esque crooners. A mellow drinking atmosphere at the eastern end of the Mitte.

Over in Savigny Platz, **Quasimodo** *(Kant Str. 12a; Tel 030/312-80-86; S-Bahn 3, 5, 7, 75, 9 or U-Bahn 2, 9, 12 to Zoologischer Garten, Bus 147 to Uhland Str.; Box office open from 5pm daily, shows begin at 10pm daily; 5-40DM admission which includes a drink; www.quasimodo.de; No credit cards)*, Berlin's blues and jazz temple since 1974, draws the biggest names in the biz, both domestic and imported. While artists like Ruben Blades, Taj Mahal, and Chaka Kahn command hefty covers, poorer music enthusiasts can enjoy free jam sessions on Tuesday nights, and the 5DM admission on Wednesdays includes a complimentary beer. Soul, disco, and rock shows designed to snare a younger crowd are hit-and-miss, but the cheap ones are worth the risk.

The strictly all-jazz lineup at Charlottenburg's **A Trane** *(Pestalozzi Str. 105; Tel 030/313-25-50; S-Bahn 3, 5, 7, 75, 9 to Savigny Platz, Bus 149 to Schlüter Str.; 9pm-1am daily; 30-150DM admission; www.a-trane.de; No credit cards)* brings in an older, more sophisticated, more music-literate crowd. Dim lighting and a decor of stylishly blended steel, cherry-stained woods, and burgundy leather give the bar a cozy jazz lounge ambiance, and artists like Arthur Blythe, Ray Brown, Gary Peacock, and Ravi Coltrane deliver on the promise. The free "Jazz After Midnight" jam session on Saturdays draws the hottest local artists and visiting performers and lasts until 3am or later.

Kind of a cultural center with a party attitude, **Pfefferberg** *(Schön-hauser Allee 176; Tel 030/44-38-31-10; U-Bahn 2 to Senefelder Platz; www.pfefferberg.de/berg.htm; No credit cards)* draws a crazy program of Gypsy music, jazz, African beats, hip-hop, and gothic rock to its home near Prenzlauer Berg. In its big sweaty pit of a dance hall, such hot bands as Spearhead play to the city's most discerning music freaks. The grounds, in a former brewery, also house a beer garden *(Open 3pm-2am May-Sept)*, techno joint *(11pm-8am Fri, Sat; 12DM cover)*, and art gallery.

club scene

Berlin clubs don't screw around: They kick in after 1am and don't stop until the sun is well above the horizon. Dancing ranges from pastime to way of life, from metal to sex-trance bizarre. In this colossal city, there's a club tailored to meet every kinky taste. Most places aren't tough to get into: Just have your money ready and stand in line with the rest of the scenesters.

Fancy duds or beat-up sneaks alike are welcome at **WMF** *(Johannis Str. 20-21; Tel 030/08-38-88-50; U-Bahn 6 to Oranienburger Tor; Midnight-7am Thur-Sun; www.wmf-club.de; 18DM cover; No credit cards)*, the city's consistently best get-down joint, where twentysomethings kick it to a high-energy mix of house, drum 'n' bass, and reggae. Conveniently near the intersection of the hopping Oranienburger and Friedrich strasses. There are two chill-out lounges and two dance floors, but by far the best space is the open-air dance hall to the rear. It feels like you're in a huge party box, as a disco ball suspended six stories up tosses dancing lights onto the walls and the star-filled sky glints above. The crowd is representing all over the place: gay and straight, gorgeous and schlumpy, dressy and scrubby. Sunday from 9pm to 3am is the GMF gay party night, with a cover that's 10DM before 10pm and 15DM after.

From headbanger's ball to technoid's delight, the well-hidden **Sage Club** *(corner of Köpenicker Str. and Brücken Str.; Tel 030/278-50-52; U-Bahn 8 to Heinrich-Heine-Str.; 10pm-7am Thur, 11pm-11am Fri-Sun; www.sage-club.de; 10-20DM cover, free entrance 10-10:30pm Thur; V, MC)* caters to a wide spectrum of scenes. Tucked away into the Heinrich-Heine Strasse U-Bahn entrance in the southwestern corner of the Mitte, this unmarked dance joint is distinguishable only by the red velvet rope and the hordes of party-goers in front. The crowd changes with the music: Leather-clad bad-asses nod their mangy heads to crossover big beat to grunge and metal on Thursdays; Adidas-wearing hip-hoppers bust out the fresh moves for the funk 'n' soul Friday nights; hipsters fill the joint for the house music on Saturdays; and techno freaks in yellow glasses, gyrating like Daniel-san waxing on, waxing off Mr. Miyagi's cars, pack the place on Sunday nights for a crazy gay night. One room, appointed with psychedelic patterns and colors, is clearly made for trippers, and occasional bursts of flame in the dance hall keep you on your toes.

Bergwerk *(Berg Str. 68; Tel 030/280-88-76; Noon-3am Sun-Thur, noon-6am Fri, Sat; 9DM cover for disco; No credit cards)*, at the eastern end of the Mitte, is the neighborhood dive here, where it doesn't matter who the hell you are or what you're wearing. If you're in the mood to mosh or groove to early-'90s grunge, head downstairs to the tiny candlelit cellar dance floor. Upstairs, the simple bar is a deliciously mixed bag, where preppy coeds sip merlot alongside shaved heads and ripped fishnets. Ask the bartender for a B-52, a flaming Sambuca-Kahlúa-Bailey's shot that you slurp down with a straw.

The city's hard-core technoids follow the nomadic beats pumped out by **No UFOs** *(various locations; www.no-ufos.de; usually a 20DM cover)*, a group of organizers who throw parties wherever they find a building. The crowd is on the intense side, most pierced and some adorned with colored horns shaved into their hair. Look for flyers in the club-gear shops around town [see *stuff*, below].

arts scene

Since the fall of the Wall, cheap-to-free studio space has become plentiful in East Berlin and the city's arts scene has been in full stride. Hordes of Austrian, Swiss, and German artists have set up shop in the tenements of the former communist quarter. The Mitte's August Strasse and vicinity boasts the densest cluster of galleries in town; it's your best bet for a quick tour of the Berlin avant-garde.

Good hangouts to find your starving artists include **Café Zapata** [see *wired*, below], an art project in itself, situated on the ground floor of the Kunsthaus Tacheles complex.

▶▶VISUAL ARTS

The visual arts world in Berlin is so active, it has spilled over the confines of the traditional gallery scene and found a home in any number of bars, clubs, and restaurants. The most experimental of the city's artists can only be found off the beaten path. Mitte, and increasingly Prenzlauer Berg, make up the new center for contemporary art in all of Germany, and, some might argue, all of Europe.

Once the center of the Berlin artistic community, **Kunsthaus Tacheles** *(Oranienburger Str. 54-56a; Tel 030/282-61-85; S-Bahn 1, 2 to Oranienburger Str., U-Bahn 6 to Oranienburger Tor; Galleries open 2pm-midnight Mon-Fri, 11am-midnight Sat, Sun; www.tacheles.de)* has become an establishment supporting the edgier arts. Located in East Berlin's nucleus, the Tacheles complex houses 40 artists' studios, several exhibition spaces showcasing anything from conventional paintings to works in digital media, a wood workshop, a silkscreen workshop, an avant-garde cinema [see *performing arts*, below], a dance and theater performance space [see *performing arts*, below], and two cafes. Built into the shelled-

west berlin

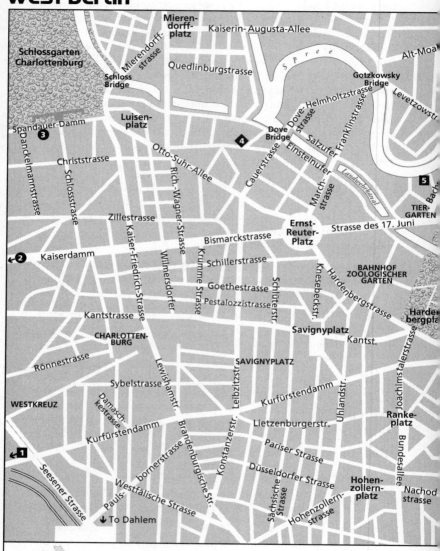

Mieren-dorff-platz

Kaiserin-Augusta-Allee

Schlossgarten Charlottenburg

Mierendorff-strasse

Quedlinburgstrasse

Spree

Gotzkowsky Bridge

Alt-Moa

Levetzowstr

Schloss Bridge

Dove-Helmholtzstrasse strasse

Franklinstrasse

Spandauer-Damm

Luisen-platz

Dove Bridge

Salzufer

Danckelmannstrasse

Christstrasse

Otto-Suhr-Allee

Cauerstrasse

Einsteinufer

Landwehrkanal

Schlossstrasse

Rich.-Wagner-Strasse

March-strasse

Bach

TIER-GARTEN

Zillestrasse

Bismarckstrasse

Ernst-Reuter-Platz

Strasse des 17. Juni

Kaiser-Friedrich-Strasse

Kaiserdamm

Schillerstrasse

Knesebeckstr.

Hardenbergstrasse

BAHNHOF ZOOLOGISCHER GARTEN

Wilmersdorfer

Krumme Strasse

Goethestrasse

Schlüterstr.

Harden-bergpla

Kantstrasse

Pestalozzistrasse

CHARLOTTEN-BURG

Savignyplatz

Kantst.

Rönnestrasse

Lewishamstr.

SAVIGNYPLATZ

Joachimstalerstrasse

Sybelstrasse

Leibzitzstr.

Kurfürstendamm

Uhlandstr.

Rankeplatz

WESTKREUZ

Damasch kettrasse

Konstanzerstr.

Lietzenburgerstr.

Bundesallee

Kurfürstendamm

Brandenburgische Str.

Pariser Strasse

Seesener Strasse

bornerstrasse

Düsseldorfer Strasse

Hohen-zollern-platz

Nachod strasse

Pauls-

Westfälische Strasse

Sächsische Strasse

Hohenzollern-strasse

↓ To Dahlem

Berlin ★

GERMANY

BARS/CLUBS ▲
Bar Am Lützowplatz **7**
Cafe Am Neven See **6**

CULTURE ZOO ●
Funkturm **2**
Sammlung Berggruen **3**
Hamburger Bahnhof, Museum Für
  Gegenwart **8**

Kleiner
Tiergarten

LEHRTER
STADT-
BAHNHOF
8
Invaliden

Alt-Moabit

Wash-
ington-
platz

Stromstrasse

Paulstrasse

Moltke
Bridge

Lessing
Bridge

Moabiter
Bridge

Luisenstrasse

Lessing-
strasse

BELLEVUE

Bellevueufer

Spree

Platz
der
Republik

Hansa-
viertel

Englischer
Garten

Spreeweg

John-Foster-Dulles-Allee

Entlastungsstrasse

Altonaerstrasse

Toleranzstrasse

Platz
vor dem
Branden-
burger
Tor

asse des 17. Juni

Grosser
Stern

Strasse des 17. Juni

Hofjägeralleestrasse

TIERGARTEN

Potsdamerstrasse

Potsdamerstrasse

6

gartenufer

Stülerstrasse

Klingelhöfer-
strasse

Tiergartenstrasse

Pots-
damer-
platz

ologischer
Garten

Budapesterstrasse

Reichpietschufer

Lützowufer

Schönebergerstrasse

Bernburger
Strasse

Linkstrasse

ergerstrasse

Lützow-
platz

Lützowstrasse

Flottwellstrasse

Kurfürstenstrasse

Einemstrasse

7

Potsdamer Strasse

Tauentzienstrasse

Nollendorf-
platz

Bülowstrasse

Goebenstrasse

Martin-Luther-
Strasse

Winterfeldtstrasse

Str.

Ansbacherstr.

Motzstrasse

Pallasstrasse

ohenstaufenstrasse

EATS ◆

Woolloomoolloo **4**

CRASHING ■

Hotel Hansablick **5**
St. Michaels-Heim **1**

0   1/4 mi

0   1/4 km

out hull of a pre-war department store (saved from demolition back in '90 by a group of artists/squatters), Kunsthaus Tacheles has a post-apocalyptic sort of charm.

Perhaps the coolest addition to the Kunsthaus Tacheles behemoth is its metal workshop, **Metalwerkstatt Im Tacheles** (*Oranienburger Str. 54-56; No phone; S-Bahn 1, 2 to Oranienburger Str., U-Bahn 6 to Oranienburger Tor; Open daily 2pm-midnight*), a combined studio and showroom in a large garage-like space. Dodging flying sparks as you stroll through the collection of mammoth welded steel sculpture keeps you on your toes. Getting in can be tricky—the studio is open only when an artist decides to work—but mid-afternoon is usually a good bet.

Hidden down a back alley and up some stairs west of Alexanderplatz in Mitte, **Helen Adkin's Museumsakademie** (*Rosenthaler Str. 39; Tel 030/308-72-580; S-Bahn 3, 5, 7, 75, 9 to Hackescher Markt, U-Bahn 8 to Weinmeister Str., 2-6pm Tue-Sat*) is a remarkably large and well-lit commercial gallery showing the works of young, highly political Berlin-based artists. Recent exhibitions include a series of pieces displaying the innovatively disfigured faces of '90s supermodels, hidden video documenting people's irritated responses to coins glued to the floor in a Wall Street office building; and a tremendous block of ice transported from the North Pole, never before seen by human eyes, that took three months to melt.

Like something from a Jim Henson nightmare, the **Dead Chickens** (*Rosenthaler Str. 39; Tel 030/30-87-25-73; S-Bahn 3, 5, 7, 75, 9 to Hackescher Markt, U-Bahn 8 to Weinmeister Str.; 6pm-midnight Fri, 4pm-midnight Sat, 4-10pm Sun; 8DM admission; www.deadchickens.de; No credit cards*) exhibit is even more bizarre than its name suggests. Appropriately situated in a dank basement, this freak show of larger-than-life mechanized monsters is so unholy and grotesque, they should keep an exorcist on hand. Buttons and levers on the scattered exhibits make these beaked, bug-eyed horrors inflate, breathe fire, and perform other unnatural feats...all in all, as cool as it is weird.

rules of the game

On the heels of its totalitarian history, Berlin has become quite forgiving when it comes to those healthy habits of yours. Drinking: The legal age is 18. Marijuana possession: technically illegal, but if somebody's caught with a small amount (under 10 grams), the worst they can expect is that the cops will snatch their stash. Particularly popular herb-friendly venues include parks and the outdoor movie theaters that open up in the summer. Harder substances, like ecstasy and coke: There are fines for having small quantities, but nobody's doing hard time for it. Ecstasy is common in clubs and especially during the **Love Parade** [see *festivals and events*, below].

a survey of berlin oddities

Begin from the southern exit of Mitte's Oranienburger T or U-Bahn 6 station. Facing north, the abandoned lot on your right reveals a view of a wildly grafittied building and the shattered backside of the **Kunsthaus Tacheles** complex [see *arts scene*, above]. Walk north and take your first right onto Oranienburger Strasse. As you pass the front of Kunsthaus Tacheles, take a peek at the giant, twisted sculptures inside the metalwork shop on the ground floor. Continue down Oranienburger Strasse, following the long procession of bars and cafes lining East Berlin's hottest strip. Two blocks down, take a left onto Tucholsky Strasse. Before the next intersection you will pass **Penthesileia**, purveyor of Berlin's funkiest/scariest bags and purses. Bang your next right onto August Strasse, the heart of the city's gallery scene. Continue past the sun-shaped wrought-iron gate on your left until you reach Grosse Hamburger Strasse, marked on the far left corner by Shiva's dayglo orange storefront. Take a right down "Fat Burger Street" and notice **Hanf Haus** (Hemp House) on your right, peddler of water pipes, hemp clothing, and cannabis beer. Continue to the end of the street and go left at the T onto Oranienburger Strasse. Check out the Sputnik-sized disco ball spinning in **Orlando**, one of Berlin's grooviest shoe stores. When you come to a fork in the road, veer left and you will quickly pass **Die Hackeschen Höfe** [see *stuff*, below] and arrive at a long alley on your left where you can find the **Dead Chickens** [see *arts scene*, above] exhibit. For a quick taste, walk down to the end where a monstrous mechanical bird head greets visitors. Continue on and pay a visit to the "musée" at the far right corner of Rosenthaler Strasse and Neue Schonhauser Strasse, an odd and unattended assortment of grafittied junk assembled on a scruffy patch of lawn. A rickety seat perched atop a pile of cinder block, crudely labeled "speaker's corner," provides the courageous and the lunatic alike a place to vent. One block up Rosenthaler Strasse you can catch the U-Bahn 8 at Wienmeister Strasse.

▶▶PERFORMING ARTS

For those of you who think the performing arts in Berlin are all black turtlenecks and grimaces, à la Sprockets, guess again. Dance, theater, and film in Germany's capital are about as staid as a Scotsman with Tourette's. Berlin is home to a ton of off-theater venues that are hit-and-miss, but will take your dollar further. Unfortunately, hardly any of it is in English, and your chances of seeing a big-budget movie that hasn't been dubbed

festivals and events

Love Parade *(Second Saturday in July):* Now the mother of all block parties, the Love Parade began in 1989 as a tiny procession of revelers dancing along West Berlin's Ku'-Damm. Ten years later, the annual festival fills Strasse des 17 Juni and the Tiergarten with over a million screaming, gyrating techno-fans. Bars and clubs throughout the city host raves this weekend to draw the crowds before and after the parade.

Berlinale International Film Festival *(Late February):* Second in size only to the Cannes festival, the Berlinale screens some 800 films across Berlin. Separated into a number of different sections, the selections for Panorama and the International Forum of Young Cinema are largely independent films leaning toward the avant-garde, while the International Competition is more mainstream Hollywood.

Jazzfest Berlin *(End of Oct; Haus der Kulturen Welt, John-Foster-Dulles Allee 10):* Still swingin' after 35 years, this four-day jam in Tiergarten brings artists from all over the world. While Jazzfest no longer brings in the banner names it once commanded, the lineup still packs a punch.

Berliner Festwochen *(Sept; Information at Berliner Festspiele, Budapester Str. 50; Tel 030/254-890):* Throughout September all of Berlin plays host to a barrage of classical music concerts, performances from international theater groups, and various readings and exhibitions.

Carnival of Cultures *(Late May):* A four-day party with exotic themes that change daily. Culminating in a parade that winds its way through the heavily Turkish Kreuzberg in the East, this festival of food, music, and dance is one of Berlin's most colorful multicultural events.

into German are slim to nada. The good news: There is a wide variety of indie cinemas that screen films in their original language, which is often English. And hey, there's always dance, right? Call box offices or check listings in *Tip* or *Zitty* for info.

Cinema Central *(Rosenthaler Str. 39; Tel 030/28-59-99-73; S-Bahn 3, 5, 7, 75, 9 to Hackescher Markt, U-Bahn 8 to Weinmeister Str.; Box office open 6pm-end of last showing Mon-Fri, from 3pm Sat, Sun; 7DM Mon, 8.5DM Tue-Wed, 12DM Thur-Sun; www.cine-berlin.de; No credit cards),* a small two-screen joint in eastern Mitte, runs a mix of Hollywood features and independent films. The current schedule includes Sunday screenings of new "South Park" episodes, betraying the youth of the crowd running the theater.

One of the smallest avant-garde theaters in Berlin, Mitte's **Kino Camera** *(Oranienburger Str. 54-56a; Tel 030/283-14-98; S-Bahn 1, 2 to Oranienburger Str., U-Bahn 6 to Oranienburger Tor; Box office open 6:30pm-end of last showing; 8-18DM admission, depending on the day of week; www.tacheles.de; No credit cards)*, an appendage of the **Tacheles** compound [see *visual arts*, above], is a bit more exotic than **Cinema Central. Kino Camera**'s program includes many experimental films and shorts, in addition to more mainstream indie productions. Worth checking out are the occasional traditional silent German films, shown with live piano accompaniment.

Despite its misleading moniker, **Friends of Italian Opera** *(Fidicin Str. 40; Tel 030/691-12-11; U-Bahn 6 or Bus 119 to Platz der Luftbrücke; Show times vary, box office opens one hour before show time; Ticket prices vary; www.thefriends.de; No credit cards)* is in fact Berlin's only English-language stage dedicated to English, Irish, Scottish, and occasionally American theater. The small, rather poorly maintained space hosts performances of plays ranging from Shakespeare's *Venus and Adonis* to more modern works like *Say Nothing* by Belfast drama troupe Ridiculousness. Look out for events and performances hosted elsewhere by Friends of Italian Opera.

Hallesches Ufer *(Hallesches Ufer 32; Tel 030/251-09-41; U-Bahn 1, 7, 12, 15 to Möckernbrücke; Box office opens two hours before performances; 20-27DM admission, 18-20DM for students; www.thub.de; V, MC)*, a large-ish open space dedicated mostly to modern dance, has evolved into a free-production venue since its birth in 1962, making its stage available to Berlin-based dance and theater groups. Productions like *The Last Dancing Communist From Prenzlauer Berg* by locally famous artist Jo Fabian teeter on the edge of existing conventions; they're more choreographed than theater and more visual than dance. Most spoken theater here is bound to be in German; but the experimental dance is worth the ticket.

Surprise, surprise; another groovy venue for contemporary dance is the theater in **Kunsthaus Tacheles** [see *visual arts*, above]. Shows staged include: *Butoh*, Japanese avant-garde dance/performance that draws, in part, from Buddhist monastic tradition, and a *Festival of Ghosts*, where spiritualism was explored through various expressive forms. Ticket prices range from 18 to 25DM.

gay scene

As active politically and socially as New York or San Francisco, Berlin is truly one of the queer capitals of the world. Nollendorf Platz, in the West's Schöneberg, is ground zero for gay life in Berlin. Motz Strasse, the main strip, has a little something for everyone, from leather bars to restaurants with topless beefcake waiters. Over in East Berlin, the streets surrounding Schönhauser Allee are home to a number of gay cafes and bars. Before you paint the town pink, arm yourself with a copy of *Sergej* (gay mag) or *Siegessäule* (gay and lesbian mag), available at most gay establishments. While both monthly publications are in German, they are free and the included calendars of upcoming events and nightlife are easy to figure out.

Berlin's most visited gay and lesbian bookstore, **Prinz Eisenherz** (*Bleibtreu Str. 52; Tel 030/313-99-36; S-Bahn 3, 5, 7, 75, 9 or Bus 149 to Savigny Platz; 10am-7pm Mon-Fri, 10am-4pm Sat; www.prinz-eisen herz.com, prinz-eisenherz@t-online.de; V, MC)* offers a well-diversified lineup of nearly 20,000 titles covering the spectrum from literature to porn. A traveler-friendly shop, with nearly 25 percent of their collection in English and an English-speaking owner, this is a good place to get the lowdown on the Berlin gay scene. Ask for a *Fun Map*, a guide to many of the city's hotter spots with some English notations thrown in. You can grab copies of *Sergej* and *Siegessäule* here as well. They also have every gay newspaper from all over Germany here.

The young twenties and thirties crowd at **Café Berio** (*Maassen Str. 7; Tel 030/216-19-46; U-Bahn 2, 15 or Bus 119, 219 to Nollendorf Platz; 8am-1am daily; No credit cards)* is a happy mix of good- and even-better-looking gay and lesbian folks. Prime seating is outside, where the social-izing and boy and girl watching is best, especially on Saturday mornings when the **Winterfeld Platz market** [see *stuff*, below] has the pre-dominantly gay Schöneberg neighborhood in full swing. Busy all day long, the house tortes and American '50s tunes keep business humming in the afternoons, while Latin and reggae beats heat things up after dark.

Lenz...Die Bar (*Eisenacher Str. 3; Tel 030/217-78-20; U-Bahn 1, 2, 4 to Nollendorf Platz, Bus 146 to Motz Str. or 219 to Urania Platz; 7pm-4 or 5am daily; V, MC, AE, Diners)*, in a mellow, softly lit room, draws a mostly gay and slightly older clientele sporting a noticeably high Lacoste alligator quotient. Tasty cocktails and the happy cocktail hour from 8-9:30pm Tue-Thur generate a lively early-evening crowd. All told, Lenz is a good warmup joint where a pleasant blend of jazz, house, and vodka and tonics can help you kick off a festive, if expen-sive, night out.

One of the oldest hangouts on Berlin's most active gay strip, **Tom's Bar** (*Motz Str. 19; Tel 030/213-45-70; U-Bahn 1, 2, 4 to Nollendorf Platz, Bus 146 to Motz Str.; 10pm-6 or 7am daily; No credit cards)* has evolved from a leather bar into its new incarnation as the scene's most popular cruising spot. A young, jeans-and-T-shirt crowd mill about outside drinking cheap beer (the bar doesn't serve mixed drinks) waiting for 12:30pm, when the dark room opens and the real action gets underway. Grungy and black lit, Tom's isn't much to look at, but for what it is, it's the place to be. The best nights are weekends and also Mondays, when drinks are two-for-one.

CULTURE ZOO

In a city constantly on the make and on the move, one can take comfort in the fact that some things will never change—like history, for example. And Berlin has got that in spades. Even in the midst of frantic reconstruction, reminders of the war still scar city monuments, memorials, landmarks, and the many gutted, fractured remains of shelled buildings. There are enough museums to keep you looking at display glass for weeks. But, we figured you'd want to save some time for beer glasses so we picked out the best of the best of the best. Or at least the ones we dig.

Sammlung Berggruen (*Westlicher Stülerbau, Schloss Str. 1; Tel 030/326-95-80; U2 to Sophie-Charlotte Platz; 10am-6pm Tue-Fri, 11am-6pm Sat, Sun; 8DM, 4DM students*): The impressive permanent exhibit "Picasso and his Time" spans the master's life, and includes works by Braque, Matisse, Klee, Laurens, and Giacometti.

Hamburger Bahnhof, Museum für Gegenwart (*Invalidenstr. 50-51; Tel 030/397-83-40; S-Bahn to Lehrter Stadtbahnhof; 10am-5pm Tue, Wed, Fri, 10am-10pm Thur, 11am-6pm Sat, Sun; 8DM, 4DM students*): Contemporary art fans will find lots to love in Berlin, especially at this place, a former train station converted in '96 to house the National galerie's contemporary collection. Warhol, Cy Twombly, Robert Rauschenberg, Roy Lichenstein, Jeff Koons...they're all there.

Deutsche Guggenheim Berlin (*Unter den Linden 13; U2 to Stadtmitte, U6 to Französische Strasse, S1, S2 to Unter den Linden, S3, S5, S7, S9, S75 to Friedrich Strasse, Buses 100, 157, 348, 200 to Unter den Linden; noon-8pm daily; www.deutsche-guggenheim-berlin.de; 8DM, free Mon*): Designed by Richard Gluckman, architect of the Dia Center in New York and the Andy Warhol Museum in Pittsburgh, the fifth Guggenheim aims to show four major exibitions each year, including one specifically commissioned for the space. Recent installations include works by Dan Levin, Amazonen der Avante Garde, Yves Klein, James Torrelle, and James Rosenquist.

Haus am Checkpoint Charlie (*Friedrich Str. 43-45; Tel 030/253-72-50; U-Bahn 6 to Koch Str.; 9am-10pm daily; 12DM admission*): Located just off the site of the infamous border gate of the same name, Haus am Checkpoint Charlie chronicles the history of the Berlin Wall, the people who managed to escape, and those who died trying. The array of wall remains alone are worth the price of admission.

Pergamon Museum (*Am Kupfergraben; Tel 030/20-90-55-55; U-Bahn 2, 5, 8 or S-Bahn 3, 5, 7, 75, 9 to Alexanderplatz; 10am-6pm Tues, Wed, Fri, till 10pm Thur, 11am-6pm Sat, Sun; 8DM admission, free first Sun of each month*): Situated on Museum Island, the Pergamon Museum houses a staggering collection of historic architectural monuments and classical antiques, including the Gate of Ishtar and the museum's awe-inspiring namesake, the Pergamon Altar (the altar of Zeus and Athene), dating from 180-160 B.C.

Funkturm (*Messedamm 22; Tel 030/30-380; U-Bahn 2 to Theodor-Heuss-Platz or to Kaiserdamm; 10am-11pm daily; 6DM admission, 3DM students*): Berlin's radio spire stands nearly 500 feet high and hosts a restaurant and decent views of the city. Overall, the Funkturm isn't much to write home about, but we dig it because, well, it's the *tower of funk.*

12 hours in berlin

1. Go on a gallery crawl: August Strasse and the surrounding streets of Mitte are chock-full-o' gallery spaces, displaying an endless stream of contemporary German and international artists. There's way too much to swallow in a single serving, so just take your time and enjoy what you find.

2. Put some history in your diet: The **East Side Gallery**, the largest remaining stretch of the Berlin Wall, runs along the river Spree on Mühlenstrasse near Ostbahnhof. Artists from around the world have painted the 28 segments in the gallery, one for each year the wall stood as a monument to totalitarianism.

3. History, part deux: Once again the seat of the German government, the rebuilt **Reichstag** [see *culture zoo*, below] is an architectural wonder. The brilliant glass-domed structure in the northeast corner of the **Tiergarten** is intended to prefigure an era of openness and moral clarity...but, to hell with symbolism, it just looks damn cool.

4. Hit the Berlin outback: Sample the hearty grub at **Woolloomoolloo** [see *eats*, below], a real Aussie BBQ joint, complete with kangaroo, crocodile, ostrich, and Fosters. Crocodile Dundee would approve.

Reichstag *(Platz der Republik Tiergarten; Tel 030/22-70; S-Bahn 1, 2 to Unter den Linden):* One of the most spectacular highlights of the heavily remodeled Berlin, the new-and-improved Reichstag (recently rebuilt after burning down in 1933), comes complete with glass dome and German Parliament. Batteries not included.

Hanf Museum *(Mühlendamm 5; Tel 030/242-48-27; U-Bahn 2 to Kloster Str. or to Alexanderplatz; 10am-8pm Tue-Fri, noon-8pm Sat, Sun; 5DM admission, 3.50DM for groups of 6+):* Yes, an entire museum dedicated to all things hemp. Explores the history and cultures surrounding the use of hemp in cooking, crafts, beauty products, and of course for medicinal/recreational purposes. Sorry, no samples, but still fun.

modification

With this many punks and hipsters, Berlin offers about any type of hair cutting you might want, from Euro-chic to wild and woolly. Haircuts are expensive, but the scissor-wielders usually do good work and offer coffee or mineral water to drink while you get coiffed. Grolmanstrasse and Schlüterstrasse, both to the west of Uhlandstrasse on the west side of the city, are loaded with stylishly upscale places. At Charlottenburg's **Art of Hair**

5. Freak nouveau: You need to check out the **Dead Chickens** [see *arts scene*, above] exhibit. You won't understand until you see it...just go.

6. Explore the Kunsthaus Tacheles complex [see *arts scene*, above]: With an avant-garde cinema, two floors of galleries, a dance and theater space, a bar, and an Internet cafe, this place is a phone call to Disney away from being a theme park.

7. Have a martini...shaken, not stirred: The vibe at **Bar am Lützowplatz** [see *bar scene*, above] is very 007, boasting the longest bar in Germany, a champagne and cocktail menu that could go toe-to-toe with the Yellow Pages, and some of the snazziest clientele since Monte Carlo back in the day.

8. Party at Gartenhaus: If Mad Max threw a beach party, this is what it would look like. Held Friday and Saturday nights in the post-apocalyptic Kunsthaus Tacheles courtyard [see *arts scene* and *hanging out*, above], this get-together packs a student-heavy crowd who come to drink and smoke up under the stars. And for 1DM, there's little to complain about.

(Schlüter Str. 34; Tel 030/885-16-16; U-Bahn 15 to Uhland Str. or U-Bahn 2 to Adenauerplatz; 10am-7pm Mon, 9am-8pm Tue-Fri, 10am-6pm Sat; 50-110DM cut for women, 40-110DM cut for men; No credit cards), two stylists will fuss over your melon and work with you to design a style before giving you a scalp-tingling shampoo and busting out the shears.

For the zany styles you would expect in Berlin, try **Hair Affair** *(Solms Str. 27; Tel 030/691-90-89; U-Bahn 7 to Gneisenau Str.; 10am-7pm Tue-Fri, 9am-2pm Sat, closed Sun, Mon; 45-65DM cut for women, 35-45DM cut for men, 35-70DM for color, varied price for crazy stuff; No credit cards)* in Kreuzberg. This place has been around for 25 years but changes its style with the alternative fashions. Right now, they're into dyeing hair in colors not found in nature, tying dreadlocks, and adding extensions. They'll also give the standard cut, but hell, that's not as much fun. Check out their hilarious window displays; recent ones have included bones hung from string over a dog house, replete with piles of fake dog crap.

If these don't work for you, and you're too shy to ask those oh-so-cool kids where they got their do's, check the *ein000* guide [see *stuff*, below] for some listings.

For more permanent modifications, head to Friedrichschain to **Für**

Immer *(Revaler Str. 11; Tel 030/29-00-49-47; 1-7pm Tue-Sat, but call for tattoo appointment as there is normally a month-long wait; www.fuerim mertattoo.de, www.provocativepiercings.de; No credit cards)*, where an award-winning body artist can tattoo you with any design you want, from tribal patterns to colorful tigers to sophisticated paintings. The shop also offers body piercing, with prices for nipples or tongues starting at about 120DM.

great outdoors

To the dismay of skate rats, The Man has outlawed in-line skating on the streets of Berlin. It's still legal to skate in public parks and skate parks, though, so head to the **Tiergarten** [see below] or one of the many half-dozen skate parks that open and close every few months. For a list of skate parks and in-line rentals, head to **Strawberry** *(Emser Str. 45; Tel 030/881-30-96; U-Bahn 1 to Hohenzollernplatz; 11am-8pm Mon-Fri, 11am-4pm Sat; 15DM/day, 25DM/weekend, all including pads; V, MC, AE)*, a store in the Wilmersdorf district run by two cool women that also stocks surfer clothes, skate gear, and snowboard gear for chicks only, as well as swimwear. You can also stop by the less personal **360°** *(Pariser Str. 23-24; Tel 030/883-85-96; 11am-7:30pm Mon-Fri, 10am-4pm Sat; They do not hire out equipment here; V, MC)*.

But the real skinny on local city sports is a surprising one: wakeboarding, where you're strapped to a pseudo-snowboard and pulled behind a speedboat. The hottest place to wakeboard is at **Velten**, a lake about an hour north of Berlin. If you're a rookie or need a ride, call **California** *(Emser Str. 45; Tel 030/882-37-28; U-Bahn 1 to Hohenzollern-platz; V)*, where 32DM will rent you a board, two hours behind a towrope, and an informal lesson. The guys from California can also give you a lift to Velten if you call ahead; excursions leave every Monday night between 7 and 9pm in the summer. On Tuesday evenings, 360° takes trips to Velten, but they charge 20DM more and give rides to fewer people.

When Berliners seek refuge from the industrial grind of their post-modern city, they have several city parks to choose from. The **Tiergarten** *(S-Bahn 3, 5, 7, 75, 9 to Tiergarten or Bus 100, 187, 341)*, a huge expanse of green in the center of the city, is perfect for joggers and bikers. (It's also a notorious gay prowling ground after dusk, so don't make eye contact with strange men if you don't feel like being followed.) On the west side of the city, **Lietzensee** *(S-Bahn 4, 45, 46 to Witzleben or Bus 139, 149, X34, X49 to Witzleben)* is a much smaller park around a banana-shaped lake, where locals sit and sunbathe or lounge on the shore under weeping willows. **Volkspark** *(U-Bahn 4 to Rath Schöneberg or U-Bahn 7 to Blisse Str.)*, to the south, is more recreational, with tennis courts, joggers, and outdoor ping-pong tables. To the southeast of the city lies **Grunewald** *(S-Bahn 7 to Grunewald)*, a massive forest with tons of hiking and biking trails. **Berlin by Bike** [see *need to know*, below] offers mountain biking tours of the Grunewald.

STUFF

If you're having Gap withdrawal, head over to West Berlin—Ku'Damm is the most touristy stretch, with loads of international clothing chains. As a general rule, the funkier stuff is in East Berlin: art and expensive fashion trends in Mitte, record shops and streetwear stuff in Prenzlauer Berg and Kreuzberg. For stylin' second-hand duds and vinyl, hit Bergmann Strasse or Oranien Strasse in Kreuzberg. A new mag called *ein000,* available free in Planet and other stores, lists—in German *and* English—trendy little boutiques where you can pick up records, board and in-line equipment, club- and streetwear, and second-hand duds. Check them out on the web at ***www.ein000.de***. All shops are open until 4pm on Saturday and closed Sunday.

▶▶DUDS

The funkiest of Berlin's footwear can be found at Kreuzberg's **Luccico** *(Bergmann Str. 97; Tel 030/691-77-14; U-Bahn 7 to Gneisenau Str.; 11am-8pm Mon-Fri, 11am-4pm Sat; No credit cards),* which carries the latest rages, from neon go-go boots and platforms to flowered Mary Janes or space-age, Italian clubbing sneakers. One typical customer we spotted was a gay, dreadlocked American expat who "just had to come back" for the beige pimp-daddy loafers he'd been eyeing the week before. There are two other branches: *(Zossener Str. 32; Tel 030/691-32-57)* and *(Goltz Str. 34; Tel 030/216-65-17).*

To round out that outrageous clubbing outfit, head just up the street to **City Market** *(Bergmann Str. 94; Tel 030/696-61-20; U-Bahn 7 to Gneisenau Str.; 10:30am-6:30pm Mon-Fri, 11am-4pm Sat; V, MC).* Shaggy faux fur coats, nylon cargo and leather pants, and tiny flowered tube tops can all be found in this crowded little boutique.

Scruffier hipsters should hit **Blue Møøn** *(Wilmersdorfer Str. 80; Tel 030/323-70-88; U-Bahn 7 to Wilmersdorfer Str.; Noon-8pm Mon-Fri, noon-4pm Sat; V, MC, AE),* also in Kreuzberg, which features everything from techno to slacker chic. Look for vinyl and plaid mini-skirts, fresh Spiderman sandals, flowery Hawaiian shirts, board shorts, and Doc Martens. The owners have also opened a smaller store: *(Uhland Str. 33; Tel 030/881-41-57).*

The resident technoids find their gear at **Planet Berlin** *(Schlüter Str. 35; Tel 030/885-27-17; 11am-8pm Mon-Fri, 11am-4pm Sat; V, MC, AE),* famous in certain circles across Germany for outfitting the party scene and local bands since 1985. Skin-tight shirts, platform shoes, hair paint, party flyers, and club advice are all dispensed with the requisite degree of snootiness. This shop is on an upscale street near Ku'Damm, in West Berlin, and the prices pretty much follow suit.

Outfitting the local goth, punk, and glam rock communities is **Plaste and Elaste** *(Bergmann Str. 15; Tel 030/692-47-15; U-Bahn 7 to Gneisenau Str.; 10:30am-6:30pm Mon-Wed, 10:30am-8pm Thur, Fri, 10am-4pm Sat; V, MC, AE),* where you can pick up that *Purple Rain* lace-

by foot

East Berlin's razor edge: A neighborhood on the move, Prenzlauer Berg is Mitte-in-waiting, a district torn between fun grunginess and gentrification. Nowhere else in Berlin is the massive cleanup effort more apparent than in this district. Beautifully restored buildings sit next to eyesores, trendy cafes sit across from old monuments, and young people struggle to keep their hip haunts open. Start at the Senefelderplatz U-Bahn station, and take the Saarbrücker Strasse/Fehrbelliner Strasse exit. Turn left out of the exit, cross the street, and head up Kollwitz Strasse. On the right, at Kollwitz Strasse 8, peek through the iron gate at one of the most graffiti-covered entryways ever. This leads to a little outdoor recreation center, where Prenzlauer Berg denizens play hoops and scale a climbing wall. Head back out, and turn right up Kollwitz. Pass Spielacart—a small cafe where local scrubs smoke cigs—then a vacant lot. Now turn around to behold one of Berlin's bizarre art projects: neon cows grazing on the side of the cafe's walls. They're illuminated at night. Keep walking up Kollwitz. Turn right on Knaack Strasse. Across from the super-trendy **Pasternak** [see *eats*, below] is the old Wasserturm (water tower), an ominous building where, it is said, Jews were concentrated and killed during the war. Turn left onto Ryke Strasse and watch the gentrification slowly creep in; some buildings are crumbling while others sparkle. Turn left on Wörther Strasse. If you're hungry, grab some-

collared shirt, leopard-spotted platform boots, and metal-studded belt you've been pining for. This place also caters to local fetishists, with leather and rubber accoutrements.

▶▶HOT COUTURE

Way, way outside the ballpark of Berlin fashion orthodoxy, in the eastern end of Mitte, **Lisa D's** *(Hackescher Höfe, Hof 4, Rosenthaler Str. 40-41; Tel 030/28-29-061; S-Bahn 3, 5, 7, 75, 9 to Hackescher Markt, U-Bahn 8 to Weinmeister Str.; Noon-6:30pm Mon-Sat; V, MC, AE)* fashions for women are colorful, political, and often bizarre; a recent collection used articles like McDonald's uniforms to parody the popularity of workmen's clothes among the leisure class. The designer herself is currently sporting her own bizarre yet elegant look, favouring colorful thirties-influenced dresses.

Back in the gray-scale world of the Berlin mainstream, on trendy Oranienburger Str., **NIX** *(Heckmann Höfe, Oranienburger Str. 32; Tel 030/283-855-77; S-Bahn 1, 2 to Oranienburger Str., U-Bahn 6 to Oranienburger Tor; Noon-8pm Mon-Fri, noon-6pm Sat, Sun; www.nix.de; V, MC)* designer Barbara Gephardt produces more commercial fashions for men, women, and ankle-biters alike and is known in the German media as the thing from the fruit stand that will be on your left. Continue straight, crossing Kollwitzplatz (don't be confused, each street around the park has the same name), keeping the park on your left, and prime people-watching cafes will be on your right. Cross Husemann Strasse, then turn left into the Kollwitzplatz park. Bear left on the path, then right, keeping the statue of Kollwitz (the park's namesake) on your right. You'll pass a small lawn that, on sunny days, fills with young sun-worshippers. Leaving the park, turn right on Knaack Strasse, then left on Wörther Strasse. You'll pass through a residential neighborhood where the buildings are newly renovated but not immune to the graffiti rash that has taken over Berlin. At Schönhauser Allee, turn left. As you reach Schwedter Strasse, notice the Alexanderplatz TV tower looming in the distance and the crosswalks. Protests convinced the government to halt its efforts to rid East Berlin of the pedestrian lights put up during Communist rule. The old lights feature a hatted man walking forward for a green light, and a hatted man with outstretched arms for a red light. Continue on Schönhauser Allee until you reach **Pfefferberg** [see *live music scene*, above], where you can sit in the beer garden of a former brewery. But like many things cool in East Berlin, the government is rumored to be considering kicking **Pfefferberg** out of its home in favor of an upscale establishment, so enjoy it while you can....

Donna Karan of Berlin. Sleek and simple in form, the NIX clothing line distinguishes itself through subtle variations: the integration of a knapsack into the back of a vest, folds in sheer cloth that create the illusion of layers, or reversible jackets lined with imitation rat fur. Fun stuff.

For a quick tour through the headgear twilight zone, check in at **Fiona Bennet** (*Grosse Hamburger Str. 25; Tel 030/280-96-330; S-Bahn 1, 2 to Oranienburger Str., S-Bahn 3, 5, 7, 75, 9 to Hackescher Markt, U-Bahn 8 to Weinmeister Str.; Noon-6pm Tue-Sat, closed Mon; V, MC, AE, Diners*), where hats ranging from strange to deranged sit framed in circular cubbyholes cut into the walls of this east-Mitte boutique. From dayglo orange Stetsons to mirror-studded skullcaps to black-horned wigs: This is the place to find the proper chapeau for any occasion, from your upscale costume party to your satanic cult gathering.

The jewelry showcased at **Fusion** (*Heckmann Höfe, Oranienburger Str. 32; Tel 030/28-38-46-83; S-Bahn 1, 2 to Oranienburger Str., U-Bahn 6 to Oranienburger Tor; 11am-8pm Tue-Fri, 11am-4pm Sat; V, MC AE*), in the same building as NIX, embodies the conflict between funk and elegance. The styles of the two designers, Alexandra Bart and Matthias Frank, are in stark contrast; Bart prefers soft, curvaceous, but clear pieces,

fashion

Fashion here is on the decline. The Berlin public's overall desire to look cool (read: not take fashion risks) has kept them in black and put local designers in the red. But don't despair—a city as large and on the move as Berlin still produces plenty of designer collections expensive enough to put a painful dent in any respectable trust fund.

whereas Frank's designs are heavy and more square-cut, with a penchant for spikes. While the prices are a bit high for finger fashion, it's worth a window-shopping trip.

▶▶THRIFT

Used duds in this city can be as dy-no-mite as Jimmy Walker on "Good Times." For a mix of new and used, hit the warehouse-like **Colours** *(Bergmann Str. 102; Tel 030/694-33-48; U-Bahn 6, 7 to Mehringdamm or Gneisenau Str.; 11am-7pm Mon-Wed, till 8pm Thur, Fri, 10am-4pm Sat; No credit cards)*, where the *License to Ill*-era Beastie Boys would have shopped had they known about it. Here in southwest Kreuzberg, you'll find feather boas, skanky suede, motorcycle jackets, and karate uniforms, as well as denim and bell bottoms galore. This place is tough to find—through a courtyard, in a building on your right, and up a flight of stairs (look for "Kleidermarkt" signs). For a similar selection, but with a 25DM-per-kilogram pricing system, head to Shöneberg's **Garage** *(Ahorn Str. 2; Tel 030/211-27-60; U-Bahn 1, 2, 4, 15 to Nollendorf Platz; 11am-7pm Mon-Wed, till 8pm Thur, Fri, 10am-4pm Sat; No credit cards)*, on a side street in the city's gay neighborhood.

Though older folk will recommend **Strasse des 17 Juni** *(S-Bahn 3, 5, 7, 75, 9 to Tiergarten or Bus 100, 187, 341)*, the mammoth flea market in the Tiergarten, we think the coolest is at **Arkonaplatz** *(U-Bahn 8 to Bernauer Str.)*, a little park in the northeast corner of Mitte. This Sunday-only market starts at 10am, later than most, because its trendy young clientele is usually just getting back from parties at that hour. Jostle with the hip natives for stylish secondhand duds, jewelry and crafts, old He-Man action figures, or ancient vinyl until nap-time at 4pm.

▶▶MALL RATS

If you're more into the Cary Grant look and have got the Ulysses S. Grants to back it up, head to **KaDeWe** *(Tauentzien Str. 21-24; Tel 030/21-21-0; U-Bahn 1, 2, 15 to Wittenberger Platz, Bus 19, 129, 146 to Wittenberger Platz; 9:30am-8pm Mon-Fri, 9am-4pm Sat; V, MC, AE, DC)*, which is an abbreviation of its full name, Kaufhaus des Westens, which means literally it is 'the' department store of the west, and in a way it is, because it is the biggest department store in Berlin and the largest in Europe outside of Harrods in London. At a whopping seven stories, this place has everything from fashion to furnishings to fine foods. If you're caught outside on a rainy day, its umbrella section is expensive but comprehensive.

▶▶TUNES

Local DJs in search of the next with-it beat head to the southwest corner of Kreuzberg to raid **Space Hall** *(Zossener Str. 33; Tel 030/694-76-64; U-Bahn 7 to Gneisenau Str.; 11am-8pm Mon, Fri, 10am-4pm Sat; V, AE, MC)*, which uses its disjointed physical space to divide up its selection. The main room features run-of-the-mill stuff, from Top 40 to mainstream dance; bins of house records, along with test-drive turntables, sit upstairs; and a little side room houses big beat, trance, Goa, and techno. The best listening station, in this final room, sits under a cardboard cutout of Bert and Ernie cuddling. If you can't find that obscure label here, head across the street to **[rc:]** *(Zossener Str. 20; Tel 030/694-78-15; U-Bahn 7 to Gneisenau Str.; 1-8pm Tue-Wed, noon-8pm Mon, Thur, Fri, noon-4pm Sat; No credit cards)*, a hole-in-the-wall vinyl dealer specializing in experimental electronic dance music and deep house, or to **Club Sound Records** *(Eberswalder Str. 32; Tel 030/449-27-03; U-Bahn 2 to Eberswalder Str.; 11am-8pm Mon-Fri, 11am-3pm Sat; No credit cards)*, a vinyl-only shop in the west end of Prenzlauer Berg where you can find great techno as well as hip hop records and DJ bags.

For used vinyl and CDs, which will run you almost as much as new disks in the U.S., try **Logo** *(Bergmann Str. 10; Tel 030/693-19-98; U-Bahn 7 to Gneisenau Str., or U-Bahn 2, 6 to Mehringdamm, or bus 19 to Bergmann Str.; Noon-7pm Mon-Fri, 11am-3pm Sat; V, MC)*, an old-style secondhand shop, just south of the Zoologischer Garten, with a surprising range of blues, jazz, sixties beat and even punk. Just start leafing through.

▶▶BOUND

A primarily German bookstore with a sizable English collection, **Marga Schoeller Bücherstube** *(Knesebeck Str. 33; Tel 030/881-11-12; S-Bahn 3, 5, 7, 9 or Bus 149 to Savigny Platz; 9:30am-7pm Mon-Wed, 9:30am-8pm Thur-Fri, 9:30am-4pm Sat; V, MC, AE)* caters to those of you itching to get your hands onto another potboiler. There's a broad and well-fleshed-out assortment of titles and enough literary obscurity to assuage even the most hard-line thin-nosed intellectual. As long on history as on charm, this quaint shop in the Savigny Platz neighborhood has been pushing paper since 1929 (and was the first location in Germany licensed to sell Penguin books after the war).

EATS

With such a strong international presence to draw on, Berlin's restaurant scene has fabulous variety and sophistication. From steak to snails to sushi, all manner of cuisine is offered before the altar of the discerning Berliner. By all means, waste no time jumping into the culinary fray, but beware of German prices—sometimes they bite back.

▶▶CHEAP

To eat a great breakfast where all the hipsters know your name (well, if your name is Dieter or Kristina...), make a morning or afternoon stop at East Berlin's **Cafe Schwarz Sauer** *(Kastanienallee 13; Tel 030/448-56-33; 8am-6am daily, food 8am-6pm; 8-12DM for breakfast; No credit cards)*. Decked out in halter tops, pedal pushers, military pants, and yellow sunglasses, the local trendoids of Prenzlauer Berg hang on this up-and-coming drag, to eat a hearty *frühstück* (breakfast) and shoot the shit with passing cyclists. Try the *klein punkte*, a breakfast basket with fresh fruits, cheeses, meats, hard-boiled eggs, peanut butter, and pastries (you choose four).

For all other occasions, Berlin's many and varied outdoor stands, called *imbiss* locally, offer great bang for your buck. Available as hole-in-the-wall snack shacks as well as the free-standing outdoor variety, *imbiss* come in many flavors: Chinese, Thai, Lebanese...but by far the most ubiquitous (and most popular) is the Turkish variety. *Doner kebab*, the signature Turkish snack, consists of a thick grilled bread stuffed with lamb shavings and cabbage, topped with mild or spicy sauce—all for the ball-park sum of 4DM.

▶▶DO-ABLE

On first inspection, Mitte's **Goa** *(Oranienburger Str. 50; Tel 030/28-59-84-51; U-Bahn 6 or Bus 157 to Oranienburger Tor, S-Bahn 1, 2 to Friedrech Str., 10am-2am Sun-Thur, till 5am Fri, Sat; 15.50-24DM per entree; V, MC, AE, Diners)* seems a rather boring, run-of-the-mill bar and restaurant. Upstairs, yes; downstairs, no. Psychedelic trance drifts up a winding staircase, which leads down to three small rooms with only an elevated wooden platform and Thai mats to sit on. Dim lighting casts deep shadows across the vaulted brick ceiling of this couples-friendly space. Be sure to wear the cleanest socks in your arsenal; there are no shoes allowed up on the platforms. The cross-mojonated Asian cuisine ranges from dim sum to Indian curry, and the lamb stir-fry is especially tasty.

For a place in East Berlin's Friedrichshain neighborhood equally suited to bringing a date or the kids, try **Donath** *(Schwedter Str. 13; Tel 030/448-01-22; U-Bahn 2 to Senefelder Platz; 9am-1am daily; 7.50-26DM per entree; No credit cards)*, a little Italian trattoria in Prenzlauer Berg with a simple but satisfying kitchen. The antipasto (with marinated mushrooms, zucchini, mozzarella, and cherry tomatoes); *tagliatelle mit rucola, frischen tomaten*, and *pecorino* (pasta with arugula, fresh tomatoes, and sharp cheese); and *spaghetti mit calamari und pulpo* (pasta with squid in tomato sauce) are surprisingly good for the cheap prices. Grab a table with a view of the trippy mural across the street.

▶▶SPLURGE

Be sure to put aside a few dead presidents for the "Real Tucker" (aka grub) at **Woolloomoolloo** *(Röntgen Str. 7; Tel 030/34-70-27-77; U-Bahn 7 to Richard-Wagner Platz, Bus 145 to Warburgzelle; Kitchen 6-11:30pm daily but open till 1am daily; 9.50-35DM per entree; No credit* *cards*), an authentic Aussie barbecue joint where large, mouth-watering dishes like "Black Stump Chicken," "Convicts Pudding," and "Borroloola Crocodile" draw a big local crowd. Yes, you heard right, they serve croc here, and ostrich, and kangaroo too, so don't waste your time with the chicken wings. In the northeast corner of the city center, Woolloomoolloo is the perfect place to mellow out in the yard area and drown a meaty 'roo steak in Fosters.

Pasternak's (*Knaack Str. 22-24; Tel 030/441-33-99; U-Bahn 2 to Senefelder Platz; 10am-2am daily; 20-30DM per entree; V*) location just off the hyper-trendy Kollwitz Platz ensures that it is packed by 9pm. Traditional dishes like beef stroganoff capture that hearty blandness so typical of Russian cuisine. For some flavor with your filler, try the borscht or the blini. Service could use a jump, but the atmosphere is pleasantly mellow. Dining gets a touch more personal on Tuesdays at 8pm, when Russian songs of love are performed.

crashing

If you're under 25 and into finding the underworld of Berlin, suck it up and hostel it for at least one night. With hordes of young people always coming through, there are hordes of entrepreneurs eager to build the coolest, cleanest, quirkiest hostel. And, with the exception of the staid St. Michaels-Heim, the people who work in these places are young and in the know; they'll give you great tips on where to go out, which, since the scenes change so quickly around here, are priceless. Our pick for best advice goes to Globetrotter Hostel Odyssee. They know more squat bars—places that will probably be shut down the following month—than any other place.

   If you pick the hotel route, you'll find clean accommodations geared toward business travelers. You'll sleep better, but is that really why you came to Berlin?

▶▶CHEAP

Well tucked away in the Friedrichshain ghetto, the **Globetrotter Hostel Odyssee** (*Grünberger Str. 23; Tel 030/29-00-00-81; U-Bahn 1, 12, 15 or S-Bahn 3, 5, 7, 75, 9 to Warschauer Str., Bus 147, 240 to Grünberger Str. Tram 20 to Grünberger Str.; www.hostel-berlin.de; 24DM 8-bed dorm, 28DM 6-bed dorm, 32DM quad, 72DM double, 96DM double room with private shower; ISIC and STA are given 5 percent discount, no long stay discounts; No credit cards*) isn't much to look at. Communal bathrooms with locker room–style showers are a bit less private than some might like; but, aside from that, it's pretty much the perfect hostel. It's owned and run completely by twentysomethings, and the needs of the young traveler—namely, to be out all night and sleep late—are well met. Checkout isn't until 1pm, and breakfast (5DM extra) lasts just as long. On the flip side, the bar, built on a long stack of munitions boxes, hawks cheap, if not good, beer all night long. The bar's mellow candlelit ambiance in the evenings makes up for the proprietors' fondness for grunge metal in the afternoon. Ask the English-speaking staff where the best clubs and live music venues and squat bars are.

While Globetrotter is the most pleasantly chill, the **Mitte's Backpackers Hostel** *(Chaussee Str. 102; Tel 030/262-51-40 or Tel 030/28-39-09-65; U-Bahn 6 to Zinnowitzer Str.; www.backpackers.de; 25-33DM dorm, 35DM quad, 38DM triple, 42DM double, 55DM single; 2DM discount on all rooms Nov-Feb, no private bathrooms, 4DM for sheets; No credit cards)*, in East Berlin's Mitte, is the perkiest and most perfectly located. Each room has a different theme, designed and decorated by longtime guests. Check out the five-bed ocean room (papier-mâché fish hang from the green ceiling), the psychedelic room, and the Berlin room, which comes complete with an Alexanderplatz TV tower lamp and has the entire city mapped out on the ceiling. Couples should ask for the "Honeymoon Suite," a floridly decorated double with hearts and lace. This 65-bed hostel has lots of convenient bonuses, like a bike rental service and a mini-travel agency, a bar that sells 4DM beers, a public kitchen with microwave and cooking supplies, and city tours, and is open 24 hours always. Bathrooms are in the halls. It has also just opened a restaurant and bar on the second floor.

St. Michaels-Heim *(Bismarckallee 23; Tel 030/896-880; Bus 110, 129 to Hertha Str., Bus 119 to Herbert Str.; 38DM per bed, breakfast à la carte; V, MC, AE)*, which was converted in 1967 from a hospital into a combo hotel and hostel, is far outside the main stream of downtown Berlin. In the Grunewald suburb, just outside Wilmersdorf, you won't need a car to get into town, but there can be a wait for the bus at night. A screening room taken over by a neighborhood film club shows old black and white pictures on Mondays, and the church room/concert hall holds frequent performances of classical, spiritual, and folk music. All in all, the crowd is about as wild and crazy as your grandma's Wednesday mah-jongg game. Just the same, everything's well kept, and if quiet and relaxed is your bag, look no further. The extra bucks for the hotel buy a free breakfast, private toilet and shower, and a TV in your room.

▶▶**DO-ABLE**

Hotel Hansablick *(Flotow Str. 6; Tel 030/390-48-00; S-Bahn 3, 5, 7, 75, 9 to Tiergarten, U-Bahn 9 to Hansa Platz; 160DM single, 195-235DM double; www.hotel-hansablick.de; V, MC, AE, Diners)* is a charming *pensione* on a quiet tree-lined block just off the Tiergarten, still in walking distance of Zoo Station. A true turn-of-the-century marble entry hall contrasts with sharply modern Ikea-esque rooms, all 29 of which come fully equipped with private bathroom and shower. Continental breakfast is included, naturally. Buffet.

▶▶**SPLURGE**

The most playful hotel on this list, and the one stocked with the most amenities, is **Holiday Inn Center-East** *(Prenzlauer Allee 169; Tel 030/44-66-10; S-Bahn 4, 8, 10 or Tram 1 to Prenzlauer Allee; 190-280DM single, 230-320DM double, 50DM per extra bed, all with private* *bathrooms; V, MC, AE, DC).* In the last year, the management has actually toned down the decor, aiming for a slightly older crowd, but it's still funky and modern. Each room is sound-proofed, with a coffee maker and private shower. There's also a fitness center and laundry service available. The huge American-style buffet breakfast costs 25DM per person.

need to know

Currency Exchange The **Deutschmark (DM)** is the national currency, which is subdivided into *pfennig*. Most banks offer currency exchange services, but the street exchange bureaus, called **Weschelstuben**, provide the best rates.

Tourist Offices The **Berlin Tourist Information Center, Berlin Tourismus Marketing** *(Europa-Center, Budapester Str.; Tel 030/250-025; 8:30am-8:30pm Mon-Sat, 10am-6pm Sun and holidays)*, is in the Europa-Center, a quick walk from the Bahnhof Zoo, the main train station. There is another office *(Brandenburg Gate; 9:30am-6pm Mon-Sun)* in Berlin's east side, in the Mitte district. Both offices will make hotel reservations or book theater tickets, and ask for voluntary contributions of 5DM. There is a direct line for reservations *(Tel 018/05-75-*

CITY WITHIN A CITY

Arabic music undulates from open windows, olive-skinned kids career through the streets on their bikes, and there are more *doner kebab* stands than you can shake a spit at. Welcome to Kreuzberg, the Berlin neighborhood known as "Little Istanbul," which has a higher concentration of Turkish immigrants than anywhere else in Germany.

Before Russia lost the Cold War, Kreuzberg leaned against the Berlin Wall, the last neighborhood separating capitalism from communism. Its cheap rents and empty buildings made it a haven for squatters, punks, and May Day rioters. And although the district has since lost its alternative mantle to Friedrichshain, to the north, the grungy feel remains. Kreuzberg has gone trendy in some places, such as Bergmann Strasse and Oranien Strasse, but many streets are still residential and pretty run down. The Turkish denizens live in relative harmony with the remaining ruffians, tending their fruit and kebab stands, second-hand furniture shops, and neighborhood bars. To soak in the exotic atmosphere, hang out with locals clad in traditional Muslim garb at any of the small parks (such as Oranienplatz [see *great outdoors*, above]), visit the Turkish markets on **Maybach Ufer** *(U-Bahn 1, 8, 15 to Kottbusser Tor)*, or just walk through the streets.

east berlin

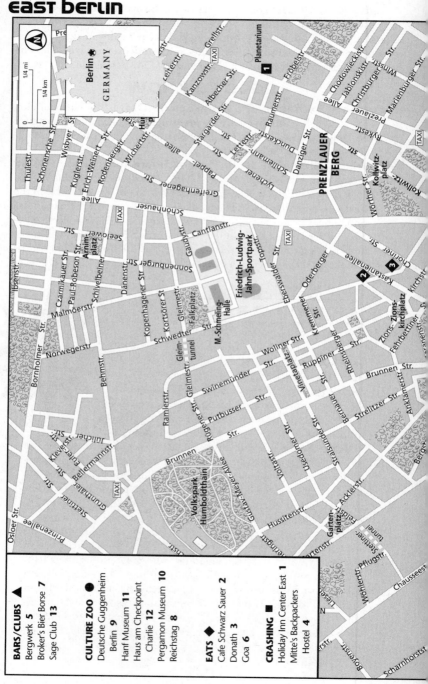

BARS/CLUBS ▲
Bergwerk **5**
Broker's Bier Borse **7**
Sage Club **13**

CULTURE ZOO ●
Deutsche Guggenheim
  Berlin **9**
Hanf Museum **11**
Haus am Checkpoint
  Charlie **12**
Pergamon Museum **10**
Reichstag **8**

EATS ◆
Cafe Schwarz Sauer **2**
Donath **3**
Goa **6**

CRASHING ■
Holiday Inn Center East **1**
Mitte's Backpackers
  Hostel **4**

40-40 *from abroad; Tel 030/25-00-25 from within Germany).* For tourist information only, ring 019/001-63-16 from within Germany.

Public Transportation Berlin and its surrounds are linked by a network of subways, trams, and buses, run by the **BVG** *(Tel 030/194-49).* Maps are available at the tourist offices, most subway stations, and within all trams and buses. U-Bahn (underground) and S-Bahn (inner-city railway) stations are identified by a large U or S. Tickets are good for any public transportation and can be purchased as single rides, in strips, good for multiple rides, or as day passes, as week passes and also for small groups. Be sure to validate your tickets as you enter a rapid transit station, tram, or bus; random spot checks can be costly (at 60DM) for the unprepared. Public transportation runs from around 4am to half past twelve at night. Taxi dispatcher: *26-10-26.*

American Express *Bayreuther Str. 37-38; Tel 032/21-47-63-01 (for queries about foreign exchange), or 069/97-97-10-00 (for lost cards); U-bahn 1 to Wittenberg Platz; 9am-6pm Mon-Fri, 10am-1pm Sat.*

Health and Emergency Police: *110*; fire/paramedic: *112*; pharmaceutical emergencies: *01-141*; poison control: *4505-3555.*

Pharmacies Pharmacies can be recognized by the red A, for *apotheke.* At least one pharmacy is open all night in each neighborhood; a sign in every pharmacy's window will give you the address of the one on call.

Telephone Country code: *49*; area code: *030*; local operator: *11-883*; international operator: *00-118.* **AT&T**: *013-000-10*; **MCI**: *013-000-12*; **Sprint**: *013-000-13.*

Airports Tegel Airport is in Reinickendorf, northwest of the city center *Tel (01805/000-186)* is served by train [see below] as well as by buses 109, 128, and X9. **Tempelhof Airport** is in Tempelhof, just south of Kreuzberg *(Information: 018/05-00-01-86).* Both airports are accessible via the **U-Bahn 6** line *(single-ride ticket 4.50DM).*

Airlines Lufthansa *(Tel 018/03-80-38-03),* and **British Airways** *(018/05-26-65-22)* both fly into Berlin.

Trains Bahnhof Zoo is Berlin's hub for points west, while **Bahnhof Lichtenberg** controls most departures and arrivals from the East. For information, call **Deutsche Bahn** *(Tel 030/194-19).*

Buses Central Bus Station *(Messedamm 8; Tel 030/301-80-28; 5:30am-9:30pm Mon-Sat).*

munich

In all its debauched glory, Munich is the place foreigners conjure up when they imagine Germany. This Bavarian capital has it all: Fat guys in *lederhosen* really do heft one-liter steins of beer and belt out songs of drunken revelry; oompah-pah bands actually honk along with meals; the average household eats more sausage than Jimmy Dean's family; and a breakfast of salty pretzels is a way of life. There is something comforting about finding the expected in foreign lands, and Munich truly lives up to its idyllic stereotype, with enough old-world charms to give you that warm and fuzzy feeling. And for the most part, this traditional stuff isn't just touristy kitsch. Hit a beer garden on a sunny day, and you'll find yourself happily clinking mugs with students and lawyers, stroller-pushing parents, and German hipsters.

But tradition alone wouldn't pull in so many culture-jonesing twenty-somethings. Munich is also home to industrial giants Siemens and BMW, countless publishing firms, and major universities. Behind Berlin, it's the place to be in Germany, drawing cool kids and wannabes from across the country. The uniformly shag-adelic *Schicki-Mickis* (i.e. chic, black-clad yuppies), the hip hop crews, the well-pierced metalheads—all find nocturnal homes here in a startling range of clubs, bars, and restaurants. Case in point: the massive **Kunstpark Ost** [see *kunstpark ost*, below], a 30-nightclub complex that keeps on chugging despite everyone's predictions that it'll get lame. So please, peel yourself away from an obligatory appearance at the legendarily overrated **Hofbräuhaus** [see *eats*, below], and see the real city. To find it, check out the English-language *Munich Found*, published 10 times a year, for restaurant and bar recommendations. Though slightly harder to find than *Munich Found*, the **Insomnia** guide gives tips on trendy hangouts (be warned: its reviews sometimes wander into the overly bubbly). Plus, it has city maps, describes places in English and German, and fits into your back pocket. Look for it in random hotel lobbies. The tourist office's **Young People's Guide** lists everything from youth hostels to skate parks to bars, in English. If none of those are working for you, pick up the biweekly German-language mag **In München**; work your way through the umlauts, and you'll find listings of upcoming concerts and club parties.

Walking past the manicured lawns and regal buildings, it's almost impossible to imagine that it was just a half-century ago that Allied bombs rained down on this city, reducing it to rubble. Out of this devastation, post-WWII Munich rebuilt itself into a handsome, stinking-rich cosmopolitan hub—and yes, that does mean that prices on everything from beer to hotel rooms are through the old roof. It's probably not a coincidence that, until you get a beer in their hands, Müncheners are uptight as hell. Bump into someone on the street and prepare for the evilest of eyes. Stand on the left side of the escalator, and you will get cursed and barreled over. But once the boozing begins, curses give way to drinking songs, invitations to sit, and, who knows, maybe even a polka.

neighborhoods

Munich looks huge on paper, but it's really pretty manageable. **Alstadt** is the historic downtown and present heart of Munich. It's shaped like a big kidney bean, fenced in by the **Hofgarten** [see *great outdoors*, below] to the north, the **Thomas Wilmer Ring Highway** to the east, **Frauenstrasse** and **Blumenstrasse** to the south, and **Sonnenstrasse** to the west (remember that *platz* means "square" and *strasse* means "street"). Hoofing it across the center would take a good 25 minutes, but the great subway system (the U-Bahn) whisks you around quickly.

Marienplatz, a cobblestone square lined with ornate government buildings, sits in the center of Alstadt. Running west to the Hauptbahnhof (the main train station) is **Kaufingerstrasse**, a 5-minute walk or one S-Bahn (tram) stop from Marienplatz, a busy pedestrian shopping street where you can buy new shoes at a trendy boutique or get conned into buying a high-tech garlic press by street vendors. Just to the north of Marienplatz, and definitely still part of the downtown glamour, lie **Theatinerstrasse** (running north-south) and **Maximilianstrasse** (running east-west), offering high-class fashions by illustrious international designers. Theatinerstrasse runs up to the well-manicured Hofgarten.

Head northeast up majestic **Ludwigstrasse** from Alstadt, and regal grandeur gives way to the gentrified-though-fun-if-you-can-afford-it district called **Schwabing** (*U-Bahn to Universität, two U-Bahn stops from Marienplatz*), which hardcore *Wayne's World* fans can gleefully pronounce *Schwa-biiiing!* Once home to starving-artist types like Thomas Mann, this area around the university is now *Schicki-Micki*-ville and is packed with pricey cafes and shops....To the south of Marienplatz is **Gärtner-**

platz *(a 10-minute walk from Marienplatz)*, a district around the square of the same name, which is, unsurprisingly, the hub of local gay life and the city's trendiest area....Head east across the **Isar River** to reach **Haidhausen** *(two S-Bahn stops from Marienplatz)*, home to most of the starving artists, both young and old, who can't afford Schwabing.

The stunning palace **Schloss Nymphenburg** [see *culture zoo*, below] and its gardens sit way to the west of downtown *(three U-Bahn stops from Hauptbahnhof)*.

The **U-Bahn** services the city proper; the **S-Bahn**, which goes through the city center, reaches into the suburbs. Added bonus for travelers: Trips on the S-Bahn are covered by your Eurail pass. If you're in town for a few days, it's best to buy a 10-pass strip ticket (it's the same ticket for both Bahns), called a *streifenkarte*, which costs 16DM. Punch one ticket for trips of less than three stops and two strips for longer rides within the city. Don't punch again for two hours unless you reverse directions. A day pass, called a *tageskarte*, will run you 9DM for city-only travel and 18DM for a pass that includes suburban trips. The subway is on the honor system, but plainclothes subway cops sometimes make the rounds. They'll fine you 60DM if you don't have a valid ticket, and no, being a dumb tourist is no excuse.

hanging OUT

There are two sure ways to find people to hang out with: Follow the food or follow the sun. Fellow travelers, from the backpacking college kid to the aging CEO, cling to the touristic **Hofbraühaus** [see *eats*, below] like flies on stank. Sure, the place is fun, just don't expect to see any real Germans hanging out here. The justly renowned **Oktoberfest** [see *festivals and events*, below] also teems with outsiders in search of that true German experience. The other 11 months of the year, travelers take their yearning for all things Bavarian to Marienplatz and the neighboring **Viktualienmarkt** [see *eats*, below], where they jostle with locals for fresh fruits and meat sandwiches.

The best place to hang with Bavarians both young and old is invariably outside. Müncheners need no excuse to hit the great outdoors, especially when the snowy winters come to a close in April, and a few travelers certainly won't keep the locals away from their city parks or beer gardens. The mammoth **Englischer Garten** [see *great outdoors*, below], bigger than New York's Central Park, is the Old Faithful of the parks. The well-groomed 17th-century royal **Hofgarten** [see *great outdoors*, below] draws old men to play *boules* in front of the historic stables. Have a beer and pretzel under leafy chestnut trees, then head to the trendy Seehaus or the more traditional **Chinesischer Turm** [see *beer gardens*, below], both in the Englischer Garten.

For a hefty afternoon *milchkaffe* (milk coffee, i.e., latte), chill with the Nietzsches-in-training at **Cafe Reitschule** *(Königin Str. 34; Tel 089/333-402; U-Bahn 3, 6 to Universität; 9am-1am daily; V, MC, AE, DC)*, a student cafe nestled on a side street between the university and the Englischer

five things to talk to a local about

1. **Bavaria** is Germany's wealthiest state, and it seems that our rich Munich friends aren't too eager to share the prosperity with their compatriots. The spendfest going on in Berlin is a great topic of conversation and an easy way to weed out the socialist holdovers from the nouveau capitalists.

2. **Skiing, canoeing, swimming, cycling, hiking**...Müncheners love it all. This would be the time to bust out that story about the time you got jacked by a bear on that kayaking trip down the Colorado River....

3. **Beer**. Right about now, you're probably asking yourself why these crazy travel writers won't shut up about German beer. Come here, and our motives will become crystal clear. Discuss the foamy head, ask questions about various ways to toast, memorize the lyrics to a drinking song.

4. **Schwabing or Haidhausen**—What kind of person are you? Schwabing is the artists' quarter of Munich legend, spawning such prolific thinkers as Thomas Mann, of *Death in Venice* fame. But an influx of fashion editors and models have driven the starving artists across the Isar River into the Haidhausen district. The university sits in the heart of Schwabing, but most students can't afford to live in Schwabing, so a thorough bitching about Schwabing's yuppie-fying will earn you brownie points.

5. **Short, chubby weisswurst vs. foot-long bratwurst** ("the slender contender"): Does size really matter?

Garten. Leaf casually through a newspaper, shoot the shit about a philosophy class, or pose with your cigarette pointed heavenward.

After most sane people have gone to bed, the hardcore partiers congregate at the **Mandarin Lounge** [see *gay scene*, below] and **Milch und Bar** [see *bar scene*, below] for weekend after-hours parties that don't break up until lunchtime. For some late-night grub ranging from French fries to sausage, head to **Nachtcafe** [see *live music scene*, below], which doesn't close until 6am.

bar scene

Beer gardens (*biergarten*) are a blast, but there are a ton of bars to pick up the slack when it rains, when you're sick of beer, or when the gardens close for the night. Munich's bars have no government-mandated closing time, so they shut down whenever they feel like it. Late weekend nights cater to the two-left-feet crowd, the people who don't feel like migrating to the discos to sweat until dawn. Cocktails are shockingly expensive, so seek out the half-price happy hours at such places as **Sausalitos** [see *eats*, below], Günther Murphy's, or Sax [see below for both].

The earnest shirt-and-tie attire of the bartenders is a sure sign that the **Havana Club** *(Herren Str. 30; Tel 089/29-18-84; Any S-Bahn to Isartor; 6pm-1am Mon-Wed, 6pm-2am Thur-Sun; V, MC, AE)* takes its cocktails seriously. This dark Cubano bar, two blocks southeast of the Hofbräuhaus, has earned a well-deserved reputation as home to the best mixed drinks in Munich. A top-ten list clues travelers in to the hottest local drinks. Try the absolutely smashing "La Floridita," made with seven-year-old Havana Club rum and maraschino, just sweet and sour enough to tweak the lips. *Schicki-Mickis* pack this place to the gills on Friday and Saturday nights; we recommend weekday evenings when it's just you, a few trendy locals, and the Hemingway portrait looking over the bartenders' shoulders.

The place where you're most likely to hear the line, "Uh, hey baby, wanna see my bratwurst?" would be **Milch und Bar** *(Grafinger Str. 6; Tel 089/49-00-35-17; 10pm-5:30am Mon, 10pm-6am Wed, Thur, 10pm-10am Fri, Sat, closed Tue, Sun; Free-10DM cover; V, MC, AE, Diners)*, Kunstpark Ost's hottest pickup scene. More raucous than Havana Club, this place is a total meat market, but only prime Grade A beef is on parade. As one local writer put it, "Only a cow is filled with more beverages and hormones." When your third wind kicks in, head here for the famous after-hours party, 5am till 9am Saturday and Sunday. Bust out the preppy button-down collars to fit in.

For a more intimate drink, head to Alstadt, venture down a steep staircase into the depths of **Master's Home** *(Frauen Str. 11; Tel 089/229-9909; U-Bahn 3, 6 or any S-Bahn to Marienplatz or S-Bahn 17, 18 to Reichenbachplatz; 6pm until 3am daily; V, MC, AE, DC)*, a dusky replica of a British Colonial manor. This Master guy's got a pretty sweet crib, with a library, bedroom, and bathroom right there for you to enjoy. Chill out on the feathery bed or the rim of the turn-of-the-century bathtub. Hit this bar later in the night or after the "After-work hour" when customers

fIVE-O

Highbrow Munich is about order and civility (Oktoberfest aside), and the cops don't dig people who forget that. There's little serious crime here, so cops preoccupy themselves with cracking down on rowdiness. With the SS days gone but not forgotten, it can be a frightening experience to have an angry, uniformed German bearing down on you. At the same time, the sensitivity about Nazi atrocities leaves cops, more than 50 years later, placing a big premium on personal rights. They're not going to haul you away unless they don't see any other way to calm you down.

get a free evening meal when they order a cocktail: The expensive cocktails (8.50-20DM) go further, and the place loses the campiness that's more apparent to the sober.

You know how some cafes just seem to draw the beautiful people? Everyone else goes to **Günther Murphy's** *(Nikolai Str. 9; Tel 089/398-911; U-Bahn 3, 6 to Gisela Str. or Münchener Freiheit; 5pm-1am Mon-Fri, 2pm-3am Sat, noon-1am Sun; www.gunther-murphys.com; V, MC, AE)*, where you can forget about crowd-watching and just have a blast. Check your pretense at the door of this brick-walled Irish pub in Schwabing. Brits and English-speaking Müncheners down Guinness pints (7.80DM) and scream over a cacophony of deafening American pop music. The kitchen, which stays open until 10 or 11 every night, serves up traditional Irish stew and American standards like cheeseburgers. Cocktails are half price during the 5 to 9pm daily happy hour. Sunday night at 9 is the kind of full-blown karaoke that only drunk Brits and Korean businessmen can pull off.

A slow, mellow hang in the afternoon, with plenty of outdoor seating, **Sax** *(Hans-Sachs Str. 5; Tel 089/268-835; U-bahn 17, 18, 27; 10am-1am Sun-Thur, till 3am Fri, Sat; No credit cards)* busies up in time for its happy hour from 10pm till 1am Sunday through Thursday, and 12pm till 3am on Fridays and Saturdays. A mixed crowd mills about this Gärtnerplatz neighborhood appreciating paintings of naked, copulating trolls and drinking beer (which is cheap at under 5DM) and *galao*, a thick Portuguese coffee. Tuesdays from 8pm till 1am a DJ spins cosmic music, an electronic blend of African percussion and native Brazilian sounds. Venture downstairs to experience Kegel Bahn, the German version of bowling that uses small balls and tall, skinny pins. You can rent the single lane by the hour, and, like bowling in any language, it straddles the line between cool and lame.

LIVE MUSIC SCENE

If you come to Munich expecting to find the next Sonic Youth, you'll go home disappointed, because there are few new music forms developing in this city. That said, it's certainly not tough to find some good tunes, in whatever genre you're craving. Musicians here, from jazz to funk to rock, do their homework and throw together some respectable party grooves. Munich's position as the ultimate cultural hub in Germany, coupled with its richesse, also pulls in top international acts nearly every weekend. Most live music spots double as DJ-led dance clubs on off nights.

A little hip-hop, a little dork rock, a little electronica, **Muffathalle** *(Zell Str. 4; Tel 089/45-87-50-00; S-Bahn to Isartor or Rosenheimer Platz, Tram-bahn 18 to Deutsches Museum; www.muffathalle.de; No credit cards)* is the multi-groove palace for indie bands and cult favorites. Recent drop-ins include the Buena Vista Social Club and Uriah Heep. London's Ninja Tune record label loves to ship drum 'n' bass groups down here for weekend stints. Lesser-known groups play in the Muffathalle Cafe, a tiny room next door to the music hall. In their programs, which are scattered throughout the city, look for the sent-from-God *Fun for Free* nights, where bands as legendary as Sebadoh play for no cover charge. On the DJ tip, reggae and ragga Tuesdays (10pm-4am) and hip-hop Thursdays (11pm-4am) draw an 18-to-30 crowd; acid jazz Fridays (11pm-5am) pull in late-twentysomethings; and drum 'n' bass Saturdays (11pm-6am) pull in a young twenties crowd.

It's all about stale leather pants and underground bands at **Backstage** *(Helmholtz Str. 18; Tel 089/126-61-00; S-Bahn to Dondnersberg-erbrüke; Opening and closing times vary, 10pm-5am Fri, Sat; www.backstage089.de; Free-10DM cover; No credit cards)*, a little club complex in an old railroad yard out to the west of Hauptbahnhof. The live music changes nightly, from hip-hop to glam rock to goth to reggae to punk rock. Famous German bands sometimes pop in incognito to rock this metal shed, playing to Lollapalooza-like crowds. The website or the concert program, available in record stores around the city, will tell you which night is your bag. Concerts usually cost from 13 to 25DM. During the Saturday *Freak Out* parties (10DM), a DJ spins Brit pop and grunge in the main shed, '60s rock moves a small crowd in the outdoor beer garden, and metalheads mosh inside a small club dubbed Aluminum. To find this place from the S-Bahn, take the first escalator on your right, turn right down the dark road, then follow the green hair and train tracks about 200 yards.

A dreaded fate has befallen **Jazzclub Unterfahrt** *(Einstein Str. 42; Tel 089/448-27-94; U-Bahn 4, 5 to Max-Weber-Platz; 7:30pm-1am Sun-Thur, till 3am Fri, Sat; 8-30DM cover; www.jazzrecords.com/unterfahrt; No credit cards)*. Once a deliciously dark and dingy musicians' hangout, it was moved by its entrepreneurial owner to a shiny-happy new club,

junge meets mädchen

Scoring with a local hottie can be a daunting task in Munich's ice-queen and ice-king culture. It's just not an outwardly sexy place. People keep their distance when they talk, and hands don't go roaming during conversations. The good news is that there's little room for mistaking someone's intentions—if they want to get it on, they'll let you know. The matchmaking scene has two very different settings: in nature or in bars. Müncheners are easily engaged in conversation while seated on the grass or a beer garden bench, but the next step is to invite them for a drink that night. That's where the real scene begins, where the alcohol gets flowin' and the locals go ho'in'. One-night stands are pretty commonplace. And the pickup scene is progressive: If *die torte* (the foxy lady) is interested, she'll ask guys for their number or invite them home.

munich bars, clubs and culture zoo

Berlin ★
GERMANY

Munich
●

BARS/CLUBS ▲
Backstage **1**
Club **3**
Havana Club **16**
Hotel Bayerischer
  Hof **13**
Jazzclub Unterfahrt **23**
Kunstpark Ost **22**
Master's Home **17**
Club Morizz **19**
Muffathalle **21**
Nachtcafe **8**
Nachtwerk **2**
New York **5**
Ododo **20**
Sax **6**
Soul City **7**
Vogler **18**

CULTURE ZOO ●
Alte Pinakothek **10**
Antikensammlungen **9**
Deutches Museum **4**
Frauenkirche **14**
Neue Pinakothek **11**
The Residenz **15**
Schloss Nymphenburg **12**

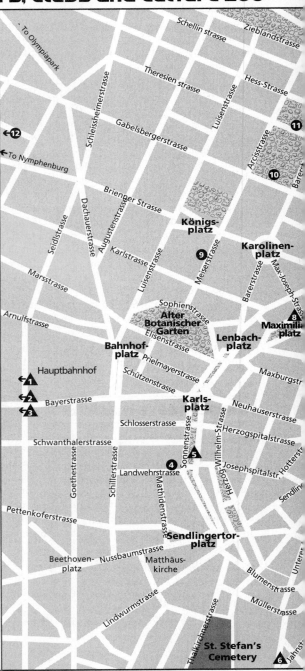

E-0253

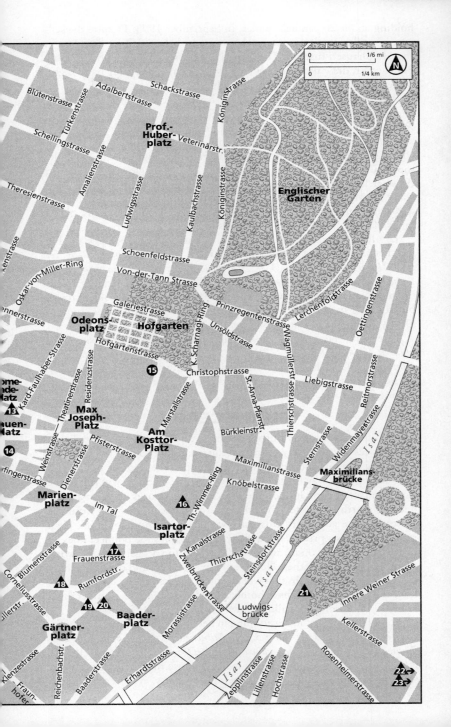

holding about 20 candlelit tables, in September 1998. Despite the sellout, it's still a good place to catch consistent bebop and modern jazz in the Haidhausen district. The Sunday night sessions, which cost only 8DM cover, draw the youngest crowds. Monday night is big band night, sometimes featuring 18-person ensembles.

The down-and-out musician scene has been transplanted to **Vogler** (*Rumford Str. 17; Tel 089/294-662; S-Bahn to Isartor or Tram 17, 18 to Reichenbackplatz; 7pm-1am Mon-Wed, till 3am Thur-Sat, closed Sun; Free-10DM cover; No credit cards*), an up-and-coming jazz bar in the up-and-coming Gärtnerplatz district. Music is free most nights—10DM is the tops you'll pay to get in. Instead of the bright white glow at Unterfahrt, the stage here is lit by dull red spots. The L-shaped club fills quickly, especially during Monday jam sessions when young cats rip through standards and on Fridays and Saturdays when live bands come and play a range of music from soul to jazz, blues to Latin.

Jazz legends making their European tours inevitably follow the big paychecks to **Hotel Bayerischer Hof** (*Promenadeplatz 2-6; Tel 089/212-09-94; U-Bahn 3, 4, 5, 6 to Odeonsplatz; 10pm-3am daily; www.bayerischerhof.de; Free-18DM; V, MC, AE, DC*), in Alstadt. This is the most upscale of the city's clubs and generally draws an older crowd, but it's tops in Munich for pulling in world-class musicians, such as Dewey Redman and Randy Brecker.

Late night, check out the usually happening **Nachtcafe** (*Maximillianplatz 5; Tel 089/59-59-00; U-Bahn 4, 5 to Karlsplatz or Odeonsplatz; 9pm-6am daily; MC, V, AE*), over on Maximillianplatz, where everyone from TV stars to leather-wearing grandmothers check in for no-cover live bands playing funk, Latin, or rock.

club scene

Munich is known for its finicky doormen and "regulars only" policies. Some places have one-way mirrors at the front door so that the bouncers can check you out and decide whether to open the door or not—good luck talking your way in when you can't even see them. If you run into a closed mirrored door, lurk on the sides until the door is open for a party deemed worthy, then tell the bouncer you came all the way from the States because you heard this club was just so damn happenin'. He'll probably say it's a private, but a glimpse of the folks the bouncer does let in you might help you formulate a game plan to try again the following night. Luckily, a lot of these "locals only" places suck, and there are plenty of really good dance clubs that will let you in on the fun. As a general rule, leave the sneakers and jeans at home, and whatever you do, don't let them know if you're bombed. Falling-down drunks won't get in anywhere.

Ebony meets ivory and everything in between at **Skyline** (*Leopold Str. 82; Tel 089/333-131; U-Bahn 3, 6 to Münchener Freiheit; 8pm-4am Tue-Thur, till 5am Fri, Sat, Sun, closed Mon; 10DM cover at weekend; V, MC, AE*). This cocktail bar, a scenic four floors above the Hertie department store in Schwabing, hosts a raging hip-hop party every Friday night.

Shortly after 12:30am, funky acid jazz is replaced by thumping hip-hop, and, in a scene reminiscent of the first awkward hour of a high-school dance, the poindexters are eventually joined on the floor by sweating masses. Saturday nights draw a smaller and slightly older crowd with standard house music, but Thursday and Sunday night's salsa party are the best jams of the week. Happy hour, when all cocktails are 8.50DM, is from 8:30 till 9:30pm daily, except for Tuesday which is Happy Night all night.

If you want to set aside the bullshit and just dance, head out west of Hauptbahnhof to **Nachtwerk** *(Landsberger Str. 185; No phone; S-Bahn to Dondnersbergerbrücke, Tram 17, 18 to same; 10pm-4am Fri, Sat, first and third Tue, Sun, only when advertised; www.nachtwerk.de; 10-13DM cover; No credit cards)*, by far the most unpretentious (and hence least stylish) dance club in Munich. The hundreds of high school and college kids bopping around to Britney Spears and the *Grease* soundtrack break no new ground, but the energized vibe is contagious. Coca-Cola and McDonald's banners give the place a relaxed, thrown-together Mcfeel. The first and third Tuesday of the month is student night, with an incredible 1DM-beer special. Forget about a dress code—if you've got the money, they'll let you in.

The jack-of-all-musics dance club, also out beyond Hauptbahnhof, is **Babylon** *(Grafinger Str. 6; Tel 089/40-00-29-28; U-Bahn 5, any S-Bahn to Ostbahnhof; 11pm-6am Fri, Sat; www.babylon-online.de; 10-15DM cover; No credit cards)*, where rubber-clad club kids come to play it cool and regular jeans-wearing party-goers come to feel cool. You enter into an enormous bar lined with seats and pinball machines that's throbbing like an irregular heartbeat, as competing sounds from the flanking dance floors leak through the walls. Head right, and you'll find yourself in a pseudo-rave, a giant techno hall complete with laser lights and go-go dancers. Head left, and you'll join the hand-waving masses singing along

RULES OF THE GAME

The legal drinking age in Munich is 18 or 16, if you're accompanied by the 'rents. Some places that score big with teeny-boppers actually do check IDs, so bring your passport with you if your boyish/girlish charms leave any doubt that you're of age. Drinking is allowed anywhere in the city: No one will bother you if you grab a seat on the grass and crack open a cold one, but it's not something regularly done here. Marijuana and hash are legal—sort of. It's legal to carry around a small amount (just enough for personal consumption), but it's illegal to sell it on the street. Müncheners tend to spark up *die tuete* (the joint) outdoors, in the fresh air of parks, or in alleys next to bars. Lighting a fat doobie after a nice meal at a restaurant is not very cool at all.

kunsтраrk ost

If you build it, they will come. Featuring more than 30 bars, clubs, skate parks, and climbing walls, **Kunstpark Ost** *(Grafinger Str. 6; U-Bahn 5 or any S-Bahn to Ostbahnhof; www.kunstpark.de)* is like a Disney World for the party generation. One club owner estimated that half of the thousands that flock here every weekend are from Munich proper; the other half are suburban kids looking for some bright lights, big city. Teeny-boppers, clubbers, hip-hoppers, and metalheads alike find it in this little youth ecosystem, set in a sprawling factory that for years processed potato dumplings. Step out of the S-Bahn or U-Bahn 5 and follow the breadcrumb trail of party fliers to Grafinger Strasse 6. From there, use signs on buildings to find places.

The biggest problem with KO is deciding which places to hit. Most have a 10DM cover, so hopping around can leave your pocket empty fast. Best to do some pre-visit homework on their website or in the free KO magazine, which is scattered around the city. Keep your eyes peeled for flyers advertising the *Party Zone*, which happens one weekend night every few months, when 17 to 20DM buys you entrance into every club and bar.

While other places are still warming up, the fake-ID and barely legal crowd is dancing on tables at **Wies'n World** *(Tel 089/40-90-72-60; 7pm-3am Thur, Fri, till 4am Sat; 10DM cover, includes a 5DM*

to '80s tunes. In the bar, a video feed lets you see what you're missing on the dance floors. The door staff isn't discriminating; just look put-together and sober.

The local house music crown goes to **Kraftwerk** *(Grafinger Str. 6; Tel 089/49-91-88-25; U-Bahn 5 or any S-Bahn to Ostbahnhof; 11pm-7am Fri, Sat; www.kw-club.de; 10-230DM cover; No credit cards)*, known as KW (pronounce Kah-Vay). This place used to be the power plant of the factory that is now Kunstpark Ost, and it's true to its history, generating hard-pumping dance tunes. Look for no fewer than nine disco balls. Friday is techno and trance night, which pulls in a smaller, more focused late teens/early twenties crowd. Saturday night is when the pulchritudinous, well-dressed posses parade in, dancing to some of the best house DJs from London, the States, and Italy—names like Tony Humphries, Junior Vasquez, and, all joking aside, the former front man for Culture Club. "Boy George throws the best parties," one employee says. "The music is very noisy, so you have to get used to it, but he just puts his hand in the air and everyone goes crazy." On Friday, leave the jeans and sneaks at home to get in. On Saturday, *really* break out the finery: Leather and rubber make you a shoo-in.

Nachtwerk's bad-boy brother, located on the same lot, is the techno drink; *No credit cards)*, aka Little Oktoberfest. Waving their beer steins and screaming along to Schlagermusic (think "99 Luftballons") and disco, these teeny-boppers are joined by an older, scruffy crowd after 10pm. Their infectious, who-gives-a-f*%k style of partying has earned this place a solid reputation at KO. Thursday is karaoke night—woo-hoo!

Der Keller *(Tel 089/49-04-21-0; 11pm-3am Mon-Sat; 8-18DM cover; No credit cards)* is home to the resident grunge and new-wave rockers, where Frank Zappa is memorialized on the walls, and the *Depeche Mode Club* spins synth classics every Tuesday night.

Incognito [see *live music scene*, above] and **Mr. Bongo's Bongo Bar** *(Tel 089/49-00-12-60; 10pm-3am Wed, Thur, till 4am Fri, Sat; 10-25DM cover; No credit cards)* draw great international bands: both ones you know and ones you'll hear about soon enough. To get your swerve on to hot DJs, check out **Kraftwerk** (aka KW) and **Babylon** [see *club scene*, above, for both]. To hear the latest in German pickup lines, hit high-class swinging **Milch und Bar** [see *bar scene*, above]. This place is at its most happening during the after-hours parties, from 6am till 10am Friday and Saturday.

joint **Club** *(Landsberger Str. 185; No phone; S-Bahn to Dondnersberger-brücke; Tram 18, 19 to Barth Str.; 10pm-4am Mon, Wed-Sat; ww.nachtwerk.de; 10-15DM cover; No credit cards)*, where a well-stocked and pricey bar sits beneath a sheet-metal balcony that looks like liquid mercury. The DJ spins house music on Wednesday nights. It's less discriminating than KW, especially on Saturday, but still draws dancers who understand what techno's all about.

gay scene

Munich, disappointingly enough, does not clock in as a gay heavyweight like Berlin or Cologne. It may be that the traditionally conservative Bavarian mind-set nurtures an unfortunate case of queer fear—in any event, be careful where you enjoy open PDA. Home base for gay citizens, the Gärtnerplatz neighborhood, between Isartor and Sendlinger Tor, is also one of Munich's youngest and fastest-growing areas. Trendy new restaurants, art galleries, and bars are popping up all along Rumford Strasse, Müller Strasse, and Baader Strasse. You can check in most bars and clubs for free copies of *Rosa Seiten* (the Pink Pages), a thick listing of the city's gay and gay-friendly establishments: piercing shops, leather bars, bathhouses, etc. It's in German, but the important words (e.g., disco, bar, cafe, sauna, sex shop) are the same as in English. Find the publication online at ***www.rosaseiten.com***.

One of Gärtnerplatz's hippest new spots, **Ododo** *(Buttermelcher Str. 6; Tel 089/260-77-41; Any S-Bahn to Isartor, U-Bahn 1, 2 to Fraunhofer Str.; 11:30am-4:30pm/6pm-1am daily, till 3am Fri, Sat; V, MC, AE, Diners)* has a young, attractive clientele that lingers somewhere between gay and straight. Cool electronic funk, like a smoothed-out mating of George Clinton and Björk, goes well with the small, metallic-gray steel-and-stucco room. Cocktails are good, but in the 15DM range, they damn well better be. An animated dinner crowd eats off of sectional, TV-dinner-style plates and ignores the tiny LCD video screens inset into the walls.

Land of the lounge lizard, Haidhauser's **Club Morizz** *(Klenze Str. 43; Tel 089/201-67-76; U-Bahn 1, 2 to Fraunhofer Str.; 7pm-2am daily, till 3am Fri, Sat; MC)* trades Ododo's steel and concrete for red leather and mirrors. The primarily gay crowd, drifting steadily out of their twenties and into money, gab in clusters to the lull of soft jazz and softer lighting. No one is going to stop you if you come in with jeans and a tank top, but most patrons will be sporting suits or blazers, so leave the buttless chaps at home. But do bring your pocketbook—mixed drinks will run you 15DM and up.

With its tacky glittering lights and disco ball, **New York** *(Sonnen Str. 25; Tel 089/561-056; U-Bahn 3, 6 to Sendlinger Tor; 11pm-4am Mon-Thur, till 8am Fri, Sat, till 5am Sun; 12DM drink required Fri-Sun only; V, MC, AE)*, in Alsadt, seems lost in an '80s time warp, but it's the only all-gay disco in Munich, so expect queers from every generation. The doorman hides behind a one-way mirror; look gay in the right way, or he won't open the door. Once you get in, you'll be surprised at how big this basement space is—that is, until you realize the walls are all mirrors. It's actually pretty tiny and fills up quickly after 2am, when the bars empty.

With nearly as many hot fag-hags as fags, the much younger and "gay-friendly" (wink wink) **Soul City** *(Maximiliansplatz 5; Tel 089/59-52-72; U-Bahn 3, 6 to Karlsplatz; Cafe 10pm-6am Wed-Sat, disco 10pm-6am Thur-Sat; www.soul-city.de; 10DM cover includes drink; V, MC, AE)*, on the northern edge of Alstadt, is a happening place for the city's young trendoids. Yellow sunglasses and wife-beaters are the costume du jour. If you can't decide whether you want to take home a guy or a gal, come here and take your pick (how about both?). The DJ spins the usual house and gay classics. Head here after midnight on Thursday or after 1am Saturday. The second Friday of the month finds the city's leather-and-fetish crowd checking in for some debauchery.

CULTURE ZOO

For its size, Munich has some of the finest art collections in the world. All of the worthwhile museums are in the city center, with the Neue Pinakothek and Alte Pinakothek just across the street from each other. If you're short on time, hit the Alte Pinakothek, the Deutsches Museum, and Schloss Nymphenburg. The Welcome Card (12DM for one day, 29DM for three days), which gives free public transportation and small discounts on attractions, is a good deal for museum hounds.

Alte Pinakothek *(Barer Str. 29; Tel 089/238-050; U-Bahn 2 to Königsplatz or Tram 27 to same; 10am-5pm daily, closed Mon, till 10pm Thur; 9DM, 6DM students; No credit cards):* Munich's pride and joy. It just reopened after a three-year renovation and houses thousands of paintings from the 14th to the 18th centuries.

Deutsches Museum *(Museumsinsel 1; Tel 089/217-91, 089/217-94-33; Any S-Bahn to Isartor or Tram 18 to Deutsches Museum; 9am-5pm daily; 12DM, 5DM students; No credit cards):* Tech geeks will lose it over this enormous museum, containing the first diesel engine, an air-and-space hall, a lightning room, and computer junk.

Schloss Nymphenburg *(Schloss Nymphenburg 1; Tel 089/17-90-86-68; U-Bahn 1 to Rotkreuzplatz, then Tram 12 toward Amelienburg Str.; 7DM admission to main palace only, 15DM admission to all parts of the estate; No credit cards):* The stunning Baroque palace and parks here are more than worth the half-hour trip, especially on a sunny day.

The Residenz *(Max-Joseph-Platz 3; Tel 089/290-671; U-Bahn 3, 4, 5, 6 to Odeonsplatz; 9am-6pm daily, till 8pm Thur; 8DM admission to the museum only, 14DM admission will also gain entry to Treasure Room; No credit cards):* Home to the Bavarian royal family from 1385 to 1918, isn't as beautiful as Nymphenburg but is easier to get to, located in the center of the city. If you stop in, check out the amazing antiquarium.

Neue Pinakothek *(Barer Str. 29; Tel 089/23-80-51-95; U-Bahn 2 to Königsplatz or Tram 27 to same; 10am-5pm daily, closed Tue, till 10pm Thur; 9DM, 6DM students; No credit cards):* The collection here isn't as impressive as the Residenz, but it's worth a trip for Van Gogh, Klimt, and Leibl.

Antikensammlungen *(Museum of Antiquities) (Königsplatz 1; Tel 089/598-359; U-Bahn 2 to Königsplatz; 10am-5pm daily, till 8pm Thur; 6DM, 3.50DM students, free Sun; No credit cards):* You guessed it: This place has ancient artifacts. If Greek vases and Mycenaean pottery are your thing, this museum is top-notch.

Frauenkirche (Cathedral of Our Lady) *(Frauenplatz 12; No phone; U-Bahn 3, 6 or any S-Bahn to Marienplatz; 7am-7pm daily; Free admission):* This beautiful 15th-century house of worship was painstakingly restored after WWII bombs practically leveled it. It's free, so poke your head inside when you're near Kaufingerstrasse.

modification

On the balance a conservative people, Munich natives are not really a body-modification kind of crowd; if you absolutely can't wait any longer to get that connected nose and nipple pierce, have it done right—go to Berlin. If you're looking to do some modifying of a less permanent nature, the Munich hairstyling scene is competitive enough to remedy an acute case of BHD. A quick stroll down Baader Strasse in the Gartnerplatz area should give you more than enough options for your styling needs. Here are our faves:

A total blast from the past, stepping into **Gemüseladen** *(Baader Str. 52; Tel 089/202-16-93; U-Bahn 1, 2 to Fraunhofer Str.; 9am-6pm Tue-Fri, till 2pm Sat; 120DM haircut; No credit cards)* is like walking onto the set of *Ozzie and Harriet.* The salon is situated in the middle of a faithfully re-created '50s living room, down to the old-fashioned wood-paneled floor radio. It's a one-man shop, so it's a good idea to make an appointment if you don't want to wait around. Even if you can't bring yourself to shell out over 100 big ones, make sure you at least poke your head in for a quick look at the decor.

Minx *(Hans-Sachs Str. 18; Tel 089/263-970; U-Bahn 1, 2 to Fraun-hofer Str.; Closed Mon, 9:30am-8:30pm Tue, 9:30am-6:30pm Tue, Wed, Fri, 12:30-8:30pm Thur, 9am-2pm Sat; 65-85DM haircut; No credit cards)*, a more modern salon, all pastels and funny angles, has an enjoy-able L.A. perkiness to it. Within the confines of the tiny salon, a group of young stylists work cheerfully on an equally young clientele. The cost of a clip can be *très cher*, however; a cut from one of the less-experienced artists will leave you a little less light in the pocketbook.

great outdoors

Even with so much to do at night, Müncheners live for the sun to come out. Pack your compass and flare gun and join the locals escaping from the world into the mammoth labyrinth of the **Englischer Garten** *(U-Bahn 3, 6 to Universität or Gisela Str.).* Find them whizzing past on bicy-cles, surfing an artificial swell in the Isar River (no kidding), and sprawled on the grass in various states of undress. It's not a pretty sight, but on summer days in the Englischer Garten, bratwurst is not the most common type of sausage on display around here, if you get my drift. The **Hof-garten** *(U-Bahn 3, 4, 5, 6 to Odeonsplatz)* feels like a French *jardin*, with well-groomed shrubbery and men playing *boules* on the gravel.

If you have a hot day to kill by the water, take a 40-minute train ride out to the woodsy lake **Starnbergersee**, where in 1865 "Mad" King Ludwig II, the Bavarian ruler who built the region's famous fairy-tale cas-tles, drowned under strange and dubious circumstances. The swarms of other bathers are largely hidden by dense trees, giving the swimming area a private feel. Take S-Bahn 6 to the town of Starnberg, then hop on a ferry to the beaches at Possenhofen or Ammerland.

The banks of the Isar River are an exercise nut's dream come true, lined with paths for bikers and in-line skaters. The paths on the east bank, which wind through a forest, feel secluded. But if you decide to stop in the middle of a route to wax poetic about the scenery, take care: Cyclists whiz around blind corners like maniacs and *will* crash into you.

If your in-line skills aren't challenged enough by the flat outdoor paths, check out the skate park in the **Olympic Ice stadium complex** *(Olympia-Eissportzentrum; Tel 089/30-67-21-50; U-Bahn 3 to Olympia-zentrum; 10am-9pm Sun-Wed, till 10pm Thur-Sat; No credit cards).*

festivals and events

What started as a royal marriage celebration nearly 200 years ago has now become the mother of all drunken parties. The **Oktoberfest** runs for 16 days, usually from the last two weeks in September into October, on the Theresienwiese, an enormous fair grounds to the west of the Hauptbahnhof. The city is invaded by hundreds of thousands of partiers, drawn by the always-flowing kegs, oompah-pah bands, and carnival rides. Book a hotel room way in advance, or you'll be sleeping on the streets. The **Starkbierzeitz** (strong beer) festival *(late March)* is Oktoberfest's wussy cousin. A heavy buzz-inspiring brew is whipped up just for the festival, which runs for two weeks.

The **Tollwood Festival** *(late June-early July; Tel 089/38-38-50-24; www.tollwood.de)* brings hordes of world-famous jazz musicians and rock groups to the Olympic Park, the complex in the north of Munich that housed the infamous 1972 Olympics.

Masked balls and boisterous parades mark **Fasching**, a four-week holiday season before Lent. The tourist office can provide specifics.

Bargain hunters will dig **Auer Dult**, an eight-day flea market royale three times a year *(last Saturday in April, end of July, and end of October)*, where peddlers spread out their wealth of antiques and junk.

Kunstpark Ost also has a climbing wall called **Heaven's Gate** *(Grafinger Str. 6; Tel 089/40-90-88-03; Any S-Bahn to Ostbahnhof; 10am-11pm daily; 16DM per session on weekdays, 21DM evenings, weekends; No credit cards)*.

After an afternoon of exercise, indulge in a little hot, sweaty action at the Haidhausen's **Mullersche Volksbad** *(Rosenheimer Str. 1; Tel 089/23-61-34-34; Tram 18; Pools 7:30am-11pm daily, steambath, sauna and sitz bath open at 9am; 22DM for 4-hour access to pools and steambath, 5.50DM for all-day pool access, 10DM deposit for key; No credit cards)*, where a steambath and two pools offer the perfect early-evening wind-down. It's not a gay bathhouse; Müncheners of all sexual persuasions have relaxed in this beautiful bath for a hundred years.

For the sedentary sports enthusiast, the hottest tickets in town are for FC Bayern München, the Jordan-era Bulls of German and international soccer. They play their matches in the **Olympiazentrum** *(U-Bahn 3 to Olympiazentrum)*. Call München Ticket *(Tel 089/54-61-81-81)*.

STUFF

With one of the largest collections of yuppies this side of the Atlantic, shopping in Munich ain't cheap, but it sure is plentiful. As a general rule, stores stay open until 7 or 8pm weekdays and 4pm on Saturdays. Almost everything's closed on Sundays.

▶▶**DUDS**

Kaufinger Strasse is the main shopping drag, housing the most affordable German and international clothing chains. If it's time to pick up a new leather jacket or retire those socks that threaten to walk away on their own, this street is your best bet. Fur shops, stuffy art galleries, and expensive-ass international designers have set up camp to the north on Maximilian Strasse and Theatiner Strasse. Sendlingerstrasse is stocked with shops that hunt for customers a few notches down the high-class food chain. It's certainly not cheap, but salespeople won't snicker if you make a beeline for the sale racks. The grooviest shop on the street is **Isy's** *(Sendlinger Str. 40; Tel 089/260-77-77; U-Bahn 1, 2, 3, 6 to Sendlinger*

by foot

Featuring surfers and nudists, drug dealers and ice cream vendors, the **Englischer Garten** ain't your ordinary town green. This 20-minute walking tour introduces you to the eccentricity that is Europe's largest public park. Pick a nice day for the stroll, and reward yourself for finishing with a beer and/or pretzel at the end.

The tour winds along the white paths of the park's verdant grounds. Begin on the **Prinzregenten Strasse bridge**, at the southern base of the **Englischer Garten**. If you're lucky, you'll find a wetsuit-clad dude catching a pseudo-wave where the water rolls through the bridge. It's a bizarre sight: The wave just swirls in place, so the surfer zips back and forth along its length, from the riverbank to the center. A "good" ride is 20 seconds.

When you're bored, head north on the woodsy path to the right of the bridge. Bear left, then cross two footbridges to reach the heart of skin city, where Helios-worshipping executives and everyday people strip down at the sun's first rays. Take a soft right at the next intersection, then a right at the next path, where a gelato vendor will usually be peddling his frosty wares. This path will take you up to the **Monopteros**, a Greek-like temple that offers a great view of the lawns and baking flesh below. When you've finished gazing, turn around and head left down the path on the backside of the **Monopteros**. You'll reach a five-way intersection; go straight, keeping the emerging buildings on your right. Fifty yards up the path, you'll see the **Chinesischer Turm** and its beer garden looming ahead.

Tor; 10am-8pm Mon-Fri, till 4pm Sat; V, MC, AE, Diners), which sells old-school New Balance, shimmering V-neck shirts, flimsy dresses, and nylon cargo pants. For you club girls, this boutique also stocks flamboyant hair dyes and nail polish.

The Eurotrash posse heads to Hohenzollernstrasse (between Leopoldstrasse and Friedrichstrasse) to get togged out before they club it. Start your Euro-makeover from the bottom up, with a pair of strappy chunkheels or polished black square-toes from **Bartu** *(Hohenzollern Str. 14; Tel 089/54-01-77-75; U-Bahn 3, 6 to Gisela Str.; 10am-8pm Mon-Fri, till 4pm Sat; V, MC).*

▶▶TUNES

Munich isn't the cheapest city in which to buy CDs or vinyl (serious DJs make trips to the States to stock up), but there are a few specialty stops here and there. **Bam Bam Records** *(Lederer Str. 10; Tel 089/222-864; U-Bahn 3, 6 or any S-Bahn to Marienplatz; 11am-7pm Mon-Fri, till 4am Sat, closed Sun; V, MC, AE)* is actually two small shops that used to be run by a couple of buddies who opened the door between their places. One specializes in hip-hop, R&B, drum 'n' bass, and acid jazz, while the other focuses more on techno, progressive, and specialized house.

For more of a grab-bag shopping experience, **Discorama** *(Baader Str. 55; Tel 089/202-19-03; Tram 27, or U-Bahn 2 to Fravenhofer Str.; 1-7pm Mon-Fri, 11am-4pm Sat; No credit cards)* has a small but broad selection of CDs and LPs, ranging anywhere from Charlie Hunter to Korn. Expect to blow 15 to 25DM for discs, slightly less for vinyl.

▶▶BOUND

In a city as staunchly Bavarian as Munich, you might expect the English lit scene to be about as happening as Scott Baio's acting career *(ba-doomp, pssssh!)*. But surprise, surprise, surprise, "gum chewers" (as some Germans describe how English speakers talk) can find refuge in a pair of bookshops. **Words' Worth** *(Schelling Str. 21a; Tel 089/280-91-41; U-Bahn 3, 6 to Universität; 9am-6:30pm Mon, Tue, Fri, till 8pm Wed, Thur, 10am-2pm Sat, closed Sun; V, MC)* is the younger yet more staid of the two, with four rooms packed neatly with new volumes of best-sellers, lit crit, poetry, and classic novels.

A group of university students studying English opened the store in 1985 and have been vying for business with the gloriously cluttered **Anglia English Bookshop** *(Schelling Str. 3; Tel 089/283-642; U-Bahn 3, 6 to Universität; 9am-6:15pm Mon-Fri, 10am-1pm Sat; No credit cards)* ever since. The shop has been around for three decades, yet the management somehow still seems to suffer brain farts when it comes to the Dewey Decimal system. Towers of books are balanced precariously around the shop; people who work here swear there's some type of order, but good luck figuring it out. There's a small secondhand collection that spills up a staircase leading to the equally cluttered loft. Used books will run you 4 to 6DM. As you face the cash register, the wall just to your left is the best place around to catch up on English-language plays and lit readings around the city.

Amerika Haus *(Karolinenplatz 3; Tel 089/552-53-70; U-Bahn 2 to Königsplatz; 1-5pm Mon, Tue, Thur, Fri, till 8pm Wed)* hosts regular poetry readings and scholarly discussions in English, featuring guest speakers as prominent as Toni Morrison and Don DeLillo. This German-American cultural center also houses a small not-for-loan library, if you're jonesing for the *Encyclopedia Britannica* or the latest issue of *Mademoiselle*.

German speakers might dig **Literaturhaus** *(Salvatorplatz 1; Tel 089/291-93-40; U-Bahn 3, 4, 5, 6 to Odeonsplatz; Gallery open noon-8pm Mon-Fri, 10am-6pm Sat, Sun; Gallery 3-5DM, lectures 12DM; No credit cards)*, the site of frequent readings and a funky literature/theater-based art gallery.

EATS

A spare-nothing attitude toward meats, a need to pack on calories for the long winter, and a complete disregard for high cholesterol levels put Munich's fare in the upper echelons of hearty heart-stopping cuisine. Potatoes, sausages, and cabbage fill most every traditional plate, though outside influences (like Italian and French) have spawned top restaurants for the more refined palate. Before you dive into your first meal, a few pointers: Though the service (aka tip) is included on most bills, either the tourists or the rich snobs here have spoiled it for all: A 10 percent tip in addition to the service has become standard. If that's just too much for you, at least round up your bill to the nearest multiple of 5, or you'll incur the wrath of a Münchener scorned. Also, don't bother asking for tap water; if you do, they'll frown and bring you the smallest cup of water they can find, just to demonstrate that tap water ain't done in Germany. It's pretty much mineral water (which they'll charge you for) or nothing.

▶▶CHEAP

Cash-strapped carnivores can't miss with the **Viktualienmarkt**, where the orange awnings of butchers beckon passersby to the meat-filled windows. Despite the slabs of raw pork and beef scattered around the shops, most butchers serve simple cooked dishes as well. A local favorite is *leberkässemmel* (literally "liver cheese," though there's neither liver nor cheese in it), a small Spam-like loaf slathered with mustard and pinched into a hard roll.

The buxom women at **Sieber** *(Bohmerwald Str. 55; No phone; Any S-Bahn or U-Bahn 3, 6 to Marienplatz; 7:30am-6pm Mon-Fri, 7am-2pm Sat, closed Sun; 3-10DM sandwiches; No credit cards)* serve up a mean *leberkässemmel* for only 3DM. If you choose not to stroll while you eat, you can stand at little communal tables while local elders scrape their plates and grunt beside you.

The American bagel chain **New York Cafe** *(Leopold Str. 43; Tel 089/38-88-98-08; U-Bahn 3, 6 to Gisela Str.; 9am-1am Mon-Sat, 10am-1am Sun; No credit cards)* brings institutional seating, crappy coffee, and decent baked goods to Bavaria. This joint, on a busy drag in Schwabing near the Englischer Garten, can be a welcome respite from the gut bomb called Bavarian food. A pastrami and mozzarella bagelwich or a bagel and lox will run you 10DM.

Vegetarians, and those who actually worry about hardening arteries, should visit **buxs** *(Frauen Str. 9; Tel 089/291-95-50; Any S-Bahn or U-Bahn 3, 6 to Marienplatz or to Isertorplatz; 11am-8:30pm Mon-Fri, till*

12 hours in munich

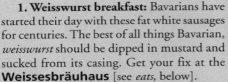

1. Weisswurst breakfast: Bavarians have started their day with these fat white sausages for centuries. The best of all things Bavarian, *weisswurst* should be dipped in mustard and sucked from its casing. Get your fix at the **Weissesbräuhaus** [see *eats*, below].

2. Make like a pastry and roll: Rent bikes or rollerblades and head for the woods. The leafy banks of the Isar River hold trails packed with joggers and cyclists. Get one with nature, man.

3. Get sloshed under the sun: There's nothing in the world quite like a beer garden—hefty liter mugs of frosty suds, pretzels, and drinking songs, all thrown together blissfully in Munich's finest tradition. Try **Seehaus** [see *beer gardens*, below], where hipsters quaff their thirst and munch on Bavarian *kuchen* (cuisine).

4. Viktualienmarkt at noon: Follow your nose through the ultimate buffet lunch, where vendors hawk everything from exotic fruits to down-home Bavarian cookin'. Take your pick from the multitude of food stands [see *eats*, above].

5. Get hot and get nekkid: Housing four beer gardens, wannabe surfers, and naked sunbathers of all shapes, the enormous **Englischer Garten** [see *great outdoors*, above] plays host to all the good, bad, and ugly Munich has to offer. Pick a nice day to shed your ambition and your clothes.

6. Oktoberfest: The craziest week of debauchery this side of Mardi Gras. Make your reservations about a year in advance and get ready for sloppiness.

7. Feed your brain for free: The **Alte Pinakothek** [see *culture zoo*, above] is one of the most important collections of 14th- to 18th-century art in Europe, and on Sundays it's as free as Bob Marley's spirit. Sure, the whole world shows up, but you can bust out the pickup line, "So, how do you like your Klimt?"

8. Club-hop in the world's biggest party mall: Choose your poison in Kunstpark Ost [see *kunstpark ost*, above], the Disney World of youth nightlife. Haunts range from techno to retro, from glam rock to German pop.

beer gardens

There is no more time-honored Munich tradition than gathering with one's fellows in the quiet embrace of Bavaria's natural splendor and drinking oneself stupid. At the first hint of sunshine, Müncheners drop their babies and abandon their computers in a mass exodus to their *biergarten* of choice. If you really want to roll like the natives, here are the rules of engagement: Order either *eine mass* (one liter) or *eine weissbier* (wheat beer: pale and tasty), along with the natural complement to an oversized glass of brew—oversized pretzels. When toasting, the German equivalent of "cheers" is *prost*. If you're drinking *weissbier*, clink the bottoms of your glasses together, tap them on the table, then down the hatch. When drinking from *masskrug*, the giant, dimpled beer steins, bring the sides of the glasses together squarely and resoundingly—don't worry, they're plenty sturdy. If you feel like taking it easy, order a *radler*, which is beer mixed with Sprite. Take care, though, there's still about a pint of suds in there.

In the shadow of a pagoda that was destroyed during World War II and rebuilt during the 1950s lies the popular **Biergarten Chinesischer Turm** *(Englischer Garten 3; Tel 089/383-87-30; U-Bahn 3, 6 to Universität or Gisela Str.; 10am-11pm daily; AE, V, MC)* which is only open on hot summery days, so make sure the sun's out before heading there! It lies smack-dab in the center of the **Englischer Garten** [see *great outdoors*, above], and the people who crowd in are impossible to categorize: tourist and local, gay and straight, old and young. A half-

3:30pm Sat; No credit cards), a cafeteria that won't serve anything that once walked. Catering to young and old veggie-heads alike, this place lets you serve yourself salads with beets, couscous, artichokes, chickpeas, spinach, and a handful of other fibrous delicacies. Be careful when loading up your tray, since you pay by the gram. Expect to pay about 10 to 20DM for a meal.

▶▶**DO-ABLE**

The world-famous **Hofbräuhaus** *(Platzl 9; Tel 089/290-13-60; U-Bahn 3, 6 or any S-Bahn to Marienplatz; 9am-11:30pm daily; www.hof braeuhaus.de; 7.90-25DM per entree; V, MC)* is a tourist's wet dream and bona fide traveler's worst nightmare, packaging everything stereotypically Bavarian into one rowdy beer hall. Regardless, this place is worth a few hours of your time (but no more...). The staged revelry is infectious; when the Japanese businessman is pulled out of his chair to conduct the oompah-pah band, you'll find yourself chewing your bratwurst in syncopation. Memo to female travelers: If you meet a charming local fellow at the Hofbräuhaus, he's probably just there to pick up foreign chicks.

liter of Helles beer costs 5.50DM, but don't be surprised when they shortchange you by 2DM. After years of losing beer steins to hoarding travelers, the entrepreneurs instituted a deposit system: Bring back your mug and you get your 2DM back.

Seehaus *(Kleinhesselohe 3; Tel 089/381-61-30; U-Bahn 6 to Dietlinden Str. or Bus 44 to Osterwald Str.; 10am-10pm daily; No credit cards)*, the hipster's beer garden, sits near the blue waters of Kleinhesseloher See, a lake in the Englischer Garten. A congregation point for in-line skaters, cyclists, and pretzel-seeking ducks, this 2,500-seat beer garden is among the prettiest you'll see. The place gets buggy at dusk, but feeding bats often perform aerial shows over the water. The Seehaus reportedly has the best *obatzter* (Camembert cheese with paprika and butter) in the city.

Located square in the heart of downtown Munich, **Augustiner-Keller** *(Arnulf Str. 52; Tel 089/594-393; U-Bahn 1, 2, 4, 5 to Hauptbahnhof, S-Bahn to Hackerbrücke; 10am-1am daily; AE, V, MC)* hosts an older Bavarian crowd. At 10.50DM per liter, the Helles Bier, reputedly the best in town, is moderately priced—for Munich. With literally thousands of seats in the garden area, the quantity of beer consumed here is so large, drained *masskrug* aren't carried from the tables—they're wheeled away on huge carts pulled by two men.

Bavarians don't eat here, but everyone else sure as hell does. This place is happening at 8pm on a Monday, for cripes sake. Try the *würstlteller* sausage sampler for 12.90DM.

Just around the corner, you'll find the beer hall where the Müncheners actually *do* show their mustard-splattered faces. The **Weissesbräuhaus** *(Tal 7; Tel 089/299-875; U-Bahn 3, 6 or any S-Bahn to Marienplatz; 8am-midnight daily; 10.90-28.80DM per entree; No credit cards)* serves up the most revered *weisswurst* in the land. These small white sausages should never be eaten after noon, and never with the skin on (dip them in mustard and suck the insides from the chewy casing). Locals of all ages pack the communal tables for the *schweinbraten* (pork loin served with boiled potatoes and cabbage salad) and the excellent Schneider *weissbier*. Stop by Hofbräuhaus for a beer, but hit Weissesbräuhaus for a real Bavarian meal.

With Milan and Venice just a short jaunt through Austria away, it's no surprise that a great Italian restaurant found its way to Munich. **Trattoria La Stella** *(Hohenstaufen Str. 2; Tel 089/341-779; U-Bahn 3, 6 to*

Gisela Str. or Bus 33 to Hohenzollernplatz or Tram 27 to Kursüstenplatz; Noon-3pm/6pm-midnight Tue-Sat, noon-midnight Sun, closed Mon; 10-35DM per entree; MC, AE) serves up authentic pasta and pizza dishes, earning it distinction as one of the best deals in Schwabing. The decor is stereotypically quaint, with black and white photos of smooching couples and cheeky kids carrying jugs of wine. Don't miss the *pizza pane alla rucola* (pan pizza with arugula), which can be ordered as an appetizer, the *fusilli al salmone* (pasta in a cream sauce with salmon chunks), or the grappa list.

▶▶SPLURGE

Leading the surge of trendy restaurants in the Gärtnerplatz region is **Rincon** *(Rumford Str. 34; Tel 089/21-93-93-40; Any S-Bahn to Isartor, Tram 17, 18 to Reichenbachplatz; 6pm-1am Mon-Fri, 10am-1am Sat, Sun; 16.50-22DM per entree; No credit cards)*, a young, modernly appointed restaurant that fuses California cuisine with Mediterranean influences. Locals from the 'hood go crazy for *zum wein*, a scrumptious appetizer of black olive paste on thick butter-soaked toast (9.50DM). Look sharp for the occasion; the clientele tends to be modish and gay, though the kitchen's quality has pulled in the business crowd as well. In the early spring, go for the *schrobenhausenerspargel mit sauce Hollandaise* (white asparagus with Hollandaise sauce), served with *salzkartoffeln* (potatoes). The *lammkrone* (lambchops) with Kenya beans and potatoes au gratin are great year-round. Their extensive collection of paintings and sculpture from local galleries is changed every month.

Though the regulars count on a sumptuous *penne a l'arrabiata* (pasta with a spicy tomato sauce) each night, the ever-changing daily menu is what keeps them coming back to **Rothmund** *(Rothmund Str. 5; Tel 089/535-015; U-Bahn 1, 2, 3, 6 to Sendlinger Tor; 10am-1am daily; 7-28DM per entree; No credit cards)*. Left to the selection of the morning market and the whims of the chef who shops there, this trendy restaurant's specials range from traditional roast beef with *spargel* (white asparagus) to an exotic ostrich filet on a bed of arugula. Rothko-like paintings hang on the walls, a potted tree sits in every window well, and the linoleum floor looks like a Magic Eye painting. The food draws a wide range of diners—it's cheap enough for the young and still refined enough for the aging gourmet—but a constant is the stream of doctors from the nearby hospital. Skip the appetizers and wine, and this place bumps down to "do-able."

Sausalitos *(Türken Str. 50; Tel 089/281-594; U-Bahn 3, 6 to Universität or Bus 53 to Türken Str.; 5pm-1am daily; 18-24DM per entree; No credit cards)*, the apex of Tex-Mex in Munich, is stuffed as full of local yupsters as its gut-wrenching fajitas are with tequila-marinated chicken and sizzling peppers. Gargantuan portions and skillfully assembled margaritas make up for the claustrophobic quarters and service you can set your calendar by. Check in for happy hour, 5 till 8pm daily, when drinks are half price, or hang around for margarita happy hour from 11pm till 1am. Make reservations or prepare for disappointment.

crashıng

Munich is packed with cheap hostels and hotels, but finding a room can be nearly impossible if you don't plan ahead, especially during the peak season in June, July, and August. Don't even think about just popping into town during Oktoberfest without reservations (which some people make two years in advance). Get help booking a bed from the Munich Information Center in the Hauptbahnhof or in City Hall, or the Munich Tourist Office website [see *need to know,* below, for both]. German hostels are always filled with young people—since guests must be 26 or younger—so they're usually pretty fun. A heavy business crowd makes for a glut of middle-priced and expensive hotels, many of which have weekend and summer discounts if you ask. And just so you know, when Germans talk about "twin beds," they're usually referring to that stage of embryonic development just *before* the twins separate. It's really nothing more than a double bed that's cracked in the middle.

▶▶CHEAP

DJH *(Wendl-Dietrich-Str. 20; Tel 089/131-156; U-Bahn 1 to Rotkeruzplatz; 36-person dormitory 26DM, 30DM/person four- or six-person room, double 34DM/person; V),* a clean, chill place to crash out in Nymphenburg, claims to be the first city youth hostel in the world. Each room in this 364-bed hostel has a sink and thin mattresses, with hallway bathrooms. The cheap price includes sheets and breakfast. An extra 10DM will get you a hot or packed lunch; 15DM extra will buy lunch and dinner in an old tram-turned-bistro. The noon check-in is another bonus, though they do ask you to clear out by 9:30am on departure day. Plan for the 20DM key deposit.

The dingy-but-happening **4 You München** *(Hirten Str. 18; Tel 089/ 552-16-60; U-Bahn or S-Bahn to Hauptbahnhof; info@4you.de, www.the4 you.de; 27DM/person 12-person room, 32DM/person four-, six-, or eight-person room, 42DM/person double, 59DM single; No credit cards)* jumps up a couple notches on the ghetto scale. Wires stick out from the walls in the front hall, and some floors have no bathrooms. Then again, you can practically roll out of bed and into the main train station. They're also looking out for our planet: The breakfasts and the cotton T-shirts they hawk are organic (maybe that's why such a low premium is put on cleaning products). Tons of American travelers make this place a blast to stay in. Breakfast is 8DM and, if you don't have a sleeping bag, sheets will run you 5DM.

Share snores with 299 other travelers underneath the parachute walls at **Das Zelt** *(Inden Kirschen 30; Tel 089/12-99-70-70; Tram 17 to Botanical Garden, then walk into Franz-Schrank-Str.; 15DM for sleeping pad and blanket, 18DM for bunk bed; No credit cards),* just south of Alstadt. The name means "The Tent," and it's like a massive slumber-party circus (it's tough to avoid meeting people when their wet socks are a few feet from your head). Sit by the bonfire or in the beer garden (yup, even campgrounds here got 'em) and enjoy the great outdoors before hitting the sack. Don't worry, there are bathrooms with plumbing and showers.

munich eats and crashing

EATS ◆

buxs **7**
New York Cafe **11**
Rincon **9**
Sausalitos **12**
Trattoria La Stella **13**
Viktualienmarkt **6**
Weissesbräuhaus **8**

CRASHING ■

Das Zelt **3**
DJH **1**
4 You München **2**
Hotel Advokat **10**
Hotel
  Europäischer Hof **4**
Hotel Uhland **5**

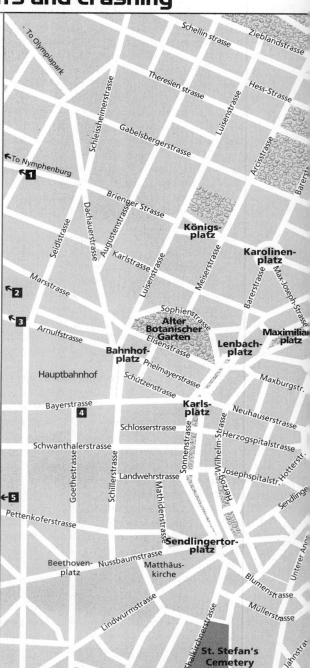

E-0253

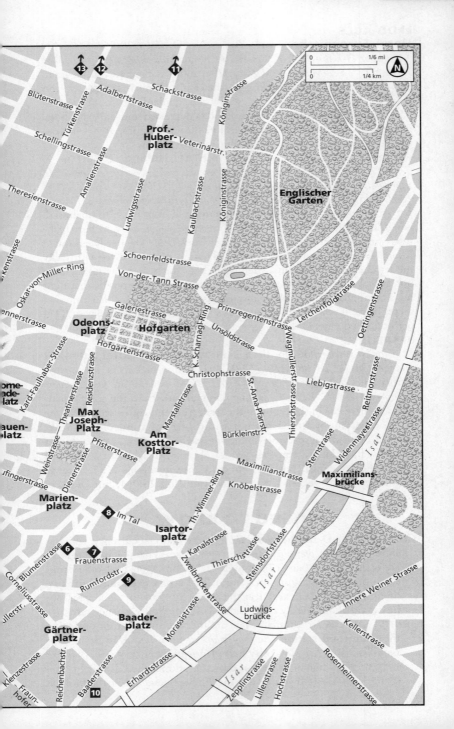

▶▶DO-ABLE

Hotel Europäischer Hof *(Bayer Str. 31; Tel 089/551-510; Any S-Bahn or U-Bahn 1, 2, 4, 5 to Hauptbahnhof; www.heh.de; 89-411DM single, 212-442DM double; V, MC, AE)* is about as close as you can get to the train station without being on the tracks. Penurious travelers can crash in bare-bones rooms that eschew the standard bathroom and TV. Though the surrounding neighborhood is depressed and dull, this hotel is only a 15-minute walk (along the city's busiest shopping street, no less) to Marienplatz. Bathtubs are available in most rooms.

As in most old hotels, each room in **Hotel Uhland** *(Uhland Str. 1; Tel 089/539-277; U-Bahn 4, 5 to Theresienwiese; www.hotel-uhland.de, info@hotel-uhland.de; 110-210DM single, 150-290DM double, 195-335DM triple; 220-380DM quad, all with private bathrooms, a TV and refrigerator; V, MC, AE, DC)*, a 10-minute walk from the Hauptbahnhof, is a little bit different from the next: Some have balconies, some have bathtubs, some have sitting rooms, some have bunk beds. The newly renovated Room 27 even features the latest in Bavarian pimpin' style, with tacky modern lamps and a double-sized water bed (the owners say it's the only hotel-owned one in Munich). A communal living room on the first floor has a computer and a machine that grinds and brews fresh coffee. Internet access is free if you use it for only a few minutes; they'll charge you 9DM per hour if you linger.

▶▶SPLURGE

Minimalist only in design, the Haidhausen district's **Hotel Advokat** *(Baader Str. 1; Tel 089/216-31-90; Any S-Bahn to Isartor; www.hotel-advokat.de; 200-290DM single, 270-330DM double, all with private bathrooms; V, MC, AE, DC)* is long on amenities, from the complimentary self-serve bar in the lobby to the fresh fruit and coffee service on the roof garden. But by far the sweetest feature of a stay at Advokat is breakfast. This elegant culinary blessing disguised as an all-you-can-eat buffet includes figs, kiwis, strawberries, raspberries, blackberries, assorted meats, cheeses, danish, pastries, and croissants, just to name a few items. Plan a visit on a weekend, when rates can drop 20DM, but check in advance.

need to know

Currency The **Deutsche mark** *(DM)* is the national currency, which is subdivided into *pfennig*. **Banks** give the best exchange rate, but most are open only 8:30am-12:30pm/1:30-3:30pm Mon-Fri (some banks stay open until 5:30pm on Thurs). The **street exchange bureaus**, many of which are in and near the Hauptbahnhof, are open later, but be careful about sneaky commission costs and low exchange rates.

Tourist Offices In Munich, there are tourism information centers at the **main train station** *(Bahnhofsplatz 2; 9am-8pm Mon-Sat, 10am-6pm Sun, holidays)* and at **city hall** *(Marienplatz; 10am-8pm Mon-Fri, till 4pm Sat)*. For information over the phone, there is a help line: 089/23-33-03-00. If you wish to make a hotel reservation, the Munich

Tourist Center will help at no extra charge. The direct line for hotel reservations is 089/23-33-01-23.

Public Transportation Munich and its surrounds are linked by a network of subways, trams, and buses, run by the **MVV** *(089/210-330)*. Maps are available at the tourist offices and are displayed in most subway stations and within all trams and buses. **U-Bahn** (subway) and **S-Bahn** (tram) stations are identified by a large U or S. Tickets are good for any public transportation and can be purchased as single rides, in strips, good for multiple rides, or as day passes. Be sure to validate your ticket as you enter a rapid transit station, tram, or bus; random spot checks can bring a costly fine (60DM) for the unprepared. Eurail pass holders ride free on the state-run S-Bahn but not the city-run U-Bahn. **Taxi dispatcher:** *194-10.*

Bike and Car Rental For bike rentals, try **Radius Bikes** *(In the Hauptbahnhof, by Tracks 27 to 36; Tel 089/596-113; U-Bahn 1, 2, 4, 5 or any S-Bahn to Hauptbahnhof; 10am-6pm daily May-mid-October, depending on weather Apr, last two weeks of Oct, closed Nov-Mar; 5-6DM/hour, 25-30DM/day, 75-90DM/week; No credit cards).* For car rentals, try **Sixt Autovermietung** *(Dr. Cal Van Linde-Str. 2; Tel 0/180-525-25-25).*

American Express *Promenadeplatz 6, Tel 089/22-80-14-65* and also at *Kaufinger Str. 24, Tel 089/22-80-13-87.*

Health and Emergency Emergency numbers: Police: *110*; Fire/paramedic: *112*; Ambulance/emergency medical: *192-22*; Pharmaceutical emergencies: *59-44-75.* The most centrally located hospital is the **University Clinic** *(Ziernssen Str. 1; Tel 089/516-00; U-Bahn 3, 6 to Goetheplatz),* and the largest hospital is **Grosshadern Hospital** *(Marchionini Str. 15; Tel 089/709-50; U-Bahn 6 to Klinikum Grosshadern).*

Pharmacies Look for the green *apotheke* sign. Pharmacies are generally open 9am-6:30pm Monday to Friday and 9am-2pm Saturday. One pharmacy is open all night in each neighborhood; a sign in every pharmacy's window will give you the address of the one on call.

Telephone Country code: *49*; city code: *089*; local directory assistance: *11-833*; international directory assistance: *11-834*. **AT&T:** *013-000-10*; **MCI:** *0-800-888-8000*; **Sprint:** *013-000-13.*

Airports Franz Josef Strauss Airport *(Erdinger Moos, 18 miles northeast of the city center; Tel 089/975-00, flight info/24-hour info 089/97-52-13-13).* An **airport bus** *(5:10am-7:50pm daily)* leaves from the Hauptbahnhof every 20 minutes. S-Bahn 1 and 8 run regularly to and from the airport for 16DM. Eurail pass holders ride free.

Airlines Lufthansa *(Ismaninger 130, Tel 089/998-383; Lenbachplatz, Tel 089/552-55-00; Ludwig Str. 11, Tel 089/281-086; Maximilian Str. 17, Tel 089/228-34-48).*

Trains Munich has one main station, the **Hauptbahnhof**, where all the trains coming into and out of the city stop. For information call *089/018-05-99-66-33.*

wired

For critical hip info, check out **www.munichfound.com**, the website of the city's English-language magazine, *Munich Found*.

You have a few choices in Internet cafes. The boldly named **Internet Café** *(Nymphenburger Str. 145; 089/1291-120; U-Bahn 1 to Rotkreuzplatz; 11am-4am daily; www.icafe.spacenet.de; V, MC, AE, Diners)* offers a seemingly innocent deal: free Internet with an order of any entree. There is a catch, however—the food. This borderline-seedy pizza and pasta place caters to American college kids, who chatter and bang away at decrepit 386-era computers. Of course, as soon as you finish eating, they kick you off the machines. But, hey, if you're just looking to grab a quick bite and check e-mail, you could do worse.

Greasy spoon meets cyberchic at **Times Square** *(Bayer Str. 10a; 089/550-88-00; Any S-Bahn or U-Bahn 1, 2, 4, 5 to Hauptbahnhof; 7am-1am daily; 12DM/hour; www.times-square.net; V, MC)*, a high-tech Internet cafe dishing out low-tech grub. Just around the corner from Hauptbahnhof, the main train station, this location is convenient for just about every traveler in town, but even with 32 terminals, be prepared to wait. The menu is filled with familiar continental dishes with a handful of Bavarian specialties thrown in. The spaghetti with Gorgonzola is worth the heartburn, but steer clear of anything more exotic...like soup.

Bus Lines Out of the City Stamberger Bahnhof, the main bus station for out-of-town trips, sits next to the Hauptbahnhof train station. For traveling around upper Bavaria, call *089/551-640*. For traveling farther afield in Germany or to other European countries, call **Deutsche Touring** *(Tel 089/54-88-70-21, www.deutschetouring.com)*.

Laundry City-SB Waschcenter *(Paul-Heyse Str. 21; Tel 089/601-40-03; U-Bahn 4, 5 to Theresienwiese or Hauptbahnhof; 7am-10pm daily; No credit cards)*.

paris

"L'art c'est la découverte de l'autre."—Ben Vautier

"Paris speaks to me through pictures, myths of romance."
—Kevin Barker, singer-songwriter, Currituck County

The first things you may notice about Paris, probably the most visited city on earth, are that the pigeons, like the people, are well-fed and plumed and that the female mannequins in the shop windows have nipples. Myths of romance hang around Paris like stale smog in Los Angeles, obscuring the dynamic reality of modern Parisian life. The couples lip-locked on park benches and the cult of femininity that Parisian women obsessively cultivate with their cooler-than-thou coiffed stares and their ever-put-together outfits only enliven the myths every person in the world seems to entertain about Paris. French advertisements use the female body sans clothing to sell everything from toothpaste to cars. It doesn't take long to realize from the way they stare at and approach women that French men are some of the last bastions of male chauvinism on the planet. In other words, they're suckers for women. Take a stroll through the sleaze of rue St.-Denis, and the beauty sheltered in the gorgeous architecture of the ritzy Right Bank will devolve into sticky peep shows and hardened prostitutes.

The mythology and even the history of Paris are steeped in its literary and artistic past, from the romantic visions of Victor Hugo and the darkness of Émile Zola, to the crazed ravings of Louis Aragon, the depressive ponderings of Sartre, and the intensely intelligent observations of Simone de Beauvoir. In modern times the cinematic has replaced the literary, and the great Jean-Pierre Melville, Jean-Luc Godard, François Truffaut, and even foreigners such as Luis Buñuel, Bernardo Bertolucci, and Woody Allen have used the city as the backdrop for their kaleidoscopic hallucinations.

Today, not only is the profile of the city transforming with the influx of immigrant populations from Africa, the Arab world, Asia, and Eastern Europe—creating both excitement and political tension—but the European Union (EU), the Chunnel, and the juggernaut of globalization have made Parisians generally more open and friendly than they've ever been. People think of the City of Light as a place for lovers, and in fact, getting to know Paris can be as intoxicating as a good love affair. Sometimes, strolling down a broad boulevard under the chestnut trees and blue sky, sun glinting off the cafe tabletops, you could swear that Paris is embracing you. But then you find yourself backed against the window of a drafty, overpriced brasserie, coldly ignored, waiting to be charged tourist rates for a cheese sandwich, and you suspect Paris might've been stringing you along the whole time. And you think, was I ever in? Was I even close?

In fact, being *in,* or *branché* (literally, "plugged in"), is what Paris is all about. A joint can be dead and dull, but still keep its rep if the right people are there, if it's *branché.* Most young Parisians will affect total ignorance about what spot is or is not *branché,* but in fact they're in constant anxiety over not being *branché.* Those who are, in fact, in, won't even use the word; they may say that a scene is trendy or say nothing about it at all.

So, if you want to be in with the in crowd, it's essential—more so than in any other place in Europe—that you meet and interact with real, live, groovy French people. There's no way in without them, unless you're wildly rich, beautiful, or powerful (in which case, who needs you?). We've scoped out the best spots for this eventuality, and then all it'll take from you is a little initiative. Parisians can seem forbidding at first, but they're not the snobs of lore. The young especially are more apt to attempt communicating in English, either to go on about the latest De la Soul album or to inform you that they're vehemently opposed (they *oppose* things *vehemently* here) to an Americanized McParis. Either way, once you crack 'em, your new friends will surprise you with their generosity and hospitality. And when you catch that look of unease on their faces ("Is this cool enough, should we be somewhere else...?") you can smile to yourself that you know you're exactly where you want to be.

The best way to find out about underground club happenings is, as ever, the old-fashioned flyer, placed in the entryways of record shops like **Marché Noir** [see *stuff,* below]. Sometimes you'll even luck out and score free entry passes if you're savvy enough to pick up the right flyer. With so much happening all at once, and new venues gaining reps with the seasons, you've got to have good resources. The best all-around listings are in *l'Officiel des Spectacles,* a weekly that comes out every Wednesday and can be had at any newsstand for 2f. It's better, cheaper,

and more exhaustive than its competitor **Pariscope,** though **Pariscope**
includes *TimeOut's* weekly listings. If you read French, even just enough
to get by, the funky monthly mag **Nova** (10f) has a "hot guide" with
day-by-day cool picks. *TimeOut* recently started putting out free
English-language quarterlies, with a sparer list of events, special features,
and decently cool venues, with a map. The free English monthly **FUSAC**
hasn't got much of anything except listings for apartment shares and
short-term digs [see *crashing,* below]; same goes for its geeky competition,
Paris Voice. Both can be found just about everywhere—try in front of
Shakespeare & Co. [see *stuff,* below]. Oh, and remember, most businesses
close for an hour or more at 1pm, so the staff can enjoy a proper *déjeuner.*
Now there's civilization for you.

neighborhoods

The Paris *arrondissement* system can appear at first to make as much sense
as the scoring system on a dartboard (the 17th is next to the 8th is next
to the 1st. Right.), but you'll get used to it. We've indicated the *arrondissement* for each venue listed after the address, below. The Seine river runs
east-west through the middle of the city. The *arrondissements* begin with
the 1st on the **Right Bank** (north) of the Seine, smack-dab in the center
of town, then swing up and out, uncoiling clockwise. The city is bounded
by the périphérique, a beltway that runs up against the far ends of the
double-digit *arrondissements*. In general, it's best to disregard the linear
order of the *arrondissements* and to think, instead, in terms of the neighborhoods associated with the number: The **1st** is the **Louvre** [see *culture
zoo* below], the **4th** is the **Marais,** the **5th** the **Latin Quarter,** the **6th**
Saint-Germain, etc.

Most of postcard Paris—the Louvre, the majestic quays along the
Seine, the **Champs Elysées,** and the **Arc de Triomphe**—is in or around
the **1st** and **8th** *arrondissements*. Needless to say, this is also tourist Paris,
more and more a spiritual extension of Disneyland Paris, and not where
you'll want to be spending most of your time. The great big megaclubs
like **Le Queen** [see *club scene,* below] are still to be found around here,
but the funkier neighborhoods pop up all over the city without warning.

The **place de la Concorde**—the broad, beautiful plaza of obelisks and
belle époque lamps on the western edge of the **Tuileries** gardens on the
Right Bank—is the center of the city, the border between the 8th and 1st
arrondissements. It is the midway point of the **Voie Triumphale,** the trail
which aligns the **Arc de Triomphe,** the Champs Elysées, and the **Palais
du Louvre.** Across the Seine from the place de la Concorde on
the **Left Bank** is the ritzy, meticulous **7th** *arrondissement,* full of min-
istries and high-price antiques shops. The massive railway-station-looking
building you'll see is the **Musée d'Orsay** [see *culture zoo,* below]. Away
and to the east you'll see the **Eiffel Tower** [see *culture zoo,* below]
standing astride the **Champs de Mars,** on the edge of the 7th. Push on
as far as the **boulevard Saint-Germain** and follow it east and you'll pass
first through the **Saint-Germain** district in the **6th** *arrondissement,* full of

paris bars, clubs and culture zoo

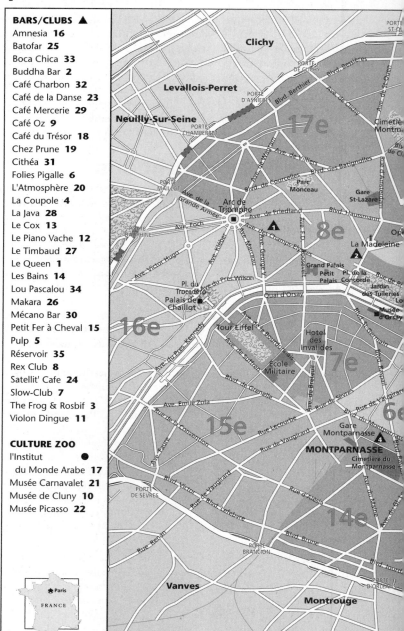

BARS/CLUBS ▲

Amnesia **16**
Batofar **25**
Boca Chica **33**
Buddha Bar **2**
Café Charbon **32**
Café de la Danse **23**
Café Mercerie **29**
Café Oz **9**
Café du Trésor **18**
Chez Prune **19**
Cithéa **31**
Folies Pigalle **6**
L'Atmosphère **20**
La Coupole **4**
La Java **28**
Le Cox **13**
Le Piano Vache **12**
Le Timbaud **27**
Le Queen **1**
Les Bains **14**
Lou Pascalou **34**
Makara **26**
Mécano Bar **30**
Petit Fer à Cheval **15**
Pulp **5**
Réservoir **35**
Rex Club **8**
Satellit' Cafe **24**
Slow-Club **7**
The Frog & Rosbif **3**
Violon Dingue **11**

CULTURE ZOO

l'Institut ●
  du Monde Arabe **17**
Musée Carnavalet **21**
Musée de Cluny **10**
Musée Picasso **22**

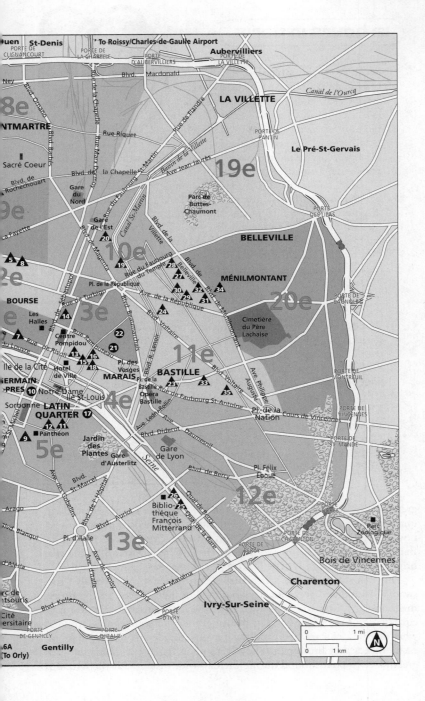

12 hours in paris

1. Walk down the Voie Triumphale from the Arc de Triomphe to the **Louvre** [see *culture zoo,* below], through the place de la Concorde and Tuileries garden.

2. Go to the Louvre after 3pm and visit the paintings section of the Richelieu wing; see Delacroix's *Liberty Leading the People* and other faves [see *culture zoo,* below].

3. Wander the two small islands in the Seine: the Île de la Cité, which was the whole of Paris c. 50 A.D., and the Île Saint-Louis.

4. Wander up into the Latin Quarter from the rue des Écoles and the little medieval streets on this side of the **Panthéon** [see *culture zoo,* below] at night, when the vampires come out.

5. Nearby, visit the **Musée de Cluny** [see *culture zoo,* below] and see the five allegorical tapestries of *The Lady and the Unicorn.*

6. Have a pot of tea and some scones at **Mariage Frères** in the Marais at 4pm, and watch the ladies who lunch pour in [see *only here,* below].

7. Wander and explore the Marais and walk elegantly around the Place des Vosges at sunset, when the galleries cast long shadows over the court.

8. After 11pm, live it up along the rue Oberkampf, at **Café Charbon, Mécano Bar,** and **Cithéa** [see *bar scene,* below, for all].

9. If it's a moody day, stroll along the banks of the Canal Saint-Martin beginning at the François le Maître Square *(Métro to République),* and soak up the atmosphere.

10. Have dinner, or at least dessert, at **Bofinger** [see *eats,* below], the extraordinary, bustling brasserie, at midnight, when the best people are only just sitting down to sup.

great little boutiques and cafes, and then the **Quartier Latin,** the student quarter, a vestige of medieval Paris, with the greatest density of tiny movie houses, cafes, and attitude in Western Europe. Cut back to the Right Bank here and you'll pass over the **Île de la Cité** and stand before the bright white facade of **Notre Dame** [see *culture zoo,* below] cathedral.

Due east along the **rue Saint-Antoine** brings you to the **Marais** ("the swamp"), a hip and gorgeous neighborhood of tight streets, 16th-century mansions, and artsy bars. This used to be the Jewish quarter, but now it is equally, if not more, the heart of the gay scene, and you begin to wonder what the trim, chic gay men and the nervous, bearded Orthodox make of each other as they brush past. The Marais offers the rare combination of a great place to poke around during the day—for instance, at the **Musée**

Carnavalet or the **Musée Picasso** [see *culture zoo,* below, for both] or at the tearoom **Mariage Frères** [see *only here,* below]—and a thumping night scene, at for instance **Petit Fer à Cheval** or **Café du Trésor** [see *bar scene,* below, for both]. Push on east along the shop-lined, aptly named, **rue de Francs Bourgeois** and you'll come to the splendid **Place des Vosges,** an enclosed plaza of perfect harmony, then brace yourself for the bustle of the **Place de la Bastille,** at the mouth of the cool **11th,** just beyond.

Bastille was the heart of the Paris night scene in the '80s and still has a mighty draw, but the glitzy crush everywhere along the **rue du Faubourg Saint-Antoine,** the **rue Charonne,** and, most of all, the bombastically over-hyped **rue de Lappe** has the hashed-over and has-been feel of a glam band of the same era that's "still rockin'." Look out for vomiting Dutch tourists. Half a mile to the north of Bastille, along the **boulevard Richard Lenoir,** you come to **Ménilmontant** and the **rue Oberkampf.** For the past few years, this nondescript little street—nothing at all to see in daylight—has reigned as uncontested king of the bar scene. It, too, shows signs of wear and creeping Disneyland Paris, but **Café Charbon** and the **Mécano Bar** [see *bar scene,* below, for both] are still the places to be seen for those of us who crave it.

East along the rue Oberkampf and along the **boulevard de Belleville** brings you to the dizzying and increasingly coolifying immigrant swirl of Belleville (now in the 20th), where West Africans, Maghrebins (North

NIQUE LES FLICS

Since the 1970s, when they were imported to work in the mines and heavy industry, North Africans have occupied a special place in French society. North African couscous and the *tagines* of delicious stewed meats seasoned with vegetables and raisins have become accepted standards of the Parisian diet, but the same acceptance cannot exactly be said of the North Africans themselves. They are French without being French, and have the brunt of the French paranoia about national and cultural identity. Films like *La Haine* only capture part of the picture. Walk certain streets of Paris, like the quays bordering the Seine and the area surrounding Pont Neuf, and you're bound to have a North African kid try to sell you some hash, but don't be suckered. High unemployment has pushed a lot of North African teenagers toward selling drugs (or pretending they have drugs to sell) and created a lot of resentment from many native-born French against all North Africans, even those who actually do hold honest, paying positions.

paris eats and crashing

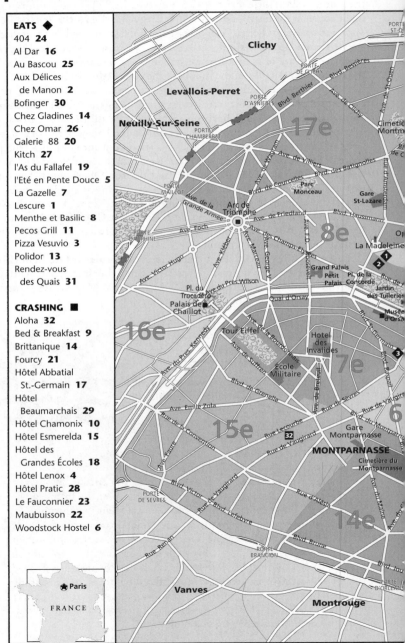

EATS ◆
404 **24**
Al Dar **16**
Au Bascou **25**
Aux Délices
de Manon **2**
Bofinger **30**
Chez Gladines **14**
Chez Omar **26**
Galerie 88 **20**
Kitch **27**
l'As du Fallafel **19**
l'Eté en Pente Douce **5**
La Gazelle **7**
Lescure **1**
Menthe et Basilic **8**
Pecos Grill **11**
Pizza Vesuvio **3**
Polidor **13**
Rendez-vous
des Quais **31**

CRASHING ■
Aloha **32**
Bed & Breakfast **9**
Brittanique **14**
Fourcy **21**
Hôtel Abbatial
St.-Germain **17**
Hôtel
Beaumarchais **29**
Hôtel Chamonix **10**
Hôtel Esmerelda **15**
Hôtel des
Grandes Écoles **18**
Hôtel Lenox **4**
Hôtel Pratic **28**
Le Fauconnier **23**
Maubuisson **22**
Woodstock Hostel **6**

★ Paris
FRANCE

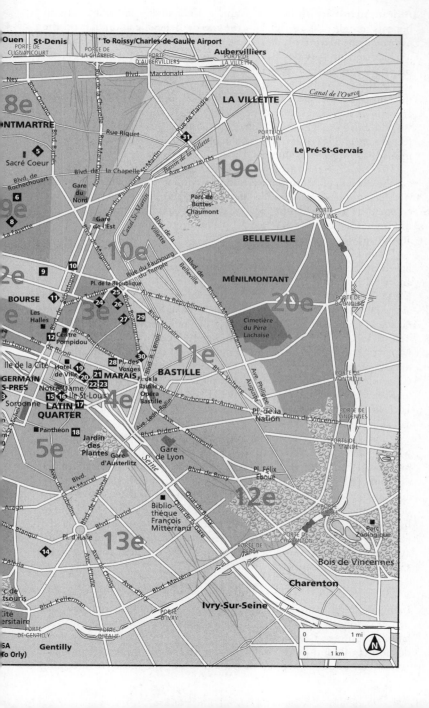

African Arabs), Sephardic Jews, Chinese, Vietnamese, and white Parisian hepcats mingle. Take a right on the rue de Belleville and a left on the **avenue Simon Bolivar,** and you'll find yourself in the **19th** and the uncharacteristic **Parc des Buttes Chaumont,** perhaps Paris's most beautiful park, with craggy cliffs, Greek temple follies, the Sublime, and that sort of thing. The 19th and the 20th, along with the 13th, way south on the Left Bank, are havens of radicalism in this otherwise solidly conservative town, and the electorate here loyally keeps the French Communist Party in business. The Paris Commune of 1871 was fueled by the disaffected here and was put down here in bloody slaughter, costing the communards upward of 3,000 lives.

To the west, in the **18th,** past the lowlands of the largely Arabic **Barbès,** are the heights of **Montmartre,** still a charming, quiet place to get lost, with a number of its wooden *moulins* (windmills) still standing, and crowned by **Sacré-Coeur** [see *culture zoo,* below], the painfully gaudy, meringue-like church perched atop the mount, and glimpsable from almost anywhere in Paris.

Far and away to the south, in the 13th, is the hilly, charming, no-frills haven of the communard spirit, the **Butte aux Cailles,** where students and workers unite. The proletarian spirit survives in simple bistros like **Chez Gladines** [see *eats,* below], where folks are likely to curse the state and sing hundred-year-old revolutionary ballads; many of the bars, in fact, take their names from the words of the Commune's anthem, "Le Temps des Cérises." West of that, through residential no-man's-lands, lies **Montparnasse,** the sometime haunt of the Lost Generation and now of aging, lost American expats. **La Coupole,** the preferred brasserie of the Gertrude Stein set, and its new salsa-pumping lower level, are worth a look, however [see *club scene,* below]. The west of Paris—the **17th** and **16th** *arrondissements* on the Right Bank, and the **15th** on the Left—you can skip with minimal loss.

Paris is served by the best public transport system in the world, the Métro. Clean, fast, convenient, it's a city planner's dream. You're never more than 5 minutes from a **Métro** stop or 30 minutes from the center of town. The suburban **RER** lines also run through the center of town and can be quicker. The only hitch is that the whole system closes down sometime around 12:30 or 1am. (The time of the last train is listed on the destination sign when you enter.) After that, you're at the mercy of Paris's pricey and underrepresented taxis. On a Saturday night, available taxis don't reappear until 3am, so be prepared to burn some shoe-leather after dancing or wait.

hanging out

In autumn and winter, Paris gets gray, dreary, and a little on edge, and people busily withdraw into their newspapers, cafes, and hot chocolates. In summer, however, you should have no trouble finding spots to do nothing in and locals to not do it with. Nearly every cafe puts out tables, and most every plaza or park is full of the most jaw-dropping

five things to talk to a local about

1. **Paris:** Parisians are more than half in love with their city, and each has a stomping ground all his or her own. Ask them about it. It's a great way to learn more about the place and its history, and listening to them go on and on is kind of endearing.
2. **Globalization:** If they're young, they're probably against the imminent decline of things French and the rise of all things American, like multinationals and fast food. Their unlikely hero is José Bove, the shepherd from the south who bulldozed a McDonald's in 1999.
3. **What a racist, terrible country France is:** The prejudice against Maghrebin (North African Arab) immigrants is often very severe, and the plight of the *sans-papiers* (illegals) is the cause célèbre of the young left.
4. **What a racist, terrible country the U.S. is:** If possible, the French are even more obsessed with race in America than the Americans. Nod your head, agree, rail freely against the States. This will bring the conversation around to...
5. **American movies:** The French don't love only Clint Eastwood, they love Westerns you've never heard of, Marilyn as a serious comedienne, and Hitchcock, and probably know far, far more than you about, say, Ernst Lubitsch. And skip the whole Jerry Lewis thing....Just let it go.

slackers you've seen. The primest spot to spark up a conversation is either the **Place de la Sorbonne**—on the Place itself or in one of its many cigarette-smoke-clogged cafes—or immediately inside the **Sorbonne** *(Sorbonne III and IV; Métro to Cluny-La Sorbonne),* in the courtyard. The gorgeous **Place des Vosges** *(Métro to Bastille or Saint-Paul),* until recently a solemn, residential cloister, is where the cool and beautiful from the Marais now come to warm themselves and spread the wealth.

With so much of the population here in cafes so much of the time, the question arises: Don't these people work? The answer to which is: sort of. With three-course lunches, 12 percent unemployment, and a freshly minted law enforcing a 39-hour-max workweek, Parisians have a lot of time to dawdle. There are also indications that some of the more picturesque cafe-dwellers are in fact paid employees of the French Tourist Bureau, strategically placed to promote the city's romantic image (no, they're not hiring). So if you're going to get in with the locals, join them at the cafes and *salons de thé* where they linger and try to look serious doing very little.

Right off the rue de Rivoli, with a view of the Seine and the dome of the Institut de France, **Le Fumoir** *(6 rue de l'Amiral-de-Coligny, 1st; Tel 01/42-92-00-24; Métro to Louvre or Louvre-Rivoli; 11am-2am daily; AE, MC, V)* is how you imagined Paris would be. With the yellow blinds shutting out any daylight, this long, ersatz-'30s speakeasy is peopled with just about everyone who's anyone: cigar-chomping suited men in leather smoking chairs; tall, gesticulating, stubble-cheeked artists; and the occasional dumbfounded onlooker. The rear room holds a reading library and the all-day-long-ers, chowing on the decent-but-pricey food.

Just the opposite effect is had at **Le Reflet** *(6 rue Champollion, 5th; Tel 01/43-29-97-27; Métro to Cluny-La Sorbonne; 10am-2am daily; MC, V)* in the Latin Quarter, a cramped little room opposite an art-house theater of the same name. It's still one of the best places in Paris to work on your novel, have an espresso, maybe a little tempeh salad, flirt with the waitstaff, and meet the coolest and most low-key of the university student set.

Right on its heels is the **Café de la Mairie** *(8 place Saint-Sulpice, 6th; Tel 01/43-26-67-82; Métro to Saint-Sulpice or Odéon; 7am-2am Mon-Sat, daily in June; No credit cards)*. Don't let the mustard-yellow ceiling or the early-'60s naugahyde banquettes and fluorescent lighting throw you—this is one of the local egghead faves. The glass-enclosed terrace has the best seats for spying on the place Saint-Sulpice, and the second level is that holy grail (for some) of Paris cafes—it has a great nonsmoking section.

The tearoom at **La Mosquée de Paris** *(210 rue des Quatre Fages, 5th; Tel 01/45-35-97-33; Métro to Place Monge; 9am-midnight daily; MC, V)*, the big exotic draw for the student set, is *hypercool* (pronounced ee-pehr-kul). The waitstaff gets a little *ee-pehr* here, and snappy, too, and you can't blame them—amazing numbers of funky students crush into the low copper tables, downing delicious spiced-almond tea and baklava under low-hung brass lamps.

A nice pit stop after a little excursion to the Pompidou, or shopping in Les Halles and the alternately chic and sleazy side streets surrounding the shopping center, is the ornately carved wood bar of **JIP's Cafe** *(41 rue St.-Denis; Tel 01/42-21-33-93; Métro to Chatelet; 11am-2am daily; MC, V)* for a taste of Kingston beer, sweetened by a bit of rich rum, or an *exotique* Caribbean cocktail. The atmosphere of the place is laid-back, attentively serviced by cutely braided help, soothed by a bit of ragga, reggae, and roots R&B, and covered by a ceiling decorated with African wood carvings.

The narrow, moody Canal Saint-Martin, with its stunted trees, tall green locks, high pedestrian bridges, and quiet, is becoming a refuge for cool Parisians fed up with cool-hunting. Before elbowing your way into **L'Atmosphère** [see *live music scene*, below] stop at **Chez Prune** *(71 quai de Valmay, 10th; Tel 01/42-41-30-47; Métro to République; 7:30am-*

2am Mon-Sat, 10am-2am Sun; V), a funky corner cafe/bar with reggae in the air, and check out the beautiful, happy inhabitants in their still-unspoiled environment.

The upper reaches of Canal Saint-Martin widen into the Basin de la Villette in the 19th, where a converted boathouse right on the wide cobblestone quay is now a small, ultra-modern multiplex movie theater. Stop in to the restaurant inside, the **Rendez-vous des Quais** *(10 quai de la Seine, 19th; Tel 01/40-37-02-81; Métro to Stalingrad; 11:30am-1am daily in winter, 10:30am-2am daily in summer; AE, MC, V)* with its awkward, sloping cement roof, low lights, and cozy atmosphere, and savor a frothy *cafe crème* while you enjoy the view (skip the food, though).

Though it's a little nasty, what with the fumes from the highway and that foaming brown city river water, the **banks of the Seine** are always elbow-to-elbow with locals sporting their little Speedos in the warmer months. A less Coney Island feel is found along the shady banks of the up-and-coming Saint-Martin Canal in the 10th and 19th *arrondissements.* Pickup ultimate frisbee games happen on the grass of the **Bois de Vincennes** (Métro to Château-Vincennes), just on the eastern edge of town.

bar scene

The bar scene is the site of Paris nightlife; it is here that Parisians feel most at home, mugging under the dim lights, dangling Gauloises and Marlboros from their puckered lips, and frightening their little dogs. Though Paris has plenty of club kids and music lovers, as everywhere, the bar allows the Parisians to show off what they've got going on, and hide away what they don't (like rhythm) [see *club scene,* below]. Dress code varies, but is generally more formal than in the States, and (big surprise) you can't go wrong with black; the bucket-jeans with dragging, shredded cuffs and sneaks (except if they're a bright pair of New Balance) probably won't wash.

Still hip after all these years, rue Oberkampf, the main drag of Ménilmontant, is lined with bar after bar, stretching toward Belleville. Mondays and Tuedays are slow here, but after that it can feel like every youth in Paris is trying to squeeze their way into this narrow little lane. The biggest and baddest of the lot are Café Charbon and Mécano Bar, only a few buildings apart from each other and both jammed full of the coolest and drop-deadest of the 18-to-25 set.

Café Charbon *(109 rue Oberkampf, 11th; Tel 01/43-57-55-13; Métro to Parmentier or Ménilmontant; 9am-2am daily; MC, V)* is a beautiful space, a belle époque dance hall with a long wide bar, gas lamps, tall mirrors, and 20-foot ceilings. The DJ spinning house and jungle gives a nice counterpoint, making this the perfect spot to linger and neck with a coquette or French loverboy before a wide audience at 3am. They also host live acts and name DJs, so call ahead to see what's on.

Mécano Bar *(99 rue Oberkampf, 11th; Tel 01/40-21-35-28; Métro to Parmentier or Ménilmontant; 9am-2am Mon-Sat, 10am-2am Sun, Wed, Sat; AE, MC, V),* despite the name, is far from a "tool shed" (though with

garçon meets fille

Are the French the seducers and seductresses they're fabled to be? They've got something, there's no denying it. Maybe it's that Paris is in some haunting way a lonelier place than you might have imagined, or maybe it's that the fear (of sex crime or insult) we know as PC has never crossed the Atlantic—but arts long-lost in the States such as innuendo, drawn-out flirtation, shameless meaningful looks between strangers, sexy PDA, and the asking-for and giving-out of phone numbers without a lot of to-do, are still alive here and charge almost every exchange with a little *frisson*. The two little kisses upon greeting and parting are not always totally innocent; nor are those lingering looks on the Métro: I heard tell of a friend of a friend, not bad-looking, who sat beside a not bad-looking total stranger, and after a 15-minute wordless ride, the two rose in unison and walked silently back to her place. Or maybe people just tell these stories to make everyone else miserable. Note: A *préservatif* is a condom, not some additive.

the bus engines and monkey wrenches hanging from the ceiling, it does overreach for the "theme bar" thing), and its more friendly layout leads to more mixing between the tables and spontaneous dancing—for more of this lip-biting, fist-pumping, endearing French phenomenon, hop across the street to **Cithéa** [see *club scene*, below]. Mécano hasn't quite got the same erotic patina as Charbon [see above], and attracts a slightly younger crowd, but is just as wildly popular.

A slightly older, more meditative crowd can be found across the street at **Café Mercerie** *(98 rue Oberkampf, 11th; Tel 01/43-38-81-30; Métro to Parmentier or Ménilmontant; 5pm-2am daily; V)*, with its oversized sewing machines, stripped walls, and back lounge.

Also located on the plain-jane-by-day, party-girl-by-night rue Oberkampf, the **Underworld Cafe** *(25 rue Oberkampf; Tel 01/48-06-35-36; Métro to Oberkampf; 6pm-2am daily; underworld@libertysurf.fr; Cover varies, free-30f; AE, MC, V)* is a good place to mellow out or get hot around the collar, but only if the moment is right. With tables, chairs and couches, three large-screen TVs, and wall projections broadcasting a range of visual stimuli, there is plenty to keep you occupied, if the beautiful girl working behind the counter or gay boys sitting alone at the bar don't. Evenings feature a mellow mix of musical styles—from pop, house, and garage to drum 'n' bass and hard techno during the week, to higher-quality DJs and events on the weekends. During the hottest all-round get-downs, the tables and chairs part to create a dance floor.

Further up along Oberkampf, just after it crosses the roundabout boulevard de Belleville and down a sneaky side street to the right, is the rue des Panoyaux, the chillest corner of Ménilmontant. Here you'll find the solid, spacious, and far calmer **Lou Pascalou** *(14 rue des Panoyaux, 20th; Tel 01/46-36-78-10; Métro to Ménilmontant; 9am-2am daily; AE, V)*, a local fave and the place to come if you're actually interested in preserving your vocal cords, and not just pretending to comprehend Jean-Claude's responses to your questions.

With all the disorienting scene-y-ness of Oberkampf, it can be shocking to realize you're a hop, skip, and stagger away from Belleville and its distinctly un-French buzz. Except for the occasional nose-ringed student here to check out "the other," Belleville (beginning, really, on the next street parallel to Oberkampf, the rue Timbaud) is a great place to wander aimlessly, but can be a bit forbidding. Though not the mecca of integration many tout it to be, Belleville does boast more genuine mingling than elsewhere in Paris.

Try the **Le Timbaud** *(99 rue Jean-Pierre Timbaud, 11th; Tel 01/49-23-08-96; Métro to Couronnes; 7:30am-2am daily, 24 hours month of Ramadan; V, MC, AE)* for just such a place, absolutely blasting West African tunes to its far-from-exclusively Arabic clientele, featuring live jazz, African, or Algerian Raï after Ramadan, and appropriately skeptical about (but nonetheless welcoming to) you.

Students who can't bother to shave and put on a tie still go out in the Latin quarter, and the student dive is **Le Piano Vache** *(8 rue Laplace, 5th; Tel 01/46-33-75-03; Métro to Maubert-Mutualité; Noon-2am Mon-Fri, 9pm-2am Sat, Sun; MC, V)*, on a medieval street on the northern slope of the Panthéon. Dingy and wonderful, its walls are all plastered and charred. A DJ spins Wednesday through the weekend, but Friday—*American Rock* night—somehow feels the most French.

British-style bars and pubs are relatively foreign to Paris's bar, brasserie, and cafe culture. Indeed, across France, Irish and British pubs tend to be more expensive and style-conscious than your average dive bar, but in Paris, kids who want to drink seriously will look to foreign-run bars or bars catering to foreigners.

Tucked off of rue Sentier in the 2nd *arrondissement,* south of boulevard

Rules of the Game

There is no enforced drinking age in France, but neither are there great drunks; people consume moderately and get drunk with great composure. It's only tourists you'll hear shouting yahoo while under the influence. As for narcotics, we would definitely not recommend you head out to the rough streets of the *banlieue,* the outskirts, the only areas in Paris where they're hawked in the street. In most public parks, like the Champ de Mars, you'll find kids sneaking a toke, though busts are extremely rare.

Poissonière, and situated (surprisingly enough) next to a police station, **Café le Port d'Amsterdam** *(20 rue du Croissant; Tel 01/40-39-02-63; Métro to Sentier; 5pm-2am; Happy hour 5-8pm; www.dutchbars.com)* is a dive bar run by a cabal of Dutch chauvinists, reputed to entice female patrons into dancing on the scarred wood tables. Music varies from Britpop to commercial Euro-dance, and at night the bar becomes a dark smoky den of sin, fueled by cheap Grolsch and testosterone.

Also located in the 2nd *arrondissement,* on the laughably sleazy rue St.-Denis, **The Frog & Rosbif** *(116 rue St.-Denis; Tel 01/42-36-34-73; Métro to Etienne Marcel; Noon-2am daily; Happy hour 6-9pm Mon-Sat; Live jazz Sun)* is the spot to gab with ex-pat Brits and butt heads with European football fans over pints and pitchers of lager and groovy microbrews. With heavy wood furniture, floors, and bar, this place has the well-trodden look and relaxed feel of an English pub, and crazy patrons to match. Remember as you settle into a booze-laden haze that they offer student discounts on their brew. Look for the live broadcasts of European football and English rugby, and watch out for that English nutter doing card and coin magic tricks. A note for the crime-weary urbanite in all of us: He's not trying to take your money, he just wants to make you smile.

And if you're feeling homesick, run around to the **Violon Dingue** *(46 rue de la Montagne Sainte-Geneviève, 5th; No phone; Métro to Maubert-Mutualité; Regular bar 6pm-1:30am Sun-Thur, 8pm-3:30am Sat, Sun, lower level 4:30pm-3:30am Fri, Sat; V, MC),* designed and run by a Minnesota local and ex-Navy man, where you can watch NFL whenever in season, and get blitzed beneath old tin Coors signs and sports pennants to the sweet sounds of James Brown on the juke.

On the western edge of the Latin Quarter, on a main street, **Café Oz** *(184 rue St.-Jacques, 5th; Tel 01/43-54-30-48; RER to Luxembourg, Métro to Cluny-La Sorbonne; 4pm-2am daily; MC, V)* is where to get your Australian fix (if the quotient was too low at the hostel). Travel yarns, sleepy 1am chess games, and Fosters is what you'll 'ave 'ere, mate.

The Marais can have a sultry, New Orleans feel at night, and a number of slick venues and American-style bars have opened up alongside the gay old-timers. The truly petite **Petit Fer à Cheval** *(28 rue Vieille-du-Temple, 4th; Tel 01/42-72-47-47; Métro to St.-Paul; 9am-2am daily; MC, V, AE),* with its tin ceiling, zinc bar, and old Paris charm, is one of the best bars in the area, if you can squeeze in. Were the talented Tom Ripley to seduce you, kill you, and steal your identity, he'd start the process here.

Just around the corner in a wide, cobbled cul de sac is the very young and very cool **Café du Trésor** *(164 Blvd. St.-Germain, 4th; Tel 01/43-26-62-93; Métro to Odéon; 7:30am-6am daily; MC, V)* with the latest house grooves playing and sultry kids on every divan.

You find an entirely different set at **Buddha Bar** *(8 rue Boissy d'Anglas, 8th; Tel 01/53-05-90-00; Métro to Concorde; 6pm-2am daily; AE, V, MC)* the transcendent shrine of the BCBGers *(bon chic bon genre),* that unique creation of modern French society: yuppies with ascots. Though not as exclusive, of course, as the *clubs privés* many of this crowd belong to, Buddha Bar is where the Donald might decline shaking hands with Lenny Kravitz or his entourage. Dominated by a huge Golden Buddha, and filled with strains of sitars, double violins, and other signals that you're firmly in France, this massive split-level, grotto-like, and hugely pricey restaurant/bar in the 8th still has to be visited at least once.

And then, of course, there's the Bastille scene, where you'll wind up despite yourself and where a good time can still be had with selective vision. The spawn of the European Union still congregate here and subject themselves to the unjustifiably snooty whims of the door along the rue du Faubourg Saint-Antoine at La Fabrique, SanZSanS, Barrio Latino, and the whole sleazy stretch of the rue de Lappe.

If you must, you might as well at **Boca Chica** *(58 rue de Charonne, 11th; Tel 01-43-57-93-13; Métro to Ledru-Rollin; 11am-2am daily; AE, MC, V)* where the "Latino" pretensions of the Bastille scene are brought to fever pitch, and the vivacity, genuine fun-lovingness, and tasty tapas make you feel hotta' than they do in Granada. Low tables, painfully loud Cesaria Evora remixes, and burnt umber are the call of the hour.

LIVE MUSIC SCENE

Paris was patron to jazz's cutting edge in the '40s and '50s, but since then we haven't consistently been able to depend on their taste, to say the least. Sometimes they treat a fledgling comer seriously—take Charlie Parker—and elevate him to his rightful place, and sometimes they elect others—say Serge Gainsbourg or Céline Dion (for whom we've got to accept partial responsibility)—and treat them with the same seriousness. The current Parisian enthusiasm is world music, that catch-all phrase that can mean anything—it can lump together respectable ska, Algerian Raï, Gypsy fiddlers, and klezmer acts, with, say, a Frenchman in red suspenders singing in Arabic to the accompaniment of a gypsy violin, a Jewish clarinet, and a tabla. It's hit-or-miss.

▶▶JAZZ

L'Atmosphère *(49 rue Lucien Sampaix, 10th; Tel 01/40-38-09-21; Métro to Gare de l'Est; Bar 11am-2am Tue-Fri, 5pm-2am Sat, Sun, sets begin 8pm Tue-Sat, 5pm Sun; No cover; No credit cards),* a tiny bistro/cafe/bar on the Canal Saint-Martin, is one of the best jazz venues out there, with the energetic blowing out of home-grown talent, and sometimes inspiring, fanciful solos, though the influence of Ornette Coleman is a little overwhelming. Linger over a glass of wine before the first set starts around 8pm—the weekend crush can be impossible—stay for the first set, and then retire to **Chez Prune** [see *hanging out,* above].

While the atmosphere at l'Atmosphère can run to the ponderous, **Cithéa** [see *club scene,* below]—whether a funk, reggae, world, or jazz show is on—makes sure its groove is front and center. With groovy bass lines and the occasional barri sax, Cithéa can make you never want to go home again—and with the DJ spinning funk faves after the set, you won't have to, till dawn.

Should you require a chiller ambiance with the possibility of release

la dı da dj

Rap has busted through the charts in France, but it pretty much remains the music of the *cité,* the generally black, Arab, and Jewish–dominated, housing project–like suburbs surrounding Paris. Paris and Marseilles, much like the East and West coasts of the United States, compete in verbal sparring contests. In the headlines of French newspapers and in the minds of many elders and young people, rap gets a bad rap and is still associated with questionable indictments of police racism, violence, and the gangster-like lifestyles prevalent in its lyrics. While the charts play host to a number of artists, often mimicking the styles of American rap, French rap has come a long way since the late '80s and the days of **MC Solaar,** one of the few French rappers to break through to the American scene. Nowadays, **NTM** is arguably one of the best and most distinguished groups on the French scene for its uncompromisingly sharp rhymes and tight beats, and the influence of American independent hip-hop is evident in the raw energy of such groups as **Supa Sian Crew.**

The obvious difference between American and French rap is the influence of ragga and dancehall (the difference between ragga and dancehall being largely one of semantics). The white dreads now sported by both girls and boys in cities like Rouen and Lille are less a statement of roots culture or Rastafarianism than a fashion statement, but they hint at larger influence in French popular culture. Afro-beat, reggae, dancehall, and ragga are wildly popular in France, as the popularity of Nigerian-born **Femi Kuti,** the son of '80s Afrobeat superstar Fela Kuti, and **Les Nubiennes,** the West African rooted R&B pop group, attest.

Ragga and dancehall have very heavily influenced rap in France and even in the most commercial of French rap, you'll hear dancehall-style backup vocals. Songs usually feature a break down, where an MC will kick a few rhymes in a dancehall-stylee flow. The inevitable result of such influence is a blurring of the genres. At the **Slow-Club,** [see *club scene,* below] you'll hear rap vocals thrown over dancehall bass lines, and dancehall vocals laid down over rap beats, often with R&B backup vocals to boot. Groups like **Raggasonic** are some of the most popular innovators of such musical miscegenation.

Essential Listening:
Supa Sian Crew, *KLR* (Virgin)
NTM, *Paris sous les Bombs* (Sony)
Premiere Classe compilation (Virgin)
Le Flow 1 & 2 compilations (Virgin & Ultra)

into the Oberkampf mayhem, check out the **Satellit' Cafe** *(44 rue de la Folie Méricourt, 11th; Tel 01/47-00-48-87; Métro to Oberkampf; 8pm-3am Tue-Thur, 10pm-6am Fri, Sat, shows at 9:30pm Tue-Thur; www. satellit-cafe.com; V, MC)* where acoustic world acts range from downright slamming to self-serious crud. The space itself, with black walls and a glow-in-the-dark solar system painting, feels like an 11-year-old's dream of an ideal club. When the friendly staff switches on the turntable on the long weekends, it can be a swinging floor, too.

The *péniches* (canal barges) **Batofar** [see *club scene*, below] and **Makara** *(quai de la Gare, 13th; Tel 01/44-24-09-00; Métro to quai de la Gare; 9pm-2am Wed-Sun; 30-50f cover; MC, V)* are rarely—at least not yet—packed, and can host everything from flamenco to funk. The multi-act shows are long, and loud.

A favorite of the *Nova*-reading set, the beguilingly eclectic **Café de la Danse** *(5 Passage Louis-Philippe, 11th; Tel 01/47-00-57-59; Métro to Bastille; Shows 8:30pm most nights; 80-120f cover; No credit cards)* is impossible to characterize, booking fast-and-furious rock acts like the Cramps as much as it pushes its Arabic character. The mood of this dank, stony place can shift from Château Dracul to Soho London between gigs. The high quality of the acts is worth the price, as are the funky young things who shell it out nightly.

Nearby, the tight but hip **Réservoir** *(16 rue de la Forge Royale, 11th; Tel 01/43-56-39-60; Métro to Faidherbe-Chaligny; Bar 8pm-2am daily, shows at 11pm Tue-Sat; No cover; AE, MC, V)*, is a slicker affair, hooked deeply into the music biz and its double-breasted, pinky-ringed sleaze factor. It's still one of the better places to hear hot labels trying out the newly signed on a beautiful, made-up clientele on Thurdays, and it's one of the Paris layover blips on the migratory path of freshly hot musicians.

If you're looking for something eclectic, take a seat on **Le Divan du Monde** (Couch of the World) *(75 rue des Martyrs; Tel 01/44-92-77-66; Métro to Pigalle; Concerts start at 7:30pm Mon-Sat, 4pm Sun; Cover varies, free-120f, 20-40f drinks; No credit cards)*. Housed in a two-tiered former cabaret club in the popping Pigalle area, this casually sized concert space hosts everything from intense drum 'n' bass, ragga, and raï events to world beat, Brit-pop, rock, and the odd hip-hop concert, and the crowd is as diverse as the music. You don't want to dally, because concerts start on time and end promptly.

club scene

The Paris club—or *boîte*—is kind of an unnatural graft onto Paris's nightlife, and this can make some of its excesses—the scoping, the over-the-top grinding, and the leaping up and down on the cushions—a little embarrassing to witness. The best dancers here are generally not nationals, but Americans, Spaniards, and the boogying huddled masses from everywhere else who flock here. Unless you are gorgeous, famous, or know someone (and, hey, don't sell yourself short), it can be hard to get into the big, *branché* clubs along the Champs Elysées or elsewhere.

There is no list you can lie and say you were left off of, and smooth-talking the bouncers is definitely harder in French. Most *branché* nighthawks get private invitations to parties in the mail in lieu of being put down on a list. If you're dying to get into one of these joints, make friends with one of the elect or get your mitts on one of those invites by whatever means necessary—the velvet rope parts the minute they check it out.

The king of these *boîtes branchées* is **Les Bains** *(7 rue du Bourg-l'Abbé, 3rd; Tel 01/48-87-01-80; Métro to Réaumur Sébastopol; 11:30pm-6am daily, restaurant 9pm-1am; 120f cover, drinks 65f; AE, MC, V),* with an upstairs restaurant that doubles as a roped-off VIP room (read: models and those who can bed 'em, like celebs). The fiftysomething prowlers stand around looking worried as those only slightly less beautiful than their sisters upstairs (or else still unsigned) cavort before their eyes. remnants of the former bathhouse, the intermittent open pools function largely as ashtrays these days. Wednesday's *Glam Parade*—when the glam beats are laid down—is the night to come, otherwise it's generally house.

If Les Bains is King, God save **Le Queen** *(102 ave. des Champs Elysées, 8th; Tel 01/53-89-08-90; Métro to Charles de Gaulle-Étoile, George V, Franklin Roosevelt; Daily midnight-dawn; Cover 100f Fri, Sat, 50f Sun-Thur; Exclusively gay Thur, Sat, Sun; V, MC, AE),* where the most outrageous element of the Paris gay scene taught its straight brothers and sisters how to get down. Still ostensibly a queer club (meaning women might be scrutinized at the door longer than they're used to), this is where the big wet kiss Paris has decided to bestow on its queer demimonde is sloppiest. Huge, with go-go dancers, six-foot transsexuals, and ear-shattering techno mixes, there is no better dance floor in Paris. For full-out delicious drag, Monday is the night to see Paris Burning. The *Respect Is Burning* party on Wednesday nights is the club's only truly mixed night, and the place kicks to the tunes of big-name house DJs like Dimitri From Paris and the occasional American import like Armand Van Helden. For much of 1999-2000, the party toured the globe as if bent on world domination. Now the party is back in town at its rightful home in the metal and slick, black industrial interior of Le Queen.

The first Thursday of the month, **Pulp** *(25 blvd. Poissonière; Tel 01/40-26-01-93; Métro to Grands Blvds; Midnight-dawn Wed-Sat; 50f Fri, Sat; AE, MC, V)* [see *gay scene,* below] tolerates unaccompanied men for a fun, mixed gay and straight party (but guys, don't expect any generosity from the less-than-*gentille* girls working the bar). While music varies from house to Latin and lacks the superstar quality of Le Queen, the vibe of this intimate place is decidedly positive.

Up in Pigalle, the seedy, Times Square–like area south of Montmartre, **Folies Pigalle** *(11 place Pigalle, 9th; Tel 01/48-78-25-56; Métro to Pigalle; Midnight-dawn daily, till noon weekends; Cover 100f; MC, V),* once a strip joint, has managed to spin tassles into gold (or at least lamé). Not nearly as plugged-in as Les Bains or Le Queen, a younger crowd comes here to enjoy itself on the runway and in the pit (rather than to hang on the pavement outside, call friends on their cell phones and *talk* about enjoying themselves). The weekends are solidly techno, while Sundays from 5:30 to 11pm see the *United Colours of Gays* tea dance, a pseudo–belly dancing event the young things just can't seem to resist in this town.

The only option for straight-ahead dancing along the Oberkampf strip is **Cithéa** *(112-114 rue Oberkampf, 11th; Tel 01/40-21-70-95; Métro to Parmentier; 10pm-5am daily, shows 11pm Wed-Sat; Admission free Mon, Tue, Sun, 40f including a drink Wed, Thur, 50f Fri, Sat; MC, V),* a small space with a '50s-marquee exterior that does triple service as a bar, a live venue [see *live music scene,* above], and a club. Cithéa feels a bit like the disco at the University Student Union, but on a good night. Here you will come to understand why Oberkampf doesn't have more dance spots, however: No matter how deep a groove is playing, the would-be Jean-Paul Belmondos from **Café Charbon** across the street [see *bar scene,* above] work the same wiggle, and that same "oh god I need a toilet" demi-crouch, tune after tune. If you have the teensiest bit of soul in your moves, you will be scoped and asked to give lessons. Great selection of acid jazz and Stevie and (he who was) Prince.

Evolving from the hair-metal nights and rock free-for-alls of the late '80s and early '90s, **Gibus** *(18 rue du Faubourg-du-Temple; Tel 01/47-00-78-88; 9pm-dawn Tue, midnight-dawn Wed-Sun; Cover 50f-100f, depending on the night)* has had a varied clientele to match its ever-changing cast of promoters. Currently under the eyes of "Bitchy Jose," the clientele is mostly gay, except for the annoying, cloying (alternately either empty or packed) VIP section. The VIP section, basically the only place to sit except for a single table tucked behind the DJ booth, features sleazy-looking guys with greasy hair holding court with their preening model girlfriends. Except for the headlining U.K. or U.S. DJ on the weekends, you will probably want to avoid this bastion of sweaty, hedonistic, over-the-top exploits, unless you want to grope or be groped.

fIVE-O

The French are, except for the occasional demonstration or revolution, a docile, law-abiding bunch. Sure, the students make a show of detesting and provoking *les flics,* reminding them of May '68 and calling them fascists; but compared to other big cities, Parisian cops are a scant, mild presence. Many people do slip in and out of the Métro or the RER without paying or park illegally, but if you get caught, good luck talking your way out of a ticket; in their religious devotion to rules and regulations, *les flics* are just like cafe waiters and every other French civil servant. Outside the city there is a separate police force, the *gendarmerie,* known to be surlier, more heavily armed, and more corrupt, so watch yourself on the highways.

A recent, slightly unholy renovation has added a Latin cafe downstairs at **La Coupole** *(102 blvd. de Montparnasse, 14th; Tel 01/43-20-14-20; Métro to Vavin; Restaurant hours: 8:30am-1am Sun-Thur, till 1:30am Fri, Sat; Club hours: 10pm-3am Tue, 10pm-5am Fri, Sat; 100f cover includes drink; AE, V, MC),* the famous Montparnasse brasserie where Hemingway and all those cats never once heard, let alone boogied to, Gypsy Kings house remixes. Yet the spacious, tiled lower level is now an all-out salsa fiesta on Tuesdays. It may be worth heading all the way down to Montparnasse to see the famous dining room, which, though slightly disfigured by the renovation, still retains the famous murals commissioned in exchange for free drinks from artist-regulars.

Should you grow weary of the Parisian craze for the traditional, with all its meandering "world" rhythms that are easier to talk about than dance to, **Rex Club** *(5 blvd. Poissonnière, 2nd; Tel 01/42-36-83-98; Métro to Bonne-Nouvelle; 11pm-dawn Wed, Thur, Fri, 11:30pm-dawn Sat; Cover 60f Wed, 70f Thur, Fri, 80f Sat; AE, MC, V)* will rev you up with techno and house, pumped out with no apologies, on a bass system so seismic you'll be asking, "What is that—do you hear that?" the whole next day. This is the house that Laurent Garnier—to many, the father of techno—built, and DJ Charles Schillings keeps the tradition hard and heavy on Friday night's *Automatik;* Garnier himself spins when the spirit in the machine moves him. Housed in a wing of the *Metropolis*-esque, Art Deco Rex moviehouse, the Rex may not be as hot as it was in the '90s, but it's true to its roots.

And if you've brought your 4-inch, electric-red patent-leather dancing shoes, you can salsa into one of Edith Piaf's haunts, **La Java** *(105 rue du Faubourg-du-Temple, 10th; Tel 01/42-02-20-52; Métro to Belleville; 11pm-5am Thur-Sat; Cover 60-80f Thur, 100f Fri, Sat; AE, MC, V),* unquestionably the best thing about Paris's Latin craze. Salsa, merengue, and tango dancers who actually know what the hell they're doing pack it into this classic old dance hall, with a great wide lacquered dance floor and period tables, lamps, and bandstand, for a sweat-drenched cha-cha-cha on the weekends. A live Latin horn band is followed by a DJ.

And a good idea whose time may have finally come are the *péniches*—small party boats—many of which have theater, live shows, and clubbing after the curtain. The vast majority are moored—and stay that way—in the distant, eastern 13th *arrondissement (Métro to quai de la Gare or Bibliothèque),* on the quay just down from the new massive Bibliothèque Nationale on the allée Arthur Rimbaud.

Batofar *(Facing 11 quai Francois-Mauriac; Tel 01/56-29-10-00; Métro to Bibliothèque; 8pm-3am Tue-Thur, Sun, till 4am Fri, Sat; Free-60f, 15-60f drinks; MC, V),* the hippest, most avant-garde bar, club, and concert space in all of Paris, hosts a consistently interesting mix of concerts and DJ gigs featuring live local, British, European, and American dub, trip-hop, hip-hop, ragga, minimal house, techno, Brit-pop, rock, post-rock, and the odd big-name heavy hitter like DJ Krush. In the smallish hull of the boat, the sound system, unencumbered by sound-wave-bending concrete pilings and bedrock, shakes the entire boat with viciously deep bass sans ugly reverb and distortion. (To test the bass, place a cigarette wrapper on the ground and watch it dance along the vibrating dance floor.) The most interesting projects are often the monthly experimental shows, throwing together live DJs and live musicians. For a complete listing of concerts, check record stores and hip shops around town for Batofar's flyers. You'll want to arrive promptly because it closes early by Parisian standards (3am) and because drinks at the well-stocked bar are cheap. Because of the club's relative isolation from the city center, ask the guys at the door to call you a taxi when you're ready to leave—taxis can be hard to come by late at night in the 13th *arrondissement*.

Kids will tell you, with forlorn faces, that Paris has no hip-hop clubs. But they're wrong. Paris *had* no hip-hop clubs, until the appearance of the **Slow-Club** (*130 rue de Rivoli; Tel 01/42-33-84-30; Métro to Chatelet; 11:30pm-4:30am Mon, Wed; 80f men, Mon free for women, Wed 50f for women; Until 12:30 admission includes a free drink; MC, V*), locßated elegantly enough across from the *grand magasin* La Samaritaine. Almost as rare as clubs in Paris with generally all-black clientele are white kids at the Slow-Club, which is not to say that they're not welcome. Quite the opposite. If you're down with the hip-hop, R&B, dancehall, and interesting percussive combinations of the three, you'll be down and you'll get down at the Slow-Club, no matter the color of your skin. Don't be intimidated by color line, the monster-sized bouncers, or the intimate frisk. While drinks are expensive at 50f a bottle, cigarette packets sit open on the coffee tables and joints move secretively around the club. Wednesdays, the club fills out with the silhouetted curves of beautiful girls singing along to their favorite R&B songs in the dim club smoke.

ARTS SCENE

▶▶VISUAL ARTS

Almost all of Paris is a giant gallery, with windows full of photographs, canvases, sculpture, antiques, and curiosities. In the Marais, Saint-Germain-des-Prés, along the rue de Rivoli in the 1st, the backstreets of the 7th, and across the Bastille, Paris serves up images of itself, its pretensions, its history, and its slightly dirty conscience everywhere.

To find the most cutting-edge of the lot, go to the northern reaches of the Marais and its extension into Beaubourg, in the 3rd *arrondissement*. There must be at least 100 galleries in this otherwise quiet area, and more opening all the time, so it's a place to get lost in.

One of the best of the area is surely the **Galerie Aréa** (*50 rue Hautevilla, 10th; Tel 01/45-23-31-52; Métro to Château d'Eau; 3-7pm Thur-Sun*) devoted exclusively to French contemporary painting. Housed in a small, two-story converted office, the Galerie shows its stuff by flouting the conceptual aesthetic conventions of many of its neighbors.

Yvon Lambert (*108 rue Vieille-du-Temple, 3rd; Tel 01/42-71-09-33; Métro to Filles du Calvaire; Open 10am-1pm/2:30-7pm Tue-Fri, 10am-*

festivals and events

Banlieue Blues *(Mar/Apr; Seine St.-Denis; 01/49-22-10-10; Free-150f):* Big funk-fest in the suburbs, known to attract nobodies and somebodies with soul.

Festival du Film de Paris *(Early Apr; Cinéma Gaumont Marignan, 27 ave. des Champs Elysées, 8th; Tel 01/42-65-12-37; Métro to Franklin Roosevelt; 35f per day, 150f per wk):* Directors, actors, and writers from all over the world come to show their films, speak about them and themselves, and look for a distributor.

Fête du Travail *(May 1):* May Day is taken very seriously, with a big parade of the proletariat and trade unions, colorfully losing their chains together.

Fête de la Musique *(June 21; Tel 01/40-03-94-70):* Every street of the city is packed with buskers playing every conceivable genre of music, while big names (James Brown and Sting have come in the past) take to the plazas for free outdoor shows.

Gay Pride March *(End of June):* Bigger by the year, if not yet on a par with New York's. Expect floats, queens, and general gaiety. Info at **Centre Gai et Lesbien** [see *gay scene,* below].

Course des Garçons et Serveuses de Cafe: *(Late June; At the Hôtel de Ville; Tel 01/42-96-60-75; Métro to Hôtel de Ville):* One of the more ridiculous contests, with cafe waiters and waitresses in full regalia racing viciously against each other, platter in hand. No tipping.

Jazz à la Villette *(Early July; 211 ave. Jean Jaurès, 19th; Tel 08/03-07-50-75; Métro to Porte de Pantin; Free-160f):* Just as venerable as the other two music fests, this is held in the Epcot Center-ish Parc de la Villette, on the Canal St.-Martin. From big names to no names.

Bastille Day *(July 14th):* The city explodes with celebrations, especially around the Place de la Bastille, and on the Champ de Mars, watching the fireworks at Trocadéro, across the water. The greatest and strangest aspect of the French independence day celebrations are the firemen's *(pompiers)* balls, held in the courtyards and streets adjacent to their firehouses.

7pm Sat) shows all the heavy hitters, like Anselm Kiefer, Nan Goldin, and Julian Schnabel, as well as video and photo shows. In its massive, well-lit warehouse space on a main thoroughfare of the Marais, Yvon Lambert is where you show once you've "arrived."

Everyone has a different opinion on the bizarre architecture of the **Centre National d'Art et de Culture Georges Pompidou** *(1 rue Beaubourg; Tel 01/44-78-12-33; Métro to Chatelet/Les Halles or Hôtel de Ville; 11am-10pm Wed-Mon, until 9pm for exhibitions; Closed May 1; Prices vary depending on exhibitions, 30-50f, 20-40f students, under 18 free),* designed

Quartier d'Eté *(Mid-July through mid-Aug; All over Paris; Tel 01/44-94-98-00):* The largely emptied city is given shows of classical and world music, circuses, and spectacles, mostly out-of-doors and free.

Le Cinéma en Plein Air *(Mid-July through mid-Aug; Parc de la Villette, 19th; Tel 01/40-03-76-92; Métro to Porte de Pantin)* Free out-door festival of classic cinema, projected onto a large screen.

La Tour de France *(End of July; Finish line on the Champs Elysées; Tel 01/41-33-15-00):* Watch 'em roll in past the **Arc de Triomphe.**

Artists' Open Studios *(Beginning in Oct):* **Artistes à la Bastille** *(Tel 01/53-36-06-73),* **Ménilmontant** *(Tel 01/40-03-01-61),* **13th** *(Tel 01/45-86-17-67).* Working studios are open for your inspection; a good time to see the work of the collectives and squats of Belleville, like **La Forge** *(32 rue de Ramponneau),* or the **Collective de Grange** *(10th; 31 rue de la Grange-aux-Belles),* and in the Barbès area of the 18th [see *arts scene,* above].

Festival FNAC-Inrockuptibles *(Early Nov):* Sponsored by *Inrockuptibles,* the French *Rolling Stone,* a big indie-music event of the year, where American alternative musicians are sold to the French market.

Armistice Day *(November 11):* Solemn commemoration of the end of WWI, which cost so many French lives.

Salon des Grands Vins *(Mid-Dec; Paris-Expo, Porte de Versailles, 15th; Métro to Porte de Versailles; 50f):* Wine expo. Great way to refine your palette and get smashed at the same time. Fifty francs buys you a glass, and from there it's just you and 1,000 vintners of France, including some of the very best; if you like, you can buy for 30 to 40 percent under retail. Spitting is classier than swallowing.

Africolor *(Late Dec; Théâtre Gérard Philippe, 59 blvd. Jules Guesde, 93200 St.-Denis; Tel 01/48-13-70-00 or 01/47-97-69-99; Métro to St.-Denis Basilique; 50f):* An African festival celebrating the cultures of the largest minority in France, held in the suburb of St.-Denis.

by Richard Rogers and Renzo Piano in the 1970s. Certainly the air-conditioner-turned-inside-out building containing the Centre d'Art Moderne—which after the **Louvre** [see *culture zoo,* below] should be the second stop of any art lover in Paris—has not aged as well as it was intended to. The glass, steel, and brightly colored plastic exterior is grayed and dirty, and the slightly seedy Place Georges Pompidou is home to throngs of pigeons, hippie bongo players, and cheesy portrait painters. But do not be put off: The center is easily navigable and always changing, displaying everything from sleek '60s Modern Braun products to Giacometti's statuary to the models of the designs of Achille Castiglioni and films of Luis Buñuel, as well as a host of temporary exhibitions. No two visits are ever quite the same.

Recently opened, **l'Espace Nouveaux Media** *(4th floor; 1-9pm)* allows the normally passive museum-goer to navigate through the multi-media computer projects of such artists as Claes Oldenburg and Chris Marker (best known for his film *La Jetée,* on which the obnoxious Terry Gilliam—Bruce Willis project *12 Monkeys* was based). Give yourself several hours to meander through the three floors of the museum, serviced by the elevators and escalators attached to the exterior of the building.

A firmly unofficial place to witness the Birth of Art is in the many collectives and squats that are generally ignored by officials. One is the converted smithy **La Forge,** in Belleville *(32 rue de Ramponneau);* another is the **Collective de Grange** in the 10th *arrondissement (31 rue de la Grange-aux-Belles).* During the *portes ouvertes* (open studios) [see *festivals and events,* above] you can get a peak inside, or try knocking anytime; providing you don't look like a narc, they'll probably let you in.

▶▶PERFORMING ARTS

The second best thing (and let's face it, sometimes the best thing) to do in a darkened room in Paris is to watch a movie. Film in Paris is venerated as nowhere else on Earth, except, sadly, as it was in the New York City of the '60s and '70s. There are megaplexes here like the Cineplex Odeon, but the number of small revival houses, art film theaters, foreign cinema theaters, festivals [see *festivals and events,* above] both official and informal, and spontaneous screenings of classics and cult classics, makes first-run films beside the point. Most foreign-language films are screened here in *version originale* (VO); that is, with the original dialogue and French subtitles. There are continual festivals of Hitchcock, Kubrick, Cassavetes, and other adored Anglo/American directors. The greatest variety and number of theaters are in the Latin Quarter (5th) and the St.-Michel area (6th).

A veritable compendium of listings for 'round-the-clock screenings can be found in *l'Officiel des Spectacles,* but you should devote a good hour to pinpointing what you want to see. Beside the title of the film (in French, even if the movie's not) are the day (*lun* = Mon, *mar* = Tue, *mer* = Wed, *jeu* = Thur, *ven* = Fri, *sam* = Sat, *dim* = Sun, *tlj* = daily) and the hour of the screening (in military time). Some of the best theaters are found on the rue des Écoles, like the **Action Ecoles** *(23 rue des Écoles; Tel 01/43-29-79-89; Métro to Maubert-Mutualité; 40f admission, 30f students; No credit cards),* the **Champo** *(51 rue des Écoles; Tel 01/43-54-51-60; Métro to Odéon or St.-Michel; 45f admission, 35f students; No credit cards),* and the **Grand Action** *(5 rue des Écoles; Tel 01/43-29-44-40; Métro to Cardinal Lemoine or Jussieu; 42f admission, 32f students; No credit cards).* The Mk2 chain, including **Rendez-vous des Quais** [see *hanging out,* above] shows arty French and foreign new releases.

Theater in Paris is thriving, owing to a devoted following, heavy government subsidies, and a French penchant for putting on a good show and being looked at. While the Comédie Française is still the height of culture and poise, performing the experimental and the classic (Shakespeare, Molière, Ibsen); the more informal dirt-on-the-floor, in-your-face pits may be more authentically French. Rather than the rise of a curtain, many of the grass-roots theater troupes signal the show's beginning as they did in the Middle Ages, with the dramaturge's repeated pounding of a pole solemnly on the ground.

For this elemental, timeless soul of French theater, head out to the avant-garde **Théâtre du Soleil** at the **Cartoucherie de Vincennes** *(Route du Champ de Manoeuvre, Bois de Vincennes, 12th; Tel 01/43-74-24-08; Métro to Chateau de Vincennes, from there shuttle bus or Bus 112; Reserve seats daily from 11am-6pm, shows 7:30pm Wed-Sat, 1pm Sun; Tickets 150f; No credit cards)* where the legendary radical Ariane Mnouchkine and her cast stage political and provocative interpretations of plays, from the contemporary to the Greek, that can border on events. Mnouchkine was known for staging productions in working-class neighborhoods before she opened in this location in 1970. The theater, just out of town on its far-eastern fringe, is in a massive overgrown industrial space—a converted military cartridge factory—a post-post-apocalyptic landscape à la *Logan's Run*. The Cartoucherie houses several companies and a number of performance spaces—with work almost always in French—and the cast even cook you dinner (reserve at the above number). Check any of the major listings mags for showtimes and ticket info.

gay scene

Increasingly, Gay Paree is openly just that, and straight Paris's fascination of the moment is watching while Paris flames. But the straight world's interest in venues like **Le Queen** [see *club scene,* above] and its mass intrusion into the Marais can feel a little obnoxious, so you may want to seek refuge at one of the many gay spots that still pride themselves on being somewhat exclusive. Gay-bashing or outright bigotry are almost unheard-of in this sophisticated city, and if there is still prejudice here, you may sense it in the over-use of the word *pédé*—"fag"—by heteros to describe a venue or style. But then again, this insensitivity may be nothing more than a nasty reflex of the straight French boys who are often mistaken for the other team, thus the refrain: "Is he gay? Maybe he's just French...."

The **Centre Gai et Lesbien** *(3 rue Keller, 11th; Tel 01/43-57-21-47; Métro to Ledru-Rollin; 2-8pm Mon-Sat, 2-7pm Sun)* is a popular meeting ground, information center, and activist HQ with a cafe where you're free to peruse the plentiful materials and flyers stashed around. Many of the main parks and public spaces become prime cruising grounds after dark. Note especially the quays of the Seine, the Parc des Buttes Chaumont, and the Tuileries gardens. The endless paths of the Bois de Boulogne are daytime cruising spots, but at night, the park is turned over to extremely gorgeous and extremely butch (no joke: blade-wielding) Brazilian transvestite prostitutes, who've driven straight trick-seekers out of the Bois almost entirely.

Even with the intrusion of straight Paris, the Marais retains that West Village or French Quarter sensuousness that characterizes the best gay neighborhoods. The main stretch, up the rue Vielle du Temple, is half-straight, half-gay, and may be yielding to the former. But the area farther west, closer to the Métro stop Hôtel de Ville, is still dominantly queer and dotted with dark-tinted windows, mysterious goings-on, and campy cabarets.

Bite your tongue and enter **Le Cox** *(15 rue des Archives, 4th; Tel 01/42-72-08-00; Métro to Hôtel de Ville; 1pm-2am daily; No credit cards)*, one of the more popular additions to the check-out and pickup scene, a roomy cafe/bar where you can, ahem, log on in the rear (with a name like that, everything seems like a double entendre).

Amnesia *(42 rue Vielle du Temple, 4th; Tel 01/42-72-16-94; Métro to Hôtel de Ville; 10am-2am daily; MC, V)* catering equally to the gay and dyke crowds, as well as to the requisite straight hangers-on, is a local favorite, split-level, with sofas and a less severely body-conscious vibe.

At night, **Le Queen** [see *club scene,* above] is still the address for lumberjacks who put on women's clothing and hang around in bars; if any boy has packed a fabulous rhinestone gown especially for Paris, here is where she can make her grand entrance.

Pulp *(25 blvd. Poissonnière, 2nd; Tel 01/40-26-01-93; Métro to Grands Boulevards; Midnight-dawn Wed-Sun; 50f cover weekends; AE, MC, V)*, the dyke club of Paris, is poised to become the next Le Queen, so brace yourself, girls. More intimate than the former, with more emphasis on Latin, and fewer robotic dance tracks.

CULTUre ZOO

You can't come to Paris and skip the museums; visiting the Louvre at least is a duty akin to getting blitzed on Saint Paddy's, or cursing at taxi drivers in New York. But as if recognizing that the clogged, stodgy museums of old and their overwhelming collections had made this duty into somewhat of a chore, Paris has revamped the old venerables over the past decade or so, and learned the importance of not just throwing everything it's got—which is, pretty much, everything—at you at once.

Musée du Louvre *(99 rue de Rivoli, 1st; Tel 01/40-20-50-50; Métro to Palais-Royal or Louvre-Rivoli, 9am-5:30pm Mon, Thur-Sun, till 9:30pm Wed, wing containing "Mona Lisa" open till 9:30pm Mon, closed Tue; 45f admission, 26f after 3pm, under 18 free, 1st Sunday of month free for all):* Divided into three wings—Richelieu, Sully, and Denon—a tenth of each of which will take you several hours. To avoid the it's-too-much-the-world-is-closing-in-on-me freakout, it's best to decide beforehand what you're going to see. Aside from the famous smilin' lady that you'll have to push through a million people to see, some ignored prizes are a Van Eyck *Madonna and Child* in the last room of Northern Painting (in Richelieu), and a Hellenistic crouching Venus in Greek Antiquities (in Denon). Go after 3pm for the cut-rate ticket and you'll still have plenty of time.

Musée d'Orsay *(1 rue de Bellechasse, 7th; Tel 01/40-49-48-14; Métro to Solférino; 10am-6pm Tue, Wed, Fri, till 9:45pm Thur, 9am-6pm Sun, closed Mon; 40f admission, 30f if 18-25, free Sun if under 18, 30f over 18):*

"Old Paris is no more. The shape of a city changes more swiftly, alas! than a man's heart." That's what Baudelaire, the preeminent *flâneur* (stroller) of all time, wrote of his town in 1857. The verb *flâner* means a kind of foot-dragging, ponderous stroll, a trance that Paris induces in the curious and restless. But following Baudelaire's lead, we can hardly send you strolling down the lacquered-up and packaged central boulevards of Paris, picturesque as they may be; the trick is to see the city as it changes. And nowhere is it changing more swiftly, in as many different directions and under as many different influences, than in the volatile, varied, and exuberant northeast corner of the city.

Start at the tourist hub of **place de La République,** where the 3rd, 11th, and 10th *arrondissements* collide, and take **rue du Faubourg du Temple,** heading east. You are still solidly in white Paris when you come to the **Square François Lemaître.** This placid retreat from République is where the Canal St.-Martin goes underground, to reemerge at Bastille. Stroll up the canal a ways, cross over the bridge, and come back up rue du Faubourg du Temple. As you continue on, you'll notice that the number of Chinese takeout places multiplies, complemented by *halal* butcher shops and, increasingly, little stores selling low-rate international phone cards for the lonesome and the far from home. When you come to the **rue Bichat,** on your left, you may want to take a quick jaunt up it to the **Hôpital Saint-Louis,** built in 1607, a massive and austere structure still penned-in by surrounding buildings, as **Notre Dame** used to be. Return on up the rue du Faubourg du Temple as it starts to climb. When it crosses the **boulevard de Belleville,** you've arrived in, yes, Belleville, now the 20th *arrondissement.* To your right is the hugely popular local Chinese restaurant **Président,** with its guardian lions and glitzy red-and-gold decor. Try to grab a seat if you're hungry; otherwise, hang a right along the boulevard de Belleville and you'll find yourself, after a few steps, deep in the Islamic neighborhood. On Tuesday and Friday mornings, this wide boulevard becomes an African market, with purchased goods carefully balanced on the buyers' heads. On your right there are many inviting pastry shops, where the goods are sold no-nonsense style in their baking trays, amid bare walls and blazing white light. Should you need to book a flight to Mecca, you'll pass several agencies that specialize in it. When you get to the **rue Timbaud,** you can turn and head down to **Le Timbaud** [see *bar scene,* above] should you so desire, or continue to **rue Oberkampf,** just beyond. If you continue on the boulevard de Belleville, it will take you to **Cimetière de Père Lachaise** [see *culture zoo,* below], where you can conclude your meditation on tradition and change.

Same deal as in the Louvre: plenty to see, many to dodge. The Impressionists and the post-Impressionists are all on the top level, and so are the mobs with their audio-phones. Off the main concourse on the ground floor, and especially off the sculpture deck on the mezzanine, are many smaller galleries of greats—like Daumier and Courbet—and wackos the curators didn't know what to do with. Don't miss the Art Nouveau wooden chamber in the rear.

The Eiffel Tower *(Champ de Mars, 7th; Tel 01/44-11-23-45, Tel 01/44-11-23-23, Métro to Bir-Hakeim; 9:30am-11pm Sept-June, 9am-midnight July-Aug; Admission charged by level, 24f Level 1 or 65f to go to the top; www.paris.org/monuments/eiffel; AE, MC, V):* Decidedly the most famous structure on earth, though the jury's still out on whether this massive erection is in good taste or not. More a showpiece of materials and engineering than a functional building—it was built to be torn down 10 years after construction—the Tower foretold the rise of steel-frame construction in the 20th century. The Jules Verne retro-restaurant on the second level is worth a gander but not for a bite. The views from the observation deck can't be beat. No tossing of monogrammed berets permitted, Rusty.

Musée Carnavalet *(23 rue de Sévigné, 3rd; Tel 01/42-72-21-13; Métro to St.-Paul; 10am-5:40pm Tue-Sun, closed Mon; 27f admission, 14.50f students and ages 18-25; AE, MC, V):* Housed in a creaky and beautiful old mansion in the center of the Marais, this is one of the best places to orient yourself to the feel of French history. Paintings and artifacts tell the story of the periodic demolition and reconstruction of the city over the past 500 years.

Musée des Arts d'Afrique et d'Océanie *(293 ave. Daumesnil, 12th; Tel 01/44-74-84-80; Métro to Porte Dorée; 10am-5:20pm Mon-Sun, closed Tue; 30f admission, 20f ages 18-25, free Sun if under 18):* It may not be the most PC of museums in terms of how they got the stuff, okay, but this storehouse of colonialist treasures is probably one of the coolest. Stored in this unfrequented corner of the city, Vanuatan slit-gongs, West African masks, and live crocs a-snappin' in the basement (just like in your nightmares) will wow you, albeit with a guilty conscience.

Musée de Cluny *(6 place Paul-Painlevé, 5th; Tel 01/53-73-78-00; Métro to Cluny-La Sorbonne; 9:15am-5:45pm Mon, Wed-Sun, closed Tue; 30f admission, 10f if 18-25, free Sun if under 18; No credit cards):* An old cloister, itself occupying the ruins of a Roman bath, has in turn been converted into a place of cool serenity. Don't miss the radiant five tapestries of *The Lady and the Unicorn,* an allegory of the five senses. Between the oh-so-delicate fondling fingers of the lady, and the collar around the neck of her pet chimp, the tapestry depicting touch gives a whole new meaning to the question, "Would you like to touch my monkey?"

Musée Picasso *(Hôtel Salé, 5 rue de Thorigny, 3rd; Tel 01/42-71-25-21; Métro to Chemin-Verte; 9:30am-5:30pm daily except Tue; 30f admission, 20f if 18-25, free Sun if under 18):* The master's progress from hard-toiling figurative nobody (until he was exactly 15) to experimental superstar is housed here at one of the best art museums in town.

only here

You've walked along the banks of the Seine, you've marveled at the endless vista of hazy roofs and shimmering domes from the **Eiffel Tower,** beheld the grandeur of the **Louvre,** and then you think...naked girls in high heels and garters. That's right, you haven't done Paris unless you've been to the one and only **Crazy Horse Saloon** *(12 ave. George V, 8th; Métro to Alma-Marceau or George V; Tel 01/47-23-32-32; Two shows nightly, 8:30pm, 11pm, three shows Sat; 560f orchestra, 450f mezzanine, 290f bar; www.crazy-horse.fr; V, MC, AE)* the tackiest (sexiest?) "erotic revue" this side of Vegas, now 45 years old. Go to the show as an expression of irony or put on an ironic expression to cover up for going to the show.

If the Crazy Horse is the French version of the Rockettes, **Mariage Frères** *(30 rue du Bourg-Tibourg, 4th; Métro to St.-Paul; Tel 01/42-72-28-11; 10:30am-7:30pm daily; 37-59f pot of tea; MC, V)* is their interpretation of teatime. With well over 200 different kinds of tea, each to be served at the correct hour, at its own precise temperature, it's kind of like a grandma-sensualism behind the potted palms. The warmed scones are scrumptious, and the tea-based *gelées* better than you dreamed they could be. Also the place to buy that classy souvenir the folks are expecting.

For the historical rubber-necker in you, head over to the **Place de l'Alma** *(Métro to Alma-Marceau),* where, in the traffic tunnel beneath a replica of Lady Liberty's torch, Lady Di was hounded to her death by paparazzi (graffiti on the gilded flame will tell you where exactly). Officials have allowed this symbol of liberty to become a *de facto* shrine to her Ladyship, and it is now plastered-over with hundreds of awfully aggrieved notes in every language.

l'Institut du Monde Arabe *(1 rue des Fossés-Saint-Bernard, 5th; Tel 01/40-51-39-53; Métro to Jussieu; 10am-6pm, closed Mon, closed May 1; 25f admission, 20f students, 18-25, or over 60, free under 18, additional 20f for exhibitions):* The structure of this museum is an uncontested success: a wedge-shaped, ultramodern metal and glass library-cum-gallery-cum-*salon de thé*-cum-cutural emblem. The whole southern facade is a reinterpretation of a traditional Arabic lattice-work screen, with light-responsive diaphragms that let through just the right amount of dappled light. There's also a museum shop and bookstore (AE, MC, V).

Cimetière du Père Lachaise *(Blvd. de Ménilmontant, 20th; Métro to Père Lachaise; 8am-6pm Mon-Fri, 8:30am-6pm Sat, 9am-6pm Sun; Free* *admission, free map at newsstand):* The ultimate shrine to the dead white male—Balzac; the dead white gay male—Proust; the dead white female—George Sand; the dead white gay female—Gertrude Stein, side-by-side with Alice B. Toklas; and, of course, the dead white lizard, Jim Morrison.

Notre Dame Cathedral *(Place du Parvis Notre Dame, 4th; Tel 01/42-34-56-10; Métro to Cité; Cathedral 8am-6:45pm daily, towers 10am-4:30pm daily; Free admission to cathedral, 35f admission to towers, 25f ages 12-25; No credit cards):* The scaffolding has just come off the facade after an elaborate "photonic disencrustation." The verdict? The old dame's white and shiny, just like in her youth, but she looks a little shorter and more commonplace after the bleach job. Still maybe the most impressive *Last Judgment* ever sculpted.

The following two monuments need to be mentioned if only for their distinctly Parisian self-importance:

Sacré-Coeur *(Place St.-Pierre, 18th; Tel 01/53-41-89-00; Métro to Abbesses, then take elevator to surface and take the funicular; Basilica 6:45am-11pm daily, Dome and Crypt 9am-6pm daily Apr-Sept, 9:15am-6pm daily Oct-Mar; Basilica free, Dome and Crypt 30f adult, 16f under 24):* A monstrosity. "Wedding cake architecture," the common epithet, doesn't go far enough; you can do better. Gaudy and inescapable when it was built, it now spoils much of beautiful Montmartre with its spillover, a massive funicular for those too feeble to scale the "mount," and the vendors it breeds, selling painting after painting of it, infecting bedrooms in Idaho or Manhattan with its likeness; plus it squanders prime real estate.

Panthéon *(Place de Panthéon, 5th; Tel 01/43-54-34-51; Métro Cardinal-Lemoine or Maubert-Mutualité; 9:30am-6:30pm daily Apr-Sept, 10am-6:15pm daily Oct-Mar; 32f adult, 21f ages 12-25):* A failure of a building named for one of the most beautiful in the world (in Rome), renowned for who's under the floor (Voltaire, Zola, Hugo, among others) and for the mathematician Foucault hanging a pendulum from its dome; a jumble of imbalanced classical elements built of flinty stone and possessed of a vast, echoing, and cheerless interior. The "gods" enshrined here are the French *grands hommes,* so you can add hubris to its list of sins, too.

modification

Hey, why not stick metal in your face and inject ink under your skin in the city that coined the term "primitivism"? From Ménilmontant to the Marais, kids are dying to be dyed like Queequeg. C'mon, everyone's doing it....

Near the hip, clubsy boutiques of the rue des Abbesses in Montmartre, **Studio Titane** *(44 rue des Abbesses, 18th; Tel 01/53-41-01-34 Métro Abbesses; 10am-7pm daily, from 50f; AE, MC, V)* is one of the newest additions, and one of the best in the area. Specializing in Polynesian patterns and delicately rendered images, Titane keeps a small, sterile, friendly shop. Plus, they'll give you a *cafe* while you bleed.

And if before going out you wouldn't feel presentable without extensions or a fresh, clotted wash of henna in your hair, stop into **Tomasso Coiffeur** *(127 bis rue de la Roquette, 11th; Tel 01/43-79-20-01; Métro*

down and out

Hemingway, when he was here, strolled through the **Jardin de Luxembourg** *(6th; RER to Luxembourg)* snatching up pigeons and wringing their necks for dinner. But that was Ernest for you. What should you do without a sou? First of all, find a place to crash. The only nest in town that won't charge a dime is the upstairs at **Shakespeare & Co.** [see *stuff*, below], where with a little charm, any broke genius can get himself a foam mattress for the night surrounded by books and an incredible view of **Nôtre Dame** [see *culture zoo*, above]. You'll have to sell your services, however, whatever you claim them to be: a poem, a drawing, a tune, a-oh, you naughty thing! At said bookstore are yellowed and broken-spined English books for 2 or 3 francs; sitting with one on the banks of the Seine, the roof of **l'Institut du Monde Arabe** [see *culture zoo*, above] overlooking the city, the **Parc des Buttes Chaumont** *(19th; Métro to Buttes-Chaumont)*, the **Place des Vosges** *(4th; Métro to Saint-Paul)*, or in the **Tuileries** gardens *(1st; Métro to Tuileries)*, you may feel that Paris is best viewed from an empty pocket.

All the churches in town are free: **Saint-Eustache** *(1st; Métro to Les Halles)* at Les Halles still stands in its unrenovated glory, and the three-tiered **Art Nouveau** gallery of the synagogue on the rue Pavée in the Marais *(Métro to Saint-Paul)*, designed by Hector Guimard himself, is definitely worth a look (but be sure to cover your head!). Many of the larger museums are free the first Sunday of the month. Any and every cafe will let you linger over a *cafe*, which at most will cost you 18f, and the sips of ambiance are absolutely free.

Voltaire; *9:30am-8pm Tue-Thur, till 9pm Fri, till 7pm Sat, 10am-7pm Mon; Men's cuts, 115f; women's from 195f; AE, MC, V)*, by the Place Leon Blum, where M. Tomasso offers funky and exotic do's at do-able prices. The narcotic pace of the stylists, and the dim lighting, will lull you into just the right state before kicking it with the new coiffure.

great outdoors

When the French say *parc*, they mean something very different than we do. They mean, "Aren't the sycamores lovely?" and "Shall we take a turn through the garden?" and most definitely, "Keep off the grass." "Let's go for a run, toss a frisbee around and blast *Regatta de Blanc*" is definitely not what they mean. At all. You'll find no release of that sort in Paris, and the huge woods traversed by paths on either end of the city, like the **Bois de Boulogne** and the **Bois de Vincennes,** can also be a real let-down because of their dull terrain and flat, featureless paths.

A more Anglo-American-style park is the **Buttes Chaumont** [see *neighborhoods,* above], once a quarry, where the craggy cliffs and steep ascents can give you a good workout.

If you're a jogger, there's nothing like the quays along the Seine; you may have to stop occasionally for tourists or traffic, but it's worth it. Otherwise, the cobblestone banks of the Canal St.-Martin and Basin de la Villette are uninterrupted and traffic-free.

The lunatic driving and cobblestones of Paris discourage biking for those of sound mind; if you're certifiable, go get yourself a cycle at **Paris à vélo, c'est sympa!** *(37 blvd. Bourbon, 4th; Tel 01/48-87-60-01; 9am-6pm daily, Nov-Mar, till 7pm Apr-Oct; 1-day rental 80f, 3-hr. guided tours 185f/person; Métro to Bastille).*

A "safer," or at least chaperoned, option is joining the shrieking mass-rollerblading horde (the record to date is 28,000 people!) with police escort, leaving from 40 place de l'Italie *(Métro to place de l'Italie)* every Friday at 10pm and returning to the same spot three hours later. Check with **Pari Roller** *(62 rue Dulong, 17th; Tel 01/43-36-89-81; www.pari-roller.com).* They rent skates, too.

It's not inconceivable that you might want to bike out of the city, and not unrealistic, either; after the *banlieue,* the suburbs of Paris, the metropolis stops abruptly, particularly to the south. A good day trip could be had by taking your bike on the train to **Chartres** and getting off wherever you decide the sprawl has sufficiently thinned, and pedaling the rest of the way. A good leaping-off point might be at Villiers, roughly the halfway point and positively rustic. The cathedral itself is, of course, extraordinary, with its famous lopsided spires, brass labyrinth, and stained glass dating to the 13th century. If you get tuckered out on the way back, hop back on the train wherever you like.

STUff

Some have called Paris the largest mall in the world, and it's true that there are more opportunities to part with cash here than almost anywhere. You can buy the very latest fashions—at the very highest prices—along the boulevard Saint-Germain (6th), or any of the designer outlets on its endless side streets, or that diamond-studded, lizard-skin pocketbook you've been hankerin' for, along with the platinum clip, at Place Vendôme. But Paris also has incredible bargains, especially considering the strength of the dollar over the past few years.

So after you've drooled outside the shops in Saint-Germain or in the 1st, it's actually very worth your while to visit the two mega-department stores **Printemps** *(64 blvd. Haussmann, 9th; Tel 01/42-82-50-00; Métro to Havre-Caumartin; 9:35am-7pm daily except Sun, till 10pm Thur; AE, MC, V)* and **Galeries Lafayette** *(40 blvd. Haussmann, 9th; Tel 01/42-82-30-25; Métro to Chausée d'Antin; 9:30am-7pm daily except Sun, till 9pm Thur; AE, MC, V),* its more veteran and expensive cousin, and pick up name brands and knock-offs at significantly less than you could find them for in the States.

The shrine of stuff is the all-in-one **FNAC** *(Forum des Halles, 1st; Tel*

01/40-41-40-00; Métro to Les Halles; 10am-7:30pm, Mon-Sat; AE, MC, V), where your one-stop shopping could snag you every CD you've ever wanted, a book from every major literature in the original language, a new stereo, and a comic book.

▶▶BIZARRE BAZAAR

For the young and impressionable traveler, the shopping experience is found at the *puces* on the outskirts of town. The *puces*—"fleas"—is where the flea market got its name. At the **Puces de Clignancourt,** the largest of the lot, there's an endless labyrinth of permanent stalls—here's where you can buy that rococo walnut four-poster bed—and bin after bin of the best and cheapest junk in France; where you can get, say, every incarnation of the Michelin man since 1970 at 10f for the bunch.

Outside the **Puces de Clignancourt,** vendors hawk pot bowls, army-navy surplus, and knockoff jeans, but also almost unbelievable vintage finds: Leather jackets that would run into the high hundreds in a Soho boutique can be gotten here for 200f.

To get to the *puces,* take Métro 4 to Porte de Clignancourt and follow the traffic signs toward the *puces.* This will take you under the *périférique* highway and into a knot of people on the other side along the avenue de la Porte de Clignancourt. Keep elbowing your way through and, on your left, a small lane will appear, and you found 'em. The *puces* are open 7am till 6pm everyday except Sunday. Get there early.

▶▶HOT COUTURE

The fashion world of Paris is everywhere you turn, but if you weren't invited to the latest catwalk show of Givenchy, Chanel, or Yves Saint-Laurent, or can't afford the very heights of haute couture, several areas will satisfy your craving for Parisian cool and sartorial savvy. The Marais, once again, has some of the best, if pricey and a bit on the conservative side, for anyone feeling desperately underdressed. Try the prophetically named rue des Francs Bourgeois for the sharpest duds. But for experimentation, the otherwise touristy lower slopes of Montmartre are the province of a number of ultracool, club/street boutiques, very often with the seamstress/designer doing triple duty as saleswoman.

Futurewear Lab *(23 rue Houden, 18th; Tel 01/42-23-66-08; Métro to Abbesses; Noon-7:30pm Mon-Sat, 2-8pm Sun; AE, MC, V)* is where ex-costume designer Tatiana Lebedev fuses industrial materials with streetwise clothes.

Bonnie Cox *(38 rue des Abbesses, 18th; Tel 01/42-54-95-68; Métro to Abbesses; 11am-8pm daily; AE, MC, V)* runs the gamut from club gear to East Village chic, at slightly steeper prices.

And incredible designer women's clothes worn only once or twice in shows are a steal at **Passé Devant** *(62 rue d'Orsel, 18th; Tel 01/42-54-75-15; Métro to Abbesses; 10:30am-7pm Tue-Sat, 1-7pm Sun, Mon; MC, V).*

The Parisian portal into the street-cum-club fashion of New York's East Village is the perfectly named **Le Shop** *(3 rue d'Argout; Tel 01/40-28-95-*

Ɥhe ꜰoꞅeꞇꞩ oꜰ Île-de-ꜰꞇance

▶▶THE FÔRET DE COMPIÈGNE

One of the most magnificent forests of Île de France, *Fôret de Compiègne,* a 200-square-kilometer district, surrounds the town of **Compiègne**, 50 miles north of Paris. Most of the trails here were originally laid out by François 1er, Louis XIV, and Louis XV as a means of facilitating their hunting parties. Outdoorspeople and novices alike hike or bike through this forest since most of it is relatively flat, with only two steep trails. Watch your footing—some of the unpaved trails are a bit sloshy when it rains. On a summer day, head for one of the oak or beech groves with a picnic basket; there are countless idyllic spots where you can pretend you're a princess out on the palatial estate....

Trains make the 50-minute trip to Compiègne from Paris's Gare du Nord several times a day. Compiègne's train station is a 10-minute walk from the center of town, across the **River Oise.** At the local **tourist office** *(Place Hôtel de Ville; Tel 03/44-40-01-00; 9:15am-12:15pm/2-6:15pm daily),* you can purchase detailed maps of the *Fôret de Compiègne,* which show all hiking and biking trails, monuments, geological oddities, bodies of water, and the general topography.

If you're not up for a big hike, take Bus 5 from the railway station to the edge of the Oise—ask your driver to let you out at *"le bord de l'Oise."* From there you can meander down a riverside promenade that, although not technically within the forest, will convey much of what the topography of the forest is all about. If you really want to delve into the hiking goodness, take STEPA bus 25—it's marked "Compiègne-Soissons"—from the train station to the Rotonda, where the German Armistice was signed. From here, paths radiate off into other parts of the forest.

▶▶THE FÔRET DE CHANTILLY

The *petit* Fôret de Chantilly, covering some 65 square miles around the town of Chantilly, lies 26 miles north of Paris. Trains leave frequently

94; *Métro to Etienne Marcel; 11am-7pm Tue-Sat, 1-7pm Mon; www.leshop-paris.com; MC, V).* A sort of department store of hip, the store is composed of 24 separate clothing vendors, each with their own phone, crammed into a medium-sized two-level space, and serviced by their own salespeople. Here you'll find hundreds of different styles of denim and polyester **Carhartt** work clothing for that Beastie Boys-circa-1989 look, **Aem'kei,** a sophisticated NYC-German rework of that skater-hip-hop look, and the environmentally conscious and free-Tibet-oriented **Komodo,** for baggy clothing that actually fits well, thanks to carefully throughout the day from Paris's Gare du Nord, arriving in Chantilly in only 30 minutes.

About a century ago, the private estate (about 15,500 acres) of the Duc d'Aumale was given (willed) to the *Institut de France,* which preserves and maintains it today, defining it as a "Private Forest." The primary motivation for the eco-folks maintaining this park involves protecting both the colonies of deer that have been the hallmark of the park since the French kings used it as their hunting grounds during the Renaissance, and the thousands of trees (especially oak, linden, elm, and various species of pine) that cover the grounds. Maintaining a good deer/sapling balance is a constant ecological battle—more than 100,000 saplings are planted every year to replace those chomped by the deer population.

Since Chantilly is "horse country," the forest is full of riding trails—as well as hiking trails—many dating from the Middle Ages. The most scenic route appears on maps as GR11. This trail links the château at Chantilly with the little town of Senlis, which is most well known for its Cathédrale Nôtre-Dame, begun in 1153. The forest is known for a series of scenic ponds and lakes. The largest of these are *les Étangs de Comelle,* the first of which were formed in the 1200s by monks who dammed local streams and rivers for irrigation of their crops. Today, they're a permanent part of the landscape. One of the most gorgeous trails in the forest is the one that winds around these bodies of water, about a 90- to 120-minute trek.

The **Chantilly tourist office** *(60 ave. Maréchal-Joffre; Tel 03/44-67-37-37, 9am-noon/2-6pm Mon-Sat, open Sun May-Sept; www.chantilly-tourisme.com)* sells maps of the forest for 58F, showing all topographical, hiking, and biking features. Bike rentals are arranged through **Orry Evasion** *(5 rue Neuve, Orry la Ville (a suburb of Chantilly); 90f per day).*

placed pleats, cool fabric choice, and hip patterns. Shoes, handbags, and all kinds of accessories are carried here for the downtown hipsters on holiday. Downstairs, there's a coffeeshop and a piercing and tattoo parlor.

But the real hip-cat b-boy or b-girl wannabe will not want to go without their own custom-made necklace or jewelry, with their name emblazoned in graffiti-like scrawl in brass, silver, or gold knuckles. Think of Run-DMC in 1984, all the Big Daddy Kanes of yesteryear, or LL Cool J yesterday. Because no one should ever have to ask you your name, contact **Anjuna Bijoux** *(Inside Le Shop, 3 rue d'Argout; Tel 01/48-39-38-39,*

fashion

Paris may not be the city of women in extravagant silk gowns, corsets, and bonnets that it once was, but there is still a latent elegance to the way people are turned out; clothes here make the man, woman, or androgyne more than almost anywhere else, and they make the man much more than most men are used to. While the American uniform of frayed baseball caps, jeans, and anoraks is forgiven as endemic, ratty T-shirts and jeans will not be. Even if you want to do the arm-the-battlements, revolutionary thing, you'd better have the right flight jacket, clean desert boots, and well-worn but not overworn jeans. The way to dress for dinner or a party is in pressed clothes and matching tones. A sports jacket is never frowned at. Dress tends toward the conservative, and real experimental outrageousness is rare, Jean-Paul Gaultier notwithstanding; but while your over-the-topness may get stares, Paris depends on people like you to set their trends.

Mobile 06-15-74-71-85, Fax 01/48-34-78-42) and arrange the production of your own "look." Be sure to negotiate the price down.

▶▶BOUND

This is the town of the revered writer. Shrines are built to Zola, Hugo, and Balzac, and even formerly fringe authors like Rimbaud and Baudelaire are now solidly ensconced in street names and public statues. It is also where most American authors of note came at least once, including Poe, Faulkner, and Dos Passos. Most girls and boys you see here will be reading finer literature and great thinkers like Lévi-Strauss or Bergson. Yikes! What to do if you're not up to cultural speed? There are several excellent English-language bookstores, with as wide selection as you'd find at the best back home, where you can find that last novel of the *comédie humaine* you've always meant to read in English, or even English books by that Paul Auster guy everyone's talking about.

Shakespeare & Co. *(37 rue de la Bûcherie, 5th; Tel 01/43-26-96-50; Métro to Maubert-Mutualité, St.-Michel; Noon-midnight daily; No credit cards)* is the heir to the famous bookstore/colony that self-published Joyce's *Ulysses* when all else failed. A swell collection of used and new books, plus free bunks [see *down and out*, above] in the attic!

The stock at **Village Voice** *(6 rue Princesse, 6th; Tel 01/46-33-36-47; 2-8pm Mon, 10am-8pm Tue-Sat, 2-7pm Sun; MC, V, AE)* is more academic than the rest with a helpful, bilingual staff that'll help you navigate the egghead terrain.

The English bookstore **WH Smith** *(248 rue de Rivoli, 1st; Tel 01/44-*

77-88-99; *Métro to Concorde; 9:30am-7:30pm Mon-Sat, 1-7:30pm Sun; MC, V, AE*) also sells American and British magazines and newspapers.

▶▶**TUNES**

You can get any CD you want for the best prices at the FNAC but if it's vinyl you crave, the major supplier for the DJ world in Paris is **Techno Import** (*16-18 rue des Taillandiers, 11th; Tel 01/48-05-71-56; Métro to Bastille; 11am-8pm Mon-Sat; MC, V*), world-renowned for its huge collection and variety of vinyl and rarities. Another resource for vinyl is the discussion boards on ***www.france-techno.com*** or on ***www.planet-tekno.com.***

Rue d'Argout is lined with hip stores from Le Shop to **Marché Noir** (*52 rue d'Argout; Tel 01/42-21-02-72; Métro to Etienne Marcel; 2-8pm Mon-Sat; MC, V*), the Parisian translation of London's Black Market record store and the place to pick up vinyl from deep to disco house to drum 'n' bass and rare groove. As at all record stores in Paris and indeed France, prices are decidedly high, so you'll want to confine yourself to strictly Parisian vinyl, which of course is reasonably cheap, even though their selection of American imports is quite cool.

Ragga and hip-hop find their home in Paris at **Sound Record** (*5 rue des Prêcheurs; Tel 01/40-13-09-45, Fax 01/45-23-03-88; Métro to Les Halles; 11am-7:30pm Tue-Sat, Mon from noon; www.sound-record.fr; MC, V*), located between rue St.-Denis and Les Halles. This nook-like store's got a decent selection of American and import releases, though the selection of French rap is limited to current releases. The staff will happily guide you through their inventory, but unfortunately will not let you listen to full-length LPs.

EATS

That the French eat so well and stay so thin and healthy is the constant gripe of the non-French. Hate the French all you want, they know something about how to eat. Take a lesson from them: Put aside, if you can, your quest for skim milk, your fear of cream sauce and butter, or any other "healthy habits" you might have, and *eat*—meaning several courses, with wine and coffee. You may even feel trim and well in the end (or bloated yet happy, which is fine, too).

Depending on the place, it's usually wise to go for one "menu" (*prix fixe* or "fixed-price" meal) for dinner. You usually have the option of a three-course menu with *entrée* (appetizer), *plat* (entree), and dessert, with wine and coffee included; or a cheaper two-course menu with choice of appetizer and entree or entree and dessert, plus wine and coffee. Tax and tip are always included, so the price you see is the price you pay. And if you just ask for water, the waitstaff will think you want mineral water—perfectly potable free tap water is brought when you order *une carafe d'eau.*

Besides the indigenous cuisine—that is, regional French and old, established, immigrant cuisine—which we've focused on here, there are of course great Chinese and Thai restaurants (particularly in the China-town in the 13th *arrondissement*), Turkish shwarma stands, and whatever other cuisine you could imagine here. If you're dying for a quick bite, the rue des Rosiers in the Marais is dotted with falafel stands side by side, each as good as the next. The same is true for the crêpe stands everywhere, with uniform prices and quality, even outside the **Louvre.**

▶▶**CHEAP**

You may have to line up for **Polidor** *(41 rue Monsieur-le-Prince, 6th; Métro to Odéon; Tel 01/43-26-95-34; Noon-2:30pm/7pm-12:30am Mon-Sat, till 11pm Sun; 60-80f per entree; No credit cards)* a popular, charming, century-old *bouillon* or brothhouse (worker's dining hall) in the Latin Quarter. Once you're seated here, choose what you want and snap out your order quick-like, and don't ask what's in what and can you get a substitution, or you'll get an earful from the *bouillon*-Nazi waitresses. Excellent down-home cooking, like tender veal in crème fraîche, or breast of duck, served in a brusque but warm-hearted atmosphere to chatty grad-student types.

garçon means "boy"

The cafe waiter—these days known as *monsieur*, not *garçon*—is one of the obnoxious fixtures of Paris life. Yes, he may mock you if you don't understand French. Yes, he will present your coffee with an exaggerated flourish that comes off as somehow even more insulting than just plopping it down. No, he will never come back with your change. Jean-Paul Sartre, the now largely ignored father of Existentialism, wrote many of his works in cafes [see *Café de la Mairie* in *hanging out,* above] and evidently got just as pissed off as us. In *Being and Nothingness,* he used the waiter as an example of someone who vanishes so completely into his role as "waiter" that he ceases to be a person. You may think you can lube him up like we do the DMV guy back home: a wink and a smile that says, "Yeah, I feel for you, crappy job." But he's not acting like that 'cause he hates his job; *au contraire,* it's 'cause he takes his job just a wee bit too seriously. This stickler mentality is what many a French lefty will unflinchingly call *petit bourgeois:* the train conductor will absolutely demand proof of age if you buy the youth-rate ticket, and the baker will give you a baker's singsong "Bon-jour" every time. Javert, the mean old inspector in *Les Misérables,* was doing the same thing when he hunted poor Jean Valjean to his death for a stolen loaf of bread. Visit the Daumier room at the **Musée D'Orsay** [see *culture zoo,* above], and see if those pinched little bureaucrats don't seem to be overplaying the part. Still true, still annoying as hell.

In the heart of the Butte aux Cailles is the teeny, rugged bistro **Chez Gladines** *(30 rue de Cinq Diamants, 13th; Métro to Corvisart or Place de l'Italie; Tel 01/45-80-70-10; Noon-3pm/7pm-midnight daily, closed Aug; 50-90f per entree; No credit cards)*. Peanut shells cover the floor, and big clay bowls full of country salads and southwestern and Basque dishes like *canard à la basquaise* (duck Basque-style) are tossed to you over the heads of that happy couple sharing the bench with you. Have a beer, put your elbows on the oilcloth, and chow down.

The minibistro **Lescure** *(7 rue de Mondovi; 1st; Métro to Concorde; Tel 01/42-60-18-91; Noon-2:15pm/7-10:15pm Mon-Fri; Closed 2 weeks in Aug; 40-80f per entree, 110f 4-course prix fixe; MC, V)* is a major find because reasonably priced restaurants near Place de la Concorde are rare. The tables on the sidewalk are tiny and there isn't much room inside, but what this place does have is rustic charm to burn. The kitchen's wide open, and the aroma of drying bay leaves, salami, and garlic hanging from the ceiling lends the room a homey vibe. House specialties include *confit de canard* (duckling) and salmon in green sauce. A favorite dessert is one of the chef's fruit tarts.

The line of hungry Parisians extending out the door of **Aux Délices de Manon** *(400 rue St.-Honoré; Tel 01/42-60-83-03, Fax 01/49-27-02-51; Métro to Concorde or Madeleine; 6:30am-10pm daily; MC, V)*, waiting to get a sandwich for take-out, speaks volumes about this small restaurant/boulangerie just a block from the Champs-Elysées. On a pretty day, pick up a sandwich *à emporter* (for take-out) and walk with it toward the Tuileries to dine on a park bench among the splendor of the gardens.

Paris may go coo-coo for couscous, but some of the best falafel outside of Jerusalem can be found along rue des Rosiers in the Marais. While the bustling street is lined with falafel joints, the best is **L'As du Fallafel** *(34 rue des Rosiers; Tel 01/48-87-63-60; Métro to St.-Paul; Noon-midnight Mon-Thur, Sun, noon-5pm Fri, 8pm-midnight Sat; MC, V)*, whose cheaply priced sandwiches are seasoned with Middle Eastern spices, dripping with tahini, and stuffed with delectable beets, lettuce, tomatoes, and other veggie goodies. The interior of the place gets super-crowded around lunch and dinner, so you may have to wait, but pay no mind and make yourself completely known to the stylish-looking family that runs the place to get the next possible seat.

The best slice of pizza for your *franc* in Paris is made in the stone ovens of **Pizza Vesuvio** *(1 rue Gozlin; Tel 01/43-54-94-78; Métro to Saint-Germain-des-Prés; Open 24 hours; 17f slice; MC, V)*, which is tucked off Boulevard St.-Germain across from the St.-Germain church. They also have two other locations around the city *(25 rue Quentin-Baucard; Tel 01/47-23-60-26, Fax 01/47-23-63-24; 6:30-midnight)* and *(144 ave. Champs-Elysées; Tel 01/43-59-68-69; 6pm-1am)*. Order your slice at the counter for take-out. Slices are delicately thin-crusted and delectably seasoned with a small amount of sauce, and the guy who molds the dough and works the oven is really Italian.

A slightly more suspect choice is the late-night window of the **Pecos Grill** *(112 rue St.-Denis; Tel 01/42-21-47-66; Métro to Etienne-Marcel; 6:30pm-2am; V, MC)*, which serves the perfect Parisian drunk fare of kebabs and *steak-frites* steps from the sketchy Les Halles. The hours generally depend on whether they have any meat left on the skewer or whether you can cajole the North African guy behind the counter to serve you one of their large steak sandwiches with lettuce and tomato topped with *pommes frites*. Order anything sounding remotely American Western from the menu at any other time besides late at night, and you put yourself in risk of fiery bowel movements—and remember, the scratchy French toilet paper isn't kind on the nether regions.

The name of **Kitch** *(10 rue Oberkampf; Tel 01/40-21-94-14; Métro to Filles du Calvaire; 5pm-2am; MC, V)* adequately describes both the fun atmosphere and the junk aesthetic interior of this hip bar-restaurant. Unwind with a snack and drink and listen to the mellow world-beat music before retiring for an afternoon siesta after a day of rigorous sightseeing. The menu is slim, but the drink list is long and includes bottles of Red Stripe for those lonesome for Jamaica's white sands. Try the tasty bagel sandwiches for an interesting commentary on the globalization of American culture.

▶▶DO-ABLE

Just north of the Marais, charming **Chez Omar** *(47 rue de la Bretaigne, 3rd; Métro to Arts et Métiers; Tel 01/42-72-36-26; Noon-2:45pm/7:45-11:30pm Mon-Sat, 7:45-11:30pm Sun; 60-100f per entree; No credit cards)* offers simple, reasonable couscous dishes for anything but a simple crowd. By 9pm every table of this unassuming, ragged old brasserie is packed with glitterati and artists from the nearby galleries. Show up early, around 7pm, stuff yourself on chicken or lamb couscous and flaky *merguez* sausage, and drink your fill of the perfumed Algerian wine, then get kicked out by Omar himself when the crush starts.

If you've wandered the streets of Montmartre, but'll be damned if you'll eat with the hordes around Sacré-Coeur, you're in luck: Wander all the way around the eastern, sheer slope of the mount along the rue Ronsard, past the little pagan grottoes cut into the rock, and you'll arrive at **l'Eté en Pente Douce** *(23 rue Muller, 18th; Tel 01/42-64-02-67; Métro to Château-Rouge; Noon-11pm daily; 60-80f per entree; MC, V)*. Here you can lunch on light, simple salads or smoked fish, or one of the fresh mushroom specialties of the proprietor, and linger for hours over a good pot of tea on a sunny, crowded terrace at the foot of the mount. Little-known to tourists but a favorite of the locals, down here you get all the charm of Montmartre without a glimmer of a single gaudy spire of the cathedral.

Al Dar *(8 rue Frédéric Sauton, 5th; Tel 01/43-25-17-15; Métro to Maubert-Mutualité; Noon-3pm/7pm-midnight daily; 85-92f per entree, prix fixe 200f; AE, DC, MC, V)* works hard to popularize Lebanon's savory cuisine. In a room lined with photographs of Lebanese architecture and scenery, you can relish their refreshing *taboulé,* and their creamier-than-thou *baba ganush* and *hummus*. Follow any of these with excellent roasted chicken; minced lamb prepared with mint, cumin, and Mediterranean herbs; and any of several kinds of *tagines* (clay pot stews) and couscous. Reservations recommended.

Tunisian and West African restaurants line Belleville and rue du Faubourg du Montmartre. Tunisian starters include *brik,* a puffed pastry with egg, cheese, and different meat fillings, and a tomato and roasted red pepper salad massaged in olive oil. Perfumed couscous and delicately spiced *tagines,* like lamb with tomato and onions, are the specialties of **La Gazelle** (*33 rue Lamartine; Tel 01/48-78-25-69; Métro to Cadet; 11am-2pm/5-11pm daily; MC, V*), a popular Tunisian restaurant nestled above the Grands Boulevards in the 9th *arrondissement.*

Just south of the Montmartre area, chef Stephane Michot serves fresh, contemporary Provençal cuisine at **Menthe et Basilic** (*6 rue Lamartine; Tel 01/48-78-12-20, Fax 01/48-78-12-21; Métro to Cadet; Noon-2:30pm/7-10:30pm daily; MC, V*). While the dining is decidedly button-down collar, the service is quite kind. The menu is light, delicious, and reasonably priced, and varies seasonally. Specialties include honey and cinnamon pork chops, exquisite fresh grilled salmon, and fresh strawberry "soup," which includes blended currants, raspberries, and strawberries with crushed fresh basil, topped with a single mint leaf.

For more eclectic dining, **Galerie 88** (*88 quai de l'Hôtel de Ville; Tel 01/42-72-17-58; Métro to Hôtel de Ville; 11am-midnight daily; No credit cards*) offers a version of vegetarian cuisine that includes fish and resembles a meatless Mediterranean–North African fusion cuisine. The Anisette 88 comes with guacamole, assorted different salads, and tabouli. Come early lest you have to wait for a seat, as the cozy yellow and red interior fills early with young Parisian trendies and unpretentiously hip cats.

▶▶SPLURGE

If you've grabbed a cheese sandwich at something that said *brasserie* on the front window, you've been duped. Just off the Place de la Bastille, **Bofinger** (*5-7 rue de la Bastille, 11th; Tel 01/42-72-87-82; Métro to Bastille; Noon-3pm/6:30pm-1am Mon-Fri, noon-1am Sat, Sun; 80-150f per entree, 119f weekday lunch menu, 189f dinner menu all week; AE, MC, V*) is the real deal, with rich dark wood paneling, brass banisters, and serious, attentive waiters in black ties standing by with hands clasped. Built in 1864, this was the first *brasserie* here, and remains one of the most magnificent examples of these Alsatian-style "brewery" restaurants, which gained popularity after the Franco-Prussian war. Come for a late-night dinner, around 11, and linger either in the bright, busy main dining room under a high stained-glass dome, or on the *1er étage* (second floor) in quiet rooms with magnificent inlaid wood tableaux. For the quality, the 189f menu is a bargain. Try the *jarret de porc* (ham hocks), served with a heaping plate of buttery *choucroute* (sauerkraut), and the *île flottant* (floating island) for dessert. Reservations are necessary on the weekends.

The literal pinnacle of hip in Paris is perhaps **Chez Georges** (*6th Floor, Centre Georges Pompidou, entrance place Georges Pompidou; Tel*

01/44-78-12-33; Métro to Les Halles/Chatelet; Noon-2am daily; Main courses 70-180f; AE, MC, V, DC). It's the perfect place to sip an *après-musée* apéritif in the sumptuous quietude of the skyline of Paris. The architecture of the restaurant is decidedly modern, but unlike the rest of the museum, it eschews right angles in favor of organic shapes and forms. Ignore the expensive, uninteresting, and poorly prepared food and check out the quietly cursing, rakishly dressed, three-button-suit-clad wait staff. Weekend evenings, DJs play to the who's who of hip Paris.

On a desolate side street full of tailors and Chinese takeout spots in the 3rd, south of République, hides the extraordinary **404** *(69 rue de Gravelliers, 3rd; Métro to Arts et Métiers; Tel 01/42-74-57-81; Noon-2:30pm/8pm-midnight Mon-Fri, noon-4pm/8pm-midnight Sat, Sun, closed 2 weeks in Aug; 80-120f per entree; AE, MC, V),* where the Arabic inscriptions in the high stone wall, the floor cushions, low tables, weepy Arab ballads, and an open stove transport you to a very comfy, if pricey, corner of the Sahara. The unusual spicy *tagines,* cooked with olives or dried fruits, are a little much at 110f, but you've got to see the dare-me-not-to-scald-you-long-distance tea pour-off at the end of the meal. Brunch is served noon to four Saturday and Sunday.

Not far from 404 in the 3rd is another gem, if not so glittery. **Au Bascou** *(38 rue Réaumur, 3rd; Métro to Arts et Métiers; Tel 01/42-72-69-25; Noon-2pm/8-10:30pm Tue-Fri, 8-10:30pm Sat, Mon, closed Sun, Aug 24, Dec 2-Jan; 90-130f per entree; AE, MC, V)* offers the salty, earthy, and rich cuisine of those independent-minded Basques in a quiet bistro setting that doesn't prepare you for the excellent food and service. Robust proprietor Jean-Guy Loustau personally oversees the presentation of dishes such as *chipiron* (baby squid and rice over crisp grilled spinach) or *axoa de veau* (a slow-cooked lamb stew). Eccentricities are revealed quietly—M. Loustau's handlebar moustache gives the first hint, then his transplanted velvet movie seats, then the free Basque liqueurs he keeps pushing on you....

crashing

Wonderful thing about Paris: Even though you know there are people—rich people—staying at the Crillon and the Plaza Athénée, with the billowing drapes, the French doors, and the silver coffee set beside the bed in the mornings, there are mid-range and budget options of such charm and taste you need never eat your heart out with envy. However, if you haven't booked months in advance for a Paris visit between June and mid-August or around Christmas, finding a place to stay can be like trying to lose your virginity in the back of your parents' Toyota Camry: Very difficult, and in the end, kind of unsatisfying. So book well in advance.

Rates may vary with the seasons, too. If you're planning on lingering, the *FUSAC* free magazine (in English) has ads for shares, apartment exchanges, and short-term sublets, many of which, in the suburbs or less-fashionable areas of Paris, might be worth your time.

▶▶**CHEAP**

The colorful, clean, well-kept interior of the centrally located **Wood-**

stock Hostel *(48 rue Rodier; Tel 01/48-78-87-76, Fax 01/48-78-01-63; Métro to Anvers or Poissonière; www.woodstock.fr; Single 147f winter, 157f summer; Bed in double 117f winter, 127f summer, bed in a 4-person room 107f winter, 117f summer, breakfast included; MC, V)* radiates that relaxed hippie vibe to receptive backpackers from around the world. Located just blocks from Gare du Nord, the hostel is the better part of the CHEAP syndicate of six hostels in Paris. The bushes adorning the exterior at first glance might be mistaken for their smokable cousins, all too familiar to actual attendees of the first Woodstock, but don't worry, the management is decidedly clean-cut and extraordinarily helpful in the event that the hostel is full, which often occurs as they don't take reservations during the summer. So show up early and try to badger your way into a room. Internet access available.

If Woodstock is full, a good bet is the less centrally located, blander **Aloha** *(1 rue Buromée; Tel 01/42-73-03-03, Fax 01/42-73-14-14; Métro to Volontaire; www.aloha.fr; Bed in double 137f winter, 137f summer, bed in 4-person 117f winter, 127f summer, breakfast included; MC, V)*, which has a similar room setup and international clientele and staff.

The cheapest choice for backpackers who don't mind slightly cramped conditions and dormitory-style triple-bunk sleeping is the no-frills, floral-wallpapered **Bed & Breakfast** *(42 rue Poissonière; Tel 01/40-26-83-08; Métro to Bonne Nouvelle; 100F bed, breakfast included; No credit cards)* run by Michel, a fluent English speaker and former resident of Queens, New York, and John, his Californian help. As with most hostels, Bed & Breakfast is reasonably safe and a good place to meet and commune with fellow trekkers. It is centrally located next to the Rex Club and a 20-minute walk from Les Halles. Like the other hostels in town, it doesn't take reservations, so show up early to snag a bed. Internet access available.

Between Notre Dame and the rue Saint-Antoine are some of the most luxuriant, pristine hostels you'll visit, run by the **Maison Internationale de la Jeunesse et des Etudiants** *(Tel 01/42-74-23-45; www.mije.com)* in three spic-and-span renovated 17th-century buildings with three addresses: **Le Fauconnier** *(11 rue du Fauconnier, 4th; Métro to St.-Paul)*, **Fourcy** *(6 rue de Fourcy, 4th; Métro to St.-Paul)*, and **Maubuisson** *(12 rue des Barres; Métro to Hôtel de Ville)*. Rates are the same for all three *(140f/person dorm, 155f/person triple, 175f/person double, 240f/person private room, plus 12f membership fee, breakfast included; No credit cards)*, and all three have the right mix of teenage tour groups, spooky loners, and attractive traveling duos, along with the indispensable attentive and efficient cleaning staff. It can be a trick to find the Fourcy address, housed in a converted convent: The huge, unmarked double doors on the rue de Fourcy have a smaller, almost hidden door that opens up into an immense courtyard. Great vaulted breakfast room in the basement, too.

Probably the best deal in the Latin Quarter is the **Hôtel Esmerelda** *(4 rue St.-Julien le Pauvre, 5th; Tel 01/43-54-19-20; Métro to St.-Michel;*

wired

Web-wise, Paris isn't quite up to speed. The official tourist site, *www.paris.org,* is functional if you want to check exhibition times or dates, but it's far simpler to buy one of the weeklies [see intro] than to go online. But when Paris catches up, it naturally does it with a lot of style. A number of portals will be opening soon which will, at the same time, function as ISPs (Internet Service Providers) free of charge—a great idea. In French, Nova has an online shadow, *www.novaplanet.com* with listings, bizarre links, a Nova radio station, and picks distinct to its online incarnation. As webspeak is largely English anyway, you should have little difficulty navigating the site.

A similarly attitude-laden site is *www.thinkparis.com,* a would-be *citysearch.com* without quite the scope, but with chatty reviews and an emphasis on the English-speaking twentysomethings of Paris. For rave and techno party news, visit the all-French but rather simple *www.france-techno.fr,* where you can find out where the local quasi-legal raves are being thrown and enter your e-mail on its mailing list. And in case you haven't run into enough drunken Anglos, *www.parispubs.com* gives an extremely Anglo-slanted portrait of "Paris's best pubs."

The cybercafe is another idea the French won't accept until they make it their own, and here are three distinct riffs:

Cyber Cafe Latino *(13 rue l'École Polytechnique, 5th; Tel 01/40-51-86-94; Métro to Maubert Mutualité; 11am-midnight Mon-Tue, 11:30am-2am Wed-Sat, 4-9pm Sun; 35f/hour; MC, V, AE),* except for the insistence on Latino-chic, is about how they do things back in the States, with fruit smoothies and tapas: Six Macs on simple work desks, in a spacious room, with the salsa turned up just

---

180-520f single, 520f double, 580f triple, 650f quad, breakfast 40f; No credit cards), which, despite its name and the view of **Notre Dame,** is the place most reminiscent of Balzac's *Maison Vauquer* that we visited, with the sickly-sweet decrepitude, the velvet, the ubiquitous plants, the cat, and the ancient, warped floors. The rooms are smaller and more rickety than at Grandes Écoles [see below], but they've got facilities, too, and less of the industrially sanitized feel.

Around the Place des Vosges in the Marais, the newly renovated **Hôtel Pratic** *(9 rue d'Ormesson, 4th; Tel 01/48-87-80-47; Métro to St.-Paul or Bastille; 525f single w/toilet, 560f double w/toilet and shower, breakfast 32f; MC, V),* with its miniature rooms painted in flowery pinks and yellow, small elevators, and small beds, gives you the vague sense that you've just eaten a little of what Alice had. With a prime location

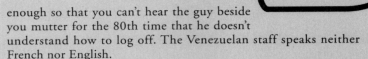

enough so that you can't hear the guy beside you mutter for the 80th time that he doesn't understand how to log off. The Venezuelan staff speaks neither French nor English.

You may think you're in an '80s arcade revival at very small, very spare **Clickside** *(14 rue Domat, 5th; Tel 01/56-81-03-00; Métro to Maubert Mutualité or Cluny-La Sorbonne; 10am-midnight Mon-Fri, 1-11pm Sat, Sun; 11 PC terminals, 30f/hour, 22f/hour with student ID; www.clickside.com; MC, V, AE),* where the future French Steve Jobses squander their intellect on the latest video games, sampled here for a small fee (at an elaborate pricing system–prorated, as opposed to the Latino). This is no-nonsense game-playing; the cafe part seems almost like an afterthought.

And the big geniuses behind the **Webbar** *(32 rue de Picardie, 3rd; Tel 01/42-72-62-50; Métro to Filles du Calvaire; 9am-2am daily; 18 PCs, 20f/hour; www.webbar.fr; MC, V, AE)* want you to understand that their complex is not a cybercafe, it's a, well, you can figure it out. Certainly more business/suit oriented, the two-level, bar/cafe/gallery also addresses the scourge of French computer illiteracy with private lessons, in a tactfully private room. The requisite salsa, jungle, and world beats laid down by, of course, DJ Replicant.

A note to the notebook carrier: Though French phone plugs may appear compatible with American ones, they're not; the order of the wires you see in the clear plastic head is reversed. There's nothing for it but an adapter, best bought at home, but findable at **FNAC** [see *stuff,* above].

on the peaceful Place du Marché Sainte-Cathérine, just a walk away from the heart of the Marais.

▶▶DO-ABLE

For an ultramodern, ultrahip option, the **Hôtel Beaumarchais** *(3 rue Oberkampf, 11th; Tel 01/53-36-86-86; Métro to Filles du Calvaire; 390-490f single Oct-Mar; 450-550f single Apr-Sept; 590f double Oct-Mar; 650f double Apr-Sept; 790f suite Oct-Mar; 850f suite Apr-Sept; breakfast 40f; AE, MC, V)* has just opened for those who simply cannot get enough Oberkampf [see *bar scene,* above] in their life. Clearly designed to be party central, it was on its way when we visited, with the sleek New York ultramodern hotel look in primary colors, albeit a little stage-set-y. Toilets and showers in every room and brand-new fixtures after a recent renovation.

A favorite hotel for the study-abroad crowd in the Latin Quarter is the **Hôtel des Grandes Écoles** *(75 rue du Cardinal Lemoine, 5th; Tel 01/43-26-79-23; Métro to Cardinal Lemoine; 560-680f single or double, 700-820f triple, 820f quad, extra cot 100f, breakfast 40f; MC, V),* shutting out the noise of the city with many large rooms with exposed rafters and other little country touches, opening onto a large cobblestone courtyard where breakfast can be taken in the summer. When fellow guests start asking if maybe you know their son, he's studying French at the Sorbonne and he's just about your age, this becomes the perfect spot to perfect your incomprehension of English. All rooms have shower, toilet, and phone.

Though the 1st *arrondissement* has better hotels, the **Britannique** *(20 ave. Victoria, 1st; Tel 01/42-33-74-59, Fax 01/42-33-82-65; Métro to Chatelet; 790f single, 950-1090f double, 70f breakfast; AE, DC, MC, V)* is a good deal. The rooms may be small, but they're clean, comfy, and have the basics. Located in the heart of Paris, near **Les Halles,** the **Centre Pompidou,** and **Notre Dame,** the Britannique was completely renovated in 1998. Bedrooms are cozy and conservatively decorated with traditional furniture. Bathrooms are small but well organized with enough shelf space for your beauty creams and a hair dryer. Minibar and TV make it positively luxurious.

The standard three-star **Hôtel Chamonix** *(8 rue d'Hauteville; Tel 01/47-70-19-49, Fax 01/45-23-14-81; Métro to Strasbourg-St.-Denis; 590f single, 700f double, 860f triple; V, MC, AE, DC)* is fully air-conditioned, recently remodeled, and centrally located between Strasbourg-St.-Denis and the place de la République. While rooms tend toward the nondescript, they are soundproofed and quite comfortable, with cable television and fully outfitted bathrooms. You'll get a 15 percent discount when you mention this guide.

▶▶**SPLURGE**

In 1996, a radical restoration of **Hôtel Abbatial St.-Germain** *(46 blvd. St.-Germain, 6th; Tel 01/46-34-02-12, Fax 01/43-25-47-73; Métro to Maubert-Mutualité; 600-720f single, 780-920f double, 1,050f triple; abba tial@clubinternet.fr; AE, DC, MC, V)* brought the six stories of this 17th-century building up to modern, smallish, but very comfortable standards. Rooms are very much French boudoir in style, with faux-Louis XVI and many lovely decorative touches. All windows are double glazed to keep out the busy and noisy surrounding neighborhood, and many rooms on the fifth—some with small balconies—and sixth floors enjoy views over **Notre Dame.** Plus AC, TV, and a minibar!

Swank and style predominate at the leather, wood, marble and leafy-ferned lobby of **Hôtel Lenox** *(9 rue de l'Université; Tel 01/42-96-10-95, Fax 01/42-61-52-63; 750-950f single or double, 50F breakfast; AE, DC, MC, V),* whose bar Hemingway was said to have hung out at. Today, for better or worse, you'll find pinch-nosed arty types at the Art Deco-ish bar. Rooms stylishly hark back to *les années folles* (the rough equivalent of the Roaring Twenties), with their hand-painted furniture and sleek bathrooms.

neeD TO KNOW

Currency Exchange Best way to change money is to use **ATMs,** which give the best rates. Both airports also have 24-hour *bureaux de change.* At the Gare du Nord, where the RER B train arrives from Charles de Gaulle Airport, there is a **Thomas Cook** *(Tel 01/42-80-11-50; 6:15am–11:25pm daily).*

Public Transportation A 48f *carnet* buys you ten **Métro** rides; if you're sticking around, a monthly, which can be used as often as you like (in Zone 1, the urban center) is 279f. The **trains** to the suburbs, the **RER** lines, also run through the center of town and can be quicker; tickets must be bought separately, and prices vary. Keep your yellow RER ticket—you'll need it to get out from the tracks. Two can—and often do—slip through the turnstiles on one ticket, but checks happen, so be careful [see *five-o,* above]. First and last train *(5–6am/12:30–1am)* are listed on the platform signs. **Taxis** are your only option then, and on Saturday nights there aren't enough.

Health and Emergency Police: *17;* Fire: *18;* Ambulance: *15.* The 24-hour **American Hospital** is just out of town in Neuilly *(63 blvd. Victor-Hugo; Bus 82; Tel 01/46-41-25-41, direct emergency line Tel 01/47-47-70-15).*

Pharmacies Pharma Presto *(Tel 01/42-42-42-50)* is a 24-hour pharmacy that delivers for a fee of 150f 8am-6pm, 250f after. Otherwise, try the **Pharmacie des Champs** *(84 ave. des Champs Elysées, 8th; Tel 01/45-62-02-41; Métro to Georges V).*

Bike/Moped/Whatever Rental **Atelier de la Compagnie** *(57 blvd. de Grenelle, 15th; Tel 01/45-79-77-24; Métro to Dupleix; 10am-7pm Mon-Fri, till 6pm Sat; MC, V, AE)* rents scooters for 190f/day, 860f/week, motorcycles from 340f/day, 1,500f/week, requires 10,000f refundable deposit, w/valid driver's license.

American Express *(38 ave. de Wagram, 8th; Tel 01/42-27-58-80; Métro to Ternes; 9am-5pm Mon-Fri).*

Telephone Country code: *33;* city code: *01;* information: *12;* international operator (USA): *00/33-12-11.* Phone cards, *télécartes,* can be bought at most tobacco shops, magazine stands, and at any post office, in 50f or 120f denominations. **AT&T:** *Tel 08-00-99-00-11;* **MCI:** *Tel 08-00-99-00-19;* **Sprint:** *Tel 08-00-99-00-87.*

Airports Charles de Gaulle (Roissy) *Tel 01/48-62-22-80;* 20 miles north of town. International flights arrive at Aérogare 1 at Charles de Gaulle; bus it to Aérogare 2, from there, catch the RER B train into town *(4-5 departures an hour 5:20am-midnight; 48f).* **Air France** buses *(4-5 departures an hour 6am-11pm daily; 60f)* leave from both Aérogares and stop at more locations. **Roissybus** *(4-5 departures an hour 5:20am-midnight; 45f)* drops you near Place de l'Opéra. **Taxis** *(around 200f w/no traffic, 300f during the day)* are the only choice in off-hours. From **Orly** *(Tel 01/49-75-15-15),* catch the **Orlyval** shuttle train

(6am-10pm Mon-Fri; 7am-11pm Sat, Sun) to RER B station **Antony** *(57f together)*, and from there into Paris. Or shuttle bus to RER C station **Pont de Rungis,** then Orlyrail train to central Paris *(Every 12 minutes 5:45am-11pm daily; 30f)*. Taxi same cost and time as from De Gaulle.

Trains General info for all trains: *Tel 08-36-35-35-35*. The six stations: **Gare d'Austerlitz, Gare Saint-Lazare, Gare Montparnasse, Gare d'Est, Gare d'Ouest,** and **Gare du Nord,** are all major Métro hubs.

Bus Lines Out of the City Most buses arrive at **Gare Routière Internationale de Paris** *(28 ave. de Général de Gaulle Tel 01/49-72-51-51; Métro to Galliéni)* in the suburb of Bagnolet. From the bus station take the Métro line 3 from Galliéni into town.

southern europe

milan

Milan is its own entity: confident, brash, sometimes a little too cool for school. It's a city that doesn't rely on the curiosity of foreigners to dictate its rhythms. You're welcome to join in, but remember, they don't really need you. Milan is big and diverse, a sprawling architectural grandiosity. It's more like London than Rome. Though it has some of the best museums around, you don't come to Milan to be a passive sightseer; you come to wander around its distinctly different neighborhoods, lose yourself in the urban funk, *shop* (exchange rates be damned!), and groove on Italy's most genuinely modern culture. Still, if you look closely at Italy's "Second City," you'll get a glimpse of old Italy tucked inside its hardcore urban veneer.

Southern Italians would have you think the secession-happy, fiercely protectionist Milanese are uptight aliens. While the people you'll meet are basically friendly and congenial, they, unlike their southern countrymen, don't communicate as much with their hands. And kids from Milan have a greater sense of purpose than those coming from other, poorer Italian towns. You won't see hordes of moped-riding students with brightly colored Invicta backpacks lounging or chatting for hours in the streets or in the neighborhood bars. Here, twentysomething culture is shaped by university classes and steady jobs. At night, kids hang out in the Ticinese, Navigli, or Garibaldi districts with friends. While Milan is one of the best cities in which to pull out your fancy clothes and play dress-up—and the few established clubs here do deliver the goods—a lovely evening can be had pursuing less-frenzied activities: seeing a flick at one of many local theaters, sipping martinis by the canal, or eating a pizza on Via Dante and then taking a long, slow, gelati-filled *passegiata* along the porticos of Corso Vittorio Emanuele.

The few slackers around mostly set up camp in the Parco Sempione, but outside the park grounds, you won't see many tie-dyed, dreadlocked street kids banging on drums or spinning a Chinese top. Other than in the Piazza del Duomo, where a sparse few trade their talents for lira, Milan isn't kind to spare-changers—the layout of the city doesn't really permit it. Unlike Rome, the city of a thousand squares, Milan is a town of grumbling boulevards—less about stopping and sitting and more about getting from here to there. But once you land wherever *there* might be, the city and its inhabitants warm up after a couple glasses of wine, inviting you to join them in their weird mix of metropolitan grit and sophisticated splendor.

The best period to visit Milan is from late April to July, when the skies are usually blue, and the sun hasn't reached its hottest. This is also the time when most outdoor events take place. In August, the city practically shuts down as residents escape to the sea and Lake Como. Whatever time of year you decide to visit, pick up a copy of **Hello Milano** at the tourist information office [see *need to know*, below] for indispensable information on what's current and happening culturally around town.

neighborhoods

One of the great things about Milan is its completely distinct neighborhoods, characterized as much by the stores and buildings as by the folks who live and/or hang out there. Milanese youth tend to bypass the bureaucratic and regal **Centro** and snobby **Brera**, heading instead to the artsy **Porta Ticinese** area or the canals of the **Navigli** district to see and be seen. Two Amsterdam-ish canals let Navigli rival Rome's Trastevere for the most happening 'hood in Italy. Late into the summer nights, the scene is like some sort of hipster boardwalk, with the streets on either side of the narrow strips of water teeming with crowded outdoor bars, restaurants, loud live music, and an unending stream of dressed-up kids. Farther down along **Corso di Porta Ticinese** and **Via Gorizia**, the snappier artsy set sits, smokes, and talks at cafes and bars like **Soup du Jour** [see *bar scene*, below]. For a slightly lower-octane experience, the Garibaldi section—especially along **Corso Como** and around **Piazza Moscova**—has a mess of scattered bars and pizzerias. Here, the lay of the land is more upscale and the prices are higher, but the mood is still casual. At about 11pm, the decked-out club kids begin to line up outside **Hollywood**, one of the hippest nightclubs in town [see *club scene*, below].

One element Milan *does* share with other Italian cities is its ability to get you lost. The centuries-old street layout has no clear pattern, and the streets themselves often change names from one block to the next. The city center is a confounding mess of Vias, Viales, and Vicolos, built around the **Piazza del Duomo**. Running from this central point are roughly 30 streets of varying size, the largest being the store-laden **Corso Vittorio Emanuelle** (eastward), **Via Mazzini** (southward), **Via Manzoni**

(northward), **Via Torino** (southwestward), and **Via Dante** (northwestward), which runs out to **Parco Sempione**. In this inner quadrangle of squares of streets you'll find most of the cultural sites, including the impressive, glass-covered mall known as the **Galleria**, the **Ambrosiana Library and Picture Gallery**, and the **Museo Civico d'Arte Contemporaneau** [see *culture zoo*, below], plus the tourist office [see *need to know*, below], which is adjacent to the Piazza del Duomo. The other major geographic hub is the **Piazza della Scala**, due north of the Duomo. From this piazza, you can walk north on **Via Verde** to the fashion district around the upscale **Via Brera** and continue on to the happenin' **Garibaldi** area. The Navigli/Porta Ticinese neighborhood is a little farther out, southwest of the Duomo by roughly 1.5 miles.

The city is connected by three efficient **Metro lines** (red: M1, green: M2, yellow: M3) and a confusing hodgepodge of orange **ATC bus** and **tram routes**. Everything you'll want to see in the city center can be walked between, but it's quicker and easier to use the Metro to get to Brera/Garibaldi (M2 to Garibaldi or Moscow), Navigli/Porta Ticinese (M2 to Stazione Genova), and off-central sites like **Chiesa di Santa Maria delle Grazie** (which houses Leonardo's *The Last Supper*) and **Cimitero Monumentale** [see *culture zoo*, below, for both].

hanging out

Milan lacks the active street life of the other big Italian cities—there really aren't any quaint piazzas made for hanging out under the stars. Your best bet at any time of day or night is **Piazza del Duomo**, where all types and ages congregate in the shadow of the great cathedral. Listen to dressed-up minstrels, watch kids chase pigeons, and browse the makeshift stands of cheap jewelry and other knickknacks. If you have a thing for riff-raff, take a seat in front of the huge and strangely appealing **Central Train Station** [see *need to know*, below], where freeloaders do their loitering thing. When the droning traffic gets to be too much for you, make for the tree-lined public gardens, or **Giardini Pubblici** *(in the northeast of the city center between Via Daniele Manin and Corso Porta Venezia)*.

bar scene

Several years ago, to help the hip young poor afford the steep drink prices that this cosmopolitan city commands—or maybe just to get them to buy more—the happy-hour phenomenon was introduced. Now almost every Milanese cafe/pub has one. Even better for the impoverished traveler are the happy-hour snacks, or *stuzzichini*. This finger food, commonly consisting of focaccia, pastas, salads, and vegetables, is better than most meals back home and goes far to calm hunger pangs.

The cool tunes on the beat-up stereo system at **Portnoy's Caffè** *(Via de Amicis 1 at Corso di Porta Ticinese; Tel 02/58-11-34-29; 8am-2pm daily; V, MC)* sound even better when you realize how cheap the drinks are here—pints are L4,000, and fresh-squeezed orange juice is just L3,000. The breezy atmosphere—plus the occasional poetry readings and art exhibits—make this *the* place to feel Euro-chic. In the morning, you'll often find coffee and beer drinkers sharing a table. A 10-minute walk south of the Duomo.

Beginning at 6:30pm, Milan's twenty- and thirtysomething crowds descend on the congenial **Diva Café** *(Via Vigevano 3; Tel 02/89-40-30-53; M2 to Porta Genova; Happy hour 6-9pm Mon-Sat; No credit cards)* in the Navigli for its delicious happy-hour buffet. There's always-packed outdoor seating, plus an open and airy inside with light-toned walls. If it's too hot, the owners may even turn on the air conditioning, a godsend in July and August. A good early-evening place.

You'll feel at home at **Antica Birreria di Porta Nuova** *(Via Solferino 56; Tel 02/659-77-58; M2 to Moscova or Garibaldi; 6pm-2am; No credit cards)*, a classic microbrewery dating from 1877, up in the Garibaldi district. The tables on the first floor are restored sewing-machine stands minus the machines, and the windows are fitted with neat English-language displays on the art of beer barrel knots and tap devices. The tapas-rich happy hour that runs from 6 till 9pm makes the very good Porretti microbrew taste even better. An ambient basement-level restaurant serves a small menu of pastas and seconds.

You can spend hours drinking coffee or beer in the flower-filled **Caffè**

la Piazzetta *(Piazza Lima at Via Ozanam; Tel 02/29-52-92-25; M1 to Lima; 7:30am-11pm; No credit cards)*, feeling oh-so-calm amid the frenetic activity of Corso Buenos Aires, to the west of the city center. Covered outdoor seating provides the shade; you do the rest.

If you want to be a part of the cocktail-toting fashion elite, just put on some fresh duds, motor over to **Radetzky Café** *(Corso Garibaldi 105; Tel 02/657-26-45; M2 to Moscova; Noon-3pm/8pm-midnight daily, closed Mon afternoon; No credit cards)* and order up a L10,000 drink. The large, open windows let you chat with your cool, cocktail-holding comrades mingling on the streets of the Garibaldi.

Word is that Indian food and slinky pumps are a great match. You'll have to go to **Maharaja Fashion Café** *(Viale Gorizia 8; Tel 02/89-42-03-19; M2 to Porta Genova; 2pm-midnight, closed Monday; No credit cards)* in the Navigli district to find out for yourself. The food's more pricey than back home, but who comes to eat? Come late, when all the other pretty boys and girls do—as the night goes on, the focus shifts more to the bar and away from the restaurant.

Loud American music streams out from **Indian Bar** *(Corso Garibaldi at Via Moscova; Tel 02/29-00-03-90; 5pm and on; No credit cards)*, a dark, two-story bar with indoor/outdoor seating just down the road from the Radetzky Café [see above]. The crowd is kind of young and definitely friendly—it's a good place to ask locals about their views on life, soccer, music, and anything else that comes to mind. Just don't fall for a 16-year-old (and if they *look* 16, they're probably 13). Strippers perform on and in the bar on Sunday nights—be sure to bring plenty of cash to cover the L10,000 entrance fee, and for tips for the ladies....

Plat du Jour 1999 *(Viale Gorizia 28; M2 to Porta Genova; 7pm-2:30am Tue-Sun, closed Mon; No credit cards)* serves yummy fruit drinks and gives overstimulated kids something different than what's offered by the more standard bars on the Navigli canals a block over. The Keith Haring-esque wall murals, tropical theme, and the dirty floor combine to create an alluringly edgy atmosphere. The slick bottle-spinning bartenders like to play loud continuous cuts of rap/rock/reggae. Wine L3,000, beer L7,000, and long drinks L9,000.

LIVE MUSIC SCENE

Most folks don't come to Milan expecting to catch a good gig, but even in a nation as music-poor as Italy (except for opera, of course), the city offers some pretty happening venues. As with many other aspects of Milan, the live music scene revolves around the Garibaldi and Navigli areas. Many bars on the major canal streets of Alzaia Naviglio Grande and Alzaia Naviglio Pavese have nightly lineups of local bands. Of these, the smaller **Charlie's** *(Via Argelati 1; Tel 02/89-40-35-60; 7am-3am Mon-Sat, closed Sun; No credit cards)* and the enormous **Naviglio Blues** *(Via Ascanio Sforza 11; Tel 02/58-10-39-29; 1pm-late daily; No credit cards)* are two of the more popular, pumping out blues, rock, and English/American covers to a young, beer-guzzling crowd. The CD shop **Supporti**

ragazzo meets ragazza

Girl travelers in Milan will have no trouble getting hit on—this is still Italy, after all. Traveling in all-female packs is one solution. While doing so will directly increase the number of catcalls received, it can also provide some protection against come-oning local goons. Guys, on the other hand, may experience problems getting chummy with local chicks. The Milanese are way more conservative than their southern brethren, which means that there is less interaction between strangers, both in the streets and in the bars. A good tactic for guys: Try frequenting the same bar for a couple days and get chummy with the *male* bartender. Tell him that you're trying to meet a local *bella donna* (not the poison kind), and he can and almost always will willingly act as matchmaker. Granted, this approach takes some time and finesse, but save for rare drunken exceptions, it's really the best way.

Fonografici and megastore **Messagerie Musicali** [see *stuff*, below, for both] are good sources of information on what's up around town.

Milan's most established music venue, **Capolinea** (*Via Ludovico Il Moro 119; Tel 02/89-12-20-24; M2 to Porta Genova; Music 10:30-1am, doors open at 8pm daily; No credit cards*), offers nightly jazz/blues/rock from accomplished local and international artists. It's slightly south of the city center, the crowd is subdued and somewhat older, and, though there's no cover, the obligatory drinks are expensive. Still, after so many tired cover bands, the high-quality licks you'll hear are worth it. The adjoining restaurant opens at 8pm for dinner, and the shows start at 10:30pm.

Bands tend to play longer sets at the more lively **Le Scimmie** (*Viale Card. A. Sforza 49; Tel 02/840-22-00; M2 to Porta Genova; Music 10:30pm-4am, doors open 8pm daily; Cover L12,000; No credit cards*), where a mix of conservative button-ups, blue-collar folk, and punky kids, local and tourist alike, come together. Unfortunately, the sound system stinks, but a couple of stage spots flicker periodically in the large-ish room to create a rock 'n' roll effect. Scimmie (which, by the way, means monkey) is a common stop for bands doing the traditional trek through Europe. On some nights a one-drink minimum replaces the cover. With dark wood paneling and music memorabilia–like photos and concert posters on the walls, this is also a good, homey place, south of the city center, to just stop in for a drink.

The spacious "Irish" pub **Blues Canal** (*Via Casale 7; Tel 02/836-07-99; M2 to Porta Genova; 6pm-3am, music starts around 9pm daily; No credit cards*), down in the Navigli, has a bizarre aquamarine interior and a nightly billing of jazz ensembles and cover bands playing English

MILAN bars, clubs and culture zoo

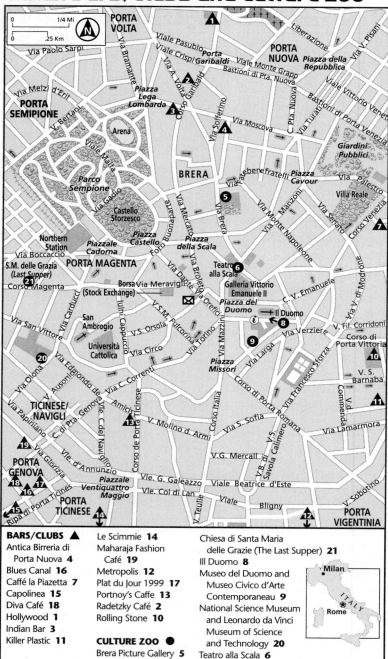

BARS/CLUBS ▲

Antica Birreria di
  Porta Nuova **4**
Blues Canal **16**
Caffé la Piazetta **7**
Capolinea **15**
Diva Café **18**
Hollywood **1**
Indian Bar **3**
Killer Plastic **11**

Le Scimmie **14**
Maharaja Fashion
  Café **19**
Metropolis **12**
Plat du Jour 1999 **17**
Portnoy's Caffe **13**
Radetzky Café **2**
Rolling Stone **10**

CULTURE ZOO ●

Brera Picture Gallery **5**

Chiesa di Santa Maria
  delle Grazie (The Last Supper) **21**
Ill Duomo **8**
Museo del Duomo and
  Museo Civico d'Arte
  Contemporaneau **9**
National Science Museum
  and Leonardo da Vinci
  Museum of Science
  and Technology **20**
Teatro alla Scala **6**

Because of the high level of commerce and great amount of wealth flaunted on every corner in the center of Milan, the police have a more austere, watchful presence than in other major Italian cities. Some actually walk a beat!

pop/rock. It's kind of a cheesy take on the House of Blues, but the hip, enthusiastic crowd is intoxicating, and you can have a blast trying to figure out the garbled words of your favorite hits from the '80s and '90s. Large wraparound sofas in the back are great for tired legs.

Rolling Stone *(Corso XXII Marzo 32; Tel 02/733-172; Tram 12 or 27; 10:30pm-4am daily, closed July, Aug; Cover L12,000-25,000 depending on the night; No credit cards)*, a youth-culture breeding ground since the '60s, has rock 'n' roll oozing out of its pores. Aggressive heavy-metal and hardcore bands take the stage and pepper the crowd with incomprehensible lyrics and mind-numbing riffs. There are about 75 seats and some cramped standing room in the black-walled space, to the east of the city center.

In addition to being a favorite local watering hole, **Indian Bar** [see *bar scene*, above], has a dirty gig pit hosting live bands and ska, funk, hip-hop, and reggae DJ nights, which the young slackerish crowd just eats right up. There are few other outlets in Milan where you can listen to such a variety of music. Call or stop by ahead of time; there's no set schedule.

club scene

For a city as classy as Milan, one of the big disappointments is the total lack of good clubs in the city center. This can be explained partly by the dirty habit locals have of keeping the best things for themselves and away from tourists, partly by the magnetic draw of the canals out in Navigli, and partly by the harsh difficulty the clubs have paying their bills and keeping their doors open in this finicky and faddish fashion scene. Fortunately, the ones that have survived do kick some ass. It's in clubs, more than in any other scene, that you'll probably smell hash wafting. A fairly snobbish vibe hangs around most clubs, but for the most part it's just a facade put on by the club owners—the clubbers themselves are cool. They're also dressed to the teeth, as you should be if you want to get in: Girls, go with the sexiest thing you can throw together. Guys, stay away from tees and shorts, and maybe gel your hair up to fit in with the local boys. The doormen are strict, but not beyond anything you would find in any other big urban place. Locals don't go out till 11 or midnight and don't pack it in till sunrise.

You'd have to be comatose to not have fun at **Hollywood** *(Corso Como 15; Doors open around 10pm Thur-Sun; Cover L20,000-25,000; No*

Rules of the game

There's no legal age limit for purchase or consumption of alcohol here—instead you're completely at the mercy of the shopkeeper and the barkeep. As long as you're not acting like a drunken fool, you shouldn't have any problem securing some hooch. Drinking and carousing in Milan is usually concentrated in ubiquitous *locali* (bars, cafes, and other going-out places), not on the streets. While you *can* bring a bottle of wine outside around the Piazza del Duomo, it's not a common thing—the general anti-intimacy of Milan's traffic-heavy streets kinda takes the allure out of it. Milan does have a local pot-smoking street scene in Parco Sempione (though marijuana is technically illegal here), where scores of bongo-playing hippie anarchists hang out.

credit cards), up in Girabaldi. The small dance floor encourages a lot of flirty nuzzling among the extremely done-up, bouncy girls and boys. The music varies from commercial to techno, and to do it right, you should stay till at least 2 or 3am. If you get drowsy, you can always grab a drink, plop down on a sofa or chair, and people-watch one of the most elite crowds in Milan's nighttime scene.

The slightly out-of-the-way location (far southeast of the city center) of Milan's hippest club, **Killer Plastic** *(Viale Umbria 120; Tel 02/733-996; M3 to Lodi TBB, then catch Bus 92 at Viale Isozno and take it north on Viale Umbria, or take the 30-minute walk up Viale Umbria from the Metro stop; Thur-Sun, gay/lesbian Thur; No credit cards)*, isn't keeping away the style-setting youth. Wear your party best and groove with the other exhibitionist trendoids in the sprawling, tropical-themed outdoor space. Music-wise, it alternates between eardrum-popping drum 'n' bass samples and more mainstream discs. No matter what the DJs have in store, you'll have a great time, especially if you're looking for pickup action. Call ahead—sometimes the schedule changes unexpectedly.

Metropolis *(Via Broni 10; Tel 02/56-81-55-70; 11pm and on nightly, gay Tue, Fri, Sat; No credit cards)* is a haven for choreographed multiple-DJ theme nights of punk, funk, drum 'n' bass, bebop, and pop. The college-age crowd likes to shake it out hard. Video and space-age doodads should keep you occupied during rest periods. Entrance is reduced for ArciGay members [see *gay scene*, below], but usually costs L15,000 to L25,000. Also slightly out of the way, south of the city center.

ARTS SCENE

▶▶VISUAL ARTS

Via Brera is quickly becoming the center of Milan's exciting gallery scene. You can cover everything from neo-post-Impressionism to post-neo-Modernism in just a few blocks.

At **Galleria Ponte Rosso** *(Via Brera 2; Tel 02/86-46-10-53; 10am-7pm Tue-Sat)*, you'll see a collection of Impressionistic canvases from local artists, as well as sculpture.

Zammarchi *(Via Brera 29; Tel 02/86-46-04-88; 9:30am-8pm Tue-Sat)* is a cozy little space featuring local and national minimalist painting and sculpture.

The bars around Corso Garibaldi are where you should go to discuss all the metaphysical values of the modernistic, anti-directional brush strokes responding to the primal need to violently re-create our ontic placement in the universe, etc. etc. etc.....

▶▶PERFORMING ARTS

Led by the world-renowned **Teatro alla Scala** [see *culture zoo*, below], the performing arts are alive and well in Milan. Scores of theaters and concert halls present music, dance, opera, and drama. The theaters in Milan are not cheap, but if you can muster up a few bucks to catch a show, it'll be worth it.

Despite what the modern and, therefore, ugly reinforced concrete frame of **Teatro Smeraldo** *(Piazza XXXV Aprile 10; Tel 02/29-00-67-67; M2 to Garibaldi or Moscova)* might lead you to think, this theater shows one of the most progressive lineups of national and international music and theater troupes. It's best to go to the theater, north of the city center, to pick up a season brochure and to purchase tickets.

Great classical and operatic programs can be heard at **Centro Culturale Rosetum** *(Via Pisanello 1; Tel 02/48-70-72-03; www.rosetum.it)*. Established in 1956, this small and quaint venue has plush seating, chan-

fESTIVALS and EVENTS

National and International Dance Festival *(Mid-June to mid-July; for info and reservations, call Comune di Trezzo sull'Adda—Ufficio Cultura 02/90-98-70-52 9am-noon, or visit www.commune.trezzo-sulladda.mi.it)*.

Festival del Teatro D'Europa *(June; held at Teatro Strehler, Largo Greppi, M2 to Lanza; Teatro Grassi, Via Rovello 2, M1 to Cordusio; and Teatro Studio, Via Rivoli 6, M2 to Lanza; For information, call the Tourist Office)*.

Festival Cinematografico Gay/Lesbico *(Early June; held in various theaters throughout town, call the Tourist Office for details. Via Sturzo 51)* held in June, is now in its 13th year.

International Cinema Competition and Festival of Milan *(Early June; Via Milazzo 9; Tel 02/659-77-32; M2 to Garibaldi or Moscova)* is hosted by Anteo Spazio Cinema [see *art scene*, below]*.

deliers, and a marble-decorated interior that offers a welcome change from the packed bars along the Brera and Navigli sections of Milan.

English-language movies are screened on various nights at: **Anteo Spazio Cinema** *(Via Milazzo 9; Tel 02/659-77-32; M2 to Garibaldi or Moscova)* Mondays, **Arcobaleno** *(Via Tunisia 11; Tel 02/29-40-60-54; M1 to Porta Venezia)* Tuesdays, and **Mexico** *(Via Savona 57; Tel 02/48-95-18-02; M2 to Porta Genova)* Thursdays. All of these are just your basic nondescript movie theaters, and all seat about 300.

gay scene

As one local put it, "Milan is the out-est Italy gets." Don't expect Chelsea or the Castro, but there's plenty to do here. In Via Sammartini (adjacent to the train station), Milan even has a so-called "Gay Street." With Groove Caffè, Libreria Babele, Afterline, and a few other stores, Via Sammartini is the place to be for gays and lesbians. The scene is also kickin' around Nuova Idea International (in the Garibaldi district) and Zip (near Parco Sempione). **ArciGay** *(Via Torricelli 19; Tel 02/58-10-03-99)* is the leading gay organization, and sponsors events, conferences, and social outings. Its gay/lesbian/trans information and help line *(02/89-40-17-49; 9am-11pm Mon, 8am-midnight Tue, Thur, Fri, 8am-11pm Wed)* is in Italian only.

To get funky with the boys of Milan, go to **Nuova Idea International** *(Via de Castillia 30; Tel 02/69-00-78-59, 02/689-27-53; M2 to Garibaldi; 10pm-4am Thur-Sun; L15,000 cover w/one drink, L25,000 Sat; No credit cards)*. This well-known dance pad north of the city center is the softcore club for gay men of all ages and types. Its two big rooms hold a lot of sweaty, muscular bodies, and you're bound to bump into one.

Even though it's a *club privato*, the raunchy, cross-dressing crowd at **Zip** *(Corso Sempione 76 at Via Salvioni; Tel 02/331-49-04; 1pm-late Thur-Sun; No credit cards)* will gladly accept you. To enter, blow a kiss to the beefy bouncer, wave your passport (make sure to bring this) and some lira in front of his face, and wiggle your butt on in there, baby. The club's in a seedy 'hood, so be alert.

In one of its ads, the gay nights at **Metropolis** [see *club scene*, above] are described in the following words: "Hi-tec, modern, megavideo, jolly self massages, and sex box." Hmm, wonder which ones caught your eye? You'll have to go to satisfy your curiosity on gay Tuesdays, Fridays, and Saturdays.

On Thursday nights, queens take over **Killer Plastic** [see *club scene*, above] for *Man2Man* night (girls are also welcome).

Next Groove *(Via Sammartini 23, Tel 02/66-98-04-52; 10am-2am daily, till 9:30pm Tue; No credit cards)*, located on "Gay Street," is advertised as the only gay bar open all day.

The name of the popular leather bar **Cocksucker** *(Via Derna 15; No phone; 10pm-whenever Wed, Fri, Sun; No credit cards)* is pretty self-explanatory.

The slightly grungy **Recycle** *(Via Calabria 5; Tel 02/376-15-31; 9pm-2am or 5am Wed-Sun, gay men allowed Wed, Thur; No credit cards)* is the oldest and perhaps the most well-known lesbian bar among locals, expats, and foreigners. The decor is pretty standard—light-brown wood and marble—and the crowd mixes between butch-grunge pierced trendoids and a variety of more sophisticated ladies. It's a good place both for coffee and for stiffer drinks. You may want to call ahead, as hours sometimes vary.

Girls can also have fun at **Cicip e Ciciap** *(Via Gorani 9; Tel 02/867-202; 8:30pm-late, closed Mon, Tue; No credit cards)*—a bar with restaurant—and **Sottomarino Giallo (Yellow Submarine)** *(Via Donatella 2; Tel 02/29-40-10-47; 10pm-2 or 3am daily, but call ahead, gay males allowed Wed-Fri; No credit cards)*, the only lesbian disco in town.

CULTURE ZOO

The strong modern-art presence in Milan is a welcome relief in this Old Master–centric country—emphasizing once again that, despite a huge stockpile of Medieval and Renaissance treasures, the city and its residents are not living on past glories. The single most important work in Milan is, obviously, Leonardo's *The Last Supper*, but in a different vein, the Museum of Torture [see below] provides a creepy antidote to your average museum excursion.

Il Duomo *(Piazza del Duomo; Tel 02/86-46-34-56; M1, M3 to Duomo; 7:15am-6:45pm daily; Free admission to cathedral floor; Roof open 9am-4:30pm daily, L6,000 stairs, L8,000 elevator; Crypt open 9am-noon/2:30-6pm daily, L2,000; Baptistery open 10am-noon/3-5pm Tue-Sun, L3,000):* With its delicately spired facade straight from a fairy tale, Milan's famous Renaissance Duomo is unlike any other in Italy. Look up to the highest pinnacle and see the superb *Madonnina*—covered in 3,900 sheets of gold leaf—watching over the piazza below.

Museo del Duomo and **Museo Civico d'Arte Contemporaneau** *(Palazzo Reale, Piazza del Duomo 12 and 14; Tel 02/860-358; M1, M3 to Duomo; 9:30am-5:30pm, closed Mon; Free admission):* The Museo del Duomo is your typical church museum, chronicling six centuries of the illustrious landmark's history. The permanent collection at the Museo Civico includes some works by Picasso and Modigliani—a welcome break from the typical Italian museum.

Chiesa di Santa Maria delle Grazie (The Last Supper) *(Piazza Santa Maria delle Grazie 2; Tel 02/498-75-88, must call 199-199-100 in advance for reservations; M1 to Cadorna, Tram 24; 8am-1pm Tue-Sun; L12,000 admission):* Making reservations in advance can be a drag, but seeing this late-15th-century da Vinci is worth the trouble. And given the painting's state of near-decay, who knows how much longer you'll have the opportunity?

Brera Picture Gallery *(Via Brera 28; Tel 02/867-518; M2 to Lanza, M1 to Cairoli or M3 to Montenapoleone; 9am-9pm Tue-Fri, till 11:40pm Sat, till 8pm Sun, holidays, closed Mon; L12,000 admission):* If you've got a one-museum limit, this has to be your choice. Relatively small, but jam-packed with masterpieces by the likes of Piero della Francesca, Raphael, Mantegna, Bellini, and Caravaggio. One of Italy's best.

by foot

At first it's just a few: Young professionals return from a hard day's work and check in to the pubs for the happy-hour haven of cheap drinks and finger food. Slowly more and more trickle in, until the place is so crowded you can hardly hear yourself think! On this walk, you get an inside look at this oh-so-Milanese post-work phenom.

Jump on the M2 line to **Porta Genova**, and as you exit the station (at 6:30pm precisely), remember that here workers get their first whiff of freedom. Take a whiff of your own and make a right on **Via Gorizia**. On your way to stop number one, **Bar Diva**, you'll pass **Maharaja Fashion Café** [see *bar scene,* above]—keep it in mind for later; it's a hot late-night spot. At **Bar Diva**, get a glass of wine, eat some munchies, and make your way across to **Porta Ticinese**. Yes, this is taking you away from the perfect pub-crawlin' of the **Navigli canals**, but don't worry, we'll get back there in a minute. Along **Corso Porta di Ticinese** you can window-shop at the clothes boutiques. Hang a right at **Via Vetere**. Here, take your choice between **Coquetel**, **Open Space**, or **Up To You**, all American-style bars. Now, back-track and make a left on P. Ticinese, and window-shop till you get to **Portnoy's Caffè** [see *bar scene,* above], where the drinks are dirt cheap. Take two cocktails. Afterward, if you want to peep around a bit, check out the incongruous Parthenon-like columned piazza, reached by walking under the **Ticinese Arch**. Now, as a finale, find a bar of your very own, and top it off with one quick shot. There, you've made it. Now high-five your friends and take the night from here....

Teatro alla Scala *(Piazza della Scala; Tel 02/72-00-37-44 for ticket info; Tickets L10,000-160,000; www.lascala.milan.it; No credit cards)*: Even if you can't imagine a bigger snorefest than a night at the opera, the overwhelming beauty of the interior of this truly grand ol' opry will blow your mind. The 200 standing-room-only tickets are sold till 30 minutes before curtain. If you're really into it, drop by the on-site La Scala museum, **Museo Teatrale alla Scala** *(9am-noon/2-5:30pm daily, closed Sun Oct-Apr; L6,000 admission)*, too.

At the **Museo della Pusterla (Torture Museum)** *(Via Carducci 14; Tel 02/805-35-05; 10am-7:30pm Mon-Sat; L10,000 admission)*, discover exactly how twisted human beings can be. The torture devices in this bizarrely kitsch museum range from a chastity belt to an elaborate pulley system used to tear victims limb from limb. The English-language descriptions are a laff riot.

National Science Museum and Leonardo da Vinci Museum of Science and Technology *(Via San Vittore 21; Tel 02/48-01-00-40; M2 to Sant'Ambrogio; 9:30am-5pm Tue-Fri, till 6:30pm Sat, Sun, closed Mon; L10,000 admission):* Housed in a former Benedictine monastery, this tribute to all things Leonardo will truly knock your mind on its proverbial butt.

Basilica di Sant'Eustorgio *(Piazza Sant'Eustorgio 1; Tel 02/58-10-15-83; M2 to Porta Genova; 7:30am-noon/3-6:30pm daily; Free admission to basilica, L5,000 admission to chapel):* Near the charming Navigli area, this simple church is notable for its 13th-century bell tower and for having the first tower clock in the world, made in 1305. Good pre-barhopping spot.

Even if you know nothing about Milanese history or the rich and famous Milanese buried here, a stroll through **Cimitero Monumentale di Milano** (Monumental Cemetery) *(Piazzale Cimitero Monumentale; Tel 02/659-99-38; M2 to Garibaldi or Tram 3, 4, 29, 30, 33; 8:30am-4:30pm Tue-Fri, till 5pm Sat, Sun, closed Mon),* a veritable hall of fame, is a nice rest from the city streets.

modification

If you want to get a big spider on your back or etch the name of your love on your bicep, call the very competent **Tatuggi di Rottino Mauro** *(Via Vigevano 9; Tel 02/58-10-21-95; M2 to Porta Genova; 3-7pm Mon-Fri)* in advance, since appointments are required.

great outdoors

The best city places for outdoor relaxation on a spot of green are the **Giardini Pubblici** [see *hanging out,* above] and **Parco Sempione**. The sprawling Sempione is not what you would call well-maintained, and has quite a few shady characters—women shouldn't go there alone past evening—but it's a good spot for a daytime jog. The better option is the public gardens, a peaceful manicured refuge with running creeks, flowers, mule rides, and playing children. The crosscutting gravel paths make for a good run or walk.

Milan's two hometown soccer teams—Milan A.C. and Inter F.C.—have a history of fierce rivalry, with each spending billions and billions of liras each year to attract the latest international star. For Milan A.C. tickets, head to **Bank Cariplo** *(Via Verdi 8; Tel 02/886-61)* or the **Milan Point Shop** *(Via Verri 8; Tel 02/796-481).* For Inter tickets, stop by **Banca Populare di Milano** *(Piazza Meda 4; Tel 02/770-01).* **Milano Ticket** *(Corso Vittorio Emanuele Pavillion)* shows no favoritism—it sells tickets for both teams. The **Meazza Stadium** *(San Siro; Via Piccolomini 5; Tel 4870-71-23; M1 to Lotto)* is where all the action goes down.

stuff

Milan definitely lives up to its reputation as a shopping megalopolis. Yeah, most goods are pricey, but there are also places to find bargains. The

12 hours in Milan

1. **Get lost in the Duomo:** The most impressive church in Italy—maybe in the world. When you finish gawking at the interior, steal a pair of binoculars and salivate over the hundreds of dazzling spires [see *culture zoo*, above].

2. **Check out the Torture Museum:** Hands-down, the best museum in Milan—a great break from the traditional Renaissance masterpieces [see *culture zoo*, above].

3. **See *The Last Supper*:** We are not worthy, and as long as it lasts, it will remain one of the world's greatest artistic treasures [see *culture zoo*, above].

4. **Barhop on the Navigli Canals:** So many happy-hour deals, so little time. Start early, end late, stumble home [see *bar scene*, above].

5. **Splurge on Something Designer:** In this fashion mecca, with Gucci, Prada, Versace, Armani, Krizia, Dolce & Gabbana, and others at your fingertips, you can't pass this up [see *stuff*, below].

6. **Chill out in Le Scimmie:** See both local and touring acts and, if you're halfway decent, maybe land a gig yourself [see *live music scene*, above].

7. **Go to a soccer game:** There's nothing better than watching the best in the world at their sport in the middle of 60,000 chanting lunatics. A change-your-life experience [see *great outdoors*, above].

8. **Opera at Teatro alla Scala:** You are completely thrust into a time warp. Standing-room-only tickets are available for some shows [see *culture zoo*, above].

9. **Party at Hollywood:** This accessible, only-somewhat-pretentious spot will get you in the groove. Wear the designer something that you bought earlier [see *club scene*, above].

10. **Eat a gelato at Rinomata Gelateria:** Nothing else in Milan compares for price, taste, and variety. You'll probably end up having two or three [see *gelati wars*, below].

best window-shopping is on the famed Via Montenapoleone and Via della Spiga—with a crush of designer boutiques like Gucci, Ferragamo, Prada, Armani, Krizia, and Sisley—Porta di Ticinese and Corso Garibaldi running a close second.

▶▶MARKET

Line up with locals at **Mercato Communale** *(Next to Piazza XXIV Maggio; 8am-7pm Mon-Sat)* for fresh fruits, vegetables, and fish. For all this, plus books, housewares, and used clothes, check out the **outdoor market along Via Marcello** *(M1 to Lima, walk west toward Stazione Centrale).*

▶▶**BOUND**

Messagerie Musicali *(Galleria del Corso 2 near Vittorio Emmanuele; Tel 02/760-551; M1 or M3 to Duomo; 9am-8pm, closed Mon; V, MC, AE)* is Milan's version of a Barnes & Noble or Tower Records superstore (there's actually a Virgin megastore near the Duomo), with a huge selection of English-language books, newspapers, magazines, and music. You can also pick up concert tickets for large events.

For all kinds of English-language reads, check the tight shelves of the **American Bookstore** *(Via Camperio 16; Tel 02/878-920; M1 to Cairoli; 9:30am-7pm Tue-Sat; No credit cards).*

▶▶**TUNES**

The collection of new and used CDs and records at **Supporti Fono-grafici** *(Corso di Porta Ticinese 100; Tel 02/89-40-04-20; 9am-7:30pm Tue-Sat, 3-7:30pm Mon; supporti@sti2.starlink.it; AE, V, MC)* will service less-mainstream music addicts.

▶▶**THRIFT**

You only wish grandma had a trunkful of clothes as hip as the ones in **Il Baule (The Trunk)** *(Ripa di Porta Ticinese 21; Tel 02/837-39-37; M2 to Porta Genova; 3:30-7:30pm Mon, 11:30am-7:30pm Tue-Thur, till 11:30pm Fri-Sun, closed two weeks in Aug; No credit cards).* This adorable shop in the Navigli sells lovely affordable vintage women's clothing.

For the best men's and women's used clothing go to **Lo Specchio di Alice** *(Corso di Porta Ticinese 84; Tel 02/58-10-34-81; 3-8pm Mon, 10am-1pm/38pm Tue-Sat, 10am-8pm Sun; V, MC),* the biggest store of its kind in Milan.

▶▶**HOT COUTURE**

Cut *(Corso di Porta Ticinese 58; Tel 02/83-94-13-5; 9:30am-7pm Tue-Sat; No credit cards)* has the most funky and original leather clothing and bags you'll see anywhere. Sexy pants, skirts, and cropped tops set the style quotient sky-high. Everything's handmade and originally designed in an amazing array of animal skins.

If that's not your thing, try **Anna Fabiano** *(Corso di Porta Ticinese 40; 10am-7pm, closed Mon; AE, V, MC),* a boutique with fun and colorful handmade women's clothing, like see-through shirts and funky floral pants.

▶▶**MULTI-TASKING**

One of the chic-est stores in Milan, multilevel **High-Tech** *(Piazza XXV Aprile 12; Tel 02/624-11-01; M2 to Garibaldi or Moscova; 10:30am-7:30pm Tue-Sun, closed Mon; AE, V, MC)* sells an assortment of housewares and neat products that showcase the multifaceted talents of Milan's artisans and designers. Everything from clocks to shoes, candles to sofas, cards to soaps, and much, much more. Walking around with a High-Tech bag shows you're an insider.

Follow the crowds veering off busy Corso Como, in the Garibaldi district, and into **10 Corso Como's** *(Corso Como 10; Tel 02/29-00-25-74;*

M2 to Garibaldi; AE, V, MC), through the verdant palazzo garden with its charming cafe to the main floor where you can browse through the gorgeous designer clothing, shoes, and jewelry, as well as their unique housewares. Upstairs there's also a bookstore that hosts readings (unfortunately not in English) and other events occasionally.

▶▶BEAUTY

Profumo *(Via Brera 6; Tel 02/7202-33-34; 9:30am-7:30pm Tue-Sat; AE, V, MC)* sells Kiehl's products, shaving materials, Listerine, and other bathroom/beauty stuff you may not be able to find elsewhere in Italy's pharmacies, so stock up.

The fantastic, fresh, and all-natural handmade soaps, shampoos, bath and beauty products carried at **Lush** *(Via Fiori Chiari 6; 9am-7pm daily; No credit cards)* are probably similar to what the Body Shop carried before it went corporate. Beat the rush and say you knew Lush when.

EATS

Like its bars, Milan's restaurants are pretty pricey—and there's no happy hour to help out here. Both pizzas and pastas usually run between L10,000 and L20,000, with meats often higher. Most restaurants serve good salads (around L10,000) that are usually big enough to be shared. Both the Navigli and Garibaldi sections have a ton of good choices and enough bars with happy hours (read: free appetizers) nearby that you'll be able to get by with only one dish at dinner. Most restaurants have per-person covers (*copertos*) ranging from L1,000 to L6,000. If this is the case, don't pay a tip; otherwise 7 to 10 percent will do. Another way to save some lira is to make sure you specify water from the tap (*aqua al rubinetto*); otherwise you'll be paying for bottled.

▶▶CHEAP

Pasticceria F.lli Freni *(Corso Vittorio Emanuele 4; Tel 02/804-871; and Piazza Duomo, corner of Via Torino; Tel 02/877-072; M1, M3 to Duomo; Both 9:30am-7pm daily; Both no credit cards)* has been making marzipan, *ciambelle*, and other Sicilian-style goodies since 1914. The glittery display window and glitzy interior may look cheesy, but trust us—this is the real deal. Both locations are just steps from the Duomo.

Princi *(Via Speronari 6; Tel 02/874-79 and Piazale Istria 1; Tel 02/606-854; Both 8am-8pm; Both no credit cards)* has so cornered the market on fresh, fast-ish food that this bright, upscale chain deserves to be on every street corner. Pizzas by the slice, focaccia, pastas, salad, fruit, vegetables, cakes, pies, tarts—try 'em all. The large central location on Via Speronari has a few stools and opens to a bakery in the back, so you can watch the workers expertly fashion new treats. A slice of mushroom pizza costs L3,500.

The self-service fresh-food chain **Brek** *(Via Lepetit 20; Tel 02/670-51-49; M2, M3 to Centrale F.S.; 9am-8pm daily; L3,500-12,000 lunch or dinner; No credit cards)*, up by the train station, is a favorite of Milan's business crowd. Ignore the suits and enjoy the mouth-watering pastas, meats, fish, and salads that are prepared right in front of your greedy face. A plate of pasta with bread and drink is around L8,000. All this, plus air conditioning.

The centrally located **Iris** *(Via Dante 7; Tel 02/877-498; M1 to Cordusio; 11am-10pm, closed Mon; L10,000-25,000 per entree; AE, V, MC)* has pretty standard fare, but the brick-oven pizza stands out, with its scrumptious crispy crust and slightly sweet sauce. The magnanimous crew of waiters loves to chat it up with the patrons, a good percentage of whom are tourists. Outdoor seating lets you keep an eye on the finely dressed locals, and, if you're lucky, you may be serenaded by a local busker.

Anywhere lots of young people roam, you'll find great options for quick, cheap meals. **Maharaja** *(Via Vetere 12; Tel 02/58-11-34-36; Noon-3pm/6pm-midnight Tue-Sun, closed Mon; L6,000-12,000 per entree; No credit cards)*, down in the Navigli, is one of them. Don't get this confused with the other **Maharaja** [see *bar scene*, above]. Including an order of the soft fresh bread *nan* (L2,000), most takeout dishes will set you back a mere L10,000—the chicken curry is especially nice. The only takeout *indiano* in Milano.

do they really look better in their armani

Fashion is to Milan as canals are to Venice, prosciutto is to Parma, and the Coliseum is to Rome: an inseparable component of its identity and the personality of its people. But on a more basic level, fashion plays out in a more complex way. Don't go to Milan looking for fashion models. Unless you're an insider or have the dough to hang at the most expensive restaurants and bars, you almost certainly won't find them. They're pretty much shielded from the rest of the city's society. So what does fashion mean to the average Milanese? In Milan, dress is a public statement, and for the most part, that translates to costly, conservative, efficient lines. The locals wear much more expensive clothing, shoes, jewelry, and accessories than do other Italians. On men, you'll see lots of smartly cut suits and Dolce & Gabbana shirts, while the women, especially in the Brera area, go for expensive suits and lots of gold. In the summer, *la moda* turns to high-cut knicker pants, tank tops, and heels or raised sandals. And just about everyone has a rich, brown tan, à la Donatella Versace. But look a little closer, and another fact becomes clear: Despite spending more, Milanese don't look any better than their more easygoing Roman or Florentine counterparts. Why? Good old-fashioned stress. What some might even call *uptightness*. Of course, covering up that stuff is what keeps the Guccis, Armanis, and Versaces in business....

With outdoor seating on wire chairs, a tidy menu of panini and salads, cheap beer (including Guinness on tap), and an old-world feel, **Osteria del Pallone** *(Viale Gorizia 30; Tel 02/58-10-56-41; M2 to Porta Genova; 11am-2am Tue-Sun, closed Mon morning; L8,000-18,000 per entree; No credit cards)* is the perfect place to chow and drink around the Navigli. The "Brillante" sandwich, with *speck* (Italian ham), cheese, and olive pulp, lives up to its name, and the vegetarian "principe," with mushrooms, lettuce, tomatoes, and mustard dashed with olive oil and salt, is tasty too. "Insalata Primavera" is a mongo salad of tuna, fresh mozzarella, tomatoes, and dressing.

Garbagnati's *(Via Dante 14; Tel 02/86-46-06-72; M1 to Cordusio; 7am-7:30pm; L8,000-20,000 per entree; AE, V, MC)* covered outdoor seating area is a great place to sit down, take a break, have a sandwich and a beer or soda, and bask in the glow of being in Europe. When you're done basking, make sure you try the gelati—made on the premises, of course. Just steps away from Iris.

▶▶DO-ABLE

The pizza and pasta are so good at **Fabbrica Pizzeria** *(Viale Pasubio 2; Tel 02/655-27-71; M2 to Garibaldi; 12:30-3pm/7:30pm-1am Tue-Sat, 7:30pm-1am Sun, closed Mon; L11,000-30,000 per entree; V, MC)* that locals sometimes wait an hour to get a table at this spot just off Porta Garibaldi. The prep area and oven are out in the middle of the dining room, so you can really check out the pizza maker's skills. There's another location at Alzaia Naviglio Grande 70 *(Tel 02/835-82-97)*. Sit back, have a carafe or two of wine, and stuff your face.

gelati wars

As soon as you walk into **Rinomata Gelateria** *(Ripa Porta Ticinese, corner of Viale Gorizia; Tel 02/58-11-38-77; M2 to Porta Genova; No credit cards)*, you know you've discovered something special: The cabinet-lined walls hold hundreds of cones and the gelati is protected by brass coverlets. Tell them to whip off those coverlets and give you a chocolate with mint or strawberry with Nutella. A few flavors are even made from soy milk for you vegans. Two close seconds to Rinomata are **Cremeria San Marco** *(Via San Marco 14; Tel 02/65-90-08-67; No credit cards)*, where the cones feature the largest scoops in all Milan, and **Venezia Gelateria** *(corner of Buenos Aires and Piazza Gugliemo Oberdan; Tel 02/29-51-39-44)* which, at L2,500 per cone, may be the most economical place to get Straciatella, Bacio, or Fragola.

Don't blink—the huge, sizzling pizzas at the Navigli's **Premiata Pizzeria** *(Via Alzaia Naviglio Grande 2; Tel 02/8940-06-48; 7:30-11:30pm; L10,000-25,000 per pizza; AE, MC, V)* will be ready in 5 minutes, which fits right in with busy Milanese schedules. Starting at 8pm, hordes of casual young people crash through the doors, sometimes making dining hard on the ears. Great place for big groups, especially out on the second-story patio. Two pizzas, one salad, and a half-carafe of wine for less than L50,000.

Though the centrally located self-service **Peck** *(Via Victor Hugo 4; Tel 02/861-040; M1, M3 to Duomo; 7:30am-9pm; L10,000-20,000 per entree; AE, V, MC)*—a sibling of the famous full-service restaurant down the street—is a bit more expensive than most *tavola calda*–type places, the rich soups, risottos, and fish dishes will satiate the traveler's appetite. With a piece of bread, the *minestrone di riso* is particularly hearty and filling. The red, twirling, butt-molded seats and modern lamps make eating here fun and relaxing. At around L5,000, panini are the best bet to not break the bank.

▶▶**SPLURGE**

Guys put on the jackets, girls slip on the heels, and all head for **Ristorante Alzaia** *(Alzaia Naviglio Grande 26; Tel 02/832-35-26; M2 to Porta Genova; 8pm-midnight daily; L40,000 and up per person per meal; AE, V, MC)*, one of the finest restaurants in the Navigli. The decor is basic white walls with wood paneling on the bottom half and some exposed brick—and the nouveau-Italian menu centers around smaller, fancier, well-thought-out gourmet dishes. The eggplant parmesan, gnocchi, ravioli, and lamb dishes are excellent. The wine list contains scores of local, Tuscan, and foreign varieties.

At first, the framed photos of Hollywood stars and others crammed onto the walls at **A Santa Lucia** *Via San Pietro all'Orto 3; Tel 02/76-02-31-55; M1 to San Babila; Lunch noon-3pm, dinner 7:30pm-midnight daily; L45,000 and up per person for a meal; AE, V, MC)* seem tacky. But hang on. The kitchen here is bad-ass—anyone who knows anything about food does not leave Milan without a stop here. The fish and meats are worth every last lira, and even the simple *spaghetti al pomodoro* will leave you obsessively sopping up the sauce. If you want to fill up for less cash, the calzones are a good deal. The service, of course, is expert. A meal like this makes staying in hostels, taking night trains, and eating bread, cheese, and jam every stinkin' day—except today—worth it. No shorts, no sneakers, no kids, and reservations are a must. Just a few blocks east of the Piazza del Duomo.

Tired of Italian? Take a break in the cool, dark, candlelit underground cantina of **El Tropico Latino** *(Corso Como 2; Tel 02/659-04-44; M2 to Garibaldi; 8pm-midnight; L15,000-35,000; AE, V, MC)*, a very un-chain-like chain. While the menu ain't traditional Tex-Mex, the entrees are well-seasoned and well-portioned, and taste even better after a couple of margaritas. Young, casual locals hang in this Garibaldi spot, both chowing in the restaurant and downing tropical drinks in the downstairs bar.

crashing

Milan will never be known for its hotels, at least not the kind your average traveler can afford. While there are tons of medium-priced and business-class choices, budget varieties are scarce and usually pretty drab. When you call a hotel, make sure to ask for the current rates—they can fluctuate greatly, especially during the high season and/or whenever there is a large convention. Because Milan is so freakin' big and spread out, it's more important here than in other cities to get a hotel close to where you're going to be hanging. Because as quick and efficient as they are—with electronic signs telling you how long you'll have to wait for the next train—subways are subways are subways, no matter what.

▶▶**CHEAP**

The long hike from the center out to the well-managed **Milan City Camping** *(M2 to Gambara, then walk to Via Triluzio and take Bus 72 to Quinto Romano, which leaves you 500 meters from campground; Check-in 8am-10pm; L12,000/person per day plus L10,000 tent fee; V, MC)* is worth it if you're budgeting—it's the cheapest option in Milan, especially if you're staying more than a few days. Sites have electricity hookups and hot showers.

With an 11:30pm curfew and location away from the bustle of the city to the northwest of the city center, **Piero Rotta Hostel (HI)** *(Via Martino Bassi 2; Tel/Fax 02/39-26-70-95; M1 to Q.T.8, then walk down Via Pogatschnig to Martino Bassi; Lockout 9am-5pm; L23,000/bed; No credit cards)* probably isn't the place you want to stay the whole time you're in Milan, but it's a good place to hole up for a couple of nights if you need to budget, or if everywhere else is full—with 388 beds, the hostel almost always has a vacancy. An HI card is required, but you can buy one there for L30,000, giving you access to other HI hostels as well.

Fancy ain't the word you'd use to describe **Pensione Cantore** *(Corso Porta Genova 25; Tel 02/835-75-65; M2 to Porta Genova; Desk open 8:30am-2am; single L40,000, double L65,000, breakfast L5,000; No credit cards)*, but it's so close to the Metro and the bar-laden Navigli/Porta Ticinese neighborhood, who cares! Plus, fairly spacious doubles start atr around L65,000. The bathrooms could use more spic-and-spanning, and if you want to party all night long, this may not be the best option—the Cantore closes at 2am every night. There are only 11 rooms, so in the high season it sometimes fills up quickly. Usually closed in August.

Close to the Brera-Garibaldi section of town, **Hotel Commercio** *(Via Mercato 1; Tel 02/86-46-38-80; M2 to Moscova; L90,000 double w/shower; No credit cards)* has got more grit than shine but, like the Cantore [see above], its location makes up for its shortcomings. Plus, the 12 rooms all come with a private bathroom—a rarity in this price range. Definitely book ahead.

Hotel Certosa *(Corso San Gottardo 7; Tel 02/89-40-21-05; M2 to Porta Genova; L65,000-85,000 doubles w/o bath; No credit cards)* is close to both Porta Ticinese and the Navigli, and there's no curfew. If that

milan eats and crashing

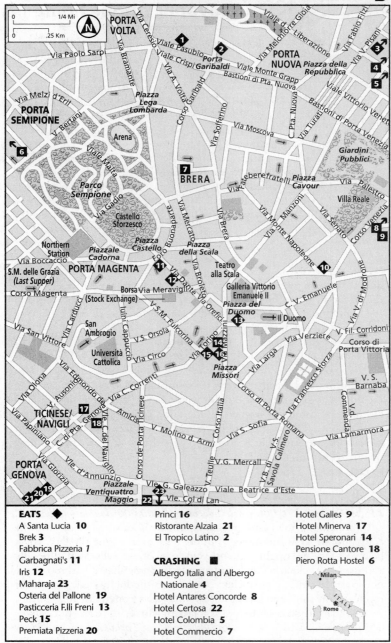

EATS ◆

A Santa Lucia **10**
Brek **3**
Fabbrica Pizzeria *1*
Garbagnati's **11**
Iris **12**
Maharaja **23**
Osteria del Pallone **19**
Pasticceria F.lli Freni **13**
Peck **15**
Premiata Pizzeria **20**

Princi **16**
Ristorante Alzaia **21**
El Tropico Latino **2**

CRASHING ■

Albergo Italia and Albergo
Nationale **4**
Hotel Antares Concorde **8**
Hotel Certosa **22**
Hotel Colombia **5**
Hotel Commercio **7**

Hotel Galles **9**
Hotel Minerva **17**
Hotel Speronari **14**
Pensione Cantore **18**
Piero Rotta Hostel **6**

giovanni, phone home

Italians are tireless consumers, always on the go, and lovers of convenience, so it's no big shocker that over 30 percent of the population owns *celluari*: cell phones. Mobile phones go off in classes, in the middle of church services, during funerals, during concerts, at the movies, on scooters, and on and on. Italians, in comparison with other cultures, do not shirk from having conversations, no matter where they are or how intrusive it may be to others. Of course, this increasing phenomenon has not gone without the classic Italian debate. Part of the population detests the little plastic nuisances and wants to pass etiquette rules dictating their use. Until this happens—and most likely it never will—Italians will continue to listen to their mamas chew them out on one end of the line while their neighbors shush them till they disconnect.

doesn't win you over immediately, here are a few more positives: Though the 26 rooms are nothing to gush about, the beds are made every day, and the friendly staff won't get too mad if you decide to—or end up having to—sleep in. Watch for price swings.

The bright rooms in the **Albergo Italia and Albergo Nazionale** *(Via Vitruvio 44/46; Tel 02/670-59-11; M2, M3 to Centrale F.S.; L55,000 single, L85,000 double; No credit cards)*, complete with sink, mirror, and green shutters, have surprisingly more character than the hotel's hole-in-the-wall exterior would betray. Between the two side-by-side establishments, owned by the same congenial proprietor, there are 42 rooms. Its proximity to the train station makes it a good late-night arrival option, but there is a catch: The curfew's at 1am and the desk doesn't reopen till 6:30am.

▶▶**DO-ABLE**

For the price and *centralissimo* location, the clean rooms at **Hotel Speronari** *(Via Speronari 4; Tel 02/86-46-11-25, Fax 02/72-00-31-78; M1, M3 to Duomo; L70,000 single w/o bath, L100,000 double w/o bath; V, MC)* are among the best bargains in Milan. Rooms that look into the courtyard are drab and muggy, but the ones overlooking the busy street below are airy and bright—choose your lesser of two evils. Staff is friendly and used to backpacker and student guests. Some shared bathrooms are not great, but the fully stocked bar next to the lobby desk is. Ask for rooms on the third and higher floors—the views from up there are lovely.

The charmless-yet-clean rooms at **Hotel Minerva** *(Corso C. Colombo 15; Tel 02/837-57-45, Fax 02/835-82-29; M2 to Porta Genova; L115,000 single, L125,000 double; V, MC)* are slightly overpriced, but all have TV and private bathrooms. About half of its 38 rooms look out onto a quiet, treeless courtyard; the others look onto side streets. Some doubles have two single beds that can be pushed together if you're traveling with a sweetie. Close to the Navigli and curfew-less, this is a good option if the cheaper pensions are booked.

The management at **Hotel Colombia** (*Via R. Lepetit 15; Tel 02/669-21-60, Fax 02/670-58-29; M2, M3 to Centrale F.S.; Closed in Aug; L100,000 single, L140,000 double; AE, V, MC*) is a bit solemn, as are the rooms, but all in all, it's not a bad choice. A private bath comes with every room, and the ground-floor sitting room, bar, and backyard garden area are nice homey touches. Northeast of the city center toward the train station.

▶▶**SPLURGE**

Hotel Antares Concorde (*Viale Monza 132; Tel 02/403-02, Fax 02/48-19-31-14; M1 to Turro; L320,000 single, L450,000 double; antares.hotel.rubens@traveleurope.it; AE, V, MC*) is part of a trio of Best Western "Antares" hotels catering to the omnipresent Milanese business crowd. The spacious, air-conditioned rooms have soundproof windows—so that businessmen can get their sleep, you know—and the bathrooms have full bathtubs. A basic continental breakfast of cereal, croissants, and coffee is included. The modern design of the gray-tone hotel falls within the Italian post-World War II guidelines—that is, must be butt-ugly—but if you want to relax and catch some CNN, this is a pretty good choice. Out to the east of the city center.

Our old friend Best Western does it right again with **Hotel Galles** (*Piazza Lima; Tel 02/204-841, Fax 02/204-84-22; M1 to Lima; L230,000 single, up to L400,000 double; galles-mi@mbox.it.net; AE, V, MC*), a renovated turn-of-the-century palazzo-esque offering. The large, air-conditioned rooms are charming but not overly charming, decorated with quasi-Victorian touches. The glistening bathrooms invite you to take long baths, the downstairs bar pours pricey-but-fun late-evening cocktails, and the rooftop garden features a solarium and Jacuzzi. The sunny terrace restaurant serves up a great American-style all-you-can-eat breakfast for L25,000 that will hold you till late afternoon; a less elaborate continental breakfast is gratis. The helpful staff speaks English better than most Americans and knows how to make you feel welcome and forget the steep prices. Keep an eye out for off-season rates which go down to L85,000 for a single. If you want to indulge, do it right—do it here. In the same area as its brother [see above].

NEED TO KNOW

Currency Exchange The currency of Italy is the **Italian Lira (L)**. Exchange currency and traveler's checks at **Stazione Centrale** or either airport for a 1-2 percent fee. ATMs or exchange machines (charging a 1 percent fee) are all over the city.

Tourist Information The great **Azienda di Promozione Turistica del Milanese** (*Piazza del Duomo at Via Marconi 1; Tel 02/725-241; 8:30am-*

8pm Mon-Fri, 9am-1pm/2-5pm Sat, 9am-1pm/3-5pm Sun) or *(Stazione Centrale; Tel 02/669-05-32; 8am-7pm Mon-Sat, 9am-12:30pm/1:30-6pm Sun)* provides priceless info as well as a place to pick up the monthly English-language *APT Events Guide* and the English/Japanese newspaper *Hello Milano*. **CTS** *(Corso Ticinese 100; Tel 02/58-47-52-23; reps Sale speak English)* is the student information center.

Public Transportation **Buses** run every 10-20 minutes 5am-1am; the **Metro** runs 6am-midnight. A bus/metro ticket costs L1,500, or get a one-day (L5,000) or two-day (L9,000) travel pass at the tourist office. The **ATM Information Offices at Stazione Centrale** *(Tel 02/800-001-68-57; 8am-8pm Mon-Sat)* or the **Metro station Duomo** *(Tel 02/480-311; 7:45am-7:15pm Mon-Sat)* both provide free bus/metro maps. Free information: *167/016-857*.

American Express *(Via Brera 3; Tel 02/72-00-36-93, 02/86-46-09-30; 9am-5pm Mon-Fri).*

Health and Emergency Police: *115*; fire, medical emergency, ambulance: *118* or *113*. The hospital **Ospedale Maggiore Policlinico** *(Via Francesco Sforza 35; Tel 02/550-31)* has English-speaking doctors.

Pharmacies There is a 24-hour pharmacy at **Stazione Centrale** *(Tel 02/669-07-35).*

Telephone Country code: *39*; city code: *02*; information: *12*; English-speaking operator: *170*. Local calls cost L200. **Phone cards** are available in denominations of L5,000, L10,000, and L15,000 (a L10,000 phone card should give you about 4 minutes of talk time to the U.S.), and are sold at cafes and *tabacchi*. Deposit a refundable L200 to use your credit card. **AT&T:** *06/172-10-11*; **MCI:** *06/172-10-22*; **Sprint:** *06/172-18-77*. You can also make credit card calls at the Telecom offices in **Galleria Vittorio Emanuele** *(between Piazza del Duomo and Piazza della Scala; Open 24 hours daily)* or **Stazione Centrale** *(8am-9:30pm daily).*

Airports General flight and airport information: *02/74-85-22-00; 7am-11pm*. **Aeroporto di Linate** is about 4 miles southeast of the city. ATM buses leave Piazza San Babila *(corner of Corso Europa; Tickets L1,500)* for Linate every 10 minutes 5:30am-12:20am. STAM buses *(02/66-98-45-09, 02/40-09-92-80; Tickets L4,500)* run between Piazza Luigi di Savoia *(Right side of Stazione Centrale)* and Linate every 30 minutes 5:40am-9:05pm. **Aeroporto della Malpensa** is 31 miles northwest. Air Pullman buses *(02/40-09-92-60)* leave Piazza Luigi di Savoia *(on the right side of Stazione Centrale)* every 20 minutes 5:20am-10pm for L13,000 one-way; STAM buses depart every half-hour for Stazione Centrale 6:30am-11pm. Tickets for both are L13,000.

Airlines **Air France** *(Tel 02/715-155)*, **Alitalia** *(Tel 02/733-335)*, **British Airways** *(Tel 02/738-20-28)*, **KLM** *(Tel 02/70-10-05-42)*, **Iberia** *(Tel 02/756-10-91)*, and **Lufthansa** *(Tel 02/70-14-52-20)* all service Milan.

Trains Stazione Centrale *(Piazza Duca d'Aosta; Tel 1478/880-88 is toll-*

The websites ***www.rcs.it/inmilano/english/benven.html*** and ***www.traveleurope.it/milano.htm*** have good general info on the city and its venues.

The site ***www.CityLightsNews.com/ztmimp2.htm*** has great maps.

The Milanese are ahead of the rest of Italy in terms of Internet usage, but that's not saying much. There are only a handful of public places to check your Internet account. The best option is **Terzo Millenio** (*Off Via Veneto; Tel 02/205-21-21; 8:30am-7:30pm Mon-Sat; L10,000/hour, L5,000/half-hour; Call ahead for times, as info changes regularly*), which has about a dozen computers and is best set up for Internet access. The friendly employees will help you with any glitches that might arise. Two other options are the centrally located **Gallery Games** (*Via S. Sisto 5; Tel 02/72-00-46-02; 10am-7:30pm/9pm-midnight daily; L18,000/hour, L11,000/half-hour; No credit cards*) and the bohemian **Netkiosk** (*Via Solari 56; Tel 02/230-003; www.netkiosk.it*), in the southwest end of the city, managed by the owners of **Sherwood Café** (*Via Solari 52; Tel 02/472-470; 7am-1pm/3-6pm*). Of these two, the computers at Gallery Games—which is really an arcade—offer better performance than the computers at Netkiosk. But if you're all for helping the little guy....

free in Italy only for bilingual information about all trains and stations; information office 7am-11pm daily; M2, M3 to Centrale F.S.; No credit cards), to the northeast of the city center, is the main station. You can catch the M3 and M2 lines from Centrale. Luggage storage open daily 4am-1:30am *(L5,000/12 hrs)*. The other two are **Stazione Garibaldi** (*Information office 6am-10pm*), to the north of the center, and **Stazione Nord** (*Piazza Cadorna 14; Tel 02/48-06-67-71; Information office 6:30am-8:30pm daily*), to the west of the city center.

Laundry Vicolo Lavanderia (*Via degli Zuccaro 2; 8am-10pm; 9am-7pm daily; L6,000 wash, L6,000 dry*) will help you look your spiffiest.

bologna

If you're looking for Partyville, Italia, you've found it. But not many others have—compared to Florence, Milan, and Rome, Bologna's a virtual secret, which, of course, makes it all that much cooler. On summer nights, it's almost impossible to escape the series of free, groovy outdoor concerts and festivals held in Piazza Maggiore and its surrounding streets. The large student population brings an edgy, carefree energy to the streets, and there's no better place to experience this than along Via Zamboni, the heavily postered main drag of the university district. Here students mingle at all hours of the day and night, talking shop, making plans, or checking out the betty on the other side of the street. With a healthy mix of slackers, skaters, straight-edgers, punks, preppies, and nerds, Bologna has a wide variety of discos, clubs, and discopubs [see *live music and club scene*, below]. Many of these, unfortunately, close for the summer when classes let out (which, combined with the humidity and heat that descend in the summer months, make July and August the worst times to visit Bologna). But it's not *all* about the students—the compact metropolis has a mood and swagger of its own. The headquarters of Italy's communist party, the city government here is one of the most forward-thinking, embracing the arts like few others in Western Europe.

While there's no big attraction like the Uffizi or Saint Peter's—which is probably why the tour groups don't swarm here—there are gorgeous ancient porticoes and crumbling towers. The outskirts of the city offer some cool diversions too, like the Ducati motorcycle factory, some neat ancient churches, and gorgeous countryside. But pretty much all of the attractions you'll want are in the *centro* (city center) and easily reached by walking. The efficient-yet-somewhat-confusing ATC bus system will take you beyond the ring road that borders the central city. Few people here, even the students, are fluent in English. Still, overall proficiency is higher than in most towns—there are quite a few English schools—but less than in a tourist haven like Florence. And, the attitude is very, very welcoming to young travelers.

neighborhoods

The historic center of Bologna is laid out like an egg-shaped wheel, with **Piazza Maggiore** in the quasi-exact center and about a dozen streets shooting off from it. The central artery is **Ugo Bassi**, which to the west turns into **Via San Felice** and to the east turns into **Via Rizzoli** and then **Via Strada Maggiore**. The **university district** is anchored by **Via Zamboni**, which runs to the northeast. The big park, **Giardini Margherita**, is situated on the northeast side of the *centro* outside the road (which changes names several times) that forms the outer circle of the egg shape. The **Stazione Centrale** is located north of Piazza Maggiore, several streets off from **Via Indipendenza**, the major north-south thoroughfare. At its largest, the *centro* is 2.5 miles (east-west) by 1.5 miles (north-south), which makes basically everything in the tightly compacted center easily walkable. Modern Bologna, with its dull yellow and tan stucco buildings, lies

five things to talk to a local about

1. **Why tourists don't come to Bologna in droves:** Just about every Bolognese has a theory why their city hasn't become a tourist hotbed on the scale of Florence or Siena.

2. **The difference between Bologna's region, Emilia Romagna, and the rest of Italy:** While a little more complex, this topic will also get the locals' vocal cords limbered.

3. How far **Bologna's soccer team** will go in Premier Division: The Bolognese are not as crazy as the Florentines, but they are loyal and, as their team has been improving, finally have something to cheer about.

4. **The role of the communist party in Bologna's history:** This will get any resident talking, red or not.

5. **Bolognese chow:** Bologna is famous for its food—tortellini, tagliatelle, lasagna verde, zampone, sausage, bolognese sauce—and hitting locals up for their fave will make ordering at a restaurant even better.

outside of the central oval and stretches on for several miles in all directions. There's not much to see out there except for the **Stadio Communale** [see *great outdoors*, below], **Made in Bo** [see *club scene*, below], and the **city cemetery**, but if you do decide to venture, it's easy to do, thanks to the remarkably efficient **ATC buses** [see *need to know*, below].

hanging out

The grandiose **Piazza Maggiore** is the perfect place to plop down and uncork a chilled bottle of wine with some friends. People of all ages pass through here throughout the day and night—walkers, bikers, and scooters using the square as a shortcut, flirty teenagers hanging around the Neptune fountain in the adjoining **Piazza del Nettuno**, jamming guitar players with their cases open for tips, and travelers like you lounging on the cathedral steps. The bar-filled **Via Zamboni** and restaurant-happy **Via delle Belle Arte** begin to get crowded in early afternoon, while **Via del Pratello** gets rolling around 8pm. Both areas are rife with stoners, by the way.

For a greener refuge, head to **Giardini Margherita**, the most popular destination for runners, rollerbladers, and sunbathers. South of the **Duomo** [see *culture zoo*, below], **Piazza Cavour** is a small, clean patch good for taking a break and eating a sandwich.

bar scene

With so many students hanging out in abject procrastination (you'll meet some who are pushing 30 and have 10 exams left till graduation), you'd better believe there is a bonanza of cafes and pubs. The most crowded street, with a variety of large English/Irish-style pubs, is Via Zamboni, where literally thousands of students swarm like busy little beer-guzzling bees. Via del Pratello and Via Mascarella are also prime streets for scoping out the leaders of slackerville.

With a great outdoor patio, the trendy **Golem Caffè D'Arte** *(Piazza San Martino 3b; Tel 051/262-620; 7pm-2:30am Tue-Sun, closed Mon; No credit cards)* provides the perfect place to sip specialty coffees or drinks and wax intellectual with your mates (and pretty much *only* your mates—the artsy crowd here isn't really outgoing). There's abstract art on the

fIVE-O

Bologna's major police congregation is usually found in the area around Piazza Maggiore, the site of large, city-sponsored, open-air concerts and the occasional demonstration. Though Bologna's police are relatively unassuming and leave you alone, with so many students, they also like to make sure things stay in order.

walls, dishes named after the likes of Gauguin and others, a range of talks and theme evenings, and sometimes even music. Mellow, if a little snooty, it's a good pre-clubbing stop, over to the east of Piazza Maggiore; cocktails L10,000.

Except for Via Zamboni, where every place is an "Irish Pub," there are few in other parts of town. One of the best is the **Celtic Druid** *(Via Caduti di Celefonia 5c; Tel 051/224-212; 6:30pm-2:30am daily; No credit cards)*, over by Piazza del Nettuno. Done up in dark wood paneling hung with Irish memorabilia, with an almost all-Irish staff, it's a favorite port of drink for English speakers, expats, students, and locals alike. Happy hour is from 6:30pm to 8:30pm—pints are only L5,000. The authenticity ends with the bar snacks, which are mostly (really good) bruschetta and pizzas.

The chic **Far Magia-Moro Moro** *(Via Isaia 4b/c; Tel 051/644-95-61; Noon-2:30pm/7pm-2am daily; No credit cards)*, east of the *centro*, has it all, including the most imaginative decor in town. Fantastic abstract murals cover the back walls, and suspended from the ceiling is a stunning Chinese dragon kite. There's even an upright piano, which offers inebriated partiers a place to practice their "skills." A restaurant in the back serves up savory lunches, dinner, and some of the fanciest happy-hour munchies in town. With Friday night DJs, the speed picks up, the bar turns dance floor at around 10:30pm, and happy souls spill out onto the street.

The no-cover **Corto Maltese** *(Via del Borgo di San Pietro 9/2a; Tel 051/229-764; 7:30pm till whenever; No credit cards)* is smack in the center of things. As with most Bologna locales, the dancing doesn't get started till past midnight, after the clean-cut regulars have downed at least a couple of drinks. Weekends can get crazy here, so if you want a more civilized crowd, show up early or during the week. Good pub grub, including sandwiches and hot dogs. Two very basic, square, fairly brightly lit rooms with live DJs playing hip-hop, commercial, and house for the one dance floor.

Primarily a disco bar, **Chalet Margherita** *(Via Meliconi 1; Tel 051/307-593; 8am-2am daily; No credit cards)* heats up in the summer with decent live music and highly entertaining karaoke and cabaret. On the northern side of **Giardini Margherita**, the whole deal is outdoors, except for the tent-like structures with seating that are scattered about. Get busy with the giddy locals on the dance floor, and order up some snacks from the gigantic menu selection to share between sets. Very laidback, a little cheesy, and a lot of fun.

Every night students spill out onto Via del Pratello, just east of the city center, from the partying going on inside **Riff Raff** *(Via del Pratello 3c; Tel 051/228-88; 10pm-5am; No credit cards)*, a hole in the wall with a makeshift bar and some tables and chairs scattered around. Sooner or later the steady stream of rap and hip-hop mixed with cups of wine, vodka, or gin will bring a new clarity to your existence. Stay a while— it only gets better as the night goes on, hitting top speed between midnight and 3am.

bologna bars, clubs and culture zoo

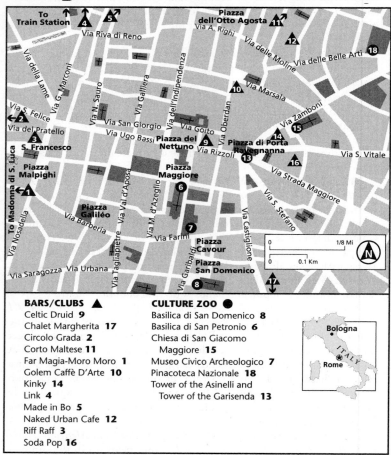

BARS/CLUBS ▲

Celtic Druid **9**
Chalet Margherita **17**
Circolo Grada **2**
Corto Maltese **11**
Far Magia-Moro Moro **1**
Golem Caffè D'Arte **10**
Kinky **14**
Link **4**
Made in Bo **5**
Naked Urban Cafe **12**
Riff Raff **3**
Soda Pop **16**

CULTURE ZOO ●

Basilica di San Domenico **8**
Basilica di San Petronio **6**
Chiesa di San Giacomo
    Maggiore **15**
Museo Civico Archeologico **7**
Pinacoteca Nazionale **18**
Tower of the Asinelli and
    Tower of the Garisenda **13**

Techno and house spun by a live DJ shake the PacMan-esque painted walls of **Naked Urban Café** *(Via Mascarella 26b; Tel 051/264-738; 10pm to late; No credit cards)*, a dark, underground bar in the city center. The funky metallic bar stools are more comfortable than they look. Chic and goth student types mix here, but make sure you go late, 'cause the scene often doesn't pick up till after midnight. Cocktails go for L8,000, beer L7,000, and wine L3,000.

live music and club scene

Bologna's nightlife is as funky as it gets in Italy. Dark industrial discos, sprawling outdoor party plazas, and screaming young instrument-bashing bands are all at the disposal of the curious sightseer. To find out what's going on in the ever-changing scene, pick up the biweekly pamphlet

Zero51 (referring to the city's area code) at local CD and music stores like **Joker** or **Casa del Disco** [see *stuff*, below, for both] and many area clubs listed below. Bologna is definitely late-night-oriented: Things usually get going *no* earlier than 10 or 10:30pm and last way into the night, till 3 or 4am on weekdays, later on weekends. The look is very casual—some girls do it up in heels, skirts, capri pants, and skimpy shirts, and some boys go for pants and button-down shirts; but for the most part, it's jeans and T-shirts across the board. In places like **Livello 57** [see below], where you're dancing on dirt and rocks in a train yard, things get even punkier and more casual. And it really doesn't matter what you're wearing; the scene is totally snob-free, completely open, and inviting. There may be a bouncer at the door of some clubs, but he's there to keep the peace, not to turn people away.

North of the train station, Bologna's best live music club, **Link** *(Via Fioravanti 14; Tel 051/370-971; 10pm-late Oct-May, closed June-Sept; No credit cards),* plays host to all the great and not-so-great local bands from rock to blues to punk to alternative. It also sponsors larger, better-known concerts, and is a central resource for finding out about other music events. From the outside, the unsightly building looks like an abandoned elementary school, but the lively acoustics and flashing stage lights inside will reassure you that this is a legitimate venue.

After Link, **Circolo Grada** *(Via della Grada; Tel 051/554-322; 10pm-whenever daily; No credit cards),* west of the *centro,* is the other major Bolognese live music spot, in a dark warehouse space with dark everything. In addition to weekly rock and/or blues nights, they throw in some funky cabaret, tango, musical theater, and even an occasional open-mike night. Usually there's no cover, so you can sample the bands before you shell out money, but odds are you'll want to stay—which is refreshing, since most Italian live music sucks.

The popular disco/discobar **Soda Pop** *(Via Castel Tialto 6; Tel*

rules of the game

As is the Italian norm, the liquor laws here are lax, which means that kids start drinking at about 16, and nobody'll bat an eyelash at a group of people passing around a bottle on the street. While plenty of hash smoking is done on Via Zamboni, it *is* illegal—though if all you have on you is what you're smoking at the moment, you'll only face "administrative sanctions" (read: fines and community service and "social reintegration" programs), not hard jail time. Many seem to stick to secluded spots, like discos, clubs, or the Giardini Margherita, which has plenty of nice, hidden nooks. As with almost anyplace in the world, a considerable amount of drugs can be found in most clubs.

ragazzo meets ragazza

As with any Italian town, foreign girls have the major upper hand in the cruising scene here. Italian men are hornier than cats in heat, and American women are considered "easy." But for brave, insistent backpacker boys, Bologna is the place where you may strike gold. Younger Bologna women are more urbane and independent than the traditional Italian damsel—though they still like a guy who will be attentive to their need to be coddled. The crowded bars on Via Zamboni, which are crawling with tipsy co-eds, are the best places to make your move. Start a conversation with a Bolognese babe interested in practicing English, which shouldn't be too difficult—English is quickly becoming an important commodity for Italians. And be sure to buy her a drink. Girls, your strategy has more to do with how to keep Bolognese guys *away*. Try holding hands with or kissing your friends—male or female—or saying *"lasciami in pace"* (leave me in peace) while giving them the frowning of a lifetime.

051/272-079; 10pm-late; No cover; No credit cards) has one of the most diverse selections of DJ-inspired theme nights from rock and funk to Brit pop to ska and reggae to hip-hop. A favorite with expats, it's also in the center of the city, which means you won't have to figure out late-night bus schedules or take a taxi. The decor is nothing special—basic wood bar and a couple of nondescript things on the wall—and it's not a big place, but they sure pack 'em in.

Okay, you're probably wondering where all the pierced punk kids you've seen on Via Zamboni go at night. **Livello 57** *(Via Maggia 6; Tel 051/246-509; Closed June-Sept; L8,000-12,000 cover; No credit cards)*, a sprawling converted industrial space next to a few abandoned tracks by the central train station, is a good bet. With weird statues made out of old railroad junk, dirt, and broken-up concrete pathways—and L5,000 liters of bottled beer—this part indoor/part outdoor club is a microcosm of what makes Bologna different from a lot of other Italian cities: There's very little pretension. Wear sneakers, ratty clothes, mess up your hair, and bang your head to the reckless, free-flow, DJ-created beats of techno, drum 'n' bass, and hardcore. All types of drugs, the least of them hash, are said to abound here.

Teatro Polivalente Occupato *(Via Irnerio 45c; Tel 051/421-07-27; Open most Fri, Sat, but call ahead, closed mid-June-Sept; L10,000 cover; No credit cards)* is another indoor/outdoor student place—actually smack dab in the university district—that has live DJs going nuts with their mixing boards and guitarists making love to the distortion pedal. There are also less-hardcore themes, from Latin to '80s nights. Whatever the kind of music, kids come here to drink, smoke hash, and dance in this big grunge-pit. For this purpose, TPO (as it's known) meets its objectives with flying colors. It would be a shame to miss out on the fun. Video and multimedia exhibits.

arts scene

In between stuffing your face, dancing, and guzzling huge quantities of wine, you can explore Bologna's other virtues, namely its very active arts culture. In the summer, on most nights, you can find a free city-sponsored outdoor theater, music, or dance event, like a Puccini opera, an outdoor art exhibit, or a fife-and-drum exhibition. Most of the festivities fall under the auspices of the well-known Bologna Sogno series, which runs from July to September. Giardini Margherita is also a site for many free outdoor concerts.

▶▶VISUAL ARTS

Bologna's not exactly known for its modern art prowess, but it does have a few worthwhile galleries in the city center. **Galleria d'Arte Maggiore** *(Via D'Azeglio; Tel 051/235-843; 10:30am-12:30pm/4:30-7:30pm)*, **Galleria d'Arte del Caminetto** *(Via Marescalchi 2; Tel 051/233-313; 4-8pm, closed Mon)*, and **Galleria Falcone-Borsellino** *(Piazza Galileo 4d; Tel 051/235-292; 10am-12:30pm/4-8pm)* show a mix of works by local and regional artists. Maggiore is the largest and has the most eclectic collection, both of abstract painting and sculpture, while the others concentrate solely on 2-D art.

▶▶PERFORMING ARTS

While **Teatro Comunale** *(Via Largo Respighi; Tel 051/529-999)*, southwest of the *centro*, is the best known venue for opera, ballet, and orchestral music, with an occasional free performance, **Teatro Perche-Compagnia d'Arte** *(Via Borgonuovo 11; Tel 051/239-221)* presents plays and readings performed by local artists southeast of the city center. Nothing in English, unfortunately.

gay scene

Though understandably small given the size of the city, gay life here is fairly active. **Arci Gay** *(Porta San Sarrogozza 2; Tel 051/644-69-02)*, the main gay organization in Bologna, organizes conferences and events concerning gay and lesbian issues, HIV/AIDS, and safe-sex awareness. In addition to the office, the historic 17th-century building, well southwest of the city center, also houses **Il Cassero** *(7pm-late daily)* a happening discobar, whose adjoining open-air terrace is open in the summer. Like the Arci Gay office, Il Cassero is a central meeting point for both the gay and lesbian communities and one of the few places in Bologna that is open year-round. June and July, when other centrally located clubs close, are its most popular months. Drinks run between L4,000 and L8,000, and there are regular theme nights and live DJs. It's a good place to either start or end an evening.

One of the local favorites is **Paquito** *(Via Polese 46c; Tel 051/243-*

festivals and events

With rides and games on one side of the hill, and vendors, bars, restaurants, discos, and live performance areas on the other, the sprawling outdoor entertainment hub **Made in Bo** *(Parco Nord-Via Stalingrado; Tel 051/264-738; Bus 25 to Parco Nord; 10pm-late July, Aug; No credit cards)* resembles a patchwork theme park. There is something for everyone here, which means attendees range from parents with crying kids to hyper teens to lovey-dovey couples to single guys and girls cruising each other. The outdoor dance floors don't get revved up till 11pm (and rage on till 4am and sometimes later), so while you wait for someone to take the plunge, try your hand at the carnival games. All types of music, live bands, and comedy.

The large classical music festival, **Bologna Festival** *(Information: Via delle Lame 58; Tel 051/649-33-97, 051/649-32-45; bofest@tin.it)*, is held each year from April to June and features national and international talent. Venues are scattered about Bologna in various churches and theaters.

998; 10:30pm-late Wed-Sat; L15,000-20,000 cover; No credit cards) a hardcore all-boys club (though brave girls sometimes go) with heavy groping, heavy gasping, and very dark near the Giardini Margherita. No one gets here before 11:30pm, so if you go, you may not be getting up before noon. It's said that they are particularly welcoming to boys from abroad. Just remember to behave yourself.

Gay Thursdays bring out an almost religious following of guys and gals to **Kinky** *(Via Zamboni 1; 10pm-late Thur-Sun; Cover varies from L15,000-25,000; No credit cards)*, as do gay-heavy Saturdays. The gregarious crowd doesn't usually go much beyond T-shirts and jeans.

Right on the Via San Felice (same thing as the Via Ugo Bassi running through the heart of the city), the **New Vigor Club** gym *(Via San Felice 6b; Tel 051/232-507; 5-minute walk from Piazza Maggiore; 2pm-2am; L18,000 cover; No credit cards)* is a great place to: a) make sure your buff build doesn't go to pot by burning off the seemingly endless mounds of carbohydrates you've been ingesting, and b) get a date! When you're done working out, you can towel off and do some more sweating in the sauna. Mostly guys, but women aren't unwelcome.

Another good relaxation venue is **Cosmos Sauna** *(Via Boldini 22, interno 16; Tel 051/255-890; 5-minute walk from train station; 2pm-late; L20,000; No credit cards)*. Larger and more modern than the New Vigor Club, the facility is for men only, which creates an unabashed cruising atmosphere.

CULTURE ZOO

For the museum- and church-weary traveler, Bologna is the place to be. There are fewer "must-see" stops, more charming nooks and crannies. Because of the almost anemic number of visitors, sightseeing is much less stressful, and, except in the high season, you might actually find yourself looking at a painting *by yourself* for a few minutes. One thing you really shouldn't miss is the climb up La Torre Asinelli. For about a buck fifty, get a great workout and an awesome skyscape view.

Pinacoteca Nazionale (National Picture Gallery) *(Via delle Belle Arti 56; Tel 051/243-222; 5-minute walk from Piazza Maggiore; 9am-1:50pm Tue-Fri, 9am-12:50pm Sun, closed Mon; L8,000 adults, under 18 free):* A one-stop tour of Bologna's greatest art offerings from the Byzantine to the Baroque.

Basilica di San Petronio (Il Duomo) *(Piazza Maggiore; Tel 051/225-442; Buses 25 and 30 from the train station to Piazza Maggiore; 7am-1:30pm/2:30-6:30pm daily Apr-Sept, 7:25am-1pm/2-6pm daily Oct-Mar; Free admission):* It's not overly impressive from the outside, but a visit to its airy and dark innards showcases one of the most beautiful and simple examples of Gothic style. Also a great way to escape the sun and heat.

Palazzo Communale and Museum of Giorgio Morandi *(Piazza Maggiore 6; Tel 051/203-526; 10am-6pm Tue-Sat; Each museum separate admission, L8,000 adults, L4,000 ages 14-18, combined tickets L12,000 adults, L6,000 ages 14-18):* Restored for the year 2000 Jubilee, the 14th-century Bologna town hall houses two small museums of artwork donated from several private collections, as well as the tourist information office.

Basilica di San Domenico *(Piazza San Domenico 13; Tel 051/640-04-11; 7am-1pm/2:15-7pm daily; Free admission):* Regardless of whether you've seen Michaelangelo's *David* in person, you'll be spellbound by his *San Procolo,* said to be the artist's "rehearsal" for his later masterpiece.

Tower of the Asinelli and Tower of the Garisenda *(Piazza di Porta Ravegnanna; 9am-6pm daily May-Sept, till 5pm Oct-Apr; L5,000):* Need a bit of exercise? After a satisfying climb up the Asinelli's wooden staircases (about 500 steps in all), you'll be rewarded with the best view in central Bologna. Looking like it may topple any day, Garisenda is closed. (Don't be afraid to get close: It's been leaning since Dante wrote the *Inferno.*)

Chiesa di San Giacomo Maggiore *(Piazza Rossini or Via Zamboni 15; Tel 051/225-970; 8am-noon/3:30-6pm daily; Free admission):* The Bentivoglio Chapel in this 13th-century structure is best known for its stunning (though somewhat dirty-looking) frescoes by Francesco Francia.

Museo Civico Archeologico *(Via dell'Archiginnasio 2; Tel 051/233-849; 9am-2pm Tue-Fri, 9am-1pm/3:30-7pm Sat, Sun, closed Mon; L8,000, L4,000 students):* All you archeology buffs will love this

12 hours in bologna

1. **Catch a free outdoor play:** In the summer, many of the piazzas in the city center become sites of free local musical and theatrical productions. Even if you can't speak Italian, it's fun to check out the scene.

2. **Climb the Tower of Asinelli:** You might get dizzy climbing the winding wood staircase, but gazing down on the red tile cityscape and confusion of Ugo Bassi are worth it [see *culture zoo*, above].

3. **Cruise the steps of Piazza Maggiore:** This is *the* place to hang out and strike up a conversation with a potential love interest. Offer to buy a coffee or gelato, and your odds increase a thousandfold [see *hanging out*, above].

4. **Party on Via Zamboni:** You'll probably be told that the student area is seedy—and it is! That, and the crush of undergrads, make it great [see *neighborhoods*, above].

5. **Dine on Via del Pratello:** One of the best, cheapest streets for restaurants, pubs, and cafes is also a student favorite [see *hanging out*, above].

6. **Go to Made in Bo:** This sprawling, outdoor nighttime carnival-disco-mall keeps the masses entertained on those hot summer

"Civic Archeological Museum," with its excellent Egyptian collection and a good showing of Greek, Etruscan, and Roman treasures.

great outdoors

Located just outside the southern rim of the city center, **Giardini Margherita** is one of Italy's most pleasant urban parks. Basketball and volleyball courts, large fields for sunbathing and frisbee, and smoothly paved pathways make this the perfect escape from the loud, scooter-filled streets. Another park option, though much less impressive, is **Giardino della Montagnola**, located in the northern half of the city. The most notable feature is a large, fish-filled fountain.

If you're visiting Bologna during the sweltering summer months, hike over to **Stadio** *(Via A. Costa 174; Tel 051/615-25-20; Bus 14, 21 from Porta San Isaia to Via A. Costa)* or **Sterlino** *(Via Murri 113; Tel 051/623-70-34; Bus 13, 96 from Porta San Stefano to Via Murri)*, two public swimming pools open every day from mid-June to Sept, 10:30am till 7pm. Entrance costs about L10,000.

stuff

Bologna is not among Italy's best shopping cities: Clothes and shoes are wicked expensive. The stylish Via d'Azeglio and Via Farini have an array

evenings when most other bars and discos in the city are closed [see *festivals and events*, above].

7. **Chill out in Giardini Margherita:** Big open fields, shaded woodsy areas, and a couple of kiddy amusement rides, and in the summer, free concerts filled with the university's soccer-playing, frisbee-chucking, rollerblading, sun-tanning student body [see *great outdoors*, above].

8. **Take a photo by the Neptune fountain:** Designed in 1566, the fountain depicts a buff Neptune with his foot on the head of a dolphin, surrounded by four very sensual sirens. Great place to take a seat and cool off [see *hanging out*, above].

9. **Headbang at Livello 57:** This place is ages ahead of the standard Bologna disco stop. Gnawed out of an abandoned train yard on the side of the central station, this mostly outdoor club is a squatter's dream. Cheap beer, great DJs, and grunge kids [see *live music and club scene*, above].

10. **Eat a Pizza:** Nicola's Pizzeria, a local favorite with students and non-students alike, is smack in the middle of town [see *eats*, below].

of designer boutiques like Gucci and Armani as well as some nifty jewelry stores, but you won't find many bargains. With a bunch of clothing and specialty shops, and a McDonald's, Via Ugo Bassi and Via Indipendenza are great window-shopping and walking streets. At the outdoor market in Piazza Aldrovandi, vendors hawk fresh fruits and vegetables, breads, Italian books, housewares, and some clothing at fair prices. Generally though, in Bologna, money is better spent on food and drink than pretty much anything else.

▶▶**BOUND**

Feltrinelli International *(Via Zamboni 7B; Tel 051/268-070; 5-minute walk from Piazza Maggiore; 9am-7pm Mon-Sat; AE, V, MC)* has an assortment of good English books, as well as magazines, travel guides, and newspapers.

▶▶**TUNES**

For relatively cheap CDs, tapes, and vinyl ("relatively" is the operative word) of basic international pop, alternative, hip-hop, rock, and the latest Italian versions of all of the above, go to **Casa del Disco** *(Via Indipendenza 30c; Tel 051/234-224; 9am-12:30pm/2:30-7:30pm, closed Thur afternoon, Sun; AE, V, MC)* or **Joker** *(Via Ugo Bassi 14e; Tel 051/265-016; 2-minute walk from Piazza di Maggiore; 9:30am-1pm/4-8pm, closed Sun; V, MC)*.

moda

The large student population here has cornered the style market on punk and grunge. Sneakers, ripped or baggy jeans, T-shirts, tank tops (for girls), and colorful Invicta backpacks are the look of choice. Blue, green, white, or purple hair is not uncommon, nor are tattoos. All of which makes fitting in easy for scrubby travelers. The best place to check out the current styles is in the university district near Via delle Belle Arte and Via Zamboni.

▶▶DUDS

For the hippest styles from Stussy, Pickwick, and Carhartt, head over to **Scout** *(Piazza VIII Agosto 28e; Tel 051/249-825; 9:30am-7:30pm; AE, V, MC)*. They also carry a wide selection of hats, Jansport and Eastpak bags, and sneakers, though some stuff like the shoes and bags are more expensive.

▶▶GIFTS

You can knock off some of your obligatory gift-shopping at **Images** *(Via delle Moline 8; Tel 051/227-630; 9am-12:30pm/3:45-7:30pm, closed Thur afternoon)*, a store full of posters, postcards, T-shirts, murals, and various souvenir knickknacks.

EATS

Bologna, famous for its sauces (ragu or bolognese), pastas, and meats, totally lives up to the hype. And you can taste them all without draining your pockets. You'll find a goldmine of cheap eats in the university district (Via delle Belle Arte) and on Via del Pratello.

▶▶CHEAP

You'll walk away from **Osteria Alle Due Porte** *(Via del Pratello 62a; Tel 051/523-565; Noon-3pm/7pm-2am, closed Tue; L10,000-25,000 per entree; V, MC)* licking your lips with gusto. If you're on a very low budget, you can make a meal of the perfectly spiced *pennette all'arrabiata* (L6,000) and a carafe of wine, but if you have a bit more dough, go for one of the scrumptious beef, veal, or fish dishes. For vegetarians, the eggplant parmagiana and caprese are heavenly. The decor is nothing special—basic white walls, wood paneling, marble floors—but the wait staff is friendly and speaks just enough English to help you get by. Arrive early to beat the student crowd for an outside table.

Also right in the heart of studentville, the Greek hole-in-the-wall **To Steki** *(Largo Respighi 4E; Tel 051/268-012; 11am-11pm, closed Sun; L6,000-15,000 per entree; No credit cards)* is a university favorite. The kitchen serves up drippy gyros, healthy moussaka, and stuffed pitas seconds after you order. There is outside seating, but you'll be hard-pressed to upend the "studious" academics.

La Mamma *(Via Zamboni 16; Noon-2:30pm/7-10pm, closed Sun; No credit cards)* is a large self-serve cafeteria a few blocks east of the Piazza Maggiore that dishes out savory-but-salty pizza, pastas, meats, and sides. The TVs in the dining room allow you a chance to catch up with Italian soap operas.

The difficulty in finding an empty table at the vegetarian **Clorofilla** *(Strada Maggiore 64c; Tel 051/235-343; 12:15-3pm for lunch, 4-7pm for tea, and 7:30pm-midnight for dinner; L8,000-20,000 per entree; AE, V, MC)* is proof that in the land of spaghetti, there *is* life after pasta. The cheerful yellow-and-green interior matches the colorful plates of rice, couscous, seitan, and tofu. At L6,000, the veggie burger makes a nutritious and light lunch or dinner. Largely full of travelers—Italians generally like their meat. Right on the Piazza di Porta Ravegnanna.

▶▶DO-ABLE

In the summer, you can't find a more sought-after outdoor table than at **Nicola's Pizzeria** *(Piazza San Martino 9a; No phone; Noon-3pm/7:30pm-midnight; L15,000-35,000 per entree; V, MC)* on the Piazza di Porta Ravegnanna. Couples, students, and families come here for the same thing: cheap and delicious food served in a great, lively atmosphere. Starting at L5,000, the brick-oven pizzas have a 100 percent satisfaction rating. The pastas (L9,000-11,000)—try the traditional bolognese or ragú sauce—won't disappoint. Everything's better with a jug of local red wine.

▶▶SPLURGE

A huge wine list, goofy wait staff, and a menu of hearty Bolognese and

down and out

Considering it's a student town, Bologna is not as cheap as you might expect. Still, there are a lot of things to do for the monetarily challenged. Sit in Piazza Maggiore or lounge in Giardini Margherita—the continual influx of all kinds of humans make these spots legendary for people-watching. Cheap eats are best found on Via delle Belle Arte and Via del Pratello. Even cheaper eats can be had by getting made-to-order sandwiches from local *alimentari*. Italians usually don't order sandwiches, so you'll have to tell the shop help exactly what you want—i.e., two slices of prosciutto *(due figlietti del proscuitto)*, one slice of cheese *(una pezza del formaggio)*, etc. Since everything is weighed separately, this will cost as much as buying bread, cheese, and meats separately and putting it together yourself, so the choice is yours....Finally, buy a couple of bottles of vino and find a stoop. It's totally legal and part of everyone's Italy experience.

gelati wars

Scoops from **Gelateria Moline** *(Via Moline 13)* are perennial favorites for students here, though the comparatively little-known **Gelateria Gianni** *(Via Montegrappa 11; Noon-1am daily, 11am-1pm Sun, closed every other Wed)*, hidden away one street north of Ugo Bassi, exceeds it in scoop size, taste, and number of flavors. Gianni also has a full bar and seating in the back and an assortment of *granita* (Italian-style slurpees) for anyone looking for a refreshing alternative to gelati. **Occhi di Venere** *(Via San Vitale 37a; 5-minute walk from Piazza Maggiore; Closed Mon)* is another good choice for big cones.

Lucan dishes are the major draws to **Trattoria Belle Arti** *(Via Belle Arte 6f; Tel 051-267-648; Lunch 11am-3pm, dinner 5-11pm; L20,000-40,000 per entree; No credit cards)*. All pastas are fresh, and meats, epecially the roast lamb, are slow-cooked and tender. Also try the *zucchine trifolate alla crema di yoghurt*—a yummy zucchini cream concoction. The one catch is that the waiters don't write down your order, so you may get something unexpected, but it's usually still delicious. The inside and outdoor tables are covered in real linen and decorated with fresh flowers. Conveniently located at the northeast corner of the *centro*.

crashing

Even in the height of summer, Bologna's center will never be crawling with disoriented map readers. You'd think this would make cheap hotel rooms and beds relatively easy to snag, but unfortunately there just isn't a big pool of low-cost options. There are a few budget hotels in the center, but virtually none by the train station, and the youth hostel is located well outside the center. Call ahead to the cheaper hotels and make a reservation, especially during the summer. Once you reach a hotel, speak up, because there is also some chance that you'll be able to negotiate a better price, as hotel owners customarily have off-season and high-season prices. Many visitors come here for the well-established business-fair circuit that runs mostly in the spring and fall, so make sure you have reservations if you're in town then.

▶▶CHEAP

Ostello per La Gioventu San Sisto (HI) *(Via Viadagola 5; Tel 051/501-810, Fax 051/391-003; Bus 93, 21B to Localita San Sisto; Desk open 7-10am/3:30-10pm, closed Dec 20-Jan 20; L21,000 per bed, L26,000 w/o HI card; V, MC)* is by far the cheapest choice in town, but you pay in other ways: There's a midnight curfew, a 10am to 3:30pm lockout, and it's a 30- to 40-minute bus ride east of the city center. Most of the rooms in the converted villa contain five beds and sinks, with (very clean) bathrooms and showers in the hallway. The young staff is eager to help. Continental breakfast included.

Due Torri *(Via Viadagola 14; Tel 051/519-202)* is run by the same folks and has all the same vitals.

Though its rooms are plain and let in a load of street noise, **Pensione Marconi** *(Via Marconi 22; Tel 051/262-832; L60,000 single w/bath; L100,000 double w/bath; No credit cards)* is a great cheap crash pad near the train station. The staff likes to point out that most rooms have ceiling fans, an absolute must in summer.

▶▶**DO-ABLE**

Sure, the rooms are antiseptic, but **Albergo Minerva** *(Via de Monari 3; Tel 051/239-652; L90,000 double w/shared bath; No credit cards)* is only a 5-minute walk from the university quarter—which makes it slightly easier to make the 2:30am curfew—and not a bad price if you share the room. The tongue-in-cheek Sicilian-born owner mans the desk for psychotically long shifts (18 hours) and likes to chat with guests. The shared bathrooms are somewhat muggy, and you may literally bump into fellow travelers in the narrow hallways.

You'll never go hungry at **Albergo Apollo** *(Via Drapperie 5; Tel 051/239-55; L55,000 single, L90,000-120,000 double, L140,000 triple; AE, MC, V)*—when you walk out the door, you're deposited in Bologna's market area, where mamas and papas hawk their tomatoes. The basic rooms are large, at least, and have cool modern furnishings. Don't bring your clothes into the bathroom with you when you shower unless you like the wet look—the showers tend to soak the whole room.

The name says it all: every room in **Albergo Panorama** *(Via Livraghi 1; Tel 051/221-802, 051/227-205; L95,000 double w/shared bath; AE, V, MC)* has a pretty view, some looking down on the hectic Via Ugo Bassi; some onto the cute and tranquil courtyard and terra-cotta roofs of its neighbors. Rooms are large and provide ample space to stretch your legs. The women who run the hotel are friendly, and operate the establishment like proud aunts. Bathrooms are clean and location can't be better. By far the best reasonably priced hotel in Bologna.

▶▶**SPLURGE**

The pleasant, three-star **Albergo Centrale** *(Via della Zecca 2; Tel 051/225-114, Fax 051/235-162; L100,000 single w/bath; L140,000 double; AE, V, MC)* puts you about a 2-minute walk from Piazza Maggiore. Ask for a top-story room—most have nice rooftop vistas. Phones and TVs found in all rooms provide good diversions, and the efficient staff keeps the lounge stocked with coffees and liquor. twenty-two rooms.

Albergo Accademia *(Via delle Belle Arte 6; Tel 051/232-318, Fax 051/263-590; L100,000 single, L150,000 double; No credit cards)* is pricier than some others in the area, but it's within earshot of the student activity and has big, yet cozy, rooms. The complimentary break-

bologna eats and crashing

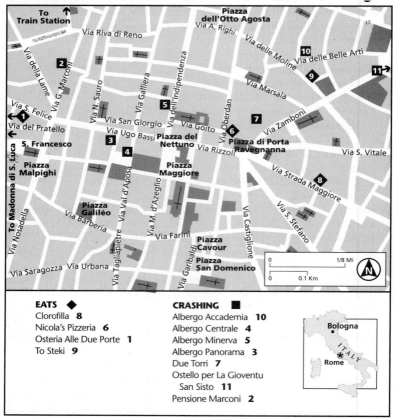

EATS ◆
Clorofilla **8**
Nicola's Pizzeria **6**
Osteria Alle Due Porte **1**
To Steki **9**

CRASHING ■
Albergo Accademia **10**
Albergo Centrale **4**
Albergo Minerva **5**
Albergo Panorama **3**
Due Torri **7**
Ostello per La Gioventu
   San Sisto **11**
Pensione Marconi **2**

fast of croissants and coffee does the belly well. twenty-eight rooms, most with private bath.

need to know

Currency Exchange The Italian currency is the **lira** (L). There are banks with **ATMs** along Via Rizzoli and Via Marconi, or at the train station, which are probably your best bet.

Tourist Information The main office of the **tourist bureau** (*Piazza Maggiore 6; Tel 051/239-660; Buses 25 and 30 from the train station to Piazza Maggiore; 9am-7pm Mon-Sat, 9am-2pm Sun, 9am-1pm holidays, closed Jan 1, Easter, Christmas, San Stefano*) provides free Internet access by reservation only, as well as the standard info, maps, and pamphlets. Or try the **Student Travel Agency (CTS)** (*Largo Respighi 2f;*

Tel 051/237-501; Buses 32-33 from Piazza Maggiore to Via San Vitale, or any other bus that makes a University stop).

Public Transportation Bologna runs on the great **ATC bus system**. Every bus stops at the centrally located Piazza Maggiore. Night buses (87-99) have limited stops. Tickets *(L1,800 for one ticket; 10-ticket packs for slightly reduced rate)* may be purchased at *tabacchi* (tobacco shops), and bus maps found at the ATC information office at the train station or at *atc.bo.it*. Buses run 5:30am-12:30am.

Health and Emergency Emergency number: *113*; fire: *115*; medical emergency: *333-333*; police: *112*. Hospitals in and near the city are **Ospedale Santa Orsola** *(Via Massarenti 9; Tel 051/636-3111)* and **Ospedale Maggiore** *(Via 1 Nigrisoli 2; Tel 051/647-8111).*

Pharmacies Farmacia Comunale Centrale *(Piazza di Maggiore 6; Tel 051/238-509; Buses 25 and 30 from train station to Piazza di Maggiore)* is always open.

Telephone Country code: *39*; city code: *51*. The red telephone booths scattered around on the squares and street corners take coins as well as phone cards, which you can buy at *tabacchi* (tobacco shops). **AT&T:** *172-1011;* **MCI:** *172-1022;* **Sprint:** *172-1877.*

Airports Aeroporto Guglielmo Marconi *(Borgo Panigale; Tel 051/647-96-15; Aerobus (L6,000) from the train station; 6am-midnight)* is 4 miles north of city center. The **Aerobus** *(6:30am-11pm; L6,000)* runs from airport to train station every half hour.

Train There's only one **train station** *(Piazza delle Medaglie d'Oro; Tel 055/630-21-11, 1478/88-088)* here. 24-hour luggage storage, L5,000 for 12 hours. Info desk open daily 8am-8pm. Buses 25 and 30 run between the station and Piazza Maggiore; Buses 11, 17, 25, 37 go to the center.

Bike/Car Rental Bikes can be rented at the **train station** *(Piazza delle Medaglie d'Oro; Tel 051/630-20-15; Buses 10, 21, 25, 30, 31, 32, 33, 35, 36, 37, 38, 39, 50, 81, 90, 91 to Piazza delle Medaglie d'Oro; 6:30am-10pm Mon-Fri; 7am-3pm Sat; L3,000/hour, L15,000/day; No credit cards).*

Laundry Wash & Dry *(Via Petroni 38; Tel 051/237-174; 9am-9pm daily; L6,000 wash, L6,000 dry)* will let you do just that.

florence

Florence is a tightly packed, hectic, scooter-crazy hub of modern northern Italian life, simultaneously creating and smashing stereotypes. The masses that come here to bask in the glow of the city's Renaissance grandeur find its beauty matched, if not surpassed, by the lively and animated locals.

Yeah, we've heard it before, but the perpetually bronzed residents *do* look better in their clothes than the rest of us. What's worse, they love to flaunt it. Second only to Milan in fashion sense—and often more put-together, thanks to a less harried city life—person for person, Florentines make great eye candy. Men, women, gay, straight, no matter, you will have a field day falling into superficial love with so many beautiful Mediterranean people about. Girls, you may have trouble keeping your boyfriends from staring putty-jawed, 'cause the Italian women love to show skin, but there's no need to be prudish, with so many hunky Giorgios, Giannis, and Fabios around. In fact, while Italian girls rarely give the white-skinned Teva-wearing tourist boys the time of day, the salivating Latin macho men are hard-wired to shower foreign women with heavenly praise. They'll do anything to get you to stop and talk so they can look and talk.

Traditional elegance aside, there's also a scrap of attitude here. Many of Florence's MTV-influenced disaffected youth have wholeheartedly embraced the spirit of grunge chic. Though not as large as Bologna's or Rome's, Florence's large T-shirt-clad university population is *unmistakably* present, especially at **Cabiria Cafe** [see *bar scene*, below] in Piazza Santo Spirito, or scattered around nearby. While this is good news for the budget traveler in dirty cutoffs and sandals, there's definitely enough Gucci and Prada around to give anyone a complex. But have no fear, the abundance of cute boutiques along vias del Corso, Magazzini, and Tournabuoni and in piazzas della Republica and Signorìa give you ample opportunity to upgrade your "wardrobe." The daily outdoor market at Piazza San Lorenzo is a must for bargain hunters and hagglers.

The city is also home to a seemingly endless list of foreign university programs (mostly American), and many centrally located hangouts are almost exclusively patronized by students from abroad. That, combined with the influx of family vacationers and package-tour sightseers, sometimes makes summer in Florence (particularly June through August) feel like an eerie burlesque, where you'll hear as many regional dialects of American English (not to mention Irish, British, and Australian) in one day as you might the rest of your life. If you want to avoid the throngs, plan on visiting in March or April or during the fall. Fewer visitors mean shorter lines, cheaper and more available rooms, and a generally mellower vibe. Cooler spring and fall temperatures are also a lot easier on the body, as the mercury during the humid summer months often hits 95° Fahrenheit and sometimes rises to 100°.

neighborhoods

Since the city itself isn't very big, and most tourist attractions are packed around **Piazza del Duomo** and the **River Arno**—which cuts the city into northern and southern areas, the latter known as **Oltrarno**—all can be easily and quickly reached on foot. While the major concentrations of popular sites such as **Santa Croce**, the **Uffizi**, and **Accademìa** [see *culture zoo*, below, for all three] are huddled in *centro storico*, the "historic center," to the north of the river, the Oltrarno features the grandiose **Palazzo Pitti** [see *culture zoo*, below] and an array of cheap *trattorìe*. Besides **Santo Spirito**, most piazza hangout areas are in the historic center. Though residential, venturing north on **Via San Zanobi** and west on **Via Palazzuolo** will lead you to some good cheap fare [see *eats*, below]. The **Ponte Vècchio**, lined with overhanging jewelry shops and packed tight with tourists, is the most famous and celebrated of Florence's eight bridges.

Finding an address in Florence can be a little tricky. The wacky Florentines use two separate street-numbering systems: one red, the other blue or black. Red is for shops and restaurants, and blue or black are for offices, hotels, and apartments and houses. In this chapter, the red addresses are noted by an "r" following the building number. It's really best to try to get a cross street or landmark if you're looking for an address that's on a long boulevard.

Though the bright orange public transportation ATC buses have extensive routes in the city center, it's best to use them for sights located outside the center such as **Piazzale Michelangelo** [see *great outdoors*, below]. That way you can save your money for the things that really count: gelati, beer, and cheap Chianti.

hanging out

Cheap nighttime—or *any*time—fun can be had chilling out in one of the city's many lovely squares. Piazzas surrounding the Duomo, Uffizi/Palazzo Vècchio, Santa Croce, and Santo Spirito are the most popular. Here you can spend hours nursing a drink with scores of locals and tourists, young and old alike. The piazza drinking scene is chatty and friendly, and if you want to speak English, you should have no problem talking with locals (keep in mind that Florentines are overexposed to the average tourist, so be fresh, dammit!). Florentines don't have the carousing spirit of the Brits or Germans, and even when the wine-drinking piazza crowds get rowdy, it's usually just harmless teenage hipsters on their scooters. In the most popular piazzas (Santo Spirito, Santa Croce, della Signorìa, della Repùbblica), the flocks peter out around 3 or 4am most summer nights, and happy boozy people walk home through the deserted narrow streets—just as they've been doing for hundreds of years. With more than 20 statues, including a replica of Michelangelo's famous stud, *David*, the classic **Piazza della Signorìa** *(3 minutes' walk south of the Duomo)* is a clear favorite for loafing. At all hours, swarms of sightseers snack on gelati, snap photographs, write postcards, and plan their next stop. During the day and early evening, **Piazza del Duomo** has pretty much the same crowd, but it clears out at night. Both piazzas are not bad for striking up conversations with locals. The restaurants, cafes, and endless stream of guitar and accordion serenaders found in the gray-stone **Piazza della Repùbblica** *(2 minutes southwest of the Duomo)* and the multicolored trade shops of the small **Piazza di Mercato Centrale** *(4 minutes east of the train station)* offer maximum relaxation, as do the steps of the **San Lorenzo** and **Santa Croce**. Via Tournabuoni, Via del Corso, and the bustling area around the mustard-yellow **Ponte Vècchio** contain hundreds of shops hawking everything from shoes, ties, underwear, posters/postcards, Duomo and Virgin Mary replicas, and Asian-made jewelry to cheesy Renaissance-style marble rip-offs. Some shops, such as **Giulio Giannini e Figlio** [see *stuff*, below], have been open for over a hundred years, and many have been in the same family for three and four generations. The **Oltrarno** is the area of Florence on the southern side of the river, where there are a number of good congregating spots led by **Piazzale Michelangelo**, which offers wonderful views of the north and west sides of the city, including the Duomo, Santa Croce, and the Ponte Vècchio. From this height you can also see **Piazza Santo Spirito**, the unanimous nighttime choice for Florentine hippie youth. With over a half a dozen outdoor restaurants and bars and perfect church steps that invite buskers, bongo players, hacky-sackers, and backpack-wielding students, this is *the* locals' evening and late-night choice for chilling, swilling, and debating. Take a relaxing stroll along either side of the Arno and enjoy wonderful views of the city and Ponte Vècchio from the Ponte San Trinità or Ponte Carraia. Located just a few minutes' walk from the Duomo, Volta di San Piero, Borgo Albizi, Via Pandolfini, and Via Faenza are all filled with eye-catching shops including sandwich bars, pubs, and a high density of travelers attracted by several Internet cafes

FIVE THINGS TO TALK TO A LOCAL ABOUT

Though friendly and helpful, Italians have a flair for making conversation that is reverential and deprecating at the same time.

1. **American Politics**—Since the U.S. alternately bombed and then saved Italy during WWII, Italians have been obsessed with the American system of politicking. The Clinton/Lewinsky thing didn't help matters; the Florida ballot debacle just made things worse.

2. **Stately Vespas vs. Moto Guzzi Crotch-Rockets**—Is it better to ride through the streets with your hair blowing gently in the wind or tear across the cobblestones striking fear into the hearts of tourists? Almost everybody's got a scooter, so almost everybody's got an opinion.

3. **Italian Food vs. Any Other Country's Food**—Bad news: It's a very short conversation. Good news: It's usually followed by a great Italian meal.

4. **Skyscrapers vs. Florentine Architecture**—Rail against decorative ornamentation in favor of glass boxes and see if you can start a fight.

5. **Italian Soccer vs. American Football**—"Ah, foootbaall, but yew Americans do not like foootbaall. We Italians looove foootbaall. We live for foootbaall. Ah, but yew have foootbaall too, 'de American kind. So fast and strong. I don't understand. But it is not like our kind of foootbaall. Gracefuull and elegant. How do you say, beautiful."

and laundromats. With the buzz of the modish cafe **La Dolce Vita** [see *bar scene*, below], Piazza del Carmine is the chosen site of the Florentine in-crowd, while the strobe lights gleaming from **Meccanò** and **Central Park** [see *club scene*, below, for both], the two summertime discos located at the easternmost edge of Viale degli Olmi *(10 minutes west of the station)*, are like laser sirens beckoning clubbers from miles away. Basically, Florence is a safe city for wandering, with a few rules: Guys, while the city center is fine for being out late into the night, don't go hanging around alone on the edges of town. Girls, don't walk anywhere at night by yourself—it's best to be with a guy or hang with a crowd. Gay guys, if you choose to dress in a majorly flamboyant way, be careful walking by yourself really late at night or in secluded areas.

bar scene

Despite having a cafe with a fully stocked bar on every corner, Italy has never traditionally had a very big drinking culture—outside of wine with dinner, of course. But with the relatively recent advent of the Irish/English/American pub and the pub-grub menu of foods like hamburgers and french fries, the landscape of Italy's drinking culture has changed somewhat. Simply by their nature, these pubs are not terribly original places, but they usually have chill atmospheres and a good selection of drinks and are popular with sightseers and Florentines alike. Despite their stock of liquor (which means you can have either espresso and/or vodka), most cafes close down around 10pm, although some do attract a late-night crowd. *Vinerìe*, which specialize in wines and also other liquors, and the pub-like *osterìe*, which offer beer, liquors, and a menu that generally consists of five to 10 meats and pastas, cater to late-night crowds. Outside the foreigner-heavy spots, Florentine-style drinking holes are relaxed; rowdiness and table-dancing are rarities. Still, as casual as the bar scene is, Florentines like to dress up when they go out, so be prepared to feel out of place if you go grungy.

One of the quickest places to get crowded is **Dublin Pub** *(Via Faenza 27r; Tel 055/293-049; 5pm-2am daily; No credit cards)*, a cozy, centrally located Guinness-sipping drinking hole. Here it's not uncommon for expats and travelers to hit the pints right at opening time. The Irish photos and Guinness memorabilia on the walls and hardy wooden stools and tables make this the most authentic of Florence's Irish pubs. The small and cozy quarters help warm up the bones in December and January, and in summer, the open front door allows spillout into the streets.

A 5-minute walk south of Il Duomo, **Angie's Pub** *(Via de' Neri 35r; Tel 055/239-82-45; 2pm and on daily; No credit cards)* is a mellow, communal pub stop where you can nurse your drink and management won't seem to mind. Drinks are cheap (around L6,000), and the menu includes burgers, hot dogs, and bagels that are amazingly tasty by any standard. The picnic tables and the small, narrow seating area can make you feel like you're on a submarine, which actually adds to the overall fun and friendly atmosphere.

Equally as relaxed but somewhat more wacky is **Public House** *(Via Palazzuolo 27r; Tel 055/290-530; 8pm-2am daily; V, MC, AE, DC)*, with an assortment of not-so-usual mobiles—tennis racket, school desk and chair, ancient horn, iron kettle, and more—suspended from the ceiling. Cleverly placed light sources create cool shadows, and flickering film projectors run a perpetual feed of nonsense video. But there's more than interior design smarts at work here. The small, intimate bar, west of the city center, is an economical place to drink (medium beer L7,000, cocktails L6,000 to L8,000, wine L3,000) and packs in crowds of both young and more "mature" Florentines.

From the late afternoon to wee in the morning, **Cabiria Cafe** *(Piazza Santo Spirito; Tel 055/215-732; 8:30am-1am Mon, Wed, Thur, till 2am Fri, Sat, closed Tue; No credit cards)* is crowded with cheery, backpack-wearing students and student types from the nearby university district who'd rather be chatting than studying. In the summer, chic herds press into the covered outdoor seating area, while the tiny bar area gets packed

dante meets beatrice

If they're breathing, foreign girls will have no problem getting picked up in any one of the major piazzas or clubs—Italian men have homing devices for women that are "more active" than their relationship-minded Italian counterparts. For traveling guys, the relationship thing *is* a major stumbling block in scoring a short-term tryst with an Italian lady. Once they come of age, Italian women are usually attached to a boyfriend or in the presence of family, which prevents them from straying too far off the traditional courtship path. The truth is that this "modesty" is an ironclad social pretense grown out of a culture where naked women are displayed just about everywhere—buses, stores, magazines, TV ads, public sculptures, museums. See, once the Florentine female gets to really *know you*, she is almost always wildly "forward" and willing to show you that she's in the know. Guys: Crack the ice by being funny and smart. Be sure to look them in the eye—they can sniff out an unworthy scoundrel from miles away (not you, of course!). Once you have their attention, you gotta shower them with gifts, praise, and kindness, and let them have their way. And remember, it's a small window before you have to meet papa and start planning the ceremony. Scared yet? The best places to make the approach are in cafes, Internet cafes [see *wired*, below], museums, and, yes, church (actually, *après* church).

in the winter. Cocktails during happy hour—everyday 6 to 9pm—are a mere L6,000. If you stay long enough, the yummy finger food could be a good substitute for dinner.

The crowds of beautiful locals at **La Dolce Vita** *(Piazza del Carmine; Tel 055/284-595; 11am-2am Mon-Sat, 5pm-2am Sun, restaurant open 12:30-2:30pm/7:30-11:30pm Mon-Sat; AE, DC)*, easily the trendiest place in Florence, conjure up images of Rome's sleekly dressed movie stars on the Via Veneto in the '60s. There may not be any Fellinis or Mastroiannis here, but the bar's all-too-hip vibe justifies the cinematic name. Olive-skinned women in Prada dresses and knickers, men in dark jackets and Dolce & Gabbana shirts, and everyone in Luxotica and Ray-Ban shades. Big after-work crowds gather at this slightly-off-the-beaten-path (south of the Arno and west of *centro storico*) spot around 6:30pm, but outdoor seating keeps it from feeling too packed. The shiny, curved bar and the mirrored walls give the patrons enough ways to check themselves and each other out shamelessly.

The relatively new **Sant'Ambrogio Caffè** *(Piazza Sant'Ambrogio 7; Tel 055/241-035; 10am-2am daily; V, MC)* is among a new generation of stylized bar/cafes with artsy, minimalist decor including high ceilings, a weird red twisty sculpture, Rothko- and Braque-style paintings, Pottery Barn–like wood and steel furniture, a long wine list, and a casual atmosphere. A few blocks west of the Duomo, it's the perfect place for an afternoon drink while discussing evening plans, catching up on reading, or whipping off a few postcards. Just remember to move in slow, tempered motions.

At **Kikuya** *(Via de' Benci 43r; Tel 055/234-48-79; 7pm-2am daily; V, MC)*, in *centro storico*, the operative words are "happy hour." Every night from 7 to 10pm, pints are L5,000. Tuesdays and Thursdays, there's over-amplified live cover music: Cat Stevens, Foreigner, Rolling Stones, and maybe even an Italian tune or two. The good pub grub—hamburgers, burritos, and sandwiches named after stops on the London underground—is cheap and satisfying. Good place to mix with the locals.

Hailed as the oldest American bar in Florence (circa 1962), the **Red Garter** *(Via de Benci 33r; Tel 055/234-49-04; Open daily; V, MC)*, a few doors down from Kikuya, is an indefatigable party place. Part small-time casino, part wood-paneled love den, the Garter pulls in American thrill-seekers in droves. Share your stories with other travelers, talk about the good ol' U.S. of A., and bitch about slow Internet connections. It's amazing how the patriotic sentiment wells up after a few Buds. Check out the mini-wall memorial to Hollywood's great femme fatales, and dance to live music (of various grades) under a disco ball. Happy hour, Friday and Saturday 9 to 9:30pm. Beer L8,000 and cocktails L10,000.

LIVE MUSIC SCENE

While Florence showcases endless artistic and architectural treasures, its modern musical tradition, though lacking in originality, can make for entertaining evenings. Be prepared to hear scores of badly sung English-language covers. Florentines who go out to hear live music tend to gravitate toward jazz, blues, and folk, and the best places for quality tunes of this variety are Chiodo Fisso and Caffè La Torre. Most rock, hip-hop, and alternative bands play at BeBop, which has a virtual monopoly on the beer-drinking grunge groupie crowd. For up-to-date information on the latest gigs in the ever-changing music and club scene, pick up a copy of the biweekly *Zero55* at local music stores like **Music Center** and **Picadilly Sound** off of Via Cavour [see *stuff*, below, for both].

Since 1979, locals and tourists have been cramming the picnic benches of the centrally located **Chiodo Fisso** *(Via D. Alighieri 16r, two blocks south of the Duomo; Tel 055/238-12-90; 11am-2pm/8pm till late; No credit cards)* to listen to traditional and original Italian folk ditties played and sung by local talent. The handwritten menu changes based on what's in the kitchen, but they always have a nice selection of cheap sandwiches and pastas that'll fill ya up. Most drinks are a steep L10,000, but there's no cover.

On Thursdays, local guitar and blues performers hit the small stage of **Eskimo** *(Via de' Canacci 12r, 3 minutes south of the train station; 8pm-*

fIVE-O

While Italy's immaculately clad *caribinieri*—Italy's royal police force—are notorious for looking the other way, they are fairly strict about public drug consumption. It's not something anyone wants to be stopped for, 'cause it is definitely, no-question-about-it, illegal. Other than that, the cops are pretty laid-back in Florence.

3am daily; No credit cards) to the delight of the twenty-to thirtysomething crowd. The establishment, which moonlights as a cultural association, also hosts live Italian pop music (Fri-Sun), ethnic and Italian folk music (Mon), and readings (Wed). In the words of the bar's promo flyer, the space is "at the disposition of everybody who would like to show their photography, paintings, sculpture—for free." If you're in Florence long enough and you're looking for a gig, give it a shot.

Come early (10pm) or come late (1am)—you'll still have fun at **Caffè La Torre** *(Lungarno Cellini 65r, 10-minute walk west of the Ponte Vècchio, 15 from the Duomo; Tel 055/680-643; 8:30pm-5am daily; No credit cards).* Jazz, pop, rock, blues, and soul are uncorked night after night by talented artists with no cover, all out under the stars. After a few drinks, you'll be feeling the vibe and convinced that you were born to get up in front of the crowd and shake your groove thang, but don't tire yourself out too much—you have to walk home, you know. Nice place to bring a date, if you've got one.

While the main draw of the overtly cheesy "American-style" **Red Garter** [see *bar scene*, above], right near the Duomo, is the chance to mingle with a sweaty American crowd, the second-best attraction is watching tireless performers entertain the even more tireless college-age audience with mostly English and American pop and the occasional Broadway show tune. The full bar doesn't hurt, either.

The stuffy basement bar **BeBop** *(Via dei Servi 76r; Tel 055/239-65-44; Music starts 10-10:30pm, open 6pm-1am daily but erratic; No credit cards),* two blocks from the Duomo, is *the* place for the heady genius of the local metalheads, garage bands, and blues dudes. The brighter rooms in the back with picnic-table seating make it a little easier to carry on a conversation over the angst-ridden guitar progressions. There's no cover, which means steep drink prices—cocktails are L16,000—but you can get around that by splitting a bottle of wine for L30,000. The crowd is a mix of grungy locals and even grungier foreigners. The music ain't great, but it's a fun time.

Every Tuesday and Thursday, **Kikuya** [see *bar scene*, above] lets the best local cover bands wail away at their English song repertoire in its cramped and musty side room. The Americans in the audience love to sing along, especially after happy hour. The splintery-wood, fully stocked bar in the main room keeps the mix of American-European

florence bars, clubs and culture zoo

BARS/CLUBS ▲
Angie's Pub **30**
BeBop **20**
Cabiria Cafe **3**
Caffè La Torre **37**
Central Park **7**
Chiodo Fisso **25**
C.S.A. RK Indianò **5**
Dublin Pub **12**
Eskimo **10**
Full Up **29**
Kikuya **32**
La Dolce Vita **4**
Maracana **36**
Meccanò **6**
Public House **9**
The Red Garter **31**
Sant'Ambrogio Caffè **35**
Space Electronic **8**

CULTURE ZOO ●
Baptistery **21**
Bargello Museum **28**
Basilica di San Lorenzo **14**
Basilica di Santa Croce **33**
Basilica di Santa Maria Novella **11**
Boboli Gardens **1**
Casa Buonarroti **34**
Cathedral of Santa Maria
  del Fiore (Il Duomo) **22**
Gallerìa degli Uffizi (Uffizi Galleries) **26**
Galleria dell'Accademìa
  (Academy Gallery) **17**
Giotto's Bell Tower **23**
Hospital of the Innocents **18**
Medici Chapels **13**
Musèo Archeòlogico
  (Archeological Museum) **19**
Museo San Marco **16**
Museum of the Duomo **24**
Palazzo Medici-Riccardi **15**
Palazzo Vècchio **27**
Pitti Palace **2**

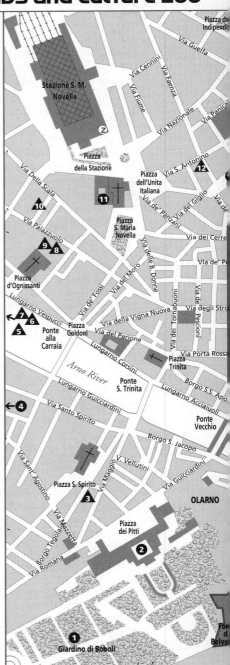

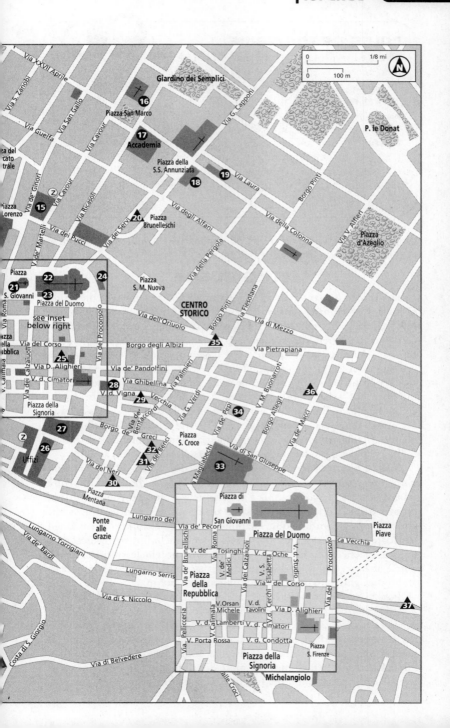

rules of the game

The age for drinking here is practically nonexistent, and you can pretty much go to any Florentine piazza and uncork a bottle of wine or beer. In fact, it's almost a cultural norm, especially on hot summer nights. If you don't get rowdy, you shouldn't have any problems (except for running out of booze too quickly). But except for clubs and large concerts and sporting venues, you're probably not gonna smell pot/hash fumes in the open air. This doesn't mean it never happens. Piazza San Spirito is reputedly the place where people snoop out buying ops. Needless to say, with jail time lurking as a possibility, care should be taken to avoid that other trip so brilliantly evoked by Dante....

tourists and locals in good spirits. The mood here is more hardcore than at the nearby teeny-bopperish Red Garter.

club scene

Italians love to dance, so naturally there are quite a few discos in the center of town. Unfortunately, many of these close during the summer, as townsfolk seek refuge from the heat in the large, open venues outside the city congestion (this is a trend all over Italy). If you're traveling during this period, it can be a bummer, but there are a few large outdoor dance arenas within walking distance of the center. Florentine clubs, though possessed by a major pop preoccupation, have the same mix of music—house, techno, hip-hop, '80s—that clubs everywhere share these days. The full range of clubdom is here, from punky and pierced to light and pop-y to sleek and exclusive. Clubs usually open between 10 and 11pm, with fashionable people arriving fashionably after midnight. Though Florence isn't known for its happening late-late-night scene, there's plenty of action around.

Space Electronic *(Via Palazzuolo 37; Tel 055/293-082; 10pm-2am daily, closed Mon in winter; L25,000 cover; V, MC, AE)*, west of *centro storico* near Via Palazzuolo, is a teenager's wet dream. You can drink, groove, drink, do karaoke, drink, hit on opposite sex, drink—just like you're a real, grown-up adult. Happily though, the club is large enough to accommodate a slightly older crowd as well, including many local men eager to practice their English (and more) with the female tourists. Playing a mix of American pop, disco, and alternative, this place, ultramodern and thoroughly hip, provides a lot of good, clean fun.

Publicized with omnipresent handouts and wall flyers, **Full Up** *(Via della Vigna Vecchia 23-25r; Tel 055/293-006; 11pm-4am Mon-Sat, closed June-Sept; No cover before midnight, L15,000 after; V, MC, AE)* is probably the most popular disco in the city center among foreigners. Digs are a bit more formal, and the music is somewhat more diverse and soulful than Space Electronic, which means a more discriminating and mature clientele. The piano bar is another big draw. If you don't want to venture outside the city, and still want to get a taste of Italian discos, this is probably your best option.

About 10 minutes west of the city center, near Viale degli Olmi, **Central Park** *(Via Fosso Macinante 2 at Parco delle Cascine; Tel 055/253-505; Bus 1, 9, 26, 27 to Parco delle Cascine; midnight-late Fri and Sat; L25,000 cover w/one drink)* is a slightly more upscale, slightly larger, just-as-popular version of its competitor, Meccanò, located across the street. Five outdoor dance floors and drinks stations keep the hordes of powdered twentysomething Florentines occupied till early morning. If you're important enough, then you can spend the evening in the exclusive, elevated V.I.P. section and literally "talk down" to the sweaty dancing serfs below. If you only want to dance, come late; the first hour or two, people like to just stand around in groups and check each other out.

Itching to dance the mambo? Wanna grind with a local? Get decked out in your cleanest, sexiest (preferably pressed) duds and check out **Maracana** *(Via Faenza 4r; Tel 055/210-298; Midnight-4am Tue-Sun, restaurant open 8:30-11:30pm, closed mid-June through Sept; L20,000 cover; MC, V)*, where you can funk to the Latin rhythms right in the center of town. The circular sunken dance floor invites shoulder-rubbing and table-dancing. When you get tired, there's ample seating, a huge bar, and a big video screen showing anything from Caribbean beach scenes to soccer matches to rock videos. On the way in or out, make sure to pay homage to the re-created Amazon jungle courtyard with an artificial creek and three very real, very loud peacocks.

If the dancing girls in high boots and low-cut dresses don't attract you to Florence's most renowned nightclub, **Meccanò** *(Viale degli Olmi 1; Tel 055/331-371; 11pm-6am Tue-Sat, restaurant 9:30pm-midnight; L20,000 cover w/one drink; AE, DC, EC, MC, V)*, about 10 minutes west of city center, then maybe the chance to sip martinis at the *Alice in Wonderland*–like table and chairs will. For those who aren't turned on by the dancing girls, there are also beefy dancing guys (sometimes dressed in chains) doing their best Chippendales renditions. Multiple dance floors—a couple indoors, a couple out—provide enough grooving options to keep even the headiest music snob happy, though Italians always seem to migrate toward mainstream pop.

If you're feeling adventurous and want to wear grungy clothes and slamdance to hardcore live music, **C.S.A. RK Indiano** *(Plaza dell'Indiano 1; Tel 055/307-210; Bus 17c to Piazzale J. Kennedy, then walk down Viale dell Indiano to the end; 10:30pm till whenever; L7,000 cover; No credit cards)*, the most active *centro sociale* in Florence, is your Shangri-La. While these "social centers" are technically illegal, they're usually overlooked by the fuzz, so you probably won't end up being deported. (Can't say we didn't warn you.) At Indiano, punk and rock bands fill up the large squatter space nightly with brain-splitting original tunes. The low entrance fees and economical drink prices (remember, these guys are communists) attract tattoos, dyed hairdos, and piercings worthy of the Lower East Side, Haight-Ashbury, and Venice Beach.

aRTS SCENE

▶▶VISUAL ARTS

It's understandable why modern visual arts in Florence have not advanced very far. It's just too damned intimidating living in the shadow of the great masters, going up against Michelangelo and Botticelli. There are, however, several modern art refuges—all in the city center—trying to make a difference.

A good place to start is Florence's premier modern art gallery, **Galleria Pananti** *(Piazza Santa Croce; Tel 055/244-931; 10am-7pm, ticket office closes at 6:30pm Mon-Sat; L12,000 admission, L10,000 students)*, east of the city center on Piazza Santa Croce. The museum-worthy exhibitions feature photography, paintings, prints, sculpture, and mixed media by Andy Warhol, Jackson Pollock, and other postmodern American masters.

A second stop is **Ken's Art Gallery** *(Via Lambertesca 15r-17r; Tel 055/239-65-87; 10am-8pm Mon-Sat; www.italink.com/kensgallery)*, where exhibits include an ever-intriguing rotation of large abstract canvases and figurative sculpture created by local and national artists.

Visit the unusual tandem galleries **Art Point Black** *(Borgo Allegri 14; Tel 055/247-97-97; 3:30-7:30pm Mon-Sat)*, showcasing abstract paintings, and **Art Point Red** *(Borgo Allegri 5)*, which specializes in figurative etchings and sculpture. Just a few blocks east of Santa Croce.

You can watch the artists paint colorful, eye-pleasing abstract canvases at the mom-and-pop **Art Studio Karan** *(Via Borgo Albizi 9; Open late mornings & afternoons daily)*.

Across Ponte alle Grazie, **Il Bisonte—International School of Specialization in Graphic Arts** *(Via San Niccolo 24r; Tel 055/234-25-85; www.ilbisonte.it)* often holds shows by the students; the large ceramics of **Akronos Gallery** *(Via dei Sapiti 18r; Tel 055/218-695; 11am-8pm Mon-Sat)* show a deep knowledge of art and fine craftsmanship.

▶▶PERFORMING ARTS

If you're looking for English-language film, theater, and classical music, you won't have trouble finding things that interest you here. Though Florence does not have as many city-sponsored events as Bologna or Rome, there's plenty to do, especially from June to September. The tourist offices [see *need to know*, below] have a ton of info on what's going on, as well as schedules for particular venues.

While most theaters feature American films, unless you know Italian, the dubbing makes it a little hard to *sapére*. To the relief of cineplexaholics, **Odeon Cinehall** *(Piazza Strozzi; Tel 055/214-068)* plays original-language films every Monday, and **Cinema Astro** *(Piazza San Simone, near Santa Croce; closed Mon)* shows English-language films every other night.

The church of **Orsanmichele** *(Via Calzaiuoli; Info 055/477-805, box office Via Faenza 139r; Tel 055/210-804)*, which plays host to the Flo-

FESTIVALS AND EVENTS

The biggest festival in Florence is the **Maggio Musicale Fiorentino** (*May-June; Biglietterìa Teatro Comunale; Corso Italia 16; Tel 055/211-158; 10am-4:30pm Tue-Fri, 9am-1pm Sat; www.maggiofiorentino.com*), now in its 62nd year. The festival presents an array of opera, dance, and classical music performances at the **Teatro Communale di Firenze**, **Teatro della Pergola**, and other venues in the city.

Dissolvenze (*June; Arena Estiva del Poggetto, Via M. Mercati 24b; Information at FLOG Centro Flog Tradizioni Popolari, Via Maestri del Lavoro 1; Tel 055/422-03-00; Tickets L8,000 per night*) is a cultural and ethnic festival featuring live music, dance, and film.

Mondo Culto! (*June-Sept; Information Tel 0339/726-37-32*) shows a series of "cult movies and incredible strange music."

On June 24, the city goes wild with **Festa di San Giovanni**, the celebration of Florence's patron saint. Parades and fireworks salute the angelic Saint John, and the crowds crunch onto the shores of the Arno. Another feature of the festival is the final match of the **Calcio Storico Fiorentino**—a competition exhibiting the medieval version of soccer played in a sandlot with small goals. Set in Piazza di Santa Croce, the spectator-filled bleachers become a rowdy foot-stomping exhibition of partisanship, chanting, and cheers. The intense action, with players diving in every direction in the sand pit, gives you a glimpse of how psychotically hard soccer was back in the day. Purchase tickets, usually around L15,000, at the box office on Via Faenza 139r (*Tel 055/210-804*).

rence Sinfonietta, is acoustically one of the best places to hear classical music—its Romanesque dome facilitates rich orchestral sounds.

Concerts of the Regional Tuscan Orchestra are often presented at **Santo Stefano al Ponte Vècchio**. Many other churches also have a regular schedule of free and low-cost concerts.

Teatro Communale di Firenze (*Corso Italia 16; Tel 055/211-158; Box office open 10am-4:30pm Tue-Fri, 9am-1pm Sat and one hour before curtain; Shows Oct-Apr; V, MC, AE, DC*) is Florence's main theater, with both opera and ballet seasons running from September to December and a concert season from January to April. Tickets cost L40,000 to L200,000 for the opera, L24,000 to L50,000 for the ballet, and L35,000 to L100,000 for concerts.

Teatro della Pergola (*Via della Pergola; Tel 055/247-96-51; Box office 9:30am-1pm/3:30-6:45pm Tue-Sat, 10am-noon Sun; Tickets L18,500-45,000*) and **Teatro Verdi** (*Via Ghibellina 99; Tel 055/212-*

320; Box office 10am-7pm Tue-Fri, 10am-1pm Sat; Tickets L10,000-35,000) also hold many theatrical and operatic performances. If you're interested in catching a show, stop by the theaters to obtain a program of the current offerings. While the Pergola is slightly larger, both theaters are elegant spaces with gold-trimmed columns and walls, excellent acoustics, and balconies.

gay scene

The gay scene in Florence is not as out as in Milan or Rome, but, save for a few stares, there should be no major problems. Still, use common-sense caution [see *hanging out*, above]. Strangely, for a city built on the glory of such Renaissance artists as Leonardo da Vinci and Michelangelo Buonarroti—both now thought to have been less than straight—there aren't many gay-oriented stores and clubs in town. In fact, the entire country's gay scene lags behind that of other Western nations. The reason for this may lie in the fact that relatively few Italians have had extensive travel experience, and a fiercely religious, and somewhat suffo-cating, patriarchal family dynamic remains rooted in the Italian culture. Even so, most youth-oriented bars and clubs have an open, casual atmos-phere that can be gay-friendly, even if they don't present themselves as gay establishments.

If you speak Italian, the local branch of the national organization **ArciGay/Lesbian** *(Via San Zanobi 54r; Tel 055/476-557)* is a good source of information on the city, gay life, and gay-friendly eateries. For more info, check out a copy of ***Quir***, Florence's bimonthly gay and lesbian magazine—available at ArciGay/Lesbian and newsstands, or ***www.dada.it/caffe/gay***.

The chic-est discopub in Florence, gay or otherwise, **Piccolo Café** *(Borgo Santa Croce 23r, right off Piazza Santa Croce; Tel 055/241-704; 5pm-late daily; No credit cards)* has neon and chrome accents and a stun-ning reflective, metallic ceiling, festooned with phallic light bulbs jutting out. Umm, what do you think? Though it opens at 5pm, the cute Italian boys (and girls) don't start showing up until 11pm. That's okay, 'cause they don't plan to go home early—and neither should you. Rotating art shows by gay and lesbian artists, live DJs. Drinks about L10,000.

Owned by the same proprietors as Tabasco Bar, the slightly softer **Tabasco Disco** *(Via dei Pandolfini 26r, 5 minutes southeast of the Duomo; People arrive 11:30pm and stay till late, daily; L15,000-25,000 cover w/one drink; No credit cards)* has only one tiny dark room and lets in women (many others don't), but that doesn't mean you can't get rau-cous. Monday nights there's cabaret and karaoke in the Flamingo Pub on the top floor, where they also have theme nights and videos playing music, movies, and porn from all over the world. Thursday through Sunday, DJs spin house, hip-hop, and techno, while on other nights they succumb to their fetishes with Madonna, Gloria Estefan, Natalie Imbruglia, and other girl pop-drops.

Hey boys, you looking for daaark rooooooms, for *molto* under-

SMOKE IT UP

Anti-smoking stalwarts are going to have a tough time in Florence (and the rest of Italy). For many Italians, smoking is as much a reflex as taking a cup or two of espresso after dinner, and people do it in all the public places: train stations, trains, airports, planes, buses (occasionally), and hotel lobbies. The thing is, Italians seem to smoke (as they do basically everything else) to *enjoy*—not to stay calm or deal with stress. It's a social custom, and they make it so natural, it's like they were born with a cig poised stylishly on their lips.

growwwnd, for a place to be lascivious and naughty? Let your libido romp at seedy **Tabasco Bar** *(To find this secret spot, from Piazza della Signorìa, with your back to Palazzo Vècchio, walk straight to Via Vacchereccia, then take a right on Vicolo Malespini, which heads into Piazza di Santa Cecilia; Tel 055/213-000; 10pm-6am Fri, Sat, till 4am other nights; L15,000 cover w/one drink; No credit cards)*, reputedly the oldest gay discobar in Italy. No girls are allowed, so there's no fear of cross-gender cruising mistakes, and you can cut loose. The irony is, it's only steps from Piazza Signorìa, yet straights, local or tourist, just don't know about it. Getting dressed up ain't that important, just gotta be gay and...oh, you know. Very hardcore.

The famous cruising skin bar **Crisco** *(Via San Egidio 43r; Tel 055/248-05-80; 9pm-3am Mon, Wed, Thur, Sun, till 5am Fri, Sat, closed Tue; No credit cards)* is the only match for Tabasco Bar, though it has a cleaner reputation and is slightly more upscale. Which may mean that you'll meet an Italian man with very deep pockets who will want to buy you and keep you for his very own. The clean dark rooms, tempting clientele, and gyrating tunes will keep your senses satiated.

La Vie en Rose *(Borgo Allegri 68r; Tel 055/245-860; Noon-3pm/7-11pm Mon-Sat; L10,000-22,000 per entree; No credit cards)* is a gay-friendly restaurant that is a great couples' place. Cozy, romantic, soft music, candles on the table—what could be better for a date? The nouveau-Italian dishes like risotto with fresh herbs (L10,000), asparagus and brie pie (L10,000), and fresh pasta with eggplant and cherry tomatoes (L12,000) are good on the stomach and the wallet. Rotating art exhibitions from local artists adorn the walls.

A number of hotels cater to the gay community, including the comfortable **Hotel Morandi alla Crocetta** *(Via Laura 50; Tel 055/234-47-47, Fax 055/248-09-54; L240,000 double; V, MC)* and the quiet, centrally located **Hotel Pensione Medici** *(Via de' Medici 6; Tel*

055/284-818, Fax 055/216-202; L200,000 double; V, MC). Both are simply decorated with medium-size rooms (most with full bath, TV, phone, and drinks bar) and serve continental breakfast.

One of the best places to relax and look at hunks is in the **Florence Bathhouse** *(Via Guelfa 93r; Tel 055/216-050; 2pm-1am Sun-Fri, 2pm-2am Sat, summer hours: 3pm-1am Sun-Fri, 3pm-2am Sat),* an exclusively gay sauna.

CULTURE ZOO

Towers and churches and frescoes and sculptures and about a billion Madonnas with Child: We've been salivating over the Renaissance-inspired masterpieces for centuries, and there's enough on every square block of Florence to keep you occupied for another century. There isn't much that hasn't been said except: Don't tire yourself out so much that you can't join in the late-night festivities. All of the following power-houses are within walking distance of each other.

12 hours in florence

1. Climb up the Duomo or Giotto's tower (don't fall off) to see stunning views of the red tile on the ancient city.

2. Eat gelati at **Gelatería Carabe** or **Vivoli** [see *gelati wars*, below]—miss this and you might as well not come.

3. Chill on the steps at San Spirito and Piazza della Signoría (*con vino*)—you'll never want to leave.

4. Browse the tombs in Santa Croce—be careful to not walk on the buried guys.

5. See the *David* at the **Accademía**—The dude is truly spell-binding—don't let the crowds bother you! [see *culture zoo*, below].

6. Club at **Full Up**, **Meccanò**, or **Central Park** [see *club scene*, above, for all three]—do it all in one night and spin with delight.

7. Eat at **Sabatino**, **Contadina**, or **Mercato Centrale** for must-eat, cheap Italian soul food [see *eats*, below, for all three].

8. Take a hike up Piazzale Michelangelo—super views of the Duomo, Santa Croce, and Ponte Vècchio will take you out of time.

9. Visit the Botticelli room in the **Uffizi**—take a seat and sali-vate at how ahead of his time Botticelli was [see *culture zoo*, below].

10. Shop at San Lorenzo market and in the shops on Via Tournabuoni and near the Duomo and Palazzo Vècchio—Prada, Gucci, Versace: Just save some money for dinner, Miss Trump.

Gallerìa degli Uffizi (Uffizi Galleries) *(Loggiato degli Uffizi; Tel 055/238-865; Bus 23, 71 to the Duomo; 8:30am-9pm Tue-Fri, till midnight Sat, till 8pm Sun, holidays, closed Mon; L12,000 admission):* Blow your mind. This famous Medici collection houses masterpiece after masterpiece, including da Vinci's *Annunciation*, Botticelli's *Birth of Venus* and *Primavera*, and *Venus of the Medici*, a 1st-century copy of the world-famous Greek sculpture.

Galleria dell'Accademìa (Academy Gallery) *(Via Ricasoli 60; Tel 055/238-86-09; Bus 1, 6, 7, 11, 33, 67, 68 to Via Alamanni; 8:30am-9pm Tue-Fri, till midnight Sat, till 8pm Sun, holidays, closed Mon; L12,000 admission):* Besides the colossal big-handed *David*, which was moved here in 1873 and is more striking than you can imagine, there's a bunch of other well-executed sculptures and paintings to check out.

The **Pitti Palace** and **Boboli Gardens** make up a massive multi-museum palace that is one of Europe's artistic treasure troves, housing the following: **Galleria Palatina (Palatine Gallery)** and **Royal Apartments** *(Palazzo Pitti; Tel 055/238-86-14; Bus D to Stazione galleria; 8:30am-9pm Tue-Fri, till midnight Sat, till 8pm Sun, holidays, closed Mon; L12,000 admission)*; **Galleria D'Arte Moderna e Galleria del Costume (Modern Art Gallery and Costume Gallery)** *(Palazzo Pitti; 8:30am-1:50pm daily; L12,000 admission)*; **Musèo degli Argenti (Silverware Museum)** *(Palazzo Pitti; Tel 055/238-87-10; 8:30am-1:50pm Tue-Sun, closed Mon; L4,000 admission)*; **Boboli Gardens** *(Piazza Pitti; Tel 055/265-171; 9am-6:30pm daily; L4,000 admission)*. Full of works by Titian, Rubens, Raphael, and Andrea del Sarto, the **Galleria Palatina** is the best-known. You can stroll through the courtyards for free.

Bargello Museum *(Via del Proconsolo 4; Tel 055/238-86-06; Bus 14, 23 to Via Alamanni; 8:30am-1:50pm Tue-Sun, closed Mon; L8,000 admission):* Dating from 1255, this fortress-turned-city-jail-with-torture-chamber now contains a bunch of important works, including sculptures by Michelangelo and Donatello.

Musèo San Marco *(Piazza San Marco 1; Tel 055/238-86-08; Bus 10, 11 to San Marco; 8:30am-1:50pm Tue-Sun, closed Mon; L8,000 admission):* The best things in this handsome palace are Fra Angelico's brilliant frescoes, altars, and panels, all of which will confirm that you are not worthy.

Cathedral of Santa Maria del Fiore (Il Duomo) *(Piazza del Duomo; Tel 055/230-28-85; Bus B, 14, 23, 36, 37, 71 to the Duomo; 10am-5pm Mon-Sat, 1-5pm Sun)*; **Cupola del Brunelleschi** *(8:30am-7pm Mon-Sat, closed Sun):* It's difficult to imagine Florence without Brunelleschi's support-free, red-tiled cupola blazing the skyline. A little sparse inside, but great views from the top. (Caution: Do not climb up into the spectacular Duomo when hung over. You'll regret it.)

Giotto's Bell Tower *(Piazza del Duomo; Tel 055/230-28-85; Bus B, 14, 23, 36, 37, 71 to the Duomo; 8:30am-4:50pm daily Apr-Sept, 9am-5:20pm daily Oct; 9am-4:20pm daily Nov-Mar, closed Jan 1, Easter, Sept,*

by foot

This walk, from **Piazzale Michelangelo** (*Bus 13 to Michelangelo*)—the Oltrarno square with picturesque views of the city—to the lovely **Piazza di Santo Spirito**, the nighttime outdoor hangout point for stylish university kids, is best from Thursday through Saturday, when all the locales are open for business.

Before you start, examine the beautiful vista. Santa Croce's right in front, the Duomo to the left, and the onion-domed Tempio Israeletico on the right. On a clear day, beyond the temple, in the camel hump formed by the rolling hills in the distance, you can make out Fiesole, a pretty town overlooking Florence. Go down the ramp, cross the road, and begin to make your way down through the terraced park. You should cross the road several times. At the bottom of the park, you will be at Piazza Giuseppe Poggi and in front of you will be the fine Poggi Tower. From there take a left on Via San Niccolo and head to **Mr. Jimmy's Bakery** [see *eats*, below], where you can fuel up on yummy American baked goods. Next, hang a right on Via dell'Olmo, then a left on Via dei Renai to the river, where you make a left toward the central city. Follow the river just past the Ponte Grazie and look across to the Florence Boating Club and mini-soccer field located on the grassy bank of the river. Dinner at the club is reputedly wonderful, but entrance is for members only. Continue to **Ponte Vècchio** [see *hanging out*, above], where you can inspect the jewelry stands, and then make a left on Via Guicciardini to Palazzo Pitti, a mega-museum with pretty **Boboli Gardens** [see *culture zoo*, above]. At Piazza San

Christmas; L10,000 admission): Awesome views atop Giotto's marble-coated tower, finished by Andrea Pisano. Worth the wait.

Baptistery (*Piazza del Duomo; Tel 055/230-28-85; Bus B, 14, 23, 36, 37, 71 to the Duomo; 8:30am-7pm Mon-Sat, till 1:30pm Sun, holidays; L5,000 admission):* Dating from the 11th and 12th centuries, this is the city's oldest structure. Its famous doors, the "Gates of Paradise," will make you cry.

Museum of the Duomo (*Piazza del Duomo 9; Tel 055/230-28-85; Bus B, 14, 23, 36, 37, 71 to the Duomo; closed at time of writing):* This museum contains sculptures removed from the Duomo and campanile including the original, restored *Gates of Paradise*, and an unfinished Michelangelo' *Pietà*.

The fresco-filled former residence of Cosmos Medici, **Palazzo Vècchio** (*Piazza della Signorìa; Tel 055/276-84-65; Bus 23, 71 to Piazza della Signorìa; 9am-7pm Mon-Wed, Fri, Sat, till 2pm Thur, 8am-1pm Sun, holidays; L10,000 admission)* has a 308-foot tower that can be seen from just about anywhere in Florence.

Felice take a left onto Via Mazzetta to the Piazza di Santo Spirito, where you can have a hard-earned drink at **Cabiria Cafe** [see *bar scene*, above].

This second tour brings you down one of the best shopping streets, Via del Corso, takes you to a series of bars, and leaves you off at Piazza della Signorìa. Start at about 5pm at **Festival del Gelato** [see *gelati wars*, below]. Buy a cone and start strolling down Via del Corso. You'll pass a number of men's and women's clothing stores as well as **Fiori dei Tempo** [see *stuff*, below], a great antique jewelry shop. Continue straight on Borgo d'Albizi (which is what Corso is now called) to Volta di San Piero, where you can snack on a delicious sandwich at **Antico Noe** [see *eats*, below]. From this first stop, continue on Borgo d'Albizi and make a right on Via Verdi. The ugly fascist Post Office building should be on your left and you should pass an *Agencia Ippica* (off-track betting) on the right: Don't do it! Continue on Via Verdi for several blocks till it turns into Via de Benci and you come to **Kikuya** [see *bar scene*, above]. Go in and have a drink. Next stop in at the **Red Garter** [see *bar scene*, above] and say hi to the American sightseers. Now continue on and make a right on Via de' Neri where you'll find **Angie's Pub** [see *bar scene*, above], which serves some pretty good bagels. Drop in for a final beer. If you want, stay for another, or head up the road to Piazza della Signorìa (it will be on your right) and rejoice in coming to the end of your journey.

Medici Chapels *(Piazza Madonna degli Aldobrandini 6; Tel 055/238-86-02; Bus 1, 6, 7, 11, 17, 33, 67, 68 to Piazza San Lorenzo; 8:30am-4:50pm Tue-Sat, till 1:50pm Sun, closed Mon; L13,000 admission):* The gaudy *Chapel of the Princes* and Michelangelo's solemn *New Sacristy* are the most popular draws to the Medici tombs.

An early Renaissance church designed by Brunelleschi and completed in 1426, the **Basilica di San Lorenzo** *(Piazza San Lorenzo; Tel 055/216-634; Bus 1, 6, 7, 11, 17, 33, 67, 68 to the Piazza; 7am-noon/3:30-6pm daily)* holds the *Old Sacristy*, a Brunelleschi marble work inspired by Donatello.

Palazzo Medici-Riccardi *(Via Cavour 1; Tel 055/276-03-40; Bus 1, 6, 7, 11, 17, 33, 67, 68 to Cavour; 9am-5:30pm, closed Mon; L6,000 admission):* Cosmos' home before relocating to the Palazzo Vècchio is a bastion of fiercely colorful frescoes.

The world's first hospital for orphans, **Hospital of the Innocents** *(Piazza della Santissima Annunziata 12; Tel 055/249-17-23; Bus 6, 31, 32 to the Piazza; 8am-4:30pm, closed Mon; L5,000 admission),* possesses a number of Botticellis, plus works by Luca della Robbia and Domenico Ghirlandaio.

The former palace that is now the **Musèo Archeològico (Archaeological Museum)** *(Via della Colonna 38; Tel 055/235-75; Bus 6, 31, 32 to Colonna; 9am-2pm Tue-Fri, till 2pm/9pm-midnight Sat, till 8pm Sun, closed Mon; L8,000 admission)* includes one of Europe's best Egyptian and Etruscan collections.

Basilica di Santa Maria Novella *(Piazza Santa Maria Novella; Tel 055/215-918; Bus 6, 9, 11, 36, 37, 68 to the Piazza):* Brunelleschi's wooden *Christ on the Cross* and the Ghirlandaio altar frescoes will keep your attention for quite a while in this often-overlooked church close to the train station.

Basilica di Santa Croce *(Piazza Santa Croce 16; Tel 055/244-619; Bus B, 13, 23 to Croce; 8am-12:30pm/3-5:45pm Oct-Easter, till 5:45pm Easter-Oct, till 1pm Sun, holidays; Free admission):* With tombs all over the place, including those of Michelangelo, Macchiavelli, Dante, and Galileo, this simple, beautiful church is a monument to dead geniuses.

Casa Buonarroti *(Via Guibellina 70; Tel 055/241-752; Bus 14 to Guibellina; 9:30am-1:30pm Wed-Mon, closed Tue; L12,000 admission):* Michelangelo bought this house for his nephew. Recently restored by the city, it now holds some of Michelangelo's fledgling sculptures as well as periodic exhibits of drawings and models.

modification

Unlike Bologna and Rome, Florence is not home to hordes of grunge and punk kids, so there aren't a lot of places to get the Florentine spin on body art. At the centrally located **Alchimista** *(Via dei Ginori 49r; Tel 055/268-305; 1-7:30pm Mon-Sat, but call ahead; No credit cards)*, the English-speaking tattoo artists will be more than willing to hip you up with original body designs.

great outdoors

In recent years, the Florentine footballers have become a feared and respected team capable of defeating perennial powerhouses Juventus of Turin and Inter of Milan. Florence's fans are equally as feared, commonly believed to be the rowdiest of Italian soccer hooligans. Tickets are available at the **Chiosco degli Sportivi** *(Via Anselmi, off Piazza della Repùbblica; Tel 055/292-363)* for as little at L30,000.

The congested nature of Florence's layout does not leave much green pasture. For grassy lawn to spread out on, go to the gardens near Fortezzo da Basso or **Boboli Gardens** [see *culture zoo*, above]. A good jog can be had by running west along the Arno, and you'll definitely get a workout hiking up to Piazzale Michelangelo [see *by foot*, above].

stuff

If your baggage isn't too heavy already, you can do well shopping in Florence, best known for hand-tooled leather goods and decorative paper and stationery. With a host of good outdoor markets led by the profusely leathery-smelling **Mercato di San Lorenzo** (*Piazza di San Lorenzo; 9am-7pm daily*), which specializes in belts, wallets, jackets, bags, jewelry, and ties, you will be able to find lots of interesting gifts.

The bohemian **Mercato La Loggia** (*Via dei Neri; 8am-7pm Thur-Sun*) has clothing, foreign handcrafted jewelry, and drums, while the market at **Sant'Ambrogio** (*Piazza Ghiberti, open weekday mornings and some afternoons*) is a pack rat's dream: Old books, light fixtures, postcards, and assorted household goods are hawked by the stall keepers. Remember, always bargain for a lower price when shopping at the markets. Many vendors will knock off 10 to 20 percent when they see you're interested (but not *too* interested).

▶▶LEATHER

For years, the very clever Santa Crocians have been making and selling beautiful handcrafted leather goods to foreign visitors through the **Scuolo del Cuoio** (*Piazza Santa Croce 16; Tel 055/244-533; 10:30am-12:30pm/3-6pm Mon-Sat Apr-Oct, 9am-12:30pm/3-6pm Sun; closed Mon Nov-Mar; leatherschool@leatherschool.it; AE, V, MC*). The bags and jackets are beautiful, but they are expensive, so you'll probably need to settle for crafty change purses or lipstick or cigar holders.

▶▶HOT COUTURE

If designer clothing is your thing, get your butt to Via Tournabuoni, home of the major boutiques such as Gucci and Ferragamo. There are also a lot of local shops you won't find elsewhere. For shoes galore, head to **Paoli** (*Via Calzaiuoli 21r; Tel 055/239-69-27; 10am-7:30pm, closed Sun; AE, V, MC*) or **Di Varese** (*Via Cerretani 49; No phone; 9am-1pm/4-7:30pm, closed Sun; AE, V, MC*). There's also a bunch of shoe and clothing stores along Via Nazionale and Via del Corso.

Even if you don't love hats, you'll have a ball trying on local designer Antonio Bramini's handmade inventions at **La Nuova Modistera** (*Via Chiara 15r; Tel 055/282-02-94; 10am-1pm/2:30-7:30pm daily; V, MC*).

▶▶THRIFT

For cheap, hip vintage boy and girl duds, **Used Clothing Store** (*Borgo Pinto 37r; No phone; 10am-6:30pm Tue-Sat; No credit cards*) is your answer.

▶▶GLAM

If you're looking for beauty aids, then makeup superstore **Profumeria Internazionale** (*Via Cavour 104r; Tel 055/239-69-61; 2:30-7:30pm Mon, 9:30am-7:30pm Tue-Sat, closed Sun; AE, V, MC*) will make you gape. Home to Christian Dior, Yves Saint-Laurent, Chanel, Clarins, and Helena Rubinstein products as well as lots of perfume and makeup samples. Look for the cellulite creams and tanning products not available in the U.S.

▶▶GIFTS

Since 1856, **Giulio Giannini e Figlio** (*Piazza Pitti 37r; Tel 055/212-621; 9:30am-7:30pm Mon-Sat, till 7pm low season Oct-Apr, closed Sun* *year-round; AE, V, MC)* have been handcrafting marbleized paper, greeting cards, and stationery.

The nifty notebooks, diaries, and other paper products at **La Tartaruga** *(Borgo Albizi 60r; Tel 055/234-08-45; 9am-7:30pm Tue-Sun, closed Mon morning, 10:30am-6pm last Sun of the month; No credit cards)* are made only from recycled paper.

You won't find just knickknacks at **Giraffa** *(Via de Ginori 20r; Tel 055/283-652; 9am-1pm/3:30-7:30pm Tue-Sat, closed Mon morning, Sun; V, MC)*, a unique store full of lava lamps, ceramics, scented candles, bags, key chains, planners, notebooks, bubble lamps, picture frames, soap, plastic inflatable furniture, and candle holders.

And finally, the mosaic-covered ceramics and lamps of **Frammenti** *(Via de' Pandolfini 11r; Tel 055/243-59-69; 10am-12:30pm/4-7:30pm, closed Sat in summer; No credit cards)* should not be missed.

▶▶BOUND

The Paperback Exchange *(Via Fiesolana 31r; Tel 055/247-81-54; 9am-7:30pm Mon-Fri, 10am-1pm/3:30-7:30pm Sat, closed Sun Apr-Oct, closed Mon Nov-Mar; papex@dada.it; V, MC, AE)* is absolutely the best English-language bookstore in Florence, boasting neatly arranged sections of books by Italian writers and books about Italy, as wells as mysteries, poetry, travel guides, romance novels, and philosophy. It also sells used books and is a good place to post notices and get information.

The English-owned **After Dark** *(Via del' Ginori 47r; Tel 055/294-203; 10am-2pm/3:30-7pm Mon-Sat, closed Sun; V, MC, AE)* also has some new and used English-language books, though it's better known for magazines.

The ubiquitous **Feltrinelli International** *(Via Cavour 12-20; Tel 055/219-524; www.vol.it/icone; V, MC, AE)* has a fair selection of both new releases and classics.

▶▶TUNES

Two of the best places to get used CDs and records are the **Music Center** *(Piazza Duomo 15a; Tel/Fax 055/211-538; 9am-7:30pm Mon-Sat, 11:30am-7:30pm Sun; AE, MC, V)* and the small, more relaxed **Picadilly Sound** *(Piazza San Marco 11; Tel 055/211-220; 9am-8pm Mon-Sat, closed Sun; V, MC, AE)*. Both stores carry the full range, from Coltrane to Britney Spears. But, sorry, no bootlegs.

€ats

Don't listen to anyone who says things like, "Florence has great museums, but the food isn't that great." If anybody says this, you have free license to knock them on the head. With an active university population, an endless flood of sightseers, and choosy locals who love fresh food, eating in Florence can be disappointing *only* if you settle for tourist dives. Otherwise, it should be top-notch. From bread to meats to pasta to fruits to vegetables, there's no reason here to settle for anything that isn't bursting with natural goodness.

Nightlife here begins with a late dinner, which winds its leisurely way through first and second courses, wine, dessert, espresso...add the casual service, and dinner can easily take an hour and a half, two hours, or more. Most spots are packed with large crowds around 8:30 or 9pm.

▶▶CHEAP

Tight budgeters will melt on entering **Mercato Centrale** *(Piazza di Mercato Centrale, next to San Lorenzo; 9am-7pm daily)*, a huge two-story fresh food market a short walk north from the Piazza del Duomo.

For the best bread and focaccia and good slices of pizza, go to **Il Fornaio** *(Via Faenza 39r; Tel 055/215-314; 8am-8pm daily; No credit cards)*, near the train station. They also specialize in cannolis, eclairs, tarts, pies, and cakes, for a morning or afternoon snack.

Gran Caffè San Marco *(Via Cavour 122; Tel 055/215-883; No credit cards)* prepares pizza in slices with bundles of different toppings a few blocks northeast of the city center near Piazza San Marco and Accademía. A quick take-out lunch of pasta or vegetables can be had at **Il Pirata** *(Via del' Ginori 56r; Tel 055/218-625; 9am-8pm Mon-Sat; L8,000 for a lunch's worth of pasta; No credit cards)* or **Chiaroscuro** *(Via del Corso 36r; Tel 055/214-247; No credit cards)*, both in the city center.

Since 1872, hordes of local workers have been coming up to Piazza del Mercato Centrale and crowding into **Nerbone** *(First floor of Mercato Centrale, make immediate left at Via S. Antonio entrance; 7am-7pm Mon-Sat; L6,000-12,000 per entree; No credit cards)* at lunchtime for sizzling, rich dishes of gnocchi, tagliatelle, sausage, or fried potatoes. Seating is across the way at communal booths. The food's so good you probably won't need to sit very long. One of Florence's secrets.

Imagine fresh rolls crammed with fresh meats, cheeses, and veggies. Think it'll taste good? *Duh.* A few steps from the Duomo, **Antico Noe** *(Volta di San Piero 6r; Tel 055/234-08-38; 8am-midnight, sandwiches till 9pm daily; closed Sat for two weeks in August; L6,000-10,000 per entree;*

gelati wars

If you're human, you'll succumb to at least one gelato (ice cream) a day. Though it's very good, **Vivoli** *(Via Isola delle Stinche 7; Tel 055/292-334)*, the most famous *gelatería* in Florence, doesn't have the best stuff. For that, go to the real gurus at **Gelatería Carabe** *(Via Ricalosi 60r; Tel 055/289-476; Open daily; No credit cards)* who bring a slightly sweeter, more robust Sicilian flair to their scoops. With over 60 flavors, **Festival del Gelato** *(Via del Corso 75r; Tel 055/294-386; Open daily; No credit cards)* easily wins the prize for most varieties. They're particularly strong on fresh fruit flavors such as pineapple, lemon, strawberry, and blackberry.

No credit cards), the best sandwich shop in Italy, has 17 panini on the menu to choose from, or you can get one custom-built just for you. The Vegetarian, with spinach, pepper, eggplant, mushrooms, and artichoke, is scrumptious, as is the turkey, brie, and sun-dried-tomato hero. Warning: Highly addictive.

The falafel sandwiches at **Il Nilo** *(Volta di San Piero 9r; No phone; Noon-midnight Mon-Sat; L6,000 per sandwich; No credit cards)* aren't award winning and neither are the gyros, but they are cheap, quick, and filling, and you can't find this sort of Middle Eastern takeout anywhere else in Florence. Across the vaultway from Antico Noe [see above].

Don't get **Trattorìa Sabatino** *(Borgo San Frediano 39r; Tel 055/284-625; L18,000 full meal w/wine, dessert; No credit cards)*, on the south side of the Arno over the Ponte alla Carraia, confused with the world-famous Sabatini's. Here, you'll sit next to strangers in a more traditional, communal setting decorated with mint-green walls and plastic tablecloths. The menu changes every day and offers some of the most delicious, economical grub in town. First courses are about L4,500 and seconds go between L5,000 and L8,000. It's patronized by lots of hungry blue-collar worker types who look like they don't have a woman at home to cook for them.

With paper and pencil, Florence's health-conscious write their orders down from the chalkboard menu at **Il Vegetariano** *(Via delle Ruote 30r; Tel 055/475-030; Lunch and dinner Tue-Fri, dinner only Sat, Sun, closed Mon; L12,000 fixed menu; No credit cards)* and anxiously await the big portions of seitan, pasta, and tofu. The lack of meat doesn't mean the dishes aren't rich and filling as hell. The desserts are downright ambrosial. Kind of a hike (north of city center), but worth it: The garden in the back is as cool, green, and crunchy as the friendly, left-leaning crowd. One of Florence's best.

There are very few things better than knowing that you can get a first course, a second course, and wine, and pay less than L18,000. With an awesome, prix-fixe menu, that's the case at **Trattorìa Contadina** *(Via Palazzuolo 69/71r; Tel 055/238-2673; 8-11pm Mon-Sat; L15,000 fixed menu; No credit cards)*. If you're staying in the center, it's well worth the 15-minute walk. If you're staying near the station, you'll probably become a regular.

With pastas at L7,000, *ribóllita* (a traditional Tuscan soup) at L5,000, most meats at L9,000, and lemon sorbet for L4,500, it's a no-brainer that by 9pm you've got to fight for a table at **Trattorìa La Casalingha** *(Via dei Michelozzi 9r; Tel 055/218-624; Noon-3pm/7-9:45pm Mon-Sat, closed Sun; V, MC, AE, DC)*, probably the Oltrarno restaurant most popular with sightseers. There's another location at Borgo Tegolaio 5r.

The teddy bear of a baker who owns **Mr. Jimmy's** *(Via San Niccolo 47, Oltrarno; Tel 055/248-09-99; 10am-8pm Thur-Sun; No credit cards)* is a savior for all the yearning-for-bagels backpackers. He's also a clever businessman. Besides bagels, he offers Rice Krispies treats, apple pie (extraordinary), carrot cake (tremendous), cheesecake, chocolate cake, chocolate-chip cookies, and an assortment of muffins. Mr. Jimmy even delivers, so you can have some American-style goodies sent to your hotel.

▶▶DO-ABLE

Despite its name—**Osteria dei Pazzi** (pazzi means crazies) *(Via dei Lavatori 3r; Tel 055/234-48-80; Noon-3pm/7-11pm; L12,000-20,000 per entree; No credit cards)*—you won't go bonkers eating their x-tra yummy pastas and quaffing their fine wines. In fact, with its large outdoor seating area, you're crazy not to try it out. Just to the east of the city center.

A longtime crowd-pleaser near the central market, **Cellini** *(Piazza del Mercato Centrale 17r; Tel 055/291-541; Noon-3pm/7:30-11pm Thur-Tue, closed Wed; L12,000; No credit cards)* has a fixed tourist menu with pasta/meat for L18,000 and brick-oven pizza from L8,000 to L14,000, making it great for afternoon or evening hunger pangs. Half-liter of wine is L6,000. The great piazza atmosphere is free.

▶▶SPLURGE

Locals and foreigners alike converge on **Il Barroccio** *(Via della Vigna Vecchia 31r; Tel 055/211-503; 7-11pm Thur-Tue, closed Wed; L24,000-35,000 per entree; AE, V, MC)*, a smallish, centrally located, elegant *trattorìa*, to sample traditional dishes like asparagus *alla parmigna*, and *pollo alla cacciatora*. The artichoke salad is served over a bed of *rucola* (arugula), a favorite green of the Italians. Pastas are a smart light-dinner option at L8,000 to L12,000. There's a good assortment of inexpensive wines, and the attentive wait staff is all smiles.

Weird name, weird water theme, weird little running fountain built into the translucent floor, and a weird-but-excellent mix of pastas, curries, grilled vegetables, and crêpes. The fun of the two-story **Hydra** *(Canto de' Nelli 38r; Tel 055/218-922; Noon-3pm/7:30-11pm; L20,000-40,000 per entree; AE, V, MC)*—besides the glowing blue ceilings—is that it doesn't fit into the common mold. The handiwork is the product of an imaginative local lady whose next idea is to move the restaurant upstairs and put a pizzeria downstairs. After dining here, a few blocks northeast of the Duomo, you can only wish her success.

crashing

With so much tourist fuss, Florence's hotel owners don't have to do much to attract visitors—usually an empty room that isn't astronomically priced will suffice. The result is that there are not many low-cost budget hotels (many *call* themselves budget), and it's almost impossible to get a single for under L54,000 or a double for under L145,000. The good news is that there are a ton of clean hostels and a few campgrounds full of groovy people. But even with this bounty, there are still times—generally between May and September—when there aren't enough beds to go around. Make reservations if you can, and definitely *don't* waltz into town late on a Friday or Saturday without a room, 'cause it might end up costing you a bundle.

▶▶CHEAP

The benefits of the congested, dusty **Camping Italiani e Stranieri** *(Viale Michelangelo 80; Tel 055/681-19-77, Fax 055/689-348; Bus 13 to Michelangelo; Check-in 7am-midnight; L13,000/person per night plus one-*

florence eats and crashing

EATS ◆
Antico Noe **23**
Cellini **13**
Gran Caffè San Marco **20**
Hydra **12**
Il Barroccio **25**
Il Nilo **22**
Il Vegetariano **15**
Mercato Centrale **14**
Nerbone **17**
Osteria dei Pazzi **24**
Trattorìa Contadina **1**
Trattorìa La Casalingha **6**
Trattorìa Sabatino **3**

CRASHING ▦
Accademìa **10**
Hotel Consigli **2**
Hotel Globus **11**
Hotel La Noce
 and Hotel Regine **18**
Hotel Le Cascine **9**
Il Perseo **19**
Institute Gould **5**
Ostello Archi Rossi **7**
Ostello Villa Camerata **21**
Pensione Pio X **4**
San Lorenzo **16**
Suore Oblato
 dello Spirito Santo **8**

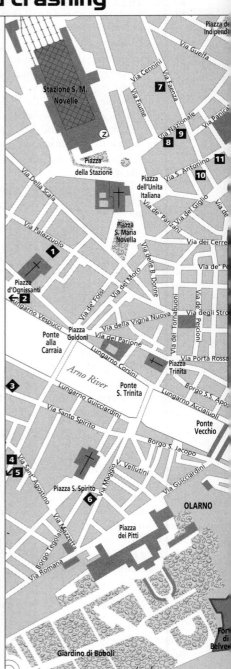

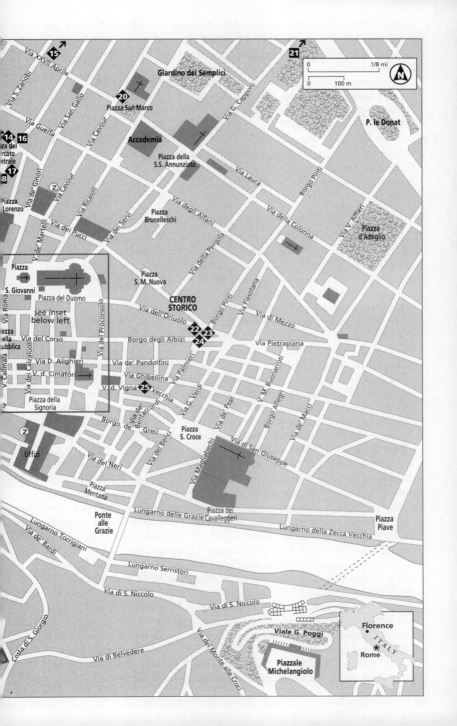

time L9,000 tent fee; No credit cards), a 10-minute walk southeast of the city center, are cheapness, great views, and camaraderie with other sweaty campers. The hot showers feel great, the toilets are kept admirably clean and de-scented, and it's only a short bus ride from the city center. Come early to grab a spot—there are always others itching to get in.

At **Institute Gould** *(Via dei Serragli 49; Tel 055/212-576, Fax 055/280-274; Office open 9am-1pm/3-7pm Mon-Fri, till 1pm Sat; L33,000 bed in quad, L48,000 single w/o bath, L72,000 double w/o bath, L105,000 triple; No credit cards)*, there are private baths, towels, clean sheets, no lockout, and no curfew. Call early to get a room—there is simply no better deal in town. In the west end of Oltrarno (about 15 minutes from the city center), Gould offers small, quaint rooms with clean, springy single beds. The bathrooms and showers are clean, too, but could use airing out.

Ostello Archi Rossi *(Via Faenza 94r, Tel 055/290-804, Fax 055/230-26-01; Lockout 11am-2:30pm; L24,000 low season, L27,000 high season; No credit cards)* is clean, smack in the city center, and fills up quickly. The self-service laundry (L10,000), cafe/bar, fax machine, and patio are added bonuses. There are 96 beds in rooms with three, four, five, six, or nine beds. Breakfast L4,000. Curfew 12:30am. Showers have good water pressure and stay hot.

Most rooms at **Pensione Pio X** *(Via dei Serragli 104-106r; Tel/Fax 055/225-044; L25,000 single, L22,000 double/triple, 2-day minimum stay; No credit cards)* are quads or quints and are clean. The generic, high-ceilinged rooms (54 beds total) don't fill up as quickly as some of the other hostels. Maybe it's because management keeps pretty good watch on things, maybe it's because of the midnight curfew, or maybe it's because it's slightly out of the way (a 15-minute walk west of center in Oltrarno). The bathrooms and showers are clean.

Depending on their mood, the sisters who preside over **Suore Oblato dello Spirito Santo** *(Via Nazionale 8; Tel/Fax 055/239-82-02; L30,000 single, L80,000 double, L90,000 triple; No credit cards)*, a short walk from the train station, may pretend that they don't run a pension at all, but persistence will show that they have a nice little business, right near the train station, going from June to September. Though rooms are technically for women, guys can get in if they play married couple with a girlfriend/girl friend. (An inexpensive ring purchased from a street vendor helps.) Two-night minimum stay, 11pm curfew.

If you can deal with the midnight curfew and the 30-minute bus ride and walk from the central train station, **Ostello Villa Camerata** *(Via Augusto Righi 4; Tel 055/601-451, Fax 055/601-300; Bus 17, ask the driver to stop at the hostel; Check-in 1-10:30pm, lockout 9am-2pm; L25,000 per bed; No credit cards)* and its verdant grounds are for you. Rooms have four, six, eight, 10, or 14 beds. Continental breakfast with croissant and coffee is included. If you want to go dirt cheap, the hostel also runs a campground. One-time tent fees are L8,000 per site plus L19,000 per person per night. Bathrooms and hot showers are available.

▶▶DO-ABLE

Most of the 23 rooms in the charming, gingerbread-ish **Hotel Globus** *(Via San Antonino 24b; Tel 055/211-062, Fax 055/239-62-25; L80,000 single w/shared bath, L110,000 double w/shared bath; hotel.globus@firen zealbergo.it; AE, V, MC)* have views of the Medici Chapel; some even have small balconies. The young couple running the place are helpful, speak English well, and are constantly thinking of new ways to attract young travelers to their nice little spot just a few minutes' walk from the train station. Their latest idea: Internet hookups in each room. Breakfast consists of eggs, cereal, pastries, yogurt, and coffee. High-season (May-Sept) and low-season (Oct-Apr) prices vary greatly, so try to negotiate.

One amiable man, Ivo, runs both **Hotel La Noce** and **Hotel Regine** *(Borgo La Noce 8; Tel 055/292-346, Fax 055/291-035; L110,000 single, L160,000 double; AE, V, MC)*, two budget-traveler-friendly lodges a few blocks north of the Duomo. Though the 18 quiet and tidy rooms look like dorm rooms with their small beds and particle-board desks, they're cooled by central air, which makes a huge difference in the summer. Continental breakfast with coffee and croissants is included, and soda can be bought in the lobby. High- and low-season prices vary by as much as L40,000. Clean, somewhat stuffy bathroom/showers.

Open since 1993, the centrally located **Il Perseo** *(Via Cerretani 1; Tel 055/212-504, Fax 055/288-377; L85,000 single w/o bath, L125,000 double w/o bath; hotel.perseo@dada.it; AE, V, MC)* is one of the best budget hotels in Florence. Aussie expat owner Louise is dripping with niceness and full of info about Florence and Tuscany. While many of their large fourth-story rooms have great views of the Duomo, a fifth-floor double has a nearly unadulterated vista of Brunelleschi's masterwork. The cheerfully decorated breakfast/lounge room is full of mags and travel guides, and all 19 rooms have ceiling or floor fans and telephones. Continental breakfast with coffee, cereal, croissants, toast, and jellies included. The only drawback: 7am church bells.

San Lorenzo *(Via Rosina 4; Tel/Fax 055/284-925; L70,000 single, L170,000 double; V, MC)* is small and quaint and so close to the bustling San Lorenzo market you can practically smell the leather stands. All eight rooms have showers, hair dryers, TVs, and telephones. Management will gladly make restaurant and tour bookings.

▶▶SPLURGE

In addition to having 16 neat, air-conditioned rooms, the three-star jewel **Accademìa** *(Via Faenza 7; Tel 055/293-451; L150,000 single, L220,000 double; AE, V, MC)* oozes character, as does its gregarious owner, Tea. She'll be quick to point out the painted wood ceilings, marble floors, crystal chandeliers, 14th-century fireplace, polished statues, and small outdoor seating area and garden. The only drawback is that the incredibly high ceilings create mini-echo chambers—ask for the large third-floor rooms where the effect is lessened. Continental breakfast with coffee, cereal/warm milk, croissants, toast, and jellies is included.

As host to an endless flow of travelers from all corners of the globe needing to get in touch with friends and family and set up travel plans, Florence has caught the Internet bug—more than any other Italian city. The Internet cafes in Florence are great meeting places, and they hold a wealth of local information, and can be cruisy for both foreigner on foreigner and foreigner on locals. *Note to guys*: If you've lost your nerve, this may be the best bet to make a local girl yours. Just lean over to the damsel's computer and tell her you like to use another Internet company. (If she uses Yahoo, say Hotmail; if she uses Hotmail, then Yahoo.) Then ask her if you can show her why, and edge over into her computer space and do your thing. You know...your *thing*, Casanova.

The centrally located **Mondial Net Firenze** *(Via de' Ginori 59r; Tel 055/265-75-84; 10am-10pm Mon-Sat, noon-4pm Sun; mondialnet@rtd.it)* is one of the most popular places with American university students and has a good message board.

@CyberOffice *(Via San Gallo 4r; Tel 055/211-103; L10,000 one hour, L5,000 half-hour; gheri.fiers@dada.it; V, MC)* is also a hit with foreign travelers, as is the ubiquitous, somewhat generic **Internet Train** *(Via dell'Oriuolo 25r; Tel 055/263-89-68; Via Guelfa 24, Tel 055/214-794; Borgo San Jacopo 30, Tel 055/265-79-35; www.fionline.it; all locations open daily till late)*.

The best deal in town is at the slightly out-of-the-way **Netik** *(Via dell'Angolo 65r, 10-15 minutes east of Duomo; Tel 055/242-645; 10am-8pm Mon-Sat; L6,000/hour)*. Coffee and soda are also served here.

Hotel Le Cascine *(Largo F.lli Alinari 15; Tel 055/211-066; L220,000 double w/bath; V, MC, AE)* has spacious and elegant Victorian rooms that look out onto a tranquil courtyard. Stall showers have easy-to-use temperature modulator, and all bathrooms have a hair dryer. Air-conditioning and TV provide added comforts. The (included) continental breakfast is served in a nook beside the reception area, where you gleefully watch the two-person staff juggle phone calls and serving duties. One of the best on this hotel-laden street.

Hotel Consigli *(Lungarno A. Vespucci; Tel 055/214-172, Fax 055/219-367; L150,000 single, L260,000 double; hconsigli@tin.it; AE, V, MC)* is a former Renaissance palace situated along the Arno that will make you feel miles away from the madness of the frenzied center. The vaulted and frescoed 25-foot ceilings and the splendid second-story rooms that open onto the terrace are so amazing that Tchaikovsky spent a year of his life boarding here, as a guest of then-owner Prince Demidoff, the First General of Peter the Great. The present owner loves to practice his English and swears that he's installing air conditioning soon. Continental breakfast included, though you can order an American-style breakfast with eggs/bacon/sausage for around L13,000. Sparkling-clean bathrooms have full tub. Free parking.

need to know

Currency Exchange Local currency is the **Italian lira (L)**. Banks have best rates; most are open 8:30am-1:30pm/2:30-3:45pm Mon-Fri. You can also exchange money at **Central Post Office**'s foreign exchange office *(V. Pellicceria 3; 8:15am-7pm Mon-Fri)*, in the heart of the city, or for no commission at the **Stazione Santa Maria Novella (S.M.N.)** [see below] *(8:20am-6:30pm Mon-Sat)*.

Tourist Information **Azienda Promozione Turistica** *(Via A. Manzoni 16; Tel 055/234-62-84, Fax 055/234-62-86; 8:30am-1:30pm Mon-Sat)*, near the train station; *(Via Cavour 1r, Tel 055/290-832, Fax 055/276-03-83; 8:15am-7:15pm Mon-Sat, till 1:45pm Sun)*, a few blocks northeast of the Duomo; or *(Borgo Santa Croce 29r; Tel 055/234-04-44; 8:30am-7:15pm Mon-Sat, till 1:45pm Sun, holidays)*, near the Piazza San Croce. The student travel organization **CTS** *(Via de' Ginori 25r; Tel 055/216-660; 9:30am-1:30pm/2:30-6pm Mon-Fri, till 12:30pm Sat)*, in the city center, helps out with reservations, tickets, maps, and advice.

Public Transportatio Florence's orange buses are operated by **ATC**. Tickets *(L1,500, 24-hr pass L6,000)* may be purchased at *tabacchi*; most buses run only until midnight or 1am. The bus station is located at **Piazza della Stazione** *(Tel 055/565-02-22)*, behind the train station. **ATC Information:** *055/56501*.

Bike/Car Rental Alinari *(Via Guelfa 85r; Tel 055/280-500; 9am-1pm/3-7:30pm Mon-Sat Nov-Apr, plus 10am-1pm/3-7:30pm Sun, Mar-Oct only)* rents both bikes and scooters. Must be over 18 with passport, driver's license, and valid credit card. **Avis** *(Borgo Ognissanti 128r; Tel 055/213-629)*, Budget *(Via Finiguerra 31r; Tel 055/287-161)*, and **Hertz** *(Amerigo Vespucci Airport; Tel 055/307-370)* will rent you cars.

American Express *(Via Dante Alighieri 20-22r; Tel 055/50981; 9am-5:30pm Mon-Fri, till 12:30pm Sat)*.

Health and Emergency **General Hospital of Santa Maria Nuova** *(Piazza Santa Maria Nuova 1; Tel 055/275-81; Bus 6 to the Duomo and walk 3 blocks east)* is open 24-7, and you can always find *someone* who speaks English.

Pharmacies **Farmacìa Comunale** *(Inside Stazione Santa Maria Novella; Tel 055/216-761)* or **Farmacìa Molteni** *(Via Calzaiuoli 7r; Tel 055/215-472)*, open 24 hrs.

Telephone City code: *055*. See Milan chapter for general telephone information.

Airports Galileo Galilei Airport *(Tel 050/500-707)* is in Pisa, 58 miles west of Florence. No direct flights to United States. **Shuttle train** every hour or two (10 or 11am to 5 or 6pm) between airport and Stazione Santa Maria Novella, L8,000 one-way. **Amerigo Vespucci Airport** *(Tel 055/373-498)* is three miles northwest of the city. **Florence Bus 62** runs between airport and Santa Maria Novella station every 20 minutes, L1,500.

Airlines Alitalia *(Lungarno degli Acciaiuoli 10-12; Tel 055/278-81)*, **Air France** *(Borgo SS. Apostoli 9; Tel 055/284-304)*, **TWA** *(Via dei Vecchietti 4; Tel 055/284-691)*.

Trains Stazione Santa Maria Novella (S.M.N.) *(Piazza della Stazione; Tel 01478/880-88)* offers fee-based hotel booking service (8:45am-8pm daily), **24-hr luggage storage** *(at Track 16, L5,000/12 hrs.)*, and a **Eurail Aid Office** *(8am-noon/3-6pm)*.

Laundry You wanna dry or you wanna go? **Wash and Dry** has seven locations, including *Via dei Servi 105r, Via della Scala 52-54r,* and *Via Ghibellina 143r.* Hours for all are 8am-10pm daily, last wash at 9pm. There's also **Wash & Go** *(Via Faenza 26r; 8am-10pm; L6,000 wash, L6,000 dry).*

rome

In *Fellini's Roma*—a lesser-known '70s must-see by the *La Dolce Vita* man himself—horrific modern traffic jams and ancient ruins play together in a way that just nails the spirit of this multi-layered city. So multi-layered, in fact, that when you party (or do anything else) here, you'll rarely lose sight of the fact that you're doing it on top of 3,000 years of history—much of which is still staring you in the face. The dichotomies here keep coming at you: ubiquitous cell phones and the Coliseum; the old-school ladies in black cardigans who think Madonna is the devil and the kids shooting by on their Vespas; the sophisticated international clerical community that runs Vatican City and the hedonistic club-goers who pile into Alpheus every Saturday night. The center of Rome is a near-inbred Mediterranean beehive of a town, yet it's also one of the most international and cosmopolitan spots on earth, and the hub of a huge exurban sprawl. During the day the city is teeming with people, local and tourist alike, but if you walk here at night you can let the watery echo of the fountains lead you from one beautiful, empty piazza to the next. In other words, just when you think you've got this place down, well, try again.

It helps that in general temperament, Romans are not unlike New Yorkers: They like to hear themselves talk, they can be a bit gruff and imposing at first glance—and underneath it all they're much nicer and more welcoming than you could have guessed. In other words, don't be surprised if at one point while you're in Rome, some drunken local grabs you in the bathroom of a bar and demands: "American?! Ah, New York? San Francisco? Los Angeles?" and invites you to come hang out with him and his friends. Go to Rome with this in mind: You are welcome here.

This really is a city that is ready and willing to grant you plenty of conversation, drink, dancing, and great meals.

Young Italians in general—and, it seems, Romans in particular—really like their pleasures, and like them most nights of the week. And the concept of "recreational" drug use actually exists in Rome. While the law is sort of wishy-washy [see *rules of the game*, below], for the most part it doesn't paint dabblers as criminals. Also, romance (read: sex) is treated with a bit more levity and less hysteria than, for example, the American there-is-no-such-thing-as-safe-sex! cultural message. And while Rome's gay and lesbian scene may not be as in-your-face (or even as visible) as the scene in, say, San Francisco or New York's Chelsea, it is also sophisticated and offers a lot of variety.

Rome could be the poster-child city for this book—it is truly one of the easier cities in which to instantly gain access to a memorably good time. Roman pop/party culture has its own flavor and style—it is energetic, outgoing, and, for the most part, lacks the nastiness and random exclusivity that a lot of big city scenes are laced with. Why? Maybe it's 'cause clubs and party promoters show a lot of talent for mixing it up, bringing in influences from all over, and constantly throwing out a variety of new themes and ideas that keep staleness and cliqueishness at bay. Maybe it's because there are a bunch of active and productive politically/socially based groups run by young partying kinds of people in Rome. Here, the Young Democrats Club isn't a bunch of aggressive yuppies, but rather a group of fun twentysomethings who sponsor clubs that promote their political views. And we're not talking debate clubs, or some geeked-out function with chips and dip and hard plastic chairs—we're talking *nightclubs*. Their attitude seems to be, hey, we'd like to have a party and go a little crazy so we might as well benefit a good cause while we're doing it. It's pretty doubtful that the crowd at **Brancaleone** or any of the other activist-minded social clubs [see *club scene*, below] has a *complete* grasp on the status of the latest UN peace talks, but hell, they'll throw in a little donation and give a shout out to the refugees of war (and so should you!). Their hearts are in the right place, and it makes a big difference.

And if you think other European cities are great for people-spying and general ogling, forget about it, Rome wins hands down. There are an inordinate number of attractive people here, blessed with good looks *and* great clothes and style. Unless you want to feel really unhip while in Rome, leave the sweatpants, ratty sweaters, and backpack at the hostel, and don't feel shy about slapping on some cool, dark sunglasses like you know you want to.

And before you arrive, try to get at least a little experience on a motorbike (not a Harley—think less power and chrome) so that you can do like the Romans do for a while. Nothing can compare with the rush of driving a motorbike when in Rome (the bus sure can't). You can zoom around these streets, pretending to race other people (*pretending*), coming up on beautiful white palaces and the glimmering water of the Tiber

12 hours in rome

1. Eat a pizza—the kind made out of two pieces of focaccia with different stuff in between, like artichokes and tuna in a creamy sauce or sun-dried tomatoes and prosciutto. You'll never even look at nasty Domino's again.

2. If it's nighttime, go for a walk along the Tevere River, cross the bridges, stroll, get lost.

3. If it's daytime, get a motorbike, look around for a mountain, ride to the top, and get a view of the whole city.

4. Eat gelato, and lots of it. Try every kind you can in small portions—amaretto, pistachio, hazelnut—and try them at different places so you can compare.

5. Go to the **Pantheon** [see *culture zoo*, below]; feel your mind expand.

6. Wander around **Vatican City** [see *Vatican Museum* in *culture zoo*, below]. No matter who your god is, it's a trip—and truly beautiful.

7. Go to **Campo de' Fiori** [see *neighborhoods*, below] at night, drink red wine until you feel really relaxed, and ask one of the strolling musicians to play you a bawdy love song.

8. Go have a sword fight with one of the gladiators at the **Foro Romano** *(Metro Line B to Colosseo)*. You can get your picture taken with them, and if you're a girl, they'll tell you your mama made you better than Michelangelo could have.

9. Make like Audrey Hepburn: Eat a chocolate bread and drink coffee while spying the display windows of all the super-beautiful, outlandishly expensive clothing stores.

10. Hang out at a cafe: Drink espresso, try to decipher the newspaper, watch couples have heated arguments at neighboring tables (*always* interesting), listen to a soccer match on the radio....

(Tevere) River at night...*aaahh*. The cost is actually not so bad if you get a cheap bike (you don't need the shiny, spanking-new Vespa) [see *need to know*, below]. Every young Italian person knows that motorbikes are really the best way to get around the city, so it's also a great way to check people out, get checked out, flirt at the gas station, etc. Gas is fairly cheap, and, being so light, scooters get good mileage. Feel free to ask the attendant for help if you need it—don't laugh, scooters are tricky little buggers. Plus the good clubs and bars are all spaced pretty far apart, so if you want the freedom to really get around at night, a bike can be key. Oh, and

only here

Okay, so you want to see something really amazing that you can't see anywhere else in the world? This is something out of a fairy tale, a perfect, beautiful view of St. Peter's Basilica, through a keyhole. But I'm not giving it away: If you want to see this one you've got to go work for it—ask around, you'll find someone who knows where it is. If it's given away, everyone would go, and then it wouldn't be so special....

Then there's the *piazzardone*, the last of his kind in Rome. He stands on a little circle platform in the middle of a crazy intersection in front of Piazza Venezia directing traffic. Wearing a big black coat, pristine white gloves, and a little white cap, and twirling his arms and hands all around, he kind of looks like Mickey Mouse in *Fantasia*.

apparently there are actual traffic laws in Rome, although to the untrained eye it looks like total freakin' chaos. Everyone seems to be doing whatever he or she wants—weaving in between cars, driving the wrong way down one-way streets. Still, keep an eye out for cops. If a bike's not in the budget, or just not your thing, the next-best way to get around is, obviously, to walk—and for those out-of-the-way clubs, the subway is a great, reliable way to go.

Most people here don't speak fluent English—many speak or at least understand a moderate amount, but a lot speak absolutely none, so there's going to be confusion or at least some challenge if you speak no Italian. But folks are real nice about it and they won't make you feel stupid if you try, even if your accent tears the hell out of their beautiful language *and* they have no clue what you're trying to say. Most people genuinely appreciate the fact that you're making an attempt—especially if you smile while you're doing it. In places like the hospital, police station, or the AMEX office, there's always somebody who speaks English, so don't freak out if you have a serious problem.

There are a few local magazine/newspaper-type things that you can check to see what's up if you're gonna be shy about it and not just ask around. They're all in Italian, but hey, "Can you translate this for me?" is a great opening pickup line....*Roma C'e* is a good one to try. Another is *Il Manifesto*, the official daily of the Italian Communist Party. Its weekly supplement, *Alias*, which you can get at most newspaper stands, contains kind of modern arty/intellectual stuff, i.e., articles about Van Gogh right next to an in-depth analysis on the theoretical significance of hip-hop. *Trova Roma*, the weekly supplement to the paper *La Repùbblica*, is another source for art shows and music performances, film festivals, dinner places, and various other entertaining whatnots. These papers can be helpful, but remember, results may vary. The "hot" party you read about may end up being nothing but weak music and a couple of stiffs; the "cutting-edge" modern art exhibit might be some guy in body paint spanking himself.

If you want to avoid flocks of tourists, schedule your trip in a non-summer month, when there are fewer tourists and better rates for hotels. The last two weeks of August are an especially bad time to be here—aside from being incredibly hot and crowded, it's also when most Romans take off for their own vacations.

No matter when you come, there's one Roman tradition you have to follow: You've got to throw a penny into a fountain (traditionally the Trevi, but your own pick will do just fine). You're supposed to stand with your back to the fountain and chuck it over your shoulder. There are about six gazillion fountains in Rome—which may actually shock you on your first couple of nights here just by being so awfully pretty—so it's not exactly a difficult tradition to carry out. Supposedly once you do this, it's guaranteed that you'll return to the city one day before you die. Lucky you.

neighborhoods

In a nutshell, you've got a city surrounded by what used to be a big wall (most has crumbled at this point), the Great Aurelian Wall, and divided by a big river, the **Tiber River** (Fiume Tevere). On the west side, you've got **Vatican City** and all of its great museums [see *culture zoo*, below], and, southeast of all that, a working-class city neighborhood called **Trastevere** that's fun to hang out in, with great bars and music spots and a generally laid-back vibe. Over on the east side of the river is where most of the action, as well as most of **ancient Rome**, lies. **Vìa del Corso**, or Il Corso, which runs north-south from the **Piazza del Popolo** to the Victor Emmanuel monument, should be your main point of reference. Starting from the Vittorio Emanuele monument, the major road going west is Corso Vittorio Emanuele. To the east of the monument, running toward the **Coliseum**, is Vìa dei Fori Imperiale. Vìa Nazionale runs from in front of the monument toward the **Termini** (train station), out on the eastern edge of the city, where you'll find a bunch of late-night spots, especially around the **Piazza della Repùbblica**. The **Spanish Steps** and the big shopping streets that surround it are at the north end of the city, a few blocks southeast of Piazza del Popolo. Ancient Rome is down at the south end of the city, starting a few blocks after Vìa del Corso ends. **Campo de' Fiori** [see *hanging out*, below], where fun young locals come to hang out, is west of Vìa del Corso, northwest of ancient Rome. At its north end is Piazza Navona, a great lounging and people-watching spot, and a few blocks east of that is the **Pantheon** [see *culture zoo*, below]. At the south end of ancient Rome is the **Piramide** area, where you'll find many clubs and bars. At the west end of Campo de' Fiori is the old Jewish ghetto.

Rome is a big, modern city, and while random crime is not a huge problem, and the weapons laws and regulations are some of the toughest, it does happen. The common sense that applies to hanging out in all cities applies here: Walk with friends or take a cab at night, and if someplace gives you an unsafe feeling, get out of there. The buses and Metro system are okay—they're not that hard to figure out, and there are night buses that keep running on the main roads *all* night [see *need to know*, below].

hanging out

Rome is host to a seemingly infinite number of hang-out spots, which makes meeting people just a matter of getting out and exploring. And it's great for your travel budget too—hanging out in a square won't cost you anything. Clubs, bars and such, on the other hand, while not exorbitant, can be a bit pricey, especially once you start drinking.

After the airport, the train, the bus, the hotel, yadda-yadda, you'll probably need a drink or six. A nice, relaxed-yet-lively, non-intimidating area for your first night is **Campo de' Fiori.** The crowd is mainly 25- to 35-year-olds, and everyone is drinking (beer or wine or coffee) and talking. This is a popular place for locals to meet up in smallish groups to mingle on the cobblestones before or after going to a club or party or to a friend's house. To whom it may concern: Skinny heels are not recom-

five things to talk to a local about

1. **Movies:** Go educate yourself at a video store before you go: *8 1/2*, *Umberto D.* (get ready to cut your wrists, but still incredible), and *Big Deal on Madonna Street* are all good places to start.

2. **Politics:** Anything but Italian issues, which no one seems willing to discuss other than to say that every politician in Italy is corrupt.

3. **Soccer:** Try to feel out what team they're for before you make any keen observations about the season.

4. **How beautiful their country is:** Italians already know it, but they really like talking about it, recommending places to go, things you must experience, delicious things to eat that you can only get in Rome, etc.

5. **Learn some Italian:** Give it a shot! It's not like you can learn the language in a single conversation, but you can pick up some funny phrases that you won't find in books, like a special saying for good luck, something about a wolf's mouth, I think....

mended here. (Actually that's a good note for the whole city—there are cobblestones everywhere, even in random bathrooms(!), so unless you want to break your ass in public, wear thick heels or platforms.) The majority of people are young, white-collar professionals who are younger, trendier, and more easy-outgoing than the kind of person that comes to mind when you hear "young white-collar professional" in other cities. If you're a club kid or have some unresolved angst, you'll still like it here, and you'll find people like yourself to hang out with. There's always at least a couple of little crews of visor-wearing kids in elephant pants, chicks with fit-and-flares and pink lipstick, and punk-rockers and squatters. Even if you don't find the Italian version of your hometown posse, it's a great place to just bliss out, talk with friends, and get loaded. There are a few wine bars, which sound fancier than they are, with some indoor seating, really crowded standing room, and outdoor seating for about 40—plus you can take your wine out into the square and soak up the fresh air.

If you're still goin' strong at 7am, stop by **Café Renault** [see *bar scene*, below] near ancient Rome. It's a great after-after spot, with DJ Pierandrea the Professor spinning everything from jazz to house at the bar. And if you're finally ready to feed your body something solid, you can grab a small breakfast of pastry, fresh orange juice, and espresso at the cafe.

Also good for lolling around at night is the Trastevere's **Piazza di Santa Maria**. It's really crowded during the day, especially in summer, but can be mellow and relaxing at night, with lots of little cafes around and a mix of people young, old, and in between. Also, people love flopping on the Spanish Steps at all hours—during the day it's completely glutted with tourists; at night it's a bit more chilled-out and quiet, with lots of teenagers and early-twenties people just hanging out, flitting around. **Piazza San Lorenzo**, in the heart of the city, is another good spot, with some really good cafes and plenty of room to just kick it, the occasional chick strumming a guitar, circles of kids hacking—you get the idea.

bar scene

No beer funnels, brawling, or throwing your bra at the bartender here—generally bars in Rome are pretty mellow. That is, unless one of the local football teams just won a really important game, and even then only if the bar is overrun with fans. Sometimes you get singing, shouting, big toasts, the occasional argument...but not often. The vibe is largely social but not cruisy, most folks relaxing with whomever they came in with or else striking up conversations with people at nearby tables, and the bartenders tend to be non-snotty.

Café Renault *(Via Nazionale 183 B; Tel 06/47-82-44-52, 06/47-82-45-48; Metro Line A to Repùbblica; 7am-2am daily; www.caferenault.com, info@caferenault.com; No credit cards)* is housed in what used to be a Renault car dealership (a few blocks north of ancient Rome), which explains the car in the cafe part downstairs. The wide-open and well-lit space has a polished, modern look, with high ceilings, glass surfaces, lots of black and steel/chrome detail, which is refreshing if you've been exploring Rome's more traditional bars and restaurants and are craving something modern. There's a bar, a cafe, and, at the top of a twisty metal staircase, a restaurant; all are a bit pricey but not outrageous. It's great for people-spying late at night, when the crowd is kind of trendy and appealing, and you can sip a drink and space out on the little objects "floating" in your table. Is it your eyes or the table playing tricks? That should keep you busy until you get your order.

If you've managed to get a wink of sleep and are ready to get started early, or need to break up that day of sightseeing, go have a couple midday drinks at the rooftop restaurant at **Hotel Forum** *(Via Tor De' Conti 25, Fori Imperiali; Tel 06/679-24-46; Metro Line B to Colosseo; 12:30pm-3pm/7:30pm-1am Mon-Sat; L25,000-60,000 per entree; forum@venere.it; AE, V, MC, DC)*. Sitting at a shaded table with a cool breeze blowing, a perfect view of the Foro Romano (Roman Forum) in front of you, and people zipping by on Via dei Fori Imperiali, it's kind of hard to leave. And who cares—it's even more gorgeous at sunset.

If you just want a nice drink before bed, try **Bar del Fico** *(Piazza del Fico; Tel 06/686-52-05; Metro Line A or Bus 95, 490, 495 to Flaminio; 9-2am Mon-Sat, noon-2am Sun; No credit cards)*, set on a quiet little street near the Piazza del Popolo, which manages to be active yet somehow still calming and comfy. Take all the time you like to drink a good glass of wine (L5,000-12,000) and soak up the night under the canopy of trees at one of the several small outdoor tables. Inside is cozy too, with marble, brass, candles, a nice, well-stocked bar, and a few tables. All kinds of people come and go from this place—young couples, families, friends—and the staff is very relaxed and sweet.

A great spot for that calming first drink in a new city—it's not intimidating, because all the employees speak your language—is the Campo de' Fiori's **St. Andrew's Pub** *(Via della Cancelleria 36; Tel 06/683-26-38; Bus 116; 7pm-3am daily; No credit cards)*, a lively, casual pub in the Scottish tradition that's a popular local hang. They serve pretty standard pub food—burgers and such—but also some simple Roman dishes like panini and other starters, plus tasty crêpes...a good place to check out if you start to tire of Italian food. The prices are fair, from L3,500 for some small fried-fish dish to L12,000 for a good-size burger. The crowd ranges in age and is mostly locals and expats or traveling Americans, Scots, and Irish.

Another good place to hang if you long to hear a language you understand is **The Drunken Ship** *(Campo de' Fiori 20-21; Tel 06/68-30-05-35; Bus 60, 64, 116; 5pm-2am daily, happy hour 5-9pm; www.drunken ship.com; V, MC, AE)*, in the Campo de' Fiori. Active—no, *packed*—at night, this place has a friendly bar staff and a gregarious crowd that spills outside on nice nights. They play American music, have drink specials every night, and offer student discounts (bust out that unflattering ID card!). Stays pretty happening until about 2am.

LIVE MUSIC SCENE

Although live music in Rome is generally not terribly original or exciting (that's the consensus even among Romans), some venues do manage to bring in cool acts. Trastevere is a good neighborhood for strolling around looking for random bars and places with live music, or the kind of combination places that play music but are really about conversation, meeting, and hanging out. Besides the places listed below, you can also intermittently find great live music at several clubs, like **Radio Londra** and **Brancaleone** [see *club scene*, below, for both].

Among the best of the live-music venues is Trastevere's **Big Mama** *(Vicolo San Francesco a Ripa 18; Tel 06/581-25-51; Tram 8 to Viale Trastevere; 9:30pm-1:30am daily Oct-June; Usually free or L20,000-30,000 cover for biggish shows, plus L20,000 membership card; www.nexus.it/bigmama; No credit cards)*, a down-to-earth place frequented by a more mature (late-twenties to mid-thirties) but very hospitable crowd. Blues, jazz, and some funk comes to this dimly lit club—they play really good music of all sorts between live sets, too. Lots of tables are cluttered in front of the stage, plus a few more spread out off to the sides in case you want to breathe. A popular place, well liked by the locals. Feel comfortable to dress up or down. Call or go by and get a schedule for show times.

Near the Piazza del Popolo, **Il Locale** *(Vicolo del Fico 3; Tel 06/687-90-75; Metro Line A to Flaminio; 10pm-3am daily, closed June-Sept 15; L10,000 cover; www.il-locale.com; No credit cards)* hosts what are considered the best local bands and is almost exclusively full of people who actually live in Rome ("Romans" sounds like history class). Think American rock 'n' roll bar, only not so predictable—there's pop/rock, grunge/alternative, funk, disco, electronica, riot grrrl rock, dance/house, and every other modern music mutation you can think of. Sometimes in English, sometimes Italian, depends on the band. The crowd ranges all over; club kids, divas, army-fatigue-ripped-T-shirt-wearing-unshavens, tomboy lesbians—wear whatever you want and feel welcome. Almost all of the gigs that show up are

ragazzo meets piccola

We've all seen it in the movies: Some young, slightly bumbling, would-be Casanova falls for a gorgeous, dark-eyed Italian beauty. Picture it—he sees her leaving the marketplace, his heart leaps, he must pursue! He trails her for blocks through winding cobblestone streets struggling to think of something to say. It starts to rain—he's got an umbrella—she doesn't—there *is* a God! They walk, they talk, she smiles, bliss, bliss, bliss! Yeah, well, that's why movies are movies and real men take Viagra. But don't let these modern times get you down. Romance is alive and well in Rome, though it's a bit more low-key than you might think based on the standard image of Italians as *the* lovers of this world. Actually, things seem to be getting on like they do elsewhere in the world: Girls ignore the occasional moron who loudly calls out what he thinks is a compliment; eye contact is made (and pretended not to be made) at coffeeshops, newspaper stands, and bakeries; people drink and kiss and grope each other on the way home. Life is good. Guys, any old notions/fears/stereotypes you might have of the ultra-protective older Italian brother are *justified*—I saw some guy get his ass beat by, like, five of 'em, just for looking at a girl too long. And women, if you're worried about that old notion/fear/stereotype of Italian guys as charming players full of pretty lies, well, you're smart enough to spot the fakes. Send them off to buy you roses, then tell them you've got an incurable VD.

good—it probably helps that they're playing for an appreciative crowd. Half-price cocktails at happy hour, which ends at 11pm.

Vatican City's chilled-out jazz club **Alexanderplatz** *(Via Ostia 9; Tel 06/39-74-21-71; Metro Line A to Ottaviano; 9pm-2am Mon-Sat, live music starts about 10pm; L12,000 membership, good for 2 months; V, MC, AE, DC)*, is much beloved by the mid- to late- twenties, stylish/bohemian/casual crowd. The full menu lists all kinds of really random, tasty Italian, Asian, and American dishes. Dress a little bit nicer—clean, unripped, unwrinkled clothes are appropriate.

club scene

Clubs offer the kind of impersonal charm that some people hate; they're too dark to see exactly who's doing what, too loud to have an actual conversation, and people don't give a crap if you're breathing their secondhand smoke. But these are also the best elements of a club: You can disappear, then reappear, get lost in a crowd of strangers, you never know who's lurking in there, you're free of the obligation of carrying on bullshit talk when you'd really rather be scamming on that guy/girl over there.

Clubs are fun, don't be old and crusty! Even if you didn't always get out and get down back home, you're away now, and the general vibe of clubs in Italy is mellow, eclectic, and non-snotty, so get your booty on the dance floor. There's enough variety and selection that you can get two or more very different kinds of parties in one night, and it's not so crazy expensive that you'll feel forced to stay someplace you don't like. Most all door policies are fine (as always, it's easier for women to get in than men), the people who work there are normal, helpful even, and the crowds are outgoing, not clique-y. It's a good idea to call ahead about a guest list, which often works if it's not a too-special occasion *and* you get someone on the phone who speaks English (which is a 50/50 chance). Get dressed around 10, find your friends, do what you gotta do to get in a good dancing mood, get there around midnight to 12:30, and try not to have any expectations—that's when good things happen.

South of ancient Rome, **Alpheus** *(Via del Commercio 36; Tel 06/541-39-85; Bus 23, 702 or Metro Line B to Pyramide; Call for information about specific parties, 10pm-4:30am Tue-Sun; L10,000-20,000 cover; AE),* one of the biggest clubs in Rome, hosts hip-hop or gay-themed parties on Friday nights. The music varies: house, '80s, commercial. There are three large rooms for dancing, connected to several other largish rooms for hanging-out and cooling off, and an area with small tables and chairs and large windows with steps leading outdoors. The crowd is mixed—gay and straight, trendy club girls with baby barrettes, lanky guys in jeans and sweaters, baby dykes in corduroys and white pocket tees, gay guys with no shirts vogueing—and very energetic.

RULES OF THE GAME

While there's no drinking age in Rome, a 12-year-old *would* get laughed out of a bar. The legal age to buy is 18, but no one enforces it, and anyone who seems to be reasonably past puberty can drink. The drug laws here are kind of peculiar. Technically speaking, the use of drugs is tolerated under criminal law, although use in public might be viewed as an "offense to the public order." Realistically speaking, small amounts of certain drugs (marijuana, hashish) are accepted. The law goes something like this: You're not permitted to buy, sell, grow, or collect these kinds of drugs for buying, selling, or growing, and if you are caught doing these things you can be prosecuted. If you have on your person only what you are consuming right then and there you might face "administrative sanctions," like having your driver's license taken away for six months or having to undergo a social reintegration program, but it seems really, really unlikely that smoking a little doob on the street is going to get anybody in any trouble, as long as they keep things discreet—while the *carabinieri* (cops) are considered morons by most Romans, they *will* bust you for flagrant behavior.

rome bars, clubs and culture zoo

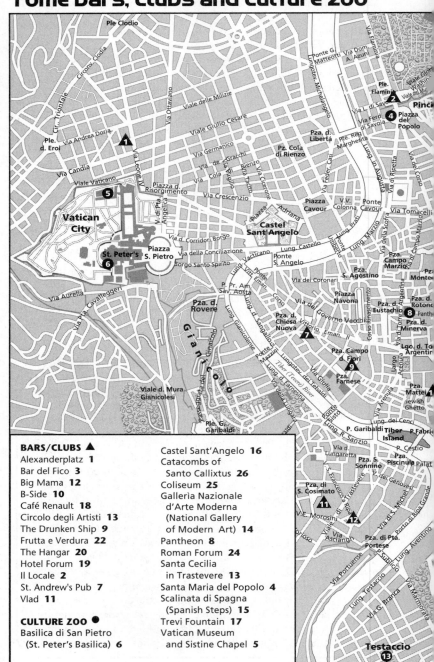

On most nights the door simply requires some patience—on Fridays and for other big parties it takes a *lot* of patience. If you're lucky you'll see a performance by the party's host, Vladimir, Rome's most celebrated guy-in-a-dress-with-better-legs-than-a-lot-of-girls. Despite the smart layout, at certain points it just gets too packed.

When the crowd has reached that critical mass, say 2 or 3am, or if you're looking for a slightly more earthy, less pop/commercial kind of place, **Goa** (*Via Libetta 13; Tel 06/574-82-77; Metro Line B to Garbatella; 10pm-5am Thur-Tue, closed May-Aug; L15,000-30,000 cover; goaclub@mclink.it; No credit cards*) has a lot of energy and an appealing tribal/Pacific Islands look going on, and (unfortunately) very expensive drinks. In the southern end of the city, the exterior is especially cool, with a section of thatched roof and burning torches. The door is a little picky but not ridiculous—wear something nice, a little bit sexy is cool, no need to go crazy. The crowd is mostly early twenties, hip, and good-looking, trendy but not hostile, with young hot things climbing onto raised levels to dance—basically a little bit more grown-up-looking/acting than the scene at Alpheus, but not *too* serious. Most important, the music is great. Claudio Coccoluto spins house, tribal, and drum 'n' bass on Thursdays, Stefano Gamma does house, funk, and groove on Fridays, Luis Radio spins American house on Saturdays, and Chicco Messina puts out funk, jungle, and house on Sundays. The bartenders actually look like they're having a good time, bopping around the well-run and well-stocked bar between drinks. The club is closed in the summer, but that's only because the club's owner is busy organizing open-air parties—call for dates and locations.

Even farther south of ancient Rome, **Ex Magazzini** (*Via dei Magazzini Generali 8; Tel 06/575-80-40; Bus 23, 702 or Metro Line B to Pyramide; Hours, days vary; Most parties free w/cash bar; No credit cards*) puts together a lot of '70s disco-revival-type stuff, like the *Velvet Goldmine Party*—think men in lipstick, tight nylon pants, and electric guitars—hosted by DJs Al Casey, Pier, and MDF. While not strictly a gay place, it's definitely gay-friendly—many of their invites note that homophobia is not admitted at the door.

B-side (*Via dei Funari 21a; Tel 06/68-80-05-24; Bus 46, 87; 11pm-4am Tue-Fri, till 6am Sat, Sun, closed July-Aug; L10,000-15,000 cover; No credit cards*), in the old Jewish ghetto, is an excellent place for dancing to new hip-hop, R&B, and house—or easing out and watching everyone else grind. The big circular dance floor usually gets packed, the whole place is lit with glowing blue light...it's all kind of sexy. The generally mid-twenties crowd dresses pretty nice—lots of fitted things and stretch fabrics on women and button-down shirts and leather shoes on guys—and you should too, or you'll wait outside for a looong time. Occasionally live rappers or R&B acts show up. Listen for Italian hip-hop like Articulo 31, kind of like a cross between Black Sheep and House of Pain, but totally different than either, 'cause they're Italian. Hang around for the good after-hours on weekends.

If you're looking for something more tripped-out, call up and find out what kind of party is in the works from **Discoteca Teatriz Baccara'** *(Vìa Provinciale Felicisio 108; Tel 054/526-120; Bus A14 to Ravenna; Hours, cover vary; No credit cards)*—or better yet, ask someone who speaks Italian to do it for you, like the guy at the hotel desk, who'll comply if you smile and ask nice. They produce big, rave-like fiestas featuring DJs from Italy, the U.S., and the UK, spinning big beat, trance, jungle, and ambient that draws club kids with glow-in-the-dark tongue toys from surrounding towns and suburbs.

On a different tip, south of ancient Rome is **Radio Londra** *(Vìa Monte Testaccio; Metro line B to Pyramide; Tel 06/575-00-44; L15,000 cover weekends includes first drink, L5,000 membership weekdays; Club 11:30am-4am Wed-Mon, bar and pizzeria 9pm-3am Wed-Mon, till 4am Sat; No credit cards)*, which is kind of cave-like, and looks like an old war bunker. Fortunately, it lacks that "more punk rock than you" attitude— anyone who wants to hear some loud, cranky, Brit-inspired garage, underground punk, or hardcore and work out some heartfelt angst through slam-dancing will feel right at home. The crowd isn't particularly outgoing, but it's not intimidating either, and it's definitely not violent (aw bollocks!). While there are a lot of safety-pin-covered, wallet-chain-wearing, spiked-with-white-glue-haired people around, not everyone sports the uniform of nonconformity, and you can feel free to dress in casual travel clothes. Obviously, you might feel a tad out of place if you show up in an Izod shirt and wing-tips (if you do, let's *hope* somebody kicks your ass). There's a lot of crossover with the gay crowd from **L'Alibi** [see *gay scene*, below] right next door (which is very straight-friendly). Live bands (mostly Italian) play occasionally, although the quality is kind of inconsistent and many just do covers, so call to see who's playing and then try to ask around. There's a patio outside where you can let your sweat dry, and, believe it or not, the pub food is really good. The weekday membership card is good for three months, although the cover thing seems kind of flexible if you arrive late.

Along similar lines is Trastevere's **Vlad** *(Piazza San Cosimato 39; Tel 06/580-08-98; Bus 44, 75, 8; About 10pm-4am, days vary; Usually no cover; No credit cards)*. Specializing in new wave, electro, goth, industrial, and post-punk—this is about as hardcore as Rome gets. Think black lipstick, Marilyn Manson, the Cure, and melancholy, angry, disillusioned youth. There's a big, dark dance floor downstairs where DJs spin to an active crowd, and a pub on the ground floor. Occasional live punk/goth bands, call and ask (again, finding an English speaker is iffy, ask your hotel desk guy to call) about shows. The crowd ranges from late teens to mid-twenties, and is nice enough, if just a bit cliqueish.

Something quite common in Rome that's completely bizarre to most travelers are the *centri sociali* (social clubs). Politically slanted, leftist, late-teens and twentysomethings form these clubs and use them for hanging out, holding concerts, throwing parties, showing films, etc. The less active clubs are less inviting for non-locals (they're mostly for people who all know each other, clustered in little groups talking about *their* stuff)—it's the ones that throw biggish open parties and show movies that are more fun for visitors, like **Brancaleone** *(Via Levanna 11; Tel 06/82-00-09-59; Bus 36, 37, 60, 366 to Piazza Sempione; 10:30pm-5am Thur-Sun; Cover varies; No credit cards)*. Friday is the best night here, and, although it officially closes at 4am, the festivities go later on the weekends. The music fluctuates: from DJs spinning drum 'n' bass, slinky lounge, and house, to live alterna-rock bands. Call for info on events. There's a mess-hall kind of barroom, with a smaller adjoining bar that also serves coffee, which is convenient if you're dragging but don't want to call it a night. This all empties outside, where there's some tables in a pretty seedy-looking courtyard, which is actually totally safe. After a little walk out, you'll pass into another building with a musty dirt floor and tripped-out black and white strobe lighting, where there's more dancing, less talking. The crowd is mainly straight, early twenties, some squatter-looking types, but mainly college-educated, left-leaning people who like to go out and party. On a recent Friday, the young people here were actually talking about UN bombings—between flirting outrageously and getting tanked, of course. Someone told me that some of these joints register as a social center instead of a nightclub just so they can legally be open after-hours.

Another *centro sociale* with a welcoming vibe is **Circolo degli Artisti** *(Via Casilina Vecchia 42; Tel 06/70-30-56-84; Bus to Via Casilina; 9pm-3am Tue-Sun; L7,000 membership good for 3 months, cover varies; No credit cards)*, near the Termini in an old milk-production center, a good-sized place with a bar, a video room, and two theaters. The music varies—although hip-hop and jungle are in abundance—as does what's going on: live performances, movie screenings, DJs....The crowd is generally early twenties, some ghetto-brat types, hip-hop kids, and guys with no shirts *and* pierced septums. No one who answers the phone here is completely with it, so the best way to get information about a particular show is to call Mondo Radio 90.9 FM *(Tel 06/207-32-32, 06/70-30-56-84)* for the pertinent details; they speak English. Oh, good note: You can find an excellent hip-hop set on that same station, called Zulu Nation *(9-10:30pm Mon-Sat; 6-8pm Sun)*.

after-hours scene

After-hours in Rome is lots of fun: The city is really empty except for the other half-wits careening around the streets and some old ladies, like, getting bread or something, so you can enjoy the splendor of the rosy glow spreading across the sky and dappling the stone of the spectacular buildings without endangering too many other people.

Frutta e Verdura *(Via Principe Umberto, Piazza Vittorio 36; Tel 0347/879-70-63; Bus 105 or Metro Line A to Vittorio Emanuele; Hours, days vary; L15,000 plus L5,000 membership; No credit cards)* consistently provides a packed and energetic party east of the city center, near the Termini. On Fridays things really get started at about 5am and go strong until at least 9am; Saturday things start a bit later, about 7am, and end around 9. Not a huge place, but big enough to make it comfortable and provide cool, dark places to slip away to. The crowd is mixed gay and straight with some trannies milling around, and a bit more sophisticated than at the *centri sociali*, but not obnoxiously so. The prompt and active bar definitely helps keep the crowd going. Once you descend the stairs to the club, it's hard to get a sense of the place, what with all the gyrating bodies and flashing lights—with stone walls and arched entries into darkened rooms where people keep on disappearing and reappearing; the main impression is of a comfortable dungeon somewhere. While the crowd is definitely not running on adrenaline alone, it's *nothing* like those nightmare sketchy after-hours scenes with depressing-looking people flopping around doing drugs. Music is mainly electronic house, with some commercial thrown in. The line to get in is a bit long, but moves fairly quickly; dressing a little bit nice—something with a little grown-up style—is appropriate. Guys, it's unfair, but it really helps to be with at least *a* girl....

If at about 7am you're feeling kind of hungry, having danced off those 5 million saturated-fat calories that you consumed at lunch, go by **Marani** *(Via dei Volsci 47; Bus 71, 492, 19, 30b; No phone; 7am-9pm daily; V, MC, AE)*, a great place to grab that milky cappuccino Italians say is good for you to drink *right* before you go to sleep (ha!) and devour fresh, flaky pastries. There's a nice little patio with tables and chairs outside where you can chill out and watch the day break in peace. A nice stop to make before you go home and pass out. Also near the Termini.

ARTS SCENE

Okay, so most people think art died when Marcel Duchamp put a signed urinal in a gallery, but believe it or not, people are still painting—with paint and brushes! On canvas! Holy crap, does Bill Gates know about this? Maybe some things never really change; there's still a whole lot of bad artists out there and a handful of interesting ones. Just think—out of the zillions of would-be greats through the centuries we've gotten, what? a couple thousand artists, if that, who can be taken seriously. The same applies to the modern art scene in Rome, although, to its credit, it's active and not very prefab or living room color coordinated.

▶▶VISUAL ARTS

Among the most interesting private art galleries is **Stefania Miscetti** *(Via delle Mantellate 14; Tel 06/68-80-58-80; Bus 23, 280; 4-8pm Tue-Fri, closed July-Sept)*, southeast of Vatican City, where Yoko Ono had work— sure, our parents still think she broke up the Beatles, but get over it. Her artwork is totally bizarre and creative and ahead of its time—and so is the work of many of the young, new sculptors who show their work here.

Also worth a look is **Gallerìa Emanuela Oddi Baglioni** *(Via Gregoriana 34; Tel 06/679-79-06; Metro Line A to Spagna; 10am-1pm/4-7:30pm, Mon-Fri, closed Aug)*. Near the Spanish Steps in the city center, the main attraction here is abstract sculpture, from big names like Marina Abramovic.

Gallerìa Gian Enzo Sperone *(Via di Pallacorda 15; Tel 06/689-*

35-25; Bus 52, 53, 56, 58b; 4-8pm Mon, 10am-1pm/4-8pm Tue-Sat, closed Aug) tends to have wilder, more experimental exhibits—it was one of the first Italian galleries to promote pop artists like Warhol and Lichtenstein.

Another good one is the **Studio d'Arte Contemporànea Pino Casagande** (Via Degli Ausoni 7a; Tel 06/446-34-80; Bus 19, 30b; 5-8pm Mon-Fri, closed Aug), exhibiting often bizarre and original sculpture and mixed-media stuff near the Termini. It walks that fine line of being almost too trendy for its own good—the work being featured becomes irrelevant at the wine, cheese, and who-is-*that*-over-your-shoulder!? party.

Near the Spanish Steps, the **Associazióne Culturale Valentina Moncada** (Via Margutta 54; Tel 06/320-79-56; Metro Line A to Spagna; 4-8pm Mon-Fri, closed Aug) is actually a series of garden-surrounded artists' studios. Well, we can't see those, but the gallery downstairs is open to the public. The work is generally semi-challenging painting and sculpture, a bit more difficult, less refined, and more intriguing than most of what's around right now.

Artists like to sit for hours and have coffee at the centrally located, quasi-trendy **Antico Caffè della Pace** (Via dell Pace 3-4-5-7; Tel 06/686-12-16; Bus 87, 280, 492; 11am-11:30pm Tue-Sun; V, MC, AE).

A bit more discreet and charming is **Cafe Notegen** [see *eats*, below], which is also just an all-around great place for lunch. It's a favorite of the older generation of local painters and poets, the kind who come every day, read the paper, and know the waitress. They have reasonably priced sandwiches, pastries, and coffees, but the real draw is the comfortable, homey atmosphere.

▶▶PERFORMING ARTS

The performing arts scene in Rome boasts a great ballet, the Rome Opera Ballet, which performs at the Teatro dell'Opera, as well as a highly praised orchestra, the RAI Symphony Orchestra, which usually performs in Vatican City at the **Academy of St. Cecilia** (Via Concillazione 4; Bus 23, 34, 64). The best bet for getting information about their shows, as well as other well-established performers', is via a ticket agent like **Termini-area Orbis** (Piazza Esquilino 37; Tel 06/474-47-76; Bus 4, 9, 16, 74; Box office 9:30am-1pm/4-7:30pm; MC, V, AE, DC)—you can usually get an English-speaker on the phone. The periodicals mentioned earlier for clubs and live-music happenings (*Trova Roma, Alias*, or *Roma C'e*), are definitely convenient for spotting something interesting, although again, quality-wise, it's hit-or-miss—look for reviews and trust word of mouth.

North of the city center, **Teatro Argentina** (Largo Argentina; Tel 06/68-80-46-01; Tickets at Via Barbieri 21; Tel 06/68-40-00-11; Box office open 10am-2pm/3-7pm Mon-Sat, performances 9pm Mon-Wed, Fri, Sat, 5pm Thur, Sat, Oct-June; V, MC, AE), run by the Teatro di Roma group, is the oldest theater in Rome. It used to be led by Luigi Ronconi, a big name in Italian theater, till he left for the bigger scene in Milan. Luckily he has a young, very talented replacement in Mario Martone, who is also known for his film work, but has remained true to his theater roots. Left-leaning and politically correct like Ronconi, but less famous and more humble, he takes on more challenging work.

Martone is also one of the many influential folks who opened the very new and rightfully hyped **Teatro India** (*Lungoteverie dei Papareschi; Buy tickets at Via Barbieri 21; Tel 06/686-56-69; No credit cards*). It's out of the center of the city (south of Trastevere, on the west side of the Tiber), not just in location but in general feel—young, more experimental. Right now it's hosting plays and also exhibitions, shows, and various multi-media perfomances.

Teatro di Roma also manages the smaller **Sala 1** (*10 Piazza di Porto San Giovanni; Tel 06/670-93-29*), which hosts dance performances, theater, poetry readings—anything that needs a more intimate space than the Argentina.

Teatro Quirino (*Via Marco Minghetti 7; Tel 06/679-06-16, 678-30-42, 678-58-02; Buy tickets at Via Minghetti; Tel 06/679-45-85; To theater, take Bus 81, 62, 85, 60; Box office 10am-1pm/3-7pm Tue-Sat, 10am-1pm/3:30-5pm Sun, performances 9pm Tue, Fri, Sat, 5pm Wed, Thur, Sun; Tickets L11,500-44,000; V, MC, DC, AE*), near the Via del Corso, is consistently lauded, hosting diverse music, dance, spoken word, and theater performances. It often presents the work of Carmelo Bene, who was once considered a great of Italian theater but now has gotten kind of tired.

During the balmier months of spring and summer, Rome hosts many beautiful open-air performances in places like the **Terme di Caracalla** (*Tickets and info: 06/481-70-03, 06/488-34-69; No credit cards*), the very impressive, huge, and beautiful ruins of baths built by Emperor Caracalla, not far from the Forum. A lot of these are live musical performances, but there is also a good dose of drama: Italian playwrights (maybe not too amusing if you don't speak Italian) for the most part, but also some American and others. There's often some Eugene O'Neill, Shakespeare (of course), or Tennessee Williams, so look around for details in the aforementioned periodicals.

For really big concerts, look out at **Teatro Olìmpico** (*Piazza Gentile da Fabriano 17; Tel 06/326-59-91; Bus 48, 280, 910; Box office 11am-7pm daily, performances 9pm daily Oct-May; Tickets L20,000-85,000*), northeast of the city center, on the eastern bank of the Tiber. Anything from string quartets to pop, rock, or alternative shows up here.

It's actually pretty easy to get cheap tickets to the opera (L20,000 for decent seats or standing room in the back), which has helped to attract a younger audience in Rome. Unfortunately, the people who really know opera, the older crowd, think it sucks right now and only mention it to complain or compare it to the *Scala* in Milan. **Teatro dell'Opera di Roma** (*Via firenze 72; Tel 06/481-601; Bus 75, 170, 64, 640; Box office 9am-5pm Mon-Sat, 9am-1:30pm Sun; Tickets L20,000-260,000; No credit cards*), east of the city center, is the place to go if you'd like to give it a shot anyhow.

At **Pasquino Cìnema** *(Vicolo de Peide 19, just off Piazza Santa Maria in Trastevere; Tel 06/580-36-22; Bus 23; L12,000; No credit cards),* you can catch either a very slightly dated new American movie or a screening of a great old classic. Most are in English with Italian subtitles (great if you're trying to learn the language). There's also a small bookstore, a cafe, and a bar that shows independent flicks on video. It's nice, comfy, air-conditioned, and usually brimming with youngish people, including lots of Italian and foreign students.

gay scene

In general, the gay scene is not exclusive *or* cut off from Rome's straight party scene. Big clubs like **Alpheus** [see *club scene,* above] regularly throw gay-friendly parties with themes like gay pride, drag divas, and AIDS awareness. Check in any of the entertainment guides to see when they're going on.

Pretty packed most nights, **The Hangar** *(Via in Selci 69; Tel 06/488-13-97; Metro Line B to Via Cavour; 10:30pm-2:30am Wed-Mon; No cover, L5,000 membership; No credit cards),* near the Coliseum, is mainly for men. Two very active and prompt bars, great music—mixed '80s like the Stray Cats and the Cure—and several screens flashing clips of music videos and stills keep the senses stimulated and thereby distracted from the squeeze of so many people in a not-huge space. Kind of half-dark, half-light, with lots of blind corners, it's a good place to check people out, invisibly or openly. Lots of cute, social twenty- and thirtysomething guys.

Women will feel more comfortable at **L'Alibi** *(Via Monte Testaccio 44; Tel 06/574-34-48; Bus 95, 673; 11pm-5am Wed-Sun; L20,000 cover; No credit cards),* where the crowd is more mixed—boys and girls, tourists and locals. One prompt bar, one big, lively dance floor, and mainly commercial dance/pop and techno-type house keep things goin'. As it's right next to **Radio Londra** [see *club scene,* above], south of the city center, there's a good deal of crossover crowd-wise, which keeps the people-watching pretty interesting.

A more strictly girl-oriented spot is **Joli Coeur** *(Via Sirte 5; Tel 06/86-21-62-40; Bus 38, 38b, 58, 58b; 10:30pm-2am Sat, Sun; L20,000 cover; No credit cards),* definitely the most popular and active club for women in the city. Some mixture in the crowd, but really a place for those of us who use tampons. Out in the northwest corner of the city.

CULTURE ZOO

Even the most jaded can't help being floored by Rome. Rome can seem almost unreal, something from a book of legends we had as kids. If your curiosity isn't piqued, even a little, to go romp around the ruins, and if the high point of centuries of art just leaves you blank, head cocked to one side saying, "Huh? I don't get it," well, at least you can tell them back home that you tried.

Vatican Museum and Sistine Chapel *(Vatican City, Viale Vati-*

FESTIVALS AND EVENTS

La Festa Di Noiantri *(July)*: Basically a great big feast in Trastevere where all the local restaurants fill the streets with tables, musicians play, and everybody stuffs themselves silly and gets drunk. It gets pretty hectic but avoids being congested to the point of suffocation.

Sagra dell'Uva *(beginning of Sept)*: The celebration of the grape! It's at the Basilica of Maxentius in the Foro Romano *(Metro Line B to Colosseo)* and the perfect setting to see grown men in skirts (ancient Roman garb). Lots of cheap, delicious grapes, and music to boot.

Carnival in Piazza Navona *(on or around Jan 5)*: We're talking games, junk food, performances, juggling, and the occasional fire-eater.

Festa della Primavera *(sometime in Apr)*: A celebration of the changing seasons, when the Spanish Steps are loaded with flowers and classical concerts are presented. Not a rockin' good time, but pretty and relaxing.

Go to the **Ente Provinciale per il Turismo** [see *need to know*, below] for details on all of these events.

cano; Tel 06/69-88-33-33; Metro Line A to Ottaviano; 7am-7pm daily Mar-Sept, till 6pm daily Oct-Feb; L18,000 admission, free last Sun of each month): Worth the big crowd and line of tourists you've gotta push through, worth the loot to get in. The place is huge and decked with treasures that the Catholic church has accumulated (try not to think *how...*): old maps, tapestries, gold everythings, Egyptian and Etruscan artifacts, and paintings (like Raphael's *School of Athens*). And unless you're dead, your jaw will drop when you see the **Sistine Chapel**. Closed on religious holidays, and there are about 500 of 'em, so call and check.

Basilica di San Pietro (St. Peter's Basilica)*(Vatican City, Piazza San Pietro; Tel 06/69-88-4466 or 06/69-88-5318; Metro Line A to Ottaviano/San Pietro, Bus 46; Basilica: 7am-7pm daily Apr-Sept, till 6pm Oct-Mar; Dome: 8am-6pm daily Apr-Sept, till 5pm Oct-Mar; Basilica: free, Dome: L5,000):* The basilica sits on one of the great architectural creations in the world, Piazza San Pietro, designed by Lorenzo Bernini. Statues of 140 saints sit on top of the 284 columns in the majestic colonnade, which curves around the square and reaches toward the basilica. The church you'll see was built in the early 16th century, when the previous one was torn down to make way for something bigger and better. The interior of the basilica is a testament to how enormously wealthy the Catholic church once was; one of the first treasures you'll see as you enter is Michelangelo's *Pietà*, which is one of his greatest works. But the most eye-catching monument in the basilica is Bernini's huge *baldacchino*, an elaborate Baroque brass canopy. You get fantastic views of Rome and the Vatican gardens from the top of the 448-ft. dome *(8am-4pm daily Nov-Mar, 7am-7pm daily Mar-Oct; L4,000 without lift, L5,000 with lift)*.

Pantheon *(Piazza della Rotonda; Tel 06/68-30-02-30; Bus 70, 81, 119, 170; 9am-6pm Mon-Sat; Free admission):* Built in 27 B.C., this is one of the undisputed architectural wonders of the world (That dome! That use of space! Those 20-ton doors!) Simply put, it is beautiful, perfect, and peaceful. If you can, go when it's raining but kind of bright; it's especially great when the rain pours in through the hole in the dome onto the stone floor.

Catacombs of Santo Callixtus *(Vìa Appia Antica 110; Tel 06/513-67-25; Bus 218 to Fosse Ardeatine; 8:30am-noon/2:30-5pm, till 5:30pm in summer, Thur-Tue; L8,000 admission):* It's worth the trek to the southwest edge of the city to see these zillions of tombs that go way, way underground. Many big-time popes are buried here, as is Santa Cecilia, the patron saint of music, a martyr who didn't die even after she got struck with the ax three times, the legal limit for a beheading.

Gallerìa Nazionale d'Arte Moderna (National Gallery of Modern Art) *(Vìale delle Belle Arte 131; 06/322-981; Bus 52, 53; 9am-10pm Tue-Sun; L8,000 admission, free if you can pass for under 18):* If you just get sick of all the old, classic, something's-wrong-with-you-if-you-don't-appreciate-this Renaissance works in the other venues, come here for the huge collection of 19th- and 20th-century paintings by de Chirico, Morandi, Manzú, Burri, Modigliani, Klee, Ernst, Pollock, Kandinsky, and the rest of 'em. It's in the Villa Borghese Gardens, at the north end of the city, so if you're gonna be there for the afternoon, it's worth the roll on over. Open surprisingly late.

Santa Cecilia in Trastevere *(Piazza di Santa Cecilia; Tel 06/589-92-89; Bus 44, 75; Church and frescoes free, L2,000 admission to excavations; 10am-noon/4-6pm daily, frescoes 10-11:30am Tue, Thur):* Get thee to a nunnery! No, really, this is a cool, random place to visit—I mean women actually *cloister* themselves here, renouncing the pleasures of the flesh and all. Sadly, you can't really ogle the nuns, although they are milling about in the background, collecting your suggested donation—just check out the church and artwork.

A few blocks east of the Corso, there's the **Trevi Fountain** *(Piazza di Trevi, Metro Line A to Barberini):* Okay, it's a totally touristy thing to go see, but amazingly beautiful just the same. The great big guy is Neptune, god of the sea (you know, Ariel's father—kidding) riding on his shell chariot.

Santa Maria del Popolo *(Piazza del Popolo 12; Tel 06/361-08-36; Metro Line A to Flaminio or Bus 90, 90B, 95, 490, 495; 7am-12:30pm/4-7pm daily; Free admission):* This place is steeped in history—we're talkin' secret burials and the church fighting against supposed demons (supposedly it is haunted by Nero, his nurse, and his

by foot

Trastevere is great for rambling around. It's not so bustling and full of tourists as other parts of the city; it's more just a normal neighborhood where people come and go about their regular lives—hence, great people-watching. Get a big bag of fresh fruit at a good price here to snack on while wandering around **Piazza di Sa Cosimato** *(Bus 44, 75, 8)*. From here make your way east, enjoying the wide-open stroll on Viale di Trastevere for a bit, and then continue over to the previously mentioned **Santa Cecilia** in Trastevere (on Piazza Mercanti) [see *culture zoo*, above]. Right around here are several cafes with outdoor seating where you can kick back for a while with a Coke or a gelato. From here continue east until you hit Porto di Ripa Grande, then make your way north and west along the Tiber. As you approach the second bridge, **Ponte Fabricio**, you'll see a small island, Tiber Island *(Isula Tiburtina)*. There's a semi-interesting church here and a hospital, but mainly it's fun just because it's a strange and kind of beautiful little island in the middle of a huge city—a nice stop if you've got the energy and the time. From here you can cross back into Trastevere and mosey over to the monument to **Santa Maria della Scala** *(Via della Scala)*, which has works by Caravaggio inside and an old-style pharmacy with herbal remedies and weird potions in glass jars from the 1700s—unfortunately, you can't get samples. And just south of there, down Via della Scala, is **Piazza di Santa Maria** in Trastevere. Although annoyingly packed during summer days, in the evening and in quieter seasons, it's great; there's a couple of fine neighboring cafes, a beautiful fountain, and a steady trickle of passersby.

mistress…). Also very old, very beautiful stained glass, chapels designed by Bernini and Raphael, two really gorgeous, famous pieces by Caravaggio, and more.

Castel Sant'Angelo *(Lungotevere Castello 50; Tel 06/687-50-36; Metro Line A to Ottaviano; L8,000 admission; 9am-3pm daily, closed last Tue of month):* This place has been a tomb for emperors, an escape hatch from the Vatican, a papal residence for popes with kids (!), and a torture chamber and prison, and is now chock-full of ancient weapons and armor—it's a true testament to the fact that real life is crazier than fiction. They pretty much give you free run of the place, and you can get a fab view of the city from the upstairs terrace.

Roman Forum *(Via del Fori Imperiali; Tel 06/699-01-10; Metro Colosseo; 9am-6pm Mon-Sat and 9am-1pm Sun Apr-Sept, 9am-sunset Mon-Sat Oct-Mar; Last admission 1 hour before closing; L12,000, 17 and* *under free):* When it came to cremating Caesar, raping Sabine women, purchasing a harlot for the night, or sacrificing a naked victim, this was where the action was. Today it's not much more than a couple arches and a bunch of boulders, but it's still pretty awe-inspiring.

Coliseum *(Piazzale del Colosseo, Via del Fori Imperiali; Tel 06/700-42-61; Metro Colosseo; 9am-7pm Mon, Tue, Thur-Sat, 9am-1pm Sun, Wed Apr-Sept ; 9am-3pm Mon, Tue, Thur-Sat, 9am-1pm Wed, Sun Oct-Mar ; Street level free, upper levels L8,000, free 18 and under):* When Titus inaugurated this joint in 80 A.D., he did it with a month-long spree in which local brutes were pitted against wild beasts while the vestal virgins screamed for blood. The party's over, and all that remains is but a shell of its former glory (no, really, it's just the shell—and only one side of it).

Scalinata di Spagna (Spanish Steps) *(Piazza di Spagna; Metro Spagna):* So, you're probably thinking, why the heck are there Spanish steps in Rome? Easy answer: The famed steps and the piazza below them, Piazza di Spagna, were named for the Spanish Embassy, which was once located here. And your second question is probably: Why would I want to spend my time checking out some stairs? Another easy answer: They're breathtaking. They curve gracefully up the hill, ending dramatically at the **Trinità dei Monte** church. At the foot of the steps is a boat-shaped fountain, which was designed by Giovanni Lorenzo Bernini and his pops, Pietro Bernini. The steps are at their best during the spring and the summer when they are filled with pots of pink azaleas. Of course, you may not be able to see all of their beauty through the masses of tourists and Italian teenagers who are constantly sprawled over them....

modification

So you're in love with a *bello Italiano* and you want his name tattooed on your arm. **Tattooing Demon Studio** *(Via dei Farnesi 72; Tel 06/687-32-06, 06/686-89-04; Bus 81 or Metro Line A to Lepanto; 1-8pm Mon-Sat, closed Sun; V, MC, AE),* near the Campo de' Fiori, can do the honors, and they also do piercing of all kinds of delicate parts. Everything's nice and sanitary and fresh and crispy out of new plastic packages (whew!). This is supposed to be the best place, with the best tattoo artists in all of Rome, so if you're gonna do it....

great outdoors

Even though Rome is a distinctly urban place, it's relatively easy to escape the city vibe and wiggle your toes in the grass. At the **Villa Borghese** [see *culture zoo,* above] you can take a relaxing walk, go jogging, take a bike ride, rollerblade, or make a picnic among its sloping green lawns. There's plenty of other folks lolling around, but it's not crowded, except on the occasional *very* beautiful Saturday or Sunday, so you can get a little solitude, meditate, do your tai chi, whatever. Almost every kind of person in the city is here, from young families to athletes to slackers to old men reading the paper.

Horseback riding is another random stay-fit thing you could give a go

forza italia

Don't be scared, there aren't *usually* riots....
Okay, Italians really love soccer, big surprise. So, predictably, a soccer match in Italy is something to see. First of all, everybody else seems to know exactly what's going on—when to sing a supportive song to the home team, when to hiss at the small section of visiting fans and make obscene hand gestures toward them as they chuck coins, plastic bottles, etc. over the Plexiglas dividers and light smoke bombs while riot police with batons and helmets keep them in check....No, really, it's a lot of fun, even if you're not a sports fan; by the second half, you'll be riveted. Rome has two major teams, Roma and Lazio. Roma is the really popular, more successful team, while Lazio is the beloved underdog that hasn't been Number One in about three decades but is getting it together these days (think Yankees and Mets). If you're in Rome between September and May, you can probably get tickets to a game; they're on Sundays at the **Stadio Olìmpico** *(Foro Italico dei Gladitori; Tel 06/368-51; Bus 32, 48, 391)*. Unless it's a big game, you can usually get tickets at the stadium (go about three hours before). Otherwise go to **Lazio Point** *(Via Farini 24; Tel 06/482-66-88; Metro Line A, B to Termini or Bus 4, 9, 14, 16)*. Tickets will run you about L42,000, more or less, depending on the game. The scalpers here are definitely to be avoided.

while in Rome. With riding grounds conveniently located in the Villa Borghese, the **Associazione Sportiva Villa Borghese** *(Via del Galoppatoio 25; Tel 06/320-04-87; Bus 95, 490, 495; Rates and hours vary, call for schedules and non-member rates)* can provide you with a decent horse and English tack if you already know how to ride—or, if you're a novice, a glue-factory candidate or a pony and a guy to lead you around comfortably while you cling for dear life to the poor animal....

After that little adventure, you could hobble next door to the open-to-the-public **Roman Sport Center** *(Via del Galoppatoio 33; Tel 06/320-16-67; Bus 95, 490, 495; Call for times and non-member rates)* and lick your wounds in one of the saunas, go swim in one of the two great big year-round swimming pools (be warned, I hear it's packed with teeny-boppers and bed-wetters in the summer months), whack a ball around in one of the squash courts, or work out at the pumping-iron-style gym.

STUFF

Rome is definitely a good place to get a fashion fix. While it's not the ultra-trendy scene that Milan is and doesn't generally target big-label bargain-hunters, that just makes it all the more appealing for those who can't afford, and wouldn't wear, but like to look at, what's coming out in haute couture and ready-to-wear. The major streets to spy or shop for clothing and accessories from houses like Armani, Valentino, Donna Karan, Versace, Gianfranco Ferré, Givenchy, Max Mara, Missoni, etc., are Vìa Condotti, Vìa Borgognona, Vìa Frattina, and, generally, all around the blocks at the foot of the Spanish Steps. Especially beautiful are the windows at Valentino; especially sexy, Missoni. A better area to check out if you actually want to *buy* something is around Vìa del Govèrno Vècchio, where there are a bundle of used-clothing shops hawking old cords, fuzzy sweaters of uncertain colors, peasant skirts, beat-up leather jackets and pants, vintage T-shirts printed with obscure messages, plus a number of less-expensive shops that sell ready-to-wear stuff, mainly from European designers.

As far as picking up some random cool souvenirs, you can get some great kitsch stuff in any number of the Catholic accessory shops near the Vatican, like plastic glow-in-the-dark rosaries or even the full priest vestments (you never know when *that* could come in handy).

▶▶HOT COUTURE

Josephine de Huertas & Co. *(Vìa del Govèrno Vècchio 68; Tel 06/687-65-86; Bus 46, 62, 64; 10am-8pm Mon-Sat; V, MC, AE)* is a small shop selling prêt-à-porter designs from Anna Sui, Bella Freud, Alberto Biani, Montana Blu, Liviana Conti, and some very sexy swimsuits (in season) from Capucine Puerari. A good selection of both funky and classic-looking stuff and not outrageously priced.

The style of **Arsenale** *(Vìa del Govèrno Vècchio 64; Tel 06/686-13-80; Bus 46, 62, 64; 3:30-7:30pm Mon, 10am-7:30pm Tue-Sat; V, MC, AE, DC)* is what you could call orphan industrial: men's wear in dark wool, beautiful scarves, elegant and sexy but comfortable-looking shoes, and funky jewelry made of plastic tubing, wire, beads, stone, glass, etc., all in a black-walled, metal-shelved store with big velvet seats.

Along the same route you can check out **Mado** *(Vìa del Govèrno Vècchio 89a; No phone; Bus 46, 62, 64; 11am-1pm/4-8pm, Mon-Sat; www.madonet.com; V, MC, DC, AE)*, a small but packed place with lots of glam clothes like silk kimonos; high-necked, full-length embroidered dresses; great accessories; big, floppy feather fans; animal-shaped brooches; and dramatic hats with gauze veils. In other words, all of the cool stuff your grandmother has in tissue paper in the back of her closet because she doesn't go work it anymore. Also great shoes and menswear.

▶▶VINTAGE

Around the corner is **Distané** *(Vìa della Chièsa Nuòva 17; Tel 06/683-33-63; Bus 46, 62, 64; 10am-8pm Mon-Sat; MC, V)*, another teeny-but-stocked place with great racks to dig through. You can find crazy lace-front bells, leather pants, every color hoodie, and great catch-all bags. Directly across from Distané is a small church and square. The church steps are a great spot for people-watching on a nice day, and there are usually a couple of people kicking around a soccer ball on the square, in case you need to catch your breath or sit and have a think.

fashion

Some people would argue that it's the French who really know fashion. Sure, they're masters at creating outlandish outfits that manage to look elegant and not ridiculous and tacky. But who wears that stuff to, say, the supermarket? When it comes to casual, it's Americans who rule, right? They invented the patched jeans/T-shirt look and the Converse-with-a-dress look, and no one seems to wear it more naturally. It's between these two extremes that the Italians have it together. For the most part, urbanized Italian people really do know how to dress well and, more important, seem to know what works on them and what doesn't. You just don't see really overweight people wearing spandex in Italy, nor do you see women with hair-sprayed poof-wing things or boys with one wind pant-leg rolled up to their calf. Nor does everyone from 12 to 35 jump on any trend, no matter how ridiculous, that shows up on models or in Hollywood. And thank god for that! While you do get the occasional 14-year-old girl who thinks she's a sex goddess in her Hello Kitty wear, or your standard shirt-unbuttoned-down-to-here-pinky-ring-wearing stud who thinks you want a real good look at his big ol' hairy belly, for the most part, people tend to wear simple, classic clothes, sometimes a little bit sexy but rarely in a look-at-me kind of way. It's really refreshing to be reminded that what is relaxed and subtle can still be extremely attractive and appealing. The only big exceptions are in clubland, where some people just go crazy—Hilfiger head-to-toe, tube tops, zebra-print bustiers—but even so, it depends on the club.

▶▶TUNES

Locals say the only real places to go for CDs are the two branches of **Disfunzioni Musicali**, one for new stuff *(Vìa Degli Etruschi 4-14; Tel 06/446-19-84; Bus 71, 492; 10:30am-7:30pm Mon-Sat; AE, MC, V, DC)* and the other for used and rare items *(Vìa deo Marruccini 1; Tel 06/445-42-63; Bus 71, 492; 10:30am-7:30pm Mon-Sat; AE, MC, V, DC)*. The new stuff branch has all of the latest in dance, house, techno, hip-hop, trance, etc., as well as a solid selection from the past. The used-and-rare store has great deals, especially on vinyl, and between the two, they either carry or can order just about anything you ask for. Both branches have helpful, knowledgeable staffs, who do their best in English or help you muddle through in Italian.

Goody Music *(Vìa C. Beccaria 2; Tel 06/361-09-59; Metro Line A to*

Flaminio; 9:30am-2pm/3:30-8pm Mon-Sat, closed 2 weeks in Aug; www.goodymusic.it; MC, V, AE, DC) caters more to the DJ set with an especially excellent selection of new hip-hop and import mixes. They also have several tables set up where you can sample. Despite its professional vibe, this shop is not snotty at all and has a great, helpful staff some; English is spoken here.

▶▶BOUND

If you want to pick up something to read while you pass the hours in a cafe or park, try **Il Manifesto** *(Via Tomacelli 144; Tel 06/68-80-81-60; Bus 81, 628; 9am-7pm Mon-Sat; md2511@mclink.it; V, MC, AE)* for a good selection of all kinds of books in Italian and a decent selection in English. They also have attractive gift books, magazines, maps, etc.

Al Ferro di Cavallo *(Via di Ripetta 67; Tel 06/322-73-03; Bus 628, 926; 9am-1pm/3-7pm Mon-Sat; V, MC, AE, DC)* is a great one for really big, glossy, beautiful books on art, photography, fashion, architecture, history, and so on. A small but well-stocked place where you can feel comfortable browsing for a while. Both located near the Via del Corso.

EATS

The Italian meal plan seems to be something like this: dessert and coffee for breakfast, pasta/carbohydrate-energy and coffee for lunch, and a fairly big, carefully selected, balanced dinner, with coffee. Most people have cappuccino or latte (both of which are usually just warm, not scalding hot) just for breakfast, but some have these later in the day or before bed—they don't keep you up as much as a straight espresso. It's not necessary to tip your waitperson in most restaurants, cafes, bars, etc., as the tip is already figured as part of the price. Still, a small tip (L500-1,000) is nice. There's excellent food to be had at very fair prices in Rome, so don't settle for mediocre meals just to fill yourself up. If the pastries look waxy or the place is completely empty, move on. And don't be intimidated if the menu is all in Italian—what you can't figure out you can ask about, or you can always just smack your hands together and lick your chops while pointing at someone else's food.

First of all, it's good to know where to get some staples. A few suggestions:

Good fruits and vegetables: **Campo de' Fiori** in the morning. From about 9am until around 1pm Monday through Saturday, it's packed with vendors selling good produce at fair—if not dirt-cheap—prices. This is where all the old people go to pick out perfect tomatoes. You can also find flowers, fish, herbs, and lots more.

Good bread: **Antico Fórno** *(Campo de' Fiori; Tel 06/68-80-66-62; Bus 42, 62, 64; 7:30am-2pm/4:45-8pm daily; No credit cards)* has all kinds of great twists of Italian, semolina, focaccia, and peasant bread with a nice, thick, crackly crust. Everything is freshly baked and consistently delicious.

Good meat: An excellent butcher is **Antica Norcineria** *(Via Campo de' Fiori; Tel 06/68-80-61-14; Bus 42, 62, 64; 7:30am-1:30pm/4:30-8pm daily; No credit cards)*. They've got just about everything here—prosciutto, salami, ham, beef, you name it. All the best quality, great cuts, and reasonably priced. The counter people are friendly and helpful, and won't get huffy if you ask for small amounts of lots of different things to get a good sampling.

Good wine: **Buccone** *(Via Ripetta 19; Tel 06/361-21-54; Bus 628, 926; 9am-8pm daily; V, MC, AE)* is a trusty place with fair prices. The staff will be glad to help you choose a good bottle in your price range.

▶▶CHEAP

The city is covered with small "bars" that sell different pastries, as well as coffee (that means espresso, cappuccino, etc.). These are also the best places to go for all three meals if you're on a really tight budget; you can get some sandwiches, maybe two or three, and a soda for under L10,000.

According to locals, **Teichner** *(Piazza San Lorenzo in Lucina 15; Bus 81, 628, 492, 70, 80; No phone; 7:30am-9pm daily; V, MC, AE, DC)* has the best coffee in the city for the best price (L1,000), as well as cheap and delicious pastries, sandwiches, candies, chocolates, and a large selection of cheeses, meats, olives, and dairy products. It's a perfect place to grab some snack supplies for later. There are also several outdoor tables and

down and out

There's plenty of stuff you can do in Rome even if you are totally, unequivocally broke, especially in the summertime. When it's warm, most of the good stuff in Rome is to be had outdoors: concerts galore, theater, art shows, and impromptu soccer games. Just look around for signs (they're *everywhere*); you can always go linger around, lie on the grass, and enjoy. All year-round, Piazza Navona is great for kicking around and people-watching; same for **Campo de' Fiori** [see *hanging out*, above]. They're old hat to locals, but for visitors, especially first-timers, the city's zillion fountains at night are truly gorgeous. With their lights making tangled, glowing reflections on the moving water and the gently bubbling sounds—which you can actually appreciate now that the noise of the city has hushed up—well, it's kind of tough not to be dumbstruck. Some dazzling ones: Bernini's Fountain at Piazza Navona, the **Trevi Fountain** at Piazza di Trevi [see *culture zoo*, above], the Fontana del Tritone at Piazza Barberini, the Naiads at Piazza della Repùbblica. The very top of the Spanish Steps, although really touristy during the day, is an amazing place to watch the sun come up.

Another fine way to live the high life on next to nothing is sneaking into private gallery openings and partaking of the wine and cheese until someone catches on, at which point you beeline for the door [see *arts scene*, above].

rome eats and crashing

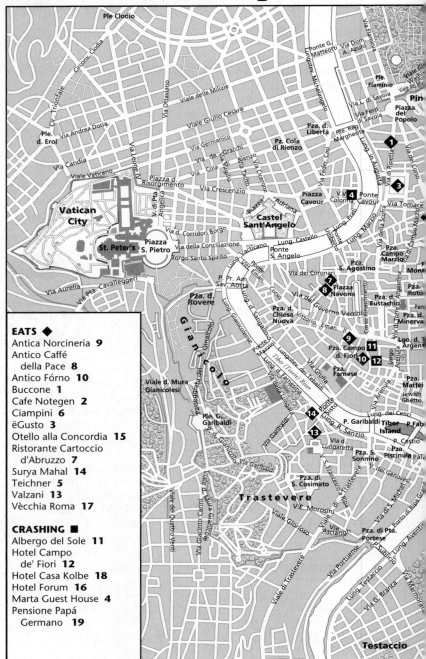

EATS ◆

Antica Norcineria **9**
Antico Caffé
 della Pace **8**
Antico Fórno **10**
Buccone **1**
Cafe Notegen **2**
Ciampini **6**
ëGusto **3**
Otello alla Concordia **15**
Ristorante Cartoccio
 d'Abruzzo **7**
Surya Mahal **14**
Teichner **5**
Valzani **13**
Vècchia Roma **17**

CRASHING ■

Albergo del Sole **11**
Hotel Campo
 de' Fiori **12**
Hotel Casa Kolbe **18**
Hotel Forum **16**
Marta Guest House **4**
Pensione Papá
 Germano **19**

one or two inside. Directly across the piazza is **Ciampini** *(Piazza San Lorenzo 'n Lucina 33; Tel 06/687-63-04; Bus 81, 628, 492, 70, 80; 7:30am-9pm Thur-Tue, closed Wed; V, MC, AE)*, which also has very good coffees, sandwiches, pastries, many kinds of tasty gelati, and indoor and outdoor seating. A bit more pricey and less intimate, but still a fine place for a simple, portable, and quick meal.

Don't ignore **Cafe Notegen** *(Via del Babuino 159; Tel 06/320-08-55; Metro Line A to Spagna; 7am-midnight Mon-Sat, 10am-midnight Sun; MC, V, DC)* just because of its location—even though it's only a few minutes' walk from the touristy Spanish Steps, it has successfully retained its charm and authenticity with dark wooden booths and old pictures on the walls. You can get a steaming, delicious *pizza margherita*—no, it's not some bizzare mozzarella cocktail (ew!), it's a straight-up pizza with sauce and cheese—for a mere L8,000.

Valzani *(Via del Moro 37 A/B; Tel 06/580-37-92; Bus 23, 280; 9am-8:30pm daily; V, MC)* has been around since 1925, so they've got all the best old-school sweet stuff: *torróne, tiramisù, pangiallo*, as well as about a hundred other homemade specialties that you can't find correctly made outside Italy. There are smaller, bite-size versions of most things for L2,000 to L3,500, if you can't decide between them.

▶▶**DO-ABLE**

For a terrific meal that's light but satisfying and delicious, particularly for lunch, try **ëGusto** *(Piazza Augusto Imperatore 9; Tel 06/322-62-73; Bus 628, 926, 81, 492; Noon-2am Tue-Sun; L14,000-45,000 per person; AE, DC, MC, V)* near the Piazza dei Popolo. There's a pizzeria that serves piping-hot thin-crust pizzas with all kinds of great toppings like artichokes, chicken, and sun-dried tomatoes, but even better is the lunch buffet with about 20 different dishes—pasta and rice salads, vegetables, cheeses, breads, baked quiches—all very fresh and very good. Scarf as much as you like for L14,000 including tax; you can't go wrong. Big rooms with high ceilings with modern/rustic/industrial-looking details are filled with small tables that the staff will gladly push together for groups. There's also a classy little wine and cigar bar, full lunch and dinner menus, and occasionally live, light, lounge-y music at night, when it's also a bit more trendy and formal.

Despite its discreet Vatican City location, most nights around dinnertime there are a bunch of people lined up at **Trattorìa da Augusto** *(Piazza de Renzi 15; Tel 06/580-37-98; 12:30-3:30pm/8-11pm Mon-Fri, 12:30-3pm Sat, closed mid-Aug to Sept; No credit cards)* for plates of perfectly turned-out lamb or mouth-watering gnocchi in tomato sauce. Just point at the menu—even if they get it wrong, you'll get something really delicious. The proprieter is brisk but welcoming, and you'll feel right at home when he writes out your check on the paper tablecloth. Somewhat nice clothing, nothing dribbled with gelato, is great. Sometimes there are gypsies wandering in with organettos or selling lighters shaped like bird cages or kissing pixies. Simple, pleasant, and comfortable, with tables inside and out.

Another place that just screams "You're in Italy!" is centrally located

Ristorante Cartoccio d'Abruzzo *(Largo Febo; Tel 06/67-70-24-27; Bus 70, 81, 87; 12:30-3pm/7:30-10:30pm Tue-Sun, closed Mon; L8,000-22,000 per entree; MC, V, DC).* Its raised patio, outlined by two pretty, quiet streets and sheltered by some wrought-iron fencing that's twined with plants and flowers, is made even more lovely at night when they light the lanterns hanging from the overhanging trees. (There's cozy indoor seating too, but why?) The menu is filled with traditional Roman and Italian dishes: tender meats like lamb and veal in savory vegetable or cream-based sauces, as well as really delicious gelato. The all-male wait staff has that white shirt/black tie thing going on. No need to go crazy, but nicer clothing is more appropriate.

The truly mellow **Surya Mahal** *(Via di Ponte Sisto 67; Tel 06/589-45-54; Bus 23, 280; 12:30-3pm/7:30-11:30pm daily; L15,000-40,000 per entree; MC, AE, V)* is set up beside a fountain in the city center with outdoor tables on gravel with standing gas torch/lamps, simple indoor bamboo wicker tables and chairs, jeweled elephants, and bowls of floating flower petals and candles. Very good, light Indian food, a selection of fruit- and yogurt-based special Indian drinks (a meal in themselves—maybe save it for dessert), tender meats, and tasty appetizers like fried cheese-fish-spice mixtures. Ask the waiter to recommend a good Indian beer to complement your meal.

▶▶SPLURGE

The antipasti at the comfortable and centrally located **Vècchia Roma** *(Via della Tribuna di Campitelli 18, Piazza Campitelli; Tel 06/68-64-66-04; Bus 44, 95, 160, 715, 716; L20,000-30,000 main courses; 1-3:30pm/8-11pm Thur-Tue; AE)* are good enough to be dinner all by themselves, but it's no excuse to miss out on the perfectly seasoned, super-tender meat dishes and delicious pastas. While eating outside at the little tables with freshly pressed tablecloths and flowers is just fine, especially at night when the candles have been lit, it's the inside of Vècchia Roma that's so surprising: a seemingly endless number of little rooms separated by drapes and a bubbling fountain.

Near the Spanish Steps, **Otello alla Concordia** *(Via della Croce 81; Tel 06/679-11-78; Metro Line A to Spagna; 12:30-3pm/7:30-11pm Mon-Sat; L12,000-28,000 main courses; AE, MC, DC, V)* serves super-tender veal that makes any qualms you had about their cruel upbringing and tragic end fly out the window, but the real draw is the possibility that some celebrity icon will show up for dinner. Also, it's an awfully pretty place at night, when the arbor and raised patio outside make it resemble a fairy-tale garden.

La Dolceroma *(Via del Portico D'Ottavia 20B; Tel 06/689-21-96; Bus 8, 44, 170, 81; 7:30am-1:30pm/4-8pm Tue-Sat, 10am-1pm Sun, closed Mon; V, MC, AE, DC)* is a bakery in the southern end of the city center that serves up American specialties, including really great choco-late-chip cookies, carrot cake, cheesecake, and brownies, as well as Aus-trian concoctions like apple strudel, marzipan, and yogurt-flavored cake. Everything is high quality and often made from organic ingredients. It's particularly nice in the late afternoon, when it's quiet and you can take your time to contemplate/resist trying all the cookies *(L2,000-5,000 each)*.

crashing

Three things to know about hotels in Rome:

1. You can check the back of your door to make sure you're not getting ripped off—the maximum that they can charge for the room is posted there.

2. If you get really desperate and can find nothing, go to a tourist booth [see *need to know*, below] and grovel; they'll usually be able to find you *something*.

3. When it comes to sneaking extra people into your room, it really depends on the reception situation. Sometimes it's possible if you're coming in during the wee hours and the receptionist has taken off to get some sleep or conked out at the desk. More often than not, it's tough to do and really not appreciated if you get caught. But hey, make friends with the manager and see what you can do.

Oh, and one last thing: Regardless of how desperate you get, it's a *really* bad idea to crash outside on some steps or something. It's illegal, so you could possibly get arrested; moreover, while Rome is a fairly safe city, it's not *that* safe. Drink coffee and sleep during the day.

While not as expensive as, say, Manhattan, Rome is not a budgeter's dream as far as accommodations go. Most places in the city center are wildly overpriced. But don't be too freaked-out—there are some good deals and even some dirt-cheap deals. In all of the inexpensive and mid-range places it's often possible to ask for and get a reduction in rate, especially if you're there in the off-season or there's some weird hole in their bookings. It's worth a shot....

▶▶CHEAP

Marta Guest House *(Vìa Marrianna Dionigi 17; Tel 06/323-01-84; Metro Line A to Ottaviano; L95,000 single w/o bath, L130,000 double w/bath; No credit cards)*, right near the Spanish Steps on the second floor of an apartment building. The fact that the rooms all have high ceilings is their saving grace.

OK, so the neighborhood is not exactly stellar, but no place near the train station is. Nevertheless, **Pensione Papá Germano** *(Vìa Calatafimi 14A; Tel 06/486-919; Metro Line A, B to Termini; L65,000 double w/o bath, L100,000 triple w/bath, phone; AE, V, MC)* is clean and decent and even kind of fun, filled with mostly young, social, college-age backpackers from all over.

Aside from these types of pension deals, the only lower-cost option in Rome is the youth hostel. It's crowded, and you get a bunk, a locker with no lock, almost no privacy, a three-day-max stay, and funky smells—hey, *that* sounds like fun, doesn't it?! The big one in Rome is the **Ostello del Foro Italico (HI)** *(Viale delle Olimpiadi 61; Tel 06/323-62-67; Metro Line A to Ottaviano; L25,000 with HI card, L30,000 for sale at the desk;*

Midnight curfew, 9am-2pm lockout, reception noon-11pm; No credit cards), well north of Vatican City. No way around it, the curfew just sucks; so does the lockout. Don't these people realize those are key sleeping hours?! It may be best to just accept the fact that you won't make curfew most nights and that your internal clock is screwed. The sunny side of the hostel thing is: You get a shower (no curtain! woo-hoo!), a place to ditch your stuff so you don't have to carry it, breakfast, and, most important, a lot of outgoing bunkmates of all varieties from all over the world (think ages 18 to 25, slanting downward) who want to hang out, get loaded, have fun, etc. Reservations are a very good idea; they've got 300-plus beds, and they still get booked out.

One more low-cost option if you're really desperate, or you just like Phish: camping! No, really, it's a perfectly fun and realistic option in the late spring through summer months. **Flaminio** *(Vìa Flaminia Nuòva 821; Tel 06/333-14-31; Bus 910 from Termini to Piazza Mancini, then Bus 200 to Vìa Flaminia Nuòva; L13,000/person per night, L8,000/per tent, bungalows L38,000-128,000; Mar-Oct; No credit cards)* isn't exactly the garden at Versailles, but the grounds are well-kept, clean, and green, and they have a clean swimming pool, a little grocery, a cafe, and a bar. The only tough thing is that it's about 5 miles north of city center, so you've got to figure out transportation—renting a bike is a good way to go.

▶▶DO-ABLE

Hotel Casa Kolbe *(Vìa S. Teodoro 44; 06/679-49-74, Tel 06/679-497; Bus 81, 160, 628, 810; L105,000 single, L135,000 double, L170,000 triple, L190,000 quad, breakfast L7,000; V, MC, AE)* has a lot going for it. First, it's right in the center of ancient Rome, which is beautiful night and day, but it's tucked away on a cozy little street. Second, lots of young people stay here, so it's really conducive to meeting small groups of people to kick around with. The rooms are simple and on the small side but comfortable, all have private baths and daily housekeeping, and many look down onto a nice garden with great big palm trees. The staff is welcoming, helpful, and largely English-speaking.

The beautiful little **Albergo del Sole** *(Vìa del Biscione 76; Tel 06/68-80-68-73; Bus 46, 62, 64; L100,000 single w/o bath, L200,000 double w/bath; AE, MC, DC, V)* is located literally right next door to Campo de' Fiori, close to a lot of great stuff, yet not so close that you can't get any sleep. While the check-in staff isn't the most warm and welcoming, they're not awful, and there's a really great marble sitting room and a classy little garden out back, complete with naked statues, where you can hang out and drink and even bring non-guest friends. The rooms are A-OK, nothing to write home about, but neat, clean, and comfortable. Mostly youngish twenty- to thirtysomethingish people. Breakfast not included.

Right across the street is **Hotel Campo de' Fiori** *(Vìa del Biscione 6; Tel 06/68-80-68-65 or 06/68-30-90-36; Bus 46, 62, 64; L150,000 single w/o bath, L180,000 single w/bath, L180,000 double w/o bath, L230,000 double w/bath, continental breakfast included; V, MC).* The nicest part about this hotel, aside from its convenient location, is the fact that it has a very cool sun roof with terra cotta tiles, lounge chairs, a garden, and a great view of St. Pete's. Again, the rooms are fine, kind of on the dark side, but hell, if you're doing most of your sleeping during the day, that's what you want. Beware, this place looks like it attracts young families, which can mean rug rats.

Hotel Delle Muse *(Via Tommaso Salvini 18; Tel 06/808-57-49; Bus 360 to Piazza dell Muse, Bus 53; L150,000 single w/bath, L260,000 triple w/bath, continental breakfast included; www.hoteldellemuse.com; info@hoteldellemuse.co; V, MC, AE, DC)*, in the northern part of Rome, is a bit out of the way (about 2 miles north of the Termini), but a good spot just the same. There's a large open garden/restaurant of the same name around back that's open in the summer, and a decent, large restaurant inside serving standard Italian fare: pasta, meat, fish, chicken, and desserts; entrees between L15,000 and L45,000. There's also a bar that closes at 10:30pm. The rooms are neat and clean, and many have little porches. Seems to attract a lot of backpackers and college students. Oh, and if you're still torn out of the frame from last night, or just plain old lazy, you can get the sweet and accommodating staff to bring your breakfast to your room for L3,000.

▶▶**SPLURGE**

Ancient Rome's **Hotel Forum** *(Via Tor Dé Conti 25, Fori Imperiali; Tel 06/679-24-46; Bus 27, 81, 85, 87, 186; L390,000-520,000/double, L550,000/triple, L630,000/suite, all including breakfast; forum@venere.it; AE, V, MC, DC)*, mentioned earlier for its stellar rooftop bar, is another swank-ass place in an easy-access location. For your money you get air-conditioning, private bath, radio, satellite TV, a continuous music system in all rooms (which, thankfully, can be shut off), garage, private parking, direct-dial phones, a bar, the roof garden, a restaurant, in-room massage, etc. The furnishings are traditional, ornate Italian/French provincial, but tasteful and not intimidating. While this hotel isn't exactly a slamming good time, there are a lot of youngish people around, especially young couples.

need to know

Currency Exchange The local currency is the **lira (L)**. *Cambio* means money change, so look for signs. The best places to change money are definitely the banks, some of which now have ATM machines outside that change bills. There's a **Banca Nazionale delle Communicazióni** right in the train station.

Tourist Information There's an information desk in the airport *(Tel 06/65-95-60-74)* where you can get a general map; for more info, contact **Ente Provinciale per il Turismo** *(Via Parigi 11; Tel 06/48-89-92-53; Metro Line A to Repùbblica)*, across the street from the train station.

Public Transportation Rome's got the *Metropolitana* **(Metro)**, which is pretty fast and not too confusing. There are two underground lines, A and B; entrances have signs with big red M's. Tickets are L1,500 and can be bought at vending machines at the stations, or you can get books of tickets at places that sell cigs, which is really the easiest thing to do if you're going to ride a lot. Trains run from 6:30am-11:30pm. The bus company is **Azienda Tramvie e Autobus del Commune di Roma** (*Vìa Volturno 65; Tel 06/46-95-44-44; Bus 3, 4, 16, 36*). The bus is also L1,500, and there are free transfers for an hour and a quarter after you use your ticket. Night buses—marked with a big ol' N before their number—run from midnight till 6am, on the main routes only. Good, clear maps for both the Metro and the buses can be gotten for free at Metro station booths or bought at the Stazione Termini. If it's late and you're too retarded to get yourself home on the bus, call 06/6645, 06/3570, or 06/4994 for a cab.

Motorbike Rental Romarent (*Vicolo dei Bovari 7a; Tel 06/689-65-55; Bus 46, 62, 64; 8:30am-7pm daily; MC, V, AE, DC*) has good package deals for several-day rentals; they also rent cars and video. An inexpensive bike will run you L100,000 for three days, and that includes tax, helmets, and insurance. Or go to **Bichi & Bachi** (*Vìa dei Viminale 5; Tel 06/48-28-84-43; Bus 70; 8am-7pm daily; V, MC, AE, DC*). An inexpensive bike here is about L40,000 per day, with all of the above also included.

American Express AMEX (*Piazza di Spagna 38; Tel 06/676-41; Metro*

wired

Fight it if you will; it is undeniable that computer networking, if not taking over the world, is at least popping up all over it. Rome is no exception, with cybercafes and Internet hookup joints abounding. If you need to get an Internet porn fix, or just feel like checking your e-mail to see if your friends have noticed you're not around lately, you can go by **Internet Cafe** (*Vìa dei Marrucini 12; Tel 06/445-49-53; Bus 11, 71, 204, 492; 9am-2am Mon-Fri, 5pm-2am Sat-Sun; www.internetcafe.it; AE, V, MC*). The place has everything a good work station should: air conditioning and a full bar. The rates are reasonable, between L8,000-10,000 per hour, cheaper before 9pm.

The **Net Gate** (*Piazza Firenze 25; Tel 06/689-34-45; Bus 116, 70, 87; 10:30am-10:30pm Mon-Sat June-Aug, 10:40am-8:30pm Mon-Sat Sept-May; www.netgate.it; V, MC*) has AC, but no bar. This place is a little bit bigger, so you'll probably never have to wait around for a computer, and they've got good package deals if you think you're going to need a couple of hours. These aren't the most happening places, but people seem nice enough. Both are located in the city center.

Line A to Spagna; Travel service and tour desk 9am-5:30pm Mon-Fri, till 12:30pm Sat Nov-Apr, plus 2-2:30pm Sat May-Oct; Financial and mail services 9am-5pm Mon-Fri, till noon Sat), near the Spanish Steps, will save your ass in so many lousy situations—they deal with money wiring, traveler's checks, and cash advances on your credit card.

Health and Emergency Emergencies: *112*; State police with an English interpreter: *113*; police hotline (for, say, a violent crime in progress): *21-21-21*. The **U.S. Embassy** has a list of English-speaking doctors, call them at *06/434-71*. All the big hospitals have 24-hour emergency rooms: **Ospedale S. Giovanni-Addolorata** *(Via dell'Amba Aradam 9; Operator 06/770-51; Emergencies 06/77-05-56-61),* **Ospedale Fatebenefratelli** *(Piazza Fatebenefratelli 2 (on the Tiburna Island); Operator 06/668-371; Emergencies 118).*

Pharmacies **Farmacia Internazionale** *(Piazza Barberini 49; Tel 06/679-46-80; Metro Line A to Barberini)* is dependable, well-stocked, and open all day and night a few blocks north of ancient Rome. Most pharmacies are open only from 8:30am-1pm/4-7:30pm and are on a rotation system, with a list posted outside of the pharmacies saying which one is open all night that night.

Telephone Country code: *39*; city code: *06*. There are orange pay phones all over the city. Local calls are L200. You can pay in coins, but phone cards are more convenient. You can get them at most places that sell cigarettes in L5,000, L10,000 or L15,000 denominations: Break the corner off and follow the directions clearly marked on the phone, in Italian and English, with pictures. For collect calls, deposit a refundable L200 and dial 170 for an English-speaking operator. To use a calling card, deposit the same L200, and dial your card's number. **AT&T:** *172-10-11*; **MCI:** *172-10-22*; **Sprint:** *172-18-77*.

Airports **Leonardo da Vinci International Airport** *(Tel 06/659-51, 06/65-95-36-40 for info),* which the locals call *Fiumincino,* handles most flights. (Charter flights arrive at **Ciampino**: *06/794-941*). The airport is about 18 unexceptional miles from the heart of the city. Follow the signs that say TRENI for the shuttle service directly to **Stazione Termini** *(arriving Track 22; 6:50am-9:20pm; about L16,000 one-way).* If you're really strapped, get a local train (L7,000 and change), running every hour to **Tiburtina Station**, and from there get the **Linea B** of the local underground for L1,000. A taxi from the airport is at least L73,000, and if you hit any traffic it can quickly go as high as L106,500.

Airlines **TWA** *(800/221-20-00; www.twa.com)*; **Delta** *(800/241-41-41; www.delta-air.com)*; **United Airlines** *(800/538-29-29; www.ual.com)*; **US Airways** *(800/428-43-22; www.usairways.com).*

Trains **Stazione Termini** *(Piazza Cinquecento; Tel 1478/880-881),* smack-dab in the city center, is the one and only big station in the city. If you want the Metro, follow the red M signs. To get a bus, go straight through the outer hall of the Termini and enter the bus lot of Piazza dei Cinquecento. You can also get a taxi here, and there's an information booth in the hall with info about trips to the rest of Italy.

Bus Lines Out of the City Depending on where you're going, check out a Metro map for the bus, underground, or combination of the two that will take you away. Buses to nearby (30 minutes to an hour away) popular excursion points run between L10,000-20,000. The bus lot is right in front of the **Stazione Termini** at Piazza dei Cinquecento *(Tel 06/465-91; Booth open 7:30am-7:30pm).*

Laundry OndaBlu *(Via Milazzo 8; Bus 492, 9, 310; 9am-10pm daily; L12,000/load, wash and dry),* a block northeast of the train station.

madrid

Folks in Madrid toss down little cups of coffee like muscle cars guzzle gas, smoke cigarettes like it was their last day on Earth, eat nothing but fried foods, and drink till—at (the very) least—three in the morning. This town is one of the true world-class capitals of late, late night fun. In fact, there are more bars and pubs here than in the other Western European capitals combined. On most nights, seemingly the whole city is drinking and dancing at an untold number of venues until the sun comes up. You can even drink in the streets. But these are just the bare facts; the actual experience of a weekend in Madrid is kind of like a 72-hour (don't forget about Sunday) bungee jump: Just give into the gravity and know that somehow you'll bounce back by Monday morning. After all, everyone else seems to be able to....

With all these vices, you would think that the average resident of this sprawling capital would have Homer Simpson's body and Keith Richards' face, but, remarkably, it isn't so. The locals are thin, healthy, and happy, smoking and drinking until a ripe old age. How do they do it? Well, if you ask a group of Madrileños, they'll tell you that their health is the result of *una vida más tranquila:* a more easygoing way of life. "Enjoy yourself here," they'll tell you, "nobody wants problems." Even though you'll have more fun in Madrid than Marilyn Manson in a latex factory, to these Spaniards the party is genuinely fueled by the desire to spend just a little more time with their friends and family.

Not surprisingly, the sunny inhabitants of this city are tolerant of all sorts. Still, young global travelers traveling in flocks are sometimes perceived here as odd birds: swooping down with baseball hats and big running shoes, demanding Internet access and rollerblades. The natives might chuckle at this sight, but mostly they're curious. Madrileños are also happy to know that visitors are interested in learning more about their language and culture, especially since an open relationship has been difficult in the past—it's only in the last 20 years or so (since the end of Franco's reign) that Spain has emerged as a significant First World nation. This is great in certain ways, but it also means that the country has opened itself up to Hollywood, Levi's, and nearly every fast-food chain that America has spawned. The result is that younger people dig Sharon Stone and Keanu Reeves; they listen to Eminem; they have cell phones; they rave. Still, even though young people are more likely than their parents to speak English, this ain't Holland or Sweden, amigo. Chances are that you won't be playing Scrabble anytime soon with any of your new Spanish friends who speak "ah leetul" English.

No matter what language you speak, with so much going on, it's hard to figure out what you're gonna do in the next 5 minutes, much less the next few days. Don't freak out, just get your hands on the all-knowing, all-powerful Buddha of nightlife, *Guía del Ocio.* This weekly magazine has got everything, man: live music, movies, performing arts, bars, clubs, and more. Buy it for 150 pesetas at any kiosk, and kneel down and worship (or read). Other good sources of info are the flyers and employees at hipster and club clothing stores (such as those on Calle Fuencarral) and also the millions of posters around town.

Finally, remember, Madrileños like to get close—really close. At first it's a little frightening when people keep putting their cheerful faces right up to yours when they're speaking, but try and stifle the urge to shove the natives back. If you look around, you'll see that Spanish guys often have a hand on their buddy's shoulders and that many women walk arm in arm with their good friends. Spanish closeness, of course, also has its own etiquette. Although men simply shake hands when meeting for the first time, women kiss each other—and men—on both cheeks when first introduced. Does this imply some lovin' later on? Absolutely not. The tradition of *dos besos* (two kisses) is as old as the culture itself, and you'll seem cold and standoffish if you don't give out *dos besos* to a woman to whom you've been introduced. So don't sweat all the Spanish physical contact. Strangers will bump into you hard without apologizing, and new friends will be holding onto you like you just saved their lives. Go with it, you'll like it.

neighborhoods

A few areas seem to stand out for a young and hopelessly cool traveler such as yourself....**Sol** is the very center of downtown Madrid. Most buses and the busiest Metro lines converge here, as do the thousands of travelers who come to gawk at the impressive **Plaza Mayor.** Good shopping (at El Calle de Preciados) and good drinking (at bar haven Plaza Santa Ana) are also in this general area. The two hundred or so bars in **Bilbao** and **Alonso Martínez** *(three Metro stops to the north and northeast of Sol)* tend to be somewhat white-bread by Spanish standards, but that's by Spanish stan-

five things to talk to a local about

1. Bullfighting: Cruel and unusual or merely unusual? Pretend to be a baby Hemingway with blood lust or a tree-hugger insisting on the use of a tofu bull and see what arguments develop. If you want to check it out first, go to the Plaza Monumental de Toros de las Ventas *(Metro Ventas)* for listings. Seats in the sun cost less.

2. Madrileños love to diss their counterparts up in Barcelona. They'll tell you that the folks in Barcelona are *más cerrado* (closed minded), *separartístas* (separatists), and *más europeos* (more European, less Spanish). Challenge them to explain how they produced so many great artists.

3. The current political party in power is El Partido Popular, which is seeking to close bars at the ungodly hour of 2am! In freakin' Madrid! Ask your local *camarero* (bartender) what he thinks about that, and you'll get an earful. Agree with him and you'll probably get a shot on the house.

4. Most young people will have at least some opinions on the ECU (which becomes "real" money in 2002) and the European Union. Some are thrilled to be able to travel more freely, others are less thrilled about the prospect of all those Europeans traveling freely here.

5. When all else fails, nothing beats an old-fashioned hash vs. marijuana symposium. Most Spanish have never smoked the green and many travelers are newcomers to the cosmically obliterating powers of *el chocolate.*

dards. **Malasaña** *(Metro Tribunal, four stops north of Sol)* is full of artists and musicians, along with the associated poetry readings, great coffeehouses, vegetarian restaurants, and down-home drinking holes. The famed, funky, and fabulous **Calle Fuencarral** begins in this neighborhood and continues right out to the Gran Vía Metro stops. Walking down **Gran Vía,** though, is kinda like eating snails: Experience the slime, excessive panhandling, and decayed greatness of this tired road at least once, just so that you can say you tried it. **Chueca** *(a few blocks south of Gran Vía and west of Calle de Fuencarral)* is the epicenter of Madrid's gay and lesbian communities. This groovy neighborhood has great coffee and shopping by day and perhaps some of the wildest bar scenes in Madrid by night. **Atocha** *(Metro stop of the same name and home of the Atocha Renfe train station),* features some cheap hostels and easy walking to **El Retiro** and **El Prado** [see *culture zoo,* below, for both], but it's special for both its blue-collar bars and its freaky youth bars. **Moncloa** and **Argüelles** (near the university, at the western end of the city) are infested with bars whose clientele all seem to take their partying cues from 1980s college frat-party movies. Definitely check out the low-rent neighborhoods of **La Latina** *(west of Sol)* and **Embajadores** *(south of Sol),* home of the El Rastro outdoor weekend market [see *stuff,* below], and then head over to the terraced, high-profile bars of the **Santiago Bernabeu** area (at the northern

only here

You'll only have to be in Madrid for a day or two before it will dawn on you that everyone here makes out anywhere and at any time. You'll be amazed at the, um, vigor with which young lovers express their affection for each other in public places such as street corners and the Metro. While walking in any of the parks (particularly El Parque del Oeste, which is right near the Complutense University), you'll see couples rolling around together in a way that will make you feel like you're on a certain street in Amsterdam. So what's with the truckloads of PDA? Well, some of it can be attributed to the more open ways of the Spanish in general, but the real reason is more likely to be the fact that most Spanish live with their parents until they get married, at age 30 or so. You'd be getting into your lover's pants in the park too, if Mom was home in the little apartment all day. Besides, as one bright Spaniard put it, it's too bad that Americans think it's OK to walk around the streets with guns but feel it's weird to hug and kiss each other in public.

Uniqueness of a slightly less physically intimate nature can be found in the sprawling, crowded weekend market, El Rastro [see *stuff,* below]. It's really not to be missed. Everything from old telephones to beautiful dresses to random squares of foam—yes, foam—can be bought here. Although a lot of the stuff here is standard (the T-shirts don't change that much from booth to booth) some of the trinkets here are more rare than Saint Stephen at a Dead show. Finally, you don't want to miss Madrid's **Teleférico (cable car)** ride *(Paseo del Pintor Rosales; Tel 91/541-74-50; Metro Argüelles; 11am-9pm daily, weekends only from Oct through Mar; 605ptas round trip),* which connects Casa de Campo and the Parque de Oeste. The slow-moving and mellow gondolas are perfect for seeing and learning more about your host city from a bird's-eye view. In your 11-minute ride, you'll get particularly good views of El Palacio Real, its regal gardens, and the taller buildings of downtown Madrid.

end of the city) to see the flip side. All of these neighborhoods have Metro stops that bear their names.

Walking between these distinct neighborhoods is easy. You'll be amazed again and again at how close they are to each other. When asking for directions, most people will guide you via one of the many *glorietas* (traffic circles) or plazas. The most common points of reference, though, are Metro stops. They're easy to see and are often named after the neighborhoods in which they're located. If you tire of walking, you might want to actually hop on the Metro, which is cheaper than candy (760ptas for 10 trips), quick, and easy to use. The **E.M.T.,** Madrid's public bus system, has the advantage of being above ground but is a whole lot more confusing and much slower. Unless you're gonna be in Madrid for several months and have an advanced degree in Busology, stick to the Metro. All lines are the same price, transfers are free, and you can pick up a pocket-sized map at the ticket booths.

As in most places that aren't the United States, it is very difficult to buy a gun in Spain. There's still crime here, obviously, but the perps are out for your wallet rather than your blood. Watch for pickpockets, especially in the crowded parts of Sol and the weekend market, El Rastro. If you can handle big North American cities, though, most parts of Madrid won't cause you any trouble: Walk in pairs or groups (especially women, although the threat is more like harassment from dirty old men than physical harm), keep track of your stuff, and use common sense. As you already guessed, there isn't a curfew in Madrid. In fact, it's rare that you'll ever hear the word "no" here.

hanging out

If your goal is to meet some actual Spanish people, you're sure to have good luck at the **Plaza Dos de Mayo** *(Metro Tribunal)*. The plaza is the focal point of Malasaña, the most artsy and with-it area in Madrid; a lot of poetry readings, skits, and live music go down here. The smallish plaza with a standard European freestanding arch, surrounded by benches and a little playground, plays host to the occasional drum circle, and young people have been known to score their hash here. Similar activities can also take place at **El Retiro** *(Metro Retiro)*. The locals enjoy running and rollerblading through this enormous park with its tall trees, peaceful lawns, and ornate fountains. It becomes a real spectacle on the weekends when the streets swell up with families, musicians, performers, and vendors. A great attraction here are the rowboats that you can rent for use in the huge man-made pond (it's a small lake, really) located in the center of the park (575ptas for 45 minutes; 10:30am-8:30pm). Although the parks in Madrid are fun, they're not a place to be at night if you are alone.

Starting at about 1am, many street vendors line up on **Gran Vía** with beer, candy, and often hot food like chicken and rice (about 300ptas). There's always groups of people around the vendors catching their breath before hitting the next disco, and since it's quieter out here, you'll usually have an easier time communicating with Juan/Juanita de España than you would in the 300-beats-per-minute din of the clubs. We're not sug-

¿donde esta el estanco?

"How the hell am I supposed to get some stamps for Mom's postcard? And man, could I use a Snickers bar right now...." If this is you or perhaps a collective "you" of friends, head on down to the nearest *estanco,* or tobacco shop. The *estancos* are those little brown stands that you see on most major streets in Madrid. Most of them say TABACO right on them with big yellow letters. These great little places will sell you stamps, postcards, phone cards, cigars, lighters, and assorted snacks. The only way they could be better is if they sold ice cream—but the ice cream stands are usually right next door.

Smoking, by the way, is an integral part of Spanish life. They love it! Unlike California (where apparently it's now illegal to even think about cigarettes while in a public place), smoking here is allowed in the food markets, stores, and hospital waiting rooms. The postal workers smoke while toting around the mail, university students smoke in class, and there is no such thing as a non-smoking section anywhere. You just have to deal with it.

gesting that you'll make friends for life while eating rice on a street corner at 3 in the morning, but you could find some amigos for the next few hours if you *habla* a little. And you shouldn't have too much trouble getting a little info on the next club (or person) that you want to check out.

What's a *guiri?* Well, you are. *Guiri* is Spanish slang for anyone who is foreign—and doesn't necessarily understand the finer points of Spanish culture. The word doesn't have bad connotations, really, it's just what they call you and your Nike-wearing friends. If you've got the urge to talk with some other *guiris* (maybe you're tired of people laughing at how you pronounce *torero*), check out one of the 15 or so Irish pubs in Madrid. **Finbar's** *(Marqués de Urquijo 10; Tel 91/548-37-93; Metro Argüelles; 10:30am-1:30am daily, till 3am Fri, Sat; No credit cards),* for example, upholds the proud tradition of Guinness (575ptas per pint), Jameson, and dark wood decor. It also features live Celtic music on Fridays and Saturdays at 10pm and English Premier League soccer on a large-screen TV during the week.

If the bar-stool scene isn't quite what you're looking for, however, put on something nice (the atmosphere is a little swank) and head over to the *Fiesta de Intercambio* that is held at the **Palacio Gaviria** *(Arenal 9; Tel 91/526-60-69; Metro Sol; 10:30pm-3am daily; V, AE, MC)* on Thursday nights *(Cover 1,500ptas).* Other nights host salsa, tango, and disco *(Cover 1,200-2,500ptas).* The Palacio is a stately club, and the place where you

madrid bars, clubs and culture zoo

BARS/CLUBS ▲
Bulevar **13**
Cafe Jazz Populart **16**
Café La Palma **5**
Cardamomo **17**
Disco Ferraz **1**
Deep **9**
El Viajero **8**
La Comedia Bar **15**
La Taberna de la Elisa **18**
Long Play **12**
Maravillas **10**
Nature **6**
Pub 900 **2**
Siroco **4**
Soma **7**

CULTURE ZOO ●
Museo de la Real
  Academia de Bellas
  Artes de San Fernando **14**
Museo del Prado **21**
Museo Nacional Centro
  de Arte Reina Sofía **19**
Palacio Real **3**
Thyssen-Bornemisza
  Museum **20**

To Bilbao

la Palma

Calle de Fuencarral

Plaza de Alonzo Martinez

Calle de Genova

SERRANO

Calle de Goya

Plaza de la Villa

Plaza de Colón

Jardines del Descubrimiento

COLÓN

Calle de El Escorial

MALASAÑA

Calle de Hortaleza

Calle Fernando VI

Calle de Gravina

Calle Bárbara de Braganza

del Pez

Corredera Baja de San Pablo

Calle de Valverde

Calle de Fuencarral

Calle de Augusto

Figueroa

del Almirante

CHUECA

Calle de Prim

Paseo Recoletos

Calle de Serrano

GRAN VÍA

Red. de San Luis

Gran Via

Calle de Barquillo

Plaza de la Independencia

SEVILLA

Plaza de la Cibeles

Calle de Alcalá

BANCO DE ESPAÑA

Calle de Montalbán

Calle Montera

Calle de Alcalá

Carrera de San Jerónimo

Paseo del Prado

Calle A. Maura

Calle de Alfonso XII

SOL

Calle de la Cruz

Plaza de las Cortes

Calle del Prado

Calle de Cervantes

Plaza de la Lealtad

Plaza C. del Castillo

Plaza Jacinto Benavente

Calle de las Huertas

Calle Atocha

Paseo del Prado

TIRSO DE MOLINA

Calle de la Magdalena

Calle de la Cabeza

ANTÓN MARTÍN

Calle de Gobernador

Calle de Espalter

Calle Jesús y María

Levapiés

Baja

Calle del Amparo

Calle Atocha

Real Jardín Botánico

Calle de Alfonso XII

Calle Mesón de Paredes

Calle de Santa Isabel

ATOCHA

Plaza Lavapies

LAVAPIES

Calle de Embajadores

Calle Miguel Servet

Sta. María de la Cabeza

Paseo de la Infanta Isabel

Estación de Atocha

Ronda de Atocha

might meet that French (or Italian or Greek or Spanish...) girl/guy that you've always dreamed of (lovin' is definitely on the menu here). Also pay a visit to La Plaza Santa Ana (Metro: Sol), where foreign students (and the Spaniards who want to meet them) crawl all over each other like ants as they try to get to the next bar via the narrow cobblestone streets. The area has bars and clubs to suit almost any taste; **La Comedia Bar** [see *bar scene,* below] is definitely a good choice if you're feeling overwhelmed.

bar scene

Madrileños call their nightlife *la marcha* (the march), because they typically prefer to have a single drink in a bar before moving on to the next (and the next, and the next...). So, trying to sum up Madrid's bar scene by describing only a few bars is like trying to tell someone about a beach by showing them only a few grains of sand. Add to the nearly limitless possibilities the fact that there are thousands of people in the streets and the bars don't close until 4am, and it's easy to see why Madrid is the undis-

boozing in madrid

You may be disappointed at first to find that mixed drinks in Madrid are about the same price as at home. But on closer inspection you'll find that the Spanish really know how to mix a drink. Keep your eye on the bartender, and you'll be psyched to see that your rum-and-Coke will almost always be 1/2 to 2/3 good stuff. None of that Puritan, one-shot crap! "Good" bartenders will give you a glass full of rum and top it off with Coke, so watch out. Mixed drinks are often served in two parts—a tall glass with ice and the liquor, and the mixer in a separate glass bottle—so that you can mix the drink to your liking. Nearly all bars will give some sort of rudimentary tapas plate, such as peanuts, chips, or olives. You usually have to pay for more elaborate sorts of snacks. Although a gratuity is included in prices you pay at bars, it's okay to give a small tip (25ptas or so) if you're happy with the service. Keep in mind that many Spanish don't drink to get drunk, at least not right away. If you want to sit at the bar and slam a pint glass against your head, that's all well and fine, but remember that the real party isn't even gonna get started till 2am or so. If you want to get the most Madrid for your money, do like the Spanish do; drink light and eat the tapas they give you until about one in the morning. From there on out, it's more acceptable to be drunker, if that's your thing, as long as you don't get too sloppy. Remember, it's life-*affirming* here.

chico meets chica

Maybe we can describe relations between *el* and *ella* by saying that being sexy is fundamental to the Spanish. Take the words *guapa* and *guapo* for example, which translate to "good-looking in a sexy way." Watching the locals in action will continuously remind you that "in a sexy way" applies to almost everything in this country. Women really are beautiful and feminine and men really are tall, dark, and handsome. The Spanish touch and talk to each other nonstop anyway, so opening conversations can contain a strong sexual charge without implying a threat or a promise. (Of course your average Spaniard could fry an egg or dial a phone with their strong sexual charge; it's what fuels the flair for which they're known.) When you get down to it, though, the general rules are more or less the same here as at home: A guy will buy a girl a drink because he digs her, and if a girl dwells on your eyes, go buy her a drink! Also remember that Spanish men are second only to the Italians when it comes to chasing booty. If you're looking good, baby, expect the whistles and come-ons. And if you're a girl of the tall and blonde variety? Brace yourself.

puted champion of European nightlife. Use the following bars as highlights and *marcha* your butt off—it's the only way to get the full effect. All of these bars have a similar prime time of around 1am on the weekends. The only exception is El Viajero, which usually sees action by 11 at night. Also, unless noted, these bars take pesetas only, no credit cards.

El Viajero *(Plaza de la Cebada 11; Tel 91/366-90-64, Fax 91/366-91-53; Metro La Latina; bar: 7:30pm-3am daily, terrace: 1pm-2:30am daily in summer, restaurant: 12:30pm-midnight daily; V, MC, AE)* is a great bar and restaurant in the very cool La Latina district of Madrid. Get an aerial view of this artist's community while eating in the third-floor terrace or relax on the second floor, which is lit almost entirely by candles—both are potentially very romantic. A little more expensive than average, but so worth it.

There's plenty of room to shake your money maker to the hip-hop playing at **La Comedia Bar** *(Príncipe 16; Tel 91/521-51-64; Metro Sol; 8pm-4am daily).* Of course you'll want to check out the entire international lovefest that is the Plaza de Santa Ana scene, but the warmth and soul of La Comedia is a step above the rest. The crowd is a little heavy on the travelers (it goes with the neighborhood), but that doesn't detract from the heat in the back dance room or the fun, hey-baby attitude that swings in the large, see-and-be-seen front room. Drinks are 900ptas.

Cardamomo *(Echegarry 15; Tel 91/369-07-57; Metro Sol; 9pm-4am daily)* is another Santa Ana bar that has got a lot of dance to it: Flamenco-pop and salsa, to be precise. The grown-up crowd here (25 and up) certainly likes to get down, and with about 300 people, it's easy to get swept up in the moment. The men favor the suit-without-tie mafioso look, while a lot of the women have got this Manhattan/Gypsy thing going on (sleek urban black clothes accessorized with tons of gypsy bangles and baubles). Located in Plaza de Santa Ana, but unique in that few foreigners come here. The drinks are 850ptas.

One final recommendation for dance is **Bulevar** *(Corner of Horteleza and Santa Theresa; Tel 91/308-34-17; Metro Antón Martín; 12:30pm-2am daily)*, which has perhaps one of the greatest DJs in any bar anywhere. On Fridays and Saturdays, DJ Antonio spins an extra-smooth mix of soul, R&B, and funk that will absolutely put you in the mood to groove. The room has several intimate booths, dark, dark wood, dim lights behind a big bar, and the feeling that Humphrey Bogart might walk in at any moment. If he doesn't, you'll still be happy to stare at the crew of good-looking twentysomethings who do come around on a regular basis.

If you don't feel like dancing, try **Pub 900** *(Benito Gutiérrez 30; Tel 91/543-14-51; Metro Argüelles; 4pm-3am Mon-Sat, till 2am Sun)*, which caters mainly to Spanish university students. Sit in a booth here with friends and play one of the many board games that 900 has to offer (and learn some more Español in the process...). Music is Smashing Pumpkins, Lauryn Hill, and Motown, and drinks are only 500ptas. Mood ranges from very chill to super-crowded.

In addition to *la marcha* (or maybe *el staggero* by the end of it) listed above, the following neighborhoods are definitely worth your carousing time. Alonso Martínez is the home of college bars for cool college students who aren't freaks or artists. Yes, many of them might be jocks, but the smart, cool, well-dressed kind of jocks. Don't confuse the bars and people here with the rowdy mayhem that frequently erupts in Moncloa and Argüelles. Santiago Bernabéu (along the Avenida de Brasil) features a fantastic, bustling terrace bar scene. The crowd is similar to the Alonso Martínez set, but more like 30- rather than 20-year-olds. Sit outside with friends, drink, and watch the (well-dressed) Spanish world talk, gesture,

fIVE-O

The Spanish philosophy of shunning complications often applies to the law, too. Cops in Madrid (like their civilian counterparts) are, for the most part, smiling (imagine that in New York!), helpful people. It probably has something to do with the fact that you can't buy a gun in Spain.... It's not uncommon to see officers in the local pubs, taking a short break from their rounds and chatting with the neighbors. As many a Spaniard will tell you, the police rarely care what you're doing if it's not bothering anyone else.

and dance on by. The best people-watching nights here are often right after a *futbol* (soccer) match at the nearby Estadio Santiago Bernabéu.

LIVE MUSIC SCENE

Yeah, the Spanish dance their flamenco, they fight their bulls, and they have their Goyas and Dalís...but they don't do rock 'n' roll very well. It's usually uninspired, unoriginal, high school–level musicianship. The blues scene doesn't bring much more to the table—many of the acts have an American frontman and a barely acceptable local backing group. But the jazz scene is a lot better, and reggae, salsa, and other world beat–style bands usually have it together. And, of course, big-name tours stop in Madrid often. R.E.M., Sugar Ray, and Maceo Parker are just a few of the big acts that have recently played in one of the football stadiums around Madrid. As always, consult the entertainment bible, *Guía del Ocio* (and the thousands of posters around the city) to see who's playing and where. For the most part, the clubs here open at about 9:30pm, the live music starts between 10 and 11 and ends at around 2am, and—in the traditional Madrid style—the clubs remain open till 6am with a DJ. Keep in mind, though, that the Spanish invented arriving fashionably late. Midnight is when things are hottest for live music in this town. You can also skip the live music and just swing by around 3am for the DJ session. These clubs also do not accept plastic unless noted otherwise.

If you're still hell-bent on seeing some Spanish rock 'n' roll, go to **Siroco** (*San Dimas 3; Tel 91/593-30-70; Metro San Bernardo; 9:30pm-6am Thur-Sat; siroco@siroco.es*). At least the venue is small, dark, and loud—the way a rock club should be. The upper floor adds some space, but the stage—and most of the action—is crammed into the basement. The 18–30 clientele is dressed in 1976 AC/DC (Back In) Black, the preferred attire of Spain's rock 'n' rollers. This is a very popular venue on weekends, and the men's room has one of the few condom machines in Madrid. Cover is anywhere from 800-2,000ptas, depending on the act.

Like Siroco, **Maravillas** (*San Vicente Ferrer 35; Tel 91/52-33-07-11; Metro Tribunal or San Bernardo; 9pm-late Fri, Sat*) is a stepping stone for many soon-to-be-bigger acts, the difference being that many of these rising stars aren't from Spain. The modest use of black lights and pink trim in this otherwise dark basement club gives it a burnt-out 1985 California feel, but the drugs aren't as heavy and not many of the 300 or so people that fit in here would recognize anything off of Jane's Addiction's first album besides "Jane Says." The Pixies, however, played here during their first European tour, and more recent FM groups that have visited here include Blur and Kula Shaker. When the occasional DJ spins, this is one of the few non-American bars where you can hear the Beastie Boys. Cover ranges from 800 to 1,500ptas, but does not include a drink because the door is the bands' pay.

Cafe Jazz Populart (*Huertas 22; Tel 91/429-84-07; Metro Sevilla or Antón Martín; 4pm-2:30am daily, till 3:30am Fri, Sat; Cover 250-1000ptas*) is the place for Madrid's lukewarm blues. But its small stage is also graced by "live music of all types," including swing, salsa, reggae, and flamenco. Decorated with old horns and photos of American blues and jazz heavy-weights, this midsized bar attracts a mix of 25-to-40-year-old yuppie types and college-age Spanish artists and musicians (many of whom can speak a little English). Upcoming acts are listed by the entrance. *Raciones* (snacks) are served, and a beer costs 450ptas. Because it's a smaller venue here, you'll want to get a good seat by showing up on time (more or less), usu-ally about 10pm. A lot of Spain was Celtic at one time, which explains why there are at least 15 Irish pubs in downtown Madrid, and there's even a Musica Celta section in the *Guía del Ocio.*

La Taberna de la Elisa *(Santa Maria 42; Tel 91/429-54-15; Metro Antón Martín; 6:30pm-3am Tue-Sun; V, MC, AE)* opened its doors in 1989 and features live traditional music every Friday and Saturday and open jam sessions on Tuesday at 10:30 (Celtic) and Sunday at 9:30 (gen-eral European folk). Although it's true that you'll meet some Irish here, it turns out that the locals (usually young professionals) stop by because they dig the ambiance at Elisa, which is almost Disney-like in its meticu-lous re-creation of an Irish street corner and pub: The bar is crammed with tarnished Irish knickknacks (including a streetlamp in the middle of the pub) and, well, many merry people (maximum of about 150).

Café La Palma *(La Palma 62; Tel 91/522-50-31; Metro Noviciado; 4pm-3am daily, till 3:30am Fri, Sat; lapalma62@hotmail.com; V, MC)* is one of the epicenters of young artist culture in Madrid. Live music is played Thursday-Sunday nights at about 10pm and is oftentimes folk or Cuban. Cover is 1,000ptas, including one drink. This kickin' venue fea-tures four separate rooms: a Moroccan-style 'chill-out' with cushions on the ground for seats, the actual stage room (holds about 250 people when they push the small tables to the back), the bar room, and the cafe room (which has beat-up comfortable booths and the bulk of the art-work). Storytelling [see *arts scene,* below] takes place on Tuesdays at 9:30 (300ptas entrance), and the eclectic artwork, which rotates every 15 days, is by local artists and is for sale.

club scene

Clubs in Madrid always have a schedule that begins at midnight, but nothing happens in any of them before 2:30am. Just accept it, like you accept lying politicians and Jesse on MTV. Although entrance prices *(entradas)* are usually 1,000ptas (or so), they always include a free drink *(consumición)*, and you can pay a little less by picking up door passes at hip clothing stores [see *stuff,* below]. The following clubs are offered as alterna-tives to Madrid's standard-dance-club scene. If you want to get on the good foot at places like **Kapital** *(Atocha 125; Metro Atocha),* **Pachá** *(Barceló 11; Metro Tribunal),* and **Joy Eslava** *(Arenal 11; Metro Sol)* then go for it. They're always crowded and sexy, and sometimes fun, but have dress codes (i.e., no sneakers), cost more, and are usually full of ugly tourists (we can't help it!). The venues below are more real: The clientele speaks Spanish and the doorman won't be wearing a freaking headset. Except for the more styled ES3 and Deep [see below for both], these clubs will not turn anyone away unless they're bleeding from the forehead or foaming at the mouth. Also, all clubs have a coat check, and unless noted, don't accept credit cards, don't have phones, and are open from midnight till 6am.

Nature *(MidDay) (Amaniel 13; Tel 93/132-78-33; Metro San Bernardo; Open Thur-Sat as Nature; 1-8pm Sun as MidDay)* (pronounced 'nah-two-ray') is absolutely worth a visit, especially on Thursdays. Unlike the normal club scene, this place is laid-back and dreddy, with a very open, hole-in-the-wall atmosphere, and DJs spinning mostly house and the occasional (relatively good) techno. The metallic decor and low red lighting makes it seem like Han Solo might show up later on. Little TVs show Japanese anime; wear your old T-shirts, sunglasses, and comfortable sneakers. Entrance is 1,000ptas, and drinks are 900ptas after that.

Although praised by many a local, **Long Play** *(Plaza Vázquez de Mella 2; No phone; Metro Gran Vía; Open Fri, Sat)* turns out to be an average club with even more average techno blaring at the white-bread clientele (aged in the low 20s). The first floor is a lot better, though, with a black and cushy salon feel and more soulful music. Sit back in one of the large semicircular booths here and take in the rich smoke and smell of about 20 *porros* (hash and tobacco joints) being smoked all at once. This club can be fun, but not mind-blowing. Entrance is 1,200ptas (free on Fridays between midnight and 3am), drinks are 900ptas.

RULES OF THE GAME

The legal drinking age in Madrid is 18, but the police certainly don't enforce that law with the same weird vigor as they can in some places. Although all other drugs are illegal, the entire city smokes *porros* like they were chewing gum. *Porros* are tobacco rolled together with hash, and it's pretty much the only way that Spaniards get high. In a small bar, use your judgment before sparking one up—if you're not sure, ask. No matter what the response, it won't include the shocked, you-must-be-a-heroin-addict look that you might get elsewhere. Hash, or *chocolate,* is legal to possess in small amounts for personal use only (a half-gram or less). Smoking and drinking on the streets or in parks is fine with the law. As long as you're cool and in control, Jose Law has got better things to do than give someone a hard time for enjoying themselves. Be forewarned, friends. There's a reason that the hash here is always smoked with tobacco: To smoke it solo in a bowl will take you to Planet WhupAss in approximately 5 minutes. The return flight, however, usually doesn't leave until the following morning. (We're totally serious, by the way.)

festivals and events

Madrid has a bunch of festivals that correspond with Christian holidays, including the **Entierro de la Sardina,** in which a sardine is placed in a small casket, paraded about Madrid, and then buried at Paseo de la Florida. This all takes place on Ash Wednesday (mid-March), for some reason, and thousands participate in the adventure. Despite the lack of ceremonial fish, however, the best festivals take place in the summertime, particularly in May.

The time of the **San Isidro festival** is when Madrid is at its very best. San Isidro is the patron saint of the city, and man, do they love him. The week-long event in his honor takes place during the third week of May (more or less) and is like New Year's, Fourth of July, and Halloween all rolled together! There are kids in costumes, a tremendous amount of hoopla (including live music, carnival food, street markets, dance performances, and more), and the drinking and dancing in the streets (particularly in the Las Vistillas neighborhood) is probably unlike anything you've ever seen. Be sure to check out the fireworks at Las Vistillas. The local tourist offices and the *Guía del Ocio* will have all the info. Also noteworthy, though not as insane, is **Festimad** *(Usually for two days in the middle of June or May; www.festimad.es),* an alternative arts festival highlighting everything from literature to photography to music and dance. Most venues listed in this chapter will have posters with all the info, but contact **Círculo de Bellas Artes** *(Marqués de Casa Riera 2; Tel 91/531-77-00; Metro Banco de España)* if for some reason you don't come across one. If you've got at least one tattoo or more than two earrings, you won't want to miss the **Dos de Mayo** celebration in the Plaza Dos de Mayo in Malasaña on, you guessed it, the 2nd of May! This holiday commemorates Madrid's rebellion against Napoleon's occupation of Spain, but the only people who bother to celebrate are those who live in the plaza of the same name. It's a neighborhood party kind of thing (with food, bands, etc.), but what a neighborhood!

If **Soma** *(Leganitos 25; Tel 91/547-74-26; soma2@mx2.redestb.es; Metro Santo Domingo; Open Thur-Sun)* were in the U.S., its license plates would read 'Live Techno or Die.' Soma hosts big-name DJs like Stacey Pullen (Detroit), but the main dance floor is a glorified hallway that gets too crowded too quick. The two smoky 'chill-out' rooms actually live up to their name, though, and there is pinball, pool, and foos in the recroom. Hardcore ravers hang here, few of whom are older than 22. The club goes by the Superfly moniker on Thursdays, when the crowd and the music both have more soul. Entrance varies from 1,000-1,500ptas.

Disco Ferraz *(Ferraz 38; Tel 91/542-53-29; Metro Argüelles; 11pm-4am Wed-Thur, 11pm-5:30am Fri-Sat; AE, V, MC)* is a salsa discotheque, baby! The girls are *guapa* (good-looking/sexy), the fellas are smooth, and everyone (aged 18 to low 30s) is dancing. Even if your clunky feet can't quite get with it, you can still have a great time watching the smooth and sexy regulars. ES3 has a mid-sized dance floor with a subdued (but effective) lighting system. This place hops on Wednesdays (and weekends), and you oughta get dressed up in your seductive best for the event. Entrance is 1,000-1,500ptas. Drinks are 950ptas.

With great house spinning in a big, beautiful venue, it's no wonder **Deep** *(Ronda de Toledo 1; Tel 90/249-99-94; Metro Puerta de Toledo; Open Thur-Sun)* is so popular. A little more expensive than other clubs, but hey, you're paying to hang with a lot of beautiful people and possibly the best electronica house DJs in town. Killer sound system, killer lights, excellent floor. Dress with taste because looking good is essential to feeling good here. Free entrance 12-3am on Friday and 12-2am on Saturday (the hardcore disco locals make a point of showing up during the last hour of these free entrance times). Although weekend nights are most popular, weeknight options are just as cool, with less crowd: Da Place plays it funky on Wednesdays, and Studio1 gives you '70s Disco on Thursdays. 1,500ptas entrance; 1,000ptas drinks.

ARTS SCENE

▶▶VISUAL ARTS

El Mercado Fuencarral mall [see *stuff,* below] and the nearby Malasaña neighborhood are the epicenters of Madrid's young and happening subcultures. The overall attitude at El Mercado Fuencarral is metallic, 21st century, and "who-the-f—k-are-you," but if you can dig—or at least get past—all that, it's a fantastic source of info on Madrid's art and club scenes. Art shows and dance parties often go down here. Malasaña, on the other hand, is more of a soul shakedown party, mon. This area is the young artists' neighborhood of choice, because it is the home of a fine arts college and a music school. Dreds and artist-types like to congregate in cafes surrounding the Plaza Dos de Mayo, the center of the Malasaña district. Malasaña features more vegetarian restaurants and literary events than any other neighborhood in Madrid [see *eats* and *stuff,* below].

Café La Palma [see *live music scene,* above] is so good we had to write it up twice. Check out this warm and buzzing place to integrate yourself with Madrid's young art scene. It's one of the preferred venues for students at El Colegio de Bellas Artes, and not only can you meet cool artists while enjoying great music or storytelling [see below], you can also buy their work. The walls of the cafe are decorated by a different artist every 15 days. A price list tells you what's what.

The **Escuela de Fotografía y Centro de Imagen** *(Fuentearrabía 4-6; Tel 91/552-99-99; Metro Menéndez Pelayo; 10am-2pm/5-10pm Mon-Fri, 11am-2pm Sat; www.efti.es; No entrance fee)* is half school and half gallery. The featured work is occasionally by students, but prize-winning photography is also often on display (such as winners from the recent Hasselblad Open, an international contest sponsored by the Swedish camera manufacturer). Displays throughout the first floor intermingle with studios, students, and a common room with some exotic image, photography, design, and style magazines that you may not have seen back home. A great way to spend an hour or two, and also a very likely place to strike up a conversation with a local art student. Set in a pleasant neighborhood with tranquil street-side cafes.

The **Facultad de Bellas Artes** *(El Greco 2; Tel 91/394-36-26; Metro Moncloa and then Bus 46 to Avenida de Juan de Herrera; 9am-10:30pm Mon-Sat, gallery 10am-1pm Mon-Sat)* is the school for fine arts at Madrid's huge Complutense University. You can get here only by bus, but it's not too bad, and the reward is that you will be right smack in the middle of the Madrid student art scene! The big, ever-changing gallery here displays paintings, sculptures, and interactive works by students. A second, smaller room hosts plays, discussions, and occasional films. In addition to a lot of books, the library here is home to nearly 300 drawings from students who studied here in the 18th and 19th centuries.

▶▶PERFORMING ARTS

Sometimes it seems like Madrid's theater and other performing arts get overshadowed by its world-class museums and 200 proof nightlife, but the performing arts scene here is alive and well, running the gamut from classical ballet to avant-garde film and theater. Meanwhile, if you want to see the latest Sandra Bullock or Mel Gibson flick dubbed into Spanish, head down to any one of the huge, old theaters at the Callao Metro stop on Gran Vía (hey, it's a great way to learn Spanish). Movies are 800-900ptas (often cheaper on Wed), and the price for snacks is not ridiculous. As always, check the *Guía del Ocio* for a complete listing of what's happening and when.

Cine Doré/Filmoteca *(Santa Isabel 3; Tel 91/369-11-25; Metro Antón Martín; 4-10:45pm for movies—check the* Guía del Ocio; *restaurant 1:30-3:30pm, cafe and cinema 4pm-midnight, closed Mon; No credit cards)* is to the movies what DJs who play the Velvet Underground are to rock 'n' roll. Filmoteca specializes in classic or off-beat films from any director at any time and for only 225ptas a flick. Especially cool in the summer months, when they screen movies out on the *terraza* (patio). All films are original versions (subtitled), and often conform to a theme or director of the week (such as Movies about Trains or Roman Polanski Week). The entire building, including the great cafe and bookstore, has a "golden era of Hollywood" feeling with marble floors and tables, large indoor plants, and subtle turquoise neon highlights. Show up early, as most showings sell out. Pick up the monthly schedule in the foyer.

The movies at **Alphaville Cinema** *(Martín de los Heros 14; Tel 91/559-38-36; Metro Ventura Rodriguez or Plaza de España; 4:30-10:45pm Mon-Sat, opens at 12:30pm Fri, Sat; 850ptas per show, 550ptas on Mon)* are a step more commercial than those at Filmoteca, but in a good, indie sort of way. Features here are usually new independent films. All movies here are shown in their original versions. The largest of the four rooms has new, comfy seating (including two-person lovers' seats). It's cool to sit—and be seen sitting—in the coffeeshop while reading over one of the free hand-outs printed for each movie. Cine de Renoir, a very similar theater, is right next door.

Ensayo 100 *(Ramundo Lulio 20; Tel 91/447-94-86; Metro Iglesia, Bilbao; Showtimes vary, Thur-Sun; No credit cards)* is half acting school and half theater. The small-but-with-it theater stages acts that range from Isaac Chocrón's *La Revolución* to Anton Chekhov's *Uncle Vanya*. The (sometimes English) productions are frequented by young actors, and it's a favorite in the Madrid alternative arts scene. Entrance is 2,000ptas, 800-2,000ptas if you've got a student card. The small pop-art bar here can be a great place to make connections and new friends after a show.

Some say that you can't see the real-deal flamenco in a heartless slab of stone like Madrid, but **Casa Patas** *(Cañizares 10; Tel 91/369-04-96; Metro Tirso de Molina or Antón Martín; Restaurant noon-5pm/8pm-3am daily; Show times: 10:30pm Mon-Thur, midnight Fri-Sat; www.visual-ware.es/guiamad/anct/patas.htm; V)* sure comes close. Skilled and heart-wrenching classical guitar will impress you even before the dancers come out. When they do come out, you'll realize that any flamenco dancer worth her salt is at least as tough as Ice T (but obviously a lot more graceful). The locals come here, and they all know that the delicous meals are definitely secondary when compared to the show. Entrance is 2,000ptas (but very worth it).

There's no confusing what **Madrid en Danza** *(Various venues; Tel 012 — that's it!; Approx May 15-June 15; www.comadrid.es; No credit cards)* is all about. For nearly 15 years, this month-long festival has brought the world's best dance to Madrid, including flamenco, ballet, modern...you name it, and they're dancing it. Over 150 performances in more than 20 different venues. Flyers and posters come out about the middle of April, and all of the events are also listed in the *Guía del Ocio*.

▶▶**CUENTA CUENTOS**

Cuenta cuentos, the traditional Spanish art of storytelling, currently has the coolness equivalent that poetry slams had in Manhattan in their heyday. The Malasaña District (Metro Tribunal) easily has the largest concentration of cafes that host these events; Pepe Botella, Café La Palma [see *live music scene,* above], and nänai [see *gay scene,* below] are just three examples of with-it, smart hangouts in the area that host *cuenta cuentos* sessions once a week. The stories told are by a single performer and usually end as a joke or moral lesson or both. These events are often free and are a definite must-see if you want to meet thoughtful Spaniards or have a truly rich cultural experience. The physical expressions of the performers will lessen the language gap as you listen uninterrupted to true orators with great voices and accents. Most sessions last for an hour or so with about three performers.

If you like *Whose Line Is It Anyway?* (the British version, of course), then you'll love **Libertad 8** *(Libertad 8; Tel 91/532-11-50; Metro Chueca; 1pm-2am Tue-Thur, till 3am Fri, Sat, 5pm-2am Mon; No credit cards),* which hosts *grupo cuentacuentos,* putting a twist on storytelling by having the audience select the topics for the performers' stories. Plus they play awesome classic Argentine tango between performances. This happening little spot also hosts live folk music acts, normal *cuenta cuentos* sessions, and even a young artists' connection night (once a month). Stop by and pick up the monthly schedule to see what's happening next at this old-time intellectuals' and artists' hangout.

Pepe Botella *(San Andrés 12; Tel 91/522-43-09; Metro Tribunal or Bilbao; 11pm-2am daily, till 3am weekends; No credit cards)* is a similar establishment in Malasaña, but with a less revolutionary look and feel. Thursday nights are reserved for poetry reading/storytelling (9:30pm, free), and other events come and go on a less-strict schedule. Check the bulletin board to see what's coming up. This big, ornate coffeehouse and bar has several rooms and many little corners and cubbies to sit quietly in. It's full of sexy bookish types who like to drink.

gay scene

The zona Chueca (chew-ey-ka) is the center of the Madrid gay scene, playing home to femme and butch alike, male or female. The Metro stop of the same name opens right in the middle of a little plaza that becomes a party dynamo at night with happening bars, dance clubs, and drag shows. Many establishments here carry solid literature on the gay community, including free magazines such as *Shangay Express. Entiendes,* a magazine with more local info, can be bought at newsstands local to the area and Gran Vía. The articles in these 'zines are in Spanish, but the advertisements for clubs and bars are occasionally in English. Chueca is more than just gay bars, of course. The bookstores, clothing stores, and many outdoor coffeehouses merit a stroll during business hours. FYI: The verb *entender* (to understand) has special significance in the gay community. If you say that you *entiendo,* you're saying that you're gay. It's kind of like saying that you "really understand."

Café Aquarela *(Gravina 10; Tel 91/522-21-43; Metro Chueca; 3pm-3am daily, till 4am Fri, Sat; No credit cards)* is fabulous. Relax in the warm ambiance and contemplate how they decorated it like grandma's living room and still made it work. Ample old chairs and little dark tables are pleasantly jumbled together, yet the cafe still exudes openness. It can become too crowded at prime time (from 10:30pm on, later on weekends) so it's better to come during daylight hours. Breakfast is served on holidays, Saturday, and Sunday beginning at 11am. Mostly young-and-beautiful gay clientele, but it also caters to a mixed crowd, too. From 250ptas for "café solo" (black) to 800ptas if you want Bailey's in it.

Chueca's Friends *(Plaza de Chueca; No phone; Metro Chueca; 5pm-4am daily; No credit cards)* is just one of the many bars in the Chueca area, but is noteworthy because it has a countertop piled high with flyers and neighborhood newspapers giving you the dope, as well as foosball and electronic darts. Despite these amenities, the spare latex black walls give the big room a slightly cold feeling. The generally mixed gay/lesbian crowd adds its own warmth, though, talking and dancing to a good combination of modern rock and electronica (though you might hear k.d. lang a little more often than you'd like...). Drinks are about 500ptas.

If you don't understand already that **Ovlas** *(Augusto Figueroa 1; Tel 91/522-73-27; Metro Gran Vía; 10:30am-2pm/5-9pm Mon-Sat; V, AE, MC)* is a clothing store for the gay male, the TVs embedded in the floor playing male strip shows will clue you in pretty quickly. You can buy an anatomically correct "Carlos" doll here along with your standard array of dance-club clothes. It also has a small leather section. Ovlas carries a lot of info on the gay community, including local newsletters, club, and bar info.

Although it's not as outrageous as some of the queen clubs, **Ohm** *(Plaza de Callao 4; No phone; Metro Callao; Midnight-6am Thur-Sat; www.interocio.es/ohm; No credit cards)* spins good house and trance, and certainly sees its share of boys in dresses. The single-floor venue is big, with good lights, good sound, and red velour everywhere. On Sundays, the name changes to *Weekend,* and is the preferred hangout for Madrid's bar and club staff (of any orientation) that had to work all weekend. Sunday nights are unbelievably crowded and fun from about 2:30am until when most people are getting ready to start the workweek. Entrance is 1,000ptas, with little trouble from the doorman, unless your pants are on your head or something. Drinks are 1,000ptas.

CULTURE ZOO

Madrid's art museums are awesome, and they're half-off if you have a Spanish student card (anything from a foreign school—particularly if it doesn't have a date on it—usually won't fly). But even at full price most venues are only about 500ptas. The following days are free for all museums: May 18 (International Day of Museums), Oct 12 (Fiesta Nacional de España), and Dec 6 (Día de Constitución Española). If you're walking everywhere, you may want to do the three biggies (Prado, Reina Sofía, Thyssen) together because they form a surprisingly small triangle with each other. The Palacio Real and the Museo de la Real Academia de Bellas Artes de San Fernando are also relatively close to each other. The other museums listed here are a little farther out and may not be worth your time if you don't have a lot of it. It depends on how much of an art-fiend you really are.

Museo del Prado *(Paseo del Prado; Tel 91/330-29-00; Metro Banco de España or Atocha; 9am-7pm Tue-Sat, 9am-2pm Sun; 500ptas, 250ptas students, free under 18, free 2:30-7pm Sat, 9am-2pm Sun):* Where does an 800-pound Museo del Prado sit? Anywhere it wants. Miss the enormous collection of medieval and Renaissance work in this top-notch museum, and your parents will never send you anywhere again. Miss the moody Goyas and trippy Boschs and you only cheat yourself.

Thyssen-Bornemisza Museum *(Palacio de Villahermosa, Paseo del Prado 8; Tel 91/420-39-44; Metro Banco de España; 10am-7pm Tue-Sun, 800ptas adults, 500ptas students):* If you were going to be stranded on a desert island for the rest of your life, which museum would you want with you? Well, the Thyssen would make good company because

by FOOT

To get a whole lot of angry young Madrid in your eye, it's hard to beat a stroll down Calle de Fuencarral. Start at the McDonald's on **Gran Vía** *(Metro Gran Vía)* (for God's sake don't go in!), cross the street, and never look back at that horrible place. The turbulent sights, smells, and fashions of Fuencarral await you on the other side of Gran Vía, and so begins your walk on the wild side. We mention this street often in other sections of this chapter, but we swear that it's sub-Madrid at its best. In the first block or so, you'll pass cramped stores selling everything from wristwatches and walkmans to pornography, but the street quickly transforms itself into a hipster's wet dream. You'll first come across clothing stores of all shapes and sizes. Many of the windows have gallery-style displays, including mannequins with TV-heads and far-out latex fantasies. As you continue, the stores will be joined by restuarants and bars where the fashions being sported by the clientele transform them into living mannequins. Both the stores and the cafes come to a climax at the plaza right next to **Mercado Fuencarral,** which is full of cafe tables, more stores, and a whole lot of people just hanging out.

A few more blocks will bring you to the **Metro Tribunal.** Located here is the **Museo Municipal,** an ugly building whose haunting facade you will not forget anytime soon. Taking a left on any of the streets across from the museum will bring you into Malasaña, our favorite part of the city. Proceeding forward will bring you to a handful more restuarants, and finally, **La Glorieta de Bilbao,** where you can sit at the sidewalk tables of **Café Comercial** [see *wired,* below] and enjoy a small cup of good coffee.

Twenty minutes southwest of Bilbao is **Plaza de España,** the starting point of your second walk. Before beginning, though, you might want to check out some modern—decidedly unhip—Madrid consumer culture: Plaza de España borders **Calle de Princesa** (whose name changes to Gran Vía as you get closer to Sol), which is full of fast food, movie theaters, a VIPS, and—about 2 minutes east of the plaza—one of Madrid's best arcades (featuring the newest pinball machines,

it's got a little bit of everything: from Renaissance to Realism and Cubism to Pop Art.

Museo Nacional Centro de Arte Reina Sofía *(Santa Isabel 52; Tel 91/467-50-62; Metro Atocha; 10am-9pm Wed, Sat, Mon, 10am-2:30pm Sun; 500ptas adults, 250ptas students, free Sat after 2:30pm and Sun all day):* With a whole lot of Picasso, Dalí, and Miró, it's like a modern art supermarket. Price check on the *Guernica* at register 6....

Palacio Real *(Plaza de Oriente; Bailén 2; Tel 91/542-00-59; Metro*

virtual racing, pool tables, and a general level of cleanliness that you won't find elsewhere in this city). Once you get to the Plaza de España proper, take it slow. The beautiful fountains and trees offer a welcome place to sit and relax a few moments. There's often hordes of young people here, too, playing soccer, smoking cigarettes, and otherwise letting time pass by. Continue walking through the plaza lengthwise, toward the southwest, until you come to **Calle de Ferraz.** Think of this busy street as a commercial during your favorite TV show.... Walk 2 minutes to the right (NW), cross the street, and climb up to **El Templo de Debod.** The Egyptian artifacts here were given to Spain and other countries in exchange for financial assistance in the building of Egypt's Aswan Dam. You can pay to go into the small museum at the top of the hill, but you'll have just as much fun taking in the view of the city below, including El Palacio Real and its gardens. There are also pay telescopes to check out the details. If it's a hot day (and it often is in Madrid in the summer) you'll be particularly happy to let the wind cool you down with droplets from the small fountain here. Now that you've been refreshed, walk down the steps on the opposite side of the hill that you climbed up (the western side) and take a right onto the **Paseo del Pintor Rosales.** This shady, windy pathway runs through the end of **El Parque del Oeste** and is a great place to hold hands with a new "friend." Now that you're in the mood, you will be happy to notice that Madrid's **Teleférico** [see *only here,* above] is right in front of you. Climb into one of the cable cars and relax. You'll be dropped off at the eerily bare **Casa de Campo,** which is supposed to be a nature reserve, but don't let the scrub brushes and dirt paths drag you down. Go to the *cafetería* and have a drink; you've earned it. Walk around a bit more if you like, and then return via the gondolas. When you return, cross Calle de Ferraz again and walk down **Calle de Marqués de Urquijo,** where most of the trendy little pubs accept credit cards and serve authentic Spanish cuisine.

Opera; 9:30am-5pm Mon-Sat, 9am-2pm Sun and holidays; 900ptas): Real? Royal? No matter how you spell it, it means splendor and opulence on a level you never thought possible. The nifty clocks alone make it worth a visit, but the official tour can make it all seem big, beautiful, and boring.

Museo de la Real Academia de Bellas Artes de San Fernando *(Alcalá 13; Tel 91/522-14-91; Metro Sol or Sevilla; 9:30am-2:30pm Sat-Mon, 9:30am-7:30pm Tue-Fri):* If it's Spanish, they've got it

12 hours in madrid

1. **Rastro Sunday Market:** The constant physical contact with the crowds, the hawking of bizarre goods, and the various smells make this a must. Buy a can of beer from one of the shops and walk, baby [see *stuff,* below].

2. **Retiro Park on the weekend:** Promenade along the main pool and check out the dozens of musicians, puppeteers, mimes, and other freaks [see *hanging out,* above].

3. **Plaza Mayor lunch:** Lunch doesn't begin in Spain till about 2pm, but if you show up a little earlier, you'll be sure to get a ringside seat at one of the several restaurants that keep shop in the Plaza Mayor. Tourists? Oh yeah. But also the most toothless, rowdiest, weirdest, panhandlers in all of Madrid. It's a freakin' circus.

4. **Disco nite till dawn:** Madrid cannot be messed with in the world of the Late Night. Choose from any one of our fine selection of nightclubs [see *club scene,* above], or seek out something new, but whatever you do, make it last till dawn. The whole rest of the city will be dancing and drinking right there with you.

5. **Malasaña dinner and drinks:** Malasaña is distinctly young, artsy, and bohemian—and distinctly Spanish. Enjoy authentic Spanish cuisine and atmosphere at Albur [see *eats,* below] before hitting the Plaza Dos de Mayo [see *hanging out,* above] and the bottle.

6. **Las Vistillas:** Metro Opera will bring you within a few minutes' walk of this lovely little neighborhood that happens to have a spectacular view of El Palacio Real. Pleasant gardens with fountains

here. Sculpture, 18th-century painting, and photography are only a few steps away from Puerta del Sol.

Ermita de San Antonio de la Florida Panteón de Goya *(Glorieta de San António de la Florida; Tel 91/542-07-22; Metro Príncipe Pío; 10am-2pm/4-8pm Tue-Fri, 10am-2pm Sat-Sun; 300ptas):* Goya painted the ceiling of this church shortly before his death. Although considered his finest moment, it is, after all, only one moment. Unless Goya is your god, if your time is limited, best stick to the museums downtown.

modification

You certainly could get a few extra holes in your body while running with the bulls, but you're less likely to get an infection if you go to a professional. **El Rastrillo** *(Montera 17; Tel 91/532-28-48; Metro Sol; 11am-9pm Mon-Thur, 11am-9:30pm Fri-Sat; V, MC, AE)* has a tattoo and piercing parlor above and a headshop/used clothing store below. The good folks upstairs are licensed, sterile, and will pierce anything (you can point at the pictures if you

and great outdoor seating under shady trees (and on real grass) make this little place an island of tranquility in the otherwise loud and paved sea of Madrid. Directions: Get yo ass to the Royal Palace. Walk south along Calle de Bailén. Cross the big bridge. Turn right immediately after the bridge and you're there.

7. **Walk on the wild side at Calle de Fuencarral:** This street begins at Gran Vía with all the grime, heavy traffic, and lost souls that you'd expect from a city of 5 million. From there it becomes starving artists and club chic [see *by foot,* above].

8. **One floor of the Thyssen-Bornemisza Museum:** Although it's probably the least known of Madrid's big three museums, the Thyssen easily has the best variety. Get in the mood, maybe bring a walkman, and enjoy the show [see *culture zoo,* below].

9. **Sol Survivor:** You'll probably wind up in Puerta del Sol whether you like it or not. It's the epicenter of downtown Madrid. There's a political demonstration of some sort most days of the week here. Be sure to check out the military guys with the wacky hats on the south end of the plaza (opposite Gran Vía).

10. **Get some PDA, baby!:** Yes, that's right. We're suggesting that a higlight of Madrid is to make out on a street corner while surrounded by strangers. It's liberating, it's a rush, and it feels right [see *only here,* above].

don't know the word for clitoris...). They charge 2,000ptas to add some weight to your ears or nose, but the jewelry itself begins at 2,400ptas.

Mao & Cathy *(Corredera Alta de San Pablo 6; Tel 91/523-13-33, Fax 91/531-19-73; Metro Tribunal; 3:30-8pm Mon (no tattooing on Mon), 11am-2pm/3:30-8pm Tue-Sat; No credit cards)* is Madrid's oldest and, according to many, best tattoo parlor. The place just has the right feel to it: You know you're in good hands the moment you walk in. A tattoo will cost you 5,000ptas and up. Piercing costs about 5,500ptas for your ear or nose, but the jewelry costs a lot less: starting from 600ptas. Mao & Cathy will also pierce anything in your pants, starting at 10,000ptas.

great outdoors

Of course the easiest place to go running is the huge city park, El Retiro *(Metro El Retiro).* The only problem is that you might be running from pickpockets and panhandlers as much as for your health. The Calle de Moyano is the best entrance for running and rollerblading, because it is far from all of the pond-related hype that goes down in the central part of the park. The high altitude of the **Parque Juan Carlos I** *(Metro Campo de las Naciones; 9am-11:30pm daily),* and its removal from the city makes it worth the half-hour Metro ride from downtown. A weird mix of nature and huge modern statues and bridges gives the park a postapocalyptic, *Planet of the Apes* vibe that is somehow very calming. Without a doubt, this is Madrid's best location for biking, running, rollerblading, skateboarding, kite flying, frisbee throwing, and day tripping [see *need to know,* below, for bike rental info]. You might even enjoy the *espectáculos* on Thursday-Sunday nights at 10:30pm; they include music, fireworks, and synchronized fountains. As with most things, consult the *Guía del Ocio* for specific times and prices. FYI: Parque Juan Carlos I is completely safe for single women during the day. Nobody hangs out here unless they've come for one of the specific activities listed above. The weirdness/sliminess factor is zero.

The bulletin board at **Central Vegetariana** [see *eats,* below] has great information on acupuncture, yoga, and other healthy activities in the Madrid area, and the friendly staff is more than happy to chat with you about the holistic happenings in Madrid. If you actually want to interact with nature, it's best that you hop on the magic bus *(Bus 724 from Plaza de Castilla, 130ptas)* and travel north for an hour toward the village of **Manzares el Real.** This small village is the base point for the enormous **Pedriza National Park.** On weekends, the main road becomes polluted with Madrileños driving their cars to a central area of the park for a picnic, but they're clearly missing the point. You'll be much happier with the fantastic hiking trails (over 1,000 of them), lush and green scenic views, and fresh air.

STUff

What are you going to bring home to your folks and friends? A flamenco dancer doll? A little keychain that says "I ♥ España?" An unabridged *Don Quixote?* If you're looking for gifts, your friends might dig one of those infamous "Italian recordings" of a favorite band in concert. Or if it's fashion you want, whip out your plastic and get on down to Puerta del Sol, where stores such as **Zara,** and even **El Corte Inglés** (both on Calle de Preciados) will be more than happy to help you spend your money fast. Only slightly less expensive, but a lot more club-oriented, are the nearly 30 clothing stores on Calle Fuencarral between Gran Vía and the Tribunal Metro Stops. This street has also got plenty of information on which clubs you want to see tonight. At its epicenter is the three-story-high mall **Mercado Fuencarral** *(Fuencarral 45; Tel 91/521-59-85; Metro Tribunal, Gran Vía, Chueca; Stores and cybercafe open from 10am-11pm Mon-Sat, till 2am Thur-Sat; A few stores take plastic),* a must-see for those who wanna get with it in Madrid. This throbbing core of coolness features nearly 50 stores that sell clothes, jewelry, smoking equipment, music and other (sub)culturally relevant items. Also has a (sometimes free) movie theater, two bars (one of them with internet a la Net Café [see *wired,* below] and a hair stylist, all of them named a variation of Fuencarral.

▶▶**BOUND**

The huge, corporate-feeling, **Casa Del Libro** *(Gran Vía 29; Tel 91/521-22-19,*

moda

If you're *de moda,* you're in style, and in Madrid, like in any other city that has publicly elected officials and Lenny Kravitz on the radio, moda is what you make of it: hippie, chic, metal, whatever. Although they're always well dressed (i.e. prep), the run-of-the-mill Madrileños are clearly not in touch with the edgy fashion scene from Paris or New York. One distinguishing characteristic, though, seems to be that the fashion here is tighter, particularly—but not exclusively—for the girls. Of course, women from all over will wear little tank tops and dresses in the summer, but Madrid women really go for the "butt" look. Really. The attitude here is that any butt, from "too-flat-to-pedal-a-bike" and all the way to "juicy fruit," is looking good when wrapped up in black stretch pants or small jeans. And the club gear? Well...it's club gear, friends. The Spanish sorority-girl types will wear the international S.P. (sorority pants) and white tops until they die, and, as in the rest of the world, fellas in the know are currently wearing the Adidas running pants with a T-shirt or tanktop that's clean.

Fax 91/522-77-58; 9:30am-9:30pm Mon-Sat; www.casadellibro.com) will have any book that you could ever want, especially maps and dictionaries. They have some titles in English, too. Much like Borders or Barnes & Noble, you can sit and read for as long as you want without anyone bothering you. Large posters in the stairwell quote famous people from the Marx Brothers to Einstein to Cervantes; reading them is a great way to practice your *Español.*

Calle de los Libreros *(Off of Gran Vía; Metro Callao; Most stores open from 9am-12:30/4-8pm Mon-Sat; Most don't accept credit cards)* is more than just a name. Yup, it really is a street that's full of booksellers. Makes for a great stroll, but many of these stores cater to university courses, meaning that a few of the *librerias* here have only chemistry or biology books. The majority, however, carry cool philosophy titles and the usual assortment of literary greats. If you want to get *The Iliad* or *The Sun Also Rises* in Spanish, this is the place. (If you want something in English, though, you best head back to Casa Del Libro or wait till you get home.) Most stores also have a small used-book section.

Cuesta de Moyano *(Outdoor vendors on Calle de Moyano; Metro Atocha; 10am-2pm/6-9pm Mon-Fri, 9-3pm Sat, Sun; No credit cards)* is the emotional, silly Stimpy to the academic, loveless Calle de los Libreros' Ren. More than 30 vendors line up along this tree-lined slope of a street to buy and sell any book you can imagine. Romances, kids' titles, and popular novels fill each vendor's booth to the brim with possibilities. If chance is on

madrid eats and crashing

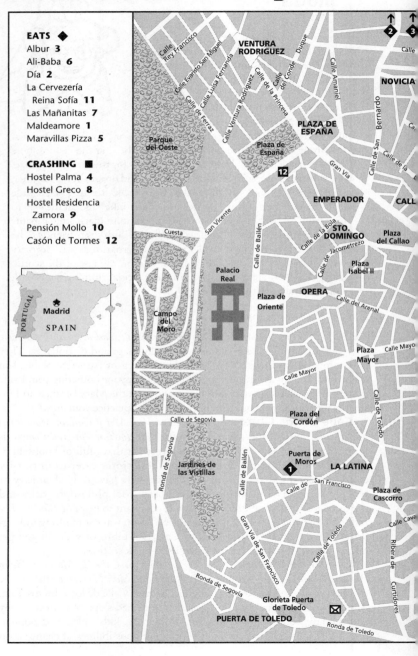

EATS ◆
Albur **3**
Ali-Baba **6**
Día **2**
La Cervezería
  Reina Sofía **11**
Las Mañanitas **7**
Maldeamore **1**
Maravillas Pizza **5**

CRASHING ■
Hostel Palma **4**
Hostel Greco **8**
Hostel Residencia
  Zamora **9**
Pensión Mollo **10**
Casón de Tormes **12**

your side (bring your lucky rubber nipples), you might find some real treasures here.

▶▶PAYING RETAIL

No Comment *(Fuencarral 39; Tel 91/531-19-57; Metro Gran Vía; 10:30am-9pm Mon-Sat; nocomment@nc-f39.es; V, MC, AE)* is one of literally dozens of cool clothing shops on Calle de Fuencarral and Calle de Hortaleza between the Gran Vía and Tribunal Metro stops. All-new, all-hip clothing and accessories for guys and girls. Very friendly staff and lots of club information.

Get wedding gifts and things for grandma at **Casa Talavera** *(Isabel Católica 2; Tel 91/547-34-17; Metro Santo Domingo; 10am-1:30pm/5-8pm Mon-Fri, 10am-1:30pm Sat; No credit cards)*. One thing that Spain does well is ceramics, and Casa Talavera sells only the best. The small store is stuffed with soup bowls, vases, tiles, lamp shades, etc. Take your time looking, because many treasures are semi-hidden throughout the store's clutter. From 800ptas for a single tile to 14,000ptas or higher for enormous, ornate vases that could hide a monkey.

▶▶TUNES

Club Amigos del Disco *(Fernandez de los Ríos 93; Tel 91/543-05-03; Metro Islas Filipinas; 10am-2pm/5-8pm Mon-Fri, 10am-2pm Sat; No credit cards)* is also amigos with vinyl, cassettes, and posters. They buy and sell CDs. This place is not exactly downtown, but is worth checking out because it's loaded with those legal-only-in-Italy live recordings of your favorite bands. The atmosphere here is exactly like your favorite local record store back home: posters covering the walls, Beck on the stereo, and scruffy musician-types flipping through the records for their find-of-the-week.

If, by some remarkable twist of fate, you cannot find what you're looking for here, you can always head over to **FNAC** *(Preciados 28; Tel 91/595-61-00; Metro Callao; Bus 44, 75, 133, 146, 147; 10am-9:30pm Mon-Sat, noon-9:30pm Sun; AE, MC, V)*, located in Sol's Calle de Preciados. FNAC is the musical equivalent of Casa del Libro: very corporate, very big selection (featuring too much Top 40 and a good selection of world music), and very many listening centers. They also carry a huge selection of videos, magazines, software, and international newspapers.

▶▶THRIFT

The infamous **El Rastro** *(Various streets; Metro La Latina and Tirso de Molina; 9am-2pm Fri-Sun; Credit cards? Yeah, right)* outdoor market is a seething concoction of bootlegged T-shirts, questionable antiques, and won't-find-anywhere gifts for friends back home. It's one of the most fun things you'll see in Madrid. There are some true artisans mixed in with the homeless people selling a few rusty nuts and bolts, and there's also plenty of bars to have a bite to eat and maybe a small *caña* of beer. Watch your pockets here, and try and check out the scene on Sundays before noon. Friday and Saturday are only half as much fun, as the place becomes unbearably crowded by 12:30.

EATS

Madrid is well known for the richness of its nightlife, but the cuisine is surprisingly bland in comparison. In general, your options are 1) Something that came from a pig; 2) Spanish *tortilla* (a tasty, thick, omelet kind of thing made of eggs and potatoes); and 3) Fast food (like everywhere). Even the mighty Spanish *paella* (yellow rice topped with meat and seafood in a spicy, brothy sauce) is less common than one would think. If you want something cheap, take three steps in any direction and walk into the nearest...pub! Nearly all bars and *cafeterías* are open from about 7am till 2am and serve *tapas* (small sandwiches or portions of food) like *tortilla,* calamari, olives, or something with bacon. Tortilla is always a safe bet for breakfast or a snack; it's served with bread and costs only 250-350ptas. In the afternoon, usually from around 1-4pm, the larger of these *cafeterías* will serve *El Menu del Día* (about 1,000-1,500ptas), which consists of bread, an appetizer (usually a vegetable), two main plates (usually pasta, soup, or a meat dish), dessert, and a drink (beer, water, or wine). Other inexpensive options are the *alimentación* stores (a Spanish 7-11), outdoor markets, and even supermarkets. **Día** *(San Bernardo 83; Metro San Bernardo)* is a particularly low-cost chain with several locations. If you aren't finding a whole lot of vegetarian options in the restaurants and your protein count is running low, try the cozy **Central Vegetariana** *(La Palma 15; Tel 91/447-80-13; Metro Tribunal; 10am-2pm/5-8pm Mon-Fri, 10am-1:30pm Sat)*. The friendly staff at this market is happy to answer your questions about soy chorizo or any other vegetarian/vegan food, supplement, or drink that they sell.

A handful of restaurants at **Plaza Emperador Carlos V/Ronda de Atocha** *(Metro: Atocha)* stay open for 24 hours on the weekends, but other than that, you will have to settle for a 7-11 or the Spanish equivalent, VIPS, after you've sampled the local *chocolate* and are red-eyed and starving. Also remember that you can drink in any restaurant in Spain; even Burger King and KFC serve beer!

▶▶CHEAP

La Cervezería Reina Sofía *(Atocha 108; Metro Atocha; 6am-2am daily; No credit cards)* is one of a handful of restaurants at Metro Atocha that stays open practically 24 hours. 'Nuff said. La Reina is here for your drunken needs with food (250ptas for a Spanish *tortilla* sandwich) and beer. If you're experiencing Madrid properly, you'll arrive at this otherwise average corner bar too late at night for the fluorescent lights and typically dirty floors to make an impact. Besides, this place is really nothing more than a human gas station; it's best to get your food and get out. If you want atmosphere, hit the bars and clubs.

Ali-Baba *(Velarde 8; Tel 91/448-55-20; Metro Tribunal; 12:30-4pm/8pm-midnight Mon-Thur, till 2am Fri-Sat, 8pm-midnight Sun; No credit cards)* is located in another drinking district, Malasaña. Yes, you came to Spain to experience Spanish culture and cuisine, but how much pig can you eat? Ali-Baba's got the Middle Eastern flava, so get a falafel or some hummus. The simple restaurant is too small to offer anything more than standup counters and a few posters of Israel, but the music is always fun Middle Eastern pop, and—at only 350ptas—the food is delicious and authentic.

▶▶**DO-ABLE**

Maravillas Pizza *(Plaza 2 de Mayo 9; Tel 91/523-19-73; 12:30pm-2am/3:30am on weekends, evenings only (from 5pm) Oct-May; pepitilla @olemail.com; No credit cards)* offers great pizza, casseroles, and several vegetarian dishes as well as huge salads from 700ptas. The outdoor seating opens up onto the plaza and offers fantastic people watching (including the other patrons). This is one of the best hangouts for young artists and people who just want to look that way.

If you're feeling a little New World, try **Las Mañanitas** *(Fuencarral 82; Tel 91/522-45-89; Metro Bilbao or Tribunal; 1:30-4pm/9-11:30pm Mon-Fri, 1-4pm Sat, Sun; V, MC)*. Despite the common language, many Mexican restaurants in Spain are, well, crappy. Las Mañanitas, however, is *muy bueno*. The maize-colored floor tiles, mariachi music, and simple (but comfortable) furniture—along with great nachos, quesadillas, and margaritas—will make you happy to be there. Meals cost around 800-1,500 ptas.

For local tastes, check out **Albur** *(Manuela Malasaña 15; Tel 91/594-27-33; Metro Bilbao; Noon-1am daily, till 2am on weekends; V, AE, MC)*. They serve their fantastic *paella* on weekends only, but the traditional Spanish cuisine served the rest of the week is also right on the money. Albur has a fun, neighborhood-restaurant atmosphere, Spanish-style: small tables crammed together (be prepared to make friends with some fellow diners), a staff that's truly *gracioso* (witty, funny), and wine that flows as quickly as the locals' animated Spanish chatter. Plus you get a free shot of cider liquor at the end of your meal. *Plato del Día* is 1,100ptas.

▶▶**SPLURGE**

A perfect atmosphere with a beautiful menu and...sushi!! **Maldeamore** *(Don Pedro 6; Tel 91/366-55-00; Metro La Latina; Noon-2am Tue-Sun, Dinner 9pm-12:30am only; AE, V, MC, DC)* also offers you many fantastic salads, Gil Gilberto on the stereo, and the coolest bar stools you ever saw. It's all very uptown: Hardwood floors and old, old brick walls sit agreeably with fresh flowers and the stainless-steel bar. The building is historically protected; its lower level is created from arches and walls that were built in Moorish times. Prices run 1,200 to 2,500ptas for an entree; the sushi combo platter is 3,000ptas.

crashing

Don't sweat trying to find a hostel in the "right" area. Yeah, Madrid's a big city, but it's physically squished. The various zones are surprisingly close together, and if you're centrally located you'll never have to walk for more than 20 minutes to get to your destination (5 or 10 is usually more like it). If you're a big lazy-ass who doesn't feel like walking, the Metro will obviously make any trip a lot shorter. If all else fails, cabs breed like flies in

wired

Most of us know that using e-mail is the best way to keep up with latest gossip back home, but who knew that the Internet cafes in Madrid would be prime locations to create some gossip of your own? When you walk into an e-mail center, be prepared to get checked out. Not like a quick-turn-of-the-head look, but more of a "mmm, mmm, mmm..." look. Seriously, forget the bars and discos, and never mind all those small cafes and museums; 90 percent of the people in Internet cafes are foreigners between 20 and 30 years old. Add the fact that—like with everything else in Spain—you can smoke and drink at these locations, and you've got yourself a regular little scene. Common lines include "Do you know how to use hotmail?," "Did your computer stop working, too?," and "Where'd you learn to type like that?" Perhaps the best place for said lines is the **Net Café** *(San Bernardo 81; Tel 91/594-09-99; Metro San Bernardo; 10am-2am daily, till 3am Fri, Sat; www.net-café.es; No credit cards),* which plays loud modern rock, displays random movies on a projector screen, and mixes stiff drinks. It's a dark bar first and Internet station second, with eight computers ingeniously recessed into Star Wars–style bar tables that function as computer screens and, well, bar tables. Internet use is free for 45 minutes if you buy one drink worth 500ptas or more. Although **Café Comercial** *(Glorieta de Bilbao 7; Tel 91/521-56-55; Metro Bilbao; 8am-1:30am Sun-Thur, 8am-2:30am Fri-Sat; No credit cards)* is a lot quieter, you can still buy drinks and food from the cafeteria downstairs. Computer use is a mere 500ptas per hour, but, because the computers are coin-op(!), there is no technical support here. Café Comercial is also a great place to study in general, as there are huge windows and always many vacant tables here. If you've got actual work to do, you best head down to **Gopher Web** *(Cea Bermúdez 66; Tel 91/399-34-39; Metro Islas Filipinas; 7:30am-12:30am daily; información@www.gopherweb.com, www.gopherweb.com; No credit cards).* The rates here are nearly double the other places (700ptas for an hour—although there are bulk-time discounts), but you can use Word and its MS Office brethren, save to floppy disks, and print. Plus, they have 20 machines, and the staff knows what it's talking about.

Madrid and are safe, honest, and very cheap, especially if you're traveling with a few people. Although impostor cabs are extremely rare, be sure that your cab is white with the little green light on top. Your ride will be metered with extra charges for luggage, of course, and you can tip a little (5 percent) if you like; tipping for any service is not a big part of Spanish culture.

Most hostels in Madrid keep their main doors locked and buzz their tenants in. Although totally annoying and inconvenient, it's true that your backpack is a lot safer this way. So, even though most hostels will tell you that they don't have a curfew, be patient when you are ringing the bell to be let in at 6am!

Though we think the places we've picked are the best, if they're all booked and you need more choices, go to any bookstore and pick up the **Guia Oficiale de Hotels,** which is a comprehensive list of all the hotels in Madrid. It's in Spanish, but addresses and phone numbers are the same in any language. Or, if you're the plan-ahead type, log on to *www.hotelsearch.com* or *http://madrid.hotels.ru/spain/madrid/hotall/asp,* either of which will give you a list of Madrid hotels and let you book a room on line at no charge.

▶▶**CHEAP**

The small, pleasant **Hostel Palma** *(Palma 17, 1st floor; Tel 91/447-54-88; Metro Tribunal or San Bernardo; 2,000ptas single; 3,500 double; No credit cards)* is right where the action is: Malasaña. Because it is clean, accessible, and on a relatively quiet street, you get much more than your money's worth here. Each room has a sink and a simple desk, chair, and closet. Many rooms also have balconies. The common bathroom is clean. The best thing about this hostel is that they give you a key to the building, allowing you to come and go whenever (and with whomever) you please.

The building and main hallway at **Pensión Mollo** *(Atocha 104, 4th floor; Tel 91/528-71-76; Metro Atocha; 2,000ptas single; 3,600ptas double, 5,100ptas triple; No credit cards)* are dark and dingy, but the rooms are very bright and pleasant. Along with a basic chair, desk, and closet, many rooms also have a small balcony. All triples and some doubles have private bath, singles have only a sink. For 300-800ptas, the staff'll do your laundry. Close to the **Prado** [see *culture zoo,* above], Atocha Renfe train station, and the Atocha bar district.

These two all full-up? Never fear, there are a couple other good, cheap options: **Albergue Santa Cruz de Marcenado** *(Calle de Santa Cruz de Marcenado 28; Tel 91/547-45-32; Dorm bed 1,200ptas under 26, 1,820ptas over 26, no private baths, breakfast included; 1:30am curfew; No credit cards),* with 72 beds; and **Hostal-Residencia Mondragon** *(Calle San Jeronimo 32, 4th floor; Tel 91/429-68-16; single 2,000ptas, double 3,000ptas, triple 3,900ptas, no private baths; No credit cards).* Cool fact: The first Spanish motion picture ever, *Ría en un Café,* was filmed in the Residencia Mondragon!

▶▶**DO-ABLE**

Hostel Residencia Zamora *(Plaza Vázquez de Mella 1, 4th floor; Tel 91/521-70-31; Metro Gran Vía; 4,500ptas single, 7,000ptas double, 9,000ptas triple, 12,000ptas quad; V)* was renovated only a few years ago, and all the rooms now have private bath, television, heat, and air conditioning. Really nice patterned hardwood floors, too. Because the rooms overlook the Plaza Vázquez de Mella, all the rooms are bright as well as quiet. If you don't have a reservation and are worried about getting stranded, check out this hostel first because there are several others in the same building. Convenient to Gran Vía, Sol, and Calle de Fuencarral.

All rooms at **Hostel Greco** *(Infantas 3, 2nd floor; Tel 91/522-46-32; Metro Gran Vía; 4,600ptas single, 7,000ptas double, 9,000ptas triple; V, MC)* have private baths, phones, TVs, and closets. Most have a safe deposit box. One of about 25 hostels in the area, but most rooms here are big and sunny with ornate mirrors and simple desks and chairs. Very close to Gran Vía, Sol, Chueca, and the cool parts of Fuencarral and Hortaleza streets. The husband's kind of grumpy; save your questions for the wife.

Other reasonable options include **Hostal Cervantes** *(Cervantes 34, 2nd floor; Tel 91/429-27-45; 6,500ptas double, private bath; No credit cards)*, near Retiro Park; the sunny and newly renovated **Hostal-Residencia Luz** *(Calle Fuentes 10, 3rd floor; Tel 91/542-07-59; 2,500ptas single, 3,700ptas double, 5,500ptas triple, 1,000ptas extra for private bath in any room, laundry 1,000ptas; No credit cards)*, in the center of town; and **Hostal-Residencia Rober** *(Calle Arenal 26, 5th floor; Tel 91/541-91-75; 3,600ptas single w/shower, 4,500ptas w/ bath, 5,700ptas double w/bath, 7,000ptas triple w/bath, all rooms have TV and A/C; No credit cards)*, which offers non-smoking rooms.

▶▶**SPLURGE**

The rooms at **Casón de Tormes** *(Río 7; Tel 91/541-97-46; Metro Plaza de España; 14,100ptas single, 17,000ptas double; V, MC, AE)* have private baths, air conditioning, TVs, and telephones, but it might be the laundry service that you appreciate most. Located near the start of one of our two walks at the **Plaza de España** [see *by foot*, above]. This hotel also offers a bar for your traveling pleasure....

If you're looking for something with a little more spice (wink, wink), check yourself into the funky **Hotel Monaco** *(Calle Barbieri 5; Tel 91/552-46-30, Fax 91/521-16-01; 7,500ptas single, 10,700ptas double, 13,500ptas triple, 15,000ptas quad, private baths; V, MC, AE)*. This swanky hotel is housed in a former bordello and the owners have parlayed that fact into a whole theme, with R-rated frescoes and big ol' mirrors everywhere. Even if you don't have the bucks to stay here, stop by their hip lounge, bar, or cafe.

need to know

Currency Exchange The local currency is the *peseta*. You can exchange money in the airport and in Cambio booths around the Sol neighborhood, but a bank, ATM, or credit card will always get you the best rates and the lowest service charge.

Tourist Information It's not the main Tourist Office *(Tel 91/429-49-51)*, but the one located in the **Plaza Mayor** *(Tel 91/588-16-36; Metro Sol; 10am-8pm Mon-Sat)*, is by far the easiest to get to and has adequate information on Madrid. The office will reserve a room for you for the same night only, and they can also give you a list of all the accommodations in Madrid.

down and out

Diving for butts? Tumbleweed blowing through your wallet? Well...if **Filmoteca** [see *arts scene,* above] has already sold out its 225ptas shows, and you've gotten all you can out of the **Thyssen museum** [see *culture zoo,* above], then maybe you ought to hop on the city bus, route Circular, and get a 50-cent tour of the city. This route can be picked up at the bus stops in Sol, and will last about an hour and 15 minutes.

Public Transportation It all boils down to the **Metro** (subway) and the **EMT** (buses). Both use the same tickets, but the Metro is infinitely easier to use. Plus, it's (usually) fast, safe, and clean. Buy your 10 trip MetroBus pass in the subways or select news/tobacco stands for only 760ptas (about 50 cents a ride). Metro system *planos* (maps) are located at the ticket windows. The subways are closed from 1:30am till 6am.

American Express *(Tel 91/572-03-20, Plaza de las Cortes 2; Metro Banco de España).*

Health and Emergency Emergency: *112.* The two main hospitals in Madrid are **Ciudad Sanitaria la Paz** *(Paseo de la Castellana 261; Tel 91/727-70-00; Metro Begoña)* and **Hospital General Gregorio Marañón** *(Doctor Esquerdo 46; Tel 91/586-80-00; Metro Ibiza or O'Donnell).*

Pharmacies Every little neighborhood in Madrid has at least one *farmacia,* marked by big **green neon crosses**. *Farmacias* rotate the all-night responsibility. Each one posts a schedule of who will be open on which night, as do the major newspapers like *El País*. Plus there's an always-24-hour one in **Plaza Antón Martín** *(Metro Antón Martín).*

Telephones City code: *91;* operator: *1003;* international operator: *1005.* They do have to dial 00 (like everybody else), so the operator knows it's an international call, then dial the area code and number. Note that recent changes in Spain's phone system now require that all local calls within Madrid be dialed with the 91 prefix. Nearly all pay phones in Madrid have a chart that lists all that info, so don't worry about committing it to memory. All pay phones in Spain can use *tarjetas telefónicas* (phone cards), which can be bought at tobacco stores and *estancos*. Remember to take your card out of the phone after your call! **AT&T:** *900/990-011;* **MCI:** *900/990-014,* **Sprint:** *900/990-013.*

Airport Barajas International Airport *(Tel 91/393-60-00)* is about 13km northeast of the city. Metro service runs directly from the airport via line 8. A bus runs about every 15 minutes from the airport to **Plaza de Colón** (350ptas); you can switch to the Metro or a taxi from there.

Trains Renfe *(Tel 90/224-02-02)* is Spain's national train line. The two main stations are **Atocha** *(Metro Atocha Renfe)* and **Chamartín** *(Metro Chamartín)*. Both are adorned with easy-to-read signs that will direct you to the Metro, but you should really take the *"cercanías"* commuter train if you're going from station to station—it's much faster than the Metro. Going to a hostel near Chamartín isn't the best idea; it's nearly 20 minutes from downtown. Instead, get on the Metro and get off at Tribunal, Antón Martín, Sol, or Gran Vía to put yourself in the center of town. Although you can walk to a few places from Atocha Station (exit to Rhonda de Atocha), you might as well use the cheap, fun Metro to get to those same stops.

Bus Lines Out of the city The main station is **Estación Sur de Autobuses** *(Mendéz Alvaro; Tel 91/468-42-00; Metro Mendéz Alvaro)*. There are many compaines; try **ALSA-Entacar** *(Tel 90/242-22-42)* for most destinations. The main office phone is more often busy or unattended than not.

Bike, Moped, and Car Rental If you're thinking about moving around on wheels, remember that gas is expensive and hard to find in the city, parking is scarce, and the roads are crammed and disorienting. OK, having said that, call **europcar** *(Tel 91/721-12-22)* for a car, and **Motoalquiler** *(Tel 91/542-06-57)* for a cycle or scooter. Good luck....

Internet See *wired,* above.

barcelona

If you took the all-out party power of Parliament's George Clinton and mixed in equal parts of the more refined tastes of Sting, then shook them up and poured them over ice, you'd be pretty close to the trippy, wild, and refined flavors that make Barcelona such a delicious drink. Now, we'll be up front and tell you that Barcelona cannot compete with Madrid when it comes to per-capita party animalism—but who can? A smallish nation like Spain would probably have to admit its entire population into rehab if it had two cities like Madrid. However, Barcelona is gonna give you everything you want: fantastic bars and clubs, a fun and funky local population, more art and culture than Oasis has eyebrow, and a real, live beach.

Want to see the artwork, homes, and architecture of some of this century's greatest artists? Can do. Want to party from Thursday through Monday morning? *Sí, Señorita.* Want to sit around and drink coffee all day and watch the beautiful world pass by? Not a problem. Young folks like ourselves come here from all over Europe for these exact reasons, so maybe the first thing you should know before you drink down that big glass of electric kool-aid that is Barcelona is that you'll be surrounded by travelers and expats. Its location on the Mediterranean and its northern latitude has always kept Barcelona better connected with Europe than other parts of Spain, so this city has been dealing with travelers of one sort or another for the better part of the last 1,500 years. You're just as likely to meet cool people from, say, Denmark or Australia as a local from B-town (as we like to call Barcelona). Well, not just as likely, but it will happen quite a bit. This is not a bad thing. Barcelona is a legitimately international town, so meeting and becoming friends with out-of-towners (as well as people who grew up here but are of an ethnicity other than Spanish) really is part of the authentic local experience. It happens to natives all the time too, especially in the summer when people come pouring into town like Jeep Cherokees and ganga goo-balls into a Phish show. But unlike in Madrid, here international is a lot less likely to equal uncool.

In addition to travelers and expats, Barcelona now deals with its evil twin, the Commercial Tourist. (The difference between a traveler/expat and a tourist put simply: Bob Dylan is to travelers/expats as Billy Joel is to tourists.) Yes, 'twas the summer of 1992 when the Olympics came to town and brought with it a lot of money, a lot of revitalization, and a lot of people in white baseball hats. Some of the results of the XXV Olympiad are not, in our minds, so great. A whole lot of lame commercial venues sprouted up here that are as exciting and fun as a pimple before the prom. But some good things have come out of the age of the Commercial Tourist as well: You can now use your credit card nearly everywhere, and you'll be able to get by more easily with English—not only with the pre-conditioned locals, but also with the Germans, Swiss, and Dutch you'll be tripping over.

And speaking of speaking, remember that the national (or regional, depending on your politics) language here is not Spanish, it's Catalan, a language that is more or less half-Spanish and half-French. If you speak either, you'll probably be able to understand Catalan in the same way that you see things without your glasses: The general shapes and colors will be understood, but you'll miss out on most of the details. Understanding spoken Catalan is not usually something that's gonna happen for the newcomer, but the French or Spanish you learned in high school will help you out some, we hope. Even though Barcelona is in Spain, the locals have a lot of regional pride, and all of the signs, menus, and TV and radio shows are in Catalan. The flip side is that everyone in Barcelona also speaks perfect Spanish. It's totally kosher to address someone in *castellano* (Castilian, aka Spanish) without first asking if they speak it. Catalans are usually sympathetic to foreigners who speak only Spanish because a) that's better than speaking only English, and b) they know that Catalan isn't spoken anywhere else on Earth. We asked many locals to translate Catalan flyers and menus into Spanish for us, and they were all thrilled to translate words like "Tuesday," "free admission," and "happy hour."

The language in Barcelona is not its only distinctive feature—Catalan culture is unique, too. Most notably, the people here are a little more...cool, a bit more savvy. Barcelona will take anything and make it a piece of art: the sidewalks, the buildings, the bicycles; not to mention hair, shoes, and skirts. Authentic Vespa mopeds park alongside beautifully ornate water fountains. The serene streets and buildings of the Barri Gòtic district are only a few steps from the beautiful tile and glasswork of the Modernist architecture along Passeig de Grácia. Most of the streetlights in this town are good-looking, for chrissake! Each step these people take is imbued with a bit of style, and the look in their eyes—if you don't mind our generalizing—reflects an appreciation for the finer things in life. Even if it's just the young folks having coffee, their hipster look is more, well, hip.

So while the rest of the country accuses Barcelona of being too European (read: cold and standoffish), it's only because your new friends here aren't ravenous in-your-face party maniacs. (And we mean that literally: In Madrid people will get so close to you in conversation that your vision blurs, but here the locals—although still as animated and friendly—are slightly less thrilled to death by every passing moment.) Don't get the wrong idea—Barcelona is still a freakin' blast. You and your kind will probably party hard in this young people's town, but the locals don't do it with quite the sense of urgency and dedication that keeps Madrid throbbing till 6am. Barcelona has always had a better business sense than Madrid, and some folks here even seem to be more interested in being clear-headed for work the next day than they are in a sixth rum-and-Coke. Everything you like about Spain is still here—namely liberal drinking, dancing, and so on—but Barcelona is better-dressed and just a little calmer when it does these things. And despite the wild times you'll experience here, this town still somehow has more of a...homey feel. A lot of the venues are right downtown, and are an easy walk or cab ride from where you're gonna be staying, so you get a neighborhood vibe. Plus, most of the nightspots here host more than one kind of party—places like **Suborn** [see *bar scene,* below], **La Boîte** [see *live music scene,* below], and **Club Apolo** [see *club scene,* below] switch from live music to a DJ after 2am on most nights—so you'll keep coming back to the same spots.

August, by the way, is the worst month to visit Barcelona—tourists are rampant, and many locals literally head for the hills, so your chances of hanging with locals diminishes considerably. And finding a place to stay becomes a real pain in the rump.

So how do you find the cool and keep away from the drool? As in Madrid, the *Guía del Ocio* is also available here (in *castellano* only, but easy to navigate), and it's as all-knowing here as it was there. Barcelona is home to several other very groovy magazines too, most notably *A Barna (aB), Punto H, Micro,* and a very trendy magazine called *b-guided.* All three have a lot of good reading (with articles in both Spanish and Catalan, although *b-guided* is in English and Spanish) about club scenes, fashion, movies, etc. But you'll probably like them best for club and bar "window shopping"—when you see something that looks cool in any of them, look it up in the *Guía* to make sure the event is still on (*A Barna* and *Micro* both come out only monthly).

neighborhoods

Barcelona's most obvious landmark is the Mediterranean Sea, its coastline running from southwest to northeast. The Barcelona you'll want to experience lies largely in the **Ciutat Vella** ("old city"), situated along the southeastern edge of the city close to the Mediterranean. **Las Ramblas** is the big avenue that splits the Ciutat Vella in two equal halves, with the **El Raval** neighborhood on the southwest and the **Barri Gòtic** on the northeast. You're gonna get a whole lot of Las Ramblas, friends—it runs from the **Plaça Catalunya** at the north straight down to the **Mirador de Colón** [see *culture zoo,* below] at the edge of the sea (about a 20-minute walk from end to end), and everything you'll be looking for in the **Ciutat Vella** will be conveniently located to one side or the other of it. There's no way to avoid this street, which, like the Spin Doctors, you'll totally love at first, but soon will wish just wasn't around so often.

The cobblestone streets in the Barri Gòtic are narrow and winding; you'll come upon cool little plazas and beautiful hidden buildings. The traditionally bohemian **El Born** neighborhood is also located here (on the northeastern edge of the Barri Gòtic, about a 15-minute walk northeast from the center of Las Ramblas), along with several great bars and restaurants, as well as the **Picasso Museum** [see *culture zoo,* below].

A few minutes' walk along the shore to the east of **Mirador de Colón** is the **Maremagnum,** a "waterfront development area" (read: a mall with a boardwalk) spawned by the Olympic-related hoopla. It is remarkably like a North American mall and therefore not really given a lot of air time in this guide. There's a whole lot of Olympic and tourist hype here in general. It's great to walk along the water here, but the restaurants in this area are overpriced, and the only locals you'll meet will be the ones serving you dinner. Maremagnum's also got a whole lot of clubs that offer free admission and a free drink or two—but unless you're really broke, they're best avoided. If you continue walking northeast along the coast for another 5 minutes or so, you'll come to the **Port Olímpic,** which is even more hyped than Maremagnum. The beach begins here, though, and for that reason it is worth checking out.

Other enormous but uninteresting streets that people will direct you to are the east-west **Gran Vía** (runs through **Plaça de Espanya,** and is just a few blocks north of **Plaça de Catalunya**), **Avenida Diagonal** (runs northwest to southeast and cuts the whole city in half, 10 blocks northwest of the **Ciutat Vella**), and **Passeig de Grácia,** which begins at Plaça de Catalunya and runs north to Avenida Diagonal.

Grácia, about an hour's walk to the northwest of the Ciutat Vella, is like the Norman Rockwell portrait of Barcelona. It's an idyllic neighborhood with a sense of community distinct from downtown Barcelona. Be sure to check out the **Plaça del Sol,** the centerpiece of the neighborhood, for a relaxing drink among the natives.

East of the Barri Gòtic and El Raval is **L'Eixample** (often divided into **L'Eixample Izquierdo**—the left half—and **L'Eixample Derecho**—the right half), which means "the enlargement," and is nothing more than a big grid of commercial streets that is void of any detectable character—the coolest thing about this area is the octagonal intersections and **La Raspa** [see *hanging out,* below]. The neighborhood of Grácia was once a separate little village outside the old city walls (erected by the Romans). They were knocked down, however, to make way for the modern streets of L'Eixample.

The **Sants-Montjuïc** neighborhood (**Mont Juïc** is the big mountain in the southwest part of town) is an otherwise unremarkable middle-class city neighborhood at the northwest end of the city. The **Plaça de Espanya,** at its southeastern corner, is the most important thing about this area. Be sure to check out the fountains here one night [see *down & out,* below]. The **Poble Espanyol** area is notable too, if only for the EPCOT-esque culture park of the same name [see *culture zoo,* below] and a handful of clubs—most notably **La Terrrazza** [see *club scene,* below], and yes, it has three r's.

Parallel/Poble Sec, between El Raval and Mont Juïc, is considered the theater district by the natives but is really more like off-Broadway. The best theaters [see *arts scene,* below] are sprinkled throughout town. Poble Sec is home to **Club Apolo** [see *club scene,* below], and that's about it.

El Raval, bordering the southwest side of Las Ramblas, used to be the worst part of town, complete with hookers, hard drugs, and a lot of muggers waiting for naive or lost tourists. But, like John Travolta, this neighborhood has experienced a remarkable comeback in recent years. Although first cleaned up by throwing everyone in jail (in preparation for the Olympics), El Raval has since been populated by artists and musicians in need of low rent. Several museums, coffeeshops, and thrift shops can be found here, too, but you should still use caution on **L'Arc del Teatre** and points south. This area of El Raval is known as **Barre Xinés,** which, translated literally, means China Town, but in Catalan slang, means red light district. Since the cleanup, though, the worst that will probably happen to you here is that an aging prostitute might proposition you, but you should still be wary of your wallet, and women should not travel here alone.

Can't figure out why everyone was staring at you as you slid your metro card through the reader to your right? Well, maybe after you've rammed your crotch into an ungiving subway turnstile you'll figure it out. When your breath returns, take a closer look at the card readers and you'll notice that they're on the *left* side of the turnstiles, contrary to every other turnstile in the free world. Once you've made it to the platform, you'll realize that Barcelona's efficient and clean subway system is like the anti-Visa: It's almost never where you want to be. We can only assume that they didn't want to dig up the Ciutat Vella to set up metro stops there, so the stops closest to where you wanna get are on Las Ramblas and over by the Port Olímpic. You'll find that it's a lot easier to walk to a lot of destinations. But that's cool—the architecture here is beautiful and, if you're here in the summer, the weather isn't as overbearing as it is in towns to the south. One thing to check out, though, is Line 1 (red line) on the metro. This subway train is ONE BIG CAR, man! It's too freaking much!! One big, bendy tube of a train! Whoooo-hoo!

hanging out

El Café que pone Muebles Navarro (aka **Muebles Navarro, Café Muebles,** etc.) *(Riera Alta 4-6; Tel 607/188-096; Metro to Liceu; 4pm-midnight Tue-Thur, 5pm-2am Fri, Sat, 5pm-midnight Sun; No credit*

five things to talk to a local about

1. **Language skills:** The Catalans truly are bilingual. They float in and out of Spanish and Catalan as easily as grandma weaving her 1984 Buick between two lanes on the highway. If you want to get on someone's good side, simply ask "Do you really speak Catalan as well as Spanish?" Then sit back and listen to your new Barcelona friend expound upon his or her mad language skills and those of the community at large.

2. **Madrid vs. Barcelona:** In the Madrid chapter, we told you how the Madrileños consider those in Barcelona to be closed minded. Here in Barcelona, they'll tell you how in Madrid, they have no sense of fashion, art, or business. Especially business. Catalunya has been an epicenter of trade for the better part of 2,000 years, and the thriving trade of this region has continually been circumvented by political bungles in Madrid.

3. **El Raval:** We've given you a few warnings here and there about the El Raval neighborhood, but ask a local what this (and other) parts of Barcelona were like before the Olympics. If you're lucky, you'll get a tour and hear the story about the police officer who used to stand where L'Arc del Teatre meets Las Ramblas, warning travelers not to enter that neighborhood.

4. **Cultcha:** Ask a local why Barcelona likes its theater and art so much. The locals here lean toward the philosophical anyway, and a question like this is bound to get them thinking.

5. **More Cultcha:** Ask your local what his or her favorite museum is—maybe they'll take you there. If your new friend doesn't have a favorite, dump him/her quick. Barcelona's got more museums than NASCAR's got bad sunglasses. In the home of some of the last century's most influential artists, everyone ought to have a favorite museum.

cards) is an absolute must-see on your quest for cool Barcelona. Like its XL name (which refers to a past life as a table factory), this building's physical size will give you vertigo if you've become accustomed to the little tiny bars and cafes (and, let's face it, everything else) of Europe. Texas-sized space between tables, many couches, and authentic NYC cheesecake. For-sale artwork, Barcelona's only poetry slam (in Catalan, Spanish, and occasionally English), plays, and live acoustic music are enjoyed by young folks, 20 to 32, wearing anything from combat boots and lip rings to button-down shirts and hair gel. Very Greenwich Village.

The **Jardins Rubio i Lluch** *(Metro to Liceu; 10am-sunset Mon-Sat)* at the **Escola Massana** [see *arts scene,* below] would be a cool place to hang out even if it wasn't usually full of art students smoking cigarettes between classes. Plenty of benches, steps, archways, and colorful trees keep you company while you sit and read. Afterward, walk into the *escola* and check out the (usually impressive) works on display in the two-room student gallery. If you're looking to meet María or José de la Arte, keep in mind that their midday break runs from noon till 3.

An *intercambio* (interchange) is when people from different nations get together to practice speaking each other's languages. It's a great way to learn a language and to make friends, too, and not in the least as cheesy as it might sound. As with everything in Spain, these events usually involve a drink. Enter **La Raspa** *(Mallorca 188; Tel 93/451-16-31; Metro to CLOT; 7pm-2:30am daily; No credit cards),* a fantastic place to meet people from all over the globe (including worldly Catalans). Although relocated internationals stop by the bar every day of the week, Wednesday at 9:30pm is the official *intercambio* time. If you're a stranger, you'll be greeted by the hostess. Tell her what you'd like to speak, and you'll be brought to a table with like-minded individuals (who come from all walks of coolness, but are always under 35 years of age). Because most people are here to try something different, be prepared to speak Spanish with Swiss, Japanese, and other Americans; the actual Spanish will be trying their luck at the English or French tables. The booze (about 350ptas per beer) helps to make the talk easier and more fun, but the vibe here is unmistakably cerebral.

Impress friends and family back home by telling them about how you saw the sun rise on the Mediterranean Sea. If you don't dig the crowds, continue walking past all the hotel lounge chairs, bar-huts, and other assorted Olympic hoopla until things thin out a bit. Outdoor parties pop up on the beach during the summer months—check the *Guía del Ocio.*

Plaça George Orwell, in the Barri Gòtic, is worth checking out for the name alone. But, as you might have guessed, this *plaça* is anything but Big Brother. You'll find a whole lot of cool bars and restaurants (almost 30 if you count the adjoining streets), and, on Saturdays and Sundays, small markets offering clothes, CDs, etc. There's a big weird-looking Picasso statue and lots of artists and other cool young folks in black sitting around drinking and enjoying a cool night breeze (the sea is only a few minutes away) before hitting the clubs for the night. Occasional drum circles happen here, but it's not a hippie scene, though it has achieved the nickname "Plaza del Trippy"—perhaps from the sculpture? Many locals say that this is the best place to meet young artsy types of all varieties.

The big, tree-lined Las Ramblas is full of street performers, artisans, outdoor bars and restaurants, gift shops, people from all over the world, and Spain's only sex museum. Begin at **Plaça de Catalunya** at the top of the street and start struttin', baby. You'll wind up at Colón and then the Port Olímpic and then (more importantly) the Mediterranean! Give yourself a good two to three hours so that you can take in the dozens of trinket shops and statue performers [see *only here,* below], along with top-notch architecture-sighting and eating/drinking. All of this is true, by the way, whether you're here at 9am or 3am.

bar scene

Barcelona is a drinker's town. With a rich tradition of spending time with friends and family (and occasionally plotting anti-Madrid revolutions) in pubs, the opportunities for a beer here have evolved into something of an art form. Whether you want small and dark or modern and vibrant, we had a hard time picking out the bars that we liked best. In general, the best bars are in El Raval and El Born. Also check the **Plaça George Orwell** [see *hanging out,* above]. Like Madrid, the bars here stay open till 3 or 4am. The one downside to the B-town bars, however, is that they're not very tapas-centric—unless they're serving actual meals, anything beyond peanuts or chips is simply not part of Catalunya culture. Without further ado, below are some truly great Barcelona bars.

If the starship Enterprise was stuffed into a blender with Deee-lite, you'd get **Dot** (*Nou de Sant Francesc 7; Tel 933/027-026; Metro to Drassanes; 9pm-2:30am Mon-Thur, Sun; 9pm-3am Fri, Sat; No credit cards*). Teleporter-style lights, subtle neon, and Japanese Godzilla movies on the projector TV create a futuristic, edgy look that, incredibly, still somehow exudes "neighborhood pub." In the back room, *el DJ residente,* Professor Angel Dust, spins a good mix of electronica most nights of the week, but never so loud that you can't talk with the young, style-y, and (semi-) international crowd here. The two-room venue becomes too crowded Thursday through Saturday, but the weekdays, honestly, are very right-on. Wear cosmo-black, prep, goth, club...this place is right out of a Levi's ad. Beer costs 300ptas. And you're only seconds away from **Harlem** [see *live music scene,* below].

Suborn (*Ribera 18; Tel 933/101-100; Metro to Jaume I; 9pm-2:30am Tue-Sat, noon-1:30am Sun, closed Mon; V, MC*) offers DJs, live music, art exhibitions, free movies, and food. But regardless of the event, you can always have a drink—that's why we put it in *bar scene.* Although Suborn's modern, metallic look contrasts with the historically bohemian (and hardwood) El Born neighborhood, this new kid on the block still has a familiar feel, thanks mainly to a kitchen that's run by the mom of one of the owners and the 10 or so terrace tables facing the **Parc de la Ciutadella** [see *great outdoors,* below]. Wednesday and Thursday nights are often the best here. The regulars, who are in their twenties, like their pants corduroy and their hair spiked. The unique hipster sports bar scene that develops here when Barcelona is on the soccer pitch is worth checking out, even if you're not into soccer.

When you've had enough of the "polished" side of Barcelona, it's time for **Kentucki** (*Arco del Teatro 11; Tel 933/182-878; Metro to Drassanes; 8pm-3am Mon-Sat; No credit cards*), where the dress code and drink prices are so prole that you expect to see Billy Bragg playing "From Red to Blue" in the corner. It's warm and communal, despite a rough Raval facade.

Amenities include a working pinball machine (!), a jukebox with only 10 discs (including Cher, early Wailers, and ABBA), and absinthe [see *only here,* below]. Crowded, lively, and young on weekends, with a dominating local crowd. Weeknights are just about the same, after the soccer matches end at 11:30pm and the old men go home. This place is a trip, full of wackos and very real people with good stories to tell.

Plaça del Sol *(In the Grácia neighborhood; Most restaurants open till midnight, bars till 3am)* is the perfect evening place in spring and summer. The scene here is formed by the tables and chairs from the eight or nine bars surrounding the plaza. Although the crowd is older than in other places we liked, the place is hardly uptight (it *is* Spain we're talking about here...). You're guaranteed a real-deal Barcelona neighborhood experience. As always, there are foreigners, too, but at least they're the ones who live and work here. Wear what you like—you won't stand out for looking "going-out" good or for wearing sandals and a two-day shadow. Beers usually cost 300ptas.

LIVE MUSIC SCENE

Barcelona is just as much a greenhouse for music as it is for art. It just seems to grow and grow here, needing little else besides water, air, and sunlight. Barcelona has a long history as a city with a deep love for jazz. Consequently, the jazz clubs are the most established and well known. However, this hardly means it is the only thing going on. While you'll definitely want to check out one of the many jazz clubs, also keep your eye out for flyers and posters advertising other kinds of live music. There are plenty of shows and local bands here. This city has it all—the only trouble is, much of it is underground. Barcelona and its cosmopolitan self has an indie-rock music movement going on, many experimental fla-

NOE MEETS NOEA

Barcelona is a whole lot less sexually charged than Madrid, so the rules are pretty much as they are in the States. Buy someone a drink, say "hola," ask for directions or a translation, or "accidentally" brush up against them on the dance floor. Travelers aren't much of a novelty here, so you're gonna get fewer points for uniqueness than you might in more remote parts of Europe, but on the other hand, a local is more likely to know what they're in for when they're talking to somebody wearing a NY Yankees hat. Keep in mind, too, that there's a chance you might actually make it into someone's apartment in Barcelona, because young folks here (many of whom have been travelers just like you) have a better shot than their Madrileño counterparts of moving out of Mom and Dad's and into their own places.

menco groups and possibly the most thriving electronic music scene in Spain. The moral of the story is: If live music is what you want, you can get it. You may just have to work a little harder for it.

Jamboree *(Plaça Reial 17; Tel 933/017-564; Metro to Drassanes; 10pm-3am daily; www.masimas.com; No credit cards)*, pronounced yamboree, is a historic Barcelona jazz mecca in El Raval. Chet Baker, Ella Fitzgerald, and newcomers like Danilo Pérez have all played this small, smart venue. As would be expected with the music, the crowd is older and quieter, but certainly not old and quiet. The stone arches, low lighting, and tiny tables will nicely complement a dress or clean shirt. Entrance is between 1,500 and 1,800ptas, which includes a drink.

There's a gig at the small and comfortable **La Boîte** *(Diagonal 477; Tel 934/195-950; Metro to Hospital Clínic; 11pm-5:30am daily; www.masimas.com; No credit cards)* seven nights a week. Although the management at this L'Eixample spot claims to offer an "eclectic" program, a lot of the music here leans toward jazz. To that end, though, some serious names have played here, including Jimmy Smith, Lou Donaldson, and Elvin Jones. For whatever reason, this place is a magnet for young couples who know they're listening to some of the best and behave and dress accordingly. Cover is usually between 1,000 and 1,500ptas; a gin and tonic goes for 800ptas. After 2am, the live music stops and the place goes *discoteca*.

Penúltimo *(Passeig del Borne 19; Tel 933/102-596; Metro to Jaume I; 10pm-2:30am daily; 500-1,000ptas cover; penultimo@hotmail.com; No credit cards)* is very El Born—cramped, dark, and small enough that you can watch the guitarist's fingering, if you want. The clientele consists mostly of artists in their late twenties who seem to be going somewhere with their careers and artists in their mid-forties who never got on the train. The music (which comes from all over Europe and the Americas) is usually quality and includes everything from Latin funk to pop and reggae. Skits and poetry readings are also part of the itinerary.

Sidecar *(Heures 4-6, Plaça Reial; Tel 933/021-586; Metro to Drassanes; 10pm-3am Tue-Sun; No credit cards)*, pronounced *see-day-car*, is a cornerstone of the Barcelona live music scene, supplying the locals with everything from (you guessed it) jazz to thrash-metal monkeys and most things in between. Unless the band is big (as in FM-radio big), entrance is only 300ptas (which also gets you a ticket for a free beer). Because Sidecar is on the Plaça Reial, right off Las Ramblas, many a young traveler winds up here. But the locals show up for the ample downstairs music venue, pool table, and chill upstairs (as well as for the saucy international pickup scene).

Although the price is right *(Free Tue-Thur and Sun, only 600ptas Fri, Sat)* for jazz and blues at the **Harlem Jazz Club** *(Comtessa de Sobradiel 8; Tel 933/100-755; Metro to Liceu or Jaume I; 10pm-4am Tue-Sun; No credit cards)*, the vinyl floor, dropped ceilings, and cheap photos of sheet music resting on top of piano keys don't exactly give the Harlem feel. But the college-student crowd is cool with that; they're all wearing sneakers and T-shirts anyway. And even though Harlem isn't pretty, the music is usually good, drinks are cheap, and you'll make friends here with more ease than at any other music venue in town.

For even more jazz, check out the **Pipa Club,** in the Teatre Malic [see *arts scene,* below].

club scene

The Barcelona club scene can't compete with Madrid's in terms of numbers, but the attitude is still right: Drink late, stay awake by any means possible, and dance, dance, dance. Although both cities warm up around midnight, hit their prime time at about 2am, and only begin to let up around 4:30am, Barcelona is a little less ferocious about the whole thing: There are fewer clubs fighting for your time, and the bouncers are generally more relaxed. B-Town outdoes Madrid, however, in that its 'zines have got it together. *A Barna (aB)* and *Micro* are both published here, both by former students of the **Escola Massana** art school [see *arts scene,* below], and give you the live, ground-level look at what your friends would be wearing, playing, doing, and watching if you had friends in Spain. (Of course there's also the Barcelona edition of the omniscient *Guía del Ocio*.) Keep in mind that the many clubs of the Port Olímpic are often populated by young obnoxious internationals and older businessmen who are looking a little too hard for some monkey business.

There's a great student culture in this town—stay away from the harbor and have a great time with great people at places like Galaxy and Club Apolo and Moog [see below]. Barcelona club prices are usually the same as Madrid (usually 1,200-2,000ptas, including a free drink), and you can find the same range of clubs, from meat market (Port Olímpic) to hipster/sophisticated (Galaxy).

Locals use words like "mythic" and "legendary" when describing **Moog** *(Arc del Teatre 3; Tel 933/017-282; Metro to Drassanes; 11:30pm-5am daily; www.masimas.com; No credit cards),* the El Raval club that is home away from home for many of Europe's biggest DJs. But the truth is that the "big" house DJs that spin on weekends don't cut it. Instead, experience the Moog's past glory on Wednesday nights, when an international DJ (who will probably favor hardcore techno) takes the tables. The young crowd fills up the 300-person-capacity dance floor at about 3am. The small upstairs room plays early-'80s pop and is exactly like the fifth-grade basement parties you went to (if you're from the suburbs). Unless you've had at least five drinks and are wearing dark sunglasses, avoid this room at all costs. Cover charge 800 to 1,500ptas, beers for 500ptas.

Club Apolo *(Nou de La Rambla 113; Tel 934/414-001; Metro to Parallel; Midnight-6am Thur-Sun; No credit cards)* hosts Nitsa Club, which is at the opposite end of the DJ spectrum from Moog: It features very good DJs who have small cult followings (kind of like Ani DiFranco had back in '92). Two additional rooms play ambient and pop music. The young movers and shakers of B-town hang out here, wearing of-the-moment sub-fashions like softball shirts and metallic turquoise eye shadow. Apolo

only here

Barcelona, in itself, is one of a kind. They'd have to paint the parking meters like rainbows and put clown shoes on the cops to make the place any more festive and happy than it already is.

One specific example: the statue performers along Las Ramblas. These silver and bronze people stand perfectly still until you put some money in their box, and then they move like Disneyland robots. Most of these guys are cool, and each one has his or her gimmick—just be sure to give them money if you're gonna take a picture or video.

Another unique thing (in Spain, at least): absinthe. Yes, absinthe, friends, the legendary, hallucinogenic drink of yore. Is it real? Is it legal? Is it simply anise and a whole lot of talk? Well, we did our best to get the lowdown on this elusive drink. Although the owner of **Marsela** (*Sant Pau 65; No phone; Metro to Liceu; 9pm-2:20am Sun-Thur, 6pm-2:30am Fri, Sat; No credit cards*) claims that only his establishment serves "real" absinthe, a variety of other bars, including **Kentucki** [see *bar scene,* above] and **Bar Patsís** (*Santa Mónica 4, El Raval; No phone; Metro to Sant Antoni; 7:30pm-2:30am daily; No credit cards*) will also serve you something that, if not absinthe, is still pretty lethal. When you buy the absinthe, you get a bottle of water and two sugar cubes with it. Rest a fork over the top of a glass and put a sugar cube on top. Pour a bit of water on the cube so that it slowly dissolves into the absinthe below. When it's done, add a little more water (a glass of absinthe tastes like a handful of black licorice–flavored Altoids) and toss it back, baby. Be careful. The effects (akin to the fringe of a hallucinogenic fever) take a minute or two to kick in. Some people, notably Brazilians, pour a bit of it into a saucer, then mush up the sugar cubes into the absinthe. They do not add water; instead, they light it on fire! (Fire! Fire!) They wait a minute as the potent mixture begins to crystallize, then jab their hand into the blue flames, pull the red-hot glob out quick, and put it in their mouth! The hand won't get burned, but the head might.

(like most venues in Barcelona) plays host to a variety of arts, such as international cinema on Mondays or (disco) salsa and live rock on other nights. Check the papers to learn more. (Also make sure you sample the abundant pinball offerings at the arcade next door.) Slightly out of the way, over in Poble Sec.

If it's all-out dance you want, stop by **La Terrrazza** (*Poble Espanyol;*

barcelona bars, clubs and culture zoo

Barcelona

PORTUGAL

★ **Madrid**

SPAIN

BARS/CLUBS ▲

Capitán Banana **19**
Club Apolo **5**
Dietrich **20**
Dot **9**
El Coño Tu Prima **21**
Galaxy **24**
Harlem Jazz Club **10**
Kentucki **11**
La Terrrazza **2**
Jamboree **8**
Mezzanine **6**
Moog **12**
Satanassa **15**
Sidecar **13**
Suborn **25**
Tijuana **23**

CULTURE ZOO ●

Catedral de Barcelona **16**
Fundació Joan Miró **4**
La Sagrada Familia **17**
Mirador de Colón **14**
Museu d'Art Contemporània
   de Barcelona (MACBA) **7**
Museu Nacional
   d'Art de Catalunya **3**
Museu Picasso **22**
Parc Güell **18**
Poble Espanyol **1**

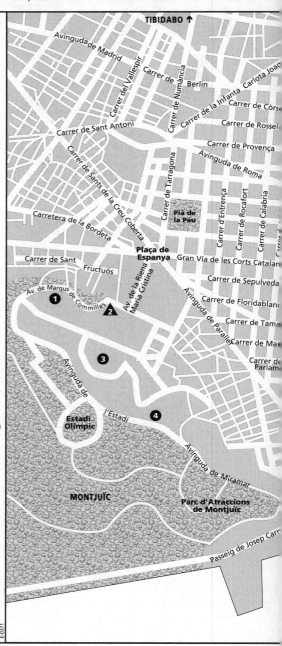

E-0371

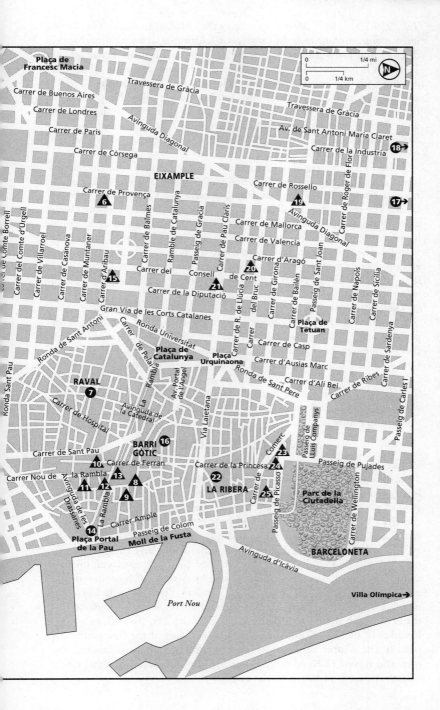

Plaça de
Francesc Macia

Carrer de Buenos Aires

Carrer de Londres

Carrer de Paris

Carrer de Còrsega

Travessera de Gràcia

Travessera de Gràcia

Av. de Sant Antoni Maria Claret

Carrer de la Industria

18→

17→

EIXAMPLE

Carrer de Provença

Avinguda Diagonal

Carrer de Rossello

Avinguda Diagonal

Carrer de Roger de Flor

6

Carrer del Comte Borrell

Carrer del Comte d'Urgell

Carrer de Villarroel

Carrer de Casanova

Carrer de Muntaner

Carrer d'Aribau

Carrer de Balmes

Ramble de Catalunya

Passeig de Gracia

Carrer de Pau Claris

Carrer de Mallorca

Carrer de Valencia

Carrer d'Aragó

Carrer de Girona

Carrer de Bailen

Passeig de Sant Joan

Carrer de Napols

Carrer de Sicilia

Carrer de Sardenya

Carrer del
Consell de Cent

15

Carrer de la Diputació

20

21

Carrer de R. de Llúcia
del Bruc

Plaça de
Tetuan

Gran Via de les Corts Catalanes

Ronda de Sant Antoni

Ronda Universitat

Carrer de Pelaji

Carrer

Carrer de Casp

Carrer d'Ausias Marc

Carrer d'Ali Bei

Carrer de Ribes

Ronda Sant Pau

Plaça de
Catalunya

Plaça
Urquinaona

Ronda de Sant Pere

Passeig de Carles I

RAVAL

7

Carrer de Hospital

Rambla

Av. Portal
de l'Angel

Avinguda de
la Catedral

Via Laietana

Passeig de
Lluis Companys

Passeig de Pujades

BARRI
GÒTIC

16

Carrer de Sant Pau

Carrer de Ferran

Comerç

Carrer de la Princesa

23

24

Passeig de Wellington

Carrer Nou de

la Rambla

10

13

8

Carrer de

22

25

Parc de la
Ciutadella

11

12

9

LA RIBERA

Passeig de Picasso

Carrer Ample

14

Plaça Portal
de la Pau

Passeig de Colom

Moll de la Fusta

Avinguda d'Icàvia

BARCELONETA

Avinguda de les Drassanes

La Rambla

Villa Olímpica→

Port Nou

0   1/4 mi
0   1/4 km
N

Tel 934/231-285; Metro to Espanya; Midnight-6am Thur-Sun; www.nightsun-group.com; No credit cards). Although it loses points for the three r's and for being located in the tourist-centric Poble Espanyol, La Terrrazza is fun once you accept the self-indulgent decor and Ibiza-like prices (2,400ptas entrance! 1,500ptas for drinks!). The crowd is 18 to 35 and literally from all over the world—though locals enjoy the spectacle of this club, too. Dress for hot weather, hot dancing, and hot innuendo, but don't discard your sense of taste: This is one of Barcelona's more upscale clubs. When the sun's coming up, be sure you're getting down on the second, outdoor dance floor.

When La Terrrazza closes, many people head over to the after-after-hours club **Tijuana** *(Passeig Marítim 34; No phone; You'll be taking a cab, trust us; 6am-10:30am Sat, Sun May-Oct only; Cover 2,000ptas; No credit cards).* The music may be all bass and no brains, but when nothing else is open, you start not to care. The big (1,000-plus people) and dark venue, however, may do less for you than the beachside splendor of the terrace seating. The crowd can be very gay but is usually well-mixed, because anyone who is too hepped-up to fall asleep winds up here. Go once for that "nightlife-in-Spain" story that your friends back home want. Small water for 600ptas.

Galaxy *(Princessa 53; Tel 934/122-294; Metro to Jaume I; 11pm-3:30am Sat only; No credit cards),* right off the Parc de la Ciutadella, is (or perhaps was...) one of Barcelona's best-kept nightclub secrets. Although this small basement room can cram in only about 250 people, DJ Mark Ryal spins the best deep house in the city. This new club has a sophisticated, slightly older crowd that shows up for the music and not for...showing up. Dancing is great, people are sincere, there's no cover, and the whole place is lit by candles. Go with a friend or two, and wear something subtly sexy.

arts scene

Unlike Madrid, whose epicenters of art and culture are like islands in a sea of industry and bureaucracy, Barcelona emits artistry and creativity from every street corner. The quarterly Spanish/English guide *b-guided,* which can be picked up at Tribu [see below], will guide you to the city's best secrets in young and on-the-money fashion, art, restaurants, and clubs. Seek out Tribu and this magazine early in your visit, as they will lead you right into the middle of the best this city has to offer. In addition to *b-guided,* the *Guía del Ocio* will open you up to a thunderstorm of theaters, galleries, and cafes that *all* host live music *and* art exhibitions *and* small plays. The city itself (i.e., the government) brings to the party an absurd number of *festivales* dedicated to the arts, which the citizens here eat up. This city has, after all, produced the likes of Picasso, Dalí, Miró, and Gaudí. Most of the best stuff happens in the Ciutat Vella, which is split into two art hemispheres: the torn and frayed El Raval to the west and the philosophical Barri Gòtic (which includes El Born) to the east.

▶▶VISUAL ARTS

Hangar *(Marqués de Santa Isabel 40; Tel 933/084-041; Metro to Poblenou or Bus 40, 42, 71; 9am-2pm/3-6pm Mon-Fri; www.hangar.org)* is an artist-advocacy group that offers dirt-cheap studio space, fantastic connections, and a politically sharp staff. If you're an art student (in video, photography, computer animation, sculpture, acting, painting, or drawing) who will be in Barcelona for awhile, drop by. Although there are no exhibits at Hangar, the staff is well-informed on where the exhibits are. Contact Laia González (she's very friendly) at the above address for more info on how to obtain studio space or otherwise get involved. Hangar is in the northeastern area of the Poble Nou neighborhood and is best reached by any of the buses listed above.

The **Escola Massana** *(Hospital 56; Tel 934/422-000; Metro to Liceu; 10am-1pm/4-6pm Mon-Fri; www.ictnet.es/massana)* is a small school of art and design that offers a similar scene. In addition to the mellow **Jardins Rubio i Lluch** [see *hanging out,* above], the school offers bulletin boards with info on small art exhibitions, a two-room gallery that displays student work, and, of course, real, live Catalan art students! Be sure to study their look—they wear things you won't see elsewhere. Scoping time is prime at about 1pm, the midday break, so plan to be here in El Raval around then.

Near Escola Massana is the small, raw, and urban **Galleria Urania** *(Doctor Dou 19; Tel 934/122-345; Metro to Liceu or Catalunya; 11am-1:30pm/5-8:30pm Tue-Sat; artinproject@mail.cinet.es; V, MC, AE)*. Exhibitions include a "fair balance" of up-and-coming folks and more established artists. The management also runs "Art in Project," a program that was created to give art students international exposure via a network of small galleries throughout Europe.

Just a few blocks to the east is **Serrahima** *(Riera Alta 10; Tel 934/427-205; Metro to Liceu; 11am-2pm/5-8:30pm Tue-Sat; www.logiccontrol.es/serrahima)*, which is small like Urania and Tribu [see below], but has nothing to do with students or anything else low-rent. The exhibits here are generally more thought-provoking and mature than in the other, "younger" galleries, with works by established European artists. Like the art, the atmosphere at Serrahima is more refined, but that doesn't make it boring. Take a break from the secondhand clothes in El Raval's stores and the secondhand couches in its cafes and check this out. It will do your head some good.

Once you've had enough of acting academic, get youself over to **Tribu** *(Avinyó 12; Tel 933/186-510; Metro to Liceu; 11am-2pm/4:30-8:30pm Mon-Sat; V, MC, AE)*. This place is one of our Barcelona favorites. The sparse collection of club fashions that you see when you first walk in is little more than a facade for the squatter-style gallery awaiting you in the rooms beyond. The artists here are local and young, their work is usually weird and disturbing, and the staff is style-y and nice. Exhibits rotate every 6 weeks, and the majority of artists are from Spain. Tribu also runs a young artists' network but isn't affiliated with the universities.

fESTIVALS and EVENTS

Carnestoltes (carnival) *(February)* includes the *castelles,* or castles, where Barcelonians pit their strength and balance against each other in attempts to build the tallest human towers. Also freaky *gegantes* (giants) and the freaky-freaky *capgrossos* (fatheads). Watch out for the *capgrossos*—they are among the goddamn freakiest things you ever saw.

A particularly beautiful holiday is the **Día de Sant Jordi** *(April 23),* when lovers exchange gifts. Women will gripe about this holiday (in jest), because tradition dictates that the man buys the woman a rose (for three bucks or so) and the woman lays out the equivalent of 15, 20 or more dollars for the traditional gift of a book for the man. This holiday has not yet been mucked up by the corporate vultures who have ruined Valentine's Day in the States, but book and rose vendors pop up on the streets this day faster than trannie fights on *Jerry Springer.*

The **Día de Sant Joan** *(June 24)* is Barcelona at its best: bonfires, firecrackers, painted faces, and—of course—the outdoor drinking and revelry that make Spain one of the coolest countries in the world. Midway between Madrid's San Isidro festival and Mardi Gras, this whole affair is very absinthe-friendly.

The **GREC Festival** and **the Marató de L'Espectacle** both take place in July and feature a smorgasbord of theater, dance, and live music with performers from all over the world—neither festival is to be missed [see *arts scene,* below].

The **Festa Major de Grácia** *(Usually third week in Aug)* is another example of Barcelona at its most celebratory. This festival is a little bit tamer than the festival hoopla normally reserved for Las Ramblas. Featuring lots of outdoor bands on small stages throughout the decorated neighborhood, and lots of kids, fewer drugs, and more drink.

The **Festa de la Mercé** *(Sept 17-24)* is the celebration of Barcelona's patron saint, Our Lady of Mercy. It's another Mardi Gras–type celebration featuring lots of human towers, glorious fireworks, general revelry, and *gegantes.*

The **Fira del Disc de Col.Leccionista** *(Estació de França (França Railway Station); Held annually, usually in mid or late November)* is organized by Catalunya Radio. This annual Record Collectors Trade Fair offers all things vinyl to those who love records. Comb carefully, and you may find a funky Catalan recorded artifact to take home to your turntable.

▶▶PERFORMING ARTS

Realizing that Barcelona freaks on its theater is as easy as walking down Las Ramblas and checking out all the street performers. Although many productions here are in Catalan, the very best things—the festivals—are presented in several languages (or none at all) because the companies come from all over Europe. A festival here can be anything from a half-dozen companies and a theater that get together for one weekend to a size-12 bugout with 48 continuous hours of fire-eaters, contortionists, comedians, and the weirdest clowns you ever saw. If you're looking to meet theater people, anyplace in the El Born neighborhood is a safe bet, and **Hangar** is a great place to get connected to a variety of art scenes. Check out *www.telentrada.com* or call *902/101-212* for theater listings or to reserve your seat.

Although it lasts for only two days in the second week of June, the **Marató de L'Espectacle** *(Mercat de les Flors at calle de Lleida 59; Tel 902/101-212; Metro to Espanya; Most shows at 10pm; No credit cards)* packs in a whole lotta hoopla. Production companies and artists from around the world offer theater, dance, skits, animation, cinema, music, and circ (circus-related performances like fire-eating, etc.). The name fittingly means "marathon of the spectacle"—the good times begin at 10:30pm and don't end till dawn. Locals *love* this event; the inherent weirdness that transpires during these two days is always the talk of the town. Located in the historic and beautiful **Mercat de les Flors** *(Tel 934/261-875)*, which began as a flower market for the 1929 World's Fair, it has been bringing Spain's and Europe's best theater groups to Barcelona since 1985.

The **GREC Festival** *(Nearly 50 different venues, information booths at the Plaça de Catalunya; Dial general information at 010 for more info; End of June and all of July; www.grecbcn.com)* is a true juggernaut of theater, dance, and music. Usually about a month after the Marató de L'Espectacle, this 5-week event also brings in performers from all over the world. If you're here in the summertime, pick up a free schedule at the big booth in the Plaça de Catalunya. The whole town totally loves this event, and, if you're a fan of dance, theater, or live music, you're guaranteed to be impressed. Try and see at least one show at the beautiful amphitheater at Montjuïc, commonly known as **Teatre Grec.**

Teatre Malic *(Fusina 3; Tel 933/107-035; Metro to Jaume I or Arc de Triomphe; Shows at 9pm, 11pm Mon-Sun; www.daucom.es/malic; 1,500-2,000ptas; No credit cards)* is a small independent theater in El Born that began as a puppet theater. These days, the 60-seat venue plays host to mainly Spanish and Catalan productions, reserving Mondays and Tuesdays for "alternative" or up-and-coming production companies. It's also home to a pleasant cafe and an extensive collection of entertainment flyers and magazines. On Sundays at 11pm, Teatre Malic becomes the temporary home of the **Pipa Club,** Barcelona's smallest and best jazz bar.

L'Espai (*Travessera de Grácia 63; Tel 934/143-133; Metro to Provença or Diagonal; No credit cards*) is a small, government-operated theater in the northeast of the city, beyond Avenida Diagonal, that most often plays host to smaller dance companies. Don't expect tame performances, however, just because *el gobierno* is running the show—L'Espai, like so many venues here, dabbles in the avant-garde.

Since 1989, **Sala Beckett** (*Alegre de Dalt 55 bis; Tel 932/845-312; Metro to Joanic; Most shows 9:30pm; salabeckett@ctv.es; No credit cards*), out on the east end of the city, has billed itself as an alternative/experimental venue, a "theater for theater people." Although they offer playwriting courses here, they're less interested in promoting new actors than are many of the other venues in Barcelona or Madrid. Sala Beckett has received the *El Premio Max* award for alternative theater in Spain, but unfortunately, the majority of the performances are in Catalan. The foyer displays a handwritten letter by Samuel Beckett himself, agreeing to allow this theater to use his name and giving it his blessing.

Like the movie theater of the same name in Madrid, the **Filmoteca (Cine Aquitania)** (*Avda. de Sarriá 33; Tel 934/107-590; Metro to Hospital Clínic; Shows 5pm, 7:30pm, 10pm daily, check the* Guía *for listings; 400ptas; No credit cards*) here, over in L'Eixample, specializes in the greatest movies you've (probably) never seen. All movies are VO (original versions...you know, subtitled) and are taken from a variety of themes and artists, such as the works of Hitchcock or movies with Fred Astaire. Shows sell out quick because they're so cheap. Pick up the monthly schedule in the foyer and be prepared.

gay scene

"Tolerant" sometimes means separate but equal, like the gay-heavy Chueca district in Madrid. But Barcelona is *so* uninterested in creating labels or judging others, no real "gay district" exists here, and many (but not all) of the "gay" clubs and bars host very mixed crowds, especially on the weekends. If a particular group seems to stand out (like the pierced-and-eyelined at Tu Prima, see below), we note it, but that doesn't mean the whole crowd is wearing collars and combat boots. *Punto H* (it has a big H on the cover) is a great gay fashion/music/nightlife magazine, as is *Shangay Express*. Both are in Spanish.

Been waiting for just the right place to put on that wig and eye shadow you stowed away in the bottom of your backpack? Or maybe you haven't done laundry in a few weeks and the only thing you have left to wear is the tight leather underwear and dog collar you decided to bring along at the last minute. **Capitán Banana** (*Moiá 1; Tel 932/021-430; Metro to Provença; 12:30am-5am daily; No credit cards*), is all about transvestites, drag queens, leather, and disco. Like most clubs, it becomes hot and sweaty here at about 2am.

Mezzanine (*Provenza 236; Tel 934/548-798; Metro to Provença or Hospital Clínic; 1-4pm/9pm-midnight Mon-Sat, closed Sun; About 900ptas per entree; V*) is popular with the gay theater crowd (mostly guys from 22 to 32) but is a must for *anyone* who doesn't eat meat. The entrees at this beautiful, *de moda* restaurant and gallery in L'Eixample are all vegan. The menu changes daily, but selections from the juice bar don't and are absolutely worth investigating—the *zumo nocturno* packs as much energy as a six-pack of Jolt. Art exhibits rotate every two months and are usually by young local painters.

The menu at **El Colibrí** *(Corner of Riera Alta and Erasme de Janer; Tel 934/423-002; Metro to Sant Antoni; 8am-10:30pm Mon-Sat; V, MC, AE)* changes almost daily, usually to accommodate whatever fish seemed best at the market that morning. Although most of the diners here are 25 to 35 and gay, it's not like they're gonna throw you out if you're not. An interesting subset here are professors from the nearby design and literary schools. There's lots of literature on gay and music happenings in town, and drag shows happen once a month (see the posters). Very mellow and relaxing, with plenty of space between tables so that you can kick back.

The lighting at **Dietrich** *(Consell de Cent 255; No phone; Metro to Passeig de Grácia; 6pm-2:30am daily, till 3am Sat; No credit cards)* has an odd, gold quality that gives the place a bar-of-the-future kind of feel. Everything is shiny, including the roof of the huge glass atrium in the back corner. Indiscriminate jazz on the hi-fi is quiet enough that you can talk. The entirely gay clientele is professional and ranges in age from 20 up to 50. Spacious and easygoing, Dietrich touts itself as a gay *teatro* cafe, but the drag-queen shows here are not regularly scheduled. Check the *Guía* or *Punto H* for listings. Drinks are about 650ptas.

El Coño Tu Prima *(Consejo de Ciento 294; No phone; Metro Passeig de Grácia; 11pm-3am daily; No credit cards)* is a big deal, man. As in three floors, Death Star–sized disco balls, huge papier-mâché dragons, big. Tu Prima hosts (local) pop and techno/house DJs (sometimes both in the same night), usually for about a 1,000ptas cover. Mixed crowd (up to age 35) on the weekends, and The Prodigy would fit right in with the leather and pierced set that always seems represented here. Note: Be sure to ask what the name of the bar translates as....

Satanassa *(Aribau 27; Tel 934/510-052; Metro Passeig de Grácia; 9pm-5am daily; No credit cards)* was, according to the management, the first gay dance club in Barcelona. The crowd becomes more gay during the weekend and is more straight during the week. The bar is adorned with lewd paintings and statues of men and women, but the dance floor vibe is very Detroit: all concrete, dark, and ready to really party (in the let's-get-wasted-and-loud sense). Fashion for the young crowd here is a very weird mix of working-class and drag queen: We guess it just doesn't matter once you've had as much to drink as these people have. The weekday DJ is technically flawless but favors the worst flavors of dance club pop.

CULTURE ZOO

All of Barcelona is a museum—even typically mundane objects like benches and sidewalks have a subtle aesthetic quality here. Although there's no single museum that can match Madrid's Prado, Barcelona has art for every taste, from the historic (and beautiful) cave paintings in the Museu Nacional to the wild architecture of the Sagrada Familia. As with everywhere else in Spain, most museums are inexpensive (all mentioned are around 700ptas) and offer half-off to students with valid ID. The following days are free for all museums: May 18 (International Day of Museums), October 12 (Fiesta Nacional de España), and December 6 (Día de Constitución Española). Check with the tourist offices [see *need to know,* below] for "Articket," which gets you in to six museums for 2,496ptas.

If you're trying to kill two museums with one afternoon, we suggest any of the following combinations:

Museu d'Art Contemporani de Barcelona (MACBA) and Centre de Cultura Contemporania de Barcelona (CCCB) are right next to each other in El Raval (and very close to many small galleries and La Escola Massana).

Fundació Joan Miró, Poble Espanyol, and Museu Nacional d'Art

12 hours in barcelona

1. **La Sagrada Familia:** We've said it so many times, but this tower is the coolest, man. Ken Kesey would've loved this thing. If it doesn't blow your mind, go home—the trains shouldn't be wasting valuable fuel carting your boring ass around the continent.

2. **(Vamos a jugar por...) La Playa:** That is, the beach. It's free, it's fun, and you can drink without fear of the law. Don't spend too much time here, though—there's plenty in this town to see besides the sea.

3. **Galaxy:** The best of the clubs here. It's not real big physically, but its vibe is beautiful. The smaller size makes it easier to start a conversation, make friends, and get treated right when you return [see *club scene,* above].

4. **La Manzana de la Discordia:** This world-famous "Block of Discord" (a 5-minute walk from **Plaça Catalunya** on the **Passeig de Grácia**) is the home of three very modernista houses from three of the top architectural teams of this movement (including, you guessed it, Gaudí). The houses look nothing alike, as each one was meant to push the limits of design. Only five blocks up the same street is another far-out Gaudí creation, the **Casa Milá** (more often known as **La Pedrera**—"The Quarry"). Barcelona, in fact, has as much cool architecture as any city in the world. If you're interested, ask for the walking-tour-of-Barcelona-modernista-architecture brochure at the tourist office underneath **Plaça Catalunya.**

de Catalunya (MNAC) are all in the Plaça de Espanya/Montjuïc part of town.

Catedral de Barcelona and Museu Picasso are both in the Ciutat Vella.

Parc Güell and La Sagrada Familia aren't really near anything else but are worth special trips.

Museu d'Art Contemporània de Barcelona (MACBA) *(Plaça dels Angels; Tel 934/120-810; Metro to Plaça de Catalunya or Universitat; 11am-7:30pm Mon, Wed-Fri; 10am-8pm Sat, 10am-7pm Sun; 800ptas):* If you are a modern-art lover you will fall head over heels for this museum. The building's architectural design is art itself, but the painting and sculpture inside are what's really enticing. This museum is dedicated to bringing contemporary art to the masses both national and international and it generally has a photography exhibit going on.

Centre de Cultura Contemporània de Barcelona (CCCB) *(Montalegre 5; Tel 933/064-100; Metro to Catalunya or Plaça Goya; 11am-2pm/4-8pm Tue, Thur, Fri; 11am-8pm Wed, Sat; 11am-7pm Sun, holidays; www.cccb.org; 600ptas):* The CCCB focuses on the trends and technolo-

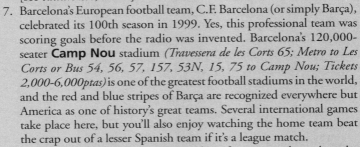

5. **Plaça George Orwell:** A great place to have a drink and meet lots of cool young people, all outside [see *hanging out,* above].

6. **Parc Güell:** We've talked about this place almost as much as Gaudí's **La Sagrada Familia.** A great way to get out of the city for a few minutes and collect your thoughts [see *culture zoo,* above].

7. Barcelona's European football team, C.F. Barcelona (or simply Barça), celebrated its 100th season in 1999. Yes, this professional team was scoring goals before the radio was invented. Barcelona's 120,000-seater **Camp Nou** stadium *(Travessera de les Corts 65; Metro to Les Corts or Bus 54, 56, 57, 157, 53N, 15, 75 to Camp Nou; Tickets 2,000-6,000ptas)* is one of the greatest football stadiums in the world, and the red and blue stripes of Barça are recognized everywhere but America as one of history's great teams. Several international games take place here, but you'll also enjoy watching the home team beat the crap out of a lesser Spanish team if it's a league match.

8. **Picasso Museum:** There are a lot of museums here, but the Picasso is cool because it tells the story of a single individual in addition to sharing captivating art. Off-hours are earlier in the morning [see *culture zoo,* above].

gies that shape modern culture and, by extension, art. The exhibits often explore themes relating to cities and art and the media and art. The CCCB has regular multimedia exhibits.

Poble Espanyol *(Marqués de Comilias, Parc de Montjuïc; Tel 935/086-330; Metro to Plaça Espanya or Bus 61 to Poble Espanyol; 9am-8pm Mon; 9am-2am Tue, Wed, Thur; 9am-4am Fri, Sat; 9-midnight Sun; www.poble-espanyol.com):* It's a tourist trap for sure, but you can get some great souvenir shopping done in this "village" in which every region of Spain is represented by miniature versions of their most recognizable attractions.

Fundació Joan Miró *(Parc de Montjuïc; Tel 934/439-470; Bus 16 from Plaça de Espanya; 10am-7pm Tue, Wed, Fri, Sat, 11am-9:30pm Thur, 10:30am-2:30pm Sun, holidays):* Miró is yet another artist to come out of Spain, one whose work strongly impacted modern art. Miró's paintings, sculptures, and tapestries will put you in a good mood and show how simple forms and shapes and bright colors collaborate to create vitality. His art was designed to stimulate the imagination and this it certainly does. Also while at the museum check out the super-cool Mercury Fountain, given to him by his longtime friend, American sculptor Alexander Calder.

Museu Nacional d'Art de Catalunya (MNAC) *(In the Palau Nacional, Parc de Montjuïc; Tel 934/237-199; Metro to Plaça de Espanya or Bus 9, 27, 30, 38, 56, 57, 65, 91 to same; www.mnac.es; 10am-7pm Tue,*

down and out

All out of pesetas? Don't let it get you down, you happen to be in one of the trippiest cities on the continent. A great place to visit (even if you do have money) is the magic fountains at **Plaça de Espanya** *(Metro to Plaça de Espanya; Shows 7-9pm weekends).* Now don't write off these fountains as something (like the Ice Capades) that only your grandma would like. We assure you that you've never seen water quite like this. The colors are beautiful, the fountain arrangements are so complex they probably require a Cray Supercomputer to run, and the music goes from classical to some Eurotrashed-out Peter Gabriel-ish theme of Barcelona.

If you want to get to know water in a more natural setting, check out the beach, only a 15-minute walk from the base of Las Ramblas. The occasional topless woman, the Mediterranean Sea, and...well, that's it. But what else do you expect from a beach? Keep in mind that the scene is more tranquil as you move farther from the Port Olímpic.

Wed, Fri, Sat; 10am-9pm Thur; 10am-2:30pm Sun) tells, through art and artifacts, the history of Catalunya. Absolutely worth checking out—learn history while appreciating the art.

Catedral de Barcelona *(Plaça de la Seu; Tel 933/151-554; Metro Jaume 1; Bus 17, 19, 40, 45 to same; 9am-1pm/4-7pm daily, closed to visitors during mass):* This place was started in the 13th century, finished in the 15th (the workers must've been union...), and is a primo example of the medieval splendor of Barcelona. Yup, it's an old cathedral all right. At least it's right near Las Ramblas, so that you can take your picture quick and get on with your day. The museum portion features *La Pietat* by Bermejo.

Museu Picasso *(Montcada 15-19; Tel 933/196-310; Metro Jaume 1; 10am-8pm Tue-Sat, holidays, 10am-3pm Sun).* People who are familiar with Picasso and the works that made him famous (i.e., Cubism, Blue and Pink period) might be disappointed by what this museum has to offer. However, if you don't expect to see his masterpieces and instead you are interested in him as a child and an old man, then this place is worth a visit. The gift shop has great Picasso paraphernalia.

Mirador de Colón *(Portal de la Pau; Tel 933/025-224; Metro to Drassanes or Bus 14, 18, 36, 57, 59, 64; 9am-8:30pm daily late June-Sept; 10am-1:30pm/3:30-7:30pm Mon-Fri, 10am-7:30pm Sat, Sun Oct-early June):* This tower with a statue of Columbus on top, built in 1888, is one of the landmarks of the city. For 250ptas, you can ascend the tower for a great view of the city and the Mediterranean.

La Sagrada Familia *(Mallorca 401; Tel 934/550-247; Metro to Sagrada Familia; 9am-6pm daily Oct-Feb; 9am-8pm Apr-Aug; 9am-7pm Mar, Sept):* This church is the coolest thing ever. If you see one "sight" in Barcelona, La Sagrada Familia, designed by Gaudí, started in 1882 and still incomplete, has to be it.

Parc Güell *(Tel 934/243-809; Metro to Vallcarca or Bus 24, 25, 31, 74; 10am-6pm daily Nov-Feb; 10am-7pm daily Mar-Oct):* Also designed by Gaudí, this park is a close second to La Sagrada Familia in terms of sheer coolness. Plus it's free! Be sure to take a tour of Gaudí's house (designed by Francesc Berenguer but full of Gaudí-designed furniture) while you're here.

modification

A man has simple criteria for a barbershop: no disco music, no neon or pastel decor, and a barber at least as old as his dad. Oh yeah, and it should cost less than $15 (U.S.) and not take all day. Gentlemen, **Pulequeria Manolo** *(Regomir 17; Tel 933/152-809; Metro to Jaume I; 9am-2pm/4-8pm Mon-Fri, 8:30am-2pm Sat; About 1,200ptas for a cut; No credit cards)* delivers. Manolo himself will cut your hair efficiently, pleasantly, and exactly how you like it (while exchanging pleasantries with every local who walks by the small front door). A great guy, a great haircut, a true cultural experience.

Barcelona isn't exactly the punk or teen-angst capital of the world

(What would they rebel against? No drinking age? The international club scene? The sexually permissive cultural norms?), but you still have the opportunity to pierce yourself silly. Several locals directed us to **L'Embruix** *(Boqueria 18; Tel 933/011-163; 10am-2pm/4-8pm Mon-Sat, 10am-8pm July, Aug; No credit cards)* because of their good artistry and cool demeanor. The several women (hence the name, which means "the witches") who run the show will charge you a minimum of 6,000ptas for a tattoo and 4,000ptas for piercings. The actual jewelry is extra (an average ring is 400ptas), as is anesthesia (1,000ptas).

great outdoors

Parc de la Ciutadella *(Metro to Ciutadella or Arc de Triomf; 8am-9pm daily)* near El Born is the main park of the city, where you can jog, rollerblade, and practice yoga amidst green grass, shady trees, fragrant gardens, tranquil ponds, and one hell of a freaky fountain. The Cascada fountain was created with a little help from Gaudí, and man, does it show....The atmosphere here can be more wholesome (especially on weekends) than expected because the city zoo (which features an albino gorilla, poor thing) is located here. Like most big-city parks, Parc de la Ciutadella is safe during daylight hours but should be traversed using common sense at night.

Barcelona by Bicycle *(Esparteria 3; Tel 93/268-21-05; Metro to Jaume I; Daily tours 10am-12:30pm Sat, Sun for 2,000ptas, evening tours 10:30pm-midnight Tue, Sat for 5,000ptas; Shop open 10am-2pm Mon-Fri)* is a guided bike tour of the Ciutat Vella and Barri Gòtic. Both day and evening tours include a stop for a drink (we love Spain...) in the Barri Gòtic, and the evening tour also includes dinner on the port. Prices include food, booze, and bike. Evening tours require an advance reservation.

Although Barcelona is no slouch as a traveler's destination, most of what it offers only fits into the "oh, that's cool" category. A few attractions and sights, like **La Sagrada Familia** [see *culture zoo*, above] and **Marató de L'Espectacle** [see *arts scene*, above] could be included in the "wow" category, but the beautiful and serene mountains of Montserrat, a 90-minute train/cable car journey from Barcelona, will probably leave you speechless. The famous monastery of the same name *(Tel 938/350-251; 9am-6pm daily, shorter hours Nov-Mar)* that sits atop this 4,000-foot wind-carved mountain was established by Benedictine monks in the 9th century. Barcelona and all of Catalunya love this place; they come to see the statue of Catalunya's patron saint, La Moreneta (the Black Madonna), which was supposedly found near the monastery sometime in the 12th or 13th century. After arriving at the monastery, you can take a funicular ride *(10am-7pm daily Apr-Oct only, 340ptas)* that will carry you (even) higher (Sly will be with you in spirit), to the top of the mountain. From here, you'll be able to see the Pyrenees Mountains to the north and Mallorca and Ibiza (which is best seen up close) to the east. Montserrat is the religious center of Catalunya, so don't go on a Sunday—

Rules of the game

The legal drinking age in Barcelona is 16, but who's keeping track? Like everywhere else in Spain, nobody cares about your drinking problem unless you're starting a fight or whizzing in the middle of Las Ramblas. Drug policies (and practices) are the same here as in Madrid [see *rules of the game*, Madrid]. When staggering out of the bars and clubs, keep in mind that the locals are very courteous to their Ciutat Vella neighbors. Bars like **Kentucki** and (particularly) **Dot** are located in residential neighborhoods where the doormen will ask you to stop shouting if you're too wasted to realize that you are....

you'll grow old waiting in line. Also remember to dress for temperatures that are about a season colder than Barcelona, and wear attire that's respectful of the monks, their monastery, and their religion (no tank tops or miniskirts). The Manresa line of the FGC (suburban) trains leaves five times a day from Plaça d'Espanya. It connects with a cable car that brings you directly to the monastery. Round-trip is 1,800ptas.

STUFF

Portal de L'Angel and the surrounding streets of Calle de la Portaferrissa, Calle de Cucurulla, and Calle Arcs are the places to go for clothes and shoes. Barcelona is much more European that Madrid, and it shows in the fashions. If it's gifts for the family and friends back home that you're looking for, **La Sagrada Familia** and the **Museo Picasso** [see *culture zoo*, above, for both] both have fantastic gift shops that offer better-than-average trinkets and posters for prices that won't keep you from that second glass of absinthe in the evening.

▶▶THRIFT

Mies & Felj *(Riera Baixa 5; Tel 934/420-755; Metro to Liceu; 11am-2pm/4:30-9pm daily; V, AE, MC)* offer the best secondhand butterfly-collar hipster shirts in the whole of Barcelona. They've got some tough competition from the handful of other retro clothing (and vinyl) stores on the same funky little block, but they take plastic here and really outdo the others' selections.

▶▶GIFT

4ART *(Boters 4; Tel 933/011-325; Metro to Liceu; 10:30am-8:30pm Mon-Sat; V, AE, MC)* has more prints and frames than Cher's had surgery. In the town that produced so many of this century's greatest painters, you're bound to find a few worthwhile gifts here. Prints start at 1,500ptas. Some artisan-type stuff is also for sale here.

ART Escudellers *(Escudellers 23-25; Tel 934/126-801; Metro to Drassanes; 11am-11pm daily; V, AE, MC)* offers a huge selection of (mainly) ceramic work created by artisans from all over Spain. A lot of expensive items here, but you can buy a lot of cool small things too, like rings, magnets, and coffee mugs. Their late hours are great for last-minute shopping.

▶▶DUDS

System *(Portaferrissa 12; Tel 933/012-526; Metro to Liceu; 10am-2pm/4:30-8:30pm, closed Mon; MC, V)* has six different stores in Barcelona, and all of their clothes are of their own label. Carrer de Porta-ferrissa, along with Portal de L'Angel, has a million women's clothing stores, but the quality and price at System are better than most. Lots of linen (about 1/3 cheaper than in the U.S.), and not your usual overdose of black and club gear. Very cool in a sexy-professional-mellow-woman kind of way, but not snobby. Few accessories and no shoes.

There are so many shops in Portal de L'Angel and nearby streets that it's easy to miss out on the one or two stores that really outshine the rest of the standard shoe-sellers and disco clothing shops. **Fantasy Shop** *(Comprising two stores that are right down the hall from each other, on the third floor of the Gallerías Gralla Hall, Portaferrissa 25; Tel 934/122-283; Metro to Liceu; 10:30am-8:30pm Mon-Sat; V, MC)* are not to be missed. The simple and elegant jewelry, shoes, and clothes in these little shops cannot be found elsewhere in Barcelona. The staff is great, and you will almost certainly walk away with a purchase of distinction. Most items are for casual wear, with an understated tone of refinement. The two stores are for him and her; his store also has some beautiful rings and bracelets, but the clothing and shoes lean more toward standard-issue club gear.

▶▶BOUND

Laie *(Pau Claris 85; Tel 933/181-739; Metro to Catalunya; Bookstore 10am-9pm Mon-Sat, cafe till 1am; V, MC)* has an overall good-bookstore feel, created by a broad selection of titles (a handful in English), semi-random stacks of books, and a cool staff. Buy your book and head upstairs to the cafe: Meals are served for around 1,000ptas, but you can just grab a cup of coffee and snack and enjoy the poet's atmosphere. Good bulletin board scene, too. A second Laie store is at the **CCCB** [see *culture zoo*, above].

Angel Battle *(Palla 23; Tel 933/015-884; Metro to Liceu; 10am-1:30pm/4-7:30pm Sun-Fri; No credit cards)* is your basic Old Europe hole-in-the-wall bookstore. Used books only, nearly all of them hardcover, and none in English. But this cluttered, dusky store is for people who love old books for their physical beauty—you half-expect to find Indiana Jones browsing the aged collection for clues on the Holy Grail. The cheapest offerings begin at around 2,500ptas. Angel Battle has also got hundreds of cool prints from Franco's Spain and earlier (very interesting stuff...).

EATS

As in most places in Europe, some of the cheapest and most interesting eats are at the markets. Late-night snacks can be purchased right from the news kiosks on Las Ramblas: Most of this stuff is like overpriced Pringles and cookies and candy. What's the biggest surprise for food in Barcelona?

An ice cream cone at McDonald's. Seriously. They're only 50ptas and are real, true ice cream (as in, delicious).

▶▶CHEAP

The Mercat Sant Josep (*On Las Ramblas between Carrer de Carme and Carrer de L'Hospital*) is like a big hockey game for the senses. Smell the fresh fruit, the raw meat, the fresh bread. Buy anything from roasted nuts and candy (at about 100ptas) to fresh olives to skinned rabbits and other animals (or not...). The best buy is the *menú del día*—a full meal for 800 to 1,200ptas.

El Taco (*Plaça Duc de Medinaceli 1; Tel 933/186-321; Metro to Drassanes; 9am-1am daily; No credit cards*) is a quick bite and drink place down by the **Mirador de Colón** that sells "grande" soft tacos (about one-and-a-half times larger than a T-Bell soft taco) for 375ptas and margaritas for 350ptas. The *Rajas con Crema de Gambas*, chock-full of shrimp,

wired

El Café de Internet (*Gran Vía de les Corts Catalanes 656; Tel 934/121-915; Metro Passeig de Grácia; 10am-midnight Mon-Wed, 10am-2am Thur-Sat; 1,000ptas per hour, 800ptas per 30 min; No credit cards*) has more than a dozen machines in a low-lit, air-conditioned, pop-rock-playing venue. A half-hour is a little pricey, but the full hour is a deal, so you might as well go for that. These prices are for students only, but the "student" policy is lax here (you look like one, you are one). Buy your drinks and food below and bring them with you upstairs. The international love quotient here is high.

The Interlight Café (*Pau Claris 106; Tel 933/011-180; Metro to Passeig de Grácia; 11am-10pm Mon-Sat, 5-10pm Sun; 700ptas per hour; interlight@bcn.servicom.es, www.gdesigners.com/interlight; No credit cards*) is one of the newer cybercafes in Barcelona and certainly one of the best. The very friendly staff speaks English well, and they serve food and coffee here. The venue itself has more sunlight and air than other e-mail locations. All 16 machines with Word. Printing is occasionally free.

While the name isn't exactly catchy, **E-mail from Spain** (*Ramblas 42/Bacardí 1; Tel 934/817-575; Metro to Drassanes; 10am-8pm Mon-Sat; 1,000ptas per hour, 600ptas per 30 min; No credit cards*) at least has a good location at the foot of Las Ramblas. The 11 machines here have Word, Excel, and an Adobe-like program that can be used with the in-house scanner. The main room can become unbearably hot in the summer and the pickup scene here is not the same as at Interlight or Café de Internet.

barcelona eats and crashing

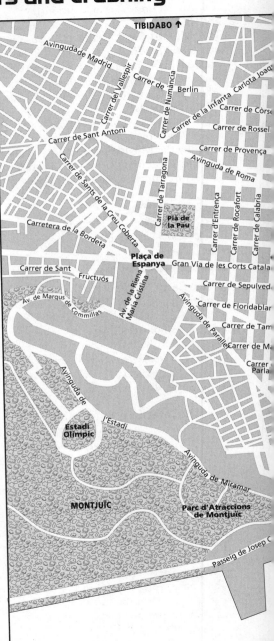

Barcelona

Madrid

SPAIN

PORTUGAL

EATS ◆

Comme Bio **3**
El Taco **11**
Kashmir **10**
Pla **9**
Venus **8**

CRASHING ■

Hostal Opera **7**
Hotel La Terrassa **5**
Hotel Peninsular **6**
Hotel Principal **4**
Pension Vitorio **2**
Turín **1**

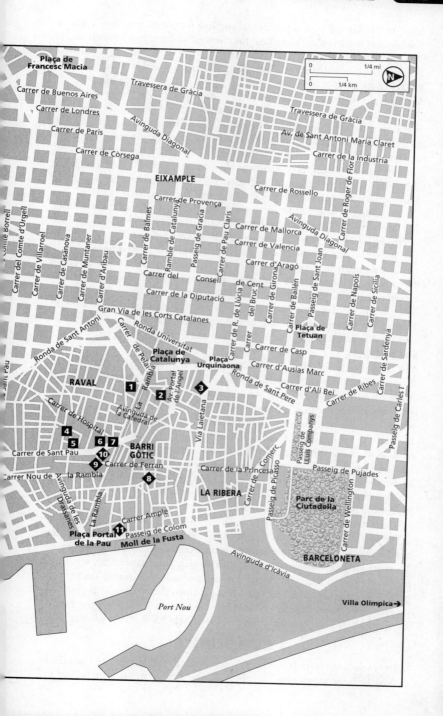

Plaça de
Francesc Macia

Carrer de Buenos Aires

Carrer de Londres

Carrer de Paris

Carrer de Còrsega

Travessera de Gràcia

Avinguda Diagonal

Travessera de Gràcia

Av. de Sant Antoni Maria Claret

Carrer de la Industria

EIXAMPLE

Carrer de Rossello

Carrer de Provença

Carrer de Mallorca

Avinguda Diagonal

Carrer de Valencia

Carrer d'Aragó

Carrer del Comte d'Urgell

Carrer de Villarroel

Carrer de Casanova

Carrer de Muntaner

Carrer d'Aribau

Carrer de Balmes

Rambla de Catalunya

Passeig de Gracia

Carrer de Pau Claris

Carrer del   Consell

de Cent

Carrer de la Diputació

Gran Via de les Corts Catalanes

Ronda Universitat

Ronda de Sant Antoni

Carrer de Pelai

RAVAL

Plaça de
Catalunya

Plaça
Urquinaona

Carrer de R. de Llúcia

del Bruc

Carrer de Girona

Carrer de Bailèn

Passeig de Sant Joan

Carrer de Napols

Carrer de Sicilia

Carrer de Sardenya

Plaça de
Tetuan

Carrer de Casp

Carrer d'Ausias Marc

Ronda de Sant Pere

Carrer d'Ali Bei

Carrer de Ribes

Passeig de Carles I

La Rambla

Av. Portal
de l'Angel

Avinguda de
la Catedral

Via Laietana

Carrer de Hospital

1

2

3

BARRI
GÒTIC

4

5

6 7

10

9   Carrer de Ferran

8

Carrer de Sant Pau

Carrer Nou de   la Rambla

Avinguda de les
Drassanes

La Rambla

11

Plaça Portal
de la Pau

Passeig de Colom

Moll de la Fusta

Carrer de la Princesa

LA RIBERA

Carrer de Comerç

Passeig de Picasso

Passeig de
Lluís Companys

Passeig de Pujades

Parc de la
Ciutadella

Carrer de Wellington

BARCELONETA

Avinguda d'Icàvia

Port Nou

Villa Olímpica→

0   1/4 mi

0   1/4 km

N

is recommended. Tropical plants and mellow flamenco-pop music soothe the hip and occasionally semi-famous clientele (whom you never heard of 'cause you're not from Spain). Also caters to the well-dressed, I-want-to-be-a-professional-already students from the nearby architecture school.

▶▶DO-ABLE

Venus *(Avinyó 25; Tel 933/011-585; Metro to Liceu; Noon-midnight Mon-Sat; Avg 500ptas per entree; No credit cards)* offers a wide variety of vegetarian dishes along with their standard, delicious menu. In addition to great food, Venus also boasts a fantastic location that is just outside the always-friendly, always-dreddy Plaça George Orwell. Chat with the exceptionally pleasant staff, take a look at the pleasant artwork, and check out the most expansive collection of flyers and free magazines that we saw in Barcelona. The chili is highly recommended for carnivores.

Barcelona is the home of many Indian and Pakistani restaurants, but nobody can touch **Kashmir** *(Sant Pau 39; Tel 934/413-798; Metro to Liceu; 1-5pm/8pm-midnight Wed-Mon, closed Tue; V, MC)* in the goodness-for-the-price category. This small, inexpensive, and delicious restaurant is recommended by locals and is perfect for lunch after checking out the Raval's galleries and secondhand shops. Tandoori chicken, artfully prepared by Chef Waseem Sarwar, goes for 750ptas. Very busy in the afternoon from 2 to 4. Although relatively safe, Kashmir is located in the roughest part of the Raval neighborhood, so you may want to make it a lunch rather than late-dinner spot.

▶▶SPLURGE

Pla *(Bellafila 5; Tel 934/126-552; Metro to Liceu; 7pm-midnight daily, till 1am weekends, bar till 3am; V, MC)* is so tucked away in the Barri Gòtic's maze of narrow cobblestone streets that most foreigners show up here only when they get lost. The establishment itself is a tall, wide-open-yet-warm-and-intimate space. Hardwood floors, candles, handwritten menus, the ever-mellow Grover Washington, Jr. on the hi-fi, and beautiful artwork combine for a serene, refined atmosphere. The clientele are late-twenty- and thirtysomethings who enjoy looking good in black. Appetizers start at 725ptas, entrees at 1,800ptas. The menu of local specialties changes almost daily, but there's usually one vegetarian dish. Reservations necessary on weekends.

Comme Bio *(Via Laietana 28; Tel 933/198-968; Metro Jaume I; About 2,500ptas dinner, 1,500ptas lunch; 9am-11:30pm daily; V, MC, AE)* has been making vegetarian tourists and health-conscious Spaniards happy for 25 years. It is a vegetarian restaurant/health food store that serves up pizzas, pastas, salads, and organic juices and sells not-tested-on-animals products, tofu, soymilk, and tasty desserts from the bakery. This place is a vegetarian's dream, but no one will be able to deny how good the food is and how all-around cool this place is. Definitely have a fruit-juice combo.

crashing

What makes the hostels in Barcelona so much more expensive than those in Madrid? Are we paying for more culture? Or for the nearby beach? Of course, the real reason might be that the population of Barcelona nearly doubles with young tourists in the summertime. Well, whatever it is, you'll be hard-pressed to find a double for 2,500ptas or a single for under 1,500ptas. Even though there are a hundred or so hostels in the Ciutat Vella, you won't get a room in one in July or August unless you start looking right around noon, when the management knows exactly who's vacated and who's sticking around another night. If you don't, you'll either wind up on the street or in a really nice hotel that you can't afford. If all else fails, go to the tourist office—they can make reservations for you. One good thing about most hostels in Barcelona is that they'll give you a key to the building, so you don't have to get buzzed in at 6 in the morning and make slurred small talk with the proprietor.

▶▶CHEAP

Pension Vitorio (*La Palla 8; Tel 933/020-834; Metro to Liceu; 2,000ptas single, 3,500-5,000ptas double, 4,500ptas triple; V, MC*) is in a good, quiet location in a beautiful old neighborhood only 2 minutes' walk from Las Ramblas and Plaça George Orwell. Singles and triples don't have their own baths, but all rooms come with bare furniture, balconies (Room 202 has three!), and are clean enough for the price.

Alberg Pere Tarrés (*Numancia 149-151; Tel 934/102-309, Fax 934/196-268, Central HI Reservations Tel 932/105-151; Metro to Les Corts; 1,500ptas/bed in a quad, linen additional 250ptas; alberg@pere tarres.org; V, MC*) isn't exactly downtown (it's over in the southwest), but we've included it in our list since lodging is so scarce in the Ciutat Vella in the summertime. There's coin-op laundry, a quiet rooftop terrace, a ground-floor terrace with a ping-pong table, and continental breakfast included in the price. A good place to meet and chill with other travelers.

Hotel La Terrassa (*Junta del Comerç 11; Tel 933/025-174, Fax 933/012-188; Metro to Liceu; 2,700-3,400ptas single, 4,000-5,200ptas double, 5,700-6,600ptas triple; V, MC, AE*) is one of the best deals in town. It's in (the good part of) El Raval, and right next to Las Ramblas and the Barri Gòtic. The second-floor terrace is a great place to meet fellow travelers. Everything is clean, and the day staff speak English.

▶▶DO-ABLE

Hotel Principal (*Junta del Comerç 8; Tel 933/188-970; Metro to Liceu; 9,500ptas single, 12,500ptas double, +4000ptas per extra person; hprincip@lix.intercom.es; V, MC*) is on the same quiet street as the Hotel La Terrassa but will give you a lot more in the way of creature comforts. Big ornate rooms include phone, satellite TV, air conditioning, bath, and continental breakfast. With a small, cozy pub and an actual restaurant, too!

Hostal Opera (*Carrer Sant Pau 20; Tel 933/188-201; Metro Liceu; 5,000ptas single, 7,000ptas double; No credit cards*) has 70 rooms, all of which have recently been renovated. If you want clean and comfortable as close to Las Ramblas as possible, this place is a good bet. While the decor is as bland as your freshman dorm room the day you moved in, the Spanish men chatting in the lounge and the new lobby make up for it.

For a lot of character and personality at a good price, try the **Hotel Peninsular** (*Carrer Sant Pau 34; Tel 933/023-138; Metro Liceu; 7,000ptas single, 9,500ptas double with breakfast; V, MC*). In one of its many past lives, it was part of a convent, but it's been recently renovated and restored. These days it hosts student groups and a diverse crowd of tourists in its 80 rooms. The hanging plants, black and white tiled floor, glass ceiling, iron railings, relaxing courtyard, and decent continental breakfast all make this place genuinely one of the nicest places to stay in Barcelona.

▶▶**SPLURGE**

Turín (*Pintor Fortuny 9; Tel 933/024-812; Metro to Plaça de Catalunya; 18,500ptas double, 23,000ptas triple; AE, V, MC*) is an island of luxury in the stormy waters of El Raval. The rooms aren't enormous, but they're very comfortable. They all have air conditioning, TV, telephone, and balconies. Although the restaurant below is good, you'll get more local flavor per peseta if you dine elsewhere in the Ciutat Vella.

neeᴅ ᴛo ᴋnow

Currency Exchange The local currency is the **peseta** (ptas). You can exchange money at the **airport,** both **train stations,** and at various locations along **Las Ramblas;** but a **bank, ATM,** or credit card will always get you the best rates and lowest service charge.

Tourist Information The main tourist office is located underground at the **Plaça de Catalunya** (*Tel 906/301-282; Metro to Catalunya; 9am-9pm daily*). Look for the sign with a big, red *i*. The office has lots of free magazines and fliers, including info on the big discos and bars, and will make hotel reservations for you. You can also get help from the official tourist guys wearing the red vests. They walk along Las Ramblas until 9pm.

Public Transportation Keep in mind that the metro and buses can't help you out in the ancient and narrow Barri Gòtic, where you'll spend most of your time....A 10-trip T1 pass costs only 825ptas, and it can be used on the Metro and buses throughout Barcelona. The subway shuts down at the ridiculous hour of 11pm on weekdays and 2am on Fridays and Satudays—but it opens again at 5am, if you're still up....

American Express There are two offices in Barcelona—one on Las Ramblas (*Ramblas 74; Tel 933/011-166; Metro Liceu; 10am-7pm Mon-Sat*), in the center of all the hype and happiness, and the other north of Plaça de Catalunya (*Passeig de Gràcia 101; Tel 93/217-00-70; Metro Diagonal; 9:30am-6pm Mon-Fri; 10am-noon Sat*) in a less touristy neighborhood.

Health and Emergency Emergency: *061;* ambulance: *933/00-20-20;* English-speaking police: **Turisme-Atención** (*Las Ramblas 43; Tel 933/019-060*), which is located in the heart of the tourist area.

Pharmacies Pharmacies operate here as they do elsewhere in Spain: Every little neighborhood has at least one *farmacia,* marked by **big green neon crosses.** No single one is open 24 hours all the time;

instead, *farmacias* rotate the all-night responsibility. Each one posts a schedule of which will be open on what night, as do the major newspapers like *El País*.

Telephone City code: *93;* operator: *1003;* international operator: *1005.* Recent changes in Spain's phone system now require that all local calls within Barcelona be dialed with the 93 prefix.

Airport Aeroport del Prat *(Tel 932/983-838)* is the official name of Barcelona's airport. The **Aerobús** *(5:30am-11:15pm Mon-Fri, 6am-11:20pm Sat, Sun; 475ptas)* leaves from the airport every 15 minutes and arrives at Plaça de Catalunya about 30 minutes later.

Trains RENFE *(Station 934/900-202; Info line 902/240-202)* is Spain's national train line. **Estació Sants** *(Metro to Sants-Estacio)* handles most trains traveling within Spain. If you're leaving for or arriving from France, you'll usually wind up at the **Estació de França** *(Metro to Barceloneta)*. Both stations have Metro access, so use it! Get off in the Barri Gòtic (either the Liceu or Plaça de Catalunya stops) and find a hostel there.

Buses Out of the City The main station is **Estació del Nord** *(Alí Bei 80; Tel 93/265-65-08; Metro to Arc de Triomf)*.

Boat Transmediterránea *(Moll de Barcelona; Station 93/295-91-00; Info line 902/454-645)* is the major ferry service that operates between Barcelona and the Balearic Islands (Mallorca, Ibiza, etc.). There's no Metro stop close to here, but it's only a 10-minute walk from the Drassanes Metro stop (at the base of La Rambla). If you've got a lot of stuff, a taxi would be your best bet.

Bike Rental Biciclot *(Carrer St. Joan de Malta 1; Tel 933/077-475; 9am-2pm/5-8pm Mon-Fri, 10am-2pm Sat; 500ptas/hr, 2,000ptas/day; No credit cards)* will get you mobile on a mountain bike or a 10-speed.

ibiza

Those who appreciate the finer cultural nuances of traveling abroad should not visit Ibiza during the summer months. There *are* a few points of interest that don't involve gin and strobe lights or the sounds of the tide, but they don't do much for you after you've been out all night. The discos and beaches are why everyone's here. But if you like to dance, look good, feel good, and ride excess like a bareback horse, Ibiza will knock your socks off. If Ibiza were a woman, its sunny, beautiful beaches and good-natured locals would probably remind you of Cameron Diaz. But that's during the day. When the sun goes down on this island, Ibiza becomes more like Courtney Love: wild, hard-partying, and looking for almost-scary fun. Imagine the festive feel and colorful clothes of Mardi Gras and put that together with the thumping and theatrical Studio 54—that's what Ibiza is like every day from the middle of July until the end of August. So, if you want to go to Ibiza, go now, because it might kill you (or your career, or your sanity) when you're older. If Ibiza were a water slide, it would be tall, man, real tall. Yup, grab the Balearic Bull by the horns and dig in your spurs....This is the biggest damn slip and slide of a party you ever saw.

This small island was once best-known for its beautiful beaches and the small artisan communities that grew from a European hippie invasion in the early and mid-1970s. Ibiza still holds true to this character for nine months of the year (and year-round in the inland villages). In the past decade, however, Ibiza has become a giant, fire-breathing Godzilla of a party. Each summer, this island rears its head, thumps it chest, and emits a terrifying war cry in the form of electronic music from the world's greatest DJs. Ibiza is one of the epicenters of modern disco/rave culture, and savvy Europeans and Aussies seek the sounds that came out of this island in the late '80s like your old college roommate sought Dead tapes from the early '70s. Even though most Americans have never heard of Ibiza, European youth recognize this little island as *the* place for summer holiday. How wild are the times here? Basically, if you took the formidable nightlife of Madrid, crushed it up and snorted it, you would be on Ibiza.

Even at its worst, Ibiza is fascinating to watch: Imagine an English Daytona Beach, complete with boorish young Englishmen and their screeching pale girlfriends, both refusing to speak anything other than English to the locals who put up with their antics for three months every summer so that they can live in peace during the other nine months of the year. You'll find a lot of the same type of Germans, Italians, and Spanish, too, but in fewer numbers. At its best, though, Ibiza is a beautiful, almost spiritual fun place that tolerates everything. (The gay community is so predominant here that we hardly gave it its own section in this chapter.) This is the time and place to try something that you think will make you feel good but have never had the balls to try out back home: Dress up! Dance! Talk to strangers! People here want to soak you in and check you out; they want you to *contribute* to the good times, not just watch them.

You'll be doing plenty of watching, though, if you show up here without a lot of money. A week's worth of nightlife will cost you as much as a new Hyundai. Getting into clubs can cost up to US$40, and most hotels double (and sometimes triple!) their prices in July and August. This island will take a toll not only on your wallet, but on your body and brain. For some people, being put on Ibiza is the same as sending a NASA explorer to Mars: They're gonna crash and burn. Despite the tremendous amount of wild, smiling fun that you can have here, we urge you to be just a little careful....

When you're ready to venture out, you'll have no trouble finding sources of info to help you navigate, red-eyed, through this hurricane of discos and sunshine. **DJ Ibiza** gives you the most info on clubs, bars, restaurants, beaches, and markets in the least amount of words, along with short interviews from the big DJs. **Ministry in Ibiza** is like the *Maxim* of this island: funny articles written by a staff that jumps into the whole Ibiza scene head-first. You're sure to get the inside (read: wasted) view of how the club scene operates. Two smaller magazines that we like are **Party San,** which you can pick up at the **Sunset Café** [see *bar scene,* below] and **7.** The website ***www.ibizanight.com*** gives you basic info on the clubs but is more useful for its detailed info on the Disco Bus [see *need to know,* below], restaurants, and—most importantly—reservation information (make your reservations early!). The site is in English and Spanish, although the official language of the Balearic Islands is Catalán, the language of Barcelona. But, between the heavy influence of Spain and

ibiza

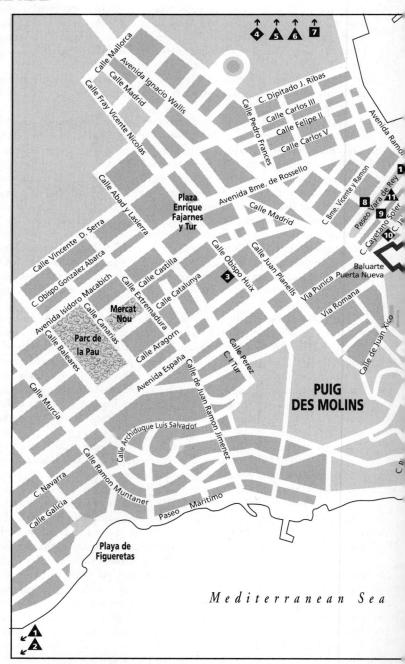

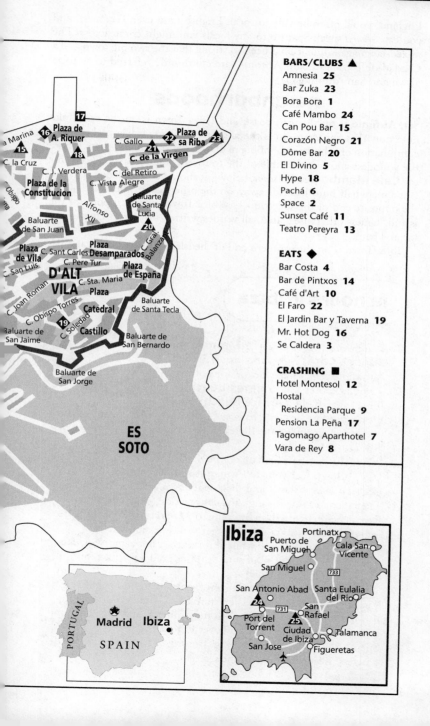

BARS/CLUBS ▲
Amnesia **25**
Bar Zuka **23**
Bora Bora **1**
Café Mambo **24**
Can Pou Bar **15**
Corazón Negro **21**
Dôme Bar **20**
El Divino **5**
Hype **18**
Pachá **6**
Space **2**
Sunset Café **11**
Teatro Pereyra **13**

EATS ◆
Bar Costa **4**
Bar de Pintxos **14**
Café d'Art **10**
El Faro **22**
El Jardin Bar y Taverna **19**
Mr. Hot Dog **16**
Se Caldera **3**

CRASHING ■
Hotel Montesol **12**
Hostal
  Residencia Parque **9**
Pension La Peña **17**
Tagomago Aparthotel **7**
Vara de Rey **8**

England, you'll often be able to speak English (and even German), and you can *always* speak Spanish to any locals you might come across. The mixed-language influence has been so strong that the two big towns—La Ciudad de Ibiza and Sant Antoni—are commonly referred to as Ibiza Town and San Antonio.

neighborhoods

San Antonio is on the west coast, and **Ibiza Town** is on the east. Take note now that San Antonio is the absolute weakest. It is a nightmarish combination of suburban shopping mall, soccer riot, and frat party, where the youngest and most terrible of the tourists come to party. Except for the **Café Mambo** [see *bar scene,* below], it should be avoided at all costs. But a mere half-hour bus ride away, on the other half of the island—and the opposite end of the spectrum—is Ibiza Town, the focal point of the island. Unless otherwise stated, all venues written up in this chapter are located here.

Ibiza Town is on the southern end of the island's eastern coast and lies

12 hours in ibiza

1. Watch the sunset at **Café Mambo** (or **Sunset Café,** right next door) in San Antonio [see *bar scene,* below, for both].
2. A day at either **Las Salinas Beach** by Ibiza Town, **Cala Xarraca Beach** up on the north coast [see *great outdoors,* below, for both], or any of the beaches in Formentera (Illetes, for example) [see *hanging out,* below].
3. Party calisthenics: Warm up on the beach at **Bora Bora** [see *bar scene,* below]. Get your full workout across the street at **Space** [see *club scene,* below], and then cool down at Bora Bora again.
4. Take a scooter ride through the countryside (pack a picnic...).
5. Experience extreme Ibiza by going to *Manumission* at **Privilege** [see *club scene,* below]. Don't forget your latex and whips.
6. Look good and feel good while at Ibiza's traditional party: *Renaissance* at **Pachá.** It's full of smart dressers and a warm, beautiful vibe [see *club scene,* below].
7. Watch the freaks go by in Sa Penya, particularly on Calle de La Virgen. Sock-and-sandaled and sunburnt German tourists, English fashion victims, loudmouth drag queens, and many, many beautiful party people from all over Europe.
8. Spend a couple hours walking around D'Alt Villa, the Old Fortress. Beautiful views of the sea.

to the south and west of the **Marina.** A small and unremarkable portion of Ibiza Town does curve around to the north of the Marina, but you won't be spending any time there. The **Sa Penya** neighborhood is where the action is—action like you may never have seen before. Dozens of bars, restaurants, street vendors, drag queens, and nationalities converge here and get warmed up for the nightly sacrifice to the disco club gods. During the day, you can find good fashion shopping, pubs, and groceries here. The beginning of Sa Penya is marked by **Plaça d'Antoni Riquer** and the street that runs through it, parallel to the Marina, which is called **Calle de Lluís Tur i Palau** to the west of the Plaça, and **Passeig des Moll** to the east. **Calle de La Virgen** is the most famous of the streets here; it is a long, narrow street that runs parallel to the Marina, from the eastern tip of the city to the equally busy **Calle de Pou,** which begins right at the Marina and runs north to south. Sa Penya continues south for about eight misshapen blocks before it runs into the foot of the elevated **D'Alt Villa** (Old Fortress). Ibiza Town more or less ends at the southern point of the Old Fortress. **Paseo de Vara de Rey** is the other major landmark in Ibiza Town—several hostels, the tourism office [see *need to know,* below], a travel agency, and a few good shops and restaurants are all on this street. Paseo de Vara de Rey is three blocks to the west of D'Alt Villa and runs northeast to southwest. Everything that we've mentioned here can be walked between in 20 minutes or less.

Other villages worthy of a day or half-day trip for some rural relaxation are **Santa Gertrudis** *(to the northwest of Ibiza Town, in the very middle of the island, about a half-hour by bus),* **Santa Eularia** *(to the east of Ibiza Town, on the coast, 20 minutes by bus),* and **San Rafael** *(directly between Ibiza Town and San Antonio).* The clubs **Privilege** and **Amnesia** [see *club scene,* below, for both] are both just outside of Ibiza Town. No point on the island of Ibiza is much more than an hour from Ibiza Town by bus, or 90 minutes by scooter. **Playa d'en Bossa** is a mere 15-minute bus ride south of Ibiza Town. This is one of the most crowded and commercial beaches on the island, but **Space** [see *club scene,* below], **Bora Bora** [see *bar scene,* below], and the **Aguamar waterpark** [see *great outdoors,* below] are all located here.

Remember that Ibiza is ridiculously small. The villages are even smaller. Venues that aren't in Ibiza Town or San Antonio simply have the village listed for the address because all of the stores/bars/etc., are located on one central street. Basic maps and road signs work just fine if you're going to scooter it between beaches and villages, and the buses go to all villages we have named and many beaches. And the clubs themselves (also reachable by bus) are landmarks that every cab driver and local knows. You'd have to work really hard to get lost on this island.

hanging out

You'll have no trouble finding the cool kids on this island, friends. The whole of Ibiza is one big party, but if you really want to "hang out," the beaches are the best for that, especially since all of them are topless (and many are nude) [see *great outdoors,* below]. Hordes of young folk don't

fiVE-0

One quick way to lose money here is by handing it over to José Law when he pulls you over for swerving around on your rented scooter. El Hombre isn't really out to get you, but let's face it: If your island were invaded each summer by two million hallucinating British Gen X-ers, you, too, would want to try to control things at least a little bit. Road blocks with breath tests are the newest attempt to keep you and your wasted friends out of harm's way. Take our advice: Use a cab at night.

really congregate in any of the plazas or squares here. With all the beautiful stretches of sand around, why would they?

Ibiza's best hangout, however, turns out to be difficult to find. Not only are these fabled **full-moon parties** hard to suss out, you also have to accept that they're only going to happen once a month. When they do go down, there will be no flyers, and the Germans and the English won't be able to help you out, but if you make friends with just a few locals, they'll be able to tell you the day and location of one of the island's best events. Drum circles, booze, bonfires, and more on secluded black-sand beaches that are beautiful enough to make you cry.

Calle de Santa Agnes, in San Antonio, is probably the last place you want to hang out, unless you're 16, belligerent, and culturally void: The scene here is vomiting and groping in the streets, 100 percent rude, 100 percent lame. If you want to get some pale English lovin', though, this street is definitely the place. We hung out for 10 minutes and then ran.

bar scene

As you would expect with a Spanish island, Ibiza has a bar for every occasion. Some are for cool beachside drinks, others are for hot late-night action, but the bulk of the bars you'll encounter in Ibiza Town are meant to operate like giant cannons that will blast your wasted ass into the disco stratosphere. Don't try and fight it, either, pal. Keep your chin up, strap on your crash helmet, and head on down to the crowded international big-top mayhem that is the Sa Penya district. It's your job to get there at about 11pm or midnight and to be ready to perform death-defying stunts of fashion and consumption. Among the feather boas, platform shoes, and glitter, you'll notice a fair number of attractive and seemingly coked-up folks who—despite all of their talking—are rather stationary. It's their job to get you into their bar. Here's how it usually goes: A sexy and fast-talking hawker approaches you and says "Hey there, mate. How about tickets for Amnesia tonight?" Be sure that you know where you want to go ahead of time, because they will always try and sell you on the less-attractive events first (e.g., a foam party [see *good clean fun,* below] instead of a hot dance scene that ends with live sex on stage). So having already done your homework, you say, "How abouts tickets for Pachá?" What usually happens next is that you'll agree to go in for a drink. Yes, that's right; if you agree to a couple of (relatively) cheap whiskey-and-Cokes, you'll get a big discount or even free admission! What a great system! Don't you wish that getting a driver's license or paying off your student loans was this easy? A good negotiating tactic is to not be shy about sticking it in the camera, baby. As so many of the twentysomething party people here already know, looking sexy and freaky will get you what you want, because the clubs want beautiful people!

Hype *(Calle d'Emile Pou 11A; No phone; 8pm-3am daily; V, MC)* is only one of the very many bars that operate in this way in the Sa Penya district. Drink your way to cheap disco and watch the freak show pass by from the terrace seating.

Bar Zuka *(Calle de la Virgen 75; No phone; 9pm-3am daily; No credit cards)* has candles, an old tile floor, a more-refined-less-hectic vibe (until they break out the tequila later at night), beautifully painted walls, and regular attendance by some of England's biggest DJs. Less queeny and painted-up than the rest of Calle de la Virgen.

When the MTV beach parties grow up, they want to be **Bora Bora** *(Playa d'en Bossa, across the street from Space; No phone; Open all the time—really; No credit cards)*. Drink, dance, and chill while coming down from nearby Space (or while gearing up for it, depending on your schedule and stamina). Along with the party people, there are many unaware beach-goers here who have a dim realization that they are not in the same state as everyone else at the bar. This is a very mellow, very appropriate, very Ibiza way to end a disco marathon: 300ptas for a beer and usually around 500 people.

In addition to alcohol, **Sunset Café** *(Plaza del Parque 3; Tel 971/394-446; 9:30am-3am Mon-Sat; No credit cards)* serves tasty chicken sandwiches (500ptas), fresh juice, and "breakfast salads" (garden salads with a lot of fruit) for 500ptas. Good house music with its own DJ from 9pm till 1am. Be sure to say hi to Stephan, the friendly German owner, and

RULES OF THE GAME

Despite their overwhelming abundance, drugs are still illegal in Ibiza. However, in traditional Spanish fashion, people don't get busted unless they get violent. So don't. The standard Spanish chill factor applies here as well, but the locals have become less patient with the rowdy English tourist in recent years, so if you do get in a bind, don't go shooting your mouth off. Also be forewarned that most people get a good searching when traveling from Ibiza to another country. Taking the boat between Ibiza and Barcelona/Valencia, however, is a cake walk.

whichever hottest-woman-ever happens to be behind the bar with him. Sitting on their pleasant plaza right off the Paseo de Vara de Rey is a great getaway from Ibiza Town nonsense.

Can Pou Bar *(Corner of Lluis Tur i Palau and Montgri; Tel 971/310-875; 9am-1am daily; Open in winter; MC, V)* has been a local favorite for over 80 years, except that the customers back then were all fishermen, not disco and clothing store owners. There are a few terrace tables and the inside is comfy (they don't try to cram people in here for the extra buck like many other places). Coffee, juice, small sandwiches, and breakfasts are served. Walls are lined with beautiful artwork that reflects the local temperament. Right on the Marina between Sa Penya and Paseo de Vara de Rey.

Café Mambo *(End of Avenida de Vara de Rey, in San Antonio; No phone; 11am-4am daily, kitchen till midnight; MC, V for purchases over 5,000ptas)* is in San Antonio, but nobody's perfect. Listen to mellow ambient music, have a drink, and watch a magnificent sunset over the water from the terrace (a must-see while in Ibiza). The rabid British party monkeys that swarm San Antonio do show up later on, but it's fun to slip slowly from the mellow sunset to that high-energy fiesta while getting sauced on gin-and-tonics. Including the surrounding beach, max capacity is about 2,000 people. 800ptas for a drink.

LIVE MUSIC SCENE

Live music? Yeah, right. Only the most popular DJs on earth spin here on a nightly basis. Save for a handful of German and Dutch expats who live inland, there's not much of a live music scene on this island. If middle-aged Germans covering the Eagles and the Dead is your thing, though, be sure to rush on over to **Teatro Pereyra** *(Corner of Calle Conde Rosellon and Calle Anibal; No phone; 7am-4am daily; No credit cards)*. The good times get rolling at 11:30pm. Despite everything, they do get points here for being open 21 hours a day and for having an enormous and beautiful bar. The big round tables can seat about six stools, and capacity is about 300 European preps. Lord knows why they came to Ibiza.

CLUB SCENE

Because they're the big business here, all of the clubs adhere to the same high prices and late schedule. Here's the lowdown (exceptions are noted in the club descriptions):

1. Clubs run from the middle of May until the end of September and are open from midnight till 6 or 8am daily.
2. Prime time is from around 3:30 to 5:30am.
3. Cover is between 6,000 and 10,000ptas! Discount flyers are easy to come by, though, and bring the price down to 4,000 to 6,000ptas [see *bar scene,* above, to learn more].
4. Little bottles of water are around 1,000 ptas and drinks are 1,500-2,500ptas. Amnesia charges 2,000ptas for water, and the owners might well go straight to hell when they die.

5. The best way to get to all of these clubs is by taxi or Disco Bus [see *need to know*, below].

6. None of the clubs are exclusive at the front door. Instead, they have exclusive rooms within.

7. All of the clubs take at least Visa and MasterCard. They want your money, in any form.

8. Each club holds between 5,000 (Pachá) and 10,000 (Privilege) people at once! They all have smaller rooms tucked away here and there (especially Pachá), so don't get put off if you don't like the feel of the main room. A little exploring will do you nice.

9. The crowds are between 19 and 30 years old. Despite the fashion blitzkrieg here, there are also thousands of preps and dorks and family men running around this island. These folks are more likely to not make it past the bar scene at Sa Penya, though.

10. English magazines *Ministry* and *DJ Ibiza* will keep you current on the club scene.

Even on Sunday at 4pm, **Space** *(Playa d'en Bossa; Tel 971/314-078; 8am-6pm—how wild is that?; www.space-ibiza.com, www.ibiza-online.com/privilege)* is still insane and happy from the night before. Whoop! This x-tensive club doesn't even open till the others close, so pretty much the whole island congregates here around 8am. A big open-air room with a semitranslucent tarp for the ceiling gives the whole club a sitting-under-a-shady-tree kind of feel. Space ties with Pachá as our favorite club. Best event: *Home*, starting Sunday at 8am.

good clean fun

Amensia and one or two other clubs host the infamous *espuma* (foam) parties that you've seen on *E!*, full of scantily clad hotties splashing around and getting it on in 6 feet of bubbly goodness. Well, color me soaking wet with soap in my eye! Who thought that being buried alive in foam was going to be a good time? Listen. If you're gonna do a foam party, do it right because—no joke—you'll wind up gagging, getting felt up (which might be what you're lookin' for), and slipping and cracking your head in 6 feet of the stuff. Being prepared, though, can make a foam party a lot more fun. The foam pros show up with backpacks containing goggles, bathing suits, beach sandals or old sneakers, and a towel. They gear up before the foam comes to town (it rains down like one of the Ten Plagues, like the fury of God himself, in terrifyingly enormous quantities), and make sure that they're a good 30 feet from the center of the dance floor.

boy meets girl

Yeah, more like boy meets boy on this island.
Or girl meets boy dressed like girl, or boy meets girl who looks like a boy dressing as a girl, or...whatever. Ibiza is not a place for the shy. The whole point of this island is that you can do whatever you want, baby. Do it loud, do it bright, do it in spandex, and do it topless— you can rest when you get home. When the summer rolls around, the local hippie types will often refer to "the colors returning," referring to the bright clothes, jewelry, and smiles that come to this island each summer. So make sure you play up the part! Believe us, you're gonna be meeting a lot of boys and girls, whether you like it or not. Of course it's easier to make small talk on the beach, but for folks of a more North American or English upbringing, it's hard to talk to someone about the weather when they're half-naked. The gay nightlife here is not a separate entity; it's all swirled together like Jell-O pudding. Our best advice on an island like this is to be safe with whomever you wind up with, because lord knows you'll have the opportunities here. The one thing we don't recommend is buying a lot of drinks for your catch-of-the-night. As the drinks regularly cost as much as US$15, you'll be broke real quick.

Privilege *(10 minutes north of San Rafael; Tel 971/198-160; 15 minutes by bus, 10 minutes by cab from Ibiza Town; Closed Tue, Sun)* is midgets and strobe lights and 10-foot drag queens on stilts, people shagging on stage (really), fire-eaters and an enormous swimming pool, and music, and lord knows what else running around all over the place. And you have to pay money for toilet paper! Now *that's* wild. Privilege tends to be more gay than other clubs, particularly for *Manumission* (Mondays), which is also its best event.

Open since 1975, **Pachá** *(Av. 8 de Agosto, on the Paseo Maritimo, a 20-minute walk southwest of Ibiza Town; Tel 971/310-959; www.pacha.com; Open year-round)* is the original Ibiza disco and is considered to be one of the finest nightclubs on planet Earth. Like Sean Connery or your favorite M.I.L.F., Pachá has aged with elegance over the years and hosts a more noticeable contingent of 30- and 40-year-olds (although they are very far from the majority). Pachá is *muy fashion,* as they say here, and the most international (read: not two-thirds English and German) of the clubs. The go-go girls are fly and the dance floor gets hot and grimy (the way you like it, baby), but the drag queens and freak-outs that keep the other clubs churning are usually not here (so don't dress out for Pachá, dress up). Famous people stop by all the time. Best nights: *Renaissance* on Wednesday and *Ministry* on Friday.

If Pachá is the Sean Connery of the clubs, **Amnesia** *(2 minutes south of San Rafael, 15 minutes by bus, 10 minutes by cab from Ibiza Town; www.amnesia.es),* which was full of hippies and liquid acid in the early '80s, is more like Mick Jagger: past its prime and blissfully unaware of it. Yes, it's as big as an airplane hangar. Yes, it has a retractable roof. Yes, it has trees and drag queens and several rooms and dancers and balconies, but big deal—where's the love? Best nights: *Godskitchen* on Tuesday and *Cream* on Thursday.

El Divino *(On the Paseo Maritimo at the Puerto de Ibiza Nueva, across the harbor from Ibiza Town; Tel 971/190-177; www.ibiza-online. com/eldevino)* is beautiful (almost opulent) and often semi-exclusive. You can get here by taking the boat that leaves every half hour from the Marina; you can't miss it, it's the one with the flashing lights and the big sign that says "El Divino." The best areas of the enormous and ornate deck on the water are usually roped off for the many VIPs that attend this club. One of the main events, *Miss MoneyPenny,* is basically the prom for a whole lot of English drag queens. *Submission,* on Saturdays, is one of the island's wildest events. Wear your latex and leather and bring a whip, because you're gonna git your freak on tonite! Be prepared for wild costumes, excessive groping, and shagging in the bathrooms. Straight out of a movie—or hell, if you're a Puritan.

gay scene

Gay life here is as prevalent as Britney Spears songs are on FM radio, so we'll just point out that a lot of mostly gay bars are on the Calle de la Virgen and Calle Mayor in Ibiza town. Check out the **Dôme Bar** *(Calle Alfonso XII 3; No phone; 8pm-3am daily; No credit cards)* for some of the trendiest and queeniest times on the island. **Corazón Negro** *(Calle de la Virgen 23; No phone; 9pm-4am daily; No credit cards)* is one of dozens of bars in a row that appeal to a more-gay clientele, but, like we said, few things here are strictly one way or the other. One exception, though, is the 95 percent gay, 100 percent nude **Es Cavellet Beach** *(15-minute bus ride south of Ibiza Town, close to the southernmost tip of the island).* Expect bad techno music, a whole lot of drugs, and *a lot* of naked gay men (and some women). Straight girls sometimes stop by for a bit of sightseeing and weird fantasizing.

ARTS SCENE

▶▶VISUAL ARTS

Besides functioning as a bookstore, **Libro Azul** *(Village of Santa Gertrudis; Tel 971/197-454; 10am-2pm/5-8pm Mon-Fri, till 2pm Tue, Sat, Sun; No credit cards)* hosts one or two readings and art expos every month. The art here leans toward the enormous, like sculptures as big as a fridge. The books (many of them secondhand) lean toward the New Age and are in German, English, Spanish, and Catalán.

▶▶PERFORMING ARTS

All the performance on this island takes place in the clubs: live sex acts, striptease, midgets, stilt freaks, fire eaters, drag queens, go-go girls, aliens, latex—and then there's all the freaks who pay to get in. Just what goes on in the bathrooms during *Manumission* at **Privilege** [see *club scene,* above] is more "performance" than most people will need in a lifetime.

modification

There are dozens of tattoo shops on the island, but they all looked iffy and none of the locals could direct us to one that stood out above the rest. In general, we recommend NOT getting a tattoo while here. That Mitsubishi symbol probably seemed like a good idea at 9am on a Saturday morning when you were still going from the night before, but the significance will be hard to explain later on when you return home and are trying to get a job that does not involve checking IDs.

great outdoors

The Ibiza tourist office claims that this tiny island has something like 56 different beaches!! If you really want to explore them, head to the tourist office [see *need to know,* below] and pick up the free *IBIZA: Playas a la Carta.* This catalog describes each of the 56 beaches and tells you how to get there, too.

To get away from the tourist hype that envelopes the beaches closer to Ibiza Town, try **Las Salinas Beach** *(about 7 miles south of Ibiza Town; follow the signs for the airport),* a full-on nudist beach that's less than 15 minutes from Ibiza Town by scooter. The attractive crowds here tend to be a little older (as in over 21), more local, and with more money. This beach is the height of cool in Ibiza.

You'll miss **Cala Xarraca Beach** unless you're looking for the restaurant of the same name. It makes sense, though, because the restaurant is the only thing here besides a few beautiful houses. The beach is more tiny pebbles and shells than sand. Surrounded by rocky cliffs, the water is very clear with tints of blue and doesn't get deep for quite a while. Topless, not a huge beach, but super-cool. Bring goggles and a snorkle for collecting stones in the water. Paddle boats are rented by the restaurant for 950ptas an hour.

The tiny island of **Formentera** is about 10 miles south of Ibiza and features dreamy and unspoilt stretches of white sand that seem to go on forever. Its three beaches, Illetes, Levant, and Es Pujols, all outdo anything on Ibiza; they're prettier and the crowds are cooler. Only 5,000 people are permanent residents on this island, and although that number jumps to 20,000 in the summer, this place is still more chill than a penguin on ice. Boats leave Ibiza Town at least once an hour from 7:45am till 10:30 at night. You'll get to Formentera in about 30 minutes and will pay about 2,500ptas each way. Contact **Baeleria Lines** *(Calle Aragón 71; Tel 971/310-711, central reservations 902/160-180; 7:30am-6:30pm daily, later in summer; V, MC)* for more info.

Ibiza has some of the best diving in the Mediterranean. Unlike you, some people come here specifically for the clear waters and the unique

SCOOT OVER

The best way to get away from some of the hype is to rent a scooter. They're cheap and they're a total blast. Try and avoid the temptation to drive your scooters when really f#@!ed up—it's hard to look good when you're picking your teeth and kneecaps up off the pavement. We don't want to sound like Nancy Reagan, but there's really no need to be driving your scooters while blinded by whiskey. The cheapest places to rent are just a little out of the tourist section [see *need to know*, below]. A short cab ride or long walk will reward you with ample savings. A little scooter that maxes out at 40mph can traverse the entire island (east to west) in about 45 minutes. And even during the crowded tourist season, many of the roads are barely populated. Bring a picnic! Find a beach! The locals inland are not likely to speak English; for them, Spanish is a second language.

marine life and mysterious shipwrecks that can be found beneath the surface. For a beautiful adventure, contact **Ibiza Diving** (*Puerto Deportivo in the village of Santa Eulária; Tel 971/332-949; www.ibiza-diving.com; 9:30am-1pm/2-6pm daily; MC, V*) or **Figueral** (*Playa de Es Figueral, 45-minute bus ride north of Ibiza Town, on the northeastern coast; Tel 971/335-079; 9am-2pm/4-6:30pm daily; V, MC*). Instructors at both places speak English. Or get reefed and hit the water slides! Just watch your language around the children. Of Ibiza's two water parks, the **Agualandia** (*near Cap Martinet*) and **Talamanca's Beach** (*15-minute bus ride northeast of Ibiza Town, way on the other side of the harbor; No phone; 10am-6pm daily; No credit cards*) has the better slides. **Aguamar** (*Playa d'en Bossa; Tel 971/396-790; 10:30am-6:30pm daily May-Oct; No credit cards*), however, is right next to **Space** [see *club scene*, above] and across the street from **Bora Bora** [see *bar scene*, above].

STUFF

Between the influence of the hippies and the already-artistic leanings of the native Ibizan culture, there's plenty of artistry, beautiful pottery, clothes, and jewelry on the island. Make sure that you set aside some money for gifts! If you don't, an empty bottle of Jack Daniels, a mostly-smoked *porro*, and a sunburn are all you'll have to bring back to Mom.

▶▶TO MARKET

If you're asking directions, don't bother translating Hippy Market into *mercadillo de hippi* or something like that. The locals themselves call the fun outdoor markets by their English name, as well. The biggest and best

fashion

Platforms, pigtails, and a Stetson will get you real far here. As will pushing yourself to the fashion limits: Dye your hair! Paint your face! Wear just a bathing suit top! The fashion here goes right with the free-wheeling and tripped-out attitude of the island. People might sneer at you if you're walking around in the middle of Iowa with a too-mini leather skirt and a quarter-ounce of glitter on your face, but people here will love it. Everyone wants you to look wild and feel good about it.

of them takes place in **Es Canar** (*northeast of Santa Eulária, 20-minute bus ride from Ibiza Town; 9:30am-7pm Wed only Apr-Oct; A few of the booths accept credit cards, but don't rely on it here*). Unlike many other outdoor markets, this one has some truly beautiful stuff: great hats and sarongs for the beach, all sorts of handmade wind chimes, instruments, ceramics, fans, and also the requisite T-shirts, bowls, and watches. The market at Es Canar is right in the middle of a hippie village and has been running since the early '70s. Get here by bus (130ptas) or by scooter (30 minutes max). It's easy to spend a few hours among the nearly 400 booths here, so give yourself some time. The bright wooden carvings of Paulo Viheira capture the warm and creative essence of non-disco Ibiza. Although he does have his own studio in Santa Eulária, you'll have an easier time tracking him down here. Prices range from about US$20 for something the size of a dinner plate to nearly US$300 for enormous carvings that you could windsurf on. Very recommended, and easy to find. Ask any of the friendly workers at the market.

▶▶DUDS

The motto at **Holala!** (*Plaza de Mercado Viejo 12; Tel 971/316-537; 10am-2pm/5-8pm daily, later in summer; MC, V*) is "unique clothing for unique people." In sticking to this creed, it has taken used clothing and brought it into the world of high fashion. Written up in nearly every fashion magazine you can think of (including *Elle, Vogue,* and *Cosmopolitan*), there's always something cooking at this trendsetting and semi-famous little shop. It sells everything from old kimonos and military surplus to modern clothing like Dickies and Adidas. But bring your wallet—those old 501s don't sell for cheap.

Mapa Mundi (*Plaza de Vila 13, at the base of the Fortress; Tel 971/391-685; 11am-2pm/6pm-midnight Mon-Sat May-Oct; V, M, AE*) is all about the shoes, which are totally unique, not too costly, and make a great gift for Mom, Sis, girlfriends, or yourself. The dresses here are beautiful, but out of the range of most travelers (they begin at 14,000ptas). If Indiana Jones and Stevie Nicks opened a store together, it might look like this place. Beautiful, flowy dresses set in an old-world setting with maps, old travel trunks, and beautiful tribal-looking jewelry.

▶▶BOUND

DK *(Ignacio Wallis 35; Tel 971/191-339; 9am-2pm/5-8:30pm Mon-Fri, 9am-2pm Sat, Sun; V, MC)* is a pleasant little bookstore that sells good maps, magazines, stationery, school supplies, and, of course, books. The friendly staff doesn't speak English.

EATS

Pills and thrills aside, try to avoid too many bellyaches by eating at least one decent meal a day. It will help you go the distance at night, too. It's sad to note that all-night food in Ibiza is only a little more common than an acoustic Happy Mondays song. Although some of the clubs sometimes have a guy in the parking lot vending pretzels and bottled water for a price that would usually get you a case of wine, you really can't count on it. Your best bet is to buy food at a local market (they're everywhere) during the day and stow it away in your hotel room for when you come back at night. Think smart and buy in advance: You'll want chips and bread to soak up some of the booze, probably some boxed juice and bottled water to un-parch your throat and calm your jittery body, and some oranges and bananas for the highs and lows (respectively). Good luck!

▶▶CHEAP

El Jardin Bar y Taverna *(Calle Mayor; Tel 971/307-328; 10am-midnight Mon-Sat, till 5pm Sun; No credit cards)* is a pleasant little restaurant tucked away within the confines of the D'Alt Villa. Beautiful, calm, and shady, with a whole lot of beautiful purple bougainvillea plants, island music, and umbrellas in your drinks. The atmosphere and desserts are better than the entrees, which run from 500ptas for a salad to 1,375ptas for a steak. Definitely not a hot spot, but that's why we recommend it. Best as a place to sit and have a drink and some ice cream after exploring the old city.

It's not like you need a travel guide to find **Mr. Hot Dog** *(At the Marina; 9:30am-4:30am daily; No credit cards)*, but we've written it up so that you know that you're getting a fair price and good food here. Mr. Hot Dog will serve you up a big-ass yummy cheeseburger for 450ptas. The French bread and chicken breast is also recommended. Their terrace seating is right in the middle of it all, providing you with some great people-watching.

▶▶DO-ABLE

Café d'Art *(Cayetano Soler 9; Tel 971/302-972; 10am-9pm Mon-Sat; V, MC)* has nothing to do with art, but this small old country store sells all kinds of semi-gourmet meats, cheeses, fresh bread, wine, and ready-made tapas. Perfect stuff for a picnic at a quiet beach of your choice, or you can sit outside at the base of the old city and eat at one of the cafe tables.

Bar de Pintxos *(Conde de Rosellon 1; Tel 971/399-559; 11:30am-*

3:30pm/8pm-2:30am daily; No credit cards) is a small outdoor cafe away from the hoopla in the harbor, right next to the old city. Pleasant staff and classic Basque tapas. 200ptas for *pinchos fríos* (small uncooked things like salmon on yummy bread) and 800ptas for calamari.

▶▶SPLURGE

Se Caldera *(Obispo Padre Huix 19; Tel 971/306-416; 1-4pm/8pm-midnight Sun-Fri, 8pm-midnight Sat; Menú del día 1,800ptas, 2,800-6,400ptas per entree, bottles of wine 1,200-3,800ptas; V, MC)* is the restaurant of choice for locals (even other restaurant owners) of Ibiza Town. Run by the same native Ibizenco couple for 15 years now: The husband cooks, the wife runs the show. All the food is "down-home," specializing in fresher-than-fresh fish. The *menú del día* costs a whopping 1,800ptas, but includes spectacular main dishes like fresh salmon. Located a little away from the port (about a 10-minute walk), so you won't see the sunset or hear the tide with your meal, but you will be treated right and get a great look at the locals in action.

El Faro *(Plaza Sa Riba 1; Tel 971/313-233; Noon-3am daily May-Oct; V, AE, MC)* is very touristy, very ritzy. Kings, presidents, rock 'n' roll stars, and famous athletes have been eating here regularly for 20 years. Choose from the living fish and lobsters for your dinner. Like Se Caldera, you can pay up to 6,000ptas for *paella* here, but unlike Se Caldera, the atmosphere here is downright swank. The restaurant is right in front of the water and a little distance from the Sa Penya hoopla a few blocks down. Reservations should be made. The owner's name is Mercedes, which totally makes sense.

crashing

The thing about Ibiza is that there's not a lot of people who are just "passing through": This is their destination. People come to this island for a wild vacation and expect to pay for it. But the prices aren't too, too crazy—it's simply finding a room here that's a big pain. Save yourself a whole lot of headaches by making a reservation for a room before you arrive on the island. A little planning ahead will get you a sweet little room at Vara de Rey or something with a view in Hotel Montesol.

▶▶CHEAP

Pension La Peña *(Calle de la Virgen 76; Tel 971/190-240; 1,500-2,400ptas single, 2,500-3,500ptas double; No credit cards)* has, as far as we can tell, the cheapest rooms in Ibiza Town. The common bathrooms are of questionable character, but many of the rooms (though small and bare) have a beautiful view of the sea. The 10 doubles and three single rooms are rented out almost exclusively to gay guys who want to be near the action that makes the Calle de la Virgen famous.

Another fairly reasonable option is **Sol y Briso** *(Avingunda B.V. 15; Tel 971/310-818; 3,500-5,000ptas double; No credit cards).*

▶▶DO-ABLE

Hostal Residencia Parque *(Calle Vicente Cuervo 3, just south of Paseo*

Vara de Rey; Tel 971/301-358; 5,000ptas single with shared bathroom, 11,000ptas triple with private bath; V, MC, AE) has 28 rooms, many with a pleasant view of the park and plaza below. Clean common bath for the singles. Most boarders at this hostel are Spanish. The stately common room has a TV, but there are better places on Ibiza to meet people than in a musty old TV room!

Pray that you can get a room at **Vara de Rey** (*Paseo de Vara de Rey 7; Tel 971/301-376; hibiza@wanadoo.es; 5,500ptas per person single or double with private bath; V, MC*). The young couple who run this hostel are beautiful to look at and to talk with. Their artists' touch makes every room a calm and serene haven from Ibiza's madness. Call ahead; many guests have been returning for years. Already a great place to make new friends, since there are only 10 rooms here, things only got more irie when the rooftop terrace was completed in the summer of 2000. Shared bathrooms only, but clean. Great, great people and beautifully painted rooms.

Hotel Montesol (*Northeastern end of Paseo de Vara de Rey 2; Tel 971/310-161; 6,740-8,700ptas single, 10,900-16,300ptas double; V*) has been *the* hotel in Ibiza Town since 1934. Private baths, phones, air conditioning, and TVs make this place worth the extra bucks. All rooms have great views (of the harbor, old city, or quaint Paseo de Vara de Rey). Big rooms and spacious closets, plus bathtubs! The sophisticated bar here is more fashionable in the off-season.

▶▶**SPLURGE**

Tagomago Aparthotel (*Paseo Maritimo, opposite side of the harbor from Sa Penya, a 5-minute cab ride from there; Tel 971/316-550; 12,000-21,000ptas single/double in June, 21,000-39,000ptas last week of July through Aug; V, MC, AE, EC*) gets jammed with Spanish coeds who have Come to Party. Bright modern rooms with a full kitchen (save cash by cooking!), living room, balcony (view of harbor), air, and TV. If you're smooth, you'll be able to get extra folks on the floor—the staff doesn't really pay attention to who's coming and going. Also, the single beds are big, and can comfortably fit two people. Hotel has cafeteria/bar and currency exchange, and will help you to rent cars and bikes. Just a 1-minute walk to **Pachá** and 5 to **El Divino.**

need to know

Currency Exchange As always, you will get the best exchange rate at an ATM. Although there aren't many of them right in **Sa Penya,** there are several scattered all around the **Paseo de Vara de Rey,** particularly at the southwestern end.

Tourist Information Tourist office *(Vara de Rey 13; Tel 971/30-19-00; 9am-1pm/5-8pm Mon-Fri, 10:30am-1:30pm Sat).* A second, smaller tourist office is located right across from where the boats let you off. They won't make hotel reservations for you—like we told you, call hotels in advance.

Public Transportation The only public transportation is the buses. They leave Ibiza Town from the **Bus Stop Bar** *(Isidoro Macabich; No phone; 9am-11pm daily; 250ptas or less per fare; No credit cards).* The service here is slower than Nyquil. Sometimes the woman behind the counter will just close up shop for 20 minutes so she can yap with her friend behind the bar, regardless of the number of people in line. You can always buy a ticket from the actual bus driver, which is recommended, since there are four different bus companies in Ibiza, and it's easy to get confused. Getting back into Ibiza Town is always easy because the buses are the biggest, loudest things to happen to the little villages and beaches to which they travel. Missing one would be like missing a marching band in your backyard.

At night, it's all about the **Disco Bus** *(Tel 971/192-456).* The fare is around 300ptas, and the destinations are every major club and hotel on the island. The Disco Bus hits each location once per hour and runs (like everything else) mid-May through end of September. See *www.ibizanight.com* to learn more about the Disco Bus and a whole bunch of other club-related info.

Cabs are available and recommended for club-hopping if you have the extra cash to spare *(Tel 971/307-000).* They're more expensive than they should be, but they're not ripping you off any worse than anyone else on the island. As in the rest of Spain, 100ptas or so is plenty for a tip. Like most of the natives here, the cabbies are mellow and safe people.

American Express AMEX is represented by **Viajes Ibiza Sa** *(Calle Vicente Cuervo 9; Tel 971/311-111; 9am-1:30pm/4:30-7:15pm Mon-Fri, 9am-1:30pm Sat).*

Health and Emergency Emergencies: *092.* Red Cross 24-hour ambulance service: *Tel 971/390-303; 971/191-009.*

Pharmacies The pharmacy on Paseo de Vara de Rey has condoms *(preservativos) (9am-1:30pm/5-9pm Mon-Sat, 5-9pm Sun).* The one in D'Alt Villa is open 24 hours for you and your horny/nauseous/sunburned friends.

Telephone City code: *971;* operator: *1003;* international operator: *1005.* Note that recent changes in Spain's phone system now require that all local calls be dialed with the 971 prefix.

Airport The **airport** *(Tel 971/809-000)* is located southwest of Ibiza Town, just above the southern coast. Buses leaving from the airport will bring you to the Bus Stop Bar in about 15 minutes. They leave by the hour, 7:30am-10:30pm, and cost 135ptas. **Iberia** *(Passeig de Vara de Rey 15; Tel 971/308-033)* is pretty much the only airline that can get you directly to the island.

Boats **Trasmediterránea** *(Andenes de Puerto Estación Maritimo; Tel 971/454-645; V, MC, AE)* is the main man. Boats from Barcelona, Valencia, and Palma de Mallorca leave all day long. If you arrive by boat, you'll be dropped off right in the middle of it all.

Bike & Moped Rental **Valentín Car/Bike** *(Avenida Bmé. Vte. Ramón 19; Tel 971/310-822; 9am-1pm/3:30-7:30pm Mon-Fri, 9am-noon/6-7pm Sat; 1,500-5,000ptas, 5,000ptas deposit if paying cash; you pay gas; V, MC)* allows you to rent by the day, and has everything from old Vespas to spanking-new 250cc Yamahas. **Bravo Rent a Car** *(Avenida de Santa Eulária; Tel 971/313-901; 9am-1pm/4-8:30pm daily; 3,500-11,750ptas, 3,000ptas deposit, you pay gas; V, MC)* brings in new cars and bikes each year. In both places, helmets are required for anything bigger than 50cc.

lisbon

The energy in Lisbon pulses like a wave up and down its seven hills. Some inhabitants come down from the more modern, northern part of the city on new Metro lines to open up their clothing stores and fruit and vegetable shops, and others go clattering up the tracks on trams to the older neighborhoods to set up postcard stands for tourists. Most Lisboetas start the morning at a *pastelería*, where they get sugared up on flaky, creamy pastries washed down with shots of espresso. The crowds overflow onto the stone sidewalks and get swept away to the next stop, a day at work, a cafe, a restaurant, a bar, a pounding club, then finally back to a *pastelería*, where it all began. The caffeine pulses through the veins of the city, and the flow moves from one neighborhood to the next as the day turns into night and the night turns into day. Lisboetas young and old live in the streets all year long.

People move to Lisbon from all over the world—mainly Brazil, Asia, and Africa—which greatly influences how the locals stuff themselves, what kind of music they groove to, and how they like to party. Travelers from all over the world also come to Lisbon. You tend to see more Europeans and Australians than people from the U.S., but they're all equally welcome. Because there's so much American and British media and music imported to Lisbon, most folks under 35 speak English, and lots speak Spanish or French. Some might even tell you they prefer to speak English or French (if only to show a little animosity toward their Spanish neighbors), so when you go up to someone, ask them, *Fala inglês?* (Do you speak English?) and go from there.

The older generation may not speak a word of English and can look like they're out of a bittersweet postwar movie. Little round men and women stroll around, picking up a baguette for the midday meal and climbing up the hills of the city with ease as you huff, puff, and stumble over the cobblestones behind them. They'll sometimes smile and try to talk to you, giving you some sort of incomprehensible advice, as you smile, nod, and almost get hit by a tram. The younger crowd in Lisbon is quite a mix of styles and attitudes—you see it all here, from Fifth Avenue (or, the local equivalent, Avenida da Liberdade) to baggy jeans and hipster bell bottoms. Young or old, they're all pretty approachable and will at least help you find your way out of the labyrinth of streets, if not lead you to their favorite bar or hangout—*everyone* here has one.

Lisbon is a comfy size—after a few days you'll start to see familiar faces around town. A lot of Lisboetas' nights have a ritual quality, as people float along from one cafe or bar to the next, where they know what and whom to expect, till around 3am when they're finally warmed up enough to go get some action at the *discotecas*. Some of the places can look intimidating, with their door buzzers and bouncers, but be brave and you definitely won't be sorry. Keeping up with the locals on a Saturday night outing is a blast, but it can be rough on the uninitiated, with after-hours parties lasting until 6pm (yes, *pm*) Sunday. You'll thank God that it's a Catholic country, where everything else shuts down, giving all ye sinners until Monday to recuperate and repent.

For info on music, cinema, theater, etc., keep an eye out for **Flirt** **(*www.ip.pt/flirt)*,** an excellent guide in English and Portuguese published by **Galeria Zé dos Bois (ZBD)** and available free at their performance and gallery space (*Rua de Barroca 59; Tel 21/343-02-05, 21/397-00-48; Metro to Baixa-Chiado, Tram 28 to Baixa-Chiado; 5-11pm Tue-Sat; www.ip.pt/zedosbois)* and at other galleries and shops in Bairro Alto. For similar info in easily decipherable Portuguese, turn to the *Vidas* section of the Saturday edition of ***Expresso***, a resource for weekly music, art, and club events, as well as cinema and book reviews. For the bigger, more commercial info in English and Portuguese on art exhibits and museums, find ***Follow Me Lisboa*** at the **Tourist Information** office [see *need to know*, below] and in the lobbies of the larger museums. Another good reference is ***Agenda Cultural Lisboa (www.consite.*** ***pt/agenda, info@hmedia.com)***, a straightforward calendar of cultural events and lists of addresses and numbers that's found free in museums, galleries, and cafes.

neighborhoods

Lisbon is flanked on the east by the **Castelo São Jorge**, Lisbon's oldest edifice, and on the west by the **25 de Abril bridge**, the longest suspension bridge in Europe. In between are about eight major neighborhoods lined up along the **Rio Tejo** (Tagus River) and perched on the seven hills of the city. The areas you'll probably be most interested in are concentrated down toward the shore, and things become less compelling for a visitor as you head north toward the **Parque Eduardo VII**.

SINTRA

Fifteen miles northwest of Lisbon, Sintra, with its lush forests and fairy-tale vibe, is considered one of the most beautiful towns in the world. To get there, catch a westbound train to Sintra from Rossio station for 200$00; the trains run every few minutes all day long. This is a great day trip, but a bit touristy for a longer visit. Don't miss the original magic castle, the **Palácio da Pena** *(Estrada da Pena, Sintra; Tel 21/910-53-40; 10am-1pm/2-5pm Tue-Sun in winter, till 6:30pm in summer, last entrance 30 mins before closing; 500$00 admission, 250$00 if under 25)*. This cartoon-looking castle was built in the 19th century for the last of the Portuguese monarchs, who you suspect were just a tad goofy. It's about 4 kilometers uphill from the train station, walkable if you have the time and inclination, but buses leave at regular intervals, and there's even a multistop tour bus for 500$00 that'll also take you through verdant, ivy-covered forests to the **Castelo dos Mouros** *(Estrada da Pena, Sintra; Tel 21/923-51-16, Fax 21/923-51-41; Bus 4343 from Sintra Station to Santa Maria; 9am-5pm daily in winter, 10am-6pm daily in summer; Free admission)* looming at the top of the mountain overlooking the town. On a clear day you can see Cabo da Roca, the westernmost point in mainland Europe, from the parapets. You can climb up and down stairs and along the wall to see truly spectacular views in every direction.

You'll probably enter the city through the **Praça do Comercio**. Most tourists do because the airport shuttle and the many buses that run from the airport into town pass through here, and because it's a 15-minute walk from the **Santa Apolónia** train station [see *need to know*, below]. This square is the gateway to the **Baixa**, **Chiado**, and **Rossio** areas, which all kind of blend together. Baixa is a gridded block of streets, and Rossio, a series of plazas full of lingering shopkeepers, is at its north end. Both have plenty of *pastelerías* and shops and are bustling with buskers. Things shut down early (around 7 or 8pm), so there's no nightlife, but it's central, and there are cheap accommodations.

Chiado, which rubs up against the west side of Baixa, just beyond the north-south-running **Rua Aurea**, is more about shopping for fat wallets. It culminates at the Metro exit and cafes at the top of its hill, warming you up for and leading you to the **Bairro Alto**, to its west. The Bairro Alto, often pronounced *Bairro alt*, has a nice boho vibe, and is full of artists, journalists, townies, and internationals. In the day, it's relaxed, with hip original shops selling hip original club clothes; at night it lights up with plenty of clubs to strut in. The **Principe** is a mainly gay area extending the groovy vibe of Bairro Alto slightly to the north, with parks and antique stores for the day and more bars and clubs for the night.

On the east side of the Baixa is the **Alfama** (which blends into Graça to the north), the oldest section of the city, with a labyrinth of narrow streets and stairways winding their way up to the **Castelo São Jorge** [see *culture zoo*, below]. This is a great place for traditional Portuguese restaurants, souvenir shopping, *fado* clubs [see *live music scene*, below], and lovely views.

South of Chiado and Bairro Alto along the water, there's **Cais do Sodré**, which is pretty sketchy and red light–esque at night. Stretching out from here to the east toward the bridge are the **Santos**, **Alcântara**, and **Docas** areas, home to nightlife of a less authentic nature. The areas in and around the old docks and harbors have been revamped recently and now house some hot, some lame, mostly expensive, discos and restaurants. Beyond the 25 de Abril bridge is **Belém**, where the Tejo meets the Atlantic and world explorers like Magellan and Vasco da Gama set sail—come here to marvel at old buildings and gaze at the distant New World....

Getting around the central area is pretty easy, cheap, and mostly walkable as the neighborhoods blend together. But if you just can't walk up one more damn hill, hop on the **Carris** (electric trams and buses that take you all over town) or the fast new Metro. The central Baixa-Chiado-Rossio areas, and parts of the Bairro Alto, are well-lit, like daylight, and women should be okay walking home alone at any hour. If you're going to Principe, Alfama, Docas, Alcântara/Santos, or Cais do Sodré at night, though, you'll want to keep out of the dark corners and travel in groups. Follow your basic safety instincts. If there aren't any buses or Metros running, take a cab. They're reliable, safe, and run you about 500$00 from the Baixa to the shore. Driving in Portugal is not for the lily-livered, so unless you're practicing for NASCAR, stick to public transportation or your feet, which will take you just about anywhere.

hanging out

One cool thing about Lisbon is that whatever time of day it is, people will be out and about in some part of town. Crowds of all ages, colors, and styles swell around the outdoor cafes and entrances to the bars. The summer weather of course clogs the arteries of the city, but the spirit is the same year-round. The main *ponto de encontro* (meeting point) for locals is the Metro stop Baixa-Chiado at the top of Rua Garrett. It's cafe central, with lots of cool galleries and shops on the side streets running perpendicular to it. Sit down for a minute, adjust to Mediterranean time (or rather, timelessness), and watch the rest of Lisbon hook up with their friends for the night. Don't be afraid to eavesdrop—they may be off to hear some heavy house beats, cool hip-hop, or sensual African and Brazilian music. Come here early evening, between 10pm and midnight (that's early for Lisbon...) to sit down at **Cafe A Brasileira do Chiado** (*Rua Garrett 120-122; Tel 21/346-95-41; Metro to Baixa-Chiado, Tram*

28 to Baixa-Chiado; 9am-2am daily; AE, MC, V), a landmark in itself, and the cafe of Lisbon since the flagrantly dissolute genius poet Fernando Pessoa graced its tables in the '20s. A bronze statue now holds his place. Drinks run around 700$00, coffee 300$00. The outdoor tables make for prime viewing of the whole scene and stay filled until closing, when the crowds move to the next destination....

As your revelry picks up steam and you're getting the munchies, you may notice that hot dog stands are everywhere you look. They're strategically placed near the bars and clubs around town: near the Largo da Trinidade in the Bairro Alto, in the square Praça Dom Luis I across from the Metro/Train stop Cais do Sodré, across the street from **Lux** [see *club scene*, below]....You can get a beer and a hot dog for close to nothin' and chat with your new Portuguese friends or the night-shift taxi drivers. The hot dog ain't quite ball-park quality, but at 4am it tastes pretty good.

Early morning, a bar opens inside the **Mercado da Ribeira** (*Avenida 24 de Julho; Metro to Cais do Sodré, Tram 15, 28, Bus 14, 32, 40; Sunrise-2pm Mon-Sat; No credit cards*) before the vendors come in to set up their stalls. It's *the* spot for post-club rejuvenation, so you get to see all the glamorous party animals by daylight, when everyone's makeup is just a little faded, their clothes a wee bit wrinkled. (Warning: This sight has been known to make some people immediately sober.)

If you want to hook up with other travelers, sit in the **Praça do Comercio.** It's the gateway for tourists both arriving and leaving the city, sitting on the benches whippin' out the maps and gazing at the cool trams and the curious modern sculptures scattered about the plaza, while the locals beeline it across the plaza to get to where they're going.

If you like to get high and hang out, Lisbon offers some choice places to do so (heh, heh). The city is famous for its seven hills, and at the top of

four things to talk to a local about

1. The relationship between **the Spanish and the Portuguese**, especially within the European Union and its move towards the Euro.

2. Ask them to teach you some **Portuguese**. Get them to slowly draw out that sexy language, showing you where to put your lips and tongue to pronounce it well.

3. **Wear a watch** and make it visible. Many here seem to have a vague sense of time, and you may be the one with all the answers.

4. **Don't say anything at all!** Dance, smile, and look your cutest. Sometimes all you need is a little body language.

almost every one, you can catch some great views of everything from the river Tejo and the 25 de Abril bridge to cluttered red-tiled rooftops, people hanging up laundry, and the big yellow umbrellas of the cafes. There are terraced lookouts (called *miradouros*) all around the Alfama, which are frequented by locals and visitors alike. A few cafes are usually set up around the *miradouros*—or at least some seats where you can rest your bones. If you take Tram 28, you'll pass the best of these lookout points, including **Miradouro de Santa Luzia** (*right off the tram track*) and the **Miradouro de Graça** (*near Igreja da Graça*). For the best panoramic view of the city, join the crowds at the top of the **Castelo São Jorge** [see *culture zoo*, below], over on the edge of the Alfama.

Other high points around the hills are the *elevadores*, two of which, **Elevador da Glória** (*Avenida de Liberdade-Restauradores to Bairro Alto-São Pedro de Alcântara; 7am-12:55am daily*) and **Elevador da Bica** (*Bairro Alto Calcada do Combro to Santos-Rua de São Paulo; 7am-12:45am Mon-Sat, 9am-10:45pm Sun, holidays*), are technically trams designed to take pedestrians up the steepest of the hills in Chiado and Bairro Alto (160$00, same as a tram ticket!). Consider the ride if you've been getting charley horses in your sleep.

Finally, the most visible lookout is the **Elevador de Santa Justa** (*Rua do Ouro to Bairro Alto-Largo do Carmo; Tel 21/342-79-44; Metro to Baixa-Chiado; 7am-11pm Mon-Fri, 9am-1am Sat, Sun; 160$00/ride*) (aka **Elevador do Carmo**), a freestanding elevator that takes you above the rooftops of the Baixa to an observation platform and cafe.

bar scene

Start in the Bairro Alto and stay there, at least until about 3am. It's the epicenter of cool. Most young (and even not-so-young) Lisboetas migrate up the hill to this neighborhood for a night out because the options are endless. During the day the neighborhood is relatively chill; the residents are out and about, and you can do some good shopping or get your belly button pierced. But on a weekend night, the place is swarming. Barhopping takes on a literal meaning here, as people move along from one to the next with drinks in hand, hardly being able to sit still long enough to get to the bottom of it. With a bar practically on every corner and in between, it's no wonder you can find everything: reggae, drum 'n' bass, mellow bossa nova, soul, jazz, hip-hop...you name it, you can hear it at some point in the night.

Neighbors often complain about the people spilling over into the streets and the vibrations rattling the windows, so cops sometimes wander around to quiet things down. Some bars and mini-*discotecas* will have a doorbell and shut door in an attempt to keep it down, which may look intimidating, but there's no need to worry—it's just a way to keep the peace (or at least the appearance of it). In this kind of concentrated mayhem, anyone can find an atmosphere to suit them, and you don't have to be decked out to enjoy it.

Toward the bottom part of the Bairro Alto slope, there are plenty of

MENINO MEETS MENINA

Occasionally a guy will pop for a drink for a beautiful exotic foreign girl, but in general, guys and girls seem to fend for themselves and rarely buy rounds, especially if they're on a twentysomething budget. Making new friends is fun, though, because you're expected to give a couple of kisses on the cheek to everyone you meet, whenever you see them (guys meeting guys, however, generally don't get to smoochie). Sometimes it doesn't take long for the question, "Posso beijá-la?" or "Can I kiss you?" to come up. This is another kind of getting-to-know-you kiss, which Portuguese men aren't afraid to ask for after some light conversation over a crowd or music. If you're a guy and feeling super-suave on the dance floor and you plan to plant one, take note of the pronunciation: *poo-soo bays-ha-ler?*

places to be hip with the boho hipsters. Swing by **Ma Jong** *(Rua de Atalaia 3; Tel 21/342-10-39; Metro to Baixa-Chiado, Tram 28 to Bairro Alto; 7pm-4am daily; No credit cards)* to surround yourself with theater, cinema, and literature buffs. Chinese food is served before 11pm, but from the looks of the sketchy kitchen, it's understandable why people skip dinner and get here around midnight to chill out and drink. The sounds on the stereo on the weekend are typically drum 'n' bass, jazz, or Brazilian, but vary with the bartenders. Grab a 700$00 mixed drink, then go work your skills on the foosball table.

Over on the next street, squeeze through the mingling crowds at **Cafe Suave** *(Rua do Diário de Noticias 6; Tel 21/342-27-93; Metro to Baixa-Chiado, Tram 28 to Bairro Alto; 10pm-2am Mon-Sat; No credit cards)*, whose green glow and jazzy music sets the scene for the arty folk leaning on the big open window, catching some air and chatting with friends who've come over from **Cafediário** *(Tel 21/343-24-34; 9:30pm-2am; No credit cards)*, a similar bar right across the street. Again, you'll be paying 700$00 to 800$00 for drinks.

Looking for something cheaper, and not interested in all that artsy-fartsy crap? Head up the street to the upper part of the slope of Bairro Alto to **Sem Nom** *(Rua do Diário de Noticias 132; Metro to Baixa-Chiado, Tram 28 Bairro Alto; 10pm-4am daily; No credit cards)* where your shoes may stick to the floor, but a beer will cost you 300$00. No velvet curtains here—they've chosen to paint them on the walls. Nirvana often heard on the stereo....

Around the upper part of the slope there's quite a few places similar to Sem Nom—with basic tile floors and short metal or plastic tables and stools—including two reggae bars, at Travessa da Cara 7 and 11, which don't seem to have names but can be found easily by tracking the sweet voice of Bob floating out into the street. Both spots are small and dark, so shuffle in through the peanut shells strewn on the floor, sit down, and get loopy. There's a "Legalize Cannabis" banner, but all you're going to find is cheap beer at 250$00 and maybe some hash floating around.

The other neighborhoods don't offer that many options. The Alfama closes up pretty early, and the Santos/Docas area feels a little forced and cheesy, like some kind of Disney World of Bars, where each spot has a different theme.

If you end up down by the river, stop by **Gringo's** *(Av. 24 de Julho 116-118; Tel 21/396-09-11, Fax 21/362-37-10; Tram 15, 18 to Cais do Sodré; 10pm-5am Mon-Sat; AE, V, MC)*, a three-story biker bar and shrine to Dean, Marilyn, and Brando that has a pool table on the top floor. Bikers actually frequent this place to chase the local workers' skirts. Wondering why it's open till 6am on Wednesday? Free drinks for girls all night! Saturdays pack 'em in too.

LIVE MUSIC SCENE

Music is a crucial part of living in Lisbon. Roots, rock, reggae, and hip-hop make appearances at various places—it's a pretty mobile scene, so keep your eyes peeled for posters and make a trip to **Godzilla** [see *stuff*, below] to pick up flyers or talk to the staff. If you've heard that your favorite big name, like Beck or the Beastie Boys, is touring Europe, check the *Agenda Cultural* or the weekend edition of the newspaper *Expresso* [see *intro*, above] to see if they're coming to town. On a smaller scale, you'll of course find the traditional *fado* [see *lisbon blues*, below], but the diverse city's diverse influences—from Africa, South America, and even the U.K.—spice up the local music scene. Taste at least a few of Lisbon's 31 flavors.

If you want to experience the full *fado*, try **Clube do Fado** *(Rua São João da Praça 92-94; Tel 21/888-26-94, 21/885-27-04, Tram 28; 8:30pm-2am daily; 1,950$00 cover includes appetizers, 6,000$00 dinner; AE, MC, V)*, a relatively new club, where you can soak in the sorrow with the local *fado* fans who often jump in. It's quite small, with arches, columns and even a Moorish-style wishing well to help you cope with your *saudade*. Located between the Baixa and the Alfama, behind the **Sé Catedral** [see *culture zoo*, below].

Cristal Fados *(Travessa da Queimada 9; Tel 21/342-67-87; Metro to Baixa-Chiado, Bus 58, 100 to same; 8:30pm-2am Tue-Sun; 1,500$00 min/per person, 1,000$00 per entree; AE, MC, V)* is a good, small, cheap, family-oriented *fado* bar in the Bairro Alto. People are often waiting for tables around 10pm as the *fadistas* (singers) readjust their clothes and up-dos, getting ready for another performance. The red-tiled doors and mirror chips plastered into the interior walls give it a cheesy charm.

Down in Santos, **B. Leza** *(Largo Conde-Barão 502º; Tel 21/396-37-35, 21/797-19-55; Tram 25, train from Cais do Sodré to Santos; 8pm-7am Tue-Sun; Free-2,000$00; No credit cards)* makes room enough for tables and a dance floor in the courtyard of this beautiful decaying old mansion.

lisbon bars, clubs and culture zoo

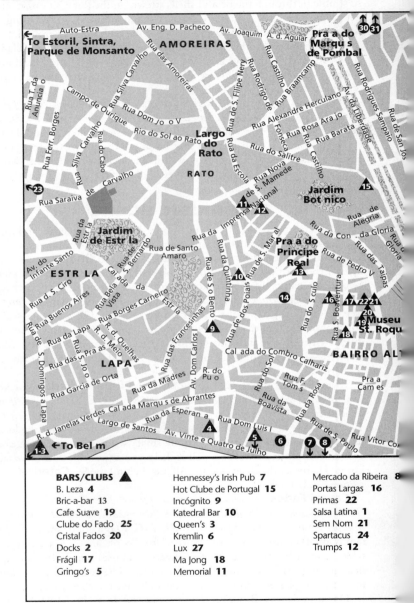

BARS/CLUBS ▲

B. Leza **4**	Hennessey's Irish Pub **7**
Bric-a-bar **13**	Hot Clube de Portugal **15**
Cafe Suave **19**	Incógnito **9**
Clube do Fado **25**	Katedral Bar **10**
Cristal Fados **20**	Queen's **3**
Docks **2**	Kremlin **6**
Frágil **17**	Lux **27**
Gringo's **5**	Ma Jong **18**
	Memorial **11**

Mercado da Ribeira **8**
Portas Largas **16**
Primas **22**
Salsa Latina **1**
Sem Nom **21**
Spartacus **24**
Trumps **12**

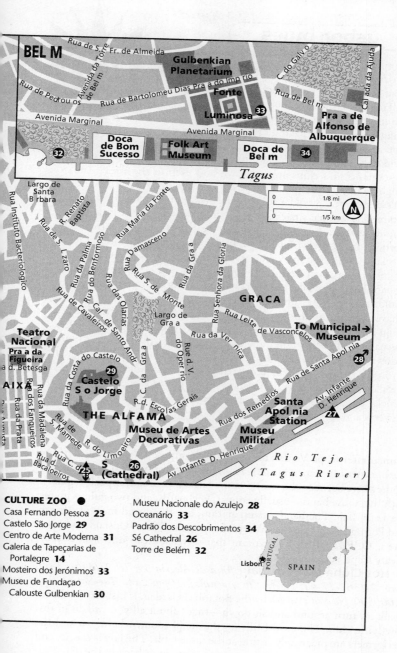

BELÉM

Rua de S. Fr. de Almeida

Gulbenkian Planetarium

Rua de Pedrouços

Avenida da Torre de Belém

Rua de Bartolomeu Dias

Praça do Império

Fonte Luminosa **33**

Rua de Belém

C. do Galvão

Calçada da Ajuda

Praça de Alfonso de Albuquerque

Avenida Marginal

Avenida Marginal

Doca de Bom Sucesso

Folk Art Museum

Doca de Belém **34**

32

Tagus

0   1/8 mi
0   1/5 km

Largo de Santa Bárbara

Rua do Instituto Bacteriologico

R. Renato Baptista

Rua de S. Lázaro

Rua da Palma

Rua do Benformoso

Rua das Olarias

Rua de Cavaleiros

Rua Cal. de Santo André

Rua María da Fonte

Rua Damasceno

Rua S. de Monte

Rua da Graça

Rua Senhora da Gloria

GRAÇA

Largo de Graça

Rua Leite de Vasconcelos

To Municipal Museum →

Teatro Nacional

Praça da Figueira

a d. Betesga

BAIXA

Rua da Costa do Castelo

Rua da Graça

Rua da Madalena

Rua dos Fanqueiros

Rua da Prata

Rua Augusta

Castelo São Jorge **29**

Rua da V. do Operário

R.d. Escolas Gerais

THE ALFAMA

Rua da Verónica

Rua dos Remédios

Santa Apolónia Station

Av. Infante D. Henrique

Rua de Santa Apolónia

28

Rua de S. Mamede

Rua d. Limoeiro

Museu de Artes Decorativas

Museu Militar

27

Rua C. d.

Rua d. Bacalhoeiros

25

Sé (Cathedral) **26**

Av. Infante D. Henrique

Rio Tejo
(Tagus River)

Lisbon
PORTUGAL
SPAIN

lisbon blues

Fado, a music unique to Portugal, was first heard in the poor neighborhoods of the Alfama. The men who left this port town to go to sea and the women they left behind both sang of *saudade*, a feeling or state that expresses the sorrow of losing loved ones, of homesickness, and of a love of Lisbon. You can bask in the fatalism of *fado* today in restaurants and clubs around town and even in the streets late at night. The *fado* club scene is like the Chicago blues scene used to be: It's dominated by older local performers rather than international stars. The women singers, fully made up in velvety outfits and costume jewelry, sing songs that can be heartbreaking, sorrowfully proud, or tainted with betrayal. In the restaurants and clubs, there's usually a small group of singers, each performing their solo, accompanied by a small, round 12-string guitar and a regular six-string Spanish guitar, while the others sit by and sing out in response to the soloist's cries. The clubs with the more professional singers usually have a minimum drink or food order and can be expensive. Dinner and a show can be up to 8,000$00—if it's in your budget, the food's usually a safe bet. In the smaller, cheaper spots, the singing is more down-home, not always in tune, but you feel closer to the song. If you can't afford a *fado* club or aren't sure if you want to invest in it, walk up the Rua do Carmo and around Chiado, and you may be lucky enough to hear some of the *fadistas* who have taken to the streets and sing all night for pocket change.

Named after Cape Verde's most famous composer, the sounds here are *funana* (African dance music), *morna* (mournful ballads), and *coladera* (somewhere between the two). Danny Silva, a local star, appears regularly with the house band—usually congas, keyboards, and two guitars giving it a Latin flair. The band sets up at 1am, but the mixed mass of African and Portuguese bodies doesn't start dancing until 3am. Upstairs and open late is **O 'Patrolho,** a restaurant that serves a mean *catchupa*, a spicy, meaty Cape Verdean stew.

Hot Clube de Portugal (*Praça de Alegria 39; Tel 21/346-73-69, Fax 21/362-17-41; Metro to Avenida; 10pm-2am Tue-Sat; Cover 1,000$00; No credit cards*), by the Botanical Garden, is Lisbon's Birdland. Walk in, turn around and sit down—that's about all you *can* do in this low-lying club. The crowd fills up the small room, where you and the performers are practically sitting at the same table. The jazz is classic, and they can even boast a Louis Armstrong appearance back in the day.

For some good Irish trad, go to **Hennessey's Irish Pub** (*Rua Cais* *do Sodré 32-38; Tel 21/343-10-64; Metro to Cais do Sodré, Bus 210, 28, 35, 83, 107, Tram 25; Noon-2am daily, till 3am Fri, Sat; No cover; AE, MC, V),* near the waterfront in Bica, on Tuesday or Saturday. It's a typical pub: a small stage, a wooden bar, Guinness, and the Irish flag in two or three places. The music gets going around 10:30pm, but it's elbow-to-elbow by then, so you may want to arrive early to eat dinner and down a few pints beforehand, especially if the British Navy is in town.

CLUB SCENE

Forget New York, Lisbon is a city that *really* doesn't sleep—and its nightlife revolves around its dance floors. The clubs' doors may unlock at 11pm, but no one sets foot on the dance floor until well after midnight. The night begins (and sometimes ends) in the Bairro Alto, where you down a little courage water and warm up in one of the smaller *discotecas*. Once you've gotten into the groove, around 2 or 3am, head down to one of the many clubs along the river in Santos or by the Santa Apolónia train station. If you're drinking, it'll usually run you around 800$00 to 1,000$00. How do they make it till dawn, you ask? Many get by with a little help from their friends.

Everyone here talks about the *beautiful people* down by the river, either

only here

Ginginha is a liquor made with a sweet brandy-like alcohol and *ginjas,* a pickled berry that's not as plump and a little more tart than its relative, the cherry. Look for it in Lisbon's plazas or in the basement of an older-generation Lisboeta. You don't find it anywhere else in the world, and anyway it loses its charm when you're not sipping it in the salty port air. The most frequented and famous places to try a shot and get your fingers sticky are around the Metro stop and plaza Rossio. **A Ginginha** *(Largo de São Domingos 8; Metro to Rossio; 9am-10:30pm daily; No credit cards)* is just one of them. It's easy to find, and since it's been here for over 150 years, people will know what you're talking about if you can't find it on your own. Even if you're shy about asking, you can't miss everyone trickling out into the little plaza in front of the bar, which is little more than a booth. The row of shoeshine booths, men on their cell phones, and workers on their breaks—not to mention their fourth shots—are all for the lookin'. You'll mostly see local working guys, but also tourists, kids in jeans, and even grandmas sipping and slugging this exotic moonshine—which just happens to be 23.5 percent alcohol.

as gods and goddesses or as monsters of materialism. All the hype—closed doors with buzzers, selective bouncers who can act as fashion police—can be intimidating. Stand tall and make eye contact—the doorman might bump the cover up to 4,000$00 if he doesn't care for you, but you should get in. Once inside, everyone's there to have a good time, and it's not as exclusive as the door makes it seem. You really shouldn't pay more than a 3,500$00 cover, though, unless it's a special event. There are usually coat checks and you can tip the bartender if you want to.

To look up special parties and raves, try ***www.ravedata.com*** and ***www.hyperreal.org.raves/grid***. Or go to almost any of the shops in Bairro Alto, especially **Eldorado** and **Raveman Records** [see *stuff*, below].

One of the mainstays of club culture since the '80s, **Frágil** *(Rua da Atalaia 126, Bairro Alto; Tel21/346-95-78, Fax 21/322-57-57; Metro to Baixa-Chiado, Tram 28 to same; 10:30pm-4am Mon-Sat; fragil@fragil.com, www.fragil.com; V)* is a gay, straight, and bi mecca where house music dominates. The door isn't left wide open, but it's not a beauty contest to get into this small lounge area and smaller dance floor, either. After 1am, the music and people (many regulars) get better.

In the Principe area, the even more intimate **Incógnito** *(Rua Poiais São Bento 37; Tram 25, 28 to Baixa-Chiado; Tel 21/390-87-55; Midnight-4am Tue-Sat; Cover free-1,000$00; V)* is where a mixed international crowd bops to everything from rap to indie pop. They pack them in on the dance floor, where bunches of dried roses hang from the ceiling.

The most praised club of the moment has to be **Lux** *(Avda. Infante D. Henrique Armazém A; Tel 21/882-08-90/8, Fax 21/882-08-99; Bus 104, 105, 107, 35 to Santa Apolónia station; 6pm-6am Tue-Sun, 4-8pm Sun; Cover 2,000$00 Fri, Sat; AE, DC, MC, V)*, apart from the rest, by the Santa Apolónia train station (a 5- to 10-minute cab ride from Bairro Alto). Downstairs you'll dance with a sexy—but not always dressed to the nines—crowd to all kinds of house and techno under the *gigundo* disco ball. Upstairs is the chill-out room, playing pop and

rules of the game

Most folks here have slugged down at least one or two Super Bock beers by the legal drinking age of 16. They'll even carry them around in the streets in transit to another bar. Drugs in Lisbon are mostly visible in the Bairro Alto and at clubs. Hash is often treated as if it were a cigarette, quickly rolled with tobacco and casually smoked in and outside certain bars and clubs. Unlike Spain, it's *illegal* here, even in personal-use quantities, but the policy seems pretty lax. Most everyone young is talking about, and waiting for, legalization, but don't exhale yet.

rock, with furniture from the '60s and '70s (even a hand chair!). Watch the sun come up from the balcony before you head to the warehouse-chic **Alcântara**.

Head east a short distance on Avenida 24 de Julho for another flourish of clubdom. **Kremlin** *(Escadinhas da Praia 5; Tel 21/395-71-01, Fax 21/395-71-02; Midnight-7am Tue-Sat, after-hours 11am-4pm weekends; Cover 2,000$00; MC, V)* seems as authentically underground as the cat-acombs. Gargantuan stone Templars hold up the ceiling, making for an apt conclusion to a day of touring medieval sites—prime time is 4 to 9am. People smoosh their way to the front to get past the door—it can make you feel like you're at recess again, hoping you won't be picked last. Puff yourself up, and try to keep your eyes focused for this somewhat degrading experience. Most don't get picked last...really. Once inside, you may wonder what all the fuss was about.

Head farther west to the Docas, a cluster of old boathouses on the Tejo that's become a posh disco strip, only if you want to spend a lot of money and see a lot of money being worn, ingested, and driven around. It's all spanking new and hyper-commercial down here and, sadly, has little charm. The crowd is mostly wealthy students and tourists who don't know any better.

If you really have to get your fix of ersatz thrills, try **Docks** *(Rua de Cintura do Porta de Lisboa, Alcântara; Tel 21/395-08-56, Fax 21/362-27-10; Restaurant 8:30-2am, bar 10pm-6am, closed Sun, Mon; V, MC, AE)*, for jungle prints and Golden Age exoticism. Tuesdays are ladies' nights, and Thursdays are Latino nights, with appropriate music and drink.

Also about a quarter mile west of Doca de Alcântara, near Doca de Santo Amaro, is **Salsa Latina** *(Gare Marítima de Alcântara, Alcântara docks; Tel 21/395-05-55, Fax 21/395-05-41; 8pm-6am Mon-Sat; Cover 2,000$00; AE, V, MC)* where merengue and salsa dancers start early on the outdoor terrace and continue until the moon sets.

arts scene

▶▶VISUAL ARTS

Lisboetas go barhopping, club-hopping, so why not gallery-hopping? After being isolated for some time, the city's visual arts scene is now flour-ishing, engaging all the shenanigans of the last 50 years, from painting and sculpture to installations, performance art, and other conceptual mischief. The arts and leisure section of the newspaper *Publico* will give you good leads on special events and openings.

If you don't have time to run around town, go directly to the two best bigger venues. **Centro Cultural de Belém—CCB**, near the **Torré de Belém**, features the **Museu do Design** *(CCB; 11am-10pm daily; 500$00 admission, 250$00 if under 25)*, where the pop-culture furniture collection is listed under three headings: Luxury, Pop, and Cool. You'll want to take home the *papasan* in the shape of a rose (complete with petal pillows) or the purple-velvet pony-shaped chair or the wood-and-metal minimalist tables.

Or try **Culturgest** *(Rua Arco do Cego 1; Tel 21/795-30-00, 21/790-54-54, Fax 21/848-39-03; Metro to Campo Pequeno; 10am-6pm Mon, Wed-Fri, 2-8pm Sat, Sun, last admission one hour before closing; 500$00 admission, 300$00 if under 25; MC, V)* inside the Caixa Geral de Depósitos building near the Praça do Toros, where you can walk through contemporary exhibits, checking out local and international photography, and watch the suits rush to and from work.

The prestige of **Galeria 111** *(Campo Grande 113A; Metro to Campo Grande; Tel 21/797-74-18, Fax 21/797-84-88; 10am-1pm/3-7:30pm Mon-Sat; Free admission)* rests in part on its relationship to Portugal's most celebrated painter, Paula Rego (b. 1935), whose early career took off here and whose current work it continues to champion. Rego's powerful portrayals of women, as both domestic workers and stiff-necked patricians, teem with social commentary.

The adventurous **Galeria Zé dos Bois-ZDB** *(Rua do Barroca, 59; Metro to Baixa-Chiado, Tram 28 to Bairro Alto; Tel 21/397-00-48; 5-11pm Tue-Sat; Free admission)* shows the work of young, totally untraditional artists. The work here tends to steer away from painting toward mixed media—sometimes even tattoo art. The dredded, pierced *Bairro Altistas* mingling around the door may even be part of the exhibit....

▶▶PERFORMING ARTS

After decades of censorship and repression under the Salazar, Lisbon's performing arts scene is happily crawling out from under a rock. Since the '70s, interest in non-traditional theater, dance, and film has been growing, but unfortunately the enthusiasm has often been greater than the availability of funds. What else is new?

The main performing arts center here, opened in 1993, is **Centro Cultural de Belém (CCB)** *(Praça do Império 1449-003; Tel 21/361-24-00, Ticket line 21/361-24-44, Fax 21/361-25-00; Tram 15, Bus 27-29, 43, 49, 51 to Belém; 11am-8pm daily, last entrance 7:15pm; Tickets 1,000-3,500$00, 25 percent discount if under 25; www.ccb.pt, ccb@ccb.pt; AE, MC, V)*. This modern marble ziggurat mimics the nearby **Torré de Belém** [see *culture zoo*, below] and has two auditoriums—one huge and one smaller—showing a wide range of stuff. It's not uncommon to see pomo jazz, symphonic performances, avant-garde dance, and classical ballet on the same monthly program. **Culturgest,** hosts performances encompassing everything from modern dance to Louisiana jazz to classical piano. Tickets run around 3,000$00. Students often stop by to study, drink coffee in the cafe, and browse the bookstore during the day.

C.E.M.: Centro em Movimento *(Praça da Alegria 27; Tel 21/342-54-22; Metro to Aucuida; Info desk 9:30am-10pm Mon-Sat; www.terravista.pt/meiapraia/3103, injs@ip.pt; No credit cards)* is a diverse performing arts center right above a firehouse off Avenida da Liberdade, offering courses in just about anything: contemporary dance, ballet, photography, script writing, acting....They put on performances from their stable and organize showings of experimental cinema, theater, art, and dance in various venues in the city. They can tell you what's going on around town and provide you with tons of info on festivals and happenings.

The Tagus Theatre group does dramatic productions in English (mostly Portuguese works translated into English) with a historical slant. They tend to work out of the **Teatro Taborda** *(Costa do Castelo 75; Tel 21/888-17-18, 21/887-37-89; Tram 12, 28, Bus 37 to Alfama; Box office Noon-2pm Tue-Sun)*, as do several other independent groups, playwrights, and actors. You can sometimes catch a free performance in this cool little theater, which is tucked away behind the Castelo in the Alfama.

Also just below the Castelo, on the same road as Taborda, with a spectacular view as the backdrop, is **A Companhia do Chapitô-Escola do Circo** *(Costa do Castelo 1; Tel 21/887-82-25, 21/886-14-10, Fax 21/886-14-63; Tram 12, 28, Bus 37 to Alfama; chapito@ip.pt)*, the school for circus performers. They put on four fun-filled productions a year—call or e-mail ahead for times.

Movie theaters are few in Lisbon. **São Jorge** *(Avenida da Liberdade 174; Tel 21/357-91-44; Metro to Restauradores; Box office 1-10pm daily; 800$00; No credit cards)* shows mainstream Hollywood fare in a beautiful old three-screen theater, only a few blocks north of the Rossio. Most flicks that make it here are action blockbusters, comedies, and Disney-style fluff, but they're usually projected with subtitles rather than dubbed. During *intermission* the concession booth serves beer (two thumbs up!) and American popcorn with salt or the European choice, sugar (eewww...).

Up Liberdade from São Jorge, a block off the avenue, **Cinemateca Portuguesa Museu do Cinema** *(Rua Barata Salgueiro 39; Tel 21/354-65-29; Metro to Marques de Pombal, Bus 1, 2, 9, 31, 36, 44-46, 90, 91 to Alfama; Shows 6:30pm, 9:30pm Mon-Fri; Tickets 400$00; No credit cards)* shows cool international art flicks. The seats are like big white clouds, and the films are never dubbed (mostly subtitled). There's also a film library *(2-7:30pm Mon-Fri)*.

The lovely **Cinema Londres** *(Avenida de Roma 7A; Tel 21/840-13-13, 21/840-04-48, 21/840-30-33, Fax 21/840-04-48; Metro to Areeiro; 1-10:15pm daily, last show 9:45; No credit cards)*, north of city center, has two theaters playing independent American movies (in American), an inexpensive vegetarian buffet, and a funky bookstore next door.

gay Scene

You can smooch your sweetie (or look for one) openly in the clubs or bars in Bairro Alto or Principe Real, but the city as a whole is still in the process of coming out. The first Gay Pride gathering a few years ago got mixed reviews and not everyone cut loose, but the ILGA (International Gay and Lesbian Organization) did succeed in repealing some harsh Catholic church–inspired laws, loosening the grip of deeply entrenched prejudices. But it still ain't totally out. For info and tips, go to **Associação Ilga Portugal, Centro Comunitário Gay e Lésbico de Lisboa** *(Rua de São Lázaro 88; Tel 21/887-39-18, Fax 21/887-39-22, help line 21/887-61-16; Metro to Martim Moniz; 4-8pm Mon-Sat, help line 9pm-midnight Wed-Sun)*. They have legal, medical, and psychological services, and a small bookstore and cafeteria. They can also give you info on the gay beaches "Praia 19" and "Praia da Bela Vista."

House music and vodka are the mix at **Frágil** [see *club scene*, above] in the Bairro Alto. This place has become a Lisbon classic, uniting gay, bi, straight, and whatever else in its newly fabricated post-industrial decor. Things only really get hopping after 1am. Right across the street, **Portas Largas** *(Rua da Atalaia 105; Tel 21/346-63-79; Metro to Baixa-Chiado, Tram 28 to Bairro Alto; 8:30pm-3:30am daily; No credit cards)*, formerly a *fado* club, maintains the classic look of an old tavern with wooden tables and stools. You can chill out to Brazilian and Portuguese music and scope the mixed crowd.

Boys, cruise over to **Bric-a-bar** *(Rua Cecílio de Sousa 82-84; Tel 21/342-89-71, 21/346-43-16; Metro to Rato; 9pm-4am daily; Cover varies on weekends; MC, V)*, in lower Rato, after 1am, where your disco experience is brightened up by the flicker of porno movies projected on the walls.

Spartacus *(Largo Trindade Coelho 2; Tel 21/322-50-18; Metro to Baixa-Chiado, Tram 28 to Bairro Alto; 3pm-9am daily; Cover 2,000$00; No credit cards)* has it all: videos, cabins, a sauna, a steam bath, a Jacuzzi, back-room action, a varied crowd, and much more! Located in the Bairro Alto, it's the best three floors of soaking and scoping in town.

This whole new scene on the Alcântara Docas draws a crossover crowd from the adjoining straight clubs, but it gets *particularly* less straight around 4am at **Queen's** *(Rua da Cintura do Porto de Lisboa, Armazém H Naves A-B; Tel 21/395-59-70; Tram 15, 17, 18, Bus 19, 28; 11pm-6am Tue-Sat; No cover; AE, MC, V)*, where the dance floor is large enough for RuPaul to do cartwheels. Strippers on Wednesdays, but no tea-bagging. There is usually a drag show on Fridays.

There isn't really an abundance of options for gay women here, but a good spot in the Bairro Alto is **Primas** *(Rua da Atalaia 152-6; Tel 21/342-*

festivals and events

With the best weather (the least rainfall and highest temperatures), spring and summer in Portugal are the seasons to party in the street. Every day Portugal celebrates a saint or two, and the festival for Lisbon's unofficial patron saint, António, makes for one of the biggest festivals in the city on June 12 and 13. It is part of the month-long **Festas dos Santos Populares,** which celebrates Anthony, John, and Peter. Anthony is the coolest of the group because he's the saint who'll help you find your lost objects, including the perfect mate to marry. It's not quite free love, but there's a free group wedding that's televised out of **Igreja de Santo António** in the Alfama next to the **Sé** [see *culture zoo,* below]. A parade begins at this church, and the people continue through the city, which is covered in lanterns and colorful decorations. They eventually return to the Alfama, Santo António's birthplace, for live music, grilled sardines, and partying. As for John and Peter, their days comes in late June and aren't such a big deal here.

Carnaval, the week before Ash Wednesday and the Lenten season of fasting, is celebrated in Lisbon by all ethnic communities with a casual parade of music and costumes leaving from the **Praça da Figueira** in Rossio. It's a party, but it's mostly limited to the Brazilian clubs and has significantly less gusto than in Rio or New Orleans.

59-25; Metro to Baixa-Chiado, Tram 28 to Bairro Alto; 10pm-4am Mon-Sat; No credit cards). It's run by four sisters (one named Prima), and the feel is local, friendly, and inviting. Have a sandwich at the bar, sit in the back at the metal tables, or play foosball, pinball, or video games up front opposite the bar. There's a jukebox with pop favorites like Madonna, Genesis, and Michael Jackson, but the sisters often play their own CDs. A good place to start the night and find out what's happening.

A hop away in Principe are a few more hangouts. **Katedral Bar** (*Rua Manuel Bernardes 22-B, off Rua da Imprensa Nacional; Tel 21/395-87-95; Metro to Rato; 8:30pm-2am Mon-Thur, till 4am Fri, Sat, 6pm-2am Sun; No credit cards*) is a comfy, mostly-women's spot with mostly South American sounds, billiards, and guitars on hand for impromptu amateur performances. The kitchen's snacks are tasty to boot. There isn't a sign out front, so look sharp, and ring to enter.

Later in the evening, travel to Rato to check out **Memorial** (*Rua Gustavo de Matos Sequira 42; Tel 21/396-88-91; Metro to Rato; 11pm-4am Tue-Sun, 4-8pm Sun; No cover, 1,000$00 per person min. during shows; No credit cards*), the main lesbian disco in Lisbon. Although this club looks like the Brady Bunch's basement playroom, it has a rough-and-tumble reputation, and you may even see a fight. It's all pop music, and the pumping and grinding gets hairy around 2am.

Or go mix with the boys at the nearby **Trumps** (*Rua da Imprensa Nacional 104 B; Tel 21/397-10-59; Metro to Rato; 10pm-6am Tue-Sun; 1,000$00 per person min.; AE, DC, MC, V*), probably the best club option—mostly for men, but frequented by women on weekends. The sounds vibrating the big dance floor range from Culture Club to techno. Plus there's a billiard room, a small bar where you can actually have a conversation, and drag shows on Sundays and Wednesdays at 2:30am.

CULTURE ZOO

Lisbon is photo-op heaven, with gorgeous architecture, laundry hanging on lines, and old-world trams. The **Tourist Office** [see *need to know*, below] sells the "Lisboa Card," which gets you discounts and entrances to most of the sites (1,900$00/24 hours, 3,100$00/48 hours, 4,000$00/72 hours, public transportation included). Another good trick is to scan the postcard racks. If you see something cool, turn it over to see what it's called, and go find it.

Castelo São Jorge (*Rua Costa do Castelo; Tel 21/886-63-54; Tram 12, 28, Bus 37 Castelo São Jorge; 9am-9pm in summer, till 7pm in winter; Free admission*): Seen at every turn, this hilltop castle is close to 1,000 years old, and has 10 towers that you can haul your butt up for the best views in town.

Sé Cathedral (*Largo da Sé, Alfama; Tel 21/886-67-52; Tram 12, 28; Church 9am-5pm daily, cloisters 10am-5pm Mon-Sat; 400$00 admission to cloisters*): Built in 1146, this is one of the oldest buildings in the city and withstood the catastrophic 1755 earthquake. History goes deep at this site, with Moorish and Roman ruins all around and under it.

Torre de Belém (*Praça da Torre de São Vicente de Belém; Tel 21/362-00-34, Fax 21/363-91-45; Tram 15, Bus 27-29, 43, 49, 51 to Belém; Commuter train to Cascais from Cais do Sodré, get off at Belém; 10am-5pm daily in winter, till 6:30pm daily in summer, last entrance a half-hour before closing; 400$00, 250$00 if under 25; No credit cards*): Looks like a rook from an *Alice in Wonderland* chess game. Climb a dizzying spiral staircase to reach the lookout deck.

Padrão dos Descobrimentos (*Av. de Brasilia; Tel 21/301-62-28; Commuter train to Cascais from Cais do Sodré, get off at Belém, Tram 15, Bus 27, 28, 43, 49 to Belém; 9:30am-6:45pm Tue-Sun; 340$00 admission*): Next door to the Torré, stand on this monument to Portuguese explorers and look off into the distance with the "discoverers" of the New World who are commemorated in stone.

Mosteiro dos Jerónimos (*Praça do Imperio; Tel 21/362-00-38, Fax 21/363-91-45; Tram 15, 17, Bus 27-29, 43, 49, 51 to Belém; 10am-5pm Tue-Sun in winter, till 6:30pm, last entrance a half-hour before closing in summer; 500$00 admission to cloisters, 250$00 if under 25*): Built between 1502 and 1551, when the explorers were bringing back bundles of gold, and architects were going crazy with late Gothic decorations. Down below, Luis de Camíes and Vasco da Gama are entombed.

Museu de Fundação Calouste Gulbenkian *(Av. de Berna 45-A; Tel 21/782-30-00, Fax 21/782-30-32; Metro to São Sebastião or Palhava, Tram 24, Bus 16, 26, 31, 46, 56 to Praça de Espanha; 10am-6pm Wed-Sun, 2-6pm Tue, last admission 30 mins before closing; 500$00 admission, free with student ID, free Sun; info@gulbenkian.pt, www.gulbenkian.pt):* This is the big one. It houses a full survey of world art, including Portuguese, lots of textiles, and a haunting collection of Art Nouveau jewelry by René Lalique.

Centro de Arte Moderna *(Rua Dr. Nicolau de Bettencourt 1050-078; Tel 21/795-02-41; Metro to Sebastião; 10am-6pm Wed-Sun, 2-6pm Tue; 500$00 admission, free Sun):* Works by Paula Rego, as well as other Portuguese contemporary and Modernist artists.

Galeria de Tapeçarias de Portalegre *(Rua da Academia das Ciências 2-J; Tel 21/346-82-02; Bus 6, 49, 58, 100 to Bairro Alta; 10am-1pm/3-7pm Mon-Sat):* Come to the Bairro Alto to view amazing handwoven textiles in patterns that haven't changed since Shakespeare was in love.

Museu Nacional do Azulejo *(Rua da Madre de Deus 4; Tel 21/814-77-47, Fax 21/814-95-34; Bus 18, 42, 104, 105; 2-6pm Tue, 10am-6pm Wed-Sun; 450$00 admission, free Sun):* Secrets of making the *azulejos* (tiles) that cover the entire city are divulged here, a half-mile east of Santa Apolónia station.

Casa Fernando Pessoa *(Rua Coelho da Rocha 16-18; Tel 21/396-81-90, Fax 21/396-82-62; Tram 25, 28, Bus 9, 18, 20, 27, 38, 74; 1-6pm Mon-Fri, 1-8pm Thur; Free admission; cfpessoa@mail.telepac.pt):* Former home of the eccentric Lisbon poet who wrote as many personae, including Alvaro de Campos, Ricardo Reis, Alberto Caiero. They even dissed one another in public! You only see his eyeglasses and a dresser that they say he wrote on, but it is one of the city's main cultural centers, and hosts writers' conferences, lectures, and art exhibits.

Oceanário *(Esplanada Dom Carlos I, Doca dosOlivias, Expo '98 site; Tel 21/891-70-06; Metro to Oriente; 10am-8pm daily in summer, 10am-7pm in winter, last entrance one hour before closing; 1,700$00 admission):* As the second-largest aquarium in the world, it's a little bit culture and a little bit zoo. It's got more varieties of shark than a talent agents' convention.

modification

It's a port town, there's got to be tattoo artists around here somewhere... lemme guess, Bairro Alto?? Walk into **Bad Bones Tattoos Body Piercing** *(Rua do Norte 73; Tel 21/346-08-88; Metro to Baixa-Chiado, Tram 28; 11am-8pm Mon-Sat; No credit cards),* and you suspect that you may get sacrificed. The green and fluorescent lights make the eyes on the hanging alien and African masks twinkle, giving you the feeling that they're watching you as you flip through the piles and piles of photo

12 hours in lisbon

1. Get jittery from shots of espresso and sugar at a *pastelería* and watch the turnover of locals. In about 10 minutes, 20 or so rush in and out of the place.

2. You may not have any *escudos* to pay for it, but at least go window-shopping in the Chiado and the Bairro Alto to admire the size-two sequined tube tops and feather boas [see *stuff*, below].

3. Go to the **Praça Rossio** in the middle of the day, down some *ginginha*, and spit out the seeds on the sidewalk like a local [see *only here*, above].

4. Hop into the time-warp of the Alfama and get lost. It gets sort of comical, more so after the *ginginha*, as you end up on the same street, one that has the same name, no name, or more than one name [see *neighborhoods*, above].

5. Point yourself in the direction of that big castle thing you keep seeing from all those little streets. It's called the **Castelo São Jorge**, and it's a perfect place around sunset to see the whole city, the river, the bridges, and snuggle with your honey [see *culture zoo*, above].

6. Go back down to the Baixa [see *neighborhoods*, above] in the

albums in the small parlor. Make an appointment, and get that penguin smoking a joint you always wanted tattooed on your butt.

great outdoors

Biking or rollerblading on the streets of Lisbon could be a serious health hazard, so if you really have a hankering, stick to the bike paths in the **Parque Florestal de Monsanto.** In the summer, you can rent from **Tejo Bike** *(an outdoor stand on the docks of Belém; No phone; Tram 15, Bus 27-29, 43, 49, 51 to Belém; 10am-8pm Sat, Sun in summer only; 750$00/hour, 5,000$00/day; No credit cards).*

Nearby in Belém, the sound of boards scraping against the pavement rings in the ears around the **Doca de Santo Amaro.** More baggy-pants skaters congregate around two worn half-pipes over on the **Passeio Marítimo de Algés,** a train hop from Cais do Sodré to Algés.

Up by the Expo '98, the site of the **Oceanário** [see *culture zoo*, above] there's also the **Parque Adrenalina** *(Parque das Nacaoes, Porta Norte; Tel 21/892-23-00, Fax 21/892-23-01; Metro to Oriente; 4pm-midnight Mon-Thur, 4pm-2am Fri, 2pm-2am Sat, 2pm-midnight Sun).* The kids in Korn T-shirts, with boards or BMXs in hand, watch some girls jump on trampolines (some things are universal). Climb on the small outdoor wall (300$00), and fly on the "PsichoSwing" (400$00). You can rent solo and tandem bikes (500$00/half hour) and blades (500$00/hour) between 10am and midnight.

early evening to watch clowns, artists, puppet shows, musicians, women selling flowers or roasting chestnuts (in winter), and the punks twirling fire and juggling. It's the greatest (free) show on earth!

7. Hang out at **Metro Baixa-Chiado** for the best glance at every kind of Lisboeta and tourist in town. Scope out the scene and get ready for the night to begin.

8. Get a secondhand high, or firsthand for that matter, while walking through Bairro Alto crowds to work up your munchies for a couscous dinner at **Pedro das Arábias** [see *eats*, below].

9. Grab a Super Bock beer, kick back, and get a buzz in the bars up in the Bairro Alto. Stretch your legs as you go in and out of the bars working your way to the mini-clubs here and get ready for the number-one thing to do in Lisbon....

10. Spend a hedonistic night dancing with the "beautiful people" of Lisbon, and be careful that your 12 hours don't mysteriously morph into 24.

The nearest beaches are about 15 miles from the center of Lisbon in **Estoril** and **Cascais.** They're easily reached by the commuter train that leaves from Cais do Sodré every 15 minutes or so. Train fare is 200$00, and the ride takes about an hour. Estoril is more upscale, with a casino and resort hotels, Cascais has a few reasonably priced hotels and better beaches. Traveling surfers and windsurfers blow into the beaches of Portugal to catch some good waves in **Guincho,** a few miles past the Cascais train stop. Winds really pick up during the day, sweeping away swimmers and providing good conditions for serious surfers. There are more visitors than locals, but we can all get along in the water—and at the Bar de Guincho, on the northern part of the beach.

Call Miguel Ruivo at the **Surfing Clube de Portugal, Guincho** *(Tel 21/466-45-16)* to find out about conditions and renting gear.

In Lisbon, contact **Associação Portuguesa De Funboard (APF)** *(Rua Coelho da Rocha 20 A; Tel 21/395-73-22, Fax 21/395-73-23; Metro to Campo de Ourique)* for information on surfing south of the Tejo in Costa da Caparica, 60 miles north in Peniche. They also have info about windsurfing on Lagoa de Obidos. **Overpower** *(Rua Coelho da Rocha 20 A; Metro to Campo de Ourique; Tel 21/395-73-22, Fax 21/395-73-23; www.100surf.pt, overpower@100surf.pt)* will clue you in on competitions, races, and events. For weather and surf conditions, call **Infopraias Beach Report** *(Tel 0601-914-914).*

stuff

The central shopping areas will take you from tacky tiles to rags to riches and back home again. In the Bairro Alto, you can shop late and find excellent music, secondhand goodies, and a mix of funky old '70s gear and new designer threads. The more upscale designer shops are in Chiado, on Avenida da Liberdade and Avenida de Roma. Campo de Ourique, one of the wealthier sections of town, is an upscale conservative choice for shopping along the shady, tree-lined streets. Also over there is Lisbon's big mall, the **Amoreiras Shopping Center** (*Avenida Engenheiro Duarte Pacheco; Tel 21/381-02-00; Metro to Marquês de Pombal, Bus 11, 18, 23, 42, 48, 51, 58*). Postmodern or not, the much-touted architectural wonder and shopping extravaganza will make you mall rats feel at home.

▶▶HOT COUTURE

The funkiest variety of fashion floats up to the Bairro Alto. **Agência 117** (*Rua do Norte 117; Metro to Baixa-Chiado, Tram 28 to Bairro Alto; Tel 21/346-12-70; 2pm-midnight Sun-Thur, till 2am Fri, Sat; MC, V, AE*) has retro, vintage, and hip-hop clothes, some books, gewgaws, a hair-stylist and make-up artist on site, a bar, and performance art and theater in the evening (after midnight). You can walk out a new person, not just externally spiffier, but more evolved, cultured even.

Fly over to **Caixa de Pandora** (*Rua de S. Boaventura 42; Metro to Baixa-Chiado, Tram 28 to Bairro Alto; Tel 21/347-79-35; 11am-8pm Tue-Wed, 11am-midnight Thur, Fri, 4pm-midnight Sat; caixapandora@ yahoo.com; No credit cards*) and walk into the web of goth capes, leather pants, candelabras, and velvet lace-up tops...everything available in black. Pointed witchy shoes will cost you 6,000$00. The staff and friends model many of the styles and will help you put on black eyeliner while reading your cards.

▶▶THRIFT

On Saturdays and Tuesdays, you can get anything you want at the **Feira de Ladra** (thieves' market) outdoor flea market, especially if you're into the hippie thing—there's tie-dye galore. Located in Campo de Santa Clara behind the Igreja São Vicente de Fora, it starts at 7am and runs all day (definitely worth getting up early for).

Remember that old velour Puma sweatsuit your dad used to wear? Well, it ended up on the racks at **Eldorado** (*Rua do Norte 23; Tel 21/347-36-51, 21/342-39-35; Metro to Baixa-Chiado, Tram 28 to Bairro Alto; AE, MC, V*), but now it's going to cost you 15,000$00! Get them to put on some of their killer vinyl (Roberta Flack, Al Green, Public Enemy), so you can see how good you look dancing in the cool duds here. There's no shortage of similar secondhand and new-stuff stores up here in Bairro Alto, so take a gander.

▶▶CLUB GEAR

Por-fi-ri-os (*Rua da Victoria 57; Tel 21/322-49-60, Fax 21/322-49-69; Metro to Rossio; 10am-7pm Mon-Fri, 10am-2pm/3-7pm Sat, Sun; MC, V*), in Baixa, is three small floors of purple neon, graffiti, and funhouse mir-

by foot

Watch Lisbon transform from old to new and escape the city life by walking up the Avenida da Liberdade to the **Estufa Fria**, Lisbon's gorgeous gardens. Take the Metro to **Restauradores**, hop out, and stroll up the mosaic median strip lined with cafes. Pass a couple of fountains and old buildings with wrought-iron balconies and stained-glass windows that could be postcards or slides from your architecture class. All of a sudden to your right, you'll start to see big fashion names like DKNY, CK, and Armani, and you'll think you're in NYC for a second. Keep hiking up the slope, and palm trees start sprouting up, and again to your right, sandwiched between it all, is a trippy bat-serpent creature flying down the mirror-windowed facade. Continue till you get to the big traffic circle, **Praça Marquês de Pombal**. Walk around it to the right and cross **Avenida Duque de Loulé** and **Avenida Fontes Pereira de Melo** to get to the **Parque Eduardo VII**. OK, I know you've been walking uphill this whole trip so far, but keep heading up the main drag of the park till you reach the top, turn around for a view of Lisbon and what you've just climbed, and get ready to step out of the city. Take a left to head down **Alameda Cardeal Cerejeira** at the edge of the park, then take the first left you can (a pedestrian walk), down to the **Estufa Fria** (*Praça Marquês de Pombal; Tel 21/388-22-78; Metro to Parque; 9am-5:30pm daily; 100$00*). Find yourself in the strange seclusion of these tropical greenhouses.

rors that you can use to check out how fly that red velvet blazer (20,000$00) or that faux-leather micro-mini (4,000$00) looks on you.

Bigger names and bigger price tags can be found in Chiado, including the designers at the two branches of **Gardenia** (*Rua Nova de Almada 96; Tel 21/322-48-00; Rua Garrett 54; Tel 21/342-50-28; Metro to Baixa-Chiado, Tram 28 to Bairro Alto; 10am-8pm Mon-Sat, 2-9pm Sun; AE, MC, V*). The shelves are lined with big spacey Destroy boots, huge foamy platforms, and a mix of clubby clothes for men and women. Who would've guessed that orange New Balance sneaks (14,000$00) would be found in the same store as hot Portuguese and international fashion designers?

▶▶**BOUND**

Ler Devagar (*Rua de São Boaventura 115; Tel 21/423-10-00, Fax 21/324-10-09; Metro to Baixa-Chiado, Restauradores; Noon-midnight daily; www.lerdevagar.com; AE, MC, V*) is a great little bookstore hidden up at the top of the Bairro Alto slope that also has a monthly program of activities involving poetry, readings, and lectures. It's a beautiful store with a nice selection, including an English section (mostly classics). People chill and read books and newspapers at the small coffee bar.

Don't despair if you need a Kathy Acker fix, **Livraria Britanica** *(Rua de São Marçal 83; Tel 21/342-84-72, Fax 21/347-82-09; Metro to Rato; 9:30am-7pm Mon-Sat; AE, MC, V)*, in the Rato, has a very cool selection of English-language books.

Over in Chiado is **Livraria Bertrand** *(Rua Garrett 73-75; Tel 21/342-19-41; Metro to Baixa-Chiado, Tram 28 Bairro Alto; 9am-8pm Mon-Thur, till 10pm Fri, Sat, 2-7pm Sun; www.bertrand-sa.pt; AE, MC, V)*, the country's oldest bookstore, founded in 1732. Once the spot for radical debate, both literary and political, the store has grown into a chain but still has its finger on the cultural pulse. Some English books.

▶▶TUNES

Raveman Records *(Travessa da Queimada 33; Tel 21/347-11-70; Tram 28 to Bairro Alto; 1-11pm Mon-Sat; www.raveman.net; AE, MC, V)* is your best source for fresh vinyl. This Bairro Alto DJ shop has imported techno, acid, trance, psychedelic, and house, as well as equipment and some CDs. Some super-friendly English-speaking guys, including DJ Blix and the Techno Militia Team, will tell you about their after-after-hours parties on Sundays.

Down in the Baixa, upstairs in the clothing store **Godzilla** *(Rua dos Douradores 120; Tel 21/886-98-45, 21/888-46-47; Metro to Rossio; 10am-8pm Mon-Fri, till 3pm Sat, Sun in summer, till 7pm Sat, Sun in winter; MC, V)*, you may find the DJ/clerk spinning Stevie Wonder, hip-hop, reggae, R&B, or dance music—all of which they'll sell you, on vinyl and CD.

For African music, try **Discoteca Ópus 222** *(Centro Comercial Mouraria, Loja 222; Tel 21/887-83-48, Metro to Martim Moniz; 10am-7:30pm Mon-Sat, 2-7pm Sun; AE, MC, V)*. Look for something you heard at **B. Leza** [see *live music scene*, above].

EATS

Since it's a port city, and the former center of an empire, there are plenty of choices for international fare in Lisbon. Portuguese cuisine itself tends to be simple and delicious, with a strong emphasis on fish. A good way to start out a meal is with the typical appetizer *caldo verde*, a kale or cabbage and potato soup usually seasoned with a little meat or sausage. Fish lovers should definitely try *bacalhau*—codfish that's been salted and dried then soaked before it's prepared a hundred different ways: roasted, stewed, creamed, and in many dishes and snacks. It's a hearty, flavorful fish, and the staple food of Portugal. Even on a budget, Portuguese wine, both red and white, is excellent and served with almost every meal. The third variety, *vinho verde* (green wine) is a cool, fresh-tasting, slightly effervescent wine for hot afternoons. If you'd rather have a *cerveja*, try a smooth Super Bock—it tastes great, and is available out of some vending machines!

▶▶CHEAP

Pastelerías—Lisbon's fast-food joints—are scattered all over the city, but

fashion

If you've been wearing the same pair of jeans for a week, walking by all the high-end chic stores in Lisbon can seem intimidating, but don't worry, you see it all here. Wearing baseball hats isn't unheard-of, and jeans aren't always worn so tight here, unlike in most European countries. You see some chunkier shoes, girls in platforms and guys in rubbery-soled aquatic sneaks. Of course there are a few punks around town in tattered black and some of the dredded hippie heads. Most of the pierced set hang at the clubs, where you'll also see more crazy feather boas, leopard prints, leather, etc. If you just can't go out dancing without your red knee-high boots and tube of body glitter, bring them along, but you can survive here without them.

the biggest concentration of them is around the Baixa. They offer not only sweet pastries and coffee but sandwiches, *salados* (pastries filled with ham, cheese, or something salty), and fried dough-wrapped meats (better than it sounds) if you're on the go. Sometimes there's a card payment system—you get a card that they run the prices on, and you take it up to the cashier when you're done. Something you ought to try are the *pastéis de nata de Belém*, crusty pastries filled with a creamy custard recipe from Belém [see *neighborhoods*, above], or a *queijada*, similar but filled with dry sweet cheese from Sintra [see *sintra*, above]. **Antiga Casa de Pastéis de Belém** *(Rua de Belém 84-92; Tel 21/363-80-77/8, Fax 21/363-74-23; Commuter train to Cascais from Cais do Sodré, get off at Belém; 8am-midnight daily; No credit cards)* is the best and most famous place for locals and tour groups to bite into the *pastéis de Belém*. Only three people in the world know the custard recipe, which has not changed since they opened in 1837.

▶▶DO-ABLE

Restaurante 1º de Maio *(Rua da Atalaia 8; Tel 21/342-68-40; Metro to Baixa-Chiado, Tram 28 to Bairro Alto; Noon-3pm/7-10:30pm Mon-Fri, till 3pm Sat; 1,500$00 per entree; AE, MC, V)* serves up delicious Portuguese plates full of fish or meat and vegetables, like melt-in-your-mouth salmon. Plenty of Lisbon families and foreigners know this comfortable and homey Bairro Alto spot and squeeze in around the tables.

The outdoor tables at **Cafe no Chiado** *(Largo do Picadeiro 10-12; Tel 21/342-30-40; Metro to Baixa-Chiado; 10am-2am Mon-Sat; AE, MC, V)* are filled till almost closing time with a mid-twenties to thirties crowd—they don't pressure you to turn over the tables. Tasty salads, sandwiches, and omelets on the menu cost around 600$00. The Tourist

lisbon eats and crashing

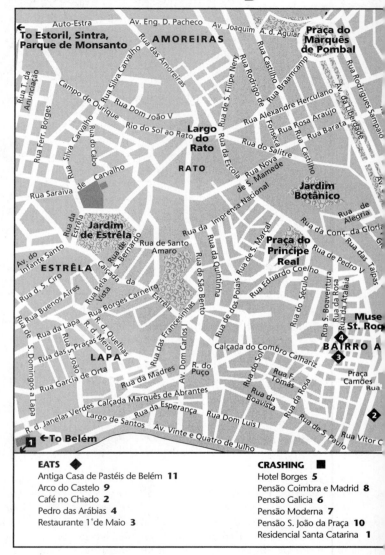

EATS ◆
Antiga Casa de Pastéis de Belém **11**
Arco do Castelo **9**
Café no Chiado **2**
Pedro das Arábias **4**
Restaurante 1°de Maio **3**

CRASHING ■
Hotel Borges **5**
Pensão Coimbra e Madrid **8**
Pensão Galicia **6**
Pensão Moderna **7**
Pensão S. João da Praça **10**
Residencial Santa Catarina **1**

Menu (3,400$00), including water, wine, soup, steak, bread, dessert, and coffee, won't disappoint. There are also flyers and info here for dance, theater, and art events. In the Chiado (if the name didn't tip you off...).

▶▶**SPLURGE**
Pedro das Arábias *(Rua da Atalaia 70; Tel 21/346-84-94; Tram 28;*

7:30pm–2am daily, kitchen closes 12:30am; 1,500$00 per entree; AE, MC, V) may at first seem like a budget place, but they give you an appetizer spread of flat bread, meatballs, eggplant salad, and olives that knocks it up 2,000$00, then after the wine, dessert, and coffee, hey, it becomes a splurge! But this Bairro Alto spot is worth it. The Arab motif, friendly staff, and scrumptious couscous served in big clay dishes bring in the mix of locals and travelers around 9pm.

Arco do Castelo *(Rua Chão da Feira 25, Alfama; Tel 21/887-65-98; 11am-midnight Mon-Sat; AE, MC, V)* is an Indian restaurant featuring the cuisine of Goa, which involves a lot of coconut, giving the spicy curries a sweet sexiness. They'll also make you excellent vegetarian curries on request. Located right at the entrance of the Castelo, this is an ideal dinner spot after watching the sun set over the city.

crashing

The standard *pensão* here is a single floor of a building with rooms equipped with a sink, a bidet, and maybe a small stall shower. There are (very clean) toilets and larger showers in the shared bathrooms. When you start to spend more money, there are bathrooms in the rooms and no curfews. Plan to pay with cash, 'cause credit cards are rarely accepted. Rates are determined by both the room and the number of occupants. The rates listed here are for the low season—most places raise their rates by 2,000 to 4,000$00 for the summer, so watch out. When you first arrive, you may be approached by owners offering to take you to their *pensão*—they're pretty honest and safe, but use your judgment. As far as cheap central pensions go, your best bet is to stay in the Baixa. It's easy to get anywhere from here, and it's a short walk from the train station. There are some good ones in Alfama, and though it looks closer on the map to the station, the hills make it actually quite a haul. Don't be tempted by the hip Bairro Alto if you're on a budget—rooms ain't cheap, the facilities can be filthy, and you may run into some shady characters. Toward the Avenida da Liberdade are some lux hotels.

▶▶**CHEAP**

Pousada de Juventude de Lisboa *(Rua Andrade Corvo 46; Tel 21/353-26-96, Fax 21/353-75-41; Metro to Picoas; 2,000$00/bed, 4,900$00 double; No credit cards)* is the main youth hostel. It's near the Parque Eduardo VII, which makes it more central than most. Call ahead (or the tourist info desk at the train station will call for you) to see if there are places available. With more than 200 beds, it's pretty noisy and social. The catch: You need to be a member of the Youth Hostel Association and have a Hostelling International Card to stay here.

Pousada de Juventude de Catalazete *(Estrada Marginal, Oeiras; Tel 21/443-06-38; Commuter train to Cascais from Cais do Sodré, get off at Oeiras; 1,500$00 in winter, 2,000$00 in summer for a dorm room, 3,700$00 in winter, 5,000$00 in summer for a double w/shower; No credit cards)* is an ideal little place to stay, but a bit of a pain to get back to after going out. It's on the Oeiras beach, halfway between Lisbon and Cascais, with a restaurant, bar, and cooking facilities on site. Turn right out of the train station and hike about a kilometer down to the beach, or pay 400$00 for a cab.

Pensão Moderna *(Rua dos Correeiros 205-4º; Tel 21/346-08-18; Metro to Rossio; 2,500$00 per person; No credit cards)*, in the Baixa, is basic

vegging out in Lisbon

Lisbon is tough territory for veg-heads. Portuguese, Brazilian, and African restaurants generally serve either fish- or meat-based dishes with little more than a garnish of vegetables. Here are some options if you don't like biting into critters.

Bairro Alto's **Celeiro** *(Rua 1º de Dezembro; Tel 21/342-24-63; Metro to Rossio; 8:30am-8pm Mon-Fri, till 7pm Sat; 1,000$00 per entree; AE, MC, V)* is a health-food chain supermarket with all your vitamin and granola needs. A macrobiotic cafeteria downstairs serves you hot meals of eggplant, tofu, seitan, rice, veggies, salads, and a selection of quiches and pastries for around 300$00 apiece. Other locations: *Av. da República 85A (Tel 21/795-28-23); Av. João XXI 22C, Areeiro (Tel 21/848-69-08);* and *Centro Comercial Vasco da Gama, Loja 21, Parque das Nacãos, Colombo Shopping Centre (Tel 21/711-10-05).*

For a heartier meal, **Os Tibetanos Restaurante Natural** *(Rua do Salitre 117; Metro to Avenida; Tel 21/314-20-38, 21/315-15-24; Noon-2pm/7:30-9:30pm Mon-Sat; 2,000$00 per meal; AE, MC, V)*, north of the Bairro Alto, is an excellent nonsmoking, completely vegetarian restaurant in the Tibetan Buddhist and Yoga center. The space is tight inside, but there's a nice patio outside to stretch out while you savor the excellent seitan and tofu dishes. There's also a wide tea selection to calm the curry-spiced plates on the menu.

and clean, with shared bathrooms and rooms that sleep one to four people from all over the world. There's no curfew, and you can sit with Dine, the Mozambican owner, in the sitting room to watch Brazilian soap operas with the others staying there.

The centrally located **Pensão Galicia** *(Rua do Crucifixo 50-4º; Tel 21/342-84-30; Metro to Baixa-Chiado; 2,500-3,000$00 single, 6,000$00 double w/bathroom, 5,000$00 triple w/o bathroom; No credit cards)* is cleaned well by a cute little old lady and has sinks in the rooms and bathrooms in some. The owners will go to the train station to pick up travelers and will also take you to two other similar, decent choices: **Royal Hostal** *(Tel 21/347-90-06)*, in the same building, or **Pension Beira-Mar** *(Tel 21/887-15-28)* in Alfama.

▶▶DO-ABLE

Near the **Sé Cathedral** [see *culture zoo*, above], **Pensão S. João da Praça** *(Rua S. João da Praça 97 2º-3ª; Tel 21/886-25-91, 21/888-13-78; Tram 12, 28, Bus 37 to Alfama; 5,500-7,500$00 double, 10,000$00 suite, extra bed 2,000$00; MC, V)* is run by an English-speaking woman

down and out

Down to your last *escudos?* Scrounge up your change and take Tram 28. The trams are made for 20 people to sit and 38 to stand (or fall all over each other grasping for anything to help them stay standing). Get on in the Baixa at the stop on Rua da Conceição, and go up through the **Alfama.** You'll spend 160$00 and see just about as much as you would on the double-decker tour bus. If you have only enough to get you to the train station, walk up **Rua Augusta** in the Baixa to see street vendors, artists, and performers, playing everything from flutes to fiddles to Casio keyboards!

and has rooms that are clean and fully equipped with TV, fridge, and telephone—some have complete shower/toilet facilities, some don't. You get your own key and have no curfew. Frequented by the French.

You enter **Pensão Coimbra e Madrid** *(Praça da Figueira 3-3º; Tel 21/342-17-60, Fax 21/342-32-64; Metro to Rossio; 3,000-5,000$00 single, 4,000-6,000$00 double, 7,000$00 triple; No credit cards)* through a tacky hallway covered in blue and green tiles and feel safe that there's a security camera to the street. Some rooms have bathrooms and a view of the **Castelo** [see *culture zoo,* above]. There's a TV room and bad machine coffee for 50$00, but you're better off going down to the nearby **Rossio** plaza to perk up.

▶▶**SPLURGE**

Residencial Santa Catarina *(Rua Dr. Luis de Almeida e Albuquerque 6; Metro to Baixa-Chiado; Tel 21/346-61-06, Fax 21/347-72-27; 7,500$00 single, 8,900-12,500$00 double, 15,800$00 triple, includes breakfast; MC, V)* on a lovely street in Chiado, has a nice breakfast room, a TV room, and a little bar you're probably not going to hang in. The basic rooms are clean, and the owner is friendly.

Hotel Borges *(Rua Garrett 108; Tel 21/346-19-51/6, Fax 21/342-66-17, 21/343-28-09; Metro to Baixa-Chiado, Tram 28 to Bairro Alto; 8,500$00 single, 9,500$00 double, 12,000$00 triple, includes breakfast; AE, DC, MC, V)* is super central, and the front rooms have a perfect perch for watching the action at **Cafe A Brasileira** [see *hanging out,* above]. All 100 rooms are spacious and clean, but the best thing about this place is you don't have to walk up any hills to get to the fun in Bairro Alto.

need to know

Currency Exchange The Portuguese currency is the **escudo** (1$00). ATMs, which give the best rates, are everywhere, and many places take cards.

Tourist Information The main office of **ICEP Investimentos, Comércio e Turismo de Portugal** is in the **Praça dos Restauradores** *(Palacio Foz; Tel 21/346-36-43; Metro to Restauradores; 9am-8pm daily)*. They're also at the Santa Apolónia train station and the airport. They will make reservations for you and/or give you a list of accommodations.

Public Transportation First, there's the **Carris**, the bus and tram system. If you buy your tickets at the Carris kiosks, they cost 155$00 for two rides, 430$00 for a day pass, and 1,000$00 for a weekly pass. If bought on the bus or tram, they're 160$00 per ride. If you hop on the newer trams, you pay a machine, which takes only coins. To figure out where each bus/tram takes you, read the lists posted at each stop from top to bottom. E before a number signifies *electrico* (tram). The Tourist Office and Carris kiosks give you maps. The Metro runs 6:30am-1am. Ticket machines at the stations give you the English option, and tickets cost 100$00 per ride, 260$00 for a daily pass, and 800$00 for 10 rides. The system is super-new, nonsmoking, and has

wired

If you have some serious work to do (god forbid), a quiet place to get it done is **Ciber Chiado** *(Largo do Picadeiro 11; Tel 21/346-67-22, Fax 21/342-82-50; Metro to Baixa-Chiado, Tram 28 to Bairro Alto; 11am-1:30am Mon-Fri, 2:30-7pm/8pm-midnight Sat; 1,000$00/minute; www.cnc.pt; No credit cards)*. It's a little study with cushy chairs and shelves full of books upstairs from **Cafe no Chiado** [see *eats*, above] in the Centro Nacional de Cultural building.

Practically next door, **Cyber.bica** *(Rua Duques de Bracaga 7; Tel 21/324-10-10; Metro to Baixa-Chiado; Noon-2am Mon-Fri, 7pm-2am Sat; 600$00/hour; www.cyberbica.pt; No credit cards)* is a fun place to eat, drink, and chill to acid jazz or R&B while using the Internet or other programs or printing. You may just want to watch space missions on the projection screen they have set up while sipping the spacey Ciber Cocktail, a colorful sweet drink whose secret ingredients can't be disclosed. One thing for sure, though, it does include booze.

Portugal for Travelers:
(http://nervo.com/pt)
(www.portugalinsite.pt)

The inside scoop on what to do: Night in Lisbon *(**www.Noitede Lisboa.com**)* is in English.

Both in Portuguese, ***www.sapo.pt*** and **AEIOU** *(**www.aeiou.pt**)* are the main Portuguese search engines.

stayed pretty clean so far. The best part is the smell of popcorn in the station—grab a cone on the way out.

Taxis are cheap, as taxis go (a trip across town will rarely cost more than 500$00), but be aware that they do add an additional charge for luggage. **Radio Taxi-Autocoope** *(Tel 21/793-27-56)* is reliable.

American Express Top Tours *(Av. Duque de Loulé 108, Marquês de Pombal; Metro to Rotunda; Tel 21/315-58-85; 9:30am-1pm/2:30-6:30pm Mon-Fri).*

Health and Emergency Emergencies: *112*. Hospitals are open 24 hours for emergency service. For an English-speaking doctor, try the **Hospital Inglês—British Hospital** *(Rua Saraiva de Carvalho 49; Tel 21/395-50-67; Tram 25, 28; 9am-noon Mon, 9am-noon/5-8pm Tue, 5pm-8pm Wed, Thur).*

Pharmacies Identified by a white cross on a green background *(9am-1pm/3-7pm Mon-Fri, 9am-1pm Sat).* There's also usually one 24-7 *far-mácia* in each neighborhood.

Telephone Country code: *351*; city code: *21* (it just came into being, so many old listings don't include it). Phone cards can be purchased at most newsstands (only a few phone booths take coins). **AT&T:** *05017-1-288*; **MCI:** *05017-1-234*; **Sprint:** *0800-800-187.*

Airports Portela Airport *(Tel 21/840-20-60; info line 21/81-37-00)* is about 4 miles northeast of Lisbon. The best way to travel to and from the airport is on the **Carris Tours Aero-Bus**, which, in town, termi-nates at Cais do Sodré and makes stops in the Rossio and Restau-radores every 20 minutes. Taxis into town are around 1,500$00.

Airlines TAP Air Portugal *(From U.S. Tel 800/221-7370, from Lisbon Tel 21/841-69-90)* flies directly to Lisbon from New York, Newark, and Boston. **TWA** *(From U.S. Tel 800/892-4141, from Lisbon Tel 21/314-71-41)* also flies to Lisbon from U.S. cities. Within Portugal, **Portugalia Airlines** *(Lisbon Tel 21/842-55-59)* flies to Porto, Faro, or the Canaries from Lisbon.

Trains There are four major train stations. Any Eurail arrival connec-tions from Spain, France, or cities north of Lisbon (Oporto, Fatima, and Braga) come into the main station, **Estação Santa Apolónia** *(Av. Infante D. Henrique; Tel 21/888-40-25, 21/881-62-42; Ticket office 6am-11:30pm daily; Luggage storage 600$00).* To get into the center of town from here, take Bus 104, 105, 107, 35 to Praça do Comerçio. **Estação Rossio** *(Tel 21/346-50-22; Metro to Rossio; 8am-11pm daily; Info office 10am-1pm/2-7pm daily; Luggage storage 500$00/48 hours),* in the **Praça Restauradores** in the center of town, offers commuter trains to Sintra [see *sintra,* above] and other destinations in the greater Lisbon area. (If you're going to the station by Metro, be aware that you have to exit the Rossio Metro stop in order to enter the aboveground Rossio station.) **Estação Cais do Sodré** *(Tel 21/347-01-81; Luggage storage 450$00/48 hours)* on the Tejo, slightly west of the **Praça do Comérçio**, offers trains west to the beaches of Estoril and Cascais and the seaside youth hostel in Oeiras. From this station, take Bus 28 to get to **Estação Santa Apolónia**, and Bus 1, 44, 45 or the Metro to **Estação Rossio**.

Ferries To go south of Lisbon, you need to cross the Rio Tejo on one of the ferries that leave every 30 minutes from the **Terreiro do Paço** dock near the **Praça do Comércio**. On the other side, they arrive at **Estação Barreiro** *(Tel 21/207-31-18)*, where you can catch a train.

Bus Lines Out of the City The main bus station, **Rodoviária da Estremadura** *(Av. Casal Ribeiro 18; Info Tel 21/54-54-35, terminal 21/55-77-15; Metro to Saldanha)* is not right off the Metro—walk through the Praça Duque de Saldanha, take the second left onto Av. Casal Ribeiro and go down it two blocks, and you're there.

Laundry Cinq a Sec is a chain of dry cleaners you'll find all over town. The most central one is at Rua dos Correeiros 105-7 *(Tel 21/342-45-27; Metro to Rossio; 8am-8pm Mon-Fri, till 6pm Sat; No credit cards)*. Self- and full-serve laundry is available at **Lava Neve** *(Rua da Alegria 37-39; Tel 21/346-61-95; Metro to Avenida; 10am-1pm/3-7pm Mon-Fri, till 1pm Sat; 800-1,400$00/load, soap included; No credit cards)*. Avoid hotel laundry services, which can be extremely expensive. *Pensão* owners will often hand-wash and line-dry clothes for a reasonable price, but most don't allow you to wash stuff yourself in their sinks.

mediterranean

THE RIVIERA

If the words "French Riviera" conjure up images of baccarat with 007, you're not far off. Casinos are still a big deal, even outside of Monaco, and there's no quicker way to win enough for dinner or lose enough to have to live off crusty baguettes for the remainder of your stay.

Something about the word "Riviera" also brings to mind glorious beaches and paradisical surroundings, right? Sorry to burst your bubble, but the Riviera's beaches are decidedly less than special. Nice has no sand at all, just big rounded rocks that take some maneuvering to lie on comfortably. *Some* sand shows up in Monaco and Cannes, but hardly enough to go around, and what little there is is obscured by rows of beach chairs and oily bodies packed together like sardines. Plus it's difficult to go to the beach for free, as most of the sand is owned by private clubs. If deserted stretches of sand are your thing, the Riviera beaches ain't it. And guys, the fantasy of bare breasts oiled for your ogling pleasure is quickly complicated by the fact that there are just as many topless grandmas as babes. Monaco's **Larvotto Beach** has these cute little platforms with diving boards on them that you can swim out to, but once you're out there, you may find it hard to psych up to swim back among the rather nasty gray fish that like to nip your toes and hands as you plough through the waves. It's not like it hurts or anything, but looking down at swarms of these things below you is kind of disconcerting. Definitely don't snorkel in the Monaco waters...better not to know what forms of pollution lurk down there. If you're bold, crash one of the big nighttime picnics on Nice's beach and practice speaking French, or just walk around hoping you look like you do.

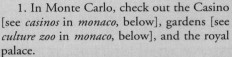

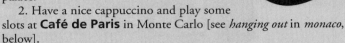

12 hours on the french riviera

1. In Monte Carlo, check out the Casino [see *casinos* in *monaco*, below], gardens [see *culture zoo* in *monaco*, below], and the royal palace.

2. Have a nice cappuccino and play some slots at **Café de Paris** in Monte Carlo [see *hanging out* in *monaco*, below].

3. Go to the beach in Nice [see *hanging out* in *nice*, below]; the crowd is larger and flashier than in Monaco or Cannes.

4. Trip out at the **Musée National Message Biblique Marc Chagall** [see *culture zoo* in *nice*, below] on the mind-blowing mural-size paintings of biblical scenes.

5. Ditto the **Musée Matisse** [see *culture zoo* in *nice*, below]; it's worth the short trek to Cimiez to check out the great one.

6. Vieux-Nice [see *hanging out* in *nice*, below] is a lovely neighborhood of charming squares and quaint cafes.

7. Groove to tunes at **Niel's Club** or learn to mambo at **La Bodéguita del Havana** [see *bar, club, and live music scene* in *nice*, below].

8. Take a flight on the wild side and go parasailing at the Monaco, Nice, or Cannes beaches.

9. Celeb-watch while you walk along La Croisette in Cannes.

10. Check out the ever-cookin' **Jimmy'z** [see *bar, club, and live music scene* in *cannes*, below] and the **Palais des Festivals** in Cannes.

If your French sucks or is nonexistent, don't worry—the Riviera is way international, and they're used to English speakers. You'll see everyone from American backpackers to European royalty on the beaches of the Côte d'Azur. And while the French aren't known for their warm and cuddly natures, local businesses know the role that tourism plays in their existence, so they won't lay on the snotty attitude that Rodeo Drive salesfolks gave Julia Roberts in *Pretty Woman*. Clubs are another story; they're not afraid to be snotty—but isn't that true of clubs everywhere? Having a lady on your arm, or being a lady, or both, is always helpful.

With plenty of compadres around, chances are you'll never feel *that* far from home. And, of course, it's nice to be able to get *Buffy* updates from fellow travelers. A handful of Internet pit stops make keeping the homesickness at bay that much easier [see *wired*, below].

In terms of where to bed down, Nice is a good base camp for dashing around the Riviera, where beds are cheaper than in Monaco and Cannes, and there's certainly plenty to do. Don't pout about missing the **Monte Carlo Casino** [see *casinos* in *monaco*, below] or the celebrity-spotting in Cannes. These two cities are only 20 minutes or so by train from Nice. On the downside, if you want to sample the nightlife in Monte Carlo or Cannes, you'll have to stay the night—trains stop running by midnight, when clubs are just opening their doors.

Now for a word on the casino thing: The French definitely don't do it Vegas-style. Forget about free drinks and comped breakfasts. You'll pay for them, and no casino employee will pat you on the back. And yes, there are plenty of men in plaid jackets from Toledo and busloads of women from New Jersey but also a pride of high rollers (mainly in private rooms in the back). If you've got money to blow, gambling can be a nice little high, but keep in mind that a lot of the people in these casinos are pros who won't appreciate your inexperience mucking up their blackjack game. And speaking of blackjack, it's much harder to win in Monte Carlo. Getting blackjack means nothing if the dealer gets it, too. Unlike in Vegas, you don't automatically win—it's a push. The slot rooms are rather unclassy dungeons of blinking lights and buzzing machines, as slot rooms are. People sit for hours, playing the same damn machine, because, hey, if you sit here for 6 hours, you may win *something*. *Bonne chance*, sucka.

NICE

Nice is nowhere near as glitzy and starstruck as its neighbor Cannes; it's a big city with an old-fashioned Provençal heart. Blocks of achingly beautiful pale-golden buildings sit like medieval townhouses on the narrow, cobbled streets of **Vieux-Nice**, the city's old town. This, as well as in the center of town, around **Place Masséna,** is where you'll find most of the nightlife in Nice.

neighborhoods

Between vendors and musicians who make up in heart what they lack in talent, the **Rue des Piétons** [see *hanging out,* below] is tourist central. Walk the street, and try to avoid having anything to do with any of the American food–wannabe restaurants—they're overpriced, and the food sucks. At the end of **Piétons** sits the fountained **Place Masséna** [see *hanging out,* below] with its rib-cage sculptures and saturated green lawn. Technically a park, this oasis also functions as the center of town, where people love to eat lunch or read the morning paper. The surrounding neighborhood houses the **Opéra de Nice** [see *arts scene,* below] and the **Museum of Modern and Contemporary Art** [see *culture zoo,* below] as well as the souvenir street market selling products of the Provence region [see *stuff,* below]. On Sundays, the over-60 crew takes over the best shaded area in Place Masséna, so be polite and don't haggle over a chair with somebody's *grand-mère*.

A block or two southeast of Masséna, you hit the old part of Nice—aptly called **Vieux-Nice**—that's filled with enough bars and pubs to fit anyone's taste, as well as galleries and shops to visit in the daylight hours. The medieval-style buildings are human-sized and charming: No building in Nice is overwhelmingly tall, except for the flashy **Casino Ruhl** [see *casinos*, below] tower, a bit of an eyesore. This is where the nightlife is in Nice. To find the party of the hour, duck in to **Mezzanine** [see *eats*, below] or **Master Home Pub** [see *bar, club, and live music scene,* below] in the afternoon to pick up some flyers and quiz the club cognoscenti about their nightly agenda. Minutes from Vieux-Nice and Place Masséna, you'll see the big blue sea bordered by the **Promenade des Anglais**, which is a glamorous name for the wide slab of concrete that runs along the water and gets its share of rollerbladers, musicians, and people lunching or stopping for coffees at outdoor cafes. The **Gare Routière** [see *need to know*, below] is just east of Place Masséna, convenient to the hotels in the Vieux-Nice area. The bus station **Station Centrale** [see *need to know*, below] is here, too.

With all the resources of a big city but the feel of a beach town, Nice is warmer and more homey and intimate than Monaco or Cannes. It's the type of place you can settle into if you have the time. If you only have a couple of days here, you'll want to stick to Vieux-Nice and the beach. You're sure to find a party somewhere—and don't worry about the etiquette involved in nursing one drink forever—bar owners prefer that their places look crowded. If you're with friends, and counting francs, take advantage of the "meter of beer" specials at **Scarlet O'Hara's** and **Jonathan's** [see *bar, club, and live music scene,* below, for both].

When you've had enough of city life and want more of a beach experience, get out of Nice and zip to the nearby towns of **Cap d'Ail** and **Juan les Pins** on the local train. Buy your tickets for anywhere along the coast from the coin- and credit card-operated machines at the train staion—no destination will cost more than 40F one way. You're only a nice (no pun intended) uphill walk away from **Cimiez**, where the museums devoted to Matisse and Chagall [see *culture zoo*, below], panoramic views, and the **Fondation Kosma** [see *arts scene*, below] await you.

hanging out

During the day, outdoor cafes in the old town's squares are popular places for people to congregate. But the most obvious hangout spot here is the beach. Look for the paler bodies on the rocks if you're trying to hook up with other travelers. Oh, and don't expect golden sand, or any sand for that matter. The Nice beach is rocks, just rocks. Wear a pair of good sandals. This beach is no snobatorium like those at Monaco and Cannes, so you won't feel out of place without a cell phone. Families, travelers, locals, young people, and old-timers mix it up at the beach, and you'll have no problem making friends with your neighbors, especially in the summer months when towels overlap for lack of space. To beat the tourist crowds, follow the locals—you'll know them by their bare chests and portable umbrellas—who prefer the less-populated strips of beach to the west.

If you're starting to get crispy, the park at Place Masséna is a great shady place for lazing around. Cool off in the nearby **Musée d'Art Moderne et d'Art Contemporain** [see *culture zoo*, below], where more than one weary soul has napped on the leather couches without being rudely awakened by a security guard.

Not much stays open on Monday and Tuesday nights, so people meet on the steps of the Palais de Justice in Vieux-Nice. Young scholarly types and scholar wannabes sip wine at the cafes that line the Place du Palais de Justice until they close at 11pm. Come in—watch the human zoo go by. After 11pm, there are plenty of nighttime choices: Locals love the Dutch pub **De Klomp** [see *bar, club, and live music scene,* below]. And Nice's **Casino Ruhl** [see *casinos*, below] stays open late-night to service the gambling addicts. It shuts down from 5am till 10am, just long enough to clean up.

Any of the Vieux-Nice pubs that stay open till 4am can satisfy your after-hours chow needs. But the only true 24-hour joint to hit after a late, late night is a little hole-in-the-wall takeout joint right off the water called **Buffet Express** (*Promenade des Anglais & rue Halevy; Tel 93/825-455; Bus 3, 6, 7 to Congrès; Open 24 hours daily; No credit cards*), an annex of the larger **Café Promenade** next door. Grab a greasy *croque-monsieur* or a selection from their huge array of American candy bars and head to the Promenade.

There's no actual chateau, but the **Parc du Château** (*Top of Castle Hill; Tel 93/856-233; Any bus to Masséna; 10am-6pm daily, 9am-8pm Aug; Free admission*) is still a great place to kick back, with its fountains set in lush gardens, miniature golf, and a human-scale chessboard. Get a group together and play some putt-putt, or just sit next to the waterfall and catch some rays. You'll run into large groups and families— the park has made it onto the must-see list of the "Tourist Trolley." These obnoxious little yellow trollies lumber around town at, like, 2 mph, full of pointing people with sunburned faces.

bar, club, and live music scene

Nice lacks what you would call a real club scene. Most bars and live music spots have dancing, too, so even the idea of clubs is different here. There are a bunch of sketchy places around town that have cartoon-like windows on the doors and require a "password." Never mind where to get the password, these places never even seem to be *open*. Ignore them. Also, don't be fooled by bouncers who usher you in, claiming "no money, no money"—cover charges are cleverly disguised by sky-high drink prices like draught beer for 100F. When it comes to entrance standards, Nice clubs adhere to the standard form: Male bouncers shepherd the ladies in and give fellas a hard time. Clubs vary in their levels of snobbery, but dressing well always helps your case.

Bars are a different story—there's no shortage of watering holes in Nice, and most of the ones worth going to are conveniently packed into Vieux-Nice, so barhopping is easy. Everyone migrates from place to place,

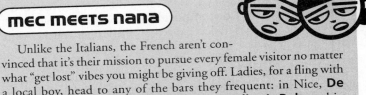

Unlike the Italians, the French aren't convinced that it's their mission to pursue every female visitor no matter what "get lost" vibes you might be giving off. Ladies, for a fling with a local boy, head to any of the bars they frequent: in Nice, **De Klomp** and **Masterhouse**; in Cannes, **Carling's Pub**; and in Monaco, **Flashman's English Pub** [see *bar, club, and live music scene* in respective cities]. Guys, it's best to use a purposeful approach when wooing the women in France. It may be tempting to cruise the beach for victims, but don't go in for the kill if the sight of a girl with no top on leaves you fumbling for words.

In Nice, **Niel's Club** [see *bar, club, and live music scene* in *nice*, below] is a good spot to meet local gals, **Jimmy'z** [see *bar, club, and live music scene* in *cannes,* below] is the place to scout them out in Cannes. In Monaco, try **Cherie's Café** [see *bar, club, and live music scene* in *monaco*, below].

and drunken fools pack the area late at night. For a slightly less "party time!" scene, try one of the many hip restaurants *not* in Vieux-Nice that transform into bars later at night: People tend to come and plant themselves in one such spot for the night. Those in the know take root at **Indyana** [see *eats*, below], but you'll be expected to order some sushi with that drink, bub. For a change of pace, immerse yourself in the pre-Castro Cuban vibe at **La Bodéguita del Havana** [see below].

Live music is definitely a part of the culture, and it pops up in even the most unassuming places. A guitar duo plays at **The Frog** [see *eats*, below] on weekend nights, and you even have a choice of karaoke spots. Jazz aficionados should plan to hit Nice during the **Jazz Festival** [see *festivals and events*, below] in July to hear jazz bigs such as pianist Herbie Hancock. The festival packs 'em in, so plan to make hotel reservations well in advance and check on the main Nice website [see *wired*, below] for ticket availability. For concert info on jazz and rock bands—and everything else, really—look on the wall outside of **Niel's Club** [see below]. And then stick around—Niel's has all kinds of shows that run the gamut from jazz to indie rock.

Master Home Pub (*11 rue de la Préfecture; Tel 93/803-382; Any bus to Masséna; 8am-2:30am Mon-Sat, 2:30pm-2:30am Sun; www.master-home.com; V, MC*) could easily transplant itself into any college town—take away the French waiters, and you're left with a bunch of baseball-capped boys in khaki shorts. During the day, the vibe and music are low-key, and French students and backpackers alike camp out in the wooden booths for hours. There are four PCs with DSL (*35F/hour*), and one has a highly coveted American keyboard. Beer lovers should get off on the 50 or so ales from a dozen countries. There are also 120 cocktails and 30 whiskies to help you along. At night, DJs spin French house and disco. If you need some fresh air, and you will, have a seat on the outdoor patio and watch the people go by.

There's a cheap happy hour at **Jonathan's Live Music Pub** *(1 rue de la Loge; Tel 93/625-762; Any bus to Masséna; 8pm-2am Tue-Sun; No credit cards)* from 8 to 9:30 pm every night, when beers are only 10F. On Tuesdays, happy hour lasts all night, and on Thursdays it's "meter of beer" at 150F. There's a definite par-tay atmosphere, with loads of Americans, and best of all, no cover. Live music (usually rock/pop-oriented) moves in to the "Cellar Cave" downstairs on the weekends.

Everyone gets the occasional urge to belt out some tunes off-key, and **Le Lagon** *(2 rue Masséna; Tel 93/877-685; Bus 7, 9, 10 to Jean-Médecin; 11pm-4am daily; V)* understands this need. With 1,600 titles and a mostly American crowd, this spot gets its karaoke going by midnight nightly. Bathe yourself in the strobe lights, order up one of their specialty cocktails named after exotic cities of the world *(50F)*, and belt out "Karma Chameleon." The purple-and-green disco decor in the big circular main room takes you back to a more polyester time, and the staff of large men with gelled hair add to the we're-still-living-in-the-early-'80s atmosphere. There's no cover, but they do charge two francs to pee.

A boisterous collegiate crew hangs out at **Scarlet O'Hara's Tavern and Ale House** *(Corner of rue Droite and rue Rossetti; Tel 93/804-322; Any bus to Masséna; 5pm-2:30am daily summer, 6pm-2:30am winter; 20-30F beers, 46-75F main courses; No credit cards)*, whose motto reads: "a pint of plain is your only man," whatever that means. O'Hara's is a traditional pub complete with a dartboard and televised sporting events and is one of the few night spots open seven days a week. Hit happy hour in the summertime for the 15F pints, or come later for dancing on the tables— yes, dancing on the tables. Live jazz sessions happen once a week (call for times), and Celtic pub grub gets served up pretty much all night. The frat-house vibe rules here when it's crowded; otherwise, a true Irish vibe prevails.

Only in Nice for a couple of hours? You could run across the street from the train station to **Paparazzi** *(26 Ave. Durante; Tel 93/885-968; Bus 12, 30 to Gare; 5pm-1am daily, No credit cards)*, the billiards-pub-restaurant joint on the corner, which clearly survives on the merits of its...location. The whole place has a Planet Hollywood–wannabe feel, with a giant movie camera, a plastic statue of Marilyn Monroe, and a jukebox full of the tired pop titles you'd expect: Nirvana, Madonna, Elton John, etc. On the upside, a game of pool or pinball is 10F, the owner plays music videos on the bar TV, and there's decent live music at night, usually rock or jazz. There's no cover per se, but drink prices are jacked up by 10F on live music nights. Then again, just hanging out in the train station isn't such a bad way to pass the time either....

Odd that the only Dutch pub in Nice is run by a couple of Brits, but that's the case at **De Klomp** *(6 rue Mascoïnat, Vieux-Nice; Tel 93/924-*

285; Any bus to Masséna; 5pm-2:30am Mon-Sat, 8:30pm-2:30am Sun; 40F pints; No credit cards). They like to watch "footy" on the "telly", so expect it to be packed during the World Cup. De Klomp, jammed with guys of all ages, is a man's place, and its hefty wooden furniture and wood paneling give it a sort of bachelor-pad feel. The 5:30 to 9:30pm happy hour brings in the students, local and foreign. It's a chill place during the day but energized later on, with live music every night and jazz on Thursdays. Expect a mainly local all-age crowd of expats and French alike. The bass player (if he's still around) is good news, as are the 18 beers on tap and 40 types of whiskey.

The *très sophistiqué* **Le Carré** *(6 Passage Emile Negrin, pedestrian zone; Tel 93/883-882; Any bus to Place Masséna and then ya gotta walk; 8pm-midnight Mon-Sat; No credit cards)* reels in the cool, black-clad Euro types. Le Carré throws lots of parties in the summer, and anything goes with the DJs: funk, soul, salsa, jazz, whatever. The decor mixes zebra-striped couches with a *Casablanca*-esque feel. Tasty tapas of salmon tartare and a martini runs about 100F. Le Carré is a restaurant, too, but you can definitely feel comfortable just having a drink. Come after 10pm to mingle with the artsy crew and pick up a party invite or two.

Niel's Club *(10 Cité du Parc, Vieux-Nice; Bus 6, 11, 16 to Gare Routière; 10pm-5am Tue-Sat; Cover 30-50F weekends only; V, MC)* has jazz every Tuesday night and by far the most live shows of any club around. Look next to the door for the schedule of weekly concerts, ranging from the Pixies to nameless electronic groovers. Indie-rock theme nights move into the cavernous underground space twice a month, where DJs blast the likes of Pavement and Superchunk. This no-nonsense place doesn't bother with any fancy-schmancy decor, and the crowd depends totally on who's playing. The cover includes one drink.

The **FNAC** ticket outlet [see *arts scene*, below] has tickets for and info on bigger jazz events around the area. Check for big rock concerts, too.

The over-glitzed **Forum** *(45 Promenade des Anglais; Tel 93/966-800; Bus 6 to Meyerbeer; 11pm-6am Thur-Sun; 100F drink minimum; No credit cards)* comes complete with a red carpet out the door and an army of beefy, suit-clad bouncers. The neon-lit interior is an electrifying mix of purple-and-red carpet with fuchsia lights. Cheesy? Perhaps. Disco? Definitely. The twentysomething touristos fill this baby up, though Forum does have a local following. Smile pretty at the four knuckleheads who stand with crossed arms outside the door—being or showing up with a girl in a tight dress doesn't hurt, either.

Le Duke *(11 rue Alexandre Mari; Tel 93/804-050; Any bus to Masséna; Midnight-5am Wed-Sun; No credit cards)* doesn't really get started till about 1am, so be fashionably late and get here at 2. This is an old-school disco, and nothing has changed: Not the cheesy decor, not the meat-market mentality, and from the taste of the beers, not the taps. There's supposedly no cover, but plan to pay 60F for a drink. The mirror-clad space is pretty small, so make reservations by phone to ensure a place on

Rules of the game

It's pretty rare to see someone openly smoking a joint on the street in Cannes, Nice, or Monaco. Monaco clubs don't see much drug use, at least not openly—that's too 1985 here. Gay clubs tend to have more of a drug thing going on, usually some E. Keep in mind that the penalty for being caught with even a joint is stiff. The French government cracked down on hash smoking about 10 years ago, and the penalty is jail time (like...seven years!!). Still, you don't see cops hanging around waiting to capture offenders. Note: Travelers should definitely refrain from carrying any sort of mind-altering substance on the train. As for booze, you're pretty safe having a drink on the beach or on the streets of Vieux-Nice or Cannes, but it's just not done in Monaco. In general, the French like their wine as much as you do, and as long as you don't cause trouble, there shouldn't be a problem. Getting rowdy at a bar or cold-cocking the casino dealer who just dealt himself blackjack is definitely a bad idea.

the dance floor, where you can get down to the hip-hop/funk and house grooves of local DJs. Dress with panache—tight is the operative word here. Wednesday is ladies' night—no cover for the girls.

If you're feeling smooth—and coordinated—**La Bodéguita del Havana** (*14 rue Chauvain; Tel 93/926-724; Any bus to Masséna; 6pm-midnight daily, possibly later in summer if the manager is in a good mood; No credit cards*) holds salsa dancing classes on Wednesday nights from 8 to 10pm—the 35F cover includes one drink. This is a hardcore dancing arena, so the lessons are definitely a good idea....The interior is what a happenin' Cuban dance club in Havana should look like: timbali and bongo drums everywhere and an upstairs that looks like a cockfighting pit.

CASINOS

There's nothing lit-up like the **Casino Ruhl** (*1 Promenade des Anglais; Tel 93/879-587; Bus 6, 2, 12 to beach; 18-30F beer, 50F cocktails; No credit cards*), Nice's homage to gambling, complete with twinkling lights and singing slot machines. The *salon des jeux* (gaming room) stays open from 8pm till 4am and charges a 75F fee to enter. Bring your passport—they require photo ID—and mind the dress code: no shorts, jeans, or untucked shirts for men; no pants for the ladies, and no sandals for anybody. They do play 21 and American craps, but some rules differ, so ask before laying down those chips. The *machines à sous* (slot machines) are open from 10am till 4am. They close for a few hours, so the house can count the money or something. Here you can walk in wearing anything but a bathing suit, and slots start at 2F.

arts scene

▶▶VISUAL ARTS

Where there are galleries, there is inevitably a cigarette-smoking, champagne-sipping, fashion-clad following. The classy **Manoir Café** [see below] has its own gallery space in addition to being a restaurant and bar. Vieux-Nice cafes [see *hanging out*, above] are sure bets for catching a bleary-eyed artist by day. The exhibitions at the galleries below change almost monthly to showcase a variety of fresh talent. None costs to get in.

The **Galerie Municipale Renoir** (*8 rue de la Loge; Tel 93/134-046; Any bus to Masséna; 10:30am-1pm/2-6pm Tue-Sat*) is far from stodgy, showing pomo-cubist work like Paul Pacatto's *Light Sculptures*.

Galerie des Ponchettes (*177 Quai des Etats-Unis; Tel 93/623-124; Bus 1, 2 to Gare Routière; 10:30am-1pm/2-6pm Tue-Sat*) and **Galerie de la Marine** (*59 Quai des Etats-Unis; Tel 93/623-711; Any bus to Masséna; 10am-noon/2-6pm Tue-Sat*), probably the two most revered galleries in Nice's small art world, often cohost international group shows. In summer months expect to see young Italian painters and sculptors like Luisa Rabbia and Enrica Borghi. Hit one of the openings, usually Fridays at 6pm, for some free grub. Such offerings as Van Gogh exhibitions (in Marine) and poetry illustrated on canvas (at Ponchettes) give these galleries the feel of scaled-back museums.

Manoir Café (*32 rue de France; Tel 93/163-616; Bus 6, 2, 17 to Meyerbeer; 7pm-midnight daily, closed Nov; 60-100F entrees, 98-150F prix-fixe menus; V, MC, AE*) has a whole different thing going on. This subdued gallery/restaurant/lounge boasts a stained-glass ceiling, leather chairs to sink your butt into, and a circular staircase that leads upstairs to the couches, coffee tables, and fashion mags. Shows include local artists' 2-D works and video installations that are enjoyable if not exceptional. Come for the atmosphere—the art is just a bonus. And the chef serves up a mean lobster and a savory artichoke salad. Now, *there's* art for ya.

▶▶PERFORMING ARTS

Theater here is in French without exception, and it's pretty commercial. Big productions at Theâtre de Nice and the Opéra include old favorites like *Hansel and Gretel* (the opera, dummy). The big-deal **Nice Jazz Festival** [see *festivals and events*, above] hits town in July. Tickets for this and most other performing arts events can be picked up at the **FNAC** *billeterie (Centre Nice Etoile 2nd floor, 30 Ave. Jean Médecin; Tel 92/177-774; Any bus to Place Masséna; 10am-7pm Mon-Sat; MC, V)*. A few movie houses show films in English—look for the magic phrase "original language." Your best bet is the homey **Cinéma Le Mercury** (*16 Place Garibaldi; Tel 08/36-68-81-06; Bus 30 to Garibaldi; Shows nightly, times vary; 42F, 28F w/student ID*), which showcases at least two pictures in English, about a year behind their opening abroad. Their phone line is an automated listing in French, so you may need to make the trek to **Mercury** for show times.

The **Nice Opera and Acropolis** (*4-6 rue Sainte Françoise de Paule;*

92/174-040; *Any bus to Masséna; Closed Mon)* hosts six operas each season along with concerts and lectures. Tickets range from 100F for a nosebleed seat to 700F for Placido Domingo's spitting range. Pick up info on shows at FNAC or the **Theater Box Office** *(9 rue de la Terrasse; 10am-6:30pm Mon-Sat)*.

There are free concerts Monday nights at **Fondation Kosma** *(Conservatoire de Nice, 24 Blvd. de Cimiez; Tel 92/267-220; Bus 15, 17 to Cimiez)* from October to April. They usually tend to be symphony-type affairs with a student following. Hey, it's music, and it's free.

Bimonthly jazz concerts are on offer at **Cédac de Cimiez** *(49 Ave. de la Marne; Tel 83/538-595; Bus 15, 17 to Cimiez; Call for times)*—a more formal setting than the clubs. Tickets can be as cheap as 25F.

Théâtre de Nice *(Promenade des Arts; Tel 93/805-260; Any bus to Masséna; 1-7pm Tue-Sat; 75F, 50F if under 25)* showcases experimental works by smaller companies. L'Etat de Siège, a mix of dance, performance art, and music, deals with (what else?) the human condition.

Cinéma Rialto *(4 rue de Rivoli; Tel 93/880-841; Bus 9 to rue Rivoli; Hours vary; 54F, 35F students)* shows a lot of indie flicks, and once in a while they have one in English. Films are only a few months old when they hit the Rialto, so you won't feel so behind the times.

If you're a film student or just a buff, call up **Cinémathèque de Nice** *(3 Esplanade Kennedy; Tel 92/040-666; Bus 25 to Acropolis; Tue-Sun)*. They know how to treat starving film junkies, charging 12F for students and 20F for the masses.

gay scene

You don't see Gay Pride flags flying on every corner, but the attitude toward men who like men and women who like women is casual and unassuming. Plenty of cafes, lounges, and dance spots cater to gay visitors and residents. Websites give out good info on gay hangouts. Local publications like *Hyzberg* and *Lesbian & Gay Pride Côte d'Azur* are free at local newsstands and at the tourist office.

The annual **Festival of Gay and Lesbian Film** takes place at **Cinéma Le Mercury** [see *arts scene*, above] in mid-June. You can also always find flyers for gallery shows by gay artists, and restaurants and bars that service gay clientele, at Mercury.

Le Blue Boy *(9 rue Spinetta; Tel 93/446-824; Bus 38 to rue Maréchal Joffre; 11pm-6am Tue-Sun; No credit cards)*, is one of the oldest gay clubs on the Riviera. Gay men of all ages show up at Blue Boy, located in a residential neighborhood between the promenade and the train station, but it's not all about sugar daddies. Disco down with the best of 'em on the multi-level, blue-neon dance floors. Plan to stay up late—Blue Boy doesn't get groovin' till well after Cinderella was due home. Spinetta is a teeny side street, so ask if you get lost. The cover varies depending on business, but usually between 40 and 70F.

Not your average bar/eatery, **Cherry's Café** *(35 Quai des Etats-Unis; Tel 93/138-545; Any bus to Masséna; 7pm-midnight Tue-Sun; V, MC)* loves

NICE

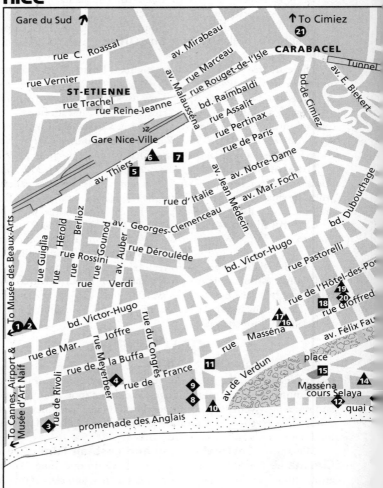

Gare du Sud ↑

↑ To Cimiez
21

CARABACEL
Tunnel

rue C. Roassal
av. Mirabeau
rue Marceau
rue Rouget-de-l'Isle
av. E. Biekert

rue Vernier
av. Malausséna
bd. Raimbaldi
bd. de Cimiez

ST-ETIENNE
rue Trachel
rue Reine-Jeanne
rue Assalit
rue Pertinax
rue de Paris

Gare Nice-Ville
6 **7**
av. Notre-Dame

av. Thiers
5
av. Jean Médecin
av. Mar. Foch

rue d'Italie
bd. Dubouchage

Berlioz
av. Georges-Clemenceau
Hérold
rue Guiglia
rue Héröld
rue Rossini
Gounod
av. Auber
rue Déroulède
bd. Victor-Hugo
rue Pastorelli

rue Verdi

bd. Victor-Hugo
rue de l'Hôtel-des-Po
19
20
rue Gioffred
18

Joffre
rue du Congrès
17
16
rue Masséna
av. Félix Fau

1 2
rue de Mar.
rue Meyerbeer
rue de la Buffa
rue de France
11
rue Masséna
av. de Verdun
place
15
14

rue de Rivoli
4
9
Masséna
cours Selaya
12

3
8
10
quai d

promenade des Anglais

To Musée des Beaux-Arts
To Cannes, Airport & Musée d'Art Naïf

0 — 1/4 mi
0 — 1/4 km
Ⓝ

BARS/CLUBS ▲
Casino Ruhl **10**
De Klomp **24**
Jonathan's
  Live Music Pub **25**
Le Blue Boy **2**
La Bodéguita del Havana **19**

Le Carré **17**
Le Duke **14**
Le Lagon **16**
Master Home Pub **28**
Niel's Club **29**
Paparazzi **6**
Scarlet O'Hara's **26**

CULTURE ZOO ●
Musée Archeologique
  de Nice Cimiez **23**
Musée des Beaux Arts
Musée Matisse **22**
Musée National Mess
  Biblique Marc Chag

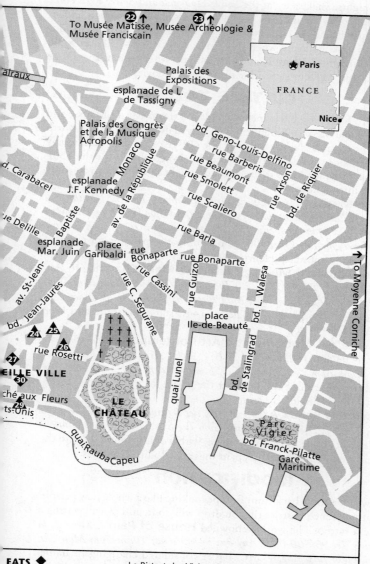

To Musée Matisse, Musée Archéologie & Musée Franciscain

Palais des Expositions

esplanade de L. de Tassigny

Palais des Congrès et de la Musique Acropolis

bd. Geno-Louis-Delfino

rue Barberis

rue Beaumont

rue Smolett

rue Scaliero

esplanade J.F. Kennedy

rue Barla

esplanade Mar. Juin

place Garibaldi

rue Bonaparte

rue Bonaparte

rue Cassini

rue Guizo

bd. L. Walesa

place Ile-de-Beauté

bd. de Stalingrad

Parc Vigier

bd. Franck-Pilatte

Gare Maritime

quai Lunel

LE CHÂTEAU

quai Rauba Capeu

ché aux Fleurs

ts-Unis

VIEILLE VILLE

rue Rosetti

Monaco

av. de la République

Baptiste

av. St-Jean-

bd. Jean-Jaurès

rue C. Ségurane

d. Carabacel

ue Delille

alraux

rue Arson

bd. de Riquier

→ To Moyenne Corniche

★ Paris

FRANCE

Nice

EATS ◆

Asia Express **9**
Bar Antoine **27**
Buffet Express **8**
Cherry's Café **13**
Indyana **20**
La Siècle **3**

Le Bistrot des Viviers **4**
Mezzanine **30**
Le Frog **12**

CRASHING ■

Hôtel Belle Meunière **5**
Hôtel de la Gare **7**
Hôtel de la Mer **15**
Hôtel Harvey **11**
Hôtel Masséna **18**

its theme nights. Shake a leg at the *Soirée Espagnole* and *Soirée Paris Nuit*. They've also got live music, eats, frothy cocktails, no cover charge, and an outdoor patio facing the ocean where most of the action happens. And if there's not a party going on when you arrive, don't worry—these guys are seriously clued into the scene and can tell you where the fun is. Dress casual-cool and you'll fit right in with the local groovies.

CULTURE ZOO

Paris it ain't. Still, Nice has some great cultural treats. Musée Matisse and Musée National Message Biblique Marc Chagall in Cimiez are both worth the trip (the Chagall is really a must). The 40F Art Pass gets you into any museum in Nice for seven days. You could also go all-out for the 130F version that provides access to every cultural sight in town, but you really need to be into sightseeing.

Musée Matisse *(164 Ave. des Arènes, Cimiez; Tel 93/810-808; Bus 15, 17 to Cimiez, get out at the Arènes stop; 10am-5pm Wed-Mon Oct-Mar, 10am-6pm Wed-Mon Apr-Sept; 25F, 15F with student ID, free on the first Sunday of every month):* Over 400 permanent works spanning the career of the famous color-saturated Henri.

Musée National Message Biblique Marc Chagall *(16 Ave. Docteur Ménard; Tel 93/538-720; Bus 15 to Cimiez; 10am-6pm Wed-Mon July-Sept, 10am-5pm Wed-Mon Oct-June; 30F, 25F if under 25):* Chagall's mural-size paintings make you just stand and stare and keep on staring. Go!

Musée d'Art Moderne et d'Art Contemporain *(Promenade des Arts; Tel 93/626-162; Bus 3, 4, 5, 6, 7, 9, 10, 16, 17, 25 to Promenade des Arts; 10am-6pm Wed-Mon; 25F, 15F with student ID):* The exterior of this steel structure alone should whet the palate for the Warhols, Lichtensteins, and installation pieces inside.

Musée des Beaux Arts *(33 Ave. des Baumettes; Tel 92/152-828; Bus 3, 5, 7, 12, 22, 38; 10am-noon/2-6pm Tue-Sun; 25F, 15F with student ID):* The most classic collection in town, with works from the 17th to the 20th centuries, including Degas paintings and Rodin sculptures.

MODIFICATION

So you want to come back from Europe looking like a whole new person? Well, eating French pastries till you drop will do it, and so will getting a freshly cut tattoo! The world-renowned **House of Pain** *(32 rue de la Préfecture; Tel 93/800-041; Any bus to Masséna; 10am-7pm Mon-Sat, 9am-midnight July, Aug; V, MC)* hasn't considered changing its name, despite the implications. The shop is as antiseptic as you can get, with no eating, drinking, or smoking allowed. Too bad—getting a tattoo is one time you'd want a shot of anything within reach. Prices start at 400F for tattoos, or 200F for body piercing, and soar from there. These guys are pros, with a wide selection of designs, and they're not averse to improvising if you want something a little bit special.

great outdoors

If the hard work of tanning your front and back evenly becomes too much for you, take a breather with some water sports. All the Nice beach clubs offer the usual parasailing, water skiing, tubing, and jet skiing. Prices are basically the same everywhere. **Sportlite** offers jet skiing at 350F/half-hour, parasailing at 200F.

If you're bent on diving in the Mediterranean, there are plenty of places dying to take you out on a boat. The **Centre International Plongée de Nice** *(Quai Lunel at the Port; Tel 92/004-386; Bus 1, 2, 9, 10 to Port; 9am-6pm Mon-Sat; No credit cards)* takes out first-timers and experienced divers. Their first-time dive, called a "baptism," will put you back 140F; regular dives are 190F. Boats leave at 9:30am and 3:30pm. If you have any doubts about your comfort or safety underwater, don't do the slightly unnerving, no-certification-required "introductory dives" that are standard in Europe and totally illegal in the U.S.

If you can tear the salesboys away from their televised boarding competitions, the aptly named **Space Cadet** *(5 Ave. Gustave V; Tel 93/825-066; Any bus to Masséna; 10am-7pm daily; V, MC)* is a convenient place to rent blades—45F will get you 4 hours of blading pleasure; a full day is 75F. If you're into the skating thing, this is a cozy little hangout with plenty of puffy/shiny gear and info on the scene. To show off your skills, skate down the Promenade des Anglais, where beginners stumble on cracks and old pros twirl on a franc. Promenade is also the best place for a jog any time of day. If you'd rather move a little faster, you can rent a bike or moped from **Nicea Location Rent** [see *need to know,* below]. For a scenic ride, nothing beats the beach for views. For a shadier locale, pedal into the hills of Cimiez and gaze at the grand old villas.

festivals and events

There are over 30 festivals yearly in Nice, but these are the most fun:

Triathlon International de Nice *(late June):* World-class athletes high-tail it to Nice for this endurance test that takes over the city.

Nice Jazz Festival *(early July):* The best from the jazz world: Herbie Hancock, among others. The festival's website *(www.nice coteazur.org/francais/culture/jazz)* is in French, but the schedule is easily decipherable.

Fête de la Vigne *(early Sept):* A wine-filled celebration of the grape harvest.

Bain de Noël: Skinny-dipping in the Mediterranean the Sunday after Christmas.

down and out in nice

Oh, what to do when the cask runs dry. Well, for starters, don't sit down at a table to eat—food to go will always save you a *centime* or two. Try the cheap local specialties [see *eats*, below], or do like the truly hard-up and buy a baguette and fruit in the morning to munch on all day, then have a decent dinner.

You can lie on the beach all day for nothing, and you won't work up an appetite on your towel. Galleries won't put a dent in your wallet, nor will strolling about the **Parc du Château** [see *hanging out*, above]. And of course you can always nurse a coffee over the course of an afternoon spent people-watching at a cafe, in traditional cheapskate fashion.

STUFF

Rue Masséna has all the designer shops you can sink your little teeth into, if you have cash to burn. Skip the street vendors selling African art, pick up a wacky wall-walker or two, and check out these more offbeat buys.

Head for the **main flea market on Cours Saleya** in Vieux-Nice from 8am till 5pm on Mondays and pick up anything from old cameras to junk jewelry. The daily **vendors' market on Rue Jean Médecin** is so-so, mainly cheap perfume and stuff made from Laura Ashley-esque fabric. There are Provençal goodies aplenty, but most of these throwaways, like quilted toilet-seat covers and milkmaid skirts, might not even qualify as kitsch.

▶▶**BOUND**

There's nothing worse than needing a good read and finding nothing but shelves of Harlequin Romances. That's not the case in Nice. There are three stores—count them—right around Place Masséna. English books are notoriously expensive everywhere in Europe, so expect to pay 30 percent more than you normally would.

The Barnes & Noble-ish **FNAC Book and Record Store** *(Centre Nice Etoile, 2nd Floor, Blvd. Jean Médecin; Tel 92/177-738; Bus 1, 2, 4, 5 to rue Pastorelli; 10am-7pm Mon-Sat; V, MC)* is the biggest. Though most of their stock is in French, they carry a bunch of books, maps, and guides in English. You can find *Bridget Jones's Diary* alongside Faulkner.

Librairie Masséna *(55 rue Gioffredo; Tel 93/809-016; Any bus to Masséna; 9am-7pm Mon-Thur, till 7:30pm Fri, Sat; V, MC)* has a decent selection of books—better than a newsstand, but no Chekhov or Bukowski. There are a rather astounding number of Agatha Christies, though.

The Groupe Sorbonne *(23 and 37 Rue Hôtel des Postes; Tel 93/137-788; Any bus to Masséna; 10am-7pm Mon-Sat; V, MC, AE)* has a few college-bookstore shops around the Place Masséna. Look for *The Pillars of Hercules* by Paul Theroux—it's set in this very same region.

▶▶HOT COUTURE

If you plan on hitting the *salon des jeux* at **Casino Ruhl** [see *casinos*, above] you'll have to dress the part. If, like most travelers, you sacrificed the dressy stuff when you packed, pass by **Zara** *(10 Ave. Jean Médecin; Tel 93/137-650; Bus 1, 2, 4, 5 along Jean Médecin; 10am-10pm Mon-Sat; V, MC, AE)* for chic men's and women's wear. Sexy little dresses run about 350 to 450F, and suave linen pants for men are 400F.

If you need to accessorize, the Parisian jewelry shop **Agatha** *(17 rue de France; Tel 93/887-644; Bus 3, 6, 7 to Meyerbeer; 10am-7pm Mon-Sat, closed Sun; No credit cards)* has fun faux rhinestone and cut-glass pieces. Handmade beaded headbands are 150F, and all sorts of jewelry and hair stuff ranges from 30 to 600F. Check out the great nail polish colors.

For the best, softest tees you'll ever wear, sail on down to **Petit Bateau** *(13 Rue Masséna; Tel 93/820-500; Bus 3, 6, 7 to Meyerbeer; 10am-7pm Mon-Sat; V, MC, AE)*. OK, it's actually a kids' store—so what? Grab the hip packaged shirts *(30-90F)* that sell for nearly twice as much in the States.

EATS

It's easy to scrimp in Nice and live off food from vendors and markets. Try the *socca*, a chickpea pancake–type thing with pepper. Anytime you sit your ass down in a chair it will cost you, so if you need to save change, take food to the promenade instead. A whole rotisserie chicken is yours for the bargain price of 20F at almost any food stand on rue des Piétons and rue Masséna. Lunch and dinner hours can be strictly adhered to, so plan to eat on the local schedule—it's damn hard to find a sit-down lunch after 2:30pm or dinner after 10:30pm.

▶▶CHEAP

The cheapest sit-down places don't serve *Niçoise* cuisine. The aptly named **Asia Express** *(5 rue Halevy; Tel 93/383-313; Bus 14 to Halevy/Promenade des Anglais; 10am-11pm daily; 18-36F per entree; V, MC)* is an ugly cafeteria serving yes, Asian cuisine, but don't let the ambiance steer you away—it pulls in a Chinese clientele, which is always a good sign. Walk right by the nasty sandwiches in the front window, head to the counter, and pick from about 30 different Chinese entrees. Ginger chicken has just the right bite to it, the dim sum is a must, but maybe skip the scary balls of paste labeled "dessert."

In the center of Vieux-Nice, the dive-y but good **Bar Antoine** *(27 rue de la Préfecture; Tel 93/852-957; Any bus to Place Masséna; 7am-8:30pm daily; 20-25F sandwiches; No credit cards)* stays open all day. The *panini Antoine* has tapenade (a tasty olive spread), mozzarella, and bacon all melted together in a gooey-but-delicious greasy treat. Take your food to go, or park it at the tables outside for a sit-down affair. We'd recommend not sitting at the indoor tables—that is, unless you really *like* fluorescent lights and chain-smoking bartenders.

▶▶DO-ABLE

Le Frog *(36 rue Milton Robbins; Tel 93/858-565; Bus 11b to Gustave; 7pm-midnight Mon-Sat; 68-85F per entree; V, MC, AE)*, a little Tex-Mex restaurant on the outskirts of Vieux-Nice, with its stucco walls and heavy wood furniture with big cushions, looks like the kind of place you could hang out in for hours, and many people do. There's live music on weekends and enough flavored margaritas to keep you sippin' all night. A little questionable on authenticity, the cuisine is sort of like Mexican food that someone's grandma might cook up: easy on the spices and with a salsa that's missing an ingredient or two.

The former hot spot **Indyana** *(Gustave DeLoye 11; Tel 04/380-67-89; Noon-2pm/7:30pm-midnight Mon-Sat; Main dishes 40-100F; V, MC)* has changed addresses and taken on a new identity, and the Riviera elite have coined it the new "it" restaurant. The look of the place—with rose petals on the floor and elaborate chandeliers hanging from the high ceiling—means more than a good meal to the flocks of fans who arrive dressed to kill. The wide slate tables are the place to see and be seen, while sipping *mojitos* or fresh melon martinis. But despite all the oh-la-la-ing that's going on in the dining room, it's what's going on in the kitchen that really matters: One side of the menu offers French standards, and the other serves up spring rolls, sushi, miso soup, and fish with ginger, soy, and tamarind. And despite the high-dollar decor, the food is reasonably priced.

▶▶SPLURGE

For the true French bistro experience, head to the charmingly informal **Le Bistrot des Viviers** *(22 rue Alphonse Karr; Tel 93/160-048; Bus 38 to Alphonse Karr; Noon-2:30pm/7-10:30pm; 75-200F per entree, 135-165F 3-course meals; V)*, a few blocks just northwest of the Place Masséna, where you read the menu off a chalkboard and the owner sits down with you to discuss anything from the food to politics. The house *foie gras* is excellent, if you're into pâté, and the salmon tartare is fresh and tasty. There's even a tank of lobsters in the front so you can choose your own critter.

A totally different type of splurge is to be had at **La Siècle** *(In the Hôtel Westend, 31 Promenade des Anglais; Tel 92/144-400; Bus 6 to Magnan; Noon-2:30pm/7-10:30pm; 180F-250F prix-fixe menus; V, MC, AE)*, a chic brasserie that looks out on the water. Careful you don't fill up on the great dense sourdough they start you off with—you definitely want to leave enough room for the cod in citrus butter and the artichoke risotto. Waiters are dressed formally, so this might not be the best place to show off your favorite cutoffs, and if it's summer, a reservation wouldn't hurt.

crashing

▶▶CHEAP

If you're in Nice for a one-night party followed by an early-morning train ride, get some melatonin and try to stay close to the station—it

may be worth an extra 15 minutes of sleep in the morning. **Hôtel de la Gare** *(35 rue Angleterre; Tel/Fax 93/821-030; Any bus to Masséna; Desk hours 7am-8pm; 150-200F single, 180-250F double, 250-300F triple, 320F quad; V, MC)* dishes up a hostel-type atmosphere at good prices. The cheaper rates are for rooms without showers, but if the grunge has accumulated to an alarming level, pay the 13F and have yourself a wash, dammit. For non-scrimpers, a room complete with bath runs about 60F more. They speak English at the desk, and rooms are basic: clean and smallish, no AC. Breakfast (bread and coffee) is yours for 20F extra.

The best deal is **Hôtel Belle Meunière** *(21 Ave. Durante; Tel 93/886-615, Fax 93/825-176; Desk open 7:30am-midnight; 78F dorm beds, 160-240F double w/shower, 336F triple w/shower; V, MC)* a converted villa even closer to the station and a bit prettier to look at. Lots of folks head to the outdoor courtyard to meet fellow travelers or just to kick back with a book. There's complimentary bread and coffee for breakfast, laundry facilities, and no lockout or curfew to kill your buzz. For the very best deal, ask about the apartment behind the hotel that has three double rooms *(190F)* with a shared bathroom and kitchenette.

▶▶DO-ABLE

Right on Place Masséna is Madame Feri's **Hôtel de la Mer** *(4 Place Masséna; Tel 93/920-910, Fax 93/850-064; Any bus to Masséna; Desk open 24 hours; 300-380F double; V, MC, AE)*. Madame Feri becomes your second mom; she takes care of her guests and gives discounts for stays of more than two nights. Rooms vary in size, but all have TV, five have AC, and some have minibars. The big rooms overlooking the park are simple and airy. Three people can squeeze into one room for a slightly increased price.

Closer to the beach and right on the rue des Piétons, the slick **Hôtel Harvey** (*18 Ave. de Suède; Tel 93/887-373, Fax 93/825-355; Bus 6 to Congrès; Desk open 24 hours, hotel closed Nov-Feb; 350-480F double, 80F extra for third person; V, MC, AE*) has a more formal atmosphere with a polished look: brass beds, glass coffee tables, etc. The rooms have satellite TV, minibars, and AC that works well. It seems like Harvey could charge a lot more and get away with it, but bless him for not doing so. You can't get rowdy at 4am here, but falling into these beds after a late night is worth it.

▶▶**SPLURGE**

Hotel prices in Nice go from reasonable to ridiculous with not much in between. That said, **Hôtel Masséna** (*58 rue Gioffredo; Tel 93/854-925, Fax 492/478-889; Bus 4 to Gioffredo; Desk open 24 hours; 650-1,000F double; V, MC, AE*) has prices that are less appalling than those of its beachfront peers. Right in the center of things, just off Place Masséna, this is a luxury hotel with its own restaurant, room service, and rooms that would be considered suites in other hotels. The terraces have great views of Nice.

need to know

Currency Exchange You can buy **French francs (F)** at **Thomas Cook Bureau de Change** (*3 locations: 13 Ave. Thiers; 2 Place Magenta; Gare SNCF de Nice, 12 Ave. Thiers*), but it charges a rip-off commission of 8 percent; competitors charge 4 to 6 percent. There are **ATM**s all over **Place Masséna.**

Tourist Information There are two offices in town, one right at the main train station (*Gare Nice Ville; Tel 93/870-707; 8am-7pm Mon-Sat*) and one right on the water near the center of town (*5 Promenade des Anglais; Tel 92/144-800; 9am-6pm Sept-June, 8am-8pm July, Aug*). The one by the train station will make hotel reservations for you.

Public Transportation All local buses start and stop at the **Station Centrale** (*10 Ave. Félix Faure; Tel 93/165-210*) in Place Masséna. Rides are 8.5F each way, day-passes are 25F, and you pay on the bus. Most lines run until 12:15am.

Bike/Moped Rental **Nicea Location Rent** (*12 rue Belgique; Tel 93/824-271; Bus 12, 30 to Gare; 9am-6pm Mon-Sat, till 2pm Sun; Bikes 120F/day, mopeds 290-340F/day; MC, V*) is near the train station, and true to their name, they rent mopeds and bikes.

American Express (*11 Promenade des Anglais; Tel 93/165-353; 9am-9pm daily in summer, till 8pm daily rest of year*).

Health and Emergency Ambulance: *15.* **Hôpital Saint Roche** (*5 rue Pierre Devoluy; Tel 92/033-375*) has 24-hour emergency service, and **Nice Médecins** (*Tel 93/524-242*) is a 24-hour on-call doctor service.

Pharmacies **Pharmacie de la Place Masséna** (*56 Blvd. Jean Jaurès; Tel*

93/85-65-45; V, MC) is centrally located and open 24 hours daily, except 8am to 7pm Sun.

Telephone Country code: *33*; city code: *4*. For local calls buy a phone card at the post office or the newspaper stands. You always have to dial **04** first when calling within the country. **AT&T:** *00/99-00-11*; **MCI:** *0-800/99-00-19*; **Sprint:** *0-800/99-00-87*.

Airports Nice Côte d'Azur Airport *(Tel 93/213-012)* is 5 miles west of Nice. Buses run from 6am till 10pm. A direct 10-minute bus ride into the city center costs 21F; a bus ride to the Nice SNCF train station costs 8.5F. Cabs into the city cost 120 to 200F.

Airlines Air France *(Tel 93/18-89-89)*, **British Airways** *(Tel 93/214-701)*.

Trains The main station is **Gare Nice Ville** *(Ave. Thiers; Tel 36/353-535)*. If you know that you're staying near the center of town, get off at **Gare Routière** *(5 Blvd. Jean Jaurès; Tel 93/800-870)*.

Bus Lines Out of the City To skip town on the bus, go to Gare Routière *(5 Blvd. Jean Jaurès; Tel 93/800-870)*. Buses depart from the Intercars Terminal.

Laundry Laverie du Mono *(8 rue Belgique)* is a self-service laundry. Wash and dry for 40F/load. **Le Panier à Linge** *(8 Ave. Durante; Tel 93/887-840)* will do the work for you, 50F/4 kilos. Both laundries are within a few blocks of the Gare Nice Ville.

monaco

It's hard to tell who's native to Monaco and who's just visiting—the hip spots are the hip spots whether you live here or are just dashing through. Also, if people have jobs here (other than serving tourists), they certainly seem to keep odd hours: Cafes are full at all times of day with groups of locals who sit for hours smoking and ordering after-lunch drinks in dizzying succession. The Monaco scene is pretty old-school, with large numbers of middle-aged partiers from all over Europe crowding in. No one will look at you funny if you're 18 and in Monaco for the first time, but you might not fit the Monaco standard of sleek and sophisticated.

Despite its über-hyped rep of being the cleanest and most polished city around, Monaco ain't pretty. The roads and ramps on the ocean side screw up the harmony of Monaco and Monte Carlo, the buildings in town are big and ugly, and the gorgeous villas set far back in the hills aren't accessible unless you have a car and plenty of time. Still, that doesn't take away from the spectacularly lush parks that lead to the Place Casino [see *down & out*, below], with their fountains, statues, and lakes, or the royal-looking exterior of the **Monte Carlo Casino** [see *casinos*, below]. And in general, Monaco is notoriously well-organized. You can count on times being accurate for any event and the **Direction du Tourisme** [see *need to know*, below] has more information than you'll ever use.

Try to avoid descending on this little principality during the second week in May when **Le Grand Prix de Monaco** takes over the town. It's a big hassle to compete for your dinner—not to mention a place to sleep—with all of Europe's racing fans.

The glamour and glitz of Monaco are only a 20-minute train ride from Nice, but keep an eye on the time, since trains stop running around midnight.

neighborhoods

There's no visible division of areas in Monaco. **The Port** is a central point, equidistant from **Monaco Ville**, the new and super-stylie train station, and the town of **Monte Carlo**. To get to the sea, walk south from the train station and stop when you see the big yachts. Up the hill from the Port lies Monte Carlo, a coil of streets that all lead back to the famed **Monte Carlo Casino** [see *casinos*, below]. The in-town Direction du Tourisme [see *need to know*, below] is located nearby on Boulevard des Moulins at the north end of the casino's gardens, so it's not a bad idea to make this an early stop.

The medieval town of Monaco Ville is situated on "the Rock," on the southwest side of the Port. Built atop the Rock, the **Palais de Monaco** [see *culture zoo*, below] rises an imposing 200 feet above the sea. **The Port** has a few good night and day spots like **Stars 'n' Bars** [see *bar, club, and live music scene*, below]. Take a gander at the ridiculous collection of yachts and ships that drop anchor in Monaco. To the west of the port, a 10-minute walk takes you to **Fontvieille**, the less-visited sports complex area of Monaco. Fontvieille hosts the **Saturday Flea Market** [see *stuff*, below] and is home to the Princesse Grace Rose Garden.

hanging out

Regular Joes and Josephines who don't want to pay 300F per person to sit at the **Monte Carlo Beach** play at the sandy public and private stretches of **Larvotto Beach**. Though not huge, and no better than decent, Larvotto is a great place to meet fellow travelers. "Crowded" is a word that comes up often when describing it, especially in the summer, when crowds can get overwhelming. There's usually a friendly mix of families, students, and travelers all looking forward to a dip in the ocean. The requisite topless ladies and Speedo'd lads strut their stuff here, but there are plenty of modestly clad beachgoers as well, so you won't feel out of place if a thong is not your thing. When hunger strikes, there's no need to go far: Larvotto is lined with cafes that actually serve decent non-junk food. **Miami Plage** (*Larvotto; 93/509-416; 8am-7pm daily; No credit cards*) has crispy pizzas for 40F and a hollowed-out pineapple fruit salad for 35F. On the public end, they've got ping-pong, foos, and volleyball courts for rent. You can use the outdoor showers and bathrooms for free, but indoor showers and changing rooms will run ya 10F.

To stay out of the sun but in the spotlight, head to the notoriously un-snobby **Stars 'n' Bars** [see *bar, club, and live music scene*, below],

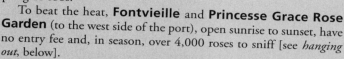

down and out in monaco

If you're out of dough, Monaco's a little rough, but you can still go to **Larvotto Beach**, where the sun will make you drowsy. Take along some water and treat yourself to a cheap game of ping-pong or foos.

To beat the heat, **Fontvieille** and **Princesse Grace Rose Garden** (to the west side of the port), open sunrise to sunset, have no entry fee and, in season, over 4,000 roses to sniff [see *hanging out*, below].

Hanging out at **Monte Carlo Casino** [see *casinos*, below] may not be something to do all day, but between the slots room, the gardens outside, and Häagen-Dazs on the corner, you can make an afternoon of it.

where Hard Rock Cafe meets boardwalk arcade/boat club by the port, to nosh on some passable "good old American food." It's a bit on the cheesy side, with a Western Americana theme in hot competition with Formula 1 racing paraphernalia, but the outdoor cafe stays open all day—a plus, since most eating establishments like to shut down at 2pm, just when midday hunger sets in, and stay closed to 7pm. If you happen to meet up with fellow wanderers, there's nothing like a "bucket of beer" *(100F)* to waste the day away.

Professional people-watchers will take to the overpriced **Le Café de Paris** (Place du Casino; Tel 92/162-124, Fax 92/163-862; Bus 1 to Place Casino; 9am-3am daily; V, MC, AE), perched right in front of the **Monte Carlo Casino** [see *casinos*, below]. Sip pricey mimosas for hours at an outdoor table amid the Monte Carlo gentry and sink into the cushioned chairs like you're right at home. The giant olives they give out free with drinks make for a nice little snack. Café de Paris and the Casino are planted on the manicured Place Casino, a good spot for a photo op or meeting up with friends.

bar, club, and live music scene

Monte Carlo is probably the only place around where clubs outnumber restaurants. Dressing well is pretty much customary across the board—funky club gear loses out to the more tastefully sleek all-black. Ladies can be spotted in gravity-defying backless tube tops, and most of the gents are in suits. Jeans are generally scoffed at, even though they're "technically" pants (as opposed to the truly declassé shorts). Best to drag out that one pair of wrinkled dress pants and steam them in the shower before you hit town. In the summer it's tough to side-step cover charges, and drink prices increase by 30 percent. Drink at a pub in the evening and head to the clubs about 1:30 or 2am when things get started. After-hours junkies will meet their match in Monaco—all the clubs stay open past 4am, so chances are you'll run out of energy before they do.

Avenue des Spelugues is home to five or six bars/clubs—if you want variety it's a good place to plant yourself on. This street is right off Place Casino [see *hanging out*, above], so you can do a pre-club warmup at the slot machines. But don't come to Monaco expecting to see the latest in indie rock. There's not a whole lot on the live music tip that's worth mentioning; lots of bars advertise "live rock" that turns out to be the kind of background noise you can deal with only after many drinks. *Bienvenue à Monaco*, which you can pick up at the Direction du Tourisme [see *need to know*, below], lists all the nightspots in town and tells you if they've got live sounds.

Cherie's Café *(9 Ave. des Spelugues; Tel 93/303-099; Bus 1, 6 to Ave. des Spelugues; 6pm-6am daily, kitchen closes at 11:30; 100F entrees; V, MC, AE, DC)* is a cafe by day and bar/club by night. Live rock, dance, or jazz music moves in several nights a week, usually around 11pm—call or stop by to see what nights have live stuff. Tons of rich-looking twenty- and

fashion

Monaco is a place where you'll need to break out the fancy duds. Next to Yves Saint-Laurent and Chanel, shorts and Birks will look decidedly out of place. It's like putting a sticker on your head telling the world that you're new in town and have no idea how to behave. Even during daylight hours, Monégasques are ready to transform themselves from beachgoers to club/casino-goers in the blink of an eye, so be sure to have some versatile clothes on hand. You can be more casual in Nice and Cannes. Nice favors cyborg-esque stretch-fabric club gear and anything black for nighttime. Cannes requires a mix of Nice and Monaco fashions. More upscale spots like **Jane's Club** [see *bar, club, and live music scene* in *cannes*, below] will make you feel like you're in Monaco, but you can wear shorts to local bars and not be snubbed.

The beaches in these three Riviera cities are all about wearing as little as possible. As a somewhat bizarre alternative to losing that bikini top, many women wear a one-piece and roll it down until it's nothing more than a bottom. Strange as that sounds, they think nothing of it. The men here love them Speedos, even thongs. If you choose to go native, don't forget to apply sunscreen to those areas that haven't seen the sun in a while.

thirtysomethings come in to dine on the Italian-French cuisine, then stay planted on the terrace until the wee hours ordering bottle after bottle of wine. This is definitely one of the hipper nightspots in town, so it's worth going to, whether there's music or not. Champagne is 65F a glass, but you can opt for 24F beers instead.

McCarthy's Pub *(7 rue du Portier; Tel 93/258-767; Bus 1 to Portier; 6pm-6am daily; AE, V, DC)* attracts more backpackers and beer lovers than locals, as most Irish pubs abroad do. It's kind of a cookie-cutter version of every Irish pub you've ever been in, with traditional Irish tunes and live music happening on Thursday, Friday, and Saturday nights. Try a big ol' Guinness *(36F)*, or an Irish Eyes, Irish Kiss, or Michael Collins *(all 60F)*, and sink into the green vinyl pub cushions with a smile.

Flashman's English Pub *(7 Ave. Princesse Alice; Tel 93/300-903; Bus 1 to Casino; 11am-5am daily; No credit cards)* isn't in any of the Monaco brochures, so it tends to be a more low-key, local hang. The interior has that seedy-bar feeling, but there's an outdoor deck if you need some air. All types congregate here, from twentysomething businessmen popping in after work to a younger crowd later at night. There are live shows on Friday and Saturday nights, a decent mix of British/American pop. Heineken draughts are 21F and a "big" whiskey is 50F.

On Avenue des Spelugues, along with a string of bars and clubs, lies the strobe-light-and-disco-ball scene at **L'X Club** *(13 Ave. des Spelugues; Tel 93/307-055; Bus 1, 6 to Ave. des Spelugues; 11pm-4am daily; No credit cards)*. Get over the purple-and-green carpet and get down with the disco/techno vibe. Wait till the outdoor terrace opens for drinks at 9pm; you'll pay less than you do inside. One of the more down-to-earth places here, the club is not into turning away good business, so there are no worries about having the door barricaded by bouncers. On weekends, 70F is supposedly the cover, but they charge at their discretion, so dress nice and hope for the best.

One of the two clubs in the Sporting d'Eté complex, **Jimmy'z** *(26 Ave. Princesse Grace; Tel 92/162-277; Bus 4, 6 to Larvotto; 11:30pm-5am daily in summer, closed Mon, Tue in winter; No credit cards)* takes the vibe of L'X Club, modernizes it, and serves it up on a much larger scale. Along with the attached **Paradise Club**, this complex can handle hundreds of people. If you don't know where to go late-night, search no longer; everyone under 50 heads out here after midnight. Again, it doesn't hurt to look nice; you'll fit in better wearing black pants than jeans, and it might get you out of the 100F cover charge.

The club at **Stars 'n' Bars** *(6 Quai Antoine I; Tel 97/979-595, Fax Tel 93/508-575; Bus 1, 2, 6 to Princesse Stephanie; 11:30pm-5am Fri, Sat; www.isp-riviera.com/starsnbars)* is 99 percent attitude-free: There's no dress code, and they won't even look at you funny for wearing flip-flops. The floor upstairs, above the bar, is devoted to all-night dancing, with plenty of space to groove the night away to a mix of techno, hip-hop, and dance vibes. When you get sick of dancing, try your skills in the game room downstairs, or sneak off for a late-night e-mail session at the club's

monaco

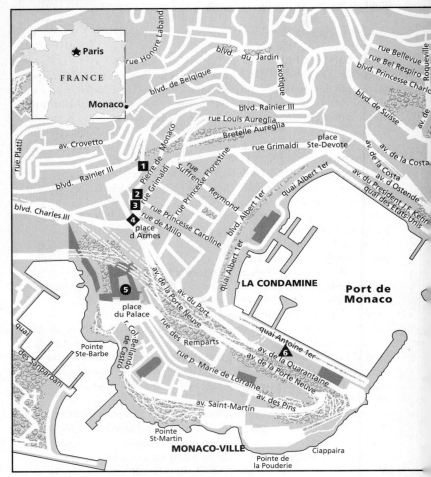

terminals. There's a cover *(20F)* only for the Friday night house party, but expect to pay 60F for a half pint and 80F for a pint when the DJ's spinning. At more reasonable hours, this is the place to watch World Cup soccer or whatever Grand Prix is on that week—the picture wall of sports heroes should put you in the mood. During the day, pints are 32F, so the 100F bucket (six mugs' worth) is a deal.

casinos

One glance at the glamorous, rococo **Monte Carlo Casino** *(Place Casino; Tel 92/162-300; Bus 1 to Place Casino; Slots from 2pm, salon des jeux from 8pm; No credit cards)* lit up in all its elegant splendor makes

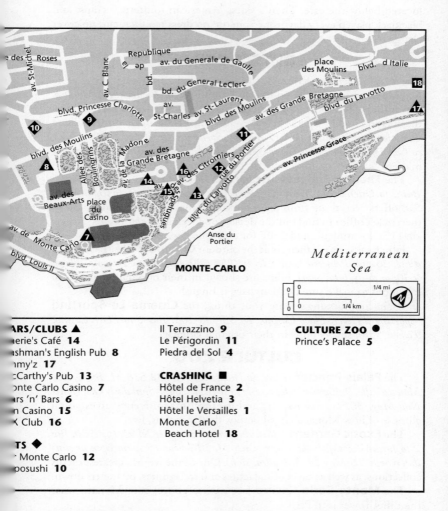

av. des Roses
av. St-Michel
Republique
av. du Generale de Gaulle
place des Moulins
blvd. d Italie
av. C. Blanc
bd. ap la Republique
bd. du General LeClerc
18
av. St-Charles
av. St-Laurent
blvd. Princesse Charlotte
av. des Moulins
av. des Grande Bretagne
blvd. du Larvotto
17
10
9
av. des Grande Bretagne
11
blvd. des Moulins
av. de la Madone
av. des Grande Bretagne
av. Princesse Grace
Allée des Boulingins
8
16
12
rue du Portier
av. des Beaux-Arts
14
av. des Citromiers
15
av. des Spelugues
13
blvd. du Larvotto
place du Casino
av. de Monte Carlo
7
Anse du Portier
blvd. Louis II
MONTE-CARLO
Mediterranean Sea

0   1/4 mi
0   1/4 km

ARS/CLUBS ▲
...erie's Café **14**
...shman's English Pub **8**
...my'z **17**
...Carthy's Pub **13**
...nte Carlo Casino **7**
...rs 'n' Bars **6**
...n Casino **15**
...K Club **16**

...TS ◆
...r Monte Carlo **12**
...posushi **10**

Il Terrazzino **9**
Le Périgordin **11**
Piedra del Sol **4**

CRASHING ■
Hôtel de France **2**
Hôtel Helvetia **3**
Hôtel le Versailles **1**
Monte Carlo
 Beach Hotel **18**

CULTURE ZOO ●
Prince's Palace **5**

Casino Ruhl [see *casinos* in *nice*, above] look like the Holiday Inn. To catch a piece of the action here, you'll need to dress well (no shorts, jeans, or sandals) and be over 21, with a passport ID to prove it. It's 50F just to enter the *salon des jeux* (gaming room) where the exotic dancer/convicted spy Mata Hari performed in the early 1900s.

If you're looking for a more laid-back scene, try the **Sun Casino** *(In the Monte Carlo Grand Hotel, 12 Ave. des Spelugues; Tel 92/162-123; Bus 1 to Ave. des Spelugues; Slots from 11am, salon des jeux from 5pm Mon-Fri, 4pm Sat, Sun; No credit cards).* There's no dress code until 8pm, and even after that it's just a no-shorts policy. And best of all, the gaming room is free.

Café de Paris [see *hanging out*, above] also has a gaming room, located below the cafe. There's slots, "American roultette," craps, and blackjack played every day from 5pm on; no dress requirement, no cover charge.

arts scene

The *Major Events* brochure at the Direction du Tourisme [see *need to know*, below] lists all the goings-on around town. *Bienvenue à Monaco*, also at the well-stocked Direction du Tourisme, gives a rundown of movie theaters and nightly opera/theater events. The **FNAC** ticket outlet *(Centre Commercial "le Metropole," 17 Ave. des Spelugues; Tel 93/10-81-99; Bus 1 to Casino; 10am-7:30pm Mon-Sat; V, MC)* has tickets to everything that matters.

The **Theâtre Princesse Grace** *(12 Ave. d'Ostende; Tel 93/253-227; Bus 2 to Ostende Supérieur; Office open 10am-12:30pm/3-6:30pm Mon-Sat)* offers everything from plays to symphonies to variety shows. Go to their ticket office to find out the details, or check in *Major Events*. Tickets are 115F for students and 230F for everyone else.

Film freaks can get their fix at the outdoor **Cinéma d'Eté** *(Le Sporting d'Eté, 26 Ave. Princesse Grace; Tel 93/258-680; Bus 4, 6 to Larvotto Plage; 9:30pm daily June-Sept)*. Films are shown in their original language, so call ahead to make sure that language is English.

If air conditioning's more your thing, the **Cinéma Le Sporting** *(Sporting d'Hiver, Place Casino; Tel 93/308-108; Bus 1 to Place Casino; Tickets 55F)*, shows films in their original languages.

culture zoo

The **Palais Princier** *(Place du Palais; Tel 377/932-518-31; Bus 1, 2 to Monaco Ville; 9:30am-6:30pm daily June-Sept, 10am-5pm daily Oct, closed Nov-May; 30F admission):* Its architectural magnificence gives you a glimpse of how Monaco's royal family, the Grimaldis, live.

The **Exotic Gardens** *(Blvd. du Jardin Exotique; Tel 93/152-980; Bus 2 to Jardin Exotique; 9am-7pm daily May 15-Sept 15, 9am-6pm or sundown Sept. 16-May 14; 38F admission):* One of the world's greatest cactus collections, as well as caves of stalactites and stalagmites, 60 meters down.

The **Monte Carlo Casino** [see *casinos*, above] is to Monaco what the Eiffel Tower is to Paris.

great outdoors

If water sports are what you crave, go down to the east end of **Larvotto Beach** and look for a sign...specifically, the one that reads, in French, "Water Sports." There's no phone, so just show up between 8am and 7pm. Pedal-boat rentals are 100F an hour, jet skis are 600F an hour, and parachuting is 350F.

Aside from the beach, Monaco isn't really an outdoorsy or fitness-focused place. You never see joggers here. If you really need a workout, try the **Columbia Tonus Center** *(7 Ave. Princesse Grace; Tel 93/250-327; Bus 1 to Portier; 9am-9pm Mon-Fri, till 2pm Sat; No credit cards)*, a small gym/spa with cardio equipment, weights, and plenty of body-pampering treatments. A one-day gym pass is 130F, and a half-hour massage is 190F.

Ambitious walkers can go for the pretty 90-minute walk along the coast to Cap Martin. If you'd rather stay in the city, hike around the **Exotic Gardens** [see *culture zoo*, above] or traipse through the olive groves in **Parc Princesse Antoinette** (*Entrance at Blvd. de Belgique or Blvd. du Jardin Exotique*).

STUff

If you've been rereading the same novel for several weeks now, **Scruples** (*9 rue Princesse Caroline; Tel 93/504-352; Bus 1, 2 to Place des Armes; 9:30am-noon/2:30-7pm Mon-Sat; No credit cards*) can help. They carry fiction and those oh-so-helpful phrase books for non-French speakers.

The bizarre **Boutique Formula 1** (*15 rue Grimaldi; Tel 93/158-244; Bus 1, 2 to Place Sainte Dévote; 10am-12:30pm/3-7:30pm Mon-Sat*) is a kick. You probably won't be *purchasing* authentic race car suits, or a car-shaped coffee table, or a full-size Formula 1 car/sculpture, but it's fun to look.

Cheap but chic outfits for the ladies can be grabbed at **Morgan** (*5 rue Grimaldi; Tel 93/256-358; Bus 1, 2 to Princesse Florestine; 9:30am-7:30pm Mon-Sat; V, MC, AE*). Put together a quick casino-worthy ensemble from Morgan's own fashions, which range from 100F to 400F.

The only flea market worth a visit is **Les Puces de Fontvieille** (*Bus 5, 6 to Fontvieille; 9am-6pm Sat*) at Espace Fontvieille, an open-air venue near the heliport in Fontvieille.

festivals and events in monaco

For details on the following events, check ***www.monaco. mc*** or ***www.visiteurope.com/Monaco/Monaco03.htm***.

International Fireworks Festival (*End of July*): Takes place at the Port, but you can see the fireworks from anywhere. Find a smooching partner, and make your own.

International Circus Festival (*Held yearly, often in Feb; Tel 92/052-345*): The best of the clowning and acrobatics world comes to Espace Fontvieille. Call for details.

Formula 1 Grand Prix (*Second week in May; Tel 93/152-600*) is one of a handful of coveted Grand Prix titles. Testosterone-pumped racing fans flock to Monaco for it.

Monte Carlo International Tennis Open (*Apr*). It's a hard-court tournament that players use as a warmup for the main season.

the monaco stroll

You can case this joint in a couple of hours, easy. Start at the train station and walk downhill, following signs to the **Palais de Monaco** on "the Rock." Hike the steps and take a tour of the royal palace, or bypass it and walk down the **Quai des Etats-Unis** and check out the **Monaco Port**. From the Port take **Boulevard Albert I** to **Avenue d'Ostende**. Hang a left up **Avenue de Monte Carlo** to the **Place Casino**. The curvy **Avenue des Spelugues**, right past the **casino**, hits **Avenue Princesse Grace**, which is the coastal road running along all beaches. **Larvotto Beach** will be on your right. Hang out on the beach and rest your tootsies.

eats

If you've tired of the regional cuisine, **Stars 'n' Bars** [see *bar, club, and live music scene*, above] has burgers and American-style breakfasts. For cheap eats, the pickings are slim. There are no vendors selling *socca* (a crepe made of chickpea flour sold on the streets of Nice), but the beach cafes like **Miami Plage** [see *hanging out*, above] do have simple fare that won't bust your wallet.

▶▶DO-ABLE

A sandwich place by day and sushi restaurant by night, **Caposushi** *(6 Impasse de la Fontaine; Tel 93/255-952; 8am-5pm Mon-Sat for sandwiches, 7pm-midnight Tue-Sun for sushi; V, MC, AE)* is a good pit stop for breakfast, lunch, or dinner. They offer giant platters of sushi for 150 to 200F, and, for those who like their meals cooked, pressed sandwiches for 39 to 74F. At night the bar gets going with 65F bottles of sake and a more obvious Japanese-y atmosphere.

It doesn't look like much from the outside, but the secluded patio at **Il Terrazzino** *(2 rue des Iris; Tel 93/502-427; Bus 1 to Place Casino; Noon-2:30pm/7:30-11pm Mon-Sat; 60-80F per entree; V, MC, AE)* has flowers and grapevines hanging overhead and an Italian peasant decor. Choose from 30 varieties of tea: *Marco Polo* is a Chinese mix of fruit and flowers, *pharoan* is perfumed by the fruits of the Nile delta. Graze at the tasty antipasto buffet, or go for one of the Italian-country-cookin' entrees.

▶▶SPLURGE

Gourmet palates will appreciate Gérard Baigue's **Le Périgordin** *(5 rue des Oliviers; Tel 93/300-602; Bus 1 to Ave. des Spelugues; Noon-2pm/ 7:30-10:30pm Mon-Sat, no lunch Sat; 98-250F per entree; gbaigue@monaco.mc; V, MC, AE)*. The business card features a dead duck, and, lo and behold, duck is the dish of choice. The duck pâté, the fillet of duck cooked in crisp pastry on a bed of apples, and the *foie gras* are all excellent. There are seafood and other meat dishes, too, but this is not a place for vegetarians. The three-course 65F prix-fixe lunch (75F w/wine) is one of the best deals in Monaco. Ask Gérard or his son Steve for a recommendation from his excellent wine selection.

crashing

Monaco does have a few hotels whose prices won't make you cringe. But, as in Nice, room rates go from do-able to unreal with not a whole lot in between.

▶▶DO-ABLE

Hôtel Helvetia (*1 bis rue Grimaldi, 1st floor; Tel 93/302-171; 290-320F single, 320-430F double, 45F breakfast; hotelhelvetia@monte-carlo.mc; V, MC, AE*) is a cute little pink hotel with balconies in front and a lovely *salon du thé* on the second floor, which doubles as the breakfast room. The plain rooms are totally sufficient with AC and TVs, and the price includes breakfast. For Helvetia, definitely book ahead; it's a hell of a lot nicer than most of the cheapish hovels and its 25 rooms fill up fast. They can also do triples and singles, so ask about pricing.

Right down the street, **Hôtel de France** (*6 rue de la Turbie; Tel 93/302-464, Fax 92/161-334; www.monte-carlo.mc/france, hotel france@monte-carlo.mc; Bus 1, 2 to Place Sainte Dévote; 370F single, 480F*

---

beat the system

Those in the know visit Monaco but stay in nearby Beaulieu Sur Mer, less than 10 miles west. Beaulieu's beach is a hell of a lot less crowded than Monaco's, and it's much easier to find cheap lodgings. And don't think that Beaulieu is some dingy suburb—far from it. Gorgeous villas along the ocean and manicured parks in town make it a much more inviting place than Monaco, with a following of Europeans who know that.

Be sure to check train times: Trains from Beaulieu Sur Mer to Monaco and back are limited and run at limited times. Less than a 5-minute walk from the train station is the quaint **Hôtel Marcellin** (*18 Ave. Albert I; Tel 93/010-169, Fax 93/013-743; Desk hours 7am-10pm; 180-360F double; V, MC*), where you follow a winding staircase up to the rooms in this villa-turned-hotel. Madame Rostaldo is a doll—she'll practice French with you and loves to serve up cocoa with breakfast. The doubles range in price because some have baths and others don't—either way, they're much cheaper than in Monaco. If Marcellin is booked, ask Madame Rostaldo to recommend an alternative.

double, 590F triple; V, MC) is a lot more modern and Holiday Inn—looking than Helvetia. It's big, with 26 track-lit rooms and plenty of amenities, like cable TV and AC. Breakfast—if you call bread and butter and coffee breakfast—is included.

Still in the same one-block radius of reasonable-hotel-land, **Hôtel le Versailles** *(4-6 Ave. Prince Pierre; Tel 93/507-934; www.monte-carlo.mc/versailles, hotel-versaille@monte-carlo.mc; Bus 1, 2 to Place Sainte Dévote; 350-500F single, 400-700F double; V, MC, AE)* has similar decor to Hôtel de France. The desk attendant wears a suit, and the furnishings are modern. There's an elevator, and rooms have a TV and mini fridge.

need to know

Currency Exchange Though independent, Monaco uses the **French franc (F)**. **Crédit Foncier de Monaco** *(11 Blvd. Albert 1 and 6 rue Comte Felix Gastaldi)* is a trustworthy spot to change money, and there are **ATMs** all along **Blvd. Albert I**.

Tourist Information Direction du Tourisme *(2a Blvd. de Moulins, Tel 92/166-116),* in the garden across from the casino, will supply all the info you need, and can reserve a hotel room for you.

Public Transportation There are five bus lines running through Monaco from 7am till 9pm Mon-Sat, with less frquent routes on Sundays. You can pick up a bus schedule at the train station or Tourist Office.

Bike Rental Auto Moto Garage *(7 rue du Millo; Tel 93/501-080).*

wired in monaco

Monaco hasn't caught on to the whole concept of Internet cafes/bars as a social prospect. You basically have two options:

The Aussies who run **Gale Force Computing** *(13 Ave. Saint Michel; Tel 93/502-092; gfc@monaco.mc; 9:30am-12:30pm/2-5:30pm Mon, Tue, Thur, Fri, 9:30am-11:30am Wed)* have only one terminal yet, but they're thinking of expanding. It's right up the winding street from the Direction du Tourisme [see *need to know*, above], so they get traffic from visiting travelers wanting to "phone" home.

The other e-mail option is back at good old **Stars 'n' Bars** [see *bar, club, and live music scene*, above]. Along with having almost everything else you need to sustain yourself, Stars has two Internet terminals. It's a bargain at 40F for a half hour.

For info about the city, go to: ***www.monaco.mc*** or ***www.visi teurope.com/Monaco/Monaco03.htm.***

American Express *(35 Blvd. Princesse Charlotte; Tel 93/257-445; 9am-6pm; Closed Sat afternoon and all day Sun).*

Health and Emergency Ambulance and fire: *18.* For medical emergencies, call **Centre Hospitalier Princesse Grace** *(Ave. Pasteur; Tel 97/989-900).*

Pharmacies **Pharmacie JPF***(1 rue Grimaldi; Tel 93/302-194; 8am-12:30pm/2-7:30pm Mon-Sat)* is in the center of town. Call the police at *17* to find out which pharmacy is on late-night duty.

Telephone Country code: *377.* **AT&T:** *800/90-288;* **MCI:** *0800/990-019;* **Sprint:** *0-800/99-00-87.*

Airports The **Nice-Côte d'Azur International Airport** is 22km (13 miles) northwest of Monaco. A shuttle service operates daily between the airport and Monaco *(Tel 97/000-700; 8am-7:30pm; 85F one-way, 65F under 25).*

Trains Monaco is served by express trains from Paris and Rome that stop at the new **Gare SNCF** *(Place Sainte Dérote, Tel 93/106-001)* and **Gare Routière**. Buses 2 and 4 stop at the **Gare SNCF**, and taxis *(Tel 93/150-101)* hang out there, too.

Bus Lines Out of the City Buses leaving Monaco travel only to the Nice airport. From there you can transfer to a bus to downtown Nice. But really, you're much better off sticking with the cheaper rail service.

cannes

Nice is an ancient city that absorbs its visitors; Cannes is a chic resort town that exists *for* them. Yes, there are the absurdly glitzy beachfront shops and hotels, but most evidence of film-festival splendor is gone by the time that last private jet splits. What remains is a classy, expensive Riviera town with amazing ocean views, narrow village streets, and plenty of good food and drink. Speaking of the infamous **Cannes Film Festival**, unless you somehow finagle a ticket to the screenings (which, by the way, is close to impossible), don't expect to schmooze with movie stars strolling down La Croisette. If you're not above star-worship, you can pick up celebrity glamour shots in local camera shops and maybe pass them off as your own. For most of us though, it's best to skip the festival. When locals leave town, they often rent out their apartments—that's how serious the hotel shortage is. Business travelers sometimes even end up in Nice for lack of lodging in Cannes. In case you're the walk-around-in-a-bikini type, be forewarned: Fines are doled out for inappropriate attire. The beach is one thing, but they prefer that you have your clothes on in this town.

neighborhoods

The part of Cannes you'll want to see is relatively small. A 5-minute walk south of the train station puts you at the beach and the sweeping waterfront promenade, **La Croisette**. Basically all the restaurants, bars, etc., are along the five streets between the station and the beach. You could take it all in in one action-packed day, on foot. Along the waterfront are the out-of-control expensive hotels and the **Palais des Festivals**, home to the better of two tourist info offices [see *need to know*, below], and the **Casino Croisette/Jimmy'z** [see *bar, club, and live music scene*, below]. You'll want to come here to visit **Limelight Records** [see *bar, club, and live music scene*, below], and pick up a week's worth of flyers for local/area parties. **Midnight Blues** and **Carling's Pub** [see *bar, club, and live music scene*, below] are right around the corner. The center of town—between the station and the beach—is a mix of bars and boutiques with a few restaurants thrown in.

hanging out

Life here revolves around the beach by day, and **Le Suquet** and **Casino Croisette** [see *casinos*, below] by night. The beach is so-so, with a small patch of public sand alongside umbrella-covered, hotel-owned sand. The public beach sees mostly tourists and families who want a few hours in the sun without having to pay the all-day fees at beach clubs. Despite space constrictions, it's still the most popular spot to laze the day away. **Plage Eden Beach** *(La Croisette; Tel 93/946-436; Bus 8 to Henri IV)* is the most reasonable in price. It has simple umbrellas and chairs and a friendly staff. **Plage du Martinez** *(73 La Croisette; Tel 92/987-422; Bus 8 to Miramar)*, with its cotton-candy pink umbrellas, is the crème de la crème of beach clubs, with the ritziest clientele.

You could easily miss **Café Poet** *(7 rue Félix Faure; Tel 93/395-958; Bus 8 to Gare Maritime; 7:30am-1am daily in summer, 7:30-9pm Mon-Fri, 8:30am-9pm Sat, Sun in winter; No credit cards)* were it not for the celeb photos hanging outside the store next door, glossy finishes gleaming. Poet is a people-watching ice cream shop/bar with a *cave à bières* serving up 30 beers from a handful of countries *(20-60F)*.

The only park-ish area is the **Square Maritime** in front of **Palais des Festivals**. It's good for picnicking or nursing a beer at night while you wait for **Jimmy'z** [see *bar, club, and live music scene*, below] to open its doors. Older locals spend their days here, and students from abroad have picnic lunches on the grass.

bar, club, and live music scene

The live music scene in Cannes is sort of lacking—train it to Nice if music is your thing—but a few worthy bars and hoppin' dance clubs make you want to stick around. **Limelight Records** *(13 rue Saint Antoine; Tel 92/991-664; Bus 8 to Mairie; 2:30-8pm daily, till midnight in summer; wwwkraft.fr./limelight-rec; V, MC)* has the word on concerts, parties, and shows for the hip-hop and house crew. This minuscule spot is the heartbeat of the Riviera's music scene, from bands to DJs to people in the know of where the best party is tonight. Stop in and browse their vinyl and CD collection, but better yet, hang out and get to know the

festivals and events in cannes

It goes without saying that the big event in Cannes is the **International Film Festival** that takes over the city in mid-May. To catch a glimpse of celebrities walking down the red carpet to a screening that you can't get a ticket for, loiter outside the **Palais des Festivals** (*Esplanade Georges Pompidou, La Croisette, on the east end of Cannes Harbor; Tel 93/390-101*). A very few passes are up for grabs at Palais des Festivals. If you can somehow produce evidence of being a film student, they might take pity on you. *Might.*

The more accessible **Festival International d'Art Pyrotechnique**, where you'll see the best that video animation has to offer, takes place at the Palais des Festivals over seven days in July and August. Go to ***www.cannes-on-line.com*** to find out exact dates.

There are also various two-day music festivals throughout the year, but the dates change annually, so it's best to check the aforementioned website.

The Cannes leg of the **Miss France Competition** is held in mid-June. Tickets are 100F and you can call *93/903-797* for more info. Yeah, we're kinda kidding.

very knowledgeable guys behind the cash register. Equip yourself with some flyers and pamphlets from the well-stocked ledge, but ask these guys their advice. They thrive on attention.

Midnight Blues (*Ave. Georges Clemenceau; Tel 93/396-626; Bus 8 to Mairie; 9pm-2am daily; No credit cards*) is plastered with black lights that don't quite mesh with the old-style bar decor. There's no cover, even for the Wednesday live rock nights, which often feature British bands doing a blues-rock mixture. Live shows sometimes show up on other nights too, so ask.

At **Carling's Pub** (*7 rue Georges Clemenceau; Tel 93/383-406; Bus 8 to Mairie; 7pm-2:30am daily; No credit cards*), the mostly local crowd spills out the door to sip drinks on the sidewalk outside. This tiny pub is packed, but if you push through to the bar, you'll be rewarded with 30F whiskeys. Girls, be prepared to be shamelessly scoped out by boys who lean on the bar waiting for their next victim. Reggae is the music of choice, and they also do live stuff on Thursday nights—usually rock or reggae played by a local band.

Studio 13 (*23 Ave. du Docteur Picaud; Tel 93/062-990; Bus 9 to Beausite; Hours and days vary; No credit cards*) is home to jazz concerts, films, techno parties, and even *Flamenco Dancing Nights*. There's something going on four or five nights a week at this classy culture house that likes to feature fresh sounds from young musicians. Tickets are usually 20 to 35F. Monthly "jam sessions" are free, and anyone can pull up a chair and rock out. Pick up Studio 13's schedule at the tourist office [see *need to know*, below].

There are Irish pubs and there are Irish pubs. This one is the real thing, with a hefty wooden bar, all Irish bartenders, and plenty of taps flowing—the French bouncer even has an Irish accent. **Morrison's** *(10 rue Teisseire; Tel 92/981-617; Bus 17 to Gare; 5pm-2am daily; V, MC, AE)* kicks up its heels to traditional Irish music (excellent) on Wednesdays and rock, blues, and jazz (not so excellent) on Thursdays. The party starts early with lots of backpackers wandering in for a before-dinner mug of draught, and the medium-sized space gets packed by midnight as more locals stop by. Beers are 30F, and seven different Irish whiskeys run 28 to 45F. Swing by between 5 and 8pm, when beers and some wines and spirits are half price.

For the ultimate club experience, you have to hit **Jimmy'z** *(Casino Croisette, Palais des Festivals; Tel 93/680-007; Bus 8 to Palais des Congrès; 11pm-5am Fri-Sun, daily July, Aug; V, MC, AE)*, where the bouncers are big and the dresses are tight. The cover charge of 100F with drink is waived for groups of ladies. People of all ages head to Jimmy'z, so expect to party with 18-year-olds and divorcees alike—as well as a large Arab contingent. Groove on the disco atmosphere: bars, mirrors, strobes, the whole bit. Music varies within the pop/'80s range with the occasional techno beat surfacing. You enter Jimmy'z via an elevator inside the casino.

The women at **Jane's Club** *(Hôtel Gray d'Albion, 38 rue des Serbes; Tel 92/997-959; Bus 8 to Hôtel Gray d'Albion; 11pm-whenever Thur-Sun,*

five things to talk to a local about

1. The **Nice Jazz Festival** is always a popular topic. Most locals have something to say about the new and old schools of jazz.

2. **How much money you lost** at the casino last night and how you can't figure out why you're going back tonight....

3. Ask about **the Monaco Grand Prix** and feign some knowledge of Formula 1 racing. Mention Williams/Renault and BMW and nod a lot.

4. Express disgust at all the **packed cafes** that cater to people-watchers (do this preferably in a cafe while people-watching).

5. Insist that **French art** died with Manet and see whether anyone will contradict you (a good way to get tips on contemporary shows—or a cold shoulder).

daily July, Aug; No credit cards) tend to like their fellas older and loaded.
Jane's has its share of pretty people dressed in the latest designer duds
lounging on cushioned seats and *chaises* and getting up for the occasonal
twirl. It's 100F to mingle with this exclusive crew. Thursdays are theme
nights, and Sundays are free for girls. You should call and make a reservation before showing up.

casinos

Good news—you don't have to travel to Monaco for a gambling fix!
Casino Croisette in the Palais des Festivals is open for business daily
from 5pm till 3am. Don't dress like a schmuck—no shorts, no sandals—
and do plan to shell out the 70F entry fee for the gaming room. If you're
just a slots player, the coin room is open from 10am till 4am, and there's
no entry fee.

arts scene

The art galleries in Cannes are all business. Most of them are part of a
hotel, with longer hours than those other galleries, and everything is
marked with a price tag. As a rule, the work isn't too interesting, and several galleries sell nothing but copies of Renoirs, Picassos, and other big
names. If you want art, make the 20-minute train trip to Nice. A hangout
tip: **Jane's Club** tends to attract the fashion/artsy people at night, and
Studio 13 [see *bar, club, and live music scene,* above, for both] has a little
bar/cafe where the younger artists hold court.

There are festivals throughout the year that spotlight the performing
arts [see *festivals and events,* above]. The **Palais des Festivals** (*Tel
92/986-277; Bus 8 to Palais des Congrès; Ticket office 10am-7pm Mon-Fri)*
is where you should go to find out specifics and buy tickets for theater,
music, or dance. The brochure *Le Mois à Cannes*—pick it up at the
tourist info office [see *need to know,* below]—gives a day-by-day
account of the cultural goings-on.

It's a little disheartening to walk past three or four theaters in the heart
of town and find that they have no movies in English. **Cinéma de Val-
bonne Sophia Antipolis** (*Salle des Fêtes du Village; Tel 93/129-188;
Hours vary)* breaks the rule, showing mainstream films in English about
once a week. Look for the telltale *VO* (original language) mark. Call
ahead for scheduling, or get their flyer from the tourist office [see *need to
know,* below].

gay scene

Cannes is the place to go on the Riviera if you're gay. The tourist info office
[see *need to know,* below] has all kinds of flyers and 'zines on gay living on
the Riviera. Or call Center Gay Associatif (*Tel 93/680-300).*

Le Zanzibar (*85 rue Félix Faure; Tel 93/393-075; Bus 17 to Maréchal
Joffre; 6:30pm-dawn daily; No credit cards),* near the Palais des Festivals,
has a really laid-back cafe atmosphere in the evening, both on the outdoor patio and in the indoor bar area. The music is on, but it's not over-

cannes

BARS/CLUBS ▲

Carling's Pub **4**
Cyber Webstation **12**
Jane's Club **13**
Jimmy'z **10**
Le Scandale **8**
Les Coulisses **14**

Limelight Records **2**
Midnight Blues **3**
Morrison's Irish Pub **16**
Studio 13 **1**
Tantra **15**
Le Zanzibar **7**

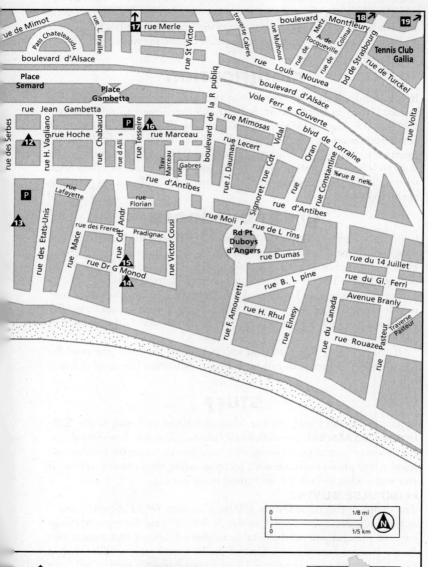

★ Paris

FRANCE

Cannes

whelming—this is the kind of place where you could actually have a conversation. Later in the night it's more bar-like, but there's still no cover, and drinks run 20 to 50F. Zanzi is sort of the "must-go" gay bar in Cannes; it's been around for ever. A few women are on the premises, but this is a mostly male joint.

modification

If you decide to commemorate your trip to Cannes with a brand-new tattoo, Danny at **Black Star Tattoo** *(39 rue Georges Clemenceau; Tel 92/992-055; Bus 8 to Mairie; 10am-7pm Mon-Sat; No credit cards)* will advise you on *tatouage* and cut some skin if you decide to go for it. But be prepared to wait—Danny is a man in demand. His mom hangs out in the shop and chats with customers to the wail of country music in a shop filled with skull & crossbones paraphernalia. Tattoos are 200F and up; piercings are 50 to 400F.

great outdoors

Scan the beachfront for the pink umbrellas of **Plage du Martinez** [see *hanging out*, above] and walk out on their dock to the water sports arena. Here you can choose from water skiing (150F), parachuting (350F), or tubing (200F). They're open for business from 8am to 8pm.

For runners or speed walkers, **La Croisette** [see *hanging out*, above] is wide enough to get in a workout while you take in the ocean view. City streets are not such a good option; they're narrow and fairly crowded at all times of day.

If you're feeling *Top Gun* (you know: You feel the need, the need for speed), bikes and mopeds can be rented at **Alliance** [see *need to know*, below].

stuff

Bypass the cheap stands on rue Maréchal Joffre and stop at the **Saturday Flea Market** *(Across from the Palais des Festivals; 9am-6pm daily)*. It's a mess of booths overflowing with used books, furniture, geodes, and jewelry. For photo buffs, there's a pretty amazing used camera section. If you know what to look for, you could make out big.

▶▶IMPULSE BUYING

The designer gadgets at **Davis** *(50 rue d'Antibes; Tel 93/990-905; Bus 7 to rue des Serbes; 10am-7pm Mon-Sat; V, MC, AE)* are the types of things you can pretend you need. Metal bean-shaped lighters that mimic Elsa Peretti designs are only 50F. One of the best trinkets is a bullet-shaped key chain that unscrews to reveal a tiny plastic vial for storing pills or a pair of earrings.

For perfumes and all sorts of accessories, head for **Reminiscence** *(56 rue d'Antibes; Tel 93/394-076; Bus 7 to rue des Serbes; 10am-7pm Mon-Sat; V, MC)*. Add to your club gear with their modern and funky earrings and rings *(300-400F)*.

▶▶DUDS

Bill Tornade *(Galerie Gray d'Albion; Tel 93/689-891; 9:30am-12:30pm/2:30-7:30pm Mon-Sat; V, MC, AE)* serves up original designs that add a funky flair to modern styles for guys and gals. Men's pants go from casual to dressy to rubberized, for 800 to 1,000F. Embroidered chiffon chemises are a hot pick for women at 395F.

▶▶BOUND

There aren't a whole lotta English bookstores in Cannes, but there is the **Cannes English Bookshop** *(11 rue Bivouac Napoléon; Tel 93/994-008; Bus 8 to Gray d'Albion; 10am-1pm/2-7pm Mon-Sat; No credit cards).* They have posters for museum exhibits on the door and a selection of English titles, from Martin Amis to Jean Genet in translation.

eats

▶▶CHEAP

Sifting through the typical sandwich stands for decent food can be a chore. Thank god for **Paul** *(572 rue Meynadier; Tel 93/381-559; 8am-7:30pm Mon-Sat, 8-1:30pm Sun; No credit cards),* an inconspicuous bread shop that sells tasty sandwiches *(15-20F)* and all sorts of breads. Several doors down on the walking-only rue Meynadier, there's a big fruit market open daily from 9am till 5pm.

    Piazza *(9 Place de l'Hôtel de Ville; Tel 92/986-080; Any bus to Mairie; Noon-2:30pm/7pm-midnight daily; piazza@iname.com; 54-78F per entree; V, MC)* is a pretty big place, with tables clad in—what else—red-and-white-checked vinyl. The pasta is made fresh on the premises, the pizza crusts are perfectly crisp, and the *spaghetti à la Fellini*, with tomatoes, olive oil, pimientos, and basil, is extra tasty.

▶▶DO-ABLE

Even if you're a meat eater, the vegetarian dishes at **Montgard** *(6 rue Maréchal Joffre; Tel 93/399-838; Bus 27 to Maréchal Joffre; Noon-2pm/7:30-10pm Tue-Sat; 118F, 128-178F prix-fixe menus; V, MC)* make it worth a visit. Mustard-colored walls and Provençal furniture provide a cozy little atmosphere, and the veggie-filled ravioli with thyme butter is super.

▶▶SPLURGE

Yes, there's the fancy Palme d'Or and its status-hungry rival restaurants. But who wants to sit in a room full of people with their eyes glued to the door on the off-chance that someone important might walk in? **La Poêle d'Or** *(23 rue des Etats-Unis; Tel 93/397-765; Bus 8 to Gray d'Albion; Noon-2pm/8-10pm Tue-Sun; 135-260F per entree; V, MC, AE)* is a no-nonsense gourmet eatery under the watchful knife of Chef Bernard Leclerc. The prix-fixe meals are a deal at 135F or 245F, and Leclerc changes menu items each month. Call the cuisine "inventive French, with an emphasis on fish."

crashing

▶▶CHEAP

Cannes has two youth hostels that are close to town and curfew-less. The hike down to the beach for either is 10 to 15 minutes—to the train station is maybe 5 minutes. **Le Chalit** *(27 Ave. Marécha Gallieni; Tel/Fax 93/992-211; le-chalit@libertysurf.fr; Bus 4 to Gallieni; Desk hours 8:30am-1pm/5-8:30pm; 85-90F dorm beds; No credit cards)* is the more homey of the two, but they do have an 11am to 5pm lockout. Rooms have a maximum of four people with shared bathrooms, and the price includes a shower. Chalit is in the suburb-ish neighborhood above the train station, which is not the most visually stimulating, but Internet access [see *wired*, below], laundry, and groceries are close by. Ask about discounts on cruises, mopeds, and cars.

Centre International de Séjour et de la Jeunesse *(35 Ave. de Vallauris; Tel/Fax 93/992-679; www.perso.wanadpp.fr/hostelling-cannes; Bus 6V to Sardoux; Desk hours 9am-12pm/5-8pm; 70-80F dorm beds; No credit cards)* is bigger and slightly closer to town, with a nice garden outside for playing cards or whatever, and a living room with a TV if the heat gets unbearable. Rooms sleep four to six people with shared bath facilities, and the friendly staff will help you get oriented.

▶▶**DO-ABLE**

If you like the idea of a cheap hotel in the hip part of town, **Hôtel Chanteclair** *(12 rue Forville; Tel/Fax 93/396-888; Bus 5 to La Ferrage; Desk hours 9am-7pm, closed Nov; 140-170F single w/o shower, 170-230F single w/shower, 200-260F double, 240-330F triple, 280-440F quad, 20F breakfast; No credit cards)* is for you. There are no cockroaches crawling around—at least I didn't see any—and there's a pretty courtyard with orange trees, but all 15 rooms are small and the beds are narrow. Monsieur Déflene is down with travelers' needs: If you're leaving late on the day you check out, he lets you leave your bags in a locker so you can come back and shower, and he has no problem with two people squeezing into a single if they can't afford anything better.

Can't hack carrying that pack? Stay right across from the train station at the quirky **Hôtel du Nord** *(6 rue Jean Jaurès; Tel 93/384-879, Fax 92/992-820; www.cannes-hotels.com; Bus 17 to Gare; Desk hours 7am-1pm; 180-250F single, 270-300F double, 360F triple, 430F quad; No credit cards)*. Rooms are unpredictable in this place; you might find that your bathroom is bigger than the bedroom. Most rooms have TVs, but be prepared to sweat in summer; this baby isn't air-conditioned.

▶▶**SPLURGE**

If you have the means, staying in a quiet villa with its own pool is always nice. **Villa Toboso** *(7 Allée des Oliviers; Tel 93/382-005, Fax 93/680-932; Bus 4 to Pont République; 250-740F double rooms/suites; V, MC, AE)* is a 10-minute walk from town, but so worth it. You won't find a party here—and they won't be too thrilled if you make one—but it's definitely nice to come back to rose-scented sheets and antique furniture after a night on the town. Some of the suites and rooms have kitchenettes and terraces or balconies, and all have cable TV and AC.

To have the fairy-tale Cannes experience, stay right on the water at

down and out in cannes

Technically, it won't cost anything to take a peek inside the **Casino Croisette** [see *casinos*, above] slots room. If you don't trust your immunity to gambling fever, get some 2F chips and try your luck at slots or video poker.

Walk along **La Croisette** [see *hanging out*, above] and try not to be envious of the luxury clientele in their luxury hotels. If it gets too hot, duck into one of said establishments and amble around their shopping arcade.

For more of an exercise, head up **rue Montfleury**, northeast of the **Gare SNCF**. You'll be on tree-lined streets that wind uphill and make you think Cannes might not be a bad place to own a house—the villas in this neighborhood will make you drool. What could be more cathartic when you're broke?

Hôtel Bleu Rivage (*61 Blvd. de la Croisette; Tel 93/942-425, Fax 93/437-492; Bus 8 to Malmaison; www.cannes-hotels.com; 500-1,000F double; V, MC, AE*), the only oceanfront hotel whose per-night prices are relatively bearable. You'll pay more to get an ocean view, but every cool, whitewashed room has a breezy feel, with AC, TV, and phone.

need to know

Currency Exchange Office Provençal (*17 Ave. Maréchal Foch; Tel 93/393-437; 8am-7pm daily*) will exchange your money without charging a rip-off fee.

Tourist Information Two offices: one at the **Gare SNCF** train station (*Tel 93/991-977; 9am-noon/2-6pm Mon-Sat*), the other in the lobby of **Palais des Festivals et des Longrés** (*Tel 93/392-453; 9am-6pm Mon-Sat*). In July and August, and during festival time, these offices are open on Sundays, too. You can call the **Centrale de Reservation** line (*Tel 97/065-307*) and have them find a hotel room for you.

Public Transportation The bus depot is at **Place de l'Hôtel de Ville** (*Tel 93/391-871*), and tickets for local buses are 7.50F.

Bike/Moped Rental Alliance (*19 rue des Frères Pradignac; Tel 93/386-262; Bus 8 to Palais des Congrès; 9am-7pm daily*) has bikes for 80F per day, mopeds for 250F per day, and cell phones for 99F per day.

Health and Emergency Police emergency: 7; medical emergency: 15. **L'Hôpital des Broussailles** is located at (*13 Ave. des Broussailles; Tel 93/697-000*).

Pharmacies AS Cannes (*9 rue Louis Braille; Tel 93/393-585; 8:30am-12:30pm/2:30-7:30pm Mon-Sat, closed Sun*) is open during regular

wired in cannes

The dark, subterranean **Cybercafe Webstation** *(26 rue Hoche; Tel 93/687-237; 10-12:30am daily; 45F per hour; No credit cards)* looks like something out of *Blade Runner*. A mixed scene of socialites, game warriors, and expats crowd into this swank little spot to drink beer, nosh on tapas and crudités, and connect with the netherworld.

www.cannes-on-line.com has everything on the city, plus links to other related sites.

pharmacy hours. On Sundays or after 7:30pm, call the main pharmacy hot line at *(Tel 93/683-333)*.

Telephone Country code: *33*; city code: *4*. For local calls buy a phone card at the post office. **AT&T:** *00-99-0011*; **MCI:** *0/800/99-00-19*; **Sprint:** *0/800/99-00-87*.

Airports The **Nice Airport** *(Tel 93/213-030)* is only 20 minutes to the northeast and is serviced by a bus that runs every 40 minutes *(48.50F)*. Or take a cab for about 350F.

Airlines Air France *(Tel 93/393-914 or 02/802-802)*.

Trains Most people reach Cannes by train. Most hotels are walkable from the station, but if you have a lot of baggage, take the bus for 9F or a cab for 30 to 50F. Nice is about 20 minutes away and trains leave hourly; they stop running at midnight. Call *(36/353-535)* for rail information or stop by the main station, **Gare SNCF**, from 9am to 6pm.

Bus Lines Out of the City For cities east of Cannes (Nice, Monaco, etc.), buses leave from **Gare SNCF**. For points north or west, you'll need to go to **Gare Routière**.

Laundry Laverie Club *(36 rue Georges Clemenceau; Tel 93/380-668; Bus 8 to Palais des Congrès; 8:30am-6:30pm Mon-Fri, 8:30am-12:30pm Sat)*, is near Le Suquet. Drop-off is 70F per load and self-service is 40F per load.

CINQUE TERRE

So, you've been burning it at both ends for awhile, and you've taken in more than you can possibly process. It's time for a little *vacation* from your way-too-active vacation. The Cinque Terre, a string of five small towns on the Italian coast, is the place to head. Cinque Terre is nothing like its French Riviera counterparts; it's all about simple pleasures: kicking back, leisurely dividing your time between sunning, hiking, tasting the local wines, and marveling at awesome cliffside views. It's all about *relaxing*. A typical day might be dragging yourself out of bed for a frothy cappuccino (Italians aren't big into the breakfast meal), heading to the beach or a rock in the sun to work on the tan, hiking some portion of the spectacular trail that runs between all five towns, and settling in to taste some of the famous Cinque Terre Sciacchetra at the local *enoteca* (wine bar) of whatever town you end up in. Gianluigi's **Cantina de di Sassarini** [see *bar scene* in *monterosso*, below] is the best—the guy's motto is "to taste is free," and he sticks to his word. Be careful not to "taste" too much if you're going hiking later on....

Cinque Terre is actually five tiny fishing villages: **Monterosso**, **Vernazza**, **Corniglia**, **Manarola**, and **Riomaggiore**, from north to south. Multicolored buildings like washed-out children's blocks improbably manage to snuggle into the steep, rocky cliffs, giving the towns a storybook look. Vernazza especially seems to sidestep gravity—the town literally hangs from a cliff. The beaches are a big draw, of course, but don't expect calm little waves lapping at a smooth, sandy shore. It's rocky, and jumping off the rocks will put you in deep water that can be dangerous

FIVE THINGS TO TALK TO A LOCAL ABOUT

1. **Wine:** These guys know their stuff. When a family has been in the business this long, they can talk vino all night long.

2. **Business:** People live and breathe their businesses. They are integral to life here, and families are always in business together.

3. **Tourism:** Locals are very interested to hear your thoughts on their homeland. There is concern about tourism dropping off after the enormous boom of the past decade. Chances are, you'll think it's plenty crowded and in need of some downsizing.

4. **Satellite TV:** The mayor of Riomaggiore has given his people a link to the outside world via cable TV, and the other Cinqueans are jealous...kinda. There's a bit of a struggle between their love of tradition and their desire to get 60 channels.

5. *Limoncina*: Everyone has a home recipe for this tangy, fermented lemon liqueur. See if you can finagle one out of someone.

if seas are rough. If water is crashing against the rocks with astounding ferocity, diving into the drink may not be the best idea.

Four of the towns have their own harbors, where local fishermen dock their boats and hang their nets out to dry. The guy trekking toward the restaurant with his bucket of fish around 4pm is in all likelihood carrying your dinner. Vino is a big deal in these parts, and many of the locals have vineyards in the hills that turn out the region's white dessert wine known as Sciacchetra. Definitely try it, even if you're more of a red wine fan, but watch out: Sciacchetra is 18 percent alcohol (versus the 10 to 12 percent of normal wines).

In recent years tourism has usurped wine and fish as the main moneymaker of Cinque. The party is on (albeit in a tourist-centric way), and you'll have no problem finding one if you need to. Each town has a centrally located bar that also functions as its information center. These are tiny one-street towns (with the exception of Monterosso), so whether it's grabbing some local wine and making your own beach party in Vernazza, or heading to the happenin' **Bar Centrale** [see *bar scene* in *riomaggiore*, below] in Riomaggiore, you'll do fine. If taking a well-earned break from the party life is on the agenda, avoid Monterosso and Vernazza in favor of the more low-key towns. Or better yet, travel to Cinque Terre when the Italians do: in April and September, when it's calmer. Cinque Terre gets packed in the summer, so take a room wherever you can get one, and don't freak out if it's not in the town you wanted—the towns are so close together it's easy to visit all five in one day. If this part of the world is on your must-see list, save yourself the finding-a-room scramble and book ahead.

The ticket to moving through—or to—Cinque Terre is the "milk run" train (it doesn't actually carry the moo juice anymore) that runs constantly from 5am till 1am. The name is a lot cuter than the train itself, which is a slow double-decker deal. Jump on the milk run in Genoa if you're coming from northern parts, or in La Spezia from the south. Schedules are posted at the station and at many local businesses—just make sure that the train you're taking stops in all five villages. Tickets are cheap, L1,800, so there's no point in wasting a punch on the Eurail Pass. Train stations in Vernazza, Corniglia, and Manarola are hardly ever staffed, so buy your ticket at the nearest newsstand or tobacco shop. It's rare that you'll even see a conductor on the trains, so tickets are essentially on the honor system. There is boat service between the four towns, but it's probably not worth the price, unless you're just dying to get on a nondescript yacht-like boat. One-way fares are from L8,000 to L15,000, and the boats run only from 10am to 5pm. Schedules can be picked up at the harbor of each town.

Walking between towns is another option [see *hiking*, below]. The trail that connects all five towns is difficult in parts, but none of the towns is more than an hour-and-a-half hike apart, plus you'll get amazing views, and it's free. The trail snakes along steep cliffs and through woodsy areas that are almost jungle-like in parts. Every 5 to 10 minutes, the greenery clears, and you get a dazzling view of the ocean crashing against the rocks below. Don't let drinking too much the night before keep you from taking a good hike—as a traveler from Miami reminded us, "The trick is to get hammered at night and sweat out the hangover with a morning hike."

Cinque Terre has a mixed crowd of travelers: hard-core backpackers in for a day and zooming out at night, lazy beach bums crashing for a week, wine connoisseurs tingling their palates, and honeymooners fresh from the altar. The local crowd is generally sweet and welcoming, but also generally older. The ideal amount of time in Cinque is probably two to three nights—just enough time to recharge with a calming break from the travel frenzy, and not enough time to get bored.

RULES OF THE GAME

Cinque Terre is so small that no one hassles you about drinking on the beach or on the street, and even if you throw up on the street they're likely to laugh it off (still, it's always preferable *not* to have to throw up on the street). Drug use seems nonexistent; what goes on behind closed doors doesn't seem to draw much attention.

MONTEROSSO

When you step off the train at Monterosso, you'll be standing on a strip of road with hotels, restaurants, and cafes that face the water. Immediately to your right is a pharmacy, and immediately to your left are an ATM and a wall with hotel and temporary residential listings. This is not the town center, however: Walking east, you'll see a tunnel with rail tracks on top. Don't bother craning your neck to see the tracks—you can't see them. Just pass through the tunnel to enter the heart of town—10 minutes or so from the train station. The largest of the five towns, Monterosso has the most amenities: sandy umbrella-ed beaches, boat rentals, real hotels rather than rooms for rent, and more than one nightspot to choose from. It tends to attract a mix of people, from vacationing Italians to American college kids. Locals are really friendly, and it's sort of a town custom to help out hard-up travelers with nowhere to crash. If you find yourself homeless, head to **Il Casello** [see *bar scene*, below] and appeal to Signore Bacco. He'll hook you up and probably offer you a drink. Monterosso gets a bad rap for being touristy and not quaint enough, but don't count it out. It definitely has the best beaches, and it's not so far gone that a McDonald's or anything of that ilk has turned up on a street corner.

bar scene

Each of the Cinque Terre towns has a multi-purpose bar that is also your link to the town. In Monterosso, **Il Casello** (*on the hill just past Piazza Garibaldi; Tel 0187/818-330; Noon-2am daily July, Aug, closed Tue rest of the year; No credit cards*) is the place to go whether you're desperate for a room or dreaming about a mug of creamy, rich "killer" draught (L4,000). Signore Bacco is the Sam Malone of Casello. As the Paul Simon tunes play, he immediately lets you know that drinks are L500 cheaper if you sit in the century-old bar interior rather than at the tables outside (although the outside ones overlook the ocean). Bacco has been known to help out room-less travelers by magically producing lodging from his myriad contacts. He tells every traveler the same thing: Make friends with the locals and go out with them! And he's right—you'll get cheaper meals and have more fun. (It's par for the course that the person who lets you a room becomes your local buddy while you're here.) Casello is the home of the *bazara*, a L6,000 adventure of liqueur and fruit juices that is Bacco's secret weapon. Casello is not about dancing on the tables singing "I Will Survive"—the atmosphere is laid-back and casual, with a generally under-35 crowd at night. Il Casello also offers cheap and fast Internet access *(L3,000 for 15 min)*.

Down the hill from Il Casello, in the center of town, is the much less chill **Il Paradiso** (*13 Via Roma; Tel 0187/817-164; 8am-2am daily; V, MC*). The walls are plastered with posters of everyone from Fishbone to the Ramones, and Cake is playing on the stereo. Paradiso has a younger crowd at night, lots of college kids doing the European adventure. The

WINE

Not *all* of Italy swears by red wine; in Cinque Terre they don't even make it. *Enotecas* do carry reds from other regions of Italy—including the rather disturbing Sieg Heil, with its picture of Hitler on the front—but if you want authentic local wine, stick to whites. Vermentina is an unusual spicy white, and sweet Sciacchetra is the dessert wine with a whopping 18 percent alcohol content. Yet another wine unique to the region is Chachetrá, a smooth sweet dessert wine locally made all along the coast. Cinque also produces lots of grappa and *limoncina*. Grappa is made from the skin of grapes that have been fermented beyond your wildest dreams. Olive- and lemon-flavored grappas are a bit smoother than the straight version, which leaves you in a sweat after a few shots. *Limoncina*, a lemon liqueur that is a result of Cinque's booming lemon-tree industry, is also shot-able, but mixing it into drinks and soda works well too. It ranges in taste from sickly candy-like lemon to the fresh stuff, so ask for a taste before you commit to a bottle. Most of the *enotecas* let you taste any of their products before you buy.

In Monterosso, pass by **Cantina di Sassarini** [see *bar scene*, below], run by Gianluigi, who is as well-versed in the English language as he is in wine. In Manarola, check out **Bramante** *(186 Via Disclovolo; Tel 0187/920-442; 9am-midnight daily, closed Thur; V, MC)*, where twentysomething Gabriel gives wine virgins tastes of his elixir.

bar is filled with tables and chairs, making it a communal party. Try one of the musical sandwiches (L6,500-8,000) like: Red Hot Chili Peppers (Parma ham and Brie cheese), Limp Bizkit (pickled veggies and cheese), Beastie Boys (raw ham and veggies), and wash it down with a cold one. This is definitely a draught beer joint: Moretti, Baffo d'oro, Labatts Extra, and La Rosa are on tap at L4,000 for a small, L12,000 for a large. If the beer and sandwiches leave you in need of a refill for your wallet, there is an ATM (or *bancomat*, in common parlance) 2 minutes up the street from the Paradiso.

Enotecas are everywhere in Cinque, but there's only one that has "To Taste Is Free" written on the door: **Cantina di Sassarini** *(7 Via Roma; Tel 0187/817-828; 10am-midnight daily; V, MC, AE)*, run by the wonderful Gianluigi. Try to hit this place during the day when he's not too busy, and he'll taste you through the wines and grappas of the area, throwing in a smattering of history about Cinque Terre's grapes and a shot of *limoncina* [see *wine*, above] to finish you off. You'll learn that the

hiking

Cinque Terre is famous for the hiking trail that connects all five towns. It's a narrow dirt trail and nothing more, so wear good shoes and don't plan to hold hands while you walk.

The annoyance about hiking in Cinque is the families and groups who insist upon walking in a little line like ducks. They walk together, they stop together, and there's never room to pass. Meditation might be a good idea in these cases: Picture yourself on a deserted backwoods trail and try to block out the explanations of local flora and fauna.

For hardcore hiking, buy a trail map at any of the newsstands for L7,000. It includes long hikes to Levanto and La Spezia, as well as the higher and more difficult hikes around Cinque Terre. Even if hiking is not your thing, the views from atop Cinque Terre's hills are worth the sweat. It's a humbling site to see monstrous waves crash against a town's breakwater while the sun sets behind the adjacent hills.

This is a breakdown of the main Cinque Terre trail, which runs roughly north-ish. All the hikes are do-able for someone who exercises regularly. Many people hike the whole damn thing, which takes about four and a half hours. There are signs along the paths so you won't get lost. Don't hike this in the rain—these trails are literally dirt on cliffs. Also, it's not good form to camp at the picnic sites along the way. Above all, bring food and water!

Monterosso to Vernazza: This one takes you about one and a half

reason the local Sciacchetra is 18 percent alcohol is a result of its 10 kilos of grapes per bottle ratio instead of the usual 1 kilo per bottle. And did you know that red wine should breathe one hour for every year that has passed since its birth? These and many other tips come courtesy of Gianluigi himself.

beaches

Monterosso's main public beach, located right below the train station, is packed with young inebriated American travelers checking each other out (picture spring break in Fort Lauderdale). If that's not your scene, walk north for about 5 minutes until you come upon a parking lot on your left. Just past the lot, you'll see the "Il Gigante" statue carved into a rock ledge. In front of that is a small public beach with clear water for snorkeling and less of a crowd. Families tend to migrate here, but the swimming is good, and you won't have to listen to drunken tales of glory for hours on end.

There are also private beaches with changing rooms in front of the train station and on the other side of the harbor. This is the same sand as the public beach, but it's sectioned off for the special people. Plots of

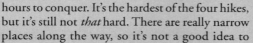

hours to conquer. It's the hardest of the four hikes, but it's still not *that* hard. There are really narrow places along the way, so it's not a good idea to walk with a big pack. Glimpses of the ocean can be had and are spectacular from these heights, but much of your time is spent in the trees.

Vernazza to Corniglia: You'll still walk for about one and a half hours, but the trail is not as steep or as narrow as the first. Lots of people like to grab a pre-hike drink at **The Blue Marlin** [see *bar scene* in *vernazza*, below]. This hike affords more ocean views, but at a slightly lower vantage point than the first.

Corniglia to Manarola: This 45-minute journey is more of a walk than a hike, and the path is actually wide enough to let you walk beside someone and chat. It's pretty level, so you won't be stopping to catch your breath, and there isn't much jungle-like tree and shrub growth, so you get to gaze at the rock cliffs and ocean spray.

Manarola to Riomaggiore: Hike? Please. This thing will take you 20 minutes. The **Via dell Amore** (lovers' lane) is the name for this stretch of the trail, as the smooching couples who come here illustrate. There are benches and gardens along the way, and even a little snack bar. The tunnel leading into Manarola is pleasantly grafittied with underwater scenes and ocean views.

sand are rented for L5,000 per person, which includes use of the shower and toilet facilities. Throw in an umbrella and two chaises, and the price is L18,000. The private beaches also rent boats; a paddleboat goes for L15,000 an hour. If the water isn't rough, you can paddle out and find a cove to hide in.

EATS

▶▶CHEAP

It's difficult to sit down in a restaurant and eat cheap in any part of Cinque Terre. One exception to this rule is **Midi Bar** *(Across Bar Centrale at Piazza Garibaldi; Tel 0187/817-003; 7am-midnight; No credit cards).* This backpackers' hangout has outdoor tables where you can grab a quick snack or sit for hours and read a book. Pizza is L2,000, focaccia is L1,000, and gelato ranges from L2,000 to L6,000, depending on size.

Il Casello and **Il Paradiso** [see *bar scene*, above, for both] also have reasonably priced food. Castello's focaccia sandwiches are really good and cheap (L5,000). Paradiso has coffee and snacks for breakfast from L1,000. If you want groceries for a beach picnic, **Super Market-Europio** *(Just* *up the street from Il Paradiso; Via Roma 61)* has a nifty selection of cheap food-stuffs.

▶▶**SPLURGE**

Expensive does not necessarily mean good. The **Ristorante Belvedere** *(38 Piazza Garibaldi; Tel 0187/817-033; Noon-2pm/7-10pm; L7,000-26,000 per entree; V, MC, AE)* is a favorite of locals (Bacco from Casello recommends it), but the food is just okay, not spectacular. It's the seafood that is worth coming for—their specialty is the *Amphora*, filled with steamed seafood for two for L75,000. Santina is the chef and owner, and her English-speaking son Frederico greets guests. The interior is kinda boring, so sit outdoors if possible. Try the house wine at L6,000 a liter and grab dessert somewhere else.

crashing

Monterosso is the place to stay if you want a real hotel room rather than a room-for-rent (read: no staff catering to your whims) or apartment. Of course, you'd better be prepared to pay real hotel prices; rooms here are way more expensive than in the other towns.

▶▶**DO-ABLE**

Just to the south of the train station is the one-star **Pension Agavi** *(30 Lungomare Fegina; 0187/817-171, Fax 0187/818-264; Desk open 9am-8pm and phone after; L80,000 single, L130,000 double; No credit cards).* Situated right on the beach promenade, it's convenient and much cheaper than the other waterfront hotels. Four people can probably pack into one of the doubles without notice—play it by ear. Rooms are plain, and there's no air-conditioning, but each has its own private bath, fridge, and phone.

▶▶**SPLURGE**

Hotel Villa Steno *(109 Via Roma; Tel 0187/817-028, Fax 0187/817-056; Desk open 7am-9pm; www.pasini.com, steno@ pasini.com; L130,000 single, L200,000 double, L240,000 triple, L260,000 quad; V, MC, AE)* is a family-run affair, with English-speaking Matteo at the helm. There is an incredibly fragrant lotus-like smell to the hotel. Fourteen rooms have balconies with ocean view, and a real breakfast of more than just bread and jam is included: You'll get hard-boiled eggs, croissants, muesli, and fruit. All rooms have AC and TVs, and the service is super-friendly, making Steno's only drawback the 10-minute uphill hike from the station.

Midway down the hill from Steno is the partially hidden **La Colonnina** *(6 Via Zuecca; Tel 0187/817-439, Fax 0187/817-778; Desk open 8am-10:30pm; L140,000 double, L190,000 triple, L225,000 quad; No credit cards).* Its shaded outdoor garden and rooftop sundeck are always nice, as are the small terraces on each floor. The room decor is a bit cheesy (vinyl surfaces, comforters, brass-edged nightstands), but chances are, you won't be in the room much, so who really cares? Each room has a satellite TV and a fridge but, alas, no AC. The breakfast buffet isn't worth the L15,000 per person unless you're really pressed for time.

Vernazza

Vernazza cannot support the numbers of tourists it gets. Because other guidebooks have touted it as their favorite, it is filled with Americans— you hardly feel like you're in Italy. Unlike Monterosso or Riomaggiore, Vernazza draws more middle-aged and older folks than wild youth. The Rick Steves tour groups, the kings of the package-deal trips, descend upon Vernazza all summer long, and you're sure to notice the clusters of 20 to 30 West Coasters who take over local establishments upon arrival. It's obnoxious, really—a group that large just dominates a town this small. If you see them at a restaurant, don't bother going in; service is sure to take forever. In terms of daylight activities, the beach at the breakwater is tiny, so you might just want to hike or train it to Monterosso for swimming. Most people sun themselves on the rocks near Vernazza's harbor; swimming is not allowed off the docks. Vernazza by night revolves around the only nightspot worth going to, **The Blue Marlin**.

bar and live music scene

In this town, **The Blue Marlin** *(43 Via Roma; Tel 0187/821-149; 6:30am-midnight, daily July, Aug, closed Thur rest of the year; bmarlin@tin.it; No credit cards)* is where it's at. Run by the boisterous Massimo and his partner Franco, this place has everything you'll need during a stay in Vernazza. Everyone shows up here at some point, and people come dressed casually, some in bathing suits. There's even Internet access (L300 per minute), but be prepared to wait a bit for the lone computer. There's live music playing nightly and plenty of drinking going on. Draught beers are L3,000 to L6,000 and cocktails are L7,000. Massimo helps people find rooms, so if you're in need, go straight to the Marlin. They also own the self-service laundry *(8am-10pm, L5,000/load)* next door.

eats

▶▶CHEAP

Once again, welcome to **The Blue Marlin** [see *bar and live music scene*, above]. Breakfast tarts and brioche go for L6,000, cappuccinos for L2,500. Massimo did an impromptu poll, and everyone agreed that the cappuccinos were cheaper and better here than at other places. For lunch try the tasty Caprese salad with tomatoes and mozzarella (L3,000) or any of the sandwiches (L5,000).

▶▶SPLURGE

All of the harbor restaurants in Vernazza are gonna set you back. The best is **Gambero Rosso** *(7 Piazza Marconi; Tel 0187/812-265; Noon-3pm/7-9:30pm daily, closed Mon; L12,000-38,000 per entree; V, MC, AE)*, which has an outdoor seating area right on the square, with white linen tablecloths, napkin rings, the whole shebang. There are five-course prix-fixe menus for L55,000 and L80,000. The *pansotti*, a tube-shaped pasta made

cinque terre

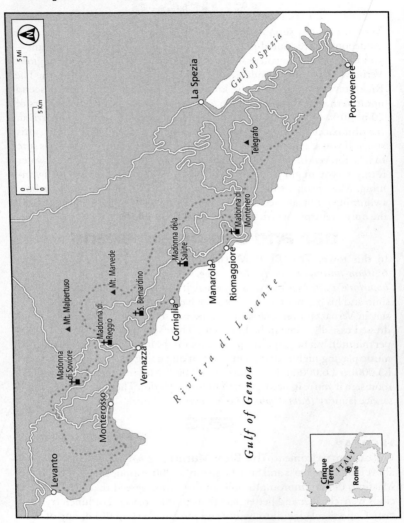

with cocoa (don't worry, it doesn't taste like chocolate) and filled with ricotta and pesto, is a house specialty. Reservations are a good idea in summer; walking in wearing your bathing suit ain't.

crashing

▶▶CHEAP
If the idea of sharing a bathroom doesn't faze you, **Albergo Barbara**

(30 Piazza Marconi, 4th floor; Tel/Fax 0187/812-398; Office open 9am-9pm; L70,000-90,000 doubles; No credit cards), on the main square, has nine decent rooms with three bathrooms between them. The rooms range in price depending on size and view, and none have AC. If you have the means, request one of the big doubles with an ocean view. Giuseppe and Patricia both speak English and like to make reservations by phone.

▶▶**DO-ABLE**

A more traditional atmosphere can be had at **Pension Sorriso** *(4 Via Gavino; Tel 0187/812-224; Desk open 8am-11pm; L90,000 single, L150,000-180,000 double; V, MC)*. Sorriso is a "real" pension, which means that the price includes breakfast and dinner. The food was described as "okay" by a visitor; still, it *is* homemade Italian fare. Try to arrive before 6pm, otherwise you're paying for a dinner you don't eat. The rooms (some with private bathroom, some with shared) are simple and spotless; none have AC, but four have balconies. A bar downstairs with drinks and ice cream is open until 11pm.

corniglia

Corniglia is the least visited of the five towns, probably because it sits on a hill rather than on the water. It's quiet except at the nudie beach, **Guvano** [see *beaches*, below], and has few restaurants, but exceptional wine. The walk to town from the train station is all uphill, and most people call Corniglia the "mountain village." You also don't see anyone hanging out on the streets here—it's a fairly reclusive place. Artsy types like the solitude here. Rounding the corners of buildings, you're bound to run into someone with watercolor paints and sketchbook having a go at re-creating the hilltops.

bar scene

Corniglia isn't the liveliest town in Cinque Terre, but there are still a few revelers about. The homey **Bar Nunzio** *(154 Via Fieschi; Tel 0187/812-138; 7am-midnight daily; No credit cards)* is *the* nightspot in town. There's a nice boar's head on the wall and trophies over the doorway, they play jazz and pop, and the bartenders are quite friendly to the young ladies. Try the strange orange cocktail *Aurora*...but don't expect to find out exactly what's in it. **Bar Matteo** [see *eats*, below] is right across the street.

beaches

To get to the nude beach, **Guvano** *(L5,000 admission)*, start at the Corniglia train station. Follow signs pointing to a tunnel, pass through it, and you'll come to the entrance. This beach has suited bathers as well, so you won't feel like an idiot if you don't strip. But there are plenty of naked, pierced (nipples and elsewhere) Europeans to stare at. The beach is far from white and sandy, so you'll want to search out the flattest rock to lie

ragazzo meets ragazza

Cinque is an easy place to meet people. When everyone is on the same beach by day and in the same bar by night, you're bound to get familiar. Riomaggiore's **Bar Centrale** [see *bar scene* in *riomaggiore*, above] is the perfect pickup spot. You don't even have to be obvious about it—conversations overlap on the wooden deck outside, and there's always room for one more at a game of cards. Nabbing an Italian love thang in these parts is not likely to happen, as there just aren't a whole lot of local young people around. If you get desperate for some lovin', hang out at the entrance to Via dell Amore [see *hiking*, above] and wait for someone to ask you to pose with them for a smooching picture.

upon. If you're pressed for time and need some George Hamilton to go, the public beach directly below the train station may or may not be there, depending on the tide. It's a narrow strip of sand, but usually not crowded, and at least there's a snack bar.

EATS

▶▶CHEAP
For snacks and a cheap lunch, check out **Bar Matteo** (*151 Via Fieschi; No phone; 7:30am-12:30am daily; L4,000-5,000 sandwiches; No credit cards*). The *panzerotto* (*L4,000*), basically a pita pocket filled with tomato and cheese, is good, and the *café fredo* (iced coffee) (*L2,500*) is exceptionally good. There's outdoor table service, but indoors is self-service. At night, this turns into a bar with shots for L3,000 to L4,000.

▶▶SPLURGE
The **Restaurant Cecio,** part of **Pensione Cecio** [see *crashing*, below], is by far the best restaurant in town. Entrees run L15,000 to L25,000, and dinner is served from 7pm (closed Wed). An outdoor garden has tables that overlook the ocean, but the restaurant interior, with exposed rock walls and log furniture, is equally impressive. The house wine is L9,000 for a half liter, and the *risotto al Cecio*, cooked in a terra cotta pot with seafood and local herbs, is the house specialty.

crashing

At almost every doorway there's a sign for *camere*—Italian for "rooms"— but if you're the kind who prefers to make reservations in advance, try **Pensione Cecio** (*Via Serra; Tel/Fax 0187/812-138; Ask about rooms in the restaurant 9am-11pm; L90,000 double; No credit cards*). The family-run Cecio is a cut above most places in Cinque Terre. Just off the town's main square, Cecio has a pension upstairs from its very solid restaurant. Rooms are whitewashed and have simple, classy furnishings and views of the water, each with its own bathroom. Included in the price is breakfast in the **Restaurant Cecio**, with a nice selection of pastries, breads, and yogurt.

manarola

Manarola is the most spread-out of the Cinque Terre villages—it has no real "center." The town is essentially an uphill road dotted with businesses and plenty of restaurants that cater to the German and Scandinavian families who make it their vacation base. The vibe can be semi-snotty in Manarola; if one of the towns were to be called "upscale," this would be the one. Dinners are expensive, and you won't find too many young people here. Keeping with the family vibe, every year at Christmas the town constructs a manger on the western slope of a hill in a vineyard adjacent to the town. The best parts of Manarola are its youth hostel and **Cantina da Zio Bramante** [see *bar scene*, below]. The nightlife is so-so—more lively than Corniglia, less lively than Monterosso and Vernazza. Finally, there's no beach at Manarola's port, so walk to Riomaggiore [see below] or train it to Monterosso [see above] if you crave sand.

bar scene

If hanging out and listening to young locals sing the "Manarola Blues" sounds like a jammin' night out, make a beeline for **Cantina da Zio Bramante** *(186 Via Disclovolo; Tel 0187/920-442; 9am-midnight daily, closed Thur; V, MC)*. Twenty-something Gabriel—not the guy from **Toretta** [see *crashing*, below]—always has a guitar on hand and loves to make up impromptu tunes to entertain his customers. "Manarola Blues" is one of his many creative efforts, and only a true curmudgeon would find his home-grown lyrics less than charming. Also charming is his willingness to let you sample his wine. In fact, if you supply the bottle, he'll fill it up with his own white for L5,000. This is the oldest cantina in Cinque Terre, so there is tradition to be had along with good music and fine wine. And Gabriel's prices are lower than the norm for bottles to go.

Across the street, the generic-as-it-sounds **Bar Gelateria** *(181 Via Disclovolo; No phone; 8am-midnight daily, closed Sun Sept-June; No credit cards)* serves up big draughts for L5,000 and a shot of whisky for L3,000. There's also an outdoor deck where locals and travelers hang out at night with picnic tables where you can plop down and make new friends.

EATS

▶▶**CHEAP**

Hankering for a hot dog? **Bar Gelateria** [see *bar scene*, above] serves up those greasy little tastes of home *(L5,000)*, along with grilled panini sandwiches filled with veggies or meat *(L4,000 to L7,000)* and splendid homemade gelato (try the coconut).

▶▶SPLURGE

Ristorante Aristide *(290 Via Disclovolo; Tel 0187/920-000; Restaurant open noon-2pm/7-10pm, snack bar open 8am-8pm; L15,000-35,000 per entree; V, MC)* is not the friendliest place, but locals love it. It has outdoor dining overlooking the water as well as an indoor restaurant with a snack bar downstairs. It's the "best restaurant in town," so to speak, so it's packed most nights in the summer. The food is gourmet-ish and expensive, and the seafood dishes—their specialty—are especially excellent.

crashing

▶▶CHEAP

Manarola has a bona fide youth hostel atop town across from the church, **Ostello Cinque Terre** *(21 Via B. Riccobaldi; Tel 0187/920-215, Fax 0187/920-218; Desk open 7am-1pm/5pm-1am; ostello@cdh.it, www.cinqueterre.net/ostello; L25,000/bed, L100,000 private quad; V, MC, AE).* There's no hanky-panky in the single-sex rooms, which hold four to six people with shared bath. The private rooms can sleep up to four and are L100,000 flat, no matter how many people. Conveniences abound: a bread, jam, and coffee breakfast for L5,000, Internet access for L4,000 per 15 minutes, and laundry for L11,000 per load. The rooms are your typical bunk-bed hostel types, but the roof terrace has a great view. The maximum reservation is three nights, and there's a 1am curfew.

▶▶DO-ABLE

Across from the youth hostel is a family-run bed-and-breakfast that is definitely worth checking out. **La Toretta** *(14 Vico Volto; Tel/Fax 0187/920-327; Desk open 8am-11pm; L70,000 double, L90,000 apartment, L150,000 large apartment for 4; toretta@cdh.it; No credit cards)* is managed by the young architect Gabriel Baldini, who designed many of the rooms. He also personally picks up guests from the train station or a nearby airport if you arrange it in advance. Toretta's rooms have ocean views, TVs, terraces, and antique-looking furniture. The apartments are a good deal, since they have a kitchen and a sitting room with a fold-out. Breakfast is L8,000 per person. There are only seven rooms, so be sure to reserve in advance.

rio maggiore

Bar Centrale [see *bar scene*, below] is an ongoing party from morning to night, the pebble beach is big enough so that you're not inhaling the suntan lotion from the sunbather next to you, *and* this is the home of Cinque Terre's scuba club. The mayor took it upon himself to cable the town to a hilltop satellite, providing residents with cable TV and views from the bizarre "spy cam" that sporadically zooms in on various parts of the town! Smaller than Monterosso, but with much more character, Rio is happy to let students take over. The buildings along the town road stay in families for generations, so any of the rooms that you stay in here are lovingly cared for and individually decorated.

bar scene

There is but one bar in town, the infamous **Bar Centrale** *(144 Via Colombo; Tel 0187/920-208; 7:30am-1am daily; barcentr@tin.it; No credit cards)*. Ivo and Alberto run this place with an iron fist. The cafe interior is where you'll place your order, but all drinking and hanging out is done on the wooden deck outside. One of the duo is always around to joke with strangers and serve up the L20,000 pitchers of beer that are guzzled down at night. On the patio outside there's drinking, late-night card games, and easy fun. They have been known, however, to blast the *Pulp Fiction* CD all night long. Internet access costs L350 per minute, and be gentle—Ivo is very protective of his PC.

beach

It's not sandy, but the sun, rocks, and pebbles grow on you. Wear shoes and walk down Via Colombo until the staircase takes you into a tunnel that goes to the harbor. The beach is around the rock to the left. In that tunnel you'll pass the **Cinque Terre Diving Center** *(Tel 0339/543-17-00; By appointment; info@acquario.ge.it; No credit cards)*, which will most likely be closed. To arrange a dive or snorkel trip, call the center's English hot line. Dives are L80,000 for students and L100,000 if school is a memory. The price includes all equipment, and you have to be scuba-certified. They may allow a shallow introductory dive without certification if it's not a full trip. Snorkeling gear is L20,000 per day. Area diving is actually good, because all of Cinque Terre's waters are protected marine land. You'll see colorful fishies and gorgeous reefs with anemones and sea sponges.

eats

Unless absolute laziness has set in, there's no reason to eat out in Riomaggiore. It's easy to pick up food from any of the five street markets and whip up an Italian feast in the kitchen. If you must have your food made for you, sandwiches are the best and cheapest option from these markets, at L2,000 for focaccia with prosciutto and cheese.

▶▶**DO-ABLE**

Dau Cila *(84 Via Colombo; Tel 0187/760-032; 8am-12:30am; L5,000 breakfast; V, MC, AE)* is a cutesy ground-level cafe with tooled iron chairs and Formica tables. This little place can help you fend off the urge for a real breakfast with its killer buffet—complete with muesli, yogurt, croissants, and the infamous Nutella (L1,500 per item). Fresh-squeezed OJ pressed right before your eyes is only L3,000, and at night they serve wine for only L3,000 a glass.

▶▶**SPLURGE**

Locals describe this waterfront eatery as chichi, but **La Lanterna** *(Marina; Tel 0187/920-589; 11am-3:30pm/7:30-11pm daily, closed Thur night; L7,000-25,000 per entree; V, MC, AE)* won't necessarily empty out your wallet. Lanterna's small outdoor terrace overlooks the harbor, so it's no surprise that fresh seafood is the house specialty. A blackboard outside lists the day's specials, which might include spaghetti cooked in cuttlefish ink or scampi roasted on a spit. The food is fine to good, but the real draw here is the atmosphere.

crashing

There are no hotels in Riomaggiore, and that's not a bad thing. Instead, locals rent out private "rooms," which are usually apartments with kitchens and living rooms. Try to get here early for a room, but if you come in on the 11pm train, go straight to **Bar Centrale** [see *bar scene*, above], and Ivo will hook you up with a place if it is at all humanly possible. More than a few sleep-deprived travelers have slumped in desperately late at night.

▶▶**DO-ABLE**

For a more traditional approach, e-mail Anna Michielini and stay in one of her flats at **Anna Michielini Rooms** *(143 Via Colombo; Tel/Fax 0187/920-411; No office, call between 8am-10pm; L80,000 double apartment, L160,000 apartment for up to six people; camichie@tin.it; No credit cards)*. Anna's daughter Daniella went to school in London and speaks perfect English, and her husband, Camillo, hooks guests up to the Net for free. The apartments vary in sizes—one is an enormous two-bedroom and another is a studio—but all have homey and simple decorations and come complete with kitchens and cookware (eating out does, in fact, get old).

    Edi Apartments *(111 Via Colombo; Tel/Fax 0187/920-325; Office open 9am-8pm; L80,000 double; edi-vesigna@iol.it; No credit cards)* are run by Edi himself, who presents guests upon arrival with bottles of his home-made *limoncina*. Don't drink it all in one sitting—this ain't lemonade. The apartments vary in size, but all have kitchens and bathrooms.

need to know

Currency Exchange Change your money in Monterosso, the only one of the five towns with **ATMs**. There's one adjacent to the train station, and another on Via Roma near **Il Paradiso** [see *bar scene* in *Monterosso*, above].

Tourist Information The only office that keeps consistent hours is the information office at Monterosso's train station *(Downstairs when you get off the train; Tel 0187/817-204; 10am-noon/3:30-7:30pm daily, closed Sun afternoon)*. The rest of the towns have information offices at their train stations too, but they're rarely open.

Public Transportation The "milk-run" train services all five towns daily from 6am until 1 or 2am [see *intro*, above]. Monterosso has a **taxi service** *(Tel 0335/616-58-42)* running from the train station, but really, you should be able to walk wherever you need to go.

Health and Emergency Medical emergencies: *118*; Police: *112*. Medical Corps on call to go to hospital in La Spezia: *800-973, 817-687, 730-500*.

Pharmacies There is no 24-hour pharmacy, so call the Medical Corps if an emergency pops up. Otherwise, regular pharmacy hours are *8am-1pm/4-7pm*, closed Sat afternoon, Sun: Monterosso *(42 Via Fegina; 817-148)*, Vernazza *(2 Via Roma; 812-396)*, Manarola *(Via Disclovolo; 949-209-30)*, Riomaggiore *(Via Colombo; 122-920-160)*.

Telephone Country code: *39*; local dialing code: *0187*.

Trains La Spezia *(714-735)* is the nearest major station. From **La Spezia**, you can reach any of the Cinque Terre towns on the **milk train**.

athens

There should be a sign posted at Athens's city limits: "PLEASE EXCUSE OUR APPEARANCE—WE'RE REMODELING!" Flying in, the city resembles a vast, gray condominium complex of drab tenements elbowing one another for precious limited space. Some of the crummier sections of town look like Beirut circa 1982. This is not a case of so-ugly-it's-cute, either. Bluntly, Athens can be uglier than Medusa on a bad hair day. Of its isolated areas of beauty, and there are many, the majority are over 2,000 years old. Architecturally, it's been downhill since the Age of Pericles.

Now that you've been warned, here's the good news: Athens is most certainly a worthwhile place to visit. Like so much compost in a thriving garden, a healthy dose of urban decay can work wonders for a culture—just look at the bygone downtown scene in Manhattan. Athens is no exception. Come for the **Acropolis**, stay for the raves. The city's grunginess lends it a perfect millennium *Road Warrior* vibe—you may not want to live here, but it's a great place to howl drunk at the moon. During the day, everyone's selling something, and it's this bustle, along with the collision of Eastern and Western influences, that makes Athens feel like the rummage sale of Europe.

Athenians tend to be a warm, talkative people. Any effort, no matter how bungling, to reach beyond your circle of traveling buddies and speak a few words of Greek will be appreciated. Yes, there's some hostility toward "American imperialism" all over Greece, but a distinction is made between people and governments.

While they're likely to tolerate your opinions, the Greeks show little of the same consideration for their Albanian population. Like Mexican immigrants in California, Albanians are scapegoated for a wealth of domestic problems, crime and joblessness topping the list. Asking someone here what they think of Albanians is a good litmus test of their politics, if you care about that sort of thing. (Just try not to ask an Albanian what he thinks of Albanians.)

On the recreational end, it's hard to know how Athenians manage it day after day, but they do not really start to party until midnight. And it can often go on until dawn, so you can make jet lag work for you here. In some of the livelier sections of town, like Kolonaki, the revelers flood the streets on weekend nights. Don't get caught with an open container of alcohol, though—it's bad form, and the cops don't mind hassling you for it.

Like the rest of the world, Greece has discovered the rave, and the ones in Athens rival the best of them. Remember, it was the Greek god Dionysus who taught the world to party, and the well-developed club culture here shows it. You can find flyers for the theme rave of your choice—from sci-fi to caveman—at some of the hipper clothing stores and used record shops in Plaka. And don't worry about crashing the smaller parties—young American and Canadian tourists abound in Athens.

Fine arts are also actually flourishing in Athens. You'll find more art galleries than you can possibly visit in a week, as well as opportunities to see classical music and opera. The **Greek Tourist Organization** near Syntagma Square [see *need to know*, below] is the easiest way to catch up on everything that's cooking while you're here. Pick up a copy of the English-language daily newspaper *Athens News*. The back page has a smattering of listings. While you're here, grab a copy of *Now In Athens*, a bimonthly glossy devoted strictly to the arts.

A word about using public transport in Athens: Don't. This is a walker's city. Except for the very fast, efficient metro between Monastiraki and Omonia squares, you're better off hoofing it than using any sort of motorized transport. Traffic during the day is dangerous and the buses and trams are packed. Late at night, however, traffic settles down a bit—play it by ear.

neighborhoods

Most of the places you'll want to get to are all within a couple of miles of each other, and navigating is fairly easy with a good map, available for free at the **Greek Tourist Organization** [see *need to know*, below]. If you can't see the **Acropolis** [see *culture zoo*, below], you can get your bearings by looking for **Lykovetos Hill**—that's the other hill in Athens, the one *without* the Parthenon sitting on top of it. Otherwise, just travel from square to square: **Kolonaki Square**, **Syntagma Square**, **Omonia Square** and countless others—they are the lily pads, you are the frog.

For gewgaws, you can while away your days in the **Plaka** district, which curls around the eastern side of the Acropolis. Besides the tourist traps, this district is home to a few hidden gems where you can buy some truly unique momentos, and an astounding number of cafes/bars for your drinking pleasure. Most visitors seem to prefer this area for their nightly carousals. Plaka also has the highest concentration of restaurants, hotels, Internet cafes, and other services for the weary traveler. Abutting Plaka's northwest border is **Monistiraki**, home of the famous **Monistiraki Flea Market** [see *stuff,* below] where you can find the bitchin'est row of used-record stores in the EU.

Psiri, just north of Monistiraki, is the hottest new party neighborhood in Athens, though you would never know it in the daytime, when it's like a ghost town. But when the sun sets, Psiri blossoms like a nocturnal party flower, awaft with aromas from some of the finest restaurants in Athens, and positively cluttered with cool bars and clubs. You might be something of a novelty at these establishments—it seems the tourist contingent hasn't discovered Psiri yet. That's right, you heard it here first, now go out and ruin it for the locals.

Kolonaki, a 15- to 20-minute walk east of Psiri, is the most classically European neighborhood, with the prettiest buildings and streets in town. This is a nice, relaxing area to while away siesta (approximately 2 till 6pm) as the rest of the city sleeps, and it's one of the most popular areas to dance the night away, too.

If you haven't the cash or time to travel to any of the Greek islands, despair not: Take the 30-minute bus ride to **Glyfada**, on the outskirts of the city. Along with a string of beaches, this area boasts some of the hottest clubs in Athens, serving up everything from traditional Greek *rebetika* music to techno.

If you want to party a little closer to your hotel, wherever that may be, you'll have no problem finding the bar or club to suit your fancy. One of the great things about Athens is its even distribution of party spots. Especially at night, Athens belongs to its youth. No matter where you are, there's probably a pretty happening place close by. And don't worry about your ID—there is no minimum drinking age in Greece.

hanging ouT

Athens, and all of Greece for that matter, is a cafe culture. The real heart of that venerable sport of people-watching and coffee-drinking is in Kolonaki, one of the wealthier neighborhoods, located on the east side of town. **Kolonaki Square** (aka Fil. Eterias Square) has more than a half-dozen outdoor cafes lining its northern edge. For round-the-clock service, sit yourself down at the **Café Peros** *(Kolonaki Sq. 7; Tel 364-70-55; Yellow Trolley Bus 3, 13, 7, 8 to the NE corner of the National Garden; 24 hours daily; 1,300-2,500Dr per entree; V, AE),* which has decent food as well as coffee and drinks. Ranks of hipsters, models, and businesspeople turn out here to preen and stare—why not join them? Sure, it can take forever to be served by the overworked, impatient help, but this place is so quintessentially Athenian, it's a must. By the way, leave the shorts and T-shirts behind and slip into something hot and stifling, unless you want to be pegged (god forbid) as an American. Or head for the cafes near Kolonaki Square, which are more laid-back.

For super espresso and cappuccino and friendly service, there's the tiny, out-of-the-way **Tiera Café** *(Othos Fokionos 12; Tel 322-39-78; Minibus 200 to the corner of Othos Perikleous and Othos Voulis; 8am-9pm Tue, Thur, Fri, 8am-6pm Mon, Wed, Sat, 10am-6pm Sun; 800Dr for double espresso; No credit cards).*

The Plaka district has a million cafes to chill out in, although the crowd here is most definitely tourist-heavy. Try **Artisimon** *(Othos Eolou 11, the corner of Othos Eolou & Othos Metropoleos; Tel 321-30-64; Minibus 150 to Eolou & Metropoleos; 8am-1am daily; 800Dr double espresso, 900Dr fresh-squeezed OJ, 500-1,000Dr sandwiches; No credit cards).* A glass of orange juice here is generous, the espresso is huge, and the sandwiches are tasty.

If it's happening young people you seek, go to the **Cultural Center** on Othos Solonos between Othos Asklipiou and Othos Massalias. Well, not actually *inside* the Cultural Center, but on its excellent green. The students from the nearby Academy of Arts and Letters like to hang out here, especially in the outdoor seating area of **Adiraiko Cafeneo** [see *bar scene*, below]. University classes must have an enforced dress code, because the students here are well-turned-out.

A more varied crowd can be found in the **National Garden**, right in the center of town. There's a cafe, a small zoo with a good wolf exhibit, and walking paths through an airy deciduous forest. On its smoother trails, you can find skateboarders doing fakies, ollies, and all that other crap. The park never closes, but while it is safe for lone women during the day, it's not safe for *anyone* alone at night.

Just west of the garden lies the **Ancient Agora**, once the center of Athenian life, now a lovely poppy-filled plot of varied ruins, perfect for meditative lounging. And finally, the **Olympic Stadium**, just south of the garden, attracts joggers, rollerbladers, obsessive stair climbers, and other health nuts [see *culture zoo*, below, for both]. It's open 8am to 8pm, technically, but visitors, gangs of kids, and strolling couples gather here at all hours. Why not take a victory lap around the 250m track? Don't cost nothing.

bar scene

Athens is a great place for a hangover. After a night of hard drinking, drag your sorry ass past the fish and meat market a quarter-mile north of Monistiraki Square—the sight and smell of carcasses and butchers in bloodied aprons will dance before your bleary, gimlet eyes like a Hieronymus Bosch painting come to life. Or just stumble aimlessly about the city in a dirty wife beater while swigging from a bottle of Pepto. There's no end to the variety of boozeterias here in the cradle of democracy, from your basic dive to the local *ouzeries* [see *the truth about ouzo*, below].

Who woulda thought you could find good hip-hop in Greece? The finest is a little bar called **Loop** *(Agiou Assomaton Sq. 3; Tel 324-76-66; 9:30-late daily; No credit cards),* in the fashionable Psiri district. Featuring the weird and priceless mixes of DJ Noiz, Loop is loud, young, casual, and way too small to even consider dancing in. The decor is unique, especially the giant Tiffany-meets-*Alice in Wonderland* lamps. Drinks are priced moderately for Athens, going anywhere from 1,000 to 2,000Dr.

The *ouzerie* is an institution in Greece. It's more than just a bar, it's a snack bar and local hangout. As its name suggests, the *ouzerie* serves up a variety of different ouzos, the licorice-flavored Greek spirit [see *the truth about ouzo*, below]. For atmosphere and quality, you can't beat **To Cafeneo** (*Othos Epikarmou 1, corner of Othos Epikarmou and Tripodon; Tel 324-69-16; 11am-2am daily; 800-2,000Dr per entree; Cash only*), run by the amiable Kostas Verigogos. His traditional Greek appetizers are excellent, and the decor is rustic without being uncomfortable. Relax at one of Kostass' handmade tables beneath the exposed beam ceiling. You can get an ouzo for less than 1,000Dr, and the beer's cheap, too. On occasion, the odd musician/band shows up here to sing for their supper.

If you want to get even more relaxed—just drinkers and their drinks— you might try **Adiraiko Cafeneo** (*Othos Akadimias 50; Tel 361-92-65; Minibus 060 to the corner of Othos Solonos & Othos Sina; 8am-1am daily; No credit cards*). First things first: Though the bar claims its address is Othos Akadimias 50, it is located in reality on Othos Solonos (a parallel street to the north) where it meets Othos Massalias. Adiraiko has large indoor and outdoor seating areas, with a mixed bag of locals (although during the day it's dominated by university students). As usual, you must dress neatly to fit in, but it's worth the small sacrifice. This is just a good, solid bar, with beers going for 600Dr and up. You also can buy an entire bottle of liquor for 2,000-5,000Dr.

Another "regular" bar is **2X3** (*Othos Ogigou 2; Tel 321-29-77; 8:30pm- whenever daily; No credit cards*), pronounced *thioepitria*, located in the chic new Psiri district. 2X3 looks like a high-ceilinged greenhouse from the outside, with a glass ceiling covering much of the seating area. The music is modern pop, with live *rebetika/laika* on Sundays and Thursdays—whether the live band is any good or not depends on who happens to show up that night, sort of like a game of pickup basketball. The friendly crowd is loud and local, in their late twenties and thirties. The cocktails here are 2,000Dr, strong, and tasty.

LIVE MUSIC SCENE

Like its Georgian sister in the United States, Athens is a hotbed of music, both local and international. Knowing all your choices is a dangerous thing here—you're likely to be frozen with indecision and end up spending the night in your hotel room reading this guide, god forbid. So whatcha, whatcha, whatcha want? If you're set on rock/pop or jazz, pay a visit to **Music Wave** [see *stuff*, below] and talk to Victor. In addition to a stack of flyers for live shows and parties, Victor offers sound advice on which acts rock and which suck. You can also pick up a copy of *Athens News* and *Now in Athens* at the **Greek Tourist Organization** [see *need to know*, below] for music listings.

For fun crowds, you can't beat the *laika/rebetika* (local Greek music) joints. *Rebetika* music has a long history combining traditional Greek folk music with styles from Asia Minor and the Arab world. The instruments include the lute and violin and songs can range from the plaintive to the very raucous, all of it pretty damn soulful. Athens has a surfeit of these places, each with its own distinct flavor. Audiences are generally 25 and up, hard-drinking, sing-along types, so don't come here for a quiet evening of Yanni music.

If you're too cheap or poor to pay for your music, take a walk around the **National Garden** [see *hanging out*, above] or **Areos Park** [see *great outdoors*, below]. You're bound to find some street musicians at either place, but you really *should* cough up a donation for the starving artists.

The premier place to rock out in Athens is **An Club** *(Othos Solomou 20-15; Tel 330-50-56; Yellow Trolley Bus 6 to the corner of Othos Tritis Septembriou & Halkokondili; 8pm-varied closing; Up to 5,000Dr cover; No credit cards)*. The cavernous warehouse space, huge enough to hold 2,000 maniacs, specializes in attracting local rock/hard rock acts as well as some strange choices from overseas. Recent lineups have included such diverse foreign acts as the Fleshtones, Lydia Lunch, the Bevis Frond, and the Flaming Stars. See a trend? This is a great venue to see those second- and third-tier groups you've always been meaning to check out. An Club is predictably big with the college set.

The **Hi-Hat Cafe** *(Othos Dragoumi 28; Tel 721-81-71; Yellow Trolley Bus 7, 8 to the Hilton Hotel; Noon-4am daily; Up to 5,000Dr cover; No credit cards)* features lesser known, more experimental rock groups, as

the truth about ouzo

Listen up. Be careful with the ouzo. The ouzo is not a toy. The ouzo is a tool. Place a few cubes of ice in a tumbler. Pour the ouzo of your choice (there are many brands, but they all taste like liquid licorice—the local fave being **No. 12**) over the ice. Observe as it changes from clear to milky white. Sip the ouzo. Do not down the ouzo. WAIT! Eat something first. The ouzo is a bitch goddess, and she'll wreak destruction on your delicate digestive tract if not treated with respect. Like all liquors on the sweet side, the ouzo can pack a hell of a hangover. The good thing about the ouzo: You don't need Binaca to cover it up. You can always claim you were just munching on some Good & Plenty. Best cure for the ouzo hangover: a sandwich from **DeliKiosk** [see *eats*, below] and a fresh-squeezed OJ.

well as some jazz and blues artists. The crowd is mostly young locals—a beer-swilling, motorhead kind of scene. The space consists of a medium-size barroom and a much smaller lounge area—altogether about enough room for 400 sloshed Greeks.

Douzeni *(Makrigianni 8; Tel 922-75-97; Yellow Trolley Bus 1, 5, 8, and 15; Midnight-5am Wed-Sat; 3,000Dr drink minimum includes one drink; No credit cards)*, a restaurant/bar/music club that pumps out the *rebetika* and *laika,* and looks like an ideal bar mitzvah space, with a similarly formal dress sensibility. The crowd here is lively and mixed, both in age and nationality, and the bands play flawlessly. The large dining room could easily fit close to 1,000 people if it were a stand-around-drinking-from-a-red-plastic-cup-of-beer kind of place. Fortunately, management decided to make this seating room only.

The least touristy *rebetika* and *laika* hangout is **Medistanes** *(Othos Lepeniotou 26; Tel 331-42-98; 9pm-whenever Tue-Sat; No cover, but one-drink minimum; No credit cards)*, located in the newest hip section of town, Psiri. Like every establishment in this part of town, the crowd is composed of locals, which means nobody's wearing shorts and a T-shirt. Contempo-casual should help you blend in nicely in this mixed-ages crowd. Medistanes is also a decent restaurant, so you could spend your whole night here. This intimate space is about 1,500 square feet, with a bar taking up one wall. There's live music every night except Wednesday and Thursday. Be prepared to sing yourself hoarse, even if you don't know what the hell the words mean.

For jazz in town the best place to start is by contacting the **Jazz Research & Promotion Center** *(Othos Tsami Karatassou 46; Tel 923-*

agori meets korits

If you're looking for a fling with a Greek goddess, Athens can be a tough nut to crack. Considering that this is the same part of the world that brought you those little goat men with giant penises, the people here are less promiscuous than you might think, especially concerning foreign men hitting on Athenian homegirls. If the degree to which feminism has taken root in a culture is a reliable gauge of sexual liberation (and it seems to be), Athens is not exactly a love-in. Take one look at the macho posturing of the city's motorcycling youth, and you know this is the type of place where the boys protect their sisters, whether they want protection or not. That said, take heart: With the city's club culture and nightly revelry, your average guy stands as good a chance as anywhere else of finding a gal who's willing to break the rules a little.

Of course, it's no problem at all for a foreign lass to find her Adonis—funny how these swords cut one-way, huh?

88-08; *jazzntzaz@prometheus.hol.gr*). They've got the lowdown on just about every gig in Athens.

Jazz in Jazz *(Othos Deinokratos 4, near Dexameni Sq.; Tel 725-83-62. Minibus 060 to Dexameni Sq.; 9pm-3am daily, No credit cards)* is, yes, a straight-ahead jazz club decorated with what appear to be the spoils of a trip to a New Orleans dump, dig? The crowd here is entirely dependent on the acts—ranging from hot trios to cool chanteuses—and dress is very casual. Cover charge varies from nothing to 5,000Dr.

For a more avant-garde selection of jazz and modern "art music," check out what's going on at the **Kinisi Art Center** *(Othos Ipatias 1B, near the corner of Othos Ipatias & Othos Metropoleos; Tel 331-29-22; Minibus 150 to the corner of Metropoleos & Voulis; Hours vary; papok@otenet.gr, http://www.otenet.gr/papok; No credit cards)*. Okay, so there's no bar and the room looks like a likely spot for an AA meeting, but the musicians are first-rate madmen producing exquisite noise and admission is always free. This place attracts a mostly twentysomething crowd of serious music fans.

club scene

Clubs in Greece do not open until 11pm at the earliest, nor do they fill up until well after midnight. This is not a bad thing. Drinks in Greek clubs tend to be overpriced and weak, so the late hours give you plenty of time to get buzzed beforehand without getting fleeced.

Most places don't specialize in any one genre; the Greeks prefer a mix of everything. It is not uncommon for a few *rebetika/laika* tunes to be thrown into an otherwise electronic lineup. In addition, most of the larger clubs are commandeered every weekend by rave promoters, so the decor can change wildly from one day to the next. If you're looking for a rave, you can find flyers amid the glow-in-the-dark club gear at **Space Om** [see *stuff*, below], a tiny, second-story boutique clothing store.

Kingsize *(Othos Amerikis 2; Tel 323-25-00; Minibus 200 to Othos Stadiou & Othos Amerikis; 12:30am-dawn Wed-Sat; No credit cards)* is a large underground space right near Syntagma Square. It's very popular with the local university students, and its music leans toward the more mellifluous, dancy end of electronica. For weekend shindigs, be prepared to pay about 5,000Dr to get in, which includes one drink. The door here can be handled by rather obnoxious clubbies, so bust out that mylar jumpsuit.

Those of you who like your music fast and inhuman, try the cavernous club they call **Loft** *(Othos Ermou & Assomaton Sq.; Tel 097-462-941; Midnight-9am Wed-Sat; No credit cards)*, in the Psiri district. The cover charge varies between 2,000 and 5,000Dr. The door has been known to turn away patrons deemed unhip, but there's no clear idea of how to dress for this place. The crowd here is very young, a raucous mix of slack-jawed skateboarders and their midriffed courtesans, privileged young hipsters who feel like slumming it, and just regular folks like you and me. Also, the place seems to be running on E (no, not empty, silly).

athens bars, clubs and culture zoo

BARS/CLUBS ▲
2X3 **4**
Adiraiko Cafeneo **16**
An Club **18**
Douzeni **7**
Hi-Hat Cafe **12**
Jazz in Jazz **15**
Kingsize (Glyfada) **8**
Kingsize **11**
Loft **2**
Loop **1**
Medistanes **3**
Next **17**
To Cafeneo **9**

CULTURE ZOO ●
Acropolis **6**
Ancient Agora **5**
National Archaeological
  Museum **19**
Byzantine Museum **13**
Museum of Greek Folk Art **10**
National Gallery and
  Alexander Soutzos Museum **14**

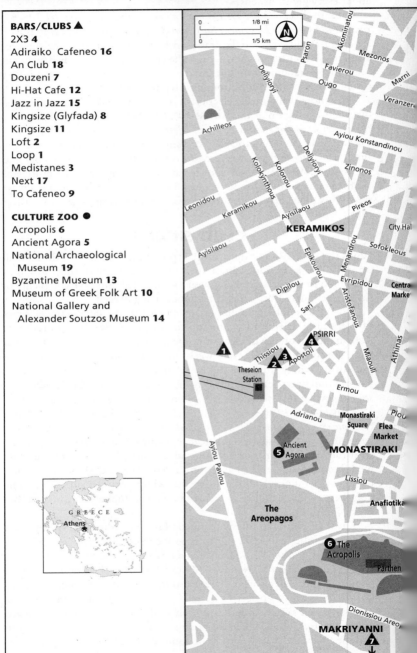

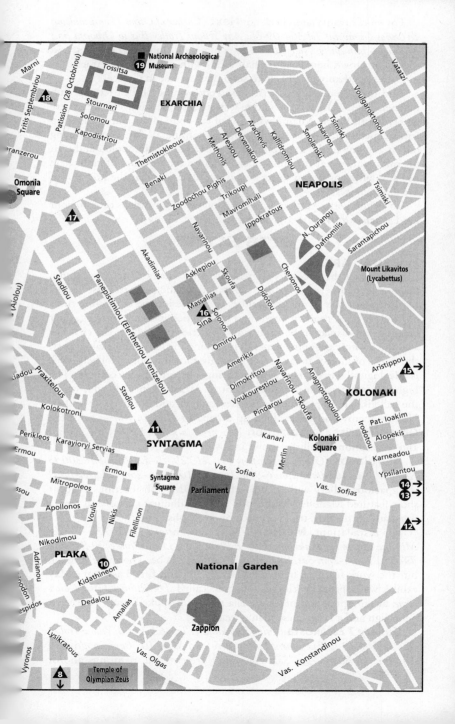

For more organic fare, check out **Next** *(Corner of Othos Themistokleous & Othos Gamveta; Tel 364-09-65; Any Yellow Trolley Bus to Omonia Sq.; Midnight-5am daily; No credit cards)*, a big, dark club that plays pop and rock. The crowd here is about half local, with more sloppy, American-style dressers than you're likely to see anywhere else in Greece.

And then there's Glyfada, Athens's very own beach district and club magnet. Take A3 Blue Bus and ride it straight to the sand. The scene here is very South Beach, Miami, with lots of fast-food joints and tourist-trap trinket merchants. After sunning and swimming all day, you can hang out in any one of the cafe/restaurants on Othos Zissimopolou and wait for midnight, when the clubs open. Because the fortunes of clubs here rise and fall from season to season, ask around for what the hot spot of the moment is.

To all you goths, you can find out which clubs in Athens cater to your kind at ***www.dark.vortex.gr/clubs/*** [see *wired*, below].

arTs scene

▶▶**VISUAL ARTS**

Athens has all the necessary ingredients for a vital artistic community: disposable income, a large student population, and perhaps most importantly, a giant pair of ancient sandals to fill. Beside the crumbling ruins of its glory days, modern artists and fashion designers are thriving, their creations on display in boutiques and galleries throughout the city. For a country whose economy depends on selling the idea of an exalted past, the artists of Greece today are surprisingly forward-looking. Their work is ideologically irreverent without being obscure or inaccessible. The highest concentration of young talent in Athens is in Kolonaki, where the galleries are as plentiful as the newsstands, and the cafes serve their Nescafé foamy and sweet. Pick up a copy of *Now in Athens* from the **Greek Tourist Organization** [see *need to know*, below] for listings and descriptions of all the shows in town.

Astrolavos *(Othos Xanthipou 11; Tel 729-43-42; Minibus 200 to Kolonaki Sq.; 10:30am-2pm/6-9pm Tue-Fri, 10:30am-2pm Sat Sept-June)* is a spacious gallery with a cool, white, MOMA-ish interior. A recent show featured Manolis Merabeliotis' electric silhouette boxes and Smara Agiakatsika's dreamy, triple-exposed photographs.

For installations, **Medusa** *(Othos Xenokratous 7; Tel 724-45-52; Minibus 200 to Kolonaki Sq.; 6:30-9:30pm Mon, 11am-2pm/6:30-9:30pm Tue-Fri, 11am-2pm Sat, Sept-June)* is the place to be. The space is small, but the work featured here is usually daring and fun. Last year's May exhibit was a piece by Yiorgos Gyparkis called *The Rubber Little Court Shoe*, an interpretation of Cinderella that looked like a cross between a neon sign and a Portuguese man o' war.

Gallery 7 Zalakosta *(Othos Zalakosta 7; Tel 362-20-50; Yellow Trolley Bus 3, 7, 8, 13 to Parliament building; 6-9pm Mon, 10:30am-2pm/6-9pm Tue-Fri, 10:30am-2pm Sat, Nov-June)* presents the paintings and/or sketches of a new artist every month or so. A recent show featured the works of Kyveli Zachariou, whose acrylic paintings combine images of feminine forms with traffic signs and maps, yet somehow look like Chagall.

If you insist on being surrounded by bohemians while you nosh, consider stopping in at **Photokoros** *(Othos Tsakalof 44; Tel 262-06-00; Minibus 200 to the corner of Othos Likavitou & Othos Skoufa; 11am-1am Mon-Sat; No credit cards)* in artsy Kolonaki. You won't pay more than 2,000Dr for a drink here, and the atmosphere is very chill. The walls are adorned with the work of featured photographers, making this an excellent place to check out the underground arts scene.

Another cafe that donates its wall space to local artists is **Aiolis** *(Othos Aiolou 23; Tel 331-28-39; Minibus 200 to the corner of Othos Athinas & Othos Evripidou; 11am-2am daily; No credit cards)*, located near the Plaka district. The art here is a little more pop-cultured, and the music can get as loud as any bar's. The coffee drinks are splendid, though, and if you happen to get lucky, you just might catch a Greek wedding procession at the church across the way (recommended wedding viewing time: Sunday at midnight).

▶▶PERFORMING ARTS

Most Athenians can speak at least a little English, but it is most certainly not the language of theater; plays are performed in Greek almost without exception. In addition, many of the opera and classical music venues sell out their seats to season-ticket holders and the like.

That being said, if you're looking for a little culture to punctuate your nights of binge drinking and meaningless, anonymous sex, there are a number of different dance companies at your disposal. Also, you might try the Megaron Musikis, which hosts recitals, concertos, and symphonies. As for film, you won't have any trouble finding English-language venues throughout the city. Find out what's going on in *Athens News* and *Now in Athens*, available at the **Greek Tourist Organization** [see *need to know*, below].

Every year from June through September, the **Athens Festival** hosts dance, music, and theater groups at the **Theatre of Herodes**

fIVE-O

Athens's police force is not a pervasive presence. The cops here are pretty laid-back when it comes to partying—although, of course, they have no choice but to enforce the mandatory seven-year sentence for drug possession. Between the unruly traffic and weekly protests/strikes, these guys have their hands full. And with the large role tourism plays in the economy, you can be certain that Athenian cops will treat you fairly. But, *seven f—ing years?*

Atticus *(At the foot of the Acropolis; Tel 323-27-71; Hours vary)*, a 2nd-century Roman amphitheater. Tickets for the shows are available at the **Athens Festival Office** *(Othos Stadiou 4; Tel 322-14-59; 8:30am-2pm/5-7pm Mon-Fri, 8:30am-1pm Sat, 10am-1pm Sun)*. Some performances, especially international rock and pop acts, are held at the **Likavitos Theater** *(Tel 722-72-09)* on Likavitos Hill.

▶▶**DANCE**
May is dance month in Athens, and no place has better shows than **Ergostasio** *(Othos Vouliagmenis 268; Tel 973-19-93; Hours vary)*. The dance companies booked here tend toward the modern, but that doesn't mean you can dress like a slacker: You wear something nice! Tickets range from 2,000Dr up.

▶▶**CLASSICAL**
The stately **Megaron Mousikis** *(Othos Vas. Sofias 89; Tel 729-03-91; Yellow Trolley Bus 3, 7, 8, 13; Box office 10am-6pm Mon-Fri, Sat till 2pm; No credit cards)* attracts international classical and jazz performers all year, with symphonies performed now and then by the State Orchestra of Athens. Tickets go from 5,000Dr and up, and the dress code is formal (dresses, dress pants, jackets, ties), so don't embarrass your country.

▶▶**FILM**
In the center of Plaka is **CineParis** *(Othos Kidathineon 22; Tel 322-20-71; Hours vary)*, an outdoor theater that shows older, mostly American films. Sure, sometimes the prints suck, but the atmosphere here is pure *Cinema Paradiso*. Tickets are 1,400Dr.

    Opera Assos Odeon *(Othos Akadimias 57; Tel 362-26-83; Yellow Trolley Bus 3, 8, 13; 5pm-midnight daily)* shows good American movies that are only 1 to 6 months old.

gay scene

Paris in the '20s it ain't, unless a handful of bars and some sleazy public-bathroom cruise spots could constitute a "scene." You'll just have to wait till Mykonos for something a little more substantial. But, what the hell, bars are a good place to meet the local family, and isn't that what our job is—bringing people together? Here's the best of the bunch. P.S., if you're interested in those public bathrooms (not that there's anything wrong with that), and certain "saunas," check out: ***http://209.67.19.99/~GayGreece***.

    LIZZARD *(Othos Apostolou Pavlou 31; Tel 346-86-70; 11pm-5am Wed-Sat; No credit cards)* is a mixed lesbian/gay bar, and very laid-back. Average-priced drinks here are anywhere from 800–2,000Dr. Except for Sunday, when Greek music dominates, electronica reigns supreme. The place is cozy and dark, with plenty of secluded nooks.

    For an all-male crowd, on an all-male street, with all-male bars, go to **Lamda Club** *(Othos Lempesi 15; Tel 922-42-02; Yellow Trolley Bus 9 to the corner of Othos Lempesi and Othos Syngrou; 10am-4am daily; No credit cards)*. The cover charge is 2,500Dr, which includes a drink. The young crowd whoops it up on two different dance floors, upstairs and downstairs. The atmosphere here is dark and a little edgy, with standard disco decor and a casual dress code (that's Greek casual, so don't come in looking like a slob).

There are several other gay bars on Othos Lempesi, including the very friendly **Granazi** *(Othos Lempesi 20; Tel 924-41-85; No credit cards)* and the cruisy **Guys/Ydrohoos** *(Othos Lempesi 8; Tel 923-02-64; No credit cards)*.

After clubbing the night away on Othos Lempesi, dry out in the day on **Limanakia Beach** *(Blue Bus A2 or A3, transfer at Glyfada square to Bus 116)*. There is not much beach to speak of, but the water's beautiful and very snorkel-able. A renowned pickup spot.

When night comes, why not stick around Glyfada and pay a visit to **Kingsize** [see *club scene*, above]? The club is an even straight/gay mix, and offers you the choice of two different theme rooms: a dark techno room and a light soft jazz/rock room. Cover is 4,000Dr, which includes your first drink.

CULTURE ZOO

You are in Greece. Take some time out from your busy party schedule, you beer-soaked, oversexed kids. You are expected to cultivate yourself. So, cuddle up in the bassinet of Western Civilization, and ponder the mysteries of a culture that could perfect the golden mean and kill Socrates at the same time.

Acropolis *(Accessible from Othos Dionissiou Areopagitou from the south or Othos Theorias from the north; Tel 321-02-19; Blue Bus 230 to Acropolis; 8am-6:30pm Tue-Fri, 8:30am-2:30pm Sat, Sun & holidays, 11am-6:30pm Mon; 2,000Dr, 1,000 students; No credit cards):* Settled thousands of years ago, the center of classical Greek life, demolished by the Persians in 480 B.C., rebuilt by Pericles, this wonder is truly a don't-miss. It's true, Lord Elgin made off to England with the best marble in the Parthenon, and smog has eaten away even more, but what's left is still pretty damn awesome.

Ancient Agora *(Accessible from Othos Adrianou; Tel 321-01-85; Admission is 1,200Dr, 600Dr students; Cash only):* Once the center of Athenian life, the beautiful, poppy-filled grounds of the Agora happen to

RULES OF THE GAME

There is no drinking age in Greece. Woo-hoo!

There is also definitely a drug culture in Athens, centered of course around the club scene, but getting a local to trust you enough to share the wealth is a task worthy of Hercules. Plus the somewhat draconian drug laws make the risks not worth the reward: Possession of narcotic substances, including marijuana and E, gets you an *automatic* seven-year-minimum sentence. Hmmmm.

house some of the finest ruins in Athens, in addition to being a righteous place to just hang.

National Archaeological Museum *(Othos Patission 44; Tel 821-77-17; Yellow Trolley Bus 2-5, 7-9, 11, 13, 15, 18 to the Museum; 8am-5pm Tue-Fri, 8:30am-3pm Sat, Sun, 11am-5pm Mon; 2,000Dr, 1,000Dr students; No credit cards):* Come and enjoy almost every piece of Attic art not stolen by the British, which is considerable.

Byzantine Museum *(Othos Vasilissis Sofias 22; Tel 723-15-70; Yellow Trolley Bus 3, 7, 8, 13 to the Museum; 8am-2:30pm Tue-Sun; 500Dr, 300Dr students; No credit cards):* A huge collection of early Christian art and iconography, including full-size-recreations of early Christian, Byzantine, and Post-Byzantine churches.

Museum of Greek Folk Art *(Othos Kidatheneon 17; Tel 322-90-31; Yellow Trolley Bus 1, 2, 4, 5, 9, 10, 11, 15, 18 to the corner of Othos Kidatheneon & Othos Filelinon; 10am-2pm Tue-Sun; Admission 500Dr, 300Dr students, free Sun; No credit cards):* If the Smithsonian put on an exhibit of Greek culture, it would look something like this.

National Gallery and Alexander Soutzos Museum *(Othos Leoforos Vassileos Konstandinou 50; Tel 721-10-10; Yellow Trolley Bus 3, 7, 8, 13 to the Gallery; 9am-3pm Mon, Wed-Sat, 10am-2pm Sun; Admission 1,000Dr; No credit cards):* Worth the trip if only for the ultramodern (hey, by Greek standards!) El Greco paintings on the first floor.

modification

There are a million different ways to desecrate the temple of your body here. Pierce it, paint it, put it through the tortures of Hercules...whatever.

"You cannot put a price on the limits of the imagination," says Paul, one of the artists in residence at **Jimmy's Tattoo** *(Othos Kyristou 13; Tel 321-97-41; 10am-6pm Mon-Sat; No credit cards)* when asked about the price range of his tattoos. Piercing is much more concrete, with belly puncturing for 10,000Dr and ears for only 2,000Dr. The studio is hygienic and very professional. Pressed for more specifics, Paul admits that tattoos start at about 9,000Dr. His intricate geometric designs are sure to please all you neopagan hedonists.

great outdoors

Want to know why you can't rent in-line skates or skateboards in Athens? Because there's no place to ride them. The streets are a mess, not to mention crowded with insane cabbies. However, you can get your natural endorphin fix at the **Olympic Stadium** [see *hanging out*, above], or head on over to **Areos Park**, just north of the Exarchia district. There are tons of little trails on which to jog. The park is always open, but it is unwise to venture here after dark. For the workout of your existence, a jog up Likavitos Hill should put the fear of Zeus in you. It's a steep 10- or 20-minute walk to the top, so be prepared to sweat. Or, if you're feeling lazy, take the funicular, which leaves every 15

fESTIVALS and EVENTS

The **Athens Festival** runs from June to September [see *arts scene*, above].

The **Annual Tattoo Expo** goes down in late May at a different club each year. It features an army of artists, hairstylists, piercers, jewelers, and live music. Ask Kostas at **Lazy Dayz Juggling** [see *stuff*, below] for the exact dates this year.

Carnival is a time in February and/or March when everybody in Athens gets wasted enough to send Dionysus into rehab.

The **Likavitos Festival** offers modern plays, dance, and musical performances in the **Likavitos Theater** *(Top of Likavitos Hill; Tel 322-14-59 for schedules and ticket info)* throughout June.

The original freakin' **Marathon** is completed at the **Olympic Stadium** [see *hanging out*, above] every October. Anyone can qualify to enter, so why not get in touch with **SEGAS** *(Othos Leoforos Syngrou 137; Tel 932-06-36)* and start training now? Or better yet, buy some beer, go to the stadium and watch the runners finish the race while you scratch your drunk, lazy self.

minutes, for 1,000Dr. The top of this hill commands an excellent view of Athens. Bring a good map, and you should be able to spot just about every major landmark there is.

For the happiest balance of activity and rest, grab your snorkel and mask and head out to **Glyfada** [see *club scene*, above] on the A3 bus, or take a cab *(approximately 2,500Dr)*. There are several different beaches to choose from here, but we liked Lagonissi—and the beaches directly surrounding it—the most (taxi required).

STUff

As with dining in Athens, shopping in Athens poses the problem of separating the half a percent of worthwhile places from the garbage. Don't get discouraged. There are some splendid little stores in Athens, you just have to follow this guide to find 'em. Plaka is glutted with a lot of useless junk, but there are some unique places sprinkled throughout. Right near Plaka is the **Monistiraki Flea Market** [see below] where you actually may find something interesting at a fair price. For those of your friends and family who have expensive taste, shop around Kolonaki, home of upscale boutiques like Machia.

▶▶**HOT COUTURE**
The foyer of **Remember The Future** *(Othos Adrianou 79; Tel 321-64-09; 9am-9:30pm Mon-Sat, 10am-1:30pm Sun; www.rememberthe future.com; No credit cards)* is covered in celebrity headshots with personal

12 hours in aThens

1. **The Acropolis:** The birth of Western Civ. A must-see, before sulphurous smog destroys all the remaining marble [see *culture zoo*, above].

2. **Likavitos Hill:** The best view of the city [see *culture zoo*, above].

3. **Monistiraki Flea Market:** This place looks like the bazaar scene in *Raiders of the Lost Ark* [see *stuff*, below].

4. **Psiri:** The coolest new neighborhood in Athens, with some of the best restaurants and bars. Make sure you go to **Loop** and **Medistanes** [see *bar scene*, above].

5. **Glyfada:** It's Miami's South Beach on the Mediterranean [see *club scene*, above].

6. **Kolonaki:** Another cool neighborhood. Between the cafes in the square and the ubiquitous art galleries, this is where the Europhiles alight [see *hanging out*, above].

7. **The National Gardens:** An enchanted little forest in the middle of a city [see *hanging out*, above].

8. **The Roman Forum:** Laze about in the scarlet poppy fields. This is one of the few places in Athens where you can just hang out among the ruins, without crowds [see *hanging out*, above].

9. **Plaka:** So it's full of tourist traps. Where else are you going to buy an authentic Greek peasant shirt to bring home to your parents?

10. **The Olympic Track:** Bring glory to your country with a lap around this turn of the century stadium. At night, they turn on the colored Olympic ring lights [see *hanging out*, above].

notes scrawled on them by the Ramones, the Scorpions, Iron Maiden—all profusely thanking the great Dmitris Tsouanatos for decking them out in the latest crotch-enhancing rock 'n' roll getups. As a mere mortal, perhaps you can find it in your wallet to buy one of the beautiful original silkscreen long-sleeve T-shirts (9,000Dr). Or, pick up a metal studded belt (3,000-15,000Dr) and accessorize, baby. Prices are negotiable here, so haggle. Even if you don't buy anything, it's worth a visit to see Dmitris's experimental clothing designs (a dress made of garden hoses, for example), as well as his original bronze sculpture garden outside.

Set on a side street of Kolonaki, **Machia** *(Othos Hartos 18; Tel 724-06-97; 10am-8pm Tue, Thur, Fri, till 3:30pm Mon, Wed, Sat; No credit cards)* is run by a native New Yorker. It's no surprise then that she's got the hottest wearable fashions from international designers. If you're going to get dressed you'll pay for it, with cashmere wraps *(180,000Dr)* and bottoms by the likes of Daryl K and Paul & Joe *(45,000-90,000Dr)*. But trinkets are abundant and not too pricey, like glass-encrusted compacts *(4,000Dr)* and dainty little hair clips *(400Dr)*.

Space Om *(Othos Pandrossou 19; Tel 324-82-31; Minibus 150 to the corner of Othos Metropoleos & Othos Karnikareas; 10am-8pm Tue, Thur-Sat, 11am-4pm Mon, Wed, 11am-6pm Sun; Shorts 6,000Dr, sarongs 8,000Dr, T-shirts 8,000-12,000Dr; Cash only)* sells handmade neon-patterned clothing, and has stacks of flyers for all the clubs and raves you may want to wear the stuff to. Styles here range from batik to surf—if that could be called a range—and it's all sexier than a mofo.

At **Morphi** *(Othos Aiolou 17; Tel 321-72-16; Minibus 150 to the corner of Othos Aiolou & Othos Ermou; 9am-2pm Mon-Sat; No credit cards)*, everything, from spaghetti-strap tops to T-shirts to skirts, is only 1,900Dr! Who cares if half the stuff is crappy? Be diligent, and you're sure to find something that suits you. Note: This store is for ladies and cross-dressing men only.

▶▶TUNES

For an eclectic selection of music on vinyl, check out **Music Wave** *(Othos Ifestou 29; Tel 325-00-57; Minibus 150 to the corner of Othos Athinas & Othos Ermou; 9:30am-5pm Mon, Wed, Sat, Sun; 10am-8pm Tue, Thur, Fri; Records & CDs 2,500Dr and up; V, MC)*, run by the admirable Victor Krisanthakis. Not only does he sell some decent new and used music, Victor also dishes the skinny on which live acts to see

cats in athens

Health alert! Athens is overrun by cats! Roaming the city in loose packs, these feral beasts are to Athens what pigeons are to New York. And unlike that cute piece of breathing furniture you left at home, Greece's stray cats have an altogether sinister appearance. Their eyes are set close together, giving them an air of menace. Their ears are wombat-like—nearly twice as big as a normal domestic cat's. And being animals of fortune, they bear countless horrible injuries and illnesses, making them a limping, snotty-eyed army of feline depravity.

Unfortunately, you most assuredly will be harassed by Greece's cats. They hang around garden and sidewalk restaurants (redundant terms in Greece), looking as pitiable as only creatures so ugly can, waiting for your scraps.

If you're a cat fancier, the place for you is the **National Garden** [see *hanging out,* above], in the center of the city. Wander around the eastern side of the park and you'll be rewarded. Bring food if you think happiness is sporting a live fur coat.

by foot

Okay, so Athens ain't the prettiest city on the map, but that doesn't mean you can't take a stroll through some greenery:

1. Stroll west down **Othos Ermou** from **Monistiraki Square**, and take a left on **Othos Apostolou Pavel**. On your left, notice the poppied expanse of the **Agora** [see *culture zoo*, above].

2. Continue moseying, and go left at the fork onto **Othos Dionissiou Areopagitou**. Look up on your left. That would be the southern facade of the **Acropolis** [see *culture zoo*, above].

3. Turn left on **Othos Amalias**, then right on **Othos Vassilissis Olgas**. You have entered the southern regions of the **National Garden** [see *hanging out*, above].

4. Look north. The **Zappeion** is pretty, yes. Take any path you choose and continue north through the **National Garden**.

5. When you come out on the northern edge of the **National Garden**, go right on **Othos Vassilissis Sofias**, then right again on **Othos Irodu Atikou**.

6. Look at the **Presidential Residence**. Note the guards with the silly pompons on their shoes.

around town. Just ask him. By the way, Othos Ifestou, just off the Monistiraki Flea Market, has several other new and used record shops on it.

▶▶**RANDOM**

Juggling isn't just a goofy pastime for bozos, it's a way of life, man. Just ask Kostas, proprietor of **Lazy Dayz Juggling** *(Othos Kyristou & Othos Erechtheos; Tel 321-60-36; Noon-10pm daily, summer only; Juggling supplies 1,500-30,000Dr; No credit cards)*. From handmade devil sticks *(7,000Dr)* to simple juggling balls *(1,500Dr)*, this store has everything you need to turn a buck in the parking lot of a Phish show. The kind folks here will even give you lessons on the finer points of juggling.

For all you rockhounds, stop by **Nikos Abandakis** *(Othos Pericleous 23; Tel 323-16-61; Minibus 200 to the corner of Othos Perikleous & Othos Voulis; 9am-4pm Mon-Fri, till 2pm Sat; Geodes 500-5,000Dr; Semiprecious ashtrays & paperweights 3,000-12,000Dr; No credit cards)* and pick up a lovely agate ashtray for the smoker in your life. Just don't weigh yourself down with a bunch of rocks, genius. There's a polar bear skeleton under glass here, rather spectacular in such a small space.

▶▶**JUNK**

The **Monistiraki Flea Market** *(Just west of Monistiraki Sq.; 8am-3pm daily, till 8pm Tue, Thur, Fri)* has the usual flea market fare, with some treasures buried amid the dross for those of you with patience....

▶▶BOUND

The one place in Athens that hosts regular poetry readings in English is **Compendium** (*Othos Nikis 28; Tel 322-12-48; Yellow Trolley Bus 1, 2, 4, 5, 9-12, 15, 18 to the SW corner of Syntagma Sq.; 9am-5pm Mon, Wed, 9am-8pm Tue, Thur, Fri, 9am-3pm Sat; No credit cards*), a small bookstore near Syntagma Square. The readings are held on the third Thursday of each month at 8pm. They include readings by published poets as well as an open mike for all you tyros. Compendium also has a decent selection of paperback classics and trash books.

The best selection of good English fiction can be found at **J. M. Pantelides** (*Othos Amerikis 9-11; Tel 362-36-73; Yellow Trolley Bus 1-5, 7, 9-13, 15, 18 to the corner of Othos Amerikis & Othos Stadiou; 9am-8pm Tue-Fri, Sun, 9am-4pm Sat; No credit cards*). It's a tiny space, but has a surprisingly complete collection of English literature. If you can't find it here, you'll have a tough time finding it in the States.

Finally, there's Greece's answer to Barnes & Noble, **Eleftherouthakis** (*Othos Panepistimiou 17; Tel 331-41-80; Yellow Trolley Bus 1-5, 7, 9-13, 15, 18 to the corner of Othos Omirou & Othos Panepistimiou; 9am-8:30pm Mon-Fri, till 3pm Sat; No credit cards*). Here you'll find a wide selection of English nonfiction, from travelogues to coffee table books. But there's no cafe inside, and there are no big comfy reading chairs.

EATS

Athens can be an incredibly frustrating place to eat, unless you know where you're going. Don't expect to just pick a random taverna and get a decent meal. The fact is, there are a lot of restaurants here, and the majority suck. Who knows why—maybe all the great short-order cooks immigrated to America. Be especially careful in Plaka, where unbelievably tenacious touts lure you in to substandard meals. Know where you're going....

fashion

Apparently, it's better to look good than to feel good in Athens. Even during their blazing summers, the young and restless dress to the nines just to sit in a cafe. How do they do it without going mad? It's one of the seven wonders of the fashion world. The code here is wear black, and if you must use color, make sure it's dark. For men, button-down shirts and black jeans are de rigueur. For the ladies, it's skirts or tight pants with a tight top. No one ever said looking good was easy, and however much they secretly suffer for it, they sure do pull it off here.

▶▶CHEAP

There are exactly 17 billion sandwich shops in Athens. Which one to choose? By far the best is the chainy-looking **DeliKiosk** *(Othos Leoforio Arditou 14-16; Tel 324-58-57; Any Yellow Trolley Bus to Syntagma Sq.; 7am-10pm Mon, Wed, Fri; 8am-10pm Sat, Sun, Tue, Thur; 600-1,000Dr sandwiches; No credit cards),* located in the northwest corner of Syntagma Square. The baguettes here have crispy golden crusts and the meat won't give you ptomaine poisoning. For Athens, that's batting a thousand.

The McDonald's of Athens, **Everest** *(Syntagma Sq. 1; Tel 331-21-00; Any Yellow Trolley Bus to Syntagma Sq.; 24 hours daily; Pressed sandwiches 500-2,000Dr; No credit cards)* is not only open 24 hours, it's everywhere (*this* one is centrally located). So no matter what bar you crawled out from, no matter when, there's probably one nearby. Just ask around. The sandwiches are tasty comfort food, and for that price, you're really not going to do better anywhere else. So shut up and eat.

For cheap, traditional Greek food, try a little snacky-wack at **To Cafeneo** [see *bar scene*, above]. Order a plate of assorted *mezedes* (appetizers), and you won't be disappointed.

▶▶DO-ABLE

In the middle of Plaka, home of the tourist-trap restaurant, sits the venerable **Hermion** *(Othos Pandrossou 15; Tel 324-67-25; Minibus 150 to the corner of Othos Metropoleos & Othos Karnikareas; Noon-2am; 1,000-5,000Dr per entree; V, MC, AE),* a traditional Greek restaurant with some international flavor. The courtyard dining area here is large yet intimate, and the food is excellent. The Wine Graver's Lamb, a specialty of the house, is a succulent, thyme-y treat. Desserts are simple but delicious.

Another Plaka surprise is **To Tristato** *(Othos Dedalou 34; Tel 324-44-72; Yellow Trolley Bus 1, 2, 4, 5, 9-12, 18 to the corner of Othos Amalias & Othos Vassilissis Olgas; Noon-1am Mon-Sat, 10am-1am Sun; Snacks & desserts 800-2,500Dr; No credit cards),* a cute little place for breakfast, light meals, and desserts. The fresh, homemade yogurt and honey here is first-class, as is the halvah. There's a wide choice of teas served in personal size pots with quaint little wicker strainers. The space is airy, with a high ceiling and a jumble of antique tables, chairs, divans, and armoires.

▶▶SPLURGE

Greek taverna fare is elevated to haute cuisine at **Krasopoulio tou Kokkora** *(Othos Essopou 4; Tel 321-15-65; Minibus 200 to the corner of Othos Athinas & Othos Athinaidos; Noon-whenever Tue-Sun, 8pm-whenever Mon; 1,200-6,000Dr per entree; No credit cards),* located in the happening new Psiri district. The S-shaped cheese pies here are flaky, aromatic wonders, and the grilled meats are juicy and tender. Choose from a wide selection of Greece's finest wines. The atmosphere inside is warm— its dark yellow walls throw a golden glow on the outdoor seating area. Best of all, there's the occasional live band playing here. You could get away without splurging here, but why would you? Reservations are recommended, unless you eat early (before 8pm).

a word about eating out

Is that waiter ignoring you? Probably. Funny thing about Greece, restaurants and cafes never rush you. You might even say the waiters snub you once you've been served. So, relax. Order a beer and sit in a nice comfy chair for as long as you like. You're practically going to have to beg the waiter to come and take your money, anyway.

Another thing: Each time a dish or drink is ordered at most places, a bill comes with it. You'll get one bill for your bread and bottled water, one bill for your appetizer, one bill for your wine, etc. Same at cafes. Each drink comes with its own bill, but you're not expected to pay until you're done. Go figure.

One more funny little restaurant custom here in the heart of Hellenism is the obligatory tour of the kitchen. Especially at seafood places, waiters may urge you to come inside and pick out precisely which little critter you want cooked. So try not to fall too much in love with the lobster fated to be your dinner.

And finally, to tip or not to tip. Locals generally don't tip unless the service is extraordinary, but rich imperialists are expected to share their wealth. Most places already have an automatic service or cover charge, but an additional 5 to 10 percent wouldn't hurt, if only to look posh. Let the drachmas flow, baby.

crashing

The funny thing about Athens is that there's no telling what kind of quality you'll get in a hotel. Never mind that it's been rated, and that it falls within a certain price range, blah blah blah. Sometimes the loveliest places turn out to be a bargain, and the expensive ones end up being dumps. One thing you can count on are cramped bathrooms, with Italian-style showers (i.e., a hand-held showerhead with no curtain to keep the water from going everywhere). A word about toilets: Do not flush your toilet paper down them, unless you feel like risking a flood. Put the soiled sheets in the baskets, please.

Generally, the price of a hotel is determined by its neighborhood. Most of your great bargains are in or near Plaka. The closer to Syntagma Square, it seems, the more expensive they become. You can book rooms at any of the travel agency desks at the airport. Do not put yourselves in the hands of a cabbie who knows "the best hotel in Athens."

▶▶**CHEAP**

The centrally located **Pension Festos** (*Othos Filellinon 18; Tel 323-24-*

athens eats and crashing

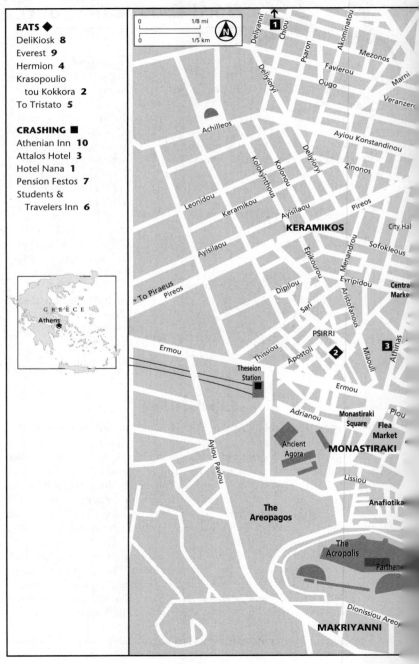

EATS ◆

DeliKiosk **8**

Everest **9**

Hermion **4**

Krasopoulio
tou Kokkora **2**

To Tristato **5**

CRASHING ■

Athenian Inn **10**

Attalos Hotel **3**

Hotel Nana **1**

Pension Festos **7**

Students &
Travelers Inn **6**

GREECE

Athens

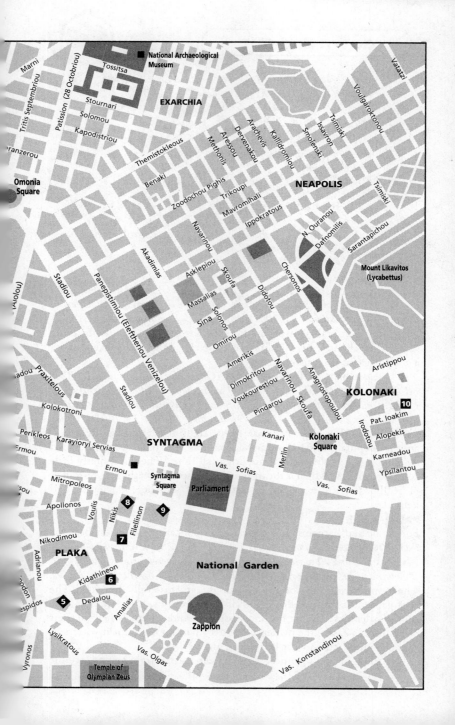

down and out

Go to the **War Museum** *(Othos Vassilissis Sofias, right next to the Byzantine Museum; Tel 725-29-75; 9am-2pm Tue-Sun; Admission free)* and take a trip through the history of Greek warfare. The jet plane in the courtyard alone is worth the trip. Inside, you'll find a fine collection of swords, guns, armor, and all things violent.

Buy a coffee/juice at any cafe in town [see *hanging out*, above] and nurse it till the cows come home. Bring a book. You won't be bothered.

Go to the **Roman Agora** [see *hanging out*, above] and lie in the fields of poppies. See if that *Wizard of Oz* thing works.

Take the A2 or A3 bus to Glyfada and lie on this tiny strip of a beach. Don't expect any surfable waves, though.

55; *Yellow Trolley Bus 1, 2, 4, 5, 9-12, 18 to the corner of Othos Filellinon & Othos Metropoleos; 24-hour desk; consolas@holo.gr; 3,000Dr/person dorm, 7,000Dr doubles, 12,000Dr triples; MC, V)* is one of the best deals in the city. The stall showers are hot, the bar is lively, and the beds are comfy. The clientele here is almost exclusively young backpackers, so it's a good place to meet fellow travelers.

The **Students & Travelers Inn** *(Othos Kidathenaion 16; Tel 324-88-02, Fax 321-00-65; Blue bus 230 to the corner of Othos Filellinon & Othos Kidathenaion; 24-hour desk; students-inn@ath.forthnet.gr; 8,000-9,000Dr single; 10,000-11,000Dr double; 12,000-13,500Dr triple, 14,000-16,000Dr quad; No credit cards)*, right in the middle of Plaka, is another popular place for young backpackers. The bathrooms are shared by all guests, but the showers are hot at all times. There is a pretty little courtyard, next to which is the in-house Internet cafe, with three terminals (1,500Dr/30 minutes, open to the public). Staff here is friendly and helpful.

▶▶**DO-ABLE**

For all-around bargains, and a great central location, you can't beat the **Attalos Hotel** *(Othos Athinas 29; Tel 321-28-01; Fax 324-31-24; Minibus 150 or 200 to the hotel; http://agn.hol.gr/hotels/attalos/attalos.htm; 24-hour desk; 15,500Dr single, 21,000Dr double, 26,400Dr triple; AE, V)*. The rooms here are air-conditioned, bright, and tastefully decorated. The roof garden has an excellent view of the Acropolis, as do many of the rooms' balconies. The staff is knowledgeable and extremely helpful. Best of all, Kostas Zissis, the owner, offers a 10 percent discount if you mention this guide (that's what he told us, anyway).

For those of you who need to stay near Larissis train station, try the

Hotel Nana *(Othos Metaxa 27; Tel 884-22-11, Fax 882-32-20; Yellow Trolley Bus 1 to Larissis station; 24-hour desk; 14,000Dr single, 18,000Dr double; Cash only)*. There's no earthly reason why you would want to stay in this area of town other than proximity to the station, but the Nana has air-conditioning and even room service, a rarity in Greece.

▶▶**SPLURGE**

Located in quaint old Kolonaki, the **Athenian Inn** *(Othos Karitos 22; Tel 723-95-52, Fax 724-22-68; Minibus 060 to the corner of Othos Patriarchi Ioakim & Loukianou; 24-hour desk; 19,700Dr single, 29,400Dr double, 36,600Dr triple, 38,400Dr 2-person suite; V, AE)* has modern, air-conditioned rooms, many with stunning views of Likavitos Hill from their balconies. The staff is friendly and informative. Best of all is the neighborhood, which is quiet and charming. Breakfast buffet is included in the price of the room.

need to know

Currency Exchange The Greek unit of currency is the **drachma (Dr)**. The best places to exchange money are **post offices**, **banks**, and the omnipresent **exchangers**. Try the **central post office**, in the southwest corner of Syntagma Square. ATMs are becoming more common, and the National Bank of Greece operates a 24-hour ATM next to the tourist information office on Syntagma Square.

Tourist Information The **Greek Tourist Organization (EOT)** *(Othos Amerikis 2; Tel 331-04-37; Yellow Trolley Bus 1-5, 7, 9, 11-13, 15, 18 to the corner of Othos Panepistimiou & Othos Amerikis; 9am-7pm Mon-Fri, 11am-5pm Sat)* provides free brochures, maps, and ferry schedules, as well as the daily *Athens News* and the bimonthly *Now in Athens*.

Public Transportation The **north-south subway line** that runs through both Omonia and Monistiraki squares costs 120Dr. Tickets, which are rarely checked, are sold from machines in the stations. **Blue buses** run throughout Athens and its suburbs. Tickets are 120Dr available at most news kiosks. Punch the ticket yourself in the machine on the bus. **Yellow Trolley Buses** run throughout central Athens. Tickets cost 120Dr and are available at most news kiosks. You are on your honor to punch it yourself on board. **Taxis** start their meters at 250Dr, and charge 70Dr/km thereafter within the city, and 120Dr/km in the outskirts 35Dr/minute of standing in traffic. Rates double between midnight and 5am. Tell the driver the general area you are going to before getting in—he may or may not agree to take you. And make sure the meter is on. There is a 300Dr surcharge for rides to and from the airport, and 50Dr for each piece of luggage that goes in the trunk. Most locals don't tip taxi drivers, but round up to the nearest convenient number.

American Express *Othos Ermou 2; Tel 324-49-75; Above McDonald's in Syntagma Sq.; 8:30am-4pm Mon-Fri; 8:30am-1:30pm Sat.*

wired

The best all-around Athens website is ***www.athensguide.com***, and the most comprehensive lists of links to websites about Athens can be found at ***gogreece.miningco.com/msub28b.htm?pid= 2753&cob=home***

The Museum Internet Cafe *(Othos Patission 46; Tel 883-34-18; Yellow Trolley Bus 2-5, 7-9, 11, 13, 14, 18 to the cafe; www.museumcafe.gr; 9am-midnight Mon-Sat; 500Dr/20min; 1,500Dr/hour)* has 15 fast computers and a damned good cappuccino. It's just north of the **National Archaeological Museum** [see *culture zoo*, above].

TaftNet *(Othos Pentelis 3; Tel 324-92-82; Yellow Trolley Bus 1, 2, 4, 5, 9, 10-12, 15, 18 to the corner of Othos Metropoleos & Othos Filellinon; 9:30am-9pm daily; www.taftnet.gr; 300Dr/15min; 1,000Dr/hour)* has a smaller selection of computers and no food or drinks. However, it's located in Plaka, and it's cheap.

Skynet *(Othos Apollonos 10; Tel 322-75-51; Yellow Trolley Bus 1, 2, 4, 5, 9, 10-12, 15, 18 to the corner of Othos Metropoleos & Othos Filellinon; 9am-8:30pm Mon-Fri, till 5pm Sat; www.skynet.gr; 1500Dr/hr, 500Dr/15min)* has seven terminals, and offers printing and network gaming services on top of the usual Internet garbage. It's a bit west of Syntagma Square.

Another good spot is the Internet cafe attached to the **Students & Travelers Inn** [see crashing, above].

Health and Emergency Ambulance: *166*; Police: *100*. **Hygeia Diagnostic and Therapeutic Center** *(Othos Erythrou 4; Tel 682-79-40)* is a competent, private hospital with English-speaking staff.

Pharmacies Generally, all pharmacies keep the same hours *(8:30am-2pm Mon, Wed, 8:30am-2pm/4:30-8:30pm Tue, Thur, Fri, closed Sat, Sun)*. However, there are always a few pharmacies open at any given time. Most pharmacies post the emergency hours schedule on the door. Or, you can phone *107*. The **emergency pharmacies** also are listed in *Athens News*, available at the **Greek Tourist Organization** [see above]. A good pharmacy with an English-speaking pharmacist is the **Farmakeio Nik. Pan. Sakellaris** *(Othos Nikis 3; Tel 322-82-48)*.

Telephone Country code: *30*; city code: *1*; local information: *134*; international operator: *161*. **Local phone cards** *(1,300Dr)* with 100 calls on them can be purchased at any **kiosk**. You cannot make a call from a public phone without one. **AT&T:** *00/800-1311*; **MCI:** *00/800-1211*; **Sprint:** *00/800-1411*.

Airports **Ellinikon Internation Airport:** Dial *144* for flight schedules. Located about 10 miles south of the center. You can take a **taxi**, which will run you about 2,200-3,000Dr, depending on how much luggage you have. If you're an **Olympic Airways** passenger, you can catch their bus from outside its international terminal to its offices in Syntagma Square *(6:30am-8:30pm every half-hour, 200Dr)*. Or, you can catch **express buses 90** or **91** in front of both the west and east terminals, running all the way to Omonia and Syntagma Squares *(On the half-hour 5am-midnight, on the hour 1am-5am; 200Dr, except for midnight-6am, when it is 250Dr)*.

Airlines **British Airways** *(Othos Othonos 10; Tel 325-06-01)*, **Delta** *(Othos Othonos 4; Tel 331-16-68)*, **Lufthansa** *(Othos Leoforos Vassilissis Sofias 11; Tel 369-21-11)*, **TWA** *(Othos Xenofondos 8; Tel 322-64-51)*, **Olympic Airways** *(Othos Leoforos Syngrou 96; Tel 926-72-51)*.

Trains **Larissa Station** *(Tel 524-06-01)* near Omonia Square and **Peloponnese Station** *(Tel 513-16-01)* in **Piraeus** are the two main train stations in Athens. From **Peloponnese Station** you can take a taxi into Athens *(about 1,500-2,000Dr)*. Or, you can take the efficient subway *(120Dr)* all the way to Omonia or Monistiraki Square. From **Rafina**, take the bus to **Areos Park** in Athens *(440Dr)*. From **Larissa Station**, walk east along Othos Filadelfias (which turns into Othos Ioulianou) all the way to Othos Patission. Walking south on Patission will take you to Omonia Square. Going southeast from there on Othos Stadiou will take you to Syntagma Square. Or, take **Yellow Trolley Bus 1** to Syntagma Square.

Bus Lines Out of the City Buses departing Athens leave from **Terminal A** *(Othos Kifissou 100; Tel 512-49-10)* and **Terminal B** *(Othos Liossion 260; Tel 831-71-81)* at **Peloponnese Station**.

greek islands

Only when you've stepped off the ferry onto island soil do you realize how stressed-out you've been. Even the most developed islands retain a mood of tranquil oblivion. It's easy to see why there are so many expats (Brits, Aussies, and Americans) in the Cyclades—if you want to get lost forever, or at least evade the IRS for a few years, this isn't a bad place for it. Although the towns all become giant, never-ending parties during the high season (July through mid-September), it's still possible to find a deserted cove with a sliver of beach on it, and not a hint of civilization in sight.

Hundreds of islands make up the Cyclades; some are mere rock outcroppings breaking the surface of the sea, and only 33 are inhabited. Together they offer some of the most spectacular island scenery on the planet. The three covered here—Mykonos, Paros, and Santorini—were chosen because each represents a different element of the quintessential Greek Island experience. All can be reached by air or ferry.

If your mind reels at the thought of booking hotels and ferry tickets throughout Greece and the islands, sit back and let **Greece Accommodation Direct** *(Tel 44-181-442-9191; sales@greecead.com, from England; www.greecead.com/gadhome/index.html)* handle it all for you. Just tell them your itinerary and budget (Greece A.D. is affiliated with 1,500 hotels in every price range), and their helpful staff will take care of every last detail, right down to having your ferry tickets dropped off at your hotel.

mykonos

Mykonos is the upscale cosmopolitan sister of the Cyclades. Fabulous people come to Mykonos, the net effect of which is higher prices, some 25 percent higher than anywhere else in the Cyclades. Mykonos is also crawling with gay men. The trick on Mykonos isn't finding a gay bar, it's finding a straight one. That's not to say that straights aren't welcomed on Mykonos. Quite the contrary; just about any gay bar, beach, or restaurant is perfectly happy to serve heteros, and the island's native population is no more gay than anywhere else. There's a lot of boy-girl macking going on here as well. Only the lesbian scene seems a bit quiet.

Being chichi, Mykonos has several purveyors of fine clothing, and even some home-grown designers. It seems like drugs are in no short supply here, for those willing to take the enormous risk [see *rules of the game*, below]. And while, according to reliable sources, there are only nine bumbling cops on patrol in Mykonos Town, the penalty of automatic prison time for possession still may not be worth it.

Travel a short distance inland, and you'll see vast expanses of stony fields. It looks as if they're farming rocks here, and the effect of seeing fields of them stretching to the horizon is pretty unsettling (you know, in a good way). As for Mykonos Town, when you get away from the hordes at the harborside cafes and shops, you'll discover a twisty maze of whitewashed splendor. So enjoy yourself when you get lost in it. Save the panic mode for when you get lost in London.

hanging out

By far the most labyrinthine of all the island ports, Mykonos Town is built on a slope leading up from the sea. It also happens to be a good deal larger than most other island towns, in size and population.

Tourists love to snap a few photos and compare notes around the windmills overlooking Little Venice on the south end of Mykonos Town. Dangle your legs over the drop-off and watch the seagulls do their hover thing into the steady northern wind. Afterward, descend into Little Venice for a seaside drink at one of its many outdoor bars. For a bit more seclusion, try the **Art Café** [see *eats*, below], which serves up tasty morsels and coffees. If you're jonesing for some wildlife, hang around the harbor—you might catch one of Mykonos's resident pelicans wallowing in the stone fountain. For the after-hours hang, check out the **Yacht Club** [see *club scene*, below] on the north side of town near the harbor.

bar scene

It comes as no surprise that the bars in Mykonos are well-decorated, but they do run the gamut from straight (i.e., hetero) tourist hangs to well-appointed gay joints. The latter are usually much more interesting than the former, with island-influenced layouts and a more eclectic range of

five things to talk to a local about

1. Ask a Mykonoan about **the fishing boat blockade** of a cruise ship in 1999 (in protest of Western involvement in Kosovo).
2. Ask any Australian shop owners **how they came to live on Santorini/Paros/Mykonos**.
3. What do you think of **Athens**? (This usually gets a more vehement response than you'd figure.)
4. Why are **German tourists** so aggressively naked?
5. **Is it hot enough for ya?**

music being played on the PA. And don't worry if you're straight—you're welcome. As elsewhere in Greece, things don't get going until after midnight, then keep going until dawn.

Please don't ask why they call a place that plays American classic rock and serves beer to its mixed crowd of locals and travelers the **Scandinavian Bar** *(Corner of Othos Yanni Barkias and Othos Kouzi Georgouli; Tel 226-69; 8:30pm-whenever daily; No credit cards)*. The music is loud, the people dance on tables, and there's a separate disco upstairs for those who prefer to do their dancing on floors (the prudes). Beers are 800 to 900Dr for a half-liter, which isn't bad on Mykonos. You'll find all kinds here, young and old, and it's always packed.

A popular place for locals, the **Paranga Beach Bar** *(Paranga Beach; Tel 253-64; 24 hours daily; No credit cards)* rocks all night long. The people here are rowdy and uninhibited, often shedding their clothes by the bonfire as the night wears on. Yow! Paranga attracts some local musicians now and then, so it may be your only chance to catch a real, live act on Mykonos.

With a long history of celebrity debauches and drag-queen spectacles, the gay-owned and -operated **Pierro's** *(Othos Mantoyianni; Tel 221-77; 10pm-6am daily; No credit cards)* may be the most esteemed bar in Mykonos. Drinks here are a bit pricey, but the atmosphere is dim and chill, the music slinky and cool. A naughty little drag show gets underway every night at 2am. Ask the bartender about this place's pedigree, and he's likely to regale you with rhinestone tales of Mick Jagger and Linda Evans getting drunk here. If it's too crowded, go next door to Manto for an uncannily similar experience.

There's no better place to cool off than the excellent **Kastro** *(Near Paraportianni Church; Tel 230-72; 6pm-2:30am daily; No credit cards)*. Classical music and a splendid breeze off the Mediterranean soothe the quiet all-ages crowd. Have a Kastro Coffee (coffee spiked with brandy and house liqueurs), sit by the window, and take in the beautiful view of the port.

There is a whole row of good bars right on the water in Little Venice, but the best bet may be **Veranda** *(Othos Venetia; Tel 262-62; 6pm-whenever daily; No credit cards)*. So what if it costs an arm and a leg to get drunk here? This is the party version of Kastro [see above]. A great place to meet people without the usual brain-jangling music.

club scene

Live music is a rarity on Mykonos. Other than a pickup band at a beach party, the only "live" music you're likely to hear is your drunken self belting out "Sweet Caroline." But Mykonos does know how to party. Check out the seriously loud Mad Club to start your evening off around midnight, then head over to strobe-lit oblivion at Down Under. Still crave a grind with a total stranger at 4am? Check out the Yacht Club for after-hours grooving right on the water. Though there's no dress code, you will stick out as a rube if you aren't fashionably attired.

Mad Club *(Taxi Sq.; Tel 242-36; 11pm-whenever daily; 1,000Dr cover; No credit cards)* is where all the hardcore clubbers go to act like a bunch of possessed savages. The music is loud enough to blast a hole through your soul, but dress nice, lest you wish to stand out as globo-trash. By the way, best drink beforehand—the drinks here are mighty pricey.

Down Under *(Othos Svoronou; Tel 228-22; 10pm-4am daily; No credit cards)* is a blazing little dance club that draws a somewhat more varied crowd (in age). Still, the majority of the people here are under 30 and drunk as hell. Don't come here if you fancy sitting. The darkness facilitates a less-stringent dress code.

When the cowards turn in at 3am, the hardcore head over to the **Yacht Club** *(At the port; No phone; 3am-whenever daily; Cover varies; No credit cards)*. Located right where the ferry comes in, this little rave-a-thon is the perfect place to spend the small hours. It's tiny and plainly decorated, but the location is excellent. Yacht supports "the best-quality techno in all its forms."

rules of the game

There is no drinking age in Greece, but drinking in the streets is frowned upon. Drugs are around in the islands' club scene, but with mandatory prison terms for small possessions, who needs it? So, all the action is a bit clandestine. And with the prison island just a 2-hour (one-way) ferry ride away, no one will take a chance dealing with a complete stranger.

gay scene

Ha! The whole island is one big gay love-in. The bars are gay. The restaurants are gay. Even the friggin' rent-a-car places are gay. If you can't connect with your brethren/sisters here, might we suggest counseling? For the most direct method, try the super-gay **Super Paradise Beach**, where the muscle men hang [see *great outdoors*, below]. Other than these pumped-up beach boys, the gay scene on Mykonos has a distinctly glammy, Euro vibe, with a healthy dose of queeniness thrown in for good measure. Interestingly, the gay bars don't seem to attract any one type of man—you'll find everyone from the strong, silent Super Paradise guys to the waif-y fashion contingent all under one roof.

culture zoo

Delos *(9am-2:30pm Tue-Sun; 1,200Dr admission, 600Dr students; No credit cards)*, a sacred island just a mile off Mykonos, is home to some of the greatest archaeological treasures in Greece, including the famous Delian Lions and the Temple of Apollo. The entire island is covered in magnificent ruins. Boats to Delos leave from the dock in town near the Paraportiannis church. Round-trips cost 1,800Dr. Guided tours are quite a bit more, so it's better to buy a map for 1,700Dr and do it yourself. Just make sure you get off the island before it closes, at 2:30pm (don't worry, they make a big announcement when the time is drawing near). And remember to bring cash—the gods don't take credit.

modification

While not exactly the mecca of body alteration you might expect it to be, Mykonos has a fair share of tattoo parlors. Naturally, water sports are the dominant motif, with scuba joints dotted all over the island.

If you must desecrate your body, pay a visit to **Mykonos Tattoos** *(Othos Ipirou; Tel 696-670; 11am-11pm daily; No credit cards)*. The artist here has worked on bods in San Francisco and New York, where degenerates are discerning, so you know you can trust him.

great outdoors

For a game of pickup basketball, go to the playground at the corner of Othos Rohari and Othos D. Koutsi. These Greeks aren't that bad, and it's free—unless you get hustled out of some drachmas.

In accordance with a recent government ordinance, all beaches on Mykonos are required to blast music at you while you're trying to relax. After all, why shouldn't you hear electronica as you lie on one of the most gorgeous slices of coastline in the world? If that sounds splendid to you, go to **Paradise** or **Super Paradise** beaches (the former has mostly straights, the latter gays, if you couldn't figure that out from the Super). If you prefer a quiet, empty beach, try **Panormos**. The wind is a bit rougher here, but the snorkeling is awesome.

There are a lot of dive centers on Mykonos, but none of them come

mykonos by foot

Mykonos isn't much of a walking island, but the seaside trail, about 3 miles, from Paradise Beach to Platis Yialos, is stunning, with many unspoiled patches of beach along the way.

Another good walk is right in Mykonos Town. Follow the sea from the windmills on the south side of town to the port on the north side. You'll pass the Little Venice section of town, and then the harbor, with its fishing boats and outdoor eateries.

close to matching the prices at the **Mykonos International Dive Center** *(Kalafatis; Tel 716-77; Call for hours; No credit cards)*. One beach dive here costs a relatively piddling 4,500Dr, while a boat dive goes for 8,500Dr. Wreck dives, cave dives, they got it all. Shop around. You won't find a better deal.

STUFF

Along with the useless baubles sold on every other island in the Mediterranean, Mykonos has some hip little clothing stores.

Milagro Fashion *(Othos Agiou Evthimiou; Tel 232-28; 9am-2:30pm/5-11pm daily; AE, MC, V)* sells sleek little Athens designs. Ladies: Get your capris here for a mere 10,000Dr, and your cute little tank tops for only 6,000Dr! The styles are beachy, yet sophisticated.

Le Poisson Bleu *(Othos Matogianni; Tel 249-85; 10:30am-4:30pm/6:30pm-midnight daily; AE, MC, V, debit cards)* sells a pricier range of duds by designers from all over the world, including Vivienne Tam, Whistles, and Stella Cadente. The styles here are sexy/funky. Pick up a sheer silk dress for a paltry 98,000Dr. For more modest budgets, colorful sarongs go for 20,000Dr. Those with no budget can make a wish in the store's in-house wishing well!

To Biblio Book Shop *(Othos Zouganelli; Tel 883-96; 9am-2pm/5-9pm Mon-Sat; No credit cards)* has an okay selection of beach reading, as well as a few classics.

EATS

One of the most difficult things to do on Mykonos is to find cheap, good food. There are plenty of excellent restaurants in the high-end range, but moderate prices for a decent meal? Fuhgeddaboutit.

▶▶CHEAP

For one of the greatest sandwiches in the world, stop by **Piccolo** *(Corner of Othos Satiros and Othos Petrou Drakopoulou; Tel 222-08; 9am-6pm Mon-Sat; About 1,000Dr sandwiches; No credit cards)*. Sandwich artist Joseph Salachas will make any concoction you can dream up. The bread is

mykonos

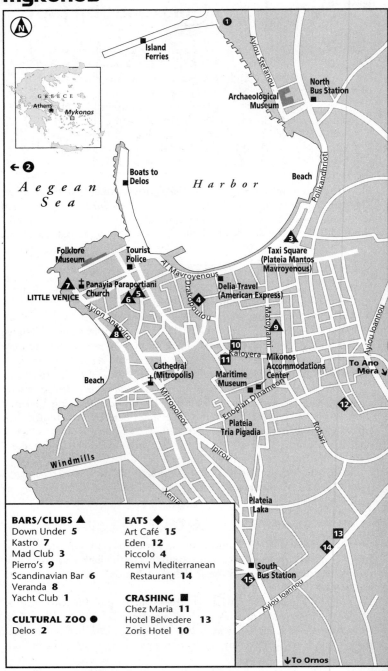

North Bus Station

Island Ferries

Archaeological Museum

Aegean Sea

Boats to Delos

Harbor

Beach

GREECE

Athens

Mykonos

Folklore Museum

Tourist Police

Taxi Square (Plateia Mantos Mavroyenous)

Panayia Paraportiani Church

LITTLE VENICE

Delia Travel (American Express)

Mikonos Accommodations Center

To Ano Mera

Cathedral (Mitropolis)

Maritime Museum

Beach

Plateia Tria Pigadia

Windmills

Plateia Laka

Plateia Laka

South Bus Station

To Ornos

BARS/CLUBS ▲
Down Under **5**
Kastro **7**
Mad Club **3**
Pierro's **9**
Scandinavian Bar **6**
Veranda **8**
Yacht Club **1**

CULTURAL ZOO ●
Delos **2**

EATS ◆
Art Café **15**
Eden **12**
Piccolo **4**
Remvi Mediterranean
 Restaurant **14**

CRASHING ■
Chez Maria **11**
Hotel Belvedere **13**
Zoris Hotel **10**

crusty and fresh and the meat and cheese, high quality. Joseph also purveys a mouth-watering array of pastries. No seating, by the way—Piccolo is a display case, a counter, and a strip of floor where you wait in line.

▶▶**DO-ABLE**

For breakfast, why not try the venerable **Art Café** (*Gialos Sq.; Tel 235-74; 9am-9pm daily; About 2,000Dr breakfast; No credit cards*), decorated with exotic flowers by the international waiter of mystery, Dagmar. The English breakfast (2,000Dr) is a good deal on this island, and the atmosphere couldn't be better for your aching head. Insulated from the hurly-burly of Mykonos, sit at the shaded tables (abstractly painted by Dagmar) and sip your OJ.

▶▶**SPLURGE**

Eden (*Near the Panahrandou Church; Tel 228-55; 7pm-1am daily; 3,500Dr and up per entree; AE, MC, V*) serves delicious continental cuisine around a large swimming pool in a courtyard. Where else in Greece can you safely order beef, let alone the absolutely succulent Chateaubriand served here? The house wine is tasty and reasonably priced, and the wait staff is very friendly. No shorts allowed here, and make reservations. And dig the restaurant's credo: "The Creator condemned man to eat so as to live, and summons upon him this task by whetting his appetite."

Part of the peerless **Hotel Belvedere** [see *crashing*, below], **Remvi Mediterranean Restaurant** (*Othos Agiou Ioannou; Tel 251-22; 1-3pm/7-11pm; 2,800-6,000Dr per entree; AE, MC, V*), serves unique, modern takes on classic Mediterranean fare. The mushrooms on a bed of arugula are pungent and meaty, and the pork in wine sauce with raisins and basmati rice is a slice of heaven. The glass of "superior red wine" (2,400Dr) is just that, and the *panacotta* is unbelievable. No casual clothing allowed. Reservations recommended here, too.

mykonos' pelicans

Have you ever looked into the eye of a bathing pelican? It's really quite extraordinary. Nothing—not spending the night wasted on whatever, not grinding with a stranger to techno until dawn's rosy fingers caress the horizon—captures the hedonist ethic of Mykonos like the sight of one of these birds lolling in the fountain near the excursion boats to Delos. Take a gander at that bird's blissed-out face, its head resting upside-down on its back, enjoying the plushness of its own feathers. Count yourself among the lucky if you happen upon this somewhat alarming spectacle of avian self-pleasuring.

festivals and events

The Balosia *(Jan 6)*. Feast traditionally held before the local merchant ships' departures out to sea.

crashing

Interesting thing about Mykonos: There seems to be none of the usual collusion here among hotels in their price schedules. A little run-down dump may charge you as much as a three-star hotel, while another may be more reasonable, so it's best to shop around. As with the restaurants, there is a good sampling of expensive places, but the bargains are tough to find.

▶▶CHEAP

Chez Maria *(Othos Kalogera; Tel 224-80; 16,000Dr double, 20,000Dr triple; No credit cards)* rents out cute, homey rooms at some of the lowest rates on the island. And Maria's flower-filled courtyard restaurant (not reviewed here, but well-liked by both locals and visitors) is a gorgeous addition to an already beautiful hotel. The rooms are decorated with an eclectic mix of furniture, and the sociable Maria is always on hand to make your stay more pleasant and lead the guests in impromptu rounds of "Doe, a Deer" (just kidding).

▶▶DO-ABLE

Run by the affable Jonathan Varnalis, the **Zoris Hotel** *(Othos Kalogera; Tel 221-67, Fax 241-69; 19,000Dr single, 24,000Dr double, 35,000Dr triple; AE, MC, V)* has beautifully appointed rooms and a great location. The bathrooms feature stall showers, plenty of room, and black and white tiling straight out of *Alice in Wonderland*. The bedrooms all have ceiling fans and big beds.

▶▶SPLURGE

Quite simply the best in Mykonos, the **Hotel Belvedere** *(Othos Agiou Ioannou; Tel 251-22, Fax 251-26; 57,000Dr single, 59,000Dr double, 73,500Dr triple, 90,000Dr suite; www.belvederehotel.com; AE, MC, V)* features (besides big, air-conditioned rooms) a health spa with Jacuzzi, an exercise room, a screening room, free Internet access, a pool and patio, and the best complimentary breakfast around (of course, you are paying for it...). Some of the bedrooms even have fireplaces, for those of you who want to winter here. All this, and the **Remvi Mediterranean Restaurant** [see *eats*, above].

need to know

Currency Exchange The currency of Greece is the **drachma (Dr)**. The **National Bank of Greece** *(Othos Akti Kambani; Tel 229-32; 8am-2pm/6-8pm Mon-Thur, 8am-1:30pm Fri, 10am-1pm Sat, Sun)* is the money changer of choice.

Tourist Information The Mykonos Tourist Office *(Near the boats to Delos; Tel 239-90; Open daily)* is the "official" tourist information bureau.

Public Transportation There is an okay bus line on Mykonos that serves the major beaches from Mykonos Town for 200 to 300Dr. The **South Bus Station**, near the windmills, has buses to Plati Yialos Beach, Paradise Beach, Ornos Beach, and Agios Ioannis. The **North Bus Station**, near the ferry port, has buses to Kalo Livadi Beach, Ano Mera, Agios Stefanos Beach, and Elia Beach.

Bike/Moped Rental Renting a car/scooter on Mykonos is an expensive but worthwhile proposition. Try **Kosmos** *(Near the ferry port; Tel 240-13)*. The cheapest car you'll find in high season is 10,000Dr/day; Scooters start at 5,000Dr/day.

American Express Delia Travel *(Othos Akti Kambani; Tel 223-22; 9am-9pm Mon-Fri, 9am-3pm/6-9pm Sat, Sun)* is Amex's local agent.

Health and Emergency Police: *227-16*; Ambulance: *166*. **Mykonos Hospital** *(Ano Mera; Tel 239-94; 9am-1pm/5-10pm daily)* has a 24-hour help line with a message stating which doctor is on duty. The **Medical Center** *(Agiou Ioannou; Tel 242-11; 8:30am-midnight daily)* is in Mykonos Town and has better hours.

Pharmacies Generally, all pharmacies keep the same hours *(8:30am-2pm/4:30-8:30pm Tue, Thur, Fri, 8:30am-2pm Mon, Wed, closed Sat, Sun)*. However, there are always a few pharmacies open at any given time. Most pharmacies post the emergency hours schedule on the door. Try **Nikos Kousathanas** *(Othos Matogianni; Tel 231-51)*.

Telephone Telephones in Mykonos require a phone card, available at almost any newsstand for 1,300Dr/100 calls. The country code for Greece is 30. Mykonos' area code is 0289. **AT&T:** *00-800-1311*; **MCI:** *00-800-1211*; **Sprint:** *00-800-1411*.

Airports Mykonos Airport *(Tel 223-27)*. Taxis to Mykonos Town, about 2 miles away, cost about 1,200Dr. Mykonos can be reached by a 35-minute small-plane air service from the Athens airport; 10 flights a day run in peak season on **Olympic Airways** [see below].

Airlines Olympic Airways *(Near the North Bus Station; Tel 224-90)*.

Ferries The ferry port in Mykonos is located just outside of Mykonos Town, at the northern jetty. If you can affort it, take a taxi. A 6-hour

wired on mykonos

There is one Internet center that mortals can afford in Mykonos, with a mere three terminals, located in the back of the **Porto Market** *(Near the ferry port; Tel 234-45; 8:30am-11:30pm daily; 1,000Dr/15 min; MC, V)*, which is a small convenience store.

ferry runs at least twice daily to Mykonos from the **Port of Piraeus** (one of Athens's two ports); in summer a hydrofoil service—what the Greeks call "The Flying Dolphin"—takes passengers to Mykonos from Piraeus and from Athens's other port, **Rafina**.

paros

Paros is Mykonos on a less glitzy, less expensive, less exclusive scale, but with the same gorgeous Aegean beaches lapped by clear turquoise water. The hub city here is most definitely the port of Parikia, with its high concentration of bars and clubs. It's your typically maze-like Greek island town, with a harbor fronted by car-rental places, travel agents, bars, and restaurants. Following the seaside road north takes you to Livadia Beach, a 5-minute walk from Parikia's harbor. There are several good **beach clubs** [see *beach club scene*, below] all around the island where you can spend the day swimming, snorkeling, or windsurfing before a night of dancing, drinking, and other distractions.

With perhaps the most wide-ranging offerings of the Cyclades islands, Paros has enough land mass that you can get away from the crowds, even at the height of summer. Young people form the huge majority of the visitors (though not overrunning it, as they do on some other islands). As in Santorini, the chosen mode of transport here is the scooter; it's convenient and a blast. But there's also a perfectly good bus system.

For more genteel pleasures, there's the pretty fishing town of Naoussa, where you can lounge in any of the harborside cafes, sucking up an iced coffee like a deranged bourgeois mosquito.

hanging out

Take a walk along **Livadia Beach** just west of Parikia. Though there are far more spectacular beaches on Paros, this is where you come to sit in a cafe and watch the parade of scandalously clad young hedonists stroll by.

A fine vantage point for all this nonsense is **Maracaibo** (*Livadia Beach; Tel 228-94; 8am-4pm daily; No credit cards*), a self-described "progressive cafe" (not code for gay, incidentally). Relax with one of Welsh owner Dylan Hawkins's fresh-squeezed juice cocktails on the trellised patio. Or, later in the season, plant yourself at one of the tables placed in the pine grove across the street, a popular pit stop for migratory sparrows. Equally popular, for natives and aliens alike, are the cafes along the main market street in the heart of Parikia.

For the all-night hang, check out **Aromas Taverna** (*Parikia; Tel 219-85; 24 hours daily June-Aug; 1,600-5,800Dr per entree; No credit cards*), where all the clubbers go at 6am after rocking all night at the nearby **Dubliner** complex [see *club scene*, below]. The food ranges from pizza to traditional Greek fare.

bar scene

If you've got a trust fund and you're looking for an island on which to drink your life away, this is it. Paros has a bar to please every palate, and they're almost invariably friendly; you feel like a regular after coming back only a couple times. All these spots are also a stone's throw from each other and easy to find.

Kitsilano *(Parikia; 6pm-2am daily; No credit cards)* is a no-shit bar that plays a nice mix of no-shit classic rock. The crowd here is young, but decidedly no-shit, as is the owner/barkeep Patrick, a good man to know on Paros. The decor is cozy—Patrick has knocked out much of the walls' white plaster facade to reveal the craggy stonework that lies below. A great place to start your night, it also wouldn't be a bad place to finish if it stayed open longer. Come here two different years, and you get to carve your name in the bar.

For a bizarre mix of locals and expats, go to **Magaya** *(Delphini Beach; Tel 237-91; 10am-4am daily; No credit cards)* and sit at the bar. If you come early, you're likely to catch the great sushi chef and character Norio [see *eats*, below] grabbing his breakfast. The bar opens up right onto the beach and features a large seating area. Beers are 600Dr for half-liters, a more-than-fair price. This is such a chill place to drink and swim the day away, you may end up spending your whole trip here. Keep your eyes peeled for a certain Coke-bottle-spectacled Brit who's fond of regaling anyone who'll listen with the merits of women from Denmark.

The **Saloon d'Or** *(Parikia; Tel 221-76; 7pm-2am daily; No credit cards)* is one of the more popular spots in Parikia. There are plenty of little nooks to tuck yourself away in, and the selection of beers is impressive. With classic rock blaring, this place attracts everyone from 18 to 50. Despite its somewhat touristy name and outward appearance, this is just a regular old bar, and a damned good one at that.

LIVE MUSIC SCENE

There are a few venues that occasionally host live music events here. For the most part, these are not bands you would see for their own sake, but

fIVE-O

Seven years for possession of illegal drugs, oh my brothers and sisters. On the plus side, the police forces on Greek islands are actually rather endearing, puttering about on their mopeds. You'll notice very few cops on the islands, and the bulk of their time is devoted to enforcing tourist-related mandates.

paros by foot

Paros has two worthwhile cave walks. In **Marathi**, halfway between Parikia and Naoussa, are the abandoned marble quarry caves. Park your car/scooter (or hop off the bus) at the gate and walk. It can be rather confusing finding the entrance to the cave, but the key is to take the path that leads up the hill. Remember to bring a couple of flashlights and wear good sneakers or hiking boots. These caves are pitch-dark and a bit creepy—in a fun way.

A bit more of a hassle but well worth your time are the gorgeous stalactite caverns of **Antiparos**, the small island off the western side of Paros *(10am-5pm daily; 400Dr admission)*. For a great day trip, take the ferry from Pounta *(170Dr/person, 1,700Dr/car, 600Dr/scooter)* to Antiparos, then hop on a bus to the south side of the island *(1,200Dr round-trip)*. Bring a camera—the stalagmites and stalactites here are among the world's most well-developed.

rather as background to the perpetual party that goes on all summer long. First, across the island from Parikia is the **Punda Beach Club** [see *beach club scene*, below], where Disneyland meets the Playboy Mansion. And near Naoussa, there's the **Monasteri Beach Club** [see *beach club scene*, below], which has a small stage surrounded by a miniature amphitheater. Call ahead for live music schedules. Finally, **Magaya** [see *bar scene*, above] hosts a local pickup jam every Sunday afternoon.

club scene

There are a good many beach-side establishments on Paros that qualify as "clubs," but these are such institutions that they've merited their own little section [see *beach club scene*, below]. Other than these places, there's really just one club you need to see here, actually a most bizarre complex of clubs flagshipped by the **Dubliner** *(Parikia; Tel 211-13; 10pm-7am daily; 1,000Dr cover; No credit cards)*. Also under this single roof are the **Down Under**, the **Scandinavian**, the **Cigar Bar**, the **Cactus Club**, the **Comma Club**, and the **Paros Rock Club**, among others. It's actually a brilliant concept: Imagine a mall in which all of the stores are bars/clubs, each catering to a different niche. The Comma Club gets the ravers, the Cactus Club has a huge selection of tequilas, and the Dubliner itself features hard house music and drunken pole dancing. Why not have a drink in each place and see if you can make it out alive?

paros

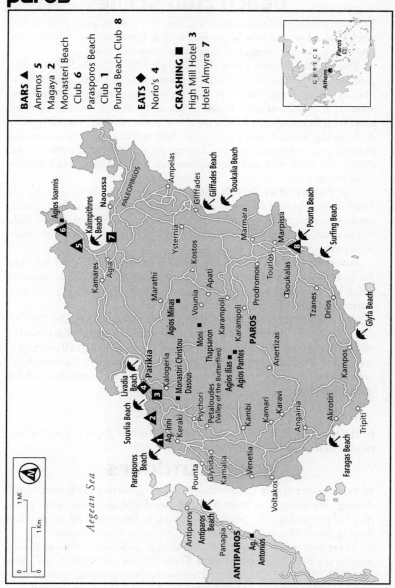

beach club scene

The beach club is a Paros institution. Basically a water park crossed with a bar crossed with a beach, the beach club phenomenon has attached itself to nearly every stretch of sand or pebbles on Paros.

The **Punda Beach Club** *(Punda Beach; Tel 417-17; 24 hours daily July/Aug; No credit cards)* looks like a place where MTV might choose to film its Spring Break show—in fact, there are apparently talks going on about that very possibility. Punda offers scuba diving, bungee jumping, massage, a flea market, a large amorphous pool, two bars, several levels of deck seating, a beach, and a restaurant. Add to that a constant soundtrack of dance and soul music, and you may get an idea of what this place is like. Punda also hosts rock and hip-hop festivals (call ahead for exact dates—these things tend to be fluid).

The **Parasporos Beach Club** *(Parasporos Beach; Tel 215-88; 24 hours daily July/Aug; No credit cards)* is a far more modest affair, but its sandy white beach kicks Punda's ass. The young and drunk crowd rocks out to much less aggressively pitched music. There's also a large bar and a restaurant.

Anemos *(Kolimbithres Beach; Tel 521-43; 9am-12am daily July/Aug; No credit cards)* is a more family-oriented place, on a small-but-beautiful beach with wind-carved rock formations. There is, thankfully, no forced music program here. All is quiet. Come, relax.

The **Monasteri Beach Club** *(Kolimbithres Beach; Tel 530-35; Noon-1am daily July/Aug; No credit cards)* attracts a mixed-age crowd of mostly Europeans with its beach volleyball court and its small amphitheater where musical acts and the occasional play show up. The beach is a pretty good size, but there's something just a little down-at-the-heels about this place.

arts scene

In the east end of Parikia is the **Cine Rex** movie theater, which shows movies in English for 1,700Dr.

great outdoors

In Paros, water sports like windsurfing and jet skiing are generally run through the ubiquitous **beach clubs** [see *beach club scene*, above]. But those of you looking for good places to jog or bike will have no problem finding them. The real action on Paros, though, is under water.

There are several scuba centers in Paros, and the one nearest to Parikia may be the best. The **Eurodivers Club** *(Punda; Tel 920-71, cell phone 093/710-77-47; AE, DC, MC, V)* leads dives into grottoes, around shipwrecks, and into reefs. They also supervise first-time dives, snorkel outings, and underwater photography expeditions. The cost for a single dive ranges between 13,000 and 18,000Dr. First-timers can do a 5-meter dive for 15,000Dr (7,000Dr if you only dive in a pool).

If you're staying in Parikia—and you probably are—there's a good run

festivals and events

Festival of the Assumption *(Aug 15)*. Feast-day celebration at the waterfront with fireworks and songs of the sea.

right outside your front door. Just take the oceanfront road west past **Livadia Beach** [see *hanging out*, above]. Keep going until the road gives out near the caves of Spileo Archilochou.

STUff

Shopping on Paros is not an overwhelming experience. The music stores have a small, expensive selection, and the market streets sell the same souvenir junk you can get anyplace in **Plaka** [see *athens*].

eats

Though not as restaurant-rich as Santorini, there's still a good variety on Paros. From the humble sandwich shop to haute Mediterranean cuisine, your tongue has no reason for complaint here. As is the case everywhere else in Greece, you just have to be careful. Walk into a place blind, and you've probably got about a one-in-four chance of getting a good meal. Ask around: Bartenders and bellboys carry a tremendous wealth of information on Grecian grub.

▶▶**CHEAP**

Mmmmm...fresh-cut sandwiches and delicious crêpes from **To Karpouzi** *(Parikia; Tel 213-16; 9am-5am daily; 700-2,500Dr crêpes, sandwiches; V, MC)*. This little hole in the wall makes 'em any way you like, and best of all, they're open 20 hours a day. Skip dessert wherever you've eaten dinner and head here for a crêpe stuffed (in season) with fresh strawberries.

For the animal-lovers (the live kind) out there, mosey on over to the **Happy Green Cow** *(Parikia; Tel 246-91; 6pm-midnight daily; 800-2,500Dr per entree; No credit cards)* and eat some plant matter. The falafel is crunchy on the outside, creamy on the inside. The joint looks like a Jefferson Airplane show at the Fillmore, and the clientele is young, young, young.

▶▶**DO-ABLE**

NOR-EE-O! NOR-EE-O! NOR-EE-O! Norio rocks. Have a beer with him at **Magaya** [see *bar scene*, above], but more importantly, check out his excellent sushi joint, **Norio's Restaurant** *(South of Parikia; Tel 236-50; 7pm-1am daily; 1,500-3,000Dr per entree; No credit cards)*. Though it's possible to end up spending a lot here, you can do just fine on the sushi plate for two (2,300Dr) and an appetizer. The locals think the world of this place, with good reason. The ambiance is charming, there's a great view of the sea, especially from the balcony seats, and the food is super. Norio also serves up Western-style desserts like pears in port wine and *tiramisù*.

▶▶SPLURGE

Levantis *(Parikia; Tel 236-13; 6:30pm–midnight daily; 1,600-4,500Dr per entree; MC, V, AE)* serves up inspired riffs on Mediterranean cuisine. For starters, try the feta cheese and pine nuts rolled inside roasted red peppers. For your main course, the fish of the day is always fresh and usually quite tasty. Wines are well-chosen and reasonably priced. The eating area is a courtyard covered by a sprawling, ancient grapevine.

crashing

For some reason, there are tons of cheap hotels in Paros. Finding a good splurge is actually a bit trickier. Also, it's easier to get away with just crashing on the beaches (a safe enough gambit here), always a favorite pastime for the indigent trust-fund traveler. As a rule, the places in and around Parikia are the best value. They're not much more expensive than hotels in the boondocks, and they're right in the middle of the action. Like everywhere else, the touts crowd the harbor here when the ferries come in, so you should have no trouble finding a room. If you prefer using more traditional middlemen, book a spot through any one of the travel agencies in the main square, right across the street from where you disembark. Or call the Room Association *(Tel 0284/245-28)* for some free assistance.

▶▶SUPER-CHEAP

The secluded little **Koula Camping** *(Parikia, near Livadia Beach; Tel 220-81, Fax 227-40; 1,400Dr/person, 1,000Dr/tent rental; No credit cards)* offers laundry service and a small store at an ideal beach location. There are bathrooms with showers.

▶▶CHEAP

The **Hotel Akropolis** *(Parikia; Tel/Fax 244-44; 14,000Dr double, 18,000Dr triple; No credit cards)* is a super-friendly place tucked away in Parikia. The rooms are clean and comfy, and have their own bathrooms.

Pension Rafaella *(Parikia; Tel 220-06, Fax 245-09; 5,000-7,000Dr/person; No credit cards)* has kitchen facilities and private baths in all of its rooms, as well as air-conditioning in a few of them (not that they need it—these rooms stay cool by themselves). The owners are friendly, knowledgeable, and eager to help.

The **High Mill Hotel** *(Parikia; Tel 235-81, Fax 234-88; 12,000Dr/ double; No credit cards)* is located just outside town, but it's well worth the short ride or walk in. There's a pool in front, and the rooms all have private patios. A cute little crowd of roosters owns the driveway.

Right in the heart of town is the **Argonauta Hotel** *(Parikia; Tel 214-40, Fax 234-42; hotel@argonauta.gr, www.argonauta.gr; 12,000-18,000Dr single; 15,000-22,000Dr double; V, MC)*, run by the feisty Chrissoulo Dmitri. The rooms are comfortable, with queen-size beds in the doubles, air-conditioning, and balconies. The range of prices we list is dependent on the season—the summer months are, of course, the most expensive.

Right outside the town of Naoussa, the **Hotel Almyra** *(Naoussa; Tel 521-16, Fax 518-23; 15,000Dr double, 18,000Dr triple, 24,000Dr quad; V, MC, AE)* commands a stunning view of the sea. More apartments than rooms, these excellent flats have kitchens, complete with refrigerators and cookware. The complex is surrounded by a pretty stone courtyard, and all the rooms have private patios. And hey: tennis courts!

need to know

Currency Exchange Exchange your money for **drachmas (Dr)** at the **National Bank** *(Mavrogenous Sq., Parikia; Tel 212-98; 8am-2pm Mon-Thur, till 1:30pm Fri).*

Tourist Information The Paros **tourist information bureau** has reportedly been embroiled in some scandal of late. Try **Orbit Travel** *(Livadia Beach; Tel 246-29; 9am-2pm Mon-Fri, 10am-1pm Sat).*

Public Transportation Buses depart from Parikia to just about anywhere on the island about every hour. How late they run depends on the time of year—in high season they go through the night. Call *211-33* for current information in English.

Scooter Rental Scooters run about 3,500-5,000Dr/day. Try **Motorplan Rent-A-Bike** *(Parikia; Tel 246-78; Open daily; V, MC).*

Car Rental Cyclades Rent-A-Car *(Parikia; Tel 210-57; Open daily; AE, DC, MC, V)* will set you up with wheels for 6,000Dr/day and up.

Health and Emergency Police: *233-33*; **Medical Center of Paros** *(Parikia; Tel 244-10)*; **Parikia Health Center** *(Parikia; Tel 225-00).*

Pharmacies Generally, all pharmacies keep the same hours *(8:30am-2pm/4:30-8:30pm Tue, Thur, Fri, 8:30am-2pm Mon, Wed, closed Sat, Sun).* However, there are always a few pharmacies open at any given time. Most pharmacies post the emergency hours schedule on the door. Try **Frangoulis Pharmacy** *(Parikia; Tel 214-49).*

Telephone Telephones in Paros require a phone card *(1,300Dr/100 calls)*, available at almost any newsstand. Country code: *30*; area code: *0284*; **AT&T:** *00-800-1311*; **MCI:** *00-800-1211*; **Sprint:** *00-800-1411.*

Airports Paros Airport; buses run frequently from the airport and cost 290Dr. Paros can be reached on daily 35-minute **Olympic Airways** [see below] flights from Athens.

Airlines Olympic Airways *(Parikia; Tel 220-92).*

Ferries Ferries (5 hours) go to Paros daily from Athens's **Port of Piraeus**, and three times a week from Rafina; a high-speed ferry (2 hours and 45 minutes) also travels to Paros from **Piraeus daily** (twice daily in the summer). You can also catch a hydrofoil service, during the summer, from Athens's **Rafina Port**.

santorini

The fiercely dramatic landscape of Santorini has been called the most stunning in the Greek Isles. The west side of the island is all steep seaside cliffs supporting whitewashed villages, while the east side flattens out onto pebbly, black-sand beaches. Santorini is somewhat more mellow than the other islands, the hard partying is largely done elsewhere, but it's still a damn good time. The key to finding the party on Santorini, and on any Cycladic island for that matter, is to follow the Australians. They work here, they play here, they live here. They're everywhere, they like to drink, and they're friendly as hell, so give 'em the third degree. Like islanders the world over, Santorinians (both Aussie and Greek) seem to be a bit more laid-back than their mainland counterparts. For nighttime activities, the place to be is Firá, the largest town on the island (not to be confused with Thira, another name for Santorini). Here you can find all the bars, clubs, and carousal that your degenerate heart could hope for.

By far the most naturally beautiful island in the Cyclades chain, Santorini is actually the tip of a submerged volcano. Its current "C" shape is the result of a massive eruption that vaporized half of its formerly donut-shaped land mass over 2,000 years ago, clouding the earth's atmosphere for a year and possibly destroying the great Minoan civilization on Crete. So show a little respect—this baby could blow again at any time. Meanwhile, don your white linens and linger along the streets of Oia, the prettiest town on the island.

There are countless beaches on the outer rim of Santorini, so it's all a question of personal taste and prevailing winds here. The Greeks call the wind *meltemi*, and its direction will probably dictate where you want to be sunning yourself. In early summer, *meltemi* blows from the north, so you want to pick a nice southern beach, like the red-sand beauty near Akrotiri [see *culture zoo*, below]. Later in the season, *meltemi* approaches from the south, pushing sun worshippers to the black gravel of Monolithos beach.

You'll probably want to rent a moped or a car to get around the island, but there is a cheap public bus if you want to save money [see *need to know*, below]. Maps of the island are sold almost everywhere, and the roads are well-maintained, for a Greek island.

hanging out

For some reason, **Kamari Beach**, located on the south side of the island *(about a 20- to 30-minute drive or bus ride from Firá)*, attracts a huge number of beautiful people, making this black sandy stretch an ideal hang during the day. If you want to rent lounging gear, which might be a good idea on this mildly uncomfortable gravel, two cozy beach chairs and an umbrella will run you about 2,000Dr.

One of the most popular spots, both day and night, is the **Dolphins**

Beach Bar *(Kamari Beach; Tel 316-08; 8am-whenever daily; V, MC)*, a large, outdoor, tiki-roofed establishment. The crowd here is international and the drinks are cheap (shooters for 200Dr, beer for 700Dr). The pop music pumps constantly, accompanied at night by surf and ski videos.

Or, just kick back in any one of the beachfront bars or cafes that line Kamari. The southernmost end of the beach has some splendid cliff diving, as well as a ferry that will take you to Perissa Beach for 1,000Dr. But, to be honest, unless Kamari is way overcrowded, Perissa just isn't worth the trip.

A more chill spot is the lovely, hard-to-reach red-sand beach near **Akrotiri** [see *culture zoo*, below], on the southwestern tip of Santorini. To get to it, go past Akrotiri toward the water, and take a right down the dirt road. After a few hundred yards, the road empties into a small parking lot. You will have to take a path around a rocky point to find the beach, but its seclusion and beauty are well worth it.

To meet like-minded American, Australian, and British back-packers, look no further than the courtyard at the **Firá Youth Hostel** [see *crashing*, below]. The place is teeming with restless revelers, so don't be a wallflower.

Like all over the rest of Greece, people in Santorini hang out in cafes. Check out the secluded **Alitana Café** *(Oia; Tel 714-04; 11am-4pm/8pm-3am daily; No credit cards)*. This courtyard cafe is a relaxing place to while away an afternoon or to spend a chill evening. The music is slinky-soulful, and the drinks are more than fairly priced for this posh area (500-800Dr for a coffee, 400Dr for a beer). **Oia** [see *by foot*, below] is on the northern tip of the island, about a 20-minute drive from Firá.

bar scene

Nightlife in Santorini tends to center around the town of Firá. While many of the beaches have bars that draw a decent crowd when the sun goes down, you can't beat Firá for sheer variety. Whether you're looking for a dive, an Irish pub, or a lounge, it's here, and it's packed to the gills. There's no need for a plan of attack in a place like this: There are really only a few long streets in Firá, making most bars within a 5-minute walk of each other. Go!

What is it about the Irish pub? Perhaps Santorinians feel a kinship toward that other island of drinkers across the wine-dark sea. The Aus-tralian-owned **Murphy's** *(Firá; Tel 222-48; Noon-4am; No credit cards)* pulls in a gigantic young crowd just about every night of the week. The decor is very college-bar, with sturdy wooden furniture and lots of mem-orabilia on the walls. The super-friendly staff seems genuinely interested in getting you as drunk as possible, even if that means fronting a few Jägermeisters to help you along the way. Each night, there is a cocktail du jour that goes for 1,000Dr, instead of the usual 1,800Dr. Happy hour runs from 9:30 till 10:30pm, during which all drinks are two-for-one. Music here runs the gamut of classic rock.

Why do they call **Kira Thira Jazz Bar** *(Firá; Tel 227-70; 9pm-4am*

santorini by foot

While there is no shortage of beautiful walks to take in Santorini, the prettiest of all may be to simply walk along the edge of the volcanic caldera in **Oia** [see *by foot*, below]. Another option: Walk to the ancient castle at the tip of the island, where you'll notice some stairs leading down to the water. Take this long walk (about an hour) down to the crystal-clear water and have a dip. The walk back up is hard on the knees, so be sure you know what you're getting into when you climb down.

daily; No credit cards) a jazz bar? Because the DJ sometimes plays jazz? Whatever—the true draw is the salty, port-town feel the place has when it's not too crowded and something quiet is playing on the PA, and the fact that beer can be had for as little as 500Dr. The crowd here is mixed ages, weighted a bit toward the thirtyish side.

Les Café *(Firá; Tel 253-83; 8pm-4am daily; No credit cards)* is a Burt Bacharach–playing little lounge with a young, hipster crowd. According to the owners, they also play Latin, acid jazz, and soul. Customers here play chess and checkers while drinking Les Cocktail (1,500Dr), a secret concoction that looks like a Rastafarian flag. The atmosphere is low-lit and intimate, with traditional Cycladic furniture (i.e., stone benches built into the walls and topped with woven cushions). Nice, nice.

club scene

Hey, party kids, do you like to writhe that body in a hormone-laden, seemingly consequence-free environment? Come to beautiful Firá, where the clubs are piled on top of each other even thicker than the Australians. As with the bars, the clubs in Firá are concentrated within a 5-minute walking radius, so you can visit every damned one before the cock crows. The dress code at most of these places is standard Greek-issue—no shorts and no flip-flops—so bring along appropriate gear. The music at most places is varied, with a definite slant toward soul and dance tunes. Clubs open at about 11pm, but true ragin' doesn't set in until about 1am, and it doesn't stop until dawn.

Enigma Club *(Othos Erithrou Stavrou; Tel 224-66; 11pm-whenever daily; No credit cards)* divides its large, sleek space equally between covered and uncovered areas. The Eurohipsters here prefer the uncovered areas, as it increases the reception on their cell phones. At 2,000Dr, the cover charge is prohibitive enough to keep out the riffraff, and drinks are no bargain either, starting at 1,500Dr. However, they do have a nice policy of letting you buy an entire bottle and holding it in your name for subsequent nights if you don't finish it right away.

Tithora *(Othos M. Danezi; Tel 235-19; 10:30pm-whenever daily; No credit cards)*, decorated in fall-of-Western-civilization style (crumbling fountains, chipped plaster busts, etc.), caters to an ostensibly more rock 'n' roll crowd, which is to say that folks here wear a bit more leather and the occasional guitar can be heard in the music. Pricing at Tithora is far more democratic: Beer starts at 500Dr, as do shots. Cover is 1,500Dr and includes a drink.

arts scene

The **Cinema Kamari** *(Kamari, north edge of town; Tickets 1,800Dr; May-Oct)* is a sweet outdoor theater that shows international films. Films are subtitled in Greek, so you'll probably want to wait for an English or American movie. Its schedule is posted at the **Dolphins Beach Bar** [see *hanging out*, above], as well as outside the theater itself.

culture zoo

Akrotiri *(Akrotiri; Buses regularly from Firá or Perissa; 8:30am-3pm Tue-Sun)* is an amazing archaeological site of an ancient Cycladic town. The site was buried under the ash of the cataclysm that wiped out half of Santorini, although the inhabitants of the town are thought to have escaped.

great outdoors

The roads on Santorini are unskatable, but there's no end to the jogging routes. Take a run on the moon at **Monolithos Beach** *(a 3-mile bus ride from Firá)*: The road on the border of this black beach sits beneath a crumbling mud bluff. It's straight and flat, perfect for a little warmup.

If you like your jogs a bit more strenuous, try the road from Monolithos to Mesaria. This winding, uphill course will kick your butt into shape.

Plunge 15 to 30 feet into the deep blue at **Kamari Beach** [see *hanging out*, above]. The cliffs are located at the southern end of the beach.

For snorkeling, there's no comparison to Monolithos Beach. About 20 yards out, a rift in the floor is home to good-sized schools of parrot fish, among others. Equipment is available for rental.

ayōpi meets kopítsi

The Greek islands attract young singles like flies to a barbecue. Translation: If you can't get lucky on a Greek island, then you have a real problem. The chances of your making it with a real, live Greek are low, however, as there are fewer natives than foreigners on most islands. Take heart though: Santorini and Paros have coteries of randy Australians and Americans, and Mykonos has the European contingent. The two biggest meat markets are the beaches by day, the clubs by night.

festivals and events

National Music Festival of Santorini *(Aug-Sept)*.

stuff

Santorini has been famed for its silversmiths for the past 2,500 years. As a result, there are so many jewelry shops in Firá, you won't know where to begin. Otherwise, shops sell either snorkel gear or the same souvenirs available in **Plaka** [see *athens*].

Nepheli *(Oia; Tel 716-12; 10:30am-2am daily Apr-Oct; V, MC, AE)* sells jewelry made by artists from all over Greece, except Santorini. Good idea—the rest of the jewelry stores are filled with Santorini-only work. The stuff here has a broad range, both in style and price, starting at 2,500Dr.

Handy Jewelry *(Othos Erithrou Stavrou; Tel 225-64; 9am-3pm/6-10pm daily; No credit cards)* is stocked with the work of owner/artist Prodromos Lipatetzoglou. His original ring designs start at 9,000Dr, and you can even check out the workshop where he fashions his creations.

Kali Bazaar *(Kamari; Tel 326-50; 10am-10pm daily; V, MC)*, run by the Aussie Charlotte Jordan, offers a wide selection of Indonesian and Thai clothing and baubles, including batik sarongs and colorful hippie shirts. There's also a small selection of used beach fiction available here.

eats

Santorini is overrun by restaurants. As in Athens, most of the dining spots here are guarded by annoyingly persistent touts, who will badger you for business. In Firá and Oia, the places with a "caldera view" (a view of the island's volcanic crater) charge way more, but are not necessarily any better than more modestly located eateries.

▶▶CHEAP

For unsurpassed brick-oven pizza and excellent souvlaki of any kind, try the deceptively silly-sounding **Casa di Pizza e Pasta** *(Othos M. Danezi; Tel 222-22; 8:30am-2am daily; 700-3,000Dr per entree; V, MC)*. The simple diner-style decor, including fluorescent lighting and booths, as well as limited seating, makes this place easy to overlook, but that would be a huge mistake.

It's breakfast time, do you know where your bottomless cup of coffee is? Try **Mama's** *(200m north of Theotokopoulos Sq., Firá; Tel 242-11; 8am-midnight daily; 700-1,500Dr breakfast; No credit cards)*, run by a feisty ball of fire known simply as Mama. Free coffee refills. Real maple syrup. Pancakes. Need you hear more? Mama routinely embarrasses newcomers as they walk in, all for the entertainment of those already seated.

Be prepared for hugs, kisses, and even reprimands for your crappy, hungover appearance. "And remember, babies, Mama loves you!"

▶▶**DO-ABLE**

Despite its prime caldera seating, **Aris Restaurant** *(Othos Agiou Mina; Tel 224-80; 8am-3pm/6pm-1am daily; 1,200-5,000Dr per entree; V, MC)* isn't overpriced. Try the tuna carpaccio appetizer or the famous moussaka for starters. Then move on to the flame-grilled fish of the day. The house red wine, made by the owner, is delicious. For best results, come at sunset and enjoy Aris' gorgeous decor: cliffs, sky, and yes, that wine-dark sea.

▶▶**SPLURGE**

Another sunset eatery, the **Kastro** *(Oia; Tel 710-45; 10:30am-2am daily; 3,300-4,000Dr per entree; V, AE)* in Oia is not to be confused with its namesake in Firá. If you can't see your way clear to spending this much on a meal, try ordering a few appetizers. The mushroom fondue is delicious and filling, and the cured salmon with mustard and apple butter melts in your mouth. If you like shellfish, try the mussels in date palm and ouzo sauce. This excellent restaurant, located on Oia's northern face, also boasts one of the greatest views on an island of great views. Come at sunset.

crashing

If you're not staying in Firá, you're likely to feel left out of the picture. Because the action is so concentrated on three or four streets here, the majority of visitors choose to bed down in the immediate environs. Then there's the safety issue: Navigating the roads of Santorini on a moped at night in a drunken stupor is the leading cause of injuries to stupid travelers.

WINERIES

Santorini has several wineries that offer cheap tastings and tours of the facilities. These manufacturers also sell bottles of their elixirs dirt cheap.

Hanging on the caldera's southern edge, with a spectacular view and outdoor seating, **Santo Wines** *(Near Pyrgos; Tel 321-28; 10am-sunset daily; Tastes 200Dr, full glasses 400Dr, tours 500Dr/person)* has the best and widest variety of wines. Go whole-hog with the plate of cheese and six tastes for 1,600Dr.

Volcan Wines *(Near Kamari; Tel 313-22; Noon-8pm daily)* offers a tour of its museum, which looks like it was designed by Edgar Allan Poe, as well as a taste of six wines, all for 500Dr. The white wine here is excellent.

▶▶CHEAP

The most excellent Yassir Abdullah runs the giant **Firá Youth Hostel** (*Othos Martiou; 223-87; Reception 9am-2pm/5-9pm; 2,500Dr dorm bed, 16,000-20,000Dr double, 24,000Dr triple; No credit cards*), located near the center of town. The hostel has a large courtyard with a cafe, and is always a good place to meet other travelers. If you happen to arrive after 1am, just grab a dorm bed and pay in the morning. Or, break out the sleeping bag and crash on the roof (2,000Dr). For dorm dwellers, the shower/toilet-to-human ratio is not very high, but what do you want for 2,500Dr?

The best camping on the island is **Santorini Camping** (*East of Firá; Tel 229-44; 1,500Dr/person, 800Dr/tent; No credit cards*), located near Firá. The crowd here is friendly and young, and its bar is a good place to hook up with others before a night of carousal in town. If you don't have a tent, they'll rent you one, and you also can wash your clothes, exchange money, and swim for free in the campground's pool. Yes, there are showers and toilets.

▶▶DO-ABLE

The **Albatros Hotel** (*Karterados; Tel 23-635, Fax 234-31; 27,600Dr single, 31,200Dr double, 42,700Dr triple; V, MC, AE*) lies just a couple of minutes (by car/bike) outside of Firá, in the town of Karterados. This is an ideal location—within walking distance to Firá, but far enough away that you can get a quiet night's sleep. The hotel has its own pool, and there's a small market across the street. The hotel is in that traditional Cycladic style—smooth white stone with vaulted ceilings. The rooms themselves, however, sport simple modern furniture.

If you want to stay in real, traditional Cycladic housing, try the **Tennis Club Apartments** (*Karterados; Tel 221-22, Fax 236-98; 24,000Dr double, 29,000Dr triple, 35,000Dr quad; AE, MC, V*), a cluster of con-

24 hours on the ıslands

1. Walk around the edge of the caldera in Oia, Santorini, at sunset, for the most spectacular view in the Mediterranean.
2. Panormos Beach, Mykonos—Excellent snorkeling.
3. The caves of **Antiparos**—The best spelunking around [see *paros*, above].
4. Naoussa, Paros—It's the Nantucket of the Cyclades.
5. Eurodivers Club, Paros—Grotto and shipwreck dives.
6. Enigma Club, Santorini—All-night carousing awaits you.
7. Paranga Beach, Mykonos—All-night naked beach carousing awaits you.
8. **Delos**, near Mykonos—An entire island full of breathtaking ruins [see *culture zoo* in *mykonos*, above].

santorini

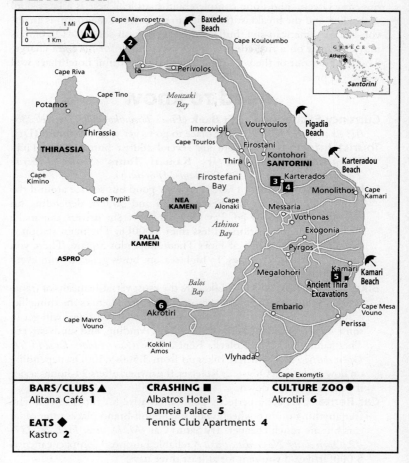

BARS/CLUBS ▲
Alitana Café 1

EATS ◆
Kastro 2

CRASHING ■
Albatros Hotel 3
Dameia Palace 5
Tennis Club Apartments 4

CULTURE ZOO ●
Akrotiri 6

---

verted houses built in the 19th century. Inside, these white stone apartments look like Luke Skywalker's pad on Tatooine, with high and vaulted ceilings over beds made of stone slabs with comfy mattresses on top. Because of their design, these structures require no air-conditioning, even in the height of summer. All this, plus two tennis courts and a good-sized pool, make this the best value on the island.

▶▶SPLURGE

If you want to get away from the hustle and bustle of Firá without having to deal with the hustle and bustle of one of the beach towns, **Dameia Palace** *(Near Kamari Beach; Tel 325-32, Fax 325-35; 70,000Dr double; AE, V, MC)* is the place for you. It's located on an almost empty road parallel to Kamari Beach, about a 20- to 30-minute walk away. The rooms are spacious, with vaulted ceilings and balconies. Bathrooms here are huge for Greece, and done completely in marble. There is a large pool with a bar, and the breakfast (included in the price of the room) is an all-you-can-eat American-style buffet, with tons of fresh-squeezed OJ. Guests may also feast on a five-course dinner every night for no extra charge. Though a bit out of the way, the Dameia is a beautiful hotel that's well worth the price.

need to know

Currency Exchange Credit Bank *(Firá's Theotokopoulos Sq.; Tel 238-01; 8am-2pm Mon-Fri)* is the place to go to get your **drachmas (Dr)**.

Tourist Information There are several tourist bureaus near Firá's Theotokopoulos Square. Try **Kamari Tours** *(South of Firá's Theotokopoulos Sq.; Tel 226-66; 8am-11pm daily)*.

Public Transportation There is a pretty good bus service around the island, with fares varying between 120 and 300Dr, depending on how far you need to go. Pay your fare in cash; drivers can make change for denominations of less than 5,000Dr. The main station is just a few blocks south of Firá's Theotokopoulos Square. There you can find current schedules. In high season, buses generally run every 15 or 20 minutes.

Bike/Moped Rental Motorbikes are the most versatile means of transport on Santorini, and also the most dangerous. There's something like a 20 percent chance that first-time or inexperienced riders will get in some kind of accident here on the windy, winding, and sandy streets. That said, check out Koletsis Rent-a-Bike *(Karterados; Tel 245-51; Open daily; MC, V)* where bikes go from 3,500-5,500Dr, depending on how many cc's. Odysseus Koletsis, the owner, offers 24-hour service if your ride breaks down.

Car Rental Cars are a perfectly good alternative for those of you who fear anything on two wheels. The small, non-brand places offer older cars but are much cheaper. Try Santo Car *(M. Danezi, Firá; Tel 237-42; Open daily; No credit cards)*. A reliable European compact car costs 5,000Dr/day, if you rent for at least three days.

Health and Emergency Police: *226-49*. The best hospital on the island is the **Firá Hospital** *(Firá; Tel 222-37)*.

Pharmacies Zacharopoulos *(Othos Decigala, Firá; Tel 234-44; 8:30am-1pm/5:30-9pm Mon, Tue, Thur, Fri, till 2pm Wed, Sat)*. Call *227-00* for emergency pharmacies.

Telephone Country code: *30*; area code: *0286*. Telephones in Santorini require a phone card, available at almost any newsstand for 1,300Dr/100 calls. **AT&T:** *00-800-1311*; **MCI:** *00-800-1211*; **Sprint:** *00-800-1411*.

Airports There is one airport on Santorini *(Tel 315-25)*. Buses to anywhere on Santorini can be caught right outside the airport terminal. Twice-daily **Olympic Airways** flights leave for Santorini from the Athens airport.

wired on santorini

There is one cyber "cafe" on Santorini: **P.C. Club** *(Theotokopoulos Sq., Firá; Tel 255-51; 10am-9pm daily; 500Dr/20min; No credit cards).* No coffee, no pastries, no amenities, but nine terminals.

Airlines Olympic Airways *(Tel 224-93)* tickets can be booked through almost any travel agency on the island.

Ferries There are two ports on Santorini: **Athinias** and **Firá**. Most ferries dock at the former. Ferries run daily from **Piraeus** (twice daily in the summer). For ferry schedules, dial *222-39.* Take the **funicular** *(800Dr)* up to Firá from **Firá Port**. It runs every 20 minutes from 6:40am-9pm. From **Athinias Port**, grab a taxi or the bus (20-30 minutes). If you have reservations at a hotel, check in advance if they will pick you up.

eastern europe

prague

Prague's reputation as an international mecca for hedonism (in all but culinary fields) is well-earned. But this little city of 1.2 million also happens to be one of the last great Old European capitals essentially untouched by the devastation of WWII. It's apparent that the strange heavenly forces are at work as you survey the Gothic arches of Old Town through a beery haze (or, for you truly brave hedonists, an absinthe blur) while getting completely lost on a pub crawl. Perfectly preserved spires, angels, Baroque onion-dome cathedrals, and Renaissance sgrafittos are your backdrop as you mix with ever-morphing Czechs at their favorite pubs—generally the grimiest and cheapest of the many beerhalls in the pedestrianized medieval center around Old Town Square. You'll encounter an initial shyness among Czechs, but if you give them their space, speak softly, and don't go on about what a bargain everything is, you'll have a dozen new friends by the end of the third round of Staropramen halfliters. Remember that their monthly wage, even in the wild free-market days of megamalls and techno parties sponsored by Lucky Strike, barely covers the rent in some shared apartment out in the boonies. Yet locals always find enough crowns for a night out at the pub and a good moan about the absurdities of a new democracy in a globalizing cyber world. These are generally held in not just the cheapest but the spookiest and most amazing drinking holes you've ever seen. Most clubs and bars are in underground Romanesque or Gothic cellars that were once at street level. An entire secret underworld lies beneath the cobblestones of Prague, owing to the city's 12th-century solution to annual flooding of the Vltava River: They just raised the city one story. Social scenes here are totally mixed up, as far as expats and Czechs go—people are much more likely to divide themselves up along crowd lines (hipsters, techno-geeks, club kids) than along lines of ethnicity. And of course the highly visible expat presence means you'll hear English spoken everywhere, from residents and visitors alike, most of whom are highly approachable.

There is no racism in the Czech Republic. Or so almost any Czech will insist, especially if he's a member of Parliament, which is your first major tip-off that racism is indeed a presence here. The upshot: Even in Prague, where violence is only a fraction of that in most Western big cities, non-whites should proceed with caution. If you're in the area called Žižkov and see a pack of drunken skinheads—whose football chants are fortunately audible quite a distance away—take another route.

Since the 1989 revolution, Prague has been so massively made over and infused with Western investment that about the only signs of the old ways are the smoked-meat shops, trams, and frozen-in-time pubs. Of course, the idea of counter *service* hasn't fully penetrated yet, and feminism, it seems, has definitely *not* caught on. Consumer fever is in full force, and the youngest generation, who barely remember pre-1989 life here, are busy exploring life's more meaningful pursuits—namely drinking, drugs, and dancing (all of which are fully tolerated, though officially a drug crackdown is growing in force, so it doesn't pay to be carrying).

The Prague Post (www.praguepost.cz) is a good English-language source on cultcha, *Think* is the hysterical party 'zine of choice, and the **Czech Tourist Authority** [see *need to know*, below] has a useful English-language info line *(187)* and a particularly good, opinionated website, *www.czech-tourinfo.cz*. When searching the site for events, remember that Europeans put their days first and months second (so, for example, October 12 is 12/10).

Finally, never forget: Ideologies may come and go, but a good half-liter of Budvar is a treasure forever.

neighborhoods

Founded a millennium ago on a bend of the **Vltava River**, Prague is a dense, though smallish, city with a medieval street plan still fully in effect in the city center. The magnificent Prague Castle [see *culture zoo*, below] overlooks all from one of the hills on the left bank, where most of the city's green space lies. Flat, Gothic **Old Town** takes up the right bank, then gives way to the more modern (and traffic-choked) streets of the **Žižkov** district to the east, **Vinohrady** to the southeast, and **New Town** to the south. The heart of the city is **Prague 1's** heavily spired Old Town, built around an open cobbled square, the perfect spot for staging executions and revolutions. Just about everything you'll want to experience is walkable from here, though the old East Bloc trams are a trip in themselves and still a damned practical way to get around. To the south of Old Town are **Prague 2's** New Town (a mere 650 years old) and **Prague 3's** Žižkov district, a pub mecca if ever there was one, with an increasingly happening music scene. Across the Vltava River, to the west, lies **Malá**

five things to talk to a local about

1. How 'bout that **Jagr**? (Jaromír, that would be, the Olympic gold–winning Czech hockey god and NHL All-Star, but of course you knew that.)

2. Seen any good deals on **potatoes**? (Works best if subject is over 40.)

3. So, gotta license for that **MS Office 2000**?

4. Do you feel better now that the Vatican has finally apologized for **the Hus burning thing**? (Jan Hus, Bohemia's greatest Protestant heretic, was martyred some 500 years ago, and a high committee in Rome only recently ruled the punishment was perhaps was a mite overzealous.)

5. You mean you like **Jablkón** (the local band that has enough bizarre African and Asian instruments to keep an ethnographer happy for years), too?

Strana, the romantic, hilly home to cafes and garret apartments, and rising above it is **Hradčany**, or **Castle Hill** (both still technically in Prague 1, though across the river from Old Town), the approach to which is predictably overrun by touristy crap.

hanging out

You sometimes get the impression that every foreigner in Prague is hanging out, especially the long-term resident aliens—including a large slice of the ones who came here to "build careers"....Most young Czechs are too busy scrambling for that little prefab concrete apartment of their own to hang out too much, though even they usually have time for a beer with a new friend. After all, there still exists a deeply held Bohemian ethic that nothing needs to happen in a hurry (and certainly your food order is usually in that category...). So things are kept in perspective, even in these wild, free-for-all capitalist days.

Islands in the Vltava River are prime hangouts in spring and fall for Praguers of all ages. One of the best for catching a sundown with a cold brew in hand is Slovanský ostrov (across a footbridge from Masarykovo nábřeži, Prague 1), just upstream of the **National Theater** [see *arts scene*, below]. This Vltava River island is the only one with its own palace, fronted and backed by green lawns, winding paths, shade trees, and folks out for a relaxing stroll. Another is Kampa (in the Malá Strana district, just downstream from the bridge called most Legii) with a big meadow of grass and shade trees much favored by hippie drummers in town for summer rockfests.

the truth about absinthe

Yes, the blue-green demon in this bottle is still illegal in most of the West, perhaps understandably, in that so many Paris artists and writers used it as a cheap ticket to cuckooville during the '20s. But the wormwood extract's no-nonsense punch is a thrill to be savored, and one you'll probably survive if you take it with a modicum of moderation. Don't just down it, though: The time-honored ritual is to take a spoonful of sugar, soak it in the stuff, set it alight until it caramelizes, then stir it back into the glass. For god's sake put it out first, though, or the whole thing will become a little hunka-hunka-burnin' love in your glass. Having proven yourself an old hand at Bohemian indulgence, you may then lift your glass, make firm eye contact with your partners in crime and say, without a trace of irony, *"Na zdraví"* (to your health). The effects aren't subtle—in fact, if you're short of cash you can achieve roughly the same sensation by whacking yourself over the head with a plank and spinning in a circle till you drop. Nevertheless, the makers of absinthe assure customers that the current version is five proof milder than the stuff that sent all those Parisians to the nuthouse back in the day. All of five proof, huh?

Striking up a conversation with fellow travelers is inevitable if you drop by **Jo's Bar and Garáž** [see *club scene*, below] during the daylight hours. This was once the only prayer in Prague for foreigners jonesing for nachos and free coffee refills. The quiet back room, done up in ochre and whatever someone didn't need when they moved, is a natural conversation pit.

Café Konvikt (*Bartolomějská 11, Prague 1; Tel 2423-2427; Metro line B to Národní třída; 9am-1am Mon-Fri, noon-1am Sat-Sun; No credit cards*), just off the main drag that encircles Old Town, is where young Czech loafers head for their perusing and caffeine fixes. This place is also more chat-friendly by day, with big pools of sunlight streaming in, friendly service, and mismatched junk-shop tables and chairs.

Káva Káva Káva (*Národní třída 37, Prague 1; Tel 268-409, 7am-9pm Mon-Fri*), hidden in a courtyard just off gallery-heavy Národní, is a quiet patio cafe that's a magnet for local creatives who are serious coffee junkies, with a global bean selection, a dozen teas, and massive carrot cake slices.

About the only 24-hour pub in the vicinity of Old Town is **U Kotvy** (*Spálená 11, Prague 1; Tel 291-161; Metro line A, B to Můstek, all-night* *tram to Lazarská crossroads on Spálená; 24 hours daily; No credit cards).* Hopefully it won't be raining when you go—the beer garden out back is much nicer than the smoky front room, which is perpetually filled with pasty-faced alcoholic zombie locals.

In New Town, your port in a late-night storm is the **Radost/FX** [see *club scene*, below] lounge. When even *that* closes (at 4 or 5am, depending on the mood), you're pretty much stuck with **U Havrana** *(Hálkova 6, Prague 1; Tel 9620-0020; Metro line C to IP Pavlova; 24 hours Mon-Fri, 6pm-6am Sat, Sun; No credit cards)*, a friendly-if-downtrodden greasy-spoon pub that's stumbling distance from Radost.

bar scene

You won't find a bunch of stylish mixed-drink bars here, Czech wine is famously bad, and pubs tend to be unapologetically smoky, fly-specked, and uncomfortable. Wait! Even if dive bars aren't your thing (which some people might see as a serious character flaw...), hold on—you do have a few positives on your side: First, there's Czech beer. With a brewing tradition spanning over 500 years, beer is the center of the drinking universe here. Plus, it's cheap, and it kicks butt. Preferred beers are the bitter Pilsner Urquell, the more mellow Budvar, the delicious Gambrinus, Radegast, and Krušovice, the up-and-coming Bernard, and Starobrno brewery's Červeny Drák, a recent Moravian award-winner. Beers can be ordered dark (*tmave*), light (*světle*), or mixed (*Řezané*), but are always preceded by the toast *"Na zdraví"* (to your health) and sometimes a clunk on the table for emphasis. (Always look whomever you're clinking mugs with straight in the eye if you want to get any respect in the beer world here.) Second, you share bench seating at the pubs with anyone who has space, so it's the perfect environment for gathering new drinking buddies. Third—and most important—whatever else might be lacking is completely made up for by absinthe, the wondrous blue-green wormwood extract that is still banned in much of Western Europe as a madness-inducing poison for degenerates [see *the truth about absinthe*, above]. Most pubs do serve food, but unless otherwise stated, you're better off eating elsewhere.

Železná dveře *(Michalská 19, Prague 1; Tel 0603/717-842; Metro line A, B to Můstek; 11am-4am daily; No credit cards)* is the hottest bar in Old Town, with a big fish tank and a coat of gold fleck paint on the walls of a cavernous cellar bar, plus occasional sushi snacks. The cool mix of veteran expats and hip Czechs who are part of the expat scene (teachers, folks who work in expat bars, writers for expat publications) will soon make you forget that anything's missing. The young, mixed crowd definitely has some money to spend, but is a long, long way from yuppie.

The nearby **Érra Café** *(Konviktská 11, Prague 1; Tel 2423-3427; Metro line B to Národní třída; 10am-midnight Mon-Fri, 11am-midnight Sat, Sun)* is another basement-level mecca of style. It's got a classy, gay-friendly atmosphere, with gold-framed mirrors, a house soundtrack, Op-Art seating, and a fireplace. Best chicken garlic sesame sandwich in town, too.

prague bars, clubs and culture zoo

BARS/CLUBS ▲
Akropolis **24**
Chapeau Rouge **9**
Delux **17**
Érra Café **14**
Fromin **19**
Jáma **26**
Jo's Bar and Garáž **2**
Karlov´y Lazné **13**
Lucerna Music Bar **18**
Marquis de Sade **10**
Mecca **22**
Rock Café **15**
Roxy **8**
U Vystřelenyho oka **23**
U Zlatéhořtygra **12**
Železné dveře **16**

CULTURE ZOO ●
Bertramka **1**
Charles Bridge **27**
Galerie Rudolfinum **6**
Golden Lane **5**
Jewish Museum **7**
National Museum **20**
Old Town Hall **11**
Prague Castle **4**
Uy´sehrad **25**
Veletrzní Palace **21**
 - National Gallery
 - Collection of Modern
   and Contemporary Art
Wallenstein Riding School **3**

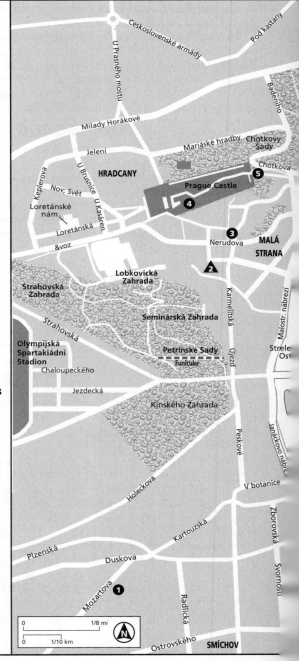

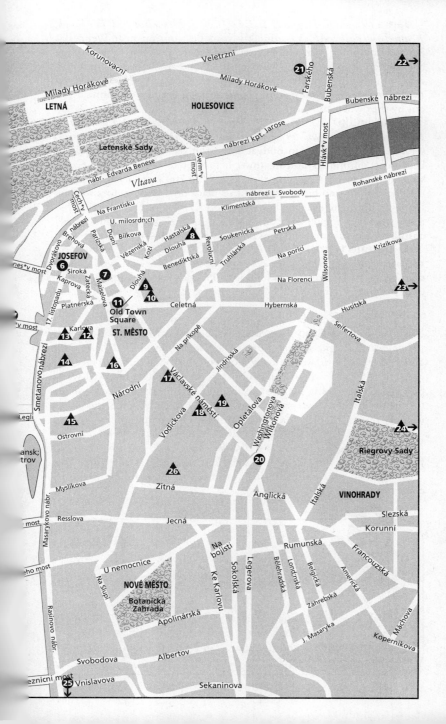

Jáma *(V jámě 7, Prague 1; Tel 242/22-383; Metro line A, B to Můstek; 11am-1am daily; AE, V)*, arguably your best option near Wenceslas Square, is hopping with a more yuppified expat crowd reliving its college bar days amid rock posters, Mexican food, and spontaneous drink specials. Sunday movie nights, a video rental counter, and *The Prague Revue* **(www.praguepivo.com/prague_revue.htm)**, a literary semiannual put out by the owners, further set this place apart.

U medvídku *(Na Perštyně 7, Prague 1; Tel 2422-0930; Metro line B to Národní třída; 11am-11pm Mon-Sat, till 10pm Sun; No credit cards)* serves up South Bohemian Budvar beer, great slabs of pork in brandy or beer sauce, dumplings, and an atmosphere loved by everyone from Czech students to American novelist wannabes. With 700 years of experience in this location, it's no big shock that this place does what it does so well. Don't sit anywhere near the hay wagon on a Friday or Saturday night— that's when the appallingly bad folk band, in their kitschy "traditional" costumes, moves into it and jams for all they're worth—which ain't much.

U Zlatého tygra *(Husova 17, Prague 1; Tel 2222-1111; Metro line A to Staroměstská; 3-11pm daily; No credit cards)* was once on every tourist map because it was the second home to Prague's favorite old crank novelist, Bohumil Hrabal. Well, he's dead now, and so is any reason to come to this bar.

The place to pick up dancing (or whatever) partners before heading down the street to **Roxy** [see *club scene*, below] is **Marquis de Sade** *(Templová 8, Prague 1; Metro line C to Náměstí Republiky; 11am-2am daily; No credit cards)*, where everybody who's anybody comes to meet up with friends and down an obligatory absinthe shot. It's a big, well-worn pub space for making plans of attack and fueling up on decent pizza (before the kitchen closes at 11pm, anyway). Despite the name, the action is pretty traditional—there's no latex or whips lying around.

Any conversation at **Chateau** *(Jakubská 2; No phone; Metro line C to Náměstí Republiky; 11am-3am daily; No credit cards)* must be shouted. Just a block from the Marquis, this hell-red bar is all contact sports: You shove through a seriously cruising crowd to the bar, grabbing whatever comes your way....

fIVE-O

Police in the Czech Republic have gotten a bad rap—a richly, richly deserved one. Once the goons of the Communist party, they've now made a proud conversion to *TJ Hooker* dress-up games. You'll invariably see them doing one of two things while robbery and corruption go unchecked and dangerous drivers gleefully blast through crosswalks: window shopping and randomly hassling people to check their papers.

KLUL MEETS HOLKA

Take a dark, winding cobbled street. Add moonlight, mist, a gargoyle or two, and cheap, sublime alcoholic beverages. Throw in the natural freedom and exuberance you feel when abroad, especially in a once-forbidden city still caught between now and then. If none of this can inspire you to make that foolish, rash move you always repress back home, maybe you should consider a life in the clergy. But for anyone who's not above a bit of bleary sin, Prague is what you'd call romantic. And don't think Czechs don't feel it, too. Modern sexual mores here are noticeably freer than in most Western cities. Feminism, if it means pay equity, might not be altogether rejected by a Prague woman, but if it means foregoing a single male overture, or heading out on a Friday night looking less than stunning, it's going to be a tough sell. Pouting to get your way is much more the style here, and PDAs are rampant, particularly on the Metro. The severe apartment crunch in Prague is probably a factor in that one, as it eliminates more private options. A bigger factor, affecting the whole romance mindset, is that the Czech Republic still has not experienced serious levels of some Western social ills like AIDS. This kind of innocence permits young Czechs, and often their partners, to get in over their heads fast (condom use is still far from the norm). Then again, there's an old Bohemian saying that Slavs just have warm hearts. And after you live through one winter here, you may just see for yourself how body heat can be a lifesaver.

The heights (or depths) of Žižkov pubbing are best experienced at either the four-bar labyrinth of **Akropolis** [see *live music scene*, below] or the far seedier underground shrine known as **U Vystřelenyho oka** (*U božích bojovníků 3, Prague 3; Tel 627-8714; Metro line B, C to Florenc, then Bus 135, 207 to Jeronýmova; 3:30pm-1am daily; No credit cards*), which serves up cheap Měštan beer in a classically run-down Žižkov pub environ, with a beer terrace outside, occasional loud, drunk bands, and surreal decor by a member of the Prague underground band Už Jsme Doma. The name of this place literally means "The Shot-Out Eye"—ask anyone here about its deeper meaning....

LIVE MUSIC SCENE

Prague may not be the next Seattle (but neither is Seattle, right?), but it does attract all the serious underground bands you'd expect in a famed capital of Bohemian living. John Cale makes regular stopovers, international global fusion groups like the Suns of Arqa turn up, and so do some of the top talents of the jazz and funk world, especially during the **Prague**

rules of the game

There's no real age limit for drinking here (as long as you can see over the table), and IDs are never required. People are allowed to drink what they choose anywhere they like, but in practice only foreign college kids ever drink on the street because everyone else prefers to do it in a pub or cafe. As throughout Europe, atmosphere and the ritual of going to the pub are just as important as what you're drinking. Besides, beer drunk from a bottle is always inferior to beer freshly tapped, and this isn't a country with a strong wine tradition of any kind. All recreational drugs are illegal but widely in circulation, with very spotty enforcement by bumbling cops. Evidence of their ineffectiveness includes the drugs dealt openly in some of the bars. But don't think drug users are completely safe. Parliament was finally forced by the explosion in drug trafficking to act and, in all their wisdom, gave the police complete powers of discretion in enforcing new zero-tolerance laws. Which means a cop can throw someone in jail for having so much as a joint or a tab of E, then let said person rot in a stinking cell for a month or more before even coming up with formal charges. Not cool at all.

Jazz Festival [see *festivals and events*, below]. Local heroes include Phil Shoenfelt, a British expat known for spooky introspection, and the legendary (in this town anyway) Iva Bittová, an avant-garde violinist with a manic art-rock following.

Akropolis *(Kubelíkova 27, Prague 3; Tel 9633-0911; Metro line A to Jiřího z Poděbrad; 10am-dawn daily; info@akropolis.cz, www.pala kropolis.cz; No credit cards)* books both of the above, plus a host of international acts, presenting them with great acoustics and lighting in its small basement theater. Slink around the labyrinth of connecting bars (four in all) to become part of the mob of students, graphic designers, local musicians, and artists from the underground scene doing the post-show-hangout thing. Definitely worth the short ride into the Žižkov district.

Lucerna *(Vodičkova 36; Tel 2421-7108; Metro line A to Můstek; 7pm-6am daily; 50-150Kč; No credit cards)*, right on Wenceslas Square, is more convenient and has a great, tattered, hastily remodeled, 1920s-club atmosphere. Neither the idols of Czech rock who play here nor their crowds of teenage fans seem to mind the awful acoustics.

Malostranská Beseda *(Malostranské náměstí 21; Tel 539-024; Tram 12, 22 to Malostranské náměstí; 1pm-1am daily; 50-80Kč; No credit cards)*, across the river in Malá Strana, is not much more than a battered bar, but has solid live music creds as the Home of Cheap Shows. Prague ska kings Sto Zvířat (100 Animals) and a whole crew of mostly Czech local rockers and blues folks rule the stage.

Rock Café *(Národní 20; Tel 2491-4416; Metro line A, B to Můstek,*

10am-3am Mon-Fri, 8pm-3am Sat, Sun; 80Kč; No credit cards) is the best Old Town live-rock alternative to the mostly DJ-ruled **Roxy** [see *club scene*, below], but it favors a bizarre lineup of Czech cover bands who "revive" everyone from Sade to the Stones by way of Janis Joplin and ABBA. The impersonal, sound-sucking hall doesn't seem to affect performance quality either way, and the big guys spilling beer on their Rutgers sweatshirts don't seem bothered by it.

American-run **U Malého Glena** *(Karmelitská 23; Tel 535-8115; Tram 12, 22 to Malostranské náměstí; 10am-2am daily; malyglen@login.cz, www.malyglen.cz; 70Kč; No credit cards)* is technically a jazz hole, but it's the major force in town for attracting new talents of *all* genres. There's a Sunday night jam, and the hottest names in local straight-up jazz play throughout the week. Watch for Najponk, a tight veteran combo that's always on point. The basement music hall is so small you'll have to stand in the doorway if you don't arrive early. If you start to freak, take a breather in the jumping-yet-less-cramped pub on the floor above.

Jazz Club Železná *(Železná 16, Prague 1; Tel 2423-9697; Metro line A, B to Můstek; 3pm-1am daily; www.mujweb.cz/www/jazz_zelezna, jazz.zelezna@mbox.vol.cz; No credit cards)* is a rock-walled Old Town cellar maze that also hosts great Sunday jams, but with more of the world beat/dub/Latin groove, which attracts a hip international crowd. The 5pm poetry slams beforehand prime the party.

The **Archa Theater** [see *arts scene*, below] goes out of its way to book fringe rock and indefinable noises from around the world, always presented in intimate digs with killer sound.

Reduta *(Národní třída 20; Tel 2491-2246; Metro line B to Národní třída; 9pm-3am daily; 120Kč; No credit cards)* is the oldest and most traditional jazz club in Prague, where Bill Clinton once blew his sax, but its seating, sound system, and acts are all pretty threadbare these days....

AghaRTA *(Krakovská 5, Prague 1; Tel 2221-1275; Metro line A, C to Muzeum; 7pm-1am daily; 2hp@arta.cz, www.arta.cz; 80Kč; No credit cards)* is where the younger jazz talents play, many of them recorded on the club's own label and available on CDs sold in the entryway. It's hip, tiny, packed with jazz buffs both Czech and foreign, and just a short walk from Wenceslas Square.

U Staré paní *(Michalská 9; Tel 2422-8090; Metro line A, B to Můstek; 7pm-1am daily; 150Kč; No credit cards)*, like Železná, is just a hop from Old Town Square, but this hotel basement, with its blasé decor, is geared more toward the younger generation of Czech jazz stars, epitomized by bassist Robert Balzar or guitar player David Doružka. Cheap wine and edible chow fuel the Saturday night jams, which usually last till 4am.

club scene

Where else in the world but Prague can you boogie in a crumbling underground former cinema like the Roxy, then stop off for the herbal wonder liqueur Becherovka in a Romanesque stone cellar? The center of this Gothic city hasn't changed much since medieval days, and clubbing is probably the best way to get into that ancient vibe. Be prepared for cramped and smoky downtown club spaces, thanks in part to their underground—literally—nature. (Prague is full of spooky subterranean spaces, because the original town was buried in the 12th century and the current one was built on top of it to provide a high-water haven during Vltava River floods.) Landlords here are still highly suspicious of clubs, which further fuels the need to be creative in finding space: hence the buttload of strange alternative spaces like out-of-business factories that open and close as clubs every summer. And it's not just the physical environment that's otherworldly, either. Attitudes toward sex and drugs tend to be very open (sometimes alarmingly so), and doormen are generally equally accommodating—if you've got the entry fee, you're in, as a rule. Club gear is fine if you've got it, but nobody really cares if you go in with sneaks and jeans, even at glammy Radost FX. A good source on the latest club spaces, raves, and parties is *Think (www.think.cz, think@terminal.cz)*, a free monthly usually found at Radost [see below]. While you're there, check out the bulletin board, which is sometimes even better. **U Malého Glena** [see *live music scene*, above] is also a nightlife nerve center that carries *Think* and sports its own bulletin board. Also try the Czech Techno site *(www.techno.cz/party/index.htm)*. Things don't really get started until after 11pm.

Old Town's best overall club, **Roxy** *(Dlouhá 33, Prague 1; Tel 2482-6390; Metro line C to Náměstí Republiky; Noon-midnight Mon-Sat, 5pm-midnight Sun; roxy@roxy.cz, www.roxy.cz; 50-250Kč; No credit cards)*, is one of the spookiest around, with potholes in the dance floor still marking where the seats were once bolted into this once-glamorous movie palace beneath the streets. As in most Prague clubs, it leans heavily toward house and techno, booking a lot of hot Berlin, Amsterdam, and London DJs, but you'll hear just about anything here. The tearoom—an intact slice of Morocco with harem-like pillow seating, hookahs, and mint tea—that used to be located off the main floor, has moved next door (check it out, it's really great), and a chill-out space has been inserted in its place. Young (and we mean *young*) club kids and twentysomething Czechs who are into the electronic music scene crowd the place all night, but don't expect to make any great conversation here—the volume is incredible, and most people are really here to dance, not talk.

Lucerna Music Bar [see *live music scene*, above] hosts mostly Czech bands and occasional hot international jazz, but there's also regular *'80s Nights* that pack this trippy balconied underground space where Josephine Baker and her ilk once played. It's all young, unpretentious Czechs here, with accordingly cheap admission and beer. Heats up late on weekend nights; other nights, go around 9 and have a plan for somewhere else later.

Mecca *(U Pruhonu 3, Prague 7; Tel 8387-0522; Tram 12, 25 to Délnicská, night tram 54 to same; 10am-11pm Sun-Thur, 10am-6am Fri, Sat; AE, MC, V)* is the hottest thing going, with packed monthly shows by funky house-master DJ Loutka, hilarious transvestite fashion nights,

fESTIVALS and EVENTS

A suspicious person just might theorize that folks are sitting around somewhere thinking up festivals to justify traveling to this crazed and beautiful city. It wouldn't be the worst idea in the world....

Days of European Film *(Apr; Tel 2423-4875)*: Cinema directors and actors from all corners of Europe, both quirky and big-budget, old and new, come to Prague with just one premise uniting them: Festival movies must never have been screened here before.

VE Day *(May 8)*: The end of World War II in Europe was just the beginning of Czechoslovakia's troubles, but survivors still pause to give thanks and lay wreaths.

Prague Spring *(Late May; Tel 530-293; www.festival.cz, festival@login.cz)*: The grandest of Prague's dozens of music festivals, dating back to the post-WWII days and attracting such global lights as the orchestras of the Met and the BBC.

Prague Jazz Festival *(May; Tel 2221-1275)*: Organized by **AghaRTA** [see *live music scene*, above], this power jam brings forces to bear with names like Maceo Parker and the Yellowjackets, usually booking them into the **Lucerna** club.

Tanec Praha *(Late June; Tel 2481-3899; www.tanecpha.cz, office@tanecpha.cz)*: Biggie modern dance festival that attracts the likes of the Martha Graham Dance Company as well as avant-garde talents from all over Europe.

Prague Autumn *(Oct; Tel 627-8740)*: The second-string classical music event of the year has nothing to apologize for with a past that has included illustrious fiddlers and stunning symphonies who jam at Prague's finest halls.

Saint Nicholas' Day *(Dec 6)*: On the evening before, Prague is overrun by men in white cotton beards, accompanied by angels and devils, who go about asking little children how they've behaved this year and offering lumps of coal to those whose stories don't jibe.

"model nights" (read: wannabe nights), and a respectable bar and restaurant running till 11pm. It may not be underground, exactly, but it is in a former factory and definitely worth the cab ride out to the inconvenient Holešovice district. A more mature (but still giddy) international crowd digs this break from the hard-edged techno scene.

Radost/FX *(Bělehradská 120, Prague 2; Tel 2425-4776; Metro line C to IP Pavlova; 11am-5am daily; radostfx@terminal.cz, www.radostfx.cz; No credit cards)*, in New Town, is much more glam, with a much less anarchistic, much more expat crowd than Roxy, but it also has its act much

down and out

Being broke, tipsy, and in Prague is a fine tradition, one practiced by some 40,000 expat foreigners (if you wanna believe the mass media reports of the early '90s). And every one of these foreigners was inspired by the local populace of 1.2 million, who, before 1989 anyway, all did the same. These days Czechs and foreigners here both seem to be working harder at making something of themselves. Screw them! You're out of money and you want to party like it's old-school Prague!

The place to start is **Old Town Square** (*Metro line A to Staroměstská*), where you can hunker down on the steps of the *Jan Hus statue*, be inspired by Bohemia's greatest heretic and martyr to religious reform, and watch the world go by all day. A more peaceful environment for the same is the island **Slovanský** [see *hanging out*, above], where you can score a rowboat for 50Kč for an hour, grab a table at the floating pub here for the 25Kč price of a beer, or claim a bench for nothing and just sit under the shade trees with a good book, watching the Vltava River flow by.

If the weather's looking sour, **The Globe Bookstore and Coffeehouse** [see *arts scene*, below] is a favorite spot to while away the hours, with comfy tattered chairs among the bookshelves tailor-made for settling into for hours while you flip through your potential purchase.

The private galleries all along Národní třída or in the cafe **Vel-ryba** [see *arts scene*, above] also make for free and stylish shelters (and even the national galleries [see *culture zoo*, below] will set you back a mere 70Kč in exchange for an afternoon of resplendent art and reverie). While you're on Národní, duck into the airy reading room of the **British Council** (*Národní 10, Prague 1; Tel 2199-1111; Metro line B to Národní třída; 10am-6pm Mon-Thur, till 4pm Fri; www.britcoun.org/czechrepublic, info@britcoun.cz*) for a complimentary look at all the latest issues of the biggest English magazines from *NME* to *TimeOut*'s weekly Prague listings. Or you can log onto ***www.timeout.com***—or anywhere else—for a half hour, gratis, on one of the Council's Internet terminals. The only catch is, they don't allow e-mail here.

more together: regular Thursday gay nights, soul on Tuesdays, beach parties in summer—sometimes with trucked-in sand—and the all-night vegetarian cafe, gallery, and lounge upstairs.

Finding the beat—plus a funky kitsch weirdness vibe—is easier at **Delux** (*Václavské náměstí 4, Prague 1; Tel 9624-9444; Metro line A, B to*

Můstek; 5pm-4am daily; www.delux.cz; No credit cards), one of Prague's hottest clubs, located smack on Wenceslas Square. A great Thai menu is in force earlier in the night, as is live jazz, all of it plopped down in a Baroque recital hall. Things get thoroughly shakin' when the funk and soul DJs take over and they clear the tables away to make dance space.

Fromin *(Václavské náměstí 21, Prague 1; Tel 2423-2319; Metro line A, B to Můstek, night tram to Národní třída; 10am-4am daily; 100Kč; No credit cards)* is another option above Wenceslas Square, with loads of glass, steel, incredible views, and blatantly commercial music and partiers. At least it's pure in its aim to be Prague's glitziest meat market....It's also got full sit-down dinner service and an outdoor terrace that's a trip, especially for late-morning coffee.

Nothing pretentious about **Jo's Bar and Garáž** *(Malostranské náměstí 7, Prague 1; Tel 9004-4151; Tram 12, 22, night tram 57 to Malostranské náměstí; 11am-2am daily; No credit cards)*, near Prague Castle, the downstairs of which is packed with foreign backpacker types by summer, boogying to free classic rock and furiously getting to know Germans/Swedes/Brits/Croatians of the opposite sex. This usually culminates in bartop dancing, often accompanied by peeling clothes....

arts scene

Any city as spooky and entrancing as Prague is bound to have an interesting visual arts movement. Still, artists in Prague, as in many former Soviet satellites, are searching for identity. Films, exhibitions, and fashions, like the Czechs, tend more toward the subtle and ironic than the in-your-face. In addition, having had free development of the arts cut off for 50 years is bound to have lingering effects on a country—especially one as small as this one, with a capital of only 1.2 million fairly homogeneous Slavs. But there are bright spots. Follow the happenings and track the openings in the pages of *Umělec* ("Artist") or *Atelier*, both of which have sections in English and can be found at Galerie Jiří Švestka [see below], or in *The Prague Post*.

▶▶**VISUAL ARTS**
Galerie Jiří Švestka *(Jungmannova 30, Prague 1; Tel 9624-50-24; Metro line A, B to Můstek; Noon-6pm Tue-Fri, 11am-6pm Sat-Sun; svestka@ok.cz)* hosts some of the most spontaneous and provocative art to be seen here, both local and international. Respected curator Jiří Švestka operates this small, quality Old Town space, showing work from the likes of Dan Graham and President Havel's decorator, Bořek Šípek.

Galerie MXM *(Nosticova 6, Prague 1; Tel 531-564; Tram 12, 22 to Malostranské náměstí; Noon-6pm Tue-Sun)* specializes in a group of 30 or so Czechs whose work you'll never see at the National Gallery—and who don't mind that fact at all. Some of them have done prank billboards on the main Czech freeway, others work in comic-strip form, and still others try anything irreverent they can think of. Near the Prague Castle.

Photography has a long, well-developed tradition in Czech art, dating back to Josef Sudek and František Drtikol, and **Prague House of Pho-**

tography *(Haštalská 1, Prague 1; Tel 2481-0779; Metro line A to Staroměstská; 11am-6pm daily)* shows off the best of it, both old and new, with shows ranging from Russian silverplate experiments to personal documents by rising new talents.

New Town's **Velryba** *(Opatovická 24, Prague 2; Tel 2491-2391; 11am-2am daily)* combines gallery space and caffeine; you just have to wander to the back room and down the spiral staircase to find it. It's predictably full of "outsider art," some of which may well require a stiff gin from the upstairs bar to really get the hang of.

Also in Old Town, **The French Institute** *(Štěpánská 35, Prague 1; Tel 2421-66-30; 9am-6pm Mon-Fri)* gallery has consistently excellent photo and painting exhibits whose openings are a must. It's also equipped with a fine patio cafe where you'll meet all the Francophiles you care to. The free screenings of Godard and the like in the downstairs theater aren't bad, either.

▶▶PERFORMING ARTS

As the old saying goes, to be Czech is to be a musician—and judging by the number of string-pickers and horn-blowers you see here, it appears to be true. Chamber music, symphonies, and opera divas perform nightly in the city's top halls: the National Theatre, the State Opera, the Estates Theatre, and the Rudolfinum, all within a 15-minute walk of each other. It's not all powdered wigs, though. Remember, Prague has always been on the cutting edge of music: The original musical bad boy, Mozart, hung out here, holed up at a friend's with lots of drugs and willing women (and you thought Keith Moon invented the concept...). Archa brings in avant-garde talents as diverse as Min Tanaka and Brian Eno (yeah, he's still cutting-edge); and Tanec Praha brings in the likes of the Martha Graham Company. Book concert tickets most easily through **TicketPro** *(Lucerna passage, Václavské nám.; Tel 2422-8455; 9am-8pm Mon-Sat, noon-8pm Sun)*.

The Archa Theater *(Na Poříčí 26, Prague 1; Tel 2171-6111; Curtain times vary; www.archatheatre.cz; 120-490Kč music and concerts, 65-120Kč theater and dance; MC, V)* sets the example for progressive booking in Prague with everyone from Siouxie and Budgie to the DV8 Physical Theater, all in a black box with prime acoustics and lighting. Bonus: You can reserve tickets online.

This city of just over a million has two top-drawer orchestras and three opera houses, all with full performance calendars from September through June. The Czech Philharmonic Orchestra gets down at the waterfront neoclassical jewel known as the **Rudolfinum** [see *culture zoo*, below], conducted by the world-renowned Vladimir Ashkenazy.

Their competition, the Prague Symphony Orchestra, plays **Municipal House** [see *culture zoo*, below], where they truly astound when performing Czech native son Smetana—or just about anything else thrown at them.

The **State Opera** *(Wilsonova 4, Prague 1; Tel 2422-7693; Metro line A, C to Muzeum; Box office 10am-5:30pm Mon-Fri, 10am-noon/1-5:30pm Sat, Sun)* is a lush 19th-century wedding cake of a performance hall that's also a slice of unadulterated Old Europe, where you can catch a stirring Verdi aria for about the price of a movie back home. Located southeast of Old Town.

The **Estates Theater** *(Ovocný trh 1, Prague 1; Tel 2421-5001; Metro line A, B to Můstek; Box office 10am-6pm Mon-Fri, 10am-12:30pm/3-6pm Sat, Sun; www.anet.cz/nd)* is where Mozart himself conducted the premiere of *Don Giovanni* in 1787, and it's still going strong with a repertoire that, not surprisingly, favors Amadeus, but also includes top Prague ballet and modern dance performances.

The **National Theater** *(Národní třída 2, Prague 1; Tel 2490-1448; Tram 6, 9, 18, 22 to Národní Divadlo; Box office 10am-6pm Mon-Fri, 10am-12:30pm/3-6pm Sat, Sun; www.anet.cz/nd)* stages its own stalwart operas—often different versions of the same piece going on at the State Opera, so don't let them play you. This is a classic 19th-century opera house, ringed with box seats and known for colorful—if not defining—productions.

The **Lucerna** *(Vodičkova 36, Prague 1; Tel 2421-69-72; Metro line A, B to Můstek; 100Kč)* is a venerated old movie palace right on Wenceslas Square that's as likely to play Bruce Willis action flicks as the latest by Czech rising-star director Saša Gideon. With its own bar, grand sweep of stairs, and a big screen in an opera-esque audience space, it usually plays a key role in any film festival that lands here [see *festivals and events*, above].

▶▶LITERARY SCENE

Prague's literary scene has been endlessly built up as the modern equivalent of Paris in the '20s—but who the hell could live up to that? Unfair expectations aside, there is a genuinely nurturing atmosphere for writers here, who inherit a long literary tradition of Praguers from Rilke to Kafka. The Globe Bookstore and Coffeehouse is at the center of things, with connections to annual PEN club events and promising new ventures like the Prague School of Poetics.

Anthologies, small presses like Twisted Spoon, and literary journals like *Trafika*, *Optimism*, and *The Prague Revue* [see *bar scene*, above] offer more outlets for mad scribblers than you'll find in any other capital of the formerly-known-as East Bloc.

Jazz Club Železná [see *live music scene*, above] hosts English-language slams in its atmospheric stony underground cellar bar every Sunday at 5pm. Competing with the original Sunday evening slam king, Radost FX, the crew here can be predictably fresher and more irreverent, though it's still a gamble on any given night.

Radost/FX [see *club scene*, above] continues to host the infamous *Beefstew* nights, Sundays at 7pm, nowadays held in the space-age basement disco, which is eerily quiet at that time of week. Like Železná, it's all very low-key and the perfect opportunity to approach a scruffy expat scribbler, buy him/her a drink, and glean all there is to know about boho life here. Don't expect to see Czechs, though, unless you look in the vegetarian cafe upstairs.

You'll certainly meet Czech literary sorts at **Literární kavárna G plus G** *(Čerchovská 4, Prague 2; Tel 627-3332; Metro line A to Jiřího z*

12 hours in prague

Faced with the excruciating choice of which two or three pubs to hit out of the hundreds of good ones in Prague, you could do worse than a noon visit to:

1. **U medvídku**—Central, cheap, with blissful but relatively rare South Bohemian Budvar brew, needed for christening any fast crawl through this city [see *bar scene*, above].

2. **Slavia**—Just up Národní, once the literary heart of this literary town (though now overmodernized, to be sure), but a fine spot for a Becherovka and castle/Vltava River view.

3. **Kampa Park**—The open green space, just across the bridge from Slavia (not the restaurant of the same name), always good for spotting a neo-hippie drum jam [see *hanging out*, above].

4. **Prague Castle**—Experience Gothic wonder in Saint Vitus' Cathedral, followed by a trip out to the castle's overlooked northside garden, where you wind down the amazing maze of paths, fountains, and frescoes back to Malá Strana proper [see *culture zoo*, above].

5. **Kampa Park** (the restaurant, not the park)—If you're on a splurge, you can't miss primo seafood by the water's edge while gazing across at Old Town spires. If not, try **Maestro**, back in Old Town [see *eats*, below], but first you'll need to cross...

Poděbrad; 10am-10pm daily), even if you only talk to the barman. Chances are he's one of the former dissidents who set up this cafe/small press, which is the country's sole publisher of books in English on Romany issues. Regular readings (not always in Czech) and acoustic music nights are scheduled here, and they stock all kinds of esoteric journals you can flip through on the comfy seating in the back room.

But when all's said and done, the **Globe Bookstore and Coffeehouse** (*Pštrossova 6, Prague 1; Tel 2491-7230; Metro line B to Národní třída; 10am-midnight daily; globe@globe1.com, AE, V)* remains the undisputed international heart of Prague's literary scene, with a cafe that everyone from Allen Ginsberg to Andrei Codrescu has paid their respects to. They stock thousands of major works in paperback, plus translations of Czech works you'll never find elsewhere, and serve a Sunday brunch that's an institution in itself. Plus, their bulletin board is an expat nerve center—all in a setting that's as cozy as it gets.

Mega Books International (*Mánesova 79, Prague 2; Tel 627-77-67; Metro line A to Jiřího z Poděbrad; 10am-9pm Mon-Fri, 2-9pm Sat; megabook@bohem-net.cz, www.megabooks.cz; No credit cards)* is about as personal as the name suggests, but it does offer a comfortable basement cafe and cheap new English-language paperback classics, right near Hlavní nádraží.

6. **Charles Bridge**—Taking you back to Old Town, this beauty is an absolute must, and offers more neo-hippie guitar riffs and a splendid assortment of soot-covered saints [see *culture zoo*, below].

7. Another two or three pubs—Choose any in Old Town and you can't really go wrong while you wait for the **Roxy** to heat up.

8. **Delux** [see *club scene*, above]—Baby-blue spotlit jazz in a red-and-gold Baroque orgy of a basement club? With Thai food and a funk DJ after 11? Why doesn't anyone ever try something *novel* in Prague?

9. **Radost/FX**—More glitzy disco action over cruising and odd food, this time vegetarian [see *club scene*, above]. If you survive both, and still wake up in time for brunch, get it at...

10. **The Globe Bookstore and Coffeehouse** [see *literary scene*, above]—Grab a nourishing meal of latte, eggs, hash browns, and muffins, and a fine translation of Czech lit on your way out. On the train or plane out of town, begin reading up on all the overwhelming reasons to come back when you've got real time to spend.

gay scene

Gay culture in Prague, much like that in the country as a whole, is growing but is still in the finding-its-feet stage. A hub of gay pubs and clubs is the working-class Žižkov district, while cross-dressing "travesty shows" both here and in Old Town have become a regular feature of nightlife. Outdoor cruising happens, appropriately, around the enormously phallic Metronome sculpture in Letná park, visible from anywhere along the Old Town riverbank. Bars are obviously the indoor places for it, though these days increasing numbers of them are dedicated more to providing a comfortable (or over-the-top) atmosphere than just being about meat markets. A bunch have put up an exclusive front, with metal doors you have to be buzzed through. But don't be intimidated—they're really pussycats if you just grin your way in. The Gayguide website is a remarkably thorough English-language source on the scene with an info line available in Prague [see below].

Amigo (Tel 684-6548, **www.amigo.cz**, *amigo@czn.cz*) is a hip monthly guide with comprehensive events listings, in Czech, but fairly decipherable. It's available at most newsstands, as is the *SOHO Absolut Revue* (*jidas.pm.cesnet.cz/~bobrik/soho*), put out by the respected gay support foundation SOHO. They also run a website where your e-mails can usually be answered in English.

Gayguide.net *(gayguide.net/Europe/Czech/Prague, prague@gay guide.net)* has updated info on every bar, cruise, gay-run accommodation, and hot line in the city.

Friends Music Video Bar *(Náprstkova 1, Prague 1; Tel 2163-5408; Metro line B to Národní třída, night tram 51, 54, 57, 58 to same destination; 4pm-3am daily; No credit cards)* is one of the classier cellar bars in Old Town, with a mellow atmosphere best summed up by the placard next to the door that welcomes "folks of every walk of life as long as they are open-minded." They've also added weekly dance parties, but keep in mind that this is a bar—don't expect any sirens or smoke machines. If you like '60s dance music, though, this is the place to be.

A-club *(Miličova 25, Prague 3; Tel 2278-1623; Tram 5, 9, 26 to Lipanská, night tram 55, 58 to same destination; 7pm-6am Mon-Sat, 3pm-midnight Sun)* is the girls' version of Friends, though smaller and dingier, with comfy couches, a postage-stamp dance floor, and women-only Fridays.

There's nothing dingy about the romantically lit **Club Stella** *(Lužická 10, Prague 2; Tel 2425-7869; Tram 4, 22, 34, night tram 57 to Jana Masaryka; 8pm-5am daily; No credit cards)*. Despite the get-it-on lighting, though, this cafe-bar is mainly for jovial hanging out, especially on the patio in summer.

U Střelce *(Karoliny Světlé 12, Prague 1; Tel 4223-8278; Metro line B to Národní třída, night tram 51, 54, 57, 58; 2pm-2am daily; No credit cards)*, hidden in a courtyard on a tiny street leading away from the front of the National Theater [see *arts scene*, above], is always a riot and welcoming to all orientations. The current reigning queen of drag shows has nightly low-budget extravaganzas that go well beyond cheesy, and a loyal audience that eats them up. The heavily mirrored basement bar accented in fire-engine red just proves you never know *what's* going on beneath the cobblestones of Old Town.

Aqua Club 2000 *(Husitská 7, Prague 3; Tel 627-89-71; Metro line B to Florenc, then Bus 135 or night bus 504; 6pm-4am daily; 150Kč; No credit cards)* is the *original* champ of the genre, though, with shows Monday, Wednesday, Friday, and Saturday in a large, industrial-looking Žižkov building hidden away behind blazing neon. Also features saunas and upstairs rooms for, well, you know....

But the true epicenter is the **New Connection After Dark** *(Rokycanova 29, Prague 3; Tel 0603-322-596; Tram 5, 6, 26 to Seifertova, night tram 57 to same destination; 9pm-4am Mon-Thur, 9pm-6am Fri-Sun; connection-praha@gayguide.net, gayguide.net/praha/connection; 80Kč; No credit cards)*. Its cramped quarters are packed on weekends, no doubt because of the copious bars, wild and dark back room, video booths, and floor shows—and in spite of the crude attempts at snazzy decor.

Fortunately, the only decor in sparkling **Sauna Babylonia** *(Martinská 1, Prague 1; Tel 2423-2304; Metro line A, B to Můstek; 2pm-3am daily; 190Kč; No credit cards)* is tilework. That is, unless you count the constant flow of studly Czech males and portly Germans into this convenient Old Town bathhouse and fitness center.

Sauna Marco *(Lublańská 17, Prague 2; Tel 229-23-07; Metro line C to IP Pavlova, night tram 51, 56, 57 to same destination; 2:30pm-3am daily; 175Kč; No credit cards)*, with steam room, Jacuzzi, bar, and video cabins, is nearly as popular, though, and is closer to the clubs listed above, located as it is on the edge of Žižkov.

CULTUrE ZOO

Thanks to the fortunes of war over the centuries, which miraculously spared Prague from destruction time and again, the whole freakin' city center is a museum, topped by an intact thousand-year-old castle straight out of your favorite bedtime story. Prague Castle and the Old Jewish Cemetery are the big must-sees, the latter being a ghostly tumble of tombstones on a tiny Old Town plot in the old Jewish Quarter.

Prague Castle *(Hradčanské náměstí, Prague 1; Tel 2437-3368; Tram 22 to Prašný most; 10am-6pm Tue-Sun):* That spike you see from all over town is the spire of the Saint Vitus Cathedral, which forms the heart of the castle, complete with tombs of martyred saints and a picture gallery full of 15th-century mannerists and erotic allegory. Don't miss the Royal Gardens or the National Gallery Gothic and Baroque collections here, in the Šternberk Palace and Saint George's Cloister (all of which are contained within the castle).

Jewish Museum *(Jáchymova 3, Prague 1; Tel 2481-0099; Metro line A to Staroměstská; 9am-5:30pm Tue-Sun, closed Saturdays and Jewish holidays; zmp@ecn.cz, www.jewishmuseum.cz):* An incredible collection of Judaica, which, along with the neighboring synagogues and the Old Jewish Cemetery, make up the heart of the Jewish Quarter tour. Even more incredibly, the museum treasures were assembled by Hitler, who intended it to be an exhibit on an extinct race.

Charles Bridge *(Karlův most, Prague 1; Metro line A to Staroměstská):* Put together with egg-yolk mortar in 1357, it's lined with stone saints, stoned guitar players, and about 12 million tourists day and night.

Old Town Hall *(Staroměstské náměstí, Prague 1; Tel 2448-2909; Metro line A to Staroměstská; 10am-6pm Tue-Sun):* The astrological tower, circa 1364, tells you things NASA can't, plus it has shows of marching apostles on the hour! The square that it sits on is where Prague's Protestant nobles lost their heads to the Catholic Hapsburgs in 1621.

Vyšehrad *(V pevnosti, Prague 2; Tel 294-900; Metro line C to Vyšehrad):* An open-air assembly of ruins that mark the original seat of the pagan Bohemian royals, one of which was Libuše, famous for chucking ex-lovers into the Vltava River below.

Veletržní Palace National Gallery Collection of Modern and Contemporary Art *(Dukelských hrdinů 47, Prague 7; Tel 2051-4599; Tram 5, 12, 17 to Strossmayerovo náměstí; 10am-6pm Tue-Sun, till 9pm Thur; 80Kč):* The city's newest modern art complex attracts regular shows of commercial heavyweights like Annie Leibovitz, and houses local treasures like the Cubist sculptures of Otto Gutfreund.

Galerie Rudolfinum *(Alšovo nábřeží 12, Prague 1; Tel 2489-3205; Metro line A to Staroměstská; 10am-6pm Tue-Sun; 30Kč):* The city's grandest concert hall is also an art gallery where hip exhibits are run, from Cindy Sherman photos to provocative explorations of myth-making and the Holocaust.

Wallenstein Riding School *(Valdštejnské náměstí 3, Prague 1; Tel 36-814; Metro line A to Malostranská; 10am-6pm Tue-Sun; 40Kč):* Top exhibitions of everything from cyberculture to romanticists and Czech modern artists like the Tvrdohlavi (hardheads) group.

Golden Lane *(Zlatá ulička, Prague 1; Tram 22 to Prašný most):* This little street adjoining Prague Castle, now totally tourist-filled, is lined with the charming little cottages where the goldsmiths, silversmiths, and wheelwrights all lived—one of them later occupied by Kafka.

National Museum *(Václavské náměstí 68, Prague 1; Tel 2449-7111; Metro line A, C to Muzeum; 10am-6pm Tue-Sun, closed the first of every month; www.nm.cz; 40Kč):* Unless you're way into rock samples, busts of forgotten heroes, or mastodon skeletons, this is as boring a museum as you'll ever find.

Bertramka *(Mozartova 169, Prague 5; Tel 543-893; Tram 4, 7, 9 to Bertramka; 9:30am-5pm Nov-Mar, 9:30am-9:30pm Apr-Oct):* Where Mozart lived while composing *Don Giovanni* in Prague—and where they say a lusty hostess locked him in and "inspired" him. Rock on, Wolfie.

great outdoors

Prague may just be the most unhealthy city in the world. It boasts the highest per-capita beer consumption globally, and if it's not in the top 10 for filterless cigarettes, then there's been a serious miscalculation. Smoking is seen as the only reasonable defense against the disgusting air quality, the argument being that the lungs need "toughening up." Sunshine is so fleeting that Czechs tend to burn themselves deep brown when it appears, or give up on the sun entirely and go through life with a pasty "pub tan." Worry is a favorite national pastime, second only to scarfing down fried pork with mayonnaise.

Perhaps because of the above, a growing number of young Czechs are forswearing beer completely (those rebels!) and spending every other evening at the gym. Prague does have some large and lovely parks good for running or blading, namely Letná and Stromovka, both in Prague 7 near **The Globe** [see *arts scene*, above], but you still see a lot more dog walkers than runners—so watch where you plant that Air Jordan.

One beauty that balances Prague's pollution is the Vltava River, which manages such grace as it cuts between Baroque facades in Old Town and Malá Strana that you forget all about what might be lurking beneath the surface. Rent an old rowboat from **Lávka** *(Novotného lávka, Prague 1; Tel 2421-4797; Metro line A to Staroměstská; 10am-6pm daily in good weather;*

OLD TOWN WALK

Prague's Old Town is blissfully free of car traffic—which, if you've seen how Czechs drive, is a double blessing.

A walk here is a trip in more ways than one, with spindly Gothic arches jumbled up against fat Renaissance palaces and seedy modern pubs blaring pop radio music squeezed in alongside crisp Baroque theaters. It's best by night, of course, when the tourist throng has vanished and ghosts begin to emerge from darkened doorways.

Starting at the **Můstek metro**, you can meander through **Old Town** and cross the **Charles Bridge** into romantic **Malá Strana** in well under an hour. You exit the metro onto **Wenceslas Square**, then want to head for the lower end of the square (so that the **National Museum** is at your back). Walk straight ahead down **Na můstku** to **Melantrichova**. On your right, you'll see a massive ornate bank that used to be a museum to **Klement Gottwald**, the first communist Czech dictator. Continue along this curving street until you can turn left into the little courtyard on **Hlavsova** (you'll notice crowds are starting to thin out here). Go left again down **Michalská** and turn into the first passage on your right. Stop off for a brew at the groovin' **Železná dveře** [see *bar scene*, above], if you like, then continue on **Michalská** to **Jilská Street**. Take a right on **Jilská** until you see the **Maximum Underground** [see *stuff*, above] music and gear shop on your right. (Actually, you'll hear it before you see it.) Take another left, down little **Jalovcová**, which turns into **Řetězová** and just keep on straight. (You'll see an airshaft near your left foot with light, smoke, and laughter pouring up from it about now and may want to divert again to find the entrance to this great hidden pub around the corner to your left.) This narrow lane is one of the quietest in the district, though it's only a block from and parallel to **Karlova**, Old Town's main tourist drag.

A block after that mysterious airshaft, you'll come to **Anenské náměstí**, where on your left you can see the little theater where Václav Havel, then a dissident playwright, worked as a stagehand. Then you're at the river. Cross over the Charles Bridge (on your right now) and take your pick of one of the pack of Malá Strana cafes.

50Kč an hour) and glide away. Just head through the 24-hour bar and club to the boat launch beneath the deck out back.

If that somehow just doesn't burn your carbs, by all means hit Letná, pick up a pair of inline skates at **Roll Skates Centrum** [see *need to know*, below], and cruise the paths under the shade trees, then reward yourself with one of the best views of Old Town from the giant ticking Metronome sculpture.

Stromovka Park *(Výstaviště exhibition grounds, Prague 7; Tram 5, 12, or 25 to Výstaviště)* is a flatter stretch of woods that used to be the personal hunting grounds of the mad Emperor Rudolf II. It now makes for pretty running scenery. Unlike their American counterparts, these parks almost never have muggings.

To join the pack at bench pressing, try the fitness center at **Hotel Axa** *(Na Poříčí 40, Prague 1; Tel 232-93-59; Metro line B to Náměstí Republiky; 6am-10pm daily; 70Kč per hour)*, where you can sweat it out to your heart's content with the full array of machines, or swim and sauna for a reasonable extra fee.

For a far more typical Prague sporting experience, try pub bowling at **Kuželky** *(Na Bělidle 25, Prague 5; Metro line B to Anděl; 4pm-2am daily; 280Kč per hour)*. It's out of the way in the Smíchov district, but these bowling simulators are a trip. They also have darts, and the brews flow cheaply here. Hopefully, you'll never even break a sweat.

modification

What better souvenir of Prague than a nice Radegast beer logo tattooed on your chest? The tattoo studio inside **Maximum Underground** [see *stuff*, below] would certainly be up to the task, and can provide any piercings you may need. It's a definite favorite among the pomo crowd, with a list of satisfied customers that includes as many Czechs as foreigners.

stuff

Shopping in Prague is an experience that has traumatized more than a few, including veteran travelers. The majority of shop clerks here have proven amazingly resilient to the tenets of capitalism and have managed to hold onto their jobs without compromising their rudeness or laziness one iota. The pre–Velvet Revolution idea that a customer is an annoyance still seems to hold sway in most of the city's stores.

One change for the better is that you can finally find just about anything you need here, including such once-impossible-to-get goods as vintage vinyl, trash fashion, and cool tunes, plus the traditional wonder fruits of the Havelská Street open market.

▶▶**HOT COUTURE**

Galerie Modá *(Štěpánská 61, Prague 1; Tel 2421-1514; Metro line A, B to Můstek; 10am-8pm Mon-Sat; MC, V)* is the place to catch the latest creations of Prague's top fashion designers, led by Helena Fejková, who has joined forces with a handful of others to open this glassed-in perch overlooking the 1920s-era Lucerna *pasáž*, a former shopping arcade glory of the First Republic on upper Wenceslas Square. Mousse and java are served to bored boyfriends and sugar daddies while their model girlfriends run rampant.

Mýrnyx Týrnyx *(Saská ulice, Prague 1; No phone; Tram 12, 22 to*

fashion

For those with the bucks, Quicksilver and mile-high shoes are it. For those making do, which is fortunately most of the rest of us, special dispensations are allowed. Thus, **Radost** will devote a night to the glam crowd, fully decked out in tight designer stuff, then hold a *Tuesday Soul Night*, at which anybody in a sweatshirt and jeans feels welcome—maybe even inconspicuous. At **Roxy**, where house and techno rules, its ethic of noncommercial underground styles also means a forgiving dress code, if any. Places like **Mecca**, where house rules, fall somewhere in between, with fashion shows on occasion but just as often a crowd in Levi's knockoffs and tees. About the only place where you may feel noticeably underdressed in Prague is at the opera or symphony, but even there the balconies are filled with young music lovers without the budget for a tux or evening gown.

Malostranské náměstí; Noon-7pm daily; No credit cards) in Malá Strana is *the* source for Day-Glo orange feather boas, red plastic shorts, and silver lamé. They've recently moved into the "alternative models" biz, and do shows at some of the hottest parties around town.

For more subdued fashions for da boys, there's the trendsetting and swank **Reporter** *(V kolkovně 5, Prague 1; Tel 232-9823; 11:30am-7:30pm Mon-Fri, 11:30am-5pm Sat; AE, MC, V)*, an Italian men's-fashions shop. Conservative stuff, but definitely with high-quality fabrics and a classy Latin flair.

▶▶**TUNES**

Maximum Underground *(Jilská 22, Prague 1; Tel 628-4009; Metro line A, B to Můstek; 11am-7pm daily; No credit cards)* doesn't just stock all the vinyl jungle and breakbeat you can shake a deck at; they also carry all the secondhand leathers, pullovers, and pants you'll ever need if and when you guest star on "That '70s Show." If the tracks you crave aren't here, they're certainly at the **Radost/FX** music shop [see *club scene*, above].

For the hottest names in Czech radio, from Lucie Bílá to Brutus, head for the **Bontonland Megastore** *(Václavské náměstí 1, Prague 1; Tel 2422-62-36; Metro line A, B to Můstek; 9am-8pm Mon-Sat, 10am-7pm Sun; AE, MC, V)* at the bottom of Wenceslas Square. Its three levels of rock, jazz, classical, and videos contain every significant and insignificant Czech recording imaginable, including some amazing deals on the local Supraphon classics label.

▶▶**BAZAAR**

Perhaps the proudest of all Czech traditions is comparison-pricing potatoes. Large numbers of Bohemian housewives have been known to go as far as Poland to buy them for a few hellers (a few hundredths of a crown) less than their local grocer charges. You only have to go as far as **Havelská Street** *(in the heart of the Old Town)* on any morning to find killer deals on mountain honey, fresh strawberries, and blueberries in midsummer. By afternoon, the trade has usually changed to hand-made wooden toys, bad art, and linens.

For true junk, you'll need to hit the *bazar,* as secondhand shops are known here. One of the best is **Rudolf Špičák Vetešnictví** *(Ostrovní 26; Tel 297-919; Metro line B to Národní třída; 10am-5pm Mon-Fri),* where you'll find everything from discarded portraits of First Working-Class President Klement Gottwald to a nice hefty *džbán* (beer jug) for your mantelpiece.

EATS

Prague restaurants have a well-earned reputation for two things: heavy, lumpy peasant food and surly service. Fortunately, things are looking up: A whole crew of places is setting new standards, both in international cuisine and in modernized Czech food. The latter really is a must, though not for vegetarians. Until you've tried roast venison in a wine and rosehip sauce at U Modré kachničky, or pork dressed in the homemade plum brandy called *slivovice*...well, basically your taste buds haven't lived.

Just remember that Czech restaurants close early (some won't take food orders after 8pm), and that even in spots with good service, the tradition is a two- or three-hour spread, so don't plan to do anything else when you're going out for a good dinner. Also, it always pays to double-check the bill—some of the, um, *less progressive* restaurants still try to scam customers by charging them absurd amounts for table snacks they never asked for.

As for tipping, just round up the nearest 10Kč unless you're in a top establishment, in which case 10 percent is usually fine. To pay just say "Za platím, prosím." Also, *The Prague Post*'s website restaurant reviews *(www.praguepost.cz/resthome.html)* are a thorough and authoritative source of info here.

▶▶CHEAP

Bohemia Bagel *(Újezd 16, Prague 1; Tel 531-102; Tram 12, 22 to Újezd; 7am-11pm daily; 150Kč per entree; No credit cards)* was the city's first source of the Yiddish wonder bread and complements it with a serious assortment of coffees and fresh-baked muffins and brownies. All the hip, non-suit expats you'd expect gather here day and night, and the bulletin board always features info on the latest happenings. The egg and salsa bagel's always a good bet.

Country Life *(Melantrichova 15, Prague 1; Tel 2421-33-66; Metro line A, B to Můstek; 9am-3pm/6-9:30pm Sun-Thur, 9am-4pm Fri; 100Kč per entree; No credit cards)* is where you'll find all the young Czech intellectuals who denounce meat and favor the sometimes-pasty vegetarian concoctions this joint sells, cafeteria-style, for almost nothing. It's a friggin' madhouse at lunch, probably because it's the fastest and cheapest spot in Old Town—watch out for scuffles at the do-it-yourself salad bar. The lumpy, arty wooden seating is, shall we say, interesting.

▶▶**DO-ABLE**

Old Town's **Palffy Palác** *(Valdštejnská 14, Prague 1; Tel 5731-22-43; Tram 12, 22 to Malostranské náměstí; 10am-11pm daily; 500Kč per entree; AE, MC, V)* is a candlelit, parquet-floored Baroque dining room run by one of the city's most charming hosts, Roman Řezníček, the man behind **Mecca** and **Érra** [see *club scene* and *bar scene*, above]. The outdoor balcony is blissfully breezy in the warmer months, so don't miss it. Try the house special veggie lasagna or crêpes, followed by homemade coconut cake.

Caffrey's Irish Bar *(Staroměstské nám. 10, Prague 1; Tel 2482-80-31; Metro line A to Staroměstská; 10am-2am daily; 500Kč per entree; AE, MC, V)* opens onto Old Town Square and yet is neither cheesy nor a rip-off. Amazing. Instead, it's a rollicking, plank-floored gathering point for well-heeled expats drawn in by the satellite sports coverage and phenomenal steaks in Guinness sauce. The traditional Irish fry, complete with black-and-white pudding, is a much-sworn-by morning hangover cure.

Maestro *(Križovnická 10, Prague 1; Tel 232-02-94; 11am-11pm daily; 350Kč per entree; MC, V)*, just two blocks from the Old Town end of Charles Bridge, is hands-down the city's best pizza, served in a big, square room with only trompe l'oeil pillars for decor.

▶▶**SPLURGE**

Kampa Park *(Na Kampě 8b, Prague 1; Tel 5731-3493; Metro line A to Malostranská; 11:30am-1am daily; www.kampapark.com; 850Kč per entree; AE, D, EC, MC)* is a modern, airy, stone-terraced spot that sits right on the Vltava River in the shadow of Charles Bridge, making for the best waterside dining in the city. A Scandinavian staff helps give their seafood in aromatic sauces solid creds, and the indoor bar is a major networking scene.

U Modré kachničky *(Nebovidská 6, Prague 1; Tel 5732-0308; Tram 12, 18, 22 to Hellichova; Noon-4:30pm/6:30-11:30pm daily; 850Kč per entree; No credit cards)*, also in Malá Strana, is a few blocks upstream on a quiet cobbled street where, if you wait long enough, you'll see every movie star shooting in Prague walk discreetly through the door. Just remodeled, the **Blue Duckling** (which is what U Modré kachničky translates to) now has a charming upstairs gallery that has the feel of a famous artist's country home. Your roast boar is served under fantastical murals painted by the owners, who've also sought out the best Czech wines to go with it.

crashing

Charming little inns may have been a Prague option in Mozart's time, but these days you'll need to shell out big-time or enlist the help of an agency to score a decent room. This city has only a handful of the small pensions

prague eats and crashing

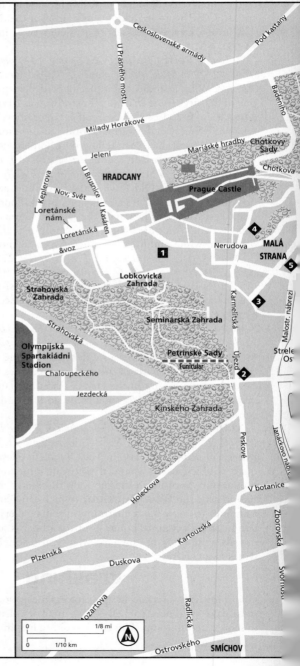

EATS ◆
Bohemia Bagel **2**
Country Life **9**
Kampa Park **5**
Maestro **7**
Palffy Palác **4**
U Modré kachnicky **3**

CRASHING ■
Cloister Inn/
  Pension Unitas **8**
The Clown and Bard **11**
Hotel Sax **1**
Hotel Sieber **12**
Na Kamp 15 **6**
Travellers' Hostels **10**

★ Prague
CZECH
REPUBLIC

Československé armády
Pod kaštany
U Prašného mostu
Milady Horákové
Badeniho
Jelení
Mariánské hradby
Chotkovy Sady
HRADČANY
Chotkova
Keplerova
Nov; Svět
U Brusnice
U Kasáren
Prague Castle
Loretánské nám.
Loretánská
&voz
Nerudova
MALÁ STRANA
Lobkovická Zahrada
Strahovská Zahrada
Karmelitská
Malostr. nábřeží
Seminárská Zahrada
Strahovská
Olympijská Spartakiádni Stadion
Chaloupeckého
Petřínské Sady
Funicular
Újezd
Strele
Os
Jezdecká
Kinského Zahrada
Peskové
Janáčkovo nábř.
Holečkova
V botanice
Zborovská
Plzenská
Duskova
Kartouzská
Svornost
Mozartova
Radlická
Ostrovského
SMÍCHOV

0   1/8 mi
0   1/10 km
N

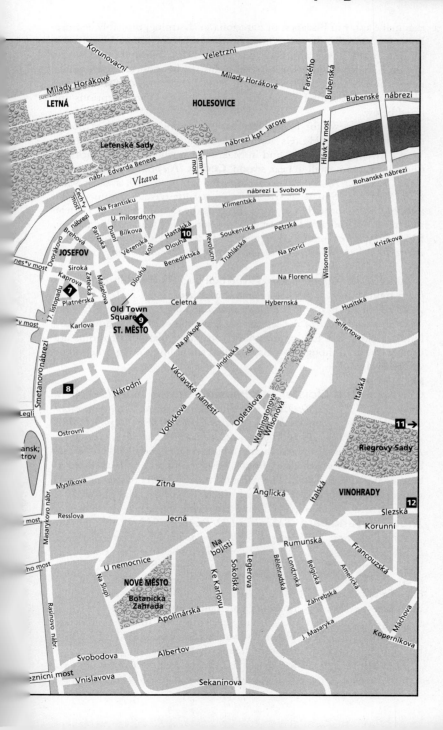

that make a stay in Budapest or Barcelona so charming, probably because Praguers themselves have been in a housing crisis for generations. If you find a pension, it will most likely be clean, comfortable, and tucked away in a grim prefab building in the semi-industrial boondocks. Small hotels tend to be overpriced, with thoroughly blasé service, and large ones charge Hilton-style rates for Holiday Inn–style facilities. The exceptions are listed below.

The good news for backpackers is an ongoing explosion of hostel options—Travellers Hostels alone have buildings on an island in the Vltava River, in Old Town, and in Malá Strana, where you'd be lucky to find a hotel room at all in peak season. **Čedok** *(Na příkopě 18; Tel 2419-7411, Fax 232-16-56; 9am-5pm Mon-Fri, till 1pm Sat)*, a short walk from Wenceslas Square, is the main agency for travel/accommodation info, but being formerly state-run, still runs the risk of long lines. A great source for self-contained apartments and rooms is the incredibly patient **Stop City** *(Vinohradská 24, Prague 2; Tel 2423-1233, Fax 2422-2497; Metro line A to Náměstí Míru; 10am-9pm daily; mail@stopcity.com; AE, MC, V)* in New Town.

A decent last-minute option as you pull into Hlavní nádraží, Prague's main train station, is **AVE** *(Wilsonova 8, Prague 2; Tel 2422-3218, Fax 2423-0783; Metro line C to Hlavní nádrazí; 6am-10pm daily; AE, MC, V, DC)*, located just to the left as you leave the platform's tunnel. Any kindly-looking old folk approaching you with Polaroids of rooms are usually fine also, though you may feel bad stumbling through their door stoned at 4am.

▶▶**CHEAP**

Old Town's **The Cloister Inn/Pension Unitas** *(Bartolomějská 9, Prague 1; Tel 232-7700; Metro line B to Národní třída; Desk open 8am-11pm; cloister@cloister-inn.cz, www.cloister-inn.cz; Pension single 1,020Kč, double 1,200Kč, Inn single 3,000Kč, double 3,800Kč, triple 4,750Kč; AE, MC, V)* is actually two places in one, a budget hotel above and an upscale hostel below, both with clean, bright, basic rooms and both attended to by the same cheerful staff. The pension has a twist: Its basement rooms were once police prison cells, one of which (P6) held Václav Havel.

You'll meet a pack of party-loving shoestring travelers from all over at **The Clown and Bard** *(Bořivojova 102, Prague 3; Tel 2271-6453; Metro Jiřího z Poděbrad; 250Kč dorm, 350Kč per person six-person apartment, 450Kč per person double; No credit cards)*. That's because they're hip to its location right in the center of pub-heaven Žižkov, where most rooms are overpriced hotels and not much different than what you get here. In fact, one of the friendliest of these pubs is in the lobby, where chess games, blues jams, and notes-comparing go on nightly until the wee hours. There is a drop-off laundry, a safe, currency exchange, and summer barbecues, but no breakfast, and no phone reservations, and you should try to arrive by 7pm. Showers and bathrooms are mostly shared.

Travellers' Hostels *(Dlouhá 33, Prague 1 (other locations as well, inquire at desk); Tel 2482-6662; Metro line B to Náměstí Republiky;*

ONLY HERE

Maybe it's backlash against the prevailing beer culture, but a lot of young Czechs won't touch the stuff. A few of the more extreme radicals among them have established a counterculture of tearooms that look like they were transplanted whole from Tibet or Sumatra. Finding one of these places, where black-robed servers are bidden by little brass bells, can be a little disorienting when you're expecting the stone cathedrals of old Prague.

Once you find **Dobrá Čajovna** *(Boršov 2, Prague 1; Tel 269-9794; 10am-midnight Mon-Sat, noon-midnight Sun)*, marked by an iron bellpull in a dark courtyard off Karoliny Světlé, you'll be glad you did. With dozens of teas from India, Africa, China, and South America, each brewed according to the tradition of its home country, you're in for a supremely mellowing experience. You sit around on little bamboo ottomans, drink at tables made of tea crates, and can ask for the hookah if you're still not far enough from the modern world. It's only loaded with scented tobacco, though.

Two other locations, in Wenceslas Square *(Václavské náměstí 14, Prague 1; Tel 2423-1480; 10am-9pm Mon-Sat, 3-9pm Sun)* and next door to the **Roxy** [see *club scene*, above], ensure that a total Eastern escape is never far in newly Westernized Prague.

hostel@terminal.cz; 580Kč per person double, 450Kč per person triple, 420Kč quad, 370Kč dorm; No credit cards) are always a bargain and always friendly, but you have a good chance of sleeping in a gymnasium in some of their many properties, so ask for details. The upside: There's laundry access, you're mere feet from great pubs, and you now have adventuresome pals from all over the world with whom you'll share showers and bathrooms.

▶▶**DO-ABLE**

The Hotel Sax *(Jánský vršek 3, Prague 1; Tel 5753-1268, Fax 5753-4101; hotelsax@bon.cz; Tram 12, 22 to Malostranské náměstí; 3,700Kč single , 4,400Kč double, 5,100Kč suite; AE, MC, V, DC)* is a rare find in Malá Strana: a clean, reasonable, and well-run option just blocks from the district's main square. The rooms are standard and the service well-above (for Prague), but the setting, amid narrow cobbled lanes, is the showstopper.

The new **Hotel Sieber** *(Slezská 55, Prague 3; Tel 2425-0025; Metro line A to Jiřího z Poděbrad; sieber@comp.cz; 4,480Kč single, 4,780Kč double, 5,480Kč suite; AE, MC, V)* is a 10-minute Metro ride from the center, but

wired

Prague is one serious cyber city, with Internet cafes popping up like mushrooms after the rain—and some highly accomplished hackers who pride themselves on the pirated software they've scored, often on the day it ships. A tremendous number of Czech websites can tell you everything from how to say something in Czech to what street runs in front of the Florenc Metro, from what's playing at the theater around the corner to whether it's likely to rain on you today.

Internet Café Spika (*Dlážděná 4, Prague 1; Tel 2421-1521; Metro line C to Náměstí Republiky; 10am-10pm daily; netcafe.spika.cz*) is the latest Czech upstart, offering a quiet atmosphere of unpretentious browsing, plus MS Office, games, and color printing and copying, all within a cool I-beamed Art Nouveau space with tile mosaics and spy balcony. Surf here for 25Kč per 15 minutes weekdays, half-price on weekends.

www.praguepost.cz: All the week's news and entertainment list-

only a 5-minute walk from Žižkov's best pubs. It's no boutique hotel, but it's solid, courteous, and reasonable. Because it's technically a business hotel, it offers big summer discounts and it's not listed with many traditional booking agencies, so it's a good spot to look into when the official word is "there's not a room free in Prague."

▶▶**SPLURGE**

The Grand Hotel Bohemia (*Králodvorská 4, Prague 1; Tel 2480-41-11, Fax 232-95-45; Metro line B to Náměstí Republiky; 9,960Kč single, 14,380Kč double, 17,020Kč, triple; AE, MC, V, DC*) was once not on the official maps, but its turn-of-the-century opulence was legendary. It's now been updated by an Austrian firm to include everything cushy, from in-room faxes to a nonsmoking *floor*. And its location, smack dab in Old Town, is impossible to beat. Breakfast included and substantial discounts off season.

Call way ahead for **Na Kampě 15** (*Na Kampě 15, Prague 1; Tel 5753-1430; Tram 12, 22 to Malostranské náměstí; archib@anet.cz; 5,400Kč single, 5,800Kč double, 7,200Kč apartment; AE, EC, MC, V*). With only 26 rooms, this enchanting, just-renovated Renaissance-era inn on Vltava Island fills up fast. Ask for a river view, the higher the better, and you might just land a raftered garret space with Old Town glowing outside your window just across the Charles Bridge. Basic breakfast is included, via the classy onsite patio pub, and discounts in the off-season are significant.

need to know

Currency Exchange The Czech national currency is the **Kč (crown or**

ings plus comprehensive restaurant reviews, tips on residency, and events calendar.

www.centraleurope.com: Wrap-ups of the regional news with countless factoids about the Czech Republic, travel features, and a link to the Czech train system's searchable timetable [see *need to know*, below].

www.radio.cz: Transcripts of daily newscasts in English plus loads of archives on questions societal.

www.kulturavpraze.cz: Searchable Czech-only listings of everything from movies to art installations.

www.ticketsbti.csad.cz/program.htm: Full schedule of all performances of the National Theater, ballet, opera, and major symphonies, and about the only way to order tickets for them in advance from abroad.

www.seznam.cz: Try out the above on this snappy Czech-language search engine for all things Bohemian.

in Czech, *koruna*). Banks are the best places to change money, but close at 5pm; otherwise there's a **CheckPoint** at train stations or any exchange desk at **Ruzyně Airport**.

Tourist Information Prague Information Service *(Staroměstské náměstí, Prague 1; Tel 264-022; 9am-7pm Mon-Fri, 9am-5pm Sat-Sun; cccr@pha.pvnet.cz, www.prague-info.cz)* has all the usual tourist info— check out their website or call their English info line *(187).*

Public Transportation A 12Kč ticket gets you a one-hour ride on any combination of metro, bus, or tram, but one-day passes at 70Kč and three-day passes at 200Kč are much less trouble. Transit maps are available at any newsstand. Inspectors will fine you 200Kč if you ride without a ticket. Metro service stops at midnight, but night trams and buses *(numbered in the 50s and 500s)* run till morning.

Bike/Moped/Whatever Rental Roll Skates Centrum *(Letenské sady, Nad Stolou 1, Prague 7; Tel 0601-296-989; Tram 1, 25, 26 to Sparta; 2-8pm Mon-Fri, 10am-8pm Sat, Sun)*, in Letná Park, rents inline skates, but bring two IDs as deposits.

American Express *(Václavské nám. 56, Prague 1; Metro line A, C to Muzeum; Tel 2280-1111; 9am-5pm Mon-Fri, till noon Sat, Sun, exchange till 7pm daily).*

Health and Emergency First Medical Clinic *(Tylovo náměstí 3, Prague 2; 2425-1319, emergency 0603-555-006; Metro line A, to IP Pavlova; 7am-7pm Mon-Fri; AE, MC, V)* has a 24-hour emergency line in English.

Telephone Prague phone numbers can be 4 to 8 digits long. Country code: *42*, city code: *02*, information: *120*, international operator: *121*. **MCI:** *0042-000-11*, **AT&T:** *0042-0087-187*, **Sprint:** *0042-087-187*. Get phone cards at any newsstand.

Airports Ruzyně *(Tel 2011-3314)* is 15km out of the city center. All airport taxis are crooked, but the **Čedaz airport shuttle** *(Tel 2011-4296; 4:30am-11:30pm)* takes you to Revoluční Street in Old Town for 30Kč, and city **Bus 119** takes you to **Dejvická Metro**.

Airlines Delta *(Národní 32, Prague 1; Tel 2494-6733)*, **Air France** *(Václavské nám. 10, Prague 1; 2422-7164)*, **British Airways** *(Ovocný trh 8, Prague 1; Tel 2211-4444)*, **Lufthansa** *(Ruzyně Airport; Tel 2011-4456)*.

Trains Hlavní nádraží, **Smíchov**, and **Holešovice** stations are the main arrival points *(Tel 2422-4200; 24 hours; www.idos.datis.cdrail.cz/default_ e.htm)*, and are all on Metro lines that run directly to **Old Town**.

Bus Lines Out of the City Florenc Station, in Prague 8, is directly on Metro lines B and C with some English-speaking info and ticket clerks *(no info line in English)*.

Taxis Rip-offs are rampant, so stick to honest **AAA** *(Tel 140-14)* or **Profi Taxi** *(Tel 1035)*.

Laundry Laundryland *(Londýnská 71, Prague 2; Metro line C to IP Pavlova; Tel 0603-411-005; 8am-10pm daily)* has laundromat or drop-off/delivery service, plus dry cleaning.

Kraków

Let's face it, Poland's never been on the top of any European "must-see" list. But like its Slavic neighbor Prague, Kraków is quickly becoming a prime destination for travelers and tourists alike, with expats from all over the world settling down here, undoubtedly attracted, among other things, to the vibrant energy of the city's 100,000 university students. Kraków also shares Prague's two great strengths: 1) It's a beautiful, medieval old town that made it through WWII essentially unscathed, complete with brilliant examples of Romanesque, Baroque, and Gothic architecture; 2) It's damn cheap!

Like their Czech neighbors, Poles are very proud of their unique cultural heritage and newly democratic nation. In comparison with many other large European cities, Kraków is, on the surface, kind of a conservative place, but there's plenty of wildness going on—you just have to know where to look. During the last decade, the conversion to a capitalist consumer-driven society and the consequential flood of American culture has reshaped Kraków. The days have passed when *everything* American was seen as a cure-all, and rapid cultural shifts are seen with a more realistic and slightly skeptical attitude. The young residents of Kraków view the increasingly powerful MTV and McDonald's culture with a mixture of fascination and disdain. Many young Poles will be spotted at McDonald's, while at the same time, just as many complain that the pace of life has sped up to unacceptable levels. You may be perplexed to sometimes even hear people express nostalgia for the oppressive regime that the Poles fought against for all those years. The logic goes something like this: Before the collapse of the old system, leisure time was abundant, leaving ample room for long lunches, vacations, and traditional marriage ceremonies lasting several days. Today, time is money, and reflective moments are scarce, vacations are short, and marriage ceremonies are often cut down to a day. Ironically, you'll find plenty of young Poles expressing their concern about the attack of fast food and prefab culture.

The soul of Kraków is deeply rooted in Catholicism. Most Poles are devout Catholics and they take religion extremely seriously. Former Archbishop of Kraków Pope John Paul II is absolutely idolized in this city, his picture plastered on storefront windows, kiosks, message boards—he's even on some phone cards. And the reverence for Catholicism or the Pope isn't just limited to the older generation. In fact, the same kids you shoot vodka with all Saturday night may roll out of bed early Sunday morning just in time for mass.

Kraków is a reasonably safe city. The area around the main market square usually has a large police/rent-a-cop presence to keep potential troublemakers at bay. But keep in mind that all the cops and security guards in the world can't stop the occasional nimble-fingered pickpocket working large unwitting crowds. You should also watch yourself more carefully in the area of the main train station and the Planty.

Kraków does have some drawbacks. The transition from the old commie insanity to the new capitalist insanity is no easy task, and is only a decade in the making. Still, it could be a lot worse, because in comparison with some of the other former Soviet-era states, Poland is a model for reform.

The few shortcomings in Kraków begin with getting there. First, if you're coming by train from Germany, be prepared for a long, long, rickety ride through Poland. Second, a rather substantial language barrier exists here, so you're going to have to be creative when attempting to communicate with locals. The younger generation—say, 17- to 25-year-olds—generally speak English a helluva lot better than the older generation, but it's still hard. Poor customer service is also something that many travelers complain about in Kraków, so don't necessarily expect first-class service just because you can afford to dine at a quality restaurant. Finally, neighborhoods outside the city center can have a melancholy aura, in part a result of hideous communist-era architecture.

So, here's the upside: old-world charm, everything you want to do within easy walking distance, super-cheap great beer, delicious meals at low-low prices, sleeping without shelling out big bucks, and the opportunity to get crazy with plenty of energetic, curious, vodka-soaked young Poles in an emerging hot spot off the typical Euro-tourist beaten path.

neighborhoods

The **town center** is within a 10-minute walk of **Kraków Główny**, the central train station. The bus station, **Dworzec PKS**, is directly across the street from the train station. As in many other cities, the train/bus station attracts a fair share of sketchy-looking, drunk, dirty men who seem to be down and out. As you get off the train and walk into town, keep an eye

THREE THINGS TO TALK TO A LOCAL ABOUT

Talking to Poles isn't going to be easy for an English-speaker. In light of this, foreign languages can definitely come in handy here, particularly if you know Russian or German. Since Russian was forced down people's throats for so long, it's well-understood by most. Breaking out in Deutsch is also an option, although (surprise!) you may not receive the warmest reception from the locals. Whatever the language, try the following ice-breakers:

1. **The transition from a totalitarian, communist society** to a market-driven, democratic society. Compare and contrast. To the surprise of many Westerners, young Poles frequently voice their ambivalence about the new lifestyle that has been thrust upon them [see *intro*]. Of course, they'll also remind you that life was no day at the beach under the Soviets.

2. **Music**—typically pop, rap, and house—is another hot topic. If you know anything about the latest craze, let the local kids know. Whether it's artists, albums, songs, concert tours, or whatever, the Poles will be interested.

3. **Polish perseverance**. The Poles are very proud that they're finally in control of their own destiny, despite getting trounced by their enemies over the centuries. Perhaps rightfully so, the Poles are somewhat nationalistic, and you'll score points by exclaiming your admiration for the Polish spirit.

out for pickpockets and the kind of losers who try to paw unsuspecting young women. There's no need to be paranoid, just be aware. When your train/bus pulls in, simply follow the crowd out of the station, and you'll quickly arrive at the main market square, the heart of **"Old Town."**

There's little reason to venture outside of the central areas of town, because the worthwhile bars, clubs, restaurants, museums, galleries, and places of interest are located in or close to the Old Town, aka **Stare Miasto**. This area is pedestrian-friendly, easily walkable, and there's virtually no automobile traffic. In the center of Stare Miasto lies **Rynek Główny**, the 13th-century main marketplace that was the largest square in medieval Europe, and is still buzzing with street sellers, locals, and tourists. Stare Miasto is very compact, and walking from one end to the other can easily be accomplished in under an hour.

The Stare Miasto is enclosed by the serene area known as the **Planty**, a ring of walking paths lined with large trees, lawns and benches, where university students and other locals go to chill out when the weather is nice

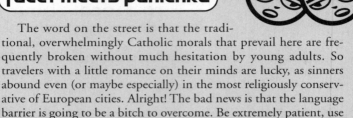

facet meets panienka

The word on the street is that the traditional, overwhelmingly Catholic morals that prevail here are frequently broken without much hesitation by young adults. So travelers with a little romance on their minds are lucky, as sinners abound even (or maybe especially) in the most religiously conservative of European cities. Alright! The bad news is that the language barrier is going to be a bitch to overcome. Be extremely patient, use plenty of body language, and speak slowly and in simple terms. But barriers can crumble after much vodka, when more primitive means of communication become possible. Here are some tips that may get you to that moment of simplicity:

Dress sharply. For guys, polished shoes and dark colors are a good bet. For better or worse, you'll automatically be associated with wealth and power. This is especially lucky for guys who like the Barbie look. But beware, gold-digging seems to top the agenda for these Barbie girls, which is why some of them appear to be attached at the hip to their shady, independently wealthy, musclehead boyfriends. Unless you like crossing paths with a potential ass-kicking mobster on his own turf, steer clear of the girls who hang out with them. Women can try to blend in with the local girls, which means high heels, very short skirts, and plenty of makeup.

If you're American and from Ohio or something, tell everyone you're from New York, L.A., Chicago, or a more exotic, warm-weather city like San Diego or New Orleans. (For the moment, American cities still rate.)

Don't even attempt to speak Polish. Yeah, it sounds ignorant, but this is only in your interest. Polish is so hard to pronounce for most native English-speakers that improvised pickup lines in Polish will only result in perplexed stares (and maybe even contempt).

Or forget about the above and chill with hipsters and degenerate expats at **Free Pub** [see *club scene*, below], and groove until dawn.

[see *by foot*, below]. Directly west of Rynek Główny is the university district clustered around the **Collegium Maius** [see *culture zoo*, below], where, naturally, you'll find the more studious types milling around the Gothic splendor. To the southwest of Stare Miasto, overlooking the river **Vistula**, lies majestic **Wawel Hill**. This is considered the heart of Polish culture, and houses an extensive collection of historical artifacts. The hill also contains a grand cathedral, royal castle, and **Zygmuntowska Tower**, which provides a remarkable view of the city [see *culture zoo*, below].

The **Kazimierz** [see *by foot*, below], the area just southeast of Stare Miasto, was predominantly populated by Jews before World War II.

Jewish life has been somewhat resurrected in this now-small community, and Kazimierz is one of the most captivating areas of the city as well as a sobering reminder of the evils of 20th-century European fascism.

The only reason you're going to have to use the city public transportation system is for getting out to an outlying hotel or private room. And since most of the student hotels and private rooms are quite a long walk from the center, you'll need public transportation. Dirt-cheap trams and buses provide you with transport services if you happen to need them [see *need to know*, below].

Tourist offices also tend to be concentrated in Stare Miasto. **Dexter Travel** will gladly supply you with detailed maps, brochures, and other info. They also help book hotel rooms and sightseeing tours. **Orbis Travel** will book bus, train, and plane tickets when you decide to take a side trip or leave town for good. **Centrum Informacji Turystycznej** is just around the corner from the main train station and will provide you with additional maps, hotel/hostel info, and tickets for tours in the city and in outlying areas. For information concerning upcoming cultural events, try Centrum Informacji Kulturalnej [see *need to know*, below, for all].

Partially in English, *Karnet* will provide you with excellent detailed descriptions of upcoming events in the city. This publication is available at tourist offices, some hotels, and bookstores.

hanging out

In the middle of Rynek Główny, on the east side of the **Sukiennice** [see *stuff*, below] Polish students and backpackers sit and watch the action from the monument memorializing poet Adam Mickiewicz. This is a good outdoor spot for people-watching or for striking up a conversation with an English-speaker. The statue is surrounded by heavy pedestrian traffic, attracting street performers, musicians, and horse-drawn carriages.

Cafe culture runs as deep in Kraków as it does in Vienna, with people literally spending their days drifting from one cafe to another. **Café Camelot** (*Sw. Tomasza 17; Tel 421/01-23; 9am-midnight; No credit cards*) is where the cute student crowd chills out, smoking cigarettes and talking about Sartre and Issey Miyake. Mostly vegetarian cuisine, excellent salads, mean Viennese-style pastries, and killer coffee keep the Prada sneaker–wearing kids happy as they casually check each other out. Cabaret Friday at 8:15pm, jazz on Wednesday and Saturday evenings, plus a very foxy wait staff.

If all that is a bit too glam for you, check out the **Catholic Intelligence Club** (*ul. Sienna 5, second floor, just off the east side of Rynek Główny; No phone; 6pm Wed; No charge*), aka "KIK." As ominous as it sounds, it's really simply an informal group of local twentysomethings interested in meeting new people, and many gather here to do just that. The meetings officially start at 6pm, and fill up around 6:30. Head upstairs, pull up a chair, introduce yourself, and take it from there. Both men and women turn up here, and often the meeting moves on to a local bar. A real mix of types gathers here, from super-squirrelly to with-it.

Probably the best place to find fellow travelers and young backpackers is at one of the Internet cafes [see *wired*, below]. Not surprisingly, a large contingent of the customers at these places is made up of travelers and tourists in Kraków for a few days. Stop in and check things out if you're hell-bent on meeting people who are in the same boat as you. It's kind of cruisy at these places, provided you can get over the fact that it's slightly unadventurous to hit a cybercafe in an attempt to pick up a fellow English-speaker.

bar scene

Locals in Kraków are quick to point out that there are about 300 bars or pubs in the Stare Miasto. So there's certainly no shortage of places to grab a beer within a stone's throw of Rynek Główny. Also be prepared to pay happy-hour prices for drinks both day and night. Large draft beers will rarely, if ever, cost more than 7zl. And unlike in so many other cities in Europe, you won't be scared to look in your wallet the morning after a long, rough night out. Young Poles, particularly on weekend nights, loosen up, hit the vodka, become much more outgoing, and eventually end up dancing around in a happy drunken stupor. If you're having a hard time meeting young Poles as a result of the language barrier, try your luck after people get trashed. Insecurities drop, the guard is let down just enough, and the natives are much more willing to give their English a try.

The Old Pub (*ul. Poselska 18; No phone; 2-minute walk southeast on ul. Grodzka from Rynek Główny, make a left onto ul. Poleska; 10am-2am Sun-Thur, till 3am Fri, Sat; MC, V*) is the choice for all you darkness-dwelling vampire types out there. The primary light sources here are single candles on each table, making it difficult to see the other side of the pub. You can barely make out reflections in the large mirrors sprinkled about the two small rooms (also good for vampires). A casual-but-not-sloppy crowd in their mid-20s quietly talks over the soft hip-hop, jazz, or rock. The ground floor entrance makes this a perfect watering hole if you've been boozing too hard and are anxious about falling downstairs while attempting to get into another basement-type deal. Palm or Zywiec beers will run you in the neighborhood of 4 to 5zl for half a liter.

When you feel the need to be transported back to your early childhood, there's always **Fischer Pub** (*ul. Grodzka 42; No phone; 3-minute walk southeast on ul. Grodzka from Rynek Główny; 1pm-2am daily; No credit cards*). With super-low stools and tables designed for Smurfs, you'll feel like you're back in the kindergarten playroom (complete with brewsky-juice before nappy-time). Old wooden kegs are strewn about the room on the crowded, higher-energy ground floor. In the basement, the vibe's calmer, chiller, maybe as a result of the normal-sized tables and chairs. A popular hangout for the somewhat serious Polish college student before, after, and during class.

When in the Kazimierz district [see *by foot*, below], a visit to the **Singer Pub** (*ul. Estery 20; No phone; Walk southeast on Stradomska, make a left onto sw. Józefa and then make a left onto ul. Estery just before the Old*

IT'S IN THE GRASS

When in Kraków, don't miss sampling **Zubrovka**, a vodka that's like an elixir. The FDA won't even allow the stuff into the U.S. because the famous piece of bison grass floating in the middle of the bottle is supposed to have certain psychotropic properties. Poles say Zubrovka tastes so good because "the bison pisses on the grass" (wherein it also derives its mysterious powers). Drink it mixed with apple juice or, better yet, knock it down straight, ice-cold: You'll find it hard to stop. Another popular drink is the "wild dog," a shot that's known to get young Poles into a crazy, frenetic mood. It's vodka, a special berry syrup, and two or three drops of Tabasco sauce. The first shot can be gut-wrenching, but they gradually become smoother (and schmooother) as the night progresses.

Synagogue; Noon-3am daily; No credit cards) is absolutely mandatory. A cozy cafe in daytime turns into an intimate, candlelit nighttime hangout. The mysterious interior is a cross between a late-19th-century Paris whorehouse and the setting of a Kafka novel, complete with sewing-machine tables. Blurred, evocative charcoal sketches cover the walls, and Billie Holiday or soulful bossa nova dominate the stereo. A single candle on every table keeps the largely local bohemian crowd staring into dark corners. With half-liters of Zywiec going for 4.50zl, it's your best option for putting your feet up after a tour of the Kazimierz district.

In Vitro *(ul. Sienna 3; No phone; Just off the east side of Rynek Główny; Noon-2am Sun-Thur, noon-5am Fri, Sat; No credit cards)* is the place in town for the high-rent, well-dressed, 21-and-over crowd. Three slide projectors on every floor, flipping through shots of New York City, are accompanied by walls and furniture that have a silvery metallic and white space-age design. Don't be misled by the snotty look of the customers, they're largely receptive to visitors, and striking up a conversation isn't too difficult. A video player in the basement bar shows anything from cartoons to avant-garde dance. Drinks are more expensive than the norm, with large Heinekens costing 7zl. There's also a large outdoor courtyard for those who prefer to hang outside. Jazz, blues, and house music are the sounds of choice, and techno is absolutely forbidden.

Klub Kulturalney *(Ulica Szewska 5; Tel 429/67-39; Noon-3 or 4am; No cover; No credit cards)*, just off the Stare Miasto, is a lovely, intimate place for the early evening. A cafe/pub located in a Romanesque cellar, the "Culture Club" has a labyrinth of small rooms, nooks, and crannies to get lost in with friends or a special sweetie. Large wooden tables,

Rules of the game

The drinking age is 18, and the open-container law is in effect citywide. Cigarette smoking is universal, meaning nearly everyone over 15 smokes, and smokes a hell of a lot. The drug scene, although largely hidden, is pretty active. Speed is reportedly the drug of choice for ravers and avid club-goers. Weed's the most popular drug, and is used by an increasingly larger and younger crew. Once semi-decriminalized for personal use, the rules have tightened up concerning marijuana. The cops used to turn a blind eye if you got nailed with a "small amount" considered to be solely for personal use. Now only 5 to 10 grams can land you in the Polish slammer.

benches, candlelight, and soul and funk music make this place perfect for a relaxed drink.

LIVE MUSIC SCENE

Jazz dominates the nightly live music scene in Kraków. There are several bars/clubs that provide live jazz on a regular basis, most of it local and pretty decent, and usually accompanied by light cover charges. On nights when live music is planned, the bands generally start up pretty early, normally around 9pm. By midnight the energy level is peaking, and the bands are performing their final number before packing it in at 1am. By this time, the bars are jammed, and the patrons tend to hang out and drink until last call. For special music events or concerts, keep an eye out for promotional posters, particularly in the area just west of Rynek Główny. For info on hip-hop or punk shows, head over to one of the relevant shops [see *stuff,* below].

If a fire ever broke out in **Harris Piano Jazz Bar** *(Rynek Główny 28; Tel 421/17-41; West side of Rynek Główny; 10am-midnight Sun-Thur, till 2am Fri, Sat; 20zl cover Sat),* the place would burn for at least three or four days. In fact, half of the remaining Polish forest may have been cut down just to decorate the interior. There's an incredible amount of thick wooden beams and wood furniture in this beautiful basement jazz club. High-quality, professional, largely local jazz acts are here at 8pm every Saturday night, playing to the slightly chic, mixed-age/nationality crowd. A wooden 10-foot trumpet player stares at you as you make your way down the stairs, black and white photos of Ray Charles and Miles hang in the back room, and small Zywiec beers sell for 4.50zl.

In the depths of a typical Kraków candlelit, brick and rock–walled basement lies a splendid weekend jazz/rock/blues bar. **U Louisa** *(Rynek Główny 13; Tel 421/80-92; East side of Rynek Główny; 11am-11pm Mon-Thur, till 2am Fri, Sat, 2-11pm Sun; 5zl cover for live music)* draws a largely young, casual international and local crowd that comes for the music and the

Polish and Czech beers for 4zl. The weekend lineup of live music is primarily jazz, with some blues and rock thrown in on occasion. The bands are mostly university-age local kids, singing in both English and Polish. If the band sounds alright—a hit-or-miss proposition—the crowd will stay put all night. There's outdoor seating on the ground level and Internet access [see *wired*, below]. Show up before 9pm if you want a drinking table. The exterior room also doubles as a small art gallery.

Although it's off the beaten path, this basic, totally unpretentious small jazz club is a great way to start your evening: **Jazz Klub Kornet** *(Al. Z. Krasińskiego 19; Tel 427/02-44; Walk west from Rynek Główny, down Smoleńsk, than make a left onto Al. Z. Krasińskiego; 11am-11pm daily; No cover for live music)* features great old-time, traditional jazz on Wednesday and Friday nights, beginning at 8:30pm sharp. Trumpets, clarinets, fiddles, and French horns hang from the ceiling as you wiggle to adjust yourself in a flimsy old chair. The local crowd, most of it over 30, can't really speak English, but are friendly enough to attempt communication anyway. The drink prices are also worth noting, because EB beers go for 3zl each. Yep, that's only 3zl a beer. Unfortunately, the bar closes at 11pm, which is always a bummer, 'cause you're not going to want to leave.

Another option for rock or jazz is **Klub Studencki Pod Jaszczurami** [see *club scene*, below].

cLub sceNe

On first glance, it may look like there are only one or two clubs on Rynek Główny. But look a little closer for the many hopping venues located below the ground floor. You can't necessarily see or hear them from the street, so you're going to have to explore. When you enter the corridors that lead between buildings, notice the signs pointing out intimidating (but don't be intimidated) staircases that lead down into basements. Depending on the venue, doormen may either be at the top or the bottom of the stairs directing customers. So yes, like many of the bars here, the vast majority of clubs are underground, creating an extraordinarily primal atmosphere. The dress requirements are pretty relaxed, especially if you

fIVE-O

In general, the cops in Kraków are trustworthy, as long as you can somehow communicate with them—Polish cops generally don't speak English. That said, doing something illegal out in the open (like smoking a joint on the street) is a bad idea, unless you'd like to do a study on Polish prison conditions. Paying off cops is a much harder proposition than it was in the past, so forget about it.

KRAKÓW bars, clubs and culture zoo

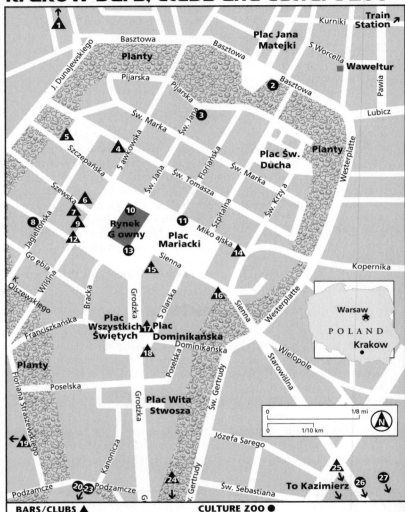

BARS/CLUBS ▲

Catholic Intelligence Club **16**
Disco Pub Pod Baranami **12**
Dwa Pstragi **1**
Fischer Pub **18**
Free Pub **4**
Harris Piano Jazz Bar **9**
Jazz Klub Kornet **19**
Kawiarnia Aperitif Bar "Pavillon" **5**
Klub Kulturalney **7**
Klub Pasja **6**
Laznia **24**
Looz Internet Cafe **14**
The Old Pub **17**
Singer Pub **25**
U Louisa **15**

CULTURE ZOO ●

Czartoryski Museum **3**
Floriańska Gate **2**
Museum of History of the City
 of Kraków Jewish Department **26**
National Museum **10**
Remu'h Synagogue/Remu'h Cemetery **27**
Royal Cathedral **20**
Royal Chambers **22**
Royal Treasury and Armory **23**
St. Adalbert's **13**
St. Mary's **11**
Sigmund's Tower **21**
University Museum **8**

head out to a club before 10pm. Unless otherwise stated, the action begins to heat up around 11pm, generally peaks at 2am, then fizzles until the 3 or 4am closing time. The clientele at the trendiest venues will be out in their Sunday best, generally a cautious, sharp, businesslike outfit that screams "I'm at the top of the food chain and have reaped the rewards of the market economy," but there are also groovier scenes where *who* you are matters more than what you've got on. Don't expect people to warm up to you, though, if you show up looking like you've been sleeping in the Planty for three nights, or if you're sporting a wacky rubber club uniform with gold epaulets.

Klub Pasja (*ul. Szewska 5; Tel 423/04-83; Just west of Rynek Główny; 7pm-2am Sun, Mon, till 3am Tue-Thur, till 4am Fri, Sat; 3-12zl cover)* is a preferred hangout for the 25-and-over, self-assured, ostentatious crowd. This is considered one of the hottest, trendiest clubs in Kraków, so expect pricey drinks (quarter-liter of Heineken for 4.50zl) and a disco full of physically attractive Poles. Getting to know these people may prove to be a tough challenge, unless: 1) You speak fluent Polish, 2) The outfit you're wearing is the latest swishy thing in Europe, or 3) You continually flash a substantial wad of Polish cash to let everyone know how rich you are. The large disco, complete with Romanesque columns reaching to the ceiling, opens its door at 8:30pm. Two billiard tables in a back room are available from 7pm, and a more level-headed, accessible crowd congregates there.

Laznia (*ul. Paulinska 28; Tel 430/74-85; 6pm-2am daily; No cover; No credit cards)* is a small club with a dance floor that's in a stylized old bath house. DJs spin hot and cool Latin music, and a dressy, hip crowd in their twenties and thirties chills in the seats, which are comfy, despite the stark and sterile decor.

Klub Studencki Pod Jaszczurami (*Rynek Główny 8; Tel 429/38-37; East side of Rynek Główny between ul. Sienna and ul. Grodzka; 9am-3am or whenever daily; 5-15zl cover after 9pm; No credit cards)*, the oldest "student club" in Kraków, is an easily noticeable, airy ground-floor spot on the main square. The mostly Polish crowd is twentyish, casual, friendly, and loves its Cracovia "wodka." During the day, a really chill pub atmosphere dominates, with outdoor seating spilling out onto the sidewalk. On Wednesday, Friday, and Saturday evenings, the tables are cleared out for disco mania. Sunday is *Disco Latina* night, featuring mostly South American DJs and Latin dance music. On Monday, Tuesday, and Thursday, cutting-edge rock, blues, or jazz bands perform. The acts are both local and out-of-towners, chiefly singing cover tunes in English and originals in Polish with predictably mixed results. This is the kind of place where the basement attracts young, rowdy Poles who sit and go shot-for-shot with each other with the Polish firewater. If you opt to pull up a chair and try to keep up with these guys, don't expect to make that morning (or evening) train out of town.

The sign at the bottom of the stairs at **Disco Pub Pod Baranami** (*Rynek Główny 27; Tel 421/39-39 West side of Rynek Główny; 6pm-3am*

fESTIVALS and EVENTS

3rd Annual Ludwig van Beethoven Easter Festival *(Easter season annually; various locations in Kraków; Tel 429/34-87):* A notable festival, among Europe's most prestigious musical events, with a number of eminent performers.

Organ Music Festival *(Late April annually; Philharmonic Hall and Kraków churches; Tel 429/13-45):* Still going strong after three decades, both Polish and foreign virtuoso organists show off their talents during this festival.

Student's Song Festival *(Early May annually; various stages in Kraków; Tel 421/75-40):* The most anticipated student event of the year, and the largest event of its kind in Poland. Musicians who make the cut in open competition get to play to enthusiastic crowds. Music ranges from rock to classical and everything in between.

Jewish Culture Festival *(Late June through early May annually; various locations in Kraków, but mainly in the Kazimierz district; Tel 421/18-84):* A grand assortment of Jewish music, meetings, lectures, theatrical productions, exhibitions and workshops, attracting top-notch musicians from Israel, the U.S.A, and Europe.

St. John's Night (Midsummer's Night) *(End of June annually; The banks of the Witsla near Wawel Hill; Tel 421/52-07):* One of the most popular annual events in Kraków. Candlelit wreaths woven with flowers float down the river as thousands of Poles party on the banks. It's a huge open-air event, with concerts, fireworks, lots of beer, and kielbasa.

Zaduszki Jazz Festival *(Late October annually; Kraków's jazz clubs; Tel 0-603-25-10-92):* The most-awaited jazz event of the year, featuring both top Polish and international jazz performers.

daily; 3-8zl cover after 9pm; No credit cards) reads: "We know how to overcome boredom," and there are plenty of attractions in this large, eerie, bomb shelter/dungeon—like atmosphere. These include a pool table (in a back room with more light), a disco floor with a crucified skeleton watching from above, and plenty of seating in a surrealist bar area. Fading wall paintings, hats that appear to be in flight, and old clocks surround you as you sit at your candlelit wooden table. Attracting an under-25 crowd, this is a good bet if you're looking to get it on with a local. The music is also pretty varied, with the likes of Lenny Kravitz in the bar area, and anything from late-'70s disco to more contemporary dancehall in the disco.

Free Pub *(ul. Slawskowska 4; Tel 222-24-06; Second entryway from the Rynek Główny, no sign, just go down the stairs; 4pm-dawn; No cover; No credit cards)* is a perfect spot to end a night on the town. A mixture of clubbies, hardcore night owls, and degenerate expats congregates at this bar and lounge with huge tables in a Roman cellar, where DJs keep things copacetic spinning trip-hop, dancehall, and trance. The place truly comes alive after 2am when other venues begin to close, and folks tend to hang till dawn drinking, puffing, dancing, or lounging. Your best bet for big fun.

ARTS SCENE

▶▶VISUAL ARTS

Since Kraków is the city of choice for young Polish artistic talents, there is an abundance of contemporary art galleries located in the city center. Also, the Kraków Academy of Fine Arts is arguably one of the finest modern art academies in Europe. A new generation of Polish and other Eastern European artists from the Academy is often promoted by well-established art galleries. Plus, most galleries are free.

Since 1989, **Format Gallery of Modern Art** (*ul. Dietla 53; Tel 422/86-31; Walk southeast on Starowišlna and make a right onto Dietla; 11am-6pm Mon-Fri, 10am-2pm Sat, closed Sun; MC, V, AE*) has been promoting artists from the Kraków Academy of Fine Arts. The multi-artist exhibitions show painting, photography, and graphic design. The work of the renowned Polish photographer Zbigniew Bajek is frequently on display. A friendly, down-to-earth, English-speaking staff greets as you enter the gallery.

Along the defensive stone wall connected to **Floriańska Gate** [see *culture zoo*, below] lies the informal gallery referred to as **"The Gate"** (*No phone; 11am-sundown daily; No credit cards*). Local artists display their paintings along the wall just off Kraków's most famous strip. Most of the better work depicts outdoor scenes in watercolor or oil. You can't miss this unique exhibition space as you walk up Floriańska Street.

Stawski Gallery (*ul. Miodowa 15; Tel 421/80-46; Just around the corner from Format Gallery of Modern Art, see above; 11am-4pm daily, closed Sun; MC, V, AE*) is one of the most prestigious modern art galleries in Kraków, showcasing solo exhibitions of new photography, sculpture, painting, and mixed media. Although the gallery concentrates on promoting artists from the Kraków Academy of Fine Arts, it also exhibits the work of already-proven Polish and international artists.

Bunkier Sztuki (*Plac Szczepański 3a; Tel 421/38-40 Just north of Rynek Główny; 11am-6pm, closed Mon; www.bunkier.com.pl; 15zl admission; No credit cards*), "The Art Bunker," the most prominent contemporary arts complex in Kraków, exhibits vital international and Polish art, and is also a great place to find out about other art venues. With several large galleries, a library, and a bookstore, it's definitely worth the minimal admission fee if you're serious about the future of imagination.

With its two slick, spectacular locations, **Starmach** (*Main Gallery, ul. Węgierska 5; Tel 656/43-17; Mon-Fri 11am-6pm; Due southwest of Rynek Główny; MC, V, AE*) is a blue-chip commercial art gallery featuring established modern and contemporary Polish and international art with a focus on postwar avant-garde and Abstract Expressionism.

Small and centrally located, **Zderzak** (*ul. Floriańska 3, walk up; Tel*

429/67-43; Just off Rynek Główny; Noon-5pm Tue-Sat closed Sun, Mon; No credit cards) is a commercial art gallery with a focus on painting and works on paper. Zderzak is an excellent place to scout emerging local talent and buy amazing art for peanuts, especially some great neo-figurative oils by the young and angry. Hot stuff.

Galeria Potocka *(Pl. Sikorskiego 10; Tel 421/02-78; Tue-Thur 4-6pm; West of Rynek Główny on the other side of the Planty; No credit cards)* is run with rare integrity and knowledge by Maria Anna Potocka (hence the name). This is an independent art space with a very small art gallery and a rare collection of conceptual Polish and European art. The work here is always smart, informed, and beautiful.

To hobnob with the artsy, head to the **Kawiarnia Aperitif Bar "Pavillon"** *(ul. Szczepańska 3a; No phone; Walk west on ul. Szczepańska from Rynek Główny; 10am-midnight daily; No credit cards)*. Artists, actors, intellectuals, and some university people come here to discuss the meaning of life. A 10-foot Pegasus wrapped in cellophane and covered in Christmas lights is the center of attention. A red velvet throne underneath Pegasus's crotch may tempt you to have a seat and snap a few ridiculous photos. Black plastic walls and angular seating add to the weirdness. Appropri-ately, great coffee and expensive beer (6zl) are also available.

▶▶PERFORMING ARTS

Polish theater certainly is not a hot topic for the overwhelming majority of English-speaking travelers. After all, nobody wants to sit through a play that they don't understand. But the venues listed below deserve your attention, because the language barrier will be less of a factor. At these places, you never know what to expect.

Theatr Buckleina *(ul. Lubicz 5; Tel 429/66-16; Across the street from Kraków Główny, the main train station; 6pm-2 or 4am daily; Occasionally, 5-10zl admission)* is a difficult place to define, as the schedules and per-formances are continually changing. Experimental theater, music con-certs, underground films and video, and poetry recitals are among the things you can see here. Every so often, a play, film, or other event is held in English, so it's possible you'll get lucky and catch one. The theater itself has a stucco ceiling, classical pilasters, and a capacity of 150 to 200 people. The usual crowd consists mainly of hospitable, creative, and English-speaking Polish students. The theater bar opens at 6pm and the events usually start between 7 and 8pm. Once the event is over, patrons stick around into the wee hours and rock all night in a bohemian disco atmo-sphere. It's best to call or swing by the theater and pick up the current monthly schedule to see what's in store.

You don't need to understand Polish to enjoy an evening listening to an excellent orchestra. **The Kraków Philharmonic Orchestra** *(ul. Zwierzyniecka 1; Tel 429/13-45; Walk south on ul. Wiślna from Rynek Główny and make a right onto ul. Zwierzyniecka; Concert times vary; 10zl symphony concert; No credit cards)* regularly fills the Kraków Philharmonic Hall with those who enjoy orchestral music. Of course, the crowd is mainly older, well-to-do folk, but don't let that discourage you from making an appearance.

gay scene

The gay capital of Europe it ain't! For some reason, the gay scene in Kraków is somewhat of a mystery, and extremely hard to locate. Maybe it's a result of commie oppression or Catholic repression, who knows? Whatever the case may be, if you ask young Poles where the gay bars/clubs are, most, after a slight blush and a delayed, hesitant reaction, say something like, "Well, I think I heard there was one, but I haven't been there and I have no idea where it is." That statement is often followed by "Well, they have more things like that in Warsaw." A serious warning, though: Kraków has had some problem with skinhead violence against gays (especially foreign gays) in the past few years, so be careful. This probably isn't the best place

12 hours in Kraków

1. Jazz Club Kornet: A very simple equation. Live old-time jazz + incredibly cheap beer + approachable, down-to-earth local crowd = good time [see *live music scene*, above].

2. Wawel Hill: Poland's royal treasure chest, and the residence of Polish kings for nearly 700 years. Truly dazzling examples of architecture, rich interior decorations, and other artistic stuff [see *culture zoo*, below].

3. Kazimierz and Schindler's Factory Walk: Discover the old Jewish quarter, then take a long stroll and explore Oskar Schindler's famous former factory [see *by foot*, below].

4. Singer Pub: The perfect rest after the tour of the Kazimierz and the Schindler Factory. Put up your feet, and let it all sink in [see *bar scene*, above].

5. Klub Studencki Pod Jaszczurami: A risk-free option for a great night out seven days a week. Throw down a few shots with local boys and girls [see *club scene*, above].

6. Theatr Buckleina: Romp with the creative crowd into the wee hours at this hopping late-night stomping ground [see *arts scene*, above].

7. Vegetarian Bar Vega: Inexpensive, charming, and downright mouth-watering, the whole city knows how attractive this place can be. Pig out and pay little [see *eats*, below].

8. Free Pub: It's very cool, it only really gets going at 2am, the dance music kicks, the crowd's wild and woolly, and...it's free! [see *club scene*, above].

by foot

1. The Planty walk

The **Planty** is an area around the perimeter of the **Old Town** lined with large trees, flower gardens, green lawns, benches, and paved walking paths. Try to do this walk in the late morning or the afternoon, because the Planty can be a bit dangerous in the evening and at night. You mostly run the risk of getting hassled or robbed, but women should, of course, take extra caution at night. Start between the **Floriańska Gate** [see *culture zoo*, below] and the **Barbakan**, make a left, and follow the path along the remnants of the city's medieval defensive walls. On your right will be the first of several lovely flower gardens, along with a fountain. As you make your way farther west under the canopy of trees, you'll soon find yourself in the old **University District**. As you cross **sw. Anny**, **Collegium Maius/University Museum** [see *culture zoo*, below] is to your left. When the path comes to a fork, bear left for a few minutes until you see the large street sign in front of you directing you right, in the direction of Wawel. On the left-hand side is **The Basilica of Saint Francis of Assisi and the Monastery of the Franciscan Order**. Make your way over to this beautiful Gothic church, which was originally constructed between 1255 and 1269. You'll soon make out **Wawel Hill** [see *neighborhoods*, above] in the distance. Walk to the end of the street and begin the climb up the hill, where you'll need a few hours to discover its many treasures [see *culture zoo*, below].

2. The Kazimierz and Schindler's Factory

This walk takes you through a few sights in the **Kazimierz**, or the old Jewish District. You'll then make your way southeast, over the river **Vis-**

to kiss your lover on the street. For the real dope, contact **Lamda Kraków** *(PO Box 249, Kraków; Tel 30-960)*, or do a web search under "gay" and "Krakow" for the latest buzz.

CULTURE ZOO

Fortunately, all the major cultural points of interest in Kraków are within a 15- to 20-minute walk from Rynek Główny. The churches in Kraków can be characterized more as places of worship than as museums for visitors to freely wander around in. You can hear a pin drop in most of them, and people of all ages will be on their knees in silent prayer.

National Museum in Kraków *(Tel 634/33-77; 10am-3:30pm Tue, Thur-Sun, till 5pm Wed, closed Mon; 5zl admission, 3zl students; No credit cards):* Located on the upper floor of **Sukiennice** [see *stuff*, below], tula and to the former site of **Oskar Schindler's famous "Emalia" enamelware factory**. From **Rynek Główny**, walk southeast on **ul. Grodzka** and **Stradomska**, and make a left onto **sw. Józefa**. Walk along sw. Józefa until it ends: **The Stara Synagogue, Museum of History of the City of Kraków Jewish Department** [see *culture zoo*, below], will be directly in front of you. When you exit the front door of the **Stara Synagogue** (which is on the other side of the building from where you will have entered from sw. Józefa), walk straight ahead on **ul. Szeroka** and the **Remu'h Synagogue/ Remu'h Cemetery** [see *culture zoo*, below] will be on your left side. Head left as you exit the Synagogue/Cemetery and then make a right onto **ul. Miodowa**. Then make a quick right onto **ul. Starowišlna** and follow it over the **river Vistula**. Make a left just on the other side of the river onto the small street just before a large, modern office building (it's easy, you can't miss it). Follow that under the train tracks and the street name is now **Lipowa Street**. On your left, at **4 Lipowa Street**, is the former "Emalia" enamelware factory (now the Telpod Electronic Works) of *Schindler's List* fame. There'll be guards manning the gate in the parking lot, and you should approach them. These guys speak only a few words of English, but are very hospitable and might give you a quick, very informal tour of some areas of the factory, the guard repeating in his best English the word "original" and walking you to such things as the staircase, portal, and the main gate. He'll also show you a bulletin board with a wartime photograph of the workers in the factory.

the main building of this museum houses a small but impressive exhibition of 19th-century Polish painting and sculpture including *Prussian Homage* by Jan Matejko. Although Polish art doesn't exactly have an international reputation, there's plenty here worth a look.

St. Adalbert's *(Noon-4pm daily; no entrance fee):* A minuscule, extremely quiet 12th-century church on the southern corner of Rynek Główny. Probably the smallest place of worship you'll ever come across, it makes you suspect there must have been a major shortage of raw materials during its original construction over 800 years ago.

Mariacki Church (St. Mary's) *(Northeast corner of Rynek Główny; 11:50am-6pm daily; 2.50zl admission through side "visitor's entrance," no fee through main entrance; No credit cards):* Easily recognizable by its two twin towers, this Gothic church traces its beginnings to 1222. Every hour on the hour, a trumpet is played from the top of the taller of the church's towers. The call is then suddenly abandoned mid-note, in remembrance of a trumpeter who was hit in the throat with an arrow while warning Kraków of an impending Tartar attack. Considered the gem of Kraków's 100 churches, St. Mary's is arguably the most beautiful church in the entire country.

Floriańska Gate (*5-minute walk up ul. Floriańska from Rynek Główny*): Built in the 1300s, this was formerly the gateway leading through the city's fortifications.

Czartoryski Museum (*sw. Jana 19; Tel 422/55-66; Just to the left as you stand at Floriańska Gate with your back to Rynek Główny; 9am-5pm Tue-Fri, 10am-3:30pm Sat, Sun, closed Mon; 5zl admission, 2.50zl students, free Sun; No credit cards*): An amazing collection of art, including heavies such as Rembrandt's *Landscape with a Good Samaritan* and da Vinci's *Lady with the Ermine*. Plus some fun ancient Greek and Egyptian stuff and Polish weaponry. The high-rolling Czartoryski family has turned over its vast collections for public viewing, leaving you no doubt that the Czartoryskis were the people to know back in the day.

Collegium Maius (University Museum) (*ul. Jagiellonska 15; Tel 422/05-49; 2-minute walk down sw. Anny Street from Rynek Główny; 11am-3pm Mon-Fri, till 2pm Sat, closed Sun; 7zl admission, 4zl students; No credit cards*): Superb guided tours are available for Copernicus's alma mater, a majestic 600-year-old university building. Complete with the famous Jagiellonska *Golden Globe*, circa 1510, featuring the earliest-known illustration of the New World. You may ask yourself, "How and why the hell is the *Golden Globe* in southeast Poland?" The knowledge-able and witty tour guides hold the answer.

The Royal Cathedral (*5- to 10-minute walk down ul. Grodzka from Rynek Główny; Tel 422/51-55 x291; 9am-5pm Mon-Sat, 2:15-5pm Sun; 6zl admission, 2zl students; No credit cards*): A heavily visited, mainly Gothic cathedral, and the final resting place of nearly every Polish monarch. Try to make it here just after 9am; you'll miss the crowds that can somewhat tarnish the mysterious mood.

Zygmuntowska Tower (Sigmund's Tower) (*5- to 10-minute walk down ul. Grodzka from Rynek Główny; Tel 422/51-55 x291; 9am-5pm Mon-Sat, 2:15-5pm Sun; Included w/admission to Royal Cathedral; No credit cards*): Accessible through the Royal Cathedral [see above]; climb the tight Renaissance-style tower staircase to an 11-ton church bell, and catch a great bird's-eye view of the city.

The Royal Castle Exhibitions (continuing restoration work may force closure of some exhibition areas noted below), all of which are on Wawel Hill:

The Royal Chambers (*5- to 10-minute walk down ul. Grodzka from Rynek Główny; Tel 422/51-55 x291; 9:30am-4:30pm Tue, Fri, till 3:30pm Wed, Thur, till 3pm Sat, 10am-3pm Sun, closed Mon; 10zl admission, 4.50zl students; No credit cards*): The 71 chambers contain a priceless collection of 14th- to 18th-century European and Polish paintings, 15th- to

17th-century Italian furniture, and 138 16th-century tapestries. Find time to take a stroll around the beautiful arcaded castle courtyard, the largest Renaissance courtyard in Europe.

The Royal Treasury and Armory *(5- to 10-minute walk down ul. Grodzka from Rynek Główny; Tel 422/51-55 x291; 9:30am-4:30pm Tue, Fri, till 3:30pm Wed, Thur, till 3pm Sat, 10am-3pm Sun, closed Mon; 10zl admission, 4.50zl students; No credit cards):* These exhibitions include the coronation sword of Polish kings and various weapons and suits of armor of Polish knights. Just picture yourself as that studly Polish knight in shining armor (even better if you're female).

The Kazimierz (Old Jewish Quarter) *(Southeast of Wawel Hill)* and **Stara Synagogue, Museum of History of the City of Kraków Jewish Department** *(ul. Szeroka 24; Tel 422/09-62; Walk southeast on Stradomska, make a left onto sw. Józefa, it's at the end of the street; 9am-3:30pm Wed, Thur, Sat, Sun, 11am-6pm Fri, closed Mon, Tue; 6zl admission, 4zl students, free Wed; No credit cards):* Restored in the late '50s, this is now a museum focusing on the history of Jewish life in Kraków. Provides a detailed account of the dynamic Jewish culture that once flourished in this district.

Remu'h Synagogue/Remu'h Cemetery *(ul. Szeroka 40; No phone; 2-minute walk straight ahead as you exit the Old Synagogue; 9am-4pm daily; 5zl admission, 2zl students; No credit cards):* A small, fully functioning, 16th-century synagogue and its neighboring, peaceful cemetery.

modification

So you've come to Eastern Europe, and for some inexplicable reason, that urge for a tattoo or piercing has overtaken you. **Tatu Tattoo** *(ul. Grodzka 50; Tel 421/53-99; Walk south on ul. Grodzka from Rynek Główny; Noon-6pm Mon-Sat; No credit cards)* will take care of you. This small, second-floor studio may be basic and somewhat scary-looking, but that just comes with the turf. The parlor seems to attract meaty, shaven-headed guys with their pit bulls, getting yet another tattoo on their chest. But the workers are really cool, speak English well, and are pretty flexible in terms of artistry. Thousands of designs are available, ranging from biomechanical to Celtic motifs.

great outdoors

A jog is always a viable option, but the poor air quality may make you feel like you've smoked one too many filterless cigarettes when you're finished. There aren't too many places to go jogging in the city center. There are simply too many people walking around, and it'd be a task in itself just dodging everyone. Your best choice is to walk down to the river Vistula, near Wawel Hill [see *neighborhoods*, above]. There are paved paths along the river making for a clear and free place to roam. Don't get too excited, though—the view isn't spectacular, and the chocolate-brown river is polluted from years of abuse.

The skateboarding/rollerblading scene in Kraków is small and largely underground. There is no particular area where you'll be able to consistently find skaters hanging out. There are occasional competitions/events sponsored by some of the skater/hip-hop–oriented shops in town.

Drop by **Cool Sport** *(ul. Loretańska 8; Tel 422/48-46; Walk west on sw. Anny from Rynek Główny until you hit ul. Loretańska; 11am-6pm Mon-Fri, till 3pm Sat; MC, V, AE)*, the largest "alternative" sports shop in town, with two floors of clothes and skateboarding, rollerblading, and snowboarding equipment. The English-speaking and very helpful staff will let you know if any kind of special skating events are planned in the near future.

STUff

It's a great idea to save all that dreaded souvenir shopping for Kraków. Not only are you going to be able to pick up something unique, but it's also gonna be affordable. Handmade sweaters and glassware are significantly cheaper than they are in the countries just to the west, amber jewelry is a hot item, and handpainted music boxes are both beautiful and abundant. If you want to go upscale, your choices are also surprisingly decent.

▶▶**GIFT**

If you're on the prowl for that perfect piece of Polish memorabilia, the ground floor of the **Sukiennice** *(Large yellow building in the middle of Rynek Główny; No phone; 11am-7:30pm Mon-Sat, till 5pm Sun; 5zl-700zl price range; Some vendors take MC, V, AE)* is the only stop you'll need to make. This is a large indoor market stretching the entire length of the building. Sweaters, furs, skins, jewelry, traditional Polish garb, handcrafted jewelry boxes, beer steins, T-shirts, handmade glassware, leather goods, and knives are just the beginning. But stay away from the three-foot battle swords, 'cause they may not let you on the plane.

▶▶**SHOP TILL YOU DROP**

The area around Rynek Główny provides more than enough options for clothes or shoe shopping, and ul. Floriańska is a good place to start. The typical store hours here are 10am till 7pm Monday through Friday, till 3pm Saturday, closed Sunday. You'll find **Benetton, Dr. Martens**, and for the jock in you, **Reebok** and **Adidas** *(Both additionally open 11am till 3pm Sunday)*.

▶▶**TUNES**

Hip-hop is trendy for high school–age Polish kids, so there are quite a few hip-hop–oriented shops in town. If you've got extra cash and are looking for rhymes and rage you can't understand, throw down some złotys for a Polish hip-hop cassette.

Record Head Shop *(Starowišlna 10; Walk southeast on Starowišlna from Rynek Główny; No phone; 11am-7pm daily, closed Sun; No credit cards)* feels like a tiny Amsterdam coffee/hip-hop store with no pot menu. It's even got the Polish version of Funkmaster Flex behind the wheels. They sell everything from hip-hop, disco, and trance vinyl to pipes, bongs, and rolling papers. There's also a small selection of skater/hip-hop clothing, like hoodies and super-baggy cargo pants.

fashion

Young Poles do not wear babushkas and are not obsessed with getting their hands on a pair of Levi's. Young women dress in stark contrast to conservative Catholic values: Skirts well above the knees, high heels, and skimpy blouses are standard in the summer. In fact, many foreign men (and some women) admit they may never see as many attractive pairs of legs as they do during a summer day on Rynek Główny. Polish men tend to dress more conservatively—black jackets and slacks giving off a professional, almost businesslike demeanor—and a look that suggests that one belongs to the new elite is preferred by the hip. Among the younger, say, under-20 crowd, the hip-hop look is the bomb. FUBU, Hilfiger, and Wu Wear seem to be the coolest thing since blue jeans in the commie days. Of course, it's weird to see Polish kids imitating American blacks—but then again, who doesn't?

Sklep Ebola *(ul. Floriańska 13; Tel 429/63-05; Walk north on Floriańska from Rynek Główny; 11am-6pm Mon-Fri, till 3pm Sat, closed Sun; No credit cards)* is the only punk music shop in Kraków. They carry a small selection of punk tapes, CDs, and vinyl along with a variety of clothes—ranging from shiny leather combat boots to more hip-hop–oriented stuff—as well as glass bongs and pipes. These guys know everything about the Polish punk scene, and will give you long-winded discourses on such things as cops, drug laws, and "the system."

Musica Antiqua *(ul. Senecka 6; Tel 411/30-00; Walk south from Rynek Główny on ul. Grodzka and make a right onto ul. Senecka; 11am-7pm Mon-Fri, till 5pm Sat, Sun; MC, V, AE)* has an excellent selection of classical vinyl, CDs, and tapes. There's also a small collection of rare live jazz CDs, used classic rock CDs, and some folk/Jewish CDs.

EATS

Very little cash will get you a fat-daddy, multi-course meal here in Kraków. Although prices are on the rise because of the increasing rate of tourism, you'll still find them pleasantly inexpensive. In other words, be prepared to eat like a Polish monarch in comparison to the more popular European cities farther west. Since eating out is quite costly for the average Pole, don't be too boisterous about how cheap you find the dining experience. The service is somewhat spotty, so don't cause a scene if you feel that the wait staff isn't up to par. If you like the service, remember to tip 15 percent, and you'll make someone's day.

▶▶CHEAP

We're talkin' really cheap. You can't get any more Polish than eating an *obwarzanki* from a street vendor located all over town. These large pretzel-like rings of bread covered with salt and sesame or poppy seeds cost just .50 to .70zl. In other words, you can eat almost three of these for the price of a U.S. postage stamp.

Vegetarian Bar Vega *(sw. Getrudy 7; Tel 422/34-94; Walk east down ul. Sienna and then make a right onto sw. Getrudy; 10am-5pm daily; 3.50-4.50zl per entree; No credit cards)* is one of the coolest places to dine in Kraków. A self-serve bar offers you an incredible array of salads, and they have great pancakes, croquettes, soy cutlets, soups, and yogurts. The servings are kind of small, so you may want to go back for seconds. A Victorian-style dining area with high ceilings, classical music, and low lighting adds to the terrific ambiance. The workers speak English, and understand vegan needs (which many people here have a hard time contemplating). The customers aren't necessarily crunchy-granola types—Polish businessmen, elderly couples, and tourists all know how great the meals are here.

Rozowy Slon *(ul. Sienna 1; Tel 421/83-22; Walk east from Rynek Główny down ul. Sienna; 9am-9pm Mon-Sat, 10am-9pm Sun; 3.80-6zl per entree; No credit cards)* is a weird mixture of colorful Polish pop-art decor and fast food. College student–age Poles sit and gossip around the pink tables and chairs. Pancakes, soups, and salads seem to be the most frequently ordered items, and don't miss the amazing pierogies. The cuisine isn't the fanciest, but it's certainly more than acceptable considering the incredibly low prices. If you're in a hurry, this is a good choice, because your food's ready in minutes.

▶▶DO-ABLE

When you're in the mood to go Greek, there's always **Akropolis** *(Grodzka 9; Tel 421/77-25; Walk southeast from Rynek Główny; 11am-midnight daily; 19zl per entree; No credit cards)*. A self-service, cafeteria-style setup greets you at the front door. Huge do-it-yourself plates of chicken, beef, and veggie dishes all cost the standard 19zl. The seating arrangement is more like an upscale restaurant, except there's no alcohol served. Ancient Greek decor and traditional Greek music temporarily make you forget you're in Poland. Outdoor seating is also available.

Slightly between a do-able and a splurge restaurant is **Restauracja Lemon** *(ul. Floriańska 53; Tel 430/01-81 between Floriańska Gate and Rynek Główny; Noon-last guest daily; 17.50-29zl per entree; MC, V)* featuring an excellent Serbian chef conjuring Balkan specialties. The evening menu focuses on delicious slabs of beef and pork cooked on the large outdoor grill. Indulge your carnivore cravings as you listen to a variety of Balkan music, including traditional, Balkan rock, and Balkan reggae (!). The atmosphere inside is spacious and colorful, with an abundance of natural light filtering through large glass windows. The soups are super, especially the house special, known as "village soup," and there's a nice selection of beer and wine to wash it all down with.

▶▶**SPLURGE**

A relaxed spot to eat hearty traditional Polish country cuisine in an elegant, rustic environment, **Cherubino** (sw. Tomasza 15; Tel 429/40-07; Directly north of Rynek Główny; Noon-midnight daily; 20-40zl per entree; MC, V) offers such savory favorites as bigos, a comfort stew of cabbage, mushrooms, and sausage. All wood and steel, the ambiance here is as calm and pleasing as the service. Cherubino also pulls off more sophisticated continental cuisine, and all of it is fresh and delicious.

To see Polish guys in kilts attempting to do their best Scottish highlander imitations, head to **Restauracja "U Szkota"** (ul. Mikošajska 4; Tel 422/15-70; Walk east on ul. Mikošajska from Rynek Główny; Noon-midnight daily; 10-34zl per entree; MC, V, AE). The idea may sound a little bizarre, but the tasty Scottish cuisine—with a concentration on meats and fish—is served to you in a quiet, chilly, rock-walled basement setting. The crowd is mostly Polish couples and businessmen, diggin' deep into their pockets for a deluxe night on the town. This is the type of place you should dress nicely for, and plan to spend an hour or two enjoying a four-course dinner.

crashing

Now that Kraków is becoming increasingly popular with young travelers, booking in advance is a very good idea. The easiest and most fun cheap lodging in Kraków is at a "student hotel." This is especially true during college summer break, from July 1 till September 25, when the number of available dorm-room beds multiplies. Beds are also available during the school season, but the numbers are considerably reduced. You can also find private rooms, either by checking out what locals offer on the street [see below], or by booking a room through a tourist office. High-end hotels, or guesthouses, often used by visiting professors, are always options for the big spenders. If you roll into town and can't find a damn thing, stop in at Centrum Informacji Turystycznej or Dexter Travel [see need to know, below, for both].

▶▶**CHEAP**

Zaczek Hotel Studencki (Maja 5; Tel 633/54-77; Tram 15 or Bus 119 to Przystankow; 90zl single w/bathroom, 70zl single w/o bathroom, 130zl double w/bathroom, 80zl double w/o bathroom, 150zl triple w/bathroom, 105zl triple w/o bathroom, 130zl quad w/o bathroom, 225zl quint w/bathroom; No credit cards) looks like a slightly run-down version of a huge student dorm at a state university in the U.S. During the summer season, an international mix of travelers on a tight budget fills up the 600 beds. When the Polish students are back for school, there are 70 beds available for those who opt to visit during the low season. Like the old college dorm, the rooms are simple, decently clean, and spacious. All the beds are twins, and since the room is designed for a full-time student, there's plenty of storage space. A restaurant, salad bar, tourist info desk, and small grocery store are all located in the building. The workers are primarily Polish students who speak English,

krakow eats and crashing

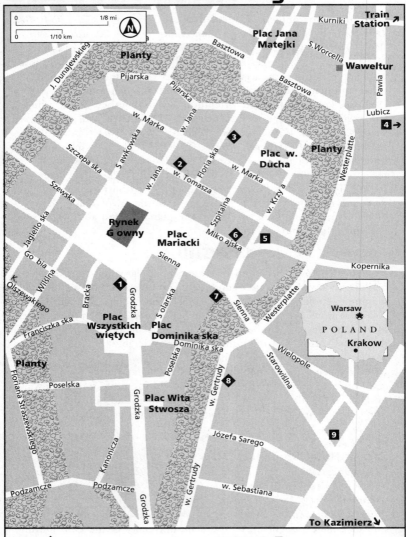

and they'll go out of their way to help you out. There's 24-hour access, and you should book two to three weeks in advance if you're the type who needs his/her own bathroom. For the most part the social vibe here is upbeat and festive, so finding drinking partners among the young dorm mates will be a snap.

Close by and nearly interchangeable is the smaller **Hotel Studencki Nawojka** *(wł. Reymonta 11; Tel 633/58-77; Tram 15 or Bus 179 to Przystankow; 59zl single w/bathroom, 85zl double w/o bathroom, 110zl triple w/bathroom, rooms w/o bathrooms available only July 1-Sept 25: single w/o bathroom 40zl, double w/o bathroom 50zl, triple w/o bathroom 69zl; No credit cards)*. It's the dorm-room setup again, including a barber, 24-hour access, TV room, small grocery store, and a bar/cafe with a pool table. The guests, workers, and young, carefree atmosphere are pretty much the same as in the other student hotels.

Studencki Hotel Piast *(ul. Piastowska 47; Tel 637/49-33 Bus 159, 173, 238, 258 to Hotel Piast, large sign for hotel at the stop; 110-140zl double w/bathroom, 150zl triple w/bathroom, 110zl single w/bathroom shared by two rooms; No credit cards)* is another large typical student hotel, popular with budget-conscious travelers from all over the world. Although a bit farther from the center, it's just like the others, with dorm-style accommodation in clean simple rooms. There's a pub/cafe on the first floor, along with a mediocre Chinese restaurant, and laundry facilities on the second floor [see *need to know*, below].

▶▶**DO-ABLE**

When you don't want to sleep in a dorm, and you don't want to spend the big bucks, try a private room. As soon as you get off the train or bus, there may be locals (usually older men and women) looking for people to rent a room in their place. Anyone with written info on their accommodations is usually legit, particularly if they have letters they can show you from previous English-speaking guests. Rooms should run in the neighborhood of 90zl for a single, 120zl for a double, and 150zl for a triple. Haggling with these people is an option, but that may be hard to do when confronted with a widow who's trying to make ends meet. Of course, basic street smarts apply, like "Don't pay until you see the place," and "Get away from this person if he/she is strange, rude, or appears untrustworthy." You can also find these potential "room dealers" hanging out in front of the **Waweltur** *(ul. Pawia 8; Tel 422/19-21; Across ul. Pawia from Kraków Główny, main train station; 75zl single, 128zl double, 171zl triple; 8am-8pm Mon-Fri, till 2pm Sat, closed Sun; No credit cards)*. Located next to the **Centrum Informacji Turystycznej** [see *need to know*, below], these helpful folks will call around and find you a room. The distance of the room from the center of the city can vary, but it's usually no more than three or four stops on a tram or bus, or a 15-minute walk.

▶▶**SPLURGE**

If you get lucky, you can land a room at the **Jagiellonian University Guest House** *(ul. Floriańska 49; Tel 421/12-25; Walk north on ul.*

Floriańska from Rynek Główny; Office open 7:30am-3pm Mon-Fri, reception open 24hrs daily; 210zl single w/private bathroom/shower, 180zl single w/shared bathroom/shower, 320zl double w/private bathroom/shower, 290zl double w/shared bathroom/shower; rybak@jetta.if.uf.edu.pl; MC, V, AE) at the last minute. But the management says it's a better idea to make a reservation at least a week in advance. You'll be quite happy you did, as the guesthouse is located right on one of Poland's most famous streets, and a few steps away from Rynek Główny. Reception is professional, sincere, and English-speaking. The rooms, usually used by visiting professors, are immaculate and classy. They're also fitted with modern furniture, hardwood floors, desks, and twin and queen beds. Some rooms have a TV, and there's a small restaurant downstairs. A simple breakfast of bread, coffee, jam, cheese, etc. is included.

If you're not strapped for cash, **Hotel Europejski** (ul. Lubicz 5; Tel 423/25-10; Across ul. Lubicz from Kraków Główny, main train station; 289zl single w/private bathroom, 349zl double w/private bathroom, 415zl triple w/private bathroom, 456zl apartment suite w/private bathroom, 197zl single w/private shower only, 179zl single w/o private shower, 229zl double w/o private shower; www.he.pl; MC, V, AE) awaits your arrival. The amenities include a cafe/bar, restaurant, outdoor garden terrace, exchange office, taxi service, satellite TV in the rooms, a substantial breakfast, and a great central location. Depending on the type of room you opt for, twin and queen beds are available. The rooms are clean and stuffed with comfortable couches, chairs, and tables. The workers are helpful, English-speaking, and cater to the largely foreign, older (over 30) patrons who frequent the hotel.

need to know

Currency Exchange The official currency is the Polish złoty (zl). Cash is the best way to pay for things, because most shops and restaurants still don't accept credit cards or traveler's checks. There are at least a dozen well-advertised exchange places within a 1- or 2-minute walk of Rynek Główny, and the rates for exchange are fairly similar. The typical hours for exchange offices are 10am-6pm Mon-Fri, till 2pm Sat. It's worth your time to take a quick 5- to 10-minute walk and check the buying/selling rates, because they are constantly changing, and shopping around can save you a little money.

Tourist Information Dexter Travel (Rynek Główny 1/3; Tel 421/77-06; Ground floor of Sukiennice; 8am-6pm Mon-Fri, till 3pm Sat, Sun May-Aug, 9am-6pm Mon-Fri, till 3pm Sat Sept-Apr; tur@dexter.com.pl) is the most centrally located. **Centrum Informacji Kulturalnej** (sw. Jana 2; Tel 421/77-87; Just off the north end of Rynek Główny; 10am-6pm Mon-Fri, 8am-4pm Sat; www.karnet.Kraków2000.pl) produces Karnet, a Kraków cultural events monthly. Tickets for many events can also be booked here. **Orbis Travel** (Rynek Główny 41; Tel 422/40-35; North end of Rynek Główny; 8am-6pm Mon-Fri, 8:30am-3pm Sat May

wired

A few Internet cafes have popped up in the center of the city over the last couple of years. If you're out to find that fellow English-speaker, these are probably the best bets in town. Unfortunately, the Polish national telecommunications company provides extremely slow connections to the Internet.

U Louisa *(11am-11pm Mon-Thur, till 1am Fri, Sat, 2-11pm Sun; 5zl/hour, 3zl/half-hour, 2zl/15 minutes)* [see *live music scene*, above] has a small room for customers who would like to jump online. The computers aren't the fastest, but the central location and low prices are right. The guys running the show are very friendly and actually seem to like the idea of customer service.

Looz Internet Cafe *(ul. Mikołajska 11; Tel 428-42-10; Walk east from Rynek Główny on ul. Mikołajska; 7zl/hour, 4.5zl/half-hour, 2zl/15 minutes; www.looz.com; MC, V, AE)* claims that their computers will soon circumvent the good ol' usual Polish low-speed connections with a satellite hookup to Sweden. But until that time comes, it seems like mailing a letter home by snail express may be faster than paying to use a computer. The lines are usually shorter here, as there are many more computers available than at U Louisa. Since there's a lot of tourist traffic using the large facility, the workers can be moody and abrasive.

www.Krakow.pl (Kraków tourism pages)
www.orbis.travel.Krakow.pl (Orbis Travel)
www.polishpages.com.pl (Polish yellow pages for foreigners)
www.karnet.Krakow2000.pl (*Karnet*, Kraków cultural events monthly)

1-Sept 31, 8:30am-5pm Mon-Fri Oct 1-Apr 31). **Centrum Informacji Turystycznej** *(ul. Pawia 8; Tel 422/60-91; Other side of ul. Pawia from Kraków Główny, main train station; 8am-6pm Mon-Fri, 9am-1pm Sat, closed Sun)* provides maps, additional hostel/hotel information (they will call around for you to see if there are any rooms available) and books tours of Kraków and the outlying areas.

Public Transportation Single **bus** and **tram** tickets cost 2.20zl. Tickets good for one hour are 2.80zl, daily tickets are 9zl, and weekly tickets 22zl. If you get on with a large backpack, suitcase, etc., that requires its own ticket. Your ticket must be activated in the machine on board the vehicle. Tickets can be purchased at kiosks or shops, or from bus or tram drivers. The drivers will make change for you, but charge an extra .50zl for their service. Daytime transportation services run from 5am-11pm. After 11pm, there are eight night bus lines.

American Express Orbis Travel [see above] provides American Express financial services.

Health and Emergency Ambulance: *999*; Fire: *998*; Police: *997*. The hospitals **Szpital im. Dietla** *(ul. Skarbowa 4; Tel 634/59-37)* and **Szpital Gabriela Narutowicza** *(ul. Pradmicka 35; Tel 633/53-99)* and the clinic **"Medycyna"** *(Rogozinskiego; Tel 412/24-59)* have English-speaking doctors.

Pharmacy Apeteka *(ul. Mogilska 21; Tel 411/01-26; 24 hours daily)*

Telephone Country code: *48*; city code: *12*. **AT&T:** *0/0800/111-11-11*; **MCI:** *0/0800/111-21-22*; **Sprint:** *0/0800/111-311*. Phone cards, or *karta telefonicza*, are available at hotels, kiosks, and post offices.

Airports John Paul II International Airport *(Balice; Tel 285-65-80)*.

Airlines LOT *(15 Basztowa; 422/42-15),* **Delta Airlines** *(36 Szpitalna St.; Tel 421/46-40)*.

Trains **Central Railway Station, Dworzec Główny** *(Plac Główny 1; Tel 422/41-82 international connections, Tel 9313 local connection line)*.

Bus Lines Out of the City Central Bus Station *(ul. Worcella, facing the railway station; Tel 9316 bus information line)*.

Laundry **Studencki Hotel Piast, 2nd Floor** *(ul. Piastowska 47; Tel 637-21-76; Bus 159, 173, 238, 258 to Hotel Piast; 10am-7pm Oct 1-June 30, 8am-8pm July 1-Sept 31; Wash 7zl, dry 7zl)*.

budapest

Over a decade into a free-market economy, Budapest is easily the most happening capital in the former Eastern Bloc. You can sense the grandeur of a former empire of the East—the center of Budapest is all wrought-iron railings, dignified bronze monuments, and crumbling apartment buildings with enormous windows—except that now, awesome Parisian-style boulevards like Andrássy út lead you straight to party heaven (and we don't mean where dead communists go). If you think this is just propaganda, wait until you've seen 'em try to fight through the pack to reach the bar at **Portside** [see *bar scene*, below], or found yourself boogying recklessly with locals at insane events like **Cinetrip** [see *club scene*, below]. By day, the rebounding spirit of this battle-scarred, oft-invaded city is just as visible at the flashy cafes of Liszt Ferenc tér, like **Incognito** [see *bar scene*, below], and especially in what girls wear (or don't) on District V's Váci utca. But, happily, some old-school Budapest traditions still hang on: There's always time for a 3-hour espresso at a grand coffeehouse, a tall cold one (or two or three) on a shady patio, or a bottle of Egri Bikavér wine in a cellar pub.

The Magyar (aka Hungarian), who may have Asian, Roman, Slavic, and/or Ottoman roots, is pretty hard to categorize physically—except maybe by a bad-ass gleam in the eye or the occasional morose mood. The average Budapester you'll likely connect with is working full-time, saving for a rickety apartment in the center, a fanatic nationalist who nevertheless gripes about everything Hungarian (but don't you try it!), a party animal of epic proportions, extremely well read, and just as well turned out. They are also usually more than willing to speak English, if only because they know their bizarre language isn't so easy to crack.

Unfortunately, you'll have trouble finding *printed* material in English. The *Budapest Sun*, the local paper you can buy at any newsstand, does have an English-language listing section, but it's lame. The NCG (Budapest Nightlife Guide) can be picked up in bars and cafes around town. For nightlife info, slogging through the Hungarian *Pesti Est*, a great entertainment weekly found in bars and cafes, may be your best bet.

If you're planning to hit Budapest's incredible museums and galleries, the **Budapest card** *(3,400 forints (Ft) for two days, 4,000Ft for three days)*, available at any Metro station, is also worth considering. It gives you unlimited public-transit rides, free entry to all museums, and dozens of discounts (15-50 percent) on shops, eats, sights, and shows. You can also pick them up at hotels, tourist offices, and the airport.

neighborhoods

Budapest is split down the center, from north to south, by the wide **Danube**, with the green hills of **Buda** to the west overlooking flat, noisy, bustling **Pest**, just opposite it. **Gellért Hill** is the king of the hills in the essentially residential, cheaper, Buda half of town. This side of the river offers nice quiet pensions and decent hostels and is home to the must-see **Royal Palace** [see *culture zoo*, below], thermal baths, and a handful of exceptional pubs and eateries. Nearly everything of interest here is in **District I**.

Then you just have to cross an ornate bridge into nice flat Pest, where all the action is. **District V** is at the heart of things, its southern end completely dominated by touristy **Váci utca** while its quieter, more stately

five things to talk to a local about

1. **VHK**, aka The Galloping Coroners, a band that's a local institution and known for prompting wild, neo-pagan dancing.

2. **Cinetrip**, the hedonistic monthly techno parties at the Rudas baths [see *club scene*, below].

3. **The 40-plus percent personal income tax** Hungarians pay. Far from a boring topic, it's guaranteed to get a Magyar, whose national religion is complaining, really going. It will also open your eyes to a few facts of life here and may raise your esteem as an informed person to locals.

4. and 5. The piss-poor state of **Hungarian soccer**/world-class state of **Hungarian water polo**.

northern half, just upstream, is humming right along with lots of new nightspots and international restaurants.

Radiating out from District V to the east is **District VII**, the once-thriving **Jewish Quarter**, which has now become home to the city's finest old-world cafes and a big chunk of its coolest clubs and bars, especially around **Liszt Ferenc tér. Dohány utca** is also a hot little block, jammed with jumping clubs, bars like **Portside** [see *bar scene*, below] and the inimitable **Fausto's** restaurant [see *eats*, below].

Also in Pest, **District VI** is another promising spoke to the northeast, with a few funky clubs and movie houses, mostly along **Teréz körút. District VIII**, to the southeast, is a bit dodgy, characterized by crumbling apartment buildings and hard-sell, down-at-the-heels street-walkers, though a handful of cool hangs like **Darshan udvar** [see *bar scene*, below] are well worth venturing to. Same goes for **District IX**, due south, with cookin' little **Ráday utca**, home to **Paris, Texas** [see *bar scene*, below] and well worth scouting out.

Addresses, like all printed information in Hungary, are a little weird, but not that hard to decode, really. Roman numerals, which tell you the city district of the place you're going, precede street addresses.

hanging out

For all the rebuilding and capitalism crash courses going on about town, Budapest is remarkably willing to just hang out, and loafers can be spotted any hour in parks and cafes, especially in roasting summer. Perhaps the attitude toward work imposed by communist times, best described as "charade," was good for something, after all. If you doubt the importance of slack time here, just try explaining the concept of "lunch at your desk" to your new Magyar friends and watch their jaws drop with horror.

Margaret Island *(XIII. Margit híd; Tram 4 or 6 to Margit híd)* is an enormous refuge from the noise and traffic of both Buda and Pest, offering peaceful gardens, Dominican cloister ruins, thousands of shade trees, the rental of truly ridiculous boneshaker bikes for its bike paths, and its own set of thermals [see *you're soaking in it*, below]. The island's open-air stage hosts some great shows, particularly during the summer **Duna** festival [see *festivals and events*, below].

Magyar champions of history watch from their pedestals as skate-boarders and trick cyclists work their technique at **Heroes' Square** *(VI. Hősök tere; Metro line 1 to Hősök tere)*, on the edge of **Városliget park** *(VI. Dózsa György út; Metro 1 to Hősök tere; currently closed for cleaning)*. Városliget itself is the kind of park worthy of a great old city, with its **Museum of Fine Arts** [see *culture zoo*, below], sprawling grassy hills, zoo, lake, terrace pubs, sauna, pool, a concert hall, and the very, very good, world-class **Gundel** [see *eats*, below].

Cafes were made for hanging out in, but some truly excel at the all-afternoon espresso-and-page-turning ritual. **Libella** *(XI. Budafoki út 7; Tel 209/47-61; Tram 18, 47, or 49 to Szent Gellért tér; 8am-1:30am Mon-Sat)* doesn't care how long you linger over your one cup of java, absorbing

java

The Budapest coffeehouse tradition is just as venerated as the Hapsburg Empire that spawned it. Whole afternoons evaporate like minutes once you're settled into this rarefied environment, seated at a corner table with a heady cappuccino and a slice of Gerbeaud liqueur cake (named after the coffeehouse below, but available everywhere), watching the world go by.

Gerbeaud *(V. Vörösmarty tér 7; Tel 429-30-00; Metro line 1 to Vörösmarty tér; 9am-9pm daily)*, is as much monument as cafe, presiding over downtown Budapest's most glitzy square, Vörösmarty tér. It's predictably high-priced and the service is unpredictable, but its 1870 pedigree is unquestionable.

A 10-minute walk from here is **Astoria Café** *(V. Kossuth Lajos utca 19-21; Tel 484-32-00; Metro line 2 to Astoria; 7am-10pm daily)*, but it's in another world. This time capsule of clinking silver, little espresso cups, and wood-paneled primness feels like a bastion against the modern world. That could be because there's a noisy traffic snarl just outside its well-draped windows, but it does make a fine spot for an elegant breakfast.

Easily the most authentic of them all is **Művész** *(VII. Andrássy út 29; Tel 352-13-37; Metro line 1 to Opera; 9am-midnight daily)*— or maybe it's just aged more gracefully. Whatever the reason, the front room is like nowhere else on earth, especially when you begin to notice the characters around you heading for the back room. Impossibly proper old lady with small dog, lonely-looking, rumpled writer-type, *nouvel entrepreneur* having discreet meeting...yep, they're all here. And the street tables on graceful old Andrássy út are hard to beat.

the works hanging on its walls, all stuff from equally unorthodox artists. Survey the pile of postcards and flyers here promoting upcoming shows. It's also a great pre- or post-**Gellért baths** [see *you're soaking in it*, below] spot, as it's just a hop away.

It's 4am, and the question is: "God, I'm hungry—what the hell could possibly be open now?" The blessed answer is **Szent Jupat** *(II. Dékan utca 3; Tel 212/29-23; Metro line 2 to Moszkva tér, night bus 6É; 5pm-midnight; 1,000Ft)*. Though inconveniently located in Buda, it's worth the taxi ride [see *need to know*, below] as it serves up the full complement of heavy, high-fat peasant fare all night long, from roast beef to schnitzel and sauerkraut, and really doesn't give a damn how long you take up table space. Which could be quite a while as you drunkenly strike up semi-coherent conversations with those English-speakers at the next table.

bar scene

Hungarians have always been champion boozers. One major tradition to have survived communism is cheap and highly drinkable wine from the sunny southern plains. The hearty red **Egri Bikavér**—Bull's Blood to you—leads the vino pack, followed in popularity by **Unicum**, a devilishly bittersweet dark liqueur that comes, appropriately, in a bomb-shaped bottle bearing the maker's label, Zwack—precisely the sound your head makes after an evening of Unicum shots. **Palinka** is Hungary's version of the fruit brandy so loved throughout Central Europe, particularly by street people in winter. If you really have to have a brew, you're welcome to try the hangover-inducing **Dreher**, which proves why Czechs, not Hungarians, are famous for their beer. A good general approach to boozing here is to start at the more outlying places (though all of the following are at least on the edge of the old city center in District V) then work your way to District VII, where the scene really picks up in the wee hours.

Incognito (*VI. Liszt Ferenc tér 3; Tel 342/14-71; Metro line 1 to Oktogon; 10am-midnight Mon-Fri, noon-midnight Sat, Sun*), whose street is that teeming pedestrian zone on your right as you walk up Andrássy út from the old city center, is a good starting point. First off, your only chance of finding an outdoor table is early on, and secondly, the bulletin board is plastered with little cards promoting every cool event in town.

fiū meets lāny

Hungarians' attitude toward romance can best be described as "incisive." So says one native who lived for years in America and has now happily returned home. There isn't an awful lot of beating around the bush, he observes, and any trip to **Portside** [see *bar scene*, above] or **Fat Mo's** [see *live music scene*, below] confirms his point. And the new freedoms in this part of Europe, which include a booming porno industry, have not been coupled with any major AIDS epidemics, which silences any arguments that young people from the East may be somehow less sophisticated about sex than their big-city counterparts in the West. In fact, just introducing yourself in certain places may be about as elaborate as your strategy needs to get. If there's something there, you'll soon find out, and if not, you'll probably find yourself on your own in about 2 minutes flat. So much for the mysteries of the East.

This little tree-lined pedestrian mall has become ground zero for the sleek young sophisticates of Budapest these days.

Paris, Texas *(IX. Ráday utca 22; Tel 218/93-23; Metro line 3 to Kálvin tér; 10am-3am Mon-Fri, 4pm-3am Sat, Sun; No credit cards)* is also a tables-on-the-street kind of spot, but with the quieter, less frantic vibe of District IX. Order an Egri Bikavér, and if there's no free spot on the sidewalk (as is typical), just meander to the rough wood-trimmed 1880s-style back rooms or smoky basement to wait your turn while chatting at the bar or shooting pool.

Another good starting point, across the river in quieter Buda, is **Rác-kert** *(I. Hadnagy utca 8-10; Tel 356/13-22; Bus 7, 7A, 5, 86 to Döbrentai tér or Rudas fürdö; 6pm-3am)*, an outdoor pub and stage next to the Rác baths on Gellért Hill. The twilight in this park setting is ushered out by a pack of beer- and underground-music-loving locals. Hungarian artists in ratty jeans and T-shirts tote African djimbes and Fender bass guitars into this noisy beer garden to jam for as long as the warm weather holds out. Double-check that it's still going before heading out, though—the anarchists who run it are the sorts who might move on at any time.

A good 'round-midnight kind of spot for quiet conversation is **Darshan Udvar** *(VIII. Krúdy Gyula utca 7-8; Tel 266/77-97; Metro line 3 to Kálvin tér or Tram 4, 6, to Baross utca; 10am-1am Mon-Fri, 4pm-1am Sat, Sun)*, actually a warren of cozy little Moroccan-style drinking nooks anchored by a lovingly mosaic-covered courtyard that leads to a vast hidden late-night pasta kitchen. What pasta has to do with these Gaudí-esque barrooms, the mellow local crowd doesn't trouble itself with. And nobody can even imagine a dress code here.

Morrison's Music Pub *(VI. Révay u. 25; Tel 269/40-60; Metro line 1 to Opera; 8:30pm-4am, closed Sun-Wed; Cover Thur-Sat after 10pm)*, just a block outside the northern District VII border, is up all night and couldn't be less elitist, with a comfortably run-down long bar and dark, dingy back room and small dance floor, where no one sees or cares what you wear and someone's always shakin' it to '80s rock. But mostly it's a quiet, talk-and-imbibe spot.

Portside *(VII. Dohány utca 7; Tel 351/84-05; Metro line 2 to Astoria; Noon-2am Mon-Thur, 11am-4am Fri-Sat, 11am-2am Sun)*, on the other hand, is the prime place to wind up a high-energy evening. Also up all night, on weekends it's so jammed with local and foreign twentysome-things you'll wish someone would throw you that rowboat hanging over the bar—that is, unless you *want* to get mashed against someone inter-esting, as most here do. Iggy on the dance floor, where the action is intense. Wear black jeans and anything breathable.

LIVE MUSIC SCENE

Sure, the international DJ conspiracy is slowly assassinating live music, but a few patches of ground are still holding out. Jazz, soul, folk, world music, and indie rock are all seemingly safe, at least for now, while much of the pop rock (both Hungarian and international) that tours here might

The Truth About Unicum

Justly a source of national pride, Unicum hits the taste buds like Coca-Cola, then magically delivers a smoky bite on swallowing. You've never tasted anything remotely like it. For over a century Budapest evenings have been christened with the stuff with mighty fine results. During the last regime, they even smuggled the secret recipe out of the country rather than risk losing it to Central Planning. So sip it or shoot it, but get it to the back of your throat fast.

actually benefit from being replaced by electronic beats....In any case, they say Hungarians are born with fiddles under their chins (and this *must* be the world capital of Gypsy bands in restaurants), so the indicators are good: There's always a jam in progress here somewhere.

Always lurking at the edges of the live music scene is the particular Budapest obsession with the neo-pagan. Personified by groups like **VHK** (Magyar initials for the Galloping Coroners), this is a firmly underground scene that you'll only hear about through word of mouth or by watching for flyers. The venues are improvised and can be anything from community centers to parks to factories. Past VHK shows have featured hayfights, mud painting, torchlight, chanting, and music that's essentially hide-drum thumping. Feeling Xena yet?

Contrary to jazz traditions everywhere, the acts at the **M4** (*VII. Dohány utca 22-24; Tel 322/00-06; Metro line 2 to Astoria; 6pm-4am daily, till 5am Fri, Sat*) play for just two hours, starting at 10pm. This oblong basement is no less hot for that, though, with smokin' straight-ahead trios and chanteuses—mostly local and on the rise—doing improv on the corner stage, framed by candy-red walls and a painted Manhattan skyline.

The **Old Man's Pub** (*VII. Akácfa u. 13; Tel 322/76-45; Metro line 2 to Blaha Lujza tér; 3pm-4am; No credit cards*) is really two places: the music pub, where hot live acts like the Cotton Club Singers, doing tight swing and scat, pack this no-cover-no-attitude-not-enough-seats place; and, a level down, the disco, which kicks in after the live show with funk and soul. It's an unpretentious, mainly Magyar crowd, but with a few veteran expats hanging out.

For that classy, sophisticated-lady feel that only a certain kind of jazz club can deliver, pony up your 300Ft cover charge and head for **Piaf** (*VI. Nagymező utca 25; Tel 312/38-23; Metro line 1 to Oktogon; 10pm-6am daily*). The upstairs lounge, if you can discreetly slip up the sometimes-roped-off stairs (no killer bouncers here), is a den of plush drapes, martini sipping, and piano tinkling Thursdays though Saturdays and Mondays.

budapest bars, clubs and culture zoo

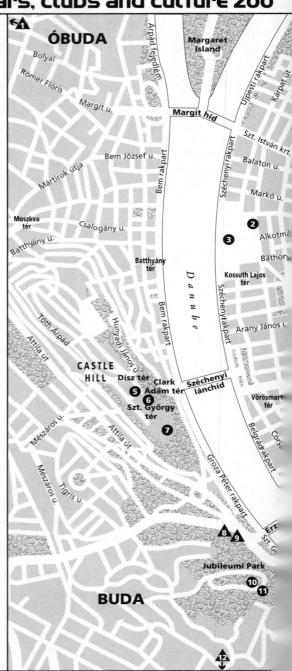

BARS/CLUBS ▲
Bamboo **28**
Budai Parkszinpad **12**
Darshan Udvar **18**
Fat Mo's Music Club **15**
Fonó **13**
Garage café **4**
Incognito **30**
Libella **14**
M4 **21**
Morrison's Music Pub **22**
Old Man's Pub **24**
Paris, Texas **19**
Petofi Csarnok **26**
Piaf **23**
Portside **16**
Rudas **9**
Rác-kert **8**
Szent Jupat **1**
Trafó **20**
Underground **29**

★ Budapest
HUNGARY

CULTURE ZOO ●
Budapest History
Museum **7**
Cave Church **11**
Hungarian National
Gallery **6**
Liberation Monument
and Citadel **10**
Ludwig Museum **5**
Museum of
Ethnography **2**
Museum of Fine Arts **27**
National Museum **17**
Parliament **3**
Saint Stephen's
Basilica **25**

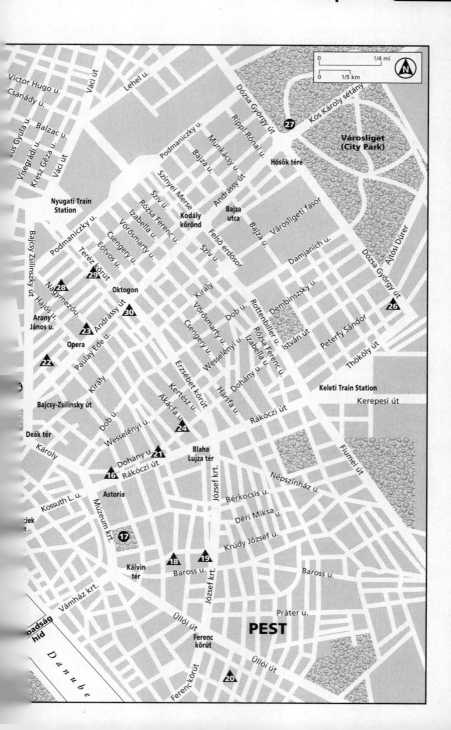

Full-on meat markets can be melded with decent soul and jazz bands, as **Fat Mo's Music Club** *(V. Nyári Pál u. 11; Tel 267/31-99; Metro line 3 to Ferenciek tere, night bus 78É; Noon-2am)* happily proves. The Chicago speakeasy theme in this brick-walled basement bar right in the heart of Budapest's old center packs in an accordingly beautiful, and only slightly obnoxious, pack. Respectable Buffalo wings and fajitas, too.

Trafó*(IX. Liliom u. 41; Tel 456/20-49; Metro line 3 to Ferenc körút or Tram 4 or 6to Ferenc körút; 5pm-midnight daily; www.c3.hu/trafo)* is a lot more into art/fringe music and dance groups, both Hungarian and international, and despite a totally institutional building (it's technically a community center), it attracts true boundary-pushers. Recent shows have included the Bang on a Can Ensemble doing Brian Eno, the *Compagnie Alentours* dance troupe, and a Magyar performance art group. All of which wins the hearts of a devoted, broke, local student crowd. It's out in blighted District IX, but you'll be glad you made the effort.

Mainstream Magyar radio rock stars (think Michael Bolton) tend to play **Budai Parkszinpad** *(XI. Kosztolányi Dezső tér; Tel 466/99-16; Bus 7 to Kosztolányi Dezső tér; Shows at 8pm; Admission varies)*, a fun but inconvenient outdoor venue out by the **Backpackers Guest House** [see *crashing,* below]. A good world-music fest that sometimes plays here in spring and summer can make it worth the trip.

Petőfi Csarnok *(XIV. Városliget, Zichy Mihály út 14; Tel 343/43-27; Metro line 1 to Széchenyi Fürdő; Shows at 8pm; Admission varies)*, up in the more accessible park meadows of Városliget [see *hanging out,* above], at the east end of District VII's Andrássy út, tends to catch the occasional touring rock band, and the **Hungarian Jazz Festival** [see *festivals and events,* below] here is a summertime must.

Something almost totally unknown outside this part of Europe is the Carpathian folk, Gypsy, and klezmer traditions of small villages to the east, and the fine souls at **Fonó** *(XI. Sztregova u. 3; Tel 246/53-33; 8pm-midnight; www.fono.hu, zenehaz.1@dpg.hu; Prices vary)* actually scour these towns, bringing musicians to Budapest, putting them on the stage, and recording and distributing them. Fonó also showcases world music, funk, and jazz with their brilliant **Duna** festival [see *festivals and events,* below] on Margaret Island every summer.

club scene

Nightclub ventures are risky even in stable, well-developed Western economies, so you can imagine how fast they open and close around here. But there's always something new on the horizon and usually you'll hear about it first at **Fotex Records** [see *stuff,* below] or at **Incognito** [see *bar scene,* above]. In summer the best, most crazed dance nights are ones that are thrown together in improvised one-time-only spaces, so watch for those flyers. One such extraordinary event that has settled into a monthly party held year-round is **Cinetrip** *(cinetrip@c3.hu)*, a house music, belly dancing, and swim night held in Budapest's most atmospheric old Ottoman bathhouse, the **Rudas** [see *you're soaking in it,* below]. Essential

rules of the game

The drinking age here might as well be 15, IDs
are never checked, nobody cares if you drink outdoors, and as for
smoking, there is virtually nowhere, outside the **Gundel** dining
room [see *eats*, below] and the Metro, where it isn't positively encouraged. All recreational drugs are illegal here, but people still do manage
it. In private settings nobody much will give you a second glance. If
you're at a rural rave, that's one thing, but in a District VII club a lot
more discretion should be exercised. Periodic raids have been known
to happen in clubs and the penalties are strict, with no presumption
of innocence. All in all, a crappy way to come down, dude.

vocabulary 101: *Ingyenes* means "free." *Köszönöm* means "thank you."
Scour cool flyers for that first word, go there, and tell them the second
word. And keep an eye out for DJ Budai on those signs, too—his house
and techno shows have become legendary.

Two little cautions: First, remember that the former East Bloc, however quickly it's rocketing toward fashionableness, ain't Soho yet. Trying
to get into places that are difficult just might cost you your health.
Bouncers in these parts are sometimes volatile, violent mafiosi whom the
local police won't touch. If you catch resistance, just politely move on.

Second, night trams and buses have been listed here, but some of
them run just once an hour, so taxis are usually a much better bet, especially in the relatively small area that makes up club mecca. These too are
uniformly corrupt, but you'll be fine if you stick to the companies listed
here [see *need to know*, below].

The ultimate Magyar club vibe may well be the techno raves held in
random meadows outside Budapest. Obviously these are summer parties,
hastily organized and promoted mostly through the grapevine. Ask
around, though, and chances are you'll hear about one, and may get a
lead on the hastily organized bus people are using to get out there—and,
just maybe, back. Don't plan on sleeping that night.

Bamboo (*VI. Dessewffy utca 44; Tel 312/36-19; Metro line 1 to
Oktogon, night bus 182É; 4pm-4am; www.extra.hu/bamboo*) is basically a
wacky, kooky, typical Hungarian tiki bar with wacky, kooky funk and
disco inferno tracks. It's also a long-lasting hit with the club kids, with a
cover charge of 200-300Ft...if they decide to charge it.

Garage café (*V. Arany János utca 9; Tel 302/64-73; Metro line 3 to
Arany János utca, night bus 50É or 14É; 11am-2am Mon-Fri, 5pm-4am
Sat, closed Sun; 800Ft Wed nights, 1,000-1,200Ft Sat*) is wacky in its own
right, though in a sleek kind of way, with all-new, open-plan, multi-
tiered, plank-floored dining space, shared with a dance floor, all lit by dis-
embodied motorcycle headlamps. The yuppified crowd probably couldn't
even start a bike.

fIVE-O

Policing is very rare here—for the most part the cops leave you alone. But when they do decide to do their jobs, *watch out*. Enforcement is strict and without a whole lotta mercy. Which has had the effect of drying up "supplies," but has somehow not yet made weed or hash any more expensive.

Later on, the cellar bar **Underground** (*VI. Teréz körút 30; Tel 296/55-66; Metro line 1 to Oktogon, night bus 6É, Tram 4, 6 to Oktogon; 11pm-1am Sun-Tue, till 3am Wed-Sat*), poses more with a dark, post-apocalyptic sewer-main decor, and a serious lineup of ambient, acid jazz, and house DJs. With cover charges even on non-DJ nights and a crowd that tries hard to look like models, it may be just a bit over the top, but it does make for good visuals.

aRTS SCENE

▶▶VISUAL ARTS

The gallery scene is hopping, with everything from Pop Art to neo-pagan on canvases, both material and electronic (for a nice taste, check out the virtual galleries found at **Artpool:** *www.artpool.hu*). The more alterna galleries tend to be scattered about the fringe of the city center, as you would expect, while the upscale ones are concentrated near the south end of District V, orbiting around Váci utca. A likely spot to catch creative types plotting, and to find flyers for their next openings, is the **Libella** cafe in Buda [see *hanging out*, above]. But the **c3** media center [see *wired*, below] bulletin board is sure to have the freshest happenings. The free monthly *Galéria (www.virtuartnet.hu)*, with a section in English (available at the **Ludwig Museum** [see *culture zoo*, below]), is also a great source for more classic private exhibitions and the skinny on the hottest shows in the Budapest state galleries and museums.

Black-Black Galéria (*IX. Balázs Bla utca 20; Tel 221/89-63; Metro line 3 to Klinikák*) loves to host the most provocative, out-there artists in Budapest, many of whom are now experimenting with multimedia and art by mail, but this place only opens periodically for specific shows. The free **Galéria 56** (*V. Falk Miksa utca 7; Tel 269/25-29; Metro line 3 to Nyugati; Noon-6pm Tue-Sat*) is ever-open, though, and ever showcasing everyone from Robert Mapplethorpe to the latest young Hungarian sensation.

Vintage Galéria (*V. Magyar utca 26; Tel 337/05-84; Metro line 2 to Astoria; 2-7pm Tue-Fri*) is a top spot for catching local photographic work that pushes the envelope, both in art and photorealism.

▶▶PERFORMING ARTS

Hungary does the cinephile's heart good with all manner of old-style movie palaces, and dozens of releases, from Hollywood blockbusters to *Lady From Shanghai* or John Waters's latest. Movies generally play in their original language with Hungarian subtitles, but the only publication to list all their titles in English is the free weekly *Pest Est*, which you can pick up in bars and cafes. Theater, at least in English, is sparse, but orchestral music, ballet, and the ultimate in European decadence, the opera, are alive and thriving.

Művész *(VI. Teréz körút 30; Tel 332/67-26; Metro line 3 to Nyugati),* the movie house so damn cool it had to expand into a club, sits atop its spawn, **Underground** [see *club scene,* above], and keeps right on showing vintage, cult, and art films in stunning movie-palace decor. The lobby cafe tends to be a filmmakers' hangout, so get there early or stay late if you've got a script that's just burning in your hands. **Toldi Stúdió Mozi** *(V. Bajcsy-Zsilinszky út 36-38; Tel 311/28-09; Metro line 3 to Arany János)* isn't as stunning visually, but its program is just as progressive and its cafe is always filled with local filmies, especially during the **Titanic International Filmpresence Festival** [see *festivals and events,* below]

festivals and events

Hungarian Film Festival *(Feb; Tel 351/77-60)* is organized by Filmunio Hungary to liven up the gray winter with a top-notch collection of Euro and world flicks, both indie-cool and Hollywood-slick, at various venues.

Budapest Spring Festival *(Late Feb; Tickets at Budapesti Fesztival kozpont, VIII. Rákóczi ut 65; Tel 333/23-37)* is the city's major classical music, dance *and* folk fest, held at venues citywide.

Revolution Day *(Mar 15):* The big break with the Hapsburg Empire in 1848, celebrated with flag-waving and flowers at the monument to Sándor Petőfi, national poet extraordinaire, on Belgrád rakpart in District V.

Budapest Autumn Festival *(Late Sept, see Budapest Spring Festival, above)* is the second-biggest culturefest of the year, with film, art, and dance thrown in [see *arts scene,* above].

Duna *(June; Margaret Island; Tram 6 to Margit híd)* is put on by **Fonó** [see *live music scene,* above]. It's a major open-air annual celebration of regional ethnic and world music.

Hungarian Jazz Festival *(June; Petőfi Csarnok; Tel 343/43-27)* is a big-time jam with local and international acts who play a three-day marathon in the city's biggest park.

St. Stephen's Day *(Aug 20, St. Stephen's Basilica):* Everyone gathers at the church of Hungary's first king, then parades around his mummified hand.

St. Nicholas's Day *(Dec 6):* Children get payback for a year of goodness/badness when St. Nick either leaves candy in their shoes or allows the demon *krampusz* to carry them away forever.

in October. If you're jonesing for more mainstream Hollywood stuff, you'll get full-screen-size projection, great sound, plush seats, and an escape from summer heat at the **Corvin Budapest Filmpalota** *(VIII. Corvin köz 1; Tel 459-5050; Metro line 3 to Ferenc körút; www.corvin.hu)*.

If actors are doing it in English, they're probably doing it at the **Merlin Theatre** *(V. Gerlóczy utca 4; Tel 317/93-38; Metro lines 1, 2, or 3 to Deák tér; 10am-6pm daily; Ticket prices vary)*, which also hosts lectures, readings, and music recitals, while acting as a magnet for expat thespian and literary types. The same folk are also likely to turn up for esoteric dance groups from all over Europe when they squeeze into the boxy experimental space at **Szkéné Theatre** *(XI. Műegyetem rakpart 3, 2nd floor; Tel 463/24-51; www.szkene.hu; Tram 18, 19, 47, 49 to Szent Gellért tér; Box office 9am-4pm Mon-Thur, 9am-2:30pm Fri and before shows)* near the Gellért Hotel. One event to watch for here is the biannual **International Meeting of Moving Theaters**, an excellent Euro fringe stage and dance fest held as part of the **Budapest Autumn Weeks** [see *festivals and events*, above].

The **MATÁV Symphony Orchestra** *(Matáv Music House, IX. Páva utca 10-12; Tel 215/79-01; Tram 4 or 6 to Boráros tér; Box office 9am-3pm Mon-Fri, closed July)* is the only major orchestra in Budapest with its own fully outfitted home concert hall. They're good, and the hall seats only 200, so buy those tickets early [for ticket agents, see *need to know*, below].

The **Zeneakadémia** *(VI. Liszt Ferenc tér 8; Tel 341/47-88; Metro line 1 to Oktogon; Box office 1-8pm Mon-Fri, 10am-noon/4-8pm Sat and Sun; Ticket prices vary)* is truly great, with all the creds of being the official hall of the Liszt music academy, where the old master himself once taught. With more splendor, far better acoustics and a location just around the corner from the Opera, this is where you'll catch all the serious Budapest state orchestras and ensembles.

The **Hungarian State Folk Ensemble** *(I. Corvin tér 8; Tel 317/27-54; Metro line 2 to Batthyány tér; Box office 2-6pm Mon-Fri)* are respected for their careful reproduction of every pattern of village folk costumes and every stomp and squeal of centuries-old dances and songs from the tiny hamlets that make up most of this country.

That massive, hulking, pillared waterfront performance hall you spotted on the main downtown square, Vörösmarty tér, is the **Pesti Vigadó** *(V. Vigadó tér 2; Tel 318/61-77; Metro line 1 to Vörösmarty tér; Box office 10am-6pm Mon-Fri, 10am-2pm Sat, 5-7pm Sun)*. Just about every major touring ensemble and orchestra lands here, but the space is so imposing it often seems to eat up their sound before it can get to your ears.

gay scene

The Magyar word for gay, *meleg*, literally means 'warm,' so it fairly sums up the current scene that's heating up here. As in most of Central Europe, gay life is emerging from underground more and more and no one seems too ruffled about it, but a macho tradition still holds sway, so

only here

Unless you count scowls from shop clerks, vestiges of the old communist regime are harder and harder to come by these days. But not to worry. All your favorite Soviet worker heroes are still on guard duty out at **Statue Park** (*XXII. Balatoni út; Tel 227/74-46; Tram 49 to Kosztolányi Dezso tér, then take the yellow bus going to Érd; 8am-8pm daily May-Sept, 10am-dusk Oct-Feb; www.szobor park.hu*). Lenin's here, front and center, along with a host of stooges, all parked safely 20 minutes away from anywhere on a suburban road where there's just one lonely bus stop. This has to be the creepiest but most hilarious museum/park you'll ever tour. The box-office clerk loves to throw on the *Best of Communism* CD when she sees curious Westerners coming—and you can even buy the damn thing if you want.

discretion seems like a good idea. Still, Gay Pride Day is a regular July event (for info contact Háttér, below) and the range of clubs, bars, and cruising spots is ever on the rise. One Internet resource, ***Gayguide (gayguide.net/Europe/Hungary/Budapest)*** is an incredibly exhaustive worldwide information fount for gays and lesbians. The English-speaking **Gay Switchboard Budapest** (*Tel 06/309-32-33-34; 4-8pm Mon-Fri; budapest@gayguide. net*) has all the dope on what's happening in town, from new cafes to advice on gay-owned accommodations, while the **Háttér Support Society for Gays and Lesbians in Hungary** (*Tel 329/33-80; 6-11pm daily; Hatter@c3.hu, http://www.c3.hu/~hatter*) has everything else.

Not everyone who ambles along Pest's Danube embankment on Belgrád rakpart in District V is there for the river view. This all-too-quaint raised walkway lined with stalls hawking folk crafts is the major gay cruise in Budapest, all happening amid unsuspecting tourists. A convenient stop-off here is the **Amstel River Café** (*V. Párizsi u. 6; Tel 266/43-34; Metro 3 to Ferenciek tere; Noon-midnight daily*), a popular gay hang right on Budapest's most fashionable (and expensive) square, with tables on the street.

Angel Club (*VII. Szövetség utca 33; Tel 351/64-90; Metro line 1 to Blaha Lujza tér, night bus 6É or 7É; 10pm till daybreak Fri, Sun, 10pm-midnight Thur; 400-600Ft*) is a glitzy three-level juggernaut that's so much fun, straights nearly outnumber gays, especially as audiences for the midnight "travesty" show Fridays through Sundays. There's intense backroom gay action on Saturdays.

Café Capella (*V. Belgrád rakpart 23; Tel 318/62-31; Metro line 3 to*

by foot

Downtown Budapest, at least on a weekday, does not inspire the thought of a stroll. Streets designed for carriages are not a pretty sight when packed with aggressive drivers who've just managed to score their first car.

A perfect antidote for this is a walk up wooded **Gellért Hill**, during which all the noise of Pest is balanced with tranquil heights just across the river in Buda—plus a nice payoff at the end. Start at the **Vörösmarty tér Metro** (*line 1*) and walk south down **Váci u.**, which takes you along a no-car zone that's lined with KFCs, tacky postcard stalls, and obvious tourists getting fleeced. Keep on toward **Szabadsajtó út** and the tackiness begins to thin out. Turn right, passing the Inner City Parish Church, the oldest in Budapest, and you'll catch sight of more regular working locals and students, especially around the side-street bars. Walk onto the **Elizabeth bridge**, and as you rise up over the Danube to Buda, check out the idlers on the banks, the working tugs and pleasure boats beneath your feet. Cross busy **Szt. Gellért Rakpart** to the waterfall on **Gellért hill**, where the path begins. Follow the path to your left, climbing until you double back to the bridge over the waterfall. Now continue in this direction down a few steps. This takes you to St. Gellért himself, the man who brought Christianity to the Magyars and who was rolled off this hill into the Danube in a spiked barrel for his trouble. From here continue your climb in the original direction, bearing right all the way. You'll soon come to an overlook where you can see the bend of the Danube below you and the peaks of Pest, highlighted by **Parliament** and **St. Stephen's Basilica.** Keep on up that hill and you end up at the **Liberty Monument** and the **Citadel**, that much-blown-up bastion of Hungarian independence. The Soviets weren't just being arbitrary when they chose this spot to put up the monument to their "liberation" of Budapest in May 1945. Now take your picture in front of the battlements and look for a cold Dreher beer at the snack stand next to the Citadel.

Ferenciek tere, night bus 78É; 9pm-4am daily; 500Ft plus 500Ft drink minimum): Drag shows here are also giddy, held Wednesdays and Fridays through Sundays. This cellar club is smaller-scale, lower-key, and a lot handier, as the main gay cruise runs just outside its door along the raised Danube embankment walk.

It's more of a chatty, drinky, hangouty kind of groove at the **Mystery Bár-Klub** (*V. Nagysándor József utca 3; Tel 312/14-36; Metro line 3 to*

Arany János utca, night bus 50É or 14É, trolley 72 or 73; 9pm-4am daily) with nonintrusive music tracks and an easygoing staff that also serves up a fair goulash.

Budapest's public baths [see *you're soaking in it,* below], around since Roman times, were probably favorite gay spots even then, but the **Gellért Gyógyfürdö** in the grand hotel at the southern base of Gellért Hill is a more recent Art Nouveau version of stained glass, marble, and blue tile dating back just to 1918. The thermal pools, where guests are divided by sex and issued tiny cloth aprons to wear, are where it's at here. At the northern base of Gellért Hill, the **Rác Gyógyfürdö**, on the other hand, is one of the original 15th-century Ottoman, stone-pillared wonders and, incidentally, gay central on men's days, Tuesday, Thursday, and Saturday.

CULTUrE ZOO

Budapest's position surrounding the most strategic hilltop on the most strategic waterway in this part of Europe has made it the prize of conquering hordes from Mongols and Romans to Hapsburgs, Nazis, and Soviets. All have left their mark, both on Gellért Hill and on the **Royal Buda Palace**, just upstream, where the throne room is long gone, having been replaced by the country's best complex of museums and galleries. They, like the rest of this city, show the richly varied prizes and the costs of being a place caught between so many powerful forces. Group tours in English are available at most.

Liberation Monument and Citadel *(XI. Gellérthegy; Bus 27 to Gellérthegy or hike from the Buda side of the Elizabeth Bridge (Erzsébet híd); Admission 200Ft):* Topping Gellért Hill, this one's a Budapest must, if not for the stunning view looking back into Pest, then for a sense of why this spot was fought for by every invading horde since hordes were invented.

Cave Church *(XI. Szent Gellérttér; Tel 385/15-29; Tram 18, 19, 47, or 49 to Szent Gellért tér; 8am-9pm daily; Free):* At the downstream base of Gellért Hill, this chapel provides an incredible glimpse into the hidden labyrinth of caves in the hill that were inhabited 4,000 years ago, formed by the same hot thermals that give the hill its Turkish baths.

Hungarian National Gallery *(I. Szent Györgytér 6, Buildings B, C, and D; Tel 375/75-33; Metro line 2 to Moszkva tér, tram 4 or 6; 10am-6pm Tue-Sun Apr-Oct, 10am-4pm daily Nov-Mar; 500Ft):* The main gallery of the Royal Palace is a treasure trove of classic tableaus and sculpture by brilliant Hungarian artists virtually unknown outside this country.

Ludwig Museum *(I. Szent Györgytér 6, Building A; Tel 375/91-75; Metro line 2 to Moszkva tér; 10am-6pm Tue-Sun; 300Ft):* A nice balance for the heavy traditional art of the National Gallery next door, with cosmopolitan collections including works by Roy Lichtenstein and Picasso.

Museum of Fine Arts *(VI. Hősök tere; Tel 343/97-59; Metro line 1 to Hősök tere; 10am-5:30pm Tue-Sun; 600Ft):* Vast collection of European masters, including a huge Spanish collection, with major shows of things like Egyptian mummies; free tours are given in English at 10:30am

down and out

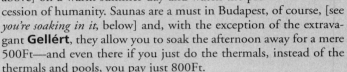

So you're broke. Don't worry, so are most Magyars—at least the honest ones. So just do like they do and head out to **Margaret Island** [see *hanging out*, above] on a warm summer day and watch the procession of humanity. Saunas are a must in Budapest, of course, [see *you're soaking in it*, below] and, with the exception of the extravagant **Gellért**, they allow you to soak the afternoon away for a mere 500Ft—and even there if you just do the thermals, instead of the thermals and pools, you pay just 800Ft.

The cafes here, of course [see *java*, above], are so refined you'd probably choose to spend an afternoon at one even if you weren't broke, but you're welcome to sit and chill for the price of an espresso (usually around 200Ft). Museums here still charge a pittance, as well, and a mere 100Ft can get you a whole day of exposure to modern art at the **Ludwig** [see *culture zoo*, above]. The **Great Market Hall** [see *stuff*, below] in District IX brings new meaning to the phrase "just looking," and costs well under 100Ft to enter.

But maybe the best of all won't cost you a cent: Exploring the back streets of **District V** and **VII**. Bring a camera along and get some incredible moments with old Gothic churches, quiet apartment courtyards (especially along **Andrássy út**), and the ghostly streets just to the south that make up the now derelict **Jewish Quarter**. But fair warning: One spot you may have to break down and drop 300Ft in is the **Fröhlich Cukrászda** *(VII. Dob utca 22; Tel 267/28-51; Metro line 2 to Astoria; 9am-6pm Mon-Thur, 7:30am-4pm Fri, 10am-4pm Sun, closed Sat)*, one of the city's last surviving kosher sweet shops, where they welcome everybody like family.

Thursday and Friday, and there's a highly cool ancient architecture and fossil garden, all just to the left of Heroes' Square.

Budapest History Museum *(I. Budavári palota, Building E; Tel 375/75-33; Metro line 2 to Moszkva tér; 10am-6pm Wed-Mon; 200Ft):* All the Roman coins, Gothic altarpieces, and Baroque sitting-room furniture you'd expect, but not so awfully much more than you'll see just running around town.

National Museum *(VIII. Múzeum körút 14-16; Tel 338/21-22; Metro line 3 to Kálvin tér; 10am-5:30pm Wed-Sun, closes at 5pm Nov-Mar; origo.hnm.hu; 300Ft):* See the 1,000-year-old coronation robe of King/St. Stephen, some super-fine communist propaganda, and everything from the years in between.

Parliament *(V. Kossuth Lajos tér; Tel 268/44-37; Metro line 2 to Kos-*

suth Lajos tér; 10am-5pm with tour in English; 800Ft): Jutting up from the waterside in District V, the Hungarian Parliament was built to be the center of the great empire that Hungary controlled before WWI—half of its rooms have been empty ever since.

Museum of Ethnography *(V. Kossuth Lajos tér 12; Tel 473/24-00; Metro line 2 to Kossuth tér; 10am-6pm Tue-Sun; info@neprajz.hv, www.nepra jz.hv; 300Ft):* Incredible collection of artifacts dating from pagan village life through contemporary folk traditions. Really, it is incredible. With helpful signs in English.

St. Stephen's Basilica *(V. Szent István tér; Tel 311/08-39; Metro line 3 to Arany János utca; Admission to church 9am-5pm Mon-Sat, 1-4pm Sun; Free, 100Ft to see St. Stephen's mummified hand):* Just blocks from Parliament and the Museum of Ethnography is this hulking Neo-Renaissance dome, visible from all around, which on August 20 comes alive with worshippers and a parade following the mummified hand of St. Stephen, Hungary's first king, which is still on display here a millennium after his reign.

Metro line 1 *(V. Vörösmarty tér-VII. Mexikói út; 5am-11:45pm daily; 90Ft):* A ride from Vörösmarty tér up to Heroes' Square, at the east end of Andrássy út, puts you on Europe's oldest and quaintest underground railroad, begun in 1872, and just renovated with historic displays in each station.

modification

Yakuza Tattoo *(V. Irányi utca 5; Tel 665-6121; Metro line 3 to Ferenciek tere; 10am-6pm Mon-Fri; 10am-1pm Sat; EC, MC, V)* is the place to get that nose ring you've been pining for—or just an arm engraving of "Mom" in Celtic. The practitioners here are said to be the best in Hungary and they specialize in pagan stuff, the chord that runs through much of the music scene here. Then again, the full line of brand-name skate baggies are in stock if you'd prefer a lifestyle statement you can change when it's out of fashion.

great outdoors

Looking around any of the Budapest baths, it's pretty obvious that the fitness plan of choice here is steaming (followed by a pack of cigarettes, a mound of schnitzel, and a round or two of Dreher beer). The rise of capitalism has created a new armada of mirror-filled fitness centers, but genuinely healthy lifestyles are still fuzzy notions in Central Europe. Because of city pollution, your only real fresh-air options are rural cycling (or caving or horseback riding), arranged through **Tourinform** [see *crashing,* below], but you'll need at least a day and night free. Another shot is staying at the **Backpacker's Guest House** [see *crashing,* below] where Attila, the owner, leads guests on caving and waterskiing trips.

Flying around Margaret Island on roller blades is a natural way to escape the city traffic and noise, but just about the only place to rent skates is at the inconvenient **Görzenál** *(III. Árpád fejedelem útja 125; Tel*

250/39-62; *Hév to Timás utca; 8am-8pm Mon-Fri, 9am-8pm Sat, Sun),* located opposite the island on the Buda side—it's a major board scene, though, with custom ramps on site.

To really build up a sweat in a non-dance-club environment (something that may classify you as a gung-ho nutball to many Magyars), you have to either hike up Gellért Hill or get out of Budapest entirely. One particularly painless and lyrical way to get some fresh small-town air is to hop a Danube excursion boat. Daily trips to Szentendre, a former artists' colony now completely ruined by tourism, or Visegrád, an enchanting medieval hilltop town that's 4-plus hours up the river, leave from the **Mahart boat terminal** *(V. Vigadó tér; Tel 318/12-23; Metro line 1 to Vörösmarty tér; call ahead for boats to Szentendre, times may vary; pass-nave@mahartpassnave.hu).*

STUff

Budapest shops are rapidly becoming more seductive these days, and you can shop here for groovy fashion. But for Westerners, it's probably the flea market and secondhand stuff that holds the most interest. Few things could make better keepsakes than communist kitsch, a one-cup stovetop espresso maker, or spices from Turkey that you found at the bazaar.

▶▶HOT COUTURE
Fashion is serious business in image-conscious Hungary, and **Emilia Anda** *(V. Váci utca 16/b; Tel 318/75-12; Metro line 3 to Ferenciek tere; 10am-6pm Mon-Fri, 10am-3pm Sat; V, MC, AE)* has made a name for herself both here and in Paris with unlikely blends of organic-toned textiles and understated flowing layers that somehow manage to look both ancient and ultramodern.

▶▶TUNES
For the latest Magyar rock sensation, it has to be **Fotex** *(V. Szerrita tér 2; Tel 318/32-95; Metro line 3 to Ferenciek tere; 10am-9pm daily; AE, V, MC, DC),* where you'll also pick up flyers for concerts. But nobody beats **Wave Music** *(VI. Révay köz 2; Tel 269/31-35; Metro line 1 to Bajcsy-Zs. út; 11am-7pm Mon-Fri, 11am-2pm Sat; No credit cards)* for true strangeness, with the full armament of trance, acid, house, breakbeat, drum 'n' bass….

▶▶BOUND
Bestsellers *(V. Október 6 utca 11; Tel 312/12-95; Metro line 3 to Arany János utca; 9am-6:30pm Mon-Fri, 10am-5pm Sat, 10am-4pm Sun; AE, V, MC, DC)* has the biggest selection of English-language books in Budapest, but even so, it's just a one-room shop and much of it's given over to guides and paperback pop stuff. Still, the staff is knowledgeable and tries its best to keep a couple of literature shelves stocked with relevant work. **Rhythm 'N' Books** *(V. Szerb utca 21-23; Tel 266/98-33, x2226; Metro line 3 to Kálvin tér; 11am-6pm Mon-Fri, closed Sat, Sun; No credit cards)* is where you'll find the secondhand English stuff, but be warned that it's very picked over. Far better is the notice board behind the cashier, where any expat lit event will appear, and the collection of

world music, including some brilliant titles by local label **Fonó** [see *live music scene,* above].

Where would a budding novelist be without java? One shudders to think, and **Litea Bookstore and Cafe** (*I. Hess András tér 4; Tel 375/69-87; Metro line 2 to Moszkva tér, then take Vár bus; 10am-6pm daily; AE, V, MC*) fortunately makes the question avoidable. Right inside the inspiring Buda palace walls, where you would least expect it, is this quiet, low-key spot with a strong art book collection.

Írók Boltja (*VI. Andrássy út 45; Tel 322/16-45; Metro line 1 from Oktogon; 10am-6pm Mon-Fri, 10am-1pm Sat May-Sept; AE, V, MC, DC*) is the center of the Magyar lit scene and feels like it, with dark paneling, author readings (once in a blue moon there's actually one in English), and little tables where you can camp out with a coffee for as long as you like and spy on the hyper-intellectual set who constantly flow through here.

▶▶**HOW BAZAAR**

The name **Great Market Hall** (*IX. Fovám tér; Tel 218/53-22; Metro line 1 to Kálvin tér; 6am-5pm Mon, 6am-6pm Tue-Fri, 6am-2pm Sat*) is no exaggeration as you'll see at this massive former railway station with well over a hundred peddlers, hagglers, and craftsfolk hawking everything from quails' eggs to hand-tooled leathers.

But for the steals of the century, head for Városliget park on weekend mornings and find **Petőfi Csarnok** (*XIV. Zichy Mihály út; Tel 343/43-27; Metro line 1 to Széchenyi Fürdö; 7am-2pm Sat, Sun*). For a pittance of an admission price, you'll discover more priceless flea market junk than you could possibly ever take home, from scythes to Lenin pins.

EATS

Hungarian food is as spicy and hearty as the Magyars themselves, and

12 hours in budapest

If you're ever forced to cram this jewel of the East into just half a day, make sure you at least have from noon to midnight. That should give you time to:

1. Cruise through an old-world coffee-house like **Művész** in District VII [see *java*, above].

2. Hit the **Royal Castle** grounds across the river in Buda to take in the view of Pest through the battlements [see *culture zoo*, above].

3. Swing a visit to the **Rudas** or **Gellért** baths for a steam and a soak before they close for the day. Once thoroughly purged of your toxins, you'll be feeling strangely hungry [see *you're soaking in it*, below].

4. Hit **Fatál** early, across the river in Pest again, and beat the crowds to order that pan full of goose and dumplings. After that, you'll surely need a walk [see *eats*, below].

5. Head up Andrássy út and enjoy that elegant 1880s feeling of boulevarding.

6. Mainline caffeine at **Incognito**, where you should sit out in the gathering twilight and ask around about what's hot tonight [see *bar scene*, above].

7. Wander to whichever of the other pubs on Dohány u. has the most interesting crowd, and cap it off by buying someone a **Unicum** shot or three. Still feel like catching that friggin' train?

they proudly heap it on with gusto. Service in touristy places can be stunningly bad, but a cheap little neighborhood hole in the wall, called an *Étkezde*, will charm you with unpronounceable noodle and goulash delights. At the other end of the spectrum are posh dining rooms with internationally renowned chefs and grand histories. Somewhere in between are the new generation of hip spots serving world cuisine, many of which have recently sprouted up in the north end of District V. A good source is the free weekly *Open*, alas in Hungarian only, but with sample menus and good color interior shots of the latest hot spots. When paying, just round up to the nearest 100Ft as there's probably a gratuity included in the bill already.

A word to the wise: The mafia presence is especially heavy in the restaurant business, and they love to prey on innocent little foreigners like you. The **U.S. Embassy** *(Tel 475/44-00, Fax 475/47-64, after hours emergency 475/47-03; V. Szabadság tér 12)* keeps a list of places that should be avoided—it's a good idea to check out the update.

▶▶**CHEAP**

Marxim *(II. Kisrókus utca 23; Tel 316/02-31, Fax 315/07-50; Tram 4 or 6 to Széna tér; Noon-1am Mon-Thur, noon-2am Fri, Sat; 450-900Ft per entree; AE, V, DC)* is always good for a grin, though its pizzas are less so. This monument to commie leftovers is festooned with red stars, socialist worker slogans, and deliberately ugly gray tables. Out of the way, but surely worth one meal.

Kisharang Étkezde *(V. Október 6 utca 17; Tel 269/38-61; Metro line 3 to Arany János utca; 11am-8pm Mon-Fri, 11:30am-4:30pm weekends; 200-700Ft per entree; No credit cards)* is a family-run place just big enough to turn around in, but the mushroom goulash and golden fruit-filled dessert dumplings are the stuff of dreams. Another Magyar-must experience is **Kulacs Étterem** *(VII. Osvát utca 11; Tel 352/13-74, 322/36-11; Metro line 2 to Blaha Lujza tér; 10am-1am daily; 1,800Ft per entree; V, MC, AE, DC)*. When the Gypsy band surrounds your table playing "Feelings," don't even think about enjoying your *kolbasz* and *nokedli* (paprika sausage and noodles in sour cream) until you've tipped them. "World-famous violinist" Sándor Járóka strikes up the band at 7pm nightly.

▶▶**DO-ABLE**

Mountainous portions of delectable peasant classics like goose leg and dumplings are the house specialty at **Fatál** *(V. Váci utca 67; Tel 266/26-07; Metro line 3 to Kálvin tér; 11:30am-2am daily; 1,500-2,500Ft per entree; No credit cards)*. The long, heavy tables, lit by stained-glass cellar windows, can just hold up the frying pans they serve you from. Reservations a must.

In the same district, but at the up-and-coming northern end, is the red-neon-lit Mexican-food mecca of **Iguana** *(V. Zoltán utca 16; Tel 331/43-52; Metro line 3 to Arany János utca; 11:30am-11pm Sun-Thur, 11:30am-midnight Fri, Sat; 800-8,000Ft per entree; reservations essential at night; AE, V)*. It's packed every night with expats and hip Hungarians, who come for two-for-one tequila specials from 4-6pm, then spill out onto street tables for Hungarian pepper quesadillas, fajitas, and fiery salsa.

▶▶**SPLURGE**

It doesn't get any classier than **Gundel** *(XIV. Állatkerti út 2; Tel 321/35-50, Fax 342/29-17; Metro line 1 to Hősök tere; Noon-4pm/6:30pm-midnight daily; 3,500-8,800Ft per entree; V, MC, AE, DC)*, an institution since 1894, with Zsolnay porcelain table settings, red marbled halls, crystal chandeliers, and velvety-cushioned seating. Let the weeping violins of the Gypsy band transport you to the turn of the century, when chef Károly Gundel whipped up his trademark foie gras, guinea hens wrapped in bacon, and *palacsinta* (crêpes) served in flaming brandy. Wines from Gundel's own vineyards accompany the above.

A quieter top contender is **Fausto's** *(VII. Dohány utca 5; Tel 269/68-06; Metro line 2 to Astoria; Noon-3pm/7-11pm daily; 1,000-3,000Ft per entree; AE, V, MC)*, one of those culinary gems always hidden away on

budapest eats and crashing

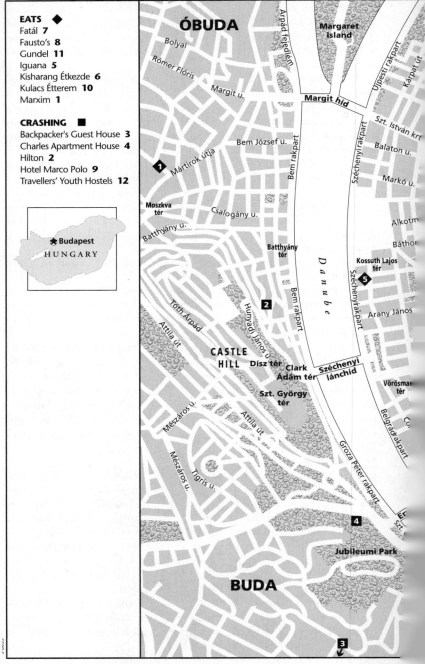

EATS ◆
Fatál **7**
Fausto's **8**
Gundel **11**
Iguana **5**
Kisharang Étkezde **6**
Kulacs Étterem **10**
Marxim **1**

CRASHING ■
Backpacker's Guest House **3**
Charles Apartment House **4**
Hilton **2**
Hotel Marco Polo **9**
Travellers' Youth Hostels **12**

★ **Budapest**
HUNGARY

ÓBUDA
Margaret Island

Bolyai
Römer Flóris
Margit u.
Margit híd
Árpád fejedelem
Újpesti rakpart
Kárpát út
Szt. István krt
Balaton u.
Markó u.
Alkotm
Báthor
Bem József u.
Bem rakpart
Széchenyi rakpart

Mártírok útja

Moszkva tér
Csalogány u.
Batthyány u.
Batthyány tér
Kossuth Lajos tér
Széchenyirakpart

Danube

Tóth Árpád
Attila út
Hunyadi János u.
Bem rakpart
Arany János

CASTLE HILL   Dísz tér
Clark Ádám tér
Széchenyi lánchíd

Szt. György tér
Attila út
Vörösmar tér
Belgrád rakpart

Mészáros u.
Mészáros u.
Tigris u.

Er
Szt.

Jubileumi Park

BUDA

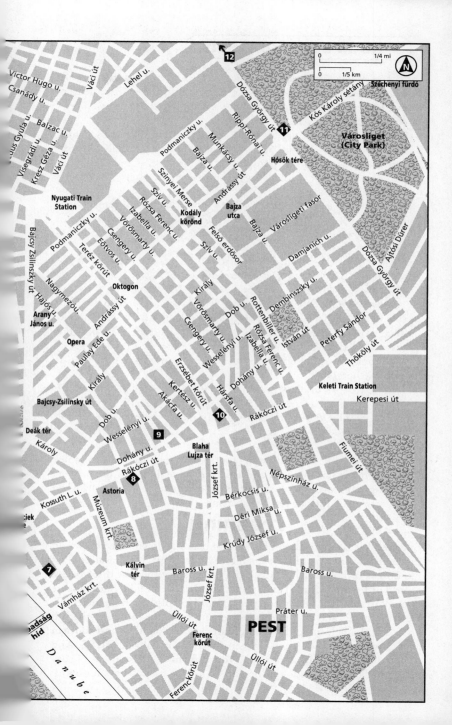

you're soaking in it

It's a moral crime to visit Budapest and not take a long soak in one of its Felliniesque bathhouses. The Romans built them, the Turks redecorated them, and conquerors have soaked in them ever since—conquerors just like you.

Budapest's baths are all built around natural thermals, which are—naturally—the star attractions here, but they usually also feature standard swimming pools and a cold plunge, the idea being to purge your toxins through steaming, then jump-start—or stop—your heart by leaping into water of widely varying temperatures.

Bathhouse terms to know: *ufdoza* (pool), *termál* (thermal pool), *fürdo* (bath), *goz fürdó* (steam bath and massage), and *pörulközó* or *lepedó* (towel). The staff at the baths aren't always responsive to English; these terms should help you out.

The grandest, if not oldest, of the bunch is the **Gellért Gyógyfürdő** (*XI. Kelenhegyi út 2-4; Tel 466/61-66; Trams 18, 19, 47, or 49 or Bus 7 to Gellért tér; 6am-6pm daily; 1,600Ft admission to the pool and bath, 800Ft after 5pm, 1,100Ft for just bath*), built into the 1918 splendor of the Gellért Hotel, all columns, skylights, tile, and marble. That would explain the number of tourists who hit these vast hot thermals and the extravagant indoor pool. More await on the grassy decks outside, and every bodily treatment, from massage to mud, is available here.

The **Rudas Gyógyfürdő** (*I. Döbrentei tér 9; Tel 356/13-22; Tram 18 to Szarvas tér; 6am-7pm Mon-Fri (pool closes at 5pm), 6am-noon Sat, Sun; 700Ft bath, 600Ft pool*) is darker and more crumbling

little streets in little muraled dining rooms that hold just a dozen tables. The homemade Italian pastas and sauces are accented with the peppery bite Hungarians love, and the fettuccini in cream sauce—especially when served with a good strong red—is amazing.

crashing

Budapest has far more decent options for bedding down than you would expect in a former East Bloc capital that's still massively renovating. Pest has dozens of hotels right in its heart (some scary socialist throwbacks, some worthy of Madonna) and, just across the river in hilly Buda, a score of comfortable little family-run pensions. Many of these have incredible views, terraces, and singing birds tweeting wake-up calls. For the full array, try the helpful and friendly state accommodation and tourism agency with a handy branch right in Keleti train station, **IBUSZ**. And though it's primarily for travel info, **Tourinform** also has dozens of cozy accommodation options on its books [see *need to know*, below, for both].

within, and only men are allowed in the thermals, but watching shafts of sunlight pierce the steam while you soak under the Ottoman stone columns is an experience you won't ever forget. And the pool is gender-mixed, at least.

The 16th-century **Király Gyógyfürdő** *(II. Fő utca 84; Tel 202/36-88; Metro line 2 to Batthyány tér; For men, 6:30am-6pm Mon, Wed, Fri, for women, 6:30am-6pm Tue, Thur, 6:30am-noon Sat; 600Ft)* has the same pasha's ruins vibe, but is also a major gay cruise.

In fact, only the 15th-century **Rác Gyógyfürdő** *(I. Hadnagy utca 8-10; Tel 356/13-22; Tram 5 or 7 to Döbrentei tér; For men, 6am-6pm, Tue, Thur, Sat, for women, 6:30am-7pm, Mon, Wed, Fri; 600Ft)*, located next to the supremely fringe outdoor music pub **Rác-kert** [see *bar scene*, above], is a bigger gay scene.

The **Lukács** *(II. Frankel Leó út 25-27; Tel 326/16-95; Tram 4 or 6 to Margit híd; 6am-6pm Mon-Sat, 6am-5pm Sun; 500Ft)*, on the Buda side opposite Margaret Island, is a mixed thermal, but is frighteningly institutional. The **Széchenyi** *(XIV. Állatkerti út 11; Tel 321/03-10; Metro line 1 to Széchenyi fürdő; 6am-7pm Mon-Fri, 6am-5pm Sat, Sun; 1,000Ft, discount for staying less than 3 hours 500Ft)* is another mixed-sex possibility if you happen to be up in the Városliget park, but it doesn't hold a candle to the **Gellért** or **Rudas**.

Then there are the inevitable hostels, sprinkled throughout the city. Noisy and bare-bones they may be, but at least they're plentiful, friendly, and none listed here have any of those ridiculous curfews.

▶▶CHEAP

The **Travellers' Youth Hostels** *(XIII. Dózsa György út 152; Tel 340/85-85, 329/86-44, Fax 320/84-25; Metro line 3 to Dózsa György út; Front desk open 24 hours; travellers@mail.matav.hu, www.travellers-hostels.com; 3,000Ft dorm, 3,300-5,700Ft per person double, 3,200-3,800Ft per person triple and quad; No credit cards)* will find you while you're still on the train to Keleti station and, if by some miracle they don't, their office in the station (to the left of the main platforms as you come in) is open 7am to 8pm daily. Ten locations all over the city, all clean and comfortable (if, well, hostels) with free shuttle service from Keleti, currency exchange, Metro passes for sale, and Internet access at some. You'll meet dozens of fellow travelers here—the only problem is that they may want to wail bad Dylan covers all night in your room. Their main location, listed above, is the only one open all year and is reasonably walkable from the clubs and bars of Pest, but locations 1 and 5, in districts V and VIII, are better still if you arrive in summer. No ISIC or Youth Hostel card required, but you'll save a few bucks if you've got one.

Breaking out of the usual backpacker orbit is what **Backpacker's Guest House** *(XI. Takács Menyhért utca 33; Tel 209/84-06, Tel/Fax 385/89-46; Bus 7 to Tétényi út; Front desk open 7am-1am; back packguest@hotmail.com, www.backpack.budapest.hu; 1,600Ft large dorm, 1,900Ft small dorm, 2,400Ft per person double; No credit cards)* is all about. Refreshingly on the fringe, it's run by Attila, a young Hungarian adventurer who loves to show visitors the lesser-known angles with caving, rock-climbing, and waterskiing trips. The hostel itself is all dorm rooms except for one double, but it's a hotbed of cheap-pubbing and clubbing info, with Internet access, a massive video collection, and an improbable Persian-carpeted bamboo temple in the backyard that's soothing to the hung-over.

▶▶**DO-ABLE**

With roomy apartments just down the road from the Gellért Hotel baths, the **Charles Apartment House** *(I. Hegyalja út 23; Tel 212/91-69, Fax 202/29-84; Bus 8 or 112 to Mészáros utca; charles@mail.matav.hu, www.charleshotel.hu; 11,000Ft single, 13,000-13,520Ft double, 16,300-23,800Ft triple; V, MC)* comes with lovely views, in-room kitchens and bathrooms, TV, laundry, some rooms with air-conditioning, a gracious staff, and 24-hour reception.

The beds at **Hotel Marco Polo** *(VII. Nyár utca 6; Tel 344/53-67, Fax 342/95-89; Metro line 2 to Blaha Lujza tér; Front desk open 6am-midnight; 4,400Ft dorm, 12,500Ft single, 8,400Ft per person double, 6,900Ft per person triple; No credit cards)* are basically bunks, but every spotless room has a bathroom. The patio, Guinness bar, and courteous staff make this the best mid-range deal in central Pest, particularly in that it's just one Metro stop from arriving trains at Keleti station—easily walkable if you haven't got massive bags—and stumbling distance from some great District VII bars. The dorm-style rooms attract a groovy young crowd.

▶▶**SPLURGE**

Towering over the city from within the walls of the Royal Palace in Buda, no one can touch the **Hilton** *(I. Hess András tér 1-3; Tel 488/66-00, Fax 156/02-85; Metro line 2 to Moszkva tér; hiltonhu@hungary.net; 485DM single; 565DM double; 650-2,500DM suite; AE, V, MC, DC)* for location and first-class service. Completely renovated and refurbished, it lays it on with solarium, sauna, pool, casino, well-stocked wine cellar, and arias in an outdoor concert hall. Weekend rates can knock $100US or more off the room price, but book well ahead.

And yes, it was the **Kempinski Hotel Corvinus** *(V. Erzsébet tér 7-8; Tel 429/37-77, Fax 429/47-77; Metro line 1, 2, or 3 to Deák tér; hotel@kempinski.hu, www.kempinski-budapest.com; 560-600DM single; 640-680DM double; 1,100-2,700DM suite; AE, V, MC, DC)* where

Madonna crashed, right in happening District V. The city's newest full-on luxury hotel offers cushy elegance with a fitness center, laundry, pool, and Art Deco wood-trimmed rooms. Satellite stations, wake-up calls, and billing information arrive via your TV, and naturally there's a phone next to the toilet for that conference call that just cannot wait.

need to know

Currency Exchange The monetary unit is the **forint**. **Banks** are best but close at 4pm, otherwise **Express Utazási** at **train stations** or any exchange desk at **Ferihegy 1** or **2** airports.

Tourist Information IBUSZ *(VII. Keleti station; Tel 349/95-72; Metro line 2 to Keleti pu.; 8am-6pm Mon-Fri, 8am-4pm weekends)* and **Tour-**

wired

Internet cafes have barely invaded Hungary, but a recent breakthough is the imaginatively named **Internet Café** *(V. Kecskemeti 5; Tel 328/02-92, Fax 328/02-94; Metro line 3 to Kálvin tér; 10am-10pm daily; info@budapest.net.hu, www. budapest.net.hu; No credit cards).* It offers three levels of Net surfing, a friendly staff, and a location in the heart of Pest, but zilch for hangout atmosphere, unless you count the network gaming, which attracts regular local kids too broke to swing their own PCs. Its walls are all blank and there are no tunes, but the rates aren't bad: just 150Ft for up to 10 minutes, lower rates for longer sessions, and they'll scan, burn CDs, or plug you into a video phone. Best deals: pre-purchased time on their Internet and game passes.

You can also try the **Vista Café** *(VII. Paulay Ede utca 7; Tel 267/86-03; Internet access 10am-10pm)* which features a restaurant, a travel agency, live music, art exhibitions, and net access for 11Ft per minute.

Also well-connected are the following Hungary websites:

www.pestiest.hu: The free weekly guide to what's happing around town, in Hungarian but with a website in English with the latest on new venues.

www.fsz.bme.hu/hungary/homepage.html: Every homepage imaginable in Hungary, organized by city or province—400 in Budapest alone.

www.hungarytourism.hu: Tourinform has it all for travels within Hungary, from rural cycling tours and wine fests to Gypsy music and thermals. E-mail: tourinform@mail.hungarytourism.hu.

www.travellers-hostels.com: The hostel kings of Budapest (and much of Europe), with detailed dope on 10 different digs here.

inform *(VII. Király u. 93; Tel 352/14-33; 9am-6pm daily; tour inform@mail.hungarytourism.hu, www.hungarytourism.hu).*

Public Transportation A 100Ft ticket gets you a one-way uninterrupted ride on any **Metro, bus,** or **tram,** but **1-day passes** (800Ft) and **3-day passes** (1,600Ft) are much less trouble. **Maps** at any newsstand. Inspectors will fine you 1,600Ft if you ride without a ticket. Metro stops at 11:25pm, but **night buses** (signs marked with **É**) run till morning.

Bike/ Moped/ Whatever Rental What little there is is around **Margaret Island** [see *hanging out,* above].

American Express *V. Deák Ferenc utca 10; Tel 267/86-73; 9am-5:30pm Mon-Fri; 9am-2pm Sat; Metro line 1, 2, or 3 to Deák tér.*

Health and Emergency Fire: *105,* Police: *107,* Ambulance: *104,* or use **R Klinika** *(II. Felső Zöldmáli út 13; Tel 325/99-99; Open 24 hours (for emergencies); Bus 29 to Szemlő-hegyi; AE, MC, V).*

Pharmacies Patika *(VI. Teréz körút 41; Tel 311/44-39; 8am-8pm Mon-Fri, 8am-5pm Sat, 8am-1pm Sun; No credit cards).*

Telephone Country code: *36*; city code: *1,* followed by local number (leave both off when dialing within Budapest); information: *198*; international operator: *190.* **MCI:** *00-800-01411*; **AT&T:** *00-800-01111*; **Sprint:** *00 800 01411.* Get **phone cards** at any newsstand.

Airports Ferihegy 2 *(Tel 296/70-00)* handles most major airlines plus **Málev; Ferihegy 1** *(Tel 296/96-96)* handles others.

Airlines Delta *(Ferihegy 2 airport; Tel 266-1400),* **Air France** *(V. Kristóf tér 6; Tel 318/04-11),* **British Airways** *(V. Rákóczi út 1; Tel 266/66-96),* **Lufthansa** *(V. Váci utca 19; Tel 266/45-11).*

Train Keleti *(Tel 333/63-42),* **Nyugati** *(Tel 349/85-03),* and **Déli** *(Tel 355/86-57)* stations are the arrival points. Expect long waits if buying a ticket here, because nothing is computerized.

Bus Lines Out of the City Erzsébet tér station is in downtown **District V** *(International info line 317/25-62).*

Getting Into Town From the airport: Airport Minibus Shuttle *(Tel 296/85-55; 4:30am-10:30pm)* takes you anywhere in Budapest for 1,800Ft...**from the ferry:** Danube ferries from Vienna stop right downtown in **District V** or **I**...**from the train station: Keleti, Nyugati** and **Déli** stations are all on **Metro** lines that run directly to **Deák tér**...**from the bus station:** the **Erzsébet tér** station is in downtown **District V.**

Taxis Rip-offs are rampant, so stick to honest **Főtaxi** *(Tel 222/22-22)* or **City Taxi** *(Tel 211/11-11).*

Ticket Agents Book concert tickets most easily through **Music Mix** *(V. Váci utca 33; Mon-Fri 10am-6pm, Sat 10am-1pm; www.musicmix. hu, jegy@musicmix.hu).*

Laundry Take it to The Home Laundry *(V. Galamb utca 9; Tel 200/53-05; 8am-7:30pm Mon-Fri, 9am-1pm Sat)* and leave it or get pickup service.

ISTANBUL

In Istanbul's crowded streets, you can sometimes see good spirits sparkling in young people's eyes. After centuries of social and economic repression, the new generation has apparently decided that it's finally time to catch up on lost merry-making, giving the city, from time to time, a high-gear, "let's live a little" feel.

When earthquakes shook neighboring cities in the second half of 1999, it created havoc. Istanbul itself doesn't lie on a major fault line, but the earth itself suddenly cracking open seems to have inspired this city to take long-term precautions and relish short-term pleasures. In Istanbul, living for today means fun is in, compromise is out, and emotions are often worn on sleeves. In short: You'll be well entertained in this port, Sailor.

This city has a lot of historical baggage to carry around, and to transform into something totally new. Half in Europe, half in Asia, Istanbul was once the capital of the Christian world and then the capital of the Muslim world and the Ottoman Empire. Today, it's a city balanced between many polarities: Culturally, it's predominantly Muslim, while the government is secular; first world–style attractions sit side by side with grinding poverty; traditional values, where many parents still arrange the marriages of their children, co-exist with blossoming liberal attitudes.

Nightlife here for the new generation is about heavy socializing (often with the clear aim of increasing horizontal accessibility), rather than drinking yourself into oblivion. Since there has never been a strong bar culture in Turkey, today's clubs dive in with enthusiasm, each happy to declare itself the most popular. The attitude toward the young traveler in the current zany sitcom mood of Istanbul is one of both endless curiosity about what *you* know (Info! Info! Info!) and the desire to show off their own culture at its best. Actually, that isn't too difficult, since Istanbul has a lot going for it: a very low crime rate, take-my-house-please hospitality, and a vibrant youth culture. Oh, and one more thing: You're the next best thing to a millionaire the minute you exchange your dollars.

To get the scoop on what's happening in town, check out the English/Turkish monthly ***Istanbul Kültür Sanat Haritasi (Istanbul Map of Culture and Arts)***, which covers new exhibitions, movies, books, and galleries. A gratis copy of ***Istanbullshit (www.beyogluweb.com/istanbull shit)***, the brainchild of a brash Aussie, provides valuable info with a "this city is nuts and so are we" attitude. ***Istanbul Classified (www.istanbul classified.com)***, the self-described "cutting-edge guide to what's in, on & out there," includes loads of ads for goods and services that make the life of the foreigner a little easier. If you want to know what the latest local and global fuss is, get a copy of ***Turkish Daily News (www.turkishdai lynews.com)***, written in crisp British English.

neighborhoods

Istanbul, the only city in the world that straddles two continents, is not known for the efficiency of its design—let's just say it wasn't mapped out with a ruler. Its layout is dictated instead by two bodies of water, the **Sea of Marmara** and the **Black Sea**, which are connected by the **Bosphorus**. European Istanbul, to the west, is further partitioned by the natural harbor known as **Haliç**, or the **Golden Horn**—the reason why the city was built here in the first place. The first of three regions, the area south of **Haliç**, is known as **Old Istanbul**, home of the ancient Sultanate, where a lot of the historical sightseeing takes place. The second, not-especially-younger area to the north, the neighborhoods of **Karaköy** (sometimes called by its former name, Galata) and **Beyoglu** (sometimes called by its former name, Pera), has become a magnet for business, and a hotbed for restaurants and entertainment. The third section, **Asian Istanbul** (east of the Bosphorus), is primarily a bedroom community. Since the city covers so much space, much of it hilly, Istanbul has been shaky on the downtown concept. It seems like everybody lives, works, and commutes all over the place in a cacophony of car horns. Lately, both slums and ultra-luxe developments have shot up, stretching the city limits far beyond these three major sections.

Centered in the historic peninsula of **Old Istanbul** is **Sultanahmet**. This is where you take pictures to prove you were in Turkey. During the day, peaceful **Sultanahmet Square** is a good place to watch clueless tourists zigzagging between countless old-but-awesome buildings [see *culture zoo*, below]. Located near **Topkapi Sarayi**, the center of the Ottoman Empire for nearly four centuries, is **Cankurtaran**, where you can see a lot of charming wooden two-story houses that have been turned into pensions. It almost has the feel of a sleepy Mediterranean village, with its cobblestone streets rarely visited by cars. Four tram stops west of

Sultanahmet is **Aksaray**, where there's a plethora of hotels, as well as some rather seedy nightlife. This area caters to Eastern European buyers, sellers, and hookers. If you want to hire the services of an Ukrainian ex-physicist for $150 a night, this is the place to be. Again four tram stops to the south of Sultanahmet is the street-vendor haven **Sirkeci**, where the train station is located. Locals in the know spend their leisure time on the north side of Haliç. To get here, take the bus across the Galata Bridge from Sirkeci on the south, where the ferry docks are, to Karaköy in the north. Then take an underground funicular railway through a funky old tunnel from Karaköy to Beyoglu. Here, there are literally hundreds of after-sunset spots tailored for various sensibilities, ages, and wallets. Even though cars are rarely allowed on its streets, the area known as **Tünel**, on the southern end of Beyoglu, has an urban vibe, with coffeeshops, galleries, and bookstores. **Istiklal Street** cuts Beyoglu from one end to the other. If you are a tiny mime, mediocre juggler, or eat live rats, then you might earn a couple of bucks here; competition isn't that intense on the street performing circuit. **Taksim Meydani** (or Taksim Square) is at the northeastern end of this pedestrian promenade. This square is a livelier center than **Sultanahmet**. Two metro stops from **Taksim Square**, is the neighborhood of **Tevikiye**, full of art galleries and luxury clothing stores. Toward the northern end of the short (six-stop) Metro line is the affluent neighborhood of **Etiler**, home to the biggest mall in Europe, **Akmerkez** [see *stuff*, below], as well as pricey nightspots like **High End** [see *club scene*, below].

Public transportation in Istanbul is extensive and can get congested, both on the streets and inside vehicles. The city bus system takes the bulk of the weight. When crossing to **Kadiköy** or anywhere else on the other side (Asia, that is), take the ferry. In terms of congestion, Times Square on New Year's Eve pales in comparison to the never-ending rush hour on the Bosphorus bridges connecting Asia with Europe. Seabuses are faster and more comfy, but the ferry is an Istanbul classic that never gets old.

The gods were ultra-generous the day they created Istanbul. The Black Sea said, "I want to go where the warmer waters are." The gods responded, "Why the hell not," broke the land in two, and let the currents travel wherever they wanted. The many natural inlets and protrusions of the shoreline on both sides led to the creation of yesterday's distinct villages and today's neighborhoods. Three thousand years of heavy history on top of that creates a view from the sea that gives commuting Turks moments of perspective and tranquility before diving back into the foray. If you're going to be here for a while, buy an *akbil*, or automatic debit card [see *need to know*, below]. It saves you money as well as the hassle of buying a different ticket for every form of public transport. The *dolmus* (dole-moosh), shared minibuses between central destinations, are another useful Turkish invention. After 11pm, or any time you don't know where the hell you are, take a cab—they're both easy to find and relatively cheap.

hanging out

Being alone is a rarity here, thanks to the sweet-natured local addiction to human interaction. There are traditional blue-collar coffeehouses in every neighborhood, where people drink cup after cup of tea and play Hearts-like card games all day, and there are cafes as the rest of world knows them sprouting up in various centers of this multi-centered city. One such, **K.V.** *(Tünel Geçidi 10, Beyoglu; Tel 0212/251-43-38; Across the street from the Tünel station; 9am-9pm daily; No credit cards)*, is full of ornamental distractions: a sphere glowing with cosmic light in one corner, purple old-lady shoes in another. Sit here for hours and suck in that Turco-European air. K.V. faces a calm courtyard in Beyoglu, but for people-watching people of all ages and income brackets, any one of the huge outdoor cafes on the **Ortaköy** *(Bus B1, B2, or 40T from Taksim to Ortaköy)* boardwalk are a better choice.

The Istanbul police are generally pretty lax about drinking in public places, including Ortakoy, and at **Hisar** *(Bus 40 from Taksim to Rumeli-hisar, walk north)*. For the regulars, meeting at Hisar—a sidewalk with benches right next to a small pier—after a stressful day is like going to a local bar. You can buy beer and wine from the **Iskele Bufe** booth here, then hang out on the sidewalk in the shadow of a 15th-century fort. The under-35 crowd here is mostly affiliated with the American-style Bogaziçi University up the hill, so language isn't going to be a problem. The atmosphere feels warmer and breezier than any you'll find inside four walls.

The colorful **Naregatsi** *(Istiklal Cad., Sakiz Agaci Sok. 3, Beyoglu; Tel 0212/243-38-69; Noon-midnight daily; No credit cards)* is a cool place to gain some depth in life. The owner is a well-known caricaturist. (Caricatures have long been a creative tool used to criticize the system in Turkey and are very popular.) An afternoon in this cafe is about drinking chamomile tea, playing absurdo-Monopoly, ignoring God, and drafting that one graphic piece that's going to end all literature.

If it's 4am and you need food, and one last stab at companionship, make a stop at **Mercan** *(Bebek Yokusu 12, Etiler; Tel 0212/265-79-72; Bus 59R from Taksim to Nispetiye; 24 hours daily; No credit cards)*. This diner specializes in fresh mussels and stuffed sheep intestines (*much* better than it sounds), appealing to Hilfiger-clad post-teens who choose to end their night of clubbing all fried out (we mean the food).

bar scene

All the bars on Kadiköy's Kadife Street close by 2am, since it's considered a residential neighborhood. In other neighborhoods, bar closing times seem to be random, but about half close by 4am. As for carding, you can get by if you have lipstick on or have some hair over your lips. (How that applies to girls or boys, I ain't saying.) There's not much variety in beers here—you'll mainly find Turkey's Bud, the mass produced Efes, which can cost 300 thousand to 2 million Turkish lira. Drinks are on the expensive end at the villas-turned-bars in Etiler, where there is a "less-dress"

OGLAN MEETS KIZ

Turkish men get high points on the hug-o-meter: firm, empathetic hugs with no pats on the back. The only problem is they sometimes won't let go. Women tend to be more reserved, but enjoy more sexual freedom than, let's say, 10 years ago. There's a lot of hanging in groups rather than couples dating. When observing couples in tea gardens, you'll see lots of that classic gal's-head-on-guy's-chest position. Relationships have short half-lives, though—turnover is pretty high. As usual, men think foreign women are easy, and local women think foreign men are interesting. Both sexes jump at the chance to practice their English. The vast majority of unmarried twentysomethings tend to live with their parents, so it can be an ordeal finding some privacy once you meet a good match.

code: The more flesh you flash, the more you fit in. Bars around Taksim Square create a darker ambiance for relaxation, inebriation, and flirtation. Remember to steer away from places that try to lure you in or seem to cover too much ground (signs in neon lights that say cafe-bar-night-club-dancing)—they're usually pretty sleazy.

Gizli Bahçe (*Nevizade Sokak 27, 3rd floor, Beyoglu; Phone unpublished; Across from the British Consulate; Walk for a hundred yards northeast on Kalyoncu Sok, make a right on Nevizade Sok, Gizli Bahce is on the right side of this street; 1pm-2am; No credit cards*) or "Secret Garden" in English, really is secret, as it's located on a restaurant row with absolutely no signs outside. Don't be afraid, walk into the apartment building; the kegs by the red saloon doors should clue you in. Nilgün, the irreverent owner who always looks like she just rolled out of bed, wants to keep the place the way it is, outside the "establishment." Like the personalities who frequent this place, each armchair here is unique, gathered from shops in the Çukurcuma area [see *stuff*, below] and flea markets. Come here for chilling out during the early evening. On a wide street off Istiklal, appealing to a similar leave-us-alone crowd, is **Peyote** (*Imam Adnan Sokak 24, Beyoglu; Tel 0212/293-32-62; Third street on the right when on Istiklal St. from Taksim Sq.; 8pm-2am Mon-Sat; No credit cards*). The miniature Hittite stage hosts—what else—underground stoner bands. The clientele are 18-to-25 close-knit art-school types. Supposedly, there's an invisible yuppie detector by the door. They play awesomely mind-boggling music here, including Mr. Bungle and their past and future followers.

If you prefer Mr. Marley to Mr. Bungle, **Ragga** (*Nispet Sokak 13, Elmadag; Tel 0212/248-49-34; Across the street from Harbiye Radyoevi (Radiohouse); 6pm-4am daily; No credit cards*) is your place. It looks and functions like a village bar in the Caribbean—don't ask for a cosmo, OK?

LION'S MILK

Raki—the original *ouzo*—magically turns an instant milky white when mixed half-and-half with aqua. Contamination of perfectly all right 100-proof alcohol is, to some, a needless American influence, to others, a smart way of giving your liver a few extra years. Of course, nobody will stop you from gulping this potent drink straight up. At first you'll behave like some chatty king or queen who loves everybody, rooting for cosmic mingling, and planting humid kisses on anything that moves. The day after…that's another story. *Raki* drinking houses are called *meyhane*. These places have tables that are set lavishly with white cheese, melon slices, and vegetarian dishes. One such place off mid-Istiklal Street is **Zindan** *(Oliva Han Geçidi 13, Beyoglu; Tel 0212/252-73-40; V, MC)*, an old dungeon housing a Gypsy band and a white-collar thirtysomething clientele. Ten million lira (about $15) buys you a fixed menu of dishes and all the *raki* you can drink. If you pace yourself, *raki* is virtually hangover-free. If you prefer not to take any chances, late-night tripe soup is just the ticket. It cleans the body of the biting anise aroma of the *raki* and pumps stomach juices *down* your system for a change. Those who have given up looking for any lasting remedy for their disillusioned souls can take doses of this earthly antidote in an all-night tripe house called **Apik Iskembe** *(Dereboyu Caddesi 79, Dolapdere; Tel 0212/250-48-04)*. Dolapdere, located northeast of Taksim, is not necessarily the safest neighborhood in the city, but that doesn't keep Apik's "loyals" (used and discarded alcohol-soaked actors, writers, etc.) away.

This come-as-you-are, cool-dred place is a meeting spot for the black population of the city—and non-black folks are made extremely welcome, too.

In Kadiköy, go up on the promenade of Bahariye Street, turn onto Sakizgulu Street, then make a left past McDonald's and Burger King and you'll find the multi-storied **Karga** *(Kadife Sokak 16, Kadiköy; Tel 0216/449-17-25; 11am-2am daily; No credit cards)*. It mainly plays avant-garde jazz and industrial, and boasts German beer, a homey patio, and a once-a-year Tom Waits theme night. Kadife Street is the "Asian side's" answer to Istiklal Street, lined with more than a dozen bars, all more or less of the same genre. Two of them, **Buddha** and **Lal**, are worth checking out.

The era of E decadence is over here, so house kids are now gulping energy drinks—definitely less empathogenic. Still, in too-tiny-to-be-a-club **Godet** *(Zambak Sokak 15, Beyoglu; Tel 0212/244-38-97; From Taksim Sq. on Istiklal St., take the first right at the corner where Aksanat is located; 8pm-4am Mon-Sat; Weekends 8,000,000TL; No credit cards)*, there's a feeling of stylish togetherness that's hard to find in electronic music spots in this city. Don't come here before 11pm. To get in, either be a girl or don't look like you're drooling to get lucky with one.

For those tired of the scene, **Cornerstone** *(Atlihan Sokak 4, Fener-bahçe; Tel 0216/345-71-01; Bus FB1, FB2 from Kadiköy to Belvu; 6pm-2am daily; AE, V, MC)* is a small neighborhood bar in a suburb on the Asian side. The house band's fondness for—and skill at—covering classic rock, the barbecues on the deck on summer weekends, and the presence of my-company-is-paying-for-this business travelers give this bar an easy, New World feel. The only thing lacking is a pool table.

For that, go back to the other side, where **Q** *(Inönü Cad. Deniz Apt. 30, Gümüssuyu; Tel 0212/251-72-51; 9am-2am daily; V, MC)* has ample tables and one of the few jukeboxes (Top 40 and King Crimson) in town. It might be a little hard to find: Take the road to the very left of **AKM** [see *performing arts*, below] as you're facing it, off Taksim Square, and go a hundred yards or so past the Chinese restaurant Guangzhou Ocean (which by the way, is actually owned by the Chinese govern-ment). Q is huge and rarely crowded—a good place to kick back and sip some booze.

LIVE MUSIC SCENE

Istanbul's live music scene hibernates in winter, countered by mostly open-air concerts in summer. **AKM** [see *performing arts*, below] offers all kinds of catalogs, flyers, and tickets for publicized events throughout the year. Check ***www.pollstar.com*** for up-to-date information on the Istanbul concert scene. For less centralized hard and heavy gigs, look for who and where at **Zihni Music Center** *(Akmar Pasaji 70, Kadiköy; Tel 0216/418-11-46; Ferry from Besiktas to Kadiköy, walk past the bus station to behind the post office; 11am-8pm daily; www.zihni.com; V, MC)*. On the electronic circuit, the staff and visiting DJs of another music store, **Simge Muzik** *(Valikonagi Cad. 109/39, Nisantasi; Tel 0212/225-92-37; Metro to Sisli or Bus 43, 43D to Valikonagi; 10am-6:30pm Mon-Sat; V, MC)* can give you insider's info. Better yet, ask the very approachable dudes who sell CDs on street corners.

The rock band that regularly plays at **Hayal Kahvesi** *(Büyük Par-makkapi Sokak 19, Beyoglu; Tel 0212/244-25-58; 11am-2am daily; Free weekdays, 5,000,000TL weekends; No credit cards)* on weekends, starting at 10:30pm, is called Bulutsuzluk Ozlemi—"longing for a cloudless sky"—a tribute to peace, love, and democracy. Their lyrics aim to con-vince the casually dressed audience (who are mostly old enough to remember Turkey's last coup, in 1980) to strive for a world where there is less surveillance and less judgment. But as soon as they're out the door, the audience is gossiping about how out-of-tune the lead singer is or how

ISTANBUL

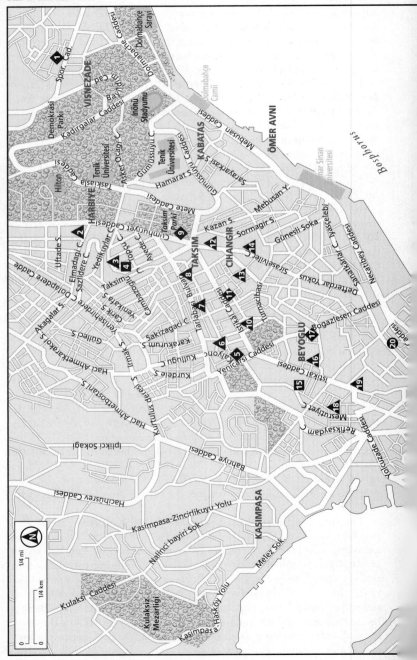

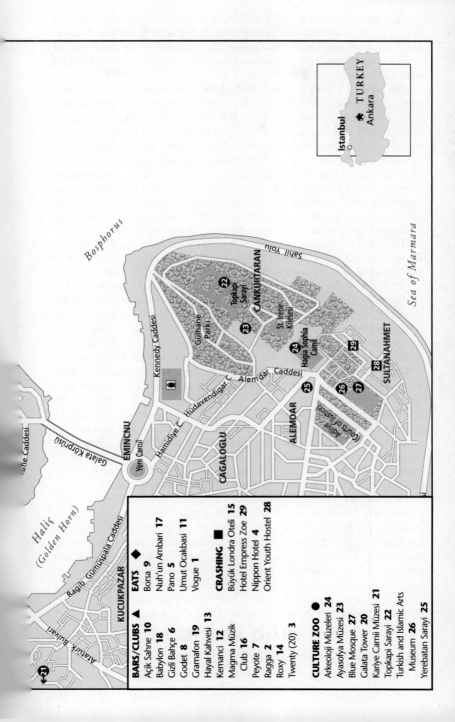

BARS/CLUBS ▲
Açik Sahne **10**
Babylon **18**
Gizli Bahçe **6**
Godet **8**
Gramafon **19**
Hayal Kahvesi **13**
Kemanci **12**
Magma Müzik
Club **16**
Peyote **7**
Ragga **2**
Roxy **14**
Twenty (20) **3**

EATS ◆
Borsa **9**
Nuh'un Ambari **17**
Pano **5**
Umut Ocakbasi **11**
Vogue **1**

CRASHING ■
Büyük Londra Oteli **15**
Hotel Empress Zoe **29**
Nippon Hotel **4**
Orient Youth Hostel **28**

CULTURE ZOO ●
Arkeoloji Müzeleri **24**
Ayasofya Müzesi **23**
Blue Mosque **27**
Galata Tower **20**
Kariye Camii Müzesi **21**
Topkapi Sarayi **22**
Turkish and Islamic Arts
Museum **26**
Yerebatan Sarayi **25**

token-babe the new bass player is. Between songs, slink out the side door that opens to a nice little alley where you can get some air and see famous old Turkish rockers chain-smoking on the corner. On the south end of Istiklal Street, Tünel is the old underground train line connecting Beyoglu with Karaköy.

Just west of Tünel Square is **Babylon** *(Seyhbender Sokak 3, Asmal-imescit, Tünel; Tel 0212/292-73-68; www.babylon-ist.com; Open sporadically; Between 5,000,000TL and 8,000,000TL; No credit cards)*, which offers a consistent lineup of live local and foreign world music. This converted carpentry shop with brick walls, high ceilings, and hardwood floors (no, sorry, they're not renting), attracts an artsy mid-twenties crowd who look like they've been in a drum circle at least once in their lives. Babylon showed some guts and chose to specialize rather than become another friggin' bar/restaurant/disco/club/concert hall/whatever. Being open only on event nights (music starts at around 10pm) prevents the scene from degenerating. Another plus: Drink prices are posted at the bar.

They play both kinds of music at **Açik Sahne** *(Turnacibasi Sokak 12, Beyoglu; Tel 0212/243-13-14; Off mid-Istiklal St. two streets northeast of Galatasaray Lycée; Noon-4am daily; www.aciksahne.com; No credit cards)*— the kind that makes you run for the closest exit and the kind that makes you slam dance till lava gushes from your veins! It depends who's on the open mic. Bands start playing early, so hang out here between 9 and 11pm. And leave the good china at home—this very young, very rowdy, very drunk crowd isn't shy about expressing its opinions about the bands.

Up the street from **Roxy** [see *club scene*, below] toward Taksim Square is **Kemanci** *(Siraselviler Cad. 69, Taksim; Tel 0212/245-30-48; Walking down Siraselviler St., it's on the last side street on the left before Alman Has-tanasi (German Hospital); 9pm-4am daily; No credit cards)*, probably the most famous live-music spot in Turkey. It has changed from the den for poor students and the mildly addicted, as it was in the '80s, to a serious moneymaker with a thousand bouncers and an attitude. The crème de la crème of Turkish rock bands play in the basement here, where a lot of Harley owners hang out, and the upstairs functions as a regular pickup bar. On both floors of the club, things get going after midnight.

Gramafon *(Istiklal Caddesi, Tünel Meydani 3, Beyoglu; Tel 0212/293-07-86; 9am-2am daily, earlier Sun; 5,000,000 to 7,000,000TL; V, MC)* is situated right next to Tünel Square. It has after-dinner regulars who look like they're in mid-life crisis and who sometimes chat rather than listen to the live jazz. Commandments: Shush everybody, and lose the friggin' cell phones. The music here is much better than at the ersatz five-star hotel jazz bars around—all of Istanbul's best jazz musicians have played here. The cover charge is added to your bill rather than taken at the door. Before you go in, ask if there's a "music charge" that night.

CLUB SCENE

Digital music culture in Istanbul climbed to prominence very quickly in

Rules of the game

All over town, men and women clutch their cancer sticks. Smoking restrictions, although on the rise, are very minimal. By law, you can't drink in public places, including parks. You have to be 18 to buy alcohol or smokes, but enforcement of these laws is not so strict. As long as you have your little brown bag to cover your container, and you keep to yourself, it's unlikely that you'll be disturbed. Just be reasonable: Don't start doing shots in a mosque courtyard. And, all recreational drugs are illegal by law.

the '90s. Both in terms of organization and DJ quality, clubs remain vigorous and in tune with the rest of Europe. Unfortunately, the kinds of clubs that draw a filthy rich clientele are not past the IMPRESS phase: You've got to put on a show to get in. You may have the bucks, but no sir, you can't go in yet. Clubs (and, as noted, even some bars) in Istanbul don't take males unaccompanied by a female. (Grandma, get your coat.) The good news, though, is that they frequently bend the rules for foreigners. Tipping generally doesn't help you at the door. Instead, look extra-confident and behave like you're doing them a favor by honoring their place. In descending importance, you'll need the right car, companion, attitude, and clothes. The dress code is generally conservative, with dark colors, and the more expensive it looks, the better. If you've got none of the above, your chances are dismal at some places, especially in Etiler.

If you're here during the summer, be on the lookout for ads about all-day and all-night techno parties in **Maslak Park Orman** *(Tel 0212/223-07-36)*, a huge park half an hour's drive from Taksim. Both Aphex Twin and Massive Attack have played here. For the latest on alternative parties on the digital circuit, get your hands on ***Partycult*** *(Tel 0212/269-70-74)*, a Turkish-language pocket-size glossy monthly that can come in handy. Get a free copy at **Vakkoroma** [see *stuff*, below].

I would like to propose marriage to the woman who designed **High End** *(Nispetiye Cad. 4, Etiler; Tel 0212/287-73-84; 11pm-6am Wed, Fri, Sat; AE, V, MC)*. Inside the door, pink leather lap-danceable couches are lit softly from above—you expect to see Captain Kirk seducing a space-babe. What you will see is large numbers of guys sporting the same mega-gellified hedgehog hair. DJs from A'dam and London often spin and on one recent night, Motor City native Juan Atkins (remember Clear? 1983?) made an appearance. Procure somebody's High End club card, issued to frequent patrons for easy entrance, to increase your chances of getting in.

Equally exclusive (this one also offers a club card), with less techno, is **Pasha** *(Muallim Naci Cad. 142, Kuruçesme; Tel 0212/227-17-11; 6pm-4am daily June-Sept; 12,000,000TL; V, MC)*. Or shall I call it Posh-a? People are so stunning here that you forget we're all just hairy bipeds.

fIVE-O

Always carry an ID with you. Border rules apply: The police have the right to search people and their belongings if they deem it appropriate. Don't act helpless when it comes to dealing with cops. On an individual basis, cops here are sensitive to the human condition, but that doesn't mean they act as social workers. As a group, they like that power-trip high, often achieved by exceeding their authority. In short, they're neither scary nor trustworthy, and generally just want to be liked by you. Some are corrupt, some are not corrupt. Cops are much nicer to travelers than to the normal citizen. If you get lost, don't ask a cop for directions—it's not that he wouldn't be helpful, but very rarely will you find a Turkish police officer who speaks English.

This outdoor complex right by the sea also has a bunch of chichi restaurants (not worth it) on the grounds. Plus fireworks, Brazilian dancers, and all that jazz. When it's crowded, it takes an hour to move 10 yards. On your way out, pretend you're famous: Start running away from the camera, and, I swear to god, a bunch of paparazzi will run after you.

Put your money—a lot of money—on number **20** *(Talimhane Cad. 20, Taksim; Tel 0212/235-61-97; 11pm-6am Mon-Sat; No credit cards)*. The only way to avoid the outrageous $25 (U.S.) cover charge might be to show up after 4am. This neighborhood, Taksim, hosted military barracks a hundred years ago. Ironically, it's now home to the straight and gay after-hours crowd. 20 is small by club standards, but it's visually exciting: industrial space theme, big pipes on the ceiling, 15-inch steps leading to platforms. Music ranges from Björk early on to some trance later in the morning, with hip- and soul-stirring techno in between. Thursdays are nostalgia nights.

On a side street off Istiklal Street, **Magma Müzik Club** *(Akarsu Sokak 5, Galatasaray; Tel 0212/292-11-19; 8pm-4am daily, till 6am Fri, Sat; 10,000,000TL; MC)*, lives up to its hot name, consistently playing the best music in town…if you like trip-hop. Magma prides itself on being the first club in town to use live instruments on top of DJ music. Either because of or in spite of the high temperatures inside, this place is a Grade-A meat market on weekends. Dress casual; combat boots are still in.

Hangar 2019 *(Atatürk Oto Sanayi Sitesi 21, Maslak; Tel 0212/285-27-30; 11pm-6am Fri, Sat; No credit cards)* is definitely less stuffy than Magma; well, it's a hangar, with a car-wreck decor. For a change, they've got a relaxed door policy. To paraphrase the Sufi poet Rumi: "You were sent to this country for one task, and that is…hmm…come and dance, whoever you are."

Roxy *(Siraselviler Cad. Arslanyatagi Sokak 9, Taksim; Tel 0212/249-48-39; 6pm-4am Tue-Sat; www.roxy.com.tr; Weekdays 4,000,000TL, weekends 10,000,000TL; No credit cards)* is a laid-back club that gathers artists, students, musicians, bankers, and the sounds of Reverend Horton Heat, Engelbert Humperdinck, Brad, and Skunk Anansie—it's a mix, is what I'm trying to say. Speaking of mixes, keep your eyes open for sex on the beach specials. Or sex period. The staff is very professional, like the great DJs who have an instinctive understanding of the mood and the crowd. Go on a weeknight—you have a better chance of getting in, there's an 8 to 10 happy hour, and a minimal cover. On weekends you'll encounter the just-past-puberty danceteria crowd (not that there's anything wrong with that!). There's a strict regulation in the city on "noise" at outdoor venues after midnight. One night, Branford Marsalis left an outdoor venue at the witching hour and started playing unannounced at this basement location, where decibel levels aren't on a curfew.

ARTS SCENE

▶▶VISUAL ARTS

Lately, it's been the in thing to open a gallery in Istanbul. This isn't necessarily the result of some undiscriminating high roller paying big dough for a chicken head in formaldehyde, it's more about the ever-increasing need to express. The paintings and sculptures in Tünel galleries tend to be atheistic, dark, and self-confident. In the evening, artists working here get together at cafes, and a little later start drinking at unpretentious restaurants in the neighborhood. Everybody knows everybody; it feels like there is an inside joke you'll never get. Nevertheless, they love to talk to travelers who have stepped aside from the tourist thing and can keep up with their slightly ironic intellectualism. While you're there, catch a show at **Babylon** [see *live music scene*, above].

You're more likely to be offered champagne from white-gloved hands when appreciating the safe art in Tesvikiye. In addition to ritzy galleries, this area has turn-of-the-century architecture, the best hairdressers in town, and people who "do" lunch. Fashion show locations in the city tend to vary. Boutique owners here might hook you up with an invite if they like your style.

A recent collage exhibition at **Pi Artworks** (*Muallim Naci Cad. 63, Ortaköy; Tel 0212/236-68-53; Bus B1, B2, 40T from Taksim to Ortaköy; 10:30am-7:30pm Tue-Sat*), consisting of letters and characters from Chinese, Finnish, and other languages, was typical of this gallery's eclectic no-brow approach to art. Shows change about once a month.

The owner of **Galeri Binyil** (*Zeytinoglu Cad. 8, Akatlar Kültür Merkezi, Akatlar; Tel 0212/357-97-13; Bus 59R, 59UC from Taksim to Akatlar; Noon-8pm Mon-Sat; Summer noon-5pm Mon-Fri*) favors the young who are lyrical and courageous. In other words, the screwier the better.

In a similar spirit, a bunch of young, idealistic artists have formed **Çekirdek Sanat Toplulugu** (*Sair Alisik Sok. 17, Kadiköy; Tel 0216/325-67-15; 11am-6pm Mon-Sat; www.cekirdeksanat.com*). The gallery is open-minded, embracing artists whether they're schooled or not, from the city or rural. Most works are sculptures in wood and marble; spac-y computer graphics are the only form of two-dimensional representation in sight.

festivals and events

Istanbul Foundation for Culture & Arts *(Tel 0212/293-31-33; www.istfest.org)* is responsible for international film, theater, music, and jazz festivals, as well as the Istanbul Biennial. In good times, sponsors are generous in their support of these festivals. When recession hits, art slides down on the list of priorities and the quality declines.

Tickets for the **International Film Festival** *(The last two weeks of April; film@istfest-tr.org)* tend to sell out fast, so purchase before the festival starts, and sneak in some wine at late-night marathons. About 150 quality films are shown overall, mostly in cinemas around **Istiklal Street**. Subtitles (English & Turkish) often take up much of the screen.

The **International Theatre Festival** *(Last week of May to first week of June; theatre.fest@istfest-tr.org)* includes contemporary multimedia-supported productions as well as classics. Recently, a Catalan theater company did *F@ust Version 3.0*, in which the stage looked like a giant web page, and a Brazilian director put on Euripides's *The Trojan Women*. The crowd is full of under-40, right-brained theater enthusiasts.

The **International Music Festival** *(Second week of June to the first week of July, music.fest@istfest-tr.org)* features classical ballet, contemporary dance, and orchestral music. A yearly highlight is Mozart's

Backed by a powerful corporation, **Borusan Sanat Galerisi** *(Istiklal Cad. 421, Tünel; Tel 0212/292-06-55; 10:30am-7pm daily; www.borusansanat.com)* keeps things sparkling, changing its exhibitions frequently: architectural projects one week, cat sculptures (of, not by) the next. There's also a CD library (with quality jazz) on the premises.

▶▶**PERFORMING ARTS**

Sure, the slackers of Istanbul subscribe to a 4-hour-a-day TV regimen. However, it's good to know that there is an able stage effort (sponsor-dependent of course) outside the tube and in the municipal theater structure. There's not much in English, so you'd better stick to things where there's enough going on without the need for linguistic comprehension.

For example, the experimental theater group **Kumpanya** *(Tarlabasi Bulvari, Dernek Sokak, 2nd floor; Tel 0212/235-54-57)* "believes in a theatrical language in which the space is the text, text is the sound, sound is the space, light is the costume, performer is the space." Don't be surprised to see young actors jumping around on plates hung from the ceiling. If they're not performing while you're in town, go say hi anyway. They'll direct you to some other nonconformist group in town, and you can have a pint in the

Abduction From the Seraglio, staged at Topkapi Palace.

The **International Jazz Festival** *(Second week of July, jazz.fest@ist
fest-tr.org)* has brought the likes of Dizzy Gillespie, Jan Garbarek, Miles Davis, and Ornette Coleman over the years. Occasionally, non-jazzers like Khaled and Suzanne Vega also perform. Most events are held at the **Open Air Theater** [see *live music scene*, above] and are immensely popular with the twentysomething crowd.

The **International Short Films Festival** *(Second week of April; Tel 0212/249-07-76; http://members.xoom.com/shortfilmist)*, offers very cool wave-of-the-future shorts to a crowd of freaky-lookin' dudes.

Galata Senligi *(Last weekend of June)* is the best neighborhood festival in the city, with folk bands, handicraft exhibitions, bohemian poetry readings, and children running around with kites (until the tails get stuck in Galata Tower).

During **Sportsfest** *(Last weekend of June; www.sk.boun.edu.tr)*, college athletes from around the globe play by day, party under the stars by night on **Bogaziçi University**'s very green central campus. You may have to leave your ID at the gate to enter the university, but once you're on campus, you're a guest to any of the parties.

almost authentic Irish bar downstairs. Kumpanya is on the right side of wide Tarlabasi Bulvari going down from Taksim Square toward the sea. For net info on theater groups, plays, and show times, check out ***www.tiyatronline.com***. The smartly named *Art-Ist* magazine might also be a good source.

If you have a taste for modern dance and multimedia art, try **Dulcinea** *(Istiklal Cad., Meselik Sokak 20, Beyoglu; Tel 0212/245-10-71; Second left on Istiklal St. from Taksim Sq.; www.dulcinea.org, art@dulcinea.org; AE, V, MC)*, a coffeeshop/performance space and "free environment for the modern arts." With icy waiters, postmodern paintings, and visitors dressed with just the right amount of elegance, the place has a continental air. During the Istanbul Theatre and Jazz festivals [see *festivals and events*, above] Dulcinea hosts live electronic music and dance shows.

A hundred yards away, **Aksanat** *(Istiklal Cad. 16; Tel 0212/252-35-00; www.akbank.com.tr/sanat)* is another multipurpose venue, minus the Colombian brew. Sculpture exhibits, classical music concerts, and movies on a laser-disc screen are all part of its heavy schedule.

When you need a hit of opera, ballet, or classical music, head to Beyoglu, to **AKM** *(Taksim Sq.; Tel 0212/251-56-00)*. The quality of events in this modern opera house is excellent. The open space in front of AKM is the number one trysting spot in the city. Steal somebody's date, then take him/her to one of the movie theaters on Istiklal Street to see a made-in-Burbank release.

For year-old avant-garde films, **Bilgi Üniversitesi** (*Inönü Cad. 28, Kustepe; Tel 0212/216-00-00; Bus 46K, 46KY from Taksim to Kustepe; www.bilgi.edu.tr/sinema*) has a strong May to September program for a mere one million lira each showing. All places in town show movies in their original language with Turkish subtitles.

gay scene

You mean there are gays in a predominantly Muslim country? It's one in ten (or was that just Masters and Johnson?), bro, no matter where the borders are. There's nothing in civil law banning homosexuality here, nor is there any evidence of organized gay-bashing, but mainstream society isn't supportive of coming out, and gay life in the city mostly stays behind closed doors. One interesting note: Since friends of the same sex in this country are very physical and warm toward each other in public displays of affection, you won't be stared at if you hold hands, kiss on the cheek, or even grab butts (like basketball players do) in public. People aren't conditioned to think that such acts are necessarily sexual. To get the 411 on being gay in Istanbul, check out ***http://qrd.tcp.com/qrd/world/europe/turkey*** and ***www.eshcinsel.net***. The first website is hosted by Lambda, a gay-rights organization in town. This site gives the virtual and the brick and mortar addresses of local gay chat rooms, gay support groups, and other gay organizations, all in English. They also help publish a bimonthly magazine called *Kaos GL*. To get a copy, check out **Mephisto** [see *stuff*, below] or any other alternative bookstore in Beyoglu.

When going out, make **Bilsak** (*Siraselviler Cad. Soganci Sokak 7, Cihangir; Tel 0212/293-37-74; Walking on Siraselviler St., take the second left past the German Hospital onto a dark street called Soganci; 5pm-1:30am Mon-Sat; V, MC*) your first stop. Take the elevators to the fifth floor. This bar offers decent sit-down food and, on weekends, free jazz. The patrons are artists, writers, ad execs, etc., in their late twenties. Have a Guinness, chat with the other laid-back single men around, and watch the Bosphorus. Before leaving, take a look at the first floor, more crowded and less discreet.

Next door to **20** [see *club scene*, above], **14** (*Abdülhakhamit Cad. 63, Talimhane; Tel 0212/256-21-21; 11pm-4am Mon-Sat; AE, V, MC*) is where you have the fun, baby. A black tank top and 501s is the uniform. Your mission is to dance on the ovoid bar and sweat at least two buckets before you leave. The under-25 crowd defines 2QT2BSTR8. Sound waves bounce back and forth between funky house, disco, Turkish pop and *sanat* (classical) music. Seeing a photograph of Zeki Muren, the most

by foot

Streets here come in all geometric shapes imaginable, and navigating them is often compared to finding one's own undiscovered brain circuits. One walk that gives a taste of these circuits is near **Sultanahmet Square**. Start on **Divanyolu Street** and make a left at **Sarayiçi**. Up this long cobblestone road, charming old women sit in their doorsteps, eyeing and making fun of each other's laundry hanging between balconies, and staring at strangers. Once you're down the hill, make a left on **Kadirga Limani Street**. The neighborhood of **Kadirga**, a former port, is built on a landfill. Walk along the right side of this urban park with its amazing trees. Make a right on **Sehsuvarbey**, a street full of cute two-story working-class wooden houses. Make the first right after **Hotel Amber** and go through another park, at the end of which you'll be greeted by a peaceful 16th-century courtyard where artists practice Ottoman calligraphy. Dire Straits and the like coming from speakers of a nearby teahouse, however, jerks you back to this century.

On another day, if you find yourself on the **Asian side**, take a walk along **Bagdat Caddesi**. "The Street," as locals call it, is at the opposite end of town from the above walk, and it makes for an interesting architectural and socioeconomic contrast. The mile stretch between the neighborhoods of **Suadiye** and **Caddebostan** is where trends in street wear generally spread to the rest of the city. People sit in street cafes and—what else—check each other out. The wide street with its wide sidewalk is youth central, optimal for auto or foot cruising, especially on spring and fall afternoons. At night, cars still race here at orgasmic speeds.

popular (dead, gay) Turkish classical singer of all time, on the wall next to murals of naked guys makes people happy: He is here in spirit. The 10 million lira (about $15) cover every day of the week makes them a little less happy.

Another after-hours alternative is **Hengame** (*Istiklal Cad. Sahne Sokak 6, Beyoglu; 2am-5:30am Mon-Sat; No credit cards*), a gender-bending club on the southwestern side of Çiçek Pasaji (Cite de Pera). It says "Musician and Guest" at the entrance, which refers to the show-business types who are a part of the clientele. The manageable cover charge buys you the first drink. Visually, it's very entertaining—I mean the people, darling—but musically, it's uninspired.

Godet, Gizli Bahçe [see *bar scene*, above], **Hangar 2019**, and the formerly gay **Roxy** [see *club scene*, above, for both] are other places with a gay/bi/lesbian following.

CULTURE ZOO

The former heart of the Byzantine Empire, and then hundreds of years later the center of the Ottoman Empire, Istanbul is layered with rich history. Yet, history is not something to sit back and look at here, it's a living part of everything you see and do. On an ordinary bus ride, you'll pass Roman arches, spectacular Ottoman mosques still used for prayer, and thousand-year-old fountains children still drink from. Unless otherwise stated, all the places below (except Kariye Museum and Galata Tower) are around Sultanahmet Square, in easy walking distance from each other.

Arkeoloji Müzeleri *(Osman Hamdi Bey Yokusu, Gülhane; Tel 0212/ 520-77-40; Tram to Gülhane; 9am-4pm Tue-Sun; 1,500,000TL):* The whole place is amazing but the *best* thing about this museum is that the overflow from the museum's collection is on display in the same yard where tea is served. Is there anywhere else in the world where you can set your feet on ancient statuary and sip tea?

Ayasofya Müzesi *(Sultanahmet; Tel 0212/522-17-50; 9am-4pm Tue-Sun; 1,500,000TL, 500,000TL students):* A genuine wonder, the amazing dome in this church/mosque/now museum is spellbinding enough to make even the most hardened atheist question things "a little." A zenith in architectural history.

Galata Tower *(Büyükhendek Sokak Sishane; Tel 0212/245-11-60; 8:30am-8pm daily; 1,000,000TL):* OK, close down that cheesy restaurant upstairs, and turn this 14th-century Genovese reconstruction, with its panoramic view, into an international club for the new millennium. Try not to get too carried away with the view and attempt to fly off the top with attached wings (as happened once in the 17th century).

Kariye Camii Müzesi *(Kariye Camii Sokak, Edirnekapi; Tel 0212/631-92-41; Bus 86 from Eminonu; 9am-4pm, closed Wed; 1,000,000TL):* A bit far from everything else, outside the old city wall, this museum is worth it for the Roman mosaics, paintings, and frescoes depicting the superstars of Christianity.

Topkapi Sarayi *(Sarayiçi, Sultanahmet; Tel 0212/512-04-80; 1,500,000TL, a million more for the harem):* Just a few minutes north of the archeological museum, this palace has room after room of spectacular treasures. Back then, it was the Sultan's sinful duo of the Harem and the Treasury, where he kept his women and his money.

Turkish and Islamic Arts Museum *(At Meydani 46, Sultanahmet; Tel 0212/518-18-05; Tram to Sultanahmet; 9am-4:30pm Tue-Sun; 1,000,000TL):* This museum, just south of the Sultanahmet (Blue Mosque) tram stop, gives a glimpse of nomadic life using stuffed mannequins. Next, please.

Yerebatan Sarayi *(Yerebatan Cad. 13, Sultanahmet; Tel 0212/522-12-59; 9am-5:30pm, closed Tue; 1,000,000TL):* The entrance to this 6th-century underground cavern is across the street from Ayasofya.

Soothing Sufi music echoing off the still water and the seductive lighting make the descent into the "Sunken Palace" an ideal environment for making out.

Blue Mosque *(Sultanahmet; Open daily 9am-6pm; Free admission):* One of the final examples of classical Ottoman architecture, this grand-daddy of a mosque was completed in 1617, after just over six and a half years of work. The overall effect is one of great harmony, grace, and power—it's impossible to walk away from this building unaffected.

modification

For your urgent piercing, body painting, henna, and dreadlock needs, **Lotus Art Factory** *(Sadri Alisik Sokak 16, Idris Bey Han 30, Beyoğlu; 11am-8pm Mon-Sat; V, MC)* is a fun spot. The staff here is patient with those undecided about their signature. For the more committed, **Indian Tattoo & Body Art Studio** *(Moda Cad., Leylek Sokak 6, Kadiköy; Tel 0216/449-04-54; 12-9pm daily; No credit cards)* offers very professional tattoo service. In Istanbul, tattoos go way back to the wild sailors coming into port, and now the youth deem them as sexy as ever. But the artist here will not do your "Winona Forever" if you show up under the influence: over-caffeinated, drunk, or in love (really).

great outdoors

To many of the city's inhabitants, athletic activity is restricted to the occasional long jump from the ferry before it touches the dock—on days when *lodos* (the city's southwest wind) hits, people get especially lethargic. Istanbul's body—both the land and the water—has been severely battered in the last few decades. A few hours' drive away, however, nature is at its best with trekking, diving, and caving opportunities. Get a copy of an *Istanbul Map of Culture and Arts* for info on organized weekend trips, a number of which are run by neo-hippie travel agencies located on Mis Sokak, off Istiklal Street.

Hills, forests, rivers, and the awesome Black Sea are for the enjoying within an hour's drive from the city in **Riva** *(Bus 137 from Beykoz)*, where villagers rent out small rowboats so you can take a peaceful ride down small creeks and lose yourself in the landscape.

Back in the city, **Mia Skate Park** *(Kennedy Cad. Yedikule Sahil Yolu; Tel 0212/529-27-80)* has one of the very few ramps in the country. A mostly inexperienced yet enthusiastic in-line and a smaller (and just as inexperienced) skateboard crowd gather at this private park. Of course, teenagers dominate the scene. There are in-line hockey pickup games in **Besiktas Square** *(right behind the ferry docks)* every Sunday, and sometimes national players show up. Such activities can't penetrate the mainstream, however: This is a football (soccer)-crazed city. **Fenerbahçe** *(Between Bagat Cad. and Recep Peker Cad., Fenerbahce; Tel 0216/345-09-40; Dolmus from Taksim (next to AKM) to Fenerbahce Stadium; Matches played Sat, Sun Sept-June)* is the country's most notorious team because of its loyal all-or-nothing fans. For most of the spectators, the weekly game is their only opportunity to unleash their inner Mr. Hyde. You can call the club the week of the game to reserve tickets for pickup at the stadium, but most people just buy them the day of the game. Watching a game (and watching those watching the game) in the Fenerbahce Stadium is a sociological study in itself.

STUff

You can load up on gifts for little money, but don't try to take a real antique out of the country—it's a serious crime. For more information on antiques and the laws associated with their purchase, take a look at the article called "The Eternal Beauty of Orientalism" posted at *http://cobe.idbsu. edu/wam/istanbul/dispatch.htm.*

▶▶BAZAAR

Another (unofficial) crime is to forego haggling in the bazaars. **Kapal-içarsi** *(Tram to Çemberlitas; 9am-7pm Mon-Sat)*, a covered bazaar with some 4,000 shops, has millions of souvenirs that'll prove to the folks back home that you actually came all the way here. This is Tourist Central, so there's a kind of pseudo-authenticity to some of the goods sold in this maze, but if you want to snoop for rugs, there's plenty here. On Tuesdays, head for a totally local scene at **Sali Pazari**. Cross to Kadiköy by ferry and start walking up Söğütlüçesme Street—you can't miss it. Thousands flock to this outdoor bazaar, set up in a six-block area between Kurbagalidere and Kadiköy Acibadem streets. The street sellers here are flat-out hilarious—these men will wear woman's panties over their heads while singing their aria-like pitches to deal-seeking housewives.

The district called **Çukurcuma** *(Right by Galatasaray Lycée, go down the hill on Yeniçarsi St., then left on Çukurcuma St.)* has a calmer vibe. People come here for great buys on anything from furniture to props used in old Turkish movies. It's a good place to get lost in time.

Pedestrian passageways lined with shops are called *pasaj.* **Aznavur Pasaji** *(Istiklal Cad. 212, Beyoglu)* has shops for flower children, vinyl detectives, and comic book junkies. **Atlas Pasaji** *(Istiklal Cad. 209, Beyoglu)* is a little more polished. At the entrance, on the right side is **Surreal** *(Atlas Pasaji 8; Tel 0212/292-43-33; 11am-8pm Mon-Sat; No credit cards)*, owned by a former belly dancer. Despite the exotic connotations, she's just a regular girl who opened up a place for club kids. Take your pick from hair dyes, polyester satin shirts, and plastic or silver accessories. Some of the goods are castaways from local pop stars. In the same *pasaj* is a small shop selling Tibetan incense, pipes, bongs, filters, and other paraphernalia. Retro seekers should take a peek at **Cav's** *(Kadife Sokak 6, Kadiköy; Tel 0216/330-42-67; 1-8pm daily; V, MC)* for vintage clothes from the '30s to the '90s and new stuff from Southeast Asia.

▶▶BOUND

There are three bookstores in Beyoglu. The loud **Mephisto** *(Istiklal Cad. 173; Tel 0212/293-19-09; 10am-10pm Mon-Sat; V, MC)* fills up with the before- and after-movie crowd. In addition to leftist books, it

fashion

Making a massive generalization, Turkish guys are Zappa-like gentlemen who look like they shower with Rogaine every morning and match their black body hair with black leather jackets. A lot of them prefer close-cropped cuts or the bald look. Platform shoes are back (for some reason…) for women, and capri pants are the new fashion. Unkempt looks are out. The young give much attention to their clothing but are amateurs in creating their individual styles. There's a lot of reliance on and display of brand names. So many people have silver rings, it's hard to tell who's engaged and who's not. One cool thing is that henna wearing is spreading, and folks are learning to apply it themselves.

sells CDs and alternative magazines that most newsstands do not care to carry—most, however, are in Turkish.

Robinson Crusoe *(Istiklal Cad. 389; Tel 0212/293-69-68; 9am-9pm Mon-Sat, 10am-9pm Sun; AE, V, MC)* is a classy place that concentrates on foreign-language publications, so it has what travelers need: maps of the city in many languages, recent newspapers from all over the world, and a bilingual staff.

Another place full of English books, **Literatur Bookshop** *(Istiklal Cad. 133, Beyoglu; Tel 0212/249-28-29; 9:30am-8pm Mon-Sat; V, MC)*, caters more to the academic crowd—not too many other places in town have an oceanography wing.

To find a concentration of secondhand bookshops, take a peek at the basement of **Moda Sinemasi** *(Bahariye Cad. 53, Kadiköy; Tel 0216/337-01-28;)*, a theater that shows art-house films. In the shops downstairs you'll find some vinyl, old *Life* magazines, truly antique books, some first-edition prints, Turkish and English pulp fiction, and penniless college students selling their grandfather's literary collection for grilled-cheese money.

▶▶HOT COUTURE

Upscale stores are concentrated in the Nisantasi area and along Bagdat Street. For classy, shameless, consumerist mall action, go to the biggest mall in Europe, **Akmerkez** *(Nispetiye Cad., Etiler; Tel 0212/282-01-70; Bus 59R, 59H, 59UL, 59UC from Taksim to Nispetiye; 10am-10pm daily; www.akmerkez.com.tr)*. The food court has all the junk food you'd find in North America. A favorite of models, the huge **Vakkorama** *(Osmanli Sokak 13, Taksim; Tel 0212/251-15-71; 10am-8pm daily; www.vakko rama.com.tr; AE, V, MC)* has hipster apparel, a fitness salon, an Internet

12 hours in istanbul

1. **Istiklal Caddesi:** Stroll along this pedestrian street from Taksim and take in the neo-Gothic churches, cafes, consulates, cinemas, and gaggles of people walking and talking. **Pano** [see *eats*, below] is a cheap wine-and-dine place come dinnertime.

2. **Back in time:** Archaic, Hellenistic, Roman, Byzantine, Ottoman—pretty much all the cultures that made this city find their place in **Arkeoloji Müzeleri** [see *culture zoo*, above]. On an autumn afternoon, the garden cafe makes you want to be a poet.

3. **Merry Ferry:** Cross to the other side (Asian side) just for the hell of it. Act incognito: Have some tea and *simit* (a savory roll covered with sesame seeds) on the boat while gazing to the horizon and beyond.

4. **20:** This underground club [see *club scene*, above] is the epitome of warehouse after-hours letting-it-all-hang-out. Home to a nocturnal, visceral, mixed crowd of homo sapiens.

5. **Aganigi Naganigi:** During the day the Sirkeci area by the train station is one of the busiest spots in the world. Walk over to its

cafe, and a ticket booth for concerts in town. For the brand fetishist, here's the lowdown on where your designer friends live in Istanbul: **Tommy Hilfiger** *(Bagdat Cad. 493, Suadiye; Tel 0216/356-27-73; 10am-8pm Mon-Sat; AE, V, MC),* **Gucci** *(Abdi Ipekçi Cad. 41, Maçka; Tel 0212/225-20-80; 10am-7pm Mon-Sat; AE, V, MC),* **Wolford** *(Tesvikiye Cad. 71, Tesvikiye; Tel 0212/261-75-52; 10am-7pm Mon-Sat; AE, V, MC),* and **DKNY** *(Bostan Sokak 4, Tesvikiye; Tel 0212/240-32-92; 10am-7:30pm Mon-Sat; AE, V, MC).*

EATS

Dear Weight Watchers, I was doing well on my diet-tuna salad three times a day. Then I stepped onto the streets of "Isnackbul." Thousands of kiosks and street carts with fresh fish sandwiches, luscious fruit, sesame rolls, corn on the cob, pistachio nuts, milk puddings. I couldn't help but try traditional Turkish foods like grape leaves stuffed with meat and rice, eggplant and artichokes cooked in olive oil, fried lamb shanks, cabbage in tomato sauce, and puff pastries with meat kebabs and vegetable fillings. Street food is cheap, relatively clean, eclectic, and accessible all day...temptation is everywhere. I'm going crazy! What do I do? The only answer is: Eat.

▶▶**CHEAP**

Sometimes you need that cafeteria-style fix: Beyoglu's **Borsa** *(Taksim Sq.; Tel 0212/252-33-22; 7:30am-midnight daily; 1-2,000,000TL per entree; V, MC)* offers traditional Turkish food and light alcohol. Take your tray spice bazaar, and look over the "natural Via-gras." Funny-sounding *Aganigi naganigi* is mild slang for sexual intercourse in Turkish.

6. **Quintessential Bosphorus:** Take a walk or jog on the European side of the Bosphorus shore, from **Rumelihisar** (*Bus 40 from Taksim to Rumeli-hisar*) northward. Buy some fish (fresh from one of the many fishing boats) and some bread on the shore to finish you off.

7. **Galata Tower:** One of the best views of the city. Pay tribute to the guy (Hazerfan Ahmet Çelebi) who glided with giant wings from the top of this tower to the Asian side. As a reward for his scientific and courageous achievement, he was jailed by the Sultan.

8. **Shop till you...: Tesvikiye** (*New Metro from Taksim Sq. to Tesvikiye*) [see *stuff,* below] provides a high-rent option for shopping. Italian-style bars around the area give you a jolt of espresso when you're ready to drop.

and gather in whatever you like. Then you may trade dishes with other travelers and students eating here.

Catty-cornered from **Hayal Kahvesi** [see *live music scene,* above], **Umut Ocakbasi** (*Hasnun Galip Cad. 6, Beyoglu; Tel 0212/245-50-05; 9:30am-midnight Mon-Sat; 400,000TL per shish kebab; No credit cards*) is a cool kebab joint catering to a blue-collar after-work crowd, blended with I-am-in-touch-with-the-people commies. In keeping with the spirit of the place, the boss hussles with the rest of the wait staff to get your *çöp sis* (small shish kebabs) hot. Just don't drink too much *raki* [see *lion's milk,* above] and start poking someone's eyeballs out. Upstairs, they'll let you cook your meat yourself on an open fire pit.

There's more variety at **Çiya** (*Güneslibahçe Sokak 48, Kadiköy; Tel 0216/336-30-13; 9am-10pm daily; 1-3,000,000TL per entree; V, MC*), but no menus. Go to the shop window and point at what you want. Try the hummus and some *kazandibi* (white pudding with a browned bottom layer baked in an oven). The otherwise friendly waiters won't tell you what kind of herbs and spices they use, so don't ask, just eat.

▶▶**DO-ABLE**

Right across from the British Consulate is the Greek wine house **Pano** (*Hamalbasi Cad. 26, Galatasaray; Tel 0212/292-66-64; 9am-2am daily; 1 million lira per appetizer; No credit cards*), in business (on and off) for more than a century. It was once used as a setting for many cheesy old Turkish movies and was a favorite watering hole of alcoholics. Today it draws upper-middle-class twentysomethings with a full range of appetizers, like fried calamari and *haydari* (thickened yogurt with garlic and dill), and table wine that's well above average.

In contrast, the nearby **Nuh'un Ambari** *(Yeniçarsi Cad. 54, Beyoglu; Tel 0212/292-92-72; Shop open 9am-9pm, cafe noon-9pm Mon-Sat; www.dhkd.org; 2-4,000,000TL per entree; V, MC)* is pretty new to the scene. Operated by the "Society for the Protection of Nature," they serve crunchy alternatives like organic dried fruit, a lot of wheat breads and pastries, herbal teas, etc.

The shop section sells soaps, breads, and posters that say "Stop me, I need to hug a tree."

Do whatever you like, just don't leave this town without eating fish by the sea. Nowhere else in the world have I seen so many fish restaurants side by side. The one with the best views is **Güzel Yer** *(Telli Baba Ustü 21, Rumelikavagi; Tel 0212/242-22-19; Bus 25A from Besiktas to Rume-likavagi; Noon-10:30pm daily; About 7,000,000TL per meal; V, MC).* Don't expect or request special sauces on your fish—let the fish speak for itself. After dinner take the 8:40 ring ferry to the Asian side (to Anadolukavagi), hang around in this village for half an hour, then ride the same ferry to Sariyer. From there, take the minibus to the nightspots in Taksim. During the half-hour ride, as the fish slowly decomposes in your stomach, pure happiness should pump into your bloodstream. Now you can build on that with (more) alcohol.

▶▶**SPLURGE**

Vogue *(Spor Cad. 92, BJK Plaza A blok, Akaretler; Tel 0212/227-25-45; Bus 30B to Akaret; 10am-2am daily; 4-10,000,000TL per entree; AE, V, MC)* is the sole occupant of the 13th floor of a business complex. This trendy, minimalist fusion spot makes excellent use of mirrors and steel. Reserve ahead, or the men in black downstairs will reduce your self-esteem to the size of a Cheerio. The idea here is to make you feel you're in Manhattan and it works, with inventive entrees, a good selection of wines, and desserts that cater to the eye and tongue. Go on a Thursday night, bar night, when, after dinner, hipsters let their bodies mo-o-ove to the music while sipping cocktails (the best margaritas in town). Open for Sunday brunch.

crashing

The law of supply and demand dictates the price of accommodations, which, by the way, is often given in US$. Especially during the winter months or when tourism goes into a cyclical downturn, I'm begging you, PLEASE PLEASE PLEASE negotiate: you might get up to 40 per-cent off and earn yourself some respect to boot. Turks admire visitors who have mastered the art of the deal. By the way, don't you believe the cabbie who tells you mouth-watering tales about the prices at his brother-in-law's carpet shop...oops, make that hotel. The Cankurtaran area, a couple of blocks from Sultanahmet Square, with its cobblestone streets and hostels/pensions left and right, has a village-y feel during the day. In the evening, you can do some mingling, and perhaps find Euro

down and out

In Istanbul, 12 million strangers compete daily for scarce space and any kind of freebies that may go with it. The artistically curious should pay a visit to **Istanbul Resim ve Heykel Müzesi** (*Dolmabahçe Cad., Akaretler, Besiktas; Tel 0212/261-42-98; 10am-4:30pm Wed-Sun*), a free-admission modern art museum that concentrates mostly on student works. It might be a little touristy, but what the hey, take a boat trip along the **Bosphorus**. On weekdays, trips originating from **Ortaköy** or **Kadiköy** cost only half a million lira. Although the music and sound system on the boats really suck, for disaster lovers there could be a bonus: About twice a year, some big ship coming from the Black Sea loses control in the unpredictable currents and goes aground, occasionally hitting one of the US$10 million houses on shore. There's a growing local protest movement aimed at prohibiting ships with dangerous cargo from entering these waters—a Valdez in the middle of Istanbul would have a disastrous effect. A little south of the Bosphorus, in the sea of Marmara, are numerous islands half an hour away by ferry (1 million lira one-way). Horse carriages and donkeys are the nostalgic forms of transport on these islands—with good bargaining, and pretty cheap rides. A couple of hours at the local bath or *hamam* (two million lira at non-touristy ones) can be an exercise in pain endurance. This is not a spa experience, however, and is locally considered either touristy or a place for people with no showers at home. A popular one is **Galatasaray Hamami**, near **Galatasaray Lycée** in mid-**Istiklal Street**. The guy or gal massaging you will turn your sore spots into flowing dough—you won't be able to decide if you feel rejuvenated or beaten down. If all else fails, the light and laser shows held on summer nights at 9pm in Sultanahmet Square may bring some color to your broke life.

boys and girls to eat/drink/hang out with. The advantage of staying in the Beyoglu area is that you're within walking distance of bars. The choice is yours. Check out ***www.hotelsofturkey.com*** for further crashing info/reservations in Istanbul. All the places listed below serve a free, tasty, typical Turkish breakfast of tea, black olives, eggs, white cheese, honey, and bread.

▶▶CHEAP

Orient Youth Hostel (*Akbiyik Cad. 13, Sultanahmet; Tel 0212/517-94-93; Front desk open 24 hours, www.hostels.com/orienthostel $3.50 dorms, $10 quads, $20 double, $35 deluxe; YHA accepted; V, MC*) is a good old hostel with a touch of the Orient (read free belly dancer and water pipe nights). The mentality is a fine balance between "It's spring break—beer me, dude" and "Let's hit the sack." Which is possible, thanks to the almost soundproof bar on the loggia. The guys who run this place go the extra mile, like picking you up from the bus station at 3am. There are some classic hostel drawbacks, like the uncooperative showers and mattresses in the corridors (yes, some people sleep in the corridors during busy times). These are compensated for by the safety and friendliness of the place, though.

Hotel Plaza (*Siraselviler Cad., Aslanyatagi Sokak 19-21, Cihangir; Tel 0212/249-79-89; $20 one person, $35 two people; V, MC*) is in reality a quiet hostel, popular with foreign students fresh out of high school who are in town for Turkish language programs. It has spacious quads with a view and a sink in addition to a couple of doubles with bathrooms. Hotel Plaza's best feature is its location: When you roll out of **Roxy** [see *club scene*, above] grotesquely drunk, your flavor of the night on your arm, you're only a stone's throw from bed.

The American sweetheart lady who owns **Hotel Empress Zoe** (*Akbiyik Cad., Adliye Sokak 10, Sultanahmet; Tel 0212/518-25-04; $55 single, $75 double, $90 triple, discount for cash/travelers checks; www.emzoe.com; V, MC*), near the Blue Mosque, has created an atmosphere that appeals more to couples than to frat brothers. She also provides a rare commodity in Istanbul: good filter coffee. Funky Greek art on the walls, queen-size beds, and especially the tranquil patio adjacent to an old, non-functioning *hamam* (Turkish bath) make me say...it's lovely.

Reserve ahead and look semi-presentable when you ring the doorbell of **Entes Apart Hotel** (*Istiklal Cad., Ipek Sokak 19, Beyoglu; Tel 0212/293-22-08; On the Taksim end of Istiklal St. behind the Lale movie theater; $400 per week, same price for 1-4 people*). They're very welcoming to young travelers here, as long as you don't invite the new headbanger friends you met last night for breakfast. Each teeny "apart" has a bedroom, a bathroom with tub, and a living room with a pullout bed, satellite TV, and a kitchen. All brand new. In theory, you can cram four people into one room. In practice, you might get to know each other better than you want to.

Although **Büyük Londra Oteli** (*Mesrutiyet Cad. 117, Tepebasi; Tel 0212/245-06-70; $60 single, $75 double, $100 triple; AE, V, MC*) or "Grand Hotel de Londres," is more than a century old, this is not a "look how cute we are" boutique hotel. Au contraire—due to lack of funds for renovation, this Beyoglu classic looks as if not much has changed since the day it opened (yes, it has hot water). A traveler told me that she once sat in the hotel's deserted Victorian lounge all night and imagined the parade of ladies and gents from the swinging times of Pera, the old name for this neighborhood, occupied by European diplomats a century ago.

▶▶**SPLURGE**

While the **Nippon Hotel** (*Topçu Cad. 10, Taksim; Tel 0212/254-99-00; $140 single, $160 double, $200 triple; AE, V, MC*) is in a nondescript

wired

Yagmur Cybercafe *(Seyh Bender Sokak 18, Asmalimescit, Beyoglu; Tel 0212/292-30-20; 11am-11pm daily; www. citlembik.com.tr; 1,000,000TL an hour; No credit cards)* serves a fine iced tea, and good, mean Turkish coffee. What else? A color scanner, laser printers, 10 computers, English-speaking young staff, and proximity to Babylon [see *live music scene*, above]. On a humid summer day though, **Surfer's Internet Cafe** *(Kadife Sokak 24, Göynük Apt., Kadiköy; Tel 0216/330-59-54; 10am-1am daily; 600,000TL an hour; No credit cards)* offers a piece of technology that's more important than two thousand and one megahertz: AC. This cafe's proximity to bars, cinemas, and fast-food joints makes it a convenient spot for late teens checking on their Hotmail.

Here's a list of websites of interest on Istanbul:
www.turkey.org, www.istanbullife.net, www.beyogluweb.com, www.milliyet.com, www.istanbulcityguide.com, www.cimko.com.tr/istanbul.htm, www.boun.edu.tr/istanbul/history.html.

building, inside it offers four-star comfort and reliability. The thing is, most of the clientele are groups who don't pay for themselves, like movie crews on location and USC students. There's a decent restaurant on the premises and a few good Japanese restaurants around the block. Guests are invited across the street to Otel Taksim Plaza (same ownership) to use the brand-new spa and pool.

need to know

Currency Exchange The **Turkish lira (TL)** is the local currency. There are hundreds of **currency-exchange bureaus** in town, offering a one-percent spread between buy and sell. The lira is devalued on average 1 percent a week, so locals change money often. A MasterCard or Visa will let you access the ATMs which are sprouting like mushrooms all over Istanbul.

Tourist Information Ministry of Tourism offices are located in the international arrivals area at **Atatürk Airport** *(Tel 0212/573-41-36)* and at the central train station, Sirkeci Gar *(Tel 0212/511-58-88)*. There's also a **Directorate of Tourism** *(Mesrutiye Cad. 57; Tel 0212/243-29-28)* office in Beyoglu. There are digital guides on the piers at Kadikoy, Usküdar, Besiktas, and Karaköy. A 24-hour **Tourist Police** *(Yerebatan Cad. 6, Sultanahmet; Tel 0212/527-45-03; Located 50 yards from Ayasofya)* office is located in Sultanahmet.

Public Transportation For information on **Metro/tram lines**, call *(Tel 0212/568-99-70)*; for ferries, *(Tel 0212/244-42-33)*; seabuses, *(Tel 0216/362-04-44)*. The *Akbil*, a prepaid fare card, is sold wherever there is a major intra-city bus station—that is, in the neighborhoods of Besiktas, Taksim, Kadiköy, and Mecidiyekoy—and can be used for all forms of public transportation. Buses, Metros, and the tram use tickets; ferries and seabuses use tokens. All five of them do a good job on punctuality, considering how full of surprises the traffic is. Unfortunately, none of them publish maps detailing the routes.

American Express Turk Ekspres *(Cumhuriyet Cad. 91, 2nd floor, Taksim; Tel 0212/230-15-15; 9am-6pm Mon-Fri)*, five blocks north of Taksim Square, deals only with lost cards and check inquiries. You can't pay your bills here.

Health and Emergency Emergency: *112*; Police: *155*; Fire: *110*. **American Hospital** *(Guzelbahçe Sokak, Nisantasi; Tel 0212/311-20-00)*, **Taksim Ilkyardim Hastanesi,** or "Emergency Hospital"*(Siraselviler Cad., Taksim; Tel 0212/252-43-00)*, here about half the doctors speak English.

Pharmacies Saglik Eczanesi *(Siraselviler Cad. 141, Taksim; 243-17-77)*, **Ece Eczanesi** *(Güzelbahçe Sokak 37, Nisantasi; Tel 0212/240-46-25)*.

Telephone Country code: *90*; city codes: *(212)* Europe, *(216)* Asia; local information: *118*; international operator: *115*. You can get **local phone cards** at a chain of stores called **PTT**, **newspaper stands**, or **some guy who sells them by the pay phone** (at a 10 percent markup). **AT&T:** *00-800-12277*, **MCI:** *00-800-11177*, **Sprint:** *00-800-14477*.

Airport Atatürk **International Airport** *(Yesilköy; Tel 0212/663-64-00)* is approximately 15 miles southwest of town. To get into town, take a **taxi** *(2,500,000TL)* to **Yesilkoy train station**. Get on the **Sirkeci** train. Get off at **Cankurtaran** to stay in **Sultanahmet**. A word: Don't follow the station list on top of the (somewhat) sliding doors. These trains were formerly used for another route, and the list is for the old route. There's also a **shared minibus** service called *Havas* from the airport. They have offices in the **International Terminal** *(to the right when you get out of customs, with a green logo)* and will beam you to Taksim in less than an hour for about 1.5 millionTL.

Trains Sirkeci Gar *(Tel 0212/527-00-50)* is the main station, and **Haydarpasa Gar** *(Tel 0216/348-80-20, 0216/366-04-75, 0216/366-20-63)*, on the Asian side, is 10 minutes west of Kadiköy on foot. From **Sirkeci** train station, take a *dolmus* (minibus) or a taxi (1,500,000TL) to **Taksim**.

Buses Out of the city Both bus lines, **Varan Turizm** *(Inönü Cad. 29, Gumussuyu; Tel 0212/251-74-74)* and **Ulusoy Seyahat** *(Inönü Cad. 59, Gumussuyu; Tel 0212/252-37-87)* leave from both stations, but **Esenler Terminali** *(20 minutes by tram from Sultanahmet; Tel*

0212/658-05-05) is by far the main terminal for buses out of the city, more so than **Harem Terminali** *(Car ferry from Sirkeci; Tel 0216/333-37-63)*. Buying tickets at the **Taksim** offices [see above] for each line is recommended; free shuttle buses will run you from here to the stations. From the **Esenler bus station**, take the tram to **Sultanahmet**. **Sirkeci Gar** (train station) is the last stop for both the tram and the train.

Laundry **Active Laundry** *(Divanyolu Cad. Dr. Eminpasa Sokak 14, Sultanahmet; Tel 0212/513-75-85; From Ayasofya toward the Grand Bazaar, on a tiny side street on the right below Arsenal Youth Hostel; 1kg laundry washed for 500,000TL, dried for 250,000TL; 8am-10pm daily)* will do the job in 3 to 4 hours.

Travel Info

Sources of Visitor Information

TOURIST OFFICES

Obviously, start with the European tourist offices in your own country; for a complete list, see the Appendix. If you aren't sure which countries you want to visit, send for a free, information-packed booklet called *Planning Your Trip to Europe*, revised annually by the 28-nation European Travel Planner *(P.O. Box 1754, New York, NY 10185, 800/816-7530; www.visiteurope.com)*.

THE INTERNET

Aside from the specific websites we've included in this book [see the *wired* section of each chapter], **Yahoo** *(www.yahoo.com)*, **Excite** *(www.excite.com)*, **Lycos** *(www.lycos.com)*, **Infoseek** *(www.infoseek.com)*, and the other major Internet indexing sites all have subcategories for travel, country/regional information, culture, and other fun stuff. One of the best hotlists for travel and destination information is Excite's **City.Net** *(www.city.net)*.

Other good clearinghouse sites for info are **Microsoft's Expedia** *(www.expedia.com)*, **Travelocity** *(www.travelocity.com)*, the **Internet Travel Network** *(www.itn.com)*, **TravelWeb** *(www.travelweb.com)*, and the **European Travel Commission** *(www.visiteurope.com)*.

TRAVEL BOOKSTORES

If you live outside a large urban area, you can order maps or travel guides from bookstores specializing in mail- or phone-order service. Some of these are **Book Passage** *(51 Tamal Vista Blvd., Corte Madera, CA 94925;*

800/321-9785 or 415/927-0960; www.bookpassage.com); and **Forsyth Travel Library** *(1780 E. 131st St., P.O. Box 48080, Kansas City, MO 64148-0800; 800/FORSYTH; www.forsyth.com)*.

Canadians can contact **Ulysses Travel Bookshop** *(4176 rue St-Denis, Montréal, PQ H2W 2M5; 514/843-9447; www.ulysses.ca)* or *(101 Yorkville Ave., Toronto, ON M5R 1C1; 416/323-3609)*.

entry requirements and customs

PASSPORTS

Protect your passport! Keep it in an inconspicuous, inaccessible place like a money belt. If you lose your passport, visit the nearest consulate of your native country as soon as possible for a replacement. You should also make a xerox of your passport (and visa, if you have one) and keep it with you, *separate* from your passport. Passport applications are downloadable from the Internet sites listed below.

U.S. Citizens If you're applying for a first-time passport, you need to do it in person at one of 13 passport offices throughout the U.S.; a federal, state, or probate court; or a major post office (though not all post offices accept applications; call the number below to find the ones that do). You need to present a certified birth certificate as proof of citizenship, and you better bring along your driver's license, state or military ID, and social security card as well. You also need two identical passport-sized photos (2 in. by 2 in.), taken at any corner photo shop (but not one of those cheapo strip photos from a photo-vending machine).

For those of you over 15, a passport is valid for 10 years and costs $60 ($45 plus a $15 handling fee); for those 15 and under, it's valid for 5 years and costs $40. If you're over 15 and have a valid passport that was issued within the past 12 years, you can renew it by mail and bypass the $15 handling fee. Make sure you allow plenty of time before your trip to apply; processing normally takes 3 weeks but can take longer during busy periods (especially spring). For general information, call the **National Passport Agency** *(202/647-0518)*. To find your regional passport office, call the **National Passport Information Center** *(900/225-5674; http://www.travel.state.gov)*.

Canadian Citizens You can pick up a passport application at one of 28 regional passport offices or most travel agencies. The passport is valid for 5 years and costs CAN$60. Kids under 16 may be included on a parent's passport but need their own to travel unaccompanied by the parent. Applications, which must be accompanied by two identical passport-sized photographs and proof of Canadian citizenship, are available at travel agencies throughout Canada or from the central **Passport Office, Department of Foreign Affairs and International Trade** *(Ottawa, Ont. K1A 0G3; 800/567-6868; www.dfaitmaeci. gc.ca/passport)*. Processing takes 5 to 10 days if you apply in person, or about 3 weeks by mail.

U.K. Citizens As a member of the European Union you need only an identity card, not a passport, to travel to other EU countries. But if you already have a passport, it's always best to carry it. To pick up an application for a regular 10-year passport (the Visitor's Passport has been abolished), visit your nearest passport office, major post office, or travel agency. You can also contact the **London Passport Office** *(020/7271-3000; www.open.gov.uk/ukpass/ukpass.htm)*. Passports are £21 for adults and £11 for children under 16.

Irish Citizens You can apply for a 10-year passport *(IR£45)* at the **Passport Office** *(Setanta Centre, Molesworth Street Dubline 2; 01/671-1633; www.irlgov.ie/iveagh/foreignaffairs/services)*. Those under 18 must apply for a 3-year passport *(IR£10)*. You can also apply at 1A South Mall, Cork *(021/272-525)* or over the counter at most main post offices.

Australian Citizens Apply at your local post office or passport office or search the government Web site *(www.dfat.gov.au/passports)*. Passports for adults are A$126, under 18 A$63.

New Zealand Citizens You can pick up a passport application at any travel agency or Link Centre. For more info, contact the **Passport Office** *(P.O. Box 805, Wellington; 0800/225-050)*. Passports for adults are NZ$80, under 16 NZ$40.

VISAS

Most of the countries covered in this guide don't require visas for U.S. or Canadian citizens for stays shorter than 90 days, but please note the specific requirements for entry into the following countries.

U.S. Citizens Czech Republic: A valid passport is required for a stay of no more than 30 days. **Hungary**: No visa is required for a stay of up to 90 days, but visitors must have both a valid passport and a valid return trip or onward ticket, as well as proof of sufficient funds. **Poland**: No visa is required, but visitors must have passports that will be valid at least one year past the date of entry. **Portugal**: Visitors can visit up to 60 days without a visa. **Turkey**: Visitors are required to have a valid passport and visa. Visas can be obtained at Turkish border crossings or Turkish consulates. They are valid for 3 months, and there is a fee of $20.

Canadian Citizens Monaco: A passport that is valid for at least three months after date of entry is required for a stay of up to 90 days. In addition, Monaco also requires Canadians citizens to have a return trip or onward ticket **Turkey**: Visitors are required to have a valid passport and visa. Visas can be obtained at Turkish border crossings or Turkish consulates. They are valid for 3 months and there is a fee of US$45.

DRIVING PERMITS

Although a valid U.S. state driver's license is usually enough, it's a good idea to get an **International Driving Permit**, which costs $12 and can be obtained from any AAA branch if accompanied by two passport size photos.

CUSTOMS

U.S. citizens Returning U.S. citizens who've been away for 48 hours or more are allowed to bring back, once every 30 days, $400 worth of merchandise duty-free. You'll be charged 10% duty on the next $1,000 worth of purchases. Have your receipts handy. On gifts, the duty-free limit is $100. You can't bring fresh foodstuffs into the United States; but canned foods are okay. For more information, contact the **U.S. Customs Service** *(1301 Constitution Ave. (P.O. Box 7407), Washington, DC 20044; 202/927-6724)* and request the free pamphlet *Know Before You Go*. It's also available on the web *(www.customs.ustreas.gov)*.

U.K. citizens U.K. Citizens returning from a European Community (EC) country will go through a separate Customs Exit (called the "Blue Exit") especially for EC travelers. Basically, there's no limit on what you can bring back from an EC country, as long as the items are for personal use (this includes gifts), and you've already paid the necessary duty and tax. But customs law sets out some guidance levels. If you bring in more than these levels, you may be asked to prove that the goods are for your own use. Guidance levels on goods bought in the EC for your own use are 800 cigarettes, 200 cigars, 1kg smoking tobacco, 10 liters of spirits, 90 liters of wine (of this not more than 60 liters can be sparkling wine), and 110 liters of beer. Enough for at least a week or two. For more information, contact **HM Customs & Excise** *(Passenger Enquiry Point, 2nd Floor Wayfarer House, Great South West Road, Feltham, Middlesex, TW14 8NP; 020/8/910-3744; www.open.gov.uk)*.

U.K. citizens returning from a non-EC country have a customs allowance of: 200 cigarettes; 50 cigars; 250g of smoking tobacco; 2 liters of still table wine; 1 liter of spirits or strong liqueurs (over 22 % volume); 2 liters of fortified wine, sparkling wine or other liqueurs; 60cc (ml) perfume; 250cc (ml) of toilet water; and £145 worth of all other goods, including gifts and souvenirs. People under 17 don't have the tobacco or alcohol allowance. For more information, contact **HM Customs & Excise** [see above].

Canadian Citizens For a clear summary of Canadian rules, write for the booklet *I Declare*, issued by **Revenue Canada** *(2265 St. Laurent Blvd., Ottawa K1G 4KE; 613/993-0534)*. Canada allows its citizens a $750 exemption, and you're allowed to bring back duty-free 200 cigarettes, 2.2 pounds of tobacco, 40 imperial ounces of liquor, and 50 cigars. Plus, you're allowed to mail gifts to Canada from abroad at the rate of Can$60 a day, provided they're unsolicited and don't contain alcohol or tobacco (write on the package "Unsolicited gift, under $60 value"). All valuables should be declared on the Y-38 form before departure from Canada, including serial numbers of valuables you already own, such as expensive foreign cameras. Note: The $750 exemption can only be used once a year and only after an absence of 7 days.

Australian citizens The duty-free allowance in Australia is A$400 or, for those under 18, A$200. Personal property mailed back should be marked "Australian goods returned" to avoid payment of duty. Upon returning to Australia, citizens can bring in 250 cigarettes or 250 grams of loose tobacco, and 1,125ml of alcohol. Enough for a day or two. If you're returning with valuable goods you already own, such as foreign-made cameras, you should file a form B263. A helpful brochure, available from Australian consulates or Customs offices, is *Know Before You Go*. For more information, contact **Australian Customs Services** (*GPO Box 8, Sydney NSW 2001; 02/9213-20-00*).

New Zealand citizens The duty-free allowance for New Zealand is NZ$700. Citizens over 17 can bring in 200 cigarettes, or 50 cigars, or 250 grams of tobacco (or a mixture of all three if their combined weight doesn't exceed 250 grams); plus 4.5 liters of wine and beer, or 1.125 liters of liquor. New Zealand currency does not carry import or export restrictions. Fill out a certificate of export, listing the valuables you're taking out of the country; that way, you can bring them back without paying duty. Most questions are answered in a free pamphlet available at New Zealand consulates and Customs offices: *New Zealand Customs Guide for Travelers, Notice no. 4*. For more information, contact **New Zealand Customs** (*50 Anzac Ave., P.O. Box 29, Auckland; 09/359-66-55*).

money

Traveler's checks, while still the safest way to carry money, are going the way of the dinosaur. The aggressive evolution of international computerized banking and consolidated ATM networks has led to the triumph of plastic throughout Europe—even if cold cash is still the most trusted currency. Odds are you can saunter up to an ATM in the dinkiest Sicilian village with your bankcard or PIN-enabled Visa and get some local cash out of it. But never rely on credit cards and ATMs alone. Although most hotels and many restaurants throughout Europe accept plastic, smaller towns and cheaper places are still wary, and occasionally the phone lines and computer networks used to verify your card can go down and render your plastic useless. Always carry some local currency and some traveler's checks for insurance.

WHAT'S UP WITH THE EURO?

In 1999, the euro, the single European currency, was launched in Austria, Belgium, the Netherlands, Finland, France, Germany, Ireland, Italy, Luxembourg, Portugal, and Spain. The other countries covered in this guide, including Greece, England, Sweden, Denmark, and the Czech Republic, among others, are not under the euro umbrella. But for the time being, you'll still be trading in the old currency of all the countries covered—that is, the peseta for Spain, the escudo for Portugal, the lira for Italy, the deutsche mark for Germany, etc. While the actual paper notes and coins won't be introduced until January 1, 2002—and the various national currencies won't be fully phased out until July 1, 2002—banks and stock exchanges are obligated in the meantime to carry out all non-cash transactions in euros, and you can make your credit card purchases in euros. This allows you to more easily compare the cost of something in Paris to the same item's cost in Rome, without having to juggle conversion rates for francs, lira, and dollars. This is good news for travelers, and even better news for Europe's economic strength as their markets can now compete on an even footing. As 2002 approaches, you'll note that more and more European shops and restaurants and so forth will list prices in euros beside the prices in francs, pesetas, or whatever. At press time, the euro had fallen 12% since its introduction and had almost reached a 1:1 conversion rate with the American dollar.

The symbol of the euro is a stylized "E,", which actually looks like an upper-case "C" with a horizontal double bar through the middle; its official abbreviation is "Eur."

ATMS

Plus, Cirrus, and other networks work on many ATMs in Europe, giving you local currency and drawing it directly from your checking account. This is the fastest, easiest, and the least expensive way to change money. You take advantage of the bank's bulk exchange rate (better than anything you'll get on your own exchanging cash or traveler's checks) and, unless your home bank charges you for using a non-proprietary ATM, you won't have to pay a commission. Make sure the PINs on your bank- and credit cards will work in Europe; you usually need a four-digit code (six digits often won't work). Keep in mind that you're usually only able to access your checking account, not savings, from ATMs abroad.

Both the **Cirrus** *(800/424-7787; www.mastercard.com/atm)* and **Plus** *(800/843-7587; www.visa.com/atms)* networks have automated ATM locators that list the banks in each country that will accept your card. Or just search out any machine with your network's symbol emblazoned upon it. Europe is getting to be like America—a bank on virtually every

what TIME IS IT anyway

Based on U.S. Eastern Standard Time, Britain, Ireland, and Portugal are 5 hours ahead of New York City; Greece is 7 hours ahead of New York. The rest of the countries in this book are 6 hours ahead of New York. (Put simply: when it's noon in New York, it's 5pm in London and Lisbon; 6pm in Paris, Copenhagen, and Amsterdam; and 7pm in Athens.) The European countries now observe daylight saving time. The time change doesn't usually occur on the same day or in the same month as in the United States.

If you plan to travel to Ireland or continental Europe from Britain, keep in mind that the time will be the same in Ireland and Portugal, 2 hours later in Greece, and 1 hour later in the other countries in this guide.

corner—and increasingly, most are globally networked. You can also get a cash advance through Visa or MasterCard (contact the issuing bank to enable this feature and get a PIN), but note that the credit card company will start charging you interest immediately, and many have begun assessing a fee every time. American Express card cash advances are usually only available from AMEX offices, which you'll find in every European city.

CREDIT CARDS:

Most middle-bracket and virtually all first-class and deluxe hotels, restaurants, and shops in Europe accept major credit cards—American Express, Diners Club, MasterCard, and Visa (not Discover). Some budget establishments accept plastic, others don't. The most widely accepted cards these days are Visa and MasterCard, but it pays to carry American Express, too. Note that you can now often choose to charge credit card purchases at either the price in euros or in the local currency—since most European currencies are now locked together, the dollar amount will always come out the same, but it may help you comparison-shop.

TRAVELER'S CHECKS:

Most large banks sell traveler's checks, charging fees of 1 to 2 percent of the value of the checks. AAA members can buy American Express checks commission-free. Traveler's checks are great travel insurance since if you lose them—and have kept a list of their numbers (and a record of which ones were cashed) in a safe place separate from the checks themselves—you can get them replaced at no charge. Hotels and shops usually accept them, but you'll get a lousy exchange rate. Use traveler's checks to exchange for local currency at banks or American Express offices. Personal checks are next to useless in Europe.

American Express *(800/221-7282; www.americanexpress.com)* is one of the largest issuers of traveler's checks, and theirs are the most commonly accepted. They'll also sell checks to holders of certain types of American Express cards at no commission. **Thomas Cook** *(800/223-7373 in the U.S. and Canada, 020/7480-7226 in London, or 609/987-7300 collect from other parts of the world; www.thomascook.com)* issues MasterCard traveler's checks. **Citicorp** *(800/645-6556 in the U.S. and Canada, or 813/623-1709 collect from anywhere else in the world; www.citicorp.com)* and many other banks issue checks under their own name or under MasterCard or Visa. Get checks issued in dollar amounts (as opposed to, say, French francs) as they will be more widely accepted abroad.

WIRE SERVICES:

American Express MoneyGram *(Wadsworth St., Englewood, CO 80155; 800/926-9400),* will let friends back home to wire you money in an emergency in less than 10 minutes. Senders should call AMEX to learn the address of the closest outlet that handles MoneyGrams. Cash, credit card, or the occasional personal check (with ID) are acceptable forms of payment. AMEX's fee is $40 for the first $500 with a sliding scale for larger sums. The service includes a short telex message and a 3-minute phone call from sender to recipient. The beneficiary must present a photo ID at the outlet where the money is received.

CURRENCY EXCHANGE:

Although currency conversions in this guide [see *currency conversion chart* at the back of the book] were accurate at press time, European exchange rates fluctuate. For up-to-date rates, look in the business pages or travel section of a any major U.S. newspaper, check online at the **Universal Currency Converter** *(www.xe.net/currency)*, or call **Thomas Cook** [see *Traveler's Checks* above].

It's more expensive to purchase foreign currency in your own country than it is once you've reached your destination. But it's a good idea to arrive in Europe with a bit of the local currency—at least enough to get you from the airport to your hotel, so you can avoid the bad rates you'll get at airport currency exchanges. Bring along about $30 to $50 in the local currencies of every European city you'll be visiting (call around to the major branches of local banks in your hometown to find the best rate).

While traveling, either withdraw local currency from an ATM [see above] or convert your cash or traveler's checks at a bank whenever possible—banks invariably give better rates than tourist offices, hotels, travel agencies, or exchange booths. You lose money every time you make a transaction, so it's often better to convert large sums at once (especially in flat-fee transactions). The rates for converting traveler's checks are usually better than those for cash, but you get the best rates by withdrawing money from an ATM with your bank or credit card.

VALUE-ADDED TAX (VAT):

All European countries charge a Value-Added Tax (VAT) of 15 to 33 percent on goods and services—it's like a sales tax that's already included in the price. Rates vary from country to country, though the goal in EU countries is to arrive at a uniform rate of about 15 %. Citizens of non-EU countries can, as they leave the country, get back most of the tax on purchases (but not services) if they spend above a designated amount (usually $80 to $200) in a single store.

Regulations vary from country to country, so ask at the tourist office when you arrive to find out the procedure— also ask what percentage of the tax will be refunded, and if the refund will be given to you at the airport or mailed to you later. Look for a "Tax Free Shopping for Tourists" sign posted in participating stores. Get the necessary forms from the storekeeper, save all your receipts, and, if possible, keep the purchases in their original packages. Save all your receipts and VAT forms from each EU country to process all of them at the "Tax Refund" desk in the airport of the last country you'll be visiting before flying home (allow an extra 30 minutes or so at the airport to process forms).

phoning around

To make a phone call **from the United States to Europe**, dial the international access code, **011**, then the **country code** for the country you're calling, then the **city code** for the city you're calling, then the regular telephone number. For an operator-assisted call, dial **01**, then the country code, then the city code, then the regular telephone number; an operator will then come on line. See the *need to know* section of individual chapters for the specific country/city codes. One note: Copenhagen and all areas within Monaco have no city code, the code is built into all phone numbers.

The easiest and cheapest way to call home from abroad is with a **calling card**. On the road, you just dial a local access code (almost always free) and then punch in the number you're calling plus the calling-card number. If you're in a non touch-tone country, just wait for an English-speaking operator, who will put your call through. The *telephone* entry in the *need to know* for each city gives the access codes for that country. Your calling card will probably come with a wallet-sized list of local access numbers in each country. You can also call any one of those companies' numbers to make a **collect call** too; just dial it and wait for the operator.

Lucky for you that calling from the U.S. to Europe is much cheaper than the other way around, so you can make a legitimate case for friends and family call you at your hotel rather than you calling them. To dial direct back **to the US and Canada from Europe**, the international access code is often, but not always, 00; the country code is 1; and then you punch in the area code and number. For **Australia** and **New Zealand**, the access code is also 00, the country codes are 61 and 64, respectively.

when to go

The peak travel period and tourist **high season**—when all tourist facilities are strained—lasts from mid-May to mid-September, with the most tourists hitting the continent from mid-June to August. In general, this is the most expensive time to travel, except in Austria and Switzerland where prices are higher in winter, during the ski season. And since Scandinavian hotels depend on business clients instead of tourists, lower prices can often be found in the summer months when business clients vacation elsewhere, and a smaller number of travellers take over.

You'll find smaller crowds, relatively fair weather, and often lower prices at hotels in the **"shoulder seasons"**: Easter to mid-May and mid-September to mid-October. **Off-season** (except at ski resorts) is November to Easter, with the exception of the Christmas season (December 25 to January 6). Much of Europe, Italy especially, takes the month of August off, and August 15 to August 30 is vacation time for many locals, so expect the cities devoid of natives but packed beaches.

CLIMATE

United Kingdom and Ireland Everyone knows that it rains a lot in Great Britain and Ireland. Winters are rainier than summers; August and September to mid-October are the sunniest months. Summer daytime temperatures average in the low to mid-60s Fahrenheit, dropping to the 40s on winter nights. Ireland, whose shores are bathed by the Gulf Stream, has a milder climate and the most changeable weather (a dark, rainy morning can quickly turn into a sunny afternoon, and vice versa). The Scottish Lowlands have a climate similar to England's, but the Highlands are much colder, with storms and snow in winter.

Scandinavia Summer temperatures above the Arctic Circle average in the mid-50s, dropping to the mid-teens during the dark winters. In the south, summer temperatures average around 70°F, dropping to the 20s in winter. Fjords and even the ocean are often warm enough for summer swimming, but it rains a lot. Above the Arctic Circle, the sun shines 24/7 in midsummer, and there's semipermanent twilight in winter. Denmark's relatively mild by comparison, with moderate summer temperatures and damp and foggy winters, with temperatures in the mid-30s.

Northern Europe In the Netherlands, the weather is never extreme at any time of year. Summer temperatures average around 67°F; winter average is about 40°F. The climate is rainy, with the driest months from February to May. The climate of northern Germany is very similar, as is Belgium's—although they get more rain.

France and Germany The weather in Paris is approximately the same as in the U.S. Mid-Atlantic states, but like most of Europe, there's less extreme variation. In summer the temperature rarely goes above the mid-70s, except along the Riviera. Winters tend to be mild, averaging in the 40s (again, it's warmer in the Riviera). Germany's climate ranges from the moderate summers and chilly, damp winters in the north to the mild summers and very cold and sunny winters of the alpine south.

Eastern Europe In Budapest, temperatures can reach 80°F in August and 30°F in January. Winter is damp and chilly, spring is mild, and May and June are usually wet. The best weather is in the late summer through October. In Prague and Bohemia, summer months have an average temperature of 65°F but are the rainiest. January and February are usually sunny and clear, with temperatures around freezing.

Southern Europe Summers are hot in Italy, Spain, and Greece, (duh) with temperatures in the high 80s (Fahrenheit), or even higher in some parts of Spain. Along the Italian Riviera, summer and winter temperatures are mild, and except in the alpine regions, Italian winter temperatures rarely drop below freezing. The area around Madrid is dry and arid, and summers in Spain are coolest along the Atlantic coast. Seaside Portugal is very rainy but has a temperature range between 50°F and 75°F year-round. In Greece there's sunshine all year, and winters are usually mild, with temperatures around 50° to 55°F. The best times to visit Greece are mid-April to June and mid-September to the end of October, when the tourists go home.

SPECIAL-INTEREST VACATIONS

CYCLING Some of the best bicycle tours are conducted by the **Cyclists' Tourist Club** *(69 Meadrow, Godalming, Surrey, England GU7 3HS; 01483/417-217; www.ctc.org.uk)*. **Holland Bicycling Tours, Inc.** *(P.O. Box 6485, Thousand Oaks, CA 91359; tel 800/852-3258, fax 805/495-8601)* leads 8-day bicycle tours throughout Europe; **Experience Plus** *(800/685-4565; www.experienceplus.com)* runs bike tours across Europe; and **Cicilsmo Clas-**

sico *(13 Marathon St., Arlington, MA 02174; tel 800/866-7314, fax 781/641-1512; www.ciclismoclassico.com)* is an excellent outfit running tours of Italy.

HIKING Wilderness Travel *(1102 9th St., Berkeley, CA 94710; 800/368-2794; www.wildernesstravel.com)* specializes in walking tours, treks, and inn-to-inn hiking tours of Europe, as well as less strenuous walking tours. **Sherpa Expeditions** *(131A Heston Rd., Hounslow, Middlesex, England TW5 ORD; 020/8577-2717; www.sherpa-walking-holidays.co.uk)* offers both self-guided and group treks through off-the-beaten-track regions of Europe; they're represented in the U.S. by **Himalayan Travel, Inc.** *(110 Prospect St., Stamford, CT 06901; 800/225-2380).*

Most European countries have associations that help out hikers and walkers. In England it's the **Ramblers' Association** *(1-5 Wandsworth Rd., London SW8 2XX; 020/7339-8500; www.ramblers.org.uk)*; in Italy contact the **Club Alpino Italiano** *(7 Via E. Fonseca Pimental, Milan 20127; 02/205-7231; www.cai.it)*; in Austria, contact **Österreichischer Alpenverein** *(Austrian Alpine Club)* *(Wilhelm-Greil-Strasse 15, Innsbruck, A-6020; 0512/595470; www.alpenverein.at)*; and in Norway, it's the **Norwegian Mountain Touring Association** *(Storgata 3, Box 7, Sentrum 0101 Oslo; tel 22-82-28-22, fax 22-82-28-55; www.turistforeningen.no).*

study abroad

The **National Registration Center for Studies Abroad (NRCSA)** *(P.O. Box 1393, Milwaukee, WI 53203; 414/278-7410; www.NRCSA.com)* and the **American Institute for Foreign Study (AIFS)** *(102 Greenwich Ave., Greenwich, CT 06830; 800/727-2437 or 203/869-9090; www.AIFS.com)* can both hook you up with study programs and summer programs abroad.

The biggest organization dealing with higher education in Europe is the **Institute of International Education** *(809 United Nations Plaza, New York, NY 10017-3580; 212/984-5400; www.iie.org)*. To order free publications, check out the IIE's online bookstore.

health and insurance

HEALTH

Aside from any pain you might inflict upon yourself, you'll hopefully encounter few health problems traveling in Europe. The tap water is generally safe to drink (except on trains, of course), and health services good to great. But you might be eating foods and spices your body isn't used to, so don't forget the Pepto....

In most cases, your existing health plan will provide all the coverage you need. Be sure to carry your identification card.

Pack prescription medications in your carry-on luggage. Carry written prescriptions in generic, not brand-name form, and dispense all prescription medications from their original labeled vials. This will help foreign pharmacists fill them—and customs officials approve them. If you wear contact lenses, pack an extra pair in case you lose one.

Contact the **International Association for Medical Assistance to Travelers (IAMAT)** *(716/754-4883 or 416/652-0137; www.sentex. net/~iamat).* This organization offers tips on travel and health concerns in the countries you'll be visiting, and it lists many local English-speaking doctors. When you're abroad, any local consulate can provide a list of area doctors who speak English. If you do get sick, you may want to ask the concierge at your hotel to recommend a local doctor.

Many European hospitals are partially socialized, and you'll usually be taken care of speedily, often at no charge for simple ailments. If you have to be admitted, most health insurance plans and HMOs will cover, at least to some extent, out-of-country hospital visits and procedures. But most make you pay the bills up front at the time of care and reimburse you once you've returned and filed out the paperwork.

INSURANCE

Comprehensive insurance programs, covering basically everything from trip cancellation and lost luggage to medical coverage abroad and accidental death, are offered by the following companies: **Access America** *(6600 W. Broad St., Richmond, VA 23286-4991; 800/284-8300);* **Travelex Insurance Services** *(P.O. Box 9408, Garden City, NY 11530-9408, 800/228-9792);* **Travel Guard International** *(1145 Clark St., Stevens Point, WI 54481; 800/826-1300; www.travel-guard.com);* and **Travel Insured International** *(P.O. Box 280568, East Hartford, CT 06128-0568; 800/243-3174; www.travelinsured.com).* British travelers can try **Columbus Travel Insurance** *(17 Devonshire Square, London EC2M 4SQ; 020/7375-0011; www.columbusdirect.com).*

Travelers with special needs

TRAVELERS WITH DISABILITIES

While Europe won't win any medals for accomodating the disabled, in the past few years its big cities have made an effort to remedy this situation.

For American Citizens *A World of Options,* a 658-page book of resources for travelers with disabilities, covers everything from biking trips to scuba outfitters. It costs $35 ($30 for members) and is available from **Mobility International USA** *(P.O. Box 10767, Eugene, OR, 97440; 541/343-1284, voice and TDD; www.miusa.org).* Annual membership for Mobility International is $35. In addition, **Twin Peaks Press** *(P.O. Box 129, Vancouver, WA 98666; 360/694-2462)* publishes travel-related books for people with disabilities.

The Moss Rehab Hospital *(215/456-9600)* has been providing friendly and helpful phone advice and referrals to travelers with disabilities for years through its **Travel Information Service** *(215/456-9603; www.mossresourcenet.org).*

You can join **The Society for the Advancement of Travel for the Handicapped (SATH)** *(347 Fifth Ave. Suite 610, New York, NY*

10016; (tel 212/447-7284, fax 212-725-8253; www.sath.org) for $45 annually, $30 for seniors and students, to gain access to their vast network of connections in the travel industry. They provide information sheets on travel destinations, referrals to tour operators that specialize in traveling with disabilities, and a quarterly magazine, *Open World for Disability and Mature Travel.* A year's subscription is $13 ($21 outside the US).

You can obtain a copy of *Air Transportation of Handicapped Persons* by writing to **Free Advisory Circular No. AC12032** *(Distribution Unit, U.S. Department of Transportation, Publications Division, M-4332, Washington, DC 20590).*

Vision-impaired travelers should contact the **American Foundation for the Blind** *(11 Penn Plaza, Suite 300, New York, NY 10001; 800/232-5463),* for information on traveling with seeing-eye dogs.

For British Citizens The **Royal Association for Disability and Rehabilitation (RADAR)** *(Unit 12, City Forum, 250 City Rd., London EC1V 8AF; 020/7250-3222),* publishes 3 holiday "fact packs." The first provides general information, including planning and booking a holiday, insurance, finances, and useful organizations and holiday providers. The second outlines transportation and rental equipment options. The third deals with specialized accommodations.

GAY & LESBIAN TRAVELERS

Much of Europe has grown to accept same-sex couples over the past few decades, and in most countries homosexual sex acts are legal. To be on the safe side, do some of research on how friendly the area that you're heading to is. As you might have guessed, smaller towns tend to be less accepting than cities. Gay centers include parts of London, Paris, Berlin, Milan, and Greece (especially the islands). Both lesbians and gays might want to pick up a copy of *Frommer's Gay & Lesbian Europe ($21.95).*

General gay and lesbian travel agencies include **Family Abroad** *(800/999-5500 or 212/459-1800; www.familyabroad.com; gay and lesbian);* and **Above and Beyond Tours** *(800/397-2681; www.abovebeyond.tours.com; mainly gay men);*

There are also two good biannual English-language gay guidebooks: ***Spartacus International Gay Guide*** and ***Odysseus.*** Both focus mainly on gay men but have information for lesbians too. Pick them up at any gay and lesbian book store, or order them from **Giovanni's Room** *(215/923-2960)* or **A Different Light Bookstore** *(800/343-4002 or 212/989-4850; www.adlbooks.com).* **Gay Travel A to Z** and **The Ferrari Guides** *(www.qnet.com)* are other good series of gay and lesbian guidebooks.

Out and About *(8 W. 19th St. #401, New York, NY 10011; 800/929-2268 or 212/645-6922; www.outandabout.com)* offers guidebooks and a monthly newsletter packed with good information on the global gay and lesbian scene. A year's subscription to the newsletter costs $35 inside U.S., $45 outside.

STUDENTS

The best resource for students is the **Council on International Educa-**

tional Exchange (**CIEE**). They can set you up with an ID card [see below], and their travel branch, **Council Travel Service** *(800/226-8624; www.counciltravel.com)*, is the biggest student travel agency operation in the world. It can get you discounts on plane tickets, rail passes, and all that. Ask them for a list of CTS offices in major cities so you can keep the discounts flowing (and help lines open).

CIEE can also hook you up with the student traveler's best friend, the $18 **International Student Identity Card (ISIC)**. It's the only officially acceptable form of student identification, good for cut rates on rail passes, plane tickets, and other discounts. Plus it provides you with basic health and life insurance and a 24-hour help line. If you're no longer a student, but still under 26, you can get a **GO 25** card from the same people, which will get you the insurance and some of the discounts but not student admission prices in museums.

In Canada, **Travel CUTS** *(200 Ronson St., Ste. 320, Toronto, ONT M9W 5Z9; 800/667-2887 or 416/614-2887; www.travelcuts.com)* offers similar services, and **Campus** USIT*(52 Grosvenor Gardens, London SW1W 0AG; 020/7730-3402; www.usitcampus.co.uk)*, opposite Victoria Station, is the place to go in Britain.

WOMEN

WomanTraveler *(www.womantraveler.com)* is an excellent woman-authored site guide with listings of women-owned hotels, hostels, etc., plus safe places for women to stay.

There are also some good books out there for the girl on the go. The **Virago Women's Travel Guides** series is excellent but new, and it covers only three cities to date: London, San Francisco, and Amsterdam. *Safety and Security for Women Who Travel*, by Sheila Swan Laufer and Peter Laufer, is well worth picking up.

GETTING THERE

FLYING FROM NORTH AMERICA

Most major airlines charge competitive fares to European cities, but price wars break out regularly and fares can change overnight. For a list of the major North American and European national airlines and their toll-free numbers and web sites, see the *Appendix*.

Tickets tend to be cheaper if you fly mid-week or off-season. **High season** for most airlines is usually June to mid-September. **Low season**—featuring the cheapest fares—is November to December 14 and December 25 through March.

You can get the best fares by planning ahead and buying low-cost advance-purchase (APEX) tickets. Usually APEX tickets have to be purchased 14 to 21 days in advance, and your stay in Europe must last between 7 and 30 days. The downside is that an APEX ticket locks you into those dates and times, and you're charged penalties for changing them [see *tips for getting the best airfare*, below, for more cheap-o options].

A more flexible—but more expensive option—is the regular economy fare, which allows for a shorter stay than the seven-day APEX minimum.

You're also usually free to make last-minute changes in flight dates and to have unrestricted stopovers.

GETTING TO THE CONTINENT FROM THE U.K.

By Train: Many different rail passes and discounts are available in the U.K. for travel in continental Europe. One of the most complete overviews on the subject is available from **Rail Europe Special Services Department** *(10 Leake St., London SE1 7NN; 0990/848-848)* or **Wasteels** *(Platform 2, Victoria Station, London SW1V 1JT; 020/7834-7066)*. Wasteels and also the London Branch of **Campus USIT** *(52 Grosvenor Gardens, London SW1W OAG; 020/7730-3402; www.usitcampus.co.uk)*, are particularly well-versed in information about discount travel as it applies to both persons under 26, full or part-time students, and senior citizens.

The most prevalent option for younger travelers, the **EuroYouth passes**, are available only to travelers under 26 and entitle the pass holder to unlimited second-class rail travel in 26 European countries.

By Chunnel The *Eurostar* train shuttles between London and both Paris and Brussels; the trip time is less than 3 hours (compared to 10 hours on the traditional train-ferry-train route). **Rail Europe** *(800/94-CHUNNEL; www.raileurope.com)* sells tickets on the Eurostar between London and Paris or Brussels (both $149 one way). You can phone for *Eurostar* reservations *(0990/300-003 in London, 01-44-51-06-02 in Paris, and 800/EUROSTAR in the U.S.; www.euro star.com)*. *Eurostar* trains arrive and depart from Waterloo Station in London, Gare du Nord in Paris, and Central Station in Brussels.

By Ferry or Hovercraft Brittany Ferries *(01705/892-200; www.brittany-ferries.com)* is the largest British ferry/drive outfit. It sails from the southern coast of England to five destinations in Spain and France. From Portsmouth, sailings reach St. Malo and Caen; from Poole to Cherbourg. From Plymouth sailings go to Santander in Spain.

P&O Stena Lines *(087/6000-0611; www.posl.com)* operates car and passenger ferries between Portsmouth and Cherbourg (with three departures a day; 5 to 7 hours); between Portsmouth and Le Havre, France (three a day; 5 1/2 hours); and between Dover and Calais, France (25 sailings a day; 1 1/4 hours).

Unless you're into leisurely sea voyages, you might be better off using the quicker, and slightly cheaper, **Hoverspeed** *(08705/240-241; www.hov erspeed.co.uk)*, which makes the 35-minute crossing between Calais and Dover 7 to 15 times per day, with fewer crossings in winter. Prices are £25 for adults, £14 for children, for one-way or five-day return.

By Bus Although travel by bus is considerably slower and less comfortable than train travel, if you're on a budget you may opt for one of **Eurolines'** regular departures from London's Victoria Coach Station to destinations throughout Europe. Contact Eurolines at 52 Grosvenor Gardens, Victoria, London SW1W OAU *(0990/143219 or 01582/404511; www.eurolines.co.uk)*.

TIPS FOR GETTING THE BEST AIRFARES

Budget Travel Agencies Before venturing into the realm of consol-

Train Trip Tips

1. Hold on to your train ticket after it's been marked or punched by the conductor. Some European railroad systems require that you present your ticket when you leave the station platform at your destination.

2. While you sleep—or even nap—be sure your valuables are in a safe place; you might temporarily attach a small bell to each bag to warn you if someone attempts to take it. If you've left bags on a rack in the front or back of the car, consider securing them with a small bicycle chain and lock to deter thieves, who consider trains happy hunting grounds.

3. Few European trains have drinking fountains and the dining car may be closed just when you're at your thirstiest, so take a bottle of water with you. Food's available on many trains, but it's super expensive, so grab some bread and cheese before you board.

4. If you want to leave bags in a train station locker, don't let anyone "help" you store them in it. Tricky thieves will help you hoist your bag in, then pocket the key to your locker while passing you the key to an empty one.

idators, virtual travel agents, and courier services, try just calling up a travel agency that specializes in budget travel. Agencies like **Council Travel** *(800/2-COUNCIL; www.counciltravel. com)*, and **STA** *(800/781-4040; www.sta.travel.com)* student travel specialists, always have the scoop on the latest cheap fares, and you don't have to be a student, under 26, or a teacher to use their services (but you'll save even more if you are).

In addition, **Cheap Tickets** *(800/377-1000; www.cheaptickets.com)*, **1-800/FLY-4-LESS**, and **1-800/FLY-CHEAP** *(www.1800flycheap.com)* all specialize in finding the lowest fares out there. You can often get discounted fares on short notice without all the advance-purchase requirements.

Charter Flights Charters book a block of seats (or an entire plane) months in advance and then resell the tickets to consumers. Always ask about restrictions: You might have to purchase a tour package and pay far in advance, and pay a stiff penalty—or forfeit the ticket entirely and lose all your money—if you cancel. Charters are sometimes canceled when the plane doesn't fill. In some cases, the charter company will offer you an insurance policy in case you need to cancel for a "legitimate" reason (not much beyond hospitalization or death in the family is considered legit).

Council Travel *(205 E. 42nd St., New York, NY 10017; 800/226-*

8624 or 212/822-2800; www.counciltravel.com) arranges charter seats on a regularly scheduled aircraft. For Canadians, good charter deals are offered by **Martinair** *(800/627-8462; www.martinair.com)* and **Travel CUTS** *(888-450-2887; www.travelcuts.com)*, which also has an office in London *(295A Regent Street; 0171/255-2082)*.

Internet Deals It's possible to get some great deals on airfare, hotels, and car rentals via the Internet. The sites highlighted below are worth checking out (especially since they're all free). Always check the lowest published fare, however, before you shop for flights online.

Arthur Frommer's Budget Travel *(www.frommers.com)*: Detailed information on 200 cities and islands around the world, and up-to-the-minute ways to save dramatically on flights, hotels, car reservations, and cruises.

The best part of **Microsoft Expedia's** *(www.expedia.com)* travel site is the "Fare Tracker": You fill out a form on the screen telling them that you're interested in cheap flights from your hometown, and, once a week they'll e-mail you the best airfare deals on up to three destinations. So cool.

Several major airlines offer a free e-mail service known as **E-Savers**, which will send you their best bargain airfares on a regular basis. The catch? These fares are usually only available if you leave the very next Saturday (or sometimes Friday night) and return on the following Monday or Tuesday. If you don't want to get 20 different emails every week, sign up with *www.smarterliving.com* which consolidates all the individual e-savers into one mailing.

ʀᴜʟᴇꜱ ᴏғ ᴛʜᴇ ʀᴏᴀᴅ

1. You drive on the left side of the road only in England, Scotland, and Ireland.

2. *Do not* ride in the left lane on a four-lane highway; it is truly only for passing.

3. If someone comes up from behind and flashes their lights at you, it's a signal for you to slow down and drive more on the shoulder so that they can pass you more easily (two-lane roads here routinely become three cars wide).

4. Except for the German Autobahn, most highways have speed limits of around 60 to 80 mph (100 to 135 kmph)

5. Remember, everything's measured in kilometers here (mileage and speed limits). For a rough conversion: 1km = 0.6 miles.

6. Gas may look cheap, but remember the price is per liter, so multiply by four to estimate the equivalent per-gallon price.

getting around

BY TRAIN

In Europe, the shortest—and cheapest—distance between two points is lined with railroad tracks. Modern high-speed trains make the rails faster than the plane for short journeys, and overnight trains get you where you're going without wasting valuable daylight hours (plus you save money on lodging). Oh, and so you know: The difference between first- and second-class seats on European trains is minor—a matter of 1 or 2 inches of extra padding and maybe a little more elbow room.

Europe has tons of different train classifications, ranging from local "milk runs" that stop at every tiny station to high-speed bullet trains that cruise at 130 mph between major cities. Many high-speed trains throughout Europe, including the popular EC (EuroCity), IC (Inter-City), and EN (EuroNight) trains, require that you pay a supplement in addition to the regular ticket fare. It's included when you buy regular tickets, but not in any of the railpasses, so check at the ticket window before boarding, otherwise the conductor will sell you the supplement on the train—and hit you with a fine.

Seat reservations are also required on some of the speediest of the high-speed runs (any train marked with an "R" on a printed train schedule). Reservations range from $15 up to $50 or more (when a meal's included). You can almost always reserve a seat within a few hours of the train's departure, but to be on the safe side, you'll probably want to do it a few days in advance. You might also need to reserve a *couchette* or sleeping berth (see below).

There are only two cases in which you need to buy individual train tickets or make seat reservations before you leave the States: For the high-speed *Artesia* run (between Paris, Turin, and Milan) you must buy a supplement. You can get a substantial discount if you have a railpass, but only if you buy the supplement in the States when you buy the pass. It's also a good idea to reserve a seat on the *Eurostar*, as England's frequent "bank holidays" (long weekends) book the train solid with Londoners taking a short vacation to Paris.

In stations you will find posters showing the track number and timetables for regularly scheduled runs that pass through (departures are often on the yellow poster). Many stations also have tourist office outposts and hotel reservations desks; banks with ATMs; and newsstands where you can buy phonecards, bus and Metro tickets, maps, and local English-language events magazines.

You can get much more information about train travel in Europe, and receive automated schedule information by fax by contacting **Rail Europe** *(800/438-7245, Fax 800/432-1329; www.raileurope.com)*. Each country's national railway web site, which includes schedules and fare information, occasionally in English, is hotlisted at **Mercurio** *(http://mercurio.iet.unipi.it)*.

RAILPASSES

The greatest value in European travel has always been the railpass, a single ticket that allows you unlimited travel (or travel on a certain number of days) within a set period of time. If you plan on doing a bunch of cities by train, a railpass will end up being much less expensive than individual tickets. Plus a railpass gives you the freedom to hop on a train whenever you feel like it, without having to wait in ticket lines. For more focused trips, you may want to look into national or regional passes or just buy individual tickets as you go.

The grand-pappy of passes is the **Eurailpass**, covering 17 countries (most of Western Europe except Britain). Now there's also the **Europass**, which covers 5 to 12 countries (depending on what version you buy)— this pass is mainly for travelers who are going to stay within the heart of Western Europe.

Railpasses are available in either **consecutive-day** or **flexipass** versions. With a flexipass, you have, say, 2 months in which to use 10 days of train travel. Consecutive-day passes are best for those taking the train every few days, covering a lot of ground, and making many short train hops. Flexipasses are better for folks who want to range far and wide but plan on taking their time over a long trip, and intend to stay in each city for a while.

If you're under 26, you can opt to buy a regular first-class pass or a second-class youth pass; if you're 26 or over, you're stuck buying a first-class pass.

You have to buy Eurail (and Eurail-offshoot) passes in the U.S. (They are available from some major European train stations but are up to 50 percent more expensive.) You can buy railpasses from most travel agents, but the biggest supplier is **Rail Europe** *(800/438-7245; www.raileurope.com)*, which also sells most national passes save a few minor British ones.

The rates quoted below are for 2000; they rise each year, usually after press time, so we can't include 2001 rates here.

Eurailpass Consecutive-day Eurail passes cost $554 for 15 days, $718 for 21 days, $890 for 1 month, $1,260 for 2 months, or $1,558 for 3 months.

Eurail Flexipass Good for 2 months of travel, within which you can travel by train for 10 days (consecutive or not) for $654 or 15 days for $862.

Eurail Saverpass A Saverpass is good for two to five people traveling together. The Saverpass costs $470 per person for 15 days, $610 for 21 days, $756 for 1 month, $1,072 for 2 months, or $1,324 for 3 months.

Eurail Saver Flexipas This is the Flexipass for two to five people traveling together. The Saver Flexipass costs $556 per person for 10 days within 2 months or $732 per person for 15 days within 2 months.

Eurail Youthpass This is the second-class railpass for travelers under 26. It costs $388 for 15 days, $499 for 21 days, $623 for 1 month, $882 for 2 months, or $1,089 for 3 months.

Eurail Youth Flexipass Only for travelers under 26, this pass allows for 10 days of travel within 2 months for $458, or 15 days in 2 months for $599.

Europass If your trip will focus on the core of Western Europe—specifically France, Germany, Switzerland, Italy, and Spain—the Eurailpass is wasteful spending. Go for the Europass, which gives you 5, 6, 8, 10, or 15 days of train travel in the five above countries for 2 months. You can expand the scope of your pass by purchasing add-on "zones"—Austria/Hungary; Belgium/the Netherlands/Luxembourg; Greece (including the ferry from Brindisi, Italy); and Portugal. The base pass ranges in price from $348 for 5 days to $728 for 15 days. You can add one zone for $60, or two zones for $100.

Europass Youth The Europass Youth is good in second-class only and is for travelers under 26. This pass grants 5, 6, 8, 10, or 15 days of unlimited train travel in France, Germany, Italy, Spain, and Switzerland, with 2 months to complete your travel. The cost is $233 for 5 days, $253 for 6 days, $313 for 8 days, $363 for 10 days, and $513 for 15 days. It costs $45 to add one associate country or $78 to add two associate countries. [See europass, above.]

EurailDrive Pass This pass offers the best of both worlds, mixing train travel and rental cars (through Hertz or Avis) for less money than it would cost to do them separately (and one of the only ways to get around the high daily car-rental rates in Europe when you rent for less than a week). You get 4 rail days and 2 car days within a 2-month period. Rates below reflect per person price for 1 adult/2 adults which vary with the class of the car. $399/$339 economy, $439/$359 compact, $459/$369 mid-size. You can add up to 5 extra rail and/or car days. Extra rail days are $59 each; car days cost $61 for economy, $80 compact, and $90 midsize. You have to reserve the first car day a week before leaving the States, but you can make other reservations as you go (always subject to availability). If there are more than 2 adults, the extra passenger gets the car portion for free but must buy the 4-day railpass for $280.

Eurodrive Pass This is a similar deal, but it's good for Europass countries only (and no add-on zones) and for shorter trips. It's good for 3 rail days and 2 car days within a 2-month period. Prices (per person for 1 adult/2 adults) are $345/$284 economy, $379/$304 compact, and $399/$314 midsize. You can add up to 7 extra rails days at $45 each and unlimited extra car days for $59 to $89 each, depending on the class of car.

Regional or National Passes There are also national railpasses of various kinds, regional passes such as ScanRail (Scandinavia), BritRail (covering Great Britain), and the European East Pass (good in Austria, Czech Republic, Slovakia, Hungary, and Poland). Some types of national passes must be bought in the U.S., some you can get on either side of the Atlantic, and still others must be purchased in Europe itself. And remember, seniors, students, and youths can usually get discounts on European trains—in some countries just by asking, in others by buying a discount card good for a year (or whatever). Rail Europe [see railpasses, above] or your travel agent can fill you in on all the details.

BritRail *(888/BRITRAIL; www.britrail.com)* specializes in railpasses in Great Britain, and **DER Tours** *(800/782-2424; www.dertravel.com)* is a Germany specialist that also sells other national passes (except French and British ones).

Another good option for travelers 26 and under, **Eurotrain** tickets are valid for 2 months and allow you to choose your own route to a final destination and stop off as many times as you like along the way. **Eurotrain "Explorer"** tickets are slightly more expensive but allow you to travel to your final destination along one route and back on another. The price includes round-trip ferry crossing as well as round-trip rail travel from London to the port. For help in determining the best option for your trip and to buy tickets, stop in London at the **International Rail Centre** *(Victoria Station; Tel 0990/848-848),* **Wasteels,** *(Victoria Station, adjacent to Platform 2; Tel 020/7834-7066),* or **Campus Travel,** *(52 Grosvenor Gardens; Tel 020/7730-3402).*

BY CAR

Many rental companies grant discounts if you reserve in advance (usually 48 hours) from your home country. Weekly rentals are almost always less expensive than day rentals. Three or more people traveling together can usually get around cheaper by car than by train (even with railpasses).

When you reserve a car, be sure to ask if the price includes the EU value-added tax (VAT), personal accident insurance (PAI), collision-damage waiver (CDW), and any other insurance options. If not, ask what these extras will cost, because at the end of your rental they can make a big difference in your final cost. The CDW and other insurance may be covered by your credit card if you use a card to pay for the rental; check with the card issuer to be sure.

If your credit card doesn't cover CDW, **Travel Guard International** *(1145 Clark St., Stevens Point, WI 54481-9970; 800/826-1300; www.travel -guard.com),* offers it for $5 per day. Avis and Hertz, among other companies, require that you purchase a theft-protection policy in Italy.

The main car-rental companies include **Avis** *(800/331-1212; www.avis.com)*; **Budget** *(800/527-0700; www.budgetrentacar.com)*; **Europcar** known as "Dollar" in the U.S. *(800/800-6000; www.europcar.com)*; **Hertz** *(800/654-3131; www.hertz.com)*; and **National** *(800/227-7368; www.nationalcar.com).*

U.S.-based companies that specialize in European car rentals are **Auto Europe** *(800/223-5555; www.autoeurope.com)*; **Europe by Car** *(800/223-1516, or 212/581-3040 in New York; www.europebycar.com)*; and **Kemwel Holiday Auto** *(800/678-0678; www.kemwel.com).* Europe By Car and Kemwel also offer a low-cost alternative to renting for periods longer than 15 days: short-term leases, in which you technically buy a fresh-from-the-factory car then sell it back when you return it. All insurance is included, from liability and theft to personal injury and CDW, with no deductible.

European drivers tend to be more aggressive than their American counterparts, and gas is generally expensive. Never rent a car just to drive around a European city—the drivers and traffic patterns can drive anyone crazy, parking is difficult and expensive, and the public transportation is usually excellent anyway. Never leave anything of value in the car overnight, and nothing visible any time you leave the car (this goes double in Italy, triple in Naples).

BY PLANE

Although trains remain the cheapest and easiest way to get around in Europe, intense competition with rail and ferry companies is slowly forcing airfares into the bargain basement. **British Airways** *(800/AIR-WAYS or 0345/222-111 in U.K.; www.britishairways.com)* and other scheduled airlines now fly regularly from London to Paris for only £98 to £105 ($167 to $179) round-trip, depending on the season. Lower fares usually apply to midweek flights and carry advance-purchase requirements of 2 weeks or so.

Lately a bunch of no-frills airline have gotten into the game, making things even cheaper. By keeping their overheads down through electronic ticketing, forgoing meal service, and flying from less popular airports, these airlines can offer low, low fares (most round-trip tickets cost from $60 to $160—in some cases that's cheaper than a train ticket). Budget airlines include **EasyJet** *(44-870/600-000; www.easyjet.com)* and British Airway's subsidiary **Go** *(44-1279/666-388)* in England; **Ryanair** *(353/1609-7800 in Ireland; 44-541/569-569 in England; www.ryanair.com)* in Ireland; and **Virgin Express** *(32-2/752-0505; www.virginexpress.com)*, an offshoot of Virgin Air, in Belgium. Be aware, though, that the names may change because these small airlines are often economically vulnerable and can fail, or merge with a big airline. Still, as quickly as one disappears, another one will pop up.

Lower airfares are also available throughout Europe on charter flights rather than on regularly scheduled ones. Look in local newspapers to find out about them. Consolidators cluster in cities like London and Athens.

Flying across Europe on regularly scheduled airlines can be super expensive. Whenever possible, book your total flight on a single ticket before leaving. For example, if you're flying from New York to Rome, but also plan to visit Palerno, Florence, and Turin, have the entire trip written up on one ticket. Don't arrive in Rome and book separate legs of the journey—it'll cost much more if you split it up like that.

Sometimes national carriers will offer amazing deals to non-European residents. For example, **Lufthansa** offers a "Discover Europe" package of three flight coupons, which vary in price, depending on the nation of origin. Another bargain is **Alitalia**'s "Europlus." First, you have to book a transatlantic flight, perhaps from New York to Rome. After that, and for only $299, you can purchase a package of three flight coupons. This will entitle you to fly on any three flights anywhere in Europe served by Alitalia. You can also purchase unlimited additional tickets, one way, for another $100 per ticket.

Go Fly Limited *(84-56-05-43-21 in London; www.go-fly.com)* offers 40 percent off standard round-trip air fares, with a two-night minimum stay. Sample round-trip air fares from London are as follows: Edinburgh £40 ($66); Copenhagen £60 ($99); Rome £70 ($115.50), and Lisbon for also £70 ($115.50).

American citizens can contact **Europe by Air** *(888/387-2479 or 512/404-1291; www.eurair.com)* to get their Europe flight pass, which serves 20 countries, 13 airlines, and 62 European cities. It costs only $90 each to travel one way between these cities.

Because discount passes are always changing on air routes within Europe, it's best to check in with **Air Travel Advisory Bureau** in London *(020/7636-5000; www.atab.co.uk)*, which offers a free service directory of suppliers of discount airfares from all major U.K. airports.

BY BUS

Bus transportation is sometimes is less expensive than train travel and covers a more extensive area, but can be slower and much less comfortable. European buses, like the trains, outshine their American counterparts, but they are still buses. **Eurolines** *(Central booking in London: 0990/143219)* serves all the countries of Western Europe (except Greece). The staff at this number can make reservations, quote prices, and give you the latest schedules for all the bus routes.

accomodations

TIPS FOR GETTING THE BEST ROOM AT THE BEST RATE

The rack rate is the maximum rate that a hotel charges for a room; it's the rate you'd get if you walked in off the street and asked for a room for the night. Hardly anybody pays these prices, since there are so many ways around them.

Don't Be Afraid to Bargain Get in the habit of asking for a lower price than the first one quoted. Most rack rates include commissions of 10% to 25% or more for travel agents, which can be cut if you make your own reservations and haggle a bit. Always ask politely whether a less expensive room is available than the first one mentioned or whether any special rates apply to you.

Dial Direct When booking a room in a chain hotel, call the hotel's local line, as well as the toll-free number, and see where you get the best deal. The clerk who runs the place is more likely to know about vacancies and will often grant deep discounts in order to fill empty rooms.

Remember the Law of Supply and Demand Resort hotels are most crowded (and therefore most expensive) on weekends; so discounts are usually available for midweek stays. To the contrary, business hotels in downtown locations are busiest during the week, so their discounts kick in over the weekend. Avoid high-season stays whenever you can: planning your trip just a week before or after official peak season can mean huge savings.

Look Into Group or Long-stay Discounts If you come as part of a large group, you should be able to negotiate a bargain, since the hotel

PUT IT IN WRITING

If you call a hotel from home to reserve a room in advance, always follow up with a confirmation fax. Not only is it what most hotels prefer, but it is proof on paper that you've booked a room. Keep the language simple; state your name, number of people, what kind of room ("double with one bed" or "double with two beds"), and the dates of your stay. Remember: Europeans abbreviate dates day/month/year not month/day/year.

can then guarantee occupancy in a number of rooms. You'll also qualify for a discount if you're planning a long stay in town (usually from five days to a week). As a general rule, you'll get one night free after a seven-night stay.

Avoid Excess Charges Find out before you dial whether your hotel imposes a surcharge on local or long-distance calls. A pay phone, however inconvenient, may save you money.

Consider a Suite If you're traveling in a group, you can pack more people into a suite, which usually comes with a sofa bed, and reduce your per-person cost. This doesn't work the same everywhere: some places charge for extra guests, some don't.

Book an Efficiency A room with a kitchenette allows you to grocery shop and eat some meals in. Especially during long stays, you're bound to save money on food this way.

Online Deal Try booking your hotel through **Arthur Frommer's Budget Travel** (*www.frommers.com*), and save up to 50 percent on the cost of your room. **Microsoft Expedia** (*www.expedia.com*) features a "Travel Agent" that will also direct you to affordable lodgings.

USING A HOTEL BOOKING SERVICE

In most cities, there is a desk at either the train station or the tourist office that will act as a central hotel reservations service. Tell them your price range and where you'd like to be in the city, and for a small fee, they'll find you a room in town from their computer database.

The advantages of using these services are that the employees always speak English, and when every hotel in town seems to be booked up—during a convention or festival, or just in high season—they can often find space for you at hotels or hostels that aren't listed in the guidebooks or other main sources. On the downside, hotels in many countries often charge higher rates to people booking through such a service.

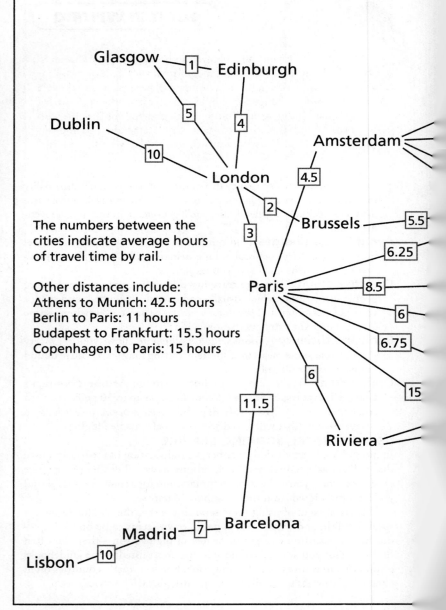

Glasgow —1— Edinburgh

Dublin

London

Amsterdam

Brussels

Paris

Riviera

Barcelona

Madrid —7— Lisbon

The numbers between the cities indicate average hours of travel time by rail.

Other distances include:
Athens to Munich: 42.5 hours
Berlin to Paris: 11 hours
Budapest to Frankfurt: 15.5 hours
Copenhagen to Paris: 15 hours

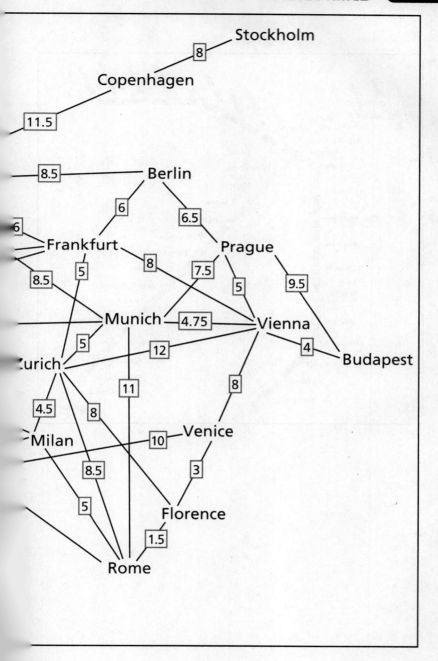

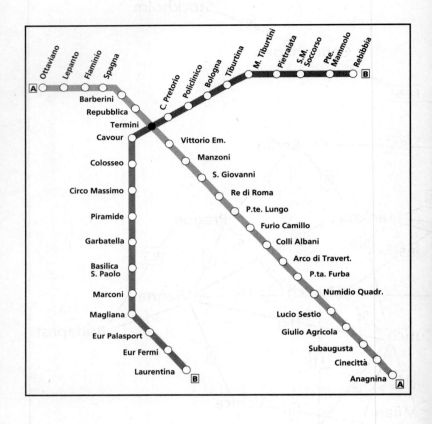

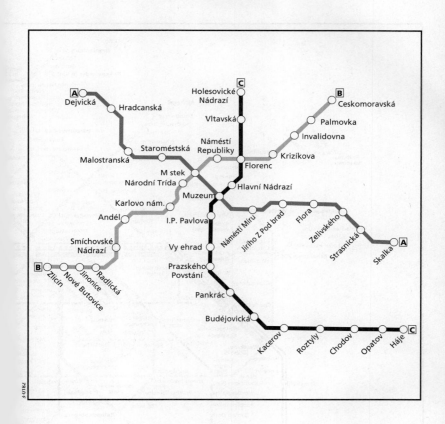

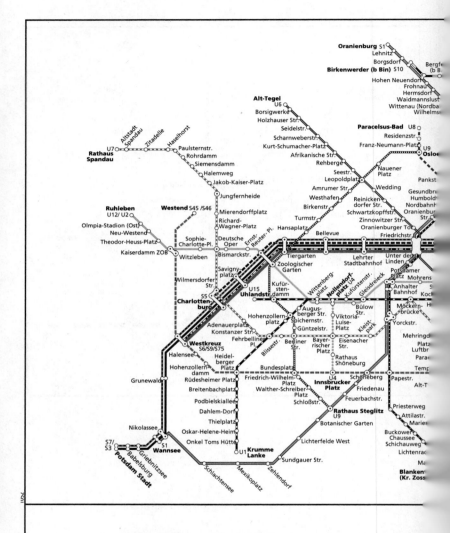

U1 Krumme Lanke/ Schlesisches Tor	**U5** Alexanderplatz/ Hönow	**U8** Leinestr./ Paracelsus-Bad
U2 Ruhleben/ Vinetastr.	**U6** Alt- Mariendorf/ Alt-Tegel	**U9** Rathaus Steglitz/ Osloer Str.
U4 Innsbrucker Platz/ Nollendorf-platz	**U7** Rudlow/ Rathaus Spandau	**U12** Ruhleben/ Schlesisches Tor
		U15 Uhlandstr./ Schelesisches

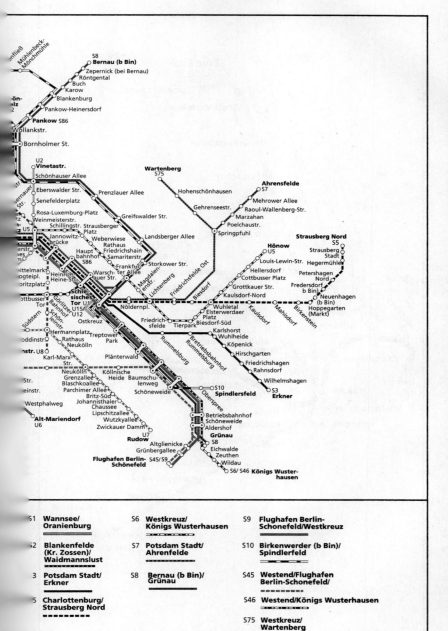

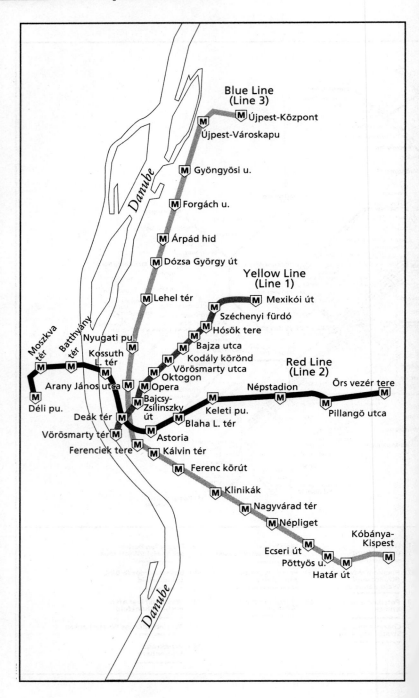

about the authors

FLORENCE, MILAN, BOLOGNA

Alexander Villari lived in Rome for a year where he explored his Italian ancestry and snacked on vine-ripened tomatoes, local cheese, olives, and bread. He has traveled extensively in northern and southern Italy and visits often. He thanks Amy Esty for her help in this project.

Florence updated by Carolyn Chapman, Milan updated by Paul Garofano,. Bologna updated by Dana and Lindsay Bowen.

COPENHAGEN

Dennis Cleary, a Hobart College graduate, works for the United Nations in Copenhagen Denmark. After a stint in Boston, the charming allure of 3pm sunsets and 50% income taxes became too great, and Dennis returned to Denmark, where he has been living on and off.

Updated by Ben Illis.

LISBON

Amanda Buttinger lives in Madrid, Spain and drinks wine with a translator. She loves to run around outside and misses being with the Rollins Outdoor Club in the tower listening to Bob. She has the coolest sister in the world in Seattle, and needs to go back soon for a haircut. Hi Mom, Dad and family! Additional research was provided by Mark and Dana Dorrity.

Updated by Amanda Buttinger.

STOCKHOLM, MUNICH, BERLIN, BRUSSELS, ANTWERP

Chris Gaither, a graduate of Wesleyan University, is a freelance writer in the Bay Area. He'd like to thank the sisters Fuchshuber and the Nilsson family for their hospitality.

Alex Blau is a writer based in New York City. He would like to thank the friends and family who bore his journey on their backs. Med varma tankar och tack till Lotta, Mats, Anton, och Amanda. Special thanks to the sisters Fuchshuber, without whose medical attentions he surely would have perished in the wilds of Bavaria. And, of course, to G—my partner and brother.

Stockholm, Brussels, and Antwerp updated by Ben Illis; Munich and Berlin updated by Tanya Datta.

ROME

Stephanie D'Ambrose graduated from NYU where she studied Philosophy and French. She had an incredible stay in Rome researching for this book and would like to give a shout out to all the great people who showed her such a good time.

Updated by Carolyn Chapman.

ATHENS AND THE GREEK ISLANDS

Jon Feldman is the author of several unsuccessful screenplays, short stories and novellas. Jon's day jobs include writing speeches for various low-level government functionaries. In his spare time, Jon likes to lie around with the lights off, biting his toenails and avoiding phone calls from his mother.

Updated by Nate Knaebel and Lauren Podis.

AMSTERDAM, KRAKOW, REYKJAVIK

Sam Anson grew up in Princeton Jct., NJ, spending most of his time fishing, canoeing, mountain biking and avoiding schoolwork, and has since traveled in over 20 countries. Sam graduated from Hobart College and is currently working at an Internet startup in New York City. Additional research was provided by Jan Baracz.

Amsterdam updated by Ben Illis. Krakow updated by Will Tizard, Reykjavík updated by Dana and Lindsay Bowen.

RIVIERA, CINQUE TERRE

Lisa Ebersole is a writer and filmmaker living in New York. In her daily work, she splits her personality between a rat, two teenage girls, an adolescent boy and his robot.

The Riviera updated by Dana and Lindsay Bowen, Cinque Terre updated by Paul Garofano.

ISTANBUL

Onur Akmehmet is an all-but dissertation doctoral student and an all-but-working actor currently residing in Istanbul. He would appreciate your comments and questions about the city at oakmehmet@hotmail.com.

Istanbul updated by Nate Knaebel, with special thanks to the Turkish Tourism Information Bureau in Manhattan.

PRAGUE, BUDAPEST

Author and screenwriter Will Tizard traded in the daily deadlines of a California crime reporter for a travel correspondent's life in Prague. His most recent script, *Could Always be Worse*, is a tale of spies, breakbeat and bad coffee. Five years after landing in Central Europe, he is nearly able to pronounce fi.

Updated by Will Tizard.

LONDON, EDINBURGH, GLASGOW

James Friedman is currently a student at Columbia University and a staff writer for *XLR8R Magazine*. He wishes to thank the Sallon family, John Featherly, and Sophie from London; Chris, Mark, Phil, Josh and Adam Queer from Edinburgh; Laura, Craig, Murray, Isaac, and Fat Mick from Glasgow.

Updated by Ben Illis.

MADRID, BARCELONA, IBIZA

International pinball star Aaron Zwas took eight weeks off from England's Professional Pinball League to research Madrid, Barcelona, and Ibiza. Sometimes, when the fame, drugs and women that come with success in the world's toughest pinball competition seem hollow, Zwas dreams of giving it all up for an anonymous day job as a corporate consultant.

Updated by Amanda Buttinger.

DUBLIN, GALWAY

Jim McCarthy is a Princeton graduate who hails from eastern Massachussetts. After completing his work on this book, Jim spent his winter living as in a hiker's shelter on the Adirondack Trail in the White Mountains.

Updated by Ben Illis.

Every year,
millions of people fly
directly over Iceland on
their way to Europe.
Many of them are asleep.
The smart ones are
flying Icelandair.

That's because Icelandair has flights to
more than 20 European cities including
Amsterdam, Frankfurt, Glasgow, London
and Paris, with easy connections through
Reykjavik. And travelers on their way
to Europe via Icelandair can stop over
"Take a Break" in Iceland for up to
three nights at no additional air fare.

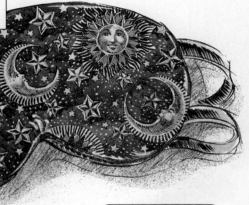

Many species of birds also stop
over in Iceland on their way
to European breeding grounds.

Typically, the birds are not sleeping.

NOTES